D1365174

SOCIOLOGY

Principles and Applications

SOCIOLOGY

Principles and Applications

James A. Inciardi
University of Delaware

Robert A. Rothman
University of Delaware

HBJ

Harcourt Brace Jovanovich, Publishers

San Diego New York Chicago Austin Washington, D.C.

London Sydney Tokyo Toronto

Cover photo: © Mike King/TSW/Click, Chicago

ISBN: 0-15-582290-X
Library of Congress Catalog Card Number: 89-85313
Printed in the United States of America

Photo Credits appear on pages P-1 and P-2, which constitute a continuation of the copyright page.

Preface

Our goal in writing this textbook was to create a work that might effectively communicate a number of things to beginning students. We wanted, first of all, to describe what sociology is, in all of its richness and variety. To do this, we have attempted to examine the kinds of questions and problems that sociologists have studied and the perspectives that they have developed in order to find answers and solutions. This objective is captured neatly in the first word of the subtitle: Principles.

We also wanted to describe what sociologists actually do—how they approach the enduring questions about how individuals have chosen to live and the problems to which such choices may lead. To do this we have tried to show that sociologists have devised certain methods of investigation, certain ways of proceeding, much as a detective might in seeking the solution to a crime. But we have also tried to illustrate this methodology without resorting to technical details that have no place in an introductory course.

Finally, we wanted to discuss what sociology as a discipline has accomplished and what relevance it has for students—as consumers, as members of families and communities, as citizens. We hope to convey our conviction that sociology is a critically important discipline in our time and for all times. It has something important to say to you, and the most obvious and most immediate part of that is also revealed in the book's subtitle: Applications.

While pursuing these goals, we hoped to accomplish a number of other things. The first was to present the theoretical underpinnings of sociology and their importance to an understanding of the dynamics of modern society. We feel, however, that detailed approaches to social theory are inappropriate for the beginning student. Therefore, we have tried to use the functionalist, conflict, and interactionist perspectives to illuminate social phenomena rather than as the basis for the study of social theory. Finally, because this is a textbook on the study of society, we feel it is important to illustrate theoretical ideas with practical examples. Therefore, the text offers students a panorama of social events.

We should point out that the components of sociology as a discipline—the objectives of this book—do not exist in isolation from each other. The great social psychologist Kurt Lewin said that there is nothing more practical than a good theory. As you read this book, you will find that principles and applications continually feed into and inform each other. It is important to keep each in mind as you read. But it is equally important to keep in mind that they should eventually come together to give you a greater understanding of human society.

ORGANIZATION OF THE BOOK

For ease of understanding, the individual topics, questions, and problems that sociologists study are gathered here under larger headings. In suggesting this organization, we do not mean to establish hard and fast rules. All institutions, for example, share certain characteristics, and it is important to understand what those characteristics are and how they have arisen. But it is also important to understand how institutions differ from each other. To this end, we hope you will constantly question our assertions as you read this book. Part One, "The Sociological Perspective," introduces sociology and explains how sociological research is conducted. Part

Two, "The Organization of Social Life," examines culture, organizations and social structures, social roles, and social groups. Part Three, "The Individual and Society," examines socialization, norms, rules, conformity, and deviance. Part Four, "Inequality and Stratification," analyzes the distribution of power in society, with emphasis on our society. Part Five, "Social Institutions," looks at the larger forms of social life. Part Six, "The Dynamics of Change," considers the events, issues, and structures that tend to ensure that things will remain as they are or that will bring about some rupture that fundamentally alters how individual lives are lived.

Within this organization, we have chosen to address some topics in depth that usually do not receive adequate coverage in an introductory textbook. Chapter 15, covering the criminal justice system, for example, discusses one of the largest institutional sectors in American society—a sector with far-reaching consequences and implications for individuals, groups, neighborhoods, and communities. Chapter 19 brings the sociological perspective to bear on the world of work—occupations, professions, careers. Chapters 18 and 20 examine two of the great tragedies of our times—the brutality of terrorism and the suffering caused by AIDS. We feel that such coverage is finally what sociology as a discipline must do. Sociology must constantly identify new problems and issues and then bring its methods and principles to bear, with the hope that the understanding gained might make a better world.

CHAPTER ORGANIZATION

Among the learning devices offered in *Sociology: Principles and Applications* are numerous boxed exhibits. Each chapter has at least one of the following exhibits.

1. *Research in Sociology*—a summary of the findings of a research study in the field of sociology that relates to a principle or problem under discussion in the chapter.
2. *Case Study*—a focused analysis of a particular phenomenon, issue, or problem that is crucial to the chapter discussion.
3. *Sociology in the Media*—an illustration of how the mass media—newspapers, newsmagazines, and television transcripts—report sociological issues or present current events related to sociological principles.
4. *Types & Stereotypes*—an examination of a stereotypically erroneous belief system related to chapter material.
5. *Sidelights on American Culture*—an illustration of some aspect of American culture that highlights a point being made in the chapter.
6. *Applied Sociology*—an illustration of the application of relevant sociological concepts to such areas as business, industry, government, or education.
7. *Sociological Focus*—an illustration of some sociological principle made using paradigms, tables, graphics, opinion polls, research findings, or current events.

In addition, each chapter also contains Social Indicators—boxed self-explanatory data (tables, graphs, opinion polls, maps, or lists) included to support points made in chapter discussions. Every chapter closes with a discussion of the applied "side" of sociological issues and principles.

ANCILLARIES AND SUPPORT MATERIALS

Because we believe strongly that materials to accompany textbooks should be an integral part of the instruction and evaluation process, we chose to develop and write these materials ourselves. We have prepared four ancillaries to accompany this textbook: a *Testbook,* a *Study Guide,* an *Instructor's Resource Guide,* and *Transparency Masters.*

1. The *Testbook,* available in both printed and disk formats, includes multiple-choice, true–false, and fill-in-the-blank questions for each chapter. At least 75 questions are included for each chapter, with each question keyed to the page in the textbook on which the answer may be found. All questions are graded with regard to degree of difficulty.

2. The *Study Guide* is designed to augment the textbook and contains at least one article per chapter illustrating ideas or concepts developed in the book and study questions for each reading. It also contains the usual complement of materials to enhance comprehension and to aid in exam preparation: objectives, lists of key concepts, and sample questions (both objective and essay).

3. The *Instructor's Resource Guide* offers suggestions for organizing and presenting material covered in the textbook, provides a narrative outline of the substance of each chapter, and includes a topical outline, key concepts, chapter objectives, and suggested discussion

questions. A key feature of this guide is a section called Supplementary Lecture Topics and Discussion Topics, which offers suggestions and ideas for developing points established in the text.

4. The *Transparency Masters* are a collection of camera-ready graphics—2 to 4 per chapter—that can easily be made into transparencies for use with overhead projectors. They are especially useful for introducing or summarizing ideas developed in the textbook. Most of the transparency masters have been taken from the textbook, but some are new.

ACKNOWLEDGMENTS

The number of debts accumulated in writing a textbook is surprisingly large. Gratitude must first go to our families, and particularly our wives—Carolyn J. Inciardi and Nancy Rothman—for their continuous support and encouragement throughout the entire process. We would also like to thank Melvin L. DeFleur, for his crucial role in the initial development of the book; our editor, Rick Roehrich, and our former editors at Academic Press and Harcourt Brace Jovanovich—Susan Loring, Warren Abraham, Marcus Boggs, and Johanna Schmid, whose input during the developmental process was invaluable; William Clements, Thomas Priest, and Allan McCutcheon for the material they contributed to the text; Alan Horowitz, for the time he devoted to the development of the testbook; and Kay Herzog, Patty Rothman, and Nancy Quillen for their assistance in editing, proofreading, and preparing a clean manuscript. We appreciate the efforts of the production team at HBJ—Helen Triller, Cheryl Hauser, Cheryl Solheid, Susan Holtz, Sarah Randall, and Eleanor Garner, who were responsible for the creation of this first edition. We are grateful to the following reviewers whose comments and suggestions resulted in the writing of a better book: Terry Arendell, Hunter College; Judith Blau, University of North Carolina, Chapel Hill; William T. Clute, University of Nebraska at Omaha; Phillip W. Davis, Georgia State University; Saul Feinman, University of Wyoming; Albeno P. Garbin, University of Georgia; Thomas F. Gieryn, Indiana University; Darnell F. Hawkins, University of Illinois at Chicago; Craig R. Humphrey, Pennsylvania State University; Janet G. Hunt, University of Maryland; William R. Kelly, University of Texas, Austin; Bruce London, Florida Atlantic University; Allan L. McCutcheon, University of Delaware; Patrick H. McNamara, University of New Mexico; Robert D. Mendelsohn, South Dakota State University; Fred Pampel, University of Iowa; T. B. Priest, Johnson C. Smith University; Harvey E. Rich, California State University, Northridge; William G. Roy, University of California, Los Angeles; Richard A. Schaffer, California Polytechnic State University; Steve Stack, Auburn University; Kenrick S. Thompson, Northern Michigan University; Bert Useem, University of Illinois at Chicago.

James A. Inciardi
Robert A. Rothman

Brief Contents

Contents

PART TWO The Organization of Social Life / 61

3 Culture / 62

4 Social Organization, Role Behavior, and Group Dynamics / 89

5 Formal Organizations / 121

PART THREE The Individual and Society / 151

6 Socialization: Self and Society / 152

7 Deviance and Crime: At Odds with Society / 181

PART FOUR Inequality and Stratification / 219

8 Socioeconomic Stratification / 220

15 Criminal Justice: Maintaining the Social Order / 466

PART SIX The Dynamics of Change / 505

16 Collective Behavior and Social Movements / 506

17 Urbanization, Industrialization, and Life in the City / 546

PART ONE

The Sociological Perspective

1 The Sociological Enterprise

Everyone understands something about life in society. Much of what we know is based on personal experience and on observations of the events that crowd into our own and other peoples' lives. Personal experience can be a valuable and important teacher that enables people to understand the society in which they live and how they function in it. Through personal experience, for example, even very young children can learn to anticipate the behavior of family members. Toddlers quickly grasp an elementary understanding of what pleases or angers parents and how to win their approval. Later on, children learn how to get along with playmates and teachers, and the importance of getting good grades and winning at sports. This process continues throughout adolescence and on into adulthood. In short, as people confront life's many new and differing situations, personal experience provides them with an ever-expanding storehouse of knowledge about society and social relationships.

But personal experience does have its shortcomings. First, it does not provide individuals with any understanding of social worlds other than their own, even within their own culture. Most law-abiding citizens, for example, have no firsthand experience with the murky worlds of heroin addiction, cocaine trafficking, or street prostitution. Most people are equally uninformed about what life would be like working on an automobile assembly line in Tokyo or Detroit, attending the elite boarding schools of the super-rich, or living in the gay and avant-garde communities of San Francisco's North Beach. Growing up on the streets of New York City's South Bronx does not teach much about the beliefs and values that dominate life in Iowa farm country and even more obscure are social patterns of the remote societies in Sri Lanka, Nepal, Tasmania, and the Solomon Islands.

Personal experience also tends to mask larger social patterns. Whether a family moves from Dayton to Houston or from Philadelphia to Miami is an individual event, but such single events are often part of broader social trends that transform the social landscape. American society is currently experiencing immigration and dramatic population shifts, profound changes in the composition of the work force and the nature of jobs, fluctuating rates of crime, and the emergence of new religions. Thus, personal experience must be considered within a broad social context.

Finally, using personal experience as a gauge by which to measure life in society may lead to the acceptance of errors of fact that impede understanding. For example, many of America's "homeless" are considered to be lazy, shiftless drunks. It probably is impossible to identify a "typical" homeless person. Some are indeed unmotivated, but a major portion of the homeless population has been driven to the streets by unemployment, lack of affordable housing, or domestic abuse. Many are children, while others are the mentally ill who have nowhere else to live. It is easy to see how such "common knowledge" can be flawed.

In sum, personal experience is an imperfect, narrow, and very selective teacher. It usually provides firsthand knowledge of only a limited segment of one society, often leaving many unanswered questions and troublesome errors. By contrast, the value of sociology is its broad focus on social relations and events. Sociology offers a unique way of looking at the world and posing crucial questions. For example, consider the following:

Most Americans lack an understanding of the plight of the homeless, who are often reduced to washing and drying their clothing in public restrooms.

- On the afternoon of December 22, 1984, four youths aboard a New York City subway car approached a well-dressed man by the name of Bernhard Hugo Goetz. They asked him for $5. Goetz, a 37-year-old electrical engineer, pulled a silver revolver from his pocket, fired on the youths at point-blank range, and fled from the train, while the rest of the passengers scrambled to the floor in terror. In the aftermath of the incident, millions across the nation applauded Goetz. He became an instant American folk hero: songs were sung about him; he was the topic of tens of thousands of television editorials, radio commentaries, and newspaper columns; donations began to accumulate for his legal defense; and politicians used the event as a prod to push for tough new anticrime legislation. What can explain this sudden and rather peculiar mass reaction to an isolated subway shooting?

- In previous generations conventional norms dictated very specific family arrangements in American society. The acceptable pattern included a man and a woman who were legally married to one another, and generally two or more children. While the father worked to support the family, the mother stayed home to cook, clean, and care for the children. Sex before marriage, the birth of children out of wedlock, working mothers, and divorce were viewed with disdain. Today, the norms are considerably different, and a variety of alternative life-styles not only are tolerated but have become accepted as common practice. What factors contributed to the changing patterns and values concerning marriage, the family, and intimate living?

- Societies are divided into a variety of different class levels. People with diverse social and occupational positions have alternative amounts of wealth, power, and prestige. Moreover, they seem to act differently and share different sets of attitudes and values. In the United States, the boundaries between the classes tend to be loosely defined, and people readily can move from one social level to another. Yet in other places, people generally spend their entire lives in the class position into which they were born. Why are power, wealth, and social position distributed so differently? How does such a distribution occur? What explains the differences between the classes? Why does social mobility exist in some societies and not in others?
- Throughout the 1960s and 1970s, there was a nationwide increase in crime rates in the United States. This increase was so alarming that "law and order" and "crime control" became political slogans in local and national elections. Then suddenly, in 1981, crime rates appeared to shift. A downward trend developed that lasted for several years. Surprisingly, this shift in the crime rates during the early 1980s had been predicted by sociologists almost two decades earlier. Not only had their forecasts indicated that there would be a decline, but they also accurately projected that it would begin in approximately 1980. Why did the rising crime rate suddenly reverse, and how was it possible to anticipate it accurately?
- During the first half of the twentieth century, students were told to stay in school. "Get your high-school diploma," their parents argued. "It's the key to success." By the 1950s and 1960s, however, people had begun to stress the link between a college degree and rapid career mobility. But in the 1980s, many college graduates began having difficulty finding meaningful work, and this problem seemed to persist in spite of the increased number of positions requiring higher education. How has the occupational structure changed to produce this situation? Has higher education failed to keep up-to-date with the changes? What is the future of work in America?

SOCIAL INDICATOR

Rates of Violent Crime (per 100,000 population)

Year	Rate	Year	Rate
1960	159.0	1974	461.1
1961	156.4	1975	487.8
1962	160.5	1976	467.8
1963	166.2	1977	475.9
1964	188.2	1978	497.8
1965	197.6	1979	548.9
1966	217.2	1980	596.6
1967	250.0	1981	594.3
1968	294.6	1982	571.1
1969	324.4	1983	537.7
1970	360.0	1984	539.2
1971	396.0	1985	556.2
1972	401.0	1986	617.3
1973	417.4	1987	609.7

Source: Federal Bureau of Investigation, *Uniform Crime Reports*, 1987.

Sociology encourages us to look beyond individual cases and immediate events and to seek to understand them in the broader context of the society in which they occur. A specific crime, family break-up, or unemployment problem is placed in the context of larger social events. In addition to posing questions in its own unique way, sociology plays two other important roles: it provides the tools and mechanisms through which social phenomena can be investigated, and it provides a variety of perspectives within which information about social behavior can be interpreted.

UNRAVELING THE SOCIOLOGICAL ENTERPRISE

Sociology generally is defined as the scientific study of society, including the relationships between people and patterns of social life. This brief definition is hardly satisfactory, however, for it says little about the subject matter of sociology and nothing about how sociologists approach their work. To begin with, sociology involves a certain way of doing research. That is, sociology is a discipline that makes use of the scientific method for studying social phenomena. Sociological research may comprise using questionnaires and conducting interviews to uncover attitudes, values, and behavior patterns. The study of religious beliefs or drug use might proceed in this manner. An alternative strategy could focus on the examination of specific kinds of documents, such as census data, unemployment figures, or police records. In other cases sociologists might rely on systematic observation of groups in action. With this technique researchers have traced the evolution of prison riots, documented the formation and destruction of religious sects, and examined the structure and distribution of urban street gangs (see Exhibit 1.1).

Exhibit 1.1

Case Study

The Gang

Sociological research at the University of Chicago during the 1920s was profoundly influenced by the thinking of sociologist Robert E. Park and his conception of the "natural areas" of the city. Natural areas were the various subcommunities that Park noted in Chicago and other cities with which he was familiar, that served as vehicles for urban freedom as well as urban disorganization. As noted by Park:

> The urban community turns out, upon closer scrutiny, to be a mosaic of minor communities, many of them strikingly different from one another, but all more or less typical. Every city has its central business district; the focal point of the whole urban complex. Every city, every great city has its more or less exclusive residential suburbs; its areas of light and heavy industry, satellite cities, and casual labor mart, where men are recruited for rough work on distant frontiers, in the mines and in the forests, in the building of railways or in the borings and excavations for the vast structures of our modern cities. Every American city has its slums; its ghettos; its immigrant colonies, regions which maintain more or less alien and exotic culture. Nearly every large city has its bohemias and hobohemias, where life is freer, more adventurous and lonely than it is elsewhere. These are the so-called natural areas of the city.[a]

The natural areas were the key to Park's view of the city and the initial thread of his theory of urbanization. His students went out to study the natural areas of Chicago, and among the students was Frederic M. Thrasher, who can be credited with the first extensive sociological study of gangs.[b]

Thrasher studied 1,313 different gangs (containing 25,000 members) that were concentrated around Chicago's Loop—the central business district. He concluded that gangs are characteristically found in geographically and socially "interstitial" areas. Interstitial areas are transitional urban localities typically found between industrial and residential districts. The interstitial areas of Chicago where Thrasher's gangs were found were situated in sections where expanding industrial plants were encroaching upon the city's older residential quarters, resulting in a high degree of cultural isolation.

The gangs were found to have formed spontaneously, representing mechanisms whereby slum children and adolescents achieved satisfaction not otherwise accessible in their underprivileged environments. In general, a loose internal structure, a common spirit of devotion and enthusiasm, solidarity, group awareness, and an attachment to some local territory characterized the gangs.

Thrasher presented detailed descriptions of many diverse types of gangs to illustrate his findings. A typical "tough" gang that he observed was the "Murderers":

> Shortly after the race riots of 1919, residents in the vicinity south of the stockyards were startled one morning by a number of placards bearing the inscription "The Murderers, 20,000 Strong, 48th & Ada." In this way attention was attracted to a gang of thirty Polish boys, who hung out in a district known as the Bush.
>
> The pastimes of the boys were loafing, smoking, chewing, crap-shooting, card-playing, pool, and bowling. Every morning they would get together at their corner or in their shack nearby to "chew the rag" and talk over the events of the day. . . .
>
> They broke into boxcars and "robbed" bacon and other merchandise. They cut out wire cables to sell as junk. They broke open telephone boxes. They took autos for joyriding. . . .
>
> Most of them were habitual truants, and they acknowledged their commitments to the parental school (house of detention) with great pride. Many of them had been in the juvenile detention home and the jail. Their "records" were a matter of considerable prestige in the group.

Although Thrasher's study of juvenile gangs was conducted more than a half century ago, it is significant nevertheless for its contribution as a portrayal of gang activities and the satisfactions obtained therein that still are applicable to many contemporary slums.[c]

SOURCES:

a. Robert E. Park, *Human Communities* (Glencoe, IL: Free Press, 1952), p. 196.

b. Frederic M. Thrasher, *The Gang* (Chicago: University of Chicago Press, 1926).

c. See Maurice R. Stein, *The Eclipse of Community* (Princeton: Princeton University Press, 1960), p. 36.

The scientific method (discussed in greater detail in Chapter 2) involves rules for the collection and analysis of data—rules that are not altogether unlike those found in physics, chemistry, and the other natural sciences. But in contrast with these so-called "hard sciences," social science research faces a special set of problems because it deals with people and human behavior, which is very complex and sometimes difficult to understand.

Concepts, Theories, and Hypotheses

All research, regardless of the scientific discipline to which it is related, is organized around concepts, hypotheses, and theories.

A **concept** is a term or label that describes or identifies a category of behaviors, characteristics, or events. In sociology, "suicide," "violence," and "arrest" are easily understood concepts. However, more useful are those concepts that focus on social arrangements and forces that influence the behavior of groups of people. *Prestige,* for example, a concept indicating the respect that people accord to others, is of considerable use to sociologists because of the ways it can shape patterns of behavior. It has been demonstrated that people value the respect of their peers and superiors, with the result that they act in ways they feel will improve their status.[1]

Sociological research is guided and directed by social theories. A **theory** in the most general sense is an attempt to describe or explain relationships among concepts. Some theories focus on very limited areas of human behavior, such as the causes of drug addiction or the rising rates of teenage suicide. More ambitious theories seek to explain the structure of whole societies or to uncover the sources of human motivation.

The accuracy of social theories is determined by formulating and testing hypotheses. A **hypothesis** is a statement of anticipated relationships between concepts. It is an "educated guess" about connections between two or more concepts. Although they may not always be recognized as such, many of the "common-sense" ideas about life that people often cling to are rudimentary hypotheses implying social theories of human behavior. Drawing on the remarks in Exhibit 1.2, consider the hypothesis that "the death penalty deters homicide." This hypothesis proposes a causal relationship between two concepts—a certain type of punishment and the occurrence of murder. The theory underlying the hypothesis, however faulty, is that the certainty of paying the ultimate penalty will discourage people from killing one another. This hypothesis has been tested many times. The fact that sociological research fails to confirm this common-sense notion hints at the contribution that sociology can make in understanding social behavior.[2]

SOCIAL INDICATOR

Teenage–Young Adult Suicide Rates

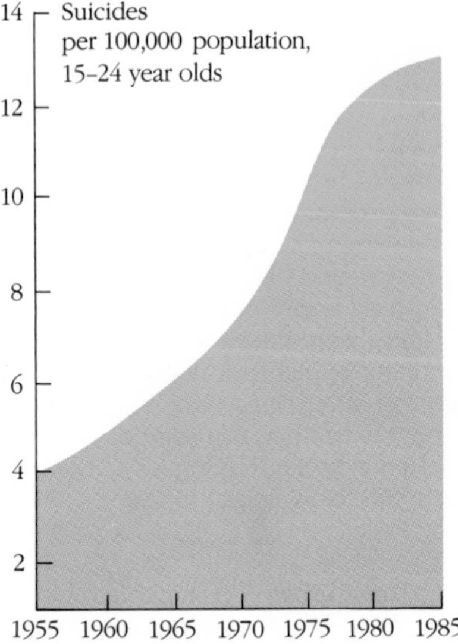

Source: National Center for Health Statistics, 1985.

The Sociological Perspective

The complexity of human behavior and the many factors influencing how people behave make it necessary for theory and research in sociology to have a unique perspective, a distinct way of looking at the world.

The sociological perspective can be illustrated by focusing on a particular element of behavior—performance in school, for example. A popular explanation (hypothesis) involving school performance is that intelligence explains school achievement. Intelligence is usually measured by IQ tests and school performance by grades. Certainly intelligence makes a difference, but it alone fails to tell the whole story. Many students with high IQs get low grades and never finish school, while others with considerably lower IQ scores are able to succeed. The sociological perspective insists that many other factors be considered: the social environment in which children are nurtured; their experiences with parents, friends, and teachers; their race and gender; the organization of schools and classrooms; and the structure of the entire educational system.

Thus, the **sociological perspective** is an approach to social phenomena that takes into consideration the group context of individual behaviors, patterned social interactions, and the impact of social structure.

Exhibit 1.2

Types & Stereotypes

It Is a Known Fact That the Death Penalty Deters Homicide!

The perceived "common-sense" relationship between homicide and the deterrent effects of the death penalty is so strong that the majority of Americans fully support the execution of convicted murderers. However, what does sociological research have to say on the matter?

A number of studies have examined the deterrent effects of capital punishment. One strategy compared the homicide rates in states that have death penalty provisions to the rates in states that do not. Another approach examined murder rates in given areas both before and after an execution. Still a third approach analyzed crime rates and murder rates in various jurisdictions both before and after the abolition of capital punishment. Regardless of the nature and logic of the inquiry conducted, the studies consistently have failed to produce evidence that the death penalty deters homicide.

On the contrary, strong evidence suggests that the death penalty may have a "brutalization" effect—that is, that executions prompt *more* rather than *fewer* murders. Researchers William J. Bowers and Glenn L. Pierce examined the effects of the death penalty on homicides in New York state. Their data included monthly homicide figures from January 1907 through August 1964 (a year after New York's last execution) and monthly execution figures from January 1906 through August 1963. Their findings indicated that a brutalizing effect did indeed occur with at least two extra homicides taking place in the month following an execution and a small carry-over effect continuing into the next month.

SOURCES: William J. Bowers, *Legal Homicide: Death as Punishment in America, 1864–1982* (Boston: Northeastern University Press, 1984); William J. Bowers and Glenn L. Pierce, "Deterrence or Brutalization: What Is the Effect of Executions?" *Crime and Delinquency*, 26 (1980), pp. 453–84.

The Group Context of Individual Behaviors

Social groups are collections of people who live or work together for extended periods of time. Most, if not all, members of any given group develop similar values and behavior patterns. This simple observation seems to be true not only of such small social groups as families, street-corner gangs, and dormitory residents, but also of larger aggregations such as religious groups and entire societies. Each group influences the ways in which its members experience and respond to the world at large. In this context, sociological research focusing on the progress of students through the American educational system has found that some students perform unusually well. A case in point involves the children of Asian-American parents. Is their superior scholarship the result of biology? Quite to the contrary, an examination of the early childhood experiences of many Asian-American children has revealed that these youngsters were exposed early to the virtues of hard work and academic success. This training manifested itself in the amount of time spent studying—fourteen hours per week, or double that of other students.[3] Here, the sociological perspective suggests that educational performance is probably influenced by group-based values and behaviors, irrespective of the gender, ethnic affiliation, or social class of the individuals involved.

Patterned Social Interactions

Relationships among individuals develop and progress through a process of social interaction. The concept of **patterned social interaction** refers to the observation that people respond to others not only as individuals, but also on the basis of group membership and social position. It is unlikely that the classroom experiences of the children of the poor are the same as those of the sons and daughters of senators, bank presidents, and corporate executives. Moreover, research has indicated that the encounters of male students tend to be quite different from those of female students, even among those in the same social position. Systematic classroom observation has indicated that teachers consistently give preferential treatment to male students. Males are called on more often, they are given more time to answer, and they

SOCIAL INDICATOR

Percent of Degrees Awarded to Women

Degree	1970	1985	1987
Bachelors	43%	50%	51%
Masters	40	53	50
Doctorate	14	37	36

Source: National Center for Education Statistics, 1987.

are coached more and interrupted less than female students. "All too often," the research concluded, "neither faculty nor students are aware of these patterns of behavior—and it is then that they can do the most harm. Without knowing precisely why, individual women students may come to feel and to behave as though they are marginal participants in the academic enterprise."[4]

A more thorough sociological analysis requires an understanding of the origins of these patterns of group social interaction, the cultural ideas about men and women that support such patterns, the meanings people attach to them, and the reactions to unequal treatment. Nevertheless, a basic observation of the sociological perspective seems to be valid: in all human interaction, social relationships are patterned on the basis of group membership and social position.

The Impact of Social Structure

Social structure is a concept that refers to stable and enduring social arrangements. It involves the more or less consistent patterns of *personal* (individual) and *interpersonal* (between people) action and relationships that serve as the organizing framework of the social life of a whole society or one of its integral parts. The social structure of contemporary schools, for example, is characterized by a variety of features, including systems of authority and promotion. The authority system places the responsibility for conducting classes in the hands of teachers, rather than in those of students. The promotion system is generally based on academic performance. One structural element that is common in most secondary schools is *tracking*—an arrangement whereby students are grouped on the basis of ability and/or career goals.[5] While there is a sound educational rationale for organizing the system in this way as a means of preparing students for alternative careers, tracking also has implications for students that are not necessarily intended.

The most enduring consequence of tracking is permanence. Students in any given track—be it college prep, business, vocational/technical, or general—almost never leave it, except to move downward. Tracking socially segregates track members. Students in any given track typically attend the same classes and socialize only with their classmates. Track placement also produces changes in measured IQ scores. The scores of those in higher tracks tend to rise, while those of students in the lower tracks are likely to fall. Moreover, lower track students receive fewer As, even when they are at the top of their sections.[6] In short, the social structure of the American educational enterprise can have a lasting impact on students in a variety of ways. This relationship raises a number of questions of considerable sociological interest. Why, for example, do such social structures exist, and who really benefits from them?

THE SOCIAL SCIENCES: CONSENSUS AND DIVERSITY

When combined with the efforts of the other social sciences—anthropology, political science, economics, psychology, and history—sociology offers the opportunity for a broad and balanced understanding of social behavior.

All of the social sciences evolved separately, with each one developing its own unique perspectives, concepts, and theories. These separate evolutionary patterns, combined with the fact that each of the social sciences generally constitutes a separate department in American colleges and universities, tend to give the impression that none of the social sciences has anything in common with any of the others. Although they tend to differ in terms of their basic orientations toward social behavior, however, they do indeed have much in common.

Anthropology

Anthropology is literally the scientific study of humanity, but what distinguishes it from the other social sciences is not so much *what* is being studied as *the manner in which* it is studied. Anthropologists generally focus on small-scale, primitive societies, often living among the members of such groups in order to observe them directly. Anthropology has, furthermore, a variety of branches. *Cultural* anthropologists scrutinize the social inheritance of existing societies that is passed on through social and cultural experiences; *physical* anthropologists examine human evolution through the analysis of fossils; and researchers in *archeology* attempt to reconstruct extinct societies through an interpretation of their artifacts.

Cultural anthropology is by far the largest branch of anthropology. Moreover, it is related closely to sociology in that both disciplines study "society." Cultural anthropology originated with the study of small, nonindustrialized societies, often located in out-of-the-way regions of the world. Part of the original fascination with these societies was rooted in the unusual beliefs and customs that separated them from Western civilization. The observation of these customs led to the development of the concept of culture, the study of how cultures emerge, and how they change and interact with other cultures. Modern cultural anthropologists continue to examine nonindustrial cultures, but their research also extends to contemporary subgroups and communities of larger societies, such as religious groups, farmers, heroin users, steel workers, or Mexican-Americans.

Political Science

The field of **political science** deals primarily with the ways in which governmental power is acquired, channeled, and used in society. Historically, political scientists have concentrated on the formal organization of governments. More recently, these researchers have broadened their objectives to include inquiries into the nature of political behavior at all levels of society: how individuals acquire and exercise political knowledge and the consequences of particular political policies and programs. As a result, some contemporary political science research is almost indistinguishable from that undertaken in sociology.

A significant contribution made by political science has been the popularization of opinion polling. Such polls, which now go well beyond the measurement of voting preferences to gauge a wide variety of social attitudes, also play a central role in sociology. Sample surveys conducted in the same manner as political polls have permitted sociologists to examine the strength and parameters of opinion on such issues as abortion, gun control, the death penalty, and women's rights, and to isolate the factors that contribute to the formation of these opinions.

Economics

Perhaps the most highly specialized of the social sciences, **economics** focuses on the production and distribution of goods and services, and patterns of consumption throughout society. Major issues include supply and demand, profit and loss, costs, interest, taxes, and income.

Much of what modern economists do can be committed to numbers, and as a result, economics is by far the most statistically sophisticated of the social sciences. Through mathematical models, for example, economists can chart the dollar value of all of the goods and services produced by a nation in a given year (the gross national product or GNP, which tells sociologists about comparative living standards); they can record the value of all imports and exports to calculate the flow of money (the balance of payments) and its implications for employment; and they can determine the amounts of money people have to spend freely after the payment of bills and taxes (the disposable income).

Although such economic issues as poverty levels, unemployment rates, and consumer behavior also attract the interest of sociologists, the central working assumption of economics is often at odds with the sociological perspective. The premise of economics that individuals and groups act rationally to maximize their self-interest (usually expressed as income) does not appear to pertain equally to all areas of human endeavor. People regularly sacrifice monetary rewards in the pursuit of prestige and

SOCIAL INDICATOR

Per-Capita GNP of Selected Nations

Australia	$11,910	Japan	$12,860
Bolivia	540	Laos	83
Canada	14,100	Libya	6,663
China	300	Mexico	1,860
Ethiopia	120	South Africa	1,800
Greece	3,680	Uganda	191
Haiti	330	**U.S.**	**17,500**
India	270	U.S.S.R.	7,400

Source: Population Reference Bureau, 1988.

In the holy war between Iran and Iraq, parents were apparently willing to sacrifice even their children in the name of religion.

social approval and often sacrifice even their lives in the name of patriotism, nationalism, or religion.

Psychology

While the focus of sociological research is on groups and societies, **psychology** research is concerned primarily with human mental processes and individual behavior. Psychologists seek to understand how the senses work, how individuals learn habits of behavior, why some individuals are more intelligent than others, how a person gives meaning to life's events, how the memory operates, and what motivates some people to act in particular ways.

In its attempts to answer these questions, psychology encompasses a broad range of research that goes well beyond the purview of sociology, most notably to the biological and physiological bases of human behavior and the study of animal species for inferences to humans. But sociology and psychology do overlap in an area known as *social psychology*. Developed during the early years of the twentieth century, social psychology represents an attempt to understand how social experiences impact on the mental activities of the individual. In many colleges and universities, courses in social psychology are taught in both sociology and psychology departments.

History

Scholars have debated for many years whether **history,** defined broadly as the study of the past, is a social science or one of the humanities. Early historians displayed little interest in science. Historians recorded, recounted, and reinterpreted the events of the past, focusing exclusively on the facts of what had taken place. In that sense, history was purely descriptive and was similar to the humanities. It was seldom that any two historians agreed on how an event occurred, and research rarely was grounded in the rigors of scientific inquiry. By contrast, modern historical research reflects objective methods for studying the events of the past and has adopted the scientific orientation. Moreover, many contemporary historians have extended their discipline into the realm of sociology by examining the social forces that influenced historical events.

In retrospect, sociology, along with anthropology, political science, economics, psychology, and history can be grouped together as social sciences in that they study human behavior and share a commitment to the scientific method. Although the social sciences may examine many of the same topics, however, each approaches them in its own unique way (see Exhibit 1.3).

THE HISTORICAL CONTEXT OF MODERN SOCIOLOGY

Although sociology emerged as an independent social science in the relatively recent past, the study of society began more than twenty centuries ago. Yet for the better part of these many years, the history of social thought was an embarrassment of riches. From Plato and Aristotle of ancient Greece to the philosophers of seventeenth- and eighteenth-century Europe, there was extensive commentary on *what* the ideal society ought to be like and *how* it might be achieved, but there was no concrete mechanism for objectively determining what recommendations were most appropriate.

The origins of modern sociology can be traced to the middle of the nineteenth century when the people who were to define the field were attempting to make sense of the many sudden disruptions that were occurring in the world around them. It was a time of rapid social change. The founders of sociology were among those who attempted to understand the nature of that change and to alleviate the suffering it had caused.

Sociology and the Dual Revolutions

It was hardly an accident that sociology emerged when it did. As the eighteenth century drew to a close, European society found itself amidst the chaos of dual revolutions. The *French Revolution* and the Napoleonic Wars had torn apart the ancient monarchies that had ruled for so many centuries, and the *Industrial Revolution* had accelerated the transition from a stable agricultural and commercial society to modern industrialism. The result was a series of relatively abrupt social, political, and economic transformations.

Along with the decline of the agrarian way of life and the growth of worldwide commerce, the invention of steam-powered machinery initiated the proliferation of numerous industries, coal mining, and the use of steel. Families from rural areas, uprooted from their traditional life-styles, sought work in the greatly enlarged factory sector by migrating to the spreading cities. There, housing shortages were acute and living standards were dismal. In the factories, where people from many different backgrounds were thrown together under one roof for low and uncertain wages, working conditions were grim. In the midst of this disorder and disruption, the nature of family life was affected as well. Factory wages were generally so low that husband, wife, and children had to spend 12–18 hours a day working, often 6 or 7 days a week. The consequences of all of these changes included poverty, rising crime rates, a declining life expectancy for the urban poor, and the emergence of

An immigrant family of seven shared this crowded tenement room in 1910. They were typical of the new urban poor produced by the Industrial Revolution.

a new social class of impoverished industrial workers. Within such a setting, it is no wonder that nineteenth-century social philosophers and reformers began looking for new ways to understand and deal with the chaos and deprivations of the new industrial society.

The Foundations of Modern Theory

Many individuals contributed to the development of sociology, yet the names of most are lost to all but those who specialize in the history of sociology. However, several individuals must be singled out for their lasting impact on the discipline.

Auguste Comte (1798–1857)

The French social philosopher **Auguste Comte** is generally credited as the "founder of sociology." In 1839 he gave sociology its name, and he was among the first to believe that the scientific method could be directly applied to the study of society. His major work, *The Positive Philosophy,* broadly outlined the subject matter of sociology and explained how the methods of science could be used to study social organization and behavior. Comte's treatise also formulated two major areas of sociological investigation: *social statics* (the structure and order of society) and *social dynamics* (the patterns of social evolution and change).[7]

Although the development of sociology evolved from Comte, he was in many ways an idealist and a romantic social dreamer. As a result, many of his ideas were considerably flawed. He believed, for example, that there were absolute "laws" of social behavior. Once these laws were learned, Comte maintained, sociologists could predict or even control, social events. Therefore, he argued sociology should be regarded as the "queen of the sciences." He envisioned the emergence of a "priesthood of positivism" in which sociologists would be both scientists and elite leaders. In fact, this new spiritual elite, headed by Comte himself, would run the new social order. With their specialized knowledge, they would right the wrongs of their chaotic society and guide humanity on its march to utopia.

Herbert Spencer (1820–1903)

Herbert Spencer, perhaps the most respected of the nineteenth-century British social philosophers, was strongly influenced by Charles Darwin's theory of biological evolution and suggested that like animal species, human societies gradually changed from simple to complex forms. The application of evolutionary theory to human social life is called **social Darwinism.** As societies evolved, only those individuals and institutions that could successfully compete would survive. Thus, the principles of "natural selection" and "survival of the fittest," when applied to the social universe as Darwin had applied them to the animal world, eliminated the weak in accordance with immutable laws of nature.[8]

The significance of Spencer's analysis was that it led him to a number of seemingly logical conclusions about the wisdom of interfering with the processes of social change. He reasoned that if society was indeed following evolutionary laws along its path of development, then any attempt to alter its inevitable course would be sheer madness. Therefore, Spencer strongly advocated the adoption of a policy of **laissez faire** (a doctrine adopted from the field of economics that holds that systems work best when there is no government interference), believing that a better society would evolve naturally if simply left alone. In fact, Spencer fought strongly against such measures as free public education, welfare programs, and any other assistance that would serve to benefit those that he considered to be "the weak." Not surprisingly, this position was found profoundly acceptable by the wealthy and powerful of Spencer's day because it gave "scientific" approval to both inequality and capitalistic enterprise.

Contemporary sociologists continue to view society as undergoing a process of evolutionary change. This approach is particularly evident in the structural-functionalist school of sociological theory, which is discussed later in this chapter. However, Spencer's elaborate organic analogy and his conclusions about the immutable laws of nature, natural selection, and the survival of the fittest as inevitably leading to utopian

Exhibit 1.3

Sociological Focus

Cocaine-Use Research and the Social Sciences

Cocaine is derived from the leaves of *erythroxylum coca,* one of some 250 species of coca plants that are native to the Andean region of South America. In recent years cocaine has become the all-American drug. Once the sinful secret of the moneyed elite and the exotic indulgence of high-gloss entrepreneurs, cocaine is now the drug of choice of millions of conventional middle-class Americans.

The current popularity of cocaine stems from the fact that many perceive it to be a relatively risk-free drug. Just one snort in each nostril and the user is flying high—alert, witty, and "with it" for 20 minutes or more—no hangover, no physical dependence, no holes in the arms or burned-out brain cells, and no need to constantly increase the dosage to achieve the desired effect. Instead, the drug yields drive, sparkle, energy, and that emblem of conspicuous consumption so often associated with wealth and status. Yet despite its popularity, cocaine is illegal. Cocaine possession is a felony in all fifty states. Moreover, of all the drugs in the United States, cocaine is the largest producer of illicit income—estimated in 1987 to involve as much as $100 billion annually.

The widespread use of cocaine has stimulated considerable research in all of the social sciences, each from its own unique perspective.

Bolivian women sell the coca leaves from which cocaine is made.

Anthropology researchers, with their focus on peasant societies, have examined the practice of coca-leaf chewing among the Indian laborers of Bolivia and Peru. Noted early in the sixteenth century by Dominican missionaries, coca chewing has been a cultural pattern in the Andes for centuries. It is common even today, for the mild stimulation engendered by the leaves enables workers to endure the burdens of their long days at hard labor in the mines and fields. Recent studies among Peruvian Indians have investigated the rituals and beliefs associated with the chewing of coca and have suggested that since coca chewing tends to raise the blood-sugar level, the practice probably emerged as an aspect of peasant folk medicine.[a]

Political science researchers, given their concern with the ways in which power is acquired and used, have examined the effects of cocaine trafficking on legislation, government functioning, and international relations. Recent research in this regard has focused attention on the political problems that cocaine has produced in South America—the securing of power by traffickers or their representatives at all levels of government; the indirect control of government posts through corruption and violence; the political instabilities that result from the unwillingness to arrest and imprison traffickers; the antigovernment terrorism that cocaine dollars finance; and the loss of government control in areas of coca production and smuggling.[b]

Economics research has typically focused on cocaine trafficking, with particular emphasis on the drug's effects on inflation, government economic planning, exchange rates and black market currency values, and wages in the coca- and cocaine-producing nations. In one study, for example, it was found that more than $3 billion entered the economy of Colombia in 1979 directly through trafficking and illicit crop cultivation and processing. Investment of these drug dollars was generally limited to luxury housing and resort hotel construction. The result was the bidding up of prices in the building industry well beyond their already inflationary levels, thus pricing lower- and middle-income families out of the housing market.[c]

Psychology researchers have concentrated on the reasons why people use cocaine and the effects of the drug on thinking, emotions, motivation, and personality. It has been found that although cocaine does not cause addiction in the physical sense, psychic dependence does indeed occur. After long-term involvement with cocaine, the user tends to compulsively seek the extreme mood elevation, elation, and grandiose feelings of heightened physical and mental prowess that the drug induces. When the drug's effects begin to diminish, a deep depression develops, which constitutes such a marked contrast to the user's previous state that he or she is strongly motivated to repeat the dosage and restore the euphoria.[d]

History researchers have been examining coca and cocaine for more than a century. Early studies documented the role of coca in the lives of the Incas of Peru, its subsequent spread throughout South America, and the eventual use of coca and cocaine during the latter part of the nineteenth century. More recent efforts have looked at cocaine use in the current century as well as legislative efforts to control it.[e]

Sociology investigators have been particularly active in studying cocaine use as an American social pattern. Research has attempted to measure the incidence and prevalence of cocaine use in the United States, explain the popularity of cocaine as a recreational drug, and document the drug's differing patterns of abuse. One of the more interesting studies examined the many beliefs and myths about cocaine—that it is an aphrodisiac, that it increases creative and physical performance, that it has no bad effects, that its cost is related to its purity and potency, and that a cold shower is a good antidote for cocaine intoxication.[f]

SOURCES:

a. Roderick E. Burchard, "Coca Chewing: A New Perspective," in Vera Rubin (ed.), *Cannabis and Culture* (The Hague: Mouton, 1975), pp. 463–84; June Nash, *We Eat the Mines and the Mines Eat Us: Dependency and Exploitation in Bolivian Tin Mines* (New York: Columbia University Press, 1979).

b. Harvey F. Kline, "New Directions for Colombia," *Current History,* 84 (February 1985), pp. 65–68; David L. Strug, "The Foreign Politics of Cocaine: Comments on a Plan to Eradicate the Coca Leaf in Peru," *Journal of Drug Issues,* (Winter 1983), pp. 135–45.

c. Peter A. Lupsha, "The Political Economy of Drug Trafficking," paper presented at the annual meeting of the Latin American Studies Association, Bloomington, IN, October 16–20, 1980.

d. James V. Spotts and Franklin C. Shontz, *Cocaine Users: A Representative Case Approach* (New York: Free Press, 1980).

e. Gerald T. McLaughlin, "Cocaine: The History and Regulation of a Dangerous Drug," *Cornell Law Review,* 58 (1973), pp. 537–72; W. G. Mortimer, *Peru: History of Coca, the Divine Plant of the Incas* (New York: J. H. Vail, 1901).

f. James A. Inciardi, *The War on Drugs: Heroin, Cocaine, Crime, and Public Policy* (Palo Alto, CA: Mayfield, 1986); Ronald K. Siegel, "Changing Patterns of Cocaine Use," in John Grabowski (ed.), *Cocaine: Pharmacology, Effects, and Treatment of Abuse* (Rockville, MD: National Institute on Drug Abuse, 1984), pp. 92–110.

society have long since been abandoned. Moreover, few sociologists would agree that a policy of laissez faire would be wise or morally acceptable.

Karl Marx (1818–1883)

Most Americans think of **Karl Marx** as a political writer and radical activist who formulated the philosophical basis of communism. In many respects that is exactly what he was, for he never thought of himself as a sociologist. In sharp contrast to the laissez-faire approach urged by Spencer, Marx sought a more just society. Conscious of the disorder the Industrial Revolution created, his intent was to change society by wresting political control from those who owned the factories and other means of production and placing power in the hands of the workers. However, his writings were almost immediately recognized as important to the emerging science of sociology.

Marx maintained that the changes in the nature of production brought about by the Industrial Revolution had separated laborers from all the rewarding aspects of work. Factory owners determined *what* would be produced, *to whom* products would be sold, *what* prices would be charged, and *how much* a laborer's effort was worth. Workers had no say in these decisions. Moreover, by breaking up the production of every item into a series of easily performed tasks—a procedure demanded by the very essence of machine manufacturing—workers were even denied the satisfaction of accomplishment. In such a situation, work had become impersonal and demeaning; in contrast with all past human experiences, machines were suddenly in control of people. Moreover, for the sake of garnering profits for themselves, factory owners "exploited" the workers as completely as they did the machines and raw materials. Working hours were long and wages were kept as low as possible to maximize profits. Marx argued that the owners got rich while the workers barely survived.

With his collaborator, Friedrich Engels, Marx supported the notion of **economic determinism**—the contention that every aspect of social life is patterned on economic relationships. More specifically, Marx stated that societies are characterized by competition and conflict among groups possessed of unequal power that are attempting to foster their own interests. Thus, it was ultimately a question of economic power that explained the structure of societies and social relationships. Marx noted that even the social planning Comte advocated would be ineffective in alleviating the problems of the urban worker, for privileged groups would not willingly concede their advantaged positions. Thus, meaningful social change could result only from a struggle between the competing groups.

As a general theory of human history, the Marxist view focused on revolutionary rather than evolutionary change. Social classes were seen as the central agents of change. In an industrial society, as the conditions of the *proletariat* (the disadvantaged workers) worsened, they would eventually organize to overthrow the *bourgeoisie* (the owners or capitalists).[9] Ultimately, Marx believed, after the laborers took control of the means of production for themselves, there would be no more social classes and no more struggle; humanity would at last be free. Under a new system of socialism, there would be public, collective ownership of the means of production, distribution, and exchange, operated for *use* rather than for *profit,* thus assuring to each member of society an equitable share of the available goods and services.

Many people have found it fashionable to dismiss Marx because of his association with a particular political ideology—one that is linked with the totalitarianism of Soviet-bloc countries. That tendency, however, ignores the importance of Marx's perspective at a broader level. Few would argue that history has not witnessed instances of domination and exploitation or conflict and competition among individuals and groups in society.

As a final note here, it is important to comment further on the contribution of Marx's collaborator,

---

Capitalism is not merely the production of commodities; it is essentially the production of surplus value.

—Karl Marx

The growth of a large business is merely the survival of the fittest.

—John D. Rockefeller

The word Capitalism is misleading. The proper name of our system is Proletarianism.

—George Bernard Shaw

Under capitalism man exploits man; under socialism the reverse is true.

—Polish proverb

If Karl, instead of writing a lot about Capital, made a lot of Capital, it would have been much better.

—Henrietta Marx (Karl's mother)

Friedrich Engels. Although Engels is generally not considered to be a "founder" of sociology, the publication of his *The Origin of the Family, Private Property and the State* in 1884 was an important event for the discipline because this work stands as the first sociological theory of gender inequality. Engels claimed that the basis of the sexual domination of men over women was to be found in the economic and power relations within society. His basic theme was that before private property existed, women shared political and economic power. However, the partriarchal (male-headed) family and monogamous (one spouse) marriage evolved as ways of guaranteeing the transfer of wealth from fathers to sons. Contemporary anthropological research does not support this position, but the link between economic and political power cannot be ignored.

The practical implications of Engels' work on the subordination of women became apparent in German politics. The socialist party in late nineteenth-century Germany was strongly influenced by both Engels and Marx, and in 1891 it initiated the first large-scale political movement to endorse full legal, economic, and political equality for women.

Emile Durkheim (1858–1917)

For **Emile Durkheim,** a professor at the Sorbonne in Paris, the social order existed as a reality in its own right and was not merely a by-product of economic or biological causes. The basic unit of sociological analysis, in Durkheim's view, was the **social fact**—an element in the overall pattern of social structure that shaped human behavior. Social facts included laws, customs, traditions, rituals, and all of the social rules that governed life in society. In addition, social facts included social regularities. Durkheim pointed out that the concern of sociology was not unique events. Thus, in a study of suicide, the reasons why a particular friend took his or her own life would not be an appropriate inquiry. However, the growing trend of teenage suicide (mentioned earlier) would indeed be a *social fact* and therefore an appropriate subject for sociological investigation. Durkheim noted further that social facts could be explained by other social facts.

One of Durkheim's fundamental assumptions was that some minimal level of integration and unity had to exist among the parts of society in order for it to function properly. He concluded that a society was held together by its common bonds. Integration came from participation in shared activities and beliefs, and a sense of trust and belonging and mutual obligation—what he called a "collective conscience." Durkheim observed the workings of the collective conscience as it related to religion, where shared beliefs and joint participation in sacred ceremonies promoted and reaffirmed the solidarity of the group.

Durkheim's concern with the functioning of society should not suggest that he had lost sight of the individual. The recognition that an individual's integration into society (or any social group) is a decisive factor in understanding human behavior led him to undertake one of the first major research studies in sociology. Focusing on suicide, his research suggested that the phenomenon could be understood as something more than a personal act of self-destruction. Durkheim felt that it could also be viewed as a reflection of the state of society and the victim's relationship to it. His *Suicide (Le Suicide),*[10] published almost a century ago, continues to receive attention from social scientists as a classic application of the sociological perspective (see Exhibit 1.4).

Max Weber (1864–1920)

The work of the German sociologist **Max Weber** is often characterized as a running debate with the ghost of Karl Marx. Like Marx, Weber was convinced that economic conditions shaped the social order, but he was unwilling to exclude the possibility that economic systems might not, in turn, be influenced by other institutions. Weber demonstrated this theory in one of his major works, *The Protestant Ethic and the Spirit of Capitalism,*[11] by exploring the possibility that the Puritan religious ideals of thrift and hard work had actually set the stage for the emergence of capitalism. In short, capitalism was a specific social form with roots in a combination of social, economic, and religious factors.

Weber's view of society focused on other areas as well. He was concerned with the future of Western society and saw a long-term trend toward the rationalization of social relations. This trend was most evident in the large-scale organizations—government and industry—that were beginning to dominate society at the time of Weber's work. Rational principles of organization were supplanting those of force and tradition, and Weber produced one of the first systematic analyses of the "bureaucratic" organization. Contemporary sociologists in this tradition have examined how the social structure of bureaucratic organizations can stifle creativity and ambition, and foster mindless attention to detail.[12]

Finally, in contrast to Durkheim's functional view and Marx's economic determinism, Weber argued that it was necessary to understand the way in which people experience social relationships. He utilized the term ***verstehen*** (from the German word that translates to

Exhibit 1.4

Research in Sociology

Emile Durkheim's Suicide

When Emile Durkheim focused on the topic of suicide during the latter part of the nineteenth century, his philosophical purpose was to demonstrate that sociology could, should, and must be an independent science of human interaction. Thus, his work was intended as a weapon in the intellectual warfare of his time.

Using the official statistics of the European nations, Durkheim formulated an explanation as to why suicide seemed to occur more often among some groups of people than among others. He looked for correlations between suicide rates and the rates of various social factors such as marriage, divorce, occupation, and religion. Suicide, he found, was more common among single adults than among married individuals. He further noted that suicide was more prevalent during periods of social and economic upheaval than during more stable times. And other variations and conditions seemed to influence the rates of suicide among particular categories of people at various times.

In his classic work, *Le Suicide,* first published in 1897, Durkheim conceived of suicide as a function of three major social factors, which in turn identified his three basic types of suicide.

Altruistic suicide is characterized by high social cohesion, dogmatic acceptance of the goals of society, and an involvement with the values and perspectives of a group to the extent that its members are willing to sacrifice themselves for the good of the whole. Durkheim noted that this type of suicide was characteristic in the military as well as in societies and communities with strong codes of honor. The concept of altruistic suicide helps to explain the Japanese kamikaze attacks on American naval vessels at the end of World War II and the willingness of contemporary terrorists to drive car bombs into the installations of their political opponents. In both instances, the sacrifice is made to further the cause of the group.

Egoistic suicide occurs at the opposite extreme—in societies or communities characterized by high social diffusion, low group solidarity, and a lack of social integration. In short, this type of suicide tends to be most apparent when the individual is weakly integrated into society and its institutions. Thus, Durkheim reasoned that individuals lacking group involvement and support would be vulnerable to suicide if confronted with stress. Loneliness and a commitment to personal beliefs rather than to group values would lead to egoistic suicide. This was the reason, Durkheim suggested, for higher suicide rates among single and divorced individuals as compared with married persons. Following the same reasoning, Protestants, whose religion stresses individuality, have higher suicide rates than Catholics, whose religion emphasizes group involvement.

Anomic suicide is depicted as resulting from the breakdown of an individual's guidelines and norms within the social system. Anomic suicide might occur during economic depressions and other periods when conventional norms are disrupted severely, leaving

"understanding") to describe the subjective meanings people associate with their own and others' behavior. Those meanings, he maintained, determine how people perceive and respond to situations. The American sociologist W. I. Thomas phrased this principle more succinctly some years later. "If men define situations as real," Thomas suggested, "they are real in their consequences."[13] Following this line of reasoning, if the unemployed believe there are no job opportunities, for example, then they will drop out of the labor force and stop looking for work. In the United States during one point in the 1980s, some 1.6 million men and women were classified as "discouraged workers,"—jobless but not looking for work because they believed no jobs were available.[14]

Charles Horton Cooley (1864–1929) and George Herbert Mead (1863–1931)

University of Michigan sociologist Charles Horton Cooley and George Herbert Mead of the University of Chicago are generally considered together because of their similar contributions to the development of social psychology. Both were concerned with the "self" and people's ideas of who and what they are. Mead developed a rather elaborate theory, but the most fundamental some individuals with a sense of disorientation or dislocation. Durkheim suggested that this type of suicide was typical among people experiencing radical life changes to which they were unable to accommodate themselves—adolescence, serious illnesses, divorce proceedings, criminal prosecutions, and the like.

Thus, the major conclusion coming from Durkheim's research was that the critical factor significant to the incidence of suicide was the manner and degree to which individuals were integrated into groups that were important to them, and not such other factors as mental illness, racial characteristics, heredity, or imitation.

SOURCE: Emile Durkheim, *Suicide: A Study in Sociology* (New York: Free Press, 1966).

Pennsylvania State Treasurer R. Budd Dwyer, after being convicted of bribery in 1988, shoots and kills himself at a news conference in his office. Anomic, altruistic, or egoistic suicide?

insight was summarized by Cooley in just five words: "Self and society are twin-born."[15]

Unlike those who saw individual growth and development as a self-contained process, both Cooley and Mead argued that the "self" emerges from interactions with others. People respond to the reactions of others, whether positive or negative, and develop an image of themselves in the process. Within this perspective, for example, the feelings of limited self-worth often experienced by the obese in American society can be traced to the way they believe other people view them. It is futile, Cooley and Mead argued, to attempt to understand people apart from their social environment.

THEORETICAL PERSPECTIVES IN SOCIOLOGY

Marx, Weber, Durkheim, and the other individuals we have just discussed are among the most influential people in the history of sociology. They shaped the way in which contemporary sociologists view the social world, developed the fundamental concepts and theories, refined methods of analysis, and phrased many of the important questions that needed to be asked. Clearly, each had a different view of the social order, and all demonstrated that there are many different ways of

Over 1,000 applicants line up to apply for 30 jobs at Sun Oil Company in Chester, Pennsylvania. "Discouraged workers" do not look for work because they believe that no jobs are available.

approaching the study of social interaction and the structure of society. Their works have given rise to many major and minor theories about human behavior, and their ideas serve as the basis for the three dominant theoretical perspectives in sociology: structural-functionalism, the conflict perspective, and symbolic-interactionism.[16]

Structural-functionalism

The perspective of structural-functionalism in sociology originates in a deceptively simple question: how is it possible for societies (or any social group) to function and survive? It is understandable that such a question would attract the attention of Comte's generation, faced as they were with the massive dislocations caused by the social and industrial revolutions that threatened the very fabric of society at that time. But it is also a question that has been asked on many occasions in more modern times—during the social revolution of the 1960s, for example, when the issues of civil rights and the war in Vietnam brought millions of Americans to the streets demonstrating for basic changes in the way our country was organized and run (see Exhibit 1.5).

As heirs to the legacy of Durkheim and Spencer, proponents of **structural-functionalism** view society as an integrated system in which each part contributes to the functioning of the whole. For functionalists, these parts include social groups (such as families) and the larger social institutions (such as religion). Therefore, a major goal of functional analysis centers around uncovering how each part functions within the system. Consider a concrete example—the matter of child care. Each new generation of children must be cared for, educated, and prepared to assume adult responsibilities. To accomplish this, mechanisms and structures must exist. Institutions may emerge through processes of either deliberate planning or unconscious evolution. The Israeli concept of the kibbutz is one possibility; the nuclear family with tasks divided along gender lines (a husband in the paid labor force and a wife assuming home and child-rearing responsibilities) is another. Such *structures* can be considered *functional* in the sense that they contribute to the survival of the society. At the same time, however, structures can also be *dysfunctional* for some other aspect of the system, producing negative consequences for society. It can be argued that the task-defined structure of the traditional nuclear family, for example, deprives a society of the productive capabilities of half its adult population.

Many pioneer sociologists applied this approach to total societies. They argued that structures (religion, family, education) formed a harmonious whole, with each making some contribution to the survival of the system. The parts hung in delicate balance, they maintained, and the introduction of new elements or ideas threatened social order. Societies would change, but only slowly as they evolved new and more functional forms.

Columbia University sociologist Robert K. Merton pointed out that members of a society might not always fully understand the implications of social patterns.[17] Therefore, he made a distinction between "manifest" and "latent" functions. **Manifest functions** are consequences that are intended and recognized by the participants of a society or group. **Latent functions** are consequences that are neither intended nor recognized by participants. A functional analysis of urban street gangs would result in the common-sense observation, for example, that group names emblazoned across members' jackets are badges of group identification and membership. This example would be a manifest function; the insignia are intended to be a public declaration of social position. On the other hand, in some male street gangs the members display physical violence in order to validate their membership to themselves and others. Thus, acts of personal violence and name jackets have the same function. However, most sociologists would label the acts of violence as latent functions in the sense that their consequences are not necessarily intended or recognized by the participants.

To carry functional analysis a step further would be to ask the question of the function of street gangs themselves. Sociologist William Whyte provided one answer by identifying the social characteristics of the members of Boston's Norton Street Gang during the early years of World War II.[18] The gang's members were largely unemployed white males living with their parents. Moreover, they were Italians living in an Irish neighborhood. Lacking any real claims to social status in the larger society, the gang functioned to provide its members with a focus for their lives.

A major criticism of structural-functionalists involves their tendency to seek positive functions for every social pattern, which results in a rather conservative analysis of social systems.[19] Moreover, functional analysis does not answer the question of the origins of social patterns. Understanding the positive functions of gang violence, for example, is not quite the same as explaining its origins. On the other hand, functional analysis does help to explain the consequences of social arrangements for the survival of social groups. It does not imply that all structures and patterns are desirable or beneficial to specific groups, but it does offer clarification for many social phenomena. Thus, functional analysis provides the understanding that gang violence fosters group identification, that crime provides for careers in law enforcement, and that poverty furnishes a cheap labor force by compelling the poor to perform the unsavory jobs no one else wants—all without condoning gang violence, crime, or poverty.

Conflict Perspective

While functionalism emphasizes harmony and stability, the conflict perspective focuses on the points of stress, conflict, and domination in social arrangements and the potential for instability within a society (see Exhibit 1.6)

Advocates of the **conflict** perspective, who are strongly indebted to Karl Marx, contend that society is composed of groups with divergent interests, goals, and objectives. As a result, these groups compete for scarce resources—money, jobs, land, sacred objects, power, and ideas. Conflict may be fairly polite and almost amiable, as in union-management contract negotiations or contests for political office. Conflict also can be *institutionalized,* for most struggles are guided by official or unofficial "rules." Even the conduct of war is guided by a set of rules. Nations have joined together to prohibit the use of certain weapons (chemical warfare) or practices (torture of prisoners). By contrast, the current wave of international terrorism violates commonly accepted rules for the conduct of war by involving civilians. Episodes of *overt conflict*—prison riots, rebellions, the racial conflict in the Republic of South Africa—lack rules of conduct, although they do exhibit fairly consistent patterns.

Conflict theorists argue that the potential for strife will be present for as long as different groups in society—rich and poor, black and white, powerful and powerless, or any of those countless other divisions

Victims of a 1988 gassing in Iraq's war against the Kurds indicate that wars are not always fought by the rules.

Exhibit 1.5

Sidelights on American Culture

Vietnam, Cambodia, and the New American Civil War

The decade beginning in the mid-sixties was one of the most socially turbulent periods in recent American history. It was marked by civil disorder, violence, riots, and rebellion. A general mistrust of the government establishment and widespread dissatisfaction with the way the country was being run had developed among a great many of the country's young adults. These hostilities were most evident in nationwide reactions to American involvement in the war in Vietnam.

U.S. involvement in Vietnam actually began during the 1950s. In part, the war was a legacy of France's colonial administration in Indochina, which effectively ended with the Geneva Accords of 1954. Indochina was then provisionally divided into the Democratic Republic of Vietnam (North Vietnam) and the Republic of Vietnam (South Vietnam). This division was followed by refugee movements between the two new states and by reprisals on the part of each regime against suspected enemies. Elections scheduled for 1956, which would have reunified the two states, were canceled by the South Vietnamese president. This action angered not only the Communist government of North Vietnam, but also the Viet Cong in South Vietnam—guerrilla insurgents backed by Communists in the north.

In 1954 the United States recognized the government of South Vietnam. In 1961 a military and economic aid treaty was signed that led to the deployment of the first U.S. support troops and the formation of the United States Military Assistance Command in 1962.

When President John F. Kennedy assumed office in 1961, there were said to be only 900 Americans in Vietnam. Within a year the number had risen to 3,200 and by the time of Kennedy's assassination in 1963, American troop levels in South Vietnam had increased to almost 25,000.

A turning point in American involvement in Vietnam came in August 1964, when the U.S.S. *Maddox*, a destroyer assigned to intelligence operations in the Gulf of Tonkin, was allegedly attacked by North Vietnamese PT boats while it was reportedly in international waters. An outraged Congress made the hasty decision to give President Lyndon Johnson advance approval to "take all necessary steps, including the use of armed force" to assist the South Vietnamese government. A major commitment to the conflict followed. By the end of 1965 troop levels had reached 184,300 men and by mid-year, 1968, they exceeded one-half million.

As the conflict escalated, television coverage brought the Vietnam War into American living rooms. The United States became a nation divided—over a war that had seemingly few, if any, implications for the safety of American democracy. Furthermore, it appeared to be a war that could not be won, yet one in which tens of thousands of American soldiers were losing their lives. As the number of casualties mounted, so did the numbers opposed to the war. Antiwar groups gave speeches, organized marches on the nation's capital, and fomented civil disorder in the streets. These activities led to a number of tragic conflicts between Americans, epitomized by the events in Chicago in 1968 and Kent, Ohio, in 1970.

Quite poignant for the New American Civil War was the protest rally held at the Democratic National Convention in Chicago in 1968. Anger over the war in Vietnam had led numerous antiwar groups, radicals, Yippies (an organization of primarily young political activists), members of the SDS (Students for a Democratic Society), supporters of antiwar Senator Eugene McCarthy, and thousands of others to Chicago to denounce the war, President Lyndon Johnson, the Democratic Party, and Vice President Hubert H. Humphrey.

Mayor Richard Daley's decision not to allow peace marches was backed by a force of 6,000 police officers, 6,000 Illinois National Guardsmen, and 6,000 regular Army troops armed with rifles, flame throwers, and bazookas. The final conflict resulted in tear gas attacks and the clubbing of hundreds of protesters. Both ironically and curiously, during the very moments of that conflict in Chicago on August 28, 1968, Philip M. Hauser, in his presidential address to the membership of the American Sociological Association in Boston, made the following observation on the means for resolving such conflicts of interest: No matter how laudable the goals, when force is employed by labor and management, by students, by advocates of peace, by minority groups, or in most extreme form by nations at war, its usage is incompatible with the continued viability of contemporary society.

Unfortunately, Hauser's remark was heeded by few, and the New American Civil War continued, resulting in, among other things, the massacre at Kent State. The incident in Kent was an outgrowth of the escalation of the war into Cambodia aimed at quelling the North Vietnamese buildup there. According to the President and the Pentagon, Cambodia was a second North Vietnam wherein numerous Viet Cong camps and command posts were situated. But the last thing Americans wanted to hear was news of war in yet another Southeast Asian country. On college and university campuses across the nation the reaction eclipsed all previous protests. By the end of May 1970, 415 campuses had been disrupted, representing the first general, and entirely spontaneous, student strike in the country's history.

A major disaster struck at Ohio's Kent State University on May 4, 1970. Eight thousand students shouting "One two three four, we don't want your -------- war," attacked the campus ROTC building and burned it to the ground. Governor James Rhodes of Ohio, determined to "eradicate" what he referred to as "the worst type of people that we harbor in America," responded by sending a five-hundred-man contingent of National Guardsmen equipped with M-1 rifles, Colt revolvers, and tear gas. The confrontation resulted in the bayoneting of three students and the shooting of another thirteen at a point when National Guardsmen were simply being taunted by the demonstrators. Tragically, four students had been shot dead. In the aftermath, more than 100,000 protesters stormed Washington, D.C., the following weekend, transforming the White House from the seat of government to an armed camp and epitomizing the fact that the United States was at war with itself.

SOURCES: Lawrence M. Baskir and William A. Strauss, *Chance and Circumstance: The Draft, the War, and the Vietnam Generation* (New York: Vintage, 1978); Philip M. Hauser, "The Chaotic Society: Product of the Social Morphological Revolution," (Presidential Address delivered before the 63rd Annual Meeting of the American Sociological Association, Boston, August 28, 1968), *American Sociological Review,* 34 (February 1969), pp. 1–19; Stanley Karnow, *Vietnam: A History* (New York: Viking, 1983); Mike Royko, *Boss: Richard J. Daley of Chicago* (New York: E. P. Dutton, 1971).

Clashes of beliefs symbolized by this student confronting the National Guard at Kent State in 1970 raise fundamental questions about the ability of a society to survive.

Exhibit 1.6

Sociological Focus

A Comparison of Structural-functionalism, the Conflict Perspective, and Symbolic-interactionism

Structural-functionalism	Conflict Perspective	Symbolic-interactionism
Society is composed of institutions, groups, and patterned behaviors that are mutually interdependent and functionally related.	Society is composed of groups that share different views, values, goals, and interests.	Society is composed of persons and groups that communicate through language and symbols.
Society tends to maintain the stability of its structure and organization. In the event of some disruption, efforts to restore stability arise.	These groups are in competition with one another as they pursue their own interests and valued goals.	Through language and symbols, people respond to one another, with mutual understanding of what behavior is appropriate resulting in shared rules for social life.
Patterned and persisting forms of behavior contribute to the stability of the society.	Conflicts arise from this competition as a normal part of social life.	The capacity of individuals to use language and symbols to communicate images and meanings enables them to label and interpret the physical and social world in ways similar to those of others with whom they communicate.
At least part of the patterned and repetitive activities that represent the makeup of the social structure are indispensable to its continued existence.	Social change results when one group prevails over another or when accommodations are made to resolve conflict.	Socially derived interpretations of reality and shared labels provide guides for individual behavior in responding to the physical and social world.

that tend to separate people along the lines of privilege—possess unequal resources. Thus, inequalities imply that society will be in a state of constant tension, ready to erupt into overt conflict as groups seek to improve their situations. The history of the United States, for example, reflects more than a century of struggle in the area of voting rights, first in extending the right to vote to the propertyless, blacks, and women, and then in terms of equal representation of minorities in government.

Domination for the purpose of maintaining a privileged position is typically envisioned in the forms of brute force with armies and weaponry (as seen in the military takeovers in Latin America), laws designed to render certain groups powerless (as seen in apartheid in South Africa), or even widespread election fraud and intimidation at the polls (as in the Philippines during the Marcos era and in Haiti during late 1987). But domination also can be subtle and invidious, and probably the most important contribution of the conflict perspective has been to uncover otherwise invisible patterns of subordination fostered by apparently benign social institutions. To cite but one example, Karl Marx once defined religion as "the opium of the masses." His statement was an assertion that a religious system that directs the attention of the poor to heavenly rewards for the sake of dulling their consciousness of worldly misery actually functions to foster the advantages of the ruling classes.

Few can quarrel with the importance of studying the many manifestations of conflict and competition in society. After all, most societies are composed of a mosaic of groups with diverse interests and objectives. Moreover, no society has unlimited resources; the attainment of goals by one group may often be at the expense of another; indeed, struggle frequently results in some kind of social change. This principle has been demonstrated rather conspicuously by the civil rights movement of the 1960s. However, strict adherence to a conflict perspective leaves little room for cooperation and consensus within societies or social relations. Such adherence merely fosters the assumption that all apparently amiable social relations mask attempts at domination. Thus, where a functionalist perspective tends to ignore struggles for advantage, the conflict perspective ignores harmony and shared interests.

Symbolic-interactionism

The symbolic-interactionism perspective focuses on face-to-face social relationships among members of society. Symbolic-interactionism is a rich and varied tradition, incorporating the ideas of Durkheim and Weber, as well as those of American sociologists Charles Horton Cooley and George Herbert Mead.

In accordance with the principles of **symbolic-interactionism,** relationships are *interactive* in the sense that they evolve as people respond to others and *symbolic* in that communication usually involves symbols. Because the reflections and feelings of others are not directly assessable, participants seek clues to the thoughts and intent of those with whom they interact by interpreting words, gestures, facial expressions, and posture. It is important to emphasize the ambiguity that exists in countless social relationships, both dramatic and routine. The approach of a stranger on a dark street corner, witnessing a mugging, or encountering a body huddled against a building all confront a person with great uncertainty, but so too do reporting to work for the first time, meeting the parents of a special friend, or attempting to negotiate a better grade. Interactionist analysis examines the process of interaction as people struggle to define these kinds of situations, interpret the actions of others, influence other people, and manage social relationships.[20]

Consider, for example, the interaction during a job interview. Candidate and interviewer meet, questions are posed, conversation ensues, the session ends, and the candidate departs. Symbolic-interactionists demonstrate and analyze the problems the participants must face as they negotiate their way through the encounter. Some of the obvious areas of uncertainty include the following: should the applicant extend a hand to the interviewer if he or she does not do so first? should the applicant sit down without being asked? what does the smile on the potential employer's face mean? what explains either party's failure to maintain eye contact? is there some hidden meaning to the employer's apparently innocent inquiry about the weather?

Through this process of interpretation and response, social relationships develop, and within this broad tradition are two schools of thought. Sociologist Erving Goffman has argued that social interaction is guided by an attempt to use gestures and symbols to create the best possible impression on others. Thus, Goffman has employed the term "impression management" to describe social interaction. He has deliberately drawn upon the world of the theater for the words and phrases he uses to describe this process to emphasize that people are constantly engaged in performances, not unlike players on a stage. Thus, his work is also referred to as *dramaturgical analysis.* At a singles bar, for example, Goffman observes that men are likely to arrive late (to create the impression of not being overly eager) and to adopt a somewhat swaggering posture (to convey the idea that they are worldly and sophisticated).[21] While even the most casual observer would concede that people are at least occasionally likely to posture in the presence of someone they would like to impress, Goffman offers a more constraining theory of social interaction. Since people can avoid neither the presence of other people nor the need to shape themselves to these others' expectations, they are unable to form a clear and stable self-concept.

Sociologist Harold Garfinkle also has contributed to the symbolic-interactionism perspective, primarily by demonstrating how many aspects of the social world are "invisible" and taken for granted. His approach is referred to as **ethnomethodology,** the study of the unwritten rules of social behavior.[22] Ethnomethodologists often approach their research by deliberately violating social conventions in everyday situations. For example, in supermarkets and department stores they have offered to pay only half of the ticket price on an item; in crowded elevators they have refused to face the front; in bars they have turned off sports events that customers were watching on television. Interestingly, their victims were typically amused, embarrassed, surprised, frustrated, or irritated, but never unaffected. Thus, the point of ethnomethodology is to identify and highlight the common rules of social interaction that lie below the threshold of people's awareness.

Symbolic-interactionists stress that individual behavior is not determined merely by social groups and social structure. Rather, people are active participants in the social world, acting to shape and influence it. This position strikes a balance to those of the conflict and functional theorists, who tend to ignore individual behaviors in their concern with broad patterns.

Many social conventions go unnoticed until they are violated.

An Integrated Perspective: The Case of Incest

Each of the three theoretical perspectives in sociology can offer insights into social phenomena. If used alone, however, each perspective has the potential to distort social reality somewhat. Alternatively, all three approaches are often combined to provide a more complete picture of the social world. Almost any area of sociological interest can be analyzed from all three approaches, as is evident by the study of the "incest taboo."

Virtually every known society prohibits marriage and sexual relations between close relatives.[23] The taboo typically forbids sexual contact between parents and their children and between brothers and sisters, and may exclude aunts, uncles, cousins, or even more distant kin not considered blood relatives by American definitions. Exceptions to the rule have been observed in a few societies, but only under special circumstances. Royal families in ancient Egypt, Hawaii, and pre-Columbian Peru, for example, permitted sibling incest as a means of maintaining their lineage.[24] In short, the taboo exists as a generalized prohibition in all societies, with only specific exceptions.

The functionalist perspective suggests that the rule against incest evolved because it is functional for both family and society.[25] Without it, sexual rivalries and jealousies would destroy the family as a stable and ongoing social unit, confusing authority relationships and making it impossible for parents to successfully prepare children for their adult roles. Moreover, the prohibition guarantees that children will marry into other families, thus creating social bonds that extend across families, communities, and generations, linking individuals to larger social units.

By contrast, the conflict perspective holds that incest taboos are a form of sexual property rights developed to perpetuate male domination over women.[26] By protecting husbands from potential sexual rivalries with sons and brothers, the incest taboo enables men to more effectively assert their authority within the family. Sibling incest deprives the father of his right to dispose of the sexual property of his daughters to his own advantage. This interpretation seems to fit better at an earlier, preindustrial stage in the development of Western societies.

Finally, the interactionism tradition focuses on social relationships within the context imposed by the incest taboo. The very word "incest" carries such strong negative symbolism that victims, usually young daughters, suffer deep and lasting emotional scars. Fathers who commit incest face criminal prosecution and the risk of social stigma that follows them forever.[27] Even in the absence of sexual contact, the power of the taboo is so great that it influences family relationships. Kin are likely to avoid physical contact with those protected by the rules of incest, and even innocent contacts may make relatives uncomfortable or cause them to feel twinges of guilt.[28] (See Exhibit 1.7.)

SOCIOLOGY: BASIC AND APPLIED

Sociology has evolved and matured considerably since Auguste Comte gave it its name and focus. It is now possible to identify many basic principles and generalizations about social behavior. Frequently, sociological research has been able to refute erroneous commonsense beliefs and theories. As noted earlier in this

Exhibit 1.7

Sociology in the Media

Quotelines on Incest

There is evidence that the incidence of incest—almost always between father and daughter—is phenomenally high. Because of its vulgar nature, the most awful secret is the least reported crime. It may touch as many as one out of every twelve American families.

—Editor, *USA Today*

I'll never forgive him. He was supposed to love me.

—19-year-old California Incest Victim

Frequently, the incestuous father can't sustain a relationship with a mature woman, so he turns to a child who cannot judge him like a man.

—Joyce Spencer, Sociologist

In the beginning, when I was only eight years old, my father said *it* was important. So I felt important. But as time went on, I felt guilt, fear, and disgust. I no longer have fear. Only the guilt is there, along with the nightmares.

—Anonymous Incest Victim, 1989

SOURCE: *USA Today,* January 12, 1984, p. 8A.

chapter, research over the last few decades has made it possible to assert with a great degree of confidence that there is no evidence that the death penalty deters homicide (except for those who are put to death). One goal of this textbook is to summarize many of these more important findings and principles of sociology. In numerous areas, of course, sociological knowledge remains quite tentative and uncertain, but we have included as much as is known with reference to these materials also.

An understanding of sociology and of social behavior at an abstract level has intrinsic value. Knowledge of sociological principles is a prerequisite of being an "educated" member of our complex modern society, as surely as is a sense of history, an appreciation of the arts and humanities, and a familiarity with the fundamentals of mathematics and the physical sciences. In this sense, sociology is a **basic science,** dedicated to the accumulation of fundamental knowledge about human behavior, the structure of society, and social phenomena. As basic scientists, sociologists are motivated by a curiosity about the structure and dynamics of the social worlds in which they live. For this reason, sociology occupies an important place in the liberal arts tradition of American education.

But sociology is also an applied science, one with practical applications and uses. Sociology enables individuals to analyze and comprehend the social forces that shape the structure of a society, its institutions, and its members. An awareness of the role of the mass media, for example, can sensitize people to the countless and subtle ways that the television and motion-picture industries shape our perceptions of minority groups and perpetuate stereotypes.

In a strict, technical sense, **applied science** can be defined as knowledge collected and organized to solve practical problems, guide policy decisions, or serve particular clients or groups. In fact, many sociologists are quite active in the applied area. Some 20% of contemporary sociologists with graduate degrees are employed in government, industry, or nonprofit organizations, with their work activities focusing on the specific goals and concerns of their employers.[29] The many others associated with colleges and universities frequently also are active in applied research, in addition to their teaching responsibilities.

Sociologists involved in applied research collect, analyze, and interpret data that enable manufacturers to anticipate consumer preferences, candidates to predict voting behavior, corporations to make personnel decisions, and courts to render informed and just decisions. In addition, sociologists also may serve as social engineers, actively involved in using sociology to design programs or create legislation aimed at achieving specific goals. For example, sociologists and other social scientists at the University of Michigan's Institute for Social Research collaborated in a recent television series designed to weaken the impact of sex-role stereotypes by exposing children to men and women in non-traditional adult roles.[30]

And finally, many sociologists serve as clinicians, working directly with individuals and groups to aid them in coping with problems or resolving conflicts.

Many sociologists with undergraduate degrees work in such fields as corrections and social welfare, offering counseling to individuals, families, and neighborhood groups. Thus, the applied side of sociology is broad, with potential applications in most areas of social endeavor (see Exhibit 1.8).

Exhibit 1.8 Applied Sociology

Providing Human Service Delivery

Why strive for knowledge of reality, if this knowledge cannot aid us in life? Social science can provide us with rules of action for the future.
—Emile Durkheim

If sociology was of no practical value, sociologists would have long since been confined to college and university classrooms, unemployment lines, and vocational retraining programs. Yet the vast majority are employed by the federal government, state and local service agencies, school systems, industrial firms, private research firms, nonprofit organizations, and political parties. Whatever their specific positions, the common feature of their work is the application of sociological principles and methods to practical situations.

A significant number of contemporary sociologists occupy positions in *human service delivery*—a network of public and private agencies providing assistance and services to the poor, the aged, and the handicapped; to the victims of crime and economic change; to communities displaced by natural disasters; and to patients in drug abuse and alcoholism treatment centers. Much of the work of sociologists in the human service delivery network falls into the area of planning, a process that occurs at numerous levels and stages.[a]

Needs Assessment

Effective program planning requires accurate forecasting of the needs of a population or community. Sociologists estimate potential needs by gathering data descriptive of the service population. An informed decision as to whether a community is in need of economic assistance programs for the aged, for example, requires accurate information about the age distribution, economic situation, and health characteristics of the community's population.

Resource Analysis and Allocation

Planners must also be aware of what services are currently available and how they can be used effectively. In 1972, for instance, a small city in northern Michigan requested federal funding for the establishment of both drug and alcohol treatment programs. But the request was denied when it was learned that both types of programs were already operating in the city. Michigan authorities then sent a small team of sociologists into the community to determine why the programs were being underutilized. The planners found that the city was divided by a river—one side populated by blacks, and the other by whites, with neither group venturing into the territory of the other.[b] The drug treatment program was on the black side and the alcoholism center on the white side, leaving each group in need of one type of service. Although the team of sociologists was not in a position to solve a segregation problem that had evolved over a thirty-year period, it was able to coordinate a cooperative effort between the two treatment agencies. Ultimately, part of the drug-abuse treatment staff was allocated space at the alcoholism center, which, in turn, established a mobile unit that crossed the river five nights a week to hold AA meetings.

Program Evaluation

Existing programs are evaluated continually to determine their cost effectiveness, ability to reach their target groups, and success in accomplishing their stated goals. In this regard, the tools of sociological research play the major role.

SOURCES:

a. Paul L. Johnson, "Human Services Planning," in Howard E. Freeman, Russell R. Dynes, Peter H. Rossi, and William Foote White (eds.), *Applied Sociology* (San Francisco: Jossey-Bass, 1983), pp. 106–27.

b. Carl D. Chambers, James A. Inciardi, and Harvey A. Siegal, *An Evaluation of the Drug and Alcohol Treatment System in the State of Michigan* (Washington, DC: Resource Planning Corporation, 1972).

SUMMARY

Sociology, defined as the scientific study of society, provides a unique way of looking at the world by applying the scientific method of inquiry to an examination of social phenomena. This unique perspective—the sociological perspective—is an approach to social phenomena that takes into account the group context of individual behaviors, patterned social interactions, and the impact of social structure.

When combined with the efforts of professionals in the other social sciences—anthropology, political science, economics, psychology, and history—sociology offers the opportunity for a broad and balanced understanding of social behavior.

The origins of modern sociology can be traced to the middle of the nineteenth century when the people who were to define the field were attempting to make some sense of the many disruptions that were occurring in the world around them. Auguste Comte is credited as the "founder of sociology," and the early and influential contributors to the developing science included Emile Durkheim, Karl Marx, and Max Weber.

In the years since these important figures made their contributions, three important theoretical perspectives have evolved in sociology. Proponents of the structural-functionalist perspective direct their attention to identifying the structures in society and to determining how they function. Adherents of the conflict perspective view society as being composed of groups with divergent interests and goals that compete for scarce resources. The symbolic-interactionist perspective focuses on face-to-face relationships in society and on how these relationships influence social behavior. While each perspective has made significant contributions to the understanding of society, each also has its weaknesses and no one point of view can fully explain the totality of social phenomena.

Finally, while sociology is a basic science dedicated to the accumulation of fundamental knowledge about human behavior, the structure of society, and social phenomena, it is also an applied science. Sociology has practical applications for individuals in their personal affairs and at work, for business and industry, and for managing social problems.

KEY TERMS/CONCEPTS

anthropology
applied science
basic science
Comte, Auguste
concept
conflict
Durkheim, Emile
economic determinism
economics
ethnomethodology
history
hypothesis
laissez faire
latent functions
manifest functions
Marx, Karl
patterned social interaction
political science
psychology
social Darwinism
social fact
social group
social structure
sociological perspective
sociology
Spencer, Herbert
structural-functionalism
symbolic-interactionism
theory
verstehen
Weber, Max

DISCUSSION QUESTIONS

1. What are the key elements of the sociological perspective and how might they be applied to the study of life in a student residence hall?
2. Can the conflict perspective be applied to the study of "peace"? Conversely, can structural-functionalism be applied to the study of "war"? Explain.
3. Suicide is a major cause of death among adolescents. Does Durkheim's work on suicide offer any insights into the causes of this contemporary pattern?
4. Using symbolic-interactionism as a basis for exploration, are there any differences in classroom relationships between *students and other students* as opposed to those between *students and instructors?*
5. How might sociology contribute to a better understanding of an economic problem such as unemployment?

SUGGESTED READINGS

Pauline Bart and Linda Frankel, *The Student Sociologist's Handbook,* 3rd ed. (Glenview, IL: Scott, Foresman, 1981). This source book presents useful information to students of introductory sociology in terms of library research for course work, research reports, and term papers.

Peter L. Berger, *Invitation to Sociology: A Humanistic Perspective* (Garden City, NY: Doubleday, 1963). Written more than two decades ago, *Invitation to Sociology* remains a classic introduction to what sociology is all about, how it differs from other social sciences, and how it is relevant to everyday life.

Randall Collins, *Three Sociological Traditions* (New York: Oxford University Press, 1985). The author provides a thorough review of the three major sociological perspectives that have come to dominate contemporary American sociology.

Howard E. Freeman, Russell R. Dynes, and William Foote Whyte (eds.), *Applied Sociology* (San Francisco: Jossey-Bass, 1983). An introduction to the promise and problems encountered in practical applications of sociological knowledge and methods.

C. Wright Mills, *The Sociological Imagination* (New York: Oxford University Press, 1959). Written thirty years ago by a sociologist who helped to introduce the conflict perspective into American sociology, this book provides the best discussion available of the limits of personal experience as a source of generalized knowledge.

Diane E. H. Russell, *The Secret Trauma* (New York: Basic Books, 1986). A systematic analysis of the dimensions of incest in contemporary society, focusing on the social and psychological consequences to its victims.

NOTES

1. For an innovative analysis of the quest for social prestige, see Robert H. Frank, *Choosing the Right Pond* (New York: Oxford University Press, 1985).
2. A recent summary of the literature on the death penalty and homicide appears in William J. Bowers, *Legal Homicide: Death as Punishment in America, 1864–1982* (Boston: Northeastern University Press, 1984).
3. Mayo Mohs, "IQ," *Discover* (September 1982), pp. 19–24; *USA Today,* February 12, 1986, p. 1A.
4. Data on the differential experiences of men and women in school can be found in *The Classroom Climate: A Chilly One for Women?* produced by the Project on the Status and Education of Women (Washington, DC: Association of American Colleges, 1982), pp. 6–8.
5. James E. Rosenbaum, "The Structure of Opportunity in School," *Social Forces,* 57 (September 1978), pp. 236–56; James E. Rosenbaum, "Track Misconceptions and Frustrated College Plans," *Sociology of Education,* 53 (April 1980), pp. 74–88.
6. See Jonathan Kozol, *Illiterate America* (Garden City, NY: Doubleday, 1984); Diane Ravitch, *The Troubled Crusade: American Education, 1945–1980* (New York: Basic Books, 1983).
7. Auguste Comte, *Systeme de politique positive,* 4 vols., 4th ed. (Paris: Cres, 1912); Lewis A. Coser, *Masters of Sociological Thought* (New York: Harcourt Brace Jovanovich, 1977), pp. 3–41.
8. Herbert Spencer, *The Study of Sociology* (New York: D. Appleton, 1891).
9. Karl Marx, *Selected Writings in Sociology and Social Philosophy,* translated and edited by T. B. Bottomore (London: McGraw-Hill, 1964).
10. Emile Durkheim, *Suicide: A Study in Sociology* (New York: Free Press, 1966).
11. Max Weber, *The Protestant Ethic and the Spirit of Capitalism* (New York: Charles Scribner's and Sons, 1958).
12. Julien Freund, *The Sociology of Max Weber* (New York: Random House, 1968).
13. William I. Thomas and Dorothy Swain Thomas, *The Child in America* (New York: Alfred A. Knopf, 1928), p. 572.
14. *Handbook of Labor Statistics,* June 1985, Table 14, p. 38.
15. Charles Horton Cooley, *Social Organization* (New York: Schocken, 1962), p. 5.
16. See Randall Collins, *Three Sociological Traditions* (New York: Oxford University Press, 1985).
17. Robert K. Merton, *Social Theory and Social Structure,* rev. ed. (New York: Free Press, 1957), p. 51.
18. William F. Whyte, *Street Corner Society* (Chicago: University of Chicago Press, 1955).
19. Jonathan H. Turner, *The Structure of Sociological Theory* (Homewood, IL: Dorsey, 1982).
20. Herbert Blumer, *Symbolic Interactionism* (Englewood Cliffs, NJ: Prentice-Hall, 1969), pp. 2–4.
21. See Erving Goffman, *Relations in Public* (New York: Basic Books, 1971).
22. Harold Garfinkle, *Studies in Ethnomethodology* (Englewood Cliffs, NJ: Prentice-Hall, 1967).
23. Fernando Henriques, *Love in Action* (New York: E. P. Dutton, 1960), p. 200; Margaret Mead, "Incest," in David L. Sills (ed.), *International Encyclopedia of the Social Sciences* (New York: Macmillan, 1968), pp. 115–22.
24. Rick Rubin and Greg Byerly, *Incest: The Last Taboo* (New York: Garland, 1983).
25. The functionalist interpretation is developed in Kingsley Davis, *Human Society* (New York: Macmillan, 1949); Talcott Parsons, "The Incest Taboo in Relation to Social Structure and the Socialization of the Child," *British Journal of Sociology,* 5 (June 1954), pp. 101–17; Leslie White, *The Science of Culture* (New York: Farrar, Straus and Giroux, 1969).
26. The idea of sexual property and the conflict perspective on incest is developed in Randall Collins, *Conflict Sociology: Toward an Explanatory Science* (New York: Academic Press, 1975), pp. 234–59; John R. Goody, *Comparative Studies in Kinship* (Stanford: Stanford University Press, 1969), pp. 13–38.
27. Marvin Harris, *Cultural Materialism* (New York: Vintage, 1980).
28. See Benjamin DeMott, "The Pro-Incest Lobby," *Psychology Today,* 14 (March 1980), pp. 11–16; Dorothy Wilner, "Definition and Violation: Incest and the Incest Taboos," *Man,* 18 (March 1983), pp. 134–59.
29. Employment patterns of sociologists are discussed in Bettina Huber, *Footnotes,* 11 (May 1983), pp. 1–7.
30. Sandra J. Ball-Rokeach, Milton Rokeach, and Joel W. Grube, *The Great American Values Test* (New York: Free Press, 1984).

Research Methods: Sociology and the Logic of Inquiry

It is late afternoon at the Miami Marina. As the cruise ships enter port at Dodge Island and the charter boats return from a day's fishing in the Gulf Stream, a young woman approaches a man sitting on a bench overlooking picturesque Biscayne Bay. She is only twenty, but looks much older. Her appearance is unimproved by her disheveled hair, rumpled miniskirt, and the prominent needle tracks that scar both her arms.

Her apprehension is evident. People usually do not offer her money just to talk about her drug habit or other aspects of her life. She cannot overcome her fear that the casual looking gentleman she is meeting—dressed in shorts, T-shirt, and deck shoes, with his face half-hidden by a fisherman's cap and dark sunglasses—is an undercover narcotics detective, an agent of the real "Miami Vice." But a friend had met him there the day before. Even if the individual on the bench is indeed "the Man," her friend had not been arrested. And too, she needs the money, so she might as well see what he really wants.

As it turns out, he is not a "narc" at all, but a professor from some university up north—a teacher, a researcher, an "egghead,"—a *sociologist.* As he introduces himself, he does not even ask her name, but merely explains that he is trying to understand the habits, daily activities, and life-styles of heroin users. He remarks that he already has talked with hundreds of other men and women and that he always is careful to ask questions in such a way that the answers would be considered "hearsay" in a court of law, and therefore inadmissible as evidence. In addition, he produces an official looking document. It says, "Grant of Confidentiality" and was issued by the United States Drug Enforcement Administration as a guarantee that he may not be compelled by any court, prosecutor, or grand jury in the nation to testify about anything he hears or sees during the course of his research.

Some of the questions are simple—age, education, jobs; others are about her parents and early life, but most focus on her criminal activity and drug use. They are exactly the same questions he has asked of all of the other drug users he has interviewed during the course of his research; he has memorized them and trained himself to take notes without disrupting the normal flow of the conversation.

Drug users are generally suspicious of strangers and often for good reason. Not until she was arrested did this woman learn that the "drug dealer" was an undercover police officer.

The questioning continues for some twenty minutes. At the conclusion he thanks her for her time and pays the promised ten-dollar fee. Just as she is about to leave, he asks one small favor—some help in locating other people like herself to provide the same kind of information. He tells her he will be at the same bench at the same time the next day if they want to meet with him.

As she retreats from his domain of social science research to reenter the street worlds of heroin and crime, he reflects on the history of his research project. It began months earlier when he first became interested in the question of how heroin use and street crime might be related. Since then he has met and spoken with more than 300 active heroin users—talking in bars and secluded alleys, on waterfront docks and street corners, in parked cars and rundown hotels, and in all of those other places of a questionable nature where his informants—located for him by word of mouth through an intricate social network that is invisible to the majority of people—feel most secure.

The street interviewing had begun nearly a year earlier through a heroin user/dealer whom the researcher had met years before. But it had taken him a long time to establish trust among street drug users and to convince dealers and traffickers, both petty and powerful, that he posed no danger. He had depended on contacts established over the course of many years.

Before he is finished with the interviewing phase of his research, he will have made contact with over 350 Miami heroin users. Still ahead will be the long task of organizing and analyzing the information to determine if it conforms with his hypothesis. Eventually, the findings will be published, becoming part of the complex mosaic of sociological knowledge about heroin use and street crime.[1]

In this chapter we will examine the structure and process of this particular study, along with numerous others, to explain and illustrate the method and logic of sociological inquiry. We will highlight the technical and ethical problems that must be solved, the choices and compromises that must be made, and the difficulties that must be overcome in the quest for knowledge about social behavior.

SOCIOLOGY, SCIENCE, AND THE SCIENTIFIC METHOD

Sociologists exhibit an endless curiosity about the social world. Some of their questions are narrow, others quite broad. And too, they range from the immutably abstract to the commendably practical. A number of sociological questions have already been encountered in this textbook:

> What is the relationship between heroin use and street crime?
>
> Does *anomie*—a situation in which social norms are unclear or no longer applicable—contribute to suicide?
>
> How can school systems in the United States be improved?
>
> Does capital punishment deter homicide?

All sociological research proceeds from a question. Research is the process of posing questions and seeking answers. The research process begins with a question that can be answered tentatively by systematically accumulating relevant information; it is a data-gathering enterprise governed by the rigorous and uncompromising rules of the **scientific method**—a set of procedures for gathering information about the social or physical world. The procedures apply equally to the natural and social sciences.

The Assumptions of Science

Science is a system of rational inquiry, disciplined by methodically precise testing. Moreover, scientific research proceeds on the basis of several assumptions. These assumptions are shared beliefs about the nature of the subject matter under study. For sociologists, it is particularly important to formulate and understand these assumptions. Failing to do so invites controversy and dissent. There have always been those who criticize the idea of studying social behavior scientifically—those with vested interests in maintaining the status quo; others who would rather find the sources of human motivation in religion or individual psychology; and the many who argue that human behavior does not lend itself to scientific inquiry.[2] Yet despite the sometimes strong opposition, sociologists have been successful in applying the scientific method to the examination of social behavior using the assumptions of *order, cause and effect,* and *tentative truth.*

A Miami "crack" house, knocked down after a community vigilante set it ablaze, is a phenomenon ripe for sociological inquiry.

The Assumption of Order

Scientists make the assumption that events under investigation exhibit an underlying order that can be observed. The patterns may be the orbits of planetary systems, the stages of cellular reproduction, or the rates of crime in a particular city. If there were no orbits, stages, or crime rates, the world would be random and unpredictable, and science impossible. Uncovering such patterns is the first step toward being able to understand and explain them.

The Assumption of Cause and Effect

Scientists assume that it is possible to explain why events occur—whether these phenomena be heart attacks, economic recessions, or changes in the divorce rate. Researchers accept the idea that any recurring incident is preceded by some other event (or combination of events) that consistently and repeatedly produces it. In the social sciences, the causal factors are usually quite complex; it is rare indeed to be able to specify any single cause. Rather, a set of factors typically combines to produce a given result. Social theories are developed to explain how causal factors influence subsequent events.

SOCIAL INDICATOR

The Divorce Rate
(per 1,000 population)

Year	Rate	Year	Rate
1890	0.5	1960	2.2
1900	0.6	1970	3.5
1910	0.8	1980	5.2
1920	1.6	1985	5.0
1930	1.6	1986	4.8
1940	2.0	1987	4.8
1950	2.6	1988	4.8

Source: National Center for Health Statistics, 1988.

The Assumption of Tentative Truth

Even when research consistently appears to demonstrate a cause-and-effect relationship between events, scientists are trained to be skeptical. Scientists proceed through the examination and reexamination of theory and research findings, seeking more knowledge and trying new theories. If scientists were to accept a theory as universally valid, it would spell an end to the accumulation of new knowledge.

THE LOGIC AND PROCESS OF INQUIRY

The research process is most easily grasped by dividing it into three broad steps: *formulating the research question, collecting data,* and *analyzing the data* (see Exhibit 2.1). First the question needs to be translated into a form that permits scientific examination. This initial step *always*

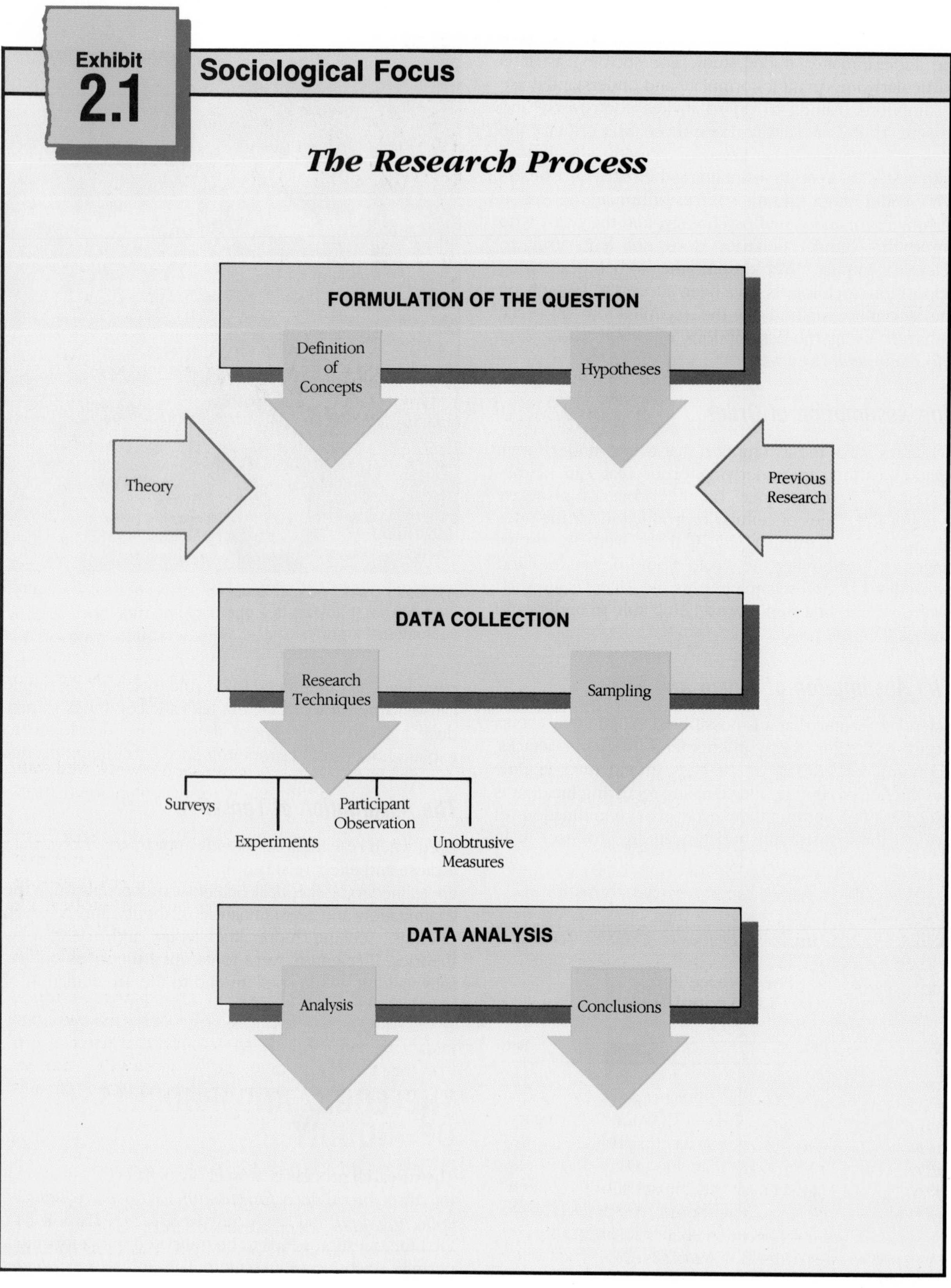
Exhibit 2.1
Sociological Focus
The Research Process
FORMULATION OF THE QUESTION
Definition of Concepts
Hypotheses
Theory
Previous Research
DATA COLLECTION
Research Techniques
Sampling
Surveys
Experiments
Participant Observation
Unobtrusive Measures
DATA ANALYSIS
Analysis
Conclusions

One goal of science is the systematic collection and analysis of evidence that will support or refute a hypothesis.

demands an identification of the concepts to be included in the study and *may* require formulation of hypotheses. Second, a plan called the "research design" must be developed. This developmental process includes the selection of a specific technique (or combination of techniques) for gathering the necessary information and deciding which individuals or groups to include in the study. Third, the information that is gathered must be analyzed, adhering to certain guidelines, and conclusions must be drawn about the original question.

Formulating the Research Question

Many research questions have their origin in the various sociological theories described in Chapter 1. For example, Karl Marx's theory was concerned with the causes and consequences of economic inequality and it has prompted sociologists to ask specific questions about the consequences of inequality. Some researchers have attempted to find links between economic inequality and religious activity as a result of Marx's suggestion that the poorer members of society would be more involved with organized religion because it would divert them from their immediate deprivation.

Moreover, since other sociologists usually have asked similar questions in the past, it is important that research build upon previous findings. Therefore, before a project is undertaken, a sociologist will review the work of others to determine what they have learned about the subject. The review of previous research will also prevent a duplication of effort.

Asking a research question is not quite as simple as posing a query about social behavior. Research questions must be worded so as to identify the exact social phenomena being studied and to specify the relationships among social phenomena. Thus, a number of rules guide the formulation of questions.

Defining and Measuring Concepts

The systematic investigation of social phenomena requires the exact identification of those aspects of the social world that are to be studied. The term *concept,* noted earlier, refers to a general category of social behavior. Suicide, homicide, drug addiction, and crime are among the many observable concepts that sociologists study. Others are abstract ideas—internal feelings that are not directly discernible. Durkheim spoke of "anomie," Marx of "alienation," and Weber of "authority"—each an abstract concept that has no direct manifestation. For the physicist, "gravity" is an abstract concept.

To be used in research, concepts must be translated into operations that allow them to be measured with some degree of precision. Hence, the process of **operationalizing concepts** involves defining them in measurable forms. For some concepts this process is relatively simple. The concepts "age" and "formal education" are measured easily in numeric terms, with data gathered either by direct questioning or a review of public records. The definition and measurement of most concepts, however, is considerably more difficult if scientific precision is to be achieved. The operational definition of something as apparently simple as "unemployment," for example, actually is plagued with many problems. Statistics collected by the government count persons as "unemployed" only if they have been jobless for at least four weeks and have actively looked for work during that period.[3] On the surface, that may appear to be a legitimate way to operationalize unemployment. But a moment's reflection reveals that adherence to the government's definition excludes all those discouraged by fruitless weeks of job hunting who have given up; those with a physical handicap that prevents them from working; and people who are involuntarily limited to part-time schedules. If they too were to be included, the number of unemployed probably would double.

The choice of measurement techniques often is determined by the purposes of the study. Economists concerned with only broad patterns of unemployment are content with government statistics. On the other hand, sociologists curious about the problems of coping with unemployment or the stresses placed by unemployment on families' social relationships need to operationalize the concept differently. After all, a basic requirement in science is to define concepts precisely, so that those who read and use the research know exactly how something was measured.

Validity and Reliability Sociologists always must be sensitive to certain inherent problems in the operationalization of concepts. The first issue involves validity. **Validity** is the extent to which research measures what the investigator claims to be measuring. If the concept is "arrest history," for example, it might be measured by the direct question, "Have you ever been taken into police custody?" But this question is phrased so that it introduces a fundamental error that compromises the validity of any respondent's answer. Since the concept of "arrest" is not defined operationally here, one cannot assume that the term will mean the same thing to everyone being questioned. Does being asked to come to the local police precinct for questioning about a crime constitute an "arrest"? One person might think so, while another might view responding to such a request as no more than doing one's duty as a citizen. A third individual might (depending upon personal factors) perceive the questioning as police harassment. Validity could be increased significantly by asking the alternative question, "Have you ever been taken into police custody, charged with the commission of a crime, and read your rights?" In this case, the concept of "arrest" is operationalized directly in the question asked.

SOCIAL INDICATOR

Alternative Indicators of Religiosity

	Member of a Church or Synagogue	Attended Services during Past Week	Religion Is "Very Important" in My Life
1965	73%	43%	70%
1979	68	40	55
1982	67	41	56
1985	71	42	55
1987	69	40	53

Source: The Gallup Poll, 1987. Reprinted by permission.

The problem of validity tends to increase with the abstractness of the concept. In studies of religious behavior, for example, "religiosity" is considered an important concept.[4] But as an indicator of a person's religious commitment, religiosity is a rather difficult concept to measure. One approach counts the frequency of attendance at religious services. This approach is a less than perfect method of measurement, however, since many extraneous factors—personal health, availability of transportation, geographic location, or weather conditions—may influence one's ability to get out to services. Moreover, it is important to consider the length of time an individual has resided in a community. Many people who change their residence need time to form attachments to a new church, synagogue, or other place of worship. Alternative approaches to the measurement of religiosity have considered how often the Bible or some other religious book is read and social reactions to those who violate important religious norms. Whatever the measure, it must be developed carefully since people's ability to attend religious services and their norms about behavior vary considerably from one religious group to the next.

The second issue in judging the quality of measurement techniques concerns **reliability**—the extent to which an operation will yield the same results every time it is repeated. This problem plagues sociologists when they study concepts that easily can be affected by certain situational factors. A good example is the concept of "job satisfaction," an obviously important matter in any research involving work roles. It is reasonable to anticipate that job satisfaction can be enhanced by such factors as wage levels, working conditions, and opportunities for advancement. The problem of reliability arises because the level of job satisfaction on any given day easily may be depressed by some minor incident—a disagreement with a supervisor, a machine breakdown, an encounter with an angry customer. This incident may produce lower levels of satisfaction than would be found on a day when work proceeded smoothly.

It is evident that designing valid and reliable measurement techniques is no easy matter. New strategies constantly are being developed as social scientists strive to improve their ability to measure social behavior with ever-increasing precision.

Working conditions may fluctuate dramatically over the course of a day, making it difficult to measure job satisfaction.

SOCIAL INDICATOR

Job Boredom Rating Scale

Assembly Line	207	Delivery Courier	86
Forklift Driver	170	Scientist	66
Machine Tender	169	Police Officer	63
Accountant	107	Air Traffic Controller	59
Engineer	100	Professor	49
—Average Score—	**100**	Physician	48
Computer Programmer	96		

Source: David Wallechinsky, Irving Wallace, and Amy Wallace, *The People's Almanac Presents the Book of Lists* (New York: William Morrow, 1977).

Hypothesis Testing

In sociology and all other sciences, the research question usually takes the form of a **hypothesis,** a precise statement of the anticipated relationship between two concepts. Importantly, there are two kinds of concepts—attributes and variables. **Attributes** sort individuals or groups into quantitatively different categories, focusing on a single property or characteristic that is either present or absent. Race, ethnic background, religious preference, political affiliation, employment status, and gender are attributes that have proven to be meaningful for explaining variations in values and behavior. People can be assigned to these categories on the basis of direct observation or self-identification.

Variables are characteristics or properties of individuals, groups, events, objects, or processes that are present in differing degrees. They can change or *vary* in some way. The science of meteorology, for example, deals with such variables as temperature, humidity, barometric pressure, and wind speed. In the sociological study of societies, industrialization, crime rates, and educational level are common variables.

When a hypothesis is being developed, one concept is the anticipated cause of the other; stated differently, one concept can bring about a change in the other. The suspected causal variable is **independent,** having an effect on one or more variables that are **dependent.** To better differentiate these two kinds of variables, it is useful to remember that one *depends* on the other.

To explain variables in more concrete terms, we can refer again to the study of Miami heroin users. The researcher in that study set out to investigate a straightforward hypothesis—the idea that the level of criminal activity increases with the frequency of heroin use. Criminal activity and heroin use are the major variables. Since the hypothesis suggests that regular users of heroin engage in more crime than sporadic users, heroin use is assumed to be the cause of crime. Therefore, *heroin use* is the independent variable and *criminal activity* the dependent variable—the second factor is the result of the first.

As already noted, hypotheses are developed from theory. This point can be illustrated by examining the theory from which the relationship between heroin use and street crime was hypothesized. Often referred to as the "enslavement theory of addiction," it suggests that given the high price of heroin on the drug black market, the otherwise law-abiding user is forced into a life of crime in order to support his or her drug habit. Stated as a formal theory, and quoting from a 1967 publication:

> First, the potential addict begins to take very small doses of some addicting drug, let us say morphine, or heroin.
>
> Second, the addict notices that the amount of the drug he has been taking does not "hold" him, and he no longer experiences the intense pleasure which he felt in the early stages of the use of the drug.
>
> Third, as the habit increases in size over a period of weeks or months, the addict who must buy his drugs from bootleg sources finds that more and more of his wages go for drugs and that he has less and less for necessities.
>
> Fourth, it becomes obvious to him that he must have increasing amounts of money on a regular basis, and that legitimate employment is not likely to supply that kind of money. . . . Therefore, some form of crime is the only alternative.[5]

It should be noted that the original hypothesis—that the level of criminal activity increases with that of heroin use—is very explicit. It identifies a specific category of people—heroin users—excluding all other types of substance abusers. Therefore, the researcher's findings in this study will not necessarily apply to those who snort cocaine or smoke marijuana. Moreover, the study is limited in its focus to heroin use and street crime, and deliberately ignores many other vital and important questions, such as the dynamics of drug trafficking or the process of being socialized into the street worlds of heroin and crime. To include these other considerations would cause the interviews to become so complex and unwieldy as to make the investigation almost impossible to accomplish.

Exploratory Studies Sometimes so little is known about a social issue or phenomenon that the investigator cannot even begin to guess at a cause-and-effect relationship. Under such circumstances, descriptive research or **exploratory studies** are conducted for the purpose of generating baseline information that can describe the social process or event in question. But even in this type of investigation, research questions must be formulated precisely. The question, "How do people become drug users?" is far too broad to yield any meaningful information, just as social life is too complex to observe and record all of it. Therefore, *precise* research questions are formulated to narrow the focus and direct attention to a manageable number of concepts.

In a study of marijuana use conducted almost four decades ago, sociologist Howard S. Becker considered the process of becoming a marijuana user.[6] Countless questions flooded his mind. How do people find drug connections? What kinds of people (men, women, young, old, wealthy, poor) use drugs? Is there a progression from the use of one substance to another? Are any social pressures involved in the initiation into drug use? Ultimately, Becker focused his attention on a very fundamental sociological question: is marijuana use a solitary act or a group-based activity? As he refined his thinking, he suggested that marijuana use was more likely to occur in some social context. Becker eventually concluded that the group played an integral part in defining how an individual user responded to the surge of euphoric experiences encountered. Without that context, he argued, marijuana use resulted in a rather bland experience.*

Becker's work is an example of exploratory research, but its "exploratory" nature should not suggest that it was an unfocused or random collection of information. As a sociologist, Becker was guided by one of the broad theoretical perspectives examined in Chapter 1. From the perspective of symbolic-interactionism, his observations centered on social interaction—how people learned the appropriate marijuana-smoking behaviors and responses. Had he used the functionalist approach, he might have focused on how smoking fostered solidarity among a group of marijuana users. From the conflict perspective, he might have looked at the discrepancies between the behaviors of marijuana smokers and the laws of the community.

The point here is that little meaningful research is not initially embedded in some theory of human behavior, however general. Becker was influenced by the knowledge that human perceptions are shaped by the group context, and therefore his research was merely an extension of that particular observation in a new situation. By contrast, the Miami heroin study was developed to examine a specific hypothesis that evolved from the enslavement theory of addiction.

---

*Interestingly, since many contemporary marijuana users experienced the drug's euphoric effects at first use and not necessarily within a group context, they probably would argue with Becker's thesis. Two factors account for this apparent contradiction: first, as the result of media portrayals of marijuana use, most novices need no instruction to know how to smoke the drug; second, today's marijuana is more than ten times stronger than that of Becker's day, making the effects readily noticeable.

Data Collection: The Research Design

A **research design** is an orderly plan for collecting, analyzing, and interpreting data. During the initial conceptualization of any research project, two crucial questions in design are encountered: exactly *how* the information should be collected, and *what* (or whom) ought to be included in the study. Frequently, the type of design is determined by the kinds of questions to be asked. In the study of heroin use and street crime in Miami, conducting interviews with actual users was the only practical method of obtaining the needed information. Had the research targeted the life-styles of street drug users, then the investigator would have needed to become a regular observer of their daily activities. Had the research interest been the arrest histories of drug users, an analysis of police records might have sufficed. If the concerns had been the structure and enforcement patterns of the drug laws, still other techniques would have been required.

In many research investigations a number of methods are available, with the final choice dependent on considerations of time, finances, contacts, validity, reliability, and the investigator's personal expertise with any given technique. Researchers interested in the process of decision making among jury members, for example, might consider observing the process as it takes place, interviewing jurors to catalogue their recollections of the process, or creating simulated jury deliberations (see Exhibit 2.2). Each approach provides useful data, but clearly different kinds of information.

Dividing the research endeavor into precise steps is a useful way of explaining the process, but it must be recognized that in practice investigators are constantly visualizing the entire study in order to anticipate later problems. It would be fruitless to develop certain kinds of hypotheses about juries if outsiders were legally prohibited from jury rooms. Thus, in many cases the variables and the formulation of the hypotheses are determined by the availability of data sources. Within this context, over the last several decades sociologists and other social scientists have refined four basic ways of gathering data about social phenomena—surveys, experiments, participant observation, and unobtrusive measures. Each offers certain advantages over the others, and all have technical limitations and raise some very real ethical questions.

Research Techniques

Survey Research The **survey,** a study in which a group of people is asked to answer a prepared list of questions, is the most familiar form of data collection in social science research. Surveys involve questions about attitudes, behavior, or beliefs, posed through an interview or mailed questionnaire.

Face-to-face interviews may be conducted in people's homes, where they work, or in the case of active heroin users, on the street. Telephone interviews are also a possibility, particularly when the subjects are widely dispersed. The advantages of the interview survey are that questions can be standardized, and if correctly formulated, can elicit the specific information needed. Moreover, respondents are more apt to answer under the direct questioning of an interviewer, as opposed to a mail survey. Mailed questionnaires are frequently lost, put aside, or simply ignored.

It is important to note at this point that the interview process involves considerably more than the simple recitation of queries drawn from a printed questionnaire. Inept questions can offend people and discourage them from responding. Poorly worded questions may confuse respondents and cast doubt on the validity of the answers. It also must be recognized that the interview process is itself a form of social interaction, and that a number of factors can distort the answers given. If interviewers are not careful, they unintentionally can influence the way people answer. Gestures or facial expressions that signal social disapproval can subtly discourage a respondent from giving a particular answer, especially if the topic under discussion involves a highly sensitive subject. Personal characteristics of the interviewer also can inhibit the interview process. For example, it is likely that questions on sexual behavior would be answered more honestly if posed by a member of the same sex. Inquiries about illegal drug use are answered more often when the age, sex, and race of the interviewer and respondent are the same.

Exhibit 2.2

Sidelights on American Culture

A Most Unpredictable Jury

The jury occupies an almost hallowed place in the American system of justice, symbolic because of the important role it often plays in the determination of innocence or guilt. The jury also has been the subject of considerable research interest, particularly in terms of its decision-making processes. Investigators from the fields of both sociology and psychology have uncovered a number of general patterns in the structure and process of jury deliberations, but it is often the exceptions to these patterns that tend to be the most interesting.

Some years ago, a man was tried in a California court for the murder of his wife. The state's case was quite convincing, but one thing was missing—the victim's body. This incongruity was the basis of the defense attorney's case, and no evidence or testimony was presented on behalf of the accused.

In a dynamic summation performance, the counsel for the defense soared to eloquent heights of oratory, repeating that given the absence of the body of the alleged victim, it could not be proven that a crime had even been committed. "You must find my client innocent for one simple reason," the attorney shouted. And then, dropping to a breathless whisper, he added, "His wife is still alive. In fact—she just walked into the courtroom!"

At once , the heads of all the jurors and spectators turned to the rear of the courtroom, only to see that not a soul had entered the chambers. But the attorney had made his point. How could proof beyond a reasonable doubt be concluded if the jurors suspected that the defendant's wife was still alive.

Everyone agreed that it had been a brilliant ploy and after less than an hour's deliberation, the jury returned with a verdict. Yet to the amazement and disbelief of all of those present, the jury had found the accused guilty of murder.

When the trial was over and the jury dismissed, the bewildered defense attorney confronted the first few jurors he saw. "How," he asked, "could you find a man guilty when you weren't even sure his wife was dead? Didn't everyone turn to look for her in the back of the courtroom?"

"Yes," answered one of the jurors, "everybody except your client."

SOURCES: Garold Stasser, Norbert L. Kerr, and Robert M. Bray, "The Social Psychology of Jury Deliberations: Structure, Process, and Product," in Norbert L. Kerr and Robert M. Bray (eds.), *The Psychology of the Courtroom* (New York: Academic Press, 1982), pp. 221–56; Melvyn Bernard Zerman, *Beyond a Reasonable Doubt: Inside the American Jury System* (New York: Crowell, 1981), pp. 10–13.

When people are scattered over large areas, it may be more efficient and less costly to use a mailed questionnaire. This allows respondents to answer at their convenience and in private. But the mailed questionnaire is generally a less desirable alternative. As noted earlier, the response rate is problematic. Moreover, in contrast with an interview, questionnaires do not give researcher's the opportunity to encourage people to complete every question or to seek clarification of an ambiguous response.

The survey has proven to be a relatively inexpensive means of collecting information from large numbers of people in a short period of time. Surveys are used to collect data on attitudes, beliefs, and behavior. Attitude surveys are designed to provide a broad general picture of the orientation or perspective of "the American public." The opinion poll, for example, which is discussed at greater length in Chapter 16, is a form of survey research that may be used to elicit attitudes toward abortion, gun control, the death penalty, and other public policy issues. Sociologists use surveys to measure beliefs, as when they seek to identify religious beliefs about the supernatural and the efficacy of prayer. Surveys also are appropriate for going beyond attitudes and beliefs to examine actual behavior. Surveys can be used to compile patterns of seat belt use, church attendance, charity work, and geographic mobility. The interview survey of heroin users in Miami focused on all three types of information—users' attitudes toward drug use, the police, and themselves; beliefs about the physiological effects of drugs; and present and past patterns of drug use and involvement in crime.

SOCIAL INDICATOR

Harmful Products Survey
Percent of college students who think these products are harmful:

Cocaine	84%
Cigarettes	70
Marijuana	62
Alcohol	10

Source: Student Watch '86 The College Stores Research and Educational Foundation.

Importantly, the survey is the most effective research tool when people are the only source of information about activities in which they themselves are involved. Why do people choose a specific career, quit a job, drop out of school, or use heroin? There is simply no other reliable source of such data other than the individuals under study. Certainly the responses of their friends or relatives would have questionable validity.

Yet surveys do have drawbacks. Human memory is not infallible, and there is always the possibility that gaps may develop in people's ability to remember details, especially about past events (see Exhibit 2.3). Moreover, the ability to recall facts does not guarantee a willingness to share them with an outsider. Much of the behavior of the heroin users studied was illegal, and neither personal assurances nor official documents could guarantee for all respondents that there would be no reprisals. Even if the behavior in question were *not* illegal, some events and activities probably were concealed because they reflected badly on some individuals, suggesting weakness or stupidity or other attributes about which human beings are frequently self-conscious. Indeed, as a result of factors of this sort, a few of the Miami heroin users contacted refused to participate in the study.

Experiments The **experiment** is a social science research technique that is used to ascertain the effects of some specific event or experience on individuals or groups. More precisely, it is a method in which independent variables are manipulated in order to test theories of cause and effect.

The word "experiment" may bring forth images of sterile laboratories, complex technical equipment, scientists in white lab coats at work with chemical formulas and steaming beakers, or perhaps even the eccentric Dr. Frankenstein anxiously waiting for a lightning bolt to breathe life into his gruesome patchwork of stolen body parts. While these images may reflect the settings in which scientific experiments originated and matured, it is only the *logic* of such trials that the sociologist utilizes.

The classic **experimental design** involves exposing two groups of people (who are similar in every respect) to alternative experiences and then making measurements of the consequences. Ideally, one cluster is an **experimental group** that is subjected to some stimulus or event. The other, the **control group,** is not. Since the composition of the two groups is the same at the outset of the experiment, it may be concluded that there is a cause-and-effect relationship between the stimulus and the reaction if the two groups react differently. Experiments of this type, furthermore, can be conducted in both laboratories and more natural settings.

Laboratory Simulations Over the years any number of laboratory experiments have been designed to understand the experiences of job applicants. In one study, the members of experimental and control groups played the role of employers evaluating the qualifications of job candidates. The job applications given to the groups were identical in every respect but one: the applications given to the control group were identified as belonging to male applicants; the same applications, when reviewed by the experimental group, were identified as applications submitted by female applicants. In the final analysis of the experiment, it was found that an application received a better evaluation when it had a man's name on it, regardless of whether the person reviewing it was a man or a woman.[7] In another simulation involving the assessment of job applications, all of the job candidates were women, with their photographs attached to their applications. Half of the applications carried snapshots of "pretty" women; the other applicants were considered "plain." Typically, the "pretty" women received the better evaluations, suggesting that physical attractiveness was the discriminating variable.[8]

The advantage of laboratory simulations is that researchers can control the physical and social environments in which experimental and control subjects are assessed. Distractions created by noise or other interruptions can be eliminated. Moreover, group members can be prevented from conferring with one another about the nature of the study or the characteristics of the research subjects—two factors that can influence the decision-making process. There may be a disadvantage to laboratory simulations as well. Nothing can guarantee that people will behave in the same manner under simulation conditions as they would in a natural setting. Consider the phenomenon known as the **Hawthorne effect** (discussed in Exhibit 2.4), which examines the possibility of influencing subjects in an experiment simply by giving them the satisfaction of being noticed and studied.

Exhibit 2.3

Case Study

Interview Surveys and the Problems of Recall

A major question that might be posed regarding the study of heroin users in Miami relates to the validity of the information gathered. Do drug users tend to distort or cover up the less admirable aspects of their lives on the street? The answer to this question is generally no. Over the years a variety of controlled studies have been undertaken to investigate the question. Addict self-reports of arrests have been compared with official records; information on drug use has been compared with urinalysis results; and intraquestionnaire safeguards and interview-reinterview procedures have been tested. In all instances, it would appear that drug users tend to tell the truth *to the best of their ability.*

We have emphasized the phrase, "to the best of their ability," to stress the fact that in a variety of situations, drug-using criminals simply cannot accurately remember everything that happens to them. Researchers in the drug field realized long ago the futility of collecting useful data on heroin users' daily drug intake. Most regular heroin users living on the streets use as much heroin as they can get their hands on. Depending on the funds they have available, their ability to "score," and the availability of heroin, some days they are able to obtain a lot of the drug, some days just a little, and on a few occasions none at all. These kinds of fluctuations, combined with the fact that users do not maintain daily records of their heroin intake, tend to make accurate recall difficult. Moreover, many heroin users, depending on whom they are talking to, may deliberately lie about heroin intake. In 1979 a woman heroin user in Miami commented on her own use level:

> When my parole officer picked me up I told her I was using only a dime bag [$10 dose] a day. She saw the fresh tracks [needle marks] on my arms so she knew I was usin' so I didn't want to lie about that. But I didn't want her to know I was usin' heavy 'cause she might take me in. But she took me in anyway. The next thing I know she's got me talkin' to a hospital social worker, tryin' to find out what I was doin' and how I was feelin' and how much I was usin'. I told her I was clean and that my P.O. [parole officer] was just tryin' to make trouble. I thought maybe she could talk my P.O. out of violatin' me. But I end up gettin' locked up anyway and when I got to detention I started screamin' that I was sick and had a $200-a-day habit and I needed medication. . . . By the time the day was over I had told so many stories that I had no idea of how much I was usin' that day or any other.

If a heroin user says that he or she shoots up six times a day or has a $300-a-day habit, a researcher should suspect that the information probably is incorrect. A more reliable indicator would be simply to determine whether use is daily, once a week, or several times a week.

Another recall problem faced by the investigator in the Miami study involved getting users to accurately recall criminal activity, which proved to be particularly difficult for those who had committed crimes with great frequency. To cite an example, when one Miami heroin user was asked how many burglaries he had committed during the previous 12 months, his response was, "Oh man, it must have been thousands." To a researcher, such an answer is of absolutely no empirical value. To aid the user in providing a more accurate estimate, the interviewer helped him to reconstruct his life events and activities for the preceding year. Several dates were found to be prominent in his mind—his birthday, Christmas, April 17 when his mother died, July 15 when he was stabbed in a fight with a connection [drug dealer], August 19 when he retaliated and shot his connection to death, December 14 when he was arrested for possession of heroin, and so forth. For each date listed, he was asked what he did on that date, and then what he did the week before and the week after. In time, a clearer picture of his criminal activity was put together, and what was originally described as "thousands" of burglaries was pared down to between 40 and 50.

Field Experiments A more difficult type of experimental design involves research conducted in natural settings, where behavior can be observed under more normal circumstances. In the "Good Samaritan" experiment, for example, sixty divinity students, divided into three groups, were instructed to report to a certain building to tape a sermon. The first group was told that it was late for the taping and had to hurry; the second group was not told to hurry; and the third group was informed that there was a delay somewhere along the line so that they had plenty of time. In addition, the students were assigned a topic for their sermon: half were to talk on the biblical parable of the Good Samaritan, while the rest were given a nonreligious topic. What the divinity students did *not* know was that the exercise was only an experiment, and that on the way to the taping each would come across a groaning man slumped in a doorway. The goal of the research was to determine if either time pressure or what people are thinking about influences "helping behavior."[9]

In the final analysis, only 40% of the divinity students stopped to help. Time pressure appeared to have the greatest influence on the decision to stop. Of those in no hurry, 63% stopped; only 10% of the rushed students stopped; and 53% of those thinking about the biblical Good Samaritan stopped. Overall, the results of the experiment clearly suggested that if people are in a hurry, they are not likely to deviate from their course.

While the Good Samaritan experiment was a fairly simple one to perform, other experiments are large, complex and expensive, sometimes involving thousands of people. Some encompass whole towns. For example, two communities of the same size and composition in the state of Washington were selected for study in what was called the Great American Values Test.[10] One was designated the "Experimental City" and the other the "Control City." All residents in both locations received mailed questionnaires designed to elicit information about their values and attitudes. Subsequently, investigators launched a massive media campaign that was directed at the residents of Experimental City, encouraging them to view a special television program. Appeals appeared in a variety of places, including *TV Guide* and local newspapers. None of this was done in Control City. The program, called "The Great American Values Test," was designed to influence viewers' attitudes toward social equality and environmental quality. Hosted by actor Ed Asner and commentator Sandy Hill of ABC's "Good Morning America," the show was carried simultaneously on all local affiliates of the three major networks.

The question of program impact was measured by sending solicitations to all residents of both communities on behalf of organizations that provided cultural opportunities for black children, that supported equal treatment for women athletes, or that lobbied for antipollution legislation. Residents were given the opportunity to be placed on the organizations' mailing lists, to donate money, and to contribute time, clothing, or equipment. Subsequent to the broadcast, it was found that the residents of Experimental City responded more positively to the solicitations. Specifically, they made monetary contributions almost six times larger than the sum contributed by residents of Control City. On the basis of this complex and elaborate field experiment, it was concluded that television did indeed have the capacity to influence social attitudes and behavior.

Field experiments also have been used in conjunction with the findings of survey research. In one such study the research question focused on whether people's *stated* behaviors toward racial minorities differed from their *actual* behaviors. It was hypothesized that people would practice discrimination against others, but would be unwilling to admit to doing so. Initially, survey data identified landlords who claimed that they would not rent to black families. Later, black couples working for the research team visited the properties of these landlords and attempted to rent apartments. Interestingly, the couples generally had no difficulties in renting, thus disproving the original hypothesis.[11]

Participant Observation As an alternative to surveys and experiments, researchers may become directly involved in the activities of those they are studying, for the sake of systematically observing and recording their behaviors. This technique, **participant observation,** was pioneered a century ago by cultural anthropologists studying preindustrial societies. These researchers lived among peoples in remote parts of the world, learning their languages and studying the subtleties of their exotic cultures. Today, sociologists who conduct observational studies focus more exclusively on urban and rural subgroups, such as heroin users, religious cults, juvenile gangs, musicians, or nudists, and on sensitive social situations.

There are varying levels of involvement in the groups being studied. Sociologist E. E. LeMasters, seeking to understand the lives of skilled blue-collar workers, limited his contacts to one neighborhood bar where such laborers congregated, talking and drinking with them as he attempted to unravel their dreams, hopes, and fears.[12] By contrast, in her attempts to understand the social world of an inner-city Chicano (Mexican-American) community, sociologist Ruth Horowitz became enmeshed in her subjects' daily routines, participating in many social and family activities, and eventually being welcomed into their homes to share meals and

Exhibit 2.4

Types & Stereotypes

The Hawthorne Experiment: Effect or Defect?

The Hawthorne experiments of the 1930s isolated a group of workers to determine the effect of working conditions on productivity.

In the folklore of the social sciences, the "Hawthorne effect" is repeatedly cited to demonstrate that mere participation in a social or behavioral experiment can have effects on the dependent variable.

The Hawthorne effect gets its name from a series of experimental studies conducted at the Hawthorne, Illinois, plant of the Western Electric Company between 1924 and 1932. The purpose of the studies was to improve worker efficiency. In their descriptions of the experiment, sociology, psychology, and social psychology textbooks over the last four decades have focused on the generally accepted results of what was called "the relay room study."

A group of women who assembled telephone relays were isolated in a small room where working conditions could be controlled. After making initial observations to determine the "normal" levels of work output, the research team began restructuring the work and manipulating the work environment in order to determine what conditions contributed to increased productivity. First, they changed the basis on which workers were paid from a seniority-based salary scale to a piecework scale that gauged the number of relays assembled by the group as a whole. Production went up. Second, three "work breaks" were introduced, and again production went up. Next, the lighting was changed. First it was improved and then made worse. Longer hours were added, followed by a shortened work week; production goals were increased, and then decreased. Still, overall production continued to increase. In fact, no matter what changes the researchers instituted, positive or negative, production continued to rise. The experiment appeared to be a failure.

Two explanations typically are presented in contemporary textbooks to account for the continuing increases in production. First, as a result of being isolated from the rest of the work force, the women relay workers had developed friendships and a group identity that strengthened their capacity to work despite adverse conditions; second, it was believed that the very presence of the research team and the workers' knowledge of the fact that they were part of an experiment had influenced the pace and quality of work. Aware that they were being studied, the relay workers changed their behavior in order to conform

festivities.[13] Total involvement in the culture under study is illustrated in the work of medical sociologist Harvey A. Siegal. In his investigations of the way of life of slum-hotel and skid-row residents in New York City, Siegal became a full participant in the culture, not only "hanging out" with his subjects, but living, working, and drinking with them—even getting arrested with them.[14]

Participant observation is no easy task. One problem involves gaining access to the group to be studied, a difficulty that can be greatly mitigated by means of a contact person. In the study of Miami heroin users, for example, the investigator had a variety of contacts, including a local drug treatment counselor who made the following introduction to a street corner group: "Listen brother, all this man wants to know is what you're doin' and what's goin' on. He's okay. He ain't gonna jive ya. . . . It's cool. . . . Just be honest for 20–30 minutes and he'll give ya 10 bucks for your time."[15]

In other circumstances, there may be no such intermediary. Ruth Horowitz described her experience:

> I chose to sit on a bench in a park where many youths gathered from noon to midnight. On the third afternoon of sitting on the bench, as I dropped a

to what they believed were the researchers' expectations. It is this latter phenomenon that has become known as the Hawthorne effect.

The foregoing description is representative of the way in which the Hawthorne experiment is reported and interpreted in contemporary literature, but subsequent investigations have suggested that what really happened in the relay room to produce the famous effect was, in fact, quite different. Various factors that have frequently been disregarded actually played an important role in the experiment's outcome. First, the relay experiment took place, from its very beginning, under better lighting and ventilation conditions than those found in the rest of the plant. Second, the supervisor in the relay room was also known to be friendlier than other supervisors in the plant. Third, during the early months of the experiment, four of the five women involved were reprimanded for excessive talking and were threatened with being returned to the main part of the plant if their production did not improve. Fourth, during the eighth month of the experiment, two women whose output rates were dropping were replaced with faster workers. And fifth, (keeping in mind that the women were being paid on a piecework basis) the relay room workers were told what their output rates were, and that the higher the rates, the more money they would earn. Hence, there was information feedback coupled with financial reward.

Aside from the fact that the experiment was invalidated by the replacement of 40% of the workers halfway through the course of the study and the added incentive of a financial motivation to perform, the Hawthorne researchers also seemed to ignore something that appears to have been quite obvious. The relay experiment persisted for five years. During that time, it is very likely that the workers were becoming more skillful at their work, and thereby faster. Moreover, seemingly forgotten in the current reports on the Hawthorne experiment is the fact that there were times when production did indeed decline. Too, there were other experiments conducted at the Hawthorne plant, similar to the one carried out in the relay room, and production in other plant areas did *not* increase. And finally, subsequent research has failed to duplicate the supposed Hawthorne effect in various experimental settings.

Within the context of these observations, is there really a Hawthorne effect?

SOURCES: H. M. Parsons, "What Happened at Hawthorne?" *Science,* 183 (March 8, 1974), pp. 922–32; Berkeley Rice, "The Hawthorne Effect: Persistence of a Flawed Theory," *Psychology Today,* February 1982, pp. 70–74; Fritz J. Roethlisberger and William J. Dickson, *Management and the Worker* (Cambridge: Harvard University Press, 1939).

softball that had rolled toward me, a young man came over and said, "You can't catch" (which I acknowledged) and "You're not from the hood [neighborhood], are you?" This was a statement, not a question. . . . When I told him I wanted to write a book on Chicano youth, he said I should meet the other young men and took me over to shake hands with eight members of the Lions [a street gang].[16]

Like the other research techniques, participant observation has several potential drawbacks. People may behave differently because they are sensitive to the fact that they are being observed—the so-called Hawthorne effect—or a subject may deliberately hide something because he or she wishes to convey the best possible image. As often occurred in the Miami heroin study, valuable time may be lost as subjects recount their experiences or seek advice from the researcher. To overcome such contingencies, some investigators have concealed their intent. To cite but one example, during the 1950s sociologist Leon Festinger and several of his colleagues learned of a small religious cult that had predicted the end of the world. The sociologists wished to study this group but faced a dilemma. To reveal themselves as sociologists automatically would have eliminated any opportunity for participant observaton. Thus, they passed themselves off as converts to the group's beliefs. This created many technical problems; they could neither openly record their observations nor ask too many obvious questions.[17]

The goal of participant observation is to systematically record the activities of a particular group or community; this task obviously demands objectivity. But observations in field settings have the built-in risk of selective perception—the potential for the researcher to develop a distorted view of the events being observed. Researchers focusing on group *conflict,* for example, may become so sensitive to the problem that they inadvertently overlook instances of *cooperation.* The threat of "going native"—losing objectivity and accepting the group's values and standards also may jeopardize objectivity. The difficulty here is that it is not always easy to maintain social distance from a group after spending a great deal of time with it. As an observer becomes accepted into a group, he or she risks losing outsider status and becoming enmeshed in group activities and values. Moreover, those under study may come to view the investigator as a "friend," instead of an "observer," placing additional strain on the need to remain objective.

Unobtrusive Measures Research on social behavior need not always involve direct contact with the people or events under study. Data collection may embrace an examination of records, communications, artifacts, and places. These sources may provide direct evidence or inferences about behavior and values. Collectively, data sources such as these are referred to as **unobtrusive measures,** because they do not impinge directly on the people involved.

Unobtrusive measures have some distinct advantages in social research. They eliminate the potential for the Hawthorne effect and deliberate or unintentional misrepresentation. Moreover, their use reduces the need for concern about many of the ethical issues associated with research on human behavior (see Exhibit 2.5).

Historians have always relied on newspapers, letters, diaries, and records to reconstruct the past. Sociologists employ the same kinds of documents but also extend their analyses to include elements of popular

Almost every product of human activity has been used as a research information source, even grafitti.

Exhibit 2.5

Sociological Focus

Ethical Dilemmas in Research

The technical requirements imposed by the scientific method are but one segment of the difficulties associated with meaningful sociological research. There are ethical dilemmas as well, principally in the areas of *privacy rights, psychological harm, deception,* and *confidentiality*.

Privacy Rights

Perhaps the most fundamental ethical question involves a subject's right to privacy. Given the very nature of sociological investigations, invasions of privacy at one level or another are a matter of natural course. Interviewers who wish to probe voting preferences, drug use, or the religious beliefs of a community do indeed encroach upon the privacy of their respondents. As a result, contemporary guidelines for research with human subjects generally demand a respondent's *informed consent.* In other words, all research subjects must be apprised of the purposes of the investigation and its possible benefits and risks. Moreover, they must be given the opportunity to decline to participate. In practice, an individual always retains the right to refuse, and it should be so, but in the process a certain level of bias may be introduced into the study. Were the heroin users who refused to participate in the Miami study, for example, significantly different from those who willingly responded to the interviewer's questions?

The Potential for Psychological Harm

Informed consent aside, researchers in sociology always must be sensitive to any chance of harming their subjects. Even the simple recollection of past events may cause a subject emotional discomfort and psychological pain. A research subject's recollection of being raped, or of the suicide of a family member, or of the aftermath of some natural disaster, for example, certainly carries with it the potential for causing emotional suffering.

The more complex ethical issues tend to emerge during the course of sociological experiments. In a series of studies designed to assess the impact of imprisonment, for example, college students were paid to play the roles of guards and prisoners in a mock jail.[a] Both groups took their jobs quite seriously, playing their respective roles with frightening veracity. Ultimately, the experiment was terminated abruptly when the "guards'" excessive harassment and verbal abuse of the "prisoners" brought about significant levels of personal disorientation. (A more complete discussion of the Zimbardo experiment appears in Chapter 4.) Was the knowledge to be gained from the experiment worth the personal cost to the participants?

It might be argued that the individual who agrees to participate in an experiment does so willingly and is free to terminate his or her involvement at any time. While this position may be logically accurate, it is sociologically invalid. Scientific research has an established level of legitimacy in American society, and this factor alone may compel some individuals to participate, despite any reservations they may have. To cite a case in point, consider the well-known studies of obedience conducted by Stanley Milgram.[b] In Milgram's experiments, a small group of research subjects was directed to administer electric shocks to another group of research volunteers. The setting had all the trappings of scientific research, and the experiments were carried out under the direction of a strong authority figure. No shocks were actually administered, but to the research subjects it appeared that electrical current was actually being conducted to the "victims," who pretended to experience acute pain and suffering. These studies had severe consequences. Those who had complied with the order to administer the shocks exhibited clear symptoms of anxiety, nervousness, guilt, and stress. They actually believed that they had administered severe shocks. When informed at the conclusion of the experiment as to the true nature of the situation, many of the subjects indicated that they had felt compelled to follow the directions given, despite the apparent physical harm involved. (Milgram's experiments are also discussed in the section on authority relations in Chapter 4.)

Deception

Subjects in field experiments and participant-observation studies do not always have the option to decline involvement in research. Sometimes they are included merely at the discretion of the investigator. The residents of Experimental City, for example, had not consented to participate in the Great American Values Test, mentioned earlier in this chapter.

(Continued)

Exhibit 2.5 (continued)

It can be argued with some justification that need for deception is legitimate when revealing the purpose of the research would either bias the results or prevent scientific investigation. To announce that job applications are being examined for the purpose of uncovering vestiges of gender discrimination would render the research results inconclusive. To reveal their identity as sociologists would have prevented Leon Festinger and his associates from gaining access to the religious group they wished to study. To report the nature of the Great American Values Test in Experimental City would have biased the experiment.

There is no easy answer to this issue. Most sociologists would argue that in the examples noted the deception was harmless and the understanding of social dynamics acquired from the experiments outweighed any minor invasions of personal privacy. This may be so, but at the very least research subjects should be notified at the conclusion of the observation period as to the true nature of the project.

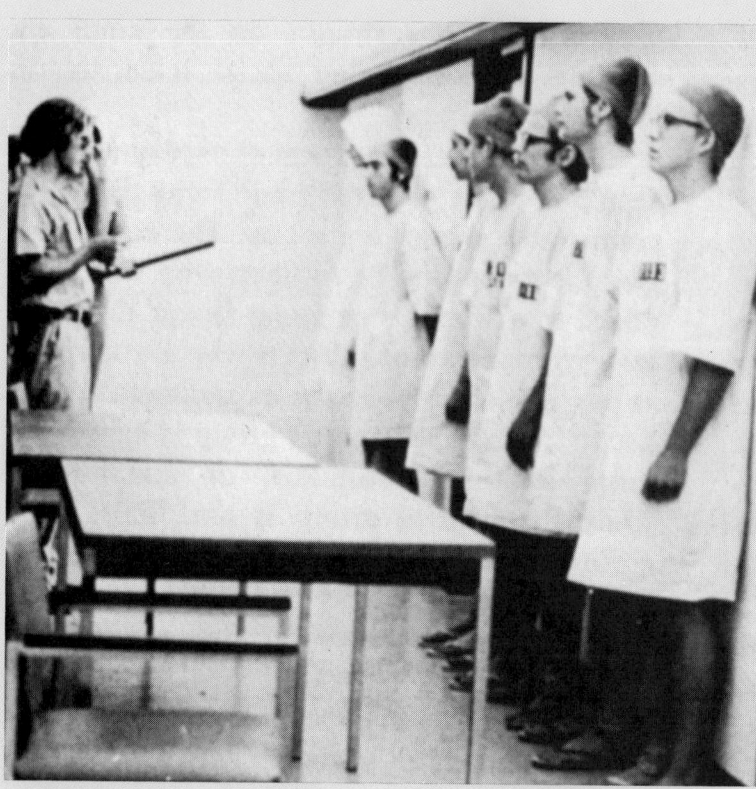

Confidentiality

The process of accumulating information about individuals or groups raises the issue of confidentiality. Most research is conducted in a manner that guarantees the confidentiality of its subjects. Names are not associated with a particular answer without the explicit permission of the respondent; data are handled in a way that makes it impossible to connect any answer (or behavior) with a specific individual; and fictitious names are used when reporting on the characteristics or behaviors of particular subjects. As was the case with Experimental City in the Great American Values Test, sometimes even the names of research cities are disguised.

Despite the many safeguards, the mere possession of confidential information about people introduces certain risks. One study that generated a considerable degree of controversy in sociological circles some years ago involved an investigation into the life-styles of homosexual males.[c] In 1965, sociologist Laud Humphries initiated his research by observing homosexual encounters in public restrooms. Subsequently, he followed the men involved to their cars, copied their license numbers, and identified them with the help of a contact at the local bureau of motor vehicles. Later, he changed his appearance and went to the subjects' homes and interviewed them—all without revealing how he had selected them for inclusion in his study or his prior knowledge of their sexual activity. The research provided Professor Humphries with data that were highly charged to cause personal embarrassment, not to mention the risks of family disruptions or threats to careers.

Numerous questions have been raised as to the ethics of

College students acted out the roles of "guard" and "prisoner" in Philip Zimbardo's famous study on the impact of imprisonment.

Humphries' research. The technique used to identify the research subjects was clearly an invasion of privacy. But there was also the issue of maintaining confidentiality. Humphries had no intention of revealing the names of his subjects. In fact, his notes were hidden, records were physically burned at the conclusion of the study, and he was prepared to go to jail rather than identify his sources. In short, he was sensitive to the ethical requirement of social research that stipulates that data must be protected from use by others.

The issue of whether or not a sociologist can be compelled to reveal information is far from resolved. Communications with certain professionals are not necessarily privileged, as they are with physicians, attorneys, and members of the clergy. This is the same problem that journalists face in safeguarding the anonymity of their sources.

SOURCES:

a. Philip P. Zimbardo, "The Pathology of Imprisonment," *Society,* 9 (April 1972), pp. 4–8.

b. Stanley Milgram, *Obedience to Authority* (New York: Harper & Row, 1974).

c. Laud Humphries, *Tearoom Trade: Impersonal Sex in Public Places* (Chicago: Aldine, 1970).

culture—novels, films, television, and music—subjecting these sources to systematic study. This technique—known as **content analysis**—examines communications in an objective and quantitative way for the purpose of measuring certain variables. The focus may be on the frequency of occurrence of words, themes, ideas, events, people, or attributes. Studies of suicide notes have been among the more interesting applications of the content-analysis technique.[18] The inspection of hundreds of messages left behind by people who committed suicide has revealed that victims' thoughts in the last moments included not just themselves but also the important people in their lives. In addition to the many expressions of guilt, hostility, and sorrow, the messages also contained advice, instructions, and requests to friends and relatives.

Public records collected by government agencies also can be quite useful in social research. For example, researchers have used marriage certificates to chart the movement of immigrant groups in the United States over time, to trace the patterns of intermarriage among religious and ethnic groups, and to estimate family size and dispersion of birth-control techniques.[19] Other researchers relying on unobtrusive measures have utilized a variety of truly creative techniques to measure social activity. One sociologist ransacked people's garbage, counting throwaways as a means of estimating beer consumption; another measured the wear on the floor in museums to determine the popularity of certain exhibits; and a third analyzed the graffiti on public restroom walls to uncover gender and cultural differences in style and content.[20] In short, any product of human activity can be used as a source of information.

In the final analysis, an endless variety of possible sources of information about social phenomena is available for study. Each source has its advantages and disadvantages. All other things being equal, researchers choose the technique that offers the greatest validity and reliability (see Exhibit 2.6).

Data Collection and the Norm of Objectivity The need for objectivity enters into the research process at many points, but it is most crucial at the data-collection phase. The **norm of objectivity** demands that the collection of information (and its subsequent analysis) not be influenced by the values and beliefs of the investigator. Objectivity has several practical requirements:

> First, subjects must not be selected (or excluded) on the basis of personal preferences or with the idea of selecting only those who conform to preconceived ideas.
>
> Second, questions must not be phrased to lead people into giving certain preconceived answers.
>
> Third, all information must be recorded, not just the information that supports the beliefs of the investigator or confirms the hypotheses.

Objectivity does not imply that personal values and preferences have no place in the research process. Obviously, interests, concerns, and values often dictate the selection of research topics. Sociologists dissatisfied with the progress of race relations may very well direct their efforts toward uncovering the sources of discrimination. Conflict theorists convinced that a small number of people control the political decision-making process may focus on the subtle exercise of power that operates beyond traditional political channels. Indeed, these are legitimate and important research topics, and sociology has a long and distinguished history in the study of these and other social problems. However, objectivity requires that once the research is initiated, personal values must not bias the collection and analysis of the data.

Sampling

Sociologists generally focus their research on broad categories or populations—Americans, blacks, women, men, Democrats, automobile workers, college students, Protestants, heroin users, and so forth. Yet it is rare for a research effort to interview or collect information from all or even most members of the population under consideration. The alternative is to use the **sample,** a smaller number of people selected to represent an entire group. The decision to sample generally is imposed by the constraints of time and money. The resources needed to measure every American's attitude toward abortion, for example, would be prohibitive. Moreover, attitude measurement is virtually an impossible logistical task when large groups are involved. Even the Bureau of the Census, which counts the population of the United States every ten years, cannot reach every person, despite a staff of thousands of people and a budget of millions of dollars.

The decision to sample involves more than just time, money, or logistics. Simply put, sampling is appropriate when it would be an unnecessary waste of effort to contact everyone, because a properly selected sample can be representative of an entire population. Moreover, statistical techniques are available that make it possible to estimate how accurately the sample describes the entire population.[21] Sampling is a mainstay of political polling, and in almost every poll conducted by news organizations a *range* is announced that indicates the maximum possible error caused by sampling. A range of "plus or minus 5%," for example, means that nineteen

Exhibit 2.6

Research in Sociology

Advantages and Disadvantages of Alternative Research Strategies

Technique	Characterization	Advantages	Disadvantages
Surveys	Best method for self-reports of behavior, attitudes, and values	Questions can be standardized Probability samples are possible	Complex issues must often be simplified Non-responses may bias results
Interviews		Researchers can follow-up vague answers	Answers may not be clear, complete Respondents may give socially acceptable answers
Questionnaires		Geographically dispersed groups can be reached	Non-responses may bias results
Experiments	Best method for determining the impact of a single variable	Extraneous factors can be controlled	Results may be influenced by the Hawthorne effect
Laboratory		Experiments can be replicated repeatedly	Behavior, reactions may be influenced by artificial conditions
Field		Behavior can be observed in natural settings	Researchers cannot control extraneous factors
Participant Observation	Best method for learning about the values, beliefs, and social organization of small groups	Researchers can observe behavior in real-life situations Researchers may record actual behavior Researchers may observe wide range of activity	People may alter their behavior Precise measurement of concepts is difficult Selective perception is possible A large investment of time and effort is required Results cannot be generalized
Unobtrusive Measures	Best method for historical research	Subjects are not influenced by data collection Research can be used in historical and cross-cultural context	Researchers must use available sources Samples may not be representative Actual behavior may not be observable Measures must depend upon available data Precise measurement is difficult

Exhibit 2.7

Sociology in the Media

Newsweek's Poll on Pot and Public Officials

When U.S. Supreme Court nominee Douglas H. Ginsburg admitted in late 1987 that he had smoked marijuana as a college student in the 1960s and again in the 1970s, the controversy this revelation caused led him to withdraw his bid for the nation's highest court. To determine the public's position on the matter, the Gallup Organization interviewed a national sample for *Newsweek* magazine. In the results reported below, percentages do not total 100 for each question due to the elimination of many "don't know" responses from the tabulations.

Thinking about people under the age of 50 in public office today, what percentage would, you say have used marijuana at least several times?

Almost All	6%
More than Half	19
About Half	32
A Quarter	21
A Tenth or Less	10

What percentage of your friends and people you know well have used marijuana at least several times?

Almost All	10%
More than Half	12
About Half	15
A Quarter	12
A Tenth or Less	41

If you knew that somebody was using marijuana occasionally, what would you do?

Report Them to Authorities	4%
Ask Them Personally to Stop	32
Avoid Them	18
Accept Their Personal Decision	40

Do you think that marijuana use is increasing, decreasing, or remaining about the same?

	CURRENT	1982
Increasing	31%	58%
Decreasing	22	8
The Same	37	24

Do you think the use of marijuana should be made legal or not?

	CURRENT	1982
Yes	17%	20%
No	77	74
Don't Know	6	6

Source: *Newsweek,* November 16, 1987, p. 52. For this Newsweek Poll, the Gallup Organization interviewed 507 adults by telephone on November 6, 1987. The margin of error is plus or minus 6 percentage points. The Newsweek Poll © 1987 by Newsweek, Inc.

times out of twenty the results from the sample could deviate by a maximum of 5% from what would have been found had every member of the population been surveyed (see Exhibit 2.7).

Since a sample does not include every member of a population, the risk of bias always is a possibility. The task then becomes one of reducing the opportunity for error as much as possible. The ideal is the **representative sample,** so-named because it represents a grouping and can be used to generalize research findings to an entire population. One type of representative sample is the **random sample,** a selection method that assures that every person in the population under study has an equal chance of being included. To draw a 10% random sample from a college population would be a relatively easy task. Researchers would need to obtain a complete list of all students from the registrar and to select 10% of the names by some random method. Thus, every student would have an equal chance of inclusion in the study, and standard statistical techniques could estimate the size of the potential error.

Unfortunately, however, there is no master list for every population that sociologists wish to study. There is no enumeration of Protestants, automobile workers, or Democrats. Strategies do exist, however, that enable researchers to generate representative samples of such groups. One approach involves identifying the places where these groups live or work, or the organizations to which they belong, and sampling within those communities or organizations.

In some kinds of research it is highly unlikely that representative samples can be structured or are even needed. Under these circumstances other techniques are available that can guarantee meaningful levels of accuracy. One approach is the use of *key informants,* who by virtue of their position in a community or group are able to provide information others will not possess. Obviously, the administrative officers of Exxon would know more about the corporation's finances and policy than would the workers in its oil fields. Or similarly, in studies of the distribution of power and influence in communities, sociologists typically interview political office holders and business leaders.

And there are other techniques. The study of heroin users on the streets of Miami made use of a **snowball sample,** wherein each person selected the next. The users, dealers, and drug counselors with whom the investigator made contact over the years served as "starting points." That is, they went to the streets with the investigator, introduced him to an active heroin user, and explained that he was conducting a research project in which there would be no reprisals from law enforcement officials. During or after each interview, at a time when the researcher felt that the rapport between him and the user was at its highest level, the researcher asked each user to identify other drug users with whom he or she was acquainted. These individuals, in turn, were located and interviewed, and the process repeated until the social network surrounding each user was exhausted.

It might be argued that the heroin users interviewed were not necessarily representative of those in other cities, or even those in other parts of Miami. That charge may indeed be true, but snowball sampling—the only technique available for doing street studies—can be structured to include mechanisms for reducing bias. In the Miami study, the networking technique restricted the pool of users to those who were currently active in the street subculture. In addition, it eliminated former users as well as those who were only peripheral to the mainstream community of street drug users. Moreover, the use of several different "starting points" in the same locale eliminated the problem of drawing all users from only one social network.

Given the fact that many populations *cannot* be accessed in any representative way, nonrepresentative samples are important sources of data in sociology and other social sciences. By themselves they are of little value in generalizing to wider populations—such as all heroin users in the United States. However, when data accumulated from equivalent samples in other cities or geographic regions reveal similar patterns, then the significance and ability to generalize about the data are considerably enhanced.

Data Analysis

Regardless of the methods of data collection utilized in sociological research, the next step in the research process is to organize the information gathered into a form appropriate for drawing conclusions and evaluating hypotheses. The ways in which the Miami heroin user data were examined illustrate the rudiments of data analysis in sociology.

Analysis

The information that is collected will not be of much use until it is organized and presented in a form that reveals what has been learned. This formatting process usually requires developing a way of summarizing the data, and at this point sociologists rely on statistics. Statistical techniques are also used to evaluate hypotheses.

Descriptive Statistics Although mention of the term "statistics" suggests complex formulas and odd-looking mathematical symbols, useful interpretations of data can be generated by some very basic, simple, and easily

Exhibit 2.8

Sociological Focus

Selected Characteristics of 356 Active Heroin Users Compared with Those of the General Population of the United States

Characteristic	Active Miami Heroin Users		General Population	
	Males	**Females**	**Males**	**Females**
Age (Median)	27.9 years	26.9 years	28.8 years	31.3 years
Ethnic Background:				
White	53.3%	55.6%	82.2%	83.9%
Black	33.5	24.8	11.2	12.1
Hispanic	14.2	16.2	6.5	6.4
Other	—	3.4	1.7	2.6
Years of Schooling (Median)	11.8	11.7	12.6	12.4
Employment Status:				
Employed	49.3%	41.9%	70.3%	47.7%
Unemployed	48.5	53.8	6.9	7.4
Not in Labor Force	2.2	4.3	22.0	48.3
Marital Status:				
Never Married	45.6%	46.2%	23.5%	17.0%
Married	25.9	13.7	68.6	63.1
Divorced/Separated	26.4	36.8	5.2	7.1
Widowed	1.7	2.6	2.7	12.8
No Data	.4	.9	—	—

Note: Percentages may not total 100 due to rounding.

Sources: James A. Inciardi, "Heroin Use and Street Crime," *Crime and Delinquency,* 25 (July 1979), p. 336; *Statistical Abstract of the United States, 1981,* (Washington DC: U.S. Department of Commerce, 1981), pp. 26, 33, 38, 142, and 380.

mastered statistical procedures. **Descriptive statistics** are arithmetic methods of reporting general patterns of social behavior. Simple percentages and averages, for example, are varieties of descriptive statistics. The majority of research reports in sociology provide some general descriptive data as a means of informing readers about the general characteristics of the sample, and it is in this context that descriptive statistics can be extremely useful. Exhibit 2.8, for example, summarizes the age, sex, marital status, education, ethnicity, and employment status characteristics of the Miami heroin users sampled. In addition, it provides a comparison of these variables for the Miami users with those of the general population of the United States.

Descriptive statistical techniques can also demonstrate how widespread the criminal activity was within this sample of heroin users. During the course of data collection, all of the research subjects were asked to indicate their sources of income. Their responses were totaled and expressed as percentages. As illustrated in the data table in Exhibit 2.9, 97.4% of the males and 94.9% of the females in the heroin study engaged in some form of criminal activity as a source of income. Interestingly, almost 50% of the men and over 40% of the women also had legal employment, while only about 20% were receiving some form of public assistance. A limited proportion also derives cash from relatives and friends.

Although these data indicate that heroin users commit crimes to support themselves, the numbers say nothing about the nature and extent of such crime, or anything about the relationship between heroin use and crime—only that most of the heroin users studied do indeed commit crimes. However, these other issues were dealt with in other segments of the data. All of the users were asked, for example, about the number and types of crimes they had committed during the 12-month period prior to their interview. As is apparent in Exhibit 2.10, their criminal activities were both frequent and diverse. Although much of this criminality involved the "less serious" crimes of drug sales and prostitution, the 356 heroin users were nevertheless responsible for almost 4,100 violent offenses (assaults and robberies) and over 23,000 thefts.

Descriptive statistics also can be employed to test hypotheses. The fundamental research question in the Miami heroin study centered on the relationship between drug use and criminal behavior, with a focus on when users initiated criminal activity. If the subjects had initiated their criminal activity after the onset of heroin use, then the evidence would offer some support for the enslavement hypothesis. The interviewer asked addicts how old they were when they first used various drugs and how old they were when they committed their first crime. Then the answers were merely averaged. As indicated in the table below, alcohol use among the participants in the Miami study began during their early teens, and both drug use and criminal activity had started by age 15—all some years prior to the first exposure to heroin. Continuous heroin use was the final step in a process that had begun at age 12 or 13. The picture that emerges is one of people who got an early start in both drugs and crime, suggesting that a generalized career in deviant behavior may have more to do with lawbreaking than with drug use. Therefore, we see that the enslavement hypothesis is not supported. This section illustrates how averages are used to indicate overall patterns, and that is a goal of sociological research—to discover general patterns of social behavior. It is quite logical to assume that this approach might conceal the fact that some individuals drifted into crime later in life to support a heavy drug habit, but that is not the more general pattern revealed by the data.

Drug/Criminal Activity	Males	Females
First Alcohol Use	12.8	13.8
First Alcohol Intoxication	13.3	13.9
First Marijuana Use	15.2	15.2
First Criminal Act	15.1	15.9
First Barbiturate Use	15.5	15.4
First Arrest	17.2	18.3
First Heroin Use	18.7	18.2
Continuous Heroin Use	19.2	18.4

Source: James A. Inciardi, "Heroin Use and Street Crime," *Crime and Delinquency*, 25 (July 1979), pp. 335–46.

Science cannot provide definite answers for every question. Source: *Science*, drawing by John Chase, reprinted by permission.

Correlational Statistics We have learned quite a bit up to this point about the results of the Miami heroin study, without examining the data using any of the sophisticated statistical methods available for data analysis. The next step in the study was a somewhat more rigorous analysis of the drugs-crime question, for which correlational techniques were used. **Correlational techniques** focus on the extent to which concepts vary together, or to put it another way, the degree to which a change in the independent variable is accompanied by a change in the dependent variable.

In Exhibit 2.11, the heroin users were classified as either "high" or "low" on *level of criminal involvement*. They were classified in the "high" category if they had committed more than the average number of crimes for the entire group (331), and in the "low" category if they fell at or below that point—a common way of subdividing large groups. This classification scheme is obviously a simplistic one, but it is also a potentially useful one. A different classification was structured for categorizing *frequency of heroin use*. The subjects' actual heroin use varied from occasional to daily: "light" was defined as use twice a week or less often, and "heavy" was defined as more than twice a week (both based on reported average use).

To demonstrate a relationship between the two variables (frequency of heroin use and level of criminal activity), a simple fourfold table ("Levels of Criminal Activity among Heroin Users" in Exhibit 2.11) was constructed. Each subject was classified for placement into the appropriate cell of the table on the basis of the two variables. Percentages are used in the table shown here to report the relative size of each user group.

Sociologists evaluate correlations relative to the idea of a **perfect correlation,** one in which every

Exhibit 2.9

Sociological Focus

Reading and Interpreting a Table

Tables are constructed to summarize a large amount of information in a brief, concise format. Although they sometimes appear complicated, they are actually simple to read. It is usually helpful to proceed as follows:

1. *The Title.* As obvious as it may seem, it is important to read the title carefully. The title will announce exactly what information is contained in the table. In the accompanying table, the title explains (1) who is involved (active heroin users); (2) what is being reported (sources of income); and (3) how the data were collected (self-reports).

Self-reported Sources of Income among 356 Active Heroin Users in Miami

	Sex of Respondents	
Source of Income	**Males**	**Females**
Family and Friends	12.5%	31.6%
Legal Employment	49.4	43.6
Public Assistance	20.0	18.8
Criminal Activity	97.4	94.9

n = 356

Note: Columns total more than 100% because respondents could list more than one source of income.

Source: James A. Inciardi, "Heroin Use and Street Crime," *Crime and Delinquency,* 25 (July 1979), p. 357.

2. *Notes and Sources.* Additional information about the respondents or the data-collection techniques utilized is often included in the form of "notes" at the foot of the table. The notes include information that cannot easily be incorporated into the title. In this exhibit's sample table the investigator alerts the reader to the fact that respondents could name more than a single source of income.

The source of the data is usually included at the end of the table. Anyone who anticipates doing research on the topic treated in the table (including those preparing term papers) will be able to locate the original research report, which will provide full details of the research project and methodology.

3. *Column and Row Labels.* These brief labels identify exactly what kind of information is summarized in the table. Columns are read down, and rows are read across. The column on the left in the sample table lists four different possible sources of income, while the next two columns subdivide the subjects by gender. It is common to find tables reporting data separately by gender, race, socioeconomic status, and age.

4. *The Numbers.* Possibly the single most important number in the table is the total number of observations included. This total is usually recorded in the following

change in the independent variable is accompanied by a change in the dependent variable. Had the correlation for the data in Exhibit 2.11 been "perfect," all light users would also have had low criminal involvement, and all heavy users would have had high criminal involvement. If there were no relationship, half of each user group would have fallen into each cell. In these data, neither situation exists. However, since 90.6% of the heavy users have *high* criminal involvement and 74.4% of the light users have *low* criminal involvement, a strong correlation is evident. Numerous statistical tests of varying degrees of sophistication are used to measure the magnitude of the correlation—the extent to which one variable increases with an accompanying increase in the other—but these go somewhat beyond the scope of an introductory course in sociology.

Drawing Conclusions

The norms of scientific inquiry have already imposed several limitations on the applicability of the heroin study research. The sample of Miami heroin users is not a format: n = 356. Generally, the total number of observations can be used as a rough indication of the dependability of the data. A study claiming to represent the population of the United States, but based on only 356 cases, should be expected to have a wide margin of error, but 356 cases is a much more reasonable sample for a study of heroin users in a single community. The interpretation of the data will also be influenced by the size of the base number. In a sample of 20, every person represents 5% of the total, and a shift of the answers of just four people would have a 20% effect on the data.

The data may be reported in percentages, central tendencies, actual numbers of cases, or some combination of these. Central tendencies (means, medians, and modes) are frequently encountered in social research, and all three forms convey information about the typical or central score of a group. The **mean** is the arithmetic average, computed by adding all scores and dividing by the number of cases. This figure will be distorted if one very large or one very small score is added to the rest. The **median** is the value that divides a group exactly in half. Numbers are arranged from high to low, and the score that is exactly in the middle is the median. The **mode** is the number that occurs most frequently in a collection of scores.

5. *The Conclusions.* Readers often overlook the fact that tabular data provide them with the opportunity to draw their own conclusions *and* to recognize the limitations of the data. There is not much room for disagreement here in our sample table with the conclusion that crime is an important source of money for heroin users. However, there are also certain conclusions that cannot be derived from the data shown. There is no indication of the amount of money involved in any category, meaning that there is no way to know how much money is derived from crime by this group of heroin users; it could be large or small amounts, gained on a regular or sporadic basis. Nor is there any indication of the kinds of criminal activity involved. Is the table chronicling property crimes, personal crimes, petty theft, or robbery on a large scale? It is a good habit to review the data in a table to confirm the investigator's conclusions.

representative one because of the impossibility of identifying the entire heroin-using population in that city. Moreover, since the investigation focused on heroin users, any conclusions derived do not apply with equal certainty to users of other drugs.

With these limitations in mind, it is still possible to draw some conclusions about the data. At the outset, it is important to note that the data do not "prove" the hypothesis. Scientific inquiry is both tentative and cumulative. The findings of one investigation must be reconfirmed in a number of different studies before scientists will accept them as being accurate. Consider how much biochemical research has been done on the link between smoking and cancer, and *still* some respected scientists question the findings. In this drug study, various sources of measurement error exist; more precise measures of drug use and crime may be possible than those that were utilized.

With respect to the relationship between heroin use and crime, the original hypothesis—that the level of criminal activity increases with the level of heroin use—may be said to be confirmed. It also must be

Exhibit 2.10

Sociological Focus

Criminal Activity among 356 Active Heroin Users during a One-year Period, Miami, Florida

	Men (N = 239)		Women (N = 117)	
Crime	**Total Offenses**	**Percentage of Offenses Resulting in Arrest**	**Total Offenses**	**Percentage of Offenses Resulting in Arrest**
Robbery	3,328	0.3 (*n* = 11)	573	0.5 (*n* = 3)
Assault	170	0.6 (*n* = 1)	26	11.5 (*n* = 3)
Burglary	4,093	0.7 (*n* = 30)	185	1.1 (*n* = 2)
Vehicle Theft	398	0.5 (*n* = 2)	5	—
Theft from Vehicle	877	0.7 (*n* = 6)	182	0.5 (*n* = 1)
Shoplifting	9,685	0.2 (*n* = 15)	5,171	0.3 (*n* = 13)
Pickpocketing	11	—	162	—
Prostitute Theft	62	1.6 (*n* = 1)	1,345	—
Other Theft	1,009	0.5 (*n* = 5)	182	0.5 (*n* = 1)
Forgery/Counterfeiting	1,711	0.4 (*n* = 6)	888	0.3 (*n* = 3)
Con Games	1,267	—	251	—
Stolen Goods	6,527	<0.1 (*n* = 3)	1,006	<0.1 (*n* = 4)
Prostitution	2	—	14,307	0.3 (*n* = 37)
Procuring	2,819	<0.1 (*n* = 1)	1,153	—
Drug Sales	40,897	0.2 (*n* = 93)	11,289	0.2 (*n* = 23)
Arson	65	—	88	—
Vandalism	58	1.7 (*n* = 1)	3	—
Fraud	185	1.1 (*n* = 2)	34	—
Gambling	6,306	<0.1 (*n* = 3)	574	—
Extortion	648	—	41	—
Loan Sharking	463	—	1	—
Alcohol Offenses	58	10.3 (*n* = 6)	22	22.7 (*n* = 5)
All Other	5	60.0 (*n* = 3)	2	100.0 (*n* = 2)
Total	80,644	0.2 (*n* = 189)	37,490	0.3 (*n* = 97)
Mean Number of Offenses per Subject	337		320	

Source: James A. Inciardi, "Heroin Use and Street Crime," *Crime and Delinquency*, 25 (July 1979), pp. 335–46.

remembered, however, that the investigator merely demonstrated a relationship, not a *causal* relationship. Causation is implied by the enslavement theory of addiction, but both of these variables may, in reality, have been caused by a still unknown third factor. And in fact, the data fail to provide confirmation of the enslavement theory. Drug use and criminal activity within the sample of Miami heroin users emerged during early adolescence. Furthermore, most had been involved in crime prior to any experimentation with heroin. This certainly casts doubt on the validity of the enslavement theory, and alternative explanations must be considered. Perhaps

Exhibit 2.11

Applied Sociology

The Drugs–Crime Connection

To what extent do the findings of the Miami heroin user study have practical use for understanding and dealing with the nature and extent of crime among heroin users? Without question, the data do indeed suggest that, at least within the population of heroin users examined in this study, criminality is extensive. (After all, as indicated in Exhibit 2.11, these heroin users committed over 100,000 crimes during a one-year period.) Beyond this, can these data be used for reducing the magnitude of drug-related crime?

Since the early 1970s, research in the drug-abuse field has been demonstrating that, contrary to popular notions, not all heroin users are alike. Some are only sporadic or "weekend users," while others are so heavily involved that all of their waking hours are spent in drug taking and drug-seeking activities. Moreover, research has indicated that while most heroin users do indeed commit crimes, the majority of these offenses are petty thefts, prostitution, and drug sales. Yet on the other hand, the same research has suggested that within the total population of drug users in the street community, a significant proportion are highly dangerous, predatory, and violent offenders who are responsible for an unknown number of armed robberies, aggravated assaults, and brutal homicides. Dispersed within all of these groups are some, as the enslavement theorists suggest, whose criminal acts are the result of the users' attempts to support their drug habits. Others are enmeshed in pervasive deviant life-styles, while still others are strongly committed to violence.

The findings of the Miami study represent an early stage in the identification of the various types of drug users, and as is apparent in the table below, there are differences in the criminality levels of the two groups classified in the study. Subsequent research in Miami and other cities may help to extend the findings of this study to determine (1) the characteristics of those heroin users who are likely to respond to treatment and (2) those criminal addicts who, for the sake of the long-term protection of society, would best be incarcerated.

Levels of Criminal Activity among Heroin Users

	Frequency of Heroin Use	
Level of Criminal Activity	Heavy	Light
High	90.6%	25.6%
Low	9.4	74.4

drug use and criminal activity are indeed just two aspects of a generally deviant life-style adopted during early adolescence. What is needed, then, is some theoretical point of view that will explain the origins of both variables. Perhaps drug use and crime are caused by childhood or family experiences, the social conditions common to those neighborhoods where rates of drug use and crime are high, or a variety of other factors.

This specific study provides many insights into the research process. The investigator devoted several years of time and effort to the project, not to mention the funds provided by the federal government. Hundreds of drug users spoke freely, revealing countless details of their lives and behavior. All these interviews had to be sorted and summarized within the framework of the larger goals of the study. The results were subsequently published so that they could be made available to other sociologists doing similar work. The knowledge gained in this study is valuable, but in the larger context of scientific research the findings add just one small segment to the body of knowledge about one social phenomena. It is still premature to conclude that one hypothesis has been demonstrated beyond doubt. Additional research is called for, and the investigator will continue with his work, as will other sociologists who will incorporate these findings in their own work. In a very real sense this study illustrates the manner in which sociological knowledge evolves—slowly, tentatively, incrementally—always with room for growth, change, and revision.

SUMMARY

Research in sociology is conducted according to the rules and procedures of the scientific method in order to generate systematic information about social phenomena. Research may be exploratory (when its purpose is to detail some previously unexplored social event or process), or explanatory (when it serves to discover or explain cause-and-effect relationships among variables).

Research in sociology is a process, an array of procedures set out in a series of logical and orderly steps. This research enterprise begins with the formulation of research questions and the definition of concepts. Alternative research designs are available for collecting data, each having its own peculiar advantages and shortcomings. In many instances, the nature of the research design is dictated by the content of the research question, the available data, or the population to be examined. Sample size and method of selection influence the investigator's ability to extrapolate from the research results for groups other than the specific group studied. Finally, as the observations are made, they are transformed into data that address the original question and suggest interpretations and conclusions.

Ethical issues impinge upon the research process at every step. Sociologists must be alert to the potential for invasion of their subjects' privacy and the infliction of psychological harm. Moreover, the research process must balance the goal of understanding social behavior against the problematic nature of deception, misrepresentation, and violations of confidentiality.

KEY TERMS/CONCEPTS

attributes
content analysis
control group
correlational techniques
dependent variable
descriptive statistics
experiment
experimental design
experimental group
exploratory studies
Hawthorne effect
hypothesis
independent variable
mean
median
mode
norm of objectivity
operationalizing concepts
participant observation
perfect correlation
random sample
reliability
representative sample
research design
sample
science
scientific method
snowball sample
survey
unobtrusive measures
validity
variables

DISCUSSION QUESTIONS

1. This chapter describes how one sociologist interviewed heroin users. Do you feel that the heroin users' responses met the criteria of validity and reliability? Why or why not?
2. Was Laud Humphries behaving in an ethical manner when he secretly identified the homosexual subjects in his study? Could he have accomplished his research in any other way?
3. What do you think would be the most effective means of selecting an unbiased sample of sociologists? Of lawyers? Of parents with children in day-care facilities? Of victims of muggings?
4. Formulate a testable hypothesis on the relationship between "substance abuse" and "broken homes." How would you operationalize your concepts? What population would you study? What kinds of data would you collect?
5. Is it possible for social scientists to be totally objective about the topics they are studying?
6. Can the research findings on heroin users be employed to generalize about the users of other types of drugs, such as marijuana or cocaine?

SUGGESTED READINGS

Irving Crespi, "Surveys as Legal Evidence," *Public Opinion Quarterly,* 51 (1987), pp. 84–91. Reprinted in the student *Study Guide* that accompanies this textbook, this essay examines both the shortcomings and relevance of survey data in legal issues.

Kenneth R. Hoover, *The Elements of Social Scientific Thinking* (New York: St. Martin's, 1984). Intended for those taking their first steps as social science researchers, this short paperback examines such issues as thinking scientifically, the elements of science, research strategies and refinements, and the measurement of variables.

Ruth Horowitz, *Honor and the American Dream: Culture and Identity in a Chicano Community* (New Brunswick, NJ: Rutgers University Press, 1983). Nominated in 1984 for the C. Wright Mills Award for the best book in sociology, this study of a Mexican-American community in Chicago illustrates the structure and process of the participant-observation technique.

James A. Inciardi and Anne E. Pottieger, "Drug Use and Crime Among Two Cohorts of Women Narcotics Users: An Empirical Assessment," *Journal of Drug Issues,* 16 (1986), pp. 91–106. Reprinted in the student *Study Guide* that accompanies this textbook, this paper focuses on the drug use and criminal activities of women heroin users contacted in Miami during the 1980s. In addition, it compares these women with a subsample of those already discussed in the textbook chapter.

NOTES

1. James A. Inciardi, "Heroin Use and Street Crime," *Crime and Delinquency,* 25 (July 1979), pp. 335–46.
2. On this latter point, a government official is reported to have said: "Though there's been some excellent work, there's great unhappiness in general with what we've been getting from our investment in social science research . . . there's just no intellectual capital to draw upon." Quoted in Tom Alexander, "The Social Engineers Under Fire," *Fortune,* October 1972, p. 32.
3. U.S. Bureau of the Census, *Handbook of Labor Statistics* (Washington, DC: U.S. Government Printing Office, 1985), p. 38.
4. See Rodney Stark and W. S. Bainbridge, *The Future of Religion* (Berkeley: University of California Press, 1985).
5. David W. Maurer and Victor H. Vogel, *Narcotics and Narcotic Addiction* (Springfield, IL: Charles C. Thomas, 1967), pp. 286–87.
6. Howard S. Becker, *Outsiders: Studies in the Sociology of Deviance* (New York: Free Press, 1963), pp. 41–58.
7. See R. D. Arvey, E. M. Passino, and J. W. Lounsbury, "Job Analysis Results as Influenced by Sex of Analyst," *Journal of Applied Psychology,* 62 (1977), pp. 411–16.
8. M. E. Hellman and L. Saruwartari, "When Beauty is Beastly: The Effects of Appearance and Sex on Evaluations of Job Applicants for Managerial and Nonmanagerial Jobs," *Organizational Behavior and Human Performance,* 23 (1979), pp. 360–73.
9. J. M. Darley and C. D. Batson, "From Jerusalem to Jericho: A Study of Situational and Dispositional Variables in Helping Behavior," *Journal of Personality and Social Psychology,* 27 (1973), pp. 100–108.
10. Sandra J. Ball-Rokeach, Milton Rokeach, and Joel W. Grube, *The Great American Values Test* (New York: Free Press, 1984).
11. See Peter Jackson and Susan J. Smith, *Social Interaction and Ethnic Segregation* (London: Academic Press, 1981).
12. E. E. LeMasters, *Blue-Collar Aristocrats: Life-Styles at a Working-Class Tavern* (Madison: University of Wisconsin Press, 1975).
13. Ruth Horowitz, *Honor and the American Dream: Culture and Identity in a Chicano Community* (New Brunswick, NJ: Rutgers University Press, 1983).
14. Harvey A. Siegal, *Outposts of the Forgotten: Socially Terminal People in Slum Hotels and Single Room Occupancy Tenements* (New Brunswick, NJ: Transaction, 1978).
15. James A. Inciardi, *The War on Drugs: Heroin, Cocaine, Crime, and Public Policy* (Palo Alto, CA: Mayfield, 1986), p. 120.
16. Ruth Horowitz, *Honor and the American Dream*, p. 7.
17. Leon Festinger, Henry W. Rieken, and Stanley Schacter, *When Prophesy Fails* (New York: Harper & Row, 1956).
18. See, for example, Stuart L. Cohen and Joan E. Fiedler, "Content Analysis of Multiple Messages in Suicide Notes," *Suicide and Life-Threatening Behavior,* 4 (Summer 1974), pp. 75–79; Valerie J. Hanken, "Banality Reinvestigated: A Computer-Based Content Analysis of Suicidal and Forced Death Documents," *Suicide and Life-Threatening Behavior,* 6 (Spring 1976), pp. 36–43.
19. Paul R. Ehrlich, Anne H. Ehrlich, and John P. Holdren, *Human Ecology* (San Francisco: Freeman, 1973).
20. Eugene J. Webb, Donald T. Campbell, Richard D. Schwartz, Lee Sechrest, and Janet Belew Grove, *Nonreactive Measures in the Social Sciences* (Boston: Houghton Mifflin, 1981).
21. Helena C. Kraemer and Sue Theimann, *How Many Subjects?* (Newbury Park, CA: Sage, 1987).

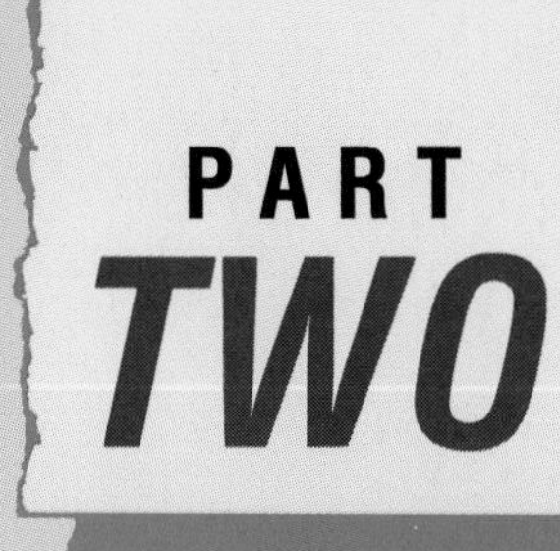

The Organization of Social Life

Culture

In the shallow light of dawn the airfield is like thousands of others; there is a runway, a hangar, and a radio-transmission tower. But here there are no planes. There is no activity except near a huge fire that burns at one end of the field, where the flames serve as a beacon to guide incoming planes. The fire is tended through the night, as it has been for many years, by a young Vanuatu tribesman with a bone ornament through his nose. The hangar is bamboo and thatch; the runway is covered with the stubble of an encroaching jungle; the radio transmitter is but a tin can.

This "airfield," quite unlike all others, is maintained with the sure knowledge that one day the great silver aircraft will return, loaded with radios, ice cream, jeeps, plates and forks, tents, firearms, and other awe-inspiring objects. Such an event happened once before, decades earlier when the Americans came to the New Hebrides Islands of the southern Pacific Ocean during World War II. The Americans left suddenly, taking their magic and riches with them, but tribal prophets reminded the people of ancient legends that explained how the ghostly white spirits of their ancestors would one day return, bearing riches once again.

The prophets also had warned that the old wartime airfield might confuse their ancestors. They felt that it was necessary to prepare a new landing strip in a more sacred place. Ground was consecrated, the landing area cleared, and the buildings erected. No one doubted what would eventually happen and the people faithfully devoted their energies to tending the beacon, often neglecting their own homes and gardens in the process. The members of this New Hebrides "cargo cult" took comfort from the words of visiting missionaries who explained that Christians had been waiting nearly two thousand years for the return of Christ. The people of the tribe hoped, however, that the ancestors would not take quite that long.[1]

New Hebridians worship The Red Cross, hoping for the return of the material wealth brought by soldiers during World War II.

CULTURE: CONSENSUS AND DIVERSITY

To outside observers from a nation where television, sports cars, space travel, and organ transplants are commonplace, the peoples of the jungle airfield—the New Hebrides cargo cult—might appear unusual or even bizarre. But in that remote section of the South Pacific, as in the United States and everywhere else in the world, people are born and nurtured into a system of customs, beliefs, rules, and ideas that define and organize their physical, social, and supernatural worlds. Regardless of whether people live on tropical islands or in the crowded cities of New York, Rome, or Shanghai, they all confront common problems—they all must eat, shelter themselves, and raise children to take their place and perpetuate their way of life. But although people everywhere share common problems, their solutions to those problems vary. The distinctive ways that groups think and act to deal with the problems of everyday existence are shaped by what social scientists call *culture.* As anthropologist Edward B. Tylor defined it more than a century ago, culture is "that complex whole which includes knowledge, belief, art, law, morals, customs and other habits acquired by [an individual] as a member of society."[2] In other words, **culture** is the customary manner in which human groups learn to organize their behavior in relation to their environment.

Although Tylor was an anthropologist, his definition of culture continues to be used by sociologists because it points out that *society* and *culture* are different concepts. While culture focuses on customs, traditions, and behaviors, most sociologists would agree that **society** refers to a group of interacting individuals who share the same territory.*

At the time of Tylor's writing during the nineteenth century, descriptions of exotic cultures singled out their unusual customs and practices. Polygamy and ancestor worship, for example, were then considered rather bizarre forms of behavior by Western standards. Yet today it is well recognized that culture is a more complex and subtle phenomenon than it appears to be. A distinctive language, a religious system, laws, and customs all form readily identifiable parts of a culture. And too, culture is far more pervasive than such surface differences alone might suggest. It also involves many "hidden dimensions"—habitual ways of thinking, acting, and feeling that often operate below typical levels of awareness (see Exhibit 3.1).

Culture Shock

It is one thing to read about other peoples' customs, but quite another to experience them firsthand—perhaps the only way to understand the full meaning of culture. As people move from one culture to another, differences become apparent to them. Moreover, they frequently experience a psychological state known as **culture shock**—the psychic stress brought on by the strain of adjusting to a different culture.

Culture shock is not something that is restricted just to students of the exotic. Even ordinary tourists feel a certain amount of isolation and vulnerability when first confronted by someone who speaks no English. Culture shock occurs in situations when people are separated from systems of cultural meanings that they are familiar with or when they find themselves in circumstances in which the meanings of acts and words are either changed or totally alien.

Even cultures that appear quite similar on the surface may reflect many subtle contrasts—some of which can be confusing. Americans traveling in Great Britain find it rather simple to adjust to the fact that *gasoline* is "petrol," a *truck* is a "lorry," a *child's stroller* is a "push chair," and a *large glass of warm beer* is a

*It should be pointed out here that there are variations on this general definition. The functionalist perspective in sociology stresses that members of a society are linked together by interdependence. Conflict sociologists emphasize that some societies are created on the basis of political views, with members from a variety of cultural backgrounds. Symbolic-interactionists note that social boundaries are a matter of peoples' awareness, and as such, society is identified by a shared feeling of common identity.

"pint." On the other hand, Americans feel that Britons insist on driving on "the wrong side" of the road, a custom about which it is rather easy to feel insecure. Too, many Americans are surprised at the way the British use knives and the way they hold their forks. Consequently, most American tourists in Britain will experience a vague sense of disorientation and uncertainty in simple social situations.

In contrast to the rather minor differences between the United States and Great Britain, culture shock can also be quite dramatic. In the Sudan, the largest country in Africa, which is situated at the eastern end of the Sahara desert zone, strict Islamic law has prevailed since 1983. Criminal codes there prescribe execution for heresy, whipping for the sale or consumption of alcohol, and stoning for adultery. Americans visiting the Sudanese capital of Khartoum experience considerable culture shock when approached by beggars who lack hands and feet as the result of amputations ordered by the courts for those convicted of theft.[3] Citizens of India raised in the orthodox Hindu tradition may never cope with the shock encountered through certain dealings with Western cultures. For Europeans and Americans, the cow is a source of food, yet the orthodox Hindu would rather die of starvation than eat one of these sacred animals.[4]

Culture shock is inevitable, but it can even happen within one's own society when confronting new situations in which different norms and beliefs prevail. A person can experience culture shock merely by changing jobs or moving to another part of the country. The reaction to culture shock tends to be a withdrawal from interaction, the maintenance of some familiar kind of human communication (writing letters to family and friends), or association with others who share common roots.

Showing respect for the dead is common to all cultures, but it may be expressed differently. The Toraja of Indonesia erect effigies of their ancestors outside the caves where they are buried. Floral offerings in a cemetery in northern Mexico are much more familiar to most Americans.

Ethnocentrism and Cultural Relativity

Unusual customs are often viewed with amusement, and people all too frequently make value judgments about the beliefs and practices of other cultures. Few members of today's generation of Americans, for example, could comfortably witness a ritual that was once common within a small society in the Pacific Northwest. Among the Kwakiutl tribe many years ago, youths being initiated into their "Cannibal Society" threw themselves into a frenzied dance that culminated with the biting of mouthfuls of flesh from the arms of the onlookers.[5] Most outsiders would label the behavior as uncivilized, repulsive, unnatural, and barbaric. Yet this reaction would be an illustration of **ethnocentrism,** the tendency to judge other cultures by the standards of one's own.

Anthropologist I. M. Lewis once remarked that "ethnocentrism is the natural condition of mankind."[6] Lewis was referring to the fact that people are indoctrinated from childhood in how to think and act. During this lifelong process the values and standards of culture are continuously reinforced through religion, at public ceremonies, in the media, and at social events. For example, people's belief that there is one all-powerful "God" renders every religion that worships many spirits a "pagan" culture. This word, along with such terms as "primitive"or "uncivilized" are sure indicators of ethnocentrism in most usages. In short, ethnocentrism is cultural chauvinism—the attitude that one's own customs and beliefs are automatically superior to those of all others. Extreme ethnocentrism is at the heart of bigotry and discrimination, and often underlies war as well.

Ethnocentrism is sometimes confused with patriotism, yet they are quite different. *Patriotism* is devotion to one's country. It was patriotism that drew Americans together when their amateur hockey team upset the Soviet Union in the 1980 Winter Olympics. It was

Exhibit 3.1

Research in Sociology

The Hidden Dimensions of Culture

Human communication is typically associated with language, but there are other ways that individuals transmit ideas to one another during the course of a conversation. Voice tones, gestures, facial expressions—even style of dress and grooming may be interpreted as messages by others.

Kinesics, the study of gestural communication or "body language," is important to people who research patterns of culture and cultural differences. Since people are physically alike for the most part, certain aspects of body language have universal meaning. A smile, for example, conveys the same message in any part of the world. But kinesic communication is heavily influenced by culture, with the result that certain gestures and postures can have radically different meanings in different parts of the world. Positioning the thumb and index finger into a circle means "OK" in the United States, but it means "worthless" in southern France, "money" in Japan, and constitutes an obscene gesture in many parts of Latin America. Similarly, tapping a finger to one's head may mean "he's crazy" to Americans, but to a Brazilian it says "I'm thinking."

While most people are aware of how communication and interaction can be influenced by body language, there are many hidden dimensions of culture about which people are less aware. The hidden dimensions of culture are best illustrated in the works of Edward T. Hall, who demonstrated how people are largely unaware of deeply ingrained cultural assumptions they hold about the physical and social world around them. Hall focused on *proxemics,* a term that is best understood as the cultural use of space in personal interactions. He pointed out, for example, that every person carries a "little bubble of space" with him that separates him from others. The size and shape of this space vary from one culture to the next. Northern Europeans and Americans, for instance, are uncomfortable with people from the Middle East who prefer to stand quite close to one another when they talk—to share their breath with others. The Middle Eastern concept of the dimensions of the "bubble" are small compared to Western standards. Thus, Middle Easterners violate the Western notion of a comfortable conversational distance of approximately 21 inches.

Bedouin men stand quite close to one another to exchange greetings, but most Americans would feel uncomfortable at this distance.

To carry this concept further, Hall noted that American culture has taught people that the space under their feet belongs to *them,* an idea that does not jibe with beliefs in the Arab world. There, because a person does not have a right to underfoot space, others may encroach upon it at will. Significantly, Hall observed, Arabs have no word for "trespass."

The social organization of Arab interaction, perfectly normal within the context of their culture, is likely to be interpreted as rude, aggressive, threatening, or even hostile by Americans. Because the Arab view violates Westerners' unconscious ideas of space, the reaction of backing off to establish a more comfortable distance seems natural to us. But to the Arab, this would be considered an unfriendly gesture. This brief discussion of proxemics suggests how subtle the influence of culture can be and how easily misunderstandings can arise.

SOURCES: Ray L. Birdwhistell, "Kinesics and Communication," in E. Carpenter and M. McLuhan (eds.), *Explorations in Communications* (Boston: Beacon, 1960), pp. 54–64; Edward T. Hall, *The Hidden Dimension* (Garden City, NY: Doubleday, 1966); Desmond Morris, Peter Collett, Porter Marsh, and Marie O'Shaugnessy, *Gestures, Their Origins and Distribution* (New York: Stein and Day, 1979).

Standards of appropriate attire for women in Morocco (where purdah is practiced by Moslem women) and California reflect diverse cultural beliefs and values.

patriotism that made Sylvester Stallone's *Rambo* and *Rocky IV* so successful at the box office during the mid-eighties.

To counter ethnocentrism, social scientists favor the standard of **cultural relativity,** the principle that any culture must be understood in terms of its own values and in its own context. Cultural relativists would argue that the Kwakiutl ritual was, in fact, a reaffirmation of their repugnance of cannibalism. No human flesh was actually consumed and the dancers were socially isolated for months afterward as a symbolic gesture of how terrible their acts were.

Cultural relativity is an easily defensible position when it comes to matters of dietary habits or social space, but it can be a difficult stance to sustain when more complex matters are involved. Is cultural relativity appropriate when a society violates human rights, endorses torture, condones slavery, or engages in terrorism? This question is not easy to answer since the definitions of "human rights," "slavery," and "terrorism" are themselves relative concepts whose definitions vary from one culture and society to the next. Consider, for example, the ideology of Moammar El-Gadhafi* and many of his followers in Libya. Gadhafi considers himself an advocate of the world's oppressed peoples. With the goals of Arab unification and the creation of a Palestinian state, Gadhafi sees Western imperialism as the real "terrorism." He views U.S. aid to the contra rebels in Nicaragua as terrorism. His own behavior, on the other hand, is not terrorism, but part of a holy war in pursuit of the salvation of the masses.[7]

Cultural Universals

Anthropologists have identified hundreds of human societies, each with its own unique culture. Despite the rich diversity, there are a good many **cultural universals**—traits and patterns that are found in all known societies. A partial list includes body adornment, interpretation of dreams, magic, marriage, language and gestures, funeral ceremonies, games, courtship, gift giving, calendars, religious systems, and luck.[8]

Universals are reminders of the common humanity of people throughout the world. Such striking uniformity suggests that members of societies everywhere must confront the same problems if they are to survive as a group. Of course, cultures have developed many alternative ways of dealing with similar situations. With respect

*Curiously, for many years no one actually new how to spell the name of the "tiger of Tripoli," as he has been called, and the Libyan leader ended up with more aliases than bank robber John Dillinger. The *New York Times* and *Washington Post* used "Qaddafi," while *Time* put its money on "Gaddafi," and *Newsweek* rendered it "Kaddafi." *U.S. News & World Report* countered with "Qadhafi," as did the *Wall Street Journal,* the White House, and the State Department. Other media representatives used "Gadhafi," "Khadaffi," "Khadafy," and "Quaddafi." The problem was that Libyans write the name in Arabic. In the Roman alphabet, however, it can be spelled many different ways. But the mystery was finally solved in 1986 when the Libyan leader personally responded to a letter from a class of second graders in Minnesota. Typed under his Arabic signature was the name "Moammar El-Gadhafi." See *U.S. News & World Report,* June 9, 1986, p. 5.

Exhibit 3.2 Case Study

"Ghost Marriages," "Wife Marriages," and "Ghost Brides" among the Nuer

The Nuer, a pastoral society living on the upper reaches of the Nile River in the African Sudan, were first studied at length during the 1930s. At that time, the Nuer had evolved a society in which patrilineal descent (descent through the males) was so important to the cultural heritage of the group that special types of marital unions were established to ensure heirs to all males in the tribe.

The "ghost marriage" was structured to provide offspring to every man or boy who had died before having any children. In such cases, it was the duty of one of his kinsmen to marry a wife on his behalf. The sons of such a union were legally the children of the dead man and would inherit the social or ritual privileges that he would normally pass on to his sons. The custom was based on the deeply held feeling that a man should not lie in his grave unremembered. He needed male offspring to whom he could make his wishes known in his afterlife. If his kinsmen failed in their duty to marry a wife for him, it was believed that he could bring evil upon them.

In the "wife marriage," an elderly woman, beyond the childbearing years, could use the property of her dead husband to set up a marriage in his and her name. The children of the marriage belonged to her and to her deceased husband, and they inherited accordingly.

The "ghost bride marriage" also existed for the sake of patrilineal descent. An old woman, whose family was about to die out because she had no living male relatives, could marry another woman to the name of a deceased male of her family. Then she invited some unrelated male to have intercourse with the "ghost bride," thus establishing a line of heirs.

Practiced for generations by the Nuer, this system of marriage variations tended to be self-perpetuating. Many men died prematurely in tribal fighting. If a man who had married a wife for a dead kinsman also died without having a wife of his own, another "ghost marriage" or other variant would be necessary. During the 1940s, the "ghost," "wife," and "ghost bride'" marriages were outlawed by the government of the Anglo-Egyptian Sudan. However, the marriage patterns persisted. Moreover, in recent years the Nuer have expanded into other parts of East Africa, bringing with them features of their culture that were subsequently adopted by neighboring tribes.

SOURCES: E. E. Evans-Pritchard, *Kinship and Marriage Among the Nuer* (London: Oxford University Press, 1951); Ralph Piddington, *Social Anthropology* (Edinburgh: Oliver and Boyd, 1952); Marshall D. Sahlins, "The Segmentary Lineage: An Organization of Predatory Lineage," *American Anthropologist,* 63 (1961), pp. 322–45.

to the institution of marriage, for instance, cultures may condone various forms of plural marriage, and in some cases even marriages in honor of the deceased (see Exhibit 3.2).

The link between universals and common group problems is often direct and straightforward. The need for a standardized means of communication underlies the adoption of a common language, calendars mark the passage of time, and courtship provides a uniform procedure for choosing a marriage partner. Other universals play a less obvious role in human affairs, often not fully recognized by participants in the culture. The meaning of "funerals" may be obscure until it is examined in a social context. Emile Durkheim pointed out, for instance, that religious ceremonies associated with the grief suffered at the death of a family member are not only acts of respect for the deceased but also serve to help the survivors cope with their loss through participation in group ritual.[9]

THE COMPONENTS OF CULTURE

When studying cultures, social scientists analyze them in terms of their principal aspects—behavioral, perceptual, and material. The *behavioral* aspect refers to how people act, particularly how they interact with one another. The

SOCIAL INDICATOR

The Logo

A *logo* (short for "logogram") is a symbol used to designate some word or name. The blue and white GM logo, for example, immediately brings General Motors Corporation to mind and is used to convey the idea of a strong, efficient company.

The logo is a part of corporate culture in industrialized nations. In fact, logos have become so important and coveted that they are protected by copyright laws. When NBC decided to modernize its corporate logo in 1980, replacing the 29-year-old NBC peacock, they settled on a geometric "N" design. Although they purchased certain rights for the "N" from a small midwestern broadcasting firm, which had begun using the "N" shortly before NBC, they only used the pure geometric form for about a year. In 1981 the company decided that they would renew their use of the peacock because its image was so clearly identified with NBC. A new composite mark was created by superimposing the peacock over the geometric "N" design.

The GM and NBC logos might be compared with that of ZB, a Miami cocaine dealer who devised his own logo for the same reason as corporate America: symbol recognition.

perceptual aspect refers to the views of the world that people have regarding how they and others should act. Some symbols are designed to create a perception. Corporate logos are an example. The *material* aspect of a culture refers to the objects that its people produce. These three aspects or components, however, do not exist independently of one another. For this reason, cultures are often more easily understood by examining their components at a more discrete level, focusing on systems of language, the symbolism of material objects, norms, values, and the beliefs that people acquire as members of their societies. Each of these factors can be examined separately to reveal how it shapes human behavior.

Language

Whether written or verbal, language is basic to all cultures. It is the mechanism through which people communicate with one another. Beginning students of a foreign language often start with the simple nouns and verbs that have an equivalent in their native tongue. They learn, for example, that the word for *house* is "casa" in Spanish or "haus" in German. Words used in this way are simply alternative names for the same things. Problems begin to emerge when students are confronted with words for which there are no equivalents in the foreign tongue. As noted in Exhibit 3.1, for example, in Arabic there is no word for *trespass.* Similarly, Eskimos have no word for *war.*[10] In many instances it is almost impossible to communicate ideas in one language that are easily expressed in another. The English sentence, "I gave it to him," cannot be directly translated into Navajo since that language does not have a verb with the general meaning of *to give.* The Navajo have twelve verb forms that suggest *giving,* but each is complicated by the inclusion of additional meanings referring to the size, shape, or current state of the object involved. About the best that can be used is *baaniskaah,* which says, "I cause a container with contents to move toward him in a manner that will complete the action."[11]

These examples suggest that language is something more than just a convenient way to communicate. Once created, language shapes the way people perceive and experience the world around them. This concept, called the **Sapir-Whorf hypothesis** after the two linguists who developed it into a formal theory, implies that the tyranny of language goes well beyond the mere influencing of the way people relate to their experiences. The power of language also forces people to perceive the world on terms that are built into the language that they speak.[12] If this theory is indeed so, then speakers of different languages never experience quite the same realities.

What this means in practice is that since Arabs have no word for *trespass,* they cannot experience an invasion of territory in the same way that Americans do. To suggest another example, Americans identify the space between two objects as *empty,* while the Japanese equivalent is *full of nothing.*[13]

Material Culture and the Symbolic Dimension

Material culture includes manufactured goods, factories, houses, tools, automobiles, arrow heads, clay pots—in short, all the tangible objects that a society produces and uses. Thus, the standard of living of any given culture can be roughly measured through an inventory of its various material artifacts. Congested with factories and awash in electronic gadgets, fast food restaurants, and millions of other material items, American culture reflects a rather high standard of living. By contrast, that of the New Hebrides cargo people, noted earlier, appears sparse, dominated by an artificial airfield and an everlasting bonfire.

An important point to make about material culture is that physical objects are seldom just "things." Since they are produced by members of a culture, they have shared symbolic meanings. The cargo cult's airfield fire is there to guide their ancestors' journey. As such, it is a sacred object. An outsider, unaware of that special role, would be unable to understand the people's single-minded dedication to the flame. Or similarly, the cargo peoples would find it difficult to comprehend why Americans respond the way they do to the Vietnam Veterans Memorial in Washington, D.C. But citizens of the United States understand the memorial to be considerably more than a massive wall etched with names. On any given day it is visited by as many as 30,000 people, many of whom fall strangely silent as they approach, reaching out to touch the granite form or the statue that looms over it. When they depart, they leave behind other aspects of their material culture—letters, flowers, photographs, and once, even a teddy bear.[14] Like the airfield fire, the war memorial, too, is a sacred object.

A visitor to the Vietnam Veterans Memorial traces an etching—an activity that the people of the cargo cult would not understand.

Failure to realize the symbolic meanings of material objects can have unusual consequences. One of the more often repeated examples occurred several decades ago among the Yir Yoront of Australia.[15] This aboriginal tribe's work of clearing land and building was done with stone axes, which were painstakingly fashioned by hand. In misguided efforts to increase agricultural productivity, missionaries distributed metal axes to all members of the tribe. The results were totally unforeseen. What the missionaries did not realize was that the stone axes were not merely tools but had traditionally served as symbols of authority and social standing for adult males. Women and children had been denied ownership of axes and the knowledge of how to make them. Construction followed an elaborate ritual. The distribution of steel axes disrupted social relations, and the survival of the culture was threatened. Another example of symbol misinterpretation appears in Exhibit 3.3.

The Normative Order

As children mature, they confront a bewildering array of rules for living in their society. Parents and peers, teachers and police officers, and a host of other individuals instruct them on how to walk, speak, dress, eat, treat their friends, play games, drive cars, and do countless other things—both important and trivial. They also learn their society's **norms,** the various rules, standards, and expectations that regulate their interactions with other members of their culture and society.

Folkways

Almost a century ago, sociologist William Graham Sumner coined the term **folkways** to designate the norms that guide the customary, normal, and habitual ways in which the peoples of a society or group do things.[16] Thus, folkways are the conventions and customs that people are expected to follow in everyday situations. The norms of shaking the hand of a new acquaintance, the rules of grammar and syntax, the tradition of mowing one's lawn when the grass begins to grow, and wearing black at funerals and burying the dead in caskets are American folkways.

Sumner argued that most people follow folkways out of habit more than for any other reason, because they have been reared in a culture that defined such conventions as "normal" ways of behaving. In fact, folkways are typically "invisible" until people deviate from them. As

Exhibit 3.3

Sociology in the Media

Bedeviled P&G Drops Trademark

Frustrated by the hellish persistence of rumors about corporate satanism, Procter & Gamble is stripping the moon-and-stars trademark from its products.

The logo—a bearded man-in-the-moon under 13 stars—has helped fuel various rumors linking the packaged-goods giant to devil worship.

The stories first surfaced in 1981; they reappeared recently in the East.

As P&G tries with mixed success to root out the source, it fields an average of 25,000 satan-related inquiries a year. So,

gradually over the next year, the logo will disappear.

"This is not going to be an immediate solution," said spokesman William H. Dobson. But eventually, P&G will eradicate the most visible element of the rumor. The trademark stays on P&G stationery, signs, and publications.

The mark evolved in the 1860s and was registered in 1882. The stars represent the 13 colonies; the moon is just that.

SOURCE: Robert Garfield, *USA Today,* April 25, 1985, p. 1A.

already noted in Chapter 1, ethnomethodologists violate folkways as part of their research. Violations of folkways are seldom ignored, although the reactions to such violations are generally relatively mild.

People who inadvertently violate their society's folkways typically feel uncomfortable.[17] For example, they might feel some embarrassment if their clothing fails to match the dress of others at certain events. Too, there are those who deliberately go against convention in order to express their individuality or to draw attention to themselves. By doing so, they are affirming that a folkway does indeed exist, but that they do not choose to follow it. Folkway violators are also noticed—there may be smirks or whispered comments.*

An interesting set of responses to folkway violation occurs when individuals break into a line of sports fans who are waiting to purchase tickets.[18] The rule breakers may be met with boos, jeers, and whistles. Some people may make loud comments about how "rude" or "pushy" some people are, and the victims directly in front or behind the line crashers may insist that the transgressors go to the end and wait their turn like everyone else. However, other than verbal disapproval, direct action is uncommon, and fights are exceedingly rare.

The point of such examples is that folkways govern behavior in many everyday situations. Departures from conventional activity disrupt the smooth flow of human interaction. Violators experience some discomfort, and victims show irritation. Yet in these circumstances, the labels "immoral" or "criminal" are not applied.

Mores

In contrast to folkways, **mores** (pronounced more-ays) are strongly held norms that generally have a moral connotation and are based on a culture's central values. Violation of cultural mores generates powerful emotions and demands for severe punishment. In the United States, for example, child abuse, theft, robbery, incest, forcible rape, murder, and cannibalism represent violations of society's mores. Resentment, perhaps even hatred and calls for retribution, are generated against the offenders. Moreover, there are punishments sanctioned by the state—fines, imprisonment, and sometimes execution.

*On some occasions folkway violation may draw considerable attention. During the summit of 1987, for example, Mikhail Gorbachev refused to wear the traditional black tie to the state dinner hosted by President Ronald Reagan. Gorbachev's stance attracted media attention nationwide.

Violations of cultural mores produce these harsh responses because the transgressions threaten the very fabric of society. Rapes, robberies, and street muggings make communities unsafe; random murders, such as the Tylenol poisonings, make life dangerous and unpredictable; incest destroys families; child molesters prey upon the vulnerable and defenseless. Societies could not effectively survive for any significant length of time under conditions that permitted such behaviors.

Laws

Many social norms have the status of law. **Laws** are norms that are enacted and enforced by a specific group within a society. Legislatures, the police, and court systems combine to carry out this function in modern industrial societies, while less complex cultures rely upon a council of elders, chief, or high priest.

There is no perfect correspondence between folkways or mores, on the one hand, and laws on the other. Many laws reflect a society's mores, but others have to do with folkways, and some are related to neither. The laws prohibiting rape, murder, and robbery are clear reflections of social mores. By contrast, it would be considered tyranny if the folkways regulating eating habits or common courtesy among friends were placed under the jurisdiction of the police and courts. Yet some folkways *are* a matter of law. Spitting in the street and smoking in public places are violations of the public health codes of many jurisdictions, and in New York City, failing to curb one's dog is a punishable offense.

Saving another person's life is the number-one fantasy of Americans. Lennie Skutnik became a national hero when he saved an airliner crash victim from drowning in the Potomac River in 1982.

One might think it difficult to come up with a law that is unrelated to a society's folkways *and* mores, but in the areas of civil and administrative law there are probably thousands. Do American's really care, for example, that the term *Kelly Green* is copyrighted by R. H. Macy and Company, or that Abercrombie and Fitch is the only firm that can legally use the word *Safari* to describe a type of jacket? Recreational marijuana use constitutes a totally different extreme. Considerably more than a few Americans feel that smoking a reefer is perfectly acceptable behavior—even *expected* behavior in certain social situations. Moreover, while the possession of even small amounts of marijuana for personal use may result in a prison sentence in most jurisdictions, in New York, Ohio, and a few other states, it does not even fall within the parameters of criminal law.*

Some of the most complex dilemmas for individuals and society arise when there are discrepancies between mores and laws. Coming to the aid of a person in distress, for example, can have powerful implications. Americans confer immediate hero status on those who rush into burning buildings, leap into freezing waters, or in some other way risk their lives to save total strangers. In fact, saving another person's life is the number-one fantasy of Americans, chosen by 78% of those surveyed in a 1985 poll.[19] But coming to the aid of a person in distress is generally *not* a legal mandate. Most state laws require people to come to the aid of a police officer in distress (*when* the officer requests it and *if* it does not place the complying citizen's life in jeopardy). But the law is silent on the issue of coming to a person's aid in almost all other circumstances. If you walked into a room and found a man dying of a heart attack, would the law require you to call a physician? The answer is no, and the law is quite specific in this regard. In the early twentieth-century case of *People v. Beardsley,*[20] for example, a man and his mistress were having a weekend affair. After a serious argument, the woman took an overdose of morphine tablets and her lover made no attempt to obtain medical help to save her life. She died, and the

*Interesting contrasts take place in this regard. Under Alaska statutes, no criminal sanctions are attached to the possession of *any* amount of marijuana, provided such possession occurs within a person's home. Compare that with the case of Roger Trenton Davis, convicted by a Virginia court in 1973 for the possession (with intent to distribute) of nine ounces of marijuana. Davis was sentenced to 40 years in prison. In 1982, the Supreme Court of the United States ruled that Davis' sentence was *not* in violation of the Sixth Amendment ban against cruel and unusual punishment. See Hutto v. Davis, 454 U.S. 372 (1982).

Exhibit 3.4

Sociological Focus

A Cross-cultural Comparison of Values

Competitiveness is a powerful force in American society. The drama of athletic competition is instilled in children as young as age five when they are fully outfitted for baseball or football and struggle in organized league competition. Later, as youths they learn the value of competing for grades, material wealth, jobs, and power. There is little social approval for the person who fails to devote his or her full energies to the quest for success.

Within this context, consider the dismay of track coaches in the American Southwest some years ago, when they encountered athletes who lacked the drive to win. One of the coaches remarked, "I had a relay team which had three runners with three of the best times in the state. They started getting publicity and two quit. . . . Hell, I had one kid who won the state championship and he carried his head down for weeks."

Another offered a simple explanation: "These kids just don't have the killer instinct . . . they don't have what it takes to keep poring it on when you've got 'em down."

The explanation was actually more complex than either coach realized. The young men in question were Navajo, raised in a culture that rejects competitiveness. Their culture places the highest value on cooperation and group solidarity. Anthropologist Ruth Benedict described it in this way:

> The ideal man is a person of dignity and affability who has never tried to lead and has never called forth any comment from his neighbors. Any conflict, even though right is on his side, is held against him. Even in contests of skill like their foot races, if a man wins habitually he is debarred from running. They are interested in a game that any number can play with even chances and an outstanding runner spoils the game.

Caught in a conflict between two values systems, the Navajo athletes reverted to the ideals of their native culture, rejecting personal recognition by performing at a level less than that of which they were capable.

SOURCES: Maria T. Allison, "Competition and Cooperation: A Sociological Perspective," *International Review of Sport Sociology*, 5 (1980), p. 93–104; Ruth Benedict, *Patterns of Culture* (New York: Mentor, 1955), p. 95.

court ruled that his failure to assist her did not constitute a crime. Although he may have had a *moral* obligation to help her, he had no *legal* duty to do so. There was no contractual relationship between the two parties such as might exist between parents and a child-care center or between a patient and a hospital; there was no status relationship that imposed a legal duty, such as that between spouses or between parents and children. Yet despite the status of the law, failing to help a person in distress in such circumstances can bring on strong social disapproval. A case of this type made national headlines during the early 1980s when a man refused to be a donor for a bone marrow transplant to save the life of his brother.

Value Systems

American athletes preparing for an important game are likely to be reminded, "Winning is not the most important thing, it is the *only* thing!" Would this admonition seem unusual or unacceptable to Americans? Probably not, for it is consistent with deeply held values that stress the importance of competition and individual effort. Yet by contrast, such behavior might be incomprehensible to members of other societies. (For a comparison of value systems across cultures, see Exhibit 3.4.)

Cultural values are shared standards of desirability, defining what is "good and bad," "important and unimportant," "vital and trivial." Material objects (automobiles), behavior (competition, courage), political ideals (democracy), and social relationships (a good family life) are among the more obvious values in contemporary American society.

The Study of Values

Researchers may approach the study of values in a number of ways. First, surveys may be used to uncover the relative importance of different values. Surveys (as

Exhibit 3.5 Sidelights on American Culture

Values in the 1980s

A national sample of 1,483 Americans was asked to rate the importance of 19 social values. The percentages reflect the number who rated each value as "extremely important."

A Good Family Life	82%
Physical Health	81
A Good Self-image or Self-respect	79
Personal Satisfaction or Happiness	77
Freedom of Choice to Do What One Wants	73
Living Up to One's Potential	71
Having an Interesting Job	69
Having a Sense of Accomplishment	63
Following God's Will	61
Having Many Friends	54
Helping People in Need	54
Helping to Better America	51
Having an Exciting, Stimulating Life	51
Following a Strict Moral Code	47
Being Active in Church or Synagogue	40
Having a Nice Home, Car, and Other Belongings	39
Having a High Income	37
Having Enough Leisure Time	36
Social Recognition	22

Source: Gallup Poll, "What's Important to Americans?" Report No. 198, March, 1982. Reprinted by permission.

already noted in Chapter 2) are popular because they can be used to gather information on a systematic basis. As outlined in Exhibit 3.5, a poll of Americans conducted in the early 1980s indicated that their values included a strong emphasis on social relationships, health, and personal attributes. Social recognition and material possessions, on the other hand, were assigned the lowest priorities. These data should not suggest, however, that there are no variations. Older people and black Americans place more value on religious activity than do younger people or white Americans. People under thirty rate personal satisfactions (interesting jobs, a stimulating life) as being more important than do those over the age of fifty. Women stress religious, ethical, and altruistic values more often than men. "Helping the needy" received a high rating from women, while only 47% of the men surveyed ranked it as being important. Overall, however, similarities between men and women and among respondents of different ages outnumber differences, suggesting a high degree of consensus on the relative priority of these values.

The findings of surveys must be interpreted with some caution, of course, for there is always the potential for some distortion. In the Gallup survey outlined in Exhibit 3.5, people could choose only from a prepared list of values, and there were probably others that may have been important to them. Moreover, survey research always raises questions about the relationship between attitudes and actual behavior. Field observation permits researchers to study values without concern for such questions.

Observational research often authenticates verbal responses. Americans indicate that they place a high value on physical health, and their behavior certainly confirms this. More and more Americans each year give up cigarette smoking, limit their intake of cholesterol, improve their diets, and participate in regular exercise programs. On the other hand, it always is possible that survey data contain what are considered to be the most socially acceptable answers. For example, "social recognition" ranked low in the Exhibit 3.5 survey, but it is readily evident that status considerations often influence many people's choices of homes, cars, and clothing. The point is that values may be so deeply ingrained that they are not obvious, even to those who possess them.

Field observation, too, is not without problems. An investigator might need to make inferences about people's motives for answering in one way or another, and this would be difficult under any circumstances. The issue is further complicated by the fact that when it comes to values, people tend to contradict themselves quite often. In a series of surveys conducted during the early 1970s, more than 15,000 people were questioned as to their attitudes and values concerning drug use. Some three-fourths of the respondents agreed that education is the best way of preventing drug abuse. Curiously, however, almost half of these same respondents concurred with the idea that strict and harsh punishment of drug abusers keeps others from using drugs.[21]

Yet despite contradictions and methodological problems, we can, nevertheless, outline what amounts to a uniquely American value system. It includes the following concepts:

- *political freedom*—freedom from arbitrary governmental intervention in personal affairs
- *personal autonomy*—freedom from social constraints (by parents, peers, or co-workers) on personal values and life-styles
- *self-reliance*—personal independence and self-direction
- *success*—personal achievement measured by external criteria such as income, status, occupational attainments, or life-style
- *competition*—dedication to the highest levels of effort and accomplishment
- *work*—the production of meaningful goods and services
- *physical beauty*—an attractive physical presence[22]

Extravagant ceremonies marked the centennial of the Statue of Liberty, emphasizing the importance of this national symbol.

Values and Symbols

In a letter written on Independence Day, 1776, John Adams commented that the occasion should be remembered "with pomp and parade, with games, sports, parades, guns, bells, bonfires and illumination from one end of this continent to the other."[23] Echoing Adams' sentiment, on the July 4th weekend in 1986, Americans held what was called "the party of the century." To celebrate the 100th birthday and restoration of the Statue of Liberty, festivals were held across the nation. In New York Harbor, the event was capped by a naval review, a parade of tall ships and military aircraft, a 40,000-shell fireworks display that turned night into day, and closing ceremonies that left spectators breathless. Some observers from foreign nations, however, misunderstood the meaning of the festivities, considering them to be exercises in extravagance held in honor of an ugly monument.[24] What they did not realize was that the exuberance of Liberty Weekend was a celebration of the essence of the American value system. The spirit of the occasion was summed up quite well by journalist Kurt Anderson of *Time* magazine:

> Who cares about the Statue of Liberty? By modern high-rise standards, it is dinky, a dozen stories from head to toe. And by the standards of statuary, Lady Liberty is absurdly huge, unnecessarily literal, a giant trinket as vulgar as a sign on the Las Vegas strip. Except for Richard Morris Hunt's pedestal, the thing was not even Made in America. (Perfect protectionist irony: an imported patriotic icon.)
>
> Who cares about the Statue of Liberty? Everyone, it seems, over the age of two from sea to shining sea. For whether the statue is too small or too big or too corny, it is by far the most American of all the country's patriotic shrines: unabashedly showy, technically impressive, evangelically democratic, erected with private funds—and now privately restored as well, with $70 million from a quarter-billion-dollar treasury raised by a showy, impressive, all-American son of immigrants named Lee Iacocca.[25]

The Quest for Attractiveness

The influence of cultural values is pervasive, affecting behavior in a variety of ways. Values instigate certain courses of action, they bias how people feel about themselves, and they shape social relationships. Nowhere is this fact more evident than in the enduring American quest for attractiveness.

Standards of physical beauty are easy to notice in industrial societies. They are announced on magazine covers, acted out in television commercials, and glorified in contests seeking to crown a Miss, Mrs., and Mr. America each year. "Beautiful people" are persons who are young, tall, trim, and have pleasing features with taut skin and good muscle tone. The devotion to the realization of this ideal can be estimated by annual expenditures for cosmetics, designer fashions, manuals promising slim thighs, flat stomachs, or magical weight loss. The distribution of clothing in any big-city department store subtly reinforces the image: "regular" sizes are available in abundant supply, are offered in more styles, and are easily accessible. Customers who require outsize garments, deviating from the norm, are forced to search for a separate department (usually located at the back of the store), where they will find fewer choices, not necessarily in the latest fashions. Moreover, clothing available in sizes for heavy people is labeled with mildly depreciating terms such as "matronly" (for women), "portly" (for men), "chub-deb" (for girls), and "husky" (for boys).*

*In recent years advertising has attempted to combat these negative images through the creation of some rather unique euphemisms. Most notable in this regard are the many television commercials directed at "full-figured" women.

It is not surprising that many, if not most, Americans are dissatisfied with their bodies, or at least parts of them. Unwanted fat is apparently the formidable enemy, particularly for women. In fact, eight out of ten American women indicated in 1986 that they would like to lose weight,[26] actively working at it with crash diets and exercise regimes. Most disturbing is the fact that many people carry this to an extreme. Recent medical research has demonstrated that one in eight high-school students has tried to lose weight by self-induced vomiting or the consumption of laxatives or other drugs.[27] The demand for plastic surgery is also considerable. In 1984, 2,700 certified surgeons performed 477,000 cosmetic procedures—tucking stomachs, enlarging breasts, lifting faces, eradicating wrinkles.[28] Formerly, fewer patients were men, but the demand for cosmetic surgery has been increasing at a faster rate for men than women in the last ten years.

For men, shortness is the most serious physical imperfection, with nearly half of all American males expressing the desire to be taller.[29] The value placed on height, furthermore, is apparent in numerous areas of American life. Some short men feel ill at ease when dating taller women. Many occupations, among them police work, fire fighting, and the military, at one time had height restrictions, until such standards came to be viewed as discriminatory against women and were relaxed. Moreover, research on employment practices has demonstrated that tall men that meet all of the job criteria are hired more often than are their shorter counterparts.[30]*

An oddity in the great American quest for attractiveness is an apparent conflict between beauty and physical fitness. Dermatologists have demonstrated that anyone who has experienced a severe sunburn at some time in their lives *will* very likely get skin cancer and that repeated exposure to sunlight hastens the onset of the

*It is interesting to note that prior to every Presidential campaign debate in recent years, the speakers' podiums are measured and adjusted to convey the impression that both candidates are exactly the same height.

SOCIAL INDICATOR

Percent Distribution of American Men, by Height

Height	Percent
Under 5′6″	14%
5′6″ to 5′8″	36
5′9″ to 6′1″	47
6′2″ and Over	3

Source: *American Demographics,* May 1986, p. 8.

SOCIAL INDICATOR

Skin Cancer's Sharp Rise

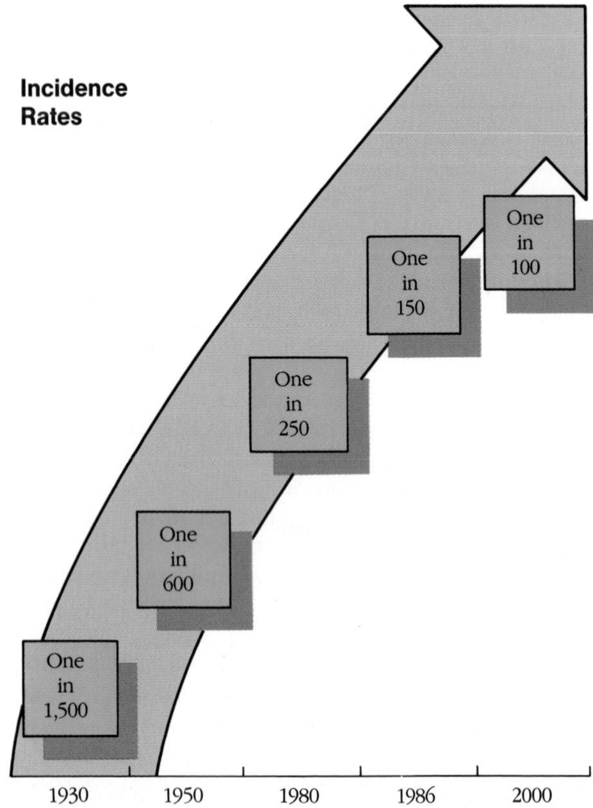

Source: Skin Cancer Foundation, American Cancer Society, 1986.

disease.[31] The only unknowns are *when* it will occur, *how bad* it will be, and *what variety* of skin cancer will develop. Yet despite the numerous warnings about the potential for skin cancer, even those most concerned with physical fitness and good health frequently visit tanning booths (referred to by many dermatologists as "cancer machines") or head for the seashore to bask in the damaging ultraviolet rays. This behavior is very much a cultural phenomenon. Prior to the 1920s, pale, white skin was the norm. A tanned body, characteristic of farmers and other laborers who worked outdoors, was associated with the working class. During the roaring twenties, however, tans became chic. They signified "tennis at the club" and quickly became a badge of the leisure class. And since 1930, the lifetime incidence of skin cancer has skyrocketed. By 1986 the incidence rate had mushroomed from one in every 1,500 people to one in every 150 people.

Beliefs

Cultural beliefs are the convictions that define social and physical reality for members of a society. Beliefs refer to what people have learned to be real whether or not it can be verified. The progress of history is often marked by a discrediting of old beliefs and the substitution of newer ones. Every elementary-school student learns with a sense of amusement that mapmakers in the days of Christopher Columbus filled unexplored areas with the warning, "Here Be Monsters." It was this threat, plus the widespread notion that the world was flat that made Columbus' journey so noteworthy. Moreover, it is important not to forget that such fears were quite real to people of the fifteenth century.

People of most cultures accept the existence of a supreme being, for example, even though this cannot be demonstrated scientifically. In the United States, beliefs are learned and shaped by contacts with peers, parents, and the mass media. As the result of wide publicity in recent years, for instance, Americans have come to believe that Halloween is a dangerous time, with innocent children the potential victims of deranged neighbors who poison candy or insert razor blades in apples. And there have indeed been incidents of this type. A case in point was the "trick-or-treat" murder of 1974 in Pasadena, Texas.[32] The victim was an eight-year-old boy, poisoned by his father for the sake of an insurance policy covering the child's life. But the Pasadena case was one of but a few isolated events. Recent research has clearly demonstrated that instances of poisoned candy and razor blades in apples are rare indeed.[33] Yet each Halloween, parents organize their lives and those of their children around the belief that danger lurks behind every door the children approach. It may even be that parents knowingly foster this belief in their children as a means of teaching other lessons about the risks of urban living.

The Convergence of Values, Norms, and Beliefs

Values, norms, and beliefs often complement and reinforce one another, but they may also exist more or less independently. Cultural norms refer to specific behavioral rules, while values are more abstract ideals. Norms often have their origins in the value system of a society. Sociologist Robin Williams has noted that "personal autonomy is one of the most deeply cherished values in American society, and norms have evolved to protect individual rights."[34] Laws and mores assert the right to express ideas, however unpopular, and to worship as people see fit. They also guarantee that individuals will not be deprived of their freedom without due process. In such cases, values and norms are deeply interwoven.

Americans place a high value on individual freedoms and our laws protect citizens' rights to express their ideas, even if their views are unpopular.

People think and act on the basis of their beliefs. Many Americans seem to accept that anyone, however poor, can become rich by working hard.[35] A logical consequence of this belief is to consider those who remain in poverty to be lazy or inept. In this way we tend to lose sight of the social handicaps of poverty.

THE ORIGINS OF CULTURE

The concept of culture emphasizes that certain patterns of behavior are shared by most, if not all, members of a society. As a result, every society has a **core culture,** the kaleidoscope of values, norms, beliefs, and practices that are ascribed to by the majority of its constituents. Few Americans would, for example, disavow the sanctity of human life or the repulsiveness of cannibalism.

The notion of a shared core culture has important implications for understanding the organization of social life. Culture makes behavior highly *predictable.* Culture is sometimes referred to as a "blueprint for living,"—a blueprint that provides people with ready-made patterns which relieve the individual of having to work out adaptations to problems alone. In the United States, for example, adult men wishing to express some degree of pleasure at seeing an old acquaintance need not invent new ways to express their feelings. They merely follow the convention of a handshake or the slapping of palms. By contrast, the norms of many European countries dictate a greeting of ritual kissing on both sides of the face. The fact that people can anticipate how others will behave is one of the things that makes cooperative group life possible. Some very simple actions are based on the assumption, often unrecognized, that people behave in very predictable ways. The ability to drive an automobile from one place to another in relative safety is such a system, one that depends on all other drivers' following the rules of the road.

The Evolution of Core Cultures

Cultures are in a state of continual flux, shifting and changing, growing and evolving, being added to and taken away from constantly. Yet the sources of cultural patterns are often difficult to unravel; the origins of any given motif may be buried in antiquity. Nevertheless, it is still possible to isolate several different processes through which core cultures tend to develop.

Adaptation: The Functionalist Approach

In their attempts to solve the riddle of cultural evolution, functional theorists stress the role of adaptation to physical and social environments. Every society is faced with coping with a given geographical setting. If it cannot move or change the environment, it must adapt to it. As a result, certain cultural patterns reflect adaptations that evolved over a period of time. Practices that prove to be effective spread throughout the society and become part of the culture, while the rest are eventually discarded.

Within this context, it is logical that members of societies in hot, desert areas would learn to avoid eating foods likely to spoil quickly. It is for this reason that pork is often taboo in desert cultures. Over time, this adaptation became a firm rule, even part of religious beliefs. Similarly, this functionalist approach can be used to explain why every part of a bull or cow—from its brains to its stomach lining, intestines, and testicles—is used in Sicilian cuisine. For almost two thousand years, Sicily was plagued by tyranny, invasion, feudal exploitation, and corruption, with the result that its people lived in a constant state of poverty and economic disorder. The development of a cuisine that made use of every part of cows, bulls, and other domesticated animals represented a repudiation of waste—one aspect of a cultural adaptation to economic hardship.

Imposition: The Conflict Approach

Conflict theorists stress the importance of power and coercion in cultural evolution. Consequently, the roots of numerous patterns of culture may be the result of impositions by the more powerful segments of a society. To some extent, criminal law in the United States reflects this situation with regard to religious practice. Despite the constitutional guarantee of freedom of religion, the norms and traditions of the more dominant religions often infringe upon those of minority religions. The Mormon Church, for example, was forced to abandon polygamy after Congress prohibited the practice in 1862. More recently, an Indiana couple was convicted of child neglect and reckless homicide as an outgrowth of their religious practices.[36] Rather than obtaining medical help when their son fell ill in 1986, they had prayed over him. The child subsequently died. The couple's religious beliefs forbade secular medical care, stipulating instead that faith and prayer be used to aid the child.

Borrowing, Diffusion, and Evolutionary Growth

In contrast with the functionalist and conflict explanations of cultural development, the evolutionary approach suggests that patterns of culture are *borrowed* through contacts with other groups and *diffused* from one subgroup in a society to all others. Thus, **diffusion** is the movement of cultural traits from one group or culture to another. The "hero sandwich,"* for example, now a part of mainstream American culture, was borrowed from nineteenth-century Italian factory workers.[37] They had created the sandwich as a way of having traditional meats and cheese during lunch breaks. An interesting aspect of American culture is that some things that people believe to be borrowed are actually American inventions (see Exhibit 3.6).

The "typical American breakfast"—bacon and eggs, waffles, coffee with cream and sugar, and orange juice—represents perhaps the best example of the evolutionary approach to patterns of culture.[38] The consumption of thin strips of flesh taken from domesticated animals stems from an East Asian tradition, with the salting and smoking process originating in Northern Europe. Indochina (the area of Southeast Asia encompassing contemporary Vietnam, Laos, and Cambodia) contributed the idea of eating the eggs of domesticated birds, and waffles came from cakes made using a Scandinavian technique applied to a strain of wheat developed in Asia Minor. Coffee is an Abyssinian plant; the domestication of cows and the process of milking them for cream originated in the Middle East; sugar was first made in India. Even orange juice has its roots elsewhere. Although oranges are typically associated with Florida and California, the fruit originated in China and was brought to the New World by Christopher Columbus.[39]

*The "hero," also known as a "grinder," "poor boy," "submarine," or "hoagie," is a sandwich on hard Italian or French bread, sliced lengthwise and overstuffed with meats and cheeses. It is known as a *hero* in New York City, where it originated, and probably got its name from the fact that one had to be a hero of sorts to consume all of it.

SOURCES OF CULTURAL DIVERSITY

Although the term core culture is used to identify that complex of norms, values, beliefs, and practices that are widely shared, a society as large and heterogeneous as that in the United States also exhibits considerable diversity. In general, there are two major sources of diversity within a society: *clashes of values* and *subcultural variation.*

Alternative Value Systems

Cultural values are often inconsistent, and adherence to one ideal may be at odds with many others. When strongly held values collide, the result is rarely a minor matter. Those with deep emotional commitments typically rally to side with those who hold a similar position.

One of the more divisive value conflicts in the United States today involves abortion, a practice that was legalized under certain circumstances in 1973 by the United States Supreme Court in the decision of *Roe v. Wade.*[40] Supreme Court decisions do not settle such complex issues. The abortion debate played a central role in the 1988 presidential election, and the Court may revise or overturn earlier decisions. Moreover, the fact that the matter has been settled by the nation's highest court does not mean that it is resolved in the minds of the public. Activists on both sides of the issue have mobilized to advance their own position.[41] The most committed individuals among the antiabortionists work actively to change the law, lobbying in legislatures, organizing mail campaigns, and developing educational programs. Other segments of the movement have taken to the streets, distributing pamphlets, picketing abortion clinics in the hope of discouraging women from entering, and even demonstrating in front of clinic workers' homes. During the mid-eighties, the debate occasionally broke into open violence, with bombs destroying abortion clinics. Such tactics do not reflect the approach of all antiabortionists, but they suggest the intensity of the feelings involved.

National opinion polls clearly reflect a lack of consensus on the matter among the public. In fact, Americans seem to be divided into three broad groups. About half favor a woman's right to an abortion under any

Exhibit 3.6

Types & Stereotypes

That's Italian?

A great many of the foods and dishes considered to be products of "old world" Italian culture may not be Italian at all. Some of the so-called "classics" that appear on the menus of Italian restaurants in the United States include the following:

- *Pizza.* Originally a Neapolitan poor people's food, pizza literally means "savory bun." The roots of pizza are unknown, but in its most common form it was a small piece of pie-shaped bread served with tomatoes. Prior to World War II, Americans were more familiar with pizza as it is known today than were Italians. Pizza "all the way," "with the works," and deep dish pizza are still unknown in Italy—except where they have been introduced by Americans.
- *Spaghetti and Meatballs.* More *Franco-American* than Italian and likely as well known to Mediterraneans as *Chef Boyardee,* spaghetti and meatballs *is* served in Italy—in restaurants catering to American tourists.
- *Shrimp Scampi.* Best known to Americans as shrimp sautéed in olive oil, butter, garlic, and white wine, the name "shrimp scampi" is actually a redundancy. *Scampi,* the plural of "scampo," is a Venetian term for prawn, not a dish, and a prawn is a generic label for several species of shellfish, including lobster and shrimp. In Italy, shrimp scampi is unknown. In the United States, *scampi* is used as an adjective. Perhaps this is why one can find a recipe for oyster scampi (oyster prawn?) in *Leone's Italian Cookbook.*
- *Caesar Salad.* This combination of Romaine lettuce, garlic, olive oil, Parmesan cheese, croutons, and sometimes anchovies was indeed named after Caesar, but not Julius Caesar. The salad's namesake was Caesar Cardini of Tijuana, Mexico, who created the dish on July 4, 1924, to feed a group of hungry American tourists.

SOURCES: Guiliano Bugialli, *The Fine Art of Italian Cooking* (New York: New York Times Books, 1977); Edward Giobbi, *Italian Family Cooking* (New York: Random House, 1971); Gene Leone, *Leone's Italian Cookbook* (New York: Harper & Row, 1967); Maril Lo Pinto and Milo Miloradovich, *The Art of Italian Cooking* (Garden City, NY: Doubleday, 1950); Mary Reynolds, *Italian Cooking for Pleasure* (London: Paul Hamlyn, 1965); *USA Today,* April 2, 1986, p. 5D.

circumstances. Another quarter are opposed to abortion under any circumstances, even when rape or valid medical issues are involved. Finally, those in the third group seem to endorse abortion for rape victims and support it when there is a valid medical need, but oppose so-called "discretionary" abortions—choices based on social, economic, or personal considerations.

Age, education, and religion exert a potent influence on public attitudes toward abortion, but opposition or support is grounded in different value systems that cut across the three identified groups.[42] Those who support a woman's right to abort a fetus under any circumstances place a high value on a woman's right to choose. Those who reject abortion under any conditions place a high value on human life and oppose the taking of life under any circumstances. Those who disapprove of "discretionary abortions" adhere to a strong moral code, holding that adultery and extra- or premarital sex are the antithesis of religious virtue. Their opposition appears to be related to the concern that abortion endorses and encourages "lax" sexual standards. In the final analysis, abortion pits three different values—human life, sexual morality, and individual freedom—against one another, and the whole issue involves assigning different priorities to these alternative values.

Subcultures

Both large and small groups within any society may adhere to distinctive patterns of learned behavior that distinguish them from the core or dominant culture. The term **subculture** refers to the way of life of a group of people whose backgrounds, experiences, and/or norms and values make them culturally distinct from the rest of the society in which they live. Every member of a complex society is exposed to the dominant culture and to one or more subcultures. The United States contains an intricate mix of regional, religious, occupational, and ethnic subcultures. In addition, **countercultures** are groups whose total system of norms, values, and lifestyles intentionally deviates from or is in conflict with those of the wider society.* Criminal subcultures, a number of radical or reactionary political groups, and several religious cults are countercultures, at least in terms of their highly divergent normative systems. By far the largest subcultural groups in American society, however, are those organized around differences in ethnicity, religion, occupation, and special interests.

*The term "counterculture" originated during the social revolution of the 1960s and was applied to the so-called *hippies* who attracted nationwide attention by challenging America's most widely held values. The hippies espoused norms counter to those associated with the pursuit of career mobility, a traditional family structure, and overall "straight" living; they did not work, lived in communes, practiced free love, and used drugs. Interestingly, America's general tolerance of hippies was in itself a norm of the wider society. See Theodore Roszak, *The Making of a Counterculture: Reflections on the Technocratic Society and Its Youthful Opposition* (Garden City, NY: Doubleday, 1969).

SOCIAL INDICATOR

The Distribution of Selected Ethnic Subcultures in the United States

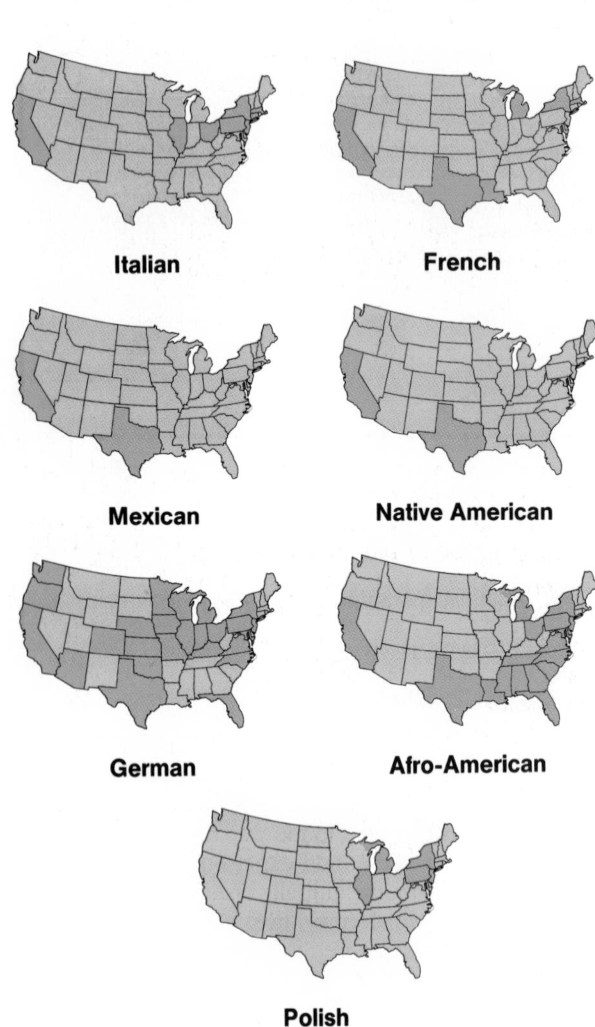

Source: U.S. Bureau of the Census, 1987.

Ethnic Subcultures

When the peoples of one society emigrate from their native lands to settle in another country, they tend to retain some elements of their native culture while accommodating themselves to the ways of their new community. The United States is populated by immigrants from no less than one hundred different countries. As a result, it is possible to identify German, Irish, Italian, Korean, Mexican, Cuban and numerous other groups that have maintained many of their original customs and traditions. These collections of people generally suffer some discrimination and are excluded from certain activities by members of the dominant culture, because of differences in the languages, customs, and beliefs that readily identify them.

Most immigrants have attempted to assimilate into the dominant culture, and many have been fully successful. However, in numerous instances membership in an ethnic subculture has brought an individual into direct conflict with the laws and mores of the dominant society. In Tarzana, California, in early 1985, for example, Fumiko Kimura attracted national attention when she led her two young daughters into the surf of the Pacific Ocean. The children drowned, but Kimura was rescued, arrested, and charged with murder.[43] A recent Japanese immigrant, she had been acting out the ancient ritual of *oyaka-shinju,* or parent-child suicide (now illegal in Japan), a response demanded when a woman's husband dishonors her by committing adultery.* Or consider the case of Jack Jones, an Eskimo, on trial in an Alaska court in 1985 on several counts of sexual abuse of children. Jones had been arrested after pulling down the pants of his son and grandson and swatting at their genitals.[44] Using what is known in legal terminology as the "traditional conduct" defense, however, Jones was found not guilty. He explained to the court that he had been partaking in a long-standing tradition of teasing behavior meant to teach young boys to laugh off adversity, protect themselves from attack, and respond quickly.

*Kimura originally faced the death penalty on charges of murder in the first degree. But the cultural conflict brought immediate support from 4,000 members of the local Japanese community. In fact, they established a Fumiko Kimura Fair Trial Committee. Ultimately, Kimura pled guilty to a reduced charge of manslaughter. At sentencing, her attorney argued that she had been raised to be submissive and passive, which made her vulnerable and led to her deteriorating mental condition. Kimura was sentenced to five years probation and reunited with her husband. See *National Law Journal,* November 4, 1985, p. 10; *USA Today,* November 22, 1985, p. 3A.

The Amish of southeastern Pennsylvania form a rural subculture within a highly industrialized society.

While most ethnic subcultures exert considerable efforts at assimilation, others marshal whatever force they can to insure the opposite result. The Old Order Amish, having first emigrated to the United States from the Netherlands during the first half of the seventeenth century, are perhaps the best example of an ethnic group that has deliberately maintained its unique identity.[45]

Along the back roads and state highways of southeastern Pennsylvania, it is not unusual to see rumbling tractor-trailers and high-performance sports cars competing for space with plodding horse-drawn carriages. The occupants of the little surreys are the Amish, the Pennsylvania Dutch, who are set apart from the rest of the local community by austere black garb that is totally without ornamentation. They live and dress as they did centuries ago. As a deliberate manifestation of their separation from the culture of the "English" (their all-inclusive term for everyone non-Amish), their drab apparel serves to affirm many diverse, yet interrelated ideals. First, it declares self-denial, a central tenet of their religion. Second, it is a reminder that God is concerned with inner attitudes, not outward appearances. Third, it is a statement of rejection of a materialistic world, and fourth, it reaffirms their group solidarity.

The distinctive dress of the Amish is easy to identify, but the underlying value system is less clear. The ban on ornamentation, automobiles, and electricity may appear to be a celebration of tradition and blind resistance to change. When an outsider asks why they live as they do, the Amish usually respond with no more than, "It has always been so." But the Amish view modern technological society as a threat to their central values of independence and self-sufficiency. They are aware of the vulnerability of mankind in modern society: rendered almost helpless by energy crises; isolated by dependence upon the whims of manufacturers and bankers and government bureaucracies; rendered spiritually weak by changing moral standards and physically weak by pesticides and processed foods.

Independence and self-sufficiency are part of the American value system, but the Amish practice it on a group basis, not just at the individual level. There are no homes for the elderly among these people; the aged and infirm are cared for within the family. The collective barn-raising is the Amish way of coming to the aid of families in financial distress, and although they pay income taxes, some years ago they managed to win an exclusion from participation in the federal Social Security system. They argued that they would refuse the benefits even if they were forced to contribute. On the whole, the Amish do not worry about the future, believing that God will take care of them in His own way.

Religious Subcultures

In addition to the many different ethnic groups that emigrated to the United States, its constitutional guarantee of freedom of religion has also made it a nation of divergent religious groups. Cults, extremely unorthodox segments of Christianity, and many lesser known religious groups are identifiable religious cultures. To many observers, their traditions and practices may be considered somewhat bizarre. The majority of contemporary religious groups, on the other hand, fully participate in most, if not all aspects of the wider society. Protestants, Catholics, Jews, and numerous others have distinctive spiritual activities and rituals during certain periods, but generally cross religious boundaries and interact with members of other groups at school, in the work place, and in their communities the rest of the time.

When it comes to understanding the influence of religious subcultures, it is important to remember that religion involves more than just ritual. Each religion also embodies a set of distinctive beliefs and values, a number of which can explain certain nonreligious behaviors. Take, for example, the problem of alcohol abuse. All Americans exposed to the mass-media celebration of social drinking are vulnerable to the same social and occupational stresses that alcohol is claimed to calm. Moreover, despite laws to the contrary, alcohol is readily available to everyone, regardless of age. Yet, observers have long noted that alcohol abuse rates vary drastically from the norm among certain religious groups. Such differences are easy to explain among Mormons, Jehovah's Witnesses, Seventh-Day Adventists, and others that ban the use of alcohol entirely. But what explains the fact that among the Jews, for whom drinking is not forbidden, rates of alcoholism are one-seventh the national average?

One explanation of this phenomenon focuses on the symbolic role of alcohol in Jewish tradition. Within mainstream American culture, alcohol has taken on a number of symbolic meanings. Advertising campaigns identify drinking as a recreational activity to be enjoyed at ball games, picnics, and when sharing intimate moments. Folk wisdom hails drinking to be a relatively harmless mechanism for escaping from the stresses of modern society. Adolescents manipulate alcohol use as a validation of adulthood and masculinity. Possibly more than anything else drinking is a symbol of sociability. The solitary drinker is considered to be on the way to alcoholism. When shared, drinking is an act of friendship, of inclusion in the group. In many homes courtesy demands that guests be offered a drink as a sign of welcome.

Among the Jews, alcohol has a religious connotation, which is emphasized beginning with almost every Jewish child's initial exposure to alcoholic beverages. Recent research among Jewish Americans has documented that Jewish children are typically introduced to alcohol at home in the form of sacramental wine.[46] Thus, from the outset, the consumption of alcohol comes to be associated with a specific purpose, and its religious symbolism is reaffirmed and reinforced as the child matures. Consequently, alternative meanings and attractions are less likely to take hold.

Sociability is considered important among Jews, but it is food, not drink, that serves as the vehicle. Hence, Jews affirm group solidarity by sharing a meal rather than a drink. Abstinence is made easier by the social context of drinking, where moderation is maintained by subtle social conventions. Rather than politely refusing offers of drinks, a "non-drinker" stance is publicly announced, thus bringing others into the process of helping the individual avoid social pressure to drink. Husbands and wives cooperate by publicly reprimanding the drinker, a device designed to discourage offers of drinks, not to embarrass.

Occupational and Work Subcultures

People who work together typically develop a distinctive subculture organized around the nature of their occupation. They create a special language to describe the things they do and the conditions under which they function. Practitioners in the medical world speak of "contusions," "abrasions," and "fractures," injuries that the general public thinks of as cuts, bruises, and broken bones. More significantly, health personnel, especially physicians, learn to place the highest value on the protection and continuation of human life. Acting on this goal produces heroic efforts to sustain life. This subcultural value that physicians champion often brings them into conflict with terminally ill patients and their families, who place greater value on the quality of that life than on its duration.

Special Interest Subcultures

All subcultures are composed of individuals who have common interests, shared ideals, and similar life-styles. There are countless political, educational, and artistic groups that develop subcultures. A case in point are the Dead Heads, a relatively small subculture united by their devotion to the Grateful Dead rock group.[47]

A product of the 1960s, like other groups of the time, the Grateful Dead attracted a loyal following of young adults exploring the new frontiers of drugs, antiwar sentiment, and countercultural life-styles. Although other rock bands attracted fans and followers during this period, the Dead Heads were among the few to develop and sustain a continuing subculture.

The popularity of most rock groups tends to be short lived, but like the Rolling Stones and the Beach Boys, the Grateful Dead still have many fans. As recently as 1985, each Grateful Dead concert attracted some 30,000, spectators—not an inconsiderable number when one considers that the group scheduled almost one hundred performances during that year. But the fellowship of the Dead Heads likely does not exceed 10,000. The members of the subculture are the young women and men who leave work on Friday to drive from Washington to Baltimore and Philadelphia to catch three concerts in as many nights and to get back for work on Monday morning. The more affluent Dead Heads attend as many as sixty concerts in a single year, following their idols all over the country by plane.

Members of the Dead Heads claim that it is the style and tone of the concerts that sets the Grateful Dead apart from all other groups. Band members have no sequins, no punk hair, no costumes. Dead Heads dress in the outdated style of the 1960s, displaying their symbols—skulls and roses. Many are teenagers, lacking any firsthand experience with the era that produced the band they follow. But they are there nevertheless, free to set up electronic equipment to record the show with the understanding (norm) that tapes may be traded, but never sold. And as a subculture, the Dead Heads have no "official" value system. Rather, they share the ideals of antimaterialism, antinationalism, antimilitarism, and anti-intolerance, thus setting themselves apart from the dominant values and perspectives of mainstream society. Although they live and work in the larger society between concerts, they never see themselves as a part of it.

A wide variety of other social groups can also be understood from the subcultural perspective—criminals, socioeconomic classes, and racial groups, to name but a few. Analyses of these subcultures appear in later chapters.

American society supports a rich mosaic of subcultures, each reflecting a diversity of customs and life-styles. At the same time a core culture provides a basic set of rules and standards. A few subcultures, such as the Amish, survive as alternatives to the prevailing system of values and beliefs. By contrast, other groups have abandoned their subcultural traditions in an effort to more fully participate in the dominant cultural order. This has been the case with each succeeding group of immigrants to the United States. But in most cases, subcultures tend to peacefully coexist and their members have been able to function in the larger society as well as within the confines of their own particular group.

CULTURE AND APPLIED SOCIOLOGY

While the study of culture can be interesting in its own right, offering perspectives on how and why different groups think and act in certain ways, does the endeavor have any pragmatic applications? Can an understanding of cultural differences be put to practical use in the business world, for example, to increase productivity, sales, or corporate profits? The answer to these questions is yes, and the reasons for this are readily apparent as the result of an analysis of some contemporary economic and political affairs involving the United States and Japan. As illustrated in Exhibit 3.7, despite Japan's history of accomplishment in the production and marketing of electronic and high-technology equipment, it failed to invade the American marketplace with home computers. What the Japanese neglected to do was to understand how computer technology and marketing had to mesh closely with patterns of American culture.

The point is that a knowledge of other cultures is of major significance to anyone who must interact with a culture other than his or her own. This lesson was learned quite painfully in 1986 by Yasuhiro Nakasone, Prime Minister of Japan. In an address to his Liberal Democratic Party, Nakasone made the following comment:

> So high is the level of education in our country that Japan's is an intelligent society. Our average [IQ] score is much higher than those of countries like the U.S. There are many blacks, Puerto Ricans, and Mexicans in America. In consequence the average score over there is exceedingly low.[48]

Unquestionably, Prime Minister Nakasone had committed an *ayamachi*—Japanese diplomatic argot for a grave social sin. Yet in his nation, an essentially monoracial society that is historically ethnocentric (with 98% of the population native born), few picked up on the implications of his remark. That was not the situation in the United States, however, and the matter was not put to rest until the Prime Minister made a personal apology. Thus, a lack of knowledge of cultural differences can have important social, economic, and political consequences.

Exhibit 3.7

Applied Sociology

A Japanese Computer Invasion?

When the personal computer industry was launched in the United States by a handful of American companies during the late 1970s, it appeared that it would be only a matter of time before the Japanese moved in to take a major market share. After all, just such a takeover had occurred with automobiles. Given the technical wizardry and marketing capabilities of the elite of Japanese consumer-electronics firms—Panasonic, Sony, NEC, Sanyo, and numerous others—it was anticipated that Japan would do with personal computers what they had done with television sets, video recorders, stereo equipment, and other electronic devices. The Japanese did indeed invade, but by the mid-eighties their personal computers were about as visible in the American market as the tiny computer chips that function as a computer's brain. In spite of intense efforts to develop innovative products and marketing strategies, in 1985 the Japanese had managed to capture only 5% of the U.S. personal computer market. What had happened, and what is still happening?

Japan's failure to translate its renowned manufacturing prowess into significant U.S. sales can be traced to a lack of understanding of certain aspects of American culture.

First, building computer sales involves not only hardware, but software as well. In the early years of the personal computer industry, computers were bundled together with various software packages. Given the differences in cultural interests, language, and accounting principles, Japanese computer programs were often of little or no use to American users.

Second, there was the matter of "documentation"—computer jargon for instruction manuals. Although these manuals had the reputation of being notoriously bad even in the American industry, the language differences made the Japanese instructional materials impossible to comprehend.

Third, there were compatibility problems. Early on, International Business Machines (IBM) had established certain standards in the computer market. Other hardware and software developers followed the IBM lead, and very quickly, anything that was not "IBM compatible" fell by the wayside. The Japanese machines required disk operating systems that had compatibility problems.

Fourth, computers cannot be plucked from a box and immediately turned on. The Japanese were slow to realize this and failed to provide users and dealers with substantial support and training.

Fifth, computer technology changes quickly. The pace of innovation among U.S. computer makers has been rapid, and the needs of users are continually evolving. With their market-research analysts and engineering departments on the other side of the world, Japanese computer makers were unable to react immediately to American market changes.

Sixth, the Japanese (along with many American computer makers), failed to understand the significance of *Big Blue*—IBM—in the American value system. Most American computer users prefer IBM products, despite the fact that other manufacturers have developed faster, more efficient, and less expensive computers.

Seventh, in the educational market, where Apple computers dominate, and in the hobby market, where Commodore and Apple hold more than a two-thirds share, Japan's problem was one of cultural differences combined with "too little, too late."

The Japanese have had considerable success with their computer printers. In fact, Japanese printers occupy the largest share of the market. But printer technology and marketing need not deal with cultural differences.

By the mid-eighties, Japanese computer manufacturers had begun to address the cultural issues that had aborted their initial efforts in the American market. Their major problem now is overcoming the IBM mystique—something that IBM's American competitors have yet to accomplish.

By contrast, American computer manufacturers made special efforts to insure that they did not fall victim to cultural differences when they planned product and marketing strategies for selling American computers overseas. IBM produces the third largest-selling computer in Japan. In addition, American corporations dominate the Japanese software market. What both industries had done was to work closely with Japanese concerns in order to develop products that could effectively deal with the unique nature of the Japanese language. Special kinds of hardware and software had to be developed to manipulate the Japanese characters.

In addition, a close examination of Japanese culture revealed that when it came to many types of software, potential computer users in Japan had a penchant for graphs and colors. In response, companies like America-based Lotus Development Corporation designed a spreadsheet program that can generate spider graphs that connect points on axes in a circular fashion. The program has been a resounding success in the Japanese market.

SOURCES: *Business Week*, July 21, 1986, pp. 122–23; *Chronicle of Higher Education*, October 10, 1984, p. 26; *CompuServe Information Service*, July 6, 1986; *Infoworld*, November 4, 1985, p. 1; *Online Today*, July 1985, p. 10; *U.S. News & World Report*, April 4, 1985, p. BC-4.

Personal Computer Market Share

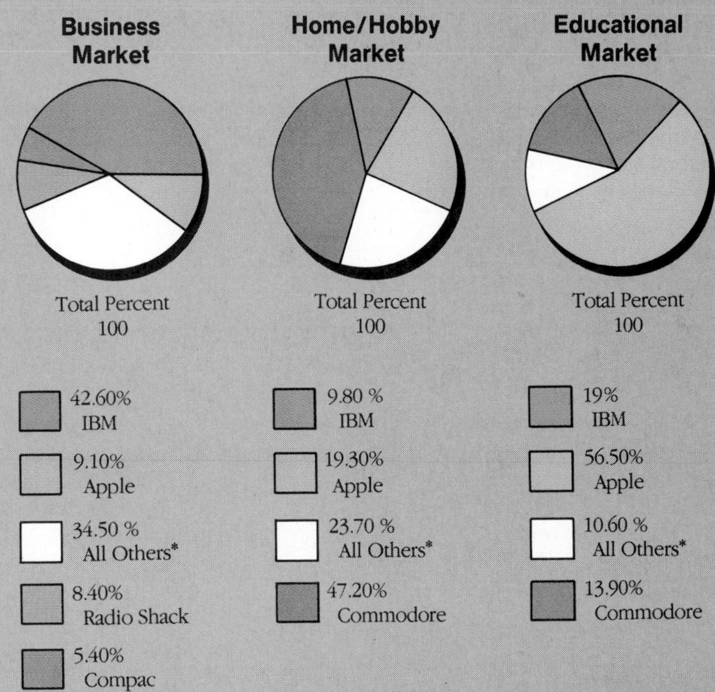

*"All Others," in which Zenith, AT&T, and Texas Instruments dominate, includes all foreign imports as well as more than 30 American manufacturers.

Sources: *Infoworld*, November 4, 1985, p. 1; International Data Corp., 1985.

SUMMARY

The concept of culture refers to the ways of thinking, acting, and feeling that people learn as members of a society. It includes language, customs, morals, habits of dress and diet, and standards of behavior. Human cultures display an endless diversity and an infinite richness. Culture is a social invention, emerging out of the unique experiences of groups of people. Sharing a culture links people together and helps to make cooperative social life possible.

Individuals are products of the culture they are exposed to while growing up. Because their own culture is so familiar to them, they often judge other people and cultures against the standards of their own—a process called ethnocentrism—and forget that different cultures must be understood in light of the history and conditions that shaped them.

Culture has several different components. Among the most obvious is language. Language is more than a device that allows people to communicate with one another; it also shapes the way in which people perceive the world and express themselves. The normative order is made up of the rules and expectations that guide social conduct. These rules or norms typically are divided into three categories. Folkways are the conventions and customs that guide much everyday behavior, such as standards of dress. More important norms are called mores, and they define the moral standards of behavior. Laws are the formal norms of a society. Shared standards of desirability and right and wrong form the cultural value system. A strong competitive spirit, the importance of the family, and the quest for physical attractiveness are all aspects of the American value system. Beliefs, or perceptions of reality are also cultural phenomena, defining how people learn to see the physical and social world.

Cultures are constantly changing, sometimes slowly and sometimes more rapidly and dramatically. They respond to environmental, technological, and demographic shifts. Cultures also evolve by borrowing elements from other cultures, as when a group of people adopts a food item that originated in another society. And in other cases, a more powerful society may impose its standards and beliefs on a weaker one.

Core culture is the term used to describe the norms, values, and beliefs shared by virtually all members of a society. Societies as large and complex as that in the United States are characterized by internal groups with ways of life that diverge somewhat from the core culture. These subcultures may be organized around ethnic background, religion, work, or some special interest such as a shared love for a particular kind of popular music.

One goal of sociology is to make people aware of cultural differences and to teach them to appreciate the meaning of such diversity. The absence of this sensitivity fosters misunderstanding and renders communication between cultures impossible.

KEY TERMS/CONCEPTS

core culture
counterculture
cultural beliefs
cultural relativity
cultural universals
cultural values
culture
culture shock
diffusion
ethnocentrism
folkways
laws
material culture
mores
norms
Sapir-Whorf hypothesis
society
subculture

DISCUSSION QUESTIONS

1. What are the differences between "patriotism" and "ethnocentrism"?
2. What might be some of the reasons why laws in American society are often inconsistent with prevailing social norms (folkways and mores)?
3. This chapter lists a number of basic American values. Do you think that those values accurately represent American society? Are there others that you feel are important?
4. Virtually everyone in the United States is a member of one or more subcultures. To how many subcultures do you belong? What are they? What are the major values and beliefs of these subcultures?
5. As a result of the racial policies of the government of South Africa, a number of Western societies have imposed economic sanctions on that nation. Is it appropriate for one culture to impose its values, beliefs, and standards on another?

SUGGESTED READINGS

Robert N. Bellah, Richard Madsen, William M. Sullivan, Ann Swidler, and Steven M. Tipton, *Habits of the Heart: Individualism and Commitment in American Life* (Berkeley: University of California Press, 1985). An examination of America's cultural history, this study focuses on the values, beliefs, and practices that have served to shape the American social character.

Ruth Benedict, *Patterns of Culture* (New York: Mentor, 1959). Perhaps the most often quoted book on culture, this work is a classic in the social sciences, examining a variety of cultures from a comparative perspective.

William M. Kephart, *Extraordinary Groups: An Examination of Unconventional Life-Styles* (New York: St. Martin's, 1987). Now in its third edition, this paperback offers interesting analyses of the Mormons, Amish, Shakers, and numerous other unusual cultural groups.

Lawrence Langer, *The Importance of Wearing Clothes* (New York: Hastings House, 1959). Originally written as a prologue to a stage play, this historical and cross-cultural perspective on clothing and bodily adornment answers such questions as why men dress differently than women, how clothing is related to sex, marriage, religious beliefs, and social activities, and why people wear clothing at all.

Betty Mahmoody, *Not Without My Daughter* (New York: Thomas Dunne/St. Martin's, 1987). This book is a moving account of an American woman's escape with her daughter from Iran after two years as a virtual hostage of her Iranian husband and his family. The significance of the book lies in its reflections on the seductive yet often misleading assumption that culture can be acquired and discarded like articles of clothing.

David W. Maurer, *Whiz Mob: A Correlation of the Technical Argot of Pickpockets with Their Behavior Pattern* (New Haven, CT: College and University Press, 1964). Originally published in the 1950s and based on research conducted a decade earlier, this book offers a glimpse into the subculture of the professional pickpocket.

NOTES

1. See Beryl Leif Benderly, Mary Gallagher, and John M. Young, *Discovering Culture: An Introduction to Anthropology* (London: John Murray, 1971); Ron Burton, "Cargo Cults and Systems of Exchange in Melanesia," *Mankind* (December 1971), pp. 115–28; Peter Worsley, *The Trumpet Shall Sound: A Study of Cargo Cults in Melanesia* (London: Macgibbon and Kee, 1957).
2. Edward B. Tylor, *Primitive Culture: Researches into the Development of Mythology, Philosophy, Religion, Art, and Custom* (London: John Murray, 1871), Vol. 1, p. 1.
3. *New York Times,* June 16, 1986, p. A5.
4. Marvin Harris, "India's Sacred Cow," *Human Nature,* (February, 1978).
5. Ruth Benedict, *Patterns of Culture* (New York: Mentor, 1959), p. 160.
6. Cited by Michael C. Howard and Patrick C. McKim, *Contemporary Cultural Anthropology* (Boston: Little, Brown, 1983), p. 12.
7. *World Press Review,* March 1986, p. 25.
8. George P. Murdock, *Social Structure* (New York: Free Press, 1949).
9. Emile Durkheim, *The Elementary Forms of Religious Life* (New York: Free Press, 1954).
10. Robert Bierstedt, *The Social Order* (New York: McGraw-Hill, 1970), p. 176.
11. Ralph Beals, Harry Hoijer, and Allan R. Beals, *An Introduction to Anthropology* (New York: Macmillan, 1977), pp. 529–30.
12. Edward Sapir, "The Status of Linguistics as a Science," *Language,* Vol. 5, (Charlottesville, VA: Linguistic Society of America, 1929), p. 209.
13. Richard T. Pascale and Anthony G. Athos, *The Art of Japanese Management* (New York: Warner, 1981), p. 142.
14. *USA Today,* May 23, 1986, p. 15A.
15. Lauriston Sharp, "Steel Axes for Stone-Age Australians," *Human Organization,* 2 (1952), pp. 17–22.
16. William Graham Sumner, *Folkways: A Study of the Sociological Importance of Usages, Manners, Customs, Mores, and Morals* (Boston: Ginn, 1906).
17. Edward Gross and Gregory P. Stone, "Embarrassment and the Analysis of Role Requirements," *American Journal of Sociology,* 70 (July 1964), pp. 1–15.
18. Leon Mann, "The Social Psychology of Waiting Lines," *American Scientist,* 58 (July 1970), pp. 390–98.
19. *USA Today,* May 13, 1986, p. 1A.
20. People v. Beardsley, 113 N.W. 1128 (1907).
21. James A. Inciardi and Sandy C. Newman, "Adolescent Attitudes Towards Drug Use: A Cross-Sectional View of Two Generations," *Addictive Diseases: An International Journal,* 1 (1974), pp. 117–30.
22. This synthesis was developed from a number of sources, and is the authors' interpretation. See Robert N. Bellah, Richard Madsen, William M. Sullivan, Ann Swidler, and Steven M. Tipton, *Habits of the Heart: Individualism and Commitment in American Life* (Berkeley: University of California Press, 1985); Christopher Lasch, *The Culture of Narcissism* (New York: W. W. Norton, 1978); David Riesman, *The Lonely Crowd: A Study of the Changing American Character* (New Haven, CT: Yale University Press, 1950); Philip Slater, *The Pursuit of Loneliness* (Boston: Beacon Press, 1976); Robin M. Williams, Jr., *American Society* (New York: Random House, 1970); Daniel Yankelovich, *New Rules: Searching for Self-Fulfillment in a World Turned Upside Down* (New York: Random House, 1981).
23. Quoted in *USA Today,* July 4, 1986, p. 8A.

24. *World Press Review,* August 1986.
25. *Time,* July 4, 1986, p. 22. Copyright 1986 The Time Inc. Magazine Company. Reprinted by permission.
26. *USA Today,* May 13, 1986, p. 1A.
27. Wilmington (Delaware) *News Journal,* March 21, 1986, p. 3A.
28. *Newsweek,* May 27, 1985, p. 64.
29. *Newsweek,* May 27, 1985, p. 64.
30. S. D. Feldman and G. W. Thielbar, *Life Styles: Diversity in American Society* (Boston: Little, Brown, 1975).
31. *Newsweek,* June 9, 1986, pp. 60–64.
32. Houston (Texas) *Post,* March 31, 1984, p. 1A.
33. Joel Best and Gerald T. Horiuchi, "The Razor Blade in the Apple: The Social Construction of an Urban Legend," *Social Problems,* 32 (June 1985), pp. 488–99.
34. Robin M. Williams, Jr., *American Society*, pp. 452–502.
35. *Public Opinion,* 5 (June-July, 1982), p. 23.
36. Hall v. State, 39 CrL 2240 (1986).
37. Edwin Eames and Howard Robboy, "The Sociocultural Context of an Italian-American Dietary Item," in Gerald Sicard and Philip Weinberger (eds.), *Sociology for Our Times* (Glenview, IL: Scott, Foresman, 1977), pp. 224–28.
38. Ralph Linton, *The Study of Man: An Introduction* (Englewood Cliffs, NJ: Prentice-Hall, 1939), pp. 326–27.
39. William H. Harris and Judith S. Levey (eds.), *The New Columbia Viking Encyclopedia* (New York: Columbia University Press, 1975), p. 2011.
40. Roe v. Wade, 410 U.S. 113 (1973).
41. *Newsweek,* January 14, 1985, pp. 20–29; *Time,* January 14, 1985, pp. 16–18.
42. Allan L. McCutcheon, "Sexual Morality, Pro-Life Values, and Attitudes Toward Abortion: A Simultaneous Latent Structure Analysis for 1978–1983," *Sociological Methods & Research,* 16 (November 1987), pp. 256–75.
43. People v. Kimura, A-091133, *National Law Journal,* November 4, 1985, p. 10.
44. State v. Jones, 4 FAS84-2933 (Alaska), *National Law Journal,* February 4, 1985, p. 6.
45. William M. Kephart, *Extraordinary Groups* (New York: St. Martin's, 1982).
46. This approach was suggested by Barry Glasser and Bruce Berg, "How Jews Avoid Alcohol Problems," *American Sociological Review,* 45 (August 1980), pp. 647–64.
47. David Gans and Peter Simon, *Playing in the Band* (New York: St. Martin's, 1985); Milton Mayer, "An Aged Deadhead," *Progressive,* 47 (May 1983), p. 66; *Time,* February 11, 1985, pp. 13–14.
48. *Time,* October 6, 1986, p. 66.

Social Organization, Role Behavior, and Group Dynamics

It had been one of the trickiest scenes to photograph. The hero, an aging actor who had virtually no experience as a stunt man, had to be filmed close-up as he fell into a deep mine shaft. Before that, the scene had been delayed by endless quibbling between the director and the "star" over exactly how the action should look. Now it was over; there would be no more endless retakes. As everyone concerned began to relax and pull themselves together, the lights dimmed; cameras were shut down; and leads and extras wandered away toward their dressing rooms.

The director turned to his assistant and began discussing the next day's shooting schedule. "I want to see the *head rat wrangler* along with the *gaffer* and the *best boy,*" he began. "Oh yeah," the director added, "better include the *key grip,* the *greensman,* and the *propmaster.*" "Yes sir," replied the assistant. "Oh," she asked, "do you want to see the *dolly grip* too?"

Is this a strange conversation? Well, yes and no. The motion picture industry operates in its own special world, one populated not only by actors, actresses, producers, directors, writers, and photographers, but also by a rather unique collection of characters known as *gaffers, greensmen, key grips, dolly grips, wranglers, propmasters,* and a host of others—each of whom is invisible to the average movie viewer.

These specialized jobs are easy to explain. Most can be traced to the beginning of the motion picture industry. Such designations as gaffer (chief electrician) and best boy (principal assistant electrician) date from the early years in Hollywood when stagehands attached spotlights to the ends of "gaffs" or booms. The key grip moved cameras and equipment and also carried the key to the grip (camera case), while the dolly grip moved photographic equipment about on a dolly. Western movies needed people to manage the horses. They were called wranglers, and now the term applies to anyone charged with the care of animals. The film the director and his assistant were discussing required that a swarm of trained rats crawl over the hero at the bottom of the mine shaft, hence the head rat wrangler. When filmmaking began, these names applied to the people actually doing the work, but today they refer to the managers of teams of specialized workers.

The division of labor on a movie set is also highly specialized, and it is regulated by an intricate set of rules that are specified in union contracts. A live plant on a set is the responsibility of a greensman, while artificial plants are handled by a propmaster. Some workers can move props only if they are touched by actors and actresses; others can move only the untouched ones. If a car is driven out of camera range by an actress, she cannot back it up for a retake; a member of the Teamster's Union must do that. Outside groups are also involved. Any time animals are used, they must be treated carefully and humanely. The American Humane Society has established a strict code and has a representative present on the set during all scenes involving animals.

Filmmaking is an intricate and complex process, requiring the participation of literally hundreds of people, sometimes even for just one short scene. The process of making a film reflects what sociologists refer to as **social organization**—the arrangement of positions within a group of people and the social relations among these positions. Each individual contributes in a unique way to the final product, and several basic observations can be made about the overall process. Each job involves certain responsibilities—gaffers do electrical work; propmasters and greensmen do not. Some positions have authority over others—gaffers coordinate the work of the best boys; producers and players do not. And finally, workers who violate these rules typically find themselves subjected to ridicule and at risk of being fired if they fail to change their behavior.

SOCIAL POSITIONS: STATUS AND ROLE

"All the world's a stage," observed William Shakespeare. "And all the men and women merely players; They have their exits and entrances; And one man in his time plays many parts."[1] There is a considerable amount of sociology in these few lines from Shakespeare's *As You Like It.* Every human society, and the social groups within these societies all have "parts" that need to be played. A

Among the many specialized jobs required to produce a film is that of the "dolly grip," who moves cameras and crew along a track.

Hollywood film production is the product of an elaborate *social organization.* The action that eventually appears on the silver screen depends not only on players acting their parts and following their scripts, but on numerous other individuals doing their jobs as well. Writers, agents, attorneys, and many other front-end people get the production started. Then various members of the film crew, followed by the editors and sound mixers, must work their magic to produce the final version of the film. Meanwhile, advertising, public relations, and other publicity agents are involved in the film's promotion. Distributors and theater-chain operators must be convinced to rent and show the film. The final success of the production also depends on delivery personnel, ticket takers, and projectionists.

Social Status

The most basic units of social organization are social statuses. A **social status** is a socially recognized position within some larger social unit such as a group, organization, or society.[2] The most easily recognized statuses are "jobs" in the conventional sense of the term. Film crews have gaffers and rat wranglers; schools have principals, students, and teachers; the American government has a president and vice-president, senators and cabinet members, representatives, judges, and ambassadors. Social status also describes a range of other social positions in every society. People occupy statuses within their families: husband and wife; mother and father; son and daughter; cousin, uncle, grandparent. To this list can be added the many statuses that each family member occupies at the societal level: citizen, woman or man, child or adult, as well as the positions people occupy on a temporary basis—job applicant, tourist, customer, pedestrian, second grader, college student.

Sociologists stress the fact that statuses are stable positions that exist for long periods of time, often with many different individuals circulating in and out of them. Thus, statuses can exist independently of the people who occupy them at any given point in time. This description certainly characterizes statuses such as president of the United States and chief justice of the Supreme Court, and applies as well to such positions as college dean and Sociology 201 student or instructor.

Every status has its rewards and expectations. Rewards usually take the form of income, social prestige, or authority. Expectations involve required behaviors. Such rewards and expectations affect the attractiveness of statuses. When people have a choice, they avoid the less desirable positions. Given the prestige, income, and power associated with the Presidency of the United States, it is a likely goal for most individuals who embark on a career in politics. Yet by contrast, witness the fact that the Catholic church in the United States has found it increasingly difficult to recruit men for the priesthood. The opportunity for service to God and the church apparently cannot compensate for the pressures of poverty, chastity, and obedience.

Social Roles

While a status is a position, it does not exist in isolation. Each position in a society is paired with one or more roles. School principals have established relationships with teachers, parents, students, and school boards. Husbands have wives, and friends have friends. Social expectations define these relationships; thus, a **social role** is the behavior expected of a person in a particular social position. Just as film actors and actresses have scripts to follow, occupants of other statuses have roles they must play.

Many social roles are more or less officially defined. On the movie set, the obligations and rights of rat wranglers, propmasters, greensmen, and electricians are spelled out either in job descriptions or union contracts. Police officers, military personnel, and Girl Scouts have rule books or manuals. Numerous books advise applicants how to behave in job interviews or tell women how to be a "good mother." On U.S. Air Force bases an *Air Force Wives' Handbook* details the dress code and rules of etiquette for civilian spouses.

Most roles, however, tend to be less formally defined. Nevertheless, they demand certain kinds of behavior. Roles are part of the cultural heritage of a

SOCIAL INDICATOR

U.S. Seminary Enrollment, 1960–1988

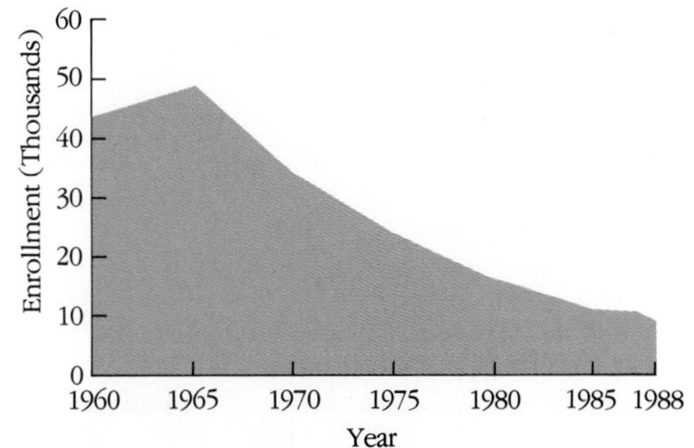

Source: *Official Catholic Directory,* 1988.

society, and they are acquired through **socialization,** the process by which people learn the behavior and attitudes appropriate to their roles in society. As children grow and mature, they absorb far more than the fundamentals taught in school. They are also exposed to many sources of information and direction. As one author put it, much is "learned without explicit, intentional instruction."[3] Thus, media presentations, folklore, children's stories, school experiences, observations of behavior, and countless other clues combine to present a consistent image of roles. No written rules or legal definitions exist for the role of "customer," for example, but through a combination of observation, trial and error, and firsthand experience, every child learns his or her part in making purchases.

The concepts of status and role are useful for understanding social behavior because they can be applied to situations that seem to be spontaneous. Expectations clearly exist with respect to "friends," and they are quite consistent. American women, when asked to explain what attributes they expect to find in a friend, list such things as reliability and trust. They seek someone with whom to share feelings and from whom to garner social and emotional support.[4] Most women impose these expectations on their friends. Men's friendships are more likely to be organized around social activities, recreational drinking, and going to sporting events. This idea of "friendship" can be carried a step further to the role of "best friend," where people demand an even higher level of trust and reliability. Because women's friendships are generally more intimate, most women can identify a "best friend," while many men cannot. When a man can, that best friend is generally a woman, and usually she is his spouse.

Ascribed and Achieved Statuses

People come to occupy social statuses by one of two processes—ascription or achievement. An **ascribed status** is assigned to an individual without regard for innate differences or abilities. The individual has no control over the decision. Every infant born into American society is ascribed numerous status positions—an age status ("baby" or "infant"), a gender status (male or female), a family status (son or daughter, and perhaps sister, brother, and cousin), religious status, racial status,

Exhibit 4.1 Sociology in the Media

Ascribing Racial Status in South Africa

The case was a textbook illustration of the absurdity of South Africa's rigid apartheid policy. In a field on the outskirts of Pretoria, a black worker came upon a two-week-old infant wrapped in a blanket, her head covered with a paper bag. The abandoned baby was taken to a nearby hospital, where nurses named her Lize.

What should have been a happy ending was only the beginning of a national controversy. By law, every South African citizen must be assigned to one of four racial categories: white, black, "colored" (mixed race), or Asian. According to the country's elaborate apartheid code, Lize should have been classified on the basis of her "appearance," along with "habits, education, and speech in general." But while Lize's complexion was darkish, because she was an infant it was impossible to apply the standard criteria.

In a hasty attempt to resolve the issue, the police suggested last week that "scientific" tests on one strand of Lize's hair proved that she was of mixed race. But South Africa's leading expert on hair immediately denounced the tentative finding as "meaningless," arguing that hair samples of infants do not reveal racial characteristics. The government then repudiated the police, calling the test "inconclusive."

As police searched for the child's parents, outrage mounted over the classification policy. Racial typing, declared the *Rand Daily Mail,* was "the cause of more human agony than any other of the South African statutes." Dr. Marius Barnard, a member of the opposition Progressive Federal Party and brother of heart surgeon Dr. Christiaan Barnard, urged the government to classify Lize as white. Said he: "It is the innocent who suffer in these matters." At week's end no one had yet decided whether Lize would go through life enjoying the privileges of white society or be a second-class citizen.

Author's Note: Lize was subsequently determined by the South African police to be of "mixed race."

SOURCE: *Time,* August 8, 1983, p. 48.

ethnic status (Italian-American, Cuban-American), and socioeconomic status (roughly divided into rich, poor, and middle class). Ascribed statuses are purely sociological accidents of birth. Over time, other statuses are ascribed—becoming an "adult," and later "old." Even without the benefit of the sociological perspective, it is clear that ascribed statuses have a lasting impact on the experiences and opportunities of a child as he or she grows up (see Exhibit 4.1).

For a variety of reasons, many people attempt to alter their ascribed statuses. Some individuals change religious affiliation because they do not agree with the doctrines espoused; people modify highly "foreign-sounding" names because they are too difficult for others to pronounce or remember, or because the ethnic group they reflect is discriminated against; a few blacks in American society have "passed" for white to avoid prejudice and segregation. Thus, an **achieved status** is acquired through personal effort, choice, or merit. It is an outgrowth of some individual action. The status of being married, for example, is achieved, as are the statuses of parent, politician, and priest.

Two important points should be noted here. The first is that achieved statuses are not always fully individual decisions. Social pressures often push people toward certain achieved statuses. Career choices, for example, frequently are shaped by parental wishes. The second point is that an ascribed status can limit opportunities to attain certain achieved statuses. A young Catholic girl, for example, may not become an "acolyte" (more typically referred to as an altar boy), and when she is an adult woman, she may not become a Catholic priest. Alternatively, being born into a poor family may involve limitations on educational attainment that children of affluent parents do not face.

A vanity license plate and a BMW are among the major status symbols of the 1990s.

Status Symbols

People regularly display **status symbols,** visible identifiers of their social status. Among the more obvious examples are the badge and blue uniform of police officers, the Roman collar of Catholic priests, and the gold stars of the army general. Similarly, a wedding band is a symbol of marital status, and a Porsche or BMW is a claim to upper-middle-class status.

Status symbols are displayed as external reminders of the rights, privileges, and duties of particular social positions. Police officers' uniforms, in combination with badge, revolver, and nightstick, emphasize the officers' authority to direct the behavior of citizens under certain circumstances. The white coats of physicians stand as reminders of their special training and expertise.

Research has demonstrated that status symbols influence how people react toward others. A recent California study indicated that people view police officers dressed in traditional uniforms as more competent, helpful, and honest than those in plainclothes or those who have adopted the "Miami Vice" look.[5] The clerical garb of priests, ministers, and rabbis implies adherence to higher standards of ethical behavior than those found in "regular" people. Because status symbols do indeed convey specific images and impressions, their display has become the subject of bitter debate and even court decisions. Not too long ago a New York lawyer-priest was prohibited from wearing his Roman collar in court on the grounds that his religious status might prejudice judges and juries.[6] Similarly, Jewish men wear the *yarmulke* as a sign of piety, but is the skullcap appropriate if the person is also a member of the uniformed armed forces? In 1986, the United States Supreme Court said that it was not. The court maintained that religious symbols undermine the need for "uniform treatment for members of all religious faiths."[7] Not all status symbols involve a positive image. Some are a stigma. As illustrated in Exhibit 4.2, a controversy recently was waged over the fairness of the "CONVICTED DUI" status symbol.

Status and Role Dilemmas

The concepts of status and role not only emphasize the complexity of social life, but also reveal areas of discord. The most common problem in this regard is **role strain,** any difficulty a person encounters in performing a particular role—an author trying to meet an unrealistic

Exhibit 4.2 Types & Stereotypes

Status Symbols, Drunk Drivers, and The Scarlet Letter

One of the more curious status symbols to emerge in recent years is the "CONVICTED DUI" bumper sticker. The idea of putting a negative symbol on the automobiles of individuals convicted of driving under the influence of alcohol began in 1981 on Vashon Island, a small community off the coast of Washington in the Pacific Northwest. Since that time the sticker has become popular elsewhere, bringing controversy because of the visible stigma associated with it.

Perhaps the most unusual DUI bumper-sticker episode occurred in 1985 when Florida Judge Becky Titus launched the program in Sarasota County. Under her plan, convicted drunk drivers, in lieu of losing their licenses, could drive their automobiles "for business purposes only," provided they displayed the sticker on their rear bumpers. Sarasota County's chief public defender, Elliott Metcalfe, objected to the practice, claiming that the red and silver reflective sticker was too much in the tradition of Nathaniel Hawthorne's *The Scarlet Letter,* and that the judge's ruling probably constituted a violation of the Eighth Amendment's ban against cruel and unusual punishment. The issue resulted in a number of court clashes between judge and public defender. And what made the episode most interesting was that Public Defender Metcalfe and Judge Titus were husband and wife.

SOURCES: *National Law Journal,* December 28, 1981, p. 35; *National Law Journal,* July 15, 1985, p. 53.

deadline, a college student preparing for three final exams scheduled for the same day, a widow having to suddenly face life alone. More complex is **role conflict,** a situation in which the expectations or demands of statuses and roles impose inconsistent, contradictory, or impossible expectations. The concept of role conflict is illustrated in a recent comment by a New York parole officer:

> Being a parole officer in this state is no easy matter. Parole in New York is defined as a casework agency. As a result, your role is one of counsellor, advisor, clinician, priest, social worker. But parole officers are also armed peace officers, charged with enforcing warrants and making arrests.
>
> Have you ever heard of a gun-carrying social worker? The two just don't compute.[8]

Status and Role Sets

Each person in a complex industrial society occupies a number of different statuses and roles in the normal course of events, easily shifting from one to another as the situation demands. If you examined a day in the life of a married, working mother, for example, you might find her breakfasting with her husband, getting the children off to school, stopping to pay the rent on her way to work, balancing her company's books, calling her aging parents to see how they are doing, preparing dinner for her husband and children, and finally straightening up the house or apartment and then doing some laundry at the end of the day. The array of positions she occupies—as spouse, parent, tenant, employee, daughter, and housewife—is termed a **status set.**

The need to juggle these various statuses may present problems, the most common of which is not having the time to pursue personal interests or maintain friendships. The matter is complicated further by the fact that in any status, an individual must interact with many **role partners,** that cluster of people that a person must relate to when performing any given role. A medical resident working in a hospital, for example, must deal with other residents, patients, relatives of patients, nurses, lab technicians, and supervising physicians.

Just as each person has a complex status set, each of those statuses is associated with a whole array of roles, collectively called a **role set.**[9] Exhibit 4.3 illustrates the role set of the married, working woman mentioned earlier. In the role as *mother,* she interacts with her children, as well as with their peers, teachers, and doctors. Her in-laws, members of the local PTA, and the parents of her children's friends are also among her role partners. As an *employee* she interacts with her boss, secretaries, other office mates, co-workers, and an assortment of business associates. Some cross-over also exists in her interactions. She deals with her in-laws, for example, not only as the mother of their grandchildren, but also as the wife of their son.

Now, as if this nexus of interaction is not complicated enough already, consider the fact that different role partners may very well have different and inconsistent expectations. The married, working woman typically is faced with the fact that her children, husband, employer, and perhaps even her parents and friends are competing for her time. Similarly, recent research on the experiences of interns during "rounds" illustrates the dilemmas and contradictions that they face in this regard.[10] Rounds involve teams of physicians and interns who visit wards to diagnose, evaluate, and discuss appropriate patient therapies. Physicians ask questions to test knowledge and they expect thorough and informed answers. Should interns raise questions that a supervising physician might not be able to answer? Should they volunteer information, showing up the ignorance of fellow students upon whom they may later have to depend? Should an intern or doctor treat a patient who is also a close friend or a relative?

Master Status

Although virtually every person in every society occupies a number of different statuses, each also has a **master status,** one that is the most important and that dominates social identity. For children, their age alone determines their master status. In many cultures, family lineage, sex, or age defines a person's master status. For most adult American men, their occupation determines their master status, as is clearly evidenced by the traditional question, "What do you do?" which always comes up at social gatherings. The answer—physician, intern, bricklayer, attorney, machine operator, police officer—helps to locate a person in the structure of society. (For an analysis of the implications of the master status of "police officer," see Chapter 15.)

In some instances a master status is self-imposed. An individual may choose to allow one aspect of his or her life to dominate all others. The so-called "workaholic," devotes all energy and time to the obligations of the job at the expense of family and friends. The intern, on the other hand, has no choice but to define his or her master status in terms of that position, in order to survive the rigors of medical school. More often than not, however, a person's master status is imposed externally. Neither George Bush nor John F. Kennedy could fail to recognize that his master status while in the White House was that of "Mr. President." For generations in the United States, when a woman married—even if she continued to work outside the home—she was assigned the master status of "homemaker," a label that served to shape people's expectations. She was expected to give priority to her husband's career or to terminate her career in favor of devoting all her energies to the home. Employers ignored women for jobs and promotions, assuming that work was unimportant to them.

Sociologist Erving Goffman explored a dramatic instance of an imposed master status by highlighting the social pain endured by people who suffer some form of

Changing social definitions of the role of homemaker are reflected in the shifting image of General Mills' Betty Crocker. The original appeared in 1936.

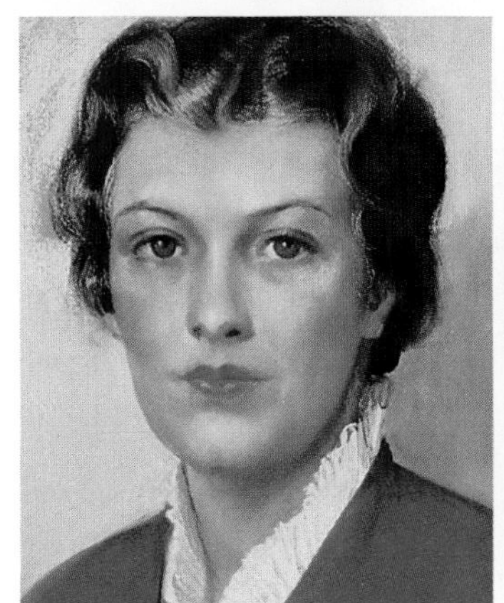

Exhibit 4.3

Sociological Focus

The Role Set of a Married, Working Mother

Married, working mother

Parent
Children
Children's Friends
Teachers, PTA

Daughter
Parents
Parents' Physician
Nursing home Staff

Wife
In-laws
Husband's Boss
Husband's Colleagues and Spouses

Employee
Boss
Clients
Colleagues
Colleagues' Spouses

Commuter
Other Commuters
Police
Parking-lot Attendant

Tenant
Other Tenants
Landlord
Doorman

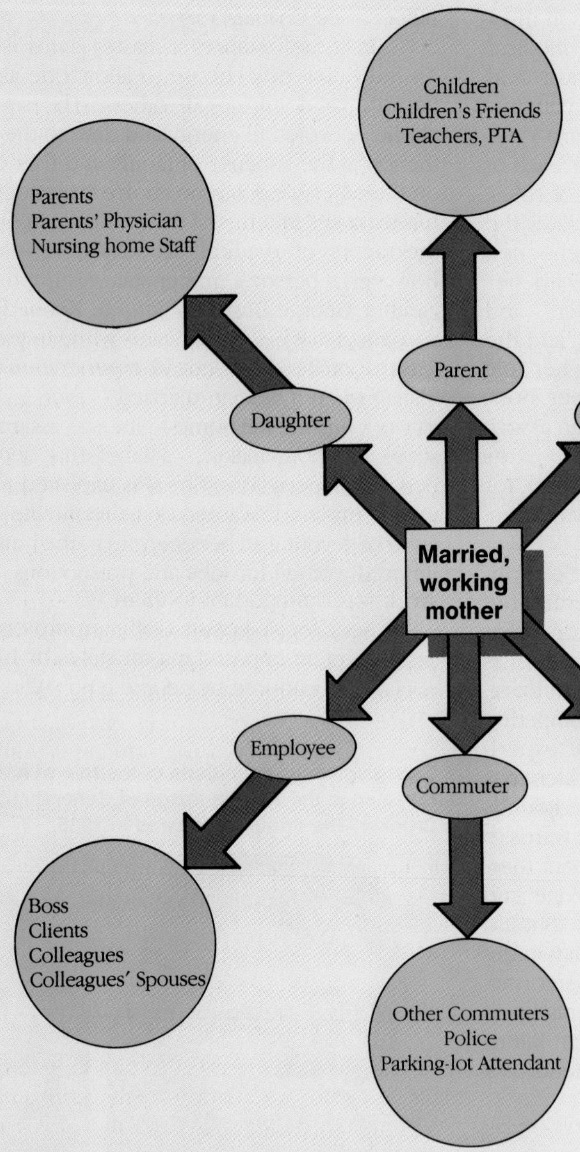

facial disfigurement. He found that the stigma of their "spoiled identity" defined the nature and direction of their every social encounter.

> Before her disfigurement [amputation of the distal half of her nose] Mrs. Dover, who lived with one of her two married daughters, had been an independent, warm, and friendly woman who enjoyed traveling, shopping, and visiting her many relatives. The disfigurement of her face, however, resulted in a definite alteration in her way of living. The first two or three years she seldom left her daughter's home, preferring to remain in her room or to sit in the backyard. "I was heartsick," she said. "The door had been shut on my life."[11]

Restructuring Social Roles

Social structures are in a constant state of flux, with socially recognized statuses and roles shifting, changing, and evolving. Although these alterations can be somewhat rapid, as has been the case with the radical reorganization of gender roles (see Chapter 10), they typically occur rather slowly and almost imperceptibly over the course of decades. In some instances, entirely new structures and positions emerge while others disappear in response to the social forces that are constantly reshaping society.

Technological Change

Redefining Motherhood New knowledge, ideas, and technologies often combine to bring new statuses and roles into being. A controversial new status that came to be defined in this way is that of "surrogate mother," a woman who is hired to carry to term and give birth to the child of its biological father, and in some cases, its biological father *and* mother. This seemingly confusing scenario is now readily manageable within the context of modern medical science. Many otherwise healthy women cannot become pregnant for a variety of biomedical reasons, but in 1976 research in the areas of animal and human reproduction made it possible for these women's husbands to artificially inseminate another female. More recent research has also made it possible for scientists to implant a fertilized egg from a married couple in the uterus of another woman. In both cases, the "surrogate" then carries the fertilized egg to term. The first child born to a surrogate mother was born in Detroit in April, 1986. The procedure cost some $40,000, including a $10,000 fee paid to the surrogate.[12]

The creation of any new status may raise complex social, moral, or legal questions, but few can compare in magnitude with those that emerged in connection with surrogate motherhood. Who, for example, is the biological mother—the woman who supplied the egg, or the woman who carried the baby to term and gave birth? Should the surrogate have the right to be paid? What should happen if a surrogate refuses to surrender the child after birth? Is this the beginning of an era in which couples too busy to have children merely hire others to do it for them? Does the surrogate have rights to visit the child? Does the child have a right to know its origins and its birth mother? Some of these questions are examined in more detail in Exhibit 4.4, which chronicles one of the most well-known cases of surrogate motherhood, the case of "Baby M."

The Rise and Fall of Computer Programmers Somewhat less dramatic, but nonetheless notable, are technological changes occurring in other sectors of society, particularly those in the occupational sphere. The introduction of modern computer technology in the 1940s created a new occupation, that of computer programmer, which has gone through several phases of development. The very first programmers were people who physically crawled around the huge mainframes, setting switches by hand. In the 1960s the next generation of computers powerfully upgraded the prestige and rewards of programmers. People with programming skills were in a position to demand large salaries, set their own hours, and pursue projects of their own choice. One corporate executive described them as "coddled and humored and pampered, . . . immune to control, discipline, and challenge." By the 1970s, technological and social changes combined to erode the privileged position of programmers. Computer languages and hardware moved toward standardization, more and more people acquired programming skills, and the availability of prepackaged software reduced demand. Programming remains a well-paid profession, but it lacks the freedom and excitement of the 1960s. Similar changes also are apparent in other occupations. The introduction of computer and robotic technology to automobile manufacturing, for example, has created new specialists in the industry, combined with a decline in the number of assembly-line workers. The health-care fields and many white-collar jobs also have been altered.

Innovation: Consumer Advocacy

In rare cases the emergence of some new status can be traced to the actions of a single individual, usually at a point in time when social conditions are ripe for change. Consider the career of Ralph Nader, the person primarily responsible for creating what is now known as "consumer advocacy." Nader's dedication to automobile safety in the 1960s crystallized public attention on the need for consumer-oriented protection and legislation. Various groups—both governmental and private—had

Exhibit 4.4

Case Study

Surrogate Motherhood and Surrogate Law

Unlike most children, "Baby M" was conceived without sex or love, under an unusual contract between a professional New Jersey couple and an unmoneyed housewife who agreed to bear the infant through artificial insemination for $10,000.

But as in any ordinary birth, the infant unleashed an outpouring of parental passion—and a novel, agonizing court battle over the child's destiny

Filed by William and Elizabeth Stern after Mary Beth Whitehead changed her mind about giving up the baby girl, the highly publicized and dramatic case tests for the first time whether surrogate-motherhood contracts are enforceable.

"What [the controversy] really boils down to is this: Is the [couple's] right to reproduce greater than or equal to the best interests of the child?" says Judianne Densen-Gerber, a New York attorney and psychiatrist surveying attitudes about surrogate motherhood.

The outcome of the New Jersey case is expected to have far-reaching implications for surrogate motherhood. Infertile couples have been relying on surrogate contracts with increasing frequency, but no court or legislature has ruled on the validity or scope of such agreements.

Courts in Michigan, Kentucky, and New York, for instance, recently reached conflicting results on the legality of the payment to the surrogate but stopped short of tackling the thornier issue of whether the contracts offend public policy.

And although other surrogates have changed their minds and refused to relinquish custody, Mr. Stern is the first biological father to legally fight that reversal.

The New Jersey case also fuels an already-charged debate among lawyers and other experts over the legal and ethical underpinnings of surrogate motherhood, first mentioned in the Bible and now dominated by a handful of family law specialists.

Attorneys who earn their living by uniting childless couples with fertile women say such work enables them to "give life." Supporters say surrogate motherhood is buttressed by the U.S. Constitution. They reason that married couples have a constitutional right to reproduce that includes the right to contract with a third party to get what they themselves are physically lacking. To them, surrogate mothers are like semen donors who receive compensation and are socially accepted.

But critics say such constitutional arguments are "silly." Paying women to have children merely to give them away is illegal, opponents say, prohibited by state laws that ban baby buying and private adoptions. They tag lawyers involved in surrogate mothering for profit "baby brokers" who exploit women, children, and the adoption laws for professional gain.

Many lawyers on both sides of the issue are looking for a legislative solution to the controversy. But lawmakers trying to regulate surrogate motherhood either remain confounded by the issue or frustrated by strong opposition from feminist and religious groups.

Biblical Example

While surrogate motherhood is new to the law, the practice dates to the Old Testament. In Genesis 16, Abraham had sexual intercourse with his wife's handmaiden, Hagar, after his wife Sarah failed to become pregnant. The encounter produced a son, Ishmael.

Modern surrogate motherhood through artificial insemination surfaced in this country in 1976, with hundreds of babies born since then. Its increasing popularity is generally attributed to a corresponding decrease in the number of white infants available for adoption through nonprofit and private agencies. . . .

In the landmark New Jersey case, 30-year-old Ms. Whitehead, who has two school-age children, agreed to donate her egg and be artificially inseminated with Mr. Stern's sperm after reading a newspaper ad inviting women to become surrogates.

$25,000 Fee

Under an elaborate, 16-page agreement, . . . Ms. Whitehead agreed "that in the best interests of the child, she will not form or attempt to form a parent-child relationship with any child . . . she may conceive . . . and shall freely surrender custody to William Stern, Natural Father, immediately upon birth of the child; and terminate all parental rights to said child pursuant to this agreement."

In exchange, Mr. Stern promised to pay roughly $25,000—$10,000 for Ms. Whitehead for "compensation for services and expenses," $5,000 for her medical, legal, and insurance costs while pregnant. . . .

But none of those promises mattered to Ms. Whitehead when the baby was born March 27, 1986.

"I signed on an egg," Ms. Whitehead told a local newspaper. "I didn't sign on a baby girl, a clone of my other little girl . . . [I]n the delivery room as my baby girl was being born, I knew I was not going to give her up."

When Ms. Whitehead ignored repeated pleas to turn over the baby, the Sterns sued the housewife and her husband, Richard, for breach of contract, specific performance, and temporary custody of the infant they call Melissa Elizabeth, the Whiteheads call Sara Elizabeth, and court papers refer to as "Baby M."

In May, 1986, Family Judge Harvey R. Sorkow of Hackensack awarded the Sterns temporary custody, but the Whiteheads evaded that order for three months by fleeing to Florida. The couple finally were picked up last July and forced by police to turn over the baby to the Sterns. This month, the judge extended his temporary custody order for the Sterns while granting Ms. Whitehead limited visitation rights, and he set trial for November 3, 1986.

At that time, the judge will be forced to decide the crucial issue of whether the surrogate-motherhood contract is valid or enforceable as a matter of public policy.

Baby Buying?

Indeed, paying a woman to turn over a child—baby buying—is prohibited in some form in every state. But those laws were passed before surrogate motherhood was envisioned and were intended to prevent women from putting their babies up for adoption because of financial pressures.

Nevertheless, lawyers and others who oppose surrogate motherhood claim the payment in that context amounts to the same thing: enticing women to terminate their parental rights. . . .

Paying for "Services"

Supporters of surrogate motherhood admit the payment is necessary to attract women, but they claim the money is not compensation for the baby but recompense for the surrogate's "services" during pregnancy. . . .

According to Noel P. Keane, a Dearborn, Michigan, lawyer who in 1976 drafted the first surrogate-mothering contract and since has handled 115 surrogate cases, most people who reject surrogate motherhood focus on the baby-buying argument when they're really objecting to the practice on moral and religious grounds. . . .

A new report by the Ethics Committee of the Washington, D.C.-based American Fertility Society attempted to answer some of the legal and ethical questions posed by surrogate motherhood and other new forms of artificial birth technologies.

But after two years of study, the eleven-member panel of lawyers, ethicists, and fertility experts concluded only that they had "serious ethical reservations about surrogacy." The panel explained it could not decide whether surrogate motherhood was ethically acceptable until additional empirical information becomes available about its risks and benefits.

In the meantime, while experts and legislatures gather data on surrogate motherhood, the judge in the New Jersey case is left facing some challenging questions with little guidance.

Author's Note: After a six-week trial early in 1987, custody of Baby M was given to the Sterns, and the child officially became Melissa Elizabeth Stern.

SOURCE: Excerpted and adapted from the *National Law Journal,* September 29, 1986, pp. 1, 8, 10.

long attempted to rid the marketplace of unsafe products and practices. But their efforts, generally passive and only in response to the most obvious crises, were ineffective at best. When Nader first began to speak out against abuses by automobile manufacturers, the general public had been fed up for some time with the difficulties that plagued the family car. Too, the 1960s were a time of social revolution, and the struggles in behalf of civil rights and environmental quality had given activists additional credibility and acceptance.

"Consumer advocates" of the 1960s and early 1970s were generally solitary individuals, like Ralph Nader, or small groups dedicated to arousing public interest. Today, many city and state governments have offices of consumer protection. Moreover, several large private groups—including one headed by Nader—work full-time to safeguard the interests of the American consumer. Thus, the consumer advocate has become a full-time, paid position, often involved with the management of large bureaucracies.

Sociocultural Change: "Living Together"

Broad social and cultural change can bring about modifications in behavior that also create new statuses, roles, and social positions. A number of trends emergent during the post-World War II era converged during the 1960s and 1970s; the result has become known as the "sexual revolution." Changing sexual mores, an increasing tolerance of open discussions of sexual practices and relationships, and the development of effective birth control strategies are all characteristics of the sexual revolution. In addition, soaring divorce rates encouraged young people to be more tentative about entering into marriage. Although many young couples had always lived together, a consequence of the "revolution" was that increasing numbers chose to do so openly and publicly. Slowly, living together became a new and socially recognized status (see the discussion in Chapter 11 under "Cohabitation").

Unlike "surrogate mother" and "consumer advocate," the status of living together involves an uncertain dimension. "Living together" has no noun equivalent; it remains a status without a convenient and generally agreed upon label. "Cohabitant" is too clinical and impersonal. "Special friend" is a bit pretentious and far too ambiguous. "Roommate" is already taken. The Census Bureau defines living together as "unmarried couples sharing the same household." The fact that there is no socially recognized label reflects the ambiguity that continues to surround the position. In fact, one study during the early 1980s suggested five different ways that living together might be designated, depending on the nature of the role partners' relationship:

- *temporary, casual*—based largely on convenience
- *affectionate dating*—defined as the most intimate form of dating
- *trial marriage*—where partners are considering a more permanent relationship
- *temporary alternative to marriage*—when schooling or other problems prevent marriage
- *permanent alternative to marriage*—the rejection, for various reasons, of traditional marriage[13]

Role Relations

With the exception of those roles that are undergoing significant change, striking elements of consistency and uniformity exist in the performance of most roles. All medical interns seem to carry out their role in more or less the same way. The same statement also can be made about school principals, senators, FBI agents, cocaine dealers, prostitutes, cashiers, and a host of other individuals. Buying a pair of shoes or a ticket to a concert is probably the most standardized and impersonal form of interaction. Salesclerks may be fired and replaced, and new customers appear constantly without having much impact on the way a sale is transacted. Thus, the nature of

Most people in routine social situations, such as forming lines in grocery stores, are unknowingly following subtle social conventions.

the role is not affected very much by the particular person who occupies that role.

In part, such consistency is due to the fact that the typical role behaviors of salesclerks, cashiers, and senators are defined as appropriate to their tasks. There are no compelling reasons to deviate from them. Other role relationships, however, are less standardized. Each pair of friends and every father and daughter, for example, have a unique personal relationship. But even in these most intimate of social liaisons, there are certain systematic patterns, and it is these regularities that attract the attention of sociologists.

Social relationships among people always occur within the context of existing social roles. In some instances the role behavior is based on the social scripts that are deemed appropriate for the situation—the sale of a pair of shoes, the purchase of a concert ticket. Under other conditions questions of power are involved, with people acting in certain ways by virtue of a position that enables them to control the actions of others. And too, the progress of social relations in many instances may be difficult to predict, serving to influence people to move beyond the constraints imposed by the existing organization of roles.

Role Playing

Roles are based on a set of expectations, and most social relationships involve simple **role playing**—people acting out socially defined roles. A familiarity with expected behaviors produces almost programmed responses—the parties involved recognize and understand the social situation and routinely play out their roles. Simple retail sales transactions illustrate this point. Customers enter places of business and make purchases from merchants without much deviation from what might be characterized as the standard sales transaction—selections are made, routine conversation takes place, money or its equivalent changes hands, the purchase is bagged or boxed, and the customer leaves. Except in unusual circumstances, the personal characteristics and demeanor of the parties involved in the transaction do not have much impact on the course of events. Polite customers may receive more courteous treatment, but anyone with enough money or a credit card will be able to complete the purchase. The roles are so well established that they barely impinge upon the consciousness of the players. We might even say that people act habitually, rather than as a matter of choice.

Many roles are knowingly chosen because they are perceived to be appropriate. Within the anonymity of a large class in an overflowing lecture hall, students voluntarily conform to the expectations of the student role—attending class, taking notes, staying awake—even when more attractive alternatives are available. Most parents attempt to adopt the behavior appropriate to the role of parent. There is evidence, for example, that women marijuana smokers cut back their use of the drug so that their use rate declines rapidly in the months prior to giving birth. Among their male counterparts, similar declines occur after they become fathers.[14] This suggests that these people view marijuana smoking as incompatible with the parental role.

Authority Relations

A significant number of role relationships involve elements of authority. In law enforcement, the military, religious orders, and numerous other institutions, each higher rank carries the authority to command those in *all* lower positions. By definition, "bosses" have authority over "workers." Workers may not enjoy being held answerable to a superior, but they accept the arrangement as a condition of employment. Thus, *authority* (a concept discussed at greater length in Chapter 14) is the "right" to command obedience and is based on willing compliance.

Lessons about authority are all part of growing up. By the time youngsters in American society reach age four, they have learned something about authority relations and key aspects of the proper roles of parents and children. In a recent research effort focusing on this phenomenon, the investigator asked a group of children to act out the roles of either "mother" or "baby." When the verbal interchanges of the children were analyzed, the researcher found that 65% of the communication from "mother" to "baby" took the form of a direct command or warning; none of the children playing the role of "baby" gave an order to a "mother."[15] This analysis held true even for communications involving children who tended to be quite verbal and demanding in other situations. The implications here are apparent: children learn at an early age that a mother's role is active and controlling while that of a child is passive and obedient.

Research also has demonstrated adults' willingness to respond to authority. During the early 1960s, psychologist Stanley Milgram convinced a number of study subjects that they should act as "teachers" in a scientific research investigation about the dynamics of memory.[16] The subjects were directed to administer "electric shocks" to "trainees" located in an adjacent room, whenever the trainees gave incorrect answers to the questions posed. The research setting had all the trappings of a scholarly endeavor: the "research director" was dressed as a scientist; the lab equipment was realistic looking, but fake; and the "trainees" were accomplices who would cry out, pound the wall, and plead for the experiment to end as the "voltage" was increased. Some two-thirds of the research subjects obeyed orders and administered what they believed to be 450-volt doses of electricity. In Milgram's later experiments, the "trainees" were placed in the same room as the subjects. Thus, the pain from the electric shocks could be witnessed in person.[17] In this situation, some 30% obeyed the order to increase the voltage, suggesting that face-to-face pain has a discouraging effect. But nevertheless, almost one-third of the subjects were willing to force a "trainee's" hand against the metal plate that produced the shock. For these individuals, *authority* was able to override any reluctance to inflict pain. All of this certainly suggests that people are generally obedient to authority.

Power, Sanctions, and Social Roles

Power (also discussed in greater detail in Chapter 14) involves a person's ability to get what he or she wants even in the face of opposition. Those with power are in a position to define and redefine roles, and as a result, they can influence others to modify their behavior for the sake of attaining rewards or avoiding sanctions.

Two important factors modify the impact of power and sanctions in social relationships. The first factor is that sanctions need not always be put to use; the mere threat of punishment is often effective. In robbery situations, for example, intimidation is typically enough to convince most victims to comply.[18] The second factor involves how people define a situation. In a study of the authority relations in an urban school district, teachers felt totally dominated by the power structure under which they worked. In consequence, they humbly followed the directives of their administrator.[19] They actually may have had some unrecognized power, but their acquiescence was based on the belief that they were without resources of power.

Sanctions, in the broadest sense, involve rewards for conformity and punishments for nonconformity. The most frequently used sanctions that affect role definitions can be organized into a variety of categories, including physical pain, monetary rewards or penalties, symbols, exclusion, and informal social sanctions.

Physical Pain

Inflicting pain has been a popular way of attempting to assure compliance. Parents spank their children; some governments routinely use torture against political dissidents; organized criminal groups rely on pain to keep their members and opponents in line. Until 1968, when the United States Supreme Court halted the practice, whipping was the major tool of inmate control in the Arkansas prison system.[20] Flogging was an official pun-

These photos of Hedda Nussbaum, taken six years apart, graphically show the physical toll of domestic abuse. Her live-in lover was convicted of manslaughter in the death of their illegally adopted child in New York in 1988.

ishment for petty thefts in Delaware until it was abolished by the state legislature in 1973.[21] In short, causing a person to suffer physically is a simple and direct mechanism for control.

During any given year, millions of wives, husbands, and children are subjected to physical abuse.[22] Many factors are at work in these cases of abuse, but role relationships enter into a significant number of them. Research has demonstrated that physical abuse is more likely to be inflicted by a man who believes that his wife's role should be subordinate to his. He uses force in an attempt to reassert his dominance, and the abusive event generally is triggered by heavy drinking, job loss, arguments over money, or generalized demands for gender equality, when the wife has more education or a higher income.[23]

Monetary Sanctions

Workers are docked in pay for absenteeism or tardiness; drivers are fined for traffic violations; and athletes run the risk of substantial fines, or even suspension, for drug use or grossly "unsportsmanlike" conduct. At one time one needed only to follow the activities of tennis star John McEnroe for a few weeks to witness the imposition of monetary sanctions in professional sports. On the other hand, monetary sanctions can also be positive—gifts, salary increases, promotions, awards. Substantial bonuses are given to executives for outstanding corporate performance, while production workers may be paid on a "piece rate" that increases their income in direct proportion to output. In short, people are often motivated by economic incentives.

Interestingly, however, monetary sanctions are not always effective. John McEnroe's repeated fines by the American Tennis Association failed for years to alter his verbally abusive treatment of spectators, officials, and opponents.[24] Despite millions of dollars in fines by the U.S. Customs Service, Colombia's Avianca Airlines carried cocaine in unmanifested cargo on 34 separate occasions during the first half of the 1980s.[25] And in the labor sector throughout most of the industrialized world, workers strike as a protest against existing working conditions, pay scales, and benefits. Strikes always mean lost wages. In general, this disregard for negative monetary sanctions is based on the sometimes realized belief that the ends justify the means, or that the potential gains outweigh the expected losses.

Symbols

Many symbols are awarded for exemplary role behavior. The military presents medals and commendations to outstanding soldiers; professional athletes strive for the distinction of Rookie of the Year or Most Valuable Player; scientists and scholars covet Nobel Prizes; journalists dream of Pulitzers. Some awards have monetary rewards attached, but the recognition of excellence that many awards symbolize appears to be the most important factor to recipients.

Exclusion

As a mechanism for instilling proper role behavior, exclusion can be either physical or social. In both cases, proper behavior is encouraged by the threat of exclusion from a group. *Physical exclusion* is put into play when parents banish recalcitrant children to their bedrooms; when teachers expel unruly students from the classroom; or when governments exercise the exclusive right to execute, deport, exile, or lock people away in prisons and mental institutions for their failure to live up to the expectations of the state.

By contrast, the Amish, one of the ethnic subcultures already examined in Chapter 3, exercise the custom of "shunning," a powerful mechanism of *social exclusion.* Amish who fail to meet their obligations to other members of their community may find themselves

The shame of homelessness in Japanese society, which places enormous value on the family, is so great that the homeless are treated as though they were "invisible."

ignored. Their neighbors and peers refuse to speak to them or do not acknowledge that they exist. This behavior is a powerful deterrent to deviance. Military academies once used a similar mechanism, called "silencing," whereby no one was permitted to speak to cadets who violated the honor code.

Social Approval and Disapproval

The many subtle social mechanisms that people use to express contentment or dissatisfaction with role performance are considerably less dramatic than pain or exclusion, but they exert a powerful influence in human affairs nevertheless. Such modest gestures as a kiss on the cheek, a pat on the back, a shake of the hand, or words given in encouragement motivate people for the simple reason that esteem is important to most individuals. Frowns and other forms of body language, on the other hand, clearly suggest disapproval.

Unquestionably, people are pleased when others show approval and dismayed by expressions of disapproval. Many sociologists contend that the quest for social approval is most powerful during an individual's adolescent years. And interestingly, every generation of parents seems surprised by the bizarre clothing worn by their adolescent children, forgetting the same stage in their own lives when their desire for peer approval found them adorned in equally strange fashions.

The Consequences of Power in Role Compliance

Whether the sanctions involve physical pain, monetary punishments, or exclusion, the use of power to influence role compliance can have unpleasant consequences for both superiors and subordinates. This point was most poignantly, although unexpectedly, demonstrated by sociologist Philip Zimbardo's mock prison experiment at Stanford University in the early 1970s (see Exhibit 4.5).

The students in Zimbardo's experiment were merely playing contrived roles, so one can imagine how difficult it may be for those enmeshed in real situations of abusive social control. Yet power is never absolute. Subordinates always have a choice; they can refuse to submit if they are inclined to pay the price. Prisoners willing to suffer torture, workers willing to be fired, and friends willing to be ostracized demonstrate the potential ineffectiveness of sheer power. Those individuals who do succumb to power become alienated, cynical, and apathetic. They act out their roles only grudgingly, putting a minimum of effort into tasks. Moreover, the risk of outright rebellion is always a possibility. Considering the implications of all types of power, the eighteenth-century French philosopher Jean Jacques Rousseau once commented: "The strongest is never strong enough to be master always, unless he transforms his strength into right, and obedience into duty."[26]

Role Making and Negotiated Relationships

An emphasis on expectations, authority, and power does not mean that individuals are passive prisoners of their roles. Social roles do not follow precise scripts; they adhere instead to general guidelines that provide more freedom to maneuver. Moreover, individuals and groups typically seek to expand their rights and rewards, protect their prerogatives, and achieve more satisfactory relationships. Symbolic interactionists refer to this process of individualizing, creating, and enlarging social roles as **role making.** Thus, the more intimate and personal social relationships (parent–child, friend–friend, husband–wife) are the least structured. They exhibit a great deal of individuality, worked out through a process of give-and-take or negotiation. Role making thus may be classified as cooperative, antagonistic, or based on a system of exchange.

Cooperative Negotiations

Cooperative negotiations occur when role partners agree on a goal and develop plans for its realization. A similar process is apparent in more formal structures, even rigid bureaucracies. Within the hospital setting, for example, in order to accomplish their respective tasks, physicians, nurses, and attendants may need to work out cooperative relationships in order to alter role expectations.[27] Overworked nurses may, for instance, negotiate the right to schedule patient care, a task formally reserved to physicians. To adhere to formalized tasks would slow the process of treatment.

Antagonistic Negotiations

Cooperative negotiations involve an accord as to the nature of the goals; in **antagonistic negotiations** the players are pursuing diverse interests that must be compromised. A common example entails the idea of what should constitute the industrial "work day." Employers have the authority to insist that workers labor until a prescribed time. Many employees, however, prefer to leave their machines a few minutes early so as to be ready to leave exactly as the whistle blows. In a large number of plants the latter arrangement becomes the negotiated order. In some instances dispute resolution emerges through interpersonal dialogue between bosses and workers, but in others it evolves by tacit agreement. And too, the same process is apparent in many white-collar operations. As a former New York City welfare investigator once commented:

> At one level there was no leeway. You absolutely *had* to clock in on time—no exceptions and no room for negotiation. If you were more than three minutes late you were docked an hour's pay. But at the end of the day it was different, and all case supervisors looked the other way. Clock-out time was 5 P.M. By 4:30 the desks would be cleared off; by 4:35 everyone had their hands washed, hair combed, and coats on; and at 4:36 they'd start lining up at the clock. It was pretty funny, watching it every day—one hundred civil service hacks standing in front of a stupid clock for almost a half hour like a bunch of jugheads.[28]

Exchange Negotiations

In **exchange negotiations,** individuals who have equal authority trade behavior.[29] Although conventional roles have assigned the tasks of cooking, house cleaning, and shopping to wives, negotiated exchanges have become common among working couples. One spouse may do the cooking, while the other looks after the house. Some exchanges involve temporary transactions: two summer campers agree to divide the tasks of keeping their cabin in shape. Other exchanges establish regular patterns that endure to become the norm—often the case in dual-career marriages.

Many of the new roles created through negotiation tend to be rather precarious. In most instances this uncertainty is due to the fact that arrangements are worked out between specific individuals and lack validation in the larger society. In others, the structure of the situation generates the potential for role negotiation. Yet when the relationship or existing structure dissolves, so too does any role behavior that had been arbitrated. Consider a recent case in point. Historically in the Texas prison system, order was maintained in the penitentiary by means of a "building-tender" system. Building tenders were prisoners who were hand-picked for controlling fellow inmates, and through corruption and brutal violence, they did indeed keep other convicts in line. A federal court decision in 1982, which declared conditions in the Texas prison system to be in violation of the Constitution, dismantled the building-tender system.[30] That corrupt and brutal prisoner control network gave rise to a new and even more violent pattern—prisoner gangs, formed along racial and ethnic lines, using methods that range from simple extortion to contract murder in their struggle for control of the penitentiaries.

SOCIAL GROUPS

Statuses and roles are but two of the primary units of social behavior. Another is the social group. A **group** is a collection of two or more people who interact with one another on the basis of a shared social identity. The film crew is a social group. The members of the crew have been together for a number of years and think of themselves as a social unit. They display a strong sense of comradeship. They have developed a democratic style whereby each individual has the right to contribute ideas about the filmmaking process. Thus, the film crew demonstrates the basic characteristics of all social groups: (1) two or more people who interact with one another on a continuous basis; (2) organized into a system of roles; (3) thinking of themselves as a unique social unit, separate from all others; and (4) sharing distinctive norms, values, and goals.

The Nature of Social Groups

Every individual participates in a vast array of social groups—families, clubs, fraternities and sororities, athletic teams, church congregations, work teams, play groups, and sometimes whole neighborhoods. Groups can come in all sizes, ranging from a doubles team in a tennis match or a pair of scientists collaborating on a research project to the membership of a professional association or trade union.

The type of interaction that takes place among the members of a group can also vary. It may be intimate and regular, such as an exchange between a husband and wife or two lovers, or it may be less personal, such as the interaction that occurs among the members of a work crew at a construction site. Regular contact is not necessary for the maintenance of a group. Tennis partners may not see each other except at their weekly match. Members of a professional association may be together only once a year at a convention. Individuals who have never had face-to-face contact may nonetheless be members of a social group. Pen pals or members of a fan club may never meet in person, but such individuals often communicate through the mail.

Group Structure and Consciousness of Kind

Every social group exhibits its own unique system of roles. The role structure in some groups is complex and formal. A sophisticated arrangement of captains, chiefs, officers, divisions, and sections characterizes law enforcement agencies. Chains and units of command assign responsibility for the accomplishment of tasks. Football teams have offensive and defensive units, special teams, coaches, coordinators, scouts, and trainers, each with designated roles. By contrast, some groups have a less

Exhibit 4.5

Research in Sociology

Pathology of Imprisonment

[An] eloquent plea for prison reform—for humane treatment of human beings, for the basic dignity that is the right of every American—came to me secretly in a letter from a prisoner who cannot be identified because he is still in a state correctional institution. He sent it to me because he read of an experiment I recently conducted at Stanford University. In an attempt to understand just what it means psychologically to be a prisoner or a prison guard, Craig Haney, Curt Banks, Dave Jaffe, and I created our own prison. We carefully screened over 70 volunteers who answered an ad in a Palo Alto city newspaper and ended up with about two dozen young men who were selected to be part of this study. They were mature, emotionally stable, normal, intelligent college students from middle-class homes throughout the United States and Canada. They appeared to represent the cream of the crop of this generation. None had any criminal record and all were relatively homogeneous on many dimensions initially.

Half were arbitrarily designated as prisoners by a flip of a coin, the others as guards. These were the roles they were to play in our simulated prison. The guards were made aware of the potential seriousness and danger of the situation and their own vulnerability. They made up their own formal rules for maintaining law, order, and respect and were generally free to improvise new ones during their eight-hour, three-man shifts. The prisoners were unexpectedly picked up at their homes by a city policeman in a squad car, searched, handcuffed, fingerprinted, booked at the Palo Alto station house and taken blindfolded to our jail. There they were stripped, deloused, put into a uniform, given a number and put into a cell with two other prisoners where they expected to live for the next two weeks. The pay was good ($15 a day) and their motivation was to make money.

We observed and recorded on videotape the events that occurred in the prison, and we interviewed and tested the prisoners and guards at various points throughout the study. Some of the videotapes of the actual encounters between the prisoners and guards were seen on the NBC News feature "Chronolog" on November 26, 1971.

At the end of only six days we had to close down our mock prison because what we saw was frightening. It was no longer apparent to most of the subjects (or to us) where reality ended and their roles began. The majority had indeed become prisoners or guards, no longer able to clearly differentiate between role playing and self. There were dramatic changes in virtually every aspect of their behavior, thinking, and feeling. In less than a week the experience of imprisonment undid (temporarily) a lifetime of learning; human values were suspended, self-concepts were challenged and the ugliest, most base, pathological side of human nature surfaced. We were horrified because we saw some boys (guards) treat others as if they were despicable animals, taking pleasure in cruelty, while other boys (prisoners) became servile, dehumanized robots who thought only of escape, of their own individual survival, and of their mounting hatred for the guards.

We had to release three prisoners in the first four days because they had such acute situational traumatic reactions as hysterical crying, confusion in thinking, and severe depression. Others begged to be paroled, and all but three were willing to forfeit all the money they had earned if they could be paroled. By then (the fifth day) they had been so programmed to think of themselves as prisoners that when their request for parole was denied, they returned docilely to

formal role structure. Among a group of homeowners drawn together for the purpose of cleaning up neighborhood trash the roles tend to evolve haphazardly. Each member gravitates toward those tasks that he or she is best equipped to handle.

In addition to roles, a sense of common identity links the members of a group. Every Girl Scout is aware of her membership in a particular troop, and the members of a police force exhibit such a strong sense of identity with their peers that they tend to isolate themselves from most other groups. This sense of identity has been referred to as **consciousness of kind,** the feeling of being bound together by common traits, views, or situations.[31]

their cells. Now, had they been thinking as college students acting in an oppressive environment, they would have quit once they no longer wanted the $15 a day we used as our only incentive. However, the reality was not quitting an experiment but "being paroled by the parole board from the Stanford County Jail." By the last days, the earlier solidarity among the prisoners (systematically broken by the guards) dissolved into "each man for himself." Finally, when one of their fellows was put in solitary confinement (a small closet) for refusing to eat, the prisoners were given a choice by one of the guards: give up their blankets and the incorrigible prisoner would be let out, or keep their blankets and he would be kept in all night. They voted to keep their blankets and to abandon their brother.

About a third of the guards became tyrannical in their arbitrary use of power, in enjoying their control over other people. They were corrupted by the power of their roles and became quite inventive in their techniques of breaking the spirit of the prisoners and making them feel they were worthless. Some of the guards merely did their jobs as tough but fair correctional officers, and several were good guards from the prisoners' point of view since they did them small favors and were friendly. However, no good guard ever interfered with a command by any of the bad guards; they never intervened on the side of the prisoners, they never told the others to ease off because it was only an experiment, and they never even came to me as prison superintendent or experimenter in charge to complain. In part, they were good because the others were bad; they needed the others to help establish their own egos in a positive light. In a sense, the good guards perpetuated the prison more than the other guards because their own needs to be liked prevented them from disobeying or violating the implicit guards' code. At the same time, the act of befriending the prisoners created a social reality which made the prisoners less likely to rebel.

By the end of the week the experiment had become a reality, as if it were a Pirandello play directed by Kafka that just keeps going after the audience has left. The consultant for our prison, Carlo Prescott, an ex-convict with 16 years of imprisonment in California's jails, would get so depressed and furious each time he visited our prison, because of its psychological similarity to his experiences, that he would have to leave. A Catholic priest who was a former prison chaplain in Washington, D.C., talked to our prisoners after four days and said they were just like the other first-timers he had seen.

But in the end, I called off the experiment not because of the horror I saw out there in the prison yard, but because of the horror of realizing that *I* could have easily traded places with the most brutal guard or become the weakest prisoner full of hatred at being so powerless that I could not eat, sleep, or go to the toilet without permission of the authorities. *I* could have become Calley at My Lai, George Jackson at San Quentin, or one of the men at Attica.

SOURCE: Philip G. Zimbardo, "The Pathology of Imprisonment." Published by permission of Transaction Publishers, from *Society,* vol. 9, no. 6 pp. 4–8. Copyright © 1972 by Transaction, Inc.

In-groups and Out-groups

Many animal species tend to establish group boundaries. Among wolves, when a pack wishes to designate its territory, the males mark it off with a trail of urine. Human groups tend to be even more explicit about boundaries. They establish such designations as family names, uniforms, badges, membership cards, and passports for this purpose. The sense of collective identity associated with boundary designations and consciousness of kind creates a social boundary between group members and nonmembers, effectively dividing the world into two, and *only* two, categories— in-groups and out-groups.

An **in-group** is any group of individuals characterized by a strong sense of identification, loyalty, and the exclusion of nonmembers. By contrast, an **out-group** is composed of the nonmembers of an in-group and may be viewed with contempt or even hostility by the in-group's constituents. This in-group/out-group distinction is ever present. Consider how the military recruiting slogan, "The few, the proud, the Marines," seeks to emphasize this divisive line between groups. And this feeling is expressed elsewhere by the cliché, "You're either with us, or against us." Or as a very cynical police officer once put it: "I hate citizens!"[32]

When in-group/out-group differentiations are carried to an extreme, there is no middle ground and the consequences can even be dangerous. Bogotá, Colombia, for instance, boasts a section that outsiders dare not enter. If stopped and confronted, strangers run the risk of being asked a fateful question: "Would you rather be stabbed or pinched?" Being pinched may not seem to be all that serious, but it tends to mutilate when done in a twisting fashion about the breast with an oversized pair of pliers. Consider also the situation in Northern Ireland, where for decades there have been battles between Protestants and Catholics. Military personnel and police have the impossible task of maintaining order, but they are the innocent victims of violence because they are not allied with one group or the other.*

Group Norms and Values

All groups develop a system of norms, values, and goals. If the group is temporary and loosely organized, the rules may be few and quite informal. Youths who have gathered on a street corner to throw firecrackers at passing cars have the same goal: to be troublesome and disruptive. Yet they have norms and values in that they generally refrain from using each other or small children as targets of their activity.

Groups that exist for any length of time tend to develop norms, values, and goals that often evolve into a unique style of life—a subculture—the content of which is passed on to new members as they join the group. This is especially true of members of high-risk occupations. Coal miners, for example, have an explicit set of norms, at the cornerstone of which is cooperation.[33] The most fundamental rule among miners demands that they assist one another when asked for help. Nothing may interfere with the provision of assistance, regardless of whether the individual of whom the request is made likes the miner requesting aid or not.

*In contrast to the in-group/out-group dichotomy, a philosopher once offered a different way of separating society into distinctive camps. "There are two groups of people in this world," he offered, "those who separate people into two groups, and those who do not." This, of course, is a paradox of double implication that cannot be resolved.

Groups and Aggregates

It is important to note that not every collection of people meets the criteria for a social group. Some are merely **social aggregates,** people who meet by chance or circumstance—who are gathered together in the same place but share little else. Travelers waiting for an overdue flight may share a common purpose (getting to Kansas City). They may chat about the latest newspaper headline or even have some awareness of a shared identity when they complain about the problems of congested air traffic and the quality of airline food. Yet they do not qualify as a social group. They lack the elements of social structure: patterned interaction, shared values and norms, and common identity. Moreover, they do not consider their temporary association to have any meaning.

The simplest and most direct test that separates a social group from an aggregate is *permanence.* Social groups have a shared history and future. If the wait at the airport becomes exceedingly long, several passengers may start a game of poker; then they will have formed a social group. They have a purpose; they share certain role expectations; they attach a level of importance to what they are doing; and they share a sense of identity when the airport police arrest them for gambling on county property.

A social group also differs from a **statistical category**—people classified together because they share certain characteristics. College students, Democrats, marijuana smokers, and the elderly are statistical categories. The members of a statistical category are generally unaware of one another and no patterned interaction occurs among them. They may however, often attempt to form social groups. The American Rifle Association tries to enlist all gun *owners,* and the American Association of Retired Persons (AARP) seeks to mobilize the *elderly,* not just retirees. The ARA and AARP are social groups. They share norms, goals, a purpose, and an identity; they have patterned interaction on an occasional basis; and their group has a past and a future.

Primary and Secondary Groups

The various characteristics of social groups do not exist in a vacuum; each is related to all others. Systematic face-to-face interaction leads to the formation of shared values and norms. These values and norms, in turn, engender a strong sense of identity. Less frequent interaction has a reduced likelihood of generating strong group norms and the same levels of identity and solidarity. To distinguish among groups on the basis of the strength of the factors linking them, sociologists classify social groups as either primary or secondary.

Primary Groups

The speaker stands and introduces himself. "My name is Fred," he begins, "and I'm an alcoholic."

"Hi, Fred," responds the small audience. Another Alcoholics Anonymous meeting has begun.

Alcoholics Anonymous is a national organization, but the key units are some 50,000 small groups. Like Fred's, each seldom numbers more than 25 people. Collectively, however, they have been instrumental in helping hundreds of thousands of people through the difficulties of problem drinking. There is a formal program, but the success of the program depends on the encouragement and social support members receive from each other.[34] Those who conquer their problems with drinking do so largely by means of the emotional support provided by *primary groups* like Fred's. A **primary group** is one characterized by intimate, face-to-face association and cooperation. Families are primary groups; pickpocket mobs and juvenile gangs are primary groups; local AA units are primary groups.

The process of welcoming a new member to an AA unit illustrates many of the key attributes of primary groups. The speaker reaffirms the collective identity of the membership—alcoholics. The inductee is Fred. His last name, job, income, family status, and what he does outside the context of AA are not important. He is accepted as an alcoholic trying to stop drinking—that is all that really matters. The goal is to create a feeling of identity with an in-group, and the unit reaffirms his membership by responding, "Hi, Fred."

AA meetings are open and friendly. At some, speakers relate their difficulties and experiences, allowing each member of the audience to recognize that they all face common problems. Other meetings are devoted to discussion sessions where each person can work through a specific dilemma. The groups are nonjudgmental and apply no formal pressures. People are free to do what they wish, even to start drinking again. But group members are a reliable source of understanding, support, and encouragement. In a way, members carry AA with them wherever they go. They are encouraged to memorize the *Twelve Steps to Sobriety* and mentally refer to them whenever they are tempted to drink. Some carry membership cards with mottoes that they can recite during times of stress. Most importantly, between meetings there are always others willing to talk in person or on the phone. Moreover, the group is always there. With a simple handshake and a "Welcome back," members are ready to accept the return of an individual who has slipped back into drinking.

Alcoholics Anonymous and other primary groups have been the subject of extensive research. They are recognized to have a powerful and profound impact on human behavior. As enunciated by sociologist Charles Horton Cooley, who originated the primary group concept:

> [Groups] are primary in several senses, but chiefly in that they are fundamental in forming the social nature and ideas of the individual. The result of intimate association, psychologically, is a certain fusion of individualities in a common whole, so that one's very self for many purposes at least is the common life and purpose of the group. Perhaps the simplest way of describing this wholeness is by saying that it is a "we."[35]

SOCIAL INDICATOR

The Twelve Steps to Sobriety

1. We admitted we were powerless over alcohol—that our lives had become unmanageable.
2. Came to believe that a Power greater than ourselves could restore us to sanity.
3. Made a decision to turn our will and our lives over to the care of God, *as we understood Him.*
4. Made a searching and fearless moral inventory of ourselves.
5. Admitted to God, to ourselves, and to another human being the exact nature of our wrongs.
6. Were entirely ready to have God remove all these defects of character.
7. Humbly asked Him to remove our shortcomings.
8. Made a list of all persons we had harmed, and became willing to make amends to them all.
9. Made direct amends to such people wherever possible, except when to do so would injure them or others.
10. Continued to take personal inventory and when we were wrong promptly admitted it.
11. Sought through prayer and meditation to improve our conscious contact with God, *as we understood Him,* praying only for knowledge of His will for us and the power to carry that out.
12. Having had a spiritual awakening as the result of these steps, we tried to carry this message to alcoholics and to practice these principles in all our affairs.

"The Twelve Steps" reprinted with permission of Alcoholics Anonymous World Services, Inc.

SOCIAL INDICATOR

Americans Who Favor a Ban on the Sale of All Alcoholic Beverages in the U.S.

Men	13%
Women	21

Source: *The Gallup Report,* 1987.

The power of primary groups is nowhere more dramatically illustrated than by research conducted among soldiers in combat.[36] During World War II, American generals continually were impressed by the efficiency of the German Army. As defeat piled upon defeat for the German forces, and while supplies ran out and the eventual loss of the war loomed clear, the soldiers continued to fight. Political ideology and patriotism might explain why men volunteer to fight or willingly submit to the draft, but what is it that compels some people to conquer their fears, risk their lives, and fight—rather than desert—in the face of certain defeat and perhaps death?

The research found that the war welded small squads of men into powerful primary groups. Squad members started together during basic training, fought side by side and survived many battles together, and provided one another with comfort and support on a daily basis. Their generals and country became a distant presence; for the foot soldiers their comrades on the front lines were real and immediate. They risked everything right to the end so as not to fail their friends.

Secondary Groups

Secondary groups are those composed of individuals who cooperate with one another for distinct, practical reasons and generally maintain few strong emotional ties. Professional associations are secondary groups; labor unions are secondary groups; a sociology class is a secondary group. In contrast with primary groups, secondary groups tend to be larger and less personal, with a weak sense of identity and commitment among their members. (See Exhibit 4.6 for an extended comparison of primary and secondary groups.)

Secondary groups bring together people who have a common interest and some common goal. Members of the American Bar Association, for example, are all lawyers. They join the ABA to share information, learn of the latest developments in their field, participate in establishing rules for the proper conduct of attorneys, and lobby for favorable treatment in the legislature. Participation is thus often called instrumental or task-oriented.

The activities of secondary groups are quite formal and organized, and are usually governed by explicit rules and sanctions. Decision making, for example, is determined by elaborate voting procedures. Meetings are conducted in adherence with *Robert's Rules of Order;* deviant members risk fines, letters of reprimand, or removal from office. And because they are formalized and structured, secondary groups often survive over long periods of time. The American Bar Association was founded in 1878, and although members continually enter and exit, the group has survived in essentially the same form for more than a century. In contrast with all primary groups, however, since members tend to participate in a very explicit way and for very specific purposes, secondary groups are generally unable to exert a strong influence on member attitudes and behavior outside the group.

Reference Groups

People need not actually be members of a particular social group for that group's standards to play a role in

Exhibit 4.6 **Sociological Focus**

Primary and Secondary Groups

	Examples	Size	Social Relations	Involvement	Group Solidarity	Social Control
Primary Groups	Families Work Teams Play Groups	Small	Continuous Personalized/Intimate	Extensive	Strong	Informal
Secondary Groups	Professional Associations Political Parties Trade Unions	Large	Occasional Contractual/Segmented	Limited	Weak	Formal Sanctions

shaping their values and activity. Groups known as reference groups can exert considerable influence. **Reference groups** are groups that exhibit attitudes and standards of behavior and provide comparison points against which people measure themselves and others. Aspiring professionals typically use their teachers as a reference group, subtly adopting their perspectives and standards.

As illustrated in Exhibit 4.7, a nineteenth-century gang of criminals called the Old Border Gang was clearly a strong reference group that was viewed as a positive force by aspiring thieves. Positive reference groups provide standards that people attempt to emulate. Little League ball players often use professional athletes as a reference group, attempting to imitate their walk, language, and batting styles. Among workers, satisfaction with pay is determined not only by how much a person actually earns but also by the pay level of their reference group—other workers with similar jobs.[37]

Astronauts are a reference group for a whole generation of young Americans.

By contrast, negative reference groups exhibit behavior that people reject and do not wish to imitate. For most Americans, the "yuppies" (young urban professionals) of the 1980s were an example of a negative reference group. A poll conducted by the Harris Organization during 1986 found that a clear majority of Americans consider many aspects of the yuppie life-style unattractive.[38] The items singled out as the least engaging were their concern with their own rather than other people's needs; a preoccupation with spending money on "trendy" foods (sushi, mousse, *Corona Extra* beer,* tofu, and Dove Bars), clothing (the latest designer fashions), and automobiles (Saab's, BMW's, and other expensive imports); their feeling of superiority; and their intense pursuit of money.

Whether viewed positively or negatively, yuppies illustrate important features of reference group behavior. But they are not a *social group*. Rather, they are a *statistical category* based on age (18 to 39), education (at least some college), spending habits, and tastes, and they lack the common identity and patterned interaction that would certify them as a social group.†

*Beer industry experts seem to be at a loss to explain the popularity of *Corona Extra*. In late 1986, however, the vice-president of Anheuser-Busch suggested that the yuppies liked it because "it looks like an imported beer, and it tastes like a domestic." See *Business Week*, September 1, 1986, p. 42.

†An important point to note here is that the negative attitudes about yuppies are based on *perceptions* of their life-style that may bear little resemblance to actual behavior. Even if these perceptions indeed describe the behavior of some yuppies, they are likely overgeneralizations that leave no room for individual differences.

SOCIAL INDICATOR

Grandparents: Group, Aggregate, or Category?

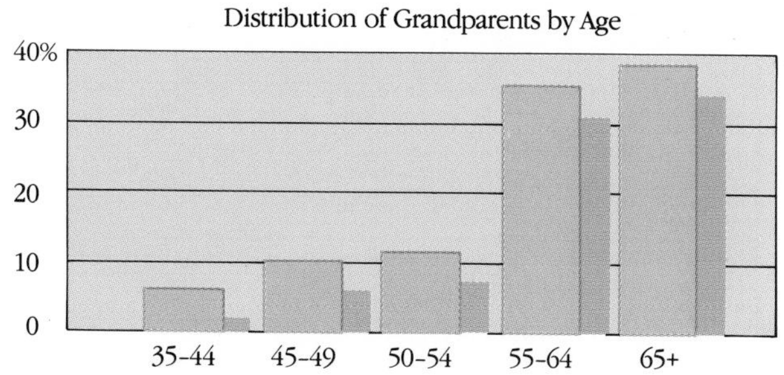

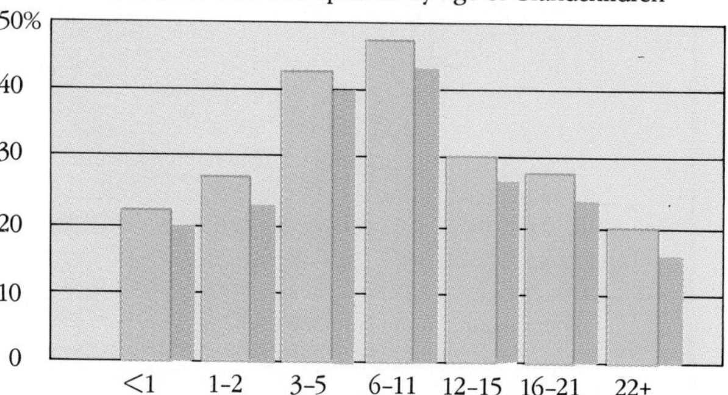

*Totals add up to more than 100 percent due to multiple mentions.

Exhibit 4.7

Sidelights on American Culture

The Old Border Gang

Unlike the street gangs of the 1980s, which are composed almost exclusively of inner-city youths who are constantly at war with one another for control of low-level drug sales and "turf," gangs of a century ago were of a different sort. Most were organized groups of thieves, many of a highly professional nature. Conspicuous among these groups was New York City's Old Border Gang, a cadre of river pirates who prowled the piers and wharves of the East and Hudson rivers. This group was a nemesis of the city's Chief of Police, George Matsell, who in 1850 commented that "they pursue their nefarious operations with the most systematic perseverence, and manifest a shrewdness and adroitness which can only be attained by long practice."

From this context comes a vivid illustration of the reference group concept, drawn from the autobiography of a turn-of-the-century professional thief who recalled his boyhood days on New York's Lower East Side during the late 1870s, with the following comments:

Members of a New York gang congregate on the docks in the 1880s.

> At the end of the block on which we lived was a corner saloon, the headquarters of a band of professional thieves. They were known as the *Old Border Gang,* and among them were several very well-known and successful crooks. They used to pass our way regularly, and boys older than I used to point the famous "guns" out to me. When I saw one of these great men pass, my young imagination was fired with the ambition to be as he was. With what eagerness we used to talk about "Juggy," and the daring robbery he committed in Brooklyn! How we went over again and again in conversation the trick by which Johnny the "grafter" had fooled the detective in the matter of the bonds!
>
> We would tell stories like these by the hour, and then go round to the corner, to try to get a look at some of the celebrities in the saloon. A splendid sight one of these grafters was, as he stood before the bar or smoked his cigar on the corner! Well dressed, with clean linen collar and shirt, a diamond in his tie, an air of ease and leisure all about him, what a contrast he formed to the respectable hodcarrier* or truckman or mechanic, with soiled clothes and no collar! And what a contrast was his dangerous life to that of the virtuous laborer!
>
> The result was that I grew to think the career of the grafter was the only one worth trying for.

SOURCES: Herbert Asbury, *The Gangs of New York* (New York: Alfred A. Knopf, 1927); Hutchins Hapgood, *The Autobiography of a Thief* (New York: Fox, Duffield, 1903), pp. 26–28; Alfred Henry Lewis, *The Apaches of New York* (Chicago: Donohue, 1912).

*A *hod* was a tray or trough with a pole handle that was borne on the shoulder for carrying mortar, cement, or brick.

Groups and Individual Behavior

Groups are an important aspect of social life for many reasons. Perhaps the most obvious is that they can mobilize the abilities of many people, allowing them to undertake tasks that could not be accomplished by a single individual. The cooperative endeavor of hunting large animals during the Neolithic era provided the impetus for the formation of preindustrial societies. Similarly, it is impossible to film a movie, publish a book, build a bridge, fight a war, explore outer space, or educate large numbers of students without the active participation of social groups.

Groups can also exert powerful influences on behavior, and a major focus in the study of groups centers on the differences in individual behavior that may occur as the result of group membership. The point is simply this: people will behave differently in the presence of others than when they are acting alone. Groups influence the kinds of things people do, the amount of individual effort they expend, and the ways in which group members react to others.

The Asch Experiment

Special interest groups have been known to change the opinions of political leaders; tenant groups have forced landlords to upgrade housing conditions; student groups even have managed now and then to effect modifications in their professors' grading policies. Perhaps the most frequently cited scientific effort to demonstrate the potency of group pressure on individual behavior is the well-known *Asch experiment.*[39] The Asch experiment was first conducted by psychologist Solomon E. Asch during the early 1950s. Small groups of people were told that they were participating in a visual perception experiment involving the relative length of lines. The assignment was simple: to tell the researcher which line on Card One matched that on Card Two. As is apparent in the sample cards reproduced in Exhibit 4.8, anyone with normal vision can easily make the correct pairing. But there was a hitch. Asch had secretly instructed all but one of his experimental subjects to choose the incorrect answer. The unsuspecting victim was confronted with a dilemma: what his senses told him was in conflict with the standards of the group. One out of every three times the experiment was repeated, the victim's answer conformed to that of the group.

The Asch experiment was significant because it was conducted with a contrived and temporary group. The research subjects were not members of a strong social group with history, traditions, or any sense of identity or involvement. Yet if one-third nevertheless conformed to group standards, one can only imagine the pressures that can be exerted *within* groups where members have a sense of identity and wish to retain group membership.

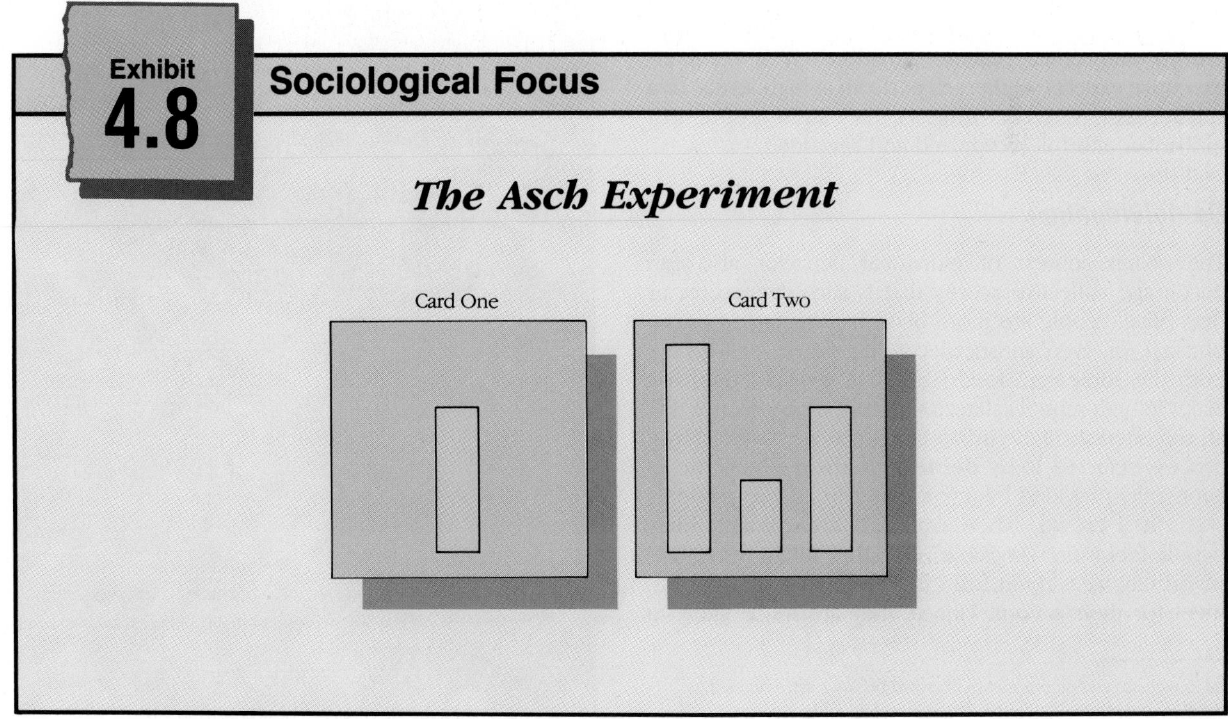

Social Loafing

The Hawthorne effect, discussed in Chapter 2, is a reminder that people may often work harder in a group context than when alone. The opposite phenomenon is known as **social loafing**—the reduced productivity of individuals as the result of participation in group activity.

Experimental studies have demonstrated on numerous occasions that individuals typically expend more effort on a task when working alone than when laboring as a member of a group.[40] One study established this point by measuring the force people exerted on a rope in a tug-of-war. The experiment found that when pulling alone, individuals averaged 63 kilograms of pressure. In groups of three, the individual effort decreased to 53 kilograms, and in groups of eight, the individual effort dropped to 31 kilograms. It appears that as groups grow larger, people become convinced that their effort has less impact on the outcome. Each participant may also feel that others are not doing their fair share, which leads to reduced personal effort. And too, some individuals believe that within the anonymity of a large group, reduced effort might not be noticed. This proclivity is readily evident in large lecture classes in many colleges and universities; fewer students come to class and keep up with their assignments.

Coping with social loafing turns out to be a relatively simple matter. When people know that their individual effort cannot be submerged into that of the group, they work at near maximum capacity. This reaction has direct implications for behavior in work groups and other real-life situations. If a company executive expects workers to perform at high levels, or a teacher assigns group projects, they must assure that individual effort is recognized and rewarded.

Deindividuation

The group context of individual behavior also can encourage collective activity that is silly, dangerous, or disruptive. People are more likely to engage in bizarre, unusual, or even antisocial conduct when in a group. Both the adolescent food fights that seem to regularly erupt in high-school cafeterias and the mob violence that all too often mars the urban landscape are fostered by a process referred to as **deindividuation,** the sense of anonymity provided by involvement in a large group.*

In a crowd, when emotions are running high, people feel more "invisible" than they might otherwise. Invisibility frees them from the threat of social punishment for their actions. Hence, they are more likely to behave in rude or even harmful ways. Yet interestingly, if the sense of anonymity can be controlled, the dangers may be reduced. Late night reruns of classic Western films often portray this point. Fearless marshals disarm angry lynch mobs by the simple expedient of calling out the names of the individual mob members and telling them to go home to their families. Contemporary law-enforcement agencies use a more technologically sophisticated version of this technique when they produce cameras and videotape equipment as a means of identifying rioters. Laboratory experiments have demonstrated that individuals exposed to their own images become more self-conscious, suggesting that disruptive crowds might indeed be dispersed by the presence of television monitors.[41]

Helping Behavior and the Bystander Effect

Almost three decades ago Americans were shocked by one of the unfortunate consequences of group dynamics. On March 14, 1964, at 3:20 A.M., 28-year-old Kitty Genovese returned home from work and parked her car only

The numbers re-create the path Kitty Genovese followed as she parked her car (1) and was attacked and killed (2–4) in her own neighborhood.

*Mob violence and other varieties of crowd behavior are examined in detail in Chapter 16, "Collective Behavior and Social Movements."

150 feet from her apartment on Austin Street in Queens County, New York, a mostly residential borough of New York City. Genovese had slowly walked only a few feet when a man came out of the shadows, stabbed her, and began to sexually assault her. She began to scream and the lights blinked on in the apartment houses along Austin Street. For the next 25 minutes, the attacker stalked, assaulted, and stabbed Genovese until she eventually died just before 3:50 A.M. Although 37 witnesses heard the woman's cries for help and watched the assault, the first call to the police did not occur until some minutes after her death, almost half an hour after the attack began. Days later, while the nation still reeled in shock over the witnesses' behavior during the crime, the *New York Times* published the following comment:

> Seldom has the *Times* published a more horrifying story than its account of how thirty-seven respectable, law-abiding middle-class Queens citizens watched a killer stalk his young woman victim in a parking lot over a half-hour period, without one of them making a call to the police department that would have saved her life. They would not have been exposed to any danger themselves; a simple telephone call in the privacy of their own homes was all that was needed. How incredible it is that such motives as "I didn't want to get involved" deterred them from this act of simple humanity. Does residence in a great city destroy all sense of personal responsibility for one's neighbors? Who can explain such shocking indifference on the part of a cross section of our fellow New Yorkers?[42]

As noted previously in Chapter 3, the American legal system rarely impels people to render assistance to others in distress. But this is not the reason why Kitty Genovese's cries for help went unanswered. Research has repeatedly demonstrated that an individual is more likely to render aid when he or she is alone than when a number of other people are present. This **helping behavior**—any positive act aimed at aiding another or preventing a criminal act—typically occurs outside the context of a social group. By contrast, Kitty Genovese was the victim of not only her assailant, 29-year-old Winston Moseley,* but also of what has become known as the **bystander effect,** the unwillingness of bystanders to "get involved" in the problems of others.

The killing of Kitty Genovese prompted research into the dynamics of helping behavior and the bystander effect, in an attempt to answer why an individual is more apt to render aid when alone than when in a group of bystanders. In one study conducted during the 1970s, a cohort of experimental subjects was led to believe they were listening to a group discussion involving one, two, or five other people via an intercom system.[43] Each subject was isolated in a separate cubicle; the other voices each individual heard were merely tape recordings. Several minutes into their "discussion," one voice began to mimic the sounds of an epileptic seizure. Eight-five percent of the subjects who thought they were the only person present other than the victim reported the emergency. Only 31% of those who believed there were others present took action to report that someone needed help. A similar pattern has emerged in experimental studies where the subjects and victims were physically present. The usual interpretation is that the

SOCIAL INDICATOR

Bystander Intervention

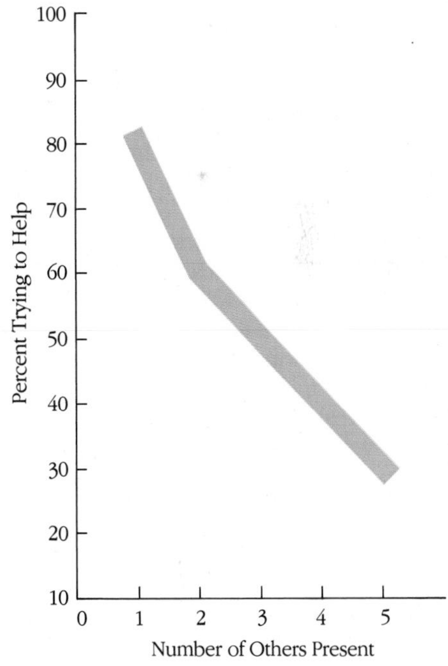

Source: Adapted from data in J. Darley and B. Latané, "Bystander Intervention in Emergencies," *Journal of Personality and Social Psychology*, 8 (1968), pp. 377–83.

*Genovese's slayer, Winston Moseley, was arrested six days after the crime. Although convicted of murder in the first degree and sentenced to death, his execution, scheduled for July 8, 1964, was delayed when the constitutionality of New York's death penalty statute was called into question. Moseley's sentence was ultimately commuted to life imprisonment, and he is now an inmate in New York's maximum-security Greenhaven Correctional Facility.

group context creates an idea of shared responsibility. Stated differently, when alone, individuals act positively, but in groups their reactions are characterized by a **diffusion of responsibility,** the tendency for no one to feel responsible for acting when others are present.

Studies also have demonstrated that bystanders are unwilling to render aid to those in distress because they fear looking stupid or incompetent in front of strangers. The results of one investigation indicated that individuals who were alone took an average of 78 seconds to provide help when confronted with an emergency (a person choking). When there were four bystanders present, the response time crept up to 150 seconds.[44] Experimental subjects who previously had been given first-aid training and were then placed in an emergency situation responded more quickly, whether or not there were bystanders present. Researchers concluded that feeling competent to handle an emergency overcomes the bystander effect.

ROLES, GROUPS, AND APPLIED SOCIOLOGY

People think about themselves not only as individuals, but also in terms of where they fit in the intricate arrangement of roles and groups that make up the social organization of society. As mentioned earlier, they act out their lives as players on a social stage, where they have roles to play as members of groups. In many cases people have no choices as to role definitions and group membership. At birth, by the process of *ascription,* people are male or female, black or white, American or Soviet. In other instances roles and group membership are a matter of choice or *achievement*—Sociology 201 student, parent, cabinet member, baseball player. Yet whether through ascription or achievement, the roles people play and the groups to which they belong consistently reveal that expectations are defined in relationships with others. We cannot escape this phenomenon, and knowledge of the dynamics of status, social relations, role behavior, and group structure can have some very practical applications.

Some four decades ago, sociologist William Whyte provided an interesting demonstration of how problem solving might be achieved through a restructuring of social relations. In a study of restaurants, he observed a level of continual conflict between waitresses and cooks that led repeatedly to emotional tension and disruption in the work process.[45] He decided that the difficulty was not a result of personality differences among the workers involved, but an outgrowth of the social structure within the restaurant. Apparently, customers were pressuring waitresses to bring meals more rapidly, and as a result, waitresses were pressuring cooks to speed up the orders. What was occurring was a situation in which low-status people were making demands of high-status people. In the social hierarchy of restaurants, cooks and chefs have the highest status, whereas that of servers is relatively low. The status problem was aggravated by the fact that the cooks were men and the servers were women, and even in today's increasingly egalitarian society, many men continue to resent taking orders from women. As an outgrowth of Whyte's findings, concerned restauranteurs solved the conflict by structuring buffers between the roles of cook and waitress. Some erected high counters to physically separate the opposing groups, while others hired supervisors to accept orders from waitresses and relay them to cooks.

Another very pragmatic application of sociological principles involves the identification of status group and statistical aggregate characteristics and preferences by business and industry. Yuppie may be a negative label, but the obvious collective purchasing power of this status group has not escaped the attention of merchandisers of all types. The media is saturated with advertisements for special lines of clothing, cosmetics, automobiles, and beer—all aimed at this particular group. Market researchers seek to understand yuppie attitudes, values, and needs in order to tap into this lucrative market. Similarly, "singles," dual-earner families, and women have been identified by many industries as important new consumer groups. However, in many cases it is not necessarily an easy task for businesses to shift away from an already entrenched customer base in the hope of replacing it with a more affluent one (see Exhibit 4.9).

Knowledge gleaned by sociologists over the decades about the impact of status differences on group solidarity has been put repeatedly to practical use. One of the more lasting contributions in this regard came about as the result of a series of studies by a team of sociologists headed by Samuel S. Stouffer. Stouffer and his colleagues researched the attitudes of enlisted men during World War II.[46] Historically, differential treatment always has been practiced in the military with regard to officers and foot soldiers. Stouffer's research indicated that although American soldiers readily accepted the legitimacy of military authority, they also resented the unequal privileges of officers and enlisted men and the insistence upon strict observance of the rituals of subordination and deference. This resentment resulted in a strong loyalty among *equals* when they were organized into fighting groups. The greater the deference and status differences between officers and enlisted men, the greater the loyalty and team work among soldiers. Stouffer's findings encouraged the armed forces to implement provisions to

Exhibit 4.9

Applied Sociology

The Sociology of the Convenience Store

Convenience stores, or "c-stores," as they are called in the merchandising industry, are relatively small retail outlets that provide snacks and staple groceries conveniently and quickly. "Conveniently and quickly" by industry definition means that these stores are open long hours and are situated along busy streets and intersections. C-store customers want stores without long lines and crowded parking lots that are not located in out-of-the-way places.

The c-store as it is known today has a history of some sixty years, dating back to "Uncle Johnny's Ice Dock" in Oak Cliff, Texas. Uncle Johnny owned the Southland Ice Company, and during the 1930s he began supplementing his ice business by selling bread, milk, and eggs. Uncle Johnny did fairly well. His Southland Ice Company later became Southland Corporation, the parent company of the well-known chain of 7-Eleven stores. Yet despite Southland's success, the c-store industry did not catch on until the 1950s, when automobile mass marketing helped stimulate America's move to the suburbs. Suburbanization, in particular, brought about dramatic expansion in the convenience-store industry. From Uncle Johnny's Ice Dock in the 1930s to some 3,500 c-stores nationally by the early 1960s—clearly the convenience store was catching on. By 1970 the figure was up to almost 12,000 outlets and by the mid-eighties some 58,000 stores were located throughout the country.

In 1985, the convenience-store business accumulated a staggering $55 billion in sales. According to a recent Gallup Poll, the c-store had seemingly locked onto a customer base dominated by blue-collar males ages 18–34 (see accompanying table). Yet the industry is attempting to alter this customer base for a number of very sound sociological reasons that include a below-average growth rate for the blue-collar population, rising numbers of middle-income households with little time to shop, and a trend toward smaller households with different shopping needs.

With these research results in mind, the convenience-store industry has determined that the key to building their clientele is to attract more women into their stores. Women as a group still do most of the food shopping—whether they are single, housewives, or members of dual-earner families. Yet as already indicated in the Gallup data table, well under half of all convenience-store customers are women. Industry surveys suggest that the major problem is "image." Convenience stores are thought of as having a crime problem, being dirty and overpriced, and serving as teenage hangouts. Further research has indicated that the keys to attracting new customers, especially women, are improved lighting, more attractive color schemes, less crowded layouts, a better product mix, and the expansion of their fast-food product lines. To date, however, convenience stores have yet to capture the new customer group that they seek in the hope of further expanding their industry.

Customers of Convenience

	C-store customers	U.S. population
Sex		
Male	57%	48%
Female	43	52
Age		
18 to 24	21	15
25 to 34	31	24
35 to 49	25	25
50+	23	35
Education		
Less Than High School	19	18
High-School Graduate	62	60
College	19	22
Annual Household Income		
<$10,000	14	13
$10,000 to $14,999	11	10
$15,000 to $19,999	12	10
$20,000+	48	48
Unknown	15	19
Race		
White	83	87
Nonwhite	17	13

Source: The Gallup Poll, December 1985. Reprinted by permission.

SOURCE: "The Sociology of the Convenience Store" adapted from "The Demographics of Convenience" by Jeremy Schlosberg. Copyright © *American Demographics*, October 1986. Reprinted with permission.

increase status differences within the military hierarchy and spurred applications of the principle within other organizations.

The practical contributions of reference group theory form the foundation of many contemporary drug treatment and drug-abuse prevention programs. The principle here is that by changing a person's reference group, the behavior of the individual might be successfully altered. In therapeutic communities for heroin and cocaine users, in education groups for high-school marijuana and alcohol users, and in therapy groups behind the walls of maximum-security prisons, the principle is applied in essentially the same way. Criminologists Rita Volkman and Donald R. Cressey outlined the principle some years ago as follows:

> The most effective mechanism for exerting group pressure on members will be found in groups so organized that criminals are induced to join noncriminals for the purpose of changing other criminals. A group in which criminal *A* joins with some noncriminals to change criminal *B* is probably most effective in changing criminal *A*, not *B*; in order to change criminal *B*, criminal *A* must necessarily share the values of the noncriminal members.[47]

Thus, some of the movement toward more conventional attitudes and behaviors among drug users and problem drinkers in therapeutic settings suggests that these support groups have become reference groups. The potential impact of the attitudes and behavior of reference groups and other "heroes" is the reason why professional athletes are used in antidrug messages and speeches, why rock and media stars have been pressured to deglamorize drinking and drug taking, and why actor Don Johnson of television's "Miami Vice" took it upon himself to quit smoking during the summer of 1985.

SUMMARY

Complex social tasks—whether filming a movie, operating a school, or fighting a war—require the active participation of many individuals, each contributing a part to the whole. The division of activities among different social positions within groups and societies represents the social organization of the group or society. Sociologists use the term "social status" to refer to the positions and the term "social role" to define the rights and obligations of people who occupy these positions.

Expectations are part of the social heritage of a society and are transmitted during the socialization process. Minor deviations from expectations are discouraged by subtle social pressures while more serious deviance may result in outright physical punishment.

Although social roles generally are stable, individuals always have room to negotiate their roles. A major consideration in the ability to negotiate is the relative influence or power that individuals have at their disposal. Social statuses and roles also change over time. Technological change, shifting social values, and broader demographic shifts can create new statuses, render others obsolete, and alter the expectations of existing roles.

Much of our time is spent in groups of one kind or another, ranging from the intimate dynamics of the family to the more impersonal relations in large organizations. Social groups exert a powerful influence on human behavior, shaping the way people perceive the world and respond to it. As a result, the behavior individuals exhibit when alone is frequently modified by interaction in a group situation.

KEY TERMS/CONCEPTS

achieved status
antagonistic negotiations
ascribed status
bystander effect
consciousness of kind
cooperative negotiations
deindividuation
diffusion of responsibility
exchange negotiations
group
helping behavior
in-group
master status
out-group
primary group
reference group
role conflict
role making
role partners
role playing
role set
role strain
sanctions
secondary group
social aggregate
socialization
social loafing
social organization
social role
social status
statistical category
status set
status symbols

DISCUSSION QUESTIONS

1. Develop a list of the ascribed and achieved statuses that you currently occupy. How do these statuses work to your advantage or disadvantage?
2. What do you think is the rationale for designating a college fraternity or sorority as a primary group? In what ways do these groups function as primary groups?
3. What are the mechanisms of social control that are used in fraternities and sororities? What forms of punishment are used? From your experience and observations, are they effective? If you have had little or no contact with these types of student groups, apply the questions to whatever types of student organizations are familiar to you.
4. Why is it that people behave differently when alone than when in groups? Provide some examples from your own experience or observations.

SUGGESTED READINGS

Helen Gouldner and Mary Symons Strong, *Speaking of Friendship: Middle-Class Women and Their Friends* (New York: Greenwood, 1987). Based on extensive interviews, this unique sociological study reveals a kaleidoscope of friendship experiences and the role that friends play in women's lives.

Ralph Linton, *The Study of Man* (New York: Appleton-Century-Crofts, 1936). A classic that puts forth definitive information on the basic concepts concerning status, role, and social groups.

Robert K. Merton, *Social Theory and Social Structure* (New York: Free Press, 1957). A collection of this renowned American sociologist's best and most insightful examinations of the nature of social organization.

Theodore M. Mills, *The Sociology of Small Groups* (Englewood Cliffs, NJ: Prentice-Hall, 1984). A useful book that provides a survey of current research on small groups and a unique perspective on group dynamics.

Robert Nisbet, *The Social Bond* (New York: Alfred A. Knopf, 1970). In this functionalist analysis of society, the author describes the "social bond" that links together a society's different statuses, roles, and groups.

Louis A. Zucher, *Social Roles, Conformity, Conflict and Creativity* (Beverly Hills: Sage, 1983). An easy-to-read exploration of the ways that people balance the expectations of their roles with their quests for freedom.

NOTES

1. William Shakespeare, *As You Like It*, Act II, Scene VII.
2. See Ralph Linton, *The Study of Man* (New York: Appleton-Century-Crofts, 1936), pp. 113–21.
3. Tamotsu Shibutani, *Social Processes* (Berkeley: University of California Press, 1986), p. 157.
4. See Joel D. Block and Diane Greenberg, *Women and Friendship* (New York: Franklin Watts, 1985); Helen Gouldner and Mary Symons Strong, *Speaking of Friendship: Middle-Class Women and Their Friends* (New York: Greenwood, 1987); Lillian Rubin, *Just Friends: The Role of Friendship in Our Lives* (New York: Harper & Row, 1985).
5. Robert Mauro, "The Constable's New Clothes: Effects of Uniforms on Perceptions and Problems of Police Officers," *Journal of Applied Psychology,* 14 (January-February 1984), pp. 42–56.
6. *New York Times,* July 13, 1980, p. 17.
7. *New York Times,* March 30, 1986, p. 6E.
8. Personal communication, July 10, 1987.
9. Robert K. Merton, "The Role-Set: Problems in Sociological Theory," *British Journal of Sociology,* 8 (1957), pp. 635–59.
10. Arnold Arluke, "Roundsmanship: Inherent Control on a Medical Teaching Ward," *Social Science and Medicine,* 14A (1980), pp. 297–302.
11. Erving Goffman, *Stigma: Notes on the Management of Spoiled Identity* (Englewood Cliffs, NJ: Prentice-Hall, 1963), p. 3.
12. *USA Today,* April 17, 1986, p. 1B.
13. Eleanor Macklin, "Unmarried Heterosexual Cohabitation on the University Campus," in Jacqueline P. Wiseman (ed.), *The Social Psychology of Sex* (New York: Harper & Row, 1976), pp. 111–36.
14. Kazuo Yamaguchi and Denise B. Kandel, "On the Resolution of Role Incompatibility: A Life Event History Analysis of Family Roles and Marijuana Use," *American Journal of Sociology,* 90 (May 1985), pp. 1284–1324.
15. William A. Corsaro, "Young Children's Conception of Status and Role," *Sociology of Education,* 52 (January 1980), pp. 46–59.
16. Stanley Milgram, "Behavioral Study of Obedience," *Journal of Abnormal and Social Psychology,* 67 (1963), pp. 371–78.
17. Stanley Milgram, *Obedience to Authority* (New York: Harper & Row, 1974).
18. David F. Luckenbill, "Generating Compliance: The Case of Robbery," *Urban Life,* 10 (April 1981), pp. 25–46.
19. Peter M. Hall and Dee Ann Spencer-Hall, "The Social Conditions of Negotiated Order," *Urban Life,* 11 (October 1982), pp. 328–49.
20. Holt v. Sarver, 309 F. Supp. 362 (E. D. Ark. 1970).
21. James A. Inciardi, *Criminal Justice* (Orlando: Academic Press, 1983), p. 673.
22. See Suzanne K. Steinmetz and Murray A. Strauss (eds.), *Violence in the Family* (New York: Harper & Row, 1974); Murray A. Strauss, Richard J. Gelles, and Suzanne K. Steinmetz, *Behind Closed Doors: Violence in the American Family* (New York: Anchor, 1980).
23. Patsy A. Klaus and Michael R. Rand, *Family Violence* (Washington, DC: U.S. Department of Justice, 1984).

24. *USA Today,* August 13, 1986, p. 3C.
25. *New York Times,* February 15, 1985, p. 6.
26. Emile Durkheim, *Montesquieu and Rosseau* (Ann Arbor: University of Michigan Press, 1960), p. 83.
27. Anselm L. Strauss, "The Hospital and Its Negotiated Order," in Eliot Freidson (ed.), *The Hospital in Modern Society* (New York: Free Press, 1963), pp. 147–69.
28. Personal communication, August 13, 1986.
29. The use of the term "exchange" here is a selected aspect of a more formal theoretical perspective known in the literature as *exchange theory.* See Peter M. Blau, *Exchange and Power in Social Life* (New York: Wiley, 1964); George C. Homans, *Social Behavior: Its Elementary Forms* (New York: Harcourt and Brace, 1961).
30. Ruiz v. Estelle, F. 2d. 115 (5th Cir. 1982).
31. Franklin H. Giddings, *Inductive Sociology* (New York: Macmillan, 1901), p. 68.
32. Elaine Cumming, Ian Cumming, and Laura Edell, "Policeman as Philosopher, Guide and Friend," *Social Problems,* 12 (Winter 1965), p. 285.
33. John B. Fitzpatrick, "Adapting to Danger: A Participant Observation Study of an Underground Mine," *Work and Occupations,* 7 (May 1980), pp. 131–58.
34. Arthur L. Greil and David R. Ruby, "Social Cocoons: Encapsulation and Identity Transformation Organizations," *Sociological Inquiry,* 54 (Summer 1984), pp. 260–78; John Lofland and Lynn Lofland, *Deviance and Identity* (Englewood Cliffs, NJ: Prentice-Hall, 1969), pp. 245–47; Milton A. Maxwell, *The AA Experience* (New York: McGraw-Hill, 1984).
35. Charles Horton Cooley, *Social Organization* (New York: Schocken, 1962), p. 23.
36. Edward A. Shils and Morris Janowitz, "Cohesion and Disintegration in the *Wehrmacht* in World War II," *Public Opinion Quarterly,* 12 (Summer 1948), pp. 280–315 Samuel A. Stouffer, *The American Soldier* (Princeton, NJ: Princeton University Press, 1949).
37. Nan Weiner, "Determinants and Behavioral Consequences of Pay Satisfaction: A Comparison of Two Models," *Personnel Psychology,* 3 (Winter 1980), pp. 741–57.
38. The Harris Survey, *Yuppie Lifestyle Felt to Be Unattractive to Americans* (Orlando: Tribune Media Services, 1986).
39. See Solomon Asch, "Opinions and Social Pressures," *Scientific American,* 193 (1955), pp. 31–35.
40. See, for example, Bibb Latané, Kipling Williams, and Stephen Harkins, "Many Hands Make Light Work: The Causes and Consequences of Social Loafing," *Journal of Personality and Social Psychology,* 37 (1979), pp. 823–32; Kipling Williams, Stephen Harkins, and Bibb Latané, "Identifiability as a Deterrent to Social Loafing: Two Cheering Experiments," *Journal of Personality and Social Psychology,* 40 (1981), pp. 303–11.
41. See Robert A. Baron and Donn Byrnes, *Social Psychology* (Boston: Allyn and Bacon, 1984), pp. 430–31; Edward Diener, "Deindividuation, Self-Awareness, and Disinhibition," *Journal of Personality and Social Psychology,* 37 (1979), pp. 1160–71; Edward Diener, "Deindividuation: The Absence of Self-Awareness and Self-Regulation in Group Members," in P. Palus (ed.), *The Psychology of Group Influence* (Hillsdale, NJ: Erlbaum, 1980).
42. Cited by Jonathan Craig and Richard Posner, *The New York Crime Book* (New York: Pyramid, 1972), p. 176.
43. See, for example, Bibb Latané and S. A. Nida, "Ten Years of Research on Group Size and Helping Behavior," *Psychological Bulletin,* 89 (1981), pp. 308–24.
44. H. M. Pantin and C. S. Carver, "Induced Competence and the Bystander Effect," *Journal of Applied Social Psychology,* 12 (1982), pp. 100–11.
45. William Whyte, "The Social Structure of the Restaurant," *American Journal of Sociology,* 54 (1949), pp. 302–10.
46. Samuel S. Stouffer, *The American Soldier.*
47. Rita Volkman and Donald R. Cressey, "Differential Association and the Rehabilitation of Drug Addicts," in John A. O'Donnell and John C. Ball (eds.), *Narcotic Addiction* (New York: Harper & Row, 1966), pp. 209–33.

Formal Organizations

Childbirth can be a unique and wondrous experience for parents. Couples generally anticipate the birth of a son or daughter with considerable exhilaration, particularly if the expected baby is their first child. They purchase diapers, receiving blankets, and a crib, and devise a list of possible names. If they have the space and money, they may transform a spare bedroom into a nursery. The expectant mother sees her physician regularly, may attend birthing classes with her husband, and rehearses the trip to the hospital in advance.

Hospitals also anticipate childbirth, but from an entirely different perspective. The birth of a child is a common event in a hospital, but it is one that requires the services of numerous health-care personnel, as well as the involvement of the technicians, administrators, and other workers needed to keep a hospital open and functioning smoothly. Admissions and finance specialists, maintenance workers, and food-service personnel all play a part in hospital routine. The birth of any given child is but one of many, all pretty much the same from the vantage point of those who work in a hospital.[1]

Routine events are best handled by strict scheduling. Rather than allow nature to take its course (and face having half the women in the maternity ward in labor at the same time), hospitals "manage" childbirth, subordinating expectant mothers to positions on a roster. To bring events into conformity with hospital schedules, doctors may administer drugs to induce, accelerate, or inhibit labor. Because childbirth is best handled by bringing patients to the medical staff, expectant mothers are moved through a series of waiting rooms, examining rooms, labor rooms, delivery rooms, and postoperative

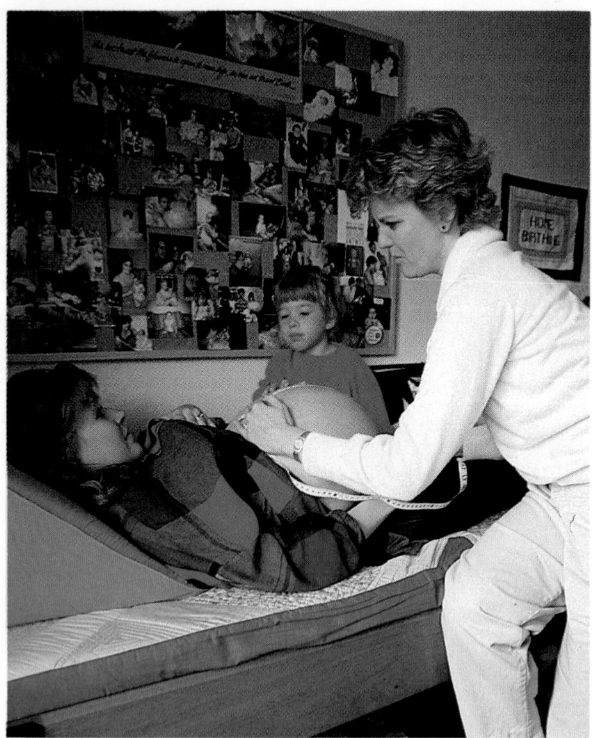

A prenatal checkup by a midwife is a more personal approach to childbirth than that encountered in many large-scale hospital settings.

rooms, in a progression not unlike that of the assembly line in an automobile factory.

Childbirth is sometimes a technical event as well, one to be witnessed by a collection of physicians, interns, residents, and nurses, who view the event as an opportunity to learn—to observe, probe, and prod the mother as she reclines in an uncomfortable and awkward position, deprived of her privacy and dignity.*

Childbirth in the hospital setting typifies the dilemma of the large formal organization in modern society. The hospital must handle many births every year, day in and day out. Although each may be unique in its own particular way, and infinitely so for the parents involved, too much time and attention to any particular case would render the hospital impossibly inefficient. The issue of striking a balance between the organizational need to coordinate and efficiently serve many people and the individual's need for personal and specialized attention dominates the study of formal organizations. Within this context, then, what are formal organizations? How are they structured? What is their impact on social life?

LIFE IN THE ORGANIZATIONAL SOCIETY

The hospital is merely one of many **formal organizations,** those relatively large social groups created to pursue specific goals. They are called formal organizations because they are characterized by explicitly prescribed positions, rules and regulations, and a system of authority, all created to contribute to the realization of the organization's goal or goals. Many different kinds of formal organizations exist in our society, and it is correct to observe that some have more formal structure than others.

Newborn infants, like virtually all members of modern American society, are destined to spend much of their lives in formal organizations of one kind or another. Most children are born in hospitals, and many spend time in organized child-care facilities or nursery schools before they are a year old. All children will be in school by age six, spending one-third of their waking hours in organizations designed to educate hundreds—and sometimes thousands—of students. By the time young people reach adolescence, many will be working in part-time jobs. In fact, almost half a million teenagers on any given day function as servers, cooks, or managers in one of the world's largest fast-food chains, producing the same basic menu for millions of people on six continents. As adults, some of these individuals later will find work with vast multinational corporations in factories and offices scattered all over the globe, but coordinated from headquarters in London, Tokyo, Bonn, or New York. Even those who never actually work in a formal organization will nevertheless depend on the products or services of such organizations to enable them to function in society. How long could society operate in the absence of telephone companies; government services, such as garbage collection, road and highway maintenance, defense and public safety, or social security; news organizations, television networks, and weather services; or the local, national, and international structures whose ultimate task is to fill the shelves of the neighborhood supermarket? The answers to this question make apparent the degree to which modern society is truly an organizational society.

*Quite obviously, not all hospitals are faceless, people-processing organizations, but enough have functioned in such impersonal ways over the years as to generate widespread criticism of the physical and social conditions of childbirth. One result has been some restructuring of hospital maternity arrangements, while another has been the reemergence of midwifery. See R. Weitz and D. Sullivan, "The Politics of Childbirth: The Re-emergence of Midwifery in Arizona," *Social Problems,* 33 (February 1986), pp. 163–75.

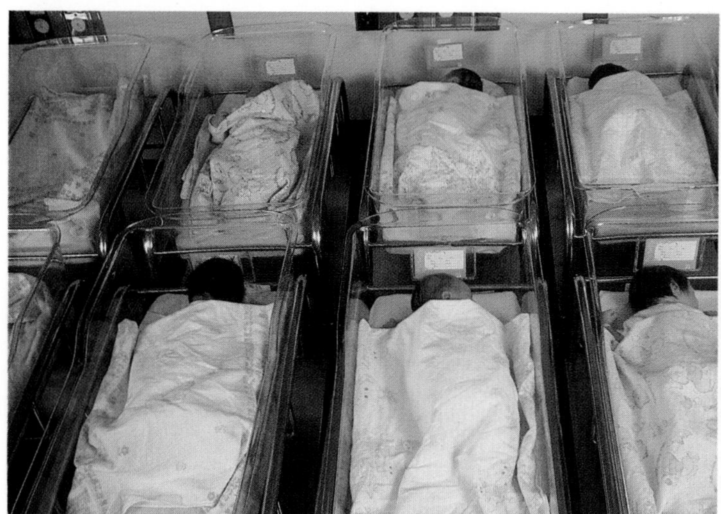

Most American children are brought into this world as ciphers shrouded in the routine of a formal organization. Many also leave it the same way.

Types of Organizations

While all organizations have a formal structure of some sort, great diversity also exists among these entities. AT&T, ABC, the Roman Catholic Church, the United States Congress, McDonald's, the Marine Corps, the Red Cross, General Foods, and the Ford Motor Company have vastly different structures. In fact, so many different types of formal organizations are evident that it quickly becomes clear that for the sake of both studying and understanding them, they must be grouped in some meaningful way.

Sociologist Amaiti Etzioni argues that one of the most useful ways of explaining the structure of formal organizations is to focus attention on an organization's lowest level participants and ask them why they are members of that organization.[2] In some cases, membership is involuntary. Prison inmates are not free to choose whether they wish to stay in prison. In contrast, people willingly join such bodies as political parties and charitable organizations because they share the organization's goals. People also make choices as to which business or industry they work for, although their motivations in this regard are probably more the pragmatic considerations of salary and career opportunities than anything else. In any case, the point of focusing on the basis of membership is that it defines the relationship of the individual to the organization, which in turn influences the kinds of social control the organization uses to manage the behavior of its members. These factors—reason for membership, nature of relationship, and nature of social control—define several very different kinds of organizations (see Exhibit 5.1).

Coercive Organizations

Membership in formal organizations, such as prisons, concentration camps, some mental hospitals, and many military units, is not a matter of choice. People often are forced into these organizations against their will, and the organizations are thus logically referred to as **coercive organizations.** Coercive organizations may lock their members away behind fences and walls and threaten punishment—creating hostility, and hence, alienation from organizational goals.* People in coercive organizations must be motivated to cooperate in their own loss of liberty. Inmates, for example, must be dissuaded from escaping, encouraged to live peacefully with others, and prevented from engaging in disruptive behavior. Many coercive organizations follow a simple rule of human behavior: a docile member is the "best" member. This rule is sometimes enforced with extreme means—keeping members drugged or weak from hunger. Observers point to considerable evidence, for example, that political prisoners in Soviet-bloc countries often are sent to "mental hospitals," where depressant drugs are utilized as a mechanism of control.[3] Critics of mental institutions in the United States maintain that strong tranquilizers or electric shock treatments are used for the same purpose. Drugs also are used in nursing homes to keep elderly patients from becoming troublesome.

*Coercive organizations also are referred to as "total institutions," a concept that is analyzed more thoroughly in Chapters 6 and 15.

SOCIAL INDICATOR

Population in Coercive Organizations, 1986

Prisoners	503,601
Mental Patients	233,400
Armed Forces	2,136,000

Inmates in American prisons have many legal rights, and as a result, they are generally protected from the threat of torture.[4] Yet they are nevertheless subject to profound controls. Many things that people who are not incarcerated take for granted, for example, are defined as "privileges" within the confines of prison walls. Personal possessions, visits from family members, mail, recreation, and numerous other activities are strictly limited—rationed out as a reward for "good" behavior.

The combination of forced membership and punishment-oriented social control characteristic of coercive organizations fosters negative attitudes, which, in turn, stimulate the emergence of subcultures, formed as a protection against the system of social control. This is most evident in prisons and other correctional institutions, where the inmate subculture encourages some sense of community. Inmates develop their own system of norms, rules, and values, as well as a communications network and bartering patterns that provide them with a degree of insulation from their repressive environment (see Chapter 15).

Although nursing homes are not coercive organizations in the sociological sense of the term, their patients are often similarly "managed" through sedation with psychoactive drugs.

Voluntary Organizations

The members of **voluntary organizations**—groups such as volunteer fire departments, the League of Women Voters, Mothers Against Drunk Driving, and parent-teacher associations—belong because they are committed to the goals of the organization. They freely join (and are equally free to leave) because they are interested in helping to achieve the goals of the organization. Since they often serve without pay, voluntary organizations must depend on persuasion or other inducements to influence their membership.

Many of the vital services in American society are provided by organizations in which volunteers do most of the work. Volunteers raise money for charity through the United Fund, offer meals for the poor and disadvantaged by means of Meals on Wheels, and attempt to create political awareness via the League of Women Voters. Countless hospitals, schools, churches, and social welfare agencies depend on volunteer workers. Some indication of the scope of volunteer work is provided by a poll taken by the Gallup Organization in 1981, which revealed that over half the American population did some type of work "to help others for no monetary pay."[5]

Management is a problem that faces all voluntary organizations. Since volunteers contribute their time and effort as a matter of choice, they cannot be controlled through the usual mechanisms. This difficulty is illustrated clearly in the case of volunteer ambulance personnel.[6] Medical professionals are firmly of the opinion that the majority of ambulance volunteers need very specific training in first aid and other emergency procedures. While this would be handled by coercion (mandatory classes) or incentive systems (time off or payment for school attendance) in other types of organizations, organizations that utilize volunteer workers do not have these options. These organizations must rely on persuasion, appealing to humanitarian goals and concern for client welfare to convince volunteer personnel to contribute additional time for training. But persuasion often fails. Volunteers have positive feelings about themselves and the work they are doing, believing that the organization has no right to make additional demands of their time and good nature, or to expect them to meet the same standards as paid personnel.

Exhibit 5.1

Sociological Focus

A Typology of Formal Organizations

Type of Organization	Reason for Membership	Basic Type of Social Control	Nature of Relationship
Coercive	Involuntary	Punishment	Alienation
Voluntary	Identification with Organization's Goals	Persuasion	Commitment
Utilitarian	Rewards	Promotions, Pay Increases	Calculation

Utilitarian Organizations

The vast majority of formal organizations in the United States—government agencies, profit-oriented businesses and corporations, hospitals, and most schools—are utilitarian in nature. **Utilitarian organizations** motivate their members by offering material rewards in the form of pay or fringe benefits. The participants are generally "employees" who approach their organization with a pragmatic or "calculating" posture, weighing the advantages and disadvantages of pay, working conditions, job security, opportunities for advancement, and other benefits. The organization, in turn, depends on this practical array of "rewards" to attract and retain its workers. While members must be willing to do what is required of them, it is not necessary that they share the organization's goals. Consequently, involvement in the utilitarian organization is based on calculation rather than on alienation or commitment. Furthermore, most members are unlikely to develop extensive loyalty to their organization and are willing to leave if other organizations (competitors) offer more lucrative rewards.

Clearly, not every formal organization fits neatly into this three-fold classification system of coercive-voluntary-utilitarian. There are mixed types. The all-volunteer army, for example, depends on recruits, but once they join they are not free to leave at will. Such exceptions, however, do not invalidate the basic typology.

Most of the organizations affecting the lives of people in modern society can be classified as "utilitarian." The vital point of the typology is that managers must be concerned continually with such issues as maintaining motivation and coordination, and integrating the work of individuals into the overall goals and objectives of the organization.

BUREAUCRACY

Attempts to plan and manage formal organizations have attracted the attention of sociologists for quite some time. The research focus has been primarily on the *formal structure* of organizations. The basic model is the **bureaucracy,** a rationally organized formal organization that emphasizes a logical and efficient pursuit of goals, achieved through a highly structured network of statuses and roles, an explicit hierarchy of authority, and clearly defined patterns of activity. Formal organizations have been a factor in social living for millennia, but the bureaucracy has but a short history, dating back less than two centuries to the beginnings of the Industrial Revolution. To most individuals, the term "bureaucracy" may conjure up images of routine, rigidity, and red tape, but to social scientists it means something quite different—a system of principles, rather than a large organization per se.

Sociologist Max Weber was among the first to study the structure and functioning of large organizations, and his research along these lines ranged from an investigation of the building of the pyramids in ancient Egypt to an examination of the civil service in his native Germany during the late nineteenth century.[7] Weber outlined the general features of bureaucracies, and noted that they exhibited a number of characteristics that distinguished them from other ways of ordering large-scale enterprises.

Bureaucracy as an Ideal Type

Weber's analysis of bureaucracy was grounded in the notion of the **ideal type,** an abstract model of a social phenomenon based on observations of actual cases. Weber argued that all knowledge was hypothetical.

What kind of bureaucracy was required for the Romans to build an entire city on the frontier?

Reality was so infinite that no single concept could wholly reconstruct the endless diversity of particular social structures and events. In his writings, "capitalism" as an ideal type represented a reflection of a specific system of economic activity. As an analytical construct, it never existed in reality in its pure form, yet it nevertheless symbolized the embodiment of those characteristics manifested by a particular economic doctrine.

The concept of the ideal type identifies the basic and essential characteristics of bureaucracy and can be used to compare specific organizations with one another or to measure how close a real organization comes to the ideal. And although the bureaucracy may be referred to as an *ideal* type, this label should not suggest that it is desirable—merely that it includes all the basic elements that distinguish it from some other form of organization. Furthermore, the bureaucracy that in actual practice fully conforms to the ideal type described by Weber probably does not exist, and for one major reason. Bureaucracy is best suited to routine, predictable tasks, yet no organization ever deals with completely predictable events.[8] Some, like hospitals, may *attempt* to impose unrelenting order in all medical cases, but they are destined to fail because of the many exceptions that persistently occur. The hospital staff may try to exercise total control over all maternity cases, but they cannot foresee emergencies—occasions when the baby just will not wait for its mother to complete the admission forms, multiple births that prolong the time spent in the delivery room, or problem births that require surgical services.

The Attributes of Bureaucracy

Weber was convinced that bureaucracy was certainly the most rational and probably the most efficient form of social organization for coordinating large numbers of people to achieve a single goal. Bureaucracy, he argued, produced a level of precision, reliability, efficiency, stability, and continuity that could not be achieved using any other structure. And bureaucracy accomplished these tasks by means of its division of labor, routinized procedures, and organizational structure (see Exhibit 5.2).

Specialized Division of Labor

Whether its purpose is to collect taxes, construct office buildings, fight wars, house convicted criminals, or deliver babies, bureaucracy builds upon the work of specialists. Each department within an organization has specific responsibilities. This aspect of bureaucracy can be observed readily in almost any large corporation. In department stores, for example, there are separate

Exhibit 5.2 Sociological Focus

The Bureaucratic Model

Division of Labor	Specialized Roles and Departments
Recruitment/Promotion	Merit
Social Relations	Impersonal
Procedures	Explicit and Written
Authority	Hierarchical and Centralized

divisions for purchasing, sales, accounting, customer service, advertising, security, maintenance, and display. Within each of these divisions, every worker has clearly defined tasks. The accounting division of the department store employs a controller, accounts receivable and accounts payable clerks, a credit manager, internal auditors, and individuals in charge of payroll, bank reconciliations, and the monitoring of cash receipts.

Selection on Merit

Recruitment for positions within a bureaucracy is based on merit, as are promotions decisions. Because specific tasks need to be accomplished, it is possible to establish

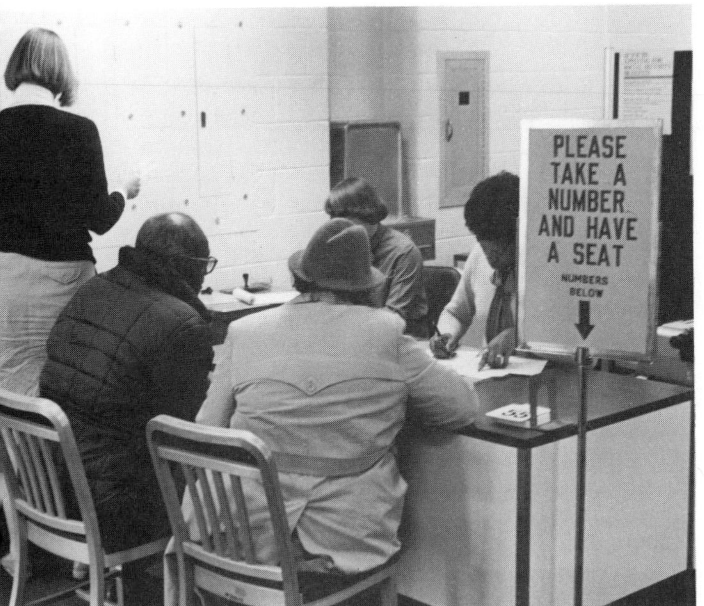

the criteria for any given position—a job description (see Exhibit 5.3)—in advance and to recruit workers on the basis of their qualifications on paper. Because they are objective, educational credentials, test scores, and previous work experience generally are considered the best indicators of a potential recruit's abilities.

Obviously, there are other ways to fill positions in organizations. National governments, for example, choose their leaders in a variety of ways, but none assure that the most qualified individuals will be selected. Democracies use elections to select presidents, prime ministers, senators, governors, and members of parliament, but this often results in the selection of the most *popular* candidate. In dictatorships, raw power determines who will govern. Monarchies, such as Iran under Reza Khan Pahlavi or Haiti under the Duvaliers, depend on the rule of inheritance in choosing a successor, but such a practice hardly guarantees that the child of a king or queen will be a capable ruler.

In many organizations recruitment and advancement sometimes are based on "connections" and "politics." Weber favored the idea of using objective measures of competence in the hiring, firing, and promotion processes, however, not only because they sidestepped the problems of "favoritism," but also because they eliminated the use of such *ascribed* criteria as race, gender, nationality, or religion.

Impersonal Orientation

Officials and subordinates in bureaucratic organizations are expected to assume an impersonal orientation in contacts with clients. Clients are to be treated as "cases" rather than as "persons." Moreover, officials are expected to disregard *all* personal considerations with regard to subordinates as well, maintaining complete personal detachment in their relations at all times.

Exhibit 5.3

Sidelights on American Culture

The Job Description

The Dictionary of Occupational Titles, a publication of the United States Department of Labor, provides detailed descriptions of all known occupations, giving the titles that identify each position, the tasks they involve, and the characteristics and skills a worker needs to fit a job well. The Department of Labor job descriptions are used by many government agencies and corporations to recruit qualified applicants. Other businesses use the Department of Labor listings as models from which to form other job descriptions. The first edition of this directory was published in 1939, and at that time, it contained some 17,000 job titles and descriptions. By 1965 this number had grown to almost 30,000, and by the 1980s over 40,000 entries were included. To demonstrate the detail and specificity of these job descriptions, we have included here those of the commonly understood position of secretary, and the more obscure position of screw inspector.

SECRETARY (clerical) Schedules appointments, gives information to callers, takes dictation, and otherwise relieves officials of clerical work and minor administrative and business detail: Reads and routes incoming mail. Locates and attaches appropriate file to correspondence to be answered by employer. Takes dictation in shorthand or on Stenotype machine [STENOTYPE OPERATOR] and transcribes notes on typewriter, or transcribes from voice recordings [TRANSCRIBING-MACHINE OPERATOR]. Composes and types routine correspondence. Files correspondence and other records. Answers telephone and gives information to callers or routes call to appropriate official and places outgoing calls. Schedules appointments for employer. Greets visitors, ascertains nature of business, and conducts visitors to employer or appropriate person. May not take dictation. May arrange travel schedule and reservations. May compile and type statistical reports. May supervise clerical workers. May keep personnel records [PERSONNEL CLERK]. May record minutes of staff meetings.

SCREW INSPECTOR (clock & watch) Examines watch screws to determine if dimensions are within specified tolerances, and facing, beveling, and polishing are according to specifications, using loupe or microscope, and tweezers: Inspects screws for defects, such as burrs and scratches. Places appropriate chart for particular screw on projector screen, positions screw beneath light so that its shadow coincides with blownup screw outline on chart, and verifies that screw dimensions are within specified tolerances. May position screws on shaker screen to expose screwhead and facilitate inspection. May be designated, according to part of screw examined as SCREW INSPECTOR, FACE AND BEVEL.

Social relations among members of a bureaucracy are structured to remain impersonal for the sake of fostering formality and preventing feelings from distorting rational judgments. Such emotions as love, hate, envy, or compassion are considered destructive in a bureaucratic organization because they tend to interfere with the free flow of communication and efficient completion of tasks. Many companies, for example, generally forbid **nepotism**—favoritism towards a relative—by means of rules that prohibit workers from supervising their spouses (or parents from supervising their children). Personal feelings, in such cases, would prevent impartial treatment within the organization. Nepotism rulings also regulate hiring and promotion decisions by a worker's relatives.

Procedures and Documents

Bureaucracy involves an elaborate system of formal procedures. Universities develop rules and regulations for admissions, course registration, the administering of examinations, student dismissal, and graduation. Hospitals create routines for elective surgery, childbirth, and out-patient care. In the absence of such procedures, each event would have to be handled as a new problem, defeating the purpose of the organization.

Whether the bureaucracy is a university, a branch of the military, a hospital, or some other type of complex organization, procedures generally are embodied in a formal document (or series of documents). Colleges and universities have a policies and procedures directory, various student manuals, and a faculty handbook. Civil service organizations have collections of official papers that detail the rules and procedures for recruitment, hiring, transfers, dismissals, salary increases, time-off requests, and a host of other functions that relate directly to the mission of the bureaucracy. The United States Army has an *SOP* (Standard Operating Procedures) manual hundreds of pages in length that describes the appropriate method of handling every possible contingency from ordering parts for a plane to the rules for conducting a court martial.

In connection with organizational manuals and SOPs, Weber noticed that bureaucracy creates an elaborate written record of its activities. Almost every action is recorded, often with countless copies to be distributed among interested parties. Endless memos are generated as divisions of the organization seek to keep in touch with other units. Clients who want something done must submit forms and applications and supporting documents. Developments in office technology often have facilitated the proliferation of paper—first offices used carbon paper, then photocopying machines, now fax machines, personal computers, and desktop publishing (see Exhibit 5.4). Written records are necessary, for without them the organization would have no past and no continuity or stability; verbal communications are easily confused or forgotten.

The members of the Commission on Federal Paperwork view 45 feet of official forms required to process aid to one dependent child.

Hierarchy and Centralization

The organization of positions in every bureaucracy follows the principle of hierarchy. A centralized authority oversees operations at the top, and each position, no matter what its purpose or role, is under the direct control and supervision of the one immediately above it. This arrangement creates a system for carrying out decisions made at the apex of the organization. Such a distribution of authority tends to slow the speed of some decision making and places limits on personal freedom, but it might be impossible to achieve complex goals if workers were free to work at their own pace or choose their own priorities. Imagine the chaos if each auto worker were free to build a car as he or she saw fit, if every soldier were permitted to attack the enemy in whatever manner they thought best, or if city governments left traffic patterns and safety regulations to the judgment of individual motorists.

The Advantages of Bureaucracy

The organizing principles of bureaucracy maximize rational decision making and administrative efficiency. Moreover, bureaucratic structure has advantages over other forms of organization because (1) experts are best qualified to make technically correct decisions, and (2) disciplined performance governed by abstract rules and coordinated by a hierarchy of authority fosters a rational and consistent pursuit of organizational objectives.

The advantages of the bureaucracy as a total system of organization are most apparent in three specific areas—magnifying individual abilities, coordination, and stability over time. First, the bureaucracy has the capacity to undertake projects that would be well beyond the capability of any single individual. No one person could possibly manage to master all the skills and knowledge necessary to design and manufacture an automobile, operate a railroad system, or launch a space shuttle.

Exhibit 5.4

Sociology in the Media

The Paper Blizzard

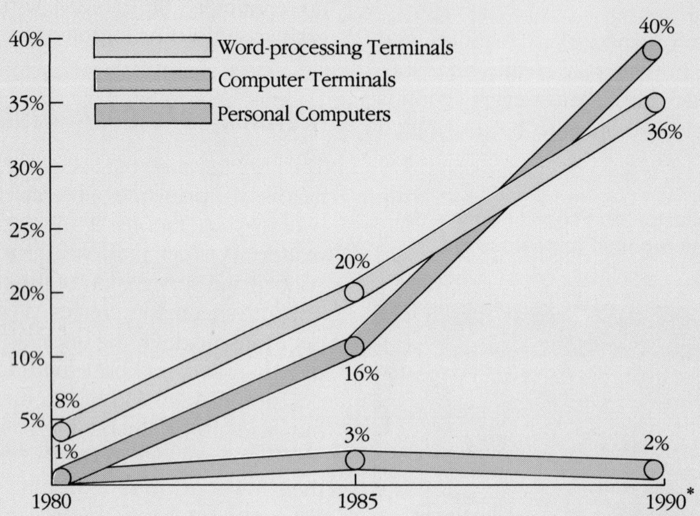

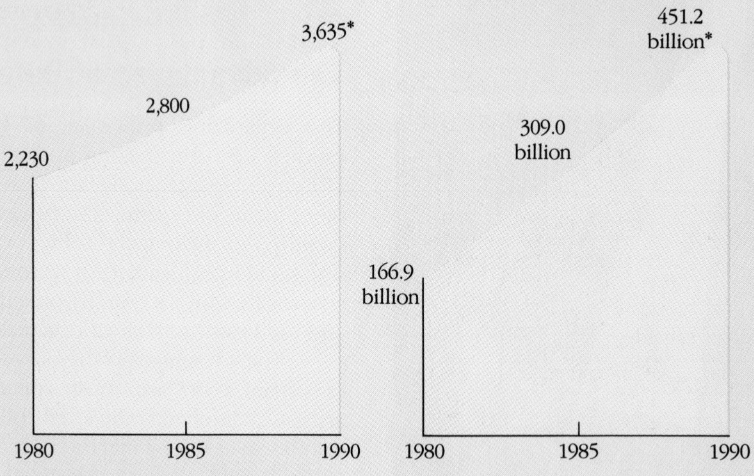

*Estimate

Source: *USA Today,* April 14, 1986, p. 1E.

Second, integrating the activities of the hundreds, and oftentimes thousands, of people involved in manufacturing automobiles, collecting taxes, or educating college students requires a systematic structure to organize their individual efforts into some larger scheme. And third, some tasks, such as issuing drivers' licenses or publishing books, remain essentially the same for long periods of time, although the specific techniques involved may change. Bureaucracy makes it possible for these tasks to be carried out over time even though the individuals involved may come and go.

The Dysfunctional Aspects of Bureaucracy

The fact that "bureaucracy" has become a pejorative term in modern society suggests that it may not be a perfect system. Social activity organized along bureaucratic lines has generated any variety of difficulties for both workers and clients, sometimes because the organization fails to live up to the ideal model. In other instances the problem lies in the very nature of bureaucratic organization.

Ritualists and the Bureaucratic Personality

The American Heritage Dictionary defines a "bureaucrat" as an official of a bureaucracy. It also defines the bureaucrat as "any official who insists on rigid adherence to rules, forms, and routines."[9] This second definition certainly brings to mind the unpleasant experience of being bogged down in the apparently endless labyrinth of bureaucratic personnel who seem more interested in following rules than in helping clients. Within this context, Columbia University sociologist Robert K. Merton has argued that strict adherence to rules is part of the very nature of bureaucracy. The result, in human terms, is many ritualists who manifest what Merton referred to as a "bureaucratic personality."[10] To use the language of functionalism, the bureaucratic personality might be termed a *latent dysfunction*—an unanticipated and negative consequence.

Drawing by Weber © 1980, *The New Yorker* Magazine, Inc.

"I'm sorry, dear, but you knew I was a bureaucrat when you married me."

Rules provide ready-made guidelines for dealing with standard and recurrent tasks, and many routine activities—processing unemployment checks and issuing drivers' licenses to list but two—are managed in this fashion. Procedural rules are originally established as a means to an end, a way of dealing with recurring situations. But they can become an end in and of themselves. The problem with bureaucratic rules is that they are formalized to deal with typical cases, but cause confusion and inefficiency when applied in an inappropriate situation. As a result, they encourage unimaginative responses, because finding creative solutions represents a break with routine—a break with the official rules. Too, creative solutions can be time-consuming. To the worker with a bureaucratic personality, creativity represents a departure from established procedure, and hence, a threat to advancement, which also is based on conformity to written rules and procedures (see Exhibit 5.5). In consequence, bureaucrats respond with ritualism, following the formal procedures to the letter rather than following the intent of the rules.

The behavior of an emergency room admissions clerk who insists on listing a Blue Cross number before summoning a physician to treat a gaping wound has become a cliché for the bureaucrat. Perhaps the most absurd illustration of unremitting adherence to bureaucratic procedure occurred in a Miami, Florida, unemployment office:

> CLERK: Sir, you did not fill out page four of your unemployment application. You must fill out every page before your application can be processed.
>
> APPLICANT: Ma'am, I filled out everything that was there.
>
> CLERK: Sir, page four of your application is blank.
>
> APPLICANT (after looking at page four): That's because there's nothing printed on page four . . . nothing even to fill out. It must be a bad form. Page four didn't get printed. Just give me a new form and I'll fill everything out all over again.
>
> CLERK: Sir, I cannot do that. All of these forms are numbered, one to a person.
>
> APPLICANT: Well, then how am I supposed to apply when the [expletive] form you sent me is a bad one and I can't get a second one?
>
> CLERK: I'm sorry, Sir, but I cannot give you a second form. All the forms are numbered. You can go

Exhibit 5.5

Research in Sociology

The Organization Man

When William H. Whyte's *The Organization Man* was published in 1956, it not only introduced the term *organization man* into the American language, but it also caused considerable controversy. Many before Whyte, then a managing editor of *Fortune* magazine, had noted the massive growth of large organizations in the financial, industrial, educational, governmental, and military sectors. President Dwight D. Eisenhower would soon warn that these organizations formed a "military-industrial complex" that concentrated incredible power in the hands of a few individuals. Whyte, however, warned of a more invisible and invidious danger—the decay of cherished American individualism brought on by the new, large, bureaucratic corporations.

Whyte observed that the organization man "not only works for the organization; he belongs to it." Thus, the dream of upward mobility and the lure of financial security were enough to convince a whole generation of junior executives that they should be willing to accept the demands of the corporation. Social acceptance became the highest value; loyalty to the organization became the criterion for success. And this ethos was readily evident in the appalling sameness of the executives' clothing and their emphasis on security, their unwillingness to challenge superiors, and their hesitancy to divulge information about unethical or illegal behavior.

One of the more poignant features of *The Organization Man* was the Appendix, "How to Cheat on Personality Tests." If you want to get ahead in the organization, Whyte pointed out, you have to do well on personality tests that seek to uncover whether you behave like everybody else. Thus, it was important that testing demonstrate that you love your parents but your father a little more, that you never worry, that you like things the way they are, and that you love your wife and children but not enough to let them get in the way of your work.

Whyte's portrait of corporate life was not a pleasant vision for a society that traditionally celebrated rugged individualism, personal freedom, and innovation. More recently, William Whyte has reaffirmed his belief that what he observed in the 1950s is still valid, commenting, "Today's MBAs and young urban professionals exhibit a faith in the system every bit as staunch as that of the junior executives of former years."

Not everyone shares his view, arguing that the domination of the organization man was swept away by the political and social changes of the 1960s and 1970s. Some evidence indicates that the organization person of the 1990s is more independent and less willing to allow the organization to dominate every aspect of life. A recent survey of middle-level managers in some of the largest corporations revealed that few felt pressures for social conformity or subservience to their bosses. Fully half said that job-hopping from one company to another was the way to succeed in today's corporate world.

SOURCES: Jerry Buckley, "The New Organization Man," *U.S. News & World Report*, January 16, 1989, pp. 41–43; William H. Whyte, *The Organization Man* (New York: Simon and Schuster, 1956); William H. Whyte, "The Organization Man: A Rejoinder," *New York Times Magazine*, December 7, 1986, p. 98.

to the second floor and speak to a supervisor. Maybe she can tell you what to do.[11]

As illustrated here, ritualists in bureaucratic organizations follow procedure to the letter; they cannot be punished for following the rules. Independent action usually is not encouraged by bureaucratic organizations. Nontypical cases are referred to a higher level for a decision. However, a new and even greater problem may arise at this point: no one in the organization may know who is responsible for handling atypical situations. And finally, the ultimate irony is that lodging a complaint may not necessarily bring about change; it may produce instead closer adherence to the rules, which is a ritualist's means of self-protection.

Communications Breakdowns

The bureaucratic ideal of dividing tasks along functional lines typically divides industrial corporations into departments of production, marketing, sales, and finance, with each headed by a vice-president. Communications flow up and down the bureaucratic hierarchy, with decisions that affect several departments coming from even higher in the bureaucratic structure. Yet as organizations grow in size and complexity, communications breakdowns occur more readily, producing a lack of coordination among the activities of different departments and their subunits.

A curious example of this type of breakdown occurred during the early part of 1986. Ford Motor Company decided to discontinue manufacturing its EXP model. The company's production department was notified, and EXPs immediately stopped coming off assembly lines. At the same time, unaware of the discontinuance decision, the sales department launched a special financing package for all new EXPs.[12] Ford ultimately was promoting automobiles that it had ceased to produce. The opposite situation occasionally occurs in the publishing industry. Production, marketing, and sales departments coordinate their efforts in the launching of a new book. Copies of the new publication are printed, bound, warehoused, and inventoried, and marketing personnel begin vigorous promotion. Yet somehow, no one tells the shipping department that the book exists. When shipping clerks cannot find the title on their computers, orders are returned stamped "out of print."

When bureaucratic rules fail to apply to a given situation, the result is frustration.

Parkinson's Law and the Peter Principle

Many of the apparent dysfunctions of bureaucracy have been popularized and have become part of conventional wisdom. A widely cited example is **Parkinson's Law,** British historian C. Northcote Parkinson's tongue-in-cheek idea that "work expands to fill the time available for its completion."[13] Parkinson argued that bureaucracies expand needlessly, and that the number of officials they utilize and the quantity of work involved are not necessarily related to one another. Consider the bureaucratic official who feels that his workload is excessive. To safeguard his position and power in the bureaucracy, the official shuns the idea of hiring someone of equal status, and hires instead two assistants who pose no threat. In time, each assistant appoints two junior assistants of his own, so that a total of seven workers now do the original job. On the surface, all appears well. Each of the seven spends a good amount of time writing memos to the others, and everyone appears to be working diligently.

The argument in the **Peter Principle** is that "in a hierarchy every employee tends to rise to his level of incompetence."[14] In other words, workers in bureaucratic organizations are promoted as long as they appear competent, but eventually they will reach positions that require talents and abilities they do not have, and there they remain frozen. In theory, at least, the Peter Principle implies that all but the lowest positions in a bureaucracy will eventually be filled by individuals who are incompetent to perform what is required of them.

Although Parkinson's Law and the Peter Principle rarely develop to reach their logical extremes, they do contain some truth nevertheless. Considerable duplication of effort occurs in many bureaucratic organizations. Bureaucracies frequently are havens for the inept, who hide their incompetence by becoming ritualistic devotees of rules, regulations, and procedures.

Red Tape, Paper Pushing, and the Sea of Memos

In British government offices, prior to the development of modern filing systems and electronic computers, presumably related documents were gathered into bundles and tied together before being placed on shelves or in cubbyholes. British bureaucrats used red ribbon, called "tape," to tie the bundles. Since that time, the term **red tape** has come to be applied to the finicky and often exasperating procedures used by bureaucrats in handling papers. To both bureaucrats and the public at large, red tape refers not only to the fussy procedures of filing, misfiling, and searching out documents, but also to the many files, reports, memos, and forms that must be typed in quadruplicate using numerous carbons. Both red tape and the proliferation of paper are outgrowths of the bureaucratic requirement for written records and centralized decision making. (And too, red tape is probably the reason why Xerox and other manufacturers of

A U.S. government official explains the many steps necessary to fire a federal employee. Due process or red tape?

electroprint copying machines have been so successful in recent decades.)

Max Weber's studies of bureaucracies concluded that records and paperwork are necessary components if formal organizations are to function effectively, and to a very great extent his observations are accurate. But as bureaucratic organizations grow ever larger, there tends to be a massive increase in the amount of information processed and circulated—particularly information in the form of memos rotating among executives and managers. This proliferation of paperwork lends considerable support to Parkinson's Law, for much of the information generated is both unimportant and unnecessary. Many bureaucratic managers write lengthy memos to impress others, to justify their jobs, and to fill spare time. To counter this trend, a number of management consultants in recent years have carved out successful careers for themselves teaching corporate personnel a communication system based on only three one-page memos—a memo to identify goals, a memo to judge progress, and a memo to evaluate subordinates.[15]

And there are other problems with bureaucracies (see Exhibit 5.6), all of which suggest that while large formal organizations may represent useful social mechanisms for integrating and coordinating the activities of large numbers of individuals, their shortcomings often combine to make them exceedingly counterproductive.

ALTERNATIVE FORMS OF ORGANIZATIONAL BEHAVIOR

Bureaucratic organizations pose a dilemma for modern societies. The ability to plan and coordinate the efforts of hundreds, thousands, and sometimes even millions of people is necessary for complex industrial societies to function. Yet the very nature and structure of bureaucracies tend to stifle the creativity, freedom, and personal fulfillment of their workers. Most organizations follow some general principles of bureaucracy, but often in alternative ways. Three approaches to management that have developed in the last several decades are known as theories X, Y, and Z.

Theory X: Scientific Management

Theory X applies an autocratic approach to managing people. It emphasizes two aspects of bureaucratic structure: narrow specialization and a hierarchy in which authority is a one-way street with workers taking orders from superiors. According to Theory X, most people dislike work and will try to avoid it whenever and wherever possible. Theory X is typified by **scientific management,** a tradition aimed at increasing produc-

Exhibit 5.6 **Case Study**

The Perpetuation of Committees

Characteristically, all bureaucracies establish various committees to handle specific tasks. The United States Senate has 23 committees and 90 subcommittees, while the House of Representatives has 27 committees and 152 subcommittees and task forces. Colleges and universities, charitable organizations, and corporations all have committees. The logic behind the establishment of committees is sound: they function to pool the talents and expertise of various people who then undertake a task that could not be accomplished by one individual alone. The Senate Judiciary Committee, for example, is composed of 18 senators who meet to monitor policies and procedures in the areas of law and the administration of justice in the United States. In the academic setting, search committees evaluate academic credentials to insure that universities hire the best-qualified new faculty members. Without these committees, such complex tasks simply would not get done.

Although committees are desirable, they have their drawbacks. One common problem involves duplication of effort. At any given time, for example, no less than 40 separate agencies within the federal bureaucracy (with several hundred committees) deal with drug-abuse issues. Oftentimes there is little interagency communication. Thus, more than one committee may be doing exactly the same thing. Once a committee is established, red tape, Parkinson's Law, the Peter Principle, and the complexity of official bureaucratic procedures seem to converge, making it difficult to end a committee's existence. Throughout bureaucratic America, for example, many government committees with large staffs never meet, outmoded projects continue to receive funding, and college and university review committees do not review anything for years. An extreme example of this sort of debacle had its roots in the British civil service system almost two centuries ago. In 1803 the British government created a job for a man to stand on the high cliffs of Dover with a spyglass. He was instructed to peer across the Straits of Dover toward northern France, to scan the horizon and be ever watchful, and to vigorously ring an alarm bell if he saw Napoleon coming. In 1805, Napoleon considered an invasion of England, but decided it was impossible. He turned his attention instead to Bavaria, Austria, and Russia. Napoleon died in 1821, but the watcher's job was not abolished until 1945.

SOURCES: Michael Barone and Grant Ujifusa, *The Almanac of American Politics, 1986* (Washington, DC: National Journal, 1985); Robert Townsend, *Up the Organization* (New York: Fawcett, 1970), p. 75.

tivity through the minute specialization of jobs and the precise specification of how jobs are to be carried out. The assumption is that workers are irresponsible while managers are not.

The principles of scientific management in American industry evolved from the ideas of Frederick W. Taylor, whose research at the beginning of the twentieth century involved time and motion studies of factory, mine, and mill workers.[16] Taylor contended that reducing the time and physical movement associated with any given task also would reduce workers' fatigue, thereby increasing production and lowering costs. Guided by the belief that workers would become more effective if they concentrated on only one task, he divided complex jobs into many different narrow and specific duties. In the Chicago slaughter houses, for example, the butcher who dressed a carcass could be replaced by almost a dozen highly specialized workers—large-stock scalper, belly shaver, crotch buster, gut snatcher, gut sorter, snout puller, ear cutter, eyelid remover, belly pumper, hind-leg toenail puller, and front-leg toenail puller.[17]

Taylor's principles of scientific management were adopted widely in major centers of light and heavy industry during the 1920s and 1930s, radically changing the structure of the American work place in the process. At the same time, the preindustrial idea of work being done by a single individual from beginning to end was replaced by specialization and routine. This principle is best illustrated in the automobile industry, where individual mechanics originally built cars one at a time. Working in one place, each mechanic started with the bare frame and added parts one by one, with a wide variety of tools, until the entire vehicle was completed.[18] This kind of procedure was replaced by assembly-line

Sorting mail, a focused and repetitive task, is organized around the principles of scientific management.

manufacturing, where each worker did a simple set of operations as the automobile slowly moved by on a conveyor belt. The result was an unprecedented spurt in productivity—mass production of automobiles.

Proponents of scientific management maintain that job specialization is not enough; it is also necessary to define in advance the exact manner in which each task should be accomplished and how long it should take to complete. Time and motion experts have studied the work habits of countless employees in a variety of settings, arriving at standards for the performance of even the simplest human tasks. The results have been printed in manuals that managers can use as a benchmark against which to evaluate any given worker. U.S. Postal Service letter sorters must even adhere to procedures that incorporate errors in using ZIP code delivery, in order to accomplish their jobs according to stipulated procedures.

SOCIAL INDICATOR

The Corporate Secretary's Time and Motion

Activity	Time Required (in seconds)
Opening (or Closing) a File Drawer	2.4
Getting up from a Chair	1.9
Turning in a Swivel Chair	5.4
Reading an Inch of Typed Words	4.8

Source: Reported in Harry Braverman, *Labor and Monopoly Capitalism* (New York: Monthly Review, 1977), p. 321.

The Dysfunctional Aspects of Scientific Management

In many ways Frederick Taylor and other pioneers in the area of scientific management were idealists, believing not only that industrial output could become more efficient, but also that workers could benefit. Taylor and the others assumed, for example, that if scientific management helped employees to work more efficiently, they would earn more money and raise their standards of living. In fact, however, history has demonstrated that scientific management has had the opposite effect. Pay scales have gone down in many instances, and in others, workers have lost jobs as efficiency levels increased.

One of the most common problems with scientific management is that those at the highest levels of the organization set the goals, and in the process, often ignore the people who use the products being produced. A case in point occurred in the military not long ago. The Pentagon wanted a sophisticated missile launcher for use by the infantry and set its designers and weapons experts to work on a design. They built the *Stinger*. Unfortunately, neither generals nor weapons experts actually ever use their products in combat; in this case they created a missile system that was too complicated for the average soldier to use.[19] Or similarly, many users of desktop computers have wondered how IBM, the maker of the world's most popular and efficient typewriters, could create a computer keyboard with misplaced keys. As all users of the popular IBM Personal Computer quickly learned after they began using their machines, the shift key was shaped and located in such a way that other keys were often touched in its place. In addition, what are known as "function keys"—all ten of them—were inefficiently placed on the left side of the keyboard (rather than across the top), making them accessible only with the left hand. The reason for the poor design, IBM engineers unofficially admit, was that the board was designed and tested not by typists, but by computer "hackers" who never use more than two fingers for typing in the first place.

Finally, while scientific management may increase productivity, specialization also often produces job dissatisfaction. "Dull, repetitive, seemingly meaningless tasks are causing discontent among workers at all occupational levels," noted one government report.[20] Other observers have found that job dissatisfaction contributes to absenteeism, high turnover rates, and

SOCIAL INDICATOR

Manufacturing: Producing More with Fewer People

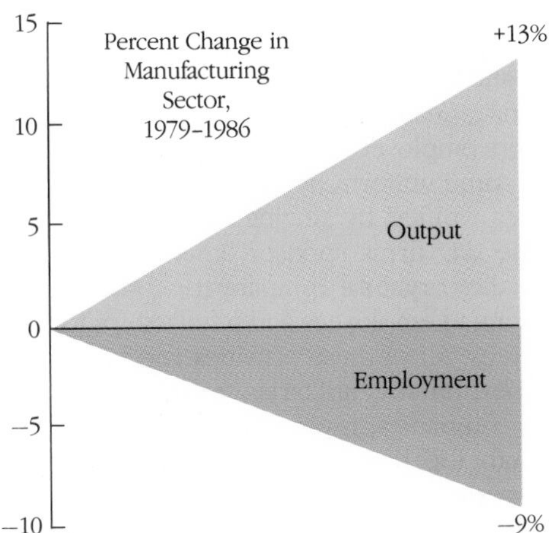

Source: *Business Week,* December 15, 1986, p. 18.

careless workmanship, rendering an organization less efficient and competitive.[21]

Scientific Management and Conflict Theory

While the functionalist approach emphasizes the positive aspects of formal organizations, conflict theorists argue that bureaucratic structures must be evaluated from the perspective of the struggles between labor and management, and that scientific management is a tool for weakening the power of workers.[22] Laborers' ability to win wage increases, for example, is based on their success at stopping production by means of strikes or work stoppages. Yet specialization and specification mean that jobs are simple and easy to learn and perform. Thus it should be easy to replace one worker with another unskilled worker who is willing to work for low wages. From this point of view, scientific management is not simply an efficient way to reduce costs and accomplish bureaucratic goals, but it is also a mechanism for exploiting workers.

Theory Y: Organizations and Human Resources

In 1960, Douglas McGregor, a professor of social psychology and industrial management at Massachusetts Institute of Technology, labeled Taylor's ideas about complex organizations, and those of other theorists who elaborated on his concepts, as Theory X.[23] McGregor maintained that workers were "human resources"; they were not necessarily inherently lazy and did not seek to avoid work, but they sometimes *developed* indolent work habits as the result of their many unpleasant experiences as employees of large-scale organizations. Arguing that all sensible people are motivated to avoid dull, repetitive, and uninteresting work, McGregor suggested an alternative management hypothesis, which he referred to as Theory Y. Theory Y was based on four fundamental principles:

1. *Work is as natural as rest or play.* According to McGregor, people do not necessarily hate work. Indeed, many derive great pleasure and satisfaction from it. McGregor's claim is confirmed by the results of a 1986 survey which found that almost two-thirds of those who had won lottery jackpots continued to work, despite the fact they no longer needed their occupational incomes.[24]
2. *Punishment is not the only way to assure that people will work toward organizational goals.* Whether they are factory workers, clerks, students, or soldiers, people need not be supervised every moment they are on the job. Most individuals will manifest considerable self-discipline if they share the goals of the organization with which they are associated.
3. *People will accept responsibility if given the opportunity.* Contrary to the ideas of Theory X, employees need not be given orders constantly. Most have the ability to work on their own and to make independent decisions when the situation calls for them to do so.
4. *People have tremendous creative potential.* Most workers have a considerable reservoir of intelligence and creativity that could be profitably developed, if they were handled properly. They should not have their occupational tasks rigidly limited by elaborate rules and regulations that inhibit them from developing their creative potential.

Theory Y can be summarized easily as a management philosophy that emphasizes directing human resources toward organizational goals. Organizations that follow the principles of Theory Y attempt to focus workers' attention on the overall goals of the organization and to encourage and reward workers as they contribute to these goals. The idea is to give employees as much responsibility as they can handle. As McGregor himself put it, "It is a process of creating opportunities, releasing potential, removing obstacles, encouraging growth, and providing guidance."[25]

Theory Z: The Japanese Model

In the post–World War II era, industrialization in Japan developed along different lines than industrialization in the United States. William Ouchi has shown that large-scale organizations in Japan are bureaucratic in broad outline, but they have a variety of different attributes that are reflections of the culture in which they emerged.[26] The Japanese model of formal organizations, often referred to as **Theory Z,** emphasizes group decision making and cooperative activities. Ouchi's analyses demonstrate clearly that the many contrasts between American and Japanese management strategies are rooted deeply in the historical and cultural differences that separate the two nations (see Exhibit 5.7).

Employee Involvement

Of the many cultural differences between the United States and Japan, two are crucial to developing an understanding of the structure of Japanese formal organizations. The first is the Japanese ability to tolerate ambiguity, uncertainty, and imperfection, which manifests itself in essentially two ways: (1) a reduced emphasis on the programming of every detail in advance of starting a project, and (2) the way in which Japanese employees were evaluated and promoted.[27] The second difference is the Japanese belief in the interdependence of human beings, which is demonstrated in many ways, ranging from the way decisions are made to the way companies treat their employees.

Perhaps the first thing about Japanese businesses that captures the attention of Westerners is the extent to which Japanese organizations will go to stimulate company morale. Many firms have badges, mottoes, and songs. Every employee, from the president to the janitor, wears the same uniform. Work days begin with opening ceremonies typified by singing and calisthenics. At the end of the day firms sponsor athletic events, and on weekends they organize company trips. Many businesses offer housing to employees and scholarships for children of employees. All of these activities and benefits, which go well beyond the utilitarian relationships found in American companies, represent efforts to integrate employees into the firm. Most American workers would probably resist an employer's incursion into areas of their lives that they consider private.

Employment Tenure

The transition from an agricultural to an industrial economy creates the need for an urban work force. In the United States a large portion of the new factory jobs were filled by the waves of immigrants who flocked to this country from Europe in search of a better life. During the years of Japanese industrialization, employers were not able to draw upon such a readily available labor force. Rather, they were faced with the problem of how to lure

Exhibit 5.7 — Sociological Focus

A Comparison of the Japanese and American Models of Organization

Characteristic	Japanese Organization	American Organization
Employee Involvement	Holistic	Utilitarian
Employment Tenure	Lifetime	Cyclical
Promotion	Slow	Competitive
Career Paths	Generalized	Specialized
Decision Making	Consensual	Hierarchical
Work Units	Groups	Individuals

SOCIAL INDICATOR

The Nippon Steel Company Song

Let's gather young power here
and light up like the hot light of the sun.
New land of green and sea.
Growing splendidly in the world.
This is Nippon Steel Kimitsu.

farmers to the cities to work in the factories. One approach was to offer secure, stable employment—*for life.* This practice was not only effective in drawing workers to the cities, but it has endured as well.

The Japanese system of lifetime employment is a two-way agreement: workers ordinarily do not move to other companies in search of higher salaries, and their employers do not lay them off when business is slow. In order to keep everyone busy, skilled craft workers may be put to work washing windows, painting, or cleaning up the factory grounds. Yet not all workers are covered by lifetime employment. By the latter part of 1986, only 25% of the Japanese labor force was composed of "core" workers who held well-paying, lifetime positions.[28] Women seldom enjoy this arrangement, and smaller companies cannot afford to pay workers when there is no business. Eight percent of the labor force in Japan now is composed of part-time workers who are subject to frequent layoffs.

Promotion

American culture emphasizes competition and individualism. In the bureaucratic setting this two-fold emphasis translates into salary increases and promotions based on merit and frequent evaluation. Thus, competition implies that there are not only "winners" but "losers" as well. Winners in the competition for advancement are motivated to even greater effort, while those who cannot advance experience discontent and low morale.

Promotions in Japanese organizations materialize rather slowly. They typically are awarded on the basis of seniority. Thus, all workers hired at the same time progress at essentially the same rate during the early part of their careers. It is only later that workers are singled out for promotion based on unusual ability. "The secret of Japanese management," comments one personnel director, "is to make everybody feel as long as possible that he is slated for the top position in the firm—thereby increasing his motivation during the most productive period of his employment."[29]

Career Paths

At the core of bureaucratic structure, as noted earlier, is specialization. This approach is central to bureaucracies in the United States where most workers seem to be specialists of one kind or another. Production workers, for example, learn a single skill to do a specific task and continue with that job for as long as work is available. Similarly, specialization for managerial personnel begins in college, where students are narrowly channeled into either accounting, marketing, finance, economics, or perhaps law. This pattern follows them into the world of work, where many spend their entire careers in a single department. Specialization teaches everything one needs to know about a particular job, but little about other aspects of an operation.

By contrast, Japanese firms focus on teaching people to be generalists. Workers are moved from one job to another, giving them experience in all phases of the company's operations. In this way they develop an intimate understanding of the entire process as well as insights into the problems of workers in all units.

Decision Making

Like American corporations, Japanese firms are arranged in a hierarchy. Executives and managers are responsible for making policy decisions, yet unless severe time pressures interfere, decisions are made only after consultation with lower level workers who will be affected by the policy change. The typical procedure employed is referred to by the Japanese as *ringi.* One individual is made responsible for making a recommendation, but he or she is required to discuss it with workers and

SOCIAL INDICATOR

Theory X vs. Theory Z in the United States

Value of Goods Produced by the Average American Worker in Plants Run by:

Americans	$ 87,000
Koreans	94,000
Japanese	115,000

Average Number of Hours Worked per Week by Managers in American Plants Run by:

Americans	50
Koreans	70–80
Japanese	60–70

Source: *Business Week,* January 19, 1987, p. 66.

supervisors, revising it until all can agree to the final plan. The objective of *ringi* is to allow everyone who is involved in a job to have his or her opinion heard.

Work Units

The Japanese model emphasizes groups rather than individuals. Specific projects generally are assigned to an entire unit, whose members have collective responsibility for planning and design, division of labor and task allocation, and final outcome. This approach is possible, in part, because each worker is a generalist, capable of working at almost every phase of an operation. If the group confronts a problem it cannot handle, experts are called in, not to solve the problem, but to teach the group the necessary skills so that they can solve the problem.

In the final analysis, Japanese organizations exhibit the basic characteristics common to any bureaucracy—specialized functions, hierarchy, and formal procedures. But bureaucracy, as Max Weber pointed out, is only a general model—an ideal type—allowing for many variations, and the Japanese pattern is one that emphasizes interdependence and group cooperation.

COLLECTIVIST ORGANIZATIONS: A NONBUREAUCRATIC APPROACH

During the past two decades, a whole array of creative new organizational structures has emerged in the United States. While different motives stimulated their growth, a deliberate antibureaucratic bias seemed to be almost universally evident. Free law clinics and food banks, for example, evolved from the desire to provide basic services to the economically disadvantaged and politically powerless who were being ignored by government and private bureaucracies. Civil, women's, and victims' rights groups were organized to redress the dilemmas of racism, sexism, and domestic violence. Still other organizations developed as responses to the impersonality of bureaucratic life. Free schools evolved, for example, because local systems had seemingly lost sight of the individual personalities and needs of children. Birthing clinics arose because public hospitals appeared to be processing expectant mothers in much the same way the food industry was preserving frozen meat.

The Nature of Collectivist Organizations

Collectivist organizations, regardless of their size or purpose, are characterized by an emphasis on participation and shared values.[30] They differ from the bureaucratic model in various ways, including systems of recruitment, social relations, authority, rules, and social control.

Recruitment

Collectivist organizations are *voluntary organizations,* with members bound together by a shared set of ideals. Achieving the goals of the organization is important, but so too is the idea of maintaining solidarity and the integrity of the group. Only those committed to the organization's values are welcome, so recruitment is accomplished on the basis of individual and highly personalized criteria—friendship, social or political values, or even personality. As a result, neighborhood law clinics, for example, will seek out only those attorneys who are willing to forego the high salaries of the elite law firms in favor of helping tenants to fight landlords or welfare clients to navigate through a local government bureaucracy. The outcome of recruitment in a collectivist organization is a cluster of conspicuously like-minded individuals.

Social Relations and Social Control

The bureaucratic ideal of submerging personal traits and maintaining formal relationships is ignored in the collectivist organization. People are encouraged to interact with one another as individuals, not as cogs in a bureaucratic machine. Time spent in getting to know a co-worker's problems, hopes, and dreams is not considered time wasted, and this philosophy extends to the clients of the organization as well.

The purpose of social control in every organization is to keep people working toward the goals of the enterprise. Even collectivist organizations, despite their selective recruitment and group decision-making procedures, need to impose some control; members' commitment may vary and sight of the collective goal might be lost. If a worker's interest in the organization's goals shows signs of weakening, others will offer a reminder of the broad moral issues that brought them all together in the first place. Attempts will be made at persuasion, but if these ultimately fail, threats of exclusion from the organization will be tendered. Exclusion is considered the ultimate punishment. The offending member loses not only material rewards (as in a utilitarian organization), but also partnership in a group of individuals who share similar values and perspectives.

Authority

A crucial aspect of the collectivist organization is the fact that authority resides with the group, not with any specific individual or office. The collectivist ideal goes well beyond the notion of democracy; it demands that everyone participate in the targeting of problems and the formulation of solutions. Moreover, all major policies and decisions—hiring, firing, promotions, work responsibilities, goals, and the distribution of profits (if any)—must be worked out and agreed upon by the group as a whole. The curricula in academic departments in most colleges and universities, for example, are worked out by faculty members, rather than being imposed by administrators. This *consensus process* is practical, emphasizing that the objective is to establish agreement among all members.

Some collectivist organizations have shown that it is possible to function without formal leadership. Specific individuals are delegated authority to deal with specific problems, but only on a temporary basis; there are no permanent authority positions such as those in a traditional bureaucracy. Most collectivist organizations probably have members with conventional titles, such as "president" or "treasurer," but their tasks do not actually involve making policy. Rather, they keep records and carry out group decisions. Often these positions exist only because state laws require all organizations to have a slate of officers in order to be incorporated.

Limitations of Collectivist Organizations

Collectivist organizations are far from perfect. Their very nature gives rise to a whole array of inherent difficulties suggesting that this form of organization may be useful only in certain situations.

Size

Most collectivist organizations are relatively small, having fewer than one hundred members. Any number larger than that makes it difficult to maintain the degree of individuality and personal involvement that these organizations strive to achieve. As a result, the nature and range of tasks they are able to undertake tends to be limited. A birthing clinic catering to healthy mothers with relatively uneventful pregnancies, for example, can be organized along collectivist lines, but a full-service hospital is faced with a complex of rather imposing tasks that are well beyond the capabilities of any small collectivist group.

Time and Efficiency

Decision making accomplished by means of the consensus model tends to be a rather slow process. Consider, for example, the procedures most universities use to hire new faculty members. Each department's faculty operates, in may ways, as a small collectivist organization. When a position needs to be filled, the faculty as a whole undertakes the recruitment effort, and every phase of the process is agreed on through *consensus.* A norm within the academic community discourages the hiring of any candidate who is unable to gain a consensus of support. In a bureaucracy, recruitment is likely to be delegated to a personnel department, which may be able to accomplish the task of hiring new employees quickly and efficiently. A collectivist organization is willing to accept higher costs as a necessary consequence of seeking consensus (see Exhibit 5.8).

On the whole, collectivist organizations have demonstrated that it is possible to realize complex tasks without resorting to bureaucracy. Some food banks and other collectivist organizations have survived for decades, fueled by members' commitment to social reform. It is this sense of commitment that distinguishes collectivist organizations from others, making it difficult, if not impossible, to transfer their principles to either utilitarian or coercive bureaucracies.

ORGANIZATIONS AND APPLIED SOCIOLOGY

Most people spend much of their time in formal organizations of one kind or another. In the interests of efficiency, coordination, and continuity, many organizations adhere to the principles of bureaucracy described by Max Weber. Bureaucratic organizations are dedicated to hierarchy, formalization, and impersonality. Creativity, individuality, and innovation are likely to be discouraged. Thus, bureaucracy can be deadening to those who must work within the narrow confines of rules and job descriptions; boredom and loss of interest in doing the best possible job are frequent consequences. Yet sociologists and other social scientists in recent years have come to play an important role in attempts to alleviate a number of these problems.

Humanizing Formal Organizations

Sociologists argue that the principles of scientific management dehumanize workers by limiting them to dull, routine, repetitive tasks. The humanizing of formal organizations involves making structural changes that give employees opportunities for challenging, creative roles. One approach, based on sociological studies of bureaucratic structure, is *job rotation,* an arrangement that allows workers to alter their tasks at regularly scheduled intervals. This idea has long been the norm at Volvo plants in Sweden, where auto workers are shifted from one phase of the production process to another

Exhibit 5.8

Types & Stereotypes

Faculty Recruitment in a Department of Sociology

College and university faculty members are recruited using a consensus process. The *faculty* of the hiring department, rather than some administrative personnel officer, controls the process from beginning to end.

The table on page 143 outlines the steps in a sociology department faculty "search" conducted during 1986, and is based on the authors' observations in a 24-person department. Columns 1 and 2 in the table indicate the type and purpose of each meeting conducted as part of the search process; column 3 designates the number of faculty members active at each phase of the search; column 4 reflects the amount of time spent at each task per faculty member, and column 5 represents the total person-hours per task or meeting.

Although the faculty as a whole usually decides what *type* of person will best meet the needs of the department—theorist, methodologist, or some other specialist—much of the work is done by a search committee appointed by the department chairperson. Generally, a national search is conducted through advertisements in educational media and association newsletters, telephone contacts, and face-to-face conversations at professional meetings. Between two and five of the top candidates are brought to campus for a two-day period, during which they deliver one or two lectures to the faculty and graduate students, meet with faculty members on an individual basis, and meet with one or more university officials.

Quite clearly, the process is a time-consuming one. In this particular example, the search took a total of 402 faculty-person hours to complete. Moreover, if one were to compute the average *daily billing rate* of the faculty (an uncommon calculation in the university setting, but a familiar computation in industry), the inefficiency and expense of the consensus process would be very apparent. The daily billing rate is the employer's *total* cost for a single day's work from the employee and includes salary, fringe benefits (paid holidays, vacation, and sick leave as well as the employer's contribution to social security, retirement, and insurance plans), and overhead (the cost of running the operation, including rents, utilities, equipment, maintenance, and administrative and clerical costs). The daily billing rate for the 24-person sociology department in this example would be calculated as follows:

Salary: with an average faculty salary of $38,000 per year, the daily rate, based on a five-day week for a nine-month academic year, totals to	$211.11
Fringe Benefits: calculated at 25% of the employee's salary	$52.78
Overhead: calculated at 58.8% of salary and fringe benefits	$155.17
Total Daily Billing Rate:	$419.06

If a faculty member's "day's work" were to be calculated at 7.5 hours, then the search process required 53.6 person-days of effort. With a daily billing rate of $419.06, the cost of faculty time totaled $22,462. Add to this figure some $4,000 in advertising costs, candidate travel expenses, telephone bills, and other miscellaneous costs, and the total comes to over $26,000 to hire one individual.

During the same time that this sociology department was conducting its national search, a 25-person corporation in Miami, Florida, was carrying on a similar national search for a $35,000-per-year managerial position. The full responsibility of locating and selecting the recruit was assigned to a $42,000-per-year executive, whose daily billing rate was calculated at $408 (salary of $175 per day based on a 12-month year, 20% fringe benefit rate, and 94.5% overhead rate). The time spent by the executive in writing an advertisement, reviewing candidate résumés, calling references, and interviewing six candidates totaled 12 hours. The 1.5 days of the executive's time came to a total cost of $612. Travel and advertising expenses came to $5,400, bringing the total cost of the search to $6,012.

As these data would suggest, the consensus process of hiring a faculty person in a university is far more time consuming and costly than the bureaucratic process of hiring a corporation manager.

Meeting	Purpose	Number of Faculty Involved	Time in Hours Per Person	Total
Full Faculty	Deciding what type of candidate and nature of advertising	18	.8	14
Miscellaneous Faculty	Discussions with potential recruits at conventions	6	2.5	15
Miscellaneous Faculty	Telephone contacts regarding potential recruits	6	2.0	12
Search Committee	Review of candidate dossiers	5	8.0	40
Search Committee	Selection of potential candidates	5	2.0	10
Full Faculty	Discussion of search committee recommendations	20	2.0	40
Search Committee Chairperson	Contacts with invited candidates	1	3.0	3
Miscellaneous Faculty	Shepherding of each candidate through interview process	4	10.0	40
Full Faculty	Individual and group contacts with *each* of 4 candidates	20	10.0	200
Search Committee	Selection of top candidate	5	1.0	5
Full Faculty	Discussion of search committee recommendation	20	1.0	20
Search Committee Chairperson	Final negotiations with selected candidate and university officials	1	3.0	3
Total Hours				**402**

Exhibit 5.9

Applied Sociology

Whistle-blowing, Frank Serpico, and the Knapp Commission

The events that led to the Knapp Commission investigation probably date back to the nineteenth century; police corruption has been widespread in New York City for well over 100 years. But the more immediate circumstances had a considerably shorter history, dating only to March 5, 1960, the day that Patrolman Frank Serpico graduated from the Police Academy.

Serpico had always wanted to be a cop; it had been his life's ambition, and he looked forward to his first assignment on the patrol squad at the "Eight-one"—cop talk for the 81st Precinct in Brooklyn, New York. But within a few short weeks Serpico found that police work was not all that he had expected it to be. And too, he found much that he had not anticipated.

It was the petty kinds of graft that his peers took part in that bothered Serpico the most. Food at the cheapest possible price seemed to be a precinct preoccupation, and he was taken around to all the local establishments that were "good to the boys at the precinct," as it was said. He was also disgusted by the fine art of *cooping,* or sleeping on duty, and the willingness of some officers to accept small bribes.

Then in August 1966, the unbelievable happened, a fellow cop handed him an envelope with "300" scribbled across it. "It's from Jewish Max," the officer said. Max, Serpico subsequently discovered, was a well-known gambler operating in the area. Jewish Max was being protected by local plainclothes officers, and $300 was to be Serpico's monthly note (payoff).

This was no traffic-ticket bribe, free meal, or petty shakedown, and he felt he had to

Frank Serpico spoke in a television interview after the Knapp Commission hearings in 1974.

(from windows, to interiors, to fuel systems, for example) every day of the week.[31]

A related approach is *job enlargement,* which involves expanding tasks rather than narrowing them. In one insurance company, for example, job satisfaction and productivity were improved when keypunch operators were given more responsibility and permitted to establish their own work schedules.[32]

Nonbureaucratic Models of Formal Organizations

A number of complex organizations have abandoned the bureaucratic structure as a result of sociological findings that suggest that such a model urges workers and clients to be passive and to accept authority uncritically. These characteristics hardly make bureaucracy a desirable model in situations where the organizational goal is to teach clients to be active, to resist attempts at the imposition of authority, and to assert control over their own lives. The structure of many shelters for battered women who are the victims of violence by husbands or boyfriends is grounded in this logic. Since men who physically abuse women generally do so for the sake of reinforcing the notion of male dominance, homes for battered women employ the nonbureaucratic, participative, collectivist model to remind their clients that they need not always submit to formal authority. In these programs women come to understand that people can live together and function effectively as a social unit without one person asserting authority over others.[33]

do something about it. Not knowing where else he could go or whom he could trust, Serpico went to Detective David Durk, a friend to whom graft was wrong anywhere and always. Durk took Serpico first to Captain Philip Foran, who at the time headed the police Department of Investigation squad. Foran, however, after hearing Serpico out, simply remarked that unless Serpico wanted to end up at the bottom of the river, he should keep his mouth shut. Durk then took Serpico to Jay Kriegel, Mayor John V. Lindsay's right-hand man. But Kriegel said that it was important not to upset the police. Months went by, and nothing was done.

In December 1966, Serpico was transferred to a plainclothes squad in the Bronx, where he found corruption to be even more widespread than in Brooklyn. At this point, he went to First Deputy Commissioner John Walsh, the number-two man in the N.Y.P.D., but again nothing was done. Still more months passed. Durk took Serpico to Arnold Fraiman, the Commissioner of Investigation, who dismissed the issue, saying that Serpico was a psycho.

By this time it was October 1967, more than a year after the $300-note from Jewish Max had surfaced. Durk had always felt that all Serpico really had was a small-time police corruption story, but he was curious that no one seemed to want to do anything about it. So he dragged Serpico everywhere. By the end of 1967 Durk had interested Bronx District Attorney Burton Roberts in a grand jury probe, if Serpico would agree to testify. Serpico agreed. During the early months of 1968, eight of Serpico's fellow officers were investigated, and indictments were handed down the following year. There were a number of trials: two cops were convicted, two were sentenced after pleading guilty, three were acquitted, and one case was still pending. Nothing really had happened that would change the system. No one was questioning the higher-ups, and there was still no investigation of the large-scale corruption that characterized the police department. But for Serpico some things *had* changed. He was an officer who broke the code of silence. He felt that his life was in danger. In January 1969 he was transferred into the midtown Manhattan prostitution detail.

Throughout 1969 Durk continued to badger Commissioner Fraiman, but still nothing happened. Durk also went back to Kriegel at the Mayor's office. Kriegel replied only that Mayor Lindsay was up for reelection, and that was their first priority.

On February 12, 1970, David Durk, Frank Serpico, and two other officers approached reporter David Burnham of the *New York Times.* They told Burnham their story, and

(continued)

Whistle-blowing

Formal organizations, as the result of inefficiency, incompetence, or deliberate intent, often engage in such unethical and illegal activities as price fixing, unsafe labor practices, the production of unsafe products, misrepresentation of goods, consumer deception, kickbacks, and other varieties of fraud.[34] Such situations produce a serious dilemma for those in the organization who are aware of the illegalities. If they remain silent, they must share the guilt, but if they speak their minds, their jobs and careers are placed at risk. Those who reveal the illegal or unethical acts of an organization are referred to as *whistle-blowers,* and they can be found in governmental, industrial, corporate, and educational bureaucracies.[35]

Perhaps the best-known whistle-blower in recent history was Frank Serpico, whose revelations during the late 1960s led to the formation of the Knapp Commission investigation of police corruption in New York City and the finding that more than half of the city's 29,600 officers had been taking part in illegal practices (see Exhibit 5.9). Another highly publicized case was that of Karen Silkwood, who had charged that her company was exposing its workers to hazardous radiation. She later died in a mysterious automobile accident. More recently, Jan Kemp was dismissed from her instructor's position at the University of Georgia for protesting the preferential treatment given to student athletes. Kemp's story made national headlines in 1986 when she won back her job and a $1-million settlement.[36] But not all whistle-blowers

Exhibit 5.9 (continued)

two months later, on April 25, it became front-page news. Burnham's story created a sensation. For weeks, police corruption was a major topic in the *Times,* the *New York Daily News,* and the *New York Post.* Coverage also was extensive on nightly radio and television broadcasts. Serpico's revelations became national news as well because the corruption was occurring in New York, and that was Mayor John V. Lindsay's city.

Lindsay was well known across the country. He was an appealing political figure, and in 1968 at age 47, one national magazine had voted him the best-looking man in America. Even more important, Lindsay was a presidential hopeful, and police corruption would hardly improve his chances. In the tradition of an astute public servant, Lindsay had made plans to protect his image, his administration, and his city even before Burnham's exposé appeared in the media. The story had taken months to prepare, and by late April the discussions between Serpico and Burnham were news all over New York. On April 23, two days before the *Times* story broke, Lindsay announced the appointment of his own special committee to investigate police corruption.

Yet, despite Lindsay's efforts, there was further turmoil and suspicion. The composition of the committee was immediately called into question. Every one of its members owed primary political allegiance to the Lindsay administration, and the most conspicuous figure on the committee was the incumbent Police Commissioner, Howard Leary, who had already vocally criticized Burnham and the *Times.*

Within a month, the committee had voted itself out of existence, recommending that the Mayor replace it with an independent body free of any official political ties. To head the new commission, Lindsay selected Percy Whitman Knapp, a 61-year-old Wall Street lawyer. Knapp was aided by fellow commission members, a chief counsel, and a staff of agents and lawyers. The city council budgeted $325,000 to the new commission. Undercover operatives were recruited from the Police Department's own ranks and sent throughout New York to entrap crooked cops. Police Commissioner Leary continued to object, until one Sunday morning when he simply walked away from his job.

During the summer of 1970, the Knapp Commission began its investigations, and at about the same time, Frank Serpico was transferred to Narcotics. On Wednesday, February 3, 1971, Serpico was shot—shot in the face by Edgar "Mambo" Echevaria, a 24-year-old drug dealer—while his partners, Patrolmen Arthur Cesare and Gary Roteman allegedly looked on. Cesare and Roteman claimed that they had gone to Serpico's aid; Serpico vowed that they did not. The new Police Commissioner,

are so fortunate. Organizations do not respond well to people who embarrass them. Usually, whistle-blowers lose their jobs, go through a period of financial stress, and eventually must embark upon a career in a different field.[37] Frank Serpico had to give up his career and his country, and Karen Silkwood may have forfeited her life. Even those who win restitution in the courts do so only after protracted and expensive litigation.

The lesson in applied sociology here is that complex organizations need to encourage workers to report illegal acts but must protect them from retaliation at the same time. The Federal Aviation Agency represents one government bureaucracy that has been effective in this regard. In 1985 it encouraged workers to report airline safety violations. An anonymous "hot line" was established, and during the first eight months of operation more than 600 calls were placed by flight and ground crew staff of numerous commercial airlines. Not all of the reports involved actual violations, but the disclosures did reveal such things as the use of unapproved spare parts and the presence of unauthorized people in the cockpit.[38]

Patrick V. Murphy, was relieved when he heard that Serpico was alive and that he had not been shot by a fellow officer, but there were rumors that Frank Serpico had been set up.

Meanwhile, Serpico lay in a hospital, partially paralyzed with a bullet in his face. As the news of the shooting spread through the department, there seemed to be little sympathy. Crudely written notices appeared anonymously on precinct bulletin boards, asking sardonically for contributions to hire a lawyer to defend "the guy who shot Serpico" and to pay for lessons "to teach him to shoot better."

Serpico, while recovering from his gunshot wound, also worked with Knapp, and public hearings began in October 1971. The Knapp Commission hearings were televised, and the public heard from narcotics informants, Commission agents, professional gamblers, and numerous other witnesses. The findings of the Commission were staggering: some 15,000 police officers were found to be involved in some form of corruption. There was a period of reform and a major overhaul of the city's entire police administration. But not all of the corruption had been routed out. In May of 1972, after the Knapp Commission had disbanded, a new scandal hit the N.Y.P.D. Twenty plainclothes officers, one police officer, and three sergeants—in the same division where Frank Serpico had been given the envelope of money some six years before—were indicted for taking a quarter of a million dollars a year in bribes from gamblers linked to organized crime.

Over the long haul, Serpico and the Knapp Commission investigation did have a positive effect on police work in New York City. Although corruption never fully disappeared, a new level of integrity began to emerge, and along with it a greater degree of police professionalism. As for Frank Serpico, his disclosures became the topic of a book, a motion picture, and a television series, but his career as a police officer was ended. In 1972, he resigned from the N.Y.P.D. and moved to Switzerland to live in seclusion.

SOURCES: Commission to Investigate Allegations of Police Corruption, *The Knapp Commission Report on Police Corruption,* August 3, 1972; Robert Daley, *Target Blue: An Insider's View of the N.Y.P.D.* (New York: Delacorte, 1973); Barbara A. Gelb, *Varnished Brass: The Decade after Serpico* (New York: G. P. Putnam's Sons, 1983); Peter Mass, *Serpico: The Cop Who Defied the System* (New York: Viking, 1973).

SUMMARY

Modern society is frequently called the "organizational society," referring to the proliferation of large-scale, formal organizations that serve to educate, govern, and care for people, and to produce goods and services.

There are three general types of organizations, differentiated on the basis of membership and social control. Voluntary organizations, such as parent-teacher associations, are those that people join freely. The members wish to achieve the organization's goals, but social control is based on persuasion and is often ineffective. Coercive organizations, such as prisons, force people into organizational life. They are able to control their members, but in the process alienate them, creating the need for more coercion. Utilitarian organizations are the most common in modern democracies and depend upon monetary incentives to ensure cooperation.

The term *bureaucracy,* first analyzed in the sociological literature by Max Weber, is used to describe a set of principles for the administration and coordination of the activities of large numbers of people. Bureaucracy is based on principles of hierarchical authority, a division of labor, appointment on merit, impersonality, and formal rules. Bureaucracies are functional in that they magnify individual abilities, coordinate and organize the efforts of people with diverse backgrounds, and remain stable over time. They are dysfunctional in that members may become ritualistic slaves to rules and procedures.

Bureaucracy represents a general set of principles, but there are actually several different versions of bureaucracy, which vary to the extent that different aspects or characteristics are emphasized. Three prominent versions are referred to as Theory X, Theory Y, and Theory Z. In the United States, Theory X took the form of a plan called *scientific management,* and it has long been the dominant perspective. It stresses very narrow specialization of jobs and the exercise of tight control over workers. It has produced dramatic increases in productivity, but the dull repetitive routine it fosters produces boredom and inattention, and encourages shoddy workmanship in the interests of speed and cost effectiveness.

Theory Y represents a different approach, one that calls for enlarging employee responsibilities within the overall organizational framework. Adherents to this approach argue that workers respond to challenge and variety, and become more productive workers as a result of being given more responsibility. Organizations that follow this model have tended to move away from the idea of narrow specialization and toward more meaningful kinds of work, so that employees have some sense of accomplishment and understand their role in the firm's operations.

Theory Z describes the approach found in many large industrial firms in Japan. There, the emphasis is on integrating the individual into the overall functioning of the organization. Perhaps the single feature that distinguishes Theory Z from other models is the idea of "consultive" decision making, where everyone is involved and consulted during the decision-making process.

Not all organizations follow bureaucratic principles. Collectivist organizations reflect group participation, shared values, and consensus decision making. Although it may not be possible to use collectivist principles in the giant corporations of complex societies, collectivist organizations nevertheless serve as reminders of the needs and goals of both workers and clients.

KEY TERMS/CONCEPTS

bureaucracy
coercive organizations
collectivist organizations
formal organizations
ideal type
nepotism
Parkinson's Law
Peter Principle
red tape
scientific management
Theory X
Theory Y
Theory Z
utilitarian organizations
voluntary organizations

DISCUSSION QUESTIONS

1. Theory Y suggests that people will be creative and inventive if given the opportunity. Can you think of situations in other areas of social behavior where this concept might be applicable also?
2. This chapter discusses a number of the problems associated with "bureaucracy." Can you provide other examples?
3. Other than bureaucracy, do you think that there is a more effective way of coordinating the activities of the thousands of workers needed to manufacture automobiles?
4. Consider the possibility of adopting Japanese methods of organization in the United States. Would they work? What are the cultural differences that might serve as barriers to adoption of the Japanese plan? How might they be overcome?
5. One problem in *voluntary organizations* is that of motivating workers. Considering the example described in this chapter, if you were the head of a voluntary ambulance group, how would you encourage your drivers to take needed courses?
6. Collectivist organizations often fail after only a few years. What sociological factors do you think account for this?

SUGGESTED READINGS

Richard H. Hall, *Organizations,* 3rd ed. (Englewood Cliffs, NJ: Prentice-Hall, 1982). A standard undergraduate textbook for the beginning student.

Rosabeth M. Kanter, *Men and Women of the Corporation* (New York: Basic Books, 1977). A view of life in the large American corporation as executives and secretaries encounter the opportunities and frustrations of organizational careers.

Charles Perrow, *Complex Organizations,* 3rd ed. (New York: Random House, 1986). A comprehensive and critical analysis of current theory and research on formal organizations. This volume is a good introduction for those interested in learning more about how large organizations actually function.

Thomas J. Peters and Robert H. Waterman, Jr., *In Search of Excellence: Lessons from America's Best Run Companies* (New

York: Warner, 1982). A national best-seller for almost two years, this book details the eight basic principles characteristic of the most successfully managed companies.

Ezra F. Voel, *Japan as Number One: Lessons for America* (Cambridge, MA: Harvard University Press, 1979). The emergence of Japanese industry is documented, along with a comparison of Japanese and American organizational systems.

William H. Whyte, *The Organization Man* (New York: Simon and Schuster, 1956). A classic portrait of the ways in which bureaucratic organizations stifle creativity and reward conformity. Although written more than three decades ago, it remains insightful and relevant.

NOTES

1. See Marian Gennaria Morris, "Psychological Miscarriage: An End to Mother Love," *Trans-action* 3 (January/February 1967), pp. 8–13; Alice Rossi, "A Biosocial Perspective on Parenting," *Daedalus,* 106 (Spring 1977), p. 1–31.
2. Amaiti Etzioni, *A Comparative Analysis of Formal Organizations* (New York: Free Press, 1975).
3. *Newsweek,* August 11, 1986, pp. 26–27.
4. See Ira P. Robbins (ed.), *Prisoners and the Law* (New York: Clark Boardman, 1985).
5. *American Volunteer* (Princeton, NJ: The Gallup Organization, 1981).
6. Jack Oldham, "Social Control of Voluntary Work Activity: The Gift Horse Syndrome," *Sociology of Work and Occupations,* 6 (August 1979), pp. 379–403.
7. Max Weber's writings on bureaucracy can be found in Max Weber, *Economy and Society,* translated and edited by Guenther Roth and Claus Wittich (New York: Irvington, 1986), vol. 1, pp. 212–25 and vol. 3, pp. 956–1001.
8. This point is made by Charles Perrow, *Complex Organizations: A Critical Essay* (New York: Random House, 1986), p. 4.
9. William Morris (ed.), *The American Heritage Dictionary of the English Language* (Boston: Houghton Mifflin, 1973), p. 177.
10. Robert K. Merton, *Social Theory and Social Structure* (Glencoe, IL: Free Press, 1957), pp. 195–206.
11. Personal observation, Miami, Florida, February 28, 1983.
12. *USA Today,* January 29, 1986, p. 2B.
13. C. Northcote Parkinson, *Parkinson's Law* (Boston: Houghton Mifflin, 1957), p. 28.
14. Laurence F. Peter and Raymond Hull, *The Peter Principle* (New York: William Morrow, 1969), p. 3.
15. *USA Today,* October 1, 1986, p. 13A.
16. Frederick W. Taylor, *Principles of Scientific Management* (New York: Harper & Row, 1911).
17. Harold Wilinsky, "The Early Impact of Industrialization on Society," in William A. Faunce (ed.), *Readings in Industrial Sociology* (New York: Appleton-Century-Crofts, 1967), pp. 78–79.
18. Eli Chinoy, *Automobile Workers and the American Dream* (Boston: Beacon, 1955).
19. *Washington Post,* August 23, 1986, p. 1A.
20. Cited in James O'Toole (ed.), *Work in America* (Cambridge: MIT Press, 1973), p. 1.
21. See, for example, Stanley Aronowitz, *False Promises* (New York: McGraw-Hill, 1973).
22. Harry Braverman, *Labor and Monopoly Capitalism* (New York: Monthly Review, 1974), p. 174.
23. Douglas McGregor, *The Human Side of the Enterprise* (New York: McGraw-Hill, 1960).
24. *USA Today,* February 4, 1986, p. 1A.
25. Douglas McGregor, *Leadership and Motivation* (Cambridge: MIT Press, 1966), p. 15.
26. William Ouchi, *Theory Z* (New York: Avon, 1982).
27. Suggested by Richard Tanner Pascale and Anthony G. Athos, *The Art of Japanese Management* (New York: Warner, 1981).
28. *Business Week,* December 15, 1986, p. 52.
29. Quoted in Nina Hatvany and Vladimir Pucik, "Japanese Management Practices and Productivity," *Organizational Dynamics,* 11 (1981), p. 13.
30. Joyce Rothschild-Whitt, "The Collectivist Organization," *American Sociological Review,* 44 (1979), pp. 509–27.
31. Pehr Gyllenhammer, "How Volvo Adapts Work to People," *Harvard Business Review,* 55 (July/August, 1977), pp. 102–13.
32. Edward M. Glaser, *Productivity Gains Through Worklife Improvements* (New York: Harcourt Brace Jovanovich, 1976), pp. 102–10.
33. Steven Wineman, *The Politics of Human Services: Radical Alternative to the Welfare State* (Boston: South End, 1984).
34. See Marshall B. Clinard and Peter C. Yeager, *Corporate Crime* (New York: Free Press, 1980); Gilbert Geis and Robert F. Meier (eds.), *White-Collar Crime: Offenses in Business, Politics, and the Professions* (New York: Free Press, 1977).
35. See Ralph Nader and Mark Green, *Whistle Blowing* (New York: Grossman, 1972).
36. *USA Today,* July 1, 1986, p. 2A.
37. *New York Times,* November 9, 1986, p. 1F.
38. *USA Today,* April 16, 1986, p. 4A.

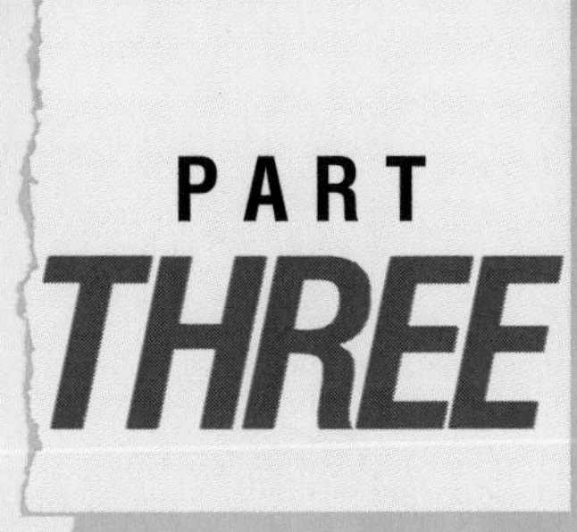

PART THREE

The Individual and Society

Socialization: Self and Society

The stories of Tarzan, Lord of the Jungle, are rather well known, having earned themselves a prominent place in both the literature and popular culture of western civilization. Tarzan first appeared in 1914 when an American pulp-fiction writer by the name of Edgar Rice Burroughs published his first novel, *Tarzan of the Apes.* The story told of an English nobleman who, lost in the jungle in infancy, was raised by apes and grew to be king of his savage domain. The epic enjoyed considerable success. A sequel, *The Return of Tarzan,* was published in 1915, and more than 65 subsequent books and films followed in the years since.

Perhaps the most curious chapter in the Tarzan saga came in 1972 with the publication of Philip José Farmer's *Tarzan Alive.*[1] Farmer, one of America's foremost science-fiction authors and a writer with a strong sense of historical continuity, claimed that the Tarzan stories had not come from the imagination of Edgar Rice Burroughs. Rather, he maintained that they were based on actual events in the life of John Clayton III, Lord Greystoke, an Englishman who in 1971 was 83 years old and still very much alive.

According to Farmer's biography of Lord Greystoke, Tarzan's parents—John Clayton II and Anne Rutherford—had set sail from England on May 11, 1888, bound for Freetown, the capital city of the British Crown colony of Sierra Leone. In the aftermath of a mutiny after but a few weeks at sea, the Claytons were stranded in the jungles of French Equatorial Africa, along a section of the West African coast now known as Gabon. The Clayton's built themselves a shelter in the trees, and on November 22, 1888, John Clayton III—the future Lord Greystoke and Tarzan, Lord of the Apes—was born. On young John's first birthday, his mother died of despair at being stranded in the jungle wilderness. Within a few hours of her death, John's father was killed by Kerchak, the head of a semisentient band of great apes that lived in the area. John was immediately adopted by Kala, a young female ape whose own baby had fallen from a tree limb and died moments earlier.

Farmer's story goes on to relate how Tarzan was raised by Kala and lived with the apes, how one day he found his parents' old camp, and how he taught himself to read, write, and speak English using his father's diary and papers. Ultimately, in Farmer's account, Tarzan was found and returned to England to go on to other adventures. He later became a Captain in the Royal Air Force during World War II.

A close reading of Philip José Farmer's *Tarzan Alive* suggests that his research was thorough and his sources exhaustive. However, regardless of whether or not one believes his story, is it possible for a human child to be raised by apes? Is it likely that an infant can be socialized by nonhumans but nevertheless have civilized characteristics? Could Tarzan have *really* taught himself English?

Tarzan books and movies have been popular for the better part of the twentieth century, not only because they are well-written, heroic adventure stories, but also because of the wonder they generate about what human beings really would be like if they were untouched by civilization. Theoretically, the best way to answer that question would be to allow a child to grow up free and unfettered. That is exactly what Burroughs did in the Tarzan novels, offering a very comfortable and reassuring portrait of the result. Tarzan was raised in the wild, yet he had the capacity to speak his parents' language; he was bound by a strong sense of conventional morality; he was capable of love; and he proved himself a tireless fighter for justice. Burroughs' work was hardly original, for speculation about what people might be like if they grew up "naturally" is an old tradition. American school children continue to be exposed to the ancient legend that attributes the founding of Rome to the brothers Romulus and Remus, who were reputedly abandoned at birth and raised by a wolf. Walt Disney also has made Rudyard Kipling's *Jungle Books* and their chief character, Mowgli, familiar to millions.

THE CONCEPT OF SOCIALIZATION

Most people realize that the stories of Tarzan are no more than mythology and speculation. At birth infants are helpless, condemned to death without the care and support of other people. Language, morals and manners, and concepts of the supernatural world are social products, transmitted from generation to generation through social relationships with parents, friends, teachers, and other individuals. This is the process of becoming a social being. In addition, some very personal attributes also are formed within the context of social interaction. A person's "self," the idea of who he or she really is, and the way that individuals really feel about themselves are also social products. Sociologists use the term **socialization** to describe this dual process of becoming a member of society and developing a self-concept.

Becoming a Social Being

One dimension of socialization is the process of acquiring the norms, values, and social skills necessary to live in groups. This acquisition process occurs by means of interaction with other members of one's society—first in the family and later with friends, neighbors, schoolmates, teachers, and the many others who provide clues to appropriate behavior. Not all socialization contacts are direct and personalized. Almost everyone also is exposed to radio, television, books, and other media that have the power to instruct. Socialization, furthermore, can be both deliberate and unintentional. Parents, teachers, and peers strive to teach children the behaviors that they consider necessary for a child to function in a group. Other individuals are extremely influential merely by providing models of behavior. Young children, for example, frequently pattern their behavior after that of athletes at a baseball park, reference groups they encounter in their neighborhood, or media stars they see on television.

Perhaps the most important question to be asked at this point is simply, what are the behaviors and traits that

In the process of developing their own identities, children take cues from the behavior of others.

a person learns as a member of society? Language? Eating habits? Facial expressions? Of course! No one today would be surprised to learn that infants, whatever the cultural origins of their biological parents, will grow up speaking the language they hear spoken around them, enjoying most of the foods they are offered regularly, and expressing themselves in much the same way that their peers do. Many of these behaviors, as we have seen in Chapter 3, are cultural. Socialization, however, goes well beyond cultural traits; in a very real sense it involves the process of becoming human. Many of the traits we often consider to be part of "human nature" are in actuality learned products of socialization. This conclusion is based on many documented instances of children growing up with a *minimum* of human contact.

The Implications of Social Isolation

Legends and myths surrounding Tarzan, and Romulus and Remus, are part of our culture because of a fascination with the idea of knowing what people would be like if they matured in a "natural state," untouched by civilization. Today, such people would be called **feral children.** Historically, various individuals have claimed that they have found true feral children.[2] In fact, it is unlikely that a child could survive from birth without the help of other humans, simply because a newborn is so completely helpless. Occasionally young children have been abandoned, later to be found in the wild.

In addition, documented cases are known of children who have been raised with the barest minimum of social contact.[3] The consequences of these instances of

Exhibit 6.1

Sociology in the Media

People in Extreme Isolation

The most widely cited cases of children raised in extreme isolation are the stories of Anna and Isabelle, first reported in the sociological literature by Kingsley David during the 1940s. Anna was discovered at the age of six. An illegitimate child, she was closed away by her grandfather in an attic room, where she received only a minimum of physical care. Having had no opportunities for social interaction, she could not walk, talk, nor clean and feed herself. She was totally apathetic to human beings and when found was erroneously believed to be retarded, blind, and deaf. Isabelle also was six years old when discovered, and like Anna, she was an illegitimate child. Isabelle and her mother, a deaf-mute, had been secluded in a dark room. While she did have interaction with her mother, Isabelle had not learned to speak and therefore was diagnosed incorrectly as feebleminded.

extreme social isolation are revealing. The picture that emerges is both direct and consistent. Almost none of these children have any recognizable language skills. Communication is limited to animal-like grunting and growling. Those who are isolated at a very early age do not walk upright. Rather, they use their hands and arms as a second pair of legs. They tear food apart with their teeth and swallow it with a minimum of chewing. Those found in the wild tend to be night creatures, sleeping during the day and prowling the world after dark. All are uncomfortable with other people and extremely suspicious of them. Exhibit 6.1 refers to several cases of people in isolation.

The sad and lonely lives of those raised in extreme isolation document the fact that people will not develop even simple human characteristics without the opportunity to interact with other people. Isabelle, briefly mentioned in Exhibit 6.1, eventually enjoyed a normal adulthood after being brought back into society. But Isabelle was an exception. She had not been as isolated as the others; she had shared her room with her deaf-mute mother. In general, efforts to rehabilitate isolated children tend to have few positive results. Most of the children prove unable to develop normally, even after living with regular families or enjoying the benefits of special education. They learn to care for themselves, but language skills are minimal, and intellectual development is never complete.

The ability to develop emotional relations with others is a very great part of being human, and this

Internationally more renowned is the "wild boy of Aveyron," whose story is told in the 1970 MGM/UA film *The Wild Child.* This child was a ten-year-old boy discovered by French peasants in 1799. His life was studied and chronicled by Dr. Jean Marc Itard, who named him Victor. The boy apparently had lived alone in the forests of rural France since early childhood. When found, he walked on all fours and was terrified of other humans.

Stories of extreme isolation continue to emerge periodically, the most recent in 1983, as reported in the accompanying article.

Although few cases of feral children have been documented, this portrayal from Truffaut's film, *The Wild Child*, reflects the human fascination with those who develop outside the boundaries of human society.

Retarded Woman Locked up and Kept Like Animal

NORTH MATEWAN, W.Va. (AP) —A magistrate, prompted by an anonymous caller, entered a locked room in an empty house and found a retarded woman who apparently had been kept for years like an animal.

The tiny, windowless room had no bathroom facilities.

"You would never in your life believe that in 1983 something like this would be going on anywhere in the world, much less in the United States," Mingo County Magistrate Ethel Pollis said Friday.

"There's not a hog anywhere in the world living in as bad a situation as she was. I do not have words to describe what I saw. It's unbelievable."

Pollis said she found the woman naked, with human feces "all over her body," in the tiny room in North Matewan Tuesday. The woman was turned over to the custody of state welfare officials.

The magistrate said she learned of the woman's confinement earlier this week from an anonymous caller. "She told me there was a woman who had been locked in a room for over 15 years and she said she could not sleep because the people who took care of her were out of town and had left her alone. She said she was worried that she wouldn't have anything to eat."

Pollis said she went to the house identified by the caller, but no one answered. A neighbor who had been asked to take food to the young woman eventually produced a key, she said.

Pollis said the woman, in her 30s, "was laying on the bed kicking on the wall, not violently, but like you had nothing to do."

"Then I saw the Clorox bottles with the tops cut off them that food had been put in," she said.

SOURCE: *Associated Press*, May 7, 1983, p. 4A. Reprinted by permission.

process also can be disrupted by social isolation during the formative years. This phenomenon was first noticed in 1945, when psychiatrist Rene Spitz compared the social and emotional development of children raised in prisons by full-time mothers with that of orphans who received only a minimum of care and spent most of the first years of their lives in tiny, separate rooms.[4] Spitz found that the orphans suffered an unusually high rate of mental retardation, physical limitations, and a lack of emotional development, failing to develop the spontaneity and curiosity that characterized the children raised by their mothers. In fact, one-third of the orphans died within two years after the original study.

Sociologists and other social scientists may not legally or ethically isolate infants from social relationships for the sake of experimental research. However, parallel studies have been conducted with animals. Particularly notable in this regard is the work of Harry and Margaret Harlow with rhesus monkeys, a group of which were taken from their mothers at birth and raised in isolation.[5] The monkeys that were raised alone were never able to join with monkeys raised in groups. The isolates either cowered in corners or became very aggressive, physically attacking others. They even failed to exhibit indications of sexual attraction. Furthermore, female monkeys raised in isolation and then artificially inseminated demonstrated no interest in their offspring. Some ignored their babies, while others tended toward violence, with a few actually killing their whelps—events that brought an abrupt end to the experiments.

Another segment of the Harlows' research offered isolated baby monkeys a choice between two different objects crafted to resemble another monkey. One was a rough wire model holding a bottle of milk; the other was a soft model without a bottle. Invariably, the babies preferred the cloth monkey to the hard wire model, in spite of the bottle of milk—a clear suggestion of the need for companionship among social animals.

The combination of human experiences and animal experiments clearly suggests that meaningful social contacts are absolutely vital if infants are to realize their potential for becoming what society has come to think of as human beings.

Baby monkeys raised in social isolation developed different traits than those who were raised by their mothers.

"Self" and "Self-concept"

The lack of social development among socially deprived children tends to confirm the decisive role that personal contact and social relationships play in the emergence of human characteristics. The other important outcome of the socialization process is the emergence of a *self* and a *self-concept*. The **self** is a person's sense of identity and awareness as a unique human being. It is a simple enough idea, but it is important to remember that this awareness of having an identity must emerge through social interaction. Most animals do not have this awareness of self. People also form **self-concepts**—perceptions, beliefs, and ideas about themselves as persons.* People, for example, think of themselves as "tall" or "short," as "bright" or "inept."

This idea of "self," in less precise form, is built into many of our linguistic conventions. A person who is overly emotional might be exhorted to "get hold of yourself." Similarly, "look at yourself" is an expression parents often use when scolding their children about certain behaviors. Or conversely, "I said to myself . . ." is a way of expressing the idea that an act had been thought-out in advance. And finally, for one to feel "self-conscious" refers to the perception of being under close scrutiny.

Charles Horton Cooley and the Looking-glass Self

Charles Horton Cooley is best known to sociologists for his suggestion that individuals' perceptions of themselves

*The most important contributions to the understanding of the self and self-concept, as already noted in Chapter 1, were made by sociologists Charles Horton Cooley and Herbert Mead, who laid the foundations of the symbolic-interactionist perspective.

are a reflection of those around them. To emphasize that people are influenced by the reactions of others, Cooley developed the concept of the **looking-glass self** to describe the fact that individuals look at themselves in the way that they assume others see them. In other words, people imagine how their actions appear to others, they imagine how others judge these actions, and then they make some sort of self-judgment based on these presumed opinions. Or as Cooley himself put it, ". . . the looking-glass self is the imagination of our appearance to the other person, the imagination of his judgment of that appearance, and some sort of self-feeling, such as pride or mortification."[6]

This formulation incorporates some of the key elements of symbolic interaction. Everyone is sensitive to those around them, particularly their friends, peers, and loved ones. Every person looks to others for clues—any actions that might reveal how others might feel about them. A word, a smile, a frown, or a nod takes on meaning from the perspective of the person receiving the clues. The person interprets such actions as signs of approval or disapproval and forms some sense of personal accomplishment or failure as a result of these interpretations. Children who are constantly told that they are stupid will eventually think of themselves as stupid. The constant boos of fans can shake the self-confidence of any athlete (except, perhaps, former baseball superstar Reggie Jackson).

If people's images of themselves are shaped by the reactions of others, then it is clear that they might sometimes wish to avoid such feedback. In situations where behavior has the potential to produce negative reactions, and in turn cause embarrassment or loss of stature, people will tend to attempt to insulate themselves from public view. The pornographic bookstore, for example, is often a setting in which men will seek privacy in a public place (see Exhibit 6.2).

Looking-glass selves?

George Herbert Mead and Role Taking

Through observations of his own children, as well as other infants and youths in homes and schools, George Herbert Mead explored the social processes involved in the development of the self. He concluded that at birth, infants have no awareness of themselves *as people* with unique traits and abilities. An image of themselves develops slowly during the first ten years of their lives as they interact with others and accumulate information about themselves and the norms and expectations of the adults that inhabit their world.[7]

Mead identified several stages in the development of a "self," starting with birth and extending over a period of years, as outlined below. While he focused mainly on the formative years, more recent theory and research have recognized that the self may continue to develop and be modified for as long as a person lives. However, it has also become clear that the basic self-image that develops during childhood remains quite stable.

The Preparatory Stage. A child is born without a sense of self as a unique person. Infants like to throw things, and some even try to grab their own feet and toss them out of the crib. Similarly, when very young children are placed in front of a mirror, they do not seem to realize that they are looking at themselves. This phase of a person's life has been referred to by many social psychologists as the preparatory stage as a reminder that it is a time when the child is first beginning to acquire fundamental skills.

The first two years of life involve a period of rapid physical growth. During this time children also slowly become sensitive to their social world, observing and imitating the behavior of those around them. They may pick up a book and hold it as though reading it, mimicking the actions of their parents or older siblings, but not understanding what the actions mean. Children also observe variations in the behavior of others in their world—affection and support, or disapproval and anger. At some point they realize that it is their behavior that is causing reactions in others. It is at this point that children have their first idea of themselves, and they soon begin to try and understand the actions of others.

The Play Stage. The first real indication that infants are developing an awareness of themselves generally occurs by the middle of the second year of life. When placed before a mirror at that age, they understand that

Exhibit 6.2

Research in Sociology

Privacy in Public Places

While George Herbert Mead and Charles Horton Cooley emphasized the value of social feedback in social relationships, research has examined many situations in which people prefer to *avoid* social contact while in the physical presence of others. A general finding has been that under certain circumstances, people do *not* wish to know what others think of them.

Research by sociologist David Karp in the pornographic bookstores of New York's Times Square area, for example, found that browsers prefer to avoid social contacts because of the potential for embarrassment. Moreover, customers choose to maintain anonymity, using a variety of strategies to safeguard their privacy in public places.

The first thing that strikes the visitor to these bookstores is the silence. No one speaks; clerks enforce this rule by ejecting customers who attempt to engage others in conversation. Customers avoid both eye contact and any physical contact. They are careful to leave plenty of physical distance between themselves and others. Each person grants every other individual his or her (but mostly, his) privacy.

While some customers may loiter at the racks of magazines, the more experienced display a studied nonchalance, wandering around the store, glancing at materials, but never stopping to actually examine the wares. After a period of time these individuals move quickly toward the exit, picking up their selections on the way. This action conveys an impression of disinterest and minimizes the time necessary to actually make purchases.

The behaviors of both clerks and customers suggest that regular patrons and employees of pornographic bookstores have developed a set of social norms that allow them to engage in legal, but unacceptable, activities without having any real social contact. In the process, they protect each other's public privacy.

SOURCE: David Karp, "Hiding in Pornographic Bookstores," *Urban Life and Culture,* 4 (January 1973), pp. 427–51.

they are seeing a reflection of themselves. When a spot of rouge is placed on a two-year-old's nose and the child is then positioned before a mirror, he or she invariably will reach up and touch the red spot.

Similarly, anyone who has a child or younger siblings knows that children love to play act. They play at being daddy or mommy, a police officer, an astronaut, or a basketball star, often imitating the appropriate dress and mannerisms. Mead interpreted this behavior as much more than simple childhood fantasy. By playing these roles children develop the ability to look at themselves from the point of view of others. They mentally project themselves into the role of people around them. Mead referred to this as **role taking**—which allows children to look at themselves from the vantage point of outsiders, and to develop a sense of personal identity. It also suggests that they are beginning to evaluate their behavior as others might. "NO, NO, NO" a child might say as he or she twists the tail of the family pet, mirroring and anticipating the reaction of a parent or older sibling.

The people who provide care during the play stage of development are very important and Mead and psychiatrist Harry Stack Sullivan referred to them as **significant others.**[8] Children learn a simple, but nevertheless vital, lesson during this phase of growing up. Significant others have standards of behavior, and by conforming to those standards children can win approval, or at least avoid punishment. Role taking allows children to get along with their parents or specific friends. But children do not as yet have an overall picture of themselves or exhibit any consistent behavior. As Mead suggested, "The child does one thing at one time and another at another, and what he is at one moment does not determine what he is at another. That is both the charm of childhood as well as its inadequacy. You cannot count on the child. . . . He is not organized into a whole. The child has no definite character, no definite personality."[9]

The Game Stage. This phase of self-development occurs when the child learns to function in groups, rather than just interacting with particular significant others. This phase of development generally begins shortly after a child enters school. According to Mead, childhood games represent the context in which group functioning is learned. To use his example, playing baseball demands knowing that a ground ball must be played to first base, not because that is what a particular manager wants, but because the rules of the game require it. The rules of baseball correspond to the general norms or expectations of a group, or society. Or, as Mead explained it, the individual must learn to take the role of a **generalized other**—the role of the composite of attitudes, values, and expectations shared by the entire group. Another way of expressing this concept is to suggest that the "generalized other" corresponds to the core culture of the group. This lesson must be learned if a child is to function correctly in social groups.

In sum, an infant is born with the capacity to think, speak, and love, but these traits do not develop spontaneously. Social development is arrested unless other people serve as role models. Much more than physical care is needed; caring social relations are a prerequisite to healthy emotional development.

Finally, Mead felt that it was necessary to include both social expectations and the uniqueness of personality in the analysis of human behavior. To accomplish this step he divided the social self into two parts. First, Mead noted, is the **me,** which represents the conventional side of human behavior and responds to the expectations of society. The other part is the creative, spontaneous side of an individual known as the **I,** the unpredictable and unique aspect of an individual's personality.

Sigmund Freud and Psychoanalytic Theory

While Mead and Cooley suggest that the development of self occurs in a fairly orderly process and that the relationship between self and society is a harmonious one, others have expressed a considerably different point of view. Most notable among these dissenters was Sigmund Freud, whose **psychoanalytic theory** held that every human action has a psychological basis, that every person has an unconscious mind, and that a function of society is to tame the savage beast within the unconscious mind.[10]

In its simplest form, Freudian theory argues that the self has three components—the id, the superego, and the ego. Humans are born with a configuration of basic drives or **instincts,** fixed and unalterable behaviors that are inherited as part of one's fundamental physical and biological makeup. Freud referred to these unconscious drives or instincts as the **id.** He viewed them as the impulsive, unsocialized side of the human animal. The primary drives are the "sexual instinctual drive" and the "aggressive instinctual drive," both of which strive for immediate gratification. These drives tend to be in conflict with the **superego,** the norms and values enforced by parents, teachers, police, and others. In other words, the superego is a product of socialization that serves as an internal censor. Id and superego are in a state of constant conflict: instinctual drives are battling societal limitations on the unfettered sex drive, in the form of the incest taboo, for example, and aggression, in the form of laws. The **ego** acts as a mediator, seeking to find socially acceptable outlets for the sex drive (marriage or consensual relations, for example) and aggression (football games).

Erik Erikson's Stages of Development

During the nineteenth century people generally ignored changes in self-concepts that occurred after childhood. Sigmund Freud was convinced that the basic personality already was formed by age five, and Mead did not carry his analysis much past the same age. Social scientists now recognize that social development is a lifelong process. Erik H. Erikson is credited with illuminating the continuing process of growth and development. He organized his theory around the idea of a series of crises.[11] Erikson argued that as people mature, they pass through specific life stages (which are detailed below and in Exhibit 6.3). In each stage they are faced with the need to resolve a number of problems that center on social relationships.

Infancy. Dependency is the chief characteristic of the first year of human life. Infants must rely on others to provide care and affection. If the people around them—parents, siblings, and relatives—treat them with love and provide a warm, stable, and secure environment, a sense of trust will build. But neglect and a lack of affection can produce a sense of mistrust and insecurity that will carry over into later social contacts.

Early Childhood. In the second and third years of life, children's worlds expand dramatically. Children grow physically—they walk, talk, and explore their environment. Social relationships will affect whether they develop a sense of autonomy or self-doubt. Autonomy is fostered by encouraging the child to attempt new things and to accept challenges without constant criticism for the inevitable failures and missteps that occur. Constant criticism or ridicule will create feelings of self-doubt and shame.

Play Age. At age four or five, children are still testing their own levels of ability, yet their social worlds have expanded to include playmates of the same age—perhaps their most important social links. Children will develop a feeling of guilt if their attempts at forging meaningful relationships are rebuffed, but they develop initiative if peers show approval and support.

School Age. Embarking upon formal schooling presents a new kind of challenge. Teachers become

Exhibit 6.3

Sociological Focus

Erikson's Eight Stages of Development

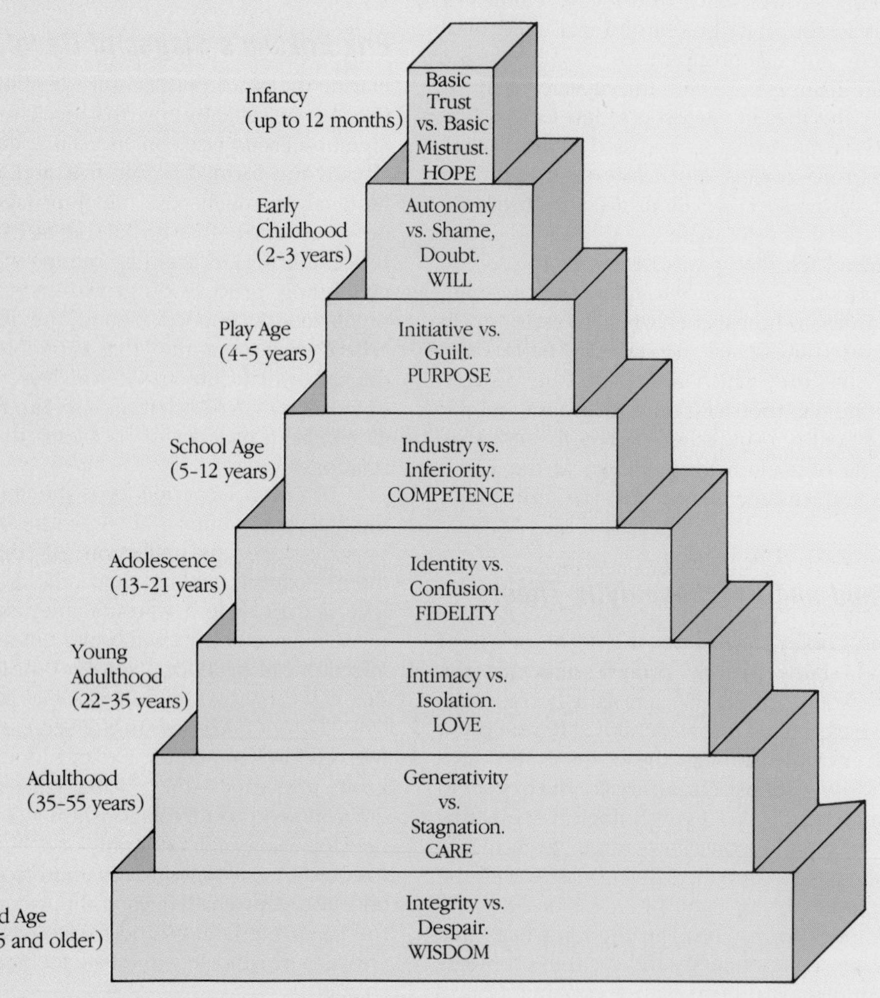

Source: "Reflections on the Last Stage—and the First" by E. H. Erikson in A. J. Solnit et al. eds., *The Psychoanalytic Study of the Child*, vol. 39, New Haven: Yale University Press, 1984.

especially important in their official roles. They are in a position to reward or punish individual effort. Schools that encourage hard work and reward people according to their ability will create a sense of industry. Feelings of inferiority will develop if the student is confronted with constant failure in competition with academically superior classmates.

Adolescence. The challenge of adolescence is one of personal identity. As Mead had pointed out, younger people have many identities that are linked to the "significant others" that occupy their social worlds. Mead calmly assumed that people could easily resolve these conflicting demands, but Erikson points out that this can be a severe crisis—an "identity crisis" to use his term—that culminates in the adolescent years. Individuals must develop *personal identities* that are consistent with their own abilities, or they will face confusion. For most adolescents, this period is an age of anomie, a time of struggle as they try to balance the capacities and desires of adults with the social franchise of children. Many fully succeed, but many also fail and then face the turbulence manifested by drug abuse, alcoholism, teen suicide, crime, and other behaviors that result in the need for psychological and psychiatric care.

Young Adulthood. The completion of formal schooling imposes the need to start upon a career, form new friendships, and institute permanent relationships. A sense of intimacy develops when a person is able to establish an emotionally close sexual relationship with another individual. Feelings of isolation develop in the absence of such interactions.

Adulthood. In adulthood, which stretches over many years, the individual faces the crisis that Erikson calls "creativity versus self-absorption." Here, the individual's perspective may focus exclusively on personal interests (self-absorption or stagnation), or it may expand to include broader social concerns, such as making a contribution to the welfare of society (generativity).

Old Age. Finally, there is the crisis of coming to grips with the aging process and the reality of human mortality. People will inevitably evaluate their lives, their accomplishments, and their failures. They will be able to face their final years and their own impending death calmly, only if they feel proud of accomplishments—only if they have a sense of integrity. However, if they focus on the failures and missed opportunities, they increase the potential for despair.

Erikson's theory has been influential in both sociology and the other social sciences. As individuals mature and confront the demands of social life, their sense of self emerges and grows, and their self-concept is shaped and reshaped in relation with an ever-expanding configuration of people and groups.

SOCIAL INDICATOR

Rise in Teen Psychological Problems

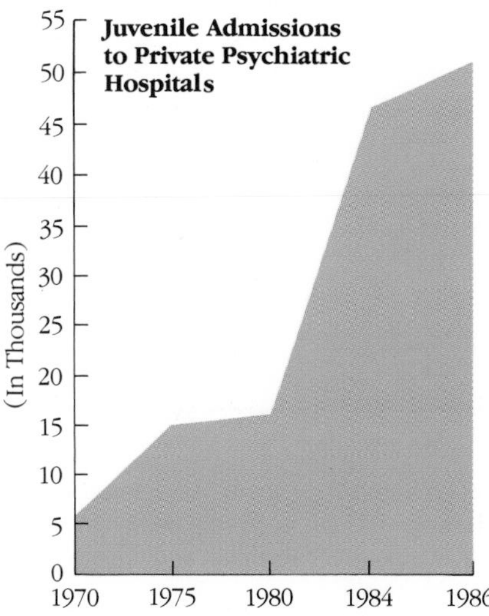

Sources: 1970–1980 National Institute of Mental Health; 1984 National Association of Private Psychiatric Hospitals.

SOCIALIZATION: HEREDITY OR ENVIRONMENT?

Social relationships are crucial in shaping human behavior, but that should not suggest that the biological component is irrelevant. When Sigmund Freud argued that humans are born with "instincts" or something called "human nature," evidence was widely available to demonstrate that people do exhibit fixed and unalterable behaviors that appear to be inherited. Consider, for example, the way in which a person always seems to "instinctively" blink as a fist approaches the eye, or the way people wave their arms in a scooping motion when falling forward or backward—two clearly protective responses.

It was a fashionable endeavor in Freud's time to compile lists of "instincts" that related to such social behaviors as sexuality or aggressiveness or territoriality (seeking to protect a specific geographic area). Moreover, theories about instincts often focused on the biological makeup of whole nations. In 1920, for example, the noted University of London physician and surgeon to the King, Wilfred Trotter, commented:

Exhibit 6.4

Case Study

From Pavlov to Cocaine, Gamblers, and Superstition: Socialization through Conditioning and Reinforcement

Ivan Pavlov often is cited in the social science literature for his contributions to the dynamics of learning. Curiously, however, he was neither a sociologist nor a psychologist, and the work that earned him a Nobel Prize in 1904 came about by accident during a study of digestive processes.

As a physiologist and member of the Russian Academy of Medicine, Pavlov experimented on dogs for the purpose of studying the role of salivation in digestion. His procedure involved cutting a slit in each laboratory dog's cheek, through which he ran a tube—one end inserted into the animal's salivary gland and the other into some sort of measuring device.

From a technical point of view, Pavlov's research seemed to work flawlessly. A piece of meat was placed in the dog's mouth. The saliva produced would flow through the tube and could be readily collected and measured. But almost immediately, Pavlov also noticed that his dogs were ruining his experiments. After but a few trials with the same dog, salivation began *before* the food went into the animal's mouth. And in many instances the dogs would salivate at the mere sight of the person who brought the food, or at the sound of the rattling of the food trays. In other words, the dogs were actually *learning* to anticipate the arrival of their food.

Undaunted, Pavlov set out to make the best of what was initially a failed experiment by examining the conditions under which a dog would come to associate a previously neutral stimulus with food. A dog would be harnessed in a soundproof laboratory; a light would be flashed and the dog would notice it, but would not salivate. Food would then be presented by remote control. The dog would eat it and salivate. After a number of trials, the dog would salivate when the light flashed, even if no food was presented at all. It soon became apparent that the dog had learned to associate the flash of light with food. Pavlov referred to the flash of light as the *conditioned stimulus* and the salivation at the sight of the light as the *conditioned response* or reflex.

In the years since Pavlov's initial experiments, his technique has been used to study a variety of learning phenomena. One of the most effective ways to study the reinforcing properties of any drug, for example, is to introduce small doses of the drug in the Pavlovian style and to measure how much work the animal being studied will do to get them. In one series of experiments, monkeys learned that by pressing a lever, they could obtain a dose of cocaine. Dr. Robert L. DuPont, a former director of the National Institute on Drug Abuse, explained the outcome of these experiments:

> In one study, for example, monkeys pressed a lever an average of 12,800 times to obtain a single dose of cocaine. Even when they were starving, the monkeys preferred cocaine to food. Male monkeys preferred to press the bar and get cocaine rather than have sex with a receptive female monkey placed in their cages. Monkeys worked for cocaine even when it was paired with severe electric shocks that were administered every time they succeeded in getting the cocaine. Monkeys hate to get electric shocks. Even given free

> When I compare German society with the wolf pack, and the feelings, desires, and impulses of the individual German with those of the wolf or dog, I am not intending to use a vague analogy, but to call attention to a real and gross identity. The aggressive social animal has a complete and consistent series of psychical reactions, which will necessarily be traceable in his feelings and his behavior, whether he is a biped or quadruped, a man or an insect. . . . The instinctive process which makes the dog among his fellows irritable, suspicious, ceremonious, sensitive to his honor, and immediately ready to fight for it is identical in the German and produces identical results.[12]

Trotter's remarks are instructive, for they reveal two problems with many of the early discussions of instincts. Social scientists note that reliance on broad traits, such as "suspicious," were so vague as to be useless in any systematic analysis of society. Moreover, many people access to cocaine, the monkeys continued to self-administer it until they had convulsions and died.

One of the major findings of this type of animal studies is that when reinforcement is only partial, as in the case of the monkeys that had to press the lever over 12,000 times to receive a single dose of cocaine, the resultant learning seems to persist for a greater length of time. In other words, an organism—animal or human—responds for a longer period of time when it has received partial reinforcement than when it has received continuous reinforcement.

Given this finding, it would appear that the designers of casino slot machines were aware of the research literature on Pavlov's experiments, socialization through conditioning, and partial reinforcement when they structured the gambling machine pay-out schedules. Consider, for example, the infamous "one-armed bandit" slot machines in Atlantic City, Las Vegas, and Reno. They are fixed to allow the gambler to win on a random and variable basis, with small payoffs coming frequently and a "jackpot" always imminent. Thus, the player can expect to win "at any time" and to "win big" with each quarter or nickel put into the slot. As a result, many gamblers will sit at the slot machines day and night, waiting to hit the jackpot, and typically losing all of their money in the process.

In an alternative direction, when behavior is *accidentally* associated with an event, superstition may be the result. A superstition is a belief founded on irrational feelings or illogical circumstances and marked by a trust in charms or practices inspired by such beliefs. The tradition that ground hogs serve as weather prophets is a superstition.

In terms of socialization, conditioning, and reinforcement, superstition is readily evident in professional baseball. After doing an exceptionally fine job on the ball field, many baseball players will isolate one specific action (or series of actions) as the cause of their success, sometimes stressing this element (or elements) to the point at which it develops into an elaborate ritual. As one observer noted:

> On each pitching day during the first three months of a winning season, Dennis Grossini, a pitcher on a Detroit Tiger farm team, arose from bed at exactly 10 A.M. At 1 P.M. he went to the nearest restaurant for two glasses of iced tea and a tuna fish sandwich. Although the afternoon was free, he changed into the sweat shirt and supporter he wore during his last winning game and he chewed a wad of Beech-Nut chewing tobacco. During the game, he touched his letters (the team name on his uniform) after each pitch and strained his cap after each ball. Before the start of each inning, he replaced the pitcher's rosin bag to the spot where it was the inning before. After every inning in which he gave up a run he would wash his hands.

SOURCES: Robert L. DuPont, *Getting Tough on Gateway Drugs* (Washington, DC: American Psychiatric Press, 1984), p. 163; G. Gmelch, "Baseball Magic," *Human Nature,* 1 (1978), pp. 32–40; Ivan P. Pavlov, *Conditioned Reflexes* (London: Oxford University Press, 1927).

feel that such discussions reflected thinly disguised racism, attempts to attribute negative traits to whole groups or nations under the guise of "science."

In contrast to the inflexibility of human behavior that the heredity/instinct approach suggests, educators and social scientists have insisted that humans are products of their environment. We noted in Chapter 3 that anthropologists emphasize the importance of culture in understanding behavior. Similarly, the work of the noted Russian physiologist Ivan Petrovich Pavlov has frequently been cited to demonstrate that both animals *and* people can be conditioned to behave in certain ways if they are systematically rewarded or punished (see Exhibit 6.4).

The debate as to whether it is biology or society that controls the socialization process continues, generally simplified into such catch phrases as "heredity *versus* environment" or "nature *versus* nurture." The term "versus" is emphasized here because theorists tend to argue fully one position against the other. The "nature" people are usually biological determinists, who claim that all behavior has biological/physiological origins, while the "nurture" advocates are cultural determinists, who see the human mind as blank at birth, free to be shaped by the environment. This debate is of more than simple historical interest. It seems to resurface constantly, with a current version focusing on sociobiology.

Sociobiology, a term coined by Harvard University's Edward O. Wilson, is the systematic study of the biological basis of social behavior.[13] Not every sociobiologist would accept the notion that *all* social behavior has its origins in biology, but all do maintain that at least some human behavior is the product of genetic evolution. Social behavior, they suggest, is transmitted through genetic material (DNA), in much the same way that such physical characteristics as eye and hair color are, and any behavior that improves the chances of the survival of individuals and their relatives will be adopted. Thus, the origins of self-sacrifice, aggression against outsiders, and the incest taboo are viewed as emerging and surviving because they increase the chances of survival of the group's gene pool.

Today, most social scientists take a different position, arguing that it is heredity *interacting with* environment that is the most promising approach to the understanding of human behavior.

People do indeed inherit certain biological characteristics—sex and race, and predispositions toward weight, height, cultural definitions of beauty, and athletic ability. Yet none of these produce totally fixed results. Consider, for example, human speech. People are born with the capacity for language in the form of vocal chords, tongue, palate, and teeth, but socially deprived children have demonstrated that speech does not develop in the absence of social contact. And too, the culture in which individuals are socialized determines the particular language learned and spoken. Biological predispositions may exist toward body build and weight, but a person's weight will nevertheless be affected by nutrition, cultural definitions of attractiveness, and lifestyle.

Perhaps the most interesting and creative way of studying the interaction between nature and nurture is to follow the lives of twins reared together or apart. If biological determinists are correct, *identical* twins (those who have inherited the same configuration of genes) should develop the same behavior patterns, even if they are raised in entirely different social environments. Obviously, no two brothers or sisters ever turn out exactly alike. Research has demonstrated that such traits as confidence, self-esteem, and leadership are influenced by hereditary factors, while ambition and aggression are more strongly social traits. But in no case is one the exclusive determining factor.[14]

AGENTS OF SOCIALIZATION

The socialization process can be visualized as exposure to an ever-expanding range of persons, groups, and institutions. Members of the family usually provide initial care and begin to introduce the child to the expectations of society. Friends and peer groups soon expand the child's range of contacts. Social relations are supplemented by the impersonal mass media, which plays a powerful role in shaping the maturing individual. Finally, in the schools, the child encounters new demands and new forms of authority. Although the socialization process continues over the life span, these agents of socialization have the most influence during the formative years.

The Family

The family—whether a single parent or an extended family of uncles, aunts, and grandparents—is the major socialization influence during the early years of life. A wide variety of skills and attributes are shaped in the home. Through a process of imitation, children pick up the language patterns heard in the family. They are also introduced to particular foods that will long influence their dietary habits. Parents expend a great deal of effort on the fundamentals of personal hygiene, constantly reminding children to make their beds, clean their rooms, or comb their hair. Basic rules of social interaction are also learned in the family, among them the rules of courtesy and self-control. These are valuable lessons, but children seldom appreciate them.[15] In fact, the major reason that children value their peers is that peers never attempt to formally instruct one another. As one youngster put it, friends are people who "never tell you to wash your hands." And, of course, children's friends are not going to be spanking them either.

Possibly the most important aspect of family socialization is that some very basic ideas about gender roles are formed within the family. Clearly, parents and siblings treat infant boys and girls differently from the moment of birth. They are, for example, likely to show greater tolerance for aggressive behavior in male children than in females, thus subtly defining adult male and female roles. Boys are more likely to be encouraged to engage in sex-typed play than girls, and fathers—when compared to mothers—place more emphasis on traditional gender roles.[16]

The emphasis on traditional sex roles is often less pronounced among young girls.

Such roles are defined further by the choice of toys provided by parents. Children may be given sex-typed toys or neutral toys, but they almost never receive toys appropriate for the other sex. Thus, while boys may be provided with weapons and sports equipment, as well as such neutral toys as arts and crafts items, they will almost never be given dolls or tea sets, unless they specifically request them. The emphasis on sex roles is not as pronounced among girls, a possible reflection of changes in the larger society. Parents of girls are certainly likely to give them "female" toys such as dolls, but toy trucks and baseball gloves are also possibilities.[17]

Peers

A **peer group** is a loose, unstable collection of individuals of roughly the same age, linked by common interests and preferences. At certain ages peers are the most powerful agents of socialization, supplanting parents and often challenging them, while also filling in the gaps left by the failure of other mechanisms of socialization.

Symbolic interactionist Victor Gecas has suggested that peer groups contribute to the development of the social self in several unique and enduring ways.[18] First, and perhaps most important, the peer group is selected by the individual, unlike the family and schools which are imposed by circumstance and accidents of birth. Consequently, the risk of expulsion or exclusion from such a group is a realistic possibility, which helps to explain why peer norms are so powerful.

Second, the peer group typifies the notion of the *generalized other,* because it is composed of people with more diverse backgrounds than the family. Individuals must learn who they *really* are, not simply who their parents think they are. Every person tests their initial self-concept (learned in the family) and makes adjustments in response to the reactions of peers. And it can be a painful adjustment, for many of the roles that are so salient in the family context—little brother or older sister—have much less meaning in the larger world of peers.

Finally, the peer group is the context for learning certain social roles that cannot (or will not) be taught elsewhere. The most obvious is that of "friend," where individuals must discover the expectations of loyalty and trust that form the basis of lasting social relations. Peers can also openly discuss matters of vital importance to them—relations with parents, school, and members of the opposite sex—with others who face the same problems and are exposed to the same lessons. And typically, it is in the peer group that deviant skills are usually, although not always, learned. Mastering how to cheat on exams, jump start a car, smoke marijuana, make a crack pipe, or acquire a fake I.D. is approached almost exclusively in the peer-group setting.

In short, peer groups play a central role in social development, particularly during adolescence. They may complement or conflict with other socialization agents. Peers are more influential among adolescents who are alienated from families and schools. However, for many youngsters, peers and family are often complementary aspects of an overall process. Parents who are conscious of generational differences typically recognize that peers will become the source of knowledge about popular music, clothing fashions, and dating customs.[19]

Schools

In the one-room school house of generations long since past, "readin', writin', and 'rithmetic" were generally viewed as the fundamentals of formal education. Today, basic communication and mathematical skills are supplemented with sex and drug education, history and social studies, typing and computer fundamentals, and a host of other courses (see Chapter 13). As a result, while the content of modern school curricula tends to be more inclusive as a socializing experience, it has also emerged as a source of conflict among divergent groups.

In 1987 the United States Supreme Court released a ruling on a state law in Louisiana. It was a decision reached after quiet deliberations in the Court chambers, a stark contrast to the sensational Scopes' Monkey Trial in Tennessee in the 1920s (see Exhibit 6.5), although the basic issue was the same. The 1987 Court struck down a state law requiring that science lessons about evolution also include "creation science," the theory based on a literal interpretation of the early chapters of the Bible that describe the creation of the universe. A 7–2 majority decided that the law was an attempt to advance a religious viewpoint and violated the First Amendment separation of church and state. This long-standing debate over religious beliefs emphasizes the difficulties of defining the schools' proper role in the socialization process in a complex society.

The Mass Media

Virtually no one in modern industrial society is beyond the reach of the mass media—television, radio, magazines, and newspapers. Television is by far the most pervasive of all forms of mass media, not only in the United States, but in many other nations as well. The average four-year-old in the United States spends more than three hours each day watching television,[20] and by the late 1980s, a television set was turned on in American homes for an average of seven hours and twelve minutes per day.[21]

Many Americans depend on their television set as a major source of entertainment (movies, drama and comedy shows, and sporting events). They also watch to learn about their world and community (local and network news broadcasts, prime-time documentaries). Viewers can garner knowledge about consumer products from commercials and can obtain religious instruction from television evangelists. And with the expansion of cable and satellite broadcasts in recent years, television also has emerged as a mechanism for participating in auctions and shopping. In fact, many television viewers spend more time interacting with a television set than they do with any other single person or group—more than with parents, teachers, spouses, or employers. A logical outgrowth of this phenomenon is the concern that television has come to replace meaningful social contacts with family and peers.

SOCIAL INDICATOR

Average Television Viewing Time per Week

Age	Men (hours:minutes)	Women (hours:minutes)
18–34	23:54	29:32
35–54	28:26	32:34
55+	39:14	43:58

Source: 1987 Nielson Report on Television.

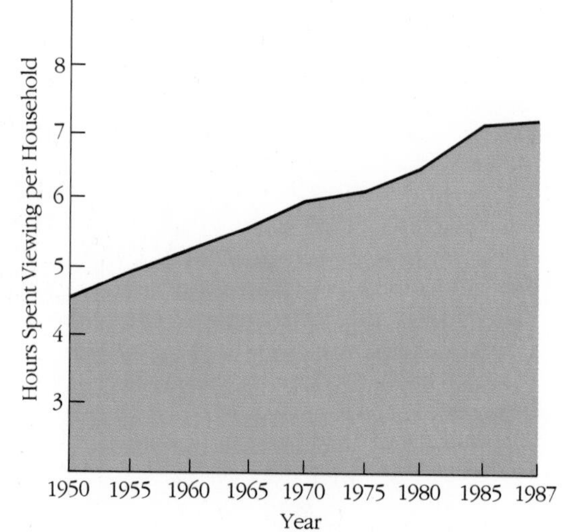

Sources: *U. S. News and World Report,* February 6, 1984; Television Bureau of Advertising; Television Information Office, 1986; 1987 Nielsen Report on Television. Copyright © 1987 Nielsen Media Research.

It is relatively easy to document the time spent viewing television, but it is more difficult to measure the impact these hours have on people. It appears that television does indeed have the power to influence intellectual skills. One study has demonstrated that six-year-olds who are heavy viewers tend to be more visually oriented, have poorer reading skills than less frequent viewers, and exhibit speech patterns lacking in the use of adjectives and adverbs.[22] Similarly, other studies have suggested that while bright children learn more from television than their less-gifted counterparts, whatever is learned by either group tends to be incidental and generally limited.[23]

Perhaps the most controversial issue associated with mass-media socialization is the debate over the impact of television violence. Television unquestionably portrays a considerable level of interpersonal violence. Some act of violence is the central theme in virtually all

Exhibit 6.5 **Sidelights on American Culture**

The Great Monkey Trial

One of the more curious and notable cases in the annals of criminal justice history occurred more than a half century ago in the remote mountain town of Dayton, Tennessee, a community of less than 2,000 persons some one hundred miles southeast of Nashville. The accused was 24-year-old John Thomas Scopes, a high-school teacher charged with a relatively minor criminal offense in violation of a Tennessee statute. The Scopes case caught the attention of the entire world, and today it is still considered by many to be among the country's most famous criminal trials.

Booksellers stand outside the courtroom of the Scopes Trial, 1925.

At the root of *Tennessee v. Scopes* was a movement of religious conservativism that had emerged during the first decade of the twentieth century in parts of the South and Midwest. This conservative movement was a reaction to a developing liberal theology that was attempting to recast Christian teaching in light of the scientific and historic thought of the time. By 1909, those who saw the orthodox truths of Christianity to be in danger organized a protest against the new "modernists" in a twelve-volume publication called *The Fundamentals.* In this work, five points of doctrine were set forth as *fundamental:* the Virgin birth, the physical resurrection of Christ, his substitutional atonement on the Cross, the physical second-coming of Christ, and the *total* infallibility of the Holy Scriptures. Those who believed in the strict letter of the Bible and refused to accept any teachings, including those of science and philosophy, which seemed to conflict with it, began in 1921 to call themselves Fundamentalists. They came primarily from the Baptists and Presbyterians, but many came from other Protestant denominations as well. The modernists, in contrast, tried to reconcile their beliefs with scientific thought—to discard that which was out of date, to retain what was essential and intellectually respectable, and generally to mediate between Christianity and the skeptical spirit of the age.

During the early 1920s, Fundamentalist politicians introduced bills into the legislatures of nearly half the states that were designed to forbid the teaching of Charles Darwin's theory of evolution. These efforts failed in most states, but in Tennessee, Oklahoma, and Mississippi, the Fundamentalists fully succeeded in writing their anachronistic views into law. The Tennessee legislature, dominated by Fundamentalists, approved a bill known as the Butler Act, which specifically provided that

> it shall be unlawful for any teacher in any of the universities, normals [colleges of education] and all other public schools of the State, which are supported in whole or in part by the public

(continued)

Exhibit 6.5 (continued)

school funds of the State, to teach any theory that denies the story of the Divine creation of man as taught in the Bible, and to teach instead that man has descended from a lower order of animals.

This statement sets the scene for the Scopes trial, which pitted the beliefs of religious fundamentalism against the principles of scientific modernism.

Shortly after the new Tennessee law had become official, the American Civil Liberties Union began agitating for a test case. They questioned the constitutionality of legislation that prohibited the teaching of evolution. After some persuasion, John T. Scopes, a biology instructor at the local Dayton, Tennessee, high school, volunteered for the challenge. It was during the late spring of 1925, and after only a few lectures on evolution, young Scopes was arrested for "undermining the peace and dignity of the State."

Attorney General A. T. Stewart of the Eighteenth Judicial Circuit of Tennessee was in charge of the prosecution. Well known to the local judiciary as a shrewd courtroom lawyer, Stewart was also an impassioned rabble-rousing orator. A number of local attorneys who had volunteered their services without pay also were attached to the state's case as lawyers *pro hac vice* (for this occasion). When the eminent statesman William Jennings Bryan offered to assist in the prosecution, what might have been only a minor criminal case in a rural county court suddenly became an international media event. At the time, Bryan was a distinguished figure in the minds of most Americans. He had been a member of the U.S. House of Representatives, the Democratic nominee for the U.S. presidency three times, and President Woodrow Wilson's Secretary of State. After his retirement from politics he had become a chief spokesman for the Fundamentalist movement, drafting legislative resolutions banning the teaching of Darwinian theory in public-school systems.

With Bryan's appearance in the case, the ACLU secured for Scopes the services of three attorneys, including the acclaimed Clarence Seward Darrow. As a defense lawyer, Darrow's abilities were considered unparalleled. His reputation had reached national proportions in 1924, when he represented Nathan Leopold and Richard Loeb in a Chicago courtroom. Although both Leopold and Loeb had been convicted and sentenced to terms of life plus 99 years for kidnapping and murder, Darrow's courtroom approaches, including the presentation of novel forms of evidence based on psychiatric examinations, had been viewed as unique for the time.

In the minds of the public the Scopes trial was characterized as a battle between religious conservativism on the one hand and twentieth-century skepticism on the other. As the day of the trial approached, revivalists of every sort flocked to Dayton, ready to defend their faith against the onslaught of "science" and "foreigners," yet at the same time curious to know what evolutionary theory was really all about. The hearings convened amidst a circus atmosphere of hot dog and lemonade vendors, booksellers, hundreds of newspaper reporters, photographers, Western Union telegraph operators, and more than 30,000 curiosity seekers. Worldwide attention focused on a small Tennessee town.

What followed was a most peculiar and bitter trial. Referred to in the media as the Scopes "monkey trial," it began on July 10, with a heated denouncement of evolutionary theory by Attorney General Stewart. He called it an "insidious doctrine" that was "undermining the faith of Tennessee's children and robbing them of their chance of eternal life." Bryan charged that Darrow's only purpose in accepting the case was to slur the Bible, and Darrow spoke of his opponent's position as simply "fool religion." The litigation continued for days, with little accomplished in terms of legal precedent.

On the afternoon of July 20, the trial finally approached its climax when the defense requested that William Jennings Bryan be placed on the stand as an expert on the Bible. Bryan consented. Popular historian Frederick Lewis Allen has described the setting:

So great was the crowd that afternoon that the judge had decided to move the court outdoors, to a platform built against the courthouse under the maple trees. Benches were set out before it. The reporters sat on the benches, on the ground, anywhere, and scribbled their stories. On the outskirts of the seated crowd a throng stood in the hot sunlight which streamed down through the trees. And on the platform sat the shirt-sleeved Clarence Darrow, a Bible on his knee, and put the Fundamentalist champion through one of the strangest examinations which ever took place in a court of law.

Soaring to awesome heights of hyperbole, Bryan declared that the Bible *must* be taken literally. Preaching fire and brimstone, he asserted that only those who believed in the letter of the Scriptures could ever be saved. What then followed was a savage encounter. Darrow asked Bryan about Jonah and the whale, Joshua and the sun, the date of the Great Flood, and the significance of the Tower of Babel. Bryan affirmed his belief that the world was created in 4004 B.C.; that it had taken the Lord but six days; that the Flood occurred around 2348 B.C.; that Eve had literally been fashioned out of Adam's rib; that the Tower of Babel was directly responsible for the diversity of languages in the world; that Joshua had moved the sun; and that a "big fish" had swallowed Jonah. He had fallen into Darrow's trap; it had quickly become clear that the naive religious faith of the Fundamentalists could not face reason as prosecutor. Bryan was laughed off the witness stand by a hooting audience. Several days later, humiliated and morose at what was an absurd end to his remarkable career, Bryan died suddenly of a heart attack.

Clarence Darrow reviews mail at the trial.

In the end, the presiding judge expunged Bryan's testimony from the record and barred Clarence Darrow from placing any scientific evidence before the jury. Scopes was convicted and fined $100. On appeal to the Tennessee Supreme Court, the antievolution law was upheld, but Scopes was exonerated on a technicality, thus preventing further appeal to the United States Supreme Court.

In theory, Fundamentalism had won. The law stood. But in reality, the conservative religious movement and the Tennessee courts and legislature had suffered a crushing defeat. Observers everywhere viewed the trial with amazement, wondering how long such ignorance would continue to control the Tennessee judicial system. It appeared too that there was another defeat as well—one involving democracy. As columnist Walter Lippman put it at the time, the people of Tennessee had used the power of democracy to prevent their own children from learning, "not merely the doctrine of evolution, but the spirit and method by which learning is possible." In so doing, he continued, they had revealed the "deep destructive confusion" that lay within the dogma of democratic majority rule.

In the decades that followed, the Scopes "monkey trial" has not been forgotten. Hundreds of books and articles have been written about the events that took place in Dayton, Tennessee, during July, 1925. As for the issue that initiated the Scopes trial, it never passed into obscurity. Even in the 1980s discussions continue as to whether both biblical and scientific explanations of creation should be taught in public-school classrooms.

SOURCES: Frederick Lewis Allen, *Only Yesterday: An Informal History of the 1920s* (New York: Harper & Row, 1931); Leslie H. Allen, *Bryan and Darrow of Dayton* (New York: Arthur Lee, 1925); L. Sprague de Camp, *The Great Monkey Trial* (Garden City: Doubleday, 1968); Louis Gasper, *The Fundamentalist Movement* (Paris: Mouton, 1963); Ronald Steel, *Walter Lippman and the American Century* (Boston: Little, Brown, 1980).

Does watching violence on television foster aggressive behavior, or are aggressive people drawn to violent shows?

police or private detective programs. Video heroes repeatedly resort to fighting or killing to settle even the most common of personal disputes. One group of researchers has estimated that between the ages of five and fifteen, the typical youthful viewer might witness the violent demise of some 13,400 characters.[24] The question is whether exposure to a constant diet of violence socializes viewers into patterns of aggression.

A variety of evidence suggests that exposure to violence may indeed have a measurable impact. One of the more ambitious studies targeted several hundred third graders, focusing on their preferences for violent forms of media and soliciting judgments of their aggressiveness from their friends.[25] Those who favored violent programs were considered more aggressive than their peers who liked less intense television. When the researchers contacted these subjects ten years later and counted their actual involvement in violent episodes, they concluded that preferences for violent media as children were predictive of aggressive conduct as young adults. Other studies have found that this pattern is the same for both girls and boys, and the findings have been reconfirmed by research in such diverse societies as those in Poland, Finland, and Australia.[26] Apparently the pattern is interactive, with television violence fostering aggressive behavior, and aggressive individuals turning to more and more violent programming.

The influence of television interacts with the other agents of socialization. As a general rule, parents who use physical punishment to discipline their children, and who express disappointment with them, have the most aggressive children. Moreover, aggressive children have less satisfactory social relationships with their peers, in part because they are aggressive. They spend more time alone watching violent television, which serves to affirm their own behavior.[27] And finally, there is the issue of the socializing effects of pornography as a form of readily available mass media (see Exhibit 6.6).

In the final analysis, socialization is a complex process. A growing, maturing individual interacts with many different people and groups that teach (directly or indirectly, intentionally or unintentionally) and define social expectations. At the same time, responses shape self-concepts. Some agents of socialization are more salient than others at different points in the life cycle, setting different or even contradictory standards.

SOCIALIZATION THROUGH THE LIFE CYCLE

The learning processes of infants and children, which occur through contacts with the family, peers, school, and the media, are generally referred to as **primary socialization.** This early learning involves the acquisition of fundamental skills—acquiring language and the ability to communicate, relating to others, understanding the fundamental values and norms of society, developing a self-concept—that are necessary for social functioning. Yet socialization does not end with childhood. Life is measured by a series of predictable transitions—formal education, embarking on a career, getting married, becoming a parent, and ultimately retiring—that require adjustments and reorientations.

Cumulative and Anticipatory Socialization

Socialization is a never-ending process. Life continues to impose the need to move into new roles, join new groups, relate to new people, and confront new sets of expectations about appropriate behavior. In many situations people experience **cumulative socialization,** when transitions build on existing social skills and abilities, such as advancing from one grade to the next or moving from one community to another. Such transitions are relatively routine and relatively easily accomplished by building on knowledge accumulated earlier in life. On entering college, students will likely encounter a wider range of peers, teachers with higher expectations, and more choices and freedom of movement. Although higher education may involve more work and tougher competition, the basic abilities and study skills learned in earlier experiences remain useful.

To cushion the impact of transitions, most people develop methods of dealing with new situations in advance. This process of preparing for new situations is termed **anticipatory socialization.** Among students leaving the elementary grades, for example, anticipatory socialization may take the form of selecting clothing deemed appropriate for high school. Students and parents may debate the *absolute* need to use the family car, for after all, as far as many high-school students are concerned, public transportation is simply out of the question. At the same time, the process may also involve observing high-school students, attempting to see how their behavior differs from that of mere eighth graders.

In short, anticipatory socialization occurs in a variety of forms and is not limited to youths entering high school. College seniors may participate in volunteer work or internships to make employment contacts or develop certain work skills; couples may live together for the sake of better understanding the demands of marriage; pregnant women and their husbands may accumulate child-rearing manuals, participate in birthing classes, or attend child-care workshops and lectures in anticipation of becoming parents.

Resocialization

Other transitions can be more dramatic, requiring that the individual abandon established patterns of behavior and adopt others. The shifts from student to employee, or from single person to spouse embrace dramatic transitions, and involve **resocialization,** the process of learning new roles that simultaneously requires the surrendering of old ones. For example, few of the experiences that average civilians encounter prepare them for the realities of military life. To survive as a soldier, an individual must learn a role that includes radically different norms, rules, and self-concepts. Other transitions also require radical changes—entering a religious order, losing a spouse, joining the ranks of the unemployed, becoming physically disabled, or being sentenced to a penitentiary.

Resocialization in Total Institutions

A number of the situations in which resocialization occurs are voluntary, while others are coerced. The most dramatic forms of resocialization occur in what sociologist Erving Goffman has referred to as **total institutions**—places that furnish barriers to social interchange with the world at large, isolating and dominating individuals' lives.[28] Prisons, the military, and monasteries are total institutions. They embrace structures that control virtually all aspects of their subjects' lives. The process of resocialization in a total institution progresses through several well-defined phases, during which significant social and psychological transformations take place.

Social and Physical Separation Prison inmates are locked away behind steel bars and high concrete walls; military recruits are sent to training camps; religious novitiates are confined to cloisters. The fences, walls, and bars are there not only to keep people in, but also to keep the rest of the world at bay. The goal is simple and direct—to segregate "subjects" from outside influences. Subjects of total institutions are isolated from friends, relatives, and any others who might represent competing loyalties, and the "managers" of total institutions censor mail and phone contacts, and limit visitors.

Suppression of Prior Statuses After the subjects have been effectively isolated from "contamination" by

SOCIAL INDICATOR

The Numbers of Military Personnel as "Subjects" in Total Institutions

Country	Number in Armed Forces	Armed Forces Personnel per 1,000 Population
China	4,100,000	4.0
U.S.S.R.	3,800,000	14.0
U.S.	**2,222,000**	**9.5**
Vietnam	1,221,000	21.4
India	1,120,000	1.5
Turkey	824,000	16.8
North Korea	784,000	41.3
South Korea	622,000	15.2
France	578,000	10.5
Italy	498,000	8.9

Source: Ruth Leger Sivard, *World Military and Social Expenditures* (1986); Carl Haub and Mary Mederios Kent, *1986 World Population Data Sheet*, (Washington, DC: Population Reference Bureau, 1986).

Exhibit 6.6

Types & Stereotypes

The Dilemma of Pornography, Violence, and the First Amendment

Rape and sexual violence directed against women constitute a social problem of major proportions in the United States, and the findings of a public opinion poll conducted in 1985 suggested that a significant number of Americans believe that sexually explicit movies, magazines, and books actually *cause* violence against women. For example:

Sexually Explicit Materials Can	Percent Agreeing
Lead to a Breakdown of Public Morals	67%
Lead Some People to Commit Rape or Sexual Violence	73

Source: *The Newsweek Poll*, March 1985.

Former Attorney General Edwin Meese presents the final report of his pornography commission under the unblinking gaze of a bare-breasted Department of Justice statue.

One of the difficulties with such a finding is that little agreement exists concerning the definition of pornography among those responding to the survey. While three-fourths labeled X-rated films as pornographic, one-third of those surveyed also held that simple female nudity in a PG or R-rated motion picture was also pornographic. Survey respondents reached greater consensus in agreeing that homosexual acts in magazines qualified as pornography, with almost 90% sharing a mutual opinion. In each case men were less likely to identify sexual material as pornographic, which reflects differences in socialization experiences among women and men in American society.

An even more complex dilemma is the question of censorship in a democratic society. The First Amendment to the Constitution of the United States guarantees that "Congress shall make no law . . . abridging the freedom of speech or of the press." Most sexually explicit media have been interpreted by both state and federal courts to fall under the First Amendment protection. So does the government have the right or obligation to ban pornography in some instances, in all instances, or not at all? Interestingly, while almost half of the men and nearly two-thirds of the women surveyed felt that pornography incited violence, 78% nevertheless supported the First Amendment safeguard that people should have the right to buy pornography, even if it *is* harmful.

The final issue in this dilemma is whether or not there is evidence confirming that pornography is a cause of violence against women. During the late 1960s the Commission on Obscenity and Pornography focused on this very question, reviewing all of the available research, conducting studies, and hearing the views of all segments of society that had an opinion on the matter. One study of college undergraduates found that both males and females were sexually aroused by sexually explicit films. Eighty percent of the men who watched the films reported partial or full arousal, and 86% of the women also experienced sensations of arousal. However, a *satiation effect* was found too, in that repeated exposure to the films diminished sexual excitement. Based on this and numerous other studies, the report of the commission concluded:

> If a case is to be made against "pornography" . . . it will have to be made on grounds other than demonstrated effects of a damaging personal or social nature. Empirical research designed to clarify [the issue] has found no reliable evidence to date that exposure to explicit sexual materials plays a significant role in the causation of delinquent or criminal sexual behavior among youth or adults.

When antipornography zeal spread across the United States during the 1980s, the Attorney General's Commission on Pornography, chaired by Edwin Meese III, was organized for another look at the purported link between portrayals of explicit sex and violence. After listening to testimony from witnesses from across the nation and reviewing more than 4,500 films, magazines, and books, the commission confessed that it had no better definition of pornography than the one offered years earlier by the late Supreme Court Justice Potter Stewart: "I know it when I see it." Moreover, although Attorney General Meese proposed an all-out war on pornography, his own commission had failed to provide any compelling evidence of the very link that it had set out to establish.

SOURCES: *Report of the Attorney General's Commission on Pornography* (Washington, DC: U.S. Government Printing Office, 1986); *Report of the Commission on Obscenity and Pornography* (Washington, DC: U.S. Government Printing Office, 1970).

the outside world, the process of stripping away old statuses commences. Goffman has used the phrase **personal identity kit** to describe the various ways in which people decorate their bodies to express their individuality—clothing, hairstyles, jewelry, and other adornments. But these distinctive decorations are all removed in total institutions. Convicts, priests, and soldiers wear identical, monotonous uniforms. Formerly nuns wore black-and-white habits, which generally suppressed their sexual identity. On military bases, barbers cut away the stylish hair of new recruits, and supply personnel issue the same nondescript uniforms to every recruit who files past. But identity kits are also more subtle. Uniqueness and individuality are evidenced in speech and posture as well. Military recruits are forced to walk with an exaggerated erectness and to speak loudly and with pronounced formality. The "lock-step" was developed in American penitentiaries years ago to make supervision easier. In this bizarre marching formation prisoners were required to line up behind one another with their hands on the shoulders of the person in front. The line moved rapidly with prisoners shuffling their feet in unison without lifting them from the ground, their eyes focused on the nearest guard.

Possibly the most intimate and unique aspect of the personal identity kit is an individual's name. Yet even these are stripped away to some degree in total institutions. Military recruits are addressed by rank (private), or some more general and derogatory term such as *swab, cootie, dud,* or *muck.* In prisons, inmates are assigned numbers. In both situations, the purpose of such depersonalizing techniques is to remind subjects that the roles they played in the outside world no longer have any relevance. In addition, the cold impersonality with which civilian statuses are rendered obsolete also reminds subjects of the power of the total institution.

Introduction of New Norms Total institutions introduce and enforce a new system of norms and values. A drill sergeant once explained Marine Corps rules to a group of new recruits on their first day at Paris Island Training Camp as follows:

> Recruits must stand at attention at all times. Recruits will not eyeball. Recruits will double time everywhere. Recruits will do nothing without permission; they will not speak or swat bugs or wipe sweat or faint without permission. Recruits will call everyone, except other recruits, "Sir." Recruits will never use the word "you" because "you" is a female sheep, and there are no ewes on Paris Island.[29]

Because total institutions are able to control rewards and apply punishments, they bring about significant changes in self-concepts. By the time Marine Corps basic training is completed, there are few recruits who still think of themselves as anything but "Marines." To use a concept introduced in Chapter 4, they have adopted the *master status* of "Marine." For most, that status survives long after they have left the military and returned to civilian life.

Many nuns live in total institutions, isolated from the larger society.

Resocialization for Disability

A tragic consequence of the many automobile accidents, shootings, and sports injuries that plague contemporary American society is the fact that thousands of people must confront the reality of permanent physical disability. Particularly catastrophic in this respect is paraplegia—complete paralysis below the waist.

Prior to World War II, a majority of the victims of such trauma did not survive, but more recent medical advances have significantly improved survival rates. Successful rehabilitation involves lengthy physical therapy, but before that can happen the victims must confront their disability and abandon the self-concept of "physical normality." This adjustment is an instance of dramatic resocialization. Sociologist Betty Cogswell followed the treatment experiences of 36 young paraplegics over a five-year period as they faced the realities of their new social role. Despite individual differences, each passed through identifiable stages, ranging from the abandonment of prior roles to the integration of totally new roles.[30]

The commonality of subjects in a total institution is apparent among these Marine recruits.

Abandoning Prior Roles The first step toward the rehabilitation of paraplegics is their psychological acceptance that the condition is irreversible. In terms of resocialization, this step is a matter of abandoning the self-concept of being "normal." However, the initial response in the subjects that Cogswell studied was denial accompanied by severe depression. Patients resisted accepting the reality of their conditions, for none could envision a style of life that was not organized around unfettered physical movement. No doubt they were also disturbed by the stigma of life in a wheelchair. Most vacillated, shifting between acceptance and denial of their new identity. Hospital personnel noted long periods of withdrawal as patients wrestled with their past and future. This step is the most difficult one; surrendering the old role means giving up that last hope of recovery—not a simple step, but one that is necessary for rehabilitation.

Identifying with New Roles Abandoning the role of physical normality is merely the first step in a long resocialization process. Unless patients accept a new social role of "disabled" or "handicapped," which means physical independence under new conditions, the only remaining alternative is a bed-ridden life. For the paraplegics in Cogswell's study, this was anything but easy. None had handicapped friends, and their experiences following their accidents were primarily those of helplessness and dependence.

Acquiring the Skills of the New Role Recently disabled persons must master two interrelated sets of new skills. First are the physical skills, some of which are entirely new (maneuvering wheelchairs or artificial limbs). Others require a restructuring of previously routine tasks (eating, bathing, and attending to other personal needs). In one sense, learning the physical skills is the easiest part of the resocialization process, for these can be practiced and refined in the sheltered and supportive hospital environment, surrounded by staff, friends, and family.

The second set of new skills are the social skills, which can be developed and mastered only in the world beyond the hospital. As the patients prepare to venture back into society, their major concern centers on the stigma of being "disabled" and of adjusting to how people will react to them. Consequently, many paraplegics become preoccupied with the problems of physical accessability—not just how to get to and into places, but also how to escape from them if things become too unpleasant. Open, uncrowded sidewalks are considered the most attractive locales. Less pleasant circumstances characterize those situations that require moving from the wheelchair to some other seat, such as a dentist's chair. And finally, the least desirable are situations that require the physical aid of others (stairs, getting on planes and other forms of public transportation). Importantly, the expansion of a paraplegic's world involves experimenting with ever-widening horizons. Again, they must develop self-confidence or their world will remain severely limited in scope.

Integrating the Role The ultimate goal in the resocialization of paraplegics is the resumption of a conventional life in which "handicapped" is merely one of many relevant roles. The goal includes resuming work, reestablishing social relationships, picking up family roles, and generally being reintegrated into the community.

During this phase of resocialization, social relationships undergo change. Paraplegics generally lose contact with the people who were their friends prior to their accidents. And this break is typically a matter of mutual disengagement. Friends are attached to old ideas of who a person was and often find it difficult to relate to an old friend in a new role. Similarly, paraplegics find it formidable to learn and "try out" their new roles before an audience of people who knew them in previous roles. Thus, many friendships wither away by a kind of unspoken yet shared agreement, almost never to be resumed. A similar phenomenon frequently has been observed among people who experience long-term unemployment.[31]

In time, new friendships develop, but paraplegics generally experiment first with people of lower social status than themselves—lower social class, younger, or

Children learn the difference between reality and the fantasy world of the media by watching the filming of a scene from a television program.

less physically attractive individuals. In a very large sense, these new friends also have a social handicap. Eventually, social relations with people of equal or higher social status are formed. If the process of resocialization is successful, the disabled role will become only one of many relevant self-concepts.

SOCIALIZATION AND APPLIED SOCIOLOGY

Over the years sociologists and other social scientists have accumulated considerable information on the process of socialization. They have developed a better understanding of the roles of various agents—parents, peers, school, and the media—in the overall process. This increased knowledge, in turn, has led to a variety of attempts to neutralize the impact of antisocial influences. In a recent controversial development, for example, sociologists have become involved in *reversing* socialization processes. The earliest applications emerged in the post-Korean War period as the military sought to overcome the systematic indoctrination of American prisoners of war with anti-American propaganda (often called "brainwashing"). More recently, distressed parents have turned to the same types of specialists in the hope of retrieving children from the grip of exotic religious cults (see Exhibit 6.7).

Similarly, because concrete research evidence shows that television can influence behavior and attitudes, especially aggression, researchers have explored ways of interrupting the cycle of television violence and aggressive behavior. One effective approach reveals the world of television to those who have been adversely affected by it as largely fantasy and illusion. Since more aggressive, more frequent television watchers are definitely more likely to believe that television is real, researchers have had some success by teaching them otherwise. For example, in one study children who engaged in high levels of violent behavior were taught how sound and visual effects are used to create the impression of violence in television fights. Four months later, there was a notable reduction in violent behavior. Such a simple technique cannot neutralize the impact of television on all groups of children, but it is one mechanism that parents and teachers can use to counteract the negative effects of violent programming.[32]

Knowledge about socialization also has been put to practical use to structure primary socialization. During

Exhibit 6.7

Applied Sociology

Cult Indoctrination and Deprogramming as Resocialization

Cults are religious movements characterized by new and perhaps unconventional spiritual ideas and practices.* Typically, cults are shepherded by charismatic leaders who expect a total commitment from their members. Cults that have made news headlines in recent years include Jim Jones' People's Temple, Sun Myung Moon's Unification Church, the Hare Krishnas, and the followers of Bhagwan Rajneesh.

Religious cults received little public notice in the United States until recently. The precipitating event occurred in 1978 at what has become known simply as "Jonestown." Jonestown was a primitive encampment in the jungles of Guyana—a small nation on the northern coast of South America—to which the Reverend Jim Jones of the People's Temple had led his American followers for the purpose of establishing a pure, new society. Among other activities, Jones conducted rituals of proclaimed "revolutionary suicide." Through brainwashing and other forms of coercion, Jones apparently convinced his followers that mass suicide would give them immortality. In 1978, the ritual became real, and 900 members of the People's Temple perished—either murdered or influenced to commit suicide.

Studies of cult activities conducted after the Jonestown tragedy indicate that many cult members become totally committed to their new religions by means of a five-phase process of aggressive conversion. In the first stage, after cult proselytizers have identified likely targets—the seemingly lonely and footloose, runaways and knapsack-carrying transients, or anyone else who appears to be beseiged with self-doubt—a potent face-to-face encounter is orchestrated. In this encounter, known as "love-bombing," the cult representative engages the potential recruit in conversation, offering acceptance, friendship, and understanding. The intent is to win the potential convert's trust and to generate the desire to continue the acquaintance. An invitation is often offered to attend a lecture, to come to dinner, or to participate in a retreat.

In the second stage, the love-bombing becomes more intense. As a guest at some isolated camp that may resemble an idyllic paradise where everyone loves and accepts everyone else at first sight, the potential recruit is welcomed as a member of a long-lost family. And there is indeed a familylike atmosphere in which all activities, even sleeping, are done in a group. Moreover, the guest encounters a strong emotional experience of community among peers.

In the third phase, after "guests" appear ready for conversion, they are isolated from their past lives—totally cut off from all emotional ties and physically separated from home, school, family, work, and peers. This isolation is symbolic as well. Cult novitiates are typically stripped of their names, belongings, and personal identities, after which they are christened with new names.

In the fourth stage, guilt and humiliation are used to convince converts to dismember their former "selves." The purpose is to force them to surrender their past lives.

In the final stage, the converts are "born again" through rituals of social death and rebirth, at which point they accept their new identities and world views.

Conversion to a cult's membership and way of life is a process of resocialization, as is *deprogramming*—the casting off of cult beliefs. Conducted primarily by sociologists, psychologists, and other behavioral scientists, deprogramming seeks to counteract conversion and indoctrination through a step-by-step process of reversal. The individual is reacquainted with his or her past and former identity—family, friends and peers, intimate relationships, objects and locations, and former interests and feelings.

Although deprogramming might appear to be a simple matter of reintegration into society, such is not the case. As deprogrammer Willa Appel once commented:

> Coming out of a cult is a difficult and protracted process. It varies, naturally, from person to person and from cult to cult. . . . The amount of time needed for rehabilitation seems to correspond directly to the amount of time spent in intensive ritual and indoctrination exercises. . . . It has been observed, too, that people belonging to cults that use rapid conversion can often be "snapped out" with relative ease, while with cults that employ a gradual conversion, getting out is also gradual.

*Cults are examined in detail in Chapter 12.

SOURCES: Willa Appel, *Cults in America: Programmed for Paradise* (New York: Holt, Rinehart and Winston, 1983); John G. Clark, Michael D. Langone, Roger C. B. Daly, and Robert E. Schecter, *Destructive Cult Conversion: Theory, Research, and Treatment* (Boston: American Family Foundation, Center on Destructive Cultism, 1981); Marcia R. Rudin, "The Cult Phenomenon: Fad or Fact," *New York University Review of Law and Social Change*, 9 (1979–1980), pp. 17–32.

the early post–World War II years, a new personality appeared on the American scene. His name was Benjamin Spock, and he offered parents *The Common Sense Book of Baby and Child Care.*[33] First published in 1946, the Spock baby book, simply referred to at the time as "Spock," ultimately sold over 30 million copies—more than any book ever printed other than the Bible. Spock served to guide a whole generation of parents through the rigors of childbirth and child rearing, primarily because of its popularity with post-war young adults who differed from their parents in two important ways. First, many were geographically mobile, cut off from their parent's advice for dealing with children. Second, post-war prosperity had significantly transformed American society, making the lessons of their depression-age parents less relevant. What Spock did was to use social science research to assist parents in the child socialization process.

In the years since the initial appearance of Spock's work, countless books, manuals, courses, videotapes, films, and demonstration projects have appeared, all designed to bring sociological and social psychological insights to bear on the child-rearing process. One of the most ambitious efforts in this respect was launched in 1978 by the Center for Parent Education to provide parents with access to research data and expert advice.[34] A key finding of the Center's project was that new middle-class parents often make the same mistake that underlies the Tarzan and Romulus and Remus legends. These young parents assume that children become civilized on their own. Furthermore, while parents may feel that the best strategy is to allow their children to behave without setting limits, the Center's findings demonstrated that children develop better social skills when limits are set on their behavior.

SUMMARY

Infants are born with the capacity to become human beings, but that potential will only be realized if they are exposed to other humans who can teach them fundamental skills and abilities. Socially isolated children display almost none of the attributes normally thought of as basic human traits, clearly illustrating that human socialization is a process that will not spontaneously occur in the absence of meaningful social contacts.

Socialization is a two-fold process. First, it involves learning the abilities necessary to function effectively in society. Among the most fundamental to later development are simple motor skills—walking, standing—and language. At the same time, individuals also must acquire the social heritage of norms, values, and beliefs of their society. This process is largely one of learning social expectations.

Through social interaction individuals also develop a self, an awareness of themselves as distinctive human beings. In addition, people develop individual self-concepts, images or perceptions of their attributes, capacities, and abilities. The work of sociologists Charles Horton Cooley and George Herbert Mead emphasizes that self-concepts emerge from the responses of the people around us. We observe and interpret the behavior of others, and mentally place ourselves in the roles of others in order to "see" ourselves as we imagine others view us.

Debate over the relative importance of heredity versus environment in social development has had a long history. This debate touches on issues such as the genetic inheritance of behavioral traits and the presence of "instincts." One current version of this issue is termed "sociobiology." Most contemporary sociologists take the position that both biology and socialization experiences influence social development, interacting in subtle and complex ways.

Social development is the outcome of the interplay of many different agents of socialization. Parents and family, peers and friends, teachers and schools are the most influential elements during the early years of life. The pervasive power of the media cannot be underestimated either. Television is especially important because it has the capacity to teach and widen horizons beyond the immediate social world, but also harbors the potential to foster undesirable social traits.

As people move into adulthood, preparation for new educational, occupational, and social roles builds on and elaborates prior socialization. Some transitions, such as the one from high school to college, are facilitated by what has gone before, but others, such as that found in going from student to employee or single to married, may involve quite significant resocialization. Each year, scores of individuals undergo very radical forms of resocialization for totally new roles. Most resocialization occurs within "total institutions" that have the capacity to reshape dramatically behavior and self-concepts.

KEY TERMS/CONCEPTS

anticipatory socialization
cumulative socialization
ego
feral children
generalized other
I
id
instincts
looking-glass self
me
peer group
personal identity kit
primary socialization
psychoanalytic theory
resocialization
role taking
self
self-concepts
significant others
socialization
sociobiology
superego
total institutions

SUGGESTED READINGS

Philip Aries, *Centuries of Childhood: A Social History of Family Life* (New York: Alfred A. Knopf, 1961). A noted social historian examines the changing concepts of the ideal child in different societies at different points in history, revealing how socialization within the family has been affected by religion, industrialization, and other external factors.

Martin Barker, *The New Racism* (Frederick, MD: University Publications of America, 1981). A critical examination of sociobiology and related theories, focusing on their potential use as modern forms of racism.

D. Pearl, L. Bouthilet, and J. Lazar, *Television and Behavior: Ten Years of Scientific Research and Implications for the Eighties* (Washington, DC: U.S. Government Printing Office, 1982). Two large volumes that attempt to summarize the mass of research on the effects of television on behavior, and suggest an agenda for the future.

Peter I. Rose (ed.), *Socialization and the Life Cycle* (New York: St. Martin's, 1979). A collection of papers that focus on socialization experiences at key points in the life cycle.

Edward O. Wilson, *Sociobiology: The New Synthesis* (Cambridge, MA: Harvard University Press, 1976). The original formulation of sociobiology, which has subsequently produced a wide variety of other studies and theories regarding the impact of biology on behavior.

Louis A. Zurcher, *The Mutable Self* (Beverly Hills: Sage, 1977). An analysis of several dimensions of self-concepts, along with a discussion of the capacity for humans to adapt and change.

DISCUSSION QUESTIONS

1. Based on the sociological insights of Cooley and Mead, is Philip Jose Farmer's thesis about Lord Greystoke plausible?
2. Is it possible that humans do indeed have "instincts"? If so, how would a sociologist go about measuring them, using the criteria of the scientific method?
3. People are exposed to many different agents of socialization in American society. How do these various agents complement and conflict with one another?
4. Students with brothers/sisters at home might want to compare the ways they are similar to/different from their siblings. What does such a comparison say about the nature versus nurture debate?
5. What does the concept of resocialization contribute to our understanding of the social barriers faced by accident victims undergoing rehabilitation?

NOTES

1. Philip José Farmer, *Tarzan Alive: A Definitive Biography of Lord Greystoke* (Garden City, NY: Doubleday, 1972).
2. There are numerous accounts of feral people in the professional and popular literature. See Roger W. Brown, "Feral and Isolated Man," in V. P. Gilbert (ed.), *Language* (New York: St. Martin's, 1972); Jean Itard, *The Wild Boy of Aveyron* (New York: Appleton-Century-Crofts, 1962, reprint of the 1801 original). An excellent review and summary of cases of feral children can be found in Lucien Malson, *Wolf Children and the Problem of Human Nature* (New York: Monthly Review, 1972).
3. Susan Curtis, *Genie: A Psycholinguistic Study of a Modern-Day "Wild Child"* (New York: Academic Press, 1977); Kingsley Davis, "Extreme Isolation of a Child," *American Journal of Sociology,* 45 (1940), pp. 554–64; Kingsley Davis, "A Final Note on a Case of Extreme Isolation," *American Journal of Sociology,* 52 (1947), pp. 432–37; Maya Pines, "The Civilizing of Genie," *Psychology Today,* 15 (September 1981), pp. 28–34.
4. Rene Spitz, "Hospitalism," *Psychoanalytic Study of the Child,* 1 (1945), pp. 53–72.

5. Harry Harlow and Margaret Harlow, "Social Deprivation in Monkeys," *Scientific American,* 207 (November 1962), pp. 137–47.
6. Charles Horton Cooley, *Human Nature and the Social Order* (New York: Schocken, 1964), p. 184.
7. George Herbert Mead, *Mind, Self, and Society* (Chicago: University of Chicago Press, 1934), pp. 134–59.
8. Harry Stack Sullivan, *The Interpersonal Theory of Psychiatry* (New York: W. W. Norton, 1953).
9. George Herbert Mead, *Mind, Self, and Society*, p. 159.
10. Sigmund Freud, "The Ego and the Id," *Standard Edition of the Complete Psychological Works of Sigmund Freud,* vol. 19 (London: Hogarth, 1923).
11. Erik H. Erikson, *Childhood and Society* (New York: W. W. Norton, 1950); Erik H. Erikson, *The Life Cycle Completed: A Review* (New York: W. W. Norton, 1982).
12. Wilfred Trotter, *Instincts of the Herd in Peace and War* (London: T. Fisher Unwin, 1920), pp. 191–92.
13. Edward O. Wilson, *Sociobiology: The New Synthesis* (Cambridge, MA: Harvard University Press, 1975), p. 4.
14. Richard J. Rose, Markku Koskenvous, Jaakko Kaprio, Seppo Sarna, and Heimo Langinvainio, "Shared Genes, Shared Experiences, and Similarity of Personality: Data from 14,288 Adult Finnish Co-Twins," *Journal of Personality and Social Psychology,* 54 (1988), pp. 161–71.
15. Zick Rubin, *Liking and Loving* (New York: Holt, Rinehart and Winston, 1973).
16. Judith Langlois and A. Chris Downes, "Mothers, Fathers, and Peers as Socialization Agents of Sex-Typed Behaviors in Young Children," *Child Development,* 51 (1980), pp. 1217–22.
17. Clyde C. Robinson and James T. Morris, "The Gender Stereotyped Nature of Christmas Toys," *Sex Roles,* 15 (1986), pp. 21–32.
18. See Victor Gecas, "Contexts of Socialization," in Morris Rosenberg and Ralph Turner (eds.), *Social Psychology* (New York: Basic Books, 1981), pp. 165–99.
19. James Youniss and Jacqueline Smoller, *Adolescent Relations with Mothers, Fathers, and Friends* (Chicago: University of Chicago Press, 1986).
20. National Institute of Mental Health, *Television and Behavior* (Washington, DC: U.S. Government Printing Office, 1982).
21. Melvin L. DeFleur and Everette C. Dennis, *Understanding Mass Communication,* 3rd ed. (Boston: Houghton Mifflin, 1989); *USA Today,* April 28, 1987, p. 1A.
22. Dorothy G. Singer, "A Time to Reexamine the Role of Television in Our Lives," *American Psychologist,* 38 (1981), pp. 815–16.
23. Sharon Lowery and Melvin L. De Fleur, *Milestones in Mass Communication Research* (New York: Longman, 1983), pp. 282–85.
24. T. B. Williams, M. L. Zebrack, and L. A. Joy, *Violence in Television Films and News* (Toronto: Queen's Printer, 1977).
25. Leonard D. Eron, L. Rowell Huesmann, Monroe M. Lefkowitz, and Leopold O. Walder, "Does Television Violence Cause Violence?" *American Psychologist,* 27 (April 1972), pp. 253–63.
26. Leonard D. Eron, "Parent-Child Interaction, Television and Violence, and Aggression of Children," *American Psychologist,* 37 (February 1982), pp. 197–211.
27. Leonard D. Eron, "Parent-Child Interaction."
28. Erving Goffman, *Asylums: Essays on the Social Situation of Mental Patients and Other Inmates* (Chicago: Aldine, 1961).
29. Steven Warner, "A Conscientous Objector at Paris Island," *Atlantic,* 229 (January 1972), p. 46.
30. Betty E. Cogswell, "Rehabilitation of the Paraplegic: Processes of Socialization," *Sociological Inquiry,* 37 (Winter 1967), pp. 11–26.
31. Douglas H. Powell and Jerry A. Jacobs, "Middle-Class Professionals Face Unemployment," *Trans-action,* 10 (May–June 1973), pp. 18–26.
32. Leonard D. Eron, "Prescription for the Reduction of Aggression," *American Psychologist,* 35 (March 1980), pp. 244–52.
33. Benjamin McLane Spock, *The Common Sense Book of Baby and Child Care* (New York: Simon and Schuster, 1946).
34. Michael K. Meyerhoff and Burton L. White, "Making the Grade as Parents," *Psychology Today,* 20 (September 1986), pp. 38–45.

Deviance and Crime: At Odds with Society

What if in New York, Chicago, Los Angeles, or the whole country for that matter, no deviants existed? Can you imagine what it would be like? At first glance, arriving at an answer would appear to be rather simple. Without question, the United States would certainly be a safer place in which to live and work. No thieves, murderers, rapists, or muggers would prowl our streets. People could walk about outdoors at any time of the day or night in complete security. No one would need locks, guard dogs, theft insurance, or any of those other devices that people use to protect their lives and property from criminals. Moreover, most communities would *look* different. No drunks would be sleeping in doorways, no junkies congregating in alleys, no hookers walking the streets or litterbugs decorating the landscape with trash. Also, the death rate would drop significantly. The drunk drivers who menace the nation's highways would be a thing of the past. People would obey traffic codes and adhere to safety laws and regulations. In short, if there were *no deviants*, there would be *no lawbreakers*, and society would indeed be a different place in which to live.

Eliminating all the lawbreakers would necessarily bring about profound changes in the structure and order of society, changes considerably more far-reaching than the few mentioned above. But is that all there is to it? Are criminals the only kinds of deviants? How about the retarded, or the eccentric, or the physically deformed? Are they deviants too? Are hermits and hobos, or strippers and nudists, or dwarfs and lesbians deviants? They are not criminals, but they are certainly *different.*

They differ from the norm, anyway. And if these people are deviants, whom do we include along with them? Are the very rich deviant because there are so few of them? Are rock singers deviants because many of them have such flamboyant life-styles? Are prison guards deviants because they work in what many believe to be a tainted profession? And taking all of this one step further, is the person who is considered deviant in one community viewed as a deviant elsewhere? When people wearing bathing suits walk across a nude beach, for example, are they the deviants?

Within this context, the focus shifts from crime and criminals to more complex questions. What is deviance? Who are the deviants? Is deviance something that is universal? Why do some people commit deviant acts while others do not? Is all deviant behavior criminal behavior, and conversely, is all criminal behavior deviant behavior? How do certain behaviors come to be defined as deviant? What are the effects of deviant behavior on a society? How do societies control their deviants?

Whereas this situation might be commonplace in some communities, it is unthinkable in others.

THE NATURE OF DEVIANCE

Apartheid is an Afrikaans term meaning "aparthood," and it denotes the official policy of racial segregation practiced in South Africa. The goal of apartheid is to deny blacks any political power, and the policy is implemented by legislation that controls places of residence, schools, universities, and recreational facilities, and prohibits mixed marriages. Apartheid practices are considered "racist" by most Americans and are violations of the law in all 50 states.

In England, the United States, and numerous other countries, persons seeking to obtain passage on a commercial aircraft generally wait their turn in a line at the ticket counter. In many parts of South America and the Middle East, however, the locals typically elbow their way to the front of the line in an effort to receive immediate service.

Homosexuality is regarded as conventional behavior for males in some communities, while in others it appears not only to be absent, but beyond imagination. Two men seen walking hand-in-hand in San Francisco, Miami's Coconut Grove, or New York's Fire Island may pass almost unnoticed. Yet in the tough steel towns of the Northeast, the rugged cowboy enclaves of the Southwest, the southern Bible Belt, or the heartland of the Midwest, the reactions of passersby would be quite different.

What accounts for these differences? What is it that makes segregation illegal in the United States but a matter of official government policy in South Africa? Why is crashing a ticket line or being a homosexual "conventional" in some communities but rude, improper, "uncivilized," or *deviant* in others? The answer lies in the folkways and mores of a culture. The customs and moral codes of a culture and society determine what constitutes crime, immorality, dishonesty, blasphemy, knavery, skulduggery, shamefulness, corruption, wickedness, malevolence, evil, or sin. Custom and morality, in short, define *deviance*.

What Is Deviance?

For most social scientists, deviance is considerably more encompassing than the concept of crime. Sociologist Kai T. Erikson has suggested that "the term, deviance, refers to conduct which the people of a group consider so dangerous or embarrassing or irritating that they bring special sanctions to bear against the persons who exhibit it."[1]

Edward Sagarin takes this definition one step further, suggesting that disvalued people (including criminals, the eccentric, and the insane) and disvalued behavior that provoke hostile reactions are "deviant."[2] Thus, **deviant behavior** is that which fails to conform to the significant social norms and expectations of society, or a group within society (see Exhibit 7.1). Important to this definition is the phrase "significant social norms and expectations." To suggest that deviance includes *any* behavior that violates social norms is not particularly useful since, as was pointed out in the discussion of culture in Chapter 3, many norms are not very important. Eating three meals a day, setting the table in a certain way, and having turkey on Thanksgiving are American folkways. Yet those who eat only one meal a day, set a table in a somewhat unconventional manner, and who may have fish on Thanksgiving because they dislike turkey, do not have special sanctions brought to bear against them.

Similarly, social deviance should not be confused with statistical rarity. Persons age 85 and older are statistically rare because they account for an extremely small proportion of the total U.S. population. The number of persons with annual incomes of $1 million or more is even smaller. Perhaps the most statistically deviant person in the United States, at least in terms of his occupational status, is the President; no one else has a similar position. Yet none of these people is "socially deviant" simply because he or she fits into a particular age, income, or occupation category.

The Kinds of Deviance and Deviants

Deviance is a universal concept. Every society has rules, and complete conformity never seems to be achieved.

Exhibit 7.1 **Sociology in the Media**

Deviance and Church Law

The following article, reprinted from *USA Today,* demonstrates how sources other than law, custom and tradition may come to define deviant behavior and deviants

Vatican: Sex Education Is Parent's Role

VATICAN CITY —A call for "positive" sex education—and affirmation of traditional church views on premarital sex and homosexuality—were hallmarks of a sweeping set of guidelines issued Thursday by the Vatican.

The 36-page statement—one of the most comprehensive by the Roman Catholic Church—said parents have the primary role in sexual education and urged them to help shape the content of such programs.

"Sex education, which is a basic right and duty of parents, must be carried out under their attentive guidance, whether at home or in educational centers chosen and controlled by them," it said.

The document also:

- Praised virginity, called masturbation a deviation reflecting immaturity, and said homosexuals should be counseled for their "disorder."
- "It will be the duty of the family and the teacher to seek first of all to identify the factors which drive toward homosexuality," it said. Possible causes to be investigated include "lack of affection, immaturity, obsessive impulses, seduction, social isolation and other types of frustration, deprivation in dress, license in shows and publications."
- Restated its position on sex outside marriage, saying it "loses its significance, exposes the selfishness of the individual, and is a moral disorder."
- Strongly repeated the church's absolute ban on artificial birth control methods.

SOURCE: *USA Today,* December 2, 1983, p. 3A.

Furthermore, when one considers the range of behaviors that are socially disapproved, it becomes clear that everyone is a likely "deviant" at one time or another.

1. *The Aberrants.* Aberrant behavior is a form of deviance that differs systematically from the norm in both its makeup and social consequences.[3] The aberrants are acting in their own private interests. They try to hide their departures from social norms from the limelight or public scrutiny, and they do so because they wish to escape the sanctions that go with deviating from existing norms. Moreover, aberrants acknowledge the legitimacy of the norms they violate; they merely find it expedient or expressive to violate them nevertheless. Much criminal activity—murder, rape, robbery, theft, assault—falls into this classification. In addition, other types of disapproved behaviors—extramarital sex, drug abuse, loafing on the job—are also marked by similar characteristics. In all instances, the aberrants are breaking rules for personal gain or satisfaction and are attempting to get away with doing so.

2. *The Nonconformists.* Nonconforming deviants differ from the aberrant variety in that they are trying to attract attention to their rule breaking. Nonconformists announce their dissent publicly. They challenge the legitimacy of the norms they reject. By denying certain rules, they hope that these will be changed or eliminated altogether. Civil disobedience in the form of sit-in participation, or membership in the Ku Klux Klan, the American Nazi Party, and similar groups exemplifies nonconforming deviance.

3. *The Aberrant-nonconformists.* Manifesting characteristics of both the aberrants and the nonconformists, these deviants are rigid idealists whose challenges to the existing social order are conducted in such an explosive manner that maintaining personal secrecy becomes necessary. Terrorist organizations that bomb public places and then take credit for the destruction are challenging the legitimacy of certain institutions. Yet the carnage often caused by their mode of dissent is so socially disapproved that their continued war against the existing order requires that they remain anonymous.

4. *The Eccentrics.* Eccentrics are nonconformists of a sort, but they rarely attempt to bring about social change. Rather, they are in many ways society's "oddballs." While they conform with most of the social norms, they ignore some of the lesser conventions, simply because they are unconcerned with them. The absent-minded professor who wears a different colored sock on each foot and those who use a spoon when eating peas are all eccentrics of a sort. Some eccentrics, such as artists, poets, rock singers, and "punkers" who wear garish clothing, attempt to advertise their own particular identity. Other eccentrics, such as hermits and hobos, drop out of society either partially or completely. In all instances, mild ridicule is the general social response to such deviance.

5. *The Socially Approved Deviants.* The infringement of any number of rules and codes throughout American history has not brought about social disapproval. This response typically occurs when the official rules fail to reflect the feelings of the community. The Prohibition Amendment to the United States Constitution, for example, was an unpopular law—so unpopular that it was broken regularly and with widespread social approval. More currently, the Saturday night poker game and other forms of petty gambling, while against the law, are accepted by most segments of society.

6. *The Involuntary Deviants.* In most communities any number of persons break the rules, sometimes quite seriously, yet many of these individuals escape sanctions because they are unable to conform for physical or mental reasons. The deviance of the mentally ill, the physically disabled, the diseased, and the extremely young, who have yet to reach the age of reason under the law, is often considered to be beyond their control. These deviants may be restrained or placed in institutions, but they are nevertheless not held accountable for their behaviors.

The identification of the many varieties of deviance serves to clarify several important points. First, deviance can be universal and engaged in by most, if not all, members of a society. The student who smokes even one marijuana cigarette is a deviant; the motorist who exceeds the speed limit is a deviant; the police officer who disregards a traffic violation is a deviant; murderers, rapists, and terrorists are deviants; absent-minded professors and the emotionally disturbed are deviants; friends who have a nickel-and-dime poker game on a Saturday night are deviants; people who have extramarital affairs

What type of deviant might this individual be?

are deviants. Although not all members of the society may consider all of these behaviors to be deviant, some will. As sociologist Howard S. Becker once commented, "Deviant behavior is behavior that people so label."[4]

Second, not all deviant behavior is criminal behavior, and conversely, not all criminal behavior is deviant behavior. As we pointed out in the discussion of cultural norms in Chapter 3, many behaviors that violate social norms do not represent violations of the law. The unconventional clothing of the poet or punker violates custom, but not law. And by contrast, although driving 56 MPH in a 55-MPH zone is technically a violation of the law, persons who violate this law are not considered deviant.

Third, and related to these distinctions between crime and deviance, deviant behavior is relative. Not only do definitions of what constitutes deviance vary within one society, but they vary across cultures as well (see Exhibit 7.2).

Deviance and Social Control

In most places and under most conditions, social behavior is remarkably orderly and predictable—so much so that most of it is taken for granted. The majority of working people report to their jobs every day and perform the tasks they are paid to do. People dress themselves before leaving their homes and generally wear the clothing that is typical of their position within their culture. Banks are open during business hours; the telephone operator answers when a zero is dialed; the police are on the streets directing traffic and patrolling; and motorists stop at red lights and do not make a practice of purposely running down pedestrians. Moreover, most individuals obey the criminal codes most of the time. In short, people generally follow the rules and fulfill their roles in accordance with social expectations. By doing so, they maintain the established order of their communities. Without this order—the *social order*—society would not be possible.

Consider what it would be like if people did not obey the rules. What kinds of chaos would ensue? Few concrete examples are known, but certain riot conditions offer a close approximation. One case in point was the Watts riots in Los Angeles during the summer of 1965.[5] Watts is a shabby district, 98% black, with a population density of 27.3 people per acre located under the approach patterns to Los Angeles International Airport. In 1965, it was a ghetto of the worst kind, characterized by poverty, crime, alcoholism, poor housing, broken glass, rusty cans, rotting chicken bones, and empty wine bottles. The quality of life in Watts was further diminished by the attitude and conduct of the typical white policeman—"The Man"—who had a way of stopping black citizens and demanding, "Let's see your I.D.!"

On August 11, 1965, a California Highway Patrol officer asked to see the I.D. of a young black suspected of driving while intoxicated. It was the fourth day of a brutal heat wave. People were on the streets, ready to assemble quickly at the promise of excitement. As the police officer took his suspect into custody, the youth's mother suddenly interfered, jumping on the patrolman's back. Other officers, who had just arrived on the scene, had to pry her loose and hold the crowd at bay with shotguns.

As the hours passed and discussion of the incident spread, the use of force employed by the police became exaggerated. In one story the police had thrown a woman against a squad car and tried to choke her. In another, an officer had struck a pregnant woman in the stomach with his nightstick. By 10 o'clock that evening, some three hours after the initial incident, the crowd of spectators had grown into a mob. They attacked passersby, overturned cars, smashed shop display windows, and looted stores. As the situation escalated, the rioters, some 2,000

Exhibit 7.2

Research in Sociology

The Cultural Relativity of Deviance

Although studies of attitudes, values, and opinions are quite common in the United States and many other countries, research that asks the same questions of national samples of people in different countries and cultures is quite rare. In one cross-cultural investigation, Graeme Newman questioned people from several countries to determine whether certain acts should be prohibited by law. The responses demonstrate the cultural relativity of deviance. The brief sampling of data presented here indicates that Americans seem to be more tolerant of homosexuality and protest than any of the other cultures surveyed. Attitudes toward homosexuality show widest variation from one country to the next. Alternatively, condemnation of air pollution emerged as almost universal, with a variation of only a few percentage points across the five cultures.

SOURCE: Adapted from Graeme Newman, *Comparative Deviance: Perception and Law in Six Cultures* (New York: Elsevier, 1976), p. 116.

Type of Act

Homosexuality in Private Between Consenting Adults

Public, Nonviolent Political Protest

Failure to Help Another Person in Danger

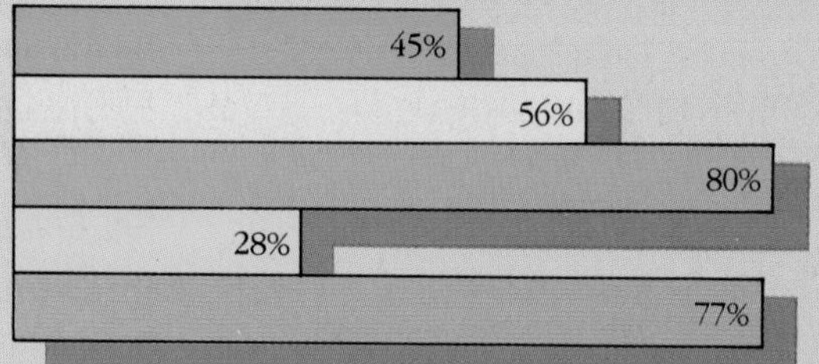

Air Pollution Caused by a Factory

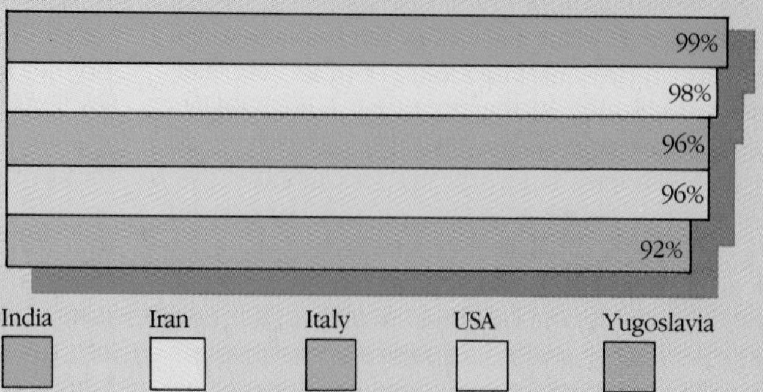

India Iran Italy USA Yugoslavia

strong, roved through Watts setting upon strangers, breaking everything in sight, fighting, stealing, and setting fires. In the days that followed, snipers fired from rooftops at the police and National Guardsmen who had been brought in to control the rioting.

Watts finally calmed down on August 18, but only after 14,000 troops were brought in and a 46-square-mile area had been placed under curfew. During the six days of madness, 34 persons had been killed, another 898 were wounded or hurt in some way, and property and other losses were put at $45 million.

What emerged in Watts was a period of *acute anomie*—a sudden state of anarchy; a situation in which the value of many of the prevailing rules and norms had faded, resulting in a collapse of the social order. But even the rioters in Watts during those six days of rebellion obeyed the majority of the social norms. Although many were involved in violence and theft, in other areas of social behavior the rules were generally followed: people dressed before going into the streets to riot; personal hygiene was taken care of in the traditional manner; food was prepared and eaten in the typical fashion; and special steps were taken to insure the safety of children and loved ones. And going well beyond the Watts of August 1965, even the most seriously violent criminals follow most of the rules the majority of the time. This conformity to rules may be attributed to two factors—*socialization* and *sanctions*.

Ideally, the socialization process, as described in Chapter 6, ensures that people learn, internalize, and follow the norms of their society. On the whole, socialization is rather successful. Almost everyone conforms to social norms most of the time through force of habit. Moreover, they do so not only when the rules are fair, sound, and useful, but also when they are petty, trivial, dogmatic, arbitrary, arrogant, outdated, contradictory, ambivalent, and even oppressive.

Nevertheless, socialization is rarely perfect and complete. People are brought into this world with varying potentials; they are exposed to alternative environments and socializing influences. They react to these influences in different ways, or they improvise new behaviors as they face new or novel situations. In a heterogeneous society like that of the United States—one peopled by many different cultural groups, each often having a variety of alternative norms, values, traits, attitudes, and traditions—no one set of rules is commonly held by all. Thus, when special circumstances arise so that socialization cannot guarantee widespread conformity—a phenomenon that exists in every known society and culture—additional mechanisms of social control become necessary. These additional mechanisms are known as **sanctions**—rewards for conformity and punishments for deviance.

Informal Sanctions

Sanctions can appear in a variety of ways. **Informal sanctions,** for example, which are spontaneous reactions or responses to certain acts, are applied with little ceremony. An *informal positive sanction* might be a pat on the back or a firm shake of the hand for a job well done. A father who lets his five-year-old daughter stay up a few minutes longer because she picked up her toys, or increases his teenage son's allowance because he got good grades in school, is applying informal positive sanctions.

Informal negative sanctions also present a diverse range of alternatives—booing an umpire when a bad call is made, insulting a neighbor who refuses to curb his dog, spreading rumors about a teacher who has unfair grading practices, or perhaps avoiding all social contact with persons who display certain kinds of deviant behavior. Informal negative sanctions can be quite severe, such as a banker's refusing to extend credit or grant loans to people simply because of the way they dress, or one individual's shooting another merely for being a member of a deviant group.

Formal Sanctions

Formal sanctions are institutionalized means of rewarding for conformity and punishing for deviance. *Formal positive sanctions* would include the awarding of a diploma upon graduation from college, the presentation of a medal of valor for some heroic deed, or the

Negative sanctions are expressed in many ways.

election of a candidate whose views are found acceptable to the majority. Among the most visible formal positive sanctions are the election of a person to the presidency of his or her country and the awarding of a Nobel Prize.

Formal negative sanctions are coercive measures employed by an organization or the state to exact compliance with the prevailing norms. Sanctions by organizations can include strikes called by labor unions in response to unsafe working conditions, the dismissal of a student from school for cheating on an examination, or the refusal of an association to endorse certain candidates because of their policies. Sanctions by the state include fines, awards, and/or judgments for civil wrongdoing, violations of health and regulatory codes, and instances of malpractice. *Criminal sanctions* involve fines, restitution, probation, incarceration, deportation, and the most extreme form of punishment—execution.

The Functions of Deviance

From a limited perspective, deviance—whether it be mental illness, crime, or some sort of "vulgar" behavior—might be construed as disruptive to a society. After all, a number of the mentally ill *are* nonproductive, burdensome, and sometimes even dangerous; criminals rape, steal, maim, and kill; and the vulgar can be repulsive affronts to social sensibilities. But from a broader view, it has been argued that deviant behavior is essential to the welfare of a society—in some ways, deviant behavior preserves the social order.

Almost a century ago, Emile Durkheim commented in his book, *The Rules of Sociological Method,* that deviant behavior is "an integral part of all healthy societies" that serves to define the boundaries of proper conduct.[6] Applying this perspective specifically to crime, others have argued:

> The social function of crime is to act as a notification of maladjustments. Just as pain is a notification to an organism that something is wrong, so crime is a notification of social maladjustment, especially when crime becomes prevalent. Crime is a symptom of social disorganization and probably can be reduced appreciably only by changes in social organization.[7]

The many negative reactions that emerge from observations of deviance establish what is both permitted and disapproved of by the conforming members of a society. Thus, when members of a community or society become aware of exactly what behaviors will and will not be tolerated by their neighbors, they can act accordingly. Moreover, as one can see in attitudes toward rapists, terrorists, traitors, and other renegades, deviance binds the "good people" together with a tighter social bond (see Exhibit 7.3). By condemning the transgressor, either through execution, banishment, excommunication, confinement in prison, or the informal act of making a person an outcast, the ties among the remaining population are strengthened. The people share a common indignation and reaffirm their own goodness, correctness, and morality.[8]

Although every system of social organization imposes discipline on its members by specifying the goals they may legitimately pursue and the means they may properly employ in pursuing those goals, some deviance is always disparaged but not rigorously repressed. This deviance can often be functional as a "safety valve" by preventing the excessive accumulation of malcontents who place strains on the legitimate order. It has been argued that prostitution, for example, performs such a "safety valve" function with respect to unsatisfied sexual needs. Unlike extramarital relationships, which can result in emotional attachments that may destroy or at least weaken the stability of a marriage, prostitution does not necessarily threaten the institution of the family.[9]

The notion that deviance can be functional to a society was taken one step further by Karl Marx. Although Marx is generally associated with conflict theories of society, he did address the ways that crime is economically related to the social order.

> The criminal produces not only crime but also the criminal law; he produces the professor who delivers lectures on this criminal law, and even the inevitable text-book in which the professor presents his lectures as a commodity for sale in the market. There results an increase in material wealth, quite apart from the pleasure which the author himself derives from the manuscript of his text-book.
>
> Further, the criminal produces the whole apparatus of the police and criminal justice, detectives, judges, executioners, juries, etc., and all these different professions, which constitute so many categories of the social division of labor.[10]

These economic and occupational functions of crime and deviance are readily apparent in the United States. In the occupational sector alone, several million persons find full-time employment in jobs that depend on the existence of deviants. Included in this group are some 550,000 lawyers and judges, 500,000 social workers, 585,000 law enforcement workers, and 450,000 prison workers and corrections officers. Many thousands of professors, social scientists, secretaries, cooks, computer operators, researchers, planners, accountants, insurance company and security personnel, and other employees whose work is related to deviance, crime, and social control also owe their livelihoods to the presence of

Exhibit 7.3

Sociological Focus

How People View the Seriousness of Various Crimes

In a nationwide survey conducted for the Justice Department in 1987 by the Population and Society Research Center at Bowling Green State University, a sample of 1,920 adults was asked to (1) rank the seriousness of 24 different crimes and (2) indicate what they felt were appropriate prison terms for persons committing each of these crimes. The rankings and average prison sentences recommended (in years) are shown here.

SOURCE: Bureau of Justice Statistics, 1987.

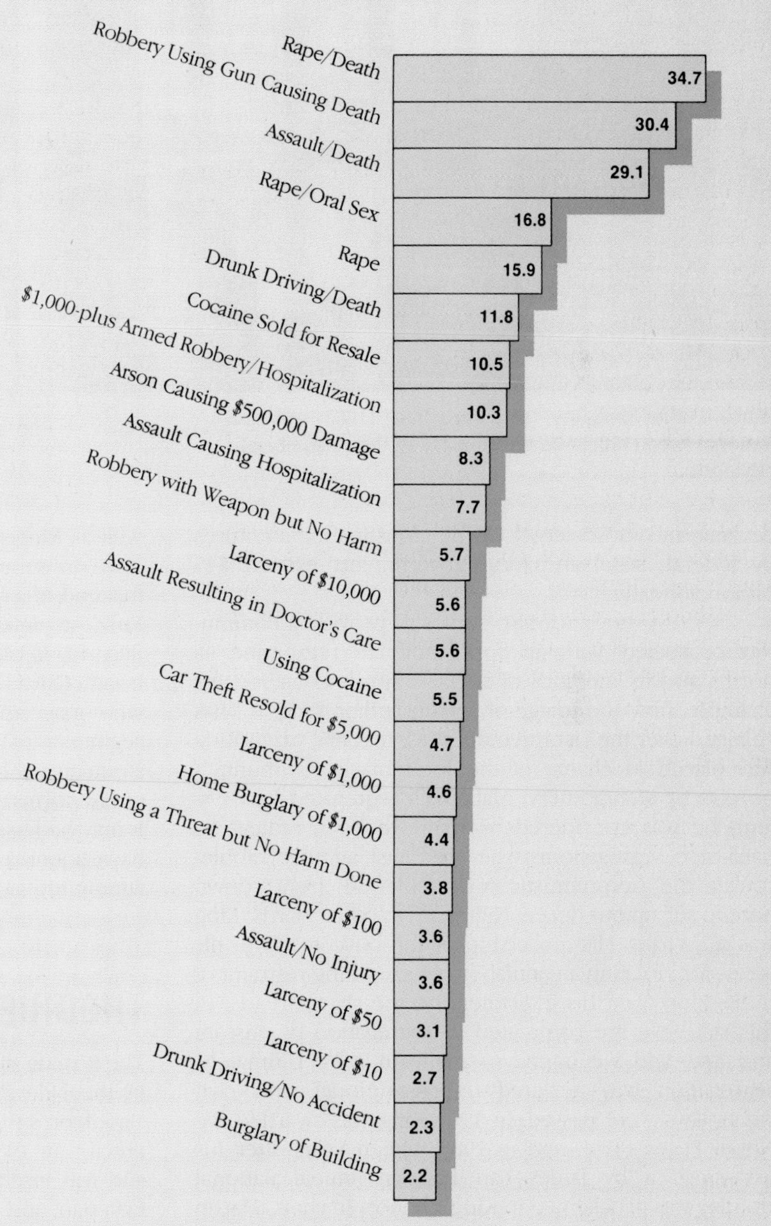

Martin Luther King, Jr.—as a "criminal" (1960) and as a national hero (1988)—is an example of the relativity of deviance.

deviants in our society.[11] Criminal justice expenditures by federal, state, and local governments exceed $45 billion annually.[12]

Finally, deviance also serves to provide a community or society with an opportunity to reexamine its norms and its methods of social control. Consider, for example, how the image of Martin Luther King, Jr., has changed over the last three decades. In 1955, when King was placed in charge of the local black community's boycott of Montgomery, Alabama's segregated bus system, he was considered by many to be a radical; to hard-core segregationists he was "just another rabble-rouser the Communistic N-double-A-C-P [sent] down here to stir up our decent Nigras."[13] In other words, King was a *deviant.* His leadership of the boycott led to his arrest for violating an antilabor law enjoining restraint of trade. Moreover, his indictment on the charge read: "In this state, we are committed to segregation by custom and law, and we intend to maintain it."[14] Ultimately, segregation was declared unconstitutional, and civil rights laws were passed. In 1964 King was awarded the Nobel Peace Prize, and in 1983, fifteen years after his assassination by James Earl Ray, an annual national holiday was proclaimed in King's honor. In short, Martin Luther King's "deviant behavior" in fighting for civil rights, along with the efforts of other black leaders, led to a reevaluation and redefinition of segregationist laws, as well as King's elevation to the status of a national hero.

In summary, deviance is not only normal to the makeup of a society, but it has functional aspects as well. First, it defines the boundaries of proper conduct. Second, it binds people together into a tighter social bond. Third, it represents a safety valve for discontents who may strain the social order. Fourth, it supports segments of the occupational structure. And fifth, it stimulates the reexamination and redefinition of many social norms. Yet deviance is troublesome, and although it may be basic to social living, researchers and theorists have spent a considerable amount of time and effort attempting to understand its roots.

THEORIES OF DEVIANCE

The Rosetta stone, now in the British Museum, was found in the Nile River delta by an engineer traveling with Napoleon's troops in 1799. It was a slab of volcanic rock erected in 195 B.C. to honor Ptolemy Epiphanes of Syria and was inscribed in three languages—Greek, demotic Egyptian, and hieroglyphic. The significance of the stone was that it furnished Egyptologists with the key by which they could decipher the meaning of Egyptian hieroglyphics, and since that time the Rosetta stone has served as a symbol for things that may unravel the more elusive mysteries of nature and human behavior. In like manner, it has been suggested that the fervent efforts of researchers in deviance and crime often reflect a belief in a *criminologists' stone*—that one monolithic approach or theory that would ultimately account for the entire range of behaviors interpreted by one society or another as deviance or crime.[15]

People have always been aware of deviance (Exhibit 7.4), but the belief in the "criminologists' stone" first became evident a century ago in the work of Italian criminologist Cesare Lombroso, who once reflected:

> Suddenly, one morning, on a gloomy day in December, I found in the skull of a brigand a very long series of atavistic abnormalities . . . analogous to those that are found in inferior vertebrates. At the sight of these strange abnormalities—as an extensive plain is lit up by a glowing horizon—I realized that the problem of the nature and generation of criminals was resolved for me.[16]

With this "revelation," Lombroso gave substance to the anthropological study of crime, criminals and deviants, suggesting that anyone who broke the rules of society was an **atavism**—a throwback to some earlier stage in human evolution.

Yet Lombroso's views failed to stand the test of time, and like Sir Walter Raleigh's pursuit of El Dorado and Juan Ponce de Leon's quest for the fountain of youth, criminologists' searches for their elusive "stone" have continued. For example, over the past one hundred years:

- a *medical* approach has sought to study the influence of physical disease on crime and deviance
- a *biological* approach has attempted to relate deviance to heredity
- *physiological* and *biochemical* approaches have correlated deviance with both normal and abnormal physiological functions and types
- a *psychological* approach has analyzed motivation and diagnosed personality deviations
- an *IQ* approach has characterized low intelligence as morphology of evil
- a *psychiatric* approach has designated mental disease the root of deviance
- a *psychoanalytic* approach has traced behavior deviations to the repression of basic drives
- a *geographical* approach has tried to demonstrate the influences of climate, topography, natural resources, and geographical location on deviance
- an *ecological* approach has investigated the impact of the spatial distribution of persons and institutions on behavior patterns
- an *economic* approach has looked for relationships between various economic conditions and deviance
- a *social* approach has considered educational, religious, recreational, occupational, and status factors as they may relate to deviance
- a *cultural* approach has examined the influence of various institutions, social values, and patterns that characterize groups, and the conflicts among cultures on deviance and crime
- a *sociological* approach has concerned itself with the nature and effects of social values, attitudes, and relationships on behavior
- a *conflict* or "critical" approach has focused on deviance and crime as consequences of the conflicts inherent in law creation
- and a *multi-factor* approach has sought to embrace the combination of any or all of these variables as they may result in the generation of deviance

Still, the criminologists' stone has not been found. Many megaliths have risen and fallen, and although the search for the root causes of deviance and crime has been an enduring and often fitful one, this should not suggest that the explanations proposed have always been without merit. An examination of the major biological and sociological theoretical perspectives will assist us to better understand the causes of deviance.

Biological Theories

Biological theories of deviance, having achieved initial prominence over a century ago, have persisted in one form or another right up to the present. These theories are grounded in the concept of **biological determinism,** a notion that suggests that the causes of deviance are the result of some biological or physical element—that deviants are "born," not made.

Criminal Anthropology

Most closely associated with the biological school of thought are the findings of Cesare Lombroso (1835–1909), an Italian army physician and prison doctor. Often referred to as the "father of modern criminology," Lombroso conducted systematic observations and measurements of the physical attributes of criminals. He believed that he saw in these individuals some of the same characteristics as those found in "savages" or

Exhibit 7.4

Sidelights on American Culture

Demonology and the Puritans of Massachusetts Bay

Prior to the beginnings of scientific criminology, no one really conducted a search for the causes of crime. People whose behavior was considered to be criminal were viewed as being possessed by some evil spirit or devil, or they were understood to have simply made the conscious choice to be "bad." The *demonological* explanation of crime has been perhaps the most enduring. Primitive and preliterate animism held that spirits infused every object or being, operating in ways that controlled the behavior of the persons and objects that served as temples or vessels housing these spirits. Hence, magic emerged as a practical procedure to change the conduct of those possessed, especially when the spirits were considered evil and disruptive.

This notion of *demonology* became more formalized during the Middle Ages; crime or criminal behavior was believed to be the result of a curse by some deity or possession by the devil. Ritual and procedure became the instruments for determining guilt or innocence. Prayer, punishment, torture, and death became tools for chasing or destroying the evil demons. Witchcraft was among the alleged behaviors associated with demonic intervention, and the history of civilization suggests that those believed to be witches were ruthlessly pursued and often conceived of as capital offenders.

The most infamous hysteria over witchcraft in America occurred in the Puritan colony of Massachusetts Bay during the latter part of the seventeenth century. History has not fully suggested how the phenomenon actually began in this small settlement, but with a legacy dating back to prehistory and a consciousness of witches and witchpriests in Britain from the fourth century, a belief in witchcraft was logically possible among the Puritans. Their rigid religious orientation included creeds that assured the fires of hell and the reality of the devil as an adversary who had the ability to possess souls for sinister purposes. The "outbreak" of witchcraft began in the home of a local minister, Reverend Samuel Parris, when several young girls were reported to have been seized by fits and convulsions. When questioned, the girls accused three village women who were then induced to confess to all manner of dealings in evil, and to indict friends and neighbors for similar practices. During 1692, trials, torture, and executions for witchcraft were common throughout the colony, and the most damaging piece of evidence that could be introduced was the *devil's mark* or *witch's mark,* which a prosecutor would reveal on the accused's body. The devil's mark took the form of a scar or strip of oddly shaped dark skin, while the witch's mark was a piece of protruding flesh, or what appeared to be a secondary pair of nipples on which the witches' imps and familiars were supposed to feed. Both witch's and devil's marks were alleged to have been awarded to the witch when initiated into the devil's evil cult, and sealed with sexual intercourse between the devil and his neophyte. While these marks are accepted today as birthmarks, moles, warts, or other imperfections, their appearance on

prehuman people. Lombroso maintained that the criminal could be identified by certain "stigmata of degeneration," such as a slanting forehead, excessive dimensions of the jaw and cheekbones, ears of unusual size, peculiarities of the eyes, abnormal teeth, excessively long arms, a sparse beard, a twisted nose, woolly hair, fleshy and swollen lips, or getting themselves tattooed. He also noted such nonphysical anomalies as a lack of morality, excessive vanity, and cruelty.

Having been heavily influenced by Charles Darwin's evolutionary doctrines, Lombroso concluded that the criminal was an atavism, a "throwback" to a more apelike ancestor.[17] Thus, he maintained, the deviant was born a deviant, defective or degenerate in some way. The atavistic features were apparent in both male and female deviants alike. Lombroso added, however, that in the case of prostitutes the typical criminal characteristics might not be immediately evident:

> The art of making up, imposed by their trade on all of these unfortunates, disguises or hides many characteristic features which criminals exhibit openly.

an accused witch meant certain conviction, followed by torture or death.

At the center of the Massachusetts witch frenzy was Cotton Mather, a zealous local clergyman, whose *Wonders of the Invisible World* epitomized Puritan fanaticism. His zeal was similar to that of Matthew Hopkins, the infamous seventeenth-century British witch finder who dedicated his life to the discovery of witchcraft and was responsible for the conviction and execution of some 200 alleged witches. Mather's efforts included experiments with those "possessed" and the collection of evidence for trial. During this reign of terror, spirited also by his father, Increase Mather, who often presided over the court cases, dozens of innocent citizens were put to death, while an even greater number were either punished, tortured, or otherwise degraded.

SOURCES: George L. Burr (ed.), *Narratives of Witchcraft Cases, 1648–1706* (New York: Charles Scribner's and Sons, 1914); Kai T. Erikson, *Wayward Puritans: A Study in the Sociology of Deviance* (New York: Wiley, 1966); Marion L. Starkey, *The Devil in Massachusetts* (New York: Alfred A. Knopf, 1949); Montague Summers, *The History of Witchcraft* (New Hyde Park, NY: University Books, 1956).

A "witch" is prosecuted in a seventeenth-century Salem court.

> If external anomalities be rare in prostitutes, internal ones, such as overlapping teeth, a divided palate . . . are more common among them.[18]

Heredity

A number of biological theorists have suggested that deviant tendencies might be inherited. Among the most frequently cited investigations in this regard is a study of the Jukes family conducted by Richard Dugdale in 1874.[19] Dugdale traced 709 members of the Jukes family back to the year 1790 and found that 20% had been either habitual thieves or prostitutes, or had been prosecuted for bastardy. He concluded that their deviance had been caused by "bad" heredity, and that the biological transmission of feeblemindedness resulted in degeneracy.[20]

Constitutional Inferiority and Body Types

Around the turn of the twentieth century, Dr. Charles Goring of Her Majesty's Prisons in Great Britain made an exhaustive study of the physical types of 3,000 English convicts.[21] His research revealed no evidence of a "physical criminal type," seemingly repudiating the whole Lombrosian doctrine. Yet in 1939, Harvard University anthropologist Earnest A. Hooton published *Crime and the Man,* a study based on the measurements of almost 14,000 prisoners in ten states, plus a large sample of noncriminals, which disposed of Goring's work as "scientifically biased" and gave some vindication to Lombroso.[22] Hooton held that criminals and other deviants exhibited a clear pattern of physical inferiority. He considered it necessary to eliminate his "criminal stock" by sterilizing their defective types and breeding a better race as a check on the growth of criminality.

Shortly after the publication of Hooton's book, William H. Sheldon and his associates at Harvard presented a body-build thesis for explaining deviant behavior.[23] They contended that all persons could be divided into roughly three basic body types, by which their personalities and their criminal potential could be predicted (see Exhibit 7.5). Thus, Sheldon was advancing the notion that behavior is a function of body structure.

Aberrant Chromosomes

Advances in the fields of molecular biology and micropathology during the last two decades have suggested a link between chromosome abnormality and deviance. Chromosomes are the parts of each living cell nucleus that carry hereditary information in the form of genes. The normal chromosomal pattern that features two similar-sized chromosomes is the female XX pattern. The normal male pattern, or the XY pattern, is characterized by two dissimilar chromosomes. The XYY pattern results in a male with an extra Y ("maleness") chromosome. In the **XYY chromosome** pattern, the particular chromosomes that control the inheritance of sex-linked characteristics are abnormal. Researchers speculate that one in every 700 males possesses an XYY chromosomal makeup, resulting in the physical characteristics of tallness, severe acne, long arms, and other skeletal irregularities. The psychological attributes of possible mental retardation or pronounced mental illness, aggressiveness, and perhaps even social isolation, sexual deviation, and criminality are also postulated.[24]

Deviance, Crime, and Human Nature

As one might suspect, the biological theories of deviance have not received widespread support, and perhaps with some justification. From the "atavistic man" to the "XYY man," the logical base for almost every theoretical posture has been structurally weak. The influences of environmental, cultural, social, and legal factors were continually ignored by proponents of biological explanations. The study samples utilized in biological research included convicted criminals, prison inmates, or certified delinquents; rarely were nondeviant control populations introduced. In addition, many of the samples were so small that conclusions drawn from them had little meaning. Finally, interpretations were often based on unsound reasoning, contorted logic, or blatant prejudice. Obvious confounding factors were invariably ignored in an effort to support the overall theoretical formulation. Yet on the other hand, a number of the biological theories have not been *dis*proven by empirical studies. Moreover, the idea that there may be some biological basis for deviance continues to have some research support.[25]

In 1985, the idea that criminals and deviants may be born, and not made, received international attention with the publication of *Crime and Human Nature.*[26] Written by prominent Harvard professors James Q. Wilson (a political scientist) and Richard Herrnstein (a psychologist), the book's central thesis was that at least a portion of crime and deviance is innate. Wilson and Herrnstein were influenced heavily by studies of IQ and constitutional inferiority, and while they rejected the idea of a specific criminal gene, they proposed the existence of a particular personality type with features that make a person more likely to value crime. These features, or "constitutional factors" as Wilson and Herrnstein referred to them, are either inborn or emerge early in life and are only minimally influenced by family. Even less influence is credited to cultural and economic factors. The authors argued, for example, that impulsiveness—the inability to contemplate the long-term consequences of one's actions—is a critical element in the criminal personality. Criminals and many other deviants are stunted in their ability to weigh either the costs that sanctions will exact or the future benefits of discipline at school, at work, or in a career. Consequently, they opt for the immediate emotional and material gratification that crime and deviance provide.

Sociological Theories

Biological theories of deviant behavior tend to focus on the makeup of the individual. The main concerns of proponents of biological theories are the characteristics of those people already classified as "deviants" or "criminals," and how they may differ from the "normals" in the population. Sociological theories, on the other hand, examine deviance in terms of how it may be related to the social system. From this perspective, the focus shifts from the individual to the society. What are the characteristics of situations in which deviance tends to occur? Why is deviance more common in certain

Exhibit 7.5 **Types & Stereotypes**

Sheldon's Body Types

William H. Sheldon identified three basic body types. The *endomorph* was characterized as having a soft and round body with short tapering limbs. The *ectomorph* was characterized by a thin and linear body with delicate bones, a small face, a sharp nose, and fine hair. The third type, the *mesomorph,* was a ruggedly muscular individual with a large trunk, heavy chest, and strong limbs. Each of the three body types had its accompanying temperament. Endomorphs were relaxed creatures of comfort who were eternal extroverts. Ectomorphs were introverts—inhibited, secretive, and restrained. Mesomorphs were assertive, aggressive, and action oriented. Sheldon held that mesomorphs were more inclined toward criminal behavior, a conclusion he stressed again years later, subsequent to his studies of juvenile delinquents.

Sheldon never denied the impact of social variables on deviance, and he held firmly that differences in body type produced differential responses to environmental pressures. In this, at least, there may be some merit to his theory. After all, heavy people (endomorphs) are expected to be jolly and good-natured; weak and skinny people (ectomorphs) are expected to be shy and withdrawn; and the large and physically powerful (mesomorphs) are often expected to be pushy and aggressive. Of course, there are exceptions, but perhaps by anticipating such behaviors, people often encourage them.

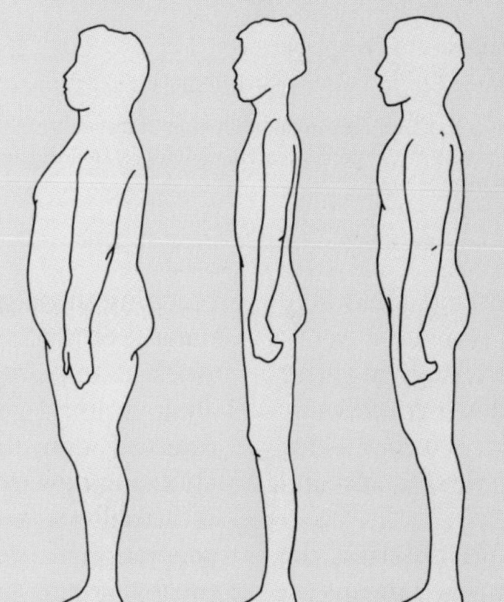

SOURCES: William H. Sheldon, Emil M. Hartl, and Eugene McDermott, *The Varieties of Delinquent Youth* (New York: Harper, 1949); William H. Sheldon, S. S. Stevens, and W. B. Tucker, *The Varieties of Human Physique* (New York: Harper, 1940).

places, within certain groups, and under certain circumstances than in others? What is the process by which some persons become deviant or criminal while others do not? Why is it that some behaviors are defined as deviant while others are not?

Anomie Theory

The concept of anomie was first introduced to modern sociology during the latter part of the nineteenth century in Emile Durkheim's study of suicide, which was discussed in Chapter 1. Durkheim described situations where social norms are weak, conflicting, or absent.[27] Thus, using Durkheim's formulation, **anomie** refers to a condition of normative confusion or "normlessness," in which the existing rules and values have little impact.

Decades later, building on Durkheim's work, Robert K. Merton used the concept of anomie to develop a general theory of deviant behavior.[28] Society, Merton suggested, has two component parts: a culture and a social structure. The culture consists of a set of norms, values, and attitudes that establishes the goals that individuals should pursue and the acceptable means and behavior patterns for achieving those goals. The social structure involves the organized set of social relationships in which the members of a society play their various roles. American society, in both its culture and social structure, places a high value on wealth, material comforts, status, and power. Too, the society specifies the rules for how to attain these valued goals properly—education, hard work, "smart" business practices, saving, and investments. While a high premium is placed on economic affluence and social ascent for all, however, the possibility for achieving material success is curtailed for many by reason of their position in the social structure. Crime and other deviant behaviors result, Merton ex-

Exhibit 7.6

Sociological Focus

Merton's Five Modes of Individual Adaptation

	Mode of Adaptation	Cultural Goals	Institutionalized Means of Achieving Goals
	Conformists	Accept	Accept
Deviants	Innovators	Accept	Reject
	Ritualists	Reject	Accept
	Retreatists	Reject	Reject
	Rebels	Accept/Reject	Reject/Accept

Source: Adapted with permission of The Free Press, a division of Macmillan, Inc. from Robert K. Merton, *Social Theory and Social Structure* (New York: Free Press, 1968), p. 194. Copyright © 1957 by The Free Press, renewed 1985 by Robert K. Merton.

plains, from this gap between aspirations and achievable goals.

Given these conditions, Merton suggests five modes of adaptation people may employ—*conformity, innovation, ritualism, retreatism,* and *rebellion*—for dealing with this conflict between cultural goals and institutionalized means (see Exhibit 7.6).

Conformity is the term used to describe the acceptance of cultural goals and the approved means for achieving them. *Most people conform!* Moreover, they do so even when the legitimate means for reaching the valued goals are out of their grasp. The indigent in American society, for example, having been exposed to many of the same cultural influences as individuals at other levels of the social structure, share more or less the same aspirations as the rest of the population. They seek secure and successful careers. They desire the same creature comforts—a safe and livable home environment, entertainment, vacations, material possessions. Yet the vast majority of Americans living in poverty have few means for satisfying these desires. Nevertheless, most poor people still conform. They play by the rules and scare up a living the best way they can. And they do so because there are other society-wide cultural influences that support conformity—religious values, belief in opportunity, public education, and the absence of formal legal restrictions against upward mobility.

Merton's other four types of adaptation relate to deviance and crime.

Innovation involves acceptance of cultural goals but rejection of the means a society deems proper for reaching those goals. The innovator selects disapproved means. Students cheating on exams, thieves, con artists, stock manipulators, drug dealers, and record pirates attain cultural goals, such as wealth or grades, but have rejected conventional routes. Rather, they innovate, choosing new means of achieving these goals. Innovation is actually a poor choice of terms for this form of adaptation.[29] Most deviants merely copy illegitimate means already known to them. Thus, using disapproved means is hardly the same thing as inventing or creating new ones.

Ritualism is the rejection of society's goals but the acceptance of society's means for achieving those goals. Ritualists accept the means for their own sake; the goals become irrelevant and are ignored. Ritualism is thus often "mindless" behavior. The example of a ritualist most often cited is the government bureaucrat, who gets bound up in "red tape" and procedure and insists on strictly enforcing every petty rule.

Retreatism describes the rejection of both the goals a culture establishes and the means society prescribes for achieving these goals. The retreatists are the alcoholics and derelicts living on skid row; they are the "street people" and "bag ladies" of the central cities; they are the tramps and outcasts in the "hobo jungles" of rural and suburban America; and they are the "junkies," psychotics, vagrants, vagabonds, and other pariahs who live on the fringes of society.

Rebellion is characterized by a rejection of the goals and the means of achieving those goals established by society. Rebels characteristically also aim to establish some new social order. They attempt to create a new set of goals and new norms governing appropriate means. The most visible and expressive examples of rebellion involve the various terrorist organizations throughout the world that resort to kidnappings, bombings, and assassinations in order to draw attention to their cause and to initiate change. Less dramatic are those individuals for whom humanistic or religious goals become paramount, and who need to develop adequate means to achieve such goals. Other rebels are the legion of adolescents who revolt in one way or another against the adult value system that has been imposed on them. Many band together into gangs, some turn "punk," while others may live in communes.

Since deviance is not altogether very easy to measure, it would be difficult to say with any degree of certainty which of the modes of adaptation accounts for the greatest number of deviants. *Innovation,* however, probably explains the greater portion of crime that comes to the attention of the criminal justice system. According to Merton, the greatest pull toward innovative deviant behavior is found in the lower income groups, where lack of education and job skills often make conventional success impossible. One must bear in mind, however, that Merton first formulated his anomie theory during the Great Depression, a time when the *means* necessary to acquire culturally approved goals, such as homes, jobs, and loans, were severely restricted by economic conditions. In addition, there were discrepancies between ends and means at other points along the socioeconomic scale—business operators on the brink of financial disaster, corporation executives under pressure to remain solvent for stockholders, entrepreneurs intent on absorbing their competitors.

Retreatism and rebellion are more genuinely deviant adaptations to anomie. The residents of skid row and the streets, the members of terrorist groups, and some religious cults have no bonds with conventional society. Some are apart from *any* society; others are meshed in a new society all their own.

Merton's theory of anomie is important to the study of deviance, for it not only offers a simple paradigm for understanding the range of deviant behaviors, but it also suggests how and why such behaviors emerge. Merton's theory does have its limitations, however. First, while it may provide a plausible interpretation of why people commit certain crimes (property crimes, for example), it fails to explain other forms of deviance, such as marijuana use, homosexuality, and sexual exhibitionism, to name but a few. Second, Merton's approach is strongly grounded in the assumption that some sort of value consensus exists in society. This assumption ignores the process through which certain behaviors come to be defined as deviant—a process that often involves a conflict in values between those who have the power to influence public opinion and policy and those who do not. And third, Merton's theory leaves a number of questions unanswered. For example, it does not explain why one mode of adaptation is chosen over another, or how norms begin to decay when goals are not achieved. In addition, it is not clear that material success ranks as high among most people as Merton seems to suggest.

Labeling Theory

Labeling theory attempts to explain why apparently similar acts are treated differently. For example, why is it that smoking dope is deviant while drinking alcohol is not? Why is it that sexual intercourse between husband and wife is called "making love," but the same act between sister and brother is called "incest"? Why is a ghetto youth caught stealing a bicycle more apt to be called a criminal than corporate executives discovered fixing prices? Why is a convicted burglar more likely to end up in jail than a convicted embezzler? Why are people with arrest records more likely to be picked up by the police than those individuals who have never been arrested? Why is it that ex-convicts are more often convicted of crimes than first offenders? And most curiously, why is it that a child who shoots a cat out of a tree on a city street with a BB gun is called "cruel," while his father, who shoots a deer in the woods with a high-powered rifle, is called a "sportsman"?

Somewhat related to these questions is the often-repeated anecdote about the colorful playwright George Bernard Shaw. Rather inebriated at a formal British dinner party, Shaw leaned over and whispered to the titled lady seated to his right, "Madam, would you sleep with me for £100,000?" After some mild quivering, the flustered woman answered, "Why possibly I just might." A moment or two later the playwright once again leaned over and asked, "Madam, would you sleep with me for £5?" The suddenly offended noblewoman indignantly replied, "Of course not! What do you think I am?!" Shaw regarded her briefly and wryly responded, "Madam, we have already established what you are. All that we are doing now is dickering about the price."

In essence, Shaw's sarcasm gets to the heart of **labeling theory.** How are definitions of deviance formulated by society? How are these definitions or labels applied to individuals? What are the consequences of these labels for those to whom the labels have been applied successfully?

In considering how the labeling process works, Howard S. Becker suggested that ". . . deviance is *not* a quality of an act the person commits, but rather a consequence of the application by others of rules and sanctions to an 'offender.' The deviant is one to whom that label has successfully been applied; deviant behavior is behavior that people so label."[30]

But the rules that might be violated do not occur automatically, nor are they brought to bear on specific actions without some reason. The mechanism through which behavior comes to be viewed as deviant was described by Becker as a process of discovery undertaken by "crusading reformers," "moral entrepreneurs," and "rule creators."[31] The reformer or crusader views certain elements in society as truly, totally, and unconditionally evil, and feels that nothing can be right until rules can be made to correct and remove the wickedness that has been perceived. The crusader's mission often becomes a holy war, for the wrongs that have been observed are a breach in the stability of the social order, and only their eradication can insure a better way of life for all. The reformer's role, then, involves bringing the evil to the attention of the public at large, to the society's opinion makers, and ultimately to the designated rule creators and rule enforcers.

The impetus for the labeling perspective came in 1951 when sociologist Edwin M. Lemert made an important distinction between *primary* and *secondary* deviations.[32] **Primary deviation** is the violation of some norm, some offensive act or characteristic. **Secondary deviation** results from the societal reaction to that violation—the behavior that people develop as the result of being labeled deviant. This distinction between primary and secondary deviation suggests that labeling can indeed have consequences, that the labeling itself adjusts peoples' perceptions of and reactions to deviants, and that these reactions can operationalize the "offender's" deviant role. Most, if not all, people break rules now and then, but they do not necessarily think of themselves as "deviant." Many even commit crimes, but again, they may not view themselves as "criminals." However, when circumstances result in their being defined and reacted to as "deviant" or "criminal," they may begin to actively fulfill those roles. For example:

> When my wife passed by and saw me having lunch with one of the secretaries, she later asked if something was going on. I told her that she was just a friend, but I guess she didn't believe a man could have an ordinary friendship with a member of the opposite sex. After a while every time she saw me even talking to another woman she'd accuse me of playing around. She even told a couple of her friends that I was having an affair. She wouldn't sleep with me anymore, so after a few months of that I did end up in bed with someone else. . . . From there things really went downhill and the marriage eventually fell apart.[33]

Similarly, many of those labeled as deviant may be forced out of a corner of conventional society into a situation or subculture that further stigmatizes them and makes the continuance of the deviant role inevitable. Persons labeled as "junkies" may lose their jobs and their friends; they are thus pushed into the drug subculture and the hustling world of the streets for companionship and financial support. And finally, secondary deviation can manifest itself in other ways. "Police work," for example, is considered by many as a "deviant" career:

> After only three months on the job I sensed that things were changing. I heard less and less from my high-school buddies, old friends didn't call me over to play some poker or have a beer, even my own brother got a little distant. . . . My wife and I didn't get invited to parties anymore—maybe they thought I'd arrest them if they pulled out a joint. . . . Enough was enough. We started hanging around with the people from Troop 6, and it was better; they were police people.[34]

It should be pointed out here that not all primary deviance results in secondary deviance. A number of factors bring about that transformation. First, how important are the norms that are being violated? People view traffic violators, pot smokers, and tax cheaters differently than they view child abusers, addicts, and thieves. Second, what is the social identity of the person violating the norm? Certain kinds of rule breaking and nonconformity by the economically powerful are more readily tolerated than are violations of the same norms by low-income minority members. Third, in what social context is the norm being violated? Marijuana smoking at a rock concert is more likely to be ignored than is marijuana smoking at a court hearing.

Labeling theory is an important concept to sociology and the study of deviance. It explains how certain behaviors come to be defined as deviant, why society will label some individuals and not others, and how the labeling process can produce future deviance. On the other hand, however, the theory does have its weaknesses. Initially, while it suggests how some kinds of deviance "come into being" as a result of moral enterprise (as was the case with narcotics addiction), it fails to explain how or why many long-standing forms of deviance emerge in the first place. Murder, for example, appears as a proscription in both the Old and New Testaments, and its designation as an offense punishable by death appears in an early chapter of the Book of Genesis. In addition, and perhaps most importantly, the labeling perspective fails to explain all of the causes of primary deviance.

Cultural Learning Theory

The beginning of cultural learning theories of deviance in the United States was influenced by Robert E. Park, the University of Chicago sociologist mentioned in

Chapter 1, who theorized that human communities were divided into "natural areas."[35] Park sent his students out to study the natural areas of Chicago—the ghetto, the ganglands, skid row, the "gold coast" (a high-income neighborhood), and the slum—and the impact of ecological structures on suicide rates, divorce rates, and crime rates.

Among Park's students was Clifford R. Shaw, who found that delinquency was concentrated in the deteriorated areas of the city, and that these areas maintained their high rates of delinquency in spite of constant population changes.[36] Through a number of case studies, Shaw and his collaborators found that slum youths were participants in a subculture where delinquency was approved behavior, and that crime and other forms of deviance were acquired in a social and cultural setting through a process of interaction.[37]

A more developed cultural learning theory is Edwin H. Sutherland's conception of **differential association.** Although this theory initially focused on "criminal behavior," its principles have been applied to other types of deviance as well. It grew from Sutherland's study of professional thieves, which suggested to him that many criminals learned the knowledge and motivations as well as all the skills necessary for engaging in criminal behavior.[38]

Specifically, the theory of differential association maintains that criminal and deviant behaviors are learned in the same way that conformity is. They are learned within the context of intimate social groups that are deviant or criminal. The learning includes the techniques of committing crimes and other deviant acts as well as the attitudes and rationalizations that serve to justify such behavior. What distinguishes these attitudes and rationalizations is that they involve a cultural rejection of legal and other social norms. Persons become criminal (or deviant), Sutherland argued, because they encounter an excess of definitions favorable to violation of the law over definitions favorable to law-abiding behavior. This excess of definitions favorable to law violation, furthermore, is due to a majority of associations with criminals over noncriminals (see Exhibit 7.7).[39]

Sutherland's theory of differential association represented a major breakthrough for the study of lawbreaking and other forms of deviance at the time it was first formulated, for it was a theoretical conception that attempted to "normalize" deviant behavior—"normal" in the sense that it was "learned" through the same

Exhibit 7.7

Sociological Focus

Sutherland's Principles of Differential Association

1. Criminal behavior is learned.
2. Criminal behavior is learned in interaction with other persons in a process of communication.
3. The principal part of the learning of criminal behavior occurs within intimate personal groups.
4. When criminal behavior is learned, the learning includes (a) techniques of committing the crime, which are sometimes very complicated, sometimes very simple; (b) the specific direction of motives, drives, rationalizations, and attitudes.
5. The specific direction of motives and drives is learned from definitions of the legal codes as favorable or unfavorable.
6. A person becomes delinquent because of an excess of definitions favorable to violation of law over definitions unfavorable to violation of law.
7. Differential associations may vary in frequency, duration, priority, and intensity.
8. The process of learning criminal behavior by association with criminal and anticriminal patterns involves all of the mechanisms that are involved in any other learning.
9. While criminal behavior is an expression of general needs and values, it is not explained by those general needs and values since noncriminal behavior is an expression of the same needs and values.

SOURCE: Edwin H. Sutherland and Donald R. Cressey, *Principles of Criminology* (Philadelphia: Lippincott, 1947), pp. 6–7. Reprinted by permission.

processes that other, nondeviant, behaviors were learned. Sutherland's ideas were not particularly unique or new, but in the way that they were presented they represented an integrated theory. They suggested a chain of interrelationships and correlates in a person's associations and learning experiences that made deviance reasonable and understandable as normal, logical behavior; they advanced a framework within which other theories of deviance might be better understood; and they suggested the simple-minded nature of those prior efforts which sought to explain deviance in terms of head size and shape, broken homes, feeblemindedness, body structure, and other factors.

Differential association theory, however, also has limitations. First, the theory seems to focus on only those kinds of criminality that are systematic in nature, such as professional theft, organized crime, certain forms of white-collar crime, and so forth. It fails to explain certain impulsive and irrational acts that result in crime, such as the majority of homicides, assaults, and forcible rapes. Second, many deviant and criminal behaviors are learned through contact with ideas, rather than with people. Furthermore, many of these same behaviors—purse snatching, shoplifting, robbery, assault, blackmail, and prostitution—require little, if any training. Third, differential association theory does not address why some persons with extensive contacts with deviants and criminals nevertheless resist deviance themselves.

Culture Conflict, Crime, and Deviance

More than 50 years ago, Jerome Michael and Mortimer J. Adler argued that crimes were no more than instances of behavior that are prohibited by the criminal law, that ". . . the criminal law is the formal cause of crime."[40] This comment gives direction to an explanation of deviance and crime as they emerge from conflicting sets of norms. In other words, if there were no laws and norms, there would be no crime and deviance.

Thorsten Sellin's *Culture Conflict and Crime* similarly regarded the criminal law as a body of rules that prohibits specific forms of conduct and has prescribed certain punishments for violations of these rules. Sellin further observed that the types of conduct the rules prohibited and the nature of the sanctions attached to their violation depended directly on the interests of those in the population who influenced legislation. According to Sellin, "in some states, these groups may comprise the majority, in others a minority, but the social values which receive the protection of the criminal law are ultimately those which are treasured by dominant interest groups."[41]

Crime, in this orientation, can emerge from, or be the result of, a conflict between the norms, values, and goal orientations of a social or cultural group and the legal codes that have been imposed by an alternative group that has the greater power to shape public policy. Yet within this framework, the crime that emerges from group conflict can occur when the purposes, interests, and valued goals of groups become competitive with one another in other ways. Albert K. Cohen's concept of the "delinquent subculture" offers an illustration.[42] Cohen suggested that working-class boys are handicapped in attaining social and economic status. Some eventually succeed, but most do not. Therefore, they band together into gangs, which provide them with an arena for striking back at the middle-class values that they oppose and give them status as a subcultural group. These subcultures are "nonutilitarian," "malicious," and "negativistic." They are

Would gun ownership in Kennesaw, Georgia, be considered a "focal concern"? In 1982, an ordinance was passed in Kennesaw mandating that *every* head of household *must* own a handgun.

nonutilitarian in that gang members defy legal codes often simply for the approval given by their peers; they are malicious in that they enjoy the discomfort of their victims because such discomfort is the result of their defiance of norms; and they are negativistic because they repudiate the standards of middle-class culture.

An alternative view that might be interpreted within the culture conflict mode was offered by Walter B. Miller, who contended that certain "focal concerns" within lower-class cultures could often lead to antisocial conduct.[43] He defined "focal concerns" as areas or issues that command widespread and persistent attention and a high degree of emotional involvement. These areas or issues could be found in the middle class, but carried higher priorities within the lower class. They included a preoccupation with "toughness," the sensitivity to "smartness," excitement, autonomy, a belief in fate, and a chronic awareness of "trouble." The illegal activity often found in lower-class areas represented an adolescent adaptation to the lower-class cultural concerns that were often in conflict with those of the wider society.

Much of what appears in culture conflict theory often seems to reflect on economic concerns. The approach focuses on the political power base occupied by those who have the influence to shape public policy and on how this base and ensuing power and influence serve to extend a criminal status to those of conflicting norms or interests. And a political power base often rests on a strong economic base, or at the very least the two are intricately interwoven. Thus, it is the "underprivileged," the "working class," or the "marginal" that so many theorists are referencing when they discuss crime in terms of culture conflict. Furthermore, much of what remains unspoken in the theoretical sphere, but which is often nevertheless apparent, is in many ways reminiscent of the early theories of economic determinism. As early as 1516 Thomas More's *Utopia* touched on the issue of crime and its relation to the poor economic status of certain groups. Similar observations were made in 1798 by Thomas Malthus in his *An Essay on the Principle of Population,* and by Karl Marx in his *A Contribution to the Critique of Political Economy* in 1859.

More recently, many public pronouncements about the causes of crime have targeted an economic base, suggesting, for example, that "poverty" is the cause of crime. But a direct cause-and-effect relationship between the two is an oversimplification that criminology has never taken seriously. Much of the statistical data on crime does suggest that high rates of certain kinds of crime appear to be more concentrated in areas of low income and that the majority of known offenders are of low socioeconomic status. But concomitants other than low income are indeed operating in these "high-crime" areas. Cultural explanations play a role in the distribution of crime and differential law enforcement in certain territories. Differential justice for those people who have the economic means for better representation in the halls of justice also figures into any equation targeting causes of crime. And finally, differential opportunity structures exist for committing crime. For example, persons of middle and high socioeconomic status have the opportunity to commit the less visible and rarely prosecuted white-collar offenses. Such opportunities are not typically available to the slum dweller, whose only opportunities for crime are the more visible offenses of burglary, robbery, and other thefts.

It should be stressed here that it would be unrealistic to expect that any one theory of deviance could explain all forms of deviant behavior. Furthermore, only a small portion of the existing theories have been discussed in this chapter. It is likely that each theory or various combinations of theories explain different kinds of deviance. In all probability, there are as many reasons for engaging in deviant behavior as there are different kinds of deviance.

THE NATURE OF CRIME

Crime is an aspect of human experience that brings forth images of evil and lawbreaking, and that has been subject to numerous interpretations and definitions. For the classical and literary scholar, crime can be drama, a presentation of conflict between elements of the good and the profane as typified so eloquently in the Greek tragedies, Shakespeare's *Macbeth,* and Dostoyevsky's *Crime and Punishment.* To the moralist and reformer, crime is a manifestation of spiritual depravity; it is that festering evil and disease of the soul that must be eradicated both fully and immediately by the powers of restraint and virtue. Crime also has been equated with sin—with violations of a "natural law," the Ten Commandments, or the proscriptions embodied in the Bible, Talmud, or Koran. And for others, crime has different meanings: to the reporter it is "news," to the detective it means "work," to the thief it is "business," and to the victim it suggests fear and loss. Given all of these varying images, then, what really is crime?

The Definition of Crime

Definitions of crime as "deviance" or "antisocial behavior" are ambiguous and lack precision. After all, not all deviant behavior is criminal behavior. Numerous kinds of acts receive social disapproval and even may be deemed blatantly antisocial but are not necessarily criminal.

Exhibit 7.8 Case Study

Sodomy Laws in the United States

Under contemporary sodomy statutes, a variety of sexual activities are prohibited, including *fellatio* (oral intercourse with the male sex organ), *cunnilingus* (oral intercourse with the female sex organ), *buggery* (penetration of the anus), *homosexuality* (sexual relations between members of the same sex), *bestiality* (sexual intercourse with an animal), *pederasty* (unnatural intercourse between a man and a boy), and *necrophilia* (sexual intercourse with a corpse).

In recent years, homosexuality has been more visible and more widely accepted. Our culture has witnessed more widespread sexual freedom among heterosexuals and a general lack of the enforcement of the sodomy laws in almost all communities in the United States. Given these changes, a variety of sexual activities that traditionally fell under the sodomy statutes for both homosexuals *and* heterosexuals have come to be considered legal per se. In 1986, however, it became quite clear to the nation at

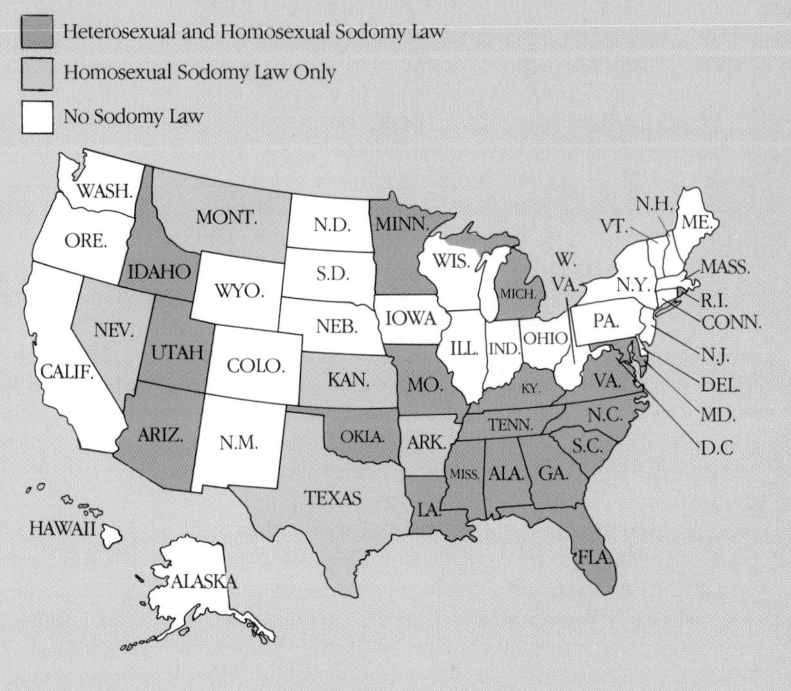

Although espousing the doctrines of nazism or communism and being an alcoholic are considered deviant by most Americans, these activities are not criminal activities and they are not treated as such. Social disapproval might even be quite strong, with the deviants subject to severe ostracism, but criminal sanctions would not be brought to bear against them.

The word "crime" has its roots in the Latin *crimen,* meaning offense, accusation, and judgment. This definition would suggest, then, that the origins of the word are legalistic—that crime pertains to violations of law. More specifically, **crime** is any intentional act in violation of the criminal law, committed without defense or justification, and sanctioned by the state as a felony or misdemeanor. Thus, crime involves violations of the **criminal law**—that collection of legal codes that deals with offenses committed against the safety and order of the state. Violations of church law, civil law, and other types of law are not crimes. The acts involved must be intentional, not accidental; the perpetrator must be acting with criminal intent. There must be no defense or justification for the prohibited act: killing in self-defense is not criminal homicide; the opening of a vault by a bank clerk under threat of harm is not complicity in a robbery. Finally, the act must be designated in the criminal codes as either a felony or a misdemeanor. A **felony** is any serious crime punishable by death or imprisonment in a state or federal penitentiary. A **misdemeanor** is any minor offense punishable by no more than a $1,000 fine and up to one year in jail, usually in a local institution.

large that this was *not* so, not only for homosexuals, but also for heterosexuals and even married couples. The announcement came from the United States Supreme Court in its decision in the case of *Bowers v. Hardwick*.

The case had begun on August 3, 1982, when an Atlanta, Georgia, police officer went to the home of Michael Hardwick to serve a warrant for failure to pay a fine for public intoxication. The man who answered the door told the officer that he was not sure whether Mr. Hardwick was at home, but that the officer could look around and check if he wished. As he walked into the house, through an open bedroom door the officer observed Hardwick and another man engaging in a homosexual act. The two were arrested and charged under the Georgia sodomy law. The charge against Hardwick was dismissed, but he decided to challenge the constitutionality of the Georgia law as a violation of his privacy rights. Two years later, the Supreme Court ruled that the statute was constitutional.

As indicated in the accompanying map, 26 states have no sodomy laws. All of the rest, as well as the District of Columbia, still do. The implication of the High Court ruling is that in those other 24 states and the District of Columbia, statutes exist under which people can be prosecuted (see table). Furthermore, in some jurisdictions even married couples run the risk of arrest and imprisonment for engaging in sexual activities that have come to be defined as "normal" and "routine."

States with Sodomy Laws	Maximum Jail Sentences for Sodomy	States with Sodomy Laws	Maximum Jail Sentences for Sodomy
Alabama	1 year	Missouri	1 year
Arizona	30 days	Montana	10 years*
Arkansas	1 year*	Nevada	6 years*
Florida	60 days	North Carolina	10 years
Georgia	20 years	Oklahoma	10 years
Idaho	5-year minimum	Rhode Island	20 years
Kansas	6 months*	South Carolina	5 years
Kentucky	12 months	Tennessee	15 years
Louisiana	5 years	Texas	$200 fine*
Maryland	10 years	Utah	6 months
Michigan	15 years (anal sex), 5 years (oral sex)	Virginia	5 years
		D.C.	10 years
Minnesota	1 year		
Mississippi	10 years		

*For homosexual sodomy only.

SOURCE: Bowers v. Hardwick, 39 CrL 3261 (1986).

The Variable and Changing Nature of Crime

Legal codes vary widely over time and from place to place. In years past criminal laws prohibited such activities as printing a book, professing the medical doctrine of circulation of the blood, driving with reins, selling coins to foreigners, having gold in the house, purchasing goods at a market for the purpose of selling them at a higher price, and writing a check for less than one dollar. More currently, certain activities that are legal in some jurisdictions in the United States are crimes in others. Prostitution is legal in Las Vegas County, Nevada (outside the city limits of Las Vegas), but illegal in all other parts of the country. Casino gambling is illegal in every state except Nevada and Atlantic City, New Jersey. Numerous variations also exist with respect to many sexual activities. Adultery, fornication, and homosexual acts between consenting adults are fully legal in some jurisdictions but criminal in others; oral sex, even when engaged in by a married couple, can result in criminal processing in some states (see Exhibit 7.8).

Within a cross-cultural perspective, even wider differences are apparent. Nudity is legally permitted on certain public beaches on several Caribbean islands, in France, and in numerous other parts of the world. In the United States, nudity is a minor misdemeanor. In Iran, public nudity is a capital offense punishable with death by torture. In all parts of the United States and most countries of the world, stealing is a crime. In Colombia, however, thieves are exempt from criminal prosecution if they have been impelled by a pressing need for food or clothing for themselves or their families, if they have no lawful means for satisfying this need, if they take no more than is necessary to sustain them, and if they avoid the use of violence during the commission of such thefts.[44]

This variable and changing nature of crime can be understood from a number of sociological points of view. Certainly, many cultural differences influence the creation of law. Emile Durkheim's conception of the **collective conscience,** those values held in common by the members of any relatively well-integrated social system, varies from one society or culture to the next. In a society as complex and heterogeneous as that in the United States, the collective conscience can vary not only from state to state but from community to community.

From an alternative perspective, Richard Quinney and other sociologists have argued that criminal definitions are often descriptive of behaviors that are in conflict not with the collective conscience, but with the interests of those segments of society that have the power to shape public policy.[45] Modern society, Quinney and those who agree with him state, is characterized by an organization of differences between social and cultural groups, with varied interests distributed among the numerous socially differentiated positions. These interests, furthermore, are organized around the activities pursued by each segment—activities usually of a political, economic, religious, kinship, educational, or civic nature. Since there is structured inequality in society, Quinney holds, characterized by an unequal distribution of power and conflict among its various divisions, the segments tend to compete with one another in terms of the priority to be assigned their respective interests. This point of view suggests how the environmental movement of the early 1970s was able to engineer the passage of many stiff pollution control laws, and how powerful corporations have been able to use their political clout to effect only minimal enforcement of those laws.

What about the many laws that remain in the criminal codes that are rarely, and sometimes never, enforced? As societies change, their social norms change,

Exxon's contingency clean-up plan of the 1989 oil spill apparently existed on paper only.

yet quite often the laws that reflected the older norms fail to change. The laws relating to homosexual relations constitute a pertinent example. The Puritan Criminal Code of 1676 included homosexuality (along with homicide and revolution) among those offenses deemed punishable by death.[46] As social norms regarding sexual relations have changed, so too have the laws. Homosexual relations are no longer subject to the death penalty, but in many jurisdictions in the United States, such activities are still a crime. Laws such as these generally are unenforced, but they remain on the books to avoid giving the impression that tacit approval is being extended to the behaviors they prohibit. In many communities it would be political suicide for a member of Congress to introduce legislation that served to condone homosexuality, adultery, or prostitution.

The Types of Crime

Literally thousands of acts are prohibited by law and designated as offenses in federal, state, and local criminal codes. In addition, **administrative law,** a branch of public law that deals with the powers and duties of government agencies, sets forth an alternative list of criminal violations. Moreover, new laws—and hence, the potential for more kinds of lawbreaking—come into being on a regular basis. A case in point occurred in California in 1983. Apparently, an assembly-line crematorium business in that state made up in volume of cremations for what it lost by charging lower prices. But as the saying goes, "you get what you pay for." It seems that the mortuary handled its backlog of bodies by cramming corpses five at a time into gas ovens built for one. The jumbled ashes were then dumped into thirty-gallon trash cans, which were then separated into boxes and labeled. The result? The remains of beloved Aunt Felicia were liberally sprinkled with the ashes of someone else's Cousin Maynard or Uncle Fred. Quite justifiably, the relatives of the deceased were not easily pacified. Someone cried, "There ought to be a law!" And soon there was one. By early 1984 a law went into effect making it a crime to conduct mass cremations or commingle ashes.[47]

The point here is that we have such a large number of laws that a catalog of behaviors defining "crime" would be so long that even their numbers would be difficult to count. On the other hand, more than 90 percent of the criminal law violations that come to the attention of state and local criminal justice agencies can be combined into two short lists of what the Federal Bureau of Investigation calls **Part I and Part II crimes** (see Exhibit 7.9). These crimes include felonies and misdemeanors—homicide, assault, burglary, disorderly conduct, drug law violations, and the like—the crimes with which most people are familiar. Part I offenses are

Exhibit 7.9 **Sociological Focus**

The FBI Crime Categories

Part I Offenses	*Part II Offenses*	
Criminal Homicide	Other Assaults	Offenses against Family and Children
Forcible Rape	Forgery and Counterfeiting	Driving under the Influence
Robbery	Fraud	Liquor Laws
Aggravated Assault	Embezzlement	Drunkenness
Burglary	Stolen Property Offenses	Disorderly Conduct
Larcency-Theft	Vandalism	Vagrancy
Motor Vehicle Theft	Prostitution/Commercialized Vice	All Other Offenses (except traffic)
Arson	Weapons Offenses	Suspicion
	Sex Offenses (except forcible rape and prostitution)	Curfew and Loitering Law Violations
	Drug Abuse Violations	Runaways
	Gambling	

considered the most serious crimes; Part II offenses are less serious.

BEHAVIOR SYSTEMS IN CRIME

Each variety of crime has two important aspects: its legal description as stated in the law, and the behavior system that brings it into being. Consider, for example, the crime of shoplifting, which penal codes define as the theft of money, goods, or other merchandise from a store or shop. The law is quite clear as to what constitutes shoplifting. But the law cannot explain the numerous behavior patterns that can be associated with shoplifting. For many students, housewives, and other individuals, an instance of shoplifting may be a first and only offense, committed out of desperation or for the sake of excitement. Department store employees pilfer merchandise on a regular basis in an attempt to supplement their legal incomes in a relatively safe manner. For street hustlers in the central cities, shoplifting is but one of many petty crimes undertaken on a sporadic basis for the sake of economic gain. And finally, professional *boosters,* a small fraternity of skilled thieves, have elevated their techniques to an art form and carry them out regularly as a full-time business or vocation. The skills and techniques utilized by these four types of shoplifters vary considerably, as do the frequency of their thefts and their methods for the disposal of the stolen goods. The first two varieties of shoplifters here rarely view themselves as criminals, while the others are proud of being hustlers and professional thieves. Within this context of the sources of deviance, then, we will examine six behavior systems in crime: (1) violent personal crime, (2) occasional property crime, (3) organized robbery and gang theft, (4) white-collar and corporate crime, (5) organized crime, and (6) professional theft.

Shoplifters are of many types. What might be this person's motivation?

Violent Personal Crime

Violent personal crime consists of criminal acts resulting from differences in personal relations in which death or physical injury is inflicted. It is a reflection of individual and personal violence, and includes specific forms of criminal homicide, assault, forcible rape, and spouse and child abuse.[48]

Several characteristics seem to distinguish violent personal crime from other forms of violent criminal behavior. First, the offenders generally have little, if any, prior involvement with crime. Second, murderers, rapists, assaulters, and child abusers generally do not view themselves as criminals, and their crimes are not part of their life organization. Third, the perpetrators of these offenses act alone; most instances of personal violence are not a reflection of some group activity. Generally, the violence is directed by the offender against a specific victim. Fourth, and a critical factor in personal violence, is the victim–offender relationship. In the majority of murders, assaults, and instances of child abuse, the victims and offenders are known to one another—spouses, children, other relatives, lovers, neighbors, and acquaintances. In cases involving forcible rape, on the other hand, greater numbers of "stranger-to-stranger" encounters occur.

Occasional Property Crime

Occasional property crime refers to those types and instances of burglary, larceny, forgery, and other thefts undertaken infrequently or irregularly, and often quite crudely. Offenders who engage in this type of property crime do not pursue it as a career. For many of these amateur thieves, urban street criminals, or youthful gangs, crime is incidental to their way of life. Their crimes are typically sprees of burglaries, auto thefts, shoplifting, or acts of vandalism undertaken as part of peer group activities or for economic gain.

Offenders of the occasional property type generally have a petty crime or noncriminal orientation. Often first-time or infrequent offenders, they do not view themselves as criminals. They are unacquainted with criminal subcultures; their techniques for committing crimes are unskilled and undeveloped; they have little or no access to structured mechanisms for the disposal of stolen property. Rather, they generally steal for their own immediate purposes and little planning is apparent. Young vandals and burglars see themselves more as "pranksters" than as thieves. Nonprofessional forgers, shoplifters, and pilferers are typically victims of temporary or desperate financial situations, or they engage in an occasional theft for the sake of adventure or excitement.[49]

Organized Robbery and Gang Theft

Organized robbery and gang theft, often called professional "heavy" crime, involves highly skilled criminal activities using or threatening force, violence, coercion, and property damage, and accomplished by planning, surprise, and speed in order to diminish the risks of apprehension.

"Heavy" criminals of this type pursue crime as a career for financial gain; they generally work in teams and are armed, sometimes heavily; their planning is careful and their timing precise; and their pursuits include armed robbery, hijacking, kidnapping, and large-scale industrial theft.

Individuals who engage in organized robbery and gang theft are usually long-term criminals who move from petty offenses to auto theft, burglary, and robbery. As young adults, their repeated experiences with police, courts, and reformatories add to their sophistication in criminality and to criminal self-conceptions. They live on the fringes of organized society, and they view the "heavy" rackets as a way to "get rich quick," to become socially mobile, or to start anew, rather than as a vocation or occupational career.[50]

White-collar and Corporate Crime

White-collar crime and **corporate crime** refer to those offenses committed by persons acting in their legitimate occupational roles. The offenders include businesspeople, members of the professions and government, and other varieties of workers who, in the course of their everyday occupational activities, violate the basic trust placed in them or act in unethical ways. Crime is neither the way of life nor the chosen career of white-collar or corporate offenders, but rather something that occurs in conjunction with their more legitimate work activities. Typical offenses include the following:

- *In the business sector*—financial manipulations, unfair labor practices, misrepresentation of goods and consumer deception by false labeling, receipt of stolen goods, shortchanging, overcharging, black marketeering
- *In the labor sector*—misuse of union funds, failing to enforce laws affecting unions, entering into collusion with employers to the disadvantage of union members, illegal mechanisms for controlling union members
- *In the corporate sector*—restraint of trade, infringement of patents, monopolistic practices, environmental contamination, misuse of trademarks, manufacture of unsafe goods, false advertising, disposal of toxic wastes
- *In the financial sector*—embezzlement, violation of currency control measures, stock manipulation
- *In the medical sector*—illegal prescription practices, fee-splitting, illegal abortions, fraudulent reports to insurance companies
- *In the legal sector*—misappropriation of funds in trusts and receiverships, procurement of prejudiced testimony, bribery, instituting fraudulent damage claims
- *In the criminal justice sector*—accepting bribes, illegal arrest and detention practices, illegal correctional practices
- *In the civil sector*—illegal commissions, issuance of fraudulent licenses, illegal tax evaluations, misuse of campaign funds, illegal campaign practices[51]

At all levels of white-collar crime, the offenders have no criminal self-concept; rather, they rationalize their behaviors as "sharp" business practices, taking advantage of an "easy *rip-off*," taking advantage of certain "unfair" laws, or gaining something that "was coming to them."

Organized Crime

The term **organized crime** designates business activities aimed toward economic gain through unlawful means.

Drawing by Richter © *The New Yorker* Magazine, Inc.

"Miss Johnson will now pass out the moral blinders."

Such crime provides illegal goods and services through activities that include gambling, loansharking, bootlegging, trafficking in narcotics and other illegal drugs, disposing of stolen merchandise, and infiltrating legitimate businesses.[52]

People who pursue organized crime as an occupational career frequently focus on this type of criminality as a mechanism for upward mobility (see Exhibit 7.10). They often are recruited on the basis of kinship, friendship, or contacts within lower income environments, where such activities are sought out as a means of achieving economic respectability. Whether individuals are within a highly structured "syndicate" or are low-level, independent prostitutes or bookies, the commitment to the career is long-term and their life organization and life-style revolve around crime.

Professional Theft

Professional theft refers to nonviolent forms of criminal occupation pursued with a high degree of skill to maximize financial gain and minimize the risks of apprehension. The more typical forms of professional theft include pickpocketing, shoplifting, safe and house burglary, forgery, counterfeiting, sneak-thieving, and confidence swindling.[53] Professional thieves are separated from other criminals who engage in the same types of offense behavior by the social, organizational, and occupational structures that define their criminal activities. Professional thieves make a regular business of stealing; it is their occupation and means of livelihood, and as such, they devote their entire working time and energy to it. Professional thieves also operate with proficiency. Like members of the legitimate professions, they have an organized body of knowledge and skills that they utilize in the planning and execution of their activities. They are graduates of a developmental process that includes the acquisition of specialized attitudes, knowledge, skills, and experience. Moreover, in identifying themselves with the world of crime, they are members of an exclusive fraternity that extends friendship, understanding, sympathy, congeniality, security, recognition, and respect. And too, as residents of this remote corner of the underworld, they have access to specialized patterns of communication, a complex system of argot (slang), and a network of contacts within the legal profession and the criminal justice system that enable them to steal for long periods of time without going to prison.

As a final note, it should be emphasized here that these six behavioral types do not represent the full spectrum of criminal behavior systems. In **political crime,** for example, which includes treason, sedition, espionage, sabotage, war collaboration, and radicalism

Exhibit 7.10

Types & Stereotypes

The New Ethnic Underworlds

During the early years of the twentieth century, organized crime represented a mechanism for upward mobility among such immigrant groups as Italians, Jews, Poles, Germans, and the Irish. In subsequent decades, organized crime was almost exclusively associated with East Coast Italian "families." In recent years, however, the early twentieth-century pattern has reemerged (see map), with an even wider variety of racial or ethnic groups represented:

- *In Miami,* Cuban gangs run illegal gambling operations and a Canadian group oversees loansharking and money laundering.
- *In Los Angeles,* Israelis dominate insurance fraud, Taiwanese control the numbers racket, and Vietnamese sell illegal drugs.
- *In New York,* Koreans sponsor the illegal massage parlors and Russian immigrants are central to crimes involving extortion and contract murder.
- *In various cities,* Mexicans, Colombians, blacks, and Asians control aspects of drug trafficking.

All of this suggests that organized crime has become an equal opportunity employer.

SOCIAL INDICATOR

Percentage of College Students Who Have Used Drugs at Least Once during the Year

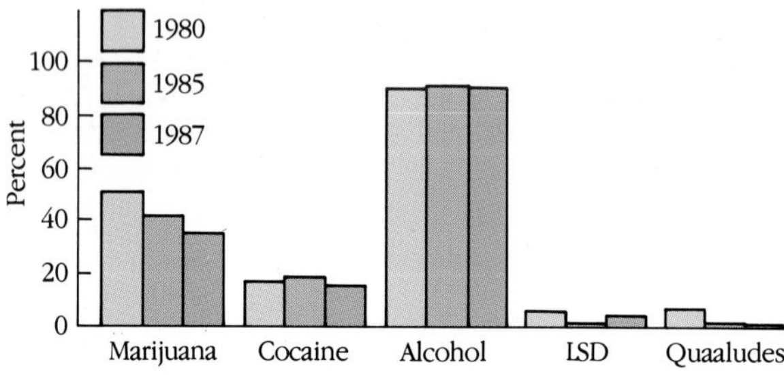

Source: Institute for Social Research, University of Michigan, 1988.

and protest, offenders violate the law when they feel that such illegal activity is essential and appropriate to achieving necessary changes in society—what Merton's theory of anomie referred to as *rebellion.* **"Victimless crime"** includes many public safety and sex offenses, drug violations, and nuisance offenses. In such crimes, no *real* injury to another person is involved, nor is the theft of goods or services. Rather, the morals, safety, and tranquility of the community are placed at risk, and the offenders are not necessarily viewed by others or themselves as criminals, per se, but rather as drunks, hookers, perverts, and junkies.

THE EXTENT OF CRIME

Crime, by its very nature, is not easily measurable. It is subject to both concealment and nonreporting—concealment by victims and offenders and nonreporting by authorities—with the result that official criminal statistics fall significantly short of the full volume and range of offenses actually perpetrated.

Official Criminal Statistics

Each year, the Federal Bureau of Investigation releases its ***Uniform Crime Reports,*** a rather lengthy compilation chronicling the magnitude and trends of crime in the United States. Two key features of the report each year are the crime index and the crime rate. The **crime index** is the total number of serious crimes—the Part I offenses listed in Exhibit 7.9—that became known to the police during the course of the year. In 1987, the crime index was 13,508,708.[54] That is, during 1987 a total of almost 13.5 million criminal homicides, forcible rapes, robberies, aggravated assaults, burglaries, larcenies, vehicle thefts, and cases of arson came to the attention of law enforcement agencies in the United States. The **crime rate** is the number of Part I offenses that occurred in any given area for every 100,000 persons living in that area. The U.S. crime rate for 1987 was 5,550.0.*

The crime index and the crime rate, usually given side-by-side in news releases, are often accepted by the general public as accurate indicators of the extent of crime. The FBI figures, however, have numerous limitations. Wide areas of criminal behavior, for example, rarely find their way into official compilations. When sex, family, and other human relationships are involved, criminal codes are often in sharp conflict with emotions and social norms, resulting in the concealment of homosexual relations, statutory rape, adultery, sodomy, illegal abortion, desertion, and nonsupport. Many white-collar crimes only rarely are brought to the attention of criminal justice officials. To these can be added the victimless crimes and syndicate rackets involving prostitution, gambling, and other illegal goods and services, which result in another group of nonreporting clientele. And finally, perhaps millions of victims of the more conventional robberies, assaults, burglaries, rapes, and thefts that occur in this country fail to report crimes to the police out of fear of publicity and reprisal, a lack of confidence in law enforcement or other criminal justice authorities, or a desire not to get involved with crime reporting and control.

At the same time, criminal statistics are also subject to concealment, nonreporting, overreporting, and other manipulations by criminal justice authorities, either for political or public relations purposes. Studies have demonstrated, for example, that law enforcement agencies wishing to secure more equipment and staff typically report (or on some occasions overreport) all known complaints. However, if such equipment or personnel has already been obtained, then the agencies may report fewer crimes, in order to suggest an efficient use of previous funding. In addition, not all complaints to police by citizens are logged into precinct files due to insufficient staffing or a receiving officer's perception that the

*Computing the crime rate is a matter of simple arithmetic. The rate indicated above was arrived at as follows:

$$\frac{\text{Total Crime Index}}{\text{Population}} \times 100{,}000 = \text{Rate}$$

$$\frac{\text{1987 Crime Index}}{\text{1987 Population}} \times 100{,}000 = \text{Rate}$$

$$\frac{13{,}508{,}708}{243{,}400{,}000} \times 100{,}000 = 5{,}550$$

SOCIAL INDICATOR

Crime in the United States, 1978–1987

Population	Crime Index Total*	Modified Crime Index Total†	Violent Crime	Property Crime	Murder and Non-negligent Man-slaughter	Forcible Rape	Robbery	Aggra-vated Assault	Burglary	Larceny-Theft	Motor Vehicle Theft	Arson†
Rate per 100,000 Inhabitants:												
1978	5,140.3		497.8	4,642.5	9.0	31.0	195.8	262.1	1,434.6	2,747.4	460.5	
1979	5,565.5		548.9	5,016.6	9.7	34.7	218.4	286.0	1,511.9	2.999.1	505.6	
1980	5,950.0		596.6	5,353.3	10.2	36.8	251.1	298.5	1,684.1	3,167.0	502.2	
1981	5,858.2		594.3	5,263.9	9.8	36.0	258.7	289.7	1,649.5	3,139.7	474.7	
1982	5,603.6		571.1	5,032.5	9.1	34.0	238.9	289.2	1,488.8	3,084.8	458.8	
1983	5,175.0		537.7	4,637.4	8.3	33.7	216.5	279.2	1,337.7	2,868.9	430.8	
1984	5,031.3		539.2	4,492.1	7.9	35.7	205.4	290.2	1,263.7	2,791.3	437.1	
1985	5,207.1		556.6	4,650.5	7.9	37.1	208.5	302.9	1,287.3	2,901.2	462.0	
1986	5,480.4		617.7	4,862.6	8.6	37.9	225.1	346.1	1,344.6	3,010.3	507.8	
1987	5,550.0		609.7	4,940.3	8.3	37.4	212.7	351.3	1,329.6	3,081.3	529.4	

Source: Federal Bureau of Investigation, 1987.

*Because of rounding, the offenses may not add to totals.
†Sufficient data are not available to estimate totals.

the offense is not important enough to log. Other complaints may be logged incorrectly or are simply lost. The end result of all these factors is a level of incompleteness, bias, and contamination that makes the accurate collection of criminal statistics impossible.[55]

DEVIANCE, CRIME, AND APPLIED SOCIOLOGY

Since the 1930s when the FBI began publishing its *Uniform Crime Reports,* social science research has been producing studies that confirm the limitations of official criminal statistics. Two mechanisms used for understanding the **"dark figure" of crime** (unknown crime) have been the study of self-reported criminal activity and the use of victimization surveys (see Exhibit 7.11). The first major effort in the study of self-reported criminal activity came in 1947, when researchers obtained completed questionnaires from 1,020 men and 678 women regarding their involvement in 49 different criminal offenses.[56] Ninety-nine percent of the respondents, who represented diverse age groups and a wide range of conventional occupations, admitted committing one or more of the offenses listed, and as indicated in the table below, the percentages of both men and women who had engaged in many types of crime were significant:

Crime	Men	Women
Petty Theft	89%	83%
Disorderly Conduct	85	76
Malicious Mischief	84	81
Assault	49	5
Tax Evasion	57	40
Robbery	11	1
Fraud	46	34
Criminal Libel	36	29
Concealed Weapons	35	3
Auto Theft	35	3
Other Grand Theft	13	11
Burglary	17	4

Exhibit 7.11

Applied Sociology

Criminal Victimization Surveys

In 1965, in an effort to determine the parameters of crime that did not appear in official criminal statistics, the President's Commission on Law Enforcement and Administration of Justice initiated the first national survey of crime victimization ever conducted. During that year, the National Opinion Research Center (NORC) of the University of Chicago surveyed 10,000 households, asking whether the person questioned, or any member of his or her household, had been a victim of crime during the preceding year, whether the crime had been reported to the police, and if not, the reasons for not reporting.[a] The 10,000 households were selected so that they would be representative of the nation as a whole, and as is the case with political polling and election forecasting, the results were considered to be essentially accurate within only a small margin of error. More detailed surveys were undertaken in medium- and high-crime areas in Boston, Chicago, and Washington, D.C.

The data from the victimization surveys quickly demonstrated that the actual number of crimes committed in the United States was probably several times that reported in the FBI's *Uniform Crime Reports* (URC). As indicated in Table 1, the NORC survey suggested that forcible rapes occurred at a rate almost four times the reported rate, larcenies were almost double, and burglaries and robberies were 50 percent greater than the reported rate. Vehicle theft was lower, but by a smaller amount than the differences between other categories of crime, and the homicide figure from the NORC survey was considered too small for accurate statistical projection.

The major reason for the differences between the NORC and the UCR rates is the fact that significant numbers of these crimes were not reported to the police. This high level of nonreporting was due primarily to the victims' beliefs that nothing could be done about the crimes or that the victimizations were simply not important enough to report. Less frequently mentioned were such reasons as fear of reprisal or publicity, inconvenience, not wanting to bother the police, or privacy concerns.

Since 1972, the national victimization surveys have been conducted on an annual basis by the U.S. Bureau of the Census. As indicated in Table 2, of the nation's 91.4 million households, some 24.4 percent were touched by crime during 1987.[b] Furthermore, 22.3 million crimes occurred, most of which were larcenies and burglaries.

In a more detailed look at rape, robbery or assault by strangers, and burglary—what the survey refers to as "crimes of high concern"—the chances of victimization were related to a household's race, family income, and place of residence. As suggested by Figure A, white households are less likely to be victimized by these crimes. Moreover, other data indicate that higher rates of rape, robbery or assault by strangers, and burglary were apparent among urban dwellers and families with incomes of less than $7,500.

The "rediscovery" of the victim as a more complete source of information on instances of criminal activity has been the chief contribution of the victimization survey. The material derived from crime victim surveys helps law enforcement agencies gauge the extent and distribution of crime in a community. In addition, since the surveys target not only victimizations but also public conceptions of the fear of crime, characteristics of the victim and the offender, conceptions of police effectiveness, and other data, victim-focused studies also are used for the following purposes:

1. to describe the characteristics of victims and high crime areas
2. to evaluate the effectiveness of specific police programs
3. to develop better insights into violent crimes through the

Households Touched by Crimes of High Concern,* by Race of Household Head, 1981–1987

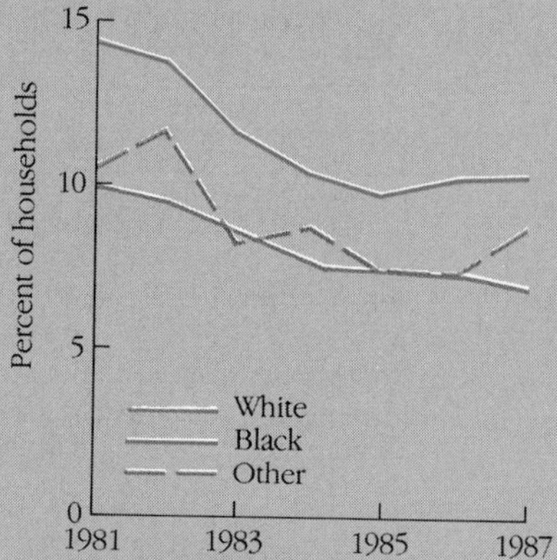

*A rape, robbery, or assault by a stranger or a household burglary analyses of victim–offender relationships

4. to structure programs for increased victim reporting of crimes to the police
5. to sensitize the criminal justice system to the needs of the victim
6. to develop training programs that stress police–victim and police–community relations
7. to structure and implement meaningful public information and crime-prevention programs

In connection with this last item, *crime prevention,* the victimization survey undertaken in a local community can have some unique applications. The data generated can be analyzed to determine *who* has the highest risk of victimization, for *which* types of crime, from *what* kinds of offenders, in *what* parts of a community, and under *what* types of circumstances. The resulting crime-prevention strategy would be *victim-* or *crime-specific,* targeting those community members whose normal behaviors and circumstances place them at high risk for certain types of crime.

SOURCES:

a. President's Commission on Law Enforcement and Administration of Justice, *Crime and Its Impact—An Assessment* (Washington, DC: U.S. Government Printing Office, 1967), p. 17.
b. *Households Touched by Crime, 1987,* Bureau of Justice Statistics Bulletin, June 1988.

Table 1 Comparison of NORC Survey and UCR Rates

Crime	NORC Survey	UCR
Homicide	3.0	5.1
Forcible Rape	42.5	11.6
Robbery	94.0	61.4
Aggravated Assault	218.3	106.6
Burglary	949.1	605.3
Larceny	606.5	393.3
Motor Vehicle Theft	206.2	251.0
Total Violent	357.8	184.7
Total Property	1,761.8	1,249.6

Source: President's Commission on Law Enforcement and Administration of Justice, *Crime and Its Impact—An Assessment* (Washington, DC: U.S. Government Printing Office, 1967), p. 17.

Table 2 Households Touched by Crime, 1987

	1987		Relative Percent Change
Households	Number of Households	Percent	1986–1987
Total	91,365,000	100%	
Touched by			
Any NCS* Crimes	22,254,000	24.4	−1.2%
Violent Crime	4,190,000	4.6	−2.1
Rape	108,000	.1	−7.7
Robbery	884,000	1.0	3.2
Assault	3,378,000	3.7	−3.9
Aggravated	1,258,000	1.4	−.7
Simple	2,374,000	2.6	−2.6
Total Larceny	15,667,000	17.1	−.9
Personal	10,074,000	11.0	−1.7
With Contact	456,000	.5	−5.7
Without Contact	9,745,000	10.7	−1.1
Household	7,236,000	7.9	−1.5
Burglary	4,717,000	5.2	−2.8
Motor Vehicle Theft	1,379,000	1.5	11.9
Crimes of High Concern (Rape, Robbery, Assault by Strangers or Burglary)	6,743,000	7.4	−3.9

*National Crime Survey

Note: Detail does not add to total because of overlap in households touched by various crimes. Relative percent change is based on unrounded figures.

Since this pioneer effort, which demonstrated that criminal activity was considerably more widespread than the police files even began to suggest, self-reported studies have become more common. In addition to their use as a check on the limitations of standard crime-reporting mechanisms and an indication of just how great the "dark figure" of crime may be, they can also be used to determine (1) how extensive criminal activity may be within the "normal" (typically noncriminal) population, (2) what kinds of crime are committed that typically remain unknown, (3) how the official system of control selects its cases, (4) whether some categories of deviants are over- or underselected by official control mechanisms, and (5) whether explanations and theories of deviance and crime developed for officially known offenders are applicable for nonregistered offenders.

One of the more dramatic examples of how great the "dark figure" can be in some communities has already been presented in Chapter 2. In Exhibit 2.10 on page 56, the extent of criminal involvement among the 356 Miami heroin users studied was strikingly high, while the rate of arrest was almost insignificant. The men, for example, had committed 80,644 crimes, or an average of 337 per individual during the one year period prior to the interviews. Although more than half of these offenses were the victimless crimes of procuring, drug sales, and gambling, the number of robberies and larcenies was also significant. Furthermore, of these 80,644 crimes, only 189 resulted in an arrest—a ratio of one arrest for every 427 crimes committed. And similarly high rates were apparent for the women as well.

Figures like these become even more interesting when one considers the number of crimes that came to the attention of the police in the same geographical area during the period of study. During 1978, for example, when the interviews were conducted, 6,385 robberies were reported to the police in the Miami metropolitan area.[57] Yet, the self-report figures alone show a one year total of 3,901 robberies perpetrated by as few as 356 individuals. Such data reinforce the idea that the "dark figure" of crime exceeds the amount of known crime.

Self-report studies do have their limitations, as is the case with official criminal statistics. Although research within certain deviant populations has demonstrated that most respondents provide valid data to interviewers,[58] self-report measures are most effective when investigating the behaviors and attitudes of select groups—drug users, delinquents, students, physicians, and the like. The method becomes cumbersome when applied to large-scale populations. As an alternative, recent research has targeted the victims of crime, perhaps the most practical method for reliably estimating the incidence of crime.

SUMMARY

Deviant behavior is behavior that fails to conform with the significant social norms and expectations of a group. Deviance includes not only crime, but other nonconforming behaviors, such as civil disobedience, nudity, littering, and adultery, as well. Deviance refers also to such disvalued persons as hermits, drunks, eccentrics, and the mentally ill. Whether acts are considered deviant depends on who is committing them, where and when they occur, and who is doing the judging.

Most people conform to the rules of their society the majority of the time. They do so because of socialization and sanctions. Socialization is the process through which people learn and internalize the norms of their society. Sanctions are rewards for conformity and punishments for deviance.

Deviance is not only normal to the makeup of a society, but it is functional as well. Deviance defines the boundaries of proper conduct, it binds people together in a tighter social bond, it represents a safety valve for discontent who may strain the social order, it supports segments of the occupational structure, and it stimulates the reexamination and redefinition of many social norms and methods of social control.

Many explanations have been offered for deviance. The biological theories receive little support. Among the sociological explanations, anomie, labeling, and differential association theory are the most frequently cited sources. Anomie theory suggests that crime and other forms of deviance are an outcome of the gap between aspirations and achievable goals. Labeling theory focuses on the processes of interaction through which certain behaviors become defined as deviant. Differential association theory holds that criminal and deviant behaviors are learned through the same processes by which nondeviant behavior is learned.

Crime, among the most visible forms of deviant behavior, is any act in violation of the criminal law, committed without defense or justification, and sanctioned by the state as a felony or misdemeanor. What constitutes crime seems to vary over place and time, and these differences are the result of varying social norms and values. Exactly how much crime exists is something that is difficult to measure, for it is subject to concealment by victims and offenders and nonreporting by authorities. Studies of both criminals and victims clearly reinforce the notion that the "dark figure" of crime well exceeds the amount of known criminal activity.

KEY TERMS/CONCEPTS

administrative law
anomie
atavism
biological determinism
collective conscience
conformity
corporate crime
crime
crime index
crime rate
criminal law
"dark figure" of crime
deviant behavior
differential association
felony
formal sanctions
informal sanctions
innovation
labeling theory
misdemeanor
occasional property crime
organized crime
organized robbery/gang theft
Part I offenses
Part II offenses
political crime
primary deviation
professional theft
rebellion
retreatism
ritualism
sanctions
secondary deviation
Uniform Crime Reports
victimless crime
violent personal crime
white-collar crime
XYY chromosome

DISCUSSION QUESTIONS

1. In the opening paragraph of this chapter we posed the question of what society would be like if there were no deviants. Now that you have a better understanding of what constitutes deviance and how it comes into being, how would you answer this question?
2. Other than the few examples mentioned in this chapter, what kinds of "socially approved deviance" exist in contemporary American society?
3. A number of sociologists and criminologists have maintained that the criminal law is the formal cause of crime? What is meant by this statement?
4. To what extent do you think that the old saying "Money is the root of all evil" is true?
5. Why do you think that certain crimes come to the attention of the police while others do not?

SUGGESTED READINGS

Howard S. Becker, *Outsiders: Studies in the Sociology of Deviance* (New York: Free Press, 1963). One of the pioneering works in the study of deviance, in a clear and interesting style, this book outlines the labeling theory of deviance, making extensive use of case materials.

Kai T. Erikson, *Wayward Puritans: A Study in the Sociology of Deviance* (New York: Wiley, 1966). A study of three "crime waves" that occurred in seventeenth-century Puritan society, from the perspectives of labeling theory and the work of Emile Durkheim.

Robert F. Meier (ed.), *Major Forms of Crime* (Beverly Hills: Sage, 1984). In a series of essays by numerous contributors, the major categories of crime (including murder and assault, forcible rape, occasional property crime, public order crime, political crime, white-collar and corporate crime, gang delinquency, organized crime, and professional theft) are analyzed in depth.

Edwin H. Sutherland, *The Professional Thief* (Chicago: University of Chicago Press, 1937). Written more than a half-century ago, this classic in criminology examines the social organization and occupational structure of stealing as a business and way of life.

James Q. Wilson and Richard J. Herrnstein, *Crime and Human Nature* (New York: Simon and Schuster, 1985). A comprehensive examination of the causes of crime, reviewing scientific evidence assembled from the fields of sociology, anthropology, economics, biology, medicine, and psychology.

NOTES

1. Kai T. Erikson, *Wayward Puritans: A Study in the Sociology of Deviance* (New York: Wiley, 1966), p. 6.
2. Edward Sagarin, *Deviants and Deviance* (New York: Praeger, 1975), p. 9.
3. Robert K. Merton, "The Sociology of Social Problems," in Robert K. Merton and Robert Nisbet (eds.), *Contemporary Social Problems* (New York: Harcourt Brace Jovanovich, 1976), pp. 29–30.
4. Howard S. Becker, *Outsiders: Studies in the Sociology of Deviance* (New York: Free Press, 1963), p. 9.
5. See Robert M. Fogelson (ed.), *The Los Angeles Riots* (New York: Arno Press, 1969); William Manchester, *The Glory and the Dream* (Boston: Little, Brown, 1974), pp. 1301–1305; National Advisory Commission on Civil Disorders, *Report of the National Advisory Commission on Civil Disorders* (New York: E. P. Dutton, 1969); Milton Viorst, *Fire in the Streets:*

America in the 1960's (New York: Simon and Schuster, 1979), pp. 309–27.

6. Emile Durkheim, *The Rules of Sociological Method* (Chicago: University of Chicago Press, 1938), pp. 65–73. See also Steven Lukes and Andrew Scull, *Durkheim and the Law* (New York: St. Martin's, 1983).
7. Edwin H. Sutherland and Donald R. Cressey, *Principles of Criminology,* 7th ed. (Philadelphia: Lippincott, 1966), p. 24.
8. Edward Sagarin, *Deviants and Deviance,* p. 372.
9. Albert K. Cohen, *Deviance and Control* (Englewood Cliffs, NJ: Prentice-Hall, 1966), p. 7.
10. Karl Marx, *Selected Writings in Sociology and Social Philosophy,* translated by T. B. Bottomore (New York: McGraw-Hill, 1956), pp. 158–59.
11. Andrew Hacker (ed.), *U.S.: A Statistical Profile of the American People* (New York: Viking, 1983), pp. 126–27; Federal Bureau of Investigation, *Crime in the United States—1986* (Washington, DC: U.S. Government Printing Office, 1987).
12. United States Department of Justice, Bureau of Justice Statistics, *Sourcebook of Criminal Justice Statistics—1986* (Washington, DC: U.S. Government Printing Office, 1987), p. 2.
13. See William Manchester, *The Glory,* p. 908.
14. William Manchester, *The Glory,* p. 909.
15. James A. Inciardi, *Reflections on Crime* (New York: Holt, Rinehart and Winston, 1978), p. 90; Nigel D. Walker, "Lost Causes in Criminology," in Roger Hood (ed.), *Crime, Criminology and Public Policy* (New York: Free Press, 1974), pp. 47–62.
16. This quotation from Lombroso's opening speech at the Sixth Congress of Criminal Anthropology at Turin, Italy, in 1906 appears in Leon Radzinowicz, *Ideology and Crime* (New York: Columbia University Press, 1966), p. 29.
17. Gina Lombroso Ferrero, *Criminal Man According to the Classification of Cesare Lombroso* (New York: G. P. Putnam's Sons, 1911), pp. 10–24.
18. Cesare Lombroso and William Ferrero, *The Female Offender* (New York: D. Appleton, 1895), p. 101.
19. Richard L. Dugdale, *The Jukes* (New York: G. P. Putnam's Sons, 1910).
20. See also Arthur H. Estabrook, *The Jukes in 1915* (Washington, DC: Carnegie Institution, 1916); Arthur H. Estabrook and Charles P. Davenport, *The Nam Family* (Cold Spring Harbor, NY: Eugenics Record Office, 1912); Henry H. Goddard, *The Kallikaks* (New York: Macmillan, 1912).
21. Charles Goring, *The English Convict* (London: Her Majesty's Stationary Office, 1913).
22. Earnest A. Hooton, *Crime and the Man* (Cambridge: Harvard University Press, 1939).
23. William H. Sheldon, S. S. Stevens, and W. B. Tucker, *The Varieties of Human Physique* (New York: Harper, 1940).
24. R. G. Fox, "The XYY Offender: A Modern Myth?" *Journal of Criminal Law, Criminology, and Police Science,* 62 (March 1971), pp. 59–73. See also Donald J. West (ed.), *Criminological Implications of Chromosome Abnormalities* (Cambridge: University of Cambridge, Institute of Criminology, 1969); "The XYY Chromosome: A Challenge to Our System of Criminal Responsibility," *New York Law Forum,* 16 (Spring 1970), p. 232.
25. For a review and discussion of the more recent studies in this regard, see Nicolas F. Hahn, "Crime and Intelligence," in James A. Inciardi and Kenneth C. Haas (eds.), *Crime and the Criminal Justice Process* (Dubuque, IA: Kendall/Hunt, 1978), pp. 67–74; C. Ray Jeffery (ed.), *Biology and Crime* (Beverly Hills: Sage, 1979).
26. James Q. Wilson and Richard J. Herrnstein, *Crime and Human Nature* (New York: Simon and Schuster, 1985).
27. Emile Durkheim, *Suicide: A Study in Sociology* (New York: Free Press, 1951).
28. Robert K. Merton, "Social Structure and Anomie," *American Sociological Review,* 3 (1938), pp. 672–82.
29. Edward Sagarin, *Deviants and Deviance,* p. 106.
30. Howard S. Becker, *Outsiders,* p. 9 .
31. Howard S. Becker, *Outsiders,* pp. 147–63.
32. Edwin M. Lemert, *Social Pathology* (New York: McGraw-Hill, 1951), pp. 75–76.
33. Personal communication, August 8, 1984.
34. James A. Inciardi, *Criminal Justice* (Orlando: Academic Press, 1984), p. 242.
35. Robert E. Park, Ernest W. Burgess, and Roderick D. MacKensie, *The City* (Chicago: University of Chicago Press, 1925).
36. Clifford R. Shaw and Associates, *Delinquency Areas* (Chicago: University of Chicago Press, 1929).
37. Clifford R. Shaw, *Brothers in Crime* (Chicago: University of Chicago Press, 1938); Clifford R. Shaw, *The Jack Roller* (Chicago: University of Chicago Press, 1930).
38. Edwin H. Sutherland, *The Professional Thief* (Chicago: University of Chicago Press, 1937).
39. Edwin H. Sutherland and Donald R. Cressey, *Principles of Criminology* (Philadelphia: Lippincott, 1947), pp. 6–7.
40. Jerome Michael and Mortimer J. Adler, *Crime, Law and Social Science* (New York: Harcourt Brace, 1933), p. 5.
41. Thorsten Sellin, *Culture Conflict and Crime* (New York: Social Science Research Council, 1938), p. 21.
42. Albert K. Cohen, *Delinquent Boys: The Culture of the Gang* (Glencoe, IL: Free Press, 1955).
43. Walter B. Miller, "Lower Class Culture as a Generating Milieu for Gang Delinquency," *Journal of Social Issues,* 14 (1958), pp. 5–19.
44. Sir Leon Radzinowicz and Joan King, *The Growth of Crime: The International Experience* (New York: Basic Books, 1977), p. 116.
45. Richard Quinney, *The Social Reality of Crime* (Boston: Little, Brown, 1970), p. 16.
46. Harry Elmer Barnes, *The Repression of Crime* (New York: George H. Doran, 1926), pp. 43–45.
47. *Time,* December 12, 1983, p. 31.
48. See Marshall B. Clinard and Richard Quinney, *Criminal Behavior Systems: A Typology* (New York: Holt, Rinehart and Winston, 1967), pp. 20–33.
49. Marshall B. Clinard and Richard Quinney, *Criminal Behavior Systems,* pp. 88–94.
50. James A. Inciardi, *Criminal Justice,* p. 104.
51. James A. Inciardi, *Reflections on Crime,* pp. 146–47.

52. For a discussion of organized crime, see Joseph L. Albini, *The American Mafia: Genesis of a Legend* (New York: Appleton-Century-Crofts, 1971); Donald R. Cressey, *Theft of the Nation* (New York: Harper & Row, 1969); Norval Morris and Gordon Hawkins, *An Honest Politician's Guide to Crime Control* (Chicago: University of Chicago Press, 1970), pp. 202–35.
53. Edwin H. Sutherland, *The Professional Thief;* James A. Inciardi, *Careers in Crime* (Chicago: Rand McNally, 1975).
54. Federal Bureau of Investigation, *Crime in the United States—1987* (Washington, DC: U.S. Government Printing Office, 1988).
55. For a detailed discussion of the problems of criminal statistics, see James A. Inciardi, "The Uniform Crime Reports: Some Considerations on Their Shortcomings and Utility," *Public Data Use,* 6 (November 1978), pp. 3–16.
56. James S. Wallerstein and Clement J. Wyle, "Our Law-Abiding Law-Breakers," *Probation,* 35 (April 1947), pp. 107–18.
57. Federal Bureau of Investigation, *Crime in the United States—1978* (Washington DC: U.S. Government Printing Office, 1979), p. 72.
58. For example, see Arthur J. Bonito, David N. Nurco, and John W. Shaffer, "The Veridicality of Addicts' Self-Reports in Social Research," *International Journal of the Addictions,* 11 (1976), pp. 719–24; Richard C. Stephens, "The Truthfulness of Addict Respondents in Research Projects," *International Journal of the Addictions,* 7 (1972), pp. 549–58.

Inequality and Stratification

Socioeconomic Stratification

Quoting from the Declaration of Independence in his address dedicating the national cemetery at Gettysburg, Pennsylvania, on November 19, 1863, President Abraham Lincoln extended a measure of immortality to the well-known phrase, "All men are created equal." These famous words have been repeated often. Some individuals have interpreted them quite literally; a few even believe them. But consider the facts. In the United States, less than 25% of the population controls most of the wealth; more than 50% of all corporate and municipal securities are in the hands of less than 2% of American families; and one out of every 230 people in the country has a net worth of at least $1 million. An individual by the name of Daniel K. Ludwig, clearly one of the richest men in America, once purchased a piece of land from the Brazilian government that was larger than the nation of Belgium. Across the Atlantic Queen Elizabeth II of England boasts a personal fortune of over £100 million. She and the rest of the royal family enjoy the comforts of eight personal residences (including the 900-room Windsor Castle), the royal yacht *Britannia,* and yearly expense accounts of millions of pounds financed by the British taxpayers. Many other nations of the world still have an aristocracy, the "society" people who can trace their ancestry back several centuries and whose great-grandparents accumulated enough capital to support their descendants for generations to come. Mere money is of little interest to these individuals and status of only minor importance; they had both at the time they were born. With their inherited rank and power, many have turned their lives into a kind of Byzantine intrigue, just to avoid simple boredom.

In contrast, consider the plight of the poor. In the United States, some 14% of the population, over 33 million people, are considered to be living in poverty—deprived of adequate shelter, health care, and nutrition. Elsewhere, "poverty" is even more life threatening. The indigent of Tunisia often survive by eating discarded bits of meat, eggshells, and fruit shavings, purchased from scavengers in local "used food markets." In Ethiopia and Chad, every child has a 1 in 5 chance of experiencing a slow death before age five, if not from disease, then from starvation.

Historians have argued that the term "equality" in the Declaration of Independence and Lincoln's Gettysburg Address referred *not* to wealth and status, but to the basic freedoms of liberty and the protection of the law. But even these basic freedoms are not always guaranteed equally. Research has repeatedly demonstrated that the probability of arrest, conviction, and execution is greater among the poor, and that access to the channels of upward mobility is structured to exclude many minority group members.

While theoretically "all men are created equal," Napoleon, the ruling pig in George Orwell's *Animal Farm,* came closer to social reality with his declaration that "some are more equal than others." In his presidential address to the membership of the American Sociological Association on August 28, 1968, Philip M. Hauser made this same point with his neologism of the "pre-conception IQ"—the IQ of a child before he or she was conceived. "The child with the high pre-conception IQ," Hauser suggested, "who selects white-skinned parents who live in the suburbs, has by this astute act guaranteed unto himself a future better than that of the child with a miserably low pre-conception IQ, stupid enough to select black-skinned parents of the inner-city slums."[1] Popular recognition of this concept is also evident in the comment of a stand-up comedian who observed that it didn't matter if you were born rich or poor, as long as you had money.

THE DIMENSIONS OF STRATIFICATION

The foregoing discussion would suggest that vast differences exist among people in terms of their wealth, status, social rank, and overall position in society. Although most Americans profess a *belief* in the concept of "equality," they also use such terms as "the rich," "the poor," and "the middle class." Value-laden designations such as "working stiffs," "welfare cases," and "fat cats" are common. It is obvious that wealth, power, income, prestige, authority, fame, and many other valued rewards are distributed unequally in society. This **structural inequality,** the unequal distribution of wealth and other rewards, is the subject matter of social stratification.

Economic Inequality

Economic or material inequality involves money, property, land, and other resources that can be translated into consumption. An almost total absence of economic inequality was common at one time in a number of nonindustrialized societies, particularly among the hunting tribes of Africa and South America when material resources were abundant and freely available. In addition, the nomadic existence of these people made the accumulation of material assets impractical.[2] A more contemporary example is to be found in the Israeli Kibbutzim, which were established to eliminate the unequal distribution of resources associated with occupational differentiation.[3] The current kibbutz structure offers a relatively homogeneous standard of living that is unaffected by the hierarchy of positions or degree of achievement an individual attains. Any differences in living conditions that do occur are based on personal criteria such as health, sex, and age.

At the other extreme are societies in which economic inequality is rampant. For example, in twelfth- and thirteenth-century England the income of the king was 24,000 times greater than that of the majority of his subjects, most of whom earned only a penny a day.[4] A number of dramatic, contemporary examples appear in the international sector. It has been estimated that prior to the end of his dictatorship in Haiti in early 1986, Jean-Claude ("Baby Doc") Duvalier had acquired a personal fortune of over $800 million, while 80% of the country's 6 million citizens earned less than $130 a year.[5] Similarly, during the twenty-year reign of Ferdinand E. Marcos as president of the Philippines, he and his family lived in unimaginable luxury while his country slipped into economic chaos. After the government takeover led by Corazon Aquino in 1986 was completed, the presidential palace doors were unhinged and an inventory of the Marcos family holdings was begun. The investigators found an impressive accumulation: a few billion dollars here, another $800 million there, an office tower in New York, a waterfront estate on Long Island, and a second

SOCIAL INDICATOR

Household Income in the U.S.

Income	Percentage of Households
Under $5,000	7.2%
$5,000–$14,999	22.7
$15,000–$24,999	20.0
$25,000–$34,999	16.5
$35,000–$49,999	16.6
$50,000–$74,999	13.3
$75,000 & Over	3.5

Source: U.S. Bureau of the Census, 1988.

palace plus a dozen or so country houses. It was estimated that, in all, Marcos had taken between $5 billion and $10 billion from his nation's treasury, while his people suffered poverty, widespread unemployment, and a worsening standard of living.[6]

In the United States, marked disparities in wealth and income are also commonplace. In 1986, the United States Bureau of the Census reported that of all the nation's 86.8 million households, just over a fourth had incomes of less than $12,500, almost two-thirds were in the $12,501 to $50,000 range, and the balance enjoyed incomes of more than $50,000 annually.[7] At the extremes were the some 4.3 million families with incomes of less than $5,000 and the small cohort of economic elites whose annual wages exceeded $1 million.

Prestige

Prestige, the honor, respectability, or worth that a person's position in society commands, is also distributed unequally in most social systems.

The assignment of prestige to various social and occupational positions in the United States seems to be based on cultural attitudes that are grounded in a peculiar mix of evaluative criteria. On the one hand, positions that are believed to require such rare or unusual abilities as physical dexterity, exceptional strength, or artistic talent, tend to be ranked as higher in prestige than those that do not demand "that something special." Simultaneously, positions that require special training also rank above the majority of others. And finally, prestige may be accorded on the basis of wealth and income.

Exhibit 8.1 shows the current prestige ranking of occupations in the U.S. The scores reflect a mix of numerous evaluative criteria.[8] Physicians, with the highest prestige ranking, occupy positions that involve all three criteria listed above; being a doctor requires special talent and training, and doctors typically garner a substantial income. College professors, on the other hand, with an overall ranking of 3, generally have lower incomes than many service and craft workers, accountants, and administrators. The prestige ranking of each society reflects its unique history, meaning that the same occupation, such as priest, will rank higher in some societies than others.

Without question, prestige is a desirable asset in most societies. Many motivational psychologists argue that the need for prestige is a basic goal that is shared by almost all people. Considerations of prestige influence decisions about food, wearing apparel, and automobiles. Prestige also enables people to obtain other kinds of rewards. Individuals who occupy prestigious positions may obtain goods and services or exercise power or political control options unavailable to most others.

Power

A third and considerably more complex form of inequality involves power. The essence of power is the capacity

SOCIAL INDICATOR

Prestige Rankings in Cross-cultural Perspective

Nigeria	Brazil
Governmental Official	Cabinet Member
Attorney	Priest
Priest	Physician
Teacher (Elementary)	Attorney
Factory Worker	Farm Owner
Police Officer	Teacher
Tailor	Auto Mechanic
Farm Owner	Police Officer
Leather Worker	Carpenter
Beggar	Garbage Collector

Czechoslovakia

Physician	Priest
Collective Farmer	Judge
Teacher (High School)	Police Officer
Mason	Sewage Worker
Cabinet Minister	

Sources: J. Michael Armer, "Intersociety and Intrasociety: Correlations of Occupational Prestige," *American Journal of Sociology,* 74 (July 1968), p. 32; Archibald O. Haller, "Variations in Occupational Prestige," *American Journal of Sociology,* 77 (March 1972), pp. 952–55; Roger Penn, "Occupational Prestige Hierarchies," *Social Forces,* 54 (December 1975), p. 355.

Exhibit 8.1

Research in Sociology

Occupational Prestige Rankings in the United States

Occupation	Score	Rank
Professional		
Physician	95.8	1
Lawyer	90.1	3
College Professor	90.1	3
Electrical Engineer	79.5	7
Registered Nurse	75.0	8
High-school Teacher	70.2	10
Elementary School Teacher	65.4	12
Social Worker	63.2	15
Administrative		
Mayor	92.2	2
Superintendent of Schools	87.8	5
Factory Owner: 2,000 Employees	81.7	6
Office Manager	68.3	11
Hotel Manager	64.1	13
Circulation Director: Newspaper	63.5	14
Supervisor: Warehouse	56.4	21
Supervisor: Assembly Line	53.8	23
Technicians		
Accountant	71.2	9
Hospital Lab Technician	63.1	16
Dental Assistant	54.8	22
Clerical		
Private Secretary	60.9	18
Stenographer	52.6	25
Office Secretary	51.3	26
Bookkeeper	50.0	28
Telephone Operator	46.2	30
Typist	44.9	32
Post-office Clerk	42.3	34
File Clerk	34.0	39
Farm Work		
Cotton Farmer	32.4	40
Fruit Harvester: For Own Family	26.0	44

Occupation	Score	Rank
Direct Service		
Stock Broker	81.7	6
Police Officer	58.3	20
Homemaker (F)	51.0	27
Salesperson: Wholesale	46.2	30
Beautician	42.1	35
Hairdresser	39.4	36
Shoe Store Salesperson	35.9	38
Waitress (F)/Waiter (M)	22.1	47
Janitor	12.5	52
Maid (F)/Household Worker (M)	11.5	53
Crafts		
Electrician	62.5	17
Plumber	58.7	19
Carpenter	53.5	24
Welder	46.8	29
Auto Mechanic	44.9	32
Butcher	38.8	37
Operatives		
Assembly-line Worker	28.3	41
Textile Machine Operator	27.9	42
Delivery Truck Driver	26.9	43
Stock Clerk	24.4	45
Coal Miner	24.0	46
Garbage Collector	16.3	48
Unskilled		
Box Packer	15.1	49
Laundry Worker	14.7	50
Salad Maker in Hotel	13.8	51
Yarn Washer	11.8	54
Parking-lot Attendant	8.0	55

Source: Based on Christine E. Bose and Peter H. Rossi, "Gender and Jobs," *American Sociological Review*, 48 (June 1983), pp. 327–28. Reprinted by permission.

to control events or to determine the behavior of other people in the face of resistance and to resist such attempts at control by others. Power is illustrated in the relationships between employers and employees, parents and children, and prison guards and inmates. One group has direct power over others because of superior force or control of jobs or money. Indirect and impersonal forms of control become apparent when individuals or groups are placed in a position in which they make far-reaching decisions that affect the lives of others. All legislators fall into this category, as do the President of the United States, the justices of the United States Supreme Court, and the members of the Federal Reserve Board, whose decisions affect interest rates, inflation, employment rates, the availability of home mortgages, and the general state of the economy.

STRATIFICATION SYSTEMS

The world is hardly a neutral place. People are continually evaluating and appraising one another, rendering judgments as to relative worth, desirability, value, and ranking in the social hierarchy. Individuals are placed into social classes, abstract categories of social position which influence how people respond to them. Depending upon a person's "class," he or she may be considered "superior" or "inferior" to others, and treated accordingly. Inequalities in wealth, income, prestige, and power reinforce this classification process. The resultant division of society into levels based on wealth, prestige, and power is known as **social stratification.** Social stratification is an integral part of the overall structure of society and is transmitted from one generation to the next.

Although some analysts have argued that social stratification is a necessary and inevitable feature of human society,[9] anthropological evidence for such an assertion is weak. The most primitive human groups, technologically speaking—the "hunting and gathering" societies whose primary activities involve the search for food—are extremely egalitarian. Inequalities in material possessions and power are minimal, if not totally absent, and these groups frequently have no permanent leader. Some differences in the prestige of members of these primitive groups do exist, but these are likely to be based on age or some personal accomplishment, such as hunting skills, valor, or generosity and are not passed on from parents to children.[10] Moreover, in contrast with Western societies, where competition is a common aspect of social life, in the hunting-and-gathering societies, sharing seems to be almost universal. In fact, sharing is often a matter of survival, particularly when drought and other natural disasters cause scarcities of food.

Types of Stratification Systems

Stratification systems vary considerably from one society to another and across time. In some systems, individuals born at the bottom of the system live their entire lives in poverty, plagued by the knowledge that the elites flourish, and the poor have no hope for themselves or for their children. In other systems, individuals have the chance to improve their positions by personal effort, or to suffer through their own failings. In all, there are four major types of stratification systems—caste, slave, estate, and industrial class.

Caste Systems

A **caste** is a ranked hereditary grouping within a rigid system of stratification. In a **caste system** of stratification, individuals are permanently positioned at a given social level on the basis of inherited characteristics. Members of any given caste are restricted severely in their choice of occupation, life-style, choice of residence, and social participation. Marriage outside of one's caste is prohibited. The caste system is associated usually with Hindu India, and social scientists who have studied castes extensively have offered two views concerning the way in which they originate. One group argues that the caste system is to be defined in terms of its Hindu attributes and rationale, and is, therefore, unique to India. The second theory is that the caste system is to be defined in terms of structural features found not only in Hindu India, but in a number of other societies as well. Those who hold this latter view maintain that caste groups exist in such widely scattered areas as the Arabian Peninsula, Polynesia, South Africa, Guatemala, Japan, aboriginal North America, and the contemporary United States. Regardless of how tenable either of these positions is, all observers agree that the caste system in India is unique—unique in its complexity, in the religious ritual that explains it, and in the degree to which the constituent groups have been cohesive and self-regulating.[11]

The Indian term for caste is *jati.* These groups vary in size from just a few members to many thousands, each with its own distinctive rules, customs, and modes of government. The origins of caste stratification in India are unknown, but an idealized version appears in a series of ancient Hindu holy books. These books describe the *varna,* a fourfold division of Hindu society into castes entitled Brahman, Kshatriya, Vaisya, and Sudra. The Brahmans were priests and holy men. As keepers of the sacred rituals, their status in the caste system was greatest. The Kshatriyas were warriors and princely rulers. The Vaisya caste was larger, and included traders, merchants, and craftsmen. The Sudra, which was composed of peasants and laborers, was also a larger grouping. These

Members of India's "untouchable" caste fill the most menial jobs in society.

four divisions, all of which were considered pure and holy, probably corresponded to large, broad, and undifferentiated social groups. Below the Sudras were the "untouchables," or Panchemas, who undertook the most menial of tasks. The outcast Panchemas were considered impure and outside the pale of Hinduism. Members of the four ritually pure castes considered contact with the Panchemas to be a kind of religious contamination—hence, the term "untouchable."

In actual practice, Indian society was composed of many thousands of castes (jatis) and subcastes. In 1901, the last year in which a complete tabulation of all castes was attempted, the number (excluding subcastes) was found to be 2,378. In 1931, moreover, some 15 million Brahmans appeared in the census, but to consider them as members of but one caste would be erroneous. In one province alone as many as 200 major castes of Brahmans were counted, none of which permitted intermarriage. These Brahman castes differed markedly in social standing. Some ranked at the top of the social scale, while others were of such low status that many of their own clients, members of low castes, would not take food in their homes.[12]

Historically, the major belief underlying the Hindu caste system was reincarnation. Rebirth into a particular caste represented a reward or punishment for an individual's behavior in a previous life or lives. This belief assured that there would be little rebellion against the caste system and its inequalities. The castes endured for some 3,000 years, but the occupational barriers they imposed have been breaking down slowly under economic pressures since the nineteenth century. The social distinctions, on the other hand, have been more persistent. Attitudes toward the "untouchables" only began to change in the 1930s, with the influence of Mohandas Gandhi's teachings. Although "untouchability" was declared illegal in 1949 , resistance to change has remained strong. As increased industrialization has produced new occupations and professions, and as new political and social functions have emerged, the caste system has adapted and persisted.

Slave Systems

Slavery is the holding of people as property or chattel, and in **slave systems** of stratification certain individuals are regarded as property and can be bought, sold, traded, or destroyed. Slave systems have a long history and have been chronicled in ancient Mesopotamia, Eygpt, Greece, and Rome. In most instances these systems were associated with agriculture, but house and personal slaves were also common. Slavery declined in Europe during the Middle Ages with the rise of feudalism, but it was reintroduced worldwide with the conquest of the New World, when it was found that blacks from Africa made effective plantation workers in warm climates. Slavery began in what is now the United States in 1619 and quickly became an institution in the South.

In slave systems of stratification, there are essentially two levels on the social ladder: *slaves* and *owners*. As disposable property, slaves are subject totally to their owners. Owners hold the rights of life or death over the slaves and are answerable to no one with regard to the treatment of their "property." Thus, slaves have no civil rights and are denied the privilege of citizenship. Although slavery typically is considered a thing of the

This drawing, the only one known to have been produced aboard a slave ship, depicts Africans en route to America to be sold into slavery. The conquest of the New World reintroduced slavery worldwide.

past, during the 1970s the United Nations Commission on Human Rights estimated that there were more than one million slaves throughout the world. Most were located in North Africa and the Middle East and were found in agrarian social networks.[13] Moreover, although the Thirteenth Amendment to the Constitution abolished slavery in the United States in 1865, the practice continues to persist in this nation as well (see Exhibit 8.2).

Estate Systems

An **estate** is a ranked division of a society whose members have rights and duties that are prescribed by law. In **estate systems** of stratification, social position is based on birth, relationship to the land, and political or military strength. The primary models of the estate system are medieval European feudal societies, in which the nobility enjoyed a privileged status and legal authority over those who tilled the land. The exact origins of the feudal estate system are difficult to trace, but according to French historian Marc Bloch, it was an outgrowth of the breakdown of centralized authority in most of Europe during the tenth century A.D.[14] Feudalism provided order and local government authority in areas where none existed.

At the center of the estate system was a feudal lord or noble who reigned supreme over a *manor,* a large area of land, sometimes as vast as several hundred square miles. Originally, the nobles claimed legal title to their manors on the basis of their strength-at-arms, often defending them against marauders and other warring lords. In time, title to a manor became a hereditary legal rank within feudal society. The bulk of the population was composed of *serfs*—peasants who worked the manor lands, providing food and other goods for themselves, the lord, and his family. Legally, peasants were bound to the land. They could leave the manor only with the permission of the lord, and they owed him various duties and obligations, such as military service should the manor come under attack, in addition to tending the fields. The lord, on the

Exhibit 8.2 **Case Study**

Slave and Peonage Systems in Contemporary America

In 1984, many viewers of prime-time television were exposed to "Angel City," a film depicting an incident of slavery in contemporary America. "Angel City" was the story of an indigent farm family that left the hills of Appalachia in search of a better life. They packed their meager belongings and traveled to South Florida, where they had heard that farm work was plentiful. When they arrived in Florida City, only a few miles south of urbane Miami Beach, the family was "hired" by the owner of Angel City, a farming complex that reportedly provided its workers with living wages and sanitary housing. As it turned out, Angel City was actually a slave camp where migrant laborers worked the fields under guard during the day and were locked up at night and prohibited from leaving under threat of death. Children too young to work were held hostage (and often raped) as a further assurance of their parents' compliance.

No doubt most viewers dismissed "Angel City" simply as television fiction. But "Angel City" was based on fact. Similar slave camps exist not only within a few miles of the winter playground of Miami Beach, but throughout Florida, the Carolinas, the Southwest, and elsewhere. In other areas *peonage systems* have been found in which victims were held in custody on the basis of alleged debts owed their keepers. For example, during the 1980s:

- In Tampa, Florida, a farm boss and his two sons were found running a farm labor camp in which workers were kept in involuntary servitude under threats of physical abuse.
- In Tyler, Texas, a group of landowners was found transporting Mexican aliens into the United States and forcing them to work their farms without compensation.
- In Ann Arbor, Michigan, sheriff's deputies discovered that two elderly men had been forced to work, without pay, on a local farm for 16 years.
- In Los Angeles, California, a number of defendants were charged with smuggling Indonesians into the United States illegally and selling them as domestic help to wealthy residents of Beverly Hills.

And these are but a few cases. In 1982, the United Nations Working Group on Slavery estimated that in the Atlantic seaboard states from Florida to New York, as many as 10,000 farm laborers were working under conditions of debt bondage or outright slavery. In 1986, the United States Department of Justice had some 49 cases of alleged slavery under active investigation.

SOURCES: Jacksonville (Florida) *Times Union,* August 14, 1983, p. B-3; United States v. Mussry, 35 Crl. 2019 (1984); *The National Law Journal,* August 29, 1983, pp. 3, 32; *Newsweek,* June 2, 1986, p. 31; *Washington Post,* August 18, 1983, pp. C1, C4; Wilmington (Delaware) *News-Journal,* August 10, 1983, p. A2.

other hand, was required to provide the peasants with protection and some measure of justice, as well as the use of the land to feed and clothe themselves.

The lords (the "first estate") ranked at the top of the social hierarchy. At the bottom were the serfs (the "third estate"). The "second estate" was composed of priests and clerics, who also had legal rank in the estate system. Clerics ministered to the spiritual needs of the other two estates, and since they were required to be celibate, they could not pass on their rank to the next generation. However, since the priesthood was open to all, regardless of rank, this "second estate" represented the source of social mobility in feudal society. For the peasants, it was a way of breaking ties with the land. For the children of nobles who would not inherit their fathers' titles or lands, it was a means of attaining a recognized social status. In actual practice, however, since positions in the church had to be purchased, it was rare for a serf to advance to the " second estate."

Feudalism began to decline in Europe during the fourteenth century as a result of the emergence of powerful monarchs, increased communication, the rise of towns, and a variety of other social and economic changes. Nevertheless, the system persisted in France until 1789, in Germany until 1848, and in Russia until 1917. And although formal estate systems of stratification have vanished, peasant-landowner relationships similar to serfdom can still be found in some agricultural regions

Exhibit 8.3 **Sociological Focus**

Agrarian Stratification in Contemporary South America

The industrialization of South America is a comparatively recent phenomenon, having begun only several decades ago. Significant progress, however, has been evident just since the 1970s. Moreover, given the steep costs of industrializing, combined with a general lack of capital resources, precarious political systems, and high rates of illiteracy and poverty, social change has been comparatively slow. As a result, agrarian social structures remain intact throughout much of South America. Particularly well entrenched in Chile, Peru, Paraguay, and parts of Brazil, these systems have at their base an aristocracy that rests on a combination of tradition, land ownership, political control, European blood, and a large dependent class of landless and illiterate peasants.

The aristocratic elite derives its wealth primarily from large estates devoted to agriculture or stockraising, and from the management of other inherited properties, often urban real estate. Many of the men in this elite group have university degrees, earned in either the United States or Colombia, and lead professional lives as politicians, lawyers, or physicians. Little of their time is spent tending their farms, plantations, and ranches.

The traditional ideals of this class of elites are those of the landed gentry, with its characteristic disdain for manual labor. Emphasis is placed on courtly manners and both verbal and written expression. These individuals have luxurious and cosmopolitan tastes, and a conservative class consciousness that is often tempered by paternalism toward their dependents. Much importance is attached to kinship ties and intermarriage between elite families as ways of preserving upper-class access to the means of production. Bloodlines are also considered important. Family genealogies are carefully traced and preserved; marriages with Indians or mestizos, however rare, are discouraged; and any dark-skinned children are encouraged to find a mate who is "lighter"—even if they must select someone from a lower social level so as to "improve the race."

Politically, the influence of the aristocracy tends to be local in nature, although some of the older families do exert influence in regional affairs and a number of landholders have accumulated such great wealth that their economic importance is of national

of Latin America (see Exhibit 8.3). Many peasants, particularly in El Salvador, Brazil, and Chile, work the lands of large estates and receive food or script in exchange for their labor. They can "spend" the script only at their master's store, where the prices are set at the owner's will.* Or similarly, a family may work to rent a small piece of estate land for their own use on a shares system under which they surrender up to half the crop.[15]

Industrial Class Systems

Social classes are abstract categories of social position composed of individuals who share similar opportunities, economic levels, life-styles, attitudes, and behavior. In **class systems** of stratification, the many, typically vague categories of social position generally are determined by individual achievement, particularly economic achievement. Thus, the potential for social mobility—both upward and downward—is considerable. Formal restrictions against marriage between persons of different classes do not exist in industrial class systems. In contrast with caste, slave, and estate systems of stratification, social classes generally are economic groups. They are not established or supported by any legal or religious rules, and membership in a particular class confers no special civil or political rights.[16] Although a person is always born into a particular class, he or she is less likely than someone born into a caste or estate system to spend an entire lifetime there. Class systems emerged with the decline of feudalism, and their development received additional stimulus from industrialization, the factory system of production, and occupation as a source of income.

*In recent years the civil war in El Salvador has brought about a decline in the serfdom of many agricultural laborers. In an effort to gain the political support of the farm and plantation workers, Marxist-led guerrillas have been forcing landowners to pay workers higher wages. In return, plantation delivery trucks roll unmolested to processing and storage mills (see *Time*, January 14, 1985, pp. 41–42).

significance. Jeremias Lunardelli of Brazil, for example, controls thousands of acres of coffee trees, numerous roasting and processing plants, and many square miles of cattle range, cut from the jungle in the eastern Amazon.

The peasant class in South American society can best be described as little better than "serfs," working the lands of the large estates as either wage laborers or tenant farmers. Most peasants are illiterate and suffer from an inadequate diet and unsanitary living habits. Their housing generally is lacking in elementary comforts and hygienic conveniences, and the infant mortality rate is high. The per-capita income of the peasant is but a few dollars a day, and as a result buying power is limited.

Since the early 1970s, a number of factors have functioned to break down the traditional positions held by the agriculturally based South American aristocracies. Industrialization has given birth to two new groups: a new upper class of corporate executives and a strata of factory and transport workers with democratic, and sometimes radical, leanings. Other forces working against the perpetuation of the old aristocratic order are the spread of popular education; the rise of a middle class whose ties are closer to the new industrial regime than to the landed gentry; and the infiltration of liberalizing influences from abroad. In addition, although most of the nations in South America now have democratic governments, the many military dictatorships that controlled these countries in the recent past deliberately worked against the power and prestige of the nobility. However, none of these changes has given much comfort to the majority of the peasants. While many have drifted to the cities in search of work, most of them now live in squatter settlements and shantytowns on the outskirts of the urban areas, in conditions far worse than those they left behind (see Chapter 17).

SOURCES: Douglas Butterworth and John K. Chance, *Latin American Urbanization* (Cambridge: Cambridge University Press, 1981); Brian Kelly and Mark London, *Amazon* (San Diego: Harcourt Brace Jovanovich, 1983); Michael Reid, *Peru: Paths to Poverty* (London: Latin America Bureau, 1985); William Lytle Schurz, *Latin America: A Descriptive Survey* (New York: E. P. Dutton, 1963); Thomas E. Skidmore and Peter H. Smith, *Modern Latin America* (New York: Oxford University Press, 1984); Byron Williams, *Continent in Turmoil* (New York: Parents' Magazine, 1971).

Most analysts suggest that there are three broad social classes in industrialized societies—upper, middle, and lower. Yet because the boundaries of the classes are not precisely defined and because mobility between them is fairly common, some argue that "classes" are not real entities.[17] Rather, critics argue, classes are simply categorical labels that are applied to aggregates of people; they do not exist beyond the eye of the observer and are really no more than statistical categories. A more pragmatic view holds that social classes are very real indeed, with each having a different history, different sources of income and levels of wealth, different attitudes and behavior patterns, and different general social characteristics. Nowhere else in Western society are these factors more evident than in contemporary Great Britain, where there are clear differences between the upper class and the majority of the rest of the population. The upper class is composed primarily of families who have been extraordinarily wealthy for generations—some for centuries. Titles are more visible in Great Britain than anywhere else. The monarchy retains numerous privileges and the hereditary House of Lords includes peers, peeresses, and high church officials. Moreover, with income tax rates as high as 86%, rarely can anyone accumulate the economic wherewithal to move into the ranks of the upper class.

THEORIES OF STRATIFICATION

Virtually every society in the world is stratified in one form or another. Some are stratified quite sharply, with rigid distinctions and barriers separating one class from another, while others are more loosely structured. Moreover, some systems of stratification are exceedingly complex, such as the caste structure of Hindu India, while others are observably simple. In any case, *stratification introduces structured inequality to a society,* a fact that has been recognized in Western thought from the time of its earliest expression. The differences between the conflict and functionalist approaches in sociology are most evident when one examines their proponents' attempts to explain stratification. Conflict theorists emphasize the struggle among groups for scarce resources and access to benefits. They stress the injustices and abuses that accompany inequality. The functionalists, on the other hand, focus on the social arrangements that maintain a society and argue that stratification is not only functional, but perhaps even necessary and inevitable.[18]

Karl Marx and the Economic Interpretation of Stratification

Perhaps the foremost theorist of social stratification was the nineteenth-century German philosopher and economist, Karl Marx. Many contemporary discussions of the topic of social stratification seem to be dialogues between Marx and his critics. Interestingly, Marx neither defined class nor developed his ideas regarding it in any systematic fashion. The idea of "class," however, is clearly implicit in his work.

Marx's theory of class and social stratification focuses on what he termed "relations of production," that is, positions in the economic structure of society. In most, if not all societies, Marx argued, some individuals or groups hold a dominant relation to production by either owning or controlling the "means of production." Under feudalism, for example, lords and nobles claimed title to the land. In capitalist societies, those individuals with the dominant relations to production own productive private property in the form of factories, land, machinery, stocks, and other corporate securities. Those with subordinate relations to production (the serfs in feudal times and the workers under capitalism) do not own or control productive property and are thus forced to exchange their labor for subsistence or wages.

For Marx, the unequal relations to production in the economic structure of society were the basis for the development of the principal social groups—social classes. Classes were not just mere categories; each had contrasting social, economic, and political interests. Marx held, furthermore, that conflict between classes with differing interests was historically common to all societies. As he stated in *The Communist Manifesto,* "The history of all hitherto existing society is the history of class struggles."[19]

Marx, of course, did not invent the concept of class. Classes were an ever-present feature of the world in

In Great Britain, members of the upper class and the working class have different leisure pursuits.

which he lived. His theoretical contribution was the way in which he identified the sources of social class in the economic fabric of society. In capitalist social structures, which Marx purposefully focused on, there were two principal classes: the **bourgeois capitalists,** the owners of the means of production, and the **proletariat,** or nonowners. The bourgeois included financiers, such as bankers, brokers, and investors, as well as the industrial capitalists who owned the factories, and agricultural landowners. The **petit bourgeois** included craftsmen and shopkeepers who owned their own tools and shops. Although Marx considered their livelihoods to be little different from those of the proletariat, as property owners he felt that they identified with the interests of the more powerful capitalists. The great mass of the proletarians were wage-workers, but Marx also pointed out the existence of a **lumpenproletariat,** the poorest and most degraded members of capitalist society.

Crucial to Marx's economic theory of social stratification is the idea of exploitation. At one time, people lived off the land, which no one owned, and presumably no one exploited anyone else. With the invention of private property came exploitation and conflict. Masters exploited slaves, nobles exploited peasants, capitalists exploited workers. What Marx meant by "exploitation" was that workers did all the labor while the exploiters—the masters, nobles, and capitalists—took the profits and paid the workers barely enough to subsist. He did believe, however, that exploitation led to conflict, and in the future, a society would be created that would be run by the proletariat and in which no one would be exploited. More specifically, over time the members of the proletariat would achieve a class consciousness that would lead to conflict and struggle. A violent revolution would result, and capitalism would be transformed into socialism—a *classless society.*

As a prophet, Marx sometimes turned out to be wrong. Certain social and economic developments in Western societies, for example, dealt somewhat harshly with a number of his predictions. Marx believed that the trade unions of his time represented the beginnings of class consciousness among the proletariat, and that this emergent phenomenon would ultimately spread to other societies and precipitate class struggle and revolution. **Class consciousness** was the recognition by a group of its role in the production process, and among the proletarians it would involve an awareness of the bourgeois' determination to live off the sweat of laborers. Revolutions did indeed come, in Russia, China, Cuba, and elsewhere. But these countries were primarily advanced

agricultural societies, and successful socialist revolutions have not yet taken place in the highly industrialized, capitalist societies.

Capitalism progressed through additional stages of development that Marx did not foresee. Individual capitalists were replaced by corporations; the wealth of industrialism led to the growth of a large middle class—professionals, white-collar workers, service workers, and highly skilled laborers—who did not own the means of production but did not identify themselves with the working class either; and the poor in industrialized nations were measurably better off than those in Marx's time. Yet despite his failure to predict the future course of capitalism accurately, in recent decades there has been renewed interest in Marx's work, particularly because of his remarkable insight into the origins of social classes and the relationships between economic power and social structure.[20]

Erik Olin Wright and a Modernization of Marx

Karl Marx witnessed the inequities and human suffering produced by the Industrial Revolution. In his time, men, women, and children often toiled twelve to eighteen hours each day in factories under the most dangerous and unsanitary conditions. That was, of course, well before the advent of labor union movements and legal protections enacted on behalf of workers. Obvious extremes in wealth and poverty were evident at the time Marx was formulating his theories, and it is easy to understand why he and his followers could visualize society as divided into a rigid two-class system.

In the late 1980s, any simple division of industrial capitalist societies into proletariat and bourgeois on the basis of "ownership of the means of production" does not make much sense. Nevertheless, Marx's insights describing work-based relationships—*ownership and control* of labor—remain useful. In recent years sociologist Erik Olin Wright and his associates at the University of Wisconsin have used the Marxist perspective to map the contemporary American class structure.[21]

At the apex of the system is a small class of individuals who own the land, capital, and factories. They also hire the employees, and hence, are able to direct and control the workers. These owners and employers qualify as the modern *bourgeois.* Almost half of the population is relegated to the *working class,* and for two reasons. First, they have no income-producing property and thus no need or reason to hire employees. Second, they are unable to make decisions about the work process.

As to the others in a capitalist society, their class positions are less clearly defined. *Managers* and *supervisors* are employees, and they are controlled by their superiors, but nevertheless have a measure of control over their subordinates. *Semiautonomous employees,* such as scientists and engineers, enjoy a great deal of freedom in the work place. And finally, the *petty bourgeois* and *self-employed* may employ a few people but lack power and control on a scale comparable to that of the large capitalists.

MODERN MARXIST CLASSES

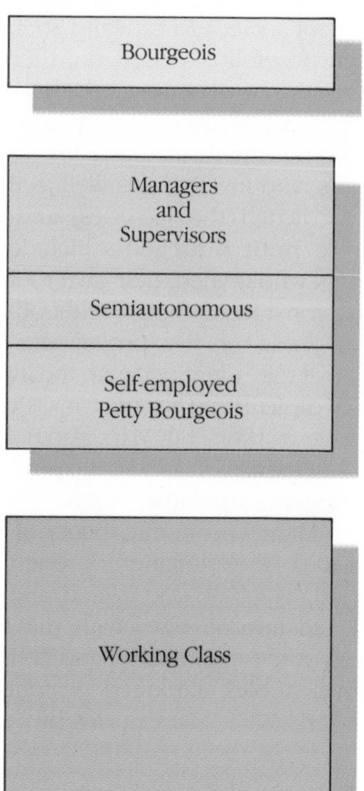

This structure, according to Wright and his associates, has two important effects. First, the existence of the mid-level social positions—the managers, supervisors, semiautonomous employees, petty bourgeois, and self-employed—offers members of the working class (or at least their children) the opportunity or dream of upward mobility. Second, because a large number of people do not occupy a definite class location, the chance of polarization between the various classes is quite limited.

The Functionalist View of Stratification

While Marx focused primarily on class, the functionalist theory of stratification targets the social and economic positions of occupations in the social structure. Stratification, according to the functionalists, is an unconsciously evolved device by which societies insure that the most important positions are conscientiously filled by the most qualified persons.[22] Stated differently, rewards are attached to all positions in the social structure. But to attract the most talented and capable people to the most important positions—those crucial to the survival of the society—and to motivate them to carry out their duties energetically, greater rewards are attached to these positions. Thus, stratification evolves from two factors: the relative importance of occupations and the scarcity of people to fill these occupations. Generals and admirals, for example, do important work, but not everyone has the ability to be a military leader. It is vital to the interests of society that people be willing to endure the training and make the effort necessary to achieve these ranks. Unless they offer significant social and economic rewards, it is likely that most societies will have ineffective military leadership.

The functionalist theory is simple and to the point, but it has been criticized heavily.[23] First, the meaning of "importance" was never made clear; how is the "importance" of a position to be determined? As far as the long-term survival of the United States is concerned, for example, the positions of farmer and garbage collector may be just as important as those of President and Secretary of Defense. Moreover, consider the positions of the highest paid ("rewarded") individuals in American society—entertainers and athletes. How crucial are their positions to the future of society? Second, the theory neglects a very central feature of most stratification systems, the inheritance of positions. Given the tendency of those in well-rewarded positions to transmit wealth and access to opportunities from one generation to the next, equality of access is unlikely. Third, studies of individuals in "important positions" have demonstrated that the correlation between responsibility and rewards is slight, while that between performance and rewards is almost nil.[24]

SOCIAL CLASS IN AMERICA

Most Americans are aware that differences exist among people at various levels of education and income and among those in different occupations. However, these

Some occupations pay much more than others, but which one is more important to society—garbage collector or baseball player?

SOCIAL INDICATOR

How We Class Ourselves

Income	Lower	Working	Middle	Upper
Under $12,500	13%	49%	35%	2%
$12,501–$25,000	3	57	39	1
$25,001–$35,000	<1	48	51	1
$35,001–$50,000	<1	33	64	3
More than $50,000	<1	14	70	15

Source: National Opinion Research Center, 1986.

distinctions generally are thought of in terms of the alternative life-styles they make possible. The conventional stereotypes suggest that "the rich" live in fine homes, drive large automobiles, wear expensive clothing, and vacation in far-off lands and exotic places. "Middle class" people live a good life. They have "nice" houses with front lawns and white picket fences; they vacation each year in the mountains or at the shore; they all have cars and some have boats and motor homes; and the majority of them have even been to Disneyland or Disney World. "The poor" live in the slums. Yet despite this awareness, most people do not consider differences of this sort to be important to self-definitions or for social action. In other words, rigid class consciousness is lacking to a great extent among the American people, and for quite a few reasons. First, the United States has no feudal past—no hereditary aristocracy, entrenched privileges, manors, "estates," or serfs. Second, since its beginnings just over two centuries ago, this country has not had royalty or a titled class that served to reinforce notions of the inferiority of the masses. Third, the egalitarianism of Protestantism and its associated norms of equality and freedom were incorporated from the start into the nation's democratic ideology. Fourth, although a strong labor movement generated a sense of working-class solidarity in opposition to a managerial class in some European countries, a similar sense of solidarity did not develop here. Fifth, the growth of the nation based on immigration from all parts of the world and the consequent population heterogeneity served to hinder the development of class-based ties. And sixth, the opportunities for social mobility made possible by expanding geographic and economic frontiers weakened ideas of firm class identity. In addition to these factors, class in America is a touchy subject. In 1980 in his book *Inequality in an Age of Decline,* sociologist Paul Blumberg referred to class as "America's forbidden thought."[25] Or even more appropriately, back in the 1930s author R. H. Tawney commented; "The word *class* is fraught with unpleasing associations, so that to linger upon it is apt to be interpreted as the symptom of a perverted mind and a jaundiced spirit."[26]

But to suggest that America is a classless society would be inaccurate. Although it is difficult to accurately measure the levels of social stratification, research indeed indicates that there are many classes in the United States, ranging from the "super rich" to the impoverished urban "underclass."[27] Yet how many social classes are there? One popular division of society separates it into the "haves" and the "have nots." Commenting on this, University of Pennsylvania English professor Paul Fussell remarked:

> The two-part division has the convenience of simplicity as well as usefulness in highlighting injustice and registering bitterness. A three-part division is popular too, because the number three is portentous, folkloristic, and even magical, being the number of bears, wishes, and Wise Men. In Britain three has been popularly accepted as the number of classes at least since the last century, when Matthew Arnold divided his neighbors and friends into upper, middle, and lower classes, or, as he memorably termed them, Barbarians (at the top, notice), Philistines (in the middle), and Populace. This three-tiered conception is the usual way to think of the class system for the people in the middle, for it offers them moral and social safety, positioning them equally distant from the vices of pride and snobbery and waste and carelessness, which they associate with those above them, and dirtiness, constraint, and shame, the attendants of those below. Upper, middle, and lower are the customary terms for these three groups, although the British euphemism *working class* for *lower class* is now making some headway here.[28]

Research suggests that American society is divided into four social classes, based on a combination of wealth, power, and prestige. At the top is a small *upper class* enjoying unusual privilege, and at the bottom is an *underclass* of chronically poor and disadvantaged. Most Americans occupy a place somewhere between these extremes. The *middle class* consists of white-collar workers, divided into upper and lower segments, and the *working class* is composed of blue-collar workers and manual laborers of various types.

The Upper Class

F. Scott Fitzgerald is reputed to have said of the rich that "they are different from you and me." No doubt they are. But exactly "how different" is another matter entirely, for no group in the United States is as difficult to identify or define as the upper class. Some confusing and contradictory messages on the issue come from the national media. In a 1983 survey by Mendelsohn Media Research of New York, the "affluence" category included families with annual incomes of $40,000 or more.[29] That figure

SOCIAL INDICATOR

The Income Elite

	All Households	Households with Incomes of $50,000+
Number (in millions)	86.8	11.1
Percent	100.0%	12.8%
Percent Distribution	100.0%	100.0%
Age of Householder		
Under 35	29.3%	15.9%
35 to 44	20.1	28.8%
45 to 54	14.6	27.6
55 to 64	15.1	19.2
65 and Over	20.9	8.5
Type of Household		
Married Couple	58.0%	84.8%
Other Families	14.2	5.7
Men Living Alone	9.1	3.5
Women Living Alone	14.6	1.6
Other Households	4.1	4.4
Size of Household		
One Person	23.7%	5.2%
Two Persons	31.6	29.5
Three Persons	17.8	23.3
Four Persons	15.7	24.3
Five or More Persons	11.2	17.7
Presence of Children		
All under 6	9.9%	7.8%
Under 6 and 6 to 17	8.0	6.5
All 6 to 17	20.1	28.2
None under 18	62.0	57.5
Earner Composition		
Husband Working, Not Wife	11.3	11.1%
Husband and Wife Only	24.2	35.9
Husband, Wife, and Other	7.9	24.7
Other Husband-wife Families	14.6	13.1
All Other Households	42.0	15.2
Education		
Grade School	14.6%	3.0%
Some High School	12.8	4.5
High-School Graduate	35.3	24.4
Some College	16.6	17.3
College Graduate	11.4	24.0
Graduate School	9.3	26.8
Occupation		
Managerial, Professional	26.9%	52.6%
Administrative, Technical, Sales	24.1	22.7
Services	10.5	3.5
Craft and Repair	16.9	12.3
Operators, Laborers	18.0	7.8
Farming, Fisheries	3.6	1.1

Source: U.S. Bureau of the Census, 1987.

worked out to 17% of all households and included 42 million American adults. More recently, the Consumer Research Center in New York City defined "The Income Elite" as that segment of the nation's households with incomes of $50,000 or more.[30] The implication is that the "affluent," the "income elite," and the "upper class" are one and the same thing. But affluence is something that is quite relative. Moreover, it is not money alone that defines a class.

The most common conception of the upper class emphasizes that its members are not only very wealthy, but have a tradition of wealth and a distinctive life-style.

A few individuals in the United States, such as Donald Trump, may be worth billions of dollars.

Exhibit 8.4

Sidelights on American Culture

Bloodlines and Behavior in the Age of "High Society"

The age of "High Society" in the United States was remarkably brief—less than the biblical lifetime—but quite colorful and peculiar. It was known as the Gilded Age and flourished between the 1870s and 1930s.

To claim a place in High Society, one had to be born both rich and with the proper bloodlines, preferably with origins in England. One had to have the "right" friends and live in the most fashionable parts of the most fashionable cities. And most importantly, men had to be "gentlemen" and women "ladies." To be a *gentleman,* one had to have inborn moral principles that made a man a person of quality—honor, integrity, generosity, and forbearance. To be a *lady* was a bit more complex. In addition to the characteristics of their gentlemen counterparts, ladies could not talk loudly, run, argue, contradict, or do anything out of the ordinary. Moreover, no matter how capable they might be, ladies had to seem helpless. Important too for ladies, as social historian Mary Cable has pointed out, was a quality that Victorians liked to call *purity:*

> The word had to do with innocence of sex—an unmarried girl knew nothing about it and a married one wished she didn't—but it went beyond that. A pure woman was like a crystal-clear pool—quiet, cool, uncontaminated, life-giving. No wind could disturb her deep serenity. She was always calm and collected. She did not sweat. She had a form, not a body; a bosom, not two breasts; and below the waist, as far as she was concerned, she had only frilly petticoats.

A characteristic of High Society was its snobbery. An infant born into the *right* family in the *right* neighborhood of the *right* city also had to be baptized in the *right* church. Episcopalian was best, in most parts of America, although in Boston it was socially acceptable to be Unitarian or Congregationalist. New York also extended acceptance to Presbyterians and Philadelphia to Quakers. But to be socially correct, the appropriate religion was not enough. One had to worship at the *right* parish. Equally important was going to the correct schools. Boys went to exclusive prep schools and girls went to the right finishing schools. And all of these were conduits to the "better" colleges. Yet the girls could not go away to school until they "came-out" as debutantes. Coming-out was a rite of passage during which young girls became young women and were presented

This description fits about 1% or less of the American population.[31] Top corporate officials and other high-level corporate managers also fit this description.[32] Most analysts agree that the members of the upper class control large accumulations of wealth, in the form of land, factories, stocks and bonds, and other investments. Yet again, wealth alone is not enough, for the upper class is also a *social* class.

As a distinctive social class the upper class has been described as those wealthy families who interact and intermarry among themselves, and share a distinctive style of life that sets them apart from the rest of society.[33] They are listed in the *Social Register* (see Exhibit 8.4); they have memberships in exclusive clubs, their behavior is elegant and mannered, and each family is concerned with the veneration of the family name and with the perpetuation of the family's position and wealth for future generations.

Historically, the upper class in the United States dominated most positions of power in the industrial, financial, and governmental sectors until World War II. Since then, their positions have been weakened considerably by the emergence of another upper class—the elites of corporate America. The new upper class is a growing body of educated professionals that began to emerge as an outgowth of the New Deal liberalism of the 1930s. Increased social spending made higher education available to larger segments of society, as is reflected in a 241% increase over the last four decades in the proportion of adults with college degrees. Among them is a growing cohort of millionaires, including a group that *Business Week* magazine has described as "capitalist outlanders"—high-technology entrepreneurs and financial engineers who created empires and fortunes from the social and economic changes of recent decades.[34] Yet little is known about this new segment of the upper class.

to their social world at some formal party or ball.

To keep track of who belonged to the exclusive network of High Society, and who did not, the *Social Register* was invented in 1887. The first edition bestowed its seal of approval on some 2,000 New Yorkers, and by 1925 editions were available in 21 different cities. Ladies of Society kept the latest edition of their *Register* beside the Bible.

To keep up with what was going on in the world of society, major newspapers had "society" columns which reported on the weddings, parties, and other comings and goings of the elites. Magazines also appeared: for the vicious gossip one read *Town Topics,* while *Town and Country* was a bit more gentle.

The Great Depression, followed by World War II and the social changes that occurred in its aftermath took their toll on the prevailing life-style of the social elite. Snobbery, the debutantes and their coming-out parties, and the social listings perservered, but to most they were no more than a curiosity. By the 1980s, High Society was all but dead in the United States. The "First Circle" of social elites still have their exclusive parties, but the general public tends to be unaware of them since the "social notes" and "society columns" have been downplayed in the newspapers.

The *Social Register* limps on—one volume covering the entire nation. To get into today's *Social Register,* aspirants must find a few people who are already listed to write letters attesting to their worthiness. Then an anonymous committee makes a decision. Some key personalities are still listed, and the *Register's* pages continue to reflect the flavor of society's foibles. Major political figures are listed, particularly if they are in favor with the country club set. During the 1980s, for example, President Reagan was listed. Senator Edward Kennedy was not. Moreover, movie stars and media personalities have long been considered tainted and are *never* listed.

SOURCES: Cleveland Amory, *Who Killed Society?* (New York: Harper & Brothers, 1960); Mary Cable, *Top Drawer: American High Society from the Gilded Age to the Roaring Twenties* (New York: Atheneum, 1984); William Davis, *The Rich: A Study of the Species* (New York: Franklin Watts, 1983); *People,* October 16, 1978, pp. 32–35; *The Wall Street Journal,* November 15, 1984, pp. 35, 46.

They do not fit the image of the hereditary and self-defined social group with a common subculture, traditions, and sense of solidarity usually envisioned as "upper class." Aside from their growing wealth and power, their habits and life-styles remain obscure.

The Middle Class

Estimates as to the size of the middle class vary widely, ranging anywhere from 25% to 50% of all American households. Regardless of its relative size, most analysts agree that the middle class has two strata—"upper" and "lower"—with the differences based largely on occupation and income.

The *upper middle class,* estimated in recent years to include some 14% of the American work force, is marked by generally high incomes when compared with the balance of the population.[35] Members of the upper middle class are business people, professionals, executives, and high government and military officials. They are among the most educated of all Americans, and a college degree has become almost an absolute requirement for entry into their ranks. Graduate and professional degrees are also not uncommon. Members of the upper middle class are active in voluntary associations, particularly those of a business or professional nature, and much of their power is exercised through these associations. Their occupations play a central role in their lives.

The *lower middle class,* perhaps 30% to 35% of the American work force by recent estimates, includes owners of small businesses, some less wealthy professionals, farm owners, sales and clerical workers, and many civil service employees. Almost all have high-school diplomas; a growing proportion have college or

SOCIAL INDICATOR

The Growing Middle Class

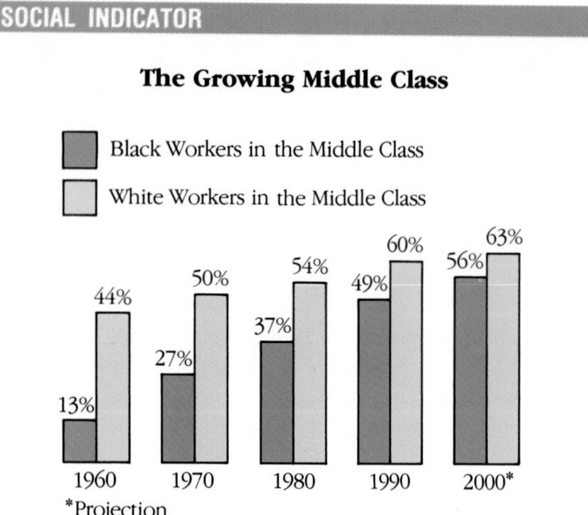

technical degrees, but few have graduate or professional education. Unlike the members of the upper middle class, who are financially secure and remain generally untouched by economic fluctuations, lower-middle-class people tend to worry about money and sometimes experience periods of unemployment.

As the result of a series of social, economic, and technological changes that gained momentum during the 1970s, it appears that the lower middle class in America is shrinking while the upper middle class is expanding. Many families fell from the middle class because of the high levels of inflation and unemployment in the 1970s and early 1980s; the increase in the trade deficit, which was brought on by foreign competition; the rising number of one-parent households; and the destruction of jobs by high technology and corporate mergers. At the same time, the emergence of high technology and an increase in the number of two-career marriages combined to push significant numbers of others into the upper middle class. Whether these trends will continue is difficult to predict. However, some analysts have argued that the ultimate outcome could be entirely negative, resulting in the replacement of the middle class with a bipolar income distribution composed of only rich and poor.[36]

In a cross-cultural perspective, the differences between the American middle class and those of other nations are often significant. In China, for example, the occupational elite—factory managers, government administrators, and those in academic teaching and research positions—have life-styles that would not be envied by their counterparts in the United States.[37] Most rent two-room apartments that they share with their immediate families, grandparents, and aunts and uncles. They work six days a week with no formally scheduled vacations. Most own television sets, but only a few have refrigerators and the ownership of an automobile is exceedingly rare (see Exhibit 8.5). Yet if contrasted with the situation for the balance of the Chinese population, this small middle class is exceedingly well off.

The "Working Class"

Although the United States has often been described as a "middle-class society," a substantial proportion of Americans can be described as "working class." Working-class occupations involve physical or manual labor. Many of these workers earn substantial wages while others in this same classification live at the edge of abject poverty. As with the higher levels on the social ladder, estimates of the size of this class vary. Some observers set the total at as high as 60% of the population. Dennis Gilbert and Joseph Kahl suggest that 32% of all Americans are in a "blue-collar–manual-labor class" and another 10% or more are "working poor."[38] As this breakdown would suggest, the working class is not a homogeneous population.

The Blue-collar or Manual-labor Class

"Blue-collar workers," as they are often termed, include craft and factory workers, and other types of skilled and semiskilled laborers. Most have high-school diplomas, but few have other credentials beyond job training and experience. Many are members of labor unions. Interestingly, significant numbers of blue-collar workers, particularly those in strong unions, earn salaries higher than those found among some members of the lower middle class. Auto workers, for example, may earn more than a college professor with a Ph.D. degree (see Exhibit 8.6). However, a characteristic of the blue-collar class is economic insecurity. The possibility of a layoff is ever present. Moreover, since most blue-collar skills are often job or plant specific, the occupational experiences of the working class are usually of little help in seeking new employment.

The Working Poor

The working poor are semiskilled and unskilled laborers—janitors, porters, ushers, elevator operators, farm hands, migrant laborers, and others in extremely low-paying positions. Many are uneducated, and some are illiterate. They are frequently laid off, they often resort to public assistance as a means of survival, and their children are sometimes unable to finish school because of their families' financial problems. A disproportionate number of minority group members are

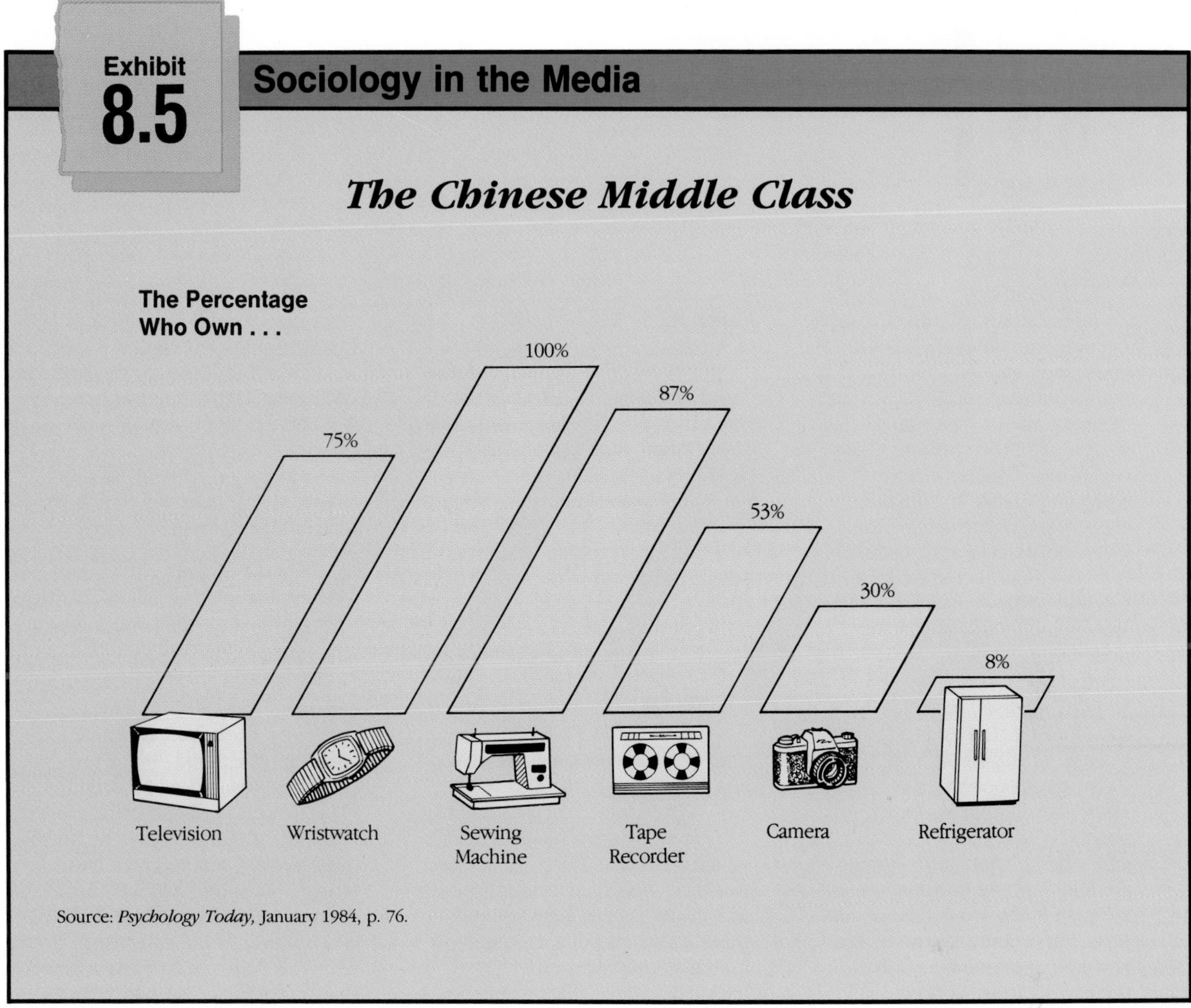

Source: *Psychology Today,* January 1984, p. 76.

among the working poor, and a great majority reside in inner-city slums. As economically insecure, powerless, and deprived people living in a social world that is far removed from what they regularly see in the mass media, they tend to develop cynical attitudes toward conventional social institutions and values. In consequence, significant numbers of the working poor do not vote or participate in other social action activities, a pattern that serves to solidify their status as outsiders in their own society.

The Underclass

The underclass is that segment of American society that is mired in deprivation. An underclass of perenially poor is produced when society fails to provide jobs, education, housing, or hope. It is also a population with many faces—welfare mothers, teenage blacks in the inner cities with no job skills, the permanently unemployable, the homeless, "skid-row" alcoholics, drug users who live on the streets, the mentally ill who have been "deinstitutionalized" with no place to go, and the destitute elderly. This group includes the 40,000 homeless people in New York City who roam the streets and jam the shelters that provide temporary places to eat and sleep; it encompasses the 20,000 native Americans who eke out a dismal existence in booming Dallas; it includes the tens of thousands of Haitian and Central American refugees who live in the mire of poverty amidst Miami's affluence; it includes the "third world" of the Texas Rio Grande valley where illegal aliens swell the many *colonias*—flyblown shantytowns whose squalor rivals that of the Palestinian refugee camps; it includes the mountain families of Appalachia, where the hillsides are decorated with dilapidated shacks, raggedly dressed people, and

Exhibit 8.6 Research in Sociology

The Blue-collar Elite

Like all other levels in the social hierarchy, the level that has become known as the "working class" is in actuality composed of many different social classes and occupational groups. Many members of the working class command incomes that are typically associated with middle class, white-collar occupations. Over the years, social scientists have periodically focused their research endeavors on this "blue-collar elite," and two studies, undertaken a decade apart, are of particular interest.

From 1967 to 1972, sociologist E. E. LeMasters of the University of Wisconsin conducted a participant observation study in a Midwestern suburban tavern that he called The Oasis. During those years, he became an irregular "regular" at The Oasis, drinking beer, shooting pool, talking, and most importantly, listening. His research subjects were some 50 members of the working class—mostly heavy equipment operators, sheet-metal workers, carpenters, plumbers, electricians, and other skilled construction workers—popularly referred to as "hard-hats" at the time. LeMasters called them "blue-collar aristocrats," because they were skilled workers who had become highly paid as the result of the successes of trade unionism during the affluent post-World War II period.

LeMasters' findings presented a rather curious picture of the blue-collar aristocrat. LeMasters suggested that this individual takes pride in his work and brings home an income that is squarely in the middle-class-income bracket. He owns a nice home in a pleasant suburb. He is free from debt and has no unfulfilled material wants. Yet his wife works and he drives an older car—both by choice.

The blue-collar aristocrat has a cocktail hour each evening, at which he drinks beer. He spends this time with his working buddies, whom he has not seen for ten minutes, while his wife waits for him at home. He neither understands nor likes most of what he sees on television, so he watches little, other than sporting events. Moreover, he does not particularly like minority groups, college students, women's liberationists, or homosexuals. He does not trust Jews, politicians, or businessmen—including the leaders of his own union—and he is convinced that white-collar workers really do not earn their salaries.

The blue-collar aristocrat does not like marriage, but he *is* married, for reasons he finds difficult to explain. He would much rather be fishing, hunting, or drinking with the boys than talking or watching television with his wife. Most of his recreation time, in fact, is spent away from the family. Moreover, he seems to have a particular disdain for women. One of the individuals in the group that LeMasters studied commented, "The trouble with American women is that they don't know their place. I was in Japan after World War II and by God those women know who is boss. When you tell one of them babes to jump, all they ask is, 'How high?' But an American woman will say, 'Why?' "

Not surprisingly, the women these men marry show an equal disdain for men. One woman commented, "These guys would

rusting automobiles.[39] These are the forgotten people of America, numbering in the millions, who are for the most part invisible to the rest of society.

POVERTY IN AMERICA

Poverty is defined simply. It is a condition in which people have too little money and too few resources to afford the basic necessities of life. In more empirical terms, various U.S. government agencies have established a **poverty line,** the designated level of income deemed necessary for the provision of basic nutrition, clothing, and shelter. Those living at or below the poverty line are the *statistically* "poor."

The official poverty line is the result of some rather curious mathematics. In 1955 Department of Agriculture analysts carried out a survey of food consumption in which they concluded that the average American family spent one-third of its after-tax income on food and the remainder on everything else. Using that statistic, the Social Security Administration multiplied by three the estimated cost of an economy food budget that relied heavily on dry beans, peas, potatoes, and grains. The resultant figure came to $3,022 for a family of four in 1960.[40] The poverty rather go deer hunting if their mother was on her death bed. They think first of themselves. When our kids were small, we could never have a birthday party on the right day for one of them because it was the week that pheasant season started."

Finally, most of the blue-collar aristocrats generally refused to face the problems of today's world. Women's rights, discrimination, poverty—these things just did not exist. These individuals wanted only to return to the world that they grew up in—to the places where they had memories of peace, quiet, and satisfaction. World War II had been a violent interruption in their lives, and they simply wanted to pick up where they had left off before the war. But the world had changed in the meantime, leaving them with the feeling that nothing in their lives, except their wages, was as good as what they had known in their youth.

More recently, from 1974 through 1981, Columbia University sociologist David Halle conducted extensive research among 121 blue-collar workers at a chemical plant in the highly industrialized Elizabeth-Linden area of New Jersey. Halle roamed through the plant at will, talking to employees and observing them at work. He also visited the workers at their homes, drank with them at neighborhood taverns, and accompanied them to ball games.

Like LeMasters' "hard hats," these chemical workers were members of the blue-collar elite, earning an average of almost $28,000 per year in 1983. Yet as Halle noted, they did not consider themselves to be part of a "working class." They actually had two distinct images of themselves. On the job, they were "working men," a term they felt set them apart from those around them, because they performed physical labor under the supervision of other people. They saw themselves as "producers," in contrast to executives and lawyers, who "just sit there and hire people who do the work," as one commented. Outside the job, however, Halle's workers identified themselves as middle class, largely because of their incomes. Their life-styles overlapped those of their white-collar, middle-class neighbors. Yet in many ways they were similar to LeMasters' blue-collar aristocrats. Many were unhappily married, and the majority obtained their greatest satisfaction and enjoyment from drinking with male buddies, fishing and hunting, and watching and betting on sports events.

Finally, Halle's study group did not accept the Marxist idea that their low position in the system of production defined them as an exploited group on and off the job. On the contrary, they all believed in the American Dream, that one can rise in social rank and occupation through individual effort and education.

SOURCES: David Halle, *America's Working Man* (Chicago: University of Chicago Press, 1984); E. E. LeMasters, *Blue-Collar Aristocrats: Life-Styles at a Working-Class Tavern* (Madison: University of Wisconsin Press, 1975).

line is recalculated each year to adjust for fluctuations in inflation and purchasing power, and in 1986 it was calculated at $11,203 for an urban family of four.[41] Using this figure, it was estimated that some 33.1 million people in the United States were living below the poverty line.

Profiling Poverty

More than 32.3 million people in the United States "officially" live in poverty. For most of them, this situation endures for years, and although some may manage to escape, their places are quickly occupied by others.

Poverty can touch almost anyone, but some groups tend to be more visible among America's poor. *Minorities* have consistently been overrepresented among the poor. As many as one-third of black Americans live in poverty, and growing numbers of Hispanics subsist under similar circumstances. The *elderly* are highly susceptible to slipping into poverty, particularly after age 70. Most elderly Americans survive on small, fixed incomes, often living alone, and many of them have had their savings depleted by illness. *Children* account for a surprising share of the poor. In fact, one out of every five children in the United States is living in poverty.[42] And finally, *women* account for a considerably disproportionate share of the poor. Almost half of all families headed by women are poor, a situation that is readily apparent in industrialized societies in all other parts of the world as well.[43]

Although poverty has always existed in the United States, except during the depression years of the 1930s when economic hardship struck most levels of society, Americans generally have been blind or indifferent to the problems of the poor. After all, the American Dream suggests that success or failure is the result of each individual's personal efforts (or lack of effort) at achievement. Thus, a substantial portion of the population has always believed that poverty is the fault of the poor. In fact, surveys conducted regularly since the 1960s have consistently shown that one-third of the population believes that "lack of effort" is the major reason why people are poor.[44]

The "Great Society" and Its Aftermath

Although Americans may have been indifferent to the plight of the poor at many points in our history, significant programs to break cycles of poverty have been attempted. During the 1960s, for example, the growing problems of crime and discrimination that had been festering for many years focused concerted attention on the plight of the nation's poor. Notable in this regard was President Lyndon B. Johnson's "Great Society" effort—a series of programs conceived and launched for the purpose of upgrading the quality of American life. As a Johnson biographer later described its agenda:

> The Great Society would offer something for almost everyone: Medicare for the old, educational assistance for the young, tax rebates for business, a higher minimum wage for labor, subsidies for the unskilled, food for the hungry, housing for the homeless, poverty grants for the poor, clean highways for commuters, legal protection for the blacks, improved schooling for the Indians, rehabilitation for the lame, higher benefits for the unemployed, reduced quotas for the immigrants, auto safety for drivers, pensions for the retired, fair labeling for consumers, conservation for hikers and campers, and more and more and more.[45]

How *great* (spelled "effective") has the Great Society effort been? Critics do not deny that it raised the living standards of many people, particularly the elderly. Medicare, food stamps, and more generous Social Security benefits helped to reduce the poverty rate for older Americans from 28.5% in 1966 to 12.6% in 1985.[46] In addition, the Head Start preschool program for the children of the poor improved their scholastic work, and federal aid for higher education enabled tens of thousands from poverty areas to enter college. Yet on the other hand, a number of Great Society programs performed erratically or failed entirely. "Model Cities," designed to improve health care, transportation, and other services in depressed communities fell victim to pork-barrel politics. Employment training projects suffered high dropout rates and were riddled with inefficiency. In fact, a single slot in the Job Corps program cost more than one year's education at Harvard University.[47]

The data in Exhibit 8.7 indicate that poverty rates have changed over the years. Between 1960, a time prior to the implementation of the war on poverty, and 1975, rates for whites and blacks were cut almost in half. The Great Society cannot account for the entire decline, however; the growing economy and the civil rights movement also served to better the lot of the poor. Yet by 1980, poverty rates were once again on the rise.

In 1981, when President Ronald Reagan's "New Federalism" pushed through the first real cuts in federal

SOCIAL INDICATOR

Perceptions about the Poor

Question: Do you think most poor people are lazy or do you think most poor people are hard-working?

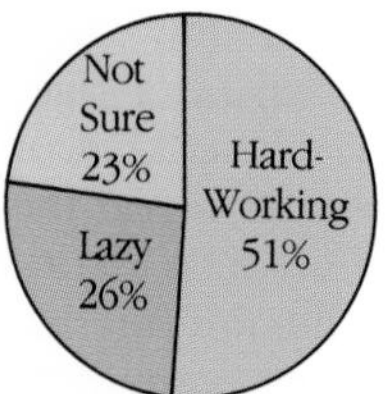

Question: Do you think we're coddling the poor—that poor people live well on welfare—or do you think poor people can hardly get by on what the government gives them?

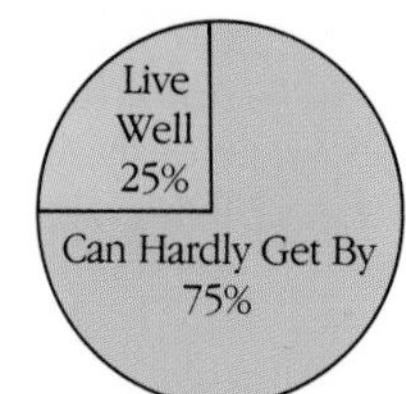

Question: Do you think poor people lack basic social and occupational skills or do you think their abilities are not all that much different from other Americans?

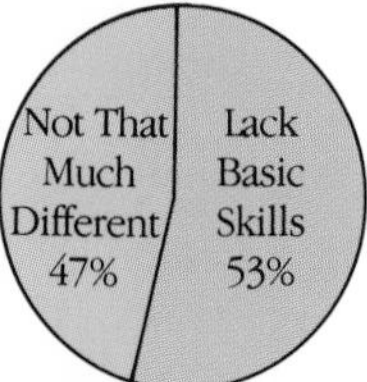

Source: Survey by the *Los Angeles Times*, April 20–25, 1985.

Thirteen million American children grow up in poverty.

aid in a quarter of a century, the Great Society programs were seriously challenged. More specifically, the federal Food Stamp program was cut by $2 billion; a change in federal guidelines served to eliminate 500,000 families from the list of those receiving aid in the AFDC (Aid to Families with Dependent Children) program; job training programs were cut by some 40%; and changes in IRS regulations increased the level of taxes paid by many poor families.[48]

By 1986, more than 32 million Americans were living below the poverty line. More than 30 million Americans have been poor every year since 1981. Additional statistics are more revealing. Although poverty rates among blacks declined appreciably, the rates increased significantly among children. In 1986, some 12.8 million children (20.5% of children 18 and under) were classified as living in poverty, an increase of 3 million children since 1968, despite the fact that the number of children in the country declined by 9 million during the same period.[49]

Is Poverty Functional?

The reasons for the emergence and persistence of poverty are numerous. Some people might argue that the poor are poor because they are unwilling to help themselves, but the main reasons lie in the structure of

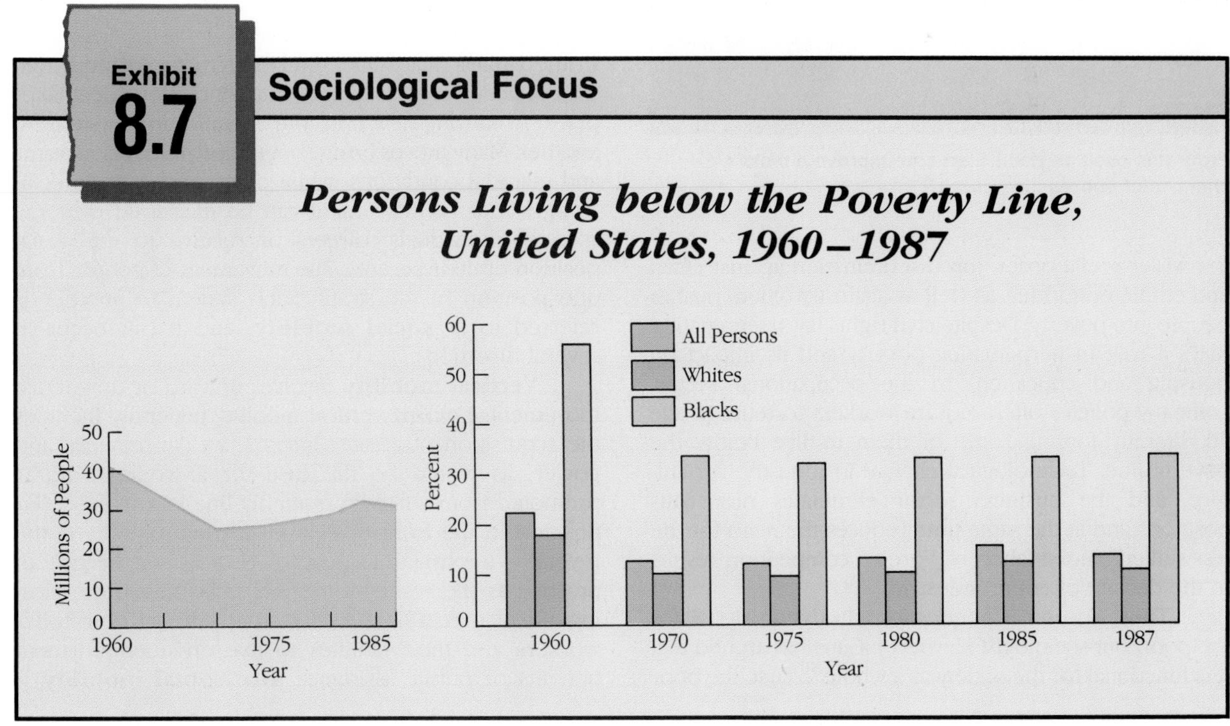

Programs such as Head Start can improve a child's chances of success in school.

the wider social order. Job discrimination against racial and ethnic minorities, as well as against women, pushes people into poverty. Despite civil rights laws, segregation plays a role in perpetuating poverty and its impact on housing and education. In the occupational sector, company policies often require workers to retire at age 70, literally forcing some of them to live below the poverty line. Technological change in industry, agriculture, and the business sector eliminates numerous positions and at the same time reduces the need for the less skilled among laborers. Foreign competition results in the decline of entire industries.

Thus, poverty is unquestionably dysfunctional for the poor, but sociologist Herbert J. Gans has argued that it is functional for the society as a whole.[50] First, the poor represent a pool of applicants for the lowest paid and most menial jobs—washing dishes, emptying hospital bedpans, waxing floors, providing janitorial services—ensuring that society's "dirty work" gets done. Second, given their low economic position, the poor provide a ready market for substandard products—stale food, slum housing, used cars, second-hand clothing—goods that would otherwise be of no value. Third, the poor create jobs for many others in society—welfare workers, public defenders, pawnbrokers, public housing officials, and all of those employed in social programs aimed at the needy. Fourth, the poor represent an opportunity for charity and altruism. By helping the poor, the better-off not only can feel good about themselves, but their donations represent desirable tax deductions. Fifth, the existence of the poorer classes improves the chances of economic success for all other groups by reducing competition for the better-paying occupations. Sixth, the poor represent a negative reference group. Just as deviance and crime are functional for society by defining the boundaries of proper conduct, poverty represents a standard for what not to become. And seventh, the poor tend to help the rich get richer. By serving in domestic and menial service roles, they free the wealthy from many of the chores of daily life. Moreover, the low incomes of the poor provide the rich with more money to invest.

SOCIAL MOBILITY

In the United States and similarly structured industrialized societies, a considerable amount of movement takes place from one level in the stratification system to another. Many moves bring about improvements in status and material conditions, while others cause declines in living standards. Movement can be measured over the span of individuals' careers or relative to the social position of their parents. The movement of people from one position in the stratification system to another is referred to as **social mobility,** and it can occur in several directions.

Vertical mobility involves upward or downward movement. *Upward* vertical mobility generally includes the acquisition of greater income, wealth, respect, and power, as would be the case for a worker who is promoted from a factory assembly line to a white-collar position in the front office. *Downward* mobility is the reverse—a physician's loss of his or her license to practice as the result of medical misconduct; the closing of a plant in a small steel town that forces blue-collar workers and their families to live on unemployment benefits or public assistance. **Horizontal mobility** is

"Everybody loves money. Too bad there isn't enough to go around."

movement from one position in the stratification system to another position at the same level. Generally, no loss or gain in wealth or prestige is involved in such lateral movement. Movements of this type are often initiated for a worker's personal convenience—a postal employee shifting from a Detroit location to the same job in Phoenix for the sake of the warmer climate; an accountant's move from one firm to another for the sole purpose of securing a better retirement program; a teller's transfer from a bank's urban headquarters to a suburban branch to shorten the daily commute. Researchers with an interest in social mobility also chart **intergenerational mobility,** movement in the stratification system from the level occupied by one's parents. Examples might include the daughter of a telephone lineman becoming a corporate accountant, or the son of a major executive living on the streets and "hustling" to support his drug habit.

In slave, caste, and estate systems of stratification, upward mobility is virtually impossible. As we noted earlier in this chapter, in these "closed systems" individuals spend their entire lives at the social level at which they were born. In "open systems," such as the class system in the United States, upward social mobility is possible, and to a certain degree, common. Yet even in the most open of societies, many barriers exist to upward social mobility.

Social Mobility, the American Dream, and the Horatio Alger Myth

The writings of Horatio Alger, Jr., during the latter part of the nineteenth century created a lasting impression on American culture and folklore. Although rather poorly written, Alger's works were immensely popular, selling more than 200 million copies over a 30-year period. In his 120 books, Alger's heroes were street waifs—bootblacks, newsboys, and other young denizens of sordid environments who valiantly struggled against poverty and adversity to be rewarded with riches and success. The stories presented the Puritan work ethic to young readers. Through the virtues of hard work, thrift, punctuality, clean living, and self-discipline, even the lowliest street boy could rise from rags to riches, or to use the phrase coined by Henry Clay, each could become a "self-made man." The idea of becoming an "Alger hero" was not altogether unthinkable, given the social climate during that part of the Industrial Revolution. After all, some of the most visible personalities of the day had accomplished it. John Wanamaker had risen from copy boy to creator of a department store chain. Andrew Carnegie started his career as a bobbin boy in a textile mill and went on to join the ranks of the richest men in America. Alger's copybook virtues of self-made wealth were also apparent in the lives of John Pierpont Morgan, William H. Vanderbilt, Jay Gould, and John D. Rockefeller.

American folklore suggests that the rags-to-riches stories of Horatio Alger, Jr., were tales of social mobility. And folklore it is, for the moral of the Alger stories is myth on several fronts. The heroes *never* actually followed the Carnegie-Wanamaker-Rockefeller pattern of gradually creating a great enterprise from small beginnings by means of vigilance, acumen, and imaginative organization. Alger's young hopefuls usually spent most of their time getting in and out of various dangers and difficulties, often the result of gratuitous malice, until *presto!*—the hero saw a runaway horse bearing down on the bank president's wife and child. He pulled her aside, thus becoming eligible for immediate silk-hatted wealth. In Alger's first story, *Ragged Dick: or, Street Life in New York,* for example, the boy-hero was indeed ragged, but fortune smiled on him and he happened to be on hand to save the small son of a properly grateful rich man from drowning.

More importantly, the Carnegies, Goulds, Vanderbilts, and Rockefellers were, and *are,* very few in number, for research on social mobility in the United States since the early part of the twentieth century has demonstrated that it is *not* the American Dream of ambition and hard work that generally leads to success. Pitirim A. Sorokin's studies during the 1920s found that few men significantly advanced beyond the occupational levels of their fathers.[51] Ely Chinoy's analysis of automobile workers at mid-century demonstrated that the chances of getting off the assembly line were minimal at best.[52] And conversely, studies of business executives have repeatedly found that few came from working-class roots.[53] We do not mean to suggest that upward social mobility is rare in the United States. Quite the contrary, it is relatively common, but seldom to the extremes or by the same means portrayed in the Alger stories.

The American Occupational Structure

The most detailed work on social mobility in the United States occurred during the 1960s with the research of sociologists Peter Blau and Otis Dudley Duncan.[54] In conjunction with ongoing surveys by the the Bureau of the Census in 1962, Blau and Duncan obtained extensive information on occupational position and intergenerational mobility for more than 20,000 males between the ages of 20 and 64. In an analysis based on a 17-category occupational scheme and job comparisons between fathers and sons, the researchers found that 49% of the respondents had been upwardly mobile, 34% had been more or less stationary, and the remaining 17% had been downwardly mobile. The fact that almost half of the respondents had been upwardly mobile would suggest that opportunities for social movement in the United States are numerous, thus allowing the fulfillment of the American Dream for many. However, as Blau and Duncan pointed out, much of the occupational mobility between fathers and sons consisted of short-distance movements—from farm labor to blue-collar work in the cities, from working class to low level white-collar work. They found, moreover, that "the closer two occupations are to one another in the status hierarchy, the greater is the flow of manpower between them."

Subsequent studies tended to confirm the findings of Blau and Duncan but suggested that much of the intergenerational mobility observed was the result of shifts in the economy that served to alter the occupational structure.[55] In recent decades, for example, while the farm-related jobs have declined, the number of new white-collar positions has expanded rapidly. Furthermore, as positions at the bottom of the occupational ladder have disappeared, those at the top have increased. And finally, despite the general alterations in the occupational structure over the years, the total amount of social mobility has remained relatively unchanged. A major exception in this regard has occurred with respect to blacks. When Blau and Duncan completed their studies in the 1960s, blacks were less likely to be as upwardly mobile as whites. In addition, education was not a particularly effective mechanism for blacks to use in achieving upward mobility. In recent years, however, successively younger cohorts of blacks have been experiencing more extensive educational and occupational mobility than their predecessors. Clearly an outgrowth of the civil rights movement, the intergenerational mobility of blacks born after about 1935 tends to compare favorably with that of the rest of the population.

America: Land of Opportunity?

In the history, literature, and folklore of many nations, the belief in America as a land of freedom and opportunity was very real. "In America," the storytellers would say, "the streets are paved with gold, and every man can live as a king." With that belief in mind, between 1855 and 1934 more than 20 million men, women, and children approached the port of New York from many parts of the world. Most were poor, and with the harshness of their past lives graphically stamped on their faces, they sought the American Dream. The feelings that many immigrants held were poignantly described in the recent recollections of Lee Iacocca:

> Nicola Iacocca, my father, arrived in this country in 1902 at the age of 12—poor, alone, and scared. He used to say the only thing he was sure of when he got here was that the world was round. And that was only because another Italian boy named Christopher Columbus had preceded him. . . .
>
> As the boat sailed into New York Harbor, my father looked out and saw the Statue of Liberty. . . . On his second crossing, when he saw the statue again, he was a new American citizen—with only his mother, his young wife, and hope by his side. For Nicola and Antoinette, America was the land of freedom—the freedom to become anything you wanted to be, if you wanted it bad enough and were willing to work for it.[56]

In their struggles to gain a foothold in the new land, some immigrants quickly found that they had changed their locales but had not altered their fortunes. Polish paupers became American paupers, as did many Jews, Germans, and Italians. But for most, particularly the Irish, the poverty and hardship that they found in the "land of opportunity" was better than what they had left behind. During the early part of the nineteenth century, Irish noblemen and landlords seeking to "improve" their lands and consolidate their estates and holdings evicted tenants by the thousands. Then came the potato rot, bringing still more evictions, famine, and starvation. Crop failures in 1845 and 1846 sent whole families wandering the countryside in a futile search for food. While the weaker died along the roads, the more resigned sat at campfires until death relieved their hunger. Despite the brutality of the factories, sweatshops, and tenements in their new land, those that found their way to America considered themselves lucky. They read the stories of Horatio Alger and dreamed the American Dream.

To the many who were lucky and energetic and ambitious, America did offer a new life, first to a few leaders, and then to more and more of the anonymous millions. Yet it was a rare individual who found the street that was paved with gold. For most it was still a hard life, but the threat of starvation was far behind them. It was the height of the Industrial Revolution, and millions of workers were needed in the factories, the mines, and in the mountains and fields to build the railroads. The frontier West, with its open spaces, free land to homesteaders, the potential for building a new life, and maybe even *gold,* also offered people a new future. In short, for many of the immigrants America was indeed a land of opportunity.

Now, in this second half of the twentieth century, can the same still be said of America? Today many upwardly mobile people live in the United States, and the democratic ideology strongly supports the belief that every individual citizen should reach out for success. Yet if "opportunity" is to be defined as the amount of upward mobility that exists in a society, then the United States does not differ dramatically from other industrialized nations. Cross-national surveys that compared the mobility patterns in the U.S. with those in Japan, France, England, and other countries in Western Europe indicated that working class Americans do have a somewhat better chance of attaining a high position in the stratification system. At the same time, however, it was clear that Americans born to high-status parents have a greater chance of inheriting an advantaged position. The similarities that exist in mobility patterns among these various nations, furthermore, are the result of the occupational structure that is generally characteristic of societies that are *industrialized*—not necessarily *American.*[57]

One could argue, nevertheless, that America remains a land of opportunity for many. The culture and social structure of the United States, more so than those in other nations, still allow for the creation of "Alger heroes," although often by different means than those employed in years past. Instant "silk-stocking" wealth seems to be an almost daily occurrence for rock artists, film and theatrical performers, professional athletes, Olympic heroes, and lottery winners. In fact, given the vast economic rewards that are attached to excellence in sports, such athletic activities as football, basketball, baseball, and boxing have become well-recognized routes out of the ghetto. The world of big business also continues to produce success stories—Lee Iacocca of Chrysler Corporation, the son of an Italian immigrant who became an American legend; William H. Gates III, a college dropout who designed IBM's first personal computer and founded Microsoft Corporation while he was still in his twenties; "kid capitalist" Steven P. Jobs, the co-founder and chairman of Apple Computer by age 29; and there are many others.[58] Although corporate leaders such as these enjoy wealth and success, the reality of life at the top can be quite routine (see Exhibit 8.8).

SOCIAL STRATIFICATION AND APPLIED SOCIOLOGY

Different social classes and prestige groups have alternative life-styles and views of the world, not only because they have more or less money to spend, but also because of differences in class-based preferences such as clothing and the image it conveys of membership in social classes (see Exhibit 8.9). As a result, many sociologists and other social scientists are employed in market research by firms producing consumer goods for the purposes of understanding these preferences, identifying and locating the various class and prestige groups, and marketing the preferred products in the appropriate manner.

Although rarely considered a theorist on the applied side of social stratification, the American philosopher and economist Thorstein Veblen offered some thoughts that are clearly reflected in contemporary advertising and marketing techniques. In his *The Theory of the Leisure Class,* written almost a century ago, Veblen described the competition for and conspicuous display of **status symbols,** material goods associated with superior social rank, as mechanisms people used to increase their prestige in the eyes of others.[59] In the United States, the most typical status symbols have included residences in particular neighborhoods, vacation homes, and particular brands of clothing, luggage, and automobiles—consumer goods that have been correctly identified by market researchers as being associated with upper-class status, and hence, are marketed as such to members of all classes.

A recent addition to the list of American status symbols, a phenomenon uncovered by the research industry, is the ZIP code. As a result of the discovery of the status value of ZIP codes, certain department stores, direct-mail firms, and other companies have targeted the more wealthy households. Living in one of the upper-class ZIP areas assures a catalog and charge card from Neiman Marcus, Bloomingdale's, or one of the many

Exhibit 8.8

Types & Stereotypes

Life at the Top

Life in the executive suite, as we all know, is the exhilarating stuff of which TV series and best-selling novels are made. Money. Power. Sex. Jet-setting glamour.

After being chauffeured to work in his limo, our typical executive begins his day with a few telephone calls to powerful politicians, cabinet secretaries, and heads of state. A brief time, of course, is spent going over the operating results of his company's far-flung divisions. Spotting some poor results, he fires a couple of division heads and lays off 2,000 or 3,000 employees.

After lunch (a tete-a-tete with a voluptuous movie star being considered for the company's latest ad campaign), the executive really gets down to work.

Three competitors are put out of business by shrewd action. Huge bribes are authorized to members of the ruling families in some backward countries, thus locking up worldwide access to crucial raw materials. And by the seventh hole of his daily golf game, our leader has already conquered his latest merger victim, convincing the head of a very successful company to sell out for 12 cents on the dollar.

On the way to the airport in his limo, our tycoon devises a revolutionary new product—a substitute for water. He then jets off to Monte Carlo, wins a few million at the roulette table and turns in early so he's rested for his monthly ceremony, at which new European employees of his multinational conglomerate offer him their first-born infants as a pledge of loyalty.

It's a great life. And, occasionally, a William Agee or a John DeLorean crops up to show that truth can be stranger than fiction.

But the truth, for most execs, is that being among the corporate elite means being in meeting after meeting after meeting. Countless "action" memoranda must be dealt with. Zillions of internal reports must be analyzed. Production schedules need to be finalized. Tax questions. Potential litigation. Employee benefit changes. Shareholder relations. Marketing and advertising. Public relations. Meetings, meetings, meetings.

All these topics can affect the corporation. And for each subject, there is a group of advocates within or outside the corporation whose views should at least be solicited, if not followed.

In the last analysis, so to speak, a successful executive is characterized less by being powerful or conniving than by having a durable posterior.

If this view of reality seems as exaggerated as the image of business conveyed by the "Dallas" oilman J. R. Ewing, consider the words of wisdom provided by Xerox Learning Systems, a Stamford (Connecticut) unit of the big office products company.

Xerox Learning, which peddles instructional material to executives, described the life of the typical executive in a recent sales brochure as follows:

"Right now, the typical highly placed executive spends more than five hours each day on the job in meetings. In fact, the higher you rise, the more time you will have to allocate each day strictly for meetings. Right now, the typical CEO [chief executive officer] logs six hours-plus in the meeting venue every livelong working day.

"From now on, you are going to spend 70 percent of every working day of your business career either leading or attending meetings. Make no mistake; that is going to be your prime responsibility from here on in. . . . From now on your business future depends more on how good you are at leading meetings than on anything else."

Xerox, of course, is interested in selling business people a sure-fire way to learn what it takes to conduct the perfect meeting. But the firm's promotional material has the perhaps unintended effect of portraying the often-dull realities of corporate leadership.

Sorry, J.R. fans, but that's the real reason corporate leaders are called chairmen.

SOURCE: Reprinted from the Baltimore *Sun*.

Although these homes in Beverly Hills lack the chic 90077 ZIP code, they make up one of America's most prestigious neighborhoods.

other highly prestigious department stores. According to a recent survey, the most chic address in the country was ZIP code 90077, the Bel Air section of southern Los Angeles, where one can find homes owned by Johnny Carson, Hugh Hefner, Barbra Streisand, and Kareem Abdul-Jabbar. At the bottom of the list was ZIP code 30313 in southwest Atlanta, Georgia.[60]

Status symbols, furthermore, are not simply the concern of adults. In a University of Utah study of elementary-school students in 1984, it was found that children appraise their peers differently, depending on what brands of jeans and shoes they wear and what bicycles they ride. For example, the grade-schoolers surveyed considered children who wore Levi's jeans to be wealthier and more popular than those wearing the Sears brand. Girls and younger children seemed to place more emphasis on status symbols than boys and older children.[61]

For students studying sociology in college and university classes, a knowledge of social stratification has an alternative value. College students are far from a random sample of the society from which they come. Most tend to be the children of parents in the upper half of the stratification scheme; a significant number are from households in the upper quarter. In consequence, students tend to have values and perspectives quite different from those held by individuals in the bottom half. Thus, they need to be aware of the problems and values of those born into less advantaged classes.

As a final note, perhaps the most important reason for studying social stratification focuses on the way that society ought to approach the problems of the disadvantaged. Extremes of poverty and inequality cannot be explained by lack of individual effort; rather we must be sensitive to the fact that they are also the result of a lack of opportunity.

Exhibit 8.9

Applied Sociology

Dress for Success

John T. Molloy, the author of the book, *Dress for Success* and *The Woman's Dress for Success Book*, conducted a series of experiments over the years with tens of thousands of executives, secretaries, and other business personnel. Using the same type of rigorous, controlled experimentation found in sociological research, Molloy sought to demonstrate that people's reactions to others, particularly in the business setting, were to a great degree controlled by a person's mode of dress. One of his conclusions was that individuals dressed in upper-middle-class clothing command more respect, are more successful, and project a greater image of authority than those dressed in lower-middle-class clothing. Since the publication of his experiments, Molloy has served as a clothing consultant to American presidents and cabinet officials, corporate executives, media personalities, and managers in all types of businesses and industries. The following excerpts from his many works reflect a number of his opinions and strategies.

About Men

Most American men dress for failure. They do so because they make one or more of four suicidal mistakes: they let their wives or girlfriends choose their clothing. They let their favorite sales clerks choose their clothing. They let designers and "fashion consultants" choose their clothing. Or they let their backgrounds choose their clothing.

We all wear uniforms and our uniforms are distinct signs of social class. We react to them accordingly. In almost any situation where two men meet, one man's clothing is saying to the other man: "I am more important than you are, please show respect;" or "I am your equal and expect to be treated as such;" or "I am not your equal and I do not expect to be treated as such."

I tested this hypothesis by using what I call the "push test." I took two men, both in their thirties, both of average height and weight, and dressed one in lower-middle-class clothes, the other in upper-middle-class apparel. On the second day of testing, we reversed the clothes so that the men's personalities and physical characteristics would not interfere with the results. We then went into the street and created minor conflict situations.

First, the man in the upper-middle-class dress stood to the side of a revolving door at the entrance to a building. When he saw someone coming, he attempted to pace his steps so that he and the approaching party would reach the door at exactly the same time. At that point we would see which man stepped aside.

In fifty-eight out of sixty-eight attempts, our man went through first without any confrontation whatsoever; the other party simply stepped aside. In the rest of the attempts, the other individual walked through first, indicating by his actions that he was more important. When the same test was conducted sixty-two times with our man in lower-middle-class clothes, he was pushed aside more often, and on three separate occasions he was threatened with physical vio-

SUMMARY

Vast differences exist among people in terms of their wealth, social rank, and overall position in society. Individuals are placed into classes of various levels, and this differential ranking and the resulting ordering of behavior is known as social stratification. Stratification is an integral part of the social structure and is generally transmitted from one generation to the next. Anthropological evidence suggests that stratification systems first emerged in horticultural societies when specialized cultivation technologies resulted in food surpluses over and above what was needed for subsistence.

Stratification systems vary considerably from one society to the next. Some systems are "closed," in that rigid boundaries are drawn between the strata with few or no mechanisms for changing one's class level. In caste, slave, and estate societies the systems of stratification are "closed." In "open" systems of stratification, such as the class system, social positions are determined by individual achievement, typically economic achievement.

lence, each time by other men wearing lower-middle-class garb.

The next day, when we reversed the clothing, the statistics held up: the man in the upper-middle-class garb was allowed to pass through the door on an average of three to one times. The man in the lower-middle-class uniform was threatened with physical violence on two occasions. We became afraid that he would be punched in the nose if we continued, so we stopped the test after twenty runs.

About Women

Most American women dress for *failure*. I have said that before about men, and research shows that it applies equally to women. Women dress for failure because they make three mistakes. 1. They let the fashion industry influence their choice of business clothes. 2. They often still view themselves mainly as sex objects. 3. They let their socioeconomic background influence their choice of clothing.

Throughout the period that I researched women's clothes, I read every article I could find on how businesswomen should dress. Most were inaccurate, some were dangerous, and all were the product of guesswork. These articles generally were based on one of two premises: that anything goes or that to get ahead in business, women should imitate men's clothes.

The "anything goes" articles were written by fashion-industry types who were not going to put themselves in a straitjacket by saying that one item worked better than another. Next year the industry might decide to manufacture and sell the other.

Everything does not go. Certain industries require certain dress. And while there is nothing morally wrong with a polyester pantsuit, research shows that it will not help you in business. A good skirted suit says you are an upper-middle-class executive-type, while an obviously cheap polyester pantsuit says you're not. My research shows that when you're wearing a good skirted suit, it is easier to give orders and have them carried out.

The "imitate men" advice usually came from women in the industry. Their articles appeared in industry-oriented magazines. They tended to base their advice on their own experience. Their experience usually came down to "I don't know what else to do, so I'll imitate men around me." And they wore things like pinstriped suits with vests.

My research shows that a three-piece pinstriped suit not only does not add to a woman's authority, it destroys it. It makes her look like an "imitation man," and that look always fails.

SOURCES: From John T. Molloy, *Dress for Success* (New York: Warner, 1975), pp. 1, 20–21; John T. Molloy, *The Woman's Dress for Success Book* (New York: Warner, 1977), pp. 15, 27–28. Reprinted by permission of the author.

Stratification introduces structured inequality to a society, a fact that has been recognized in Western thought from its earliest expression. In the view of Karl Marx, individuals' unequal relations to production in the economic structure of society were the basis for the development of the principal social classes. Max Weber also saw the economic order as the basis of class structure. However, Weber's theory additionally stressed the importance of wealth, prestige, and power to the ordering of the class structure. By contrast, the functionalist view of stratification holds that classes evolve as devices to insure that the most important positions in a society are filled only by the most qualified people.

American society is divided into four social classes, each of which can be further divided into upper and lower groups. The upper class includes those who have not only great wealth, but also a tradition of wealth and influence. A new upper class is composed of highly educated professionals, corporate officials, and others characterized by the recent acquisition of wealth. Most Americans are members of the middle class, with professionals, managers, and high ranking government and military officials in the upper portion, and small business owners, clerical workers, farm owners, and some less wealthy professionals in the lower portion. Manual workers make up the working class, and a segment of this group is classified as the working poor because of low wages and unstable employment. Finally, there is an underclass of chronically poor and disadvantaged individuals. Each class and subclass not only reflects differences in wealth, income, occupation, and prestige, but alternative life-styles as well.

A large segment of the population lives below the "poverty line," a statistical designation based on the amount of income necessary for basic nutrition, clothing, and shelter. The causes of poverty are found in the overall structure of the wider social order.

Class systems of stratification are characterized by social mobility, the movement of people from one social position to another. Mobility can be vertical and horizontal. Studies indicate that while considerable social mobility occurs in American society, short-distance movements up the social ladder are the most common.

KEY TERMS/CONCEPTS

bourgeois capitalist
caste
caste system
class consciousness
class system
estate
estate system
horizontal mobility
intergenerational mobility
lumpenproletariat
petit bourgeois
poverty
poverty line
prestige
proletariat
slavery
slave systems
social classes
social mobility
social stratification
status symbols
structural inequality
vertical mobility

DISCUSSION QUESTIONS

1. Can the various social classes in American society be considered "subcultures"? Why or why not?
2. Other than the class system, do other systems of stratification exist in the United States?
3. A number of observers maintain that black Americans are members of a "color caste." Is this really so? Can the same claim be made about Asian, Hispanic, and native Americans?
4. For Cuban, Haitian, Asian, and other immigrant refugee groups, can it be said that America is a "land of opportunity"?
5. Can the socioeconomic structure of the United States be altered to promote equality without impairing economic productivity?
6. Herbert J. Gans maintained that poverty is functional for the rest of society. With this in mind, is wealth also functional?

SUGGESTED READINGS

Richard P. Coleman and Lee Rainwater, *Social Standing in America* (New York: Basic Books, 1978). A description of the way different classes rank themselves and others, how public perceptions of social class have changed over the years, and the way these changes reflect economic and social realities.

William Davis, *The Rich: A Study of the Species* (New York: Franklin Watts, 1983). In a study based on some thirty years' experience in financial journalism, the author provides a portrait of the world's rich, focusing on their ambitions and methods, their pleasures and ego trips, their battles with tax collectors and other enemies, their fears, and the satisfactions they derive from outsmarting other people and their desire to maintain their position at the top.

Paul Fussell, *Class: A Painfully Accurate Guide Through the American Status System* (New York: Ballantine, 1984). In this irreverent description of the American class system, the author asserts that there are nine rigid castes in the United States. His ideal is what he calls the "X" class, the cosmopolitan elite who speak several languages, drink excellent cheap wine, never have to be at work on time, and whistle Beethoven quartets.

David Halle, *America's Working Man* (Chicago: University of Chicago Press, 1984). The author, a sociologist, provides a penetrating analysis of how and why blue-collar workers in a New Jersey chemical plant see themselves as "working men" when on the job but as "middle class" at all other times.

Michael Harrington, *The New American Poverty* (New York: Holt, Rinehart and Winston, 1984). A description of the nature and extent of poverty in contemporary America, including a review of the successes and failures of the various antipoverty programs and the reasons for the emergence of what the author calls the "new American poverty."

Charles Murray, *Losing Ground: American Social Policy, 1950–1980* (New York: Basic Books, 1984). A description and explanation of why, despite the expenditures on job training, welfare, food stamps, crime control, and education for the poor during the 1960s and 1970s, their poverty has become worse.

Albert Szymanski, *Class Structure: A Critical Perspective* (New York: Praeger, 1983). A conflict theorist's thoughtful analysis of social class in the United States.

NOTES

1. Philip M. Hauser, "The Chaotic Society: Product of the Social Morphological Revolution." Paper presented at the 63rd Annual Meeting of the American Sociological Association, Boston, August 28, 1968; reprinted in the *American Sociological Review,* 34 (February 1969), pp. 1–19.
2. Allan Holmberg, *Nomads of the Long Bow: The Sirionо of Eastern Bolivia* (Washington, DC: Smithsonian Institution, Institute of Social Anthropology, 1950); Herbert S. Klein, *Bolivia: The Evolution of a Multi-Ethnic Society* (New York: Oxford University Press, 1982); L. Marshall, "The Kung Bushmen of the Kalahari Desert," in Jack Gibbs (ed.), *Peoples of Africa* (New York: Holt, Rinehart and Winston, 1965), pp. 257–58.
3. Eva Rosenfeld, "Social Stratification in a 'Classless' Society," *American Sociological Review,* 16 (December 1951), pp. 766–74.
4. Gerhard Lenski, *Power and Privilege: A Theory of Stratification* (New York: McGraw-Hill, 1966), p. 212.
5. *Newsweek,* February 10, 1986, pp. 54–55; *Newsweek,* February 17, 1986, pp. 44–46; *Time,* February 17, 1986, p. 40.
6. *Newsweek,* March 10, 1986, pp. 18–37; *Time,* March 10, 1986, pp. 28–34.
7. *USA Today,* August 19, 1986, p. 4B.
8. Christine E. Bose and Peter H. Rossi, "Gender and Jobs," *American Sociological Review,* 48 (June 1983), pp. 327–28.
9. Kingsley Davis and Wilbert E. Moore, "Some Principles of Stratification," *American Sociological Review,* 10 (April 1945), pp. 242–49.
10. Rae Lesser Blumberg, *Stratification: Socioeconomic and Sexual Inequality* (Dubuque, IA: W. C. Brown, 1978); Gerhard Lenski, *Power and Privilege.*
11. Gerald D. Berriman, "Caste in India and the United States," *American Journal of Sociology,* 66 (1960), pp. 120–27; John H. Hutton, *Caste in India: Its Nature, Function and Origins* (New York: Oxford University Press, 1964); Mysore N. Srinivas, *Caste in Modern India, and Other Essays* (New York: Asia, 1962).
12. Kingsley Davis, *Human Society* (New York: Macmillan, 1949), p. 379.
13. J. Derrik, *Africa's Slaves Today* (New York: Schocken, 1975); *New York Times,* September 10, 1980, p. A2; A. M. Rosenberg, "The Middle East Slave Trade," *Middle East Review,* 9 (1977), p. 58.
14. Marc Bloch, *Feudal Society* (London: Routledge and Kegan Paul, 1961).
15. *New York Times,* May 29, 1977, p. 1; March 10, 1980, p. A3; January 6, 1981, p. 23; May 30, 1982, p. 3; Byron Williams, *Continent in Turmoil* (New York: Parents' Magazine, 1971).
16. T. B. Bottomore, *Classes in Modern Society* (London: Allen and Unwin, 1965).
17. Robert Nisbet, "The Decline and Fall of Social Class," *Pacific Sociological Review,* 2 (Spring 1959), pp. 11–17; Dennis Wrong, "Social Inequality Without Social Stratification," *Canadian Review of Sociology and Anthropology,* 1 (December 1969), pp. 1–12.
18. See Lenski, *Power and Privilege,* p. 22.
19. See R. C. Tucker (ed.), *The Marx-Engels Reader* (New York: W. W. Norton, 1979), p. 473.
20. See R. V. Robinson and Jonathan Kelley, "Class as Conceived by Marx and Dahrendorf: Effects on Income Inequality and Politics in the United States and Britain," *American Sociological Review,* 44 (March 1979), pp. 35–58; Erik Olin Wright and Luca Perrone, "Marxist Class Categories and Income Inequality," *American Sociological Review,* 42 (March 1977), pp. 32–55.
21. Erik Olin Wright, Cynthia Costello, David Hachen, and Joey Sprague, "The American Class Structure," *American Sociological Review,* 47 (June 1982), pp. 709–26.
22. Kingsley Davis and Wilbert E. Moore, "Some Principles of Stratification."
23. Walter Buckley, "Social Stratification and the Functional Theory of Social Differentiation," *American Sociological Review,* 23 (August 1958), pp. 369–75; Melvin Tuman, "Some Principles of Stratification: A Critical Analysis," *American Sociological Review,* 18 (August 1953), pp. 387–97; Dennis Wrong, "The Functional Theory of Stratification: Some Neglected Considerations," *American Sociological Review,* 24 (December 1959), pp. 773–81.
24. Leonard Broom and R. G. Cushing, "A Modest Test of an Immodest Theory: The Functional Theory of Stratification," *American Sociological Review,* 42 (February 1977), pp. 157–67.
25. Paul Blumberg, *Inequality in an Age of Decline* (New York: Oxford University Press, 1980).
26. R. H. Tawney, *Equality* (London: Allen and Unwin, 1964).
27. See Richard Coleman and Lee Rainwater, *Social Standing in America* (New York: Basic Books, 1978); Robert A. Rothman, *Inequality and Stratification in the United States* (Englewood Cliffs, NJ: Prentice-Hall, 1978).
28. Paul Fussell, *Class* (New York: Ballantine, 1984), p. 15.
29. *USA Today,* October 21, 1983, p. 1A.
30. Fabian Linden, "The Income Elite," *American Demographics,* August 1986, p. 4.
31. G. William Domhoff, *Who Rules America?* (Englewood Cliffs, NJ: Prentice-Hall, 1967).
32. Daniel Rossides, *The American Class System: An Introduction to Social Stratification* (Boston: Houghton Mifflin, 1976), pp. 24–25.
33. E. Digby Baltzell, *Philadelphia Gentlemen* (Glencoe, IL: Free Press, 1958); E. Digby Baltzell, *The Protestant Establishment* (New York: Random House, 1964).
34. *Business Week,* January 21, 1985, p. 63.
35. Dennis Gilbert and Joseph Kahl, *The American Class Structure: A New Synthesis* (Homewood, IL: Dorsey, 1982), pp. 350–52.
36. *New York Times,* February 2, 1984, p. F3.
37. *Psychology Today,* January 1984, p. 76.
38. Dennis Gilbert and Joseph Kahl, *American Class Structure.*
39. *Newsweek,* January 2, 1984, pp. 20–29; Harvey A. Siegal, *Outposts of the Forgotton: Socially Terminal People in Slum Hotels and Single Room Occupancy Tenements* (New Brunswick, NJ: Transaction Books, 1978); *U.S. News & World Report,* March 26, 1984, pp. 54–57, 64–65; *U.S. News & World Report,* September 10, 1984, pp. 75–76; *World Press Review,* April 1984, pp. 21–23.

40. Michael Harrington, *The New American Poverty* (New York: Holt, Rinehart and Winston, 1984), p. 70; Mollie Orshansky, "Counting the Poor: Another Look at the Poverty Profile," *Social Security Bulletin,* July 1965, pp. 8–10.
41. *New York Times,* August 27, 1986, p. A1.
42. U.S. Bureau of the Census, *Poverty in the United States,* Current Population Reports, Series P–60, No. 160 (Washington, DC: U.S. Government Printing Office, 1987); William P. O'Hare, *Poverty in America: Trends and Patterns* (Washington, DC: Population Reference Bureau, 1987).
43. Deborah A. Abowitz, "Data Indicate the Feminization of Poverty in Canada, Too," *Sociology and Social Research,* 70 (April 1986), pp. 209–13; Diane Pearce, "The Feminization of Poverty: Women, Work and Welfare," *Urban and Social Change Review,* February 1978, pp. 28–36.
44. Joe R. Feagin, "We Still Believe That God Helps Those That Help Themselves," *Psychology Today,* November 1972, p. 101. See also *Public Opinion,* June/July 1985, p. 28.
45. Doris Kearns, *Lyndon Johnson and the American Dream* (New York: Harper & Row, 1976), p. 216.
46. *New York Times,* August 27, 1986, p. A17.
47. See Charles Murray, *Losing Ground: American Social Policy, 1950–1980* (New York: Basic Books, 1984).
48. Center on Budget and Policy Priorities, *End Results: The Impact of Federal Policies Since 1980 on Low-income Americans* (Washington, DC: Interfaith Action for Economic Affairs, 1984).
49. *U.S. News & World Report,* August 13, 1984, pp. 5–7.
50. Herbert J. Gans, "The Uses of Poverty: The Poor Pay All," *Social Policy,* 2 (July-August 1971), pp. 21–24; Herbert J. Gans, "The Positive Functions of Poverty," *American Journal of Sociology,* 78 (September 1972), pp. 275–89.
51. Pitirim A. Sorokin, *Social Mobility* (New York: Harper & Row, 1927).
52. Ely Chinoy, *The Automobile Worker and the American Dream* (New York: Doubleday, 1955).
53. Elton F. Jackson and Harry J. Crockett, Jr., "Occupational Mobility in the United States," *American Sociological Review,* 24 (1964), pp. 5–15; Joseph A. Kahl, *The American Class Structure* (New York: Holt, Rinehart and Winston, 1957); Seymour Martin Lipset and Rinehard Bendix, *Social Mobility in Industrial Society* (Berkeley: University of California Press, 1959).
54. Peter Blau and Otis Dudley Duncan, *The American Occupational Structure* (New York: Wiley, 1967).
55. David Featherman and Robert M. Hauser, *Opportunity and Change* (New York: Academic Press, 1978); Hugh A. McRoberts and Kevin Selbee, "Trends in Occupational Mobility in Canada and the United States: A Comparison," *American Sociological Review,* 46 (August 1981), pp. 406–20.
56. Lee Iacocca, *Iacocca: An Autobiography* (Toronto: Bantam, 1984), p. 3.
57. Lucille Duberman, *Social Inequality: Caste and Class in America* (Philadelphia: Lippincott, 1976); Andrea Tyree, Mosche Semyonov, and Robert W. Hodge, "Gaps and Glissandos: Inequality, Economic Development, and Social Mobility in 24 Countries," *American Sociological Review,* 44 (June 1979), pp. 410–24.
58. *Business Week,* January 21, 1985, p. 78.
59. Thorstein Veblen, *The Theory of the Leisure Class* (New York: Modern Library, 1934).
60. *USA Today,* September 23, 1983, p. 1A.
61. *USA Today,* June 5, 1984, p. 1D.

Racial and Ethnic Relations

1883

The United States Supreme Court declares the Civil Rights Bill of 1875 unconstitutional. The bill stated that "all persons within the jurisdiction of the United States shall be entitled to the full and equal enjoyment of inns, public conveyances, theaters, and other places of public amusement." By its declaration, the High Court puts its seal of approval on segregation and discrimination against blacks.

1912

In Forsyth County, Georgia, a small community some 30 miles north of Atlanta, a white woman is beaten and raped one afternoon. She names her three alleged attackers, all of whom are black. One is lynched, and the other two are tried and hanged before a gloating crowd. So many threats are made against the county's remaining 1,000 blacks that they all move out of the county.

1920

Automaker Henry Ford begins publication of the *Dearborn Independent*, a newspaper that for the next seven years carries on a vicious and relentless campaign against Jews.

1946

Researchers at Alabama's Tuskegee Institute report that during the previous half century, more than 3,000 blacks

For renowned black artist Jacob Lawrence, the noose symbolizes decades of violent racial prejudice.

were lynched in the United States by local mobs. In many instances, the lynchings were the result of the broad southern definition of rape, which included *all* sexual relations between black men and white women.

1955

On August 28, Emmett Till, a 14-year-old black youth, is kidnapped from his Mississippi home after having allegedly whistled at a white woman. Four days later his body is found and recovered from the Tallahatchie River, and an all-white jury acquits the two white men accused of his murder.

Are these incidents reflections from long-since-forgotten chapters in America's sordid past? Hardly. Consider the following:

1980

In the aftermath of two decades of heavy immigration to South Florida by Cubans and other Hispanics, posters tacked to telephone poles and pasted on buildings along U.S. Highway 1 through Dade County ask: "Will the last American leaving Miami please take down the flag!"

1983

U.S. Attorney Dan Webb cites the town of Cicero, Illinois, for practicing "the most egregious, aggravated case of race discrimination" the Department of Justice has ever prosecuted. Although located only a few miles from Chicago, which boasts a population that is 40% black, Cicero has only 74 blacks in a population of over 61,000 people. Not one of Cicero's schoolchildren is black, nor are any of its municipal workers. Virtually all of Cicero's blacks work at a local race track, living on its grounds in cinder block huts.

1984

In an act of blatant anti-Semitism, Jewish radio-talk-show host Alan Berg of Denver, Colorado, is gunned down in a hail of machine-gun bullets—allegedly by a white supremacist hate group.

1985

Bumper stickers in Los Angeles County read: TOYOTA-DATSUN-HONDA-PEARL HARBOR. And in Philadelphia, an interracial couple is driven from an all-white neighborhood by threats and racial slurs.

1986

At The Citadel, a South Carolina military college, a black cadet is routed out of bed in the middle of the night by five whites dressed in Ku Klux Klan garb. White students at the University of Massachusetts in Amherst, angered at the World Series defeat of the Boston Red Sox by the New York Mets, attack a group of black classmates. And in West Philadelphia, California, and Washington, D.C., the homes and businesses of Vietnamese, Laotian, Korean, and Cambodian refugees are firebombed or otherwise vandalized.

1987

Charles Blackburn is the first black to return to Forsyth County, Georgia, since all of the county's blacks moved away under threat of violence in 1912. He organizes a march to protest the county's racial policies, and his group is greeted with rocks, bottles, clots of mud, and racial slurs.

The Ku Klux Klan attacked civil rights demonstrators in all-white Forsyth County, Georgia, in 1987 on the anniversary of the birth of Martin Luther King, Jr.

RELIGIOUS, RACIAL, AND ETHNIC GROUPS

The world is filled with a wide diversity of peoples, each group having its own ancestry, culture, and traditions. Yet throughout history, human beings have tended to emphasize the differences separating groups, rather than the similarities uniting them. Religion, ethnic background, and race have always been used to emphasize differences among groups. All too often these differences have been overemphasized, resulting in relations marred by hostility and conflict.

Religion

Many different views of the supernatural world exist. These views reflect the many varying religions that are practiced across the globe. Catholicism is a religion. Judaism is a religion. Islam is a religion.

A variety of cultures believe in a single, all-powerful being who has the ability to directly affect the course of human events. By contrast, other societies visualize distant and impersonal forces residing in streams and trees. Religion is a powerful force that touches some of the most intimate and awesome aspects of human existence, such as salvation and life after death. In consequence, it is not unusual for many religions to teach that their's is the "one true religion," that their's is the only true explanation of the supernatural order. And this position is understandable, for to suggest otherwise might weaken the faith. Thus, religion is often the source of deep divisions between groups.

Ethnicity

Culture, as we have seen, is a complex set of values, norms, and beliefs. However, most often in the modern world, people use language or nationality (ancestral country of origin) as an indication of broader cultural patterns. Sociologists use the terms **ethnicity** or **ethnic group** to refer to members of a group who share a distinctive cultural tradition. Thus, Italians, Koreans, and Greeks each constitute an ethnic group.

As demonstrated in Chapter 3, ethnocentrism is the tendency to use one's own culture as the standard for judging all others. The result is the inclination to rank the others as somehow inferior—creating the potential for interethnic conflict.

Race

Physical anthropologists define *race* as a population that has inbred for generations, thereby producing a set of distinctive characteristics. Although this might seem initially to be a simple definition, the concept of race requires a rather detailed explanation, for it is one of the most misunderstood terms in contemporary society. It is a mistake to look to biology or genetics to understand the concept of race, for the concept originated as, and continues to be, primarily based on an arbitrary set of features typically chosen to suit the purposes and convenience of the labeler.

Europeans first began to sort the peoples of the world into groups based on skin color and physical features as early as the 1600s.[1] This sorting process always has seemed easy because it allowed everyone in the world to be placed into one of a limited number of neat little categories based on superficial perceptions of skin color: *white* for Europeans, *red* for native Americans, *yellow* for Asians, and *black* for sub-Saharan Africans.

But is skin color alone meaningful for distinguishing among groups? If so, how does one classify the peoples of the Middle East, and southern Europe who are dark skinned? If other physical characteristics are added, such as head and nose shape, or hair texture, the problem of racial classification is no less complex, for these criteria seem to be independent of skin color. Moreover, different groups within a "color" have been identified, and groups with different colors have been judged similarly. During the 1880s in the United States, for example, Irish-Americans were described as having apelike features—a connotation that sometimes has been attributed to blacks:

> Practically every accusation that has been made against the American black was also made against the Irish: Their family life was inferior, they had no ambition, they did not keep up their homes, they drank too much, they had no morals, it was not safe to walk in their neighborhoods at night. . . .[2]

Cartoonists in the nineteenth century often stereotyped Irish immigrants as primitive and violent.

The *legal* and *administrative* definitions of race do little to clarify the concept. In the United States during slavery and the early years after emancipation, different states alternately defined people as "colored" depending on whether they had one-fourth, one-eighth, or one-twelfth "Negro blood," while in other states individuals were classified as colored if they were born with any ascertainable trace of Negro blood in their veins. The legal consequences of such determinations were significant, as poignantly illustrated by Mark Twain's description of the slave Roxy:

> From Roxy's manner of speech, a stranger would have expected her to be black, but she was not. Only one-sixteenth of her was black, and the sixteenth of her did not show. . . . Her complexion was fair. . . . To all intents and purposes Roxy was as white as anybody, but the one-sixteenth of her that was black outvoted the other fifteen parts and made her a Negro. She was a slave. . . . Her child was 31 parts white, and he, too, was a slave. . . .[3]

Prior to 1970 the U.S. Bureau of the Census classified anyone who had *any* Negro ancestry as "black," even though he or she might be indistinguishable in appearance from "white" Americans. At the same time, however, an "Indian" (native American) was anyone who was regarded by the community in which he or she lived as "Indian."[4] Since 1970, the Census Bureau has used rather loosely defined categories based on both color and ethnicity.

What all of this suggests is that **race** is an *ascribed status,* defined on the basis of *visible* physical characteristics such as skin color, facial features, hair texture, body shape, or whatever criteria people use to classify others.

PATTERNS OF INTERGROUP RELATIONS

Groups of people with different histories and traditions constantly encounter one another. Sometimes these encounters take place on a battlefield. Other contacts are more peaceful as groups emigrate to new areas in search of land, jobs, homes, or freedom. The diverse social relations between groups can be divided into three broad categories. Some situations are characterized by *pluralism,* cooperative and peaceful relations based on mutual respect. In others, contact produces conflict, resulting in attempts at *domination*—endeavors to subordinate or even destroy members of a group. Finally, various contacts are best classified as instances of *assimilation,* when one group adapts to the culture and social arrangements of another.

Pluralism

Social relations between groups with different histories and traditions need not inevitably produce problems; numerous cases of peaceful cooperation have been recognized. **Pluralism** is found in those societies in which different racial, ethnic, and religious groups peacefully coexist, with each group having the same rights and privileges. The key feature of pluralistic societies is that the various groups treat each other with respect and tolerance, allowing each to maintain its unique traditions. This type of treatment occurs at both the interpersonal level and the group level.

Most observers suggest that contemporary Switzerland is a fully pluralistic society, with Protestants, Catholics, and Jews, as well as German-, Italian-, and French-speaking groups living together in peace and harmony. Switzerland traces it origins to A.D. 1291, when the representatives of three small *cantons* (states) formed a confederation. Over time other states joined the confederation for purposes of mutual defense, but each state retained its basic independence. A true central government was not established until the nineteenth century. In 1815, the Treaty of Paris guaranteed Switzerland its perpetual neutrality. It is now a nation with three official names and languages: Schweiz (German), Suisse (French), and Svizzera (Italian). Official documents are produced in all three, and the highest court in the land includes representatives of each language group. Finally, although Switzerland was a member of the League of Nations, its current policy of strict neutrality prevents its membership in the United Nations.

Forms of Domination

Conflict, domination, exploitation, and discrimination are all too often the norm in relations among different groups. Social scientists have used the term *minority group* to identify any collectivity singled out for discriminatory treatment by some other assembly—a *majority group.* Although the terms "minority" and "majority" are used widely in American society in reference to group composition and dynamics, many sociologists would argue that "subordinate" and "dominant" are more accurate terms.

Most people think of minorities as small groups within a large society. Fewer than a million Ukrainians live in the United States, for example, and they do indeed qualify as a numerical minority. Blacks, who account for only 12% of the U.S. population, also qualify as a numerical minority. Yet this demographic approach is of limited value, for the concept of a "minority group" is more appropriately based on the idea of *unequal power.* One group can dominate or discriminate only if it is in some way stronger and more powerful—with more guns, superior jobs, or control of the government or legal system. It is for this reason that women, who constitute approximately half the population of the world, often have been referred to as a minority group. Similarly, blacks in the Republic of South Africa must be classified as a minority group, despite the fact that they outnumber whites by four to one.

Domination emerges in many forms. It can range from subtle discrimination to attempts at total elimination of a targeted minority group. Social relations based on unequal power and exploitation typically lead to confrontation and conflict as subordinated groups strive for equality. Consequently, minority-majority relations are constantly shifting and changing. Sometimes they change quite dramatically in a very short period of time; other alterations take place at a rigorously slow pace.

Extermination and Expulsion

Dominant groups may actually seek to physically eliminate minority populations, as was many times the case in the United States in encounters between Europeans and native Americans during the eighteenth and nineteenth centuries. **Extermination** involves a policy of systematically destroying the members of a particular minority group. Quite clearly, this goal was expressed by many Europeans as they pushed across the American frontier. An alternative designation describes the same policy as **genocide,** the systematic destruction of an entire ethnic or national group. Hitler's attempted "final solution to the Jewish problem" stands as history's grimmest and most pervasive episode of extermination.

A policy of **expulsion** eliminates minorities by forcibly removing them from the territory of the dominant society. American history provides many examples. During the nineteenth century, native Americans were forcibly relocated to reservations, typically to places where the land was of little value for hunting, farming, ranching, or otherwise supporting a population. In numerous instances entire tribes of native Americans

Many Cherokees died of hunger and exposure along the Trail of Tears as they were forcibly displaced from their lands in Georgia in the 1830s and relocated to Oklahoma.

were forced to march, with whatever possessions they could carry, from the east coast of the United States to the far west.[5] Similarly, the hysteria over the bombing of Pearl Harbor in 1941 led to the forced movement of thousands of Japanese-Americans into relocation camps.[6]

Extermination and expulsion usually emerge in conjunction with two sets of circumstances. Perhaps the most frequent instances occur when the minority group has valuable property. In the case of native Americans it was the land they occupied, which the frontier colonists needed for farming and cattle grazing. The other circumstance is based on a *perceived* threat to the dominant society's welfare. The internment of Japanese-Americans was considered necessary at the time for purposes of national security. Or similarly, under Hitler's Nazi philosophy, Jews were perceived as a threat to racial purity. In these circumstances, the key word is *perception.* No evidence was ever put forward, for example, that Americans of Japanese ancestry were disloyal or posed any physical danger to the United States during World War II. The United States was at war with Germany and Italy at the same time, but Americans of German and Italian ancestry in the United States were not jailed without reason. As for Hitler's "final solution," notions of "racial purity" and contamination were based on myth and bigotry.

Subjugation

Minorities are often "useful," in an exploitative sense, to members of the majority. A particular group, viewed as a convenient pool of "free" or cheap labor, may be forced, as the result of its relative powerlessness, to do a society's "dirty work"—picking cotton, cleaning streets, digging canals. This forced control of their lives and activities, combined with denial of the rights and privileges available to others, is referred to as **subjugation.** And there are essentially two forms of subjugation—enslavement and segregation.

Enslavement, as the term suggests, is the act of reducing a group to the status of property—a phenomenon that has existed for millennia. Slavery was already well established before recorded history began in Egypt and Mesopotamia. A large part of the population of the ancient Greek city-states was servile. In Roman times wealthy households boasted personal, house, and plantation slaves. The discovery and conquest of the New World created a worldwide slave trade when the Spanish and the Portuguese learned that black Africans could be used as effective workers on plantations in warm climates.

Segregation involves the physical and social separation of the members of a minority within a society. It has many faces and many names. For example, the term **apartheid,** the South African government's policy of racial segregation, means "apartness" in Afrikaans, one of the nation's official languages. The origins of the word *ghetto* may be traced to the medieval practice of forcing Jews to live in separate areas, usually surrounded by walls, with gates locked after dark.

The walls built to enforce segregation are not always constructed of stone and mortar; *social* segregation can be equally effective. Today's urban ghettos are created and perpetuated by social and economic pressures. Within this context, segregation can be both *de jure* (by law) and *de facto* (in fact, in reality).

***De jure* segregation** exists when segregationist policies are supported by law (see Exhibit 9.1). Included among the legal aspects of segregation in the United States were "restrictive covenants," which were part of the contracts signed when property was transferred. In some northern Delaware neighborhoods developed prior to 1948, for example, deeds included the following covenant:

> At no time shall the land included in said tract, or any part thereof, or any building erected thereon, be occupied by any Negro or person of Negro extraction. This prohibition, however, is not intended to include the occupancy by a Negro domestic servant or other person, while employed in or about the premises by the owner or occupant on any included property in said tract.[7]

Segregationist laws may disappear, but segregation can be maintained by custom, tradition, and social practice, a process called ***de facto* segregation.** Restrictive covenants no longer have legal standing, black codes have been repealed, and separate schools prohibited, but *de facto* segregation persists in a variety of forms, including exclusive clubs which bar entry to blacks, Hispanics, Jews, and other minorities.[8]

Segregationist policies tend to be supported by two practices, both intertwined with issues of unequal power.

SOCIAL INDICATOR

Separate Neighborhoods: Whites and Blacks in New York City*

If you could live in a neighborhood as good as the one you are living in now, would you personally prefer to live in a neighborhood with:

	Whites	Blacks
Almost All Whites	16%	-
Mostly Whites	29	3%
Half Whites/Half Blacks	29	62
Mostly Blacks	0	7
Almost All Blacks	0	3
All Races Mixed	7	10
Don't Care	20	16

Source: *New York Times,* April 1, 1987, p. B4. Copyright © 1987 by The New York Times Company. Reprinted by permission.

*Based on telephone interviews conducted March 8–11 with 1,063 New Yorkers; 57% of whom identified themselves as whites, 25% as blacks, and 18% as something else. Those who said they did not know or had no opinion are not included. A dash represents less than 1%.

SOCIAL INDICATOR

The Geography of Apartheid

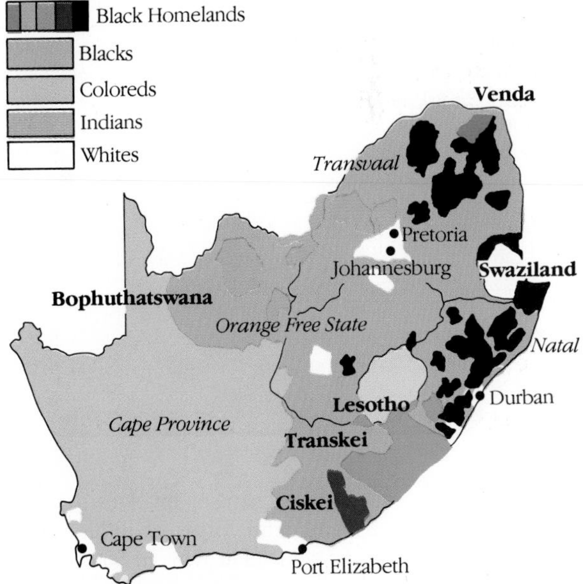

Source: *USA Today,* April 11, 1986, p. 6A.

Exhibit 9.1

Sidelights on American Culture

De Jure *Segregation: The Black Codes, Jim Crow Laws, and the United States Supreme Court*

Contrary to popular beliefs, the Emancipation Proclamation did not abolish slavery in the United States—neither in law nor in actual practice. The Emancipation Proclamation was issued by President Lincoln on September 23, 1862, and it provided that all slaves would be declared free in those states that, after January 1 of the following year, came under the control of the Union Army. Thus, the proclamation was a war measure designed to gain the support of world public opinion for the Union cause. Abolition did not actually come until 1865 with the adoption of the Thirteenth Amendment to the Constitution of the United States.

The Black Codes

Yet despite the Thirteenth Amendment, white supremacists solemnly resolved to keep repressed and separate, not just former slaves, but all blacks residing in the United States. In 1865 southern governments passed the Black Codes, a series of laws that were designed to replace slavery with a caste system that would preserve the prewar way of life as much as possible. These codes imposed severe restrictions on blacks, forbidding them to vote and (in some states) to sit on juries, limiting their right to testify against whites, requiring them to have steady work, and subjecting them to severe penalties for violations of labor contracts. The laws also included harsh vagrancy and apprenticeship legislation, draconic penal codes, and cruel and arbitrary punishments. Blacks were prohibited from bearing arms or taking certain jobs. The Black Codes affected a drastic reduction in blacks' newly granted freedoms and reduced them once more to a state of virtual peonage.

The Black Codes were short lived, officially at any rate. In 1866 Congress overrode a presidential veto from Andrew Johnson and passed the Civil Rights Act of 1866. Other legislation was subsequently approved for the purpose of strengthening and extending the intent of the Thirteenth Amendment. As part of the Fourteenth Amendment, adopted in 1867, citizenship and civil liberties were granted to former slaves. This step was accomplished by prohibiting the states from denying or abridging the privileges or immunities of citizens by depriving "any person of his life, liberty, or property without due process of law," or denying to any person the equal protection of the law. The Fifteenth Amendment, ratified in 1870, gave blacks the right to vote. Five years later, Congress passed the Civil Rights Act of 1875, which is mentioned at the beginning of this chapter.

The Jim Crow Laws

In spite of these federal efforts, white supremacist ideals and segregation prevailed. Beginning in Tennessee in 1870, Southerners enacted laws prohibiting interracial marriage in every southern state. Known as "miscegenation statutes," they were not limited to the South. A California law declared "illegal and void" all "marriages of white persons with Negroes and mulattoes." Tennessee again led the way in imposing *de jure* segregation with the Jim Crow laws. A series of these ordinances, adopted by Tennessee in 1875, required that whites and blacks be separated on trains, and other laws extended segregation to hotels, theaters, schools, restaurants, barber shops, and everywhere else that people congregated.

"Separate but Equal"

The Jim Crow laws were in direct violation of the Civil Rights

The first and most direct mechanism involves denying minorities access to meaningful forms of influence or power—in other words, political activity. In South Africa blacks do not have the right to vote, and they have no elected political representatives.[9] Elsewhere, even where minorities have the legal right to vote, countless other ways of discouraging their participation in elections are found. Heavy poll taxes or unreasonable literacy tests once were used in the United States to prevent blacks from voting. In 1985, the Supreme Court of the United States struck down a provision of the Alabama Constitution which, in effect, had been designed to deny blacks

Act of 1875, but in an 1883 ruling, the United States Supreme Court stated, "It would be running the slavery argument into the ground, to make it [the 13th Amendment] apply to every act of discrimination which a person may see fit [to commit], as to the persons he will entertain, or as to the people he takes into his coach or cab or car, or admits to his concert or theater, or deals with in other matters of intercourse or business." The Court refused to view racial discrimination as a "badge of slavery," thereby abolishing the Civil Rights Act of 1875 and suggesting a "separate but equal" doctrine with respect to blacks. Still, the matter was not fully settled as far as many blacks were concerned. Through the efforts of a group of Louisiana blacks who formed a Citizens' Committee to Test the Constitutionality of the Separate Car Law, the separate but equal question was placed directly before the Supreme Court in the case of *Plessy v. Ferguson* in 1896.

Homor Adolph Plessy was seven-eighths white, and his one-eighth "African blood" was anything but apparent. He had been selected by the Citizens' Committee to test the Louisiana separate car law, and committee members had made sure that the East Louisiana Railroad knew of his background. Plessy boarded a train in New Orleans and immediately took a seat in the "Whites Only" coach. When the conductor requested that Plessy move to the "Colored Only" section, he refused, whereupon he was arrested and charged with violating Louisiana's Jim Crow Car Act of 1890. Plessy was convicted, but appealed on grounds of Thirteenth and Fourteenth Amendment violations. When his case was brought before the Supreme Court, it was held that the object of the Constitution was to ensure absolute equality of both races before the law. But the court added:

> This is a political equality, not a social equality. The case hinges itself in the question of whether or not this is a reasonable regulation. Thus established usages, customs, and traditions, as well as the preservation of public peace and good order must be considered. Gauged by this standard, separate public conveyances are not unreasonable nor contrary to the Fourteenth Amendment.
>
> If the colored race assumes that this separation makes them inferior, it is not by reason of the act. If the civil and political rights of both races be equal, that is sufficient. The Constitution cannot put them on the same plane socially.

With these words, the Supreme Court of the United States had affirmed the "separate but equal" doctrine as the law of the land, a dogma that remained in force until *Plessy* was overturned by the Court's decision in *Brown v. Board of Education* in 1954.

SOURCES: Henry J. Abraham, *Freedom and the Court: Civil Rights and Liberties in the United States* (New York: Oxford University Press, 1977); Lawrence M. Friedman, *A History of American Law* (New York: Simon and Schuster, 1973); C. Vann Woodward, *The Strange Career of Jim Crow* (New York: Oxford University Press, 1957); Brown v. Board of Education, 347 U.S. 483 (1954); The Civil Rights Cases, 109 U.S. 3 (1883); Plessy v. Ferguson, 163 U.S. 537 (1854).

the right to vote.[10] The provision, passed by an all-white state constitutional convention in 1901, took the right to vote away from persons convicted of adultery, vagrancy, and other petty crimes. The Supreme Court held that the explicit intent of the Alabama law had been racial disenfranchisement, for blacks were convicted of the crimes specified in the provision ten times more often than whites.

Segregation is supported by a second and less obvious array of strategies which seek to assure that subsequent generations of a particular minority group will remain in the same disadvantaged position as their parents. This enforced separation is accomplished by excluding minorities from the educational system, thus guaranteeing that each new generation will be limited to poverty. A similar effect can be achieved by excluding minorities from high-paying jobs. Between the 1880s and the 1940s, blacks were excluded from such skilled craft unions as machinists and barbers. Now in the late 1980s, white supremacist groups again attempt to bar blacks from many high-paying occupations.

Minority Responses to Domination

Subordinate groups seldom passively accept their condition. Minority responses, ranging from underground subversion to social protest and open rebellion represent attempts to assert (or reassert) claims to freedom.

Rebellion

As early as 1663 in the Virginia colony the slave population gave evidence of being restive under the yoke of white domination and began conspiring against their masters.[11] In 1687 another plot was uncovered in the same colony in which slaves, during a mass funeral, had planned to kill all the whites in the vicinity in a desperate bid for freedom.[12] In both of these instances the planned revolts were thwarted by informers, but in subsequent years slave uprisings did become a reality. Between 1699 and 1845, more than 150 revolts took place aboard slave ships, and numerous bloody rebellions occurred in the Atlantic seaboard states and as far west as Texas.[13] Perhaps the best known of these was the Nat Turner Rebellion of 1831, when slaves in Southampton County, Virginia, marched from plantation to plantation, gathering adherents and killing whites. After but a few days, the Virginia militia put down the revolt, and the death toll included no less than 60 whites and 100 blacks.[14]

The Nat Turner Rebellion and similar events document the unwillingness of subordinate groups to accept their inferior status. The irony is that failed rebellions frequently serve to strengthen the hand of the oppressors, bringing on more repressive methods and rallying public support. In the aftermath of the Texas Slave Insurrection of 1860, when the business district of Dallas was burned to the ground as part of alleged abolitionist agitation to free slaves, vigilante committees were organized throughout the state to expose conspirators and ruthlessly suppress all traces of dissent.[15]

Separatist Movements

Minority groups oftentimes have responded to repressive situations with **separatist movements,** attempts to escape oppression and gain political autonomy by forming separate nations. Modern Pakistan was formed in 1947, for example, when the Moslem minority split from the Hindu majority in India. Similarly, the continuing strife in Northern Ireland centers on issues of political autonomy and minority rights for both Protestants and Catholics.

Separatist movements have flourished at many points in American history. One of the best known is Marcus Garvey's back-to-Africa movement, conceived in the 1920s for the purpose of achieving a level of success for blacks that Garvey felt could never be achieved under the legacy of slavery (see Exhibit 9.2). The 1960s witnessed the emergence of a number of similarly militant black separatist groups whose members disagreed with the nonviolent tenets of the civil rights movement of the era, which focused on reform of the existing system. Notable among these groups was the Nation of Islam (Black Muslims), a portion of whose membership continues to argue for a separate nation for blacks within the continental United States.[16]

Social Protest Movements

Social protest movements, which are discussed at greater length in Chapter 16, involve unconventional actions undertaken to show disapproval of, and the need for change in, some policy or condition. The protests challenge the system in the courts and in the streets, and can take the form of publicly violating laws that support segregation. The civil rights movement of the 1960s, for example, received its initial impetus from Rosa Parks, a 42-year-old black woman who refused to give up her seat to a white man on a Montgomery, Alabama, bus in 1955 (see Exhibit 9.3). In so doing, Parks quickly became a symbol for a whole generation of black Americans who challenged legal segregation, which deprived them of access to schools, lunch counters, rest rooms, and hotels. The 1960s and 1970s were marked by countless public demonstrations that revealed the inequities of segregation. At the same time, the laws were being challenged in the courts, leading to a series of Supreme Court decisions that more fully liberated black Americans.

Domination: The Conflict Perspective

Intergroup contact does not inevitably lead to conflict and attempts at subordination. In many cases, groups with divergent histories and backgrounds have been able to live together in harmony. The pluralism of modern Switzerland is but one instance. In what is now Manchuria, a section of northeastern China near the Soviet border, Cossaks and Tungus—two groups with radically

Exhibit 9.2

Sociological Focus

Marcus Garvey and the Back-to-Africa Movement

Marcus Moziah Garvey was born in Jamaica in 1887. He was largely a self-educated man whose career reflects one of the more ambiguous episodes in black Americans' struggle for equality. To that end he founded the Universal Negro Improvement Association (UNIA) in 1914, and by 1920 he had established branches of his organization in almost every urban area in the United States with a substantial black population.

Initially, the UNIA bore impressive fruit in the form of a series of business enterprises—a chain of grocery stores, laundries and restaurants, a hotel, a printing plant, a doll factory, and a steamship company to carry on trade between the United States and Africa—financed by the sale of stock to association members. Membership in the UNIA was estimated to be as high as 500,000 by 1923.

In 1920 Garvey convened the first UNIA international convention in New York City's Harlem. Some 25,000 delegates from 25 countries attended. Garvey delivered a series of remarkable addresses on black-American and black-African rights, urging that blacks accept a black deity, exalting African beauty, and expounding on the lives and notable achievements of blacks throughout history. Most importantly, he projected plans for blacks to resettle in Liberia—a small nation on the West African coast—in a back-to-Africa movement.

Garvey's messages exhorting black-owned, black-operated ventures began to rebuild the confidence of blacks in themselves and to prepare them for economic independence. But in the mid-twenties, the crusade faltered. In 1924, the government of Liberia, fearing that Garvey's motives were revolutionary, rejected his plans for resettlement, and the back-to-Africa movement stalled. American blacks began to demonstrate some understandable reluctance toward the idea of leaving their familiar homeland for the privations of life in the bush. The incompetence and dishonesty of Garvey's principal associates in the UNIA turned out to be damaging as well. In 1925 Garvey was convicted of fraudulent business dealings, and two years later he was deported to Jamaica. Although all evidence suggested that his subordinates were the real offenders, it is likely that the jury that convicted him and the government that deported him regarded his black nationalism as the real crime. In the years that followed, Garvey continued working in behalf of his beliefs, but his influence and prestige declined. In 1940 he died at the age of 56, obscure and impoverished.

In retrospect, it is difficult to conclude whether Garvey's back-to-Africa slogan was meant to be taken literally. Perhaps his paeans to the glories of African civilization were intended primarily to awaken black pride and self-assertion within the United States. His assertive separatism, in any event, remained as a legacy, contributing directly to the rebirth of black nationalism in the 1960s.

SOURCES: Marcus Garvey, "The Negroe's Greatest Enemy," *Current History,* 18 (September 1923), pp. 951–57; Marcus Garvey, in Amy Jacques Garvey (ed.) *The Philosophy and Opinions of Marcus Garvey* (New York: Atheneum, 1969).

different backgrounds, customs, and traditions—have peacefully coexisted for generations.[17] Similarly, Protestants and Catholics live together without incident everywhere in the United States, but seem to be at war continually in Northern Ireland. Thus, it is not just differences in religion and culture that cause exploitation. Conflict theorists argue that for domination to emerge, three factors must be present—competition for scarce resources, differences in power, and ideologies of inferiority.[18]

Competition

Differences between divergent groups may frequently be worked out, but the situation is destined to be made worse if the groups are competing for some scarce resources. A limited supply of land or jobs has time and again been the source of competition.

History has witnessed any number of struggles between competing groups over the control of land—struggles that resulted in the domination of one

Exhibit 9.3

Case Study

The Legacy of Rosa Parks

What began on the evening of December 1, 1955, in the cradle of the Confederacy served to change the course of American history, or as black activist Eldridge Cleaver later described it, "Somewhere in the universe a gear in the machinery had shifted." The place was Montgomery, Alabama, and the key player in the incident was a black seamstress named Rosa Parks.

On that Thursday evening in December, Parks prepared to take her usual ride home via Montgomery's segregated bus system. She paid her fare, went to the rear door of the bus to board, and headed for the back of the vehicle as was expected. But the rear seats were already filled, so she took a seat in the middle of the bus. At a later stop, the driver picked up several white passengers and called out, "Niggers move back." For Parks, tired after a full day of working and Christmas shopping, moving to the back meant that she would have to stand in the rear of the bus for the rest of the trip. So she did not budge, refusing to give up her seat to a white man. Her intention was not to bring a test case to the public or the courts; as she later stated: "I was just tired from shopping. I had my sacks and all, and my feet hurt."

Rosa Parks had violated both custom and law. Not only was it a southern tradition for blacks to give up their seats to whites, but it was also against the law for anyone to ignore a bus driver's instructions. Parks was arrested, charged with a misdemeanor, convicted, and fined ten dollars. She was a popular woman in her community, and these events made her many friends angry. The incident came to the attention of

Mrs. Rosa Parks, here being fingerprinted after her arrest for refusing to move to the back of a bus, precipitated events that were to change the course of American history.

group over the other. Land was at stake in many conflicts between native Americans and European settlers during the push across the trans-Mississippi West. Different groups continue to compete for the lands of the Middle East, Africa, and South America. Similarly, when jobs are in limited supply, competition and outright conflict often result. Interracial tensions in the United States were not helped when the Civil War freed many thousands of skilled black craftsmen to compete with white workers. Beginning in the early 1980s, conflicts between blacks and Hispanics developed in South Florida with the successive waves of immigrants fleeing Castro's Cuba to settle in the U.S. And more recently, much of the dissension among Americans involving Mexicans cross-local black leaders, who immediately moved to galvanize a massive protest against Parks' arrest and the Jim Crow laws that had precipitated it. Meeting in churches over the following weekend, local blacks decided to organize a boycott against the city's bus system, which was used primarily by Montgomery's large black population, who did not own automobiles. Elected to lead the boycott was the twenty-seven-year-old pastor of the Dexter Avenue Baptist Church. His name was Martin Luther King, Jr. Little did King know at the time that the Montgomery bus boycott would make him one of the most loved and most hated men in the United States.

The mathematics of the boycott was simple. Montgomery was home to some 25,000 blacks, who represented 75% of the busline's patronage. Company officials were told that they would have no more black passengers until Negroes were seated on a "first come, first served" basis *and* allowed to keep their seats. And so the boycott began.

As the weeks went by, the boycott appeared to be almost 100% effective. Montgomery's blacks were not riding the bus. And as time passed with no compromise on either side, the determination of blacks simply increased. Then the rest of Alabama began to watch Montgomery; soon the rest of the country was watching, and ultimately the rest of the world watched too.

Montgomery's Mayor, W. A. Gayle, a member of the local White Citizen's Council and a prominent segregationist leader, declared that the city would never capitulate:

> We have now pussyfooted around long enough and it has come time to be frank. There seems to be a belief on the part of the Negroes that they have the white people hemmed in a corner and they are not going to give an inch until they can force the white people of the community to submit to their demands.

Preaching nonviolence, Martin Luther King, Jr., retorted from the pulpit of his Dexter Avenue Church:

> This is not a tension between Negroes and whites. This is only a conflict between justice and injustice. We are not just trying to improve Negro Montgomery. We are trying to improve the whole of Montgomery. If we are arrested every day; if we are exploited every day; if we are triumphed over every day; let nobody pull you so low as to hate them.

After three months of deadlock, King was arrested, convicted, and fined $1,000 for conspiring to hinder a company in conduct of its business. But this action only served to further strengthen blacks' determination. Blacks had become accustomed to walking or bicycling to work. The bus company had fallen deep in debt, and its drivers were drifting to other jobs or leaving the city. The federal courts intervened late in 1956. First an injunction was handed down outlawing segregation, followed by the Supreme Court's ruling in *Gayle v. Browder,* which struck down the Montgomery statute mandating segregation on buses operated within the city. King was released, and discrimination on buses recognized as a violation of federal law. And that was how it all began. The successful Montgomery boycott set a precedent for similar actions, setting the stage for the entire civil rights movement during the 1960s.

SOURCES: Henry F. Bedford, *Trouble Downtown: The Local Context of Twentieth-Century America* (New York: Harcourt Brace Jovanovich, 1978); Douglas T. Miller and Marion Nowak, *The Fifties: The Way We Really Were* (Garden City, NY: Doubleday, 1977); J. Ronald Oakley, *God's Country: America in the Fifties* (New York: Dembner, 1986); William L. O'Neill, *American High: The Years of Confidence, 1945–1960* (New York: Free Press, 1986); Gayle v. Browder, 352 U.S. 903 (1956).

ing the Rio Grande into Texas and southern California is work related.

Power and Social Control

The ability to subordinate a population ultimately depends on power. Direct physical force has been used by invading forces to win control over native populations since the beginning of recorded history. Control also may be exercised by legal mechanisms that subordinate the minority. In the aftermath of the Civil War, more than one labor union systematically excluded blacks from membership and prohibited their participation in apprenticeship programs.[19]

Control also depends on maintaining power, and minorities can be deprived of their political power in many ways. Limits placed on voting rights and access to political office are among the most direct means of subordination. At the height of anti-Chinese feelings in the United States during the 1850s, the California legislature banned Chinese from giving testimony against whites—effectively cutting them off from the court system. And more currently, blacks in South Africa do not have the right to vote.

Ideologies of Inferiority

Discrimination and exclusionary practices are most effectively carried out if supported by some **ideology of inferiority,** a cultural belief system that suggests that minorities are somehow inferior—socially, culturally, or intellectually.

It is not all that unusual for members of one group to exhibit feelings of superiority toward others. A group's religion may teach that they are "the chosen people," superior to all others, while believers of different faiths are labeled as "pagans," or worse. As noted in the analysis of culture, members of a society often display ethnocentrism, belittling what they consider to be inferior customs and beliefs. If ethnocentrism does not exist prior to contact, it will emerge to justify the system.[20]

A rather prominent ideology of inferiority in American society is racism. Embedded in racism are *myths* of inferiority that supposedly "prove" that minorities are deserving of domination. These myths play an important role in processes of subordination. Although many individuals commonly use the word "racism" to refer to any instance of discrimination, the term actually has a different and rather precise meaning. **Racism** refers to the belief that the human population is made up of different genetic groups that can be identified by distinctive physical characteristics (facial structure, skin color, hair texture) and are distinguished by unequal intellectual capacity.[21]

An American version of racism directed against various racial and ethnic groups* was popular during the first half of the current century and featured a curious mixture of central themes. Primary among these was the idea of "polygenesis," the argument that the various "races" evolved at different times, and that some were therefore more "primitive" or otherwise less civilized than others. The second tenet was that culture was a product of intellectual capacity. Hence, lower races (for instance, blacks or the Irish) could not carry on the culture of higher races (whites). And third, because the children of any mixed racial or ethnic union would have a biological and cultural capacity midway between their parents, any complete assimilation would produce the deterioration of western civilization (see Exhibit 9.4).[22]

Quite clearly, such a system of beliefs would justify the subordination of minority groups. In addition, ideologies of inferiority can have other important consequences. In the United States, which was founded with the lofty ideals of equality and freedom embodied in the Declaration of Independence, beliefs that minority group members are culturally inferior allow members of the dominant group to reconcile inconsistencies between behavior and ideals.

Ideologies also serve to justify the allocation of minorities to inferior occupational positions and work roles. Sociologist Edna Bonacich has referred to this phenomenon as a **split labor market,** one in which the superior group monopolizes the higher paying, higher prestige jobs, while members of the minority group are limited to the less desirable positions.[23] Yet since the mere presence of the minorities represents a continuous threat to the jobs of the majority, the minorities are denied access to education, which might enable them to attain higher levels of employment.

Assimilation

The American experience of absorbing waves of immigrants points to still another form of intergroup contact—assimilation. **Assimilation** refers to the eventual disappearance of a minority group as a separate and unique culture when its members adopt the culture of the majority. Group identity is lost as minorities are absorbed into the way of life of the larger culture. Certain elements of the minority culture may survive; they may even become incorporated into the larger cultural heritage, producing some changes in the core culture, but the host culture ultimately prevails. This process of assimilation is reflected in the words of John Quincy Adams, who proclaimed during his presidency in the early part of the nineteenth century the conditions under which immigrants would be welcome:

> To one thing they must make up their minds, or they will be disappointed in every expectation of happiness as Americans. They must cast off the European skin, never to resume it. They must look forward to their posterity rather than backward to their ancestors; they must be sure that whatever their own feelings may be, those of their children will cling to the prejudices of this country.[24]

Adams' observation has turned out to be quite accurate sociologically; in it he predicted two crucial aspects of assimilation that have developed in the United

*During the nineteenth century the word "race" was often used to refer to religious groups (the Jewish race), and white ethnic groups (the Irish race), as well as blacks, Chinese, and native Americans.

States. The first was that successful acceptance into American society could be gained only through an abandoning of native cultures and certain religious customs. Social acceptance has been dependent upon adopting the English language, accommodating to the rhythm of a Christian calendar organized around Easter, Christmas, and a Sunday sabbath, monogamous marriage, and basically English culture. Hence, the cultural norm against which immigrants must often judge their beliefs, values, and behavior has been called **anglo conformity,** conformity to a style of life that has its origins in a white, middle-class, Christian, northwestern European society.

Adams was also correct in anticipating that individuals immigrating to the United States would probably not be fully accepted into the anglo society. Rather, it would be the children or grandchildren of these immigrants who could look forward to full participation. Thus, assimilation is actually a process, extending over generations. Each generation faces a somewhat different set of circumstances than their parents faced. The experiences of the waves of immigrants who flooded into America during the nineteenth century demonstrate the process.

Exhibit 9.4

Sociological Focus

William B. Shockley and the Saga of "Bad Genes"

Perhaps the most controversial proponent of the notion of racial inferiority in recent years is physicist William Bradford Shockley. Born in 1910, Shockley was educated at the California Institute of Technology and Massachusetts Institute of Technology. In later years, working as a researcher for Bell Telephone Laboratories, Shockley was instrumental in developing the junction transistor, which not only revolutionized the electronics industry, but also won him the Nobel Prize in physics in 1956. While an engineering professor at Stanford University during the mid-sixties, Shockley began developing his views on genetics, and not without considerable publicity.

The central thrust of Shockley's thesis is what he calls "dysgenics"—the notion that declining intelligence is caused by overbreeding among the "genetically disadvantaged," a category in which he includes most blacks. While holding that many individual blacks may be superior to individual whites, Shockley has claimed that because of heredity, blacks as a group suffer "intellectual and social deficits," which manifest themselves in lower scores on IQ tests, among other ways. According to the Shockley view, blacks have "bad genes," and enlightened society should intervene in limiting the spread of these genes throughout the gene pool.

To deal with the problem of declining intelligence, Shockley has proposed making payments to non-taxpayers of child-rearing age with IQs under 100 who undergo voluntary sterilization—payments of $1,000 for each IQ point below 100. Shockley has no degree in genetics, and not surprisingly, his theories are viewed as quackery by experts in the field. In ridiculing Shockley's belief that heredity alone determines intelligence, Princeton anthropologist Ashley Montagu once commented: "Had Mozart been born to a blacksmith, there never would have been a Mozart—just a blacksmith named Mozart."

Dr. Shockley has remained in the news in recent years. In 1980, at age 70 (and highlighting the superiority of his own genes), he announced that he had made a donation to a sperm bank established to produce the offspring of highly intelligent people—including Nobel Prize winners. In 1984, he filed a $1.25 million libel suit against the Atlanta *Constitution,* claiming that one of its reporters had compared his "voluntary sterilization bonus plan" with the efforts at genocide practiced by Nazi Germany during World War II. Shockley won the libel suit, but it would appear that at the same time the jury sent him a message—his damage award totaled $1.

SOURCES: Asa Briggs, Alan Isaacs, and Elizabeth Martin (ed.), *Longman Dictionary of 20th-Century Biography* (Essex: Longman, 1985), pp. 455–56; William B. Shockley, "Models, Mathematics and Moral Obligation to Diagnose Origin of Negro IQ Defects," *Review of Educational Research,* 41 (1971), pp. 369–77; William B. Shockley, "Proposed Research to Reduce Racial Aspects of Environment-Heredity Uncertainty," *Science,* 160 (1968), p. 443; *Time,* September 24, 1984, p. 62; *National Law Journal,* October 1, 1984, p. 8.

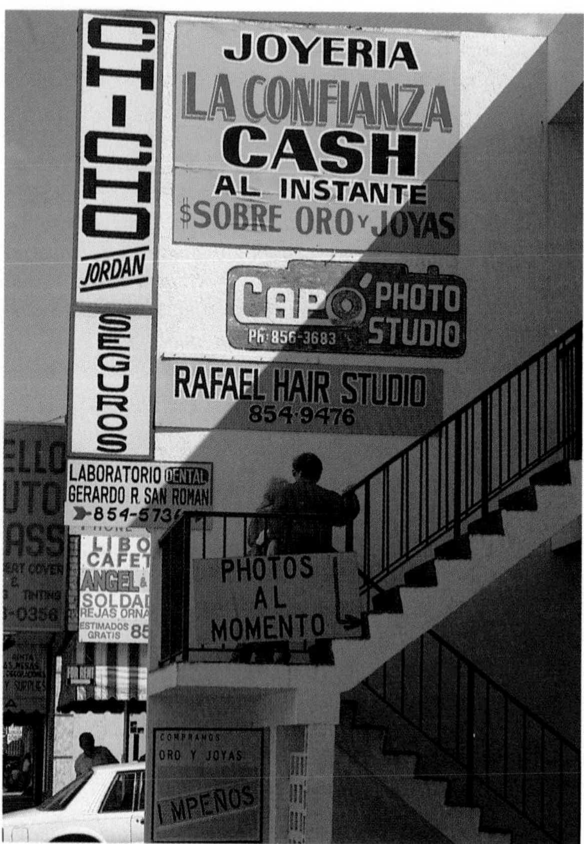

Recent immigrants frequently have been segregated in ethnic enclaves such as Miami's Little Havana.

First Generations: Discrimination and Exclusion

First-generation immigrants entering an alien culture typically face discrimination, exclusion, and outright hostility. Their language, customs, and beliefs quickly identify them, serving to set them apart from the social world of the native-born population.

Many early immigrants to the United States eventually lived in **ethnic enclaves** or **ethnic villages,** small communities or neighborhoods made up of members of a single racial or ethnic group. Countless "Little Italys" and "Chinatowns" founded in the last century survive in cities large and small. Similarly, more recent immigrations have produced their own ethnic villages—the Mexican-American "barrios" of the Southwest or Miami's "Little Havana" Cuban enclave.

It would appear that ethnic enclaves emerge in large part as responses to the discriminatory practices of the majority, who systematically exclude minorities from their neighborhoods. At the same time, however, residence in ethnic enclaves has a voluntary dimension, offering the advantages and security of association with members of the same culture.

Ethnic enclaves have advantages and disadvantages for the process of assimilation. Economics and exclusionary practices may make residence in an ethnic enclave a *forced* choice rather than a voluntary decision. The businesses and services that typically evolve in the segregated community—the churches, stores and restaurants, social clubs and other groups that cater to the needs of minority members—offer a refuge and perpetuate minority traditions, but simultaneously act as barriers to any movement into mainstream society. Enclaves become a refuge from an alien world where immigrants fail to integrate themselves into the dominant society. It is their children, the second generation, who begin the real process of integration.

Second Generations: Partial Assimilation and Marginality

Children of first-generation immigrants may be able to break away from the constraints of the ethnic village to achieve partial assimilation, but then they face a different sort of problem. Many second-generation immigrants experience **marginality,** participation in two cultures without being a full member of either.[25]

Because they are born and raised in the new society, having early exposure to the dominant culture through schools and the mass media, the members of the second generation are able to adopt many of the dominant values and behavior patterns. And yet, as children, they may use the native language of their parents, participate in old-world customs, and be exposed to the history and traditions of their ancestral homelands. Consequently, many second-generation immigrants remain visible because of accent, distinctive dress, or other ethnic characteristics, and are unlikely to achieve full acceptance. Moreover, the pull of the ethnic traditions of their parents often makes it difficult for them to identify with the new culture. And at the same time, they have become separated from the culture of their parents.

Third Generations: Full Assimilation

Second-generation parents will usually seek to give their children the advantage of full membership in the society. The features that tied these members of the second generation to the past—language, customs, and values—were barriers for them in school and later in the world of work. Therefore, they are less likely to pass on the old traditions. Their children will be reared in the mainstream culture, and most will enjoy full assimilation. Their names—whether Kawalski, or Scarpitti, or

O'Boyle—may identify their origins, but not their perspectives. The culture of their grandparents will survive in the ethnic enclaves and in the memories of their parents, but the third generation usually is made up of people who identify themselves as "Americans."

The Assimilation Dilemma: Maintaining Racial and Ethnic Identity

Representatives of many racial and ethnic groups have long sought to maintain their identities, celebrating the legacies of their past, and emphasizing the accomplishments of their group. Yet sociologist Andrew Greeley has argued that groups have become even more conscientious about reviving their cultural traditions in recent years, a phenomenon he refers to as **ethnogenesis.**[26] St. Patrick's Day and Columbus Day are long-standing manifestations of Irish and Italian ethnic pride. Newer indications of cultural consciousness include the vast popularity of books that focus on tracing ancestors to their native lands.

Ethnogenesis raises a complex problem in any society that has not as yet achieved pluralism. More specifically, ethnogenesis creates an **assimilation dilemma**—the question of how to deal with a group's social acceptance at the cost of losing its unique identity (see Exhibit 9.5). Yet to resist assimilation and acceptance for the sake of retaining group identity invites continued discrimination.

Social Distance: An Interactionist Approach to Assimilation

Patterns of acceptance among groups are acted out through social relations among members. Sociologists measure this dimension of interpersonal contact as **social distance,** the degree of closeness or intimacy people are willing to extend to members of dissimilar groups. The usual research strategy for measuring social distance is to ask people a series of questions that focus on close, more intimate social relationships with a specific group.

The patterns illustrated in Exhibit 9.6 clearly reveal underlying attitudes toward members of religious or cultural minorities. Those who are the most different from the dominant anglo culture appeared the least welcome. Arabs, Chinese, and Turks, who were seen as non-Christians as well as the possessors of an exotic culture, were at the bottom of the scale. Russians also ranked low, possibly reflecting the recent history of strained political relations with the United States, but also because of their image as representatives of a strange culture. Even Canadians, long-time friends and allies of the United States, did not win full acceptance by all Americans.

The Bogardus statements are a measure of the preferred social relations among members of different groups. They may help to explain certain kinds of concrete behavior, such as the movement of white, middle-class, urban residents away from the cities peopled by ethnic minorities, or the placement of their children in private schools to avoid social contacts with minorities. Both are examples of attempts to place social distance between two groups.

PREJUDICE, STEREOTYPES, AND DISCRIMINATION

Consider these common expressions, used to describe many different groups:

> "They all look alike."
>
> "How many of them does it take to change a light bulb?"
>
> "Never turn your back on one of them."

What these expressions reflect are prejudices and stereotypes, which shape many of the social relations between minority and majority groups.

Prejudice

Prejudice is a negative attitude toward a group or individual members of a group. Prejudice is frequently exhibited toward members of racial and ethnic minorities, different political parties, geographical regions, occupational groups, as well as homosexuals, old people, and members of various social classes.

It is easy to dismiss prejudice as a trait possessed by an individual, something unique to some narrow-minded person. Sociologists have emphasized, however, that prejudice is learned behavior, that it is more likely to be found among certain social groups, and that it may best be explained by what has often been referred to as the **frustration-aggression hypothesis.**[27] Reflecting a basic social-psychological behavior pattern, the hypothesis is very direct: aggression *is* a common response to frustration. The argument is that when people feel frustrated, they strike out, expressing their antagonism in harmful, injurious actions toward the source of their disappointment. Frustration does not necesarily *cause* aggression in all individuals, but it creates the potential

Exhibit 9.5

Sociology in the Media

The Assimilation Dilemma: Four Cases

Some "Subcommunities" Cling to Tried and True

Across the U.S., so-called "subcommunities"—holdouts from the cultural mainstream—are threatened by the powerful tide of assimilation. Yet, experts report some groups are showing renewed determination to avoid extinction and keep old ways alive.

Here are four of many remaining subgroups:

Shakers

In the 1850s, 6,000 of these pacifist Christians lived as celibates in the Northeast and Midwest. Known for their handmade furniture, Shakers grew only by converts to their simple life of prayer and hard work. Eleven groups remain—three in New Hampshire, eight in Maine.

An English preacher brought Shakerism here in 1774. "We are very sad that Shakerism will pass into history, but we feel that it is according to prophesy," says Eldress Bertha Lindsay, 89, of 600-acre Shaker Village in Canterbury, New Hampshire, which stopped taking new members in 1957. Eldress Bertha and two other Shakers tape their memoirs so future generations will know the Shakers and learn from their example.

But the community at Sabbathday Lake, Maine, still accepts new members who've proven their sincerity as true seekers. Sabbathday Lake "adheres to the view that the door must be kept open," says Gerard Wertkin, a non-Shaker who has written a book on Shakerism.

Cajuns

In a twist on the Peace Corps concept, teachers from France and Belgium are in Louisiana to help save the Cajun culture and language. Oldtimers on the bayous speak the Cajun French of their forebears, but not many younger adults. "It would be a shame to lose that . . . just because everyone feels that English is the official language," says Philippe Gustin, a Belgian who runs the Council for the Development of French in Louisiana.

The council has 100 French teachers from abroad and 200 from the U.S. teaching French in the schools.

Cajuns are descended from French peasants who came to Louisiana in 1755. Today, 500,000 Louisianans have varying degrees of French fluency. Gustin predicts students will grow up to create pockets of greater fluency and "more active bilingualism."

Along with a revival of the language has come a renaissance of Cajun music, cooking and history, which has benefited not only Cajuns, but state tourism.

Says Gustin: "Now, everyone wants to be Cajun."

Hutterites

The crisis sweeping the U.S.'s Farm Belt extends to a few Hutterite farming colonies. But the religious Hutterites are getting help—from one another.

"We keep their heads on top of water," says Paul Gross, 77, elder of the Spokane, Washington, Hutterian Brethren. Of 130 Hutterite farms in the U.S., six or so are in trouble.

Like Amish, Hutterites are Anabaptists whose European

for aggression. The frustration-aggression hypothesis is easily applied to intergroup relations. In any society some people will be harmed by social and economic conditions. The threat of unemployment serves as a good example. Massive job losses can be traced to many factors—shifting consumer preferences, technological changes, and the movement of the stock market currency exchange rates. The feature common to all of these factors is that most people have no real control over them, so personal goals of job security and providing for one's family become frustrated. Because their aggression has no direct outlet, it is then displaced to focus on some specific identifiable group, often a highly visible minority group. The minority is thus a **scapegoat,** a substitute for the real cause of the frustration.

Social historians have observed that racial discrimination is often strongest among individuals and groups harmed by broad social forces over which they have little or no control. In Germany during the 1930s, many people were harmed by deteriorating economic condi-

The Hutterites of Montana seek to preserve their cultural traditions.

forebears came here a century ago. All Hutterite possessions and duties are shared. Income from crop sales goes into the colony. Among themselves, Hutterites still speak German.

"They are the oldest, largest, and most thriving of all family-type Christian communal groups," says anthropologist John Hostetler. From 400 Hutterites in 1874, they've grown to 12,000 in the Northwest, the Dakotas and Montana.

Pineys

In the middle of New Jersey, in a wilderness called the Pine Barrens, live the Pineys, whose simple ways seem more appropriate in Appalachia.

Pineys—whose forebears settled there centuries ago—work cranberry bogs, fish, or hunt. A few make a living pulling moss or gathering pine cones for florists. Those who have jobs on the "outside," return nightly to the Pines' dirt-road security. They live in places like Woodmansie and Possum Trot.

But the Pine Barrens, which covers one-fifth of the state, has been discovered; and Pineys are colliding with newcomers, environmentalists and developers. "We can't raise chickens in our yards. . . . Neighbors don't like to hear roosters crowing in the morning," complains Piney Janice Sherwood, 54.

In 1979, the state enacted tough laws to protect the Pine Barrens and control growth. Sherwood and most Pineys support protection, but they think the laws penalize oldtimers for newcomers' sins. "I feel like we saved the Pinelands from developers and lost it to the government," says clammer Merce Ridgway, 45.

SOURCE: *USA Today,* March 24, 1987, p. 8A.

tions, the result of repressive governmental restrictions in the aftermath of that nation's loss of World War I. This, in turn, contributed to the tendency of some to be attracted to the anti-Semitic appeals of Adolf Hitler.[28]

Stereotypes

Prejudice toward racial and ethnic groups is an extremely common part of the dominant culture. By the time American students reach high school, few have not heard unflattering racial and ethnic epithets. Slurs and epithets reflect **stereotypes,** simplified, rigid beliefs and assumptions about a whole category of people. Stereotypes tend to be caricatures, a sort of mental cartoons, that describe groups in terms of one, or a few, negative traits—lazy or demanding, happy or savage, dumb or carefree. They are a cultural phenomena, learned and reinforced in the socialization process, with the more blatant examples emphasizing negative or threatening traits.[29]

Exhibit 9.6

Research in Sociology

Measuring Social Distance

In a study of social distance conducted during the 1970s, college students were asked a series of six ranked questions about social relations with Jews, Canadians, Germans, Italians, blacks, Chinese, Arabs, Turks, and Russians. For each racial or ethnic group, individual respondents were asked if they would accept that group in the contexts listed at right:

Ranked Score	Situation/ Social Relationship
6	A Resident of My Country
5	A Speaking Acquaintance
4	Members of My Work Group
3	My Neighbors
2	Very Good Friends
1	Kin by Marriage

For each racial or ethnic group the scores were averaged, with the higher numbers reflecting the greater level of social distance. The findings, broken down by gender, were as follows:

Group	Men	Women	Group	Men	Women
Canadians	1.8	1.6	Chinese	3.2	2.5
Germans	2.1	1.8	Turks	3.3	2.8
Italians	2.2	1.8	Russians	3.1	2.9
Jews	2.5	2.1	Arabs	3.5	3.1
Blacks	2.7	2.4			

Source: Sue R. Crull and Brent Bruton, "Bogardus Social Distance in the 1970s," *Sociology and Social Research: An International Journal,* 63 (July 1979), pp. 771–83. Reprinted by permission.

Stereotypes are perpetuated in many different ways—by word of mouth from one generation to the next, through circulating racial and ethnic jokes, and in countless other interpersonal transactions. The media—books, films, and television—is also a powerful force in teaching prejudice to new generations.[30] People often make the mistake of looking for a single stereotype of minorities, when in fact, a number of different stereotypes typically coexist, all of which portray minorities negatively. Each stereotype portrays a different negative trait, and thus one is always available that fits a particular situation. Three basic stereotypes can be identified, each playing a different role in the subordination of a minority group.

The Negative Stereotype

Perhaps the most common minority portrayal draws a picture of persons or groups who possess traits that violate some vital feature of the dominant culture. The seemingly harmless ethnic joke is one mechanism through which this stereotype is taught to new generations. Common phrases also serve the same purpose. The "Chinese fire drill," for example, is frequently used to describe mass disorganization. Similarly, among boating enthusiasts the term "Irish pennant" refers to the end of a rope or sail carelessly left loose or trailing from a vessel.

The "Protestant Work Ethic" in American culture, with its celebration of hard work, toil, and effort, has provided fertile ground for the "lazy" stereotype. This stereotype has been applied to workers dozing under sombreros or military and police personnel sleeping on duty. The function of such stereotypes is clear and direct. Some people consider discriminatory behavior to be justified because they feel that minorities lack the traits appropriate for full citizenship and therefore deserve to be mistreated.

The Dangerous Stereotype

Many stereotypes include exaggerated claims that a particular minority is "dangerous." As early as the seventeenth century, native Americans were described as "uncivilized" pagans and agents of the devil. The word "Indian" still conjures up images of battles between frontier settlers and red savages. It is an impression reinforced by hundreds of western movie reruns that continue to fill the early morning and late evening hours on television. Similarly, studies of school textbooks reveal the persistent image of warriors, dressed in feathers and "war paint," armed with bow and arrow.[31] The stereotype is perpetuated by athletic teams that seek to demonstrate their ferocity on the playing field by choosing "Braves," or "Redskins" or "Indians" as their namesakes.

Current stereotypes of native Americans, Italians, blacks, Colombians, and other groups also carry a clear message: these individuals represent dangerous minorities that must be suppressed before they destroy the dominant society.

The Good Stereotype

Not all minorities are considered undesirable or dangerous by members of the wider society, for some appear passive and accepting of their subordination. In a detailed history of the portrayal of blacks in American films, sociologist Donald Bogel found that it was common for a black character to be called "Tom," named for "Uncle Tom" in the novel *Uncle Tom's Cabin*.[32] This form of black stereotyping was widespread in films depicting nineteenth-century life in the American South, a popular movie genre of the 1920s through the 1940s, which included the all-time favorite *Gone With the Wind*. First depicted in these films as happy slaves, as Bogel put it, and although "chased, harassed, hounded, flogged, enslaved, and insulted . . . [they] remain hearty, submissive, stoic, generous, and selfless." Later they played the roles of servants and other menial laborers.

At the heart of the good stereotype of blacks is that some feel they possess the key social trait of "knowing their place." That is, despite shoddy treatment, they accept subordination without resistance. This role is preferred for the minority, and it has been argued that it is primarily for their own benefit: "Pay them a low wage—too much money will just confuse them or get them into trouble." If the dominant group can convince the subordinate group of the benefits of passive acceptance, they reduce considerably the risks of encountering open resistance and rebellion.

The Declining Significance of Stereotypes

Stereotyping of minorities does seem to be on the decline. A recent study, comparing the responses of samples of colleges students questioned at various different points in time during a 50-year period, shows that the percentage ascribing negative traits to blacks and Jews has declined over the past half century (see Exhibit 9.7). However, such findings must be interpreted with caution. It is not always clear whether verbal responses represent a *valid* measure of underlying attitudes or merely reflect changes in the society that have rendered the open expression of stereotypical attitudes less acceptable than they once were.

Discrimination

Prejudice is an attitude, built upon and reinforced by stereotypes. **Discrimination,** on the other hand, involves the acting out of prejudice by depriving minority group members of equal access to rights, privileges, and opportunities. Discrimination may be direct and confrontational, as in the case of racial slurs or lynchings, or it may be more subtle, as in the case of exclusion from jobs or club memberships. Discriminatory behavior may be incorporated into the legal system or it may evolve as part of the customs of the society. It also occurs as the result of some combination of these two factors.

Discrimination as Public Policy

Discrimination may be classified as public policy when the laws of a nation grant unequal rights on the basis of some social characteristic. South African apartheid divides the society into separate groups, each having different rights and privileges. Blacks have no vote and no representation in the national government; Indians and "coloreds" (mixed black, white, and Indian peoples) have the right to vote for representatives in separate chambers of the Parliament, but neither chamber has any real political voice.

The fact that laws of official policies exist does not mean that every citizen supports them. A recent poll of South African whites confirmed that a growing number are dissatisfied with their country's apartheid policies: 45% were clearly "unhappy with apartheid and more than 70% felt that the system could not survive for another decade.[33]

Any official policy of discrimination can continue to exist for some time after it loses public support, primarily because powerful segments of the society that directly

Exhibit 9.7 Types & Stereotypes

Changing Stereotypes of Blacks and Jews among College Students

Percentages Agreeing in:	1930s	1950s	1960s	1980s
Blacks Are:				
Superstitious	84	42	10	9
Lazy	75	32	18	18
Happy-go-lucky	39	17	5	1
Ignorant	38	24	8	9
Jews Are:				
Shrewd	79	47	37	15
Mercenary	49	28	8	2
Grasping	34	17	1	1
Sly	20	14	8	9

Source: Leonard Gordon, "College Student Stereotypes of Blacks and Jews on Two Campuses," *Sociology and Social Research: An International Journal,* 70 (April 1986), pp. 200–201. Reprinted by permission.

benefit from discrimination are in a position to maintain it. In South Africa, a number of major employers who are dependent on the black labor force are threatened with failure and bankruptcy should apartheid be set aside. For this reason they use their powerful influence in the Parliament to maintain the current system.

Institutionalized Discrimination

Unequal treatment does not need the support of the legal system to survive. It *can* and *does* frequently endure long after laws change. As the civil rights movement in the United States progressed during the 1960s, black Americans correctly noted that changing the laws was not, in and of itself, enough to eliminate discrimination. What they learned to recognize was what has become known as *institutionalized racism,* the informal patterns of subordination that prevailed in schools, on the job, and in housing. A subtle variety of institutionalized discrimination that has persisted was recently described by investigative journalists in New York City. They found that a few employment agencies secretly refused to refer blacks for certain kinds of jobs, thus denying them the opportunity to compete fully with whites in the occupational sector. In fact, these agencies had an informal coding system to classify members of minority groups: "5" for Jews, "6" for blacks, and "9" for gays. When discriminatory employers contacted the agencies with a job opening, to express their wishes for whites who were neither Jewish nor gay, they would simply state, "Don't send me any numbers."[34]

Prejudice, Discrimination, and Social Behavior

It should be noted here that not all prejudice is acted out, and not all discrimination is based on prejudice. The two do not *always* go hand in hand, a point first analyzed by sociologist Robert K. Merton more than four decades ago.[35] Merton noted that prejudice and discrimination are shaped by social situations and conventions, yielding the fourfold behavioral typology diagrammed in Exhibit 9.8.

Unprejudiced Nondiscriminator. Those who believe in the concept of equality and will not discriminate against minorities under any circumstances, regardless of

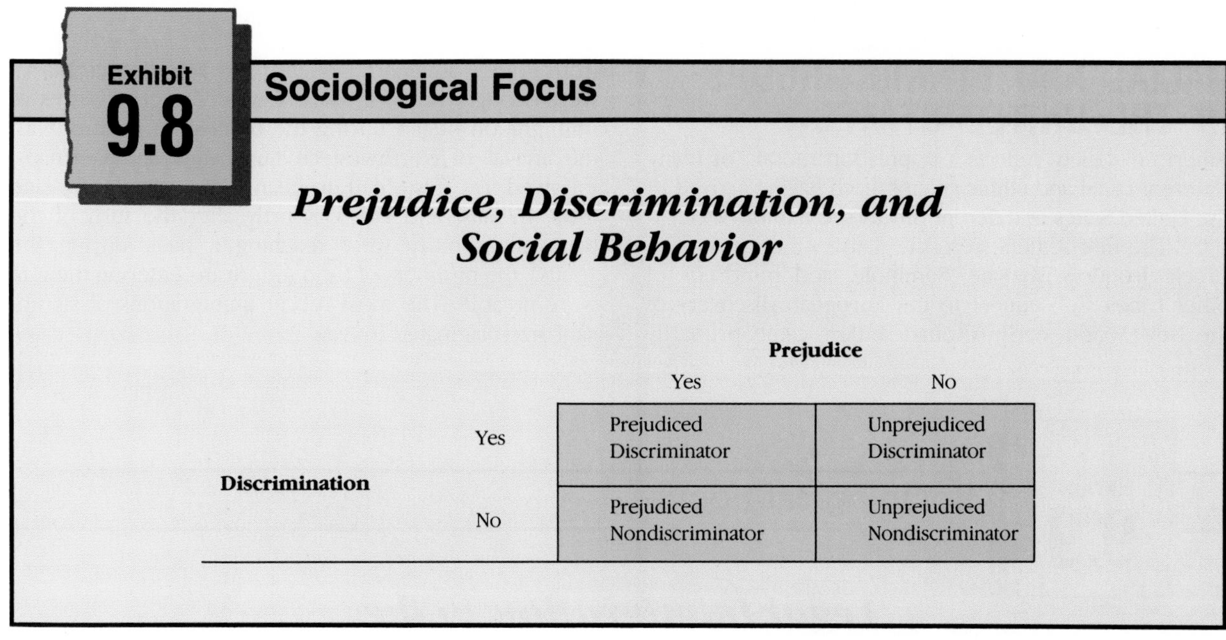

Exhibit 9.8

Sociological Focus

Prejudice, Discrimination, and Social Behavior

		Prejudice: Yes	Prejudice: No
Discrimination	Yes	Prejudiced Discriminator	Unprejudiced Discriminator
	No	Prejudiced Nondiscriminator	Unprejudiced Nondiscriminator

social pressures to do so, are termed unprejudiced nondiscriminators. Their attitudes and behavior are entirely consistent with one another.

Unprejudiced Discriminator. Those who will discriminate against others, in spite of the fact that they do not feel prejudiced, are known as unprejudiced discriminators. They find themselves in situations where group pressure is powerful. Adolescents, for example, may find themselves participating in acts of vandalism initiated by their friends against a Hispanic schoolmate. Similarly, neighborhood pressures might prevent some families from selling their homes to blacks.

Prejudiced Nondiscriminator. Social pressures can also deter discrimination, thus discouraging individuals from acting out their prejudices. People who are pressured to hide their prejudices are termed prejudiced nondiscriminators. Employers may hire and promote members of minority groups despite their own attitudes.

Prejudiced Discriminator. Those who are willing to discriminate even in the face of public opposition are termed prejudiced discriminators. Their attitudes and behavior are consistent. White supremacist groups that march against racial equality, undaunted by mass public criticism, fit into this category.

In the final analysis, prejudice and discrimination involve complex matters. People are exposed to a variety of social experiences that may create and enforce prejudiced attitudes and social pressures to discriminate. At the same time, however, they are also confronted with ideas and pressures (both social and legal) encouraging tolerance and equality. Responses are shaped by a combination of these forces in specific situations.

Prejudices toward racial and ethnic minorities are formed early in the socialization process.

RACIAL AND ETHNIC GROUPS IN THE UNITED STATES

American society reflects a population mosaic of many different racial and ethnic groups, each having arrived in the United States at different times (see Exhibit 9.9).

The first settlers were the native Americans—the Creek, Iroquois, Apache, Seminole, and hundreds of other tribes. Subsequent to the European discovery of the New World, early colonial settlers came primarily from France, England, Holland, and Scandinavia. Blacks were brought from Africa as slaves. The great waves of immigration began during the nineteenth century with the arrival of Northwestern Europeans and Germans, followed by Eastern Europeans—principally Russian Jews, Italians, and Poles. Shortly after the turn of the twentieth century (and reaching a peak during the 1960s), the numbers of Latin Americans entering the U.S. were notable. The most recent immigrations of significant size originated in Asia.

Exhibit 9.9

Sociological Focus

Legal Immigration to the United States by Region of Last Residence: 1820–1987

Intercensal Decade	Total Number	Europe Total*	North and West Europe†	South and East Europe†	Asia‡	Africa
		(percent of total)				
1820–1830	151,824	70.1	67.9	2.2	—	—
1831–1840	599,125	82.7	81.7	1.0	—	—
1841–1850	1,713,251	93.2	92.9	0.3	—	—
1851–1860	2,598,214	94.4	93.6	0.8	1.6	—
1861–1870	2,314,824	89.2	88.1	1.1	2.8	—
1871–1880	2,812,191	80.8	76.2	4.5	4.4	—
1881–1890	5,246,613	90.3	78.8	11.5	1.3	—
1891–1900	3,687,564	96.4	60.6	35.8	2.0	—
1901–1910	8,795,386	91.6	46.1	45.5	3.7	0.1
1911–1920	5,735,811	75.3	25.3	49.9	4.3	0.1
1921–1930	4,107,209	60.0	32.5	27.0	2.7	0.2
1931–1940	528,431	65.8	38.6	26.7	3.0	0.3
1941–1950	1,035,039	60.0	49.9	9.8	3.1	0.7
1951–1960	2,515,479	52.7	39.7	12.7	6.1	0.6
1961–1970	3,321,677	33.8	18.3	15.4	12.9	0.9
1971–1980	4,493,314	17.8	6.7	11.0	35.3	1.8
1981–1987	4,067,630	11.4	5.4	6.0	47.8	2.6
Total 1820–1987	53,723,582	69.8	47.2	22.5	8.8	0.4

Sources: U.S. Immigration and Naturalization Service (INS), *1984 Statistical Yearbook* (Washington, DC: 1986) Table IMM 1.2, and unpublished data for fiscal year 1985 (October 1, 1984–September 30, 1985) and *Immigration Statistics: Fiscal Year 1987*, June 1987.

*Includes all of present-day U.S.S.R., except 1931–1950, when U.S.S.R. is divided into European U.S.S.R. and Asian U.S.S.R.

†Through 1901–1910, North and West Europe includes Austria-Hungary. After 1901–1910, Austria included in North and West Europe, Hungary in South and East Europe. Immigrants recorded as "Other Europe" (57,182 altogether through fiscal year 1984) are omitted from these two regions as shown in this table.

‡Asia according to INS definition, includes Southwest Asia, for example, Iraq, Israel, Syria, Turkey.

File cabinets on Ellis Island contained the records of immigrants to the United States.

As immigrant groups, each of these has faced varied experiences at different points in the history of the nation. Most have been exposed to some prejudice and discrimination; some have even suffered through episodes of exclusion or segregation.

Native Americans

No less than one million, and probably close to ten million native Americans populated the North American continent when Europeans first arrived in the New World. The first explorers promptly called the local inhabitants "Indians"—a designation that endures even today—in the mistaken belief that they had found a passage to India. As a result of forced relocations to reservations, attempts at outright extermination, and their lack of natural immunities to European diseases, the native American population had declined to some one-quarter million by 1850.[36]

In numerous instances, native Americans and European settlers were able to peacefully coexist. In some cases intermarriage took place. Typically, however, conflict was the more common pattern. The westward expansion encroached upon the lands and traditional fishing areas of native Americans and destroyed the buffalo herds on which many depended for survival. Concerted attempts were made to impose European standards, and government policy toward native Americans was generally inconsistent and exploitative.

At first, the native tribes were approached in the manner of foreign nations. Several hundred treaties were negotiated, yet most were ignored. Official displacement of native Americans began in 1830 with the passage of the Indian Removal Act, which permitted the President of the United States to relocate tribes to the less valuable lands of the trans-Mississippi West. By 1890 the natives had become "wards" of the government and most had been removed to reservations supervised by the Bureau of Indian Affairs. It was not until 1924 that native Americans were granted citizenship.

Although only about one-third remain segregated on reservations, the legacy of reservation life has provided a dispiriting and dismal existence for contemporary native Americans. Housing is less than adequate. As many as 40% of the Navajo, for example, live without running water and sanitary facilities.[37] Such oppressive circumstances produce conditions that severely limit the future of younger generations. The school dropout rate among native Americans approaches 50%, causing many children to ultimately have few marketable skills in work environments beyond the reservation. More than half of some tribes are unemployed. Alcohol use is high, as is the suicide rate, reflecting the sense of frustration that native Americans currently face.

Those who flee the reservations are likely to encounter discrimination, which when combined with modest educational credentials relegates many to jobs at the lower end of the economic scale. Yet not all native Americans have failed to prosper under the legacy of reservation life. Some five percent of the land in the United States is owned by native Americans. More than a third of the strippable coal, half of all known uranium deposits, expansive timber stands, and 10% of domestic oil and gas reserves are located on reservation lands.[38] Although these resources are far from equally distributed throughout native American territory, many tribes have profited from them. Moreover, some 54% of the native American population resides in metropolitan areas, and a segment of these have made a successful transition from reservation life to the city, drawing on tribal traditions of sharing and looking after one another to do so.[39]

Asian-Americans

Immigration into the United States from China, Japan, and other parts of the Asian continent began on a large scale during the middle of the nineteenth century and was linked to the need for labor on the farms, mines, and railroads of the western United States. More recent immigrants have come from the area often referred to as Indo-China—Vietnam, Burma, Thailand, Laos, and Cambodia—reflecting the political instability of that region. While a segment of each group has experienced significant levels of success and prosperity, all groups have suffered periods of extreme prejudice and discrimination.

Chinese-Americans

The first major wave of Chinese immigration to the United States began just before the Civil War and continued for some three decades. The Chinese filled heavy labor jobs in the mining and railroad industries in the inhospitable terrain of the western United States, as well as low-paying restaurant and service work. In a period of severe labor shortages, the Chinese were welcomed as long as they performed the undesirable work that others sought to avoid.

Changes in the economy, however, stimulated strong anti-Chinese feelings. The completion of the railroads freed the Chinese to compete with Americans for other jobs. In California, where most of the Chinese lived at the time, their willingness to work for low pay kept wages down and caused vigilante groups to agitate for anti-Chinese riots. Organized labor also opposed the Chinese, bringing the idea of their "exclusion" to the attention of Congress. The problem reached its climax in 1882 when a shoe manufacturer in North Adams, Massachusetts, tried to break a strike by importing Chinese workers.[40] The result was passage of the **Chinese Exclusion Acts,** a series of laws passed between 1882 and 1892 that prohibited Chinese laborers from entering the United States. These acts were not repealed until 1943.

Japanese-Americans

The first Japanese immigrants arrived in the United States as contract workers on plantations in Hawaii during the 1880s. Shortly thereafter other Japanese workers were attracted to California, where a demand for unskilled labor offered them employment opportunities. Although few in number—only 25,000 by 1900—these early immigrants from Japan encountered strong anti-Japanese sentiments, to some degree an outgrowth of the discrimination against the Chinese who had preceded them. In spite of anti-Japanese feelings, Japanese immigration continued, primarily among the family members of earlier male immigrants.

The onset of World War II initiated one of the worst chapters in the history of minority relations in the United States. The growing presence of Japan as a military power in the Pacific heightened racist attitudes even before the attack on Pearl Harbor. The Japanese assault on December 7, 1941, unleashed a tidal wave of anti-Japanese sentiment, in addition to accusations of espionage and sabotage. Japanese-Americans, along with Italians and Germans, were prohibited from residing in certain military areas along the West Coast. But only the Japanese, about 100,000 of them (mostly native-born American citizens, as noted earlier in this chapter), were forcibly evacuated to relocation camps.

Other Asian Groups

Since the 1970s relatively large numbers of Koreans, Vietnamese, Laotians, and Cambodians have joined the

The children of Asian immigrants pursue assimilation through higher education.

Exhibit 9.10

Case Study

The Killing of Vincent Chin

The recent national monitoring and reporting of racially motivated actions against persons of Asian descent began in 1982 with the death of Vincent Chin, a Chinese American, in Detroit, Michigan. On June 19, 1982, two white males "began an argument" with Chin in a lounge, calling him "Chink," "Nip," and other "numerous obscenities." After being ejected from the lounge, one of the white men "obtained a baseball bat from his automobile" and, with the other man, "chased Vincent Chin out of the . . . parking lot." The two defendants located Chin, and one struck Chin with the bat "numerous times in the knee, the chest, and the head." The victim died four days later.

The two defendants, who were laid-off automobile workers, apparently believed Chin was Japanese and allegedly blamed him for the layoffs in the industry. According to one witness, one of the defendants made "an offensive racist remark" and said "because of you [Chin] . . . we're out of work."

The two defendants were charged with second degree murder by the Wayne County, Michigan, District Attorney's office. In March 1983, one defendant pled guilty to manslaughter, and the other defendant pled *nolo contendere* to the same charge. Wayne County Circuit Court Judge Charles Kaufman sentenced both defendants to 3 years' probation and fined them $3,780 each.

Asian and Pacific Island Americans were incensed about the lenient sentences, which they considered a sign that they were not considered Americans who were worthy of equal protection of the laws. Asian-American organizations joined together, galvanized by Chin's death and the light sentences received by the defendants, to demand an investigation by the U.S. Department of Justice. That department ultimately examined the case for possible federal civil rights violations. The case was referred to a federal grand jury, and on November 2, 1983, indictments were returned against both defendants, charging them with two counts of federal civil rights violations. On June 28, 1984, a U.S. district court jury found one of the defendants guilty of interference with Chin's civil rights, but acquitted him on the charge of conspiracy to violate his civil rights.

In handing down the guilty verdict, the jury found that the assault on Chin was indeed racially motivated and that a violation of his civil rights had taken place. On September 18, 1984, the U.S. District Court for the Eastern District of Michigan sentenced the guilty defendant to 25 years in prison and recommended that he be placed in an institution where he could receive treatment for alcoholism. The other defendant, who apparently was not directly involved in beating Chin, was acquitted.

SOURCE: United States Commission on Civil Rights, *Recent Activities Against Citizens of Asian Descent* (Washington, DC: U.S. Government Printing Office, 1986), pp. 43–44.

flow of Chinese and Japanese into the United States. Their experiences clearly parallel those of Asians who preceded them. They are exposed to discrimination; language barriers segregate them; many have become the targets of violence. The Vincent Chin case, elaborated in Exhibit 9.10, is but one incident, but it reveals many facets of contemporary anti-Asian sentiment.

The racial slurs directed at Chin reveal a current tendency to use physical features to identify people, and the practice of grouping diverse groups together. Vincent Chin was mistaken for Japanese, making him the target of anti-Japanese feelings that were based on the belief that Japan was responsible for economic problems in the United States. Yet Chin's antagonists were the victims of broader economic issues. Their treatment in the courts suggests that members of the criminal justice system may have shared at least some of the prejudices that caused Chin's death.

In contrast to the tragedy of Vincent Chin, Asian-Americans have also experienced individual and collective success. Their strong cultural emphases on hard work and formal education have been translated into levels of educational attainment well above the national average. In the prestigious and highly competitive Ivy League schools, for example, they accounted for some 11% of the entering freshman in 1987, even though Asian-Americans comprise only about 2% of the total population.[41]

An alternative measure of change in social relations involving Americans and Asian immigrant groups can be seen in the blurring of racial boundaries with respect to interracial marriage. Research shows that intermarriage between Asians and non-Asians in the United States has doubled during the past decade. Some interracial couples do indeed encounter discrimination, but it appears that most of the opposition to such marriages currently originates within the families of the individuals involved.[42]

Hispanic Americans

The term "Hispanic" technically refers to the peoples, language, and culture of Spain and Portugal, but in recent years it has come to identify any number of predominantly Catholic, Spanish-speaking groups. Together, they form the second largest minority group in the United States, and by the year 2000 they are projected to become the largest minority group in all of North America. Hispanics include groups with vastly different ethnic traditions, the two largest being Mexican-Americans and Puerto Ricans, followed by growing numbers emigrating from Cuba, Colombia, and parts of Central America.

Mexican-Americans

The first Mexicans to find themselves residents of the United States were not immigrants. Rather, their lands had been annexed by the United States government in the nineteenth century during the expansion of the Texas and New Mexico territories. In later years, poverty, population pressures in Mexico, and the catastrophic effects of the Mexican Revolution drew hundreds of thousands of Mexicans into the United States between 1900 and 1930. During these years, male Mexican immigrants did most of the common labor in the copper mines, picked cotton and vegetables, and laid the tracks for the railroads. The women toiled in laundries and cleaned the homes of the wealthy. Overt pay discrimination was rampant. While unskilled work generally paid other workers 40 cents an hour, Mexicans earned only 25 cents.[43]

The 1940s brought thousands of additional Mexicans into the United States as seasonal agricultural workers under the *bracero* program. A third major wave of Mexican immigration began during the 1960s, fueled by the poor employment opportunities and fragile economic circumstances that have come to be endemic in Mexico. Many in this group were illegal aliens. Large numbers of Mexicans continue to cross the border clandestinely into California and Texas.

In addition to the typical problems of discrimination and assimilation that almost all minority groups seem to encounter after arriving in the U.S., those coming from Mexico have been confronted with a whole new array of disadvantages. Because many are illegal aliens, their problems with substandard housing and employment are especially acute; their illegal status makes it difficult for them to use the courts to gain equity.

SOCIAL INDICATOR

Median Family Incomes of Selected Groups

Total U.S.	**$30,853**
White	32,274
Black	18,098
Hispanic	20,306
Families Headed by:	
College Graduates	46,533
High-school Graduates	29,937
Females	14,620
Northeast	33,938
Midwest	30,991
South	28,250
West	32,026

Source: U.S. Bureau of the Census, 1988.

Puerto Ricans

The Puerto Rican population is geographically divided between the island commonwealth and the American mainland. In contrast with other immigrant groups discussed here, Puerto Ricans are generally not referred to as "Puerto Rican-Americans" because they all have U.S. citizenship. When the Spanish-American War ended with the Treaty of Paris in 1898, Puerto Rico was ceded directly to the United States. In 1952, the island nation ceased to be a colonial possession and became a "free commonwealth." At the same time, plagued by overpopulation and an essentially one-crop economy, Puerto Ricans began migrating to the United States.

Like the minority groups arriving before them, Puerto Ricans faced prejudice, discrimination, and all the associated disadvantages. More than two million Puerto Ricans are now concentrated in the large urban centers, notably New York, Chicago, Cleveland, and Los Angeles.[44] Recent immigrants tend to have little formal education, thus limiting their occupational attainment. With the exception of native Americans, the income of Puerto Ricans is the lowest of any group in the United States.[45]

Cuban-Americans

While most Hispanic groups emigrating to the United States left their homelands because of economic hard-

SOCIAL INDICATOR

Estimates of Cuban Arrivals, 1959–1980

Immigration Stages	Manner of Transportation	Estimate
First Stage Early Departures, Castro's Takeover January 1, 1959–October 22, 1962	Commercial Flights from Havana	248,070
Second Stage Post-missile Crisis October 22, 1962 September 28, 1965	No Direct Transportation Small Boats and Rafts	55,916
Third Stage Freedom Flights, Family Reunification September 28, 1965–April 6, 1973	U.S. Airlift	297,318
Fourth Stage Third-country Arrivals April 6, 1973–October 21, 1978	Commercial Flights from Spain, Mexico, Jamaica	38,903 (January 1972/ December 1974)
Fifth Stage Ex-political Prisoners, Families and Others October 21, 1978–April 22, 1980	Flights from Cuba Small Boats and Rafts	10,000
Sixth Stage Mariel Boat Lift April 22, 1980–September 27, 1980	Boat Lift to Key West from Mariel Harbor	124,789

Source: Clyde B. McCoy and Diana Gonzalez, *Cuban Immigration and Immigrants in Florida and the United States: Implications for Immigration Policy* (Gainesville: Bureau of Economic and Business Research, University of Florida, 1985), p. 13. Reprinted by permission.

ships, for Cubans the reasons were political. In 1952, former Cuban President Fulgencio Batista seized control of the government and established a dictatorship, which eventually became harsh and corrupt. Four years later a student leader by the name of Fidel Castro assembled a rebel band to oppose the Batista regime. Late in 1958, when Castro's guerrilla forces began to erode the government structure, Batista fled the country. In the resulting political vacuum, Castro took power. His government, dominated by extreme leftists, quickly began a socialist program of drastic economic and social change. Many of the promised liberties were lacking, however. Castro ultimately established a communist state, allied with the Soviet Union. His opponents were imprisoned, and many were executed. Almost 300,000 other Cuban citizens fled to the United States.

Five subsequent waves of Cuban immigrants left Cuba over the next two decades. In what has become known as the Mariel Boat Lift of 1980, the Castro regime announced that Cuban dissidents wishing to emigrate would be permitted to board boats at the port of Mariel. What followed was the exodus of 125,000 refugees in flotillas of small boats over a five-month period.[46] Although the boat lift has long since passed, Cuban refugees continue to risk the treacherous waters of the Gulf Stream and the Florida Straits—in rowboats, life rafts, and even inner tubes—arriving in Miami and points along the Florida Keys in search of freedom in the United States.[47] Most have remained in South Florida, primarily in Miami (Dade County). As of 1985, Hispanics accounted for 43% of the Dade County population; two-thirds of that figure were Cubans and Cuban-Americans.[48]

The heavy concentration of so many Cubans and other Hispanics in the Miami area has had both positive and negative consequences. Miami has clearly become a multicultural community. In 1986, the mayor and the Dade County Manager were Hispanic, as were three of five City Council members, and two of the seven members of the county school board.[49] In terms of economic assimilation, the incomes of Anglos and Hispanics are similar, and Hispanics own some 25,000 small

The Mariel Boat Lift of 1980 brought over 100,000 Cuban refugees to the United States.

SOCIAL INDICATOR

Hispanics in Miami-Dade County

Total Population	**1,771,000**
Hispanic	768,000
By Place of Origin:	
Cuba	517,000
Puerto Rico	45,000
Colombia	25,000
Nicaragua	25,000

Source: Metropolitan Dade County Planning Department, 1987.

businesses in southern Florida, generating $2.2 billion for the local economy.[50] By contrast, however, a larger number of Hispanics are poor, and their school dropout rate remains high. The issue of language creates a considerable amount of tension in the region (see Exhibit 9.11).

Black Americans

Although a few blacks entered the American colonies as indentured servants and were freed after working for a predetermined period of time, for most individuals the black experience until the late 1860s was one of slavery. While historians debate whether slave owners were cruel or kind, the fact remains that slavery denied personal freedom and reduced humans to the status of property. Moreover, slaves were continually threatened with the possibility of being separated from their families.

The post-slavery period following the Civil War imposed new problems. Lynching gained popularity as a means of maintaining black subordination. Between 1892 and 1901, more than 1,100 blacks were lynched in the South for a variety of real and alleged crimes.[51] A lack of jobs and the overt hostility of the South encouraged migration to the industrial North. There, overt discrimination also translated into limited opportunities. As late as 1955, the eve of the modern civil rights movement, less than 15% of all black workers in the United States were in white-collar occupational positions.

The Civil Rights Act of 1964 initiated the erosion of the many legal and social barriers to blacks' full participation in American society. Since that time, although numerous positive changes have occurred, progress has been anything but rapid. An interesting measure in this regard is the number of blacks holding elective office. In 1985, for example, 6,384 black officials had positions in state and local governments, including the mayors of Chicago, Philadelphia, and 200 other cities.[52] Although this figure represents a significant increase over the days when blacks were barred from office, black officials still only constitute 1.3% of all officials in a nation where more than 12% of the total population is black.

In a more negative vein, a lack of progress and the reversal of positive trends in numerous other areas have also occurred. Many of the educational, economic, and occupational gains made by blacks during the 1970s have begun to fade in recent years. Black enrollments in colleges and universities, for example, a key to future progress, are in a period of decline, a phenomenon elaborated on in Chapter 13.

Infant mortality and poverty rates also document the difficulties currently faced by many blacks. Increasing numbers of Americans, both black and white, have been plagued by the economic dislocations of the 1980s, with

SOCIAL INDICATOR

Black Elected Officials in the United States

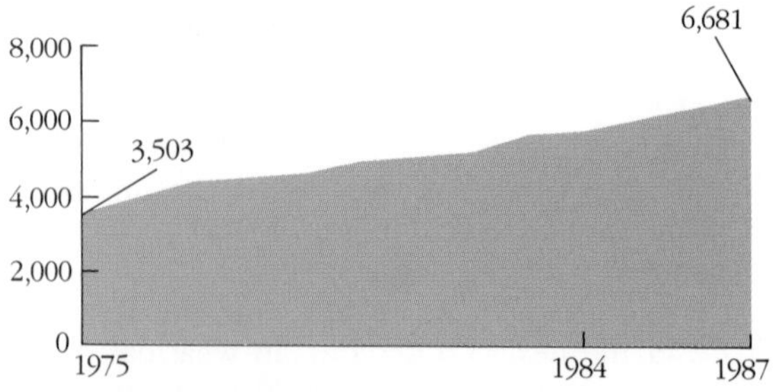

Source: *Black Elected Officials: A National Roster,* 1988.

Exhibit 9.11

Case Study

One Language or More?

In 1980, Miami's WNWS radio-talk-show host Al Rantel commented on the influx of Cubans into the city: "The idea that these people are being assimilated is ridiculous. They are absorbing us, and not the other way around." Most of Rantel's callers agreed with him, pouring out their resentment over not finding jobs or even being able to shop for groceries in Miami unless they spoke Spanish. One listener from South Miami said, "It's like we're the foreigners here!" And with the political leadership of the Miami area dominated by Hispanics, many local residents wonder why bus schedules and street signs still are printed in English.

What has been happening in Miami in recent years is far from unique. The number of Americans speaking a language other than English at home was 8 million in 1975. By the mid-eighties the figure had increased to 23 million, with a projection that the total would reach almost 40 million by the end of the century—all of which has sparked controversy over whether the United States should have one official language or two, or three, or more. Gerda Bikales, head of a lobby group known as *U.S. English,* articulated the issue in this way: "There is a trend in our government—we think unwise—toward recognizing rival languages. The principle we want to promote is that English has a special status in our society."

As the controversy continued, a number of bills were introduced in Congress seeking to repeal provisions of the Voting Rights Act that require that foreign language ballots be printed in thirty states. By 1987, eight states had adopted English as their official language. Advocates of these actions argue that a common language helps to integrate all members of society into a single unit. Moreover, they point out that non-English speaking children tend to face problems in coping with school; that non-English speaking adults are at a loss when it comes to reading street signs and various documents; and that because English is the predominant language in business, industry, education, and government, persons unable to speak it may forever be at a disadvantage.

Yet there also is considerable antagonism against the new laws. Opponents worry that the laws are merely symptoms of deep-seated racism. Many also feel that *Official English* will lead to the elimination of a variety of programs designed to facilitate Spanish-speaking participation in American society. For example, if bilingual education were to be eliminated, would this also extend to other areas of long-established custom? In New Mexico, because of its concentration of Mexican-Americans, there have been English-Spanish ballots since 1912, as well as dual-language road signs and marriage ceremonies.

How the multilingualism debate will ultimately be resolved is difficult to predict. No doubt ethnocentrism is involved on both sides of the argument. In fact, a recent *New York Times* poll on the matter found opinions rather clearly divided along racial/ethnic lines. For example, consider the responses to the question: "Should the government conduct business in English, or in English and other languages?"

Group	English Only
Hispanics	34%
Blacks	50
Whites	64

SOURCES: *Business Week,* February 4, 1985, p. 87; *New York Times,* October 26, 1986, p. 6E; *USA Today,* February 13, 1987, p. 12A; *USA Today,* June 12, 1984, p. 3A.

increasing numbers, particularly blacks, falling below the government's poverty level. In fact, throughout the 1980s, more than a third of all blacks in the United States lived in poverty. Poverty contributes heavily to infant mortality, and the rate for blacks is double that of whites.

American Jews

Jews worldwide have long been the victims of discrimination and blatant attempts at extermination. Many have sought refuge in the United States; some six million currently reside in this country.

Historically, discrimination and exclusionary practices have been aimed almost regularly at American Jews. Twelve of the original thirteen colonies limited voting rights and office holding to Christians, with many of these discriminatory laws surviving until after the Civil War. Similarly, during the 1920s and 1930s, the Ku Klux Klan directed its violence not only against blacks, but against Jews as well. Moreover, since the start of the 1980s,

SOCIAL INDICATOR

Antisemitic Incidents, 1980–1988

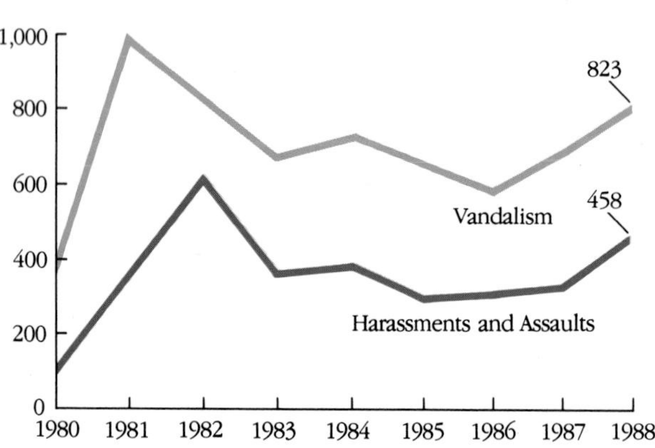

Source: Anti-Defamation League of B'nai B'rith in Philadelphia, 1988.

hundreds of incidents of violence, vandalism, and intimidation against Jews have been reported.

Upon emigrating to the United States, Eastern European Jews brought with them a forceful devotion to education and a strong sense of family. Parents were willing to make great personal sacrifices to improve opportunities for their children. High educational attainments in each succeeding generation were, in turn, translated into occupational and financial attainments. Jewish educational attainments are, on the average, above the national standards.

For the most part in the United States, Jews and Christians coexist peacefully, an example of pluralism that most Americans view with great pride. This should not suggest, however, that Anglo religion does not impinge on Jews and other non-Christians in subtle ways. It must be remembered that the calendar of holidays (Christmas and Easter) that dictates school breaks, derives from Christian custom. So too does the traditional work week, which views Saturday—the Jewish sabbath—as a day for many businesses to be open, requiring people to work in violation of their religious preferences. It must also be noted that each year several hundred instances of physical or emotional violence are perpetrated against Jews. Most involve the Nazi swastika, a hateful reminder of the horrors of the 1940s.

White Supremacy and the New Racism

Quite clearly, assimilation is not welcomed by all segments of the social order. The 1980s have witnessed an increase in incidents of violence directed against blacks and other minority groups. A number of these

Some "skinheads" have become militant white supremacists.

SOCIAL INDICATOR

The Violent Side of Bigotry

	1980	1981	1982	1983	1984	1985	1986	Total
Crossburning	36	64	59	41	32	23	46	301
Assault	44	10	42	58	18	61	69	302
Murder	39	3	10	20	12	25	12	121
Arson	11	10	9	9	28	17	14	98
Shooting	41	11	17	23	22	10	21	145
Bombing	11	14	4	10	31	32	36	138
Total	182	112	141	161	143	168	198	1,105
Other Harassment, Vandalism 1980–1986								1,814
Total Incidents, 1980–1986								2,919

Source: *Center for Democratic Renewal,* 1988.

Exhibit 9.12

Sociology in the Media

This Is a Country for White Aryans Only

HAYDEN LAKE, Idaho—The right of self-preservation for the individual, or of a racial nation composed of individuals, is an inalienable, fundamental right. Therefore, our white or Aryan nation has a right and is under an obligation to preserve itself and its members.

For these ends, the Declaration of Independence and Constitution of the [United States] became the organic law in perpetuity for their white racial "posterity." Thus was created a government of organic law and not of men or men's opinions.

The framers also noted "that when any form of government becomes destructive of these ends, it is the right of the people to alter or abolish it."

The "we the people" in the Constitution's preamble were and are the Aryan or white race of people who became the lawful de jure citizens of this new national state for our race.

Our present generation of white Aryan people living in the U.S. and the free, white immigrants constitutionally admitted are the only lawful de jure citizens as the posterity of those who framed and adopted our Constitution.

It is self-evident that a government de facto has introduced a state of war against the white racial posterity or citizens de jure, therefore also self-evident that a counterrevolution to that of 1776 has been and is now in progress.

Today, the lawful citizens are being dispossessed from farms, homes, businesses, and employment while their country is being invaded by alien hordes on a scale unprecedented in all the world's history.

John Locke said: "A conquest may be called foreign usurpation, and also usurpation is a kind of domestic conquest, with this difference, that a usurper can never have a right on his side where he gets possession to what another has a right to." Today, the de jure citizens exist under a de facto government based upon an illusion or deception that a new constitution instituted by gun and bayonet and called the 14th and 15th amendments was constitutionally adopted.

We are also asked to believe that the laws of nature and of nature's God can be repealed, and that Congress and courts can "twist a rope of sand," as Ralph Waldo Emerson put it.

The undisputed record attested by official journals and the unanimous writings of historians establish that these so-called amendments were never constitutionally ratified and that even their proposal was treason to the Constitution and the lawful citizens.

When the fate of a nation and a people is imperiled from within its own ranks and from aliens who have joined its ranks, and when within the space of one or two generations the society established by its forefathers has been riven from its frame, the guardians of that nation must take action to defend their people from their own destructive elements and repair their defects or be held responsible before God and man for their inaction.

Elected administrators of the supreme law, your nation is calling.

Note: Richard G. Butler is pastor of the Church of Jesus Christ, Christian, and leader of Aryan Nations.

SOURCE: Richard G. Butler, *USA Today,* September 26, 1986, p. 8A. Copyright 1986, USA Today. Reprinted with permission.

actions reflect the prejudice and bigotry of isolated individuals, striking out for their own private reasons. At the same time, however, many organized groups profess **white supremacy,** the doctrine that racial purity should be maintained, and that members of the "white race" are, and should be dominant. The views of one white supremacist are given in Exhibit 9.12.

No doubt the Ku Klux Klan is the most well-known of white supremacist groups. Recent estimates place its membership at six to seven thousand. Other groups—the White Patriot Party; The Order; The Covenant, the Sword, and the Arm of the Lord; and the Aryan Nations Church—are quite small, sometimes numbering but a few dozen active participants. Yet many of these smaller organizations have been the most militant. The Order, whose membership apparently has never exceeded 25, has allegedly been involved in arson, counterfeiting, armored-car holdups, and the murder of Denver radio personality Alan Berg. Moreover, the founder of the group died in a 36-hour shootout with police and FBI agents in 1984, and by 1987 all known members of the group were in prison.[53]

The central issue being debated in connection with white supremacist activities is whether they represent the isolated deeds of a few malicious individuals or indicate the reemergence of widespread racism in American society and a return to the open conflict of an earlier era. Those who worry that the United States will be swept by renewed racial tension argue that two factors are at work to produce this growing incidence of open violence. Those two factors are increasing numbers of minorities and economic competition.

Analysts have long argued that racism in the American South prior to the civil rights era was greater in areas with large concentrations of blacks.[54] Research in southern cities once demonstrated that support for the Ku Klux Klan was strongest in white neighborhoods near black and ethnic neighborhoods, where people were most likely to feel threatened.[55] Current population trends indicate that a number of minority populations in the United States are growing rapidly. More than 700,000 Southeast Asian refugees (Vietnamese, Laotians, and Cambodians) have entered the United States since 1975, and these groups continue to arrive at a rate of 4,000 each month.[56] Asians have tended to settle in a few states, notably California, Texas, and New York, creating a highly visible minority population. And as noted earlier, Hispanics constitute a growing presence in South Florida. Concentrations of minorities in any area create the potential for overt conflict.

When an economy is flourishing, more than enough work is available for everyone, with the lowest paying jobs typically relegated to minorities. However, when economic systems lose momentum, minority-group members suddenly become competitors, particularly those in the less-skilled labor sectors. An opinion

Exhibit 9.13

Applied Sociology

Brown v. Board of Education

In its 1896 decision in *Plessy v. Ferguson,* the Supreme Court sanctioned the "separate but equal" doctrine developed to justify state-imposed racial segregation. The *Plessy* ruling endured; in subsequent decades *school* segregation was challenged, but *Plessy* prevailed until the middle of the twentieth century, when Oliver Brown of Topeka, Kansas, brought a case before the Supreme Court on behalf of his daughter, Linda.

Under a Kansas law permitting cities with populations over 15,000 to operate dual school systems, Topeka had opted to segregate its primary schools. As a result, six-year-old Linda Brown was forced to walk 20 blocks to an all-black grade school rather than attend an all-white school in her neighborhood. Other black families eventually joined the challenge.

In 1951, a federal district court found Topeka's system to be detrimental to black children, but no violation of the Constitution was found. The court reasoned that black and white primary schools were substantially equal with respect to curricula, buildings, transportation, and teachers. The case was then moved to the United States Supreme Court, and on May 17, 1954, the High Court rendered a unanimous decision. The Court's "opinion" (the written document stating its decision), described by many as the most socially and ideologically significant in the Court's history, was but a few paragraphs long. At the heart of the opinion were these statements:

> In approaching this problem, we cannot turn the clock back to 1868 when the [Fourteenth] Amendment was adopted, or even to 1896 when *Plessy v. Ferguson* was written. We must consider public education in the light of its full development and its present place in American life throughout the Nation. Only in this way can it be determined if segregation in public schools deprives these [Negroes] of equal protection of the laws.
>
> Today, education is perhaps the most important function of state and local government. . . . [Education] is the very foundation of good citizenship. Today it is the principal instrument in awakening the child to cultural values, in preparing him for later professional training, and in helping him to adjust normally to his environment. . . .
>
> We come to the question presented: Does segregation of children in public schools solely on the basis of race, even though the physical facilities and other "tangible" factors may be equal, deprive the children of the minority group of equal educational opportunity? *We believe that it does.*

With these words, school segregation on the basis of race

poll conducted in nine large cities found that 47% of the target populations agreed with the statement, "Indochinese refugees take jobs away from others in my area."[57] Thus, changing economic conditions may produce conflict among groups—conflict that might not otherwise occur.

MINORITIES AND APPLIED SOCIOLOGY

Through their efforts to influence public policy, American sociologists have frequently championed attempts to eliminate discriminatory practices against minority groups. The first major legal breakthrough in minority affairs in the United States, the Supreme Court's landmark decision in *Brown v. Board of Education,*[58] was based in great part on the research and testimony of sociologists, social psychologists, and other social scientists. The High Court's decision in *Brown* stipulated that racially segregated schools were unconstitutional (see Exhibit 9.13), and the basic thrust of the sociological research that supported the Court's decision focused on the harmful effects of segregation on educational achievement by black children.

While it is one thing to discuss prejudice and discrimination, it is quite a different matter to actually experience these social phenomena. Social scientists have argued that a person who has enjoyed the luxury of being in the majority by the accident of birth can better understand the effects of prejudice and discrimination by

became a violation of federal law throughout the United States. The Court's opinion also included the famous "footnote 11," perhaps the most controversial footnote in Supreme Court history. The footnote cited seven sociological and psychological studies of the effects of racial segregation to support its contention that school segregation was detrimental to blacks. The footnote was controversial because critics of the Court's decision considered the footnote "unjudicial." As Mississippi Senator James O. Eastland stated in a speech before the United States Senate several days later:

> The Supreme Court could not find the authority for its decisions in the wording of the Fourteenth Amendment, in the history of the amendment or in the decision of any court. Instead, the Court was forced to resort to the unprecedented authority of a group of recent partisan books on sociology and psychology. If this is the judicial caliber of the Court, what can the nation expect from it in the future? What is to prevent the Court from citing as an authority in some future decision the works of Karl Marx?

In many ways, the decision in *Brown v. Board of Education* was an unfulfilled promise. In 1986, Linda Brown was in court once again. By then she was Linda Brown Smith and the mother of two children, reopening the *Brown* case on behalf of other black children in Topeka. Her argument was that Topeka had never fully integrated its schools, and that although none were all-white or all-black, many were racially identifiable. In early 1987 the federal district court rejected her charges, once again paving the way for a hearing of *Brown v. Board of Education* before the United States Supreme Court.

SOURCES: Richard Kluger, *Simple Justice: The History of Brown v. Board of Education and Black America's Struggle for Equality* (New York: Alfred A. Knopf, 1976); Brown v. Board of Education, 347 U.S. 483 (1954); *Congressional Record,* May 27, 1954, 100: 7252; *National Law Journal,* November 3, 1986, p. 6; Plessy v. Ferguson, 163 U.S. 537 (1896); *U.S. News & World Report,* April 20, 1987, p. 13.

actually being treated as an inferior. Such an experience, it is added, makes the individual more sensitive to the feelings and needs of minorities. In putting the concept of applied social science into action, an Iowa elementary school teacher divided her all-white third graders into superior and inferior groups, on the basis of their eye color.[59] For one full week, brown-eyed children were forced to wear a special collar, were denied classroom privileges, and were ridiculed openly by teacher and students. Roles were reversed during the second week with blue-eyed children treated as inferior. As might be expected, it was an unpleasant experience for all involved. Not only were the children emotionally upset, but their scores on standardized tests declined during the brief period of the experiment.

It is impossible to assess the long-term implications of such experiences. Prejudice and discriminatory behavior are learned in a social context, and the children in the Iowa classroom may have continued to be negative towards minorities, if such feelings were supported by the groups of which they were members. Perhaps, however, they also remembered the unpleasant aspects of being the victims of prejudice and became more tolerant of racial and ethnic differences.

SUMMARY

The world is a mosaic of groups. Although they worship different gods, have dissimilar customs and beliefs, and may be physically dissimilar, they nevertheless share the same human problems and joys. They show pride in their children, face the need to earn a living, and worry about life after death. Sometimes they live together in peace and harmony, and differences that do separate them do not prevent them from getting along with their neighbors. In countless neighborhoods and communities across the United States, diverse peoples live, attend school, work, and play together. Thus, it is possible to cite instances of pluralism. Many people point to modern Switzerland as the best societal instance of this.

Yet throughout history, physical, religious, and cultural differences have produced hostility and conflict. These reactions are most likely to occur when groups compete for jobs, land, or other scarce commodities. The struggle between European settlers and native Americans for control of the land was the source of some of the most unpleasant episodes in American history.

Relationships among groups reveal various forms of domination. In the most extreme cases one group may seek to displace or destroy whole populations in the name of religion or racial purity. More commonly, domination takes the form of physical and social segregation in inferior jobs, schools, and neighborhoods. Segregation may be openly supported by the power of the law and the government, or maintained by custom and informal social practices. Each succeeding wave of immigrants to the United States has experienced exploitation at the hands of the majority. However, their children and grandchildren often have fared better as they adopted the values and standards of the dominant culture. This process of assimilation benefits individuals, but results in the disappearance of the original group.

Prejudicial attitudes and discriminatory behavior toward minority-group members are forms of social behavior, learned during the socialization process. These attitudes and behaviors are perpetuated by stereotypes that classify individuals on the basis of group membership and attribute negative characteristics to them.

The United States has always been a nation of racial, religious, and ethnic minority groups—blacks, native Americans, Jews, Asians, and Hispanics. Most have suffered through periods of intense prejudice and discrimination. Even today general patterns of tolerance are often interrupted by episodes of violence and mistreatment. Instances of intolerance are seldom random events; they are instead frequently stimulated by larger social, economic, and demographic trends.

KEY TERMS/CONCEPTS

anglo conformity
apartheid
assimilation
assimilation dilemma
Chinese Exclusion Acts
de facto segregation
de jure segregation
discrimination
enslavement
ethnic enclaves/ethnic villages
ethnicity/ethnic group
ethnogenesis
expulsion
extermination
frustration-aggression hypothesis
genocide
ideology of inferiority
marginality
pluralism
prejudice
race
racism
scapegoat
segregation
separatist movementds
social distance
social protest movements
split labor market
stereotypes
subjugation
white supremacy

DISCUSSION QUESTIONS

1. Have you ever been the victim of prejudice because of your race, religion, customs, dress, physical features, or some other reason? What happened? What were your reactions to that experience?
2. In what ways do your beliefs and customs differ from those of your parents, grandparents, or great-grandparents, who may have immigrated to this country from another nation?
3. Many people have suggested that hostility toward Japanese-Americans will increase in the next few years. Why might this happen?
4. If you were in a position to change the laws of American society, what would you do to bring about better social relations among different racial and ethnic minorities?
5. Some people argue that the South African policy of apartheid is an internal matter within that country, and that outsiders have no right to impose their values and perspectives on another group. Do you see any merit to this view?
6. During the next decade, Hispanics will become the largest minority in the United States. What social changes might accompany this demographic change?

SUGGESTED READINGS

Gordon W. Allport, *The Nature of Prejudice* (Reading, MA: Addison-Wesley, 1954). This classic social-psychological study of prejudice provides a wealth of information on the social sources of prejudice and their consequences for individuals and society.

Robert Blauner, *Racial Oppression in America* (New York: Harper & Row, 1972). Blauner develops the concept of "internal colonialism," the idea that groups exploit other racial and ethnic groups for economic reasons.

Joe R. Feagin, *Racial and Ethnic Relations* (Englewood Cliffs, NJ: Prentice-Hall, 1984). An advanced text that includes sections on all major racial and ethnic minorities, including the white ethnic groups.

Nathan Glazer, *Ethnic Dilemmas* (Cambridge, MA: Harvard University Press, 1983). A well-written collection of essays that seeks to explain and understand developments in racial and ethnic relations in the years since the Civil Rights Act of 1964.

Lewis M. Killian, *The Impossible Revolution: Phase II* (New York: Random House, 1975). A useful starting point for anyone hoping to understand the meaning of black protest movements in the social context of American society.

NOTES

1. Winthrop D. Jordon, *White Over Black* (Baltimore: Penguin, 1969), p. 219.
2. Andrew M. Greeley, *That Most Distressful Nation* (Chicago: Quadrangle, 1972), pp. 119–20.
3. Mark Twain's "The Tragedy of Pudd'nhead Wilson" was first published as a series in *Century* magazine, from December 1893 through June 1894.
4. George E. Simpson and J. Milton Yinger, *Racial and Cultural Minorities* (New York: Harper & Brothers, 1958), p. 39.
5. Virgil J. Vogel, *This Country Was Ours* (New York: Harper & Row, 1972), p. 284.
6. Jacobus Ten Broek, Edward N. Barnhart, and Floyd W. Matson, *Prejudice, War and the Constitution* (Berkeley: University of California Press, 1954).
7. Wilmington (Delaware) *News-Journal,* August 16, 1986, p. C1.
8. See *USA Today,* April 15, 1985, p. 3A.
9. *The Chronicle of Higher Education,* June 11, 1986, p. 2; see also Roger Omond, *The Apartheid Handbook: A Guide to South Africa's Everyday Racial Policies* (New York: Viking, 1985).
10. Hunter v. Underwood, U.S. Ala., 105 SCt. 1916 (1985).
11. See Joe R. Feagin, *Racial and Ethnic Relations* (Englewood Cliffs, NJ: Prentice-Hall, 1984), pp. 213–17.
12. John Hope Franklin, *From Slavery To Freedom: A History of Negro Americans* (New York: Alfred A. Knopf, 1967), p. 74.
13. See Richard Hofstadter and Michael Wallace (eds.), *American Violence: A Documentary History* (New York: Random House, 1970), pp. 187–203.
14. Richard Hofstadter and Michael Wallace, *American Violence,* p. 198.
15. William W. White, "The Texas Slave Insurrection of 1860," *Southwestern Historical Quarterly,* LII (January 1949), pp. 259–85.
16. C. Eric Lincoln, *The Black Muslims in America* (Boston: Beacon, 1961). For a discussion of black nationalists' role in the 1984 Presidential election, see *Newsweek,* April 9, 1984, pp. 14–17.
17. See Ethel J. Lindgren, "An Example of Culture Contact Without Conflict: Reindeer Tungus and Cossaks in Northern Manchuria," *American Anthropologist,* 40 (October–December 1938), pp. 605–21.
18. See Donald L. Noel, "How Ethnic Inequality Begins," *Social Problems,* 16 (Fall 1968), pp. 157–72.
19. Philip S. Foner, *History of the Labor Movements in the United States,* Vol. III (New York: International, 1964), p. 238.
20. This idea, in a somewhat different form, is suggested in Manning Nash, "Race and the Ideology of Race," *Current Anthropology,* 3 (June 1962), pp. 285–88.
21. Pierre L. van der Berghe, *Race and Racism* (New York: Wiley, 1967), p. 11.
22. See Ashley Montagu, *Race, Science and Humanity* (Princeton, NJ: D. Van Nostrand, 1963).
23. Edna Bonacich, "Theory of Ethnic Antagonism: The Split Labor Market," *American Sociological Review,* 17 (October 1972), pp. 547–59; Edna Bonacich, "Abolition, the Extension of Slavery and the Position of Free Blacks: A Study of Split

Labor Markets in the United States, 1830–1863," *American Journal of Sociology,* 81 (November 1975), pp. 601–28; Edna Bonacich, "Advanced Capitalism and Black/White Relations in the United States: A Split Labor Market Interpretation," *American Sociological Review,* 41 (February 1976), pp. 34–51.
24. Quoted in Milton Gordon, *Human Nature, Class and Ethnicity* (New York: Oxford University Press, 1978), p. 187.
25. See Robert E. Park, "Human Migration and the Marginal Man," *American Journal of Sociology,* 33 (1928), pp. 888–96; Everett Stonequist, *The Marginal Man* (Chicago: University of Chicago Press, 1937).
26. Andrew M. Greeley, *Ethnicity in the United States* (New York: Wiley, 1974).
27. The frustration-aggression hypothesis was originally formulated by John Dollard and his associates in *Frustration and Aggression* (New Haven, CT: Yale University Press, 1939).
28. Hans Speier, *German White-Collar Workers and the Rise of Hitler* (New Haven, CT: Yale University Press, 1986).
29. This point was first articulated in Gordon Allport, *The Nature of Prejudice* (Reading, MA: Addison-Wesley, 1954), p. 189.
30. See, for example, Blanche Knott, *Truly Tasteless Jokes* (New York: Ballantine, 1983).
31. Jeanette Henry, "Textbook Distortion of the Indian," *Civil Rights Digest,* 1 (Summer 1968), pp. 4–8.
32. Donald Bogel, *Toms, Coons, Mulattoes, Mammies and Bucks* (New York: Viking, 1973).
33. See *New York Times,* August 3, 1986, pp. 1, 14, 23.
34. Alice Pifer, "Wanted: Employment Agencies That Don't Discriminate," *Civil Rights Quarterly,* 12 (Winter 1980–81), pp. 16–23.
35. Robert K. Merton, "Discrimination and the American Creed," in Robert MacIver (ed.), *Discrimination and National Welfare* (New York: Institute for Religious and Social Studies, 1984), pp. 99–126.
36. For recent estimates of native populations see Virgil J. Vogel, *This Country Was Ours*, p. 250.
37. Tim Giago and Sharon Illoway, "Dying Too Young," *Perspectives* 14 (Fall 1982), p. 30.
38. *Christian Science Monitor,* June 27, 1986, p. 18.
39. *Christian Science Monitor,* June 26, 1986, pp. 16–17.
40. Samuel Eliot Morison, *The Oxford History of the American People* (New York: Oxford University Press, 1965), p. 769.
41. *Newsweek,* February 9, 1987, p. 60.
42. *Newsweek,* November 24, 1986.
43. Mario Barrera, *Race and Class in the Southwest* (South Bend, IN: University of Notre Dame Press, 1979), p. 62.
44. U.S. Commission on Civil Rights, *Puerto Ricans in the United States* (Washington, DC: U.S. Government Printing Office, 1976), p. 19.
45. U.S. Bureau of the Census, *Characteristics of the Population Below the Poverty Level, 1982* (Washington, DC: U.S. Government Printing Office, 1984), Table 46.
46. Clyde B. McCoy and Diana Gonzalez, *Cuban Immigration and Immigrants in Florida and the United States: Implications for Immigration Policy* (Gainesville: Bureau of Economic and Business Research, University of Florida, 1985).
47. *Miami Herald,* April 13, 1987, p. 1A; *Newsweek,* July 21, 1986, p. 21.
48. *Miami Herald,* February 13, 1987, p. 1C.
49. *USA Today*, November 26, 1986, p. 9A.
50. *Miami Herald,* October 23, 1986, p. 1.
51. *Historical Statistics of the United States* (Washington, DC: U.S. Government Printing Office, 1960), p. 218.
52. *USA Today,* September 6, 1986, p. 5A.
53. *USA Today,* September 9, 1985, p. 6A; *USA Today,* July 11, 1986, p. 3A.
54. Valdimer O. Key, *Southern Politics* (New York: Alfred A. Knopf, 1949), p. 5.
55. See, for example, Kenneth T. Jackson, *The Ku Klux Klan in the City, 1915–1930* (Chicago: University of Chicago Press, 1965), pp. 46–54.
56. U.S. Commission on Civil Rights, *Recent Activities Against Citizens and Residents of Asian Descent* (Washington, DC: U.S. Government Printing Office, 1986), p. 18.
57. Paul D. Starr and Alden Roberts, "Attitudes Toward New Americans," *Research in Race and Ethnic Relations,* 3 (Summer 1982), p. 175.
58. Brown v. Board of Education, 347 U.S. 483 (1954).
59. Robert A. Baron and Donn Byrne, *Social Psychology* (Boston: Allyn and Bacon, 1984), p. 189.

Age and Gender: Changing Roles in Modern Society

The basic biological facts that govern all living things apply equally to humans. Two are quite obvious: people are born either male or female and eventually mature and grow old. How people will be treated, the ways they experience their lives, and the privileges and benefits they may or may not enjoy will be shaped profoundly by these two factors. Importantly, the ways that these experiences are shaped have more to do with social factors than biological ones.

From the very moment of birth the physical manifestations of sex become the basis for the different social expectations held for females and males. Parents, peers, and others will expect different things from boys than they will of girls. Moreover, members of the family, playmates and friends, teachers, and a host of others will work at molding both boys and girls to fit preexisting ideals of thought and behavior. People also respond differently to others on the basis of age. Different expectations develop as people reach certain physical stages in the aging process—adolescence, adulthood, and old age. The best way to understand these differential expectations and responses is to remember that while "sex" and "aging" are biological events, "gender" and "age" are socially defined and constructed roles.

GENDER AND AGE: SOME SOCIOLOGICAL DEFINITIONS

Although the terms "sex" and "gender" tend to be used interchangeably in the popular media, they have precise meanings in sociology. **Sex** refers to biological categories defined on the basis of chromosomes, hormones, and anatomy. **Gender** involves the sociological, psychological, and cultural aspects of being male or female. As a sociological concept, gender can be elaborated by building upon ideas introduced earlier in this textbook. **Gender identity,** for example, is the awareness of being a member of one sex or the other, and it is one element of a person's self-concept that has been forged through continuous social interaction. By contrast, the term **gender roles** refers to the social expectations held for boys and girls, and men and women in any given society. For example, sociologist Erving Goffman once offered the following portrait of the ideal male role in American society:

> In an important sense there is only one complete unblushing male in America: a young, married, white, urban, northern, heterosexual Protestant father of college education, fully employed, of good complexion, weight and height, and a recent record in sports. Every American male tends to look out upon the world from this perspective, . . . and whoever fails to qualify in any one of these ways is likely to view himself—during moments at least—as unworthy, incomplete and inferior.[1]

A wife and mother offers this additional comment on the male role: "I don't want to be him; then I would have to go and fight the world. I don't want the pressures he has to bear—supporting a family, a mortgage, putting in all those hours at the office. Ugh!"[2]

The sociological study of age is based on a similar perspective. Physical aging is a slow and continuous process, yet in virtually every human society the life cycle is marked off into **age roles**—social segments involving different rights and privileges. Anthropologists have suggested that every society divides the life cycle into age-based roles such as "infant," "child," "adult," and "elder." Socially defined age categories exist in American society, but they tend to be based more on the counting of birthdays than on particular manifestations of biological aging.

Moving from one age to the next in the United States brings alternative expectations and rights. People must begin school by age 5 or 6; they are permitted to drive at age 16; they become eligible to vote at 18; and they can legally consume alcoholic beverages when they reach age 21. The transition to "old" or "elderly" generally occurs at about age 65 or 70, when people become eligible for Social Security and were, until recently, forced to retire from work.

In short, gender and age are of vital interest to sociologists because they shape not only the ways people think, act, and feel about themselves and others, but also their social relations with others. Equally important is the fact that many forms of inequality—social, occupational, economic, and political—have their origins in gender and age differentiations.

WOMEN AND MEN: BIOLOGY, CULTURE, AND SOCIETY

People always have understood the basic biological differences between men and women, but contemporary research in the fields of medicine and molecular biology suggests the existence of genetic and biochemical variations between the sexes. For example, clear differences in the genetic makeup of the sexes are evidenced in chromosomal makeup. **Chromosomes** are the structural carriers of hereditary characteristics that are found in the nucleus of every cell. Males and females differ distinctly in the pair of chromosomes that the human species carries for determining sexual characteristics. Males have one X chromosome and one Y chromosome; females have two X chromosomes. Beginning in puberty, males have higher levels of the hormone *testosterone,* which initiates facial hair growth, voice changes, and increases in genital size, and accounts for greater muscular development. Females have higher levels of *progesterone,* which controls menstruation and prepares the mammary glands for milk production, and *estrogen,* which initiates breast growth and ovulation. Social science research suggests *behavioral* differences between the sexes as well. As infants in American society, boys tend to be more active than girls.[3] Later, on the average, men score higher on tests measuring visual-spatial abilities and mathematics, but women's average scores tend to be superior on verbal ability.[4]

In short, some basic and very tangible differences exist between males and females. However, research raises a fundamental question: do biological differences determine behavioral and attitudinal differences in the sexes? Many observers have thought so for a long time, but no clear scientific evidence supports this assertion. Behavioral differences are often minor, and averaged scores frequently conceal a great deal of overlap. Many men, for example, have better verbal skills than many women.

This endless debate over biological determinism misses the most essential point that sociology can make. From the very moment of birth, people are labeled as either "girls" or "boys" on the basis of anatomy. That single action is the most decisive factor in determining the *gender* that a person will exhibit. Culture and social organization, furthermore, can shape behavior and overcome biological predispositions. In fact, children deliberately socialized into the "wrong" sex end up with the "wrong" gender attributes, and those with undeveloped sexual organs can be socialized into roles that violate their genetic sex.[5]

As a final note here, we should stress that biology and sociology interact. The sex of a child is an anatomical fact, but responses from others are social facts. This interaction results in alternative socialization experiences for males and females. Boys and girls also may have different social and economic statuses in their culture or community. In consequence, a rather fierce debate has evolved over whether parents ought to have the right to choose the sex of their children (see Exhibit 10.1).

Gender Roles

In every society boys and girls are socialized to fit culturally defined *gender roles*. Perhaps the most widely used measure of gender roles is the **Bem Sex-Role Inventory** (BSRI), developed by psychologist Sandra L. Bem.[6] The BSRI is a list of 60 adjectives that people have identified as desirable traits for men, desirable traits for women, or sexually neutral traits. These adjectives identify a wide range of traits—specific behaviors, such as language and leadership, and feelings such as compassion and sympathy. In addition, other manifestations of common gender roles include the expectation that boys play rough and fix bikes, while girls should be neat.[7]

In spite of changing gender roles in American society, boys playing with "dolls" still seems unusual to many people.

SOCIAL INDICATOR

Socially Desirable Traits

Masculine Items	
Acts as a Leader	Has Leadership Abilities
Aggressive	Independent
Ambitious	Individualistic
Analytical	Makes Decisions Easily
Assertive	Masculine
Athletic	Self-reliant
Competitive	Self-sufficient
Defends Own Beliefs	Strong Personality
Dominant	Willing to Take a Stand
Forceful	Willing to Take Risks

Feminine Items	
Affectionate	Loves Children
Cheerful	Loyal
Childlike	Sensitive to the Needs of Others
Compassionate	Shy
Does Not Use Harsh Language	Soft Spoken
Eager to Soothe Hurt Feelings	Sympathetic
Feminine	Tender
Flatterable	Understanding
Gentle	Warm
Gullible	Yielding

Neutral Items	
Adaptable	Moody
Conceited	Reliable
Conscientious	Secretive
Conventional	Sincere
Friendly	Solemn
Happy	Tactful
Helpful	Theatrical
Inefficient	Truthful
Jealous	Unpredictable
Likable	Unsystematic

Sociological Focus

The Sex-selection Debate

Scientific advances often bring forth complex and difficult social questions. As already seen in Chapter 4, surrogate motherhood represents but one example. The development of nuclear weapons is another (see Chapter 20). In each case, science created a situation that weighed heavily upon the limits of existing norms and values. Within the past few decades medical advances have created another dilemma: researchers have made it possible not only to identify the sex of a child while the child is still in its mother's womb, but also for parents to preselect the sex of their children with a high degree of certainty.

Not surprisingly, Americans are clearly divided on the sex-selection issue, with half strongly opposing the practice. Many feel that it violates the laws of nature, while others view it as contrary to their religious or moral values. A few parents would rather wait until the child is born to know its sex, and still others worry that sex selection might produce too many children of one sex.

Worries about possibly disproportionate numbers of one sex are not an unreasonable concern. Evidence from other nations suggests that sex selection would be fatal to females. Women's groups in India, China, and South Korea claim that large numbers of pregnant women use prenatal testing to determine the sex of unborn children in order to abort females. The cultural preference for males has a long history, traceable back to the agricultural traditions wherein boys were believed to be more productive farm workers. Moreover, sons have more social status and are considered a source of family and community pride in India, China, and Korea.

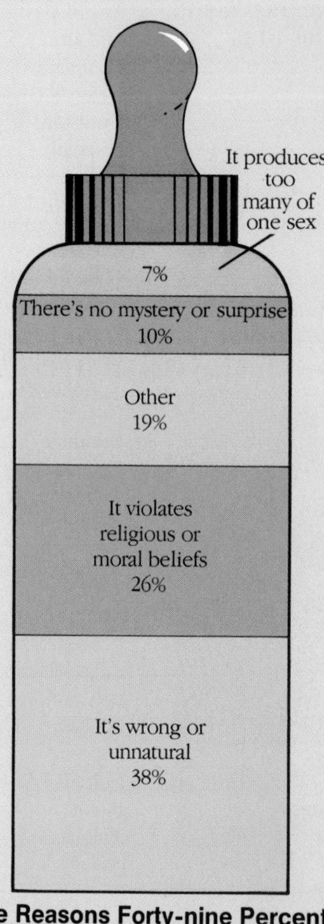

The Reasons Forty-nine Percent of All Americans oppose Pre-selection

Proponents of sex testing and sex selection consider the procedures practical solutions to the problems of world overpopulation. They argue that some parents continue to have babies until a son is born, and that the techniques will ultimately reduce the size of families by allowing a couple to plan the family they want.

Some nations have banned prenatal sex tests on the basis of evidence indicating increases in the male birth rate. South Korea prohibited the tests in 1986 after the male birth rate was found to have increased from 106 (for every 100 girls) to 117. The issue is very real in the United States as well, for there is a definite preference in this country that the first-born child be a boy. Over 90% of men who approve sex selection and 80% of the women, favor a son.

SOURCES: *New York Times,* October 26, 1986, p. 7E; *USA Today,* August 15, 1986, p. 8A; *USA Today,* November 19, 1986, p. 1D; Wilmington (Delaware) *News-Journal,* July 17, 1986, p. 9A.

During infancy the ideals of gender are taught in subtle ways, usually by treating boys and girls differently and providing discrete social environments for them. With the onset of the preschool years the emphasis shifts to shaping specific behaviors and thought patterns. Boys experience greater pressures to conform—from both parents and peers. By the time children reach school age most have learned the expectations of their gender, and these expectations become the standards by which they judge themselves and others. Many conform, bringing their behavior into line with societal expectations.

Gender roles are a part of the cultural heritage of a society and are maintained and perpetuated in many ways. Once these roles exist, people come to anticipate that males and females will exhibit different traits, to the point that the roles influence how people actually perceive or "see" others (see Exhibit 10.2). For example, sarcastic remarks are labeled "spiteful" when made by a woman but "cynical" when made by a man.[8] In a study conducted during the 1970s to examine the relationship of cultural expectations and gender roles, parents of newborn infants were contacted just 24 hours after their children were born and asked to describe their traits. The babies were far too young to show any real differences, but the parents of girls saw their children as softer, smaller, and less attentive than did the parents of boys. It appeared that the fathers' perceptions more often than the mothers' were influenced by the child's sex. Fathers used words such as "delicate" and "inattentive" to describe their daughters and portrayed their sons as "alert" and "strong."[9]

Reflections on everyday experience and research in a number of the social sciences document how children are socialized into their appropriate gender roles from almost the very moment of birth—beginning with a sex-typed name (see Exhibit 10.3). The environment to which children are exposed also reinforces gender roles. When American parents bring newborns home from the hospital, for example, girls and boys are placed in alternative surroundings—both social and physical. Girls are likely to find themselves in rooms with soft colors, surrounded by dolls and household items; boys have guns and sports equipment, typically in more brightly colored rooms.[10]

It would appear that it is in infancy as well that differences in verbal and spatial behaviors receive initial shaping. For example, boys' toys—vehicles and sports equipment—are oriented to activity and movement. By

Exhibit 10.2 **Research in Sociology**

Testing for Sex-role Strain

Researcher Joseph H. Pleck has pointed out that gender roles are often sources of both social and psychological strain. If gender roles are viewed as social expectations, it quickly becomes evident that people will approach them as guidelines for obtaining social approval—adjusting their behaviors to conform with the guidelines. Failure to conform, even perceived failure, means social disapproval. In addition, psychological stress originates with feelings of inadequacy when individuals find themselves unable to live up to these expectations.

Within this context, Pleck developed a simple, self-administered, true-false test to measure the relative levels of stress produced by gender roles. The level of sex-role strain rises with each additional *True* reponse given to the following statements.

	True	False
1. Society has very definite ideas about what men and women should be like.	___	___
2. There is no way that people can do all the things expected of them as men and women.	___	___
3. People who flaunt society's expectations about how men and women should act are usually ostracized.	___	___
4. There is greater tolerance of tomboys than sissies.	___	___
5. Many masculine and feminine traits are undesirable.	___	___
6. Many people have ideas about masculinity or femininity that they cannot live up to.	___	___
7. Many men who seem too masculine are concerned about not living up to society's expectations.	___	___
8. Probably most people fail to live up to society's expectations for men and women.	___	___
9. Masculinity does not have to exclude emotionality.	___	___
10. Masculinity and femininity would be less stressful if less stereotyped.	___	___
11. Masculinity should not require aggressiveness.	___	___

Source: Joseph H. Pleck, *Men and Masculinity* (Cambridge, MA: MIT Press, 1981), pp. 133–34. Copyright 1981 MIT Press. Reprinted by permission.

Exhibit **10.3** Sidelights on American Culture

What's in a Name?

What's in a name? Quite a bit, as it turns out. Names given to children are, like most other social phenomena, sex-typed, symbolic, and subject to the whims and fads of the times.

It is obvious that most names are sex-typed—identified with males or females. There can be little doubt that Matthew and Robert and James are appropriate for males, while Kristin, Nancy, and Carolyn are girls' names. A few names, usually designated by alternative spellings, are used for both sexes (Carroll/Carole, Brooks/Brooke, and Francis/Frances). And a few more are fully neutral, such as Lee and Leslie.

The sex-typing of names changes over time, in accordance with certain patterns. Male names lead to female variations. For example, Robert can be traced to medieval times, but the female form, Roberta, didn't appear till the 1870s. By contrast, female names have not generated male variations.

***Last Row:* Scott, Jennifer, Jennifer, Scott, Jennifer, Jennifer, Scott, Scott *Middle Row:* Jennifer, Jennifer, Scott, Scott, Jennifer, Jennifer, Scott, Jennifer, Scott *Front Row:* Jennifer, Scott, Scott, Jennifer, Mrs. Wanda Projhieki, Scott, Scott, Scott, Scott**

In rare cases, parents have been able to get away with giving traditional male names to females. The popular actresses Michael Learned and Glenn Close are among the few examples. Perhaps this kind of name is given to attract attention, to set the child above the crowd. However, once a name begins to be widely used as a female name, it is abandoned for males. Joyce, once used for both

age three for boys and age five for girls, most children are asking for sex-typed toys.[11]

> ***A little boy can play with a truck. . . . A little girl can play with a doll. But he can never play with a doll, and she can't play with a truck.***
>
> **Catherine Pollard, 69, lamenting sexual stereotyping after her loss in the Connecticut Supreme Court of a 13-year battle to become the nation's first woman Boy Scout troop leader, 1987**

As children grow and mature, parents treat boys and girls differently, attempting to mold their behaviors to conform to society's established gender roles. Nowhere is this more well defined than in the assignment of household duties. Girls' tasks tend to be located *in* the home—cleaning and cooking; boys' "chores" are oriented beyond the confines of the house—lawn mowing and other yard work.[12] This differentiation is often reinforced in schools, with teachers responding differently to certain behaviors, depending on the sex of the student. It has been found that many teachers tend to be more tolerant of boys' calling out answers than girls.[13] Thus, it would appear that teachers assume that this form of assertive behavior is more acceptable among boys.

sexes, is now almost exclusively a woman's name, as is Robin.

Names also evoke images. Professional women reportedly change their names for the sake of greater credibility and respect. Kyle and Morgan clearly evoke stronger images than Trixie and Ginger.

Also readily apparent is the fact that the popularity of specific names varies over time. The 1980s have witnessed a resurgence of biblical names, especially for boys, with Matthew, David, and Joshua among the 10 most common choices. Variations occur among various groups as well, with Catholics more likely to use the names of venerated saints, while Jews honor dead relatives. Similarly, black Americans are choosing names that reflect their African cultural heritage.

In the tables at right consider how the popularity of some names has persisted, while that of others has declined.

SOURCE: Virginia Painter and Deborah Finebaum Raub, "Choose a Name Your Child Won't Outgrow," *USA Today*, January 20, 1987, p. 4D.

The Top Ten First Names for Boys in the United States

1925	1950	1970	1982 *(white)*	1982 *(non-white)*
1 Robert	1 Robert	1 Michael	1 Michael	1 Michael
2 John	2 Michael	2 Robert	2 Christopher	2 Christopher
3 William	3 James	3 David	3 Matthew	3 James
4 James	4 John	4 James	4 David	4 Jason
5 Charles	5 David	5 John	5 Jason	5 Robert
6 Richard	6 William	6 Jeffrey	6 Daniel	6 Anthony
7 George	7 Thomas	7 Steven	7 Robert	7 Brandon
8 Donald	8 Richard	8 Christopher	8 Eric	8 Kevin
9 Joseph	9 Gary	9 Brian	9 Brian	9 David
10 Edward	10 Charles	10 Mark	10 Joseph	10 Charles

The Top Ten First Names for Girls in the United States

1925	1950	1970	1982 *(white)*	1982 *(non-white)*
1 Mary	1 Linda	1 Michelle	1 Jennifer	1 Tiffany
2 Barbara	2 Mary	2 Jennifer	2 Sarah	2 Crystal
3 Dorothy	3 Patricia	3 Kimberly	3 Nicole	3 Ebony
4 Betty	4 Susan	4 Lisa	4 Jessica	4 Erica
5 Ruth	5 Deborah	5 Tracy	5 Katherine	5 Lakisha
6 Margaret	6 Kathleen	6 Kelly	6 Stephanie	6 Latoya
7 Helen	7 Barbara	7 Nicole	7 Elizabeth	7 Nicole
8 Elizabeth	8 Nancy	8 Angela	8 Amanda	8 Candice
9 Jean	9 Sharon	9 Pamela	9 Melissa	9 Danielle
10 Ann(e)	10 Karen	10 Christine	10 Lindsay	10 Brandi

Source: Leslie Dunkling and William Gosling, *The Facts on File Dictionary of First Names* (New York: Facts on File, 1983). Copyright © 1983. Reprinted with permission.

Clearly, expectations shape the way people respond to others, creating pressures for individuals to bring their behavior into line with cultural ideas. The social pressure of peers is especially important to youths during late childhood and early adolescence, for this time is one when an appropriate gender role appears to be quite crucial. In grades three through six, children react negatively to peers who do things that violate appropriate behaviors for boys and girls.[14] A boy who chooses to wash dishes rather than mow a lawn risks being less popular than other boys. By the time people reach college age, however, living up to gender roles appears to be somewhat less important, suggesting that these roles are subject to modification.

Sex Discrimination and Institutionalized Sexism

As noted in Chapter 9, discrimination involves social practices that deprive categories of people equal access to rights, privileges, and opportunities. Within this context, **sex discrimination** refers to open and covert limitations placed on opportunities because of an individual's sex. Exclusion from specific jobs, lower pay for the same work, and denial of promotions were once common and open features of sex discrimination in American society. Recent legislation has rendered most of these practices illegal, although a few tend to linger. For example, women are currently barred from "combat" roles in the military. Yet, even when the sex discrimination is prohibited by law it may continue on a covert basis. Some branches of the military have been accused of limiting the career opportunities of women in the services by misusing the "combat" classification to reserve better jobs for men.[15]

Sex discrimination is often based on beliefs that one sex is somehow inferior to the other, or that each has different capacities and abilities. In *Muller v. Oregon,*[16] which was decided by the Supreme Court in 1908, special occupational restrictions for women were endorsed on the grounds that women were weaker than men and werethe mothers of future generations (see Exhibit 10.4).

Although the decision in *Muller* occurred almost a century ago, even today gender roles continue to produce discrimination. Research has documented that *identical* performance and achievement are evaluated lower for women than men. One way that this was demonstrated involved having groups of people evaluate an essay, a painting, or an employment résumé. Although all the materials to be evaluated were identical, some groups were told that they were the work of a man; the other groups were told that they were the work of a woman.[17] The evaluators were not *intentionally* discriminating; they actually felt the essay or painting was better when they thought it was the work of a male. No doubt their evaluations were shaped by ideas about the different characteristics of men and women contained in societal gender roles. Intentional or not, however, the outcome is the same: women are at a clear disadvantage in American society (see Exhibit 10.5).

Institutionalized sexism refers to social patterns and elements of social organization that limit opportunity and access for the members of a particular sex. The lack of paid maternity leave in many work situations, for example, has forced a large number of pregnant women to quit their jobs when their children are born. Similarly, the lack of adequate and affordable child-care facilities has resulted in many mothers' remaining home with young children longer than they had planned. In either case, work interruptions can be severe, sometimes resulting in the loss of all seniority in a particular position, job, or even career. Alternatively, institutionalized sexism is readily apparent in the inadequate child-support legislation and enforcement that often drives single mothers into poverty.

Exhibit 10.4 Sociological Focus

Muller v. Oregon: *Sex Discrimination and the Supreme Court*

The 1908 Supreme Court decision in *Muller v. Oregon* was interesting sociologically. It involved the validity of an Oregon statute that prohibited women from working in laundries for more than 10 hours a day. The statute had been challenged in an earlier court proceeding on the grounds that it bore no reasonable relation to the public health, safety, and morals of women, and therefore denied them due process of law.

Louis D. Brandeis, who was later appointed to the Supreme Court, argued the case for the state of Oregon. He filed a brief with the High Court that contained but two pages of legal arguments, followed by more than 100 pages of sociological facts and statistics demonstrating what he considered to be the "evil effect" of long working hours on women.

The Court was impressed with the Brandeis argument. It unanimously upheld the constitutionality of the Oregon statute, with the following comment:

> The two sexes differ in structure of the body, in the functions to be performed by each, in the amount of physical strength, in the capacity for long-continued labor, particularly when done standing, the influence of vigorous health upon the future well-being of the race, the self-reliance which enables one to assert full rights, and in the capacity to maintain the struggle for subsistence. This difference justifies a difference in legislation and upholds that which is designed to compensate for some of the burdens which rest upon women.

In short, the Court had relied on the argument, supported by sociological data, that longer working hours might impair the childbearing function of women.

SOURCE: Muller v. Oregon, 208 U.S. 412 (1908).

Exhibit 10.5

Sociology in the Media

Sexism in Schools Is "Alive and Well," New Study Reports

WASHINGTON—A study of America's schools released Monday by a women's group found that sexism "is alive and well" in the classroom, and back-to-basics reform has not addressed sex discrimination in education.

The Project on Equal Education Rights, part of the National Organization for Women's Legal Defense and Education Fund, said its nationwide study, conducted over the last school year, is the first to look at sexism and sex discrimination in American education.

"Sex discrimination is alive and well in America's schools," said author Theresa Cusick, whose report used privately gathered statistics and federal and state figures on education.

Among the study's key findings:

- Dropout rates are almost as high for girls as for boys but, "Too often, women are invisible in the dropout discussion." Women are assumed to have dropped out because of pregnancy, but studies show that males and females usually drop out because of alienation and poor performance.
- Female students score lower than males on Scholastic Aptitude Tests but have high first-year college grades. However, lower SAT scores limit girls' access to some scholarships.
- Sexism in schools leads to sexism in the job market. Boys are encouraged to take courses in mathematics, science, computer science, and technical vocational education, but girls are steered away from those classes.
- Women comprised only one-fourth of the elementary school principals in 1984–85, down from more than half in 1928.

Among its recommendations, the group called for state laws to protect the rights of women, minorities, and the disabled, and to assure access to a full range of academic and extracurricular programs for all students.

Florida officials were among those the group criticized—for refusing to institute fast-pitch softball for girls in high school.

Education Secretary William Bennett received his second "Lifetime Underachievement Award" for overseeing a policy that excludes pregnant teens from being eligible for some single parent and homemaker programs. Loye Miller, a spokesman for Bennett, said, "We thought our hands were bound by the legislation and the legislative history, which indicated very clearly that the [program] did not include pregnant teenagers."

SOURCE: From *Herald* Wire Services.

Theoretical Approaches to Gender

The universality of gender roles has produced deep theoretical controversy within the field of sociology. It has led some sociologists to understand gender differentiation in *evolutionary* terms, havings its origins in an earlier preindustrial period, and supported by tradition and inertia rather than contemporary conditions. Others have pointed out the *positive functions* of such differentiation, arguing that regardless of origin, gender roles have positive aspects, at least at the group or societal level. This latter approach may appear to endorse sexual inequities and to stand in the way of social change, but it is more accurately described as an attempt to place gender roles within a social, cultural, and historical context. A third point of view is *conflict analysis,* which focuses on gender inequality, seeking to uncover the social processes that tend to maintain the unequal benefits associated with sex and gender. Conflict approaches have alerted sociologists to many of the hidden costs of being female. When contrasted, the three approaches provide different insights into gender differentiation.

Gender Differentiation: An Evolutionary Approach

The evolutionary approach to gender differentiation examines modern gender roles as a legacy of the preindustrial origins of human society. Or as one observer put it not too long ago: "We are still living with the remnants of male supremacy because we have not yet emerged from the phase of human evolution in which the physical strength of males was necessary for cultural survival."[18] Within this context, warfare and the threat of war were often constant realities and the very survival of the group depended on its ability to fend off enemies. Hence, such societies needed a corps of warriors—the more aggressive the better. Gentleness in battle was a real handicap, putting the whole society at risk.

The members of preindustrial societies certainly recognized all of the biological differences between the sexes that made men better suited for warfare. Men are stronger on the average, and are not limited during pregnancy, childbirth, and lactation. Consequently, it was logical to socialize men from birth to be aggressive, brave, and dominating. Thus, the ideal traits associated with traditional masculinity are evolutionary products of socialization, rather than innate predispositions toward certain behaviors.

Gender Differentiation: A Functional Interpretation

The functional approach to gender differentiation generally has been examined within the context of family structure and organization.[19] It has been suggested that stable family units require two different forms of behavior, and that husbands' (fathers') and wives' (mothers') roles complement one another. The woman's role emphasizes emotional support and child rearing while the man's stresses providing for the material well-being of family members. The division of labor along gender lines thus enables the family to function as a group and assures the socialization of children.

This approach was developed at a time when fewer women were in the paid labor force and although it may have accurately described the situation for most middle-class families a generation ago, the American family has undergone considerable change (see Chapter 11). Thus, the "functional" arrangement of gender roles is clearly dysfunctional when both spouses are employed; in such cases conflict often arises over household tasks and other responsibilities.

Exploitation: The Conflict Perspective

Conflict theorists generally have focused on the unequal rewards associated with gender differentiation, emphasizing the exploitative nature of gender roles. Karl Marx and Friedrich Engels were among the first to place the gender role problem within the dynamics of industrialization. Men, they argued, were interested in monopolizing the upper levels of the industrial labor force and sought to exclude women from the better-paying jobs by channeling them into less important positions, such as clerical work.[20]

Women laborers in the U.S. have experienced a long history of exploitation. In the nineteenth century they comprised much of the labor force in American factories. During World War II, over 6 million women joined the work force, but many lost their jobs to returning veterans after the war.

Having won control of jobs in management and the professions, men reaped the economic benefits and used their superior occupational roles to maintain their position—a situation that modern research has confirmed.[21] Women were also relegated to *unpaid* household work, further reducing their economic independence and resources.

Regardless of the perspective that is used to explain gender differentiation, it is clear that **gender inequality** is widespread—unequal rewards and opportunities are associated with being a man or woman in contemporary society.

SOCIAL INDICATOR

The Risk of Being Murdered

	1 out of:
All Americans	133
All Men	84
White Men	131
Black Men	21
All Women	282
White Women	369
Black Women	104

Source: Bureau of Justice Statistics, *Special Report*, 1988.

Gender Inequality

Gender is a social construction, and it is important because as the result of gender differentiation, rewards and opportunities in society are distributed unequally. Women live longer, for example, an outgrowth of both their biology and the social roles they play. In addition, and also as the result of socialization, women are far less likely to be the victims of violent death. In the occupational sphere, however, women are concentrated in lower-paying occupations, and on the average, earn less than men. In the political sphere, women have made significant gains in winning elective office but continue to lag behind men in positions of power. Each of these points is worth examining in some detail, for they reveal a great deal about the functioning of American society.

Gender and Life Expectancy

A woman born in the United States during the second half of the 1980s can anticipate living 78.3 years, a full seven years longer than the average man.[22] A large part of this discrepancy can be attributed to life-styles associated with gender roles. It is true that only women face the

SOCIAL INDICATOR

Major Causes of Death in the United States (rates per 100,000 population)

Cause	Men	Women
Heart Disease	248	127
All Cancers	165	111
Stroke	35	30
Accidents	52	19
Chronic Lung Diseases	28	13
Pneumonia, Flu	18	10
Suicide	19	5
Liver Disease	13	6
Diabetes	10	9
All Other Causes	717	409

Source: *Statistical Abstract of the United States*, 1988.

life-threatening risks associated with pregnancy and childbirth, but these are generally minimal in modern industrial society. Most other major causes of death work to the advantage of women.

Men have higher rates of diseases related to smoking and drinking—two behaviors that are *learned*. Many men believe smoking and drinking to be necessary in confirming their masculinity. Heart disease, the major cause of death in the United States, strikes men at a rate twice that of women. Various forms of cancer, in addition to those linked to smoking, are also more likely to strike men, with one interesting exception. Varying rates of cancer have been tallied for different occupations, and as an "occupational group," homemakers have the highest rates—seemingly the result of exposure to a broad range of toxic substances found in the home.[23]

Finally, men are clearly at greater risk of suffering violent death, either through automobile accidents or as the victims of crime. This fact is no doubt related to traditional male roles that emphasize greater risk-taking and aggressive behaviors. And similarly, men are also more likely to be suicide victims. The unequal suicide rates are generally explained by the uneven distribution of men and women in the world of work, where men are found far more frequently in professional and managerial roles—positions that place greater levels of stress on people. In addition, these work roles typically involve a greater chance of relative "failure" than other work roles—a matter that tends to be more demoralizing for men, given the cultural emphasis on male success.

Gender and Mental Health

For some time now researchers have noted that men have lower rates of reported mental illness than women.[24] Two different explanations have been proposed. The first explanation is that the subordinate social status of women results in fewer opportunities for fulfilling their potential as total human beings. Lower average income and limited occupational opportunities produce frustration. In addition, some observers argue that marriage tends to be more difficult for women than men because of the unrewarding nature of housework and the conflicts of work and child care, which produce social stress.

The second explanation is that men are less willing to accept that they are experiencing mental problems, and even when they do they are less willing than women to admit it by seeking out professional help. Both explanations find the source of the differences in socially defined gender roles.

Work and Occupational Segregation

Women's participation in the paid labor force has been increasing steadily (see Chapter 19). Traditional barriers denying women access to careers in medicine, law, and numerous other professions and occupations have been falling in response to social and legal transformations. And yet, most women are concentrated in occupations long-defined as "women's work." Occupational segregation is the end product of many factors, but it may be illustrated best by focusing on careers in math-based work, such as science and engineering, where women have low rates of participation. This is so, in part, because women do not seem to do as well as men on their math SATs, and the reasons for this fact are curious.

The Scholastic Aptitude Test (SAT) plays a major role in the lives of all high-school students planning to continue their education. Not scoring well can have a variety of consequences. It may preclude admission to the college of one's choice or admission to any college, for that matter; it relates directly to the possibility of getting a scholarship; and it may close opportunities for careers in science, engineering, and many other occupations. Despite continuing debates over the validity of "aptitude tests," SATs remain a major criterion in the academic screening process. Systematic gender differences have been observed in the results of these tests: women in the United States consistently perform some 50 points lower than men on the mathematics sections of these examinations.[25]

This scoring phenomenon raises two questions. Are women born with less mathematical ability? Or is math performance a product of social factors? No clear way to measure innate mathematical ability has been found, but social science evidence suggests that math achievement is encouraged in men and discouraged in women.

A fundamental issue here is that mathematics is associated with male social roles. When asked to describe a "mathematician," both men and women think in terms of conventional male traits—individualistic, independent, responsible, and rational.[26] Moreover, men who are good at math also rate themselves high on "masculinity."[27] This factor suggests that performing well in math is a way for men to live up to male gender roles.

Overall, this image tends to discourage young girls in a number of different ways as they grow up. First, they do not perceive being a mathematician as a realistic career option. Second, the image promotes discouragement by others. Parents inhibit their daughters' selection of math- and science-oriented careers in a variety of subtle ways. For example, parents are more likely to buy computers for sons than daughters (see Exhibit 10.6),

Exhibit 10.6 Case Study

Women and Computers

Much has been written about the microcomputer revolution since it began a decade ago, and a frequent theme has been women's relative lack of involvement with computers. The term "female computer phobia" occasionally has been seen, leading many observers of the phenomenon to wonder why far greater proportions of women than men seem to be shunning computers.

One of the first studies undertaken to investigate this question was designed to determine whether women have the same computer aptitudes as men. Researchers at Claremont Graduate School conducted a series of investigations to clarify this issue, and the findings were rather curious. In their abilities to estimate, recognize graphic patterns, complete sentences, and solve logical analogies—common tests of computer aptitude—*women ranked as high as men*! However, the testing also gauged computer interest and knowledge, and on these measures women ranked significantly lower. Further investigations at Claremont and elsewhere found these differences to be socially based.

Computer science has an image much like that of mathematics—it is viewed as a male profession, not only by young people looking for careers but by parents of younger children as well. Researchers at Stanford University studied 87 children ages 5–8 and found that their parents were reluctant to buy home computers for their daughters, but not for their sons. More important was the fact that girls in the study lost interest in computers relatively quickly, primarily because they found the software boring. A study of both the entertainment and educational software available for children indicated that it typically was male oriented—built around action, adventure, and war games with few programs having even a marginal relationship to the interests of young girls.

The image of computer technology as a male-dominated field has not eased the situation for women. Furthermore, many women who did elect careers in computer science ultimately dropped out because of what they called the inhospitable environment of male computer hackers.

While these observations generally characterized the situation involving women and computers during the first half of the 1980s, it would appear that the trends began to change as the decade wore on. As offices were computerized, women were forced to become acquainted with the machines and the computer gender gap began to close. The San Francisco-based Women's Computer Literacy Project was founded to counter the fear that without advanced computing skills, women might lose much of the ground they had gained in the work force since 1970. The Project has sponsored seminars throughout the nation, stimulating women's interest in computer use. And simultaneously, the software industry began to recognize girls and women as viable market groups and to create products tailored to their interests and needs.

SOURCES: Gina Kolata, "Equal Time for Women," *Discover,* January 1984, pp. 24–27; *The Chronicle of Higher Education,* October 10, 1984, p. 26; *Online Today,* July 1985, p. 10; *Popular Computing,* February 1984, p. 21; *USA Today,* October 16, 1984, p. 3D.

Although parents are more likely to buy computers for their sons than for their daughters, the trend is beginning to change.

and enrollments of boys at computer camps often outnumber girls by three to one.[28] In schools, most math teachers are men, providing role models for boys, but not girls.

Observers also have pointed out that higher male achievement in mathematics becomes pronounced in the early teenage years, with females often having better scores prior to that point.[29] This observation suggests that social relationships may play a significant role in explaining the emergence of unequal performance. The teenage years are a period in which concern with social approval is acute, and it may be that girls are less willing to violate conventional gender roles by excelling in math.

The Earnings Gap

Wage discrimination based on sex (as well as race, religion, age, and national origin) is prohibited by federal law, but despite the consciousness raising generated by the women's movement (see Exhibit 10.7), American women are still generally paid less than their male counterparts—a pattern that is apparent throughout the world. Women are paid less in terms of the average earnings of all workers, and less also with regard to men and women in the *same* occupation. This **earnings gap**—the lower pay accorded to women as compared to men—is typically reported using womens' income as a percentage of mens' income. In 1986, for example, the earnings gap was 0.72; that is, women were paid some 0.72 of what men were paid (see Exhibit 10.8).

A number of factors combine to explain this form of inequality. Probably the single most important item is the fact that women in the work force are concentrated in lower-paying occupations—clerical work, teaching and nursing, retail sales, and service. By constrast, few women are employed in the well-paid skilled crafts (carpenters, electricians) or professional specialties (engineering, medicine). This pattern of occupational segregation can be traced to the gender typing of occupations.

A variety of other factors also contributes to the earnings gap.[30] Unions traditionally have been slow to include women in their recruitment efforts, thus depriving them of the advantages of collective bargaining for wage increases. Women, on the average, work fewer hours, which reduces their income levels. Finally, female workers generally have less seniority, and many jobs grant pay increases on the basis of longevity. It is important to note that these three factors—unionization, hours, and seniority—can all be traced to the competing demands of work and family roles usually faced by women in American society.

Another issue also is intricately tied to traditional social roles and gender differentiation. Women, to begin with, typically put a higher priority on family roles than do men. For this reason, women tend to work fewer hours in order to spend time taking care of chidren, or they accept lower-paying jobs that offer more flexible hours. Perhaps the greatest impact on women's wages and careers, as noted earlier in this chapter, is due to the intermittent work patterns and career interruptions initiated by pregnancy, childbirth, and child-care responsibilities. Not only are wages lost, but so too is seniority, thus rendering women more vulnerable to layoffs under the "last hired, first fired" rule. Job skills may change while women are on leave for birth and infant care. Many women returning to jobs in the banking field during the first half of the 1980s, for example, found that the industry had changed drastically during their absence, primarily as the result of the introduction of microcomputers and electronic data processing. For women in this and many other fields, the penalties for motherhood were threefold. First, just being away from the job brought on a certain level of dissatisfaction. Second, they missed out on consideration for promotions or raises. On this point, sociologist Rosabeth Kanter has observed that the peak years for child-rearing responsibilities (ages

Exhibit 10.7

Sociological Focus

The Women's Movement

Women's resistance to their socially defined subordinate status has two histories. The first history is composed of individual profiles in courage—portraits of women willing to challenge a system that denied access to property and position. This history can be written in terms of "firsts"—the *first* to breach some social or legal barrier. Elizabeth Blackwell was the first woman in the United States to earn an M.D. It should be noted that Dr. Blackwell earned this distinction in 1849 after being rejected by 29 medical schools. She was finally accepted only because program administrators assumed that she would fail to complete the program's requirements. After her graduation she could not attract patients and was refused access to hospitals. Ultimately, in order to practice medicine and promote medical careers for women, Dr. Blackwell was forced to found a hospital staffed exclusively by women (1857) as well as a medical school for women (1868).

The second history is one of women's movements—conscious and collective attempts to bring about changes in the social status of women. This history focuses on the issues and organizations that have mobilized both women and men in pursuit of major structural and social changes in society. The United States is currently in the midst of a broadly based effort, initially preceded by movements that focused on narrow and specific issues, such as labor reform and voting rights.

The contemporary women's movement, referred to by many as "women's liberation" because it focuses on the artificial constraints imposed by gender roles, is but a few decades old. Its origins cannot be pinpointed to any specific date, but its many benchmarks include the publication of Betty Friedan's *The Feminine Mystique* in 1963, the founding of NOW (the National Organization for Women) in 1966, and the failed but nevertheless vigorous first attempt at establishing an Equal Rights Amendment in the 1970s. Like all social movements (see Chapter 16), the origins of the women's movement were rooted in social conditions that generated frustration and dissatisfaction.

The 1960s were a time ripe for social change. Increasing numbers of women were entering the labor force, only to find themselves relegated to clerical and blue-collar jobs, regardless of their education and experience. Even women graduating from law schools found themselves limited to library and secretarial work—a situation once faced by Sandra Day O'Connor, the first woman to be appointed to the Supreme Court of the United States.

The 1960s were also a time when claims for social justice and equality were generating a radical critique of specific American institutions. Efforts were being pressed by black Americans for equality with whites, and antiwar protests on college campuses were calling for reexamination of American foreign policy. At a broader level, it was a period that challenged the legitimacy of social arrangements that were to facilitate the emergence of many different social movements, including those focusing on the rights of women.

The movement attracted people with different goals and agendas, and alternative strategies for initiating change. Political interest groups worked to bring about legislative changes. These groups have had a number of meaningful successes for women, including laws on equal pay for equal work. Litigation has been another tactic, challenging discriminatory laws and practices. Some of the more meaningful advances in this regard have been in the area of sexual harassment.

Perhaps the most significant accomplishment of the women's movement has been to bring the inequities and abuses to public attention. During the early stages of the movement, *consciousness raising* groups were organized to bring women together to share their dissatisfactions as a way of confirming that they were dealing with social, and not individual problems. It is probably safe to say that the women's movement has raised the consciousness of large segments of society. Not all people agree with all of the goals of the women's movement, but few today would condone instances of violence, abuse, and discrimination based on gender.

SOURCES: Jessie Bernard, *The Female World* (New York: Free Press, 1981); Barbara Sinclair Deckhard, *The Women's Movement*, 3rd ed. (New York: Harper & Row, 1983); Eleanor Flexner, *A Century of Struggle* (New York: Atheneum, 1971).

Exhibit **10.8** Sociological Focus

The Wage Gap

Figures for Full-time Workers in Selected Occupations	Women as a Percent of All Workers		Earnings Ratio, Female to Male	
	1979	1986	1979	1986
Accountants and Auditors	34%	45%	0.60	0.72
Computer Programmers	28	40	0.80	0.81
Computer Systems Analysts	20	30	0.79	0.83
Lawyers	10	15	0.55	0.63
Managers and Administrators	22	29	0.51	0.61
Sales of Business Services	28	34	0.58	0.79
Teachers, Elementary School	61	82	0.82	0.95

Source: U.S. Bureau of the Census, 1988.

25–35) coincide with the time that employers make fateful decisions about the futures of younger workers.[31] Finally, because of the computerization of the banking industry, many workers needed to be retrained.

Considering the negative consequences of intermittent work careers, it is not surprising that a number of controversial issues have arisen in the work place in recent years. Perhaps the most controversial is maternity leave. At least 10 states have enacted legislation requiring large employers to grant women unpaid maternity leave and to guarantee reinstatement at the conclusion of the leave. In 1987 the United States Supreme Court upheld the California law dealing with this issue but stopped short of requiring that all states establish similar maternity leave guarantees.[32] Many observers have supported the High Court's decision on the grounds that women no longer should be penalized for pregnancy and childbirth. But others worry that the ruling will lead to a backlash, discouraging employers from hiring women of childbearing age.

"Comparable Worth"

Women cannot be denied equal pay for equal work. In other words, people doing the same job ought to be paid at the same rate. However, as already noted, part of the earnings gap is the result of women's being concentrated in low-paying clerical occupations. In many instances jobs held by women are paid at a relatively low rate when compared to jobs having similar skill requirements that are dominated by men. In other words, does driving a truck, operating a fork lift, or collecting garbage require greater skill than taking dictation or typing? And if the skill levels and educational requirements are the same, should the salaries and benefits be comparable? These questions are the essence of the comparable worth debate. Consider some specific cases. During the mid-eighties the state of Washington compared pay scales in numerous occupations. The general finding was that patterns of unequal pay exist frequently among men and women. Although the positions of top-level secretary and electrician were given the same ranking, based on knowledge and skills required, mental demands, and accountability and working conditions, the female-dominated secretarial positions paid $600 less per month than male-dominated electrician positions.

Unequal pay is, in part, a matter of sound economics. Employers can be expected to take advantage of the opportunity to pay lower wages for work of equal value to *any* group willing to accept them or unable to prevent the practice. But a social process of **undervaluation** is also at work here, placing a lower monetary value on the work tasks of women. Undervaluation is not necessarily intentional; it may be rather, an outgrowth of subtle social images of, and assumptions about, women. In one case, for example, a male zoo keeper was paid more than a female nursery-school teacher, because child care was not considered a job-related skill, but was viewed instead as an inherent characteristic of women. In another situation, women were not given credit for typing skills, because of the assumption that "all women know how to type."[33]

This undervaluation pattern underlies the demands for **comparable worth,** best defined as "equal pay for males and females doing work requiring comparable skill, effort, and responsibility under similar working conditions."[34] Efforts to insure comparable worth are making some progress in the United States; some states have legislation in place and most others are at least studying the matter. The federal government has been slow to take action on the issue, lagging behind other nations. All ten members of the European Economic Community guarantee women equal pay for work of equal value.[35]

Gender and the Political Sphere

In 1987, Eleanor Smeal left the presidency of NOW, the National Organization of Women, to tour the country, encouraging women everywhere to enter the political arena. Smeal urged women to do so not merely as volunteers helping to elect men, but as political office seekers in their own right. Her point was that women continue to be underrepresented in politics.

In recent years several democratic nations have elevated a woman to their top political post—Indira Gandhi in India, Golda Meir in Israel, Margaret Thatcher in Great Britain, and Corazon Aquino in the Philippines. But the American political system has yet to elect a woman to the presidency of the United States, although the Democratic party did place Geraldine Ferraro on the ballot for vice-president in 1984. Women candidates have been more successful at the state and local levels. The number of women in state legislatures doubled between 1975 and the late 1980s, but they still comprise only a scant 15% of the total number of legislators nationally.[36]

A major issue with women candidates is whether gender makes a difference in attracting voters. On the one hand, public opinion polls show that some Americans express reluctance to vote for women candidates. A candidate's sex conjures up different images for voters. In one experimental situation, pictures of hypothetical

SOCIAL INDICATOR

What Other Countries Do about Maternity Leave

	Maximum Leave	Pay While on Leave	Parent on Leave
Sweden	52 weeks	90%/ 38 weeks	Either
Finland	39 weeks	80%/ 39 weeks	Either
Canada	37 weeks	60%/ 15 weeks	Mother
Italy	24 weeks	80%/ 24 weeks	Mother
Austria	20 weeks	100%/ 20 weeks	Mother
Chile	18 weeks	100%/ 18 weeks	Either
West Germany	14 weeks	100%/ 14 weeks	Mother

Source: *U.S. News & World Report,* March 10, 1986, p. 52.

SOCIAL INDICATOR

State Efforts on Pay Equity

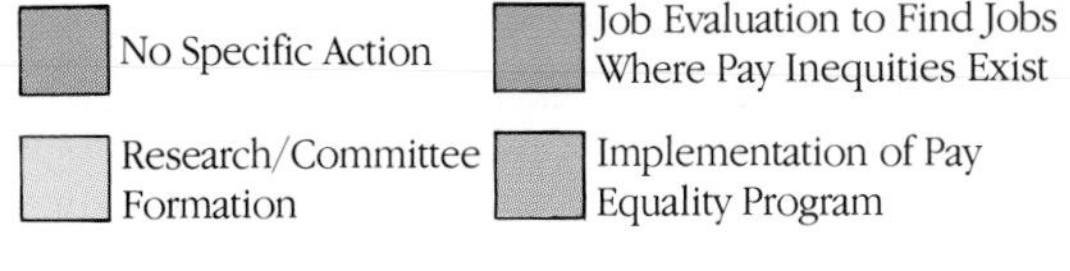

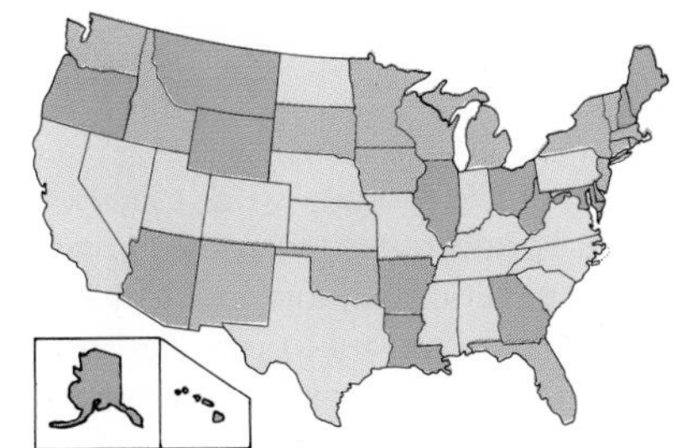

Source: National Committee on Pay Equity, February 1987.

Sexual harassment takes many forms—unwanted touching, fondling, offensive comments, or demands for sex.

male candidates were often perceived as better at handling "tough decisions"; those of female candidates were perceived as "organized, and good with details and new ideas."[37] However, research on actual voting behavior conducted after elections shows that gender does not have much of an impact in contests between qualified candidates. Political party, experience, and stance on important issues are much more important. Voters—both men and women—will support a woman who is viewed as a strong candidate and reject an unqualified one—the same process they use in evaluating men.[38]

Sexual Harassment

It would appear that men and women work together in offices, factories, schools, and numerous other environments across the nation generally without incident, but in many situations women are exposed to repeated sexual harassment. **Sexual harassment** consists of unwelcome and unreciprocated sexual advances or contacts, or requests for sexual favors, and studies document that it is an all-too-common occurrence. In a 1982 survey, for example, 30% of college women at a major university reported incidents of harassment by teachers on at least one occasion during their college careers.[39] Offensive touching, leers, and stares, and outright sexual propositions were common. Fear of retaliation kept most of these college women from reporting the incidents, which contributed to a weakening of the victims' self-confidence. In an alternative example, in 1987 the United States Navy and Marine Corps were cited for sexual harassment, including verbal abuse and *coerced* sexual relations, against female military personnel in the Pacific area. The report issued by those investigating the matter suggested that "leadership attitudes condone discriminatory behavior, in part as a means of perpetuating the 'male mystique' that is traditionally associated with military forces."[40]

Many forms of sexual harassment are known. At one extreme are blatant demands for sexual relations in return for grades, jobs, or promotions—what in the entertainment industry is still called the "casting couch" procedure. Such forms are clearly an abuse of authority, for they can be demanded only by people in positions to reward or punish subordinates. As a result, the courts have defined such requests for submission to sexual acts as a form of illegal discrimination.

A different form of harassment involves offensive physical touching (patting or fondling). *Anyone*—superior, subordinate, customer, or client—can be guilty of such advances. If the offending person is a superior, rejection can directly threaten a victim's career or employment. Whatever the source, such acts can humiliate, embarrass, disgust or threaten, creating a hostile and intimidating environment in which to study or work. Similarly, frequent sexually oriented jokes and comments can produce an unfavorable climate in which to function. A work place dominated by sexually oriented looks, conversations, and advances can also produce a hostile and intimidating social situation. And it should be added here that contrary to widespread beliefs, women are not the only victims of sexual harassment, and men are not always the offenders.

It is not likely that *all* offensive touching and demands for sex are deliberate attempts to harass. However, some of the actions that produce hostile environments originate in socially defined gender roles. As insensitive as they may be to the victims involved, leering at the female form and sexually oriented jokes are deeply ingrained aspects of the male role. Often these actions occur unconsciously. And while there is no excuse for sexual harassment of any type, many situations can be improved by informally making people aware of the negative implications of their actions. In other cases, official action in the form of written protests, grievances, or legal procedures becomes necessary.

As a final note, it should be pointed out that some unwanted advances that are defined as harassment by a victim may be something else entirely. The victim may have misread the other person's behavior. Symbolic interactionists constantly emphasize that people act on the basis of perceptions and interpretations of social acts. Evidence is plentiful that men and women often perceive the same behavior differently. Men frequently impute more sexual meaning to a social interaction than women do. For example, after viewing staged situations involving couples in photographs and video tapes, men almost always "see" more sexual intent in the activity of the female players than women do.[41] Therefore, single incidents of unwanted advances may be a case of men and women interpreting nonverbal cues differently.

Despite greater consciousness about sexual stereotyping, many lapses occur nevertheless. Consider, for example, the Beachin' Times, a color supplement from the Miller Brewing Company that appeared in campus newspapers across the nation just prior to Spring Break 1989.

AGING IN AMERICA

Although curious by contemporary standards, a rather interesting phenomenon occurred in 1776. No, we are not referring to the founding of the new American republic. Instead, in that year a population census was conducted in the states of Maryland and Connecticut in which many people apparently lied about their ages.[42] What makes this a curiosity is that they exaggerated their years, claiming to be older than they actually were! This occurrence suggests that to be old in colonial America was to enjoy high status or some other benefit. Why else would people have tried to pass themselves off as elderly? This phenomenon is supported by the literature and sermons of the period, which instructed young people to show respect for their elders. Older people in contemporary society do not enjoy the same status they once did, but the cause of this change is not clear. What has occurred in the United States during the last two centuries that might explain this status change?

Aging and Modernization

A broad theoretical approach to explaining the role of older people in contemporary society contrasts the situation of the elderly in agricultural and industrial economies.[43] In traditional agricultural societies it remains common for the elderly to enjoy unusual social status and power, but as noted above, they do not have this advantage in modern industrial societies. The decline of their position and status is but one part of a general

SOCIAL INDICATOR

Old . . . By Any Other Name

"Old" is a *social role,* and it is seldom a desirable one. Or as an anthropologist once observed:

> Among all people a point is reached in aging at which any further usefulness appears to be over and the incumbent is regarded as a living liability. "Senility" may be a suitable label for this. Other terms among primitive people are the "overaged," the "useless stage," the "sleeping period," and the "already dead." Then, without actual death, the prospects are gloomy. . . . Some do something positive about it. Others wait for nature to do it or perhaps assist nature in doing it.

Source: Leo W. Simmons, "Aging in Preindustrial Societies," in Clark Tibbitts (ed.), *Handbook of Social Gerontology* (Chicago: University of Chicago Press, 1960), p. 87.

process of social change typically referred to as **modernization**—the social, demographic, and economic changes that accompany the transition of societies from agricultural to industrial production. These changes generally tend to undermine the status of the elderly.

Land is the most valuable resource in a system based on farming, and land ownership often resides in the hands of the oldest member of a family. High birth rates combined with high death rates result in only a few people reaching old age. This fact increases the uniqueness of the elderly and raises their social status. Perhaps the most important factor contributing to high status for the elderly is that they also accumulate a lifetime of knowledge and experience, providing them with wisdom not found among the younger generations.

Industrialization weakens such claims to economic and social status. Jobs, not land, become the major source of income and wealth. Public health improves the chances of long life, making older people a common social feature. A most important consideration is the fact that modern societies are marked by rapid technological and social change. Thus, the knowledge possessed by older members of a society is often no longer relevant to current conditions, and in effect, becomes obsolete.

Modernization is often viewed as a structural and functional approach to the question of age, focusing on the idea that older people make a lesser contribution to the survival of an industrial society. But other factors also have contributed to the declining status and perceived importance and usefulness of the elderly. Perhaps the most significant have been changes in ideas about old age. At the end of the nineteenth century aging was redefined; the perception changed from one of wisdom to one of degeneration in physical and mental capacity.[44]

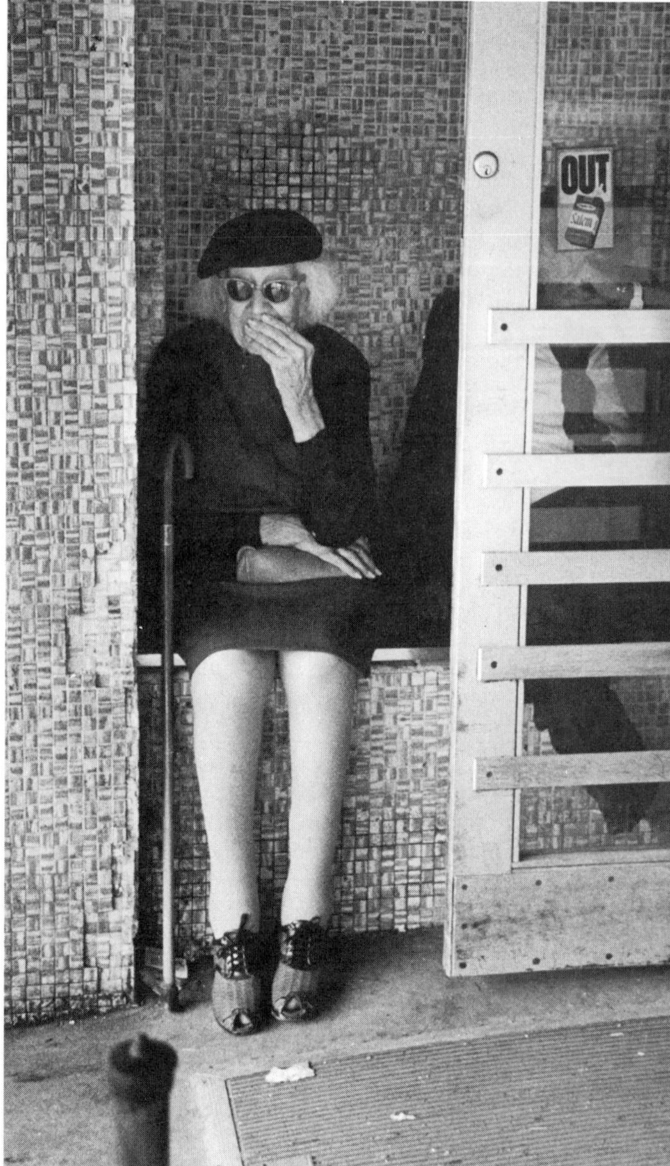

Although the elderly are looked up to in many agricultural societies, that is not necessarily the case in most industrial countries.

Aging as Degeneration

It is important to note that the idea that people are physically and mentally "different" at various points in the life cycle is a relatively new social phenomenon. For example, at one time, children were considered to be adults on a smaller scale. This idea of children as "miniature adults" existed throughout the Middle Ages, enduring until the nineteenth century. Parents and children wore the same clothing, they did the same work, participated in the same religious ceremonies, and even openly exchanged sexual jokes with one another.[45]

The notion that "growing old" was a degenerative process and that the elderly could no longer play a significant role in society began to emerge shortly after the Civil War. This attitude can be traced to events that occurred in medicine, religion, and the labor market.[46] Taken together these events set in motion a process that altered the way old age was perceived and changed attitudes toward the aged. Several examples clearly illustrate the process.

In the field of medicine, old and young had always been treated alike, until scientific research began identifying specific diseases associated with aging, such as hardening of the arteries and "gout." Most of these diseases were invariably defined as incurable. Thus, "old age" came to be designated as a stage in the life cycle—one characterized by dependency and death. A physician, writing in 1904, summarized the position of the medical profession on this point:

> For a person in their seventies, it is not worth while to make any great sacrifice in the way of money and associations to go in search of health, because the probabilities are that [treatment] will do more harm than good.[47]

And the scenario went further. Because the elderly were doomed to be unproductive as the result of their physical infirmities, it would be better to segregate them from the rest of society—they would be better off in old-age homes and institutions. Even attempts to help the aged during these years contributed to their declining social images. In 1907, for example, a veterans' pension law treated age as an official disability; that is, when people reached the age of 62, they were defined as having lost one-half of their ability.

In the area of religion, the end of the nineteenth century witnessed a strong wave of evangelical Protestantism. The emphasis was on individual self-control and self-reliance, rather than on strict adherence to church rules as the road to salvation. The degenerative model of aging emphasized dependency and the loss of mental capacity, suggesting also that the elderly lost their capacity for moral behavior.[48] Thus, while medicine emphasized physical decay, religion emphasized the moral decay of the elderly.

The last major event contributing to the segregation and degradation of the elderly was the Social Security Act of 1935. This act was one way to force older workers out of the labor market where they competed with the young for scarce jobs. Mandatory retirement meant that a person, no matter how healthy and productive he or she might be, was forced into retirement at age 65. Of course, the act also had a positive side, for it guaranteed Social Security benefits to those who had spent a lifetime working.[49]

In summary, it can be noted that the role of the elderly in modern society was undermined by two factors, both of which created social barriers between young and old. First, modernization weakened the relevance of the knowledge that the elderly had acquired during their lives. In technological societies, formal schooling replaces experience as the source of most knowledge. Modern societies increasingly are also urban societies where geographical mobility becomes common, with people moving from place to place to attend school, find jobs, or move up in their professions and occupations—thus separating each generation from parents and grandparents.

Second, the idea of aging as degeneration emphasized the chasm between the young and the old in a somewhat different way, creating an image of the old as unproductive and disabled, thus depressing their social status and segregating them (physically and socially) from the rest of society. Those who entered homes for the aged were physically segregated, and those who remained with their families were socially segregated by a role which suggested that they were so different from other people that the young and old had little in common.

Aging and Ambivalence in Contemporary America

If a single word can be used to describe the attitude toward the elderly in contemporary America, that word is *ambivalence.* Americans, young and old alike, hold

SOCIAL INDICATOR

Geographical Mobility and the Elderly

Among Persons Ages 65 and over Who Live Alone, the Time It Takes Their Nearest Child to Get to Their Home:

Child Arrives in	Minutes	72%
	Hours	25
	Days	3

Source: National Center for Health Statistics, 1988.

SOCIAL INDICATOR

Physical Segregation of the Elderly

Percent of Elderly Population Living in Homes for the Aged, by Age:

Age	Percent
65–69	1%
70–74	2
75–79	5
80–84	10
85+	22

Source: Special Committee on Aging, United States Senate, 1985.

conflicting images of age and its consequences. These images shape the role of older people in society. The social condition of the elderly is also ambivalent. In recent years fewer retired Americans have been relegated to disability and poverty, but many still suffer diminished life-styles.

Conflicting Images

The biological aging process imposes its mark on the human body. Eyesight begins to decline after age forty, wrinkles and lines mar the face, grey hairs appear, and among many men, the hairline begins to recede. Taken together these changes do not paint a very attractive picture for a culture that celebrates independence, flexibility, and physical attractiveness. The impact of these negative images is confirmed by the success of the countless ointments, creams, and other potions sold daily to fend off wrinkles, sagging skin, and balding heads.

Although these physical alterations may represent only superficial changes, they are important because they are visible clues that a person is aging, and they call to mind certain stereotypes of the elderly. It is clear that members of American society hold two different images of what it is like to be old. Old people are, on the one hand, stereotyped as dependent, rigid, and asexual. Such stereotypes are reinforced in the media where older characters usually play minor roles and are typically stubborn, irritable, and narrow-minded people. By contrast, it also is apparent that the elderly are seen to have such positive traits as friendliness, trustworthiness, and knowledge. This combination reflects a "kindly grandparent" image of an individual enjoying a happy and contented retirement, free from financial or health worries, and with a house full of happy relatives gathered around a bountiful Thanksgiving table (see Exhibit 10.9).

Yet as has been seen elsewhere in this textbook, stereotypes are often contradicted by social research, and that is certainly the case with reference to ideas about the aging process. For example, research indicates that advancing age does *not* mean that sexual activity disappears; many older Americans continue to enjoy healthy intimate relations, some well into their nineties.[50] The physical infirmities attributed to the elderly, furthermore, are frequently misconceptions, applicable only to a tiny

Exhibit 10.9 **Types & Stereotypes**

Most People over 65 Are . . .

Very Warm and Friendly	82%
Very Wise from Experience	66
Very Physically Active	41
Very Good at Getting Things Done	35
Very Bright and Alert	29
Very Open-minded and Adaptable	19
Very Sexually Active	5

Source: "A Survey of Adults 18–64" in *The Myth and Reality of Aging* (1975), a study prepared by Louis Harris & Associates for the National Council on Aging, Inc., 600 Maryland Ave. S.W., Washington, D.C. 20024. Reprinted by permission.

minority. Nine out of ten older Americans have no difficulty crossing a busy street, dressing themselves, cooking their own meals, speaking clearly, or controlling urination.[51] Studies of voting and political opinions have failed to demonstrate that the elderly are necessarily more conservative than younger people.[52]

However, as sociologists consistently have demonstrated, "objective" facts are usually less important than beliefs, and it is clear that "images" influence the manner in which the young treat the old. Symbolic interactionists have conducted some interesting research on this point, demonstrating how being old influences the way people are treated under many circumstances. In everyday social situations, for example, people are far more likely to offer help to older people.[53] This observation has been found to be especially applicable when elderly persons are stranded on street corners or in disabled automobiles. The willingness to give aid seemingly combines images of the elderly as helpless with the feeling that they are more trustworthy than younger persons.

Ageism and Health

Not all of the implications of aging stereotypes work to the advantage of the elderly. Numerous patterns of **ageism**—prejudice and discrimination directed against older people—are visible in our society. Older workers generally are no less skilled or dependable than younger workers. Indeed, they tend to be more conscientious and have better attendance records. Nevertheless, many forms of ageism are found in the American work place.[54] In 1987 alone, more than 26,000 cases of alleged age discrimination were filed with the Equal Employment Opportunity Commission.[55] Complaints center on allegations that younger people are favored over more elderly workers in decisions concerning hiring and promotion, and that older workers are denied access to training and retraining programs.

In an alternative frame of reference, **elder abuse**—physical violence directed toward older family members—is a problem of growing proportions in the

The aging process often results in generational inversion, wherein the roles of parent and child are reversed.

United States.[56] Many sociologists attribute the phenomenon to the real or perceived dependency of aging parents. Social stress is sometimes acted out by striking out at the person believed to be responsible for the stress. Having to care for an older family member frequently causes stress, but it is made more difficult by the fact that children and parents must reverse their roles, a process sociologist Suzanne Steinmetz has referred to as **generational inversion.**[57] During the early years of their lives children depend on their parents for care and emotional support, but when their parents age the roles are often reversed, and acceptance of such new responsibilities is stressful for many.

The biological aging process, in combination with changing social attitudes towards people as they grow old, may also alter the way the elderly feel about themselves. Ambivalence once again comes into play. On the whole, older people are as happy as other age groups. They are usually satisfied with their financial situations.[58] At the same time, however, older Americans believe the best years of their lives have passed. Throughout their twenties and thirties most people anticipate the future; in their forties and fifties they believe they are enjoying the most productive years of their lives. By the time they are 65, most would concede that the best years are behind them.[59]

The feeling that the best years are past may help to explain suicide rates among the elderly. These rates rise dramatically with age. As illustrated in Exhibit 10.10, vulnerability to suicide increases at two important points in the life cycle. The first crucial period occurs during the adolescent years; the second period of vulnerability begins at about age sixty. It is at about age sixty that people must confront the reality of aging, which has many implications. For some it means the onset of physical decline. For others it involves anticipation of retirement from work, and for still others, it signals increased worry about money to maintain life-styles and pay medical bills. Aging also brings with it the need to confront one's own mortality, which can raise serious fears and anxieties.[60]

GENDER, AGE, AND APPLIED SOCIOLOGY

Age and gender roles are social constructions that are not determined exclusively by biology. As such, they are significant social realities, defining the way people think of themselves and influencing the perceptions and behaviors of others. Given this, the tools and perspectives of applied sociology are significant in overcoming the artificial barriers of age and gender.

SOCIAL INDICATOR

The Time of Our Lives

Three out of every four of us say we do not want to be older or younger—we like the age we are. And most of us either think we are in the prime of life or approaching it:

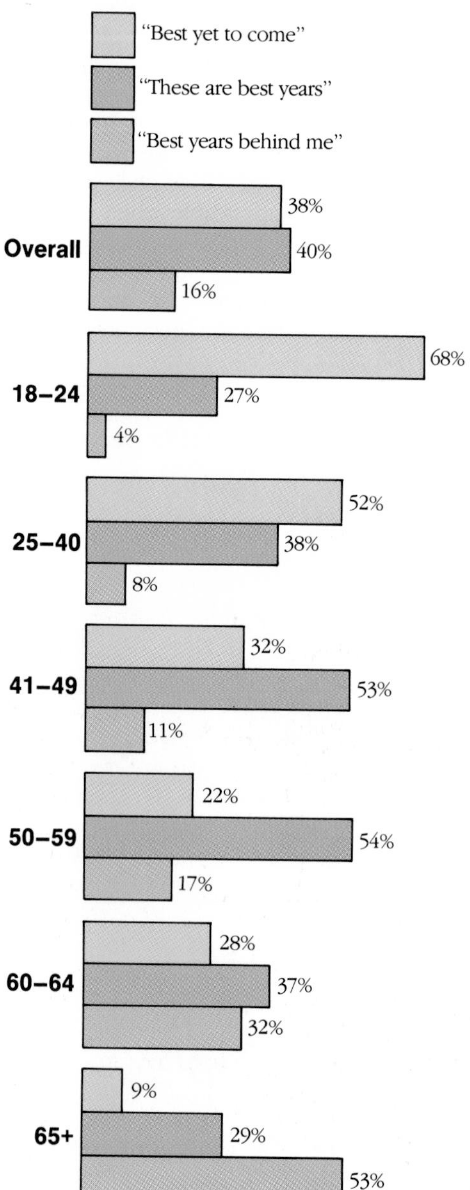

Source: *USA Today,* May 18, 1987, p. 4A.

Exhibit 10.10

Sociological Focus

Suicide Rates by Age

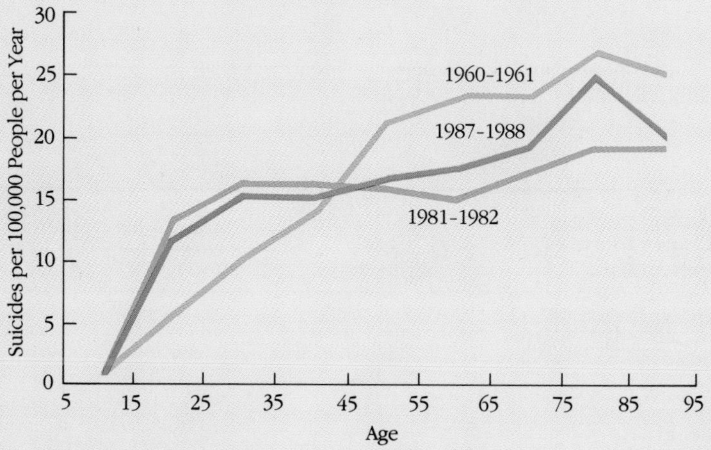

Suicides per 100,000 People per Year (0, 5, 10, 15, 20, 25, 30)

Age (5, 15, 25, 35, 45, 55, 65, 75, 85, 95)

1960-1961

1987-1988

1981-1982

Source: *Statistical Abstract of the United States,* 1989.

Recognizing the fact that age and gender groups are genuine social categories, each with different needs, interests, and expectations, the field of market research has made perhaps the widest use of sociological knowledge about men and women, old and young.[61] To cite but one specific example, measurements have been made based on data about the elderly generated by the Bureau of Labor Statistics as to approximately how much the elderly spend each year on food, housing, health care, clothing, personal care, insurance, entertainment, and charity (see Exhibit 10.11).[62] These data are not only being used for current marketing purposes, but they are being utilized to project future trends about the elderly. Many industries have recognized that as America continues to age, its elderly are becoming more affluent and better educated. Marketing personnel have begun to notice the social science data on the elderly and are expanding on it to uncover potential new markets.

In another area, employers are beginning to take more seriously the situations of their aging workers.[63] Work roles represent master statuses for many people. The drastic changes instituted by a sudden withdrawal from these statuses upon retirement tend to have negative impacts on many elderly persons. Consequently, based on the accumulated social science knowledge

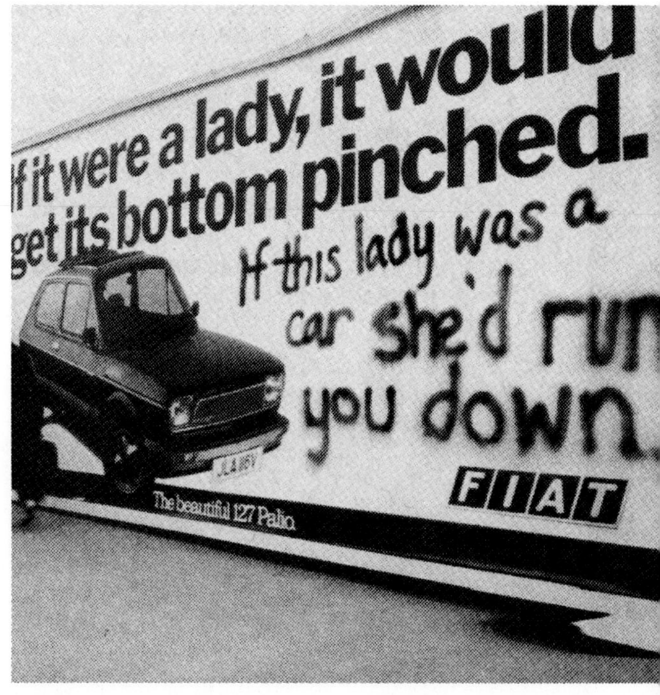

What is the applied sociology lesson here?

Applied Sociology

What Older Americans Spend

While households headed by older Americans spend less than the average household, on a per-capita basis (household spending divided by number of persons in household) older Americans spend as much or more than the average in many categories.

(Average Annual Expenditures of Households, in 1984 Dollars)	All Households	Households Headed by Older Americans			
		Total	55–64	65–74	75+
Number of Persons in Household	2.6	2.1	2.5	1.9	1.6
Food Total	$3,280	$2,900	$3,602	$2,714	$1,865
Food at Home	2,300	2,129	2,536	2,027	1,518
Grocery Stores	2,164	2,029	2,412	1,929	1,462
Convenience Stores	136	99	124	98	55
Food Away from Home	980	772	1,065	687	348
Housing Total	$6,284	$5,079	$6,195	$4,562	$3,767
Shelter	3,494	2,520	3,124	2,203	1,865
Owned Dwellings	2,066	1,526	2,049	1,264	939
Rented Dwellings	1,071	641	633	558	781
Fuels, Utilities, and Public Services	1,638	1,645	1,878	1,588	1,292
Household Operations	315	275	263	251	332
House Furnishings and Equipment	837	640	930	520	278
Furniture	270	178	283	119	69
Major Appliances	141	123	166	115	56
Small Appliances/Housewares	62	53	73	49	20
Miscellaneous Household Equipment	229	169	248	139	66
Apparel Total	$1,107	$788	$1,136	$657	$331
Males, Aged 2 and Over	285	177	265	140	66
Females, Aged 2 and Over	447	356	503	307	154
Transportation Total	$4,264	$3,226	$4,435	$2,926	$1,409
Vehicle Purchases	1,813	1,247	1,814	1,126	364
Vehicle Finance Charges	213	113	188	80	25
Gasoline and Motor Oil	1,058	842	1,134	782	386
Maintenance and Repairs	439	344	448	311	197
Health Care Total	$902	$1,256	$1,065	$1,360	$1,458
Health Insurance	291	507	329	643	636
Medical Services	454	504	524	462	529
Medicines and Medical Supplies	157	245	211	255	292
Personal Care Total	$192	$203	$243	$195	$139
Personal Services, Females	121	150	172	149	111
Personal Services, Males	66	49	66	42	27

(Average Annual Expenditures of Households, in 1984 Dollars)	All Households	Households Headed by Older Americans			
		Total	55–64	65–74	75+
Number of Persons in Household	2.6	2.1	2.5	1.9	1.6
Entertainment Total	$973	$674	$1,008	$531	$265
Fees and Admissions	313	238	312	226	118
Televisions	219	154	204	131	93
Radios and Sound Equipment	91	50	92	24	10
Other	350	233	400	149	45
Reading Total	$132	$122	$141	$123	$84
Newspapers	61	71	77	72	57
Magazines/Periodicals	33	28	32	29	18
Book Clubs	9	7	9	5	3
Encyclopedias/Other	3	1	2	1	—
Education Total	$286	$147	$237	$74	$88
Elementary and High Schools	46	15	33	3	—
Colleges and Universities	175	105	153	60	83
Other	16	10	18	5	2
Alcoholic Beverages	$286	$184	$258	$164	$76
Tobacco and Smoking Supplies	$227	$185	$264	$166	$66
Miscellaneous	$295	$232	$324	$174	$145
Contributions Total	$706	$791	$874	$681	$800
Charities	73	83	79	78	96
Religious Organizations	259	303	343	294	241
Educational Organizations	13	10	15	7	5
Political	7	12	16	9	7
Personal Insurance Total	$1,928	$1,357	$2,481	$711	$225
Life Insurance, Endowments, Annuities, etc.	300	297	462	229	90
Retirement/Pensions, Social Security	1,628	1,060	2,019	482	134
Total Expenditures*	$20,862	$17,144	$22,264	$15,038	$10,718

Source: Bureau of Labor Statistics 1984 Consumer Expenditure Survey.

*Subcategories may not sum to category total because not all subcategories are shown. Averages refer to all households, whether or not they purchased the particular item.

about work roles and the life cycle, numerous firms have established preretirement programs to help ease the transition from work to leisure. Some programs are limited to teaching coping skills, while others target a variety of areas, including social activities, health care, and financial planning.[64]

Finally, recognizing that social isolation has become a problem for the elderly in society, for example, both federal and state governments have begun to channel social research funds toward charting and solving the problems faced by the aged in America. The first wave of studies has established the parameters of the populations of concern, noting that some 30% of those over age 65 live alone. The majority of these individuals are women because of their longer life expectancy, and a fourth of them are struggling with poverty. In addition, the data show that most of the elderly maintain some ties with other people, either by phone or in person. Perhaps the most important finding is that the social contact and social support of friends and relatives turn out to be matters of life and death for the elderly; those with social contacts tend to live longer than those who lack social interaction.

SUMMARY

Aging and sexual differences are universal human characteristics. Both are based on biology in the sense that human beings belong to one of the two sexes and that all humans mature and change. Some physiological differences are obvious, but being "male," "female," or "old" is largely a social role governed by sets of expectations concerning appropriate attitudes and behavior.

It is not clear how gender and age roles originate, because they are often the legacy of a long and unclear past. Economic, demographic, cultural, and social factors all play a role in shaping them. And, like all social phenomena, they are constantly changing and evolving.

Gender roles are a product of socialization practices that expose girls and boys to different experiences, impose different norms, and lead to different treatment from others. These roles become the standards by which people judge themselves and their peers. The power of roles varies over time but seems to peak somewhere during the adolescent years. They generally become less salient after that, permitting many people to break through their confining boundaries.

The sexes are unequal in many areas—health, economics, and politics to name but the most important. In each case, social definitions are the major issue. Gender life-styles, for example, can increase or decrease life expectancy or susceptibility to accidents and violent death. In other areas, perceptions (or stereotypes) limit opportunities and impose artificial limits on earnings.

American society still exhibits many examples of sexual harassment. The abuse of power in organizations of all types results in demands for sexual favors in return for jobs, promotions, and even grades. In addition, women frequently (and men to a lesser extent) are the victims of unwanted sexual advances or situations textured with sexual innuendo.

Cross-cultural research has demonstrated that the "elders" in many nonindustrial societies occupy privileged positions. This tends not to be the case in contemporary industrial societies. The social and economic aspects of the modernization process have tended to weaken the status once accorded the elderly. Most significant have been the technological changes that render the knowledge and skills of the elderly obsolete. Current ideas about the aging process can be traced to the last century when aging came to be associated with physical and mental degeneration.

Advanced age places individuals in ambivalent positions. A general respect for age is pitted against the social image of degeneration. This ambivalence is reflected in contradictions between social stereotypes of the elderly and their own perceptions of themselves. Many elderly persons flourish as they continue to grow old, but it is a difficult time for most. Retirement, whether voluntary or mandatory, eliminates them from the labor force and forces them to cast aside the social roles associated with work. Many live alone, with few social contacts and in problematic economic circumstances.

KEY TERMS/CONCEPTS

ageism
age roles
Bem Sex-Role Inventory
chromosomes
comparable worth
earnings gap
elder abuse
gender
gender identity
gender inequality
gender roles
generational inversion
institutionalized sexism
modernization
sex
sex discrimination
sexual harassment
undervaluation

DISCUSSION QUESTIONS

1. Have you ever heard of or observed parents referring to girl babies as "soft" or boys as "firm"? How might this influence the way in which these individuals treat their children as they grow up?
2. Women in the U.S. live longer than men on the average. This element of reality may be due in part to the fact that women are physically superior to men. Other explanations may include the differences between male and female social roles. What do you think?
3. Under current federal law, most workers are no longer forced to retire at age 70. Tenured faculty members at colleges and universities in the United States represent one of the few exceptions. Do you see any advantages or disadvantages to this rule for students? faculty? schools? society?
4. Each year, the telecast of the Miss America Pageant in Atlantic City is watched by more women than men. What do you think motivates women (and men) to watch this contest?

SUGGESTED READINGS

Margaret L. Andersen, *Thinking About Women,* 2nd ed. (New York: Macmillan, 1987). This comprehensive and thorough approach to the social role of women in society covers sociological theory and research, as well as defining feminist perspectives.

Robert C. Atchley, *Social Forces and Aging,* 4th ed. (Belmont, CA: Wadsworth, 1985). The latest edition of one of the best textbooks to examine aging as a social process.

Nijole V. Benokraitis and Joe R. Feagin, *Modern Sexism* (Englewood Cliffs, NJ: Prentice-Hall, 1986). The many forms of discrimination against women in modern society, both blatant and subtle, are revealed, along with strategies for dealing with them.

Susan Brownmiller, *Femininity* (New York: Simon & Schuster, 1984). An up-to-date look at the images and social pressures that define being a woman in contemporary society.

Clyde W. Franklin, *The Changing Definition of Masculinity* (New York: Plenum, 1984). The focus here is on social change in the role of men as society faces the challenges of the 1990s.

Jack Levin and William C. Levin, *Ageism* (Belmont, CA: Wadsworth, 1980). Prejudice and discrimination against the elderly are analyzed and described, along with recommendations for methods of eliminating them.

David Van Tassel and Peter N. Sterns (eds.), *Old Age in a Bureaucratic Society* (New York: Greenwood Press, 1986). This collection of papers brings together some of the best new scholarship on the aging process in both social and historical contexts.

NOTES

1. Erving Goffman, *Stigma: Notes on the Management of Spoiled Identity* (Englewood Cliffs, NJ: Prentice-Hall, 1963), p. 128.
2. Quoted in Kathleen Gerson, "What Do Women Want From Men?" *American Behavioral Scientist* 29 (May/June, 1986), p. 625.
3. Judith Bardwick, "Infant Sex Differences," in Clarice Stasz Stoll (ed.), *Sexism* (Reading, MA: Addison-Wesley, 1973), pp. 28–42.
4. J. E. Parsons, (ed.) *The Psychobiology of Sex Differences and Sex Roles* (Washington, DC: Hemisphere, 1980).
5. John Money and Anke A. Ehrhardt, *Man, Woman, Boy and Girl: The Differentiation and Dimorphism of Gender Identity from Conception to Maturity* (Baltimore, MD: Johns Hopkins University Press, 1972), Chapter 11.
6. Sandra L. Bem, "The Measurement of Psychological Androgyny," *Journal of Clinical and Consulting Psychology,* 42 (April 1974), pp. 155–62.
7. S. G. Koblinsky, D. F. Cruse, and A. Sugawara, "Sex Role Stereotypes and Children's Memory of Story Content," *Child Development,* 49 (1978), pp. 452–58.
8. S. E. Taylor, S. T. Fiske, N. L. Etcoff, and A. J. Ruderman, "Categorical Bases of Person Memory and Stereotypes," *Journal of Personality and Social Psychology,* 36 (1978), pp. 778–93.
9. Jeffery Z. Rubin, Frank J. Provenzano, and Zella Luria, "The Eye of the Beholder: Parents' Views on Sex of Newborns," *American Journal of Orthopsychiatry,* 44 (1974), pp. 512–19.
10. Harriet L. Rheingold and Kaye V. Cook, "The Contents of Boys' and Girls' Rooms as an Index of Parents' Behavior," *Child Development,* 46 (1975), pp. 459–63.
11. Clyde C. Robinson and James T. Morris, "The Gender-typed Nature of Christmas Toys Received by 36-, 48-, and 60-month-old Children," *Sex Roles,* 15 (1986), pp. 21–32.
12. Lynn K. White and David B. Brinkerhoff, "The Sexual Division of Labor: Evidence from Childhood," *Social Forces,* 60 (September 1981), pp. 170–81.
13. Myra Sadker and David Sadker, "Sexism in the Schoolroom of the '80s," *Psychology Today,* 19 (March 1985), pp. 54–57.
14. Thomas J. Berndt and Kirbey A. Heller, "Gender Stereotypes and Social Inferences," *Journal of Personality and Social Psychology,* 50 (1986), pp. 889–98; D. B. Carter and L. A. McCloskey, "Peers and the Maintenance of Sex-Typed Behavior," *Developmental Psychology,* 18 (1982), pp. 812–14; A. Huston, "Sex Typing," in E. M. Hetherton (ed.), *Handbook*

of Child Psychology: Socialization, Personality and Child Development, (New York: Wiley, 1983), pp. 387–468.
15. *New York Times,* September 17, 1987, pp. 1, 26.
16. Muller v. Oregon, 208 U.S. 412 (1908).
17. See, for example, P. A. Goldberg, "Are Women Prejudiced Against Women?" *Transaction,* 5 (April 1968), pp. 28–30; and G. I. Peterson, S. B. Kiesler, and P. A. Goldberg, "Evaluation of the Performance of Women as a Function of Their Sex, Achievement, and Personal History," *Journal of Personality and Social Psychology,* 19 (1971), pp. 114–18.
18. Marvin Harris, "Male Supremacy Was Just a Phase in the Evolution of Culture," *Psychology Today,* 9 (January 1975), p. 66.
19. Talcott Parsons and Robert F. Bales, *Family, Socialization and Interaction* (Glencoe, IL: Free Press, 1955).
20. Friedrich Engels, *The Essential Works of Marxism* (New York: Bantam, 1965).
21. Ava Barron, "Women and the Making of the American Working Class," *Review of Radical Political Economics,* 14 (1982), pp. 23–42.
22. *Statistical Abstract of the United States, 1988* (Washington, DC: U.S. Department of Commerce, 1988), p. 70.
23. W. Morton and T. Ungs, "Cancer Mortality in the Major Cottage Industry," *Women and Health,* 4 (Winter 1979), pp. 305–54.
24. Walter Gove and Jeanette Tudor, "Adult Sex Roles and Mental Illness," *American Journal of Sociology,* 78 (1973), pp. 812–35; Barbara F. Reskin and Shelly Coverman "Sex and Race in the Determinants of Psychophysical Distress," *Social Forces,* 63 (June 1985), pp. 1038–1059.
25. Daniel Goleman, "Girls and Math: Is Biology Really Destiny?" *New York Times Education Life,* August 27, 1987, pp. 42–43.
26. Lorelei R. Brush, "The Significance of Students' Stereotype of a Mathematician for Their Career Planning," *Personnel and Guidance Journal,* 56 (December 1980), pp. 231–35.
27. N. E. Betz and G. Hackett, "The Relationship of Mathematics Self-efficacy Expectations to the Selection of Science-based College Majors," *Journal of Vocational Behavior,* 23 (1983), pp. 329–45.
28. Sara Kiesler, Lee Sproull, and Jacquelynn E. Eccles, "Second Class Citizens?" *Psychology Today,* 17 (1983), pp. 40–48.
29. L. W. Richardson, *The Dynamics of Sex and Gender* (Boston: Houghton Mifflin, 1981).
30. The earnings gap is well documented in James P. Smith and Michael P. Ward, *Womens' Wages and Work in the Twentieth Century* (Santa Monica, CA: The Rand Corporation, 1985).
31. Rosabeth Kanter, *Men and Women of the Corporation* (New York: Basic Books, 1977).
32. *U.S. News & World Report,* January 26, 1987, p. 12.
33. Ronnie Steinberg, *Comparable Worth: Issue for the '80s* (Washington, DC: U.S. Commission on Civil Rights, 1984), p. 108.
34. See Alvin O. Bellak, *Comparable Worth: Issue for the '80s* (Washington, DC: U.S. Commission on Civil Rights, 1985), p. 75.
35. Janice R. Bellace, "Comparable Worth: Proving Sex-based Wage Discrimination," *Iowa Law Review,* 69 (March 1984), p. 702.
36. *USA Today,* August 11, 1986, p. 5A.
37. *New York Times,* February 12, 1984, p. 34.
38. John F. Zipp and Eric Plutzer, "Gender Differences in Voting for Female Candidates: Evidence from the 1982 Election," *Public Opinion Quarterly,* 49 (1985), pp. 179–97.
39. Donna J. Benson and Gregg E. Thomson, "Sexual Harassment at a University Campus," *Social Problems,* 29 (February 1982), pp. 240–50.
40. *New York Times,* September 17, 1987, pp. 1, 26.
41. Antonia Abby and Christian Melby, "The Effects of Nonverbal Cues on Gender Differences in Perceptions of Sexual Intent," *Sex Roles,* 15 (1986), pp. 283–98.
42. David H. Fischer, *Growing Old in America* (New York: Oxford University Press, 1978), pp. 82–86.
43. Donald O. Cowgill and Lewelyn Holmes, *Aging and Modernization* (New York: Appleton-Century-Crofts, 1972).
44. Brian Gratton, "The New History of the Aged: A Critique," in David Van Tassel and Peter N. Stearns (eds.), *Old Age in a Bureaucratic Society* (New York: Greenwood, 1986), pp. 3–29.
45. Phillippe Aries, *Centuries of Childhood* (New York: Vintage, 1962).
46. W. Andrew Achenbaum, *Old Age in the New Land: The American Experience Since 1790* (Baltimore, MD: Johns Hopkins University Press, 1978).
47. Carol Haber, *Beyond Sixty-Five* (Cambridge, England: Cambridge University Press, 1983), p. 80.
48. Thomas Cole, *Past Meridian: Aging and the Northern Middle Class* (Rochester, NY: University of Rochester, Unpublished Ph.D. Dissertation, 1980).
49. See, for example, William Graebner, *A History of Retirement: The Meaning and Function of an American Institution, 1885–1978* (New Haven, CT: Yale University Press, 1980).
50. E. M. Brecher, *Love, Sex, and Aging: A Consumer's Union Report* (Mt. Vernon, NY: Consumer's Union, 1984).
51. *Public Opinion,* 8 (February-March, 1985), p. 35.
52. Johannes T. Pedersen, "Age and Change in Public Opinion," *Public Opinion Quarterly,* 40 (Summer 1976), pp. 143–53.
53. Arthur Weinberger, "Responses to Old People Who Ask for Help," *Research on Aging,* 3 (September 1981), pp. 345–68.
54. Reviews of research on older workers are available in Robert C. Atchley, *The Social Forces in Later Life,* 4th ed. (Belmont, CA: Wadsworth, 1985); Jon Hendricks and C. Davis Hendricks, *Aging in Mass Society,* 3rd ed. (Cambridge, MA: Winthrop, 1986).
55. Wilmington (Delaware) *News-Journal,* September 10, 1987, p. 14B.
56. Nancy R. King, "Exploitation and Abuse of Older Family Members," in J. J. Costa, (ed.), *Abuse of the Elderly* (Lexington, MA: Lexington, 1984), pp. 3–12.
57. Suzanne K. Steinmetz, "Family Violence Towards Elders," in Susan Saunders, Ann Anderson, and Cynthia Hart (eds.), *Violent Individuals and Families* (Springfield, IL: Charles C. Thomas, 1983).
58. *Public Opinion,* 8 (February–March, 1985), p. 33.
59. *USA Today,* May 18, 1987, p. 4A.
60. See, for example, Elizabeth Kubler-Ross, *On Death and Dying* (New York: Macmillan, 1969).
61. See, for example, David E. Bloom, "Women and Work," *American Demographics,* September 1986, pp. 25–30; Brad

Edmondson, "Inside the Empty Nest," *American Demographics,* November 1987, pp. 24–29; Thomas G. Exter and Frederick Barber, "What Men and Women Think," *American Demographics,* August 1987, pp. 35–37, 61–62; David B. Wolfe, "The Ageless Market," *American Demographics,* July 1987, pp. 26–29, 55; *Business Week,* October 6, 1986, pp. 50–54.

62. William Lazer and Eric H. Shaw, "How Older Americans Spend Money," *American Demographics,* September 1987, pp. 36–41.
63. *New York Times,* May 25, 1986, p. 32.
64. See Terry A. Beehr, "The Process of Retirement: A Review and Recommendations for Future Investigation," *Personnel Psychology,* 1986, pp. 31–55.

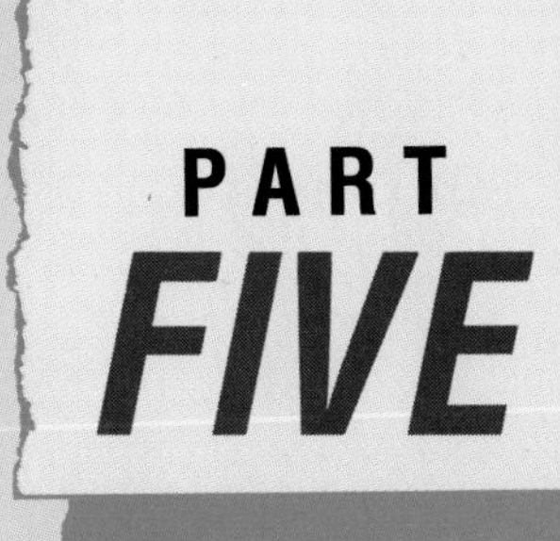

PART FIVE

Social Institutions

The American Family: Myth and Reality

On the evening of October 2, 1949, just four years after the television industry entered the business of prime-time network shows, NBC launched a new comedy series that impacted American thinking in many ways for the next four decades. October 2 marked the first telecast of "The Aldrich Family," a situation comedy about the adventures of teenager Henry Aldrich and his "typical American family." It was a rather forgettable show that quickly fell into obscurity, yet it presented a formula for the family situation comedy that has persisted ever since. In the 1950s "Father Knows Best" and "Life with Father" picked up where "The Aldrich Family" left off. Then came "My Three Sons" and "Leave It to Beaver" in the 1960s, "Eight Is Enough" and "The Brady Bunch" in the 1970s, and perhaps a hundred or so more. During the latter part of the 1980s viewers were introduced to "The Cosby Show," "Growing Pains," and "Family Ties," to name but a few.

The significant aspect of these and other situation comedies is their focus; they focus not on what the family really is, but on what many feel it *ought* to be—what it was thought to be like back in the "good old days" when it was a close-knit social unit firmly tied to the community and to generations past and future. All of these comedies portray the family when it was filled with love and self-sacrifice and represented a united front against life's hardships, when it gave its members a sense of place and personal identity. Even in the situation comedies of the 1980s, the television family often appears to be almost "perfect." It usually consists of two parents and two, three, or maybe four children. At least one of the parents works, typically at a middle-class occupation. Social relations within the family are warm, loving, intimate, and trusting. The parents can always be depended on to be fair and reasonable, so much so that they rarely lose their tempers even when provoked. The children—typically mischievous—are always fundamentally good, needing only firm guidance once in a while. Parents and children have their little difficulties—sibling rivalry, dating problems, irritating neighbors, and unreasonable bosses—but the strength and understanding of the family unit seems always to turn hardship into enthusiasm and perpetual contentment.

Quite clearly, television's "typical American family" has been largely a distorted caricature—a mythical and fictitious view of family organization. The television families that seem to dominate prime-time viewing fail to reflect the realities of today's real families. Alcoholism and drug use are not a part of the life-style, nor are extramarital sexual adventures by either parent. Child abuse, spouse abuse, and incest do not exist. Only once in a while does the specter of divorce emerge, and rarely do family members face the tragedies of fatal auto accidents, suicides, or loss of income.

Perhaps it is escapism and a longing for what many feel the family ought to be like—what it once was—that explains the popularity of television's portrayal of the typical American household. One also might argue that the traditional family is in a process of decay, and that through television the norms and values of past generations are brought back to life. Whatever the explanations, it is impossible to deny that the family is changing. In recent decades, the American family has undergone numerous transformations brought about by a variety of potent social forces. Economic and technological changes have restructured the American work place. The result has been increased geographical mobility and a greater number of families who have severed their ties with past generations and moved to new communities. Rates of divorce and teenage pregnancy have risen, and the number of single-parent households is growing steadily. The influence of changing attitudes and gender roles has increased the number of working mothers and dual-career marriages.

Yet while changes have occurred, has decay really begun? And other questions are of even greater significance. How is the family structured and what are its functions? What kinds of changes is the family undergoing? What is meant when the family is referred to as a primary social institution? Will change enable it to continue as a primary social institution? In what direction is the family going? What does the future hold for the structure and functions of the family?

Perhaps the primary question that must be addressed before pursuing other matters is what *is* the family? In considering this question, one must remember that many contemporary families lack one or more of the key members of television's "ideal" family. Many couples, for example, have deliberately chosen not to have children. As a result of death, divorce, or separation, numerous families are headed by a single individual. If we look beyond the familiar family structures characteristic of contemporary America, we find cultures in which husbands or wives may have several spouses.

Given these differential patterns, any definition of the family must be broad enough to encompass them all, in all societies. Thus, the **family** might be defined as two or more persons related by blood, marriage, adoption, or some other socially recognized arrangement, who live together and share a variety of social and economic responsibilities.

THE FUNCTIONS OF THE FAMILY

Sociologists and anthropologists whose work reflects the functionalist tradition have noted that the family in any society serves a variety of functions—both for individuals and for their society. The most obvious functions include reproduction, regulation of sexual behavior, socialization, economic support, social placement, and emotional support.[1] Quite understandably, the relative emphasis placed on each function is subject to wide variation from one culture to another.

Reproduction

In order for a society to survive and continue, it must replace members that are lost to death or emigration. The family serves as the environment in which such replication usually takes place. Defined roles are established for each parent in terms of child care within the family situation. Many children are born outside of the family context, which generally is considered a social problem when the numbers become significant (see Exhibit 11.1). Anthropologist Bronislaw Malinowski articulated the family's **principle of legitimacy,** that every child should have a legitimate father to act as the child's guardian, protector, and representative in society.[2] In contemporary American society, this principle is still taken seriously (although through adoption the legitimate father is not always the biological father). Children born outside of the family, that is, "out of wedlock," are considered "illegitimate." The stigma traditionally associated with being an "illegitimate child" or an "unwed mother" is beginning to change, however, at least in the United States. In recent years, more middle-class,

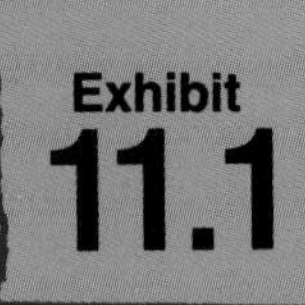

Sociological Focus

Unmarried Mothers

The rates of pregnancy and childbirth among unmarried women have increased dramatically in recent years—from 224,300 out-of-wedlock births in 1960 to over 700,000 each year by the late 1980s. Among girls under age 15, the number has more than quadrupled, with the highest rates to be found among black teenagers (top figure). The explanations for these spiraling rates include the greater sexual freedom that followed the social revolution of the 1960s and a general lack of sex and birth control education aimed at youth.

The birth rate has also increased among older unmarried women, primarily as the result of two factors—the reduced stigma associated with illegitimacy and the greater number of women foregoing marriage but nevertheless wishing to become mothers (bottom figure).

SOURCE: National Center for Health Statistics, 1988.

Pregnancy Profile

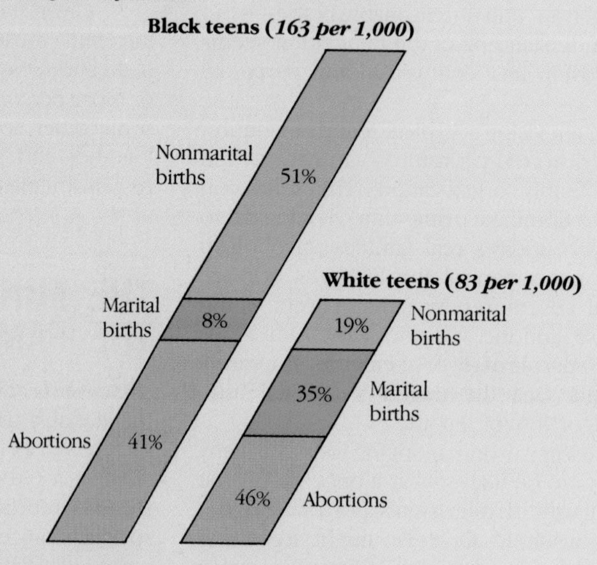

(In thousands)

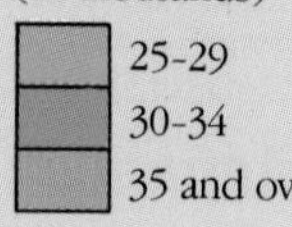

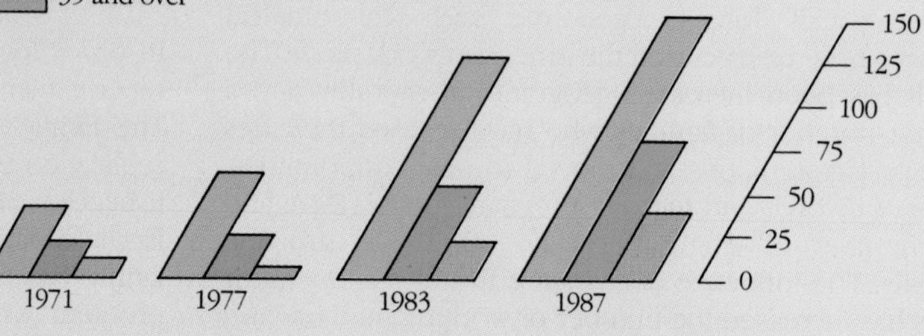

career-oriented, single women are making conscious decisions to have children. Their motivation is usually the desire for children but not marriage, and they do not look upon themselves as deviant.[3]

Sexual Regulation

In purely biological terms, almost any human, except the very young, is capable of engaging in sexual activity with any other. In actual practice, however, every known society regulates sexual contacts between its members in some way, although these patterns vary widely. These regulations typically are enforced within the context of the family. Although sexual intercourse is quite common among unmarried young people, for example, it generally is discouraged by parents as part of their task in raising children. All societies also have an **incest taboo,** a rule that forbids sexual contacts between closely related

Families may be different, but each shapes our sense of who we are and where we belong.

individuals. The determination of which individuals constitute close relatives and are therefore subject to the taboo is a matter of societal definition, but in most cultures the taboo prohibits sex between parents and their children, or between any sibling pair (brothers and sisters).

Socialization

Every new member of every society must be encouraged to master its language, accept its values and the life-styles it favors, and perform the work and other duties it requires. Children are socialized in the family more than anywhere else. It is there that they learn the language, values, norms, folkways and mores, social roles, accepted behaviors, and other important aspects of culture. Although all societies have other agents of socialization—play groups, schools, and the work place—it is the family that serves as the primary mechanism through which children acquire the knowledge and skills needed to engage in adult roles.

Economic Support

Infant human beings, more than any other species, are completely dependent on others for shelter, nourishment, and protection. The family provides the intimate atmosphere and economic entity in which these needs can be met. In many societies, the family also may represent a functioning and cooperative economic unit composed of husband, wife, and all noninfant children. Even today in the United States each member of many small-business and farm families has a role in contributing to the economic support of the whole.[4]

Social Placement

The social placement function of the family occurs at several levels. By simply being born into a family, each individual automatically inherits such attributes as social status (or perhaps caste membership), economic privilege (or disadvantage), and racial or ethnic identity. In addition, children generally assume the legal, religious, and political statuses of their family. Even a number of those statuses that individuals may achieve later in life, such as where and for how long they are educated, what occupation they choose, and whom they marry, are influenced greatly by the family in which they were reared and socialized.

Emotional Support

Beyond these generally agreed upon functions, the family performs in other areas as well. It has an important emotional function. Since people are social animals, the vast majority of whom seek companionship and choose not to live as hermits or cave dwellers, the family provides them with the affection and expressive intimacy necessary for normal emotional development. For infants especially, the family has a *protective function.* Infants have poor physical coordination and are prone to injury if not watched carefully. Before the socialization process can teach infants and children the dangers of such things as sharp objects, speeding automobiles, and fire, the family's protective role must be acutely exercised. And finally, *religious and recreational functions,* through which family bonds and unity can be realized and strengthened, are performed within the family context.

The Family as a Social Institution

The foregoing discussion suggests the family's relationship to both society and culture. In its relationship to society, the family serves as a social institution. Sociologists and other social scientists tend to apply the term **social institution** in a more technical sense than do most people, viewing it as a relatively stable organization of social groups, roles, and norms that exist to deal with fundamental issues in social living. The religious institution regulates peoples' relations to the supernatural; the educational institution is concerned with the transmission of skills and knowledge from one generation to the next; the political institution involves the legitimate use of power in society; the economic institution defines and regulates patterns of production, distribution, and consumption of goods and services; and the justice institution focuses on the management and control of those who violate a society's significant social norms.* Along with these, the family is also a major social institution, responsible for the many functional aspects described earlier.

This designation of the family as a social institution applies to broad social arrangements, not specific families. The family institution does not come into existence with the Joneses next door or the Hernandezes down the street. Rather, it exists more in the abstract, for even after the Jones and Hernandez families die out, the family institution continues.

In its relationship to culture, the family functions as a social unit. Each family is a primary group characterized by face-to-face interaction within which children learn the language, values, and cultural traditions of the family and community. As a primary group and social unit, the family also provides protection, shelter, support, and social placement for its members.

DIMENSIONS OF FAMILY ORGANIZATION

As noted earlier in Chapter 3, a characteristic trait of most members of any society is ethnocentrism—the tendency to judge other peoples, societies, and practices by the values and standards of one's own culture. Because of this ethnocentric inclination, people tend to favor the family structure found in their immediate social world. As a result, not only are other patterns of marriage and family structure and organization repeatedly overlooked, but the assumption also is made that if the familiar forms change too quickly or drastically, the institution of the family as a whole will decay and ultimately collapse. Yet it is important to recognize that historically and cross-culturally, many differences in family and marriage forms exist and the functioning of each is characterized by different norms.

Family Forms

Kinship is a socially recognized link based on ancestry, marriage, or adoption. Thus, kinship involves a cluster of social relations supported by biological ties, as well as the social norms regarding marriage, adoption, and guardianship. Within the general framework of kinship are two main types of family structure. The primary form is the **nuclear family,** composed of a husband, wife, and children, usually living apart from other relatives (see Exhibit 11.2). Nuclear families, the norm for most

*The social institutions of religion, education, politics, economics, and justice are examined in subsequent chapters in this section of the textbook.

Exhibit 11.2 **Sociological Focus**

Patterns of Family Structure

Nuclear Family

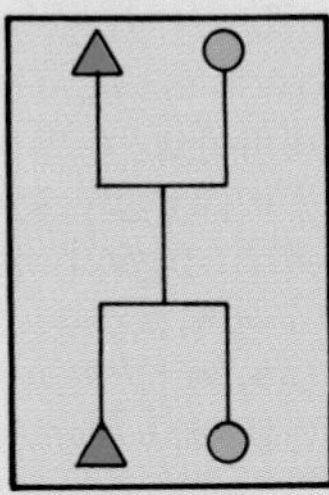

Key:
▲ Male
● Female
⊔ Marriage
⊓ Sibling Tie
| Descent

Nuclear Families Resulting from Polygamy

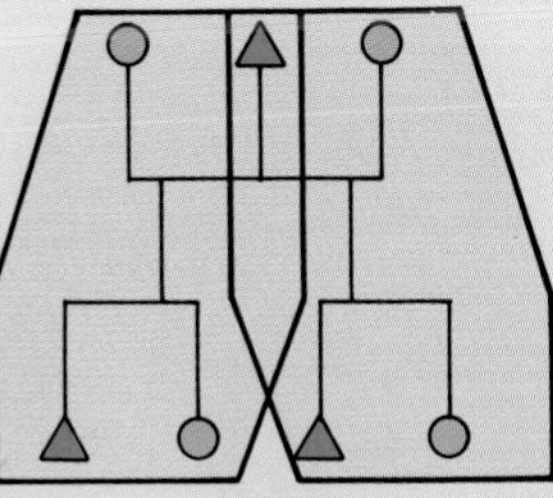

Male with Multiple Wives

(a) Polygyny

Female with Multiple Husbands

(b) Polyandry

Extended Families

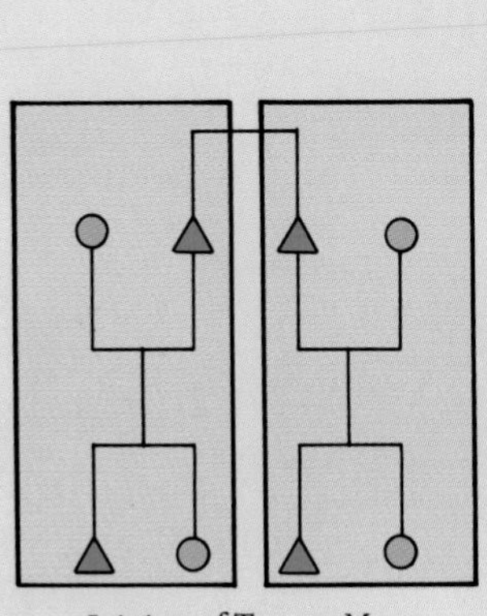

Joining of Two or More Siblings' Families

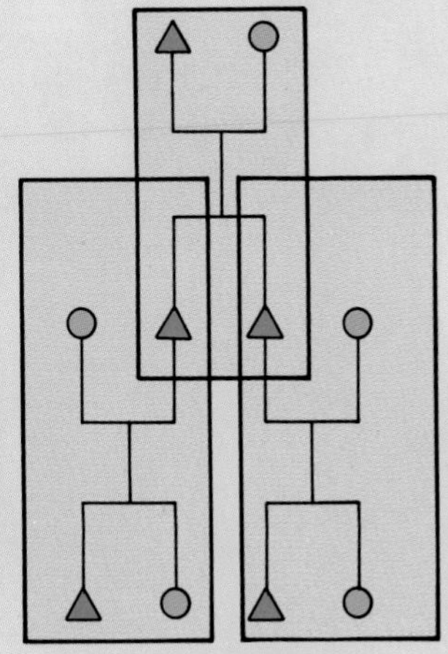

Joining of Three Generations: Parents and the Families of Some of Their Children

Americans, may often be incomplete as a result of the death of one parent, separation and divorce, or the absence of children; second marriages may unite two nuclear families into one unit. They may also be expanded by the presence of a grandparent or unmarried brother or sister living with the family. Regardless of these instances of contraction or expansion, such families are nevertheless nuclear in form.

An **extended family** is created when siblings (and their spouses and children) join together to form a single family, or when three generations (children, parents, and grandparents) live together in the same household. Cross-cultural studies have demonstrated that the nuclear family form is almost universal and the extended family form exists in about one-half of the world's societies.

Most individuals, at some point during their lifetimes, are members of two different but overlapping families. Almost everyone is born into a family composed of self, one or two parents, and perhaps siblings. This grouping is the **family of orientation.** Should an individual eventually marry, he or she leaves the family of orientation to form a new family composed of self, spouse, and perhaps children. This unit is the **family of procreation.**

Marriage Forms

Most Americans think of marriage as a relationship in which two adults of the opposite sex make a personal and legal commitment to live together as husband and wife. Yet both historically and cross-culturally, marriage has taken on many different forms. Hence, **marriage** must be thought of in a broader sense as a socially recognized and institutionalized union between males and females permitting sexual contact and childbirth.

In the majority of industrialized cultures, **monogamy**—the marriage of one man to one woman at a

Family reunions reaffirm the importance of the extended family.

Exhibit 11.3 Types & Stereotypes

"The Most Marryin' Fool"

In the 1983 edition of the *Guiness Book of World Records,* Giovanni Vigliotto is listed as "the most marryin' fool of all time." Over a 33-year span, Vigliotto had a total of 105 wives, all without the benefit of divorce or annulment. He romanced lonely, middle-aged women, married them, acquired control of their assets and, setting a date for a rendezvous in another city, simply faded away. His marrying streak endured for over three decades, primarily because of police apathy in the matter. When his victims went to local law enforcement authorities with a swindling complaint, they were told to hire a lawyer because the matter was essentially a matrimonial dispute. But wife No. 104 brought an end to Vigliotto's adventures. She pursued him vigorously for six months—from Indiana and Arkansas to Texas, Mississippi, and Florida. In February 1983, Vigliotto was convicted of bigamy and fraud, fined $336,000, and sentenced to a 34-year prison term.

SOURCES: *Newsweek,* February 21, 1983, p. 27; *Time,* April 11, 1983, p. 82.

time—is the accepted, "proper," and only legal form of marital union. In fact, the monogamous marriage is the only form that is universally recognized. Even in those societies where other forms of marriage are permitted, monogamy is the predominant type. On the other hand, only a minority of cultures consider it unacceptable to have more than one mate.

Polygamy, marriage to more than one spouse, is present in some three-fourths of the world's societies. Polygamy should not be interpreted as sexual promiscuity among several men and several women. Rather, it matches one man with several women—*polygyny*—or less often, one woman with several men—*polyandry.*

Anthropologist George P. Murdock, whose work at Yale University distinguished him as one of the most respected researchers of family life, sampled 565 societies and found polygamous marriages present in more than 80% of them.[5] The dominant form was polygyny, while polyandry was found to be quite rare, occurring only in Tibet and a few other localities.

In the United States, polygamy was practiced by the Mormans and the Crow Indians, but it was ultimately outlawed by state bigamy and polygamy statutes. Instances of polygamy do occur now and then, nevertheless (see Exhibit 11.3). Yet while some might find the idea of having numerous mates an exciting prospect, at least from a sexual point of view, polygamy presents numerous problems. First is the issue of economics. It costs considerably more to maintain several households than it does to support just one. Second is the issue of demographics. In any given society, men and women are more or less equal in number, and as a matter of simple arithmetic, only a few spouses can have more than one mate. (King Solomon's household of some 1,000 wives suggests that 999 other men in his kingdom may have been doomed to bachelorhood.) Third, the chances of strife and marital discord, numerous enough in a single marriage, can multiply alarmingly in a plural one. Thus, as a result of economic and social pressures, most persons in polygamous societies choose to remain monogamous. Quite common in the United States and other societies, however, is **serial monogamy**—the pattern of having several spouses, one after another. It is

Contemporary humor about divorce often conceals the serious difficulties that may accompany divorce.

"Good evening. I am Martha's son by a previous marriage."

both legal and socially acceptable to have more than one spouse, as long as it is done sequentially and not simultaneously. One need only look at the lives of such celebrities as Elizabeth Taylor, Mickey Rooney, and Zsa Zsa Gabor to understand the extreme to which serial monogamy can be carried.

Monogamy in its strictest sense was the norm in the United States well into the 1960s, with divorce and remarriage often having negative consequences. New York Governor Nelson Rockefeller's attempts to win the Republican presidential nomination in both 1964 and 1968 were unsuccessful largely as a result of his divorce and remarriage a few years earlier. By the 1980s, however, serial monogamy had come to be well accepted, a shift that was clearly apparent in Ronald Reagan's popularity, despite his two marriages.

Mate Selection

Every society has rules governing with whom one can mate, as well as limitations in this regard based on the principles of **exogamy**—the obligation to marry outside the group—and **endogamy**—the obligation to marry within the group. Exogamy usually applies to close relatives in the form of an incest taboo, while endogamy applies chiefly to social groups on the basis of differences in caste, race, ethnicity, religion, and social class. Rules of exogamy and endogamy often coexist. For example, marrying a cousin may be prohibited under the rules of exogamy, while marrying someone of a different race or religion may be viewed with scorn under the rules of endogamy. A principle of endogamy that was enforced by law in numerous jurisdictions in the United States for over two centuries involved **miscegenation**—the interbreeding of what are presumed to be distinctly different races. Laws prohibited marriage and sexual contact between blacks and whites. Although the statutes against intermarriage were enforced, for as long as slavery endured, black women had no rights. As a result, sexual unions with white men in the slave-owning areas were frequent.[6] Although the Commonwealth of Massachusetts repealed its antimiscegenation statute as early as 1843, the law persisted in Virginia into the 1960s. In *Loving v. Virginia,*[7] which was decided in 1967, the United States Supreme Court held that state laws providing punishment for persons who enter into interracial marriages violate both the equal protection and due process clauses of the Fourteenth Amendment. In the *Loving* opinion Chief Justice Earl Warren declared: "Under our Constitution, the freedom to marry or not marry a person of another race resides with the individual and cannot be infringed by the state."

In most Western societies, some sort of *partial endogamy* is practiced with respect to religion and race. Among numerous preindustrial societies, marriage is banned outside of the tribe. The incest taboo, however, seems to be a universal dictum. Historically, incest was forbidden in nearly all circumstances and continues to be throughout the world. The exact reason for this taboo is unknown; it has been the subject of considerable debate, and numerous sociological and psychological interpretations have been offered.[8] Some analysts hold that humans have an innate aversion to incest. Others suggest that the incest rule prevents jealousies within the family. A number of anthropologists maintain that for many societies the incest taboo fostered marriages that facilitated social alliances between kinship groups. And finally, researchers have demonstrated that family inbreeding can produce inherited genetic defects. Despite the taboo, incest is not an unheard of phenomenon. A 1975 survey by the Playboy Foundation reported that 4% of men and women had sexual contact with a sibling; a survey of 796 college students during the late 1970s found that 15% of the women and 10% of the men had experienced incest; and it has been estimated that no less than 50,000 children annually are sexually abused by a parent or guardian.[9]

SOCIAL INDICATOR

Interracial Married Couples in the United States

Year	Couples
1970	555,000
1980	1,135,000
1983	1,274,000
1986	1,473,000

Authority Patterns

Norms governing who makes the important decisions are present in all families and kinship systems. In *patriarchal* societies, men have this power and authority. In *matriarchal* societies, this authority rests with women, particularly the wives and mothers. Most societies are patriarchal, and in Iran, Thailand, and Japan, male dominance is a matter of law.

What is the family authority pattern in the United States? Some would say that it is **egalitarian authority,** a rather rare form cross-culturally in which authority is equally divided between husband and wife. Those who argue that the egalitarian form is the American way point to the fact that when husbands and wives do not make a decision jointly, each takes responsibility for different areas of concern. However, despite the advances made by women in American society in recent years, authority systems here are probably more patriarchal than egalitarian since many men still control the income and other resources of most families.

The Conflict View of the Family

While functionalist theorists have examined the family in terms of reproduction, sexual regulation, socialization, economic support, and social placement, the conflict perspective has focused on the authority patterns in families, both historically and cross-culturally. The conflict perspective emphasizes that groups have diverse interests, that many social arrangements are the result of competition or outright struggle, and that the family evolved as a form of diminution of women by men. As one sociologist explained it:

> In modern societies . . . marriage is a socially enforced contract of sexual property, as indicated by the facts that marriage is usually not legal until sexually consummated, sexual assault [was] not legally rape [until recently], and the major traditional ground for divorce was sexual infidelity. That the basis of sexual property rights is male violence is still demonstrated by the generally acknowledged dispensation of fathers and brothers to kill rapists of their daughters and sisters.[10]

Thus, adherents to the conflict view of the family reason that modern ideas of marriage evolved for the sake of ensuring exclusive rights to female sexuality. This point of view suggests that the historical foundations of sex, marriage, and the family were established during the earliest years of human society, when physical force was the major arbitrator in disputes. Since men were (and still are) generally bigger and physically stronger than women, men could be the aggressors in sexual conquests. Their strength permitted them to impose their will upon women, but they needed to compete with other males who also sought sexual satisfaction. Thus, marriage emerged as a legal and social announcement to other males that a woman was the "sexual property" of her husband. An extension of this position would hold that females born of a marital union were also the property of the father. The incest taboo evolved since husbands viewed sons and brothers as potential sexual rivals.

Although the origins of the family would be difficult to verify historically from a conflict perspective, ample evidence is available in modern societies that male domination is a fact of life in many marriages. "Battered wives" are numerous in American families. The idea of wives and daughters as "property" apparently has been institutionalized in numerous societies. Until 1974 a Texas law defined a husband's shooting and killing of his wife's lover as justifiable homicide if he found them in the act of adultery—a clear reflection of the concept of the wife as *sexual* property. A corresponding law for wives who caught their husbands being unfaithful did not exist. By contrast, the payment of a "bride-price" or "dowry" clearly indicates the idea of daughters as *economic* property (see Exhibit 11.4).

Truk society is an example of a matrilineal and matrilocal system, with descent and residence traced through the female line.

Descent and Inheritance

Three important features of kinship systems are the norms governing descent, succession, and inheritance. (For a summary of these patterns of descent and other aspects of family structure described earlier, see Exhibit 11.5.) The rules of descent regulate the birthright membership of a social group. Descent can be traced through either the father or the mother. Under the patrilineal system, kinship is traced through the male line; a person is assigned at birth to a group of kin related through males only. Thus, all children become members of the husband's family. Family titles are passed on to males *(succession),* and *inheritance* is restricted to male offspring. Under the matrilineal system, the situation is reversed; descent, relationship, succession, and inheritance are traced through the mother and the female line.

Patrilineal and matrilineal systems of descent probably make little sense to persons born into American society. Each of these systems favors one side of the family while ignoring the other, despite the fact that every child is biologically related to both parents. Americans typically adhere to the **bilateral system of descent** wherein kinship lines are traced through both of the parents equally and the sex of a child is not of consequence in determining inheritance. Descent determines little in the United States, other than the designation of a child's surname.

MARRIAGE AND THE FAMILY IN THE UNITED STATES

How are families and marriage patterns in the United States structured? At the most general level, as we have

Exhibit 11.4

Case Study

The Dowry and Bride-burning

In years past, it was quite common for the selection of mates to be guided primarily by social, economic, and political considerations aimed at the establishment of new ties or the consolidation of old ones. It was not unusual for the husband or wife to be pledged in childhood, sometimes in infancy or even before birth. Such practices were tied to the fact that the potential marriage partners were each members of distinct family groups, and their marital bond would widen the overall kinship networks.

Often connected to such social arrangements was the transfer of gifts from one family to another. When property passed from the family of the husband to that of the wife, it was known as the *bride-price;* when the exchange came from the bride's family, the gifts were called the *dowry.* The general idea behind the payment of a bride-price rested on the economic value of women in many primitive societies. Because of the division of labor between the sexes, young girls were useful to their parents, helping in the production of food, clothing, and handicrafts, and the accomplishment of domestic tasks. The loss of such services demanded some compensation. In the case of the dowry, brides in some societies were considered an economic liability for the husband's family. In others, the exchange was almost purely ritual, and its value was typically outweighed by that of the bride-price. Exchanges were carried out publicly and represented an important ceremonial event.

Although bride-price and dowry exchanges persist in numerous contemporary primitive cultures, they have all but disappeared in more modern industrialized societies. One exception is India, where the payment of a dowry to the husband's family is a concomitant to many marriages. Although a 1961 law prohibits dowries in India, they are still quite common, with some affluent Indians paying as much as $40,000 to arrange an early and suitable marriage for their daughters.

The amount of the dowry is usually fixed when the parents arrange their children's marriage. In recent years, however, India's widespread unemployment has combined with the increasingly seductive pull of consumerism to lead more and more grooms and their families to demand additional dowry payments several months after the marriage. When the bride's family is too poor or refuses to pay, the in-laws harass her, sometimes to the point of physical abuse.

Consider, for example, the events that followed the 1980 marriage between Sudha and Lakshman Kumar. At the wedding, Sudha's brothers had paid the Kumar family 23,000 rupees in cash (about $2,300), a wardrobe of new saris and suits, as well as a full array of kitchenware. Two months after the wedding, Lakshman and his mother demanded more—an additional 10,000 rupees, a refrigerator, and a motor scooter. But Sudha's family had no more to give, and harassment failed. On December 1, 1980, Lakshman, his mother, and brother poured five liters of kerosene on Sudha, set her on fire, locked her in the family's enclosed back yard, and watched the blaze from a back window. Sudha, just days from giving birth to her first child, was burned over 70% of her body and died nine hours later.

Bride-burning by in-laws became common in India in the early 1980s. Killing a daughter-in-law paved the way for a second marriage and a second dowry. During 1982 in New Delhi alone, 260 young women were the victims of bride-burning. In one of the few cases to ever reach the courts, the trio responsible for Sudha's death was convicted and sentenced to hang, but they were released by an appeals court several months later on grounds that the evidence against them was inconclusive.

SOURCES: *Miami Herald,* June 6, 1983, pp. 1A, 4A; *Miami Herald,* July 10, 1983, p. 11A; *Philadelphia Inquirer,* November 6, 1983, p. 3D.

seen, the "typical" American family has a number of obvious features. It is *monogamous* and generally *nuclear,* increasingly *egalitarian* in authority, and *bilateral* in descent. Beyond these few generalities, marriage and family patterns become rather complex.

Love and Marriage

Americans believe in "love" as the basis of choosing a marriage partner. The media has socialized them into believing that "love conquers all" and that no rules exist

Exhibit 11.5 Sociological Focus

Summary of Family Structures and Institutional Patterns

Dimension	Form	Description
Family Type	Nuclear	Parents and Children (if any)
	Extended	More than Two Generations
Marriage	Monogamy	One Husband/One Wife
	Polygamy	More than One Spouse
	Polygyny	One Husband/Two or More Wives
	Polyandry	One Wife/Two or More Husbands
Authority	Patriarchal	Male Decision Making
	Matriarchal	Female Decision Making
Descent	Patrilineal	Descent Traced through Males
	Matrilineal	Descent Traced through Females
	Bilateral	Descent Traced through Males/Females

for mate selection. Americans choose their own mates and view romantic love as essential for a successful marriage. But is the process all that clear-cut? Are Americans fully free to choose whomever they wish to marry?

Mate Selection and Homogamy

Marriage statistics suggest that many social and religious constraints foster a pattern of **homogamy,** the tendency of an individual to choose a spouse with a similar background. Although the laws of bigamy and incest are the only rules that formally interfere with the free choice of a mate, Americans most often marry persons of the same racial, religious, ethnic, educational, age, and socioeconomic backgrounds as themselves. One study demonstrated that 93% of Jews marry Jews, 91% of Protestants marry Protestants, and 78% of Catholics marry Catholics.[11] Although the number of interracial marriages has increased during the last two decades, in 1980 only three-tenths of one percent of the nation's 48 million married couples consisted of interracial pairs.[12] Furthermore, most people marry within their own age group. As of 1980, 12% of all married couples involved persons of the same age as their spouse and of the remainder, the median number of years separating partners was less than three.[13] Social norms seem to be so potent in

Most Americans marry someone of the same age, but if they do not, the woman almost always will be younger.

influencing people to marry someone of a similar age that age homogamy is characteristic of both blacks and whites, the rich and the poor, and laborers and professionals.[14] Finally, most Americans choose a mate from the same educational level, the same intelligence level, and the same general height and health.

Is romantic love alone the best basis for a lasting marriage? Perhaps not, given the high divorce rates in the United States. Romantic love is certainly a noble and wonderful ideal, and it has been fully endorsed in Western societies by all aspects of the popular media. When people meet and fall in love, they expect the excitement and romance to last forever despite any differences they have or hardships they may face; they believe that love not only conquers all, but that it is blind as well. In reality, studies suggest that romantic love is an important basis for a successful marriage, but by itself it is not sufficient to insure that a marriage will survive the years of domestic and economic routine. More crucial factors include mutual support, social similarity, respect, trust, maturity, and a compatibility of social values—factors conducive to the optimal development of both partners.[15] Unfortunately, few young couples in love look beyond physical attraction and romance to the more mundane aspects of love that make for a lasting relationship.

SOCIAL INDICATOR

Median Age at First Marriage

1900
1910
1920
1930
1940
1950
1960
1970
1980
1987

20 21 22 23 24 25 26

Men Women

Marriage Rates

The great majority of Americans marry and spend most of their lives in a family group. In fact, the marriage rate in the United States is the highest among the industrialized nations of the world. The **marriage rate** is the number of marriages per 1,000 population, and this figure has fluctuated somewhat throughout this century. As indicated in Exhibit 11.6, the marriage rate reached a high of 12.2 per 1,000 population in 1945, dropped to 8.5 in 1960, and rose to 10.6 in 1985. By 1988 it had dropped back to 9.9. These figures would suggest that marriage has become more popular in recent decades, but the numbers are misleading. Actually, the reverse situation has occurred. More than a third of the marriages included in these data are remarriages. Since 1960, a steady decline has taken place in the number of first marriages. Part of this has to do with the fact that people are slower to marry. From 1950 to 1960, the median ages of first marriage for men and women were 22.8 and 20.3, respectively. By 1987, the median ages for both sexes had increased by three years. In addition, more young adults have chosen to remain single. In 1960, 28% of the women between the ages of 20 and 24 had never been married. By 1980 this figure had risen to 50%, and toward the close of the decade it was up over 60%.

Marital Adjustment

For all newlyweds, the marriage ceremony represents an endorsement of their relationship. It also represents the initiation of a new nuclear family. Unless a couple has lived together prior to marriage, when they do decide to marry, they find themselves suddenly propelled into a situation for which they are rarely prepared. For the first time in their lives they must adjust to a physical and emotional intimacy that lasts 24 hours a day, day after day, week after week, and month after month. It is a rather traumatic transition for most.

Every married couple is faced with the need to work out a satisfactory balance between personal and emotional needs on the one hand, and instrumental needs on the other. On the personal and emotional side they must deal with values and expectations regarding

Exhibit 11.6 Sociological Focus

Marriage Rates in the United States, 1910–1988

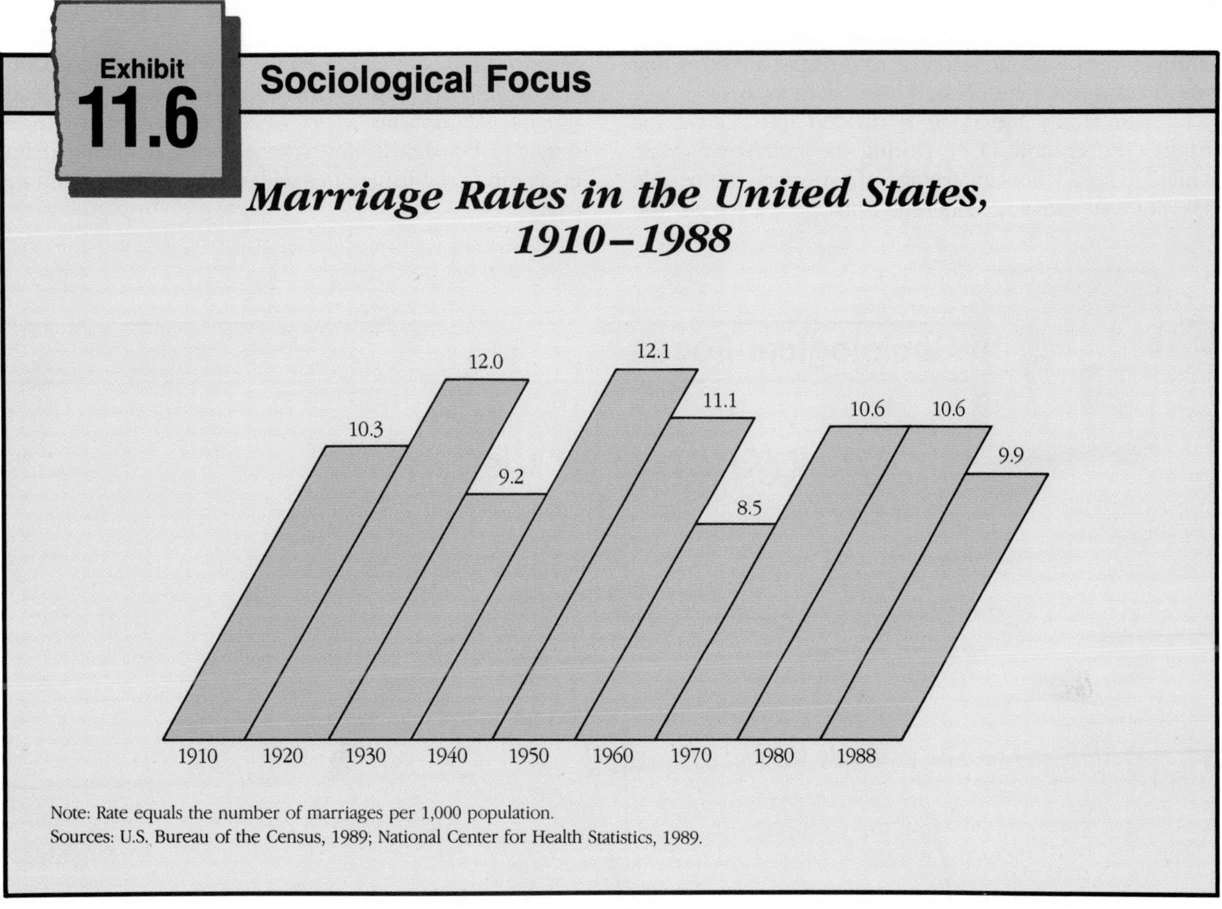

Note: Rate equals the number of marriages per 1,000 population.
Sources: U.S. Bureau of the Census, 1989; National Center for Health Statistics, 1989.

affection, companionship, personal development, and self-expression. On the instrumental side the issues include work and economic security, physical health, and the couple's position in the community. At one time in the majority of marital relationships, the roles and statuses of each spouse were rather clearly defined. Those of the wife focused on socioemotional issues—home, children, and kin; those of the husband dominated instrumental matters—family support and representation in the community. In recent years, however, the boundaries between these statuses and roles have become less clearly defined, and modern couples are faced with the added burden of sorting out each other's respective position in the family.

After they are married and have established a nuclear household (assuming that adjustment was sufficient to let the relationship continue), couples begin to contemplate the question of children. Over 90% of all American couples raise at least one child, and many have two, spaced rather closely together during the first ten years of marriage. The advent of the first child brings profound changes to the couple's life-style and often severe strains. Prior to becoming parents, both partners are usually in the labor force, and they enjoy an active social life, but babies have a way of changing things for new parents. The wife-mother loses a portion of her mobility and freedom, the husband-father is in competition for his wife's attention, and both suffer the loss of her income.

The Family Life Cycle

The establishment of a new nuclear family and the initial adjustments to married life represent but one stage in what has become known as the **family life cycle.** Every couple is unique in many ways. They may not be the same age when they marry; some choose not to have children, although most do; family size tends to vary; and in many cases both spouses will have careers, while in others the wife remains at home with the children. The cycle may, of course, be disrupted by death, divorce, or separation. Yet despite the potentially numerous patterns, research has demonstrated that almost every family undergoes a fairly predictable progression of expansions and contractions during the course of time.[16] Moreover, along with changes in the size and complexity of the family comes a progression of role responsibilities that are thrust upon a couple and later taken away.

The family life cycle is divided into four basic stages (see Exhibit 11.7). During the *newlywed stage,* which generally lasts an average of two years, the couple has not yet had any children. Both spouses have the responsibilities of taking on the new roles of "husband" and "wife," working out the discrepancies between each other's assumptions as to what these respective roles ought to be, developing strategies for resolving differences, and establishing ties with one another's family and friends.

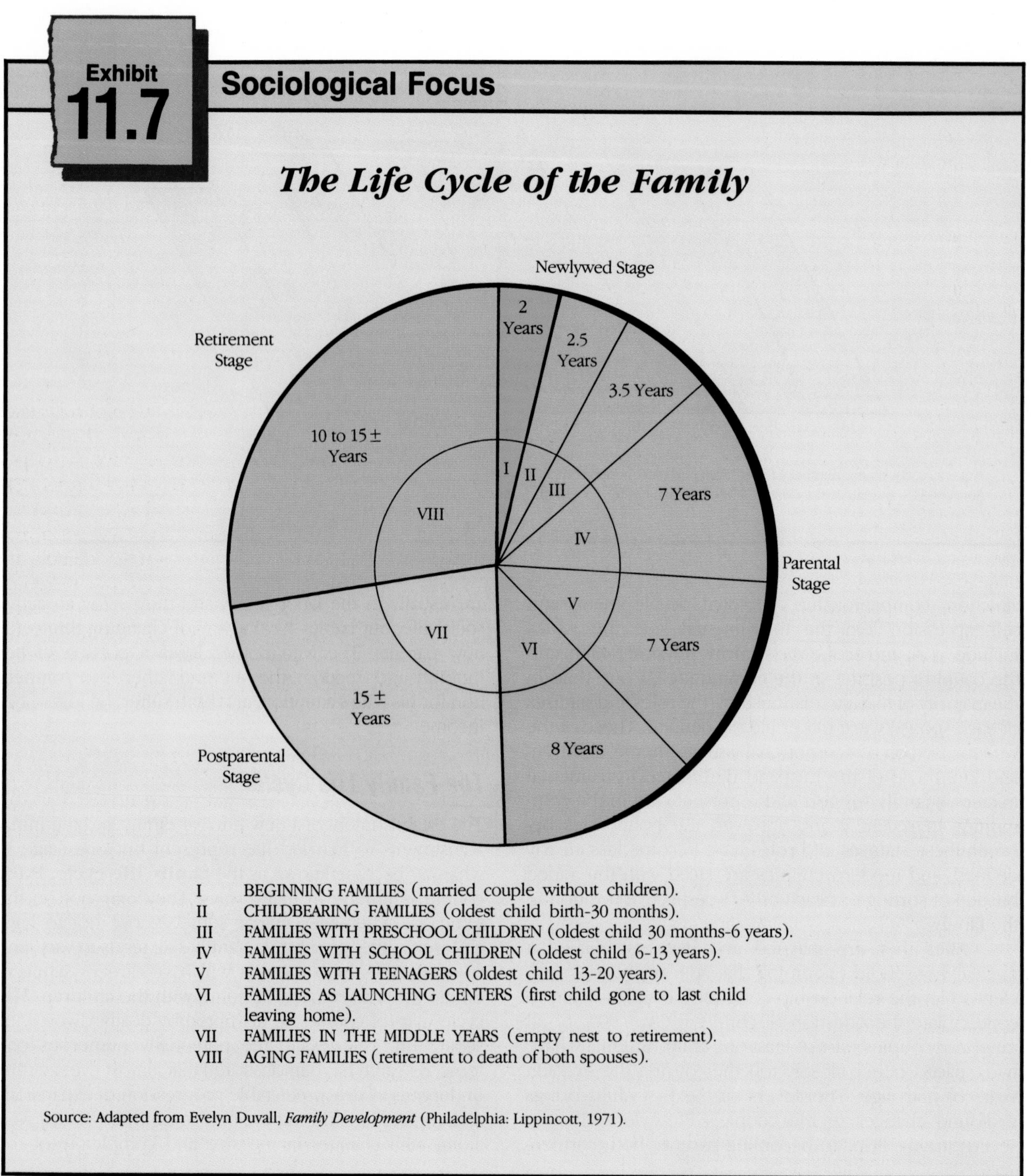

I BEGINNING FAMILIES (married couple without children).
II CHILDBEARING FAMILIES (oldest child birth-30 months).
III FAMILIES WITH PRESCHOOL CHILDREN (oldest child 30 months-6 years).
IV FAMILIES WITH SCHOOL CHILDREN (oldest child 6-13 years).
V FAMILIES WITH TEENAGERS (oldest child 13-20 years).
VI FAMILIES AS LAUNCHING CENTERS (first child gone to last child leaving home).
VII FAMILIES IN THE MIDDLE YEARS (empty nest to retirement).
VIII AGING FAMILIES (retirement to death of both spouses).

Source: Adapted from Evelyn Duvall, *Family Development* (Philadelphia: Lippincott, 1971).

The *parental stage* generally lasts from 22 to 28 years, proceeding through five separate substages: the childbearing years, lasting from the birth of the first child and enduring for two-and-a-half years; the preschool years, enduring until the oldest child reaches age six; the elementary school years, until the oldest child reaches age thirteen; the teenage years, until the oldest child reaches age twenty; and the launching center years, lasting until the youngest child leaves home.

Each segment of the parental stage brings with it a series of abrupt changes and new roles and conflicts. Couples must adjust to their new roles as parents; domestic, recreational, and work commitments must be balanced; and the financial burdens of parenthood must be addressed. As couples progress through each segment of this stage, roles and relationships continue to shift. Preschool children require constant care and attention. If the wife has a career, the matter of child care must be considered. School-age children have emotional, academic, and social needs—homework, PTA meetings, car pools, band practice, difficulties with teachers and peers—that require attention. During the teenage years generational differences in attitudes, values, and interests invariably place stresses on even the most cohesive of family units. And when the children pass into young adulthood and begin to move away from home, roles and responsibilities are altered once more.

After all of the children have moved away and established residences of their own, the *postparental stage* begins. This stage lasts until retirement age and is also characterized by changes. Some of these changes create new problems while others allow new freedoms and a renewed sense of companionship.

Given the factors of longer life expectancy, a compressed childbearing period, and fewer children that characterize contemporary American families, couples whose marriages remain intact generally spend more than 40 years together. Moreover, half of this time is spent with no children in the house. As one observer noted, "This phase of the family cycle is seen by the majority of middle-aged spouses as a time of new freedoms. . . ."[17] In a study of role shifts in the postparental stage, sociologist Marvin B. Sussman found that couples started spending more time with one another and doing more things together.[18] On the other hand, studies also have demonstrated that strong dissatisfactions may emerge during this time. Often referred to as "mid-life crisis," the postparental stage is a time when many men feel that a good bit of their lives has ebbed away with few achievements and satisfactions, and many women, particularly those who remained at home with the children, experience depression and a feeling of uselessness.

The last segment in the family life cycle is the *retirement stage,* which lasts from retirement to the death of both spouses. Once again, a redefinition of roles takes place. At retirement, spouses who made heavy time investments in their occupational roles have the opportunity to reorient their activities and interests. The abruptness of retirement, however, whether mandatory or voluntary, represents the loss of a major social role and function, and often initiates periods of idleness and feelings of depression and lack of self-worth. Moreover, retirement requires a redefinition of household routines and responsibilities, combined with an adjustment to the fact that husband and wife are suddenly spending more hours together each day than they ever did before—even more hours than they spent during the newlywed stage of their marriage.

Differences in male and female life spans mean that many aging widows will form groups that provide emotional support and serve as an outlet for social activity.

After the husband's retirement, 10–15 years remain until the death of the last spouse. Overall, wives outlive their husbands and are forced to cope with the roles associated with widowhood. The man who retires at age 70 has a life expectancy of some 12 years. If his wife is age 65 at the time, her life expectancy is 19 years.[19]

In summation, sociologists differ in their views of the "typical" marriage and family relationship. The *functionalist perspective* suggests that everyone benefits from family life. In return for staying at home to care for the house and the children, the wife receives economic support and social status; in return for the daily routine at work, the husband is cared for and given children to carry on his name. Adherents of the *conflict perspective* argue that the contemporary family is not particularly well-suited to modern economic life. Its very structure oppresses women; the husband is the powerful bourgeois and the wife is the powerless proletariat. The *exchange perspective* holds that every relationship has its costs and rewards. Thus, a marriage can thrive in a spirit of bargaining and exchange. The *interactionist perspective* views marriage as a process of reciprocal interactions wherein each partner affects the other in a cycle of continual adjustment.

Violence in the Family

Conflict is associated with virtually all role adaptations and expectations in the family. Each year in the United States more than eight million men, women, and children are the victims of severe physical attacks at the hands of their spouses, parents, siblings, and children. Even more astonishing is the number of murders that take place that involve family members. As illustrated in Exhibit 11.8, some three thousand persons are intentionally killed each year by a family member—spouses kill one another, parents kill their children, children kill their parents, and brothers and sisters kill each other. Most often, it is wives who are killed by their husbands, but some husbands are murdered by their wives. It would appear, then, that physical violence is not uncommon in American families, and that the family is not necessarily a haven from aggression.

Marital Violence

Spouse abuse is not new. Although it has received considerable attention in the media in recent years, no reason exists that should lead people to believe that the situation was any different in previous generations. Spouses probably always have been pushed, shoved, slapped, bitten, spanked, punched, kicked, knocked down, struck with an object, choked, stabbed—and since the invention of firearms, shot. Studies suggest that 16% of all couples come to blows with each other annually, and more than a third of these violent confrontations are rather severe. Over the course of a marriage the chances are greater than one in four (28%) that a couple will experience an interspousal assault.[20]

The picture that comes to mind almost immediately when one thinks of marital violence is the "battered wife syndrome." Conventional mythology does not seem to allow for "battered husbands." But studies and court

Exhibit 11.8 Sociological Focus

Homicides by Family Members, United States, 1980–1987

	1980	1984	1987
Total Homicides	21,860	16,689	17,859
Family Victim			
Husband	3.6%	3.2%	2.7%
Wife	4.7	5.2	5.2
Mother	.6	.8	.6
Father	.8	1.2	.9
Daughter	.9	1.3	1.3
Son	1.2	1.6	1.7
Brother	1.1	1.3	1.1
Sister	.2	.3	.3
Other	3.0	2.6	2.7
Total Family Homicides	3,519	2,921	2,946
Percentage of All Homicides	16.1%	17.5%	16.5%

Source: FBI, *Uniform Crime Reports,* 1980–1987.

records demonstrate that both partners can be violent. In one survey of physical violence in the American family, 4.9% of the men said they were the victims of abuse and 4.2% of the women admitted to abusing their husbands. In the same study, 4% of the women reported being abused by their husbands and 3.4% of the men acknowledged assaults on their wives.[21] Yet in spite of the reported greater frequency of abuse by wives, it was women who were more often seriously hurt. Some two million wives are abused each year by their husbands, and one in four of these victims are abused while pregnant.[22]

A recent topic in the discussions of "wife abuse" is *marital rape*. According to the laws of most states, there is no such thing as marital rape. As Sir Matthew Hale, the English jurist and Member of Parliament, explained to his peers in the seventeenth century, "A husband cannot be guilty of rape upon his wife for by their mutual matrimonial consent and contract the wife hath given up herself in this kind to her husband, which she cannot retract."[23] This attitude is reflected in the statutes of a number of state jurisdictions. In the West Virginia Criminal Code, for example:

> A person is guilty of sexual assault in the first degree [rape] when he engages in sexual intercourse with another person by forcible compulsion. . . .
>
> "Sexual intercourse" in this article means any act *between persons not married to each other* involving penetration of the female sex organ by the male sex organ. . . .[24]

Thus, legal codes in some jurisdictions reflect certain ideas about women and the relationship between spouses, suggesting that married women are expected to be submissive and have no recourse in the courts. The laws in some states have changed recently, and in 1979 an Oregon woman became the first to charge her husband with rape. (The husband was found not guilty and the couple reconciled their differences but later separated.)

What explains widespread marital violence? This question is as difficult to answer as the question of what causes violence in general. Marital violence seems to be an accepted, pervasive attribute of American life. Whatever the reasons, prevailing attitudes add to the problem. Not too long ago the National Commission on the Causes and Prevention of Violence estimated that between one-fourth and one-fifth of all adult Americans held that it was acceptable for spouses to strike one another under certain circumstances.[25]

Child Abuse

Most people may find it shocking to know that small children are far more likely to be injured by their parents than by anyone else. Physicians not uncommonly find themselves treating children with unexplained fractures, severe bruises, or multiple abrasions. It is difficult to estimate the number of children who are the victims of physical violence at the hands of their parents, but studies suggest that roughly 2 million children are beaten up in any given year. More than 2,000 die as a result of these attacks, and at least 1 million are threatened with a gun or knife.[26]

Many parents hit their children when they will not behave, and they have a legal right to do so. Some people see spanking for the sake of eliciting compliance with a parental rule as child abuse, while others do not. Studies indicate that parental violence against children goes well beyond ordinary physical punishment, however, and is not only extensive but is also a patterned phenomenon in parent-child relations. Mothers are more likely to abuse a child, in large part because they more often have the everyday responsibilities of child care and its attendant frustrations. Sons and young children are the more common victims.[27] Evidence is now fairly conclusive that many abusive parents usually were raised in an atmosphere similar to that they re-create in the rearing of their own children.[28] That is, child-abusing parents were themselves abused as children. It should be emphasized, however, that not all child abusers were abused as children, and not all of those abused as children become abusers themselves later in life.

Although no single instance of a child being abused by a parent can be considered "routine," child abuse, as such, does manifest itself in a number of "typical" forms—hitting, punching, and throwing something at the child. The use of a knife or gun is less common. However, more bizarre episodes arise now and then. In 1983, for example, a prominent Miami attorney and former chief counsel for the U.S. Environmental Protection Agency beat his son with a baseball bat at a school playground because the boy had failed to "hustle" during a local league game.[29] A Camden, New Jersey, woman murdered her four children in 1984 by placing them in a rain-swollen river while they slept.[30]

Other forms of child abuse by parents also have been construed as being in the realm of family violence—parent-child incest, rape, and other sexual abuses; the use of children in pornographic films; and the promotion of child prostitution.[31] Perhaps the most extreme case in this regard came to the attention of the U.S. Attorney General's Task Force on Family Violence in 1983 when a woman from Media, Pennsylvania, testified that from age 2 to 16, she was repeatedly raped and sexually assaulted by her brother, father, and grandfather.[32] And finally, although not "family violence" in the traditional sense of the term, baby selling by parents, a practice incident to illegal adoption procedures, may also be seen as an abusive practice.[33]

Other Forms of Family Violence

The data in Exhibit 11.8 clearly indicate that family violence is not limited to spouse and child abuse. Children commit acts of violence against one another and against their parents. Often, the assault of a parent by a child is in defense of, or in retaliation for, the parent's violent behavior. Such was the case in a Cheyenne, Wyoming, homicide in 1982, when a brother and sister, ages 16 and 17, ambushed their father with a 12-gauge shotgun and a .30-cal. automatic carbine to take revenge for the many severe beatings they had received for what had been only minor infractions.[34]

Many incidents of family violence evolve from the combination of arguments and bad tempers to climax in assault or homicide. One need only remember the 1984 killing of singer Marvin Gaye, the Prince of Motown, who was shot twice by his father during an argument over insurance.

Divorce

It would appear that the American courtship system does not work very well. The reason for this may be that the choice of partners, which is based on romantic love and freedom of choice, encourages young people who fall in love to marry even though they may not be ready for marriage or be well-suited for one another. Or perhaps the problem is rooted elsewhere. Is the human condition compatible with the expectation of a life-long marital union? We do not know if perhaps the difficulty is with marriage itself—with its expectations and with its responsibilities. Whatever the reasons, divorce rates are high in the United States.

The Frequency of Divorce

Divorce was relatively rare in colonial America and remained so until after the Civil War. In 1867 the **divorce rate** was .3 per 1,000 population, and by the year 1900 it had reached .7. Since the turn of the century the rate has increased steadily and by 1981 it had grown to 5.4 per 1,000 population (see Exhibit 11.9). In 1986 the divorce rate slipped to slightly below 5.0, but this figure still meant that a divorce was occurring somewhere in the United States about every 30–40 seconds and that of every 100 couples getting married during 1986 almost half would ultimately separate and divorce.[35] As indicated in Exhibit 11.10, the largest proportion of divorces (9.2%) occur during the third year of marriage,* and half

SOCIAL INDICATOR

Percent of Newly Married Couples Who Will Celebrate the Following Anniversaries:

10th	63%
25th	41
40th	25
50th	13

of all divorces occur before six years of marriage. If a marriage lasts 10 years, statistically it has a 2 to 1 chance of continuing—certainly better than the 50-50 odds a couple has on the day of their wedding.

The Causes of Marital Breakdown

Why do so many marriages end in divorce? Actually, this question is difficult to answer; people have almost as many reasons for divorce as there are divorces. Nevertheless, some general patterns characterize a great many contemporary divorces. First, romantic love fades. It seems that Americans, and the peoples of many other societies as well, are fully socialized to believe that romantic love will last forever. For some it does, but for most the heady joys of romantic love are short-lived; they become lost in the daily routines of housework, fatigue, job pressures, diapers, commuting, doing the laundry, getting the kids to school, PTA meetings, home mortgages, bills, and installment payments. With such a hectic daily routine, the frequency of sex also declines. Or as an elderly Russian-American woman once put it:

> During your first year of marriage, put a bean in a jar every time you and your wife make love. I am sure your jar will begin to fill quickly. Starting with the second year, take a bean out every time the two of you make love. I bet that in all the remaining years of your marriage you'll never empty that jar.[36]

Studies have documented that the frequency of marital sex does indeed diminish with age (and hence, with length of time married). The "average" American married couple has intercourse about three times a week in their twenties and thirties, after which it slowly declines, dropping to about once a week or less past age 50.[37] However, diminished sexual activity or the dulling of "romantic love" should not suggest that a husband and wife no longer love one another. The relationship may have changed, having evolved into something more mature and perhaps very fulfilling. Many Americans, however, have not been socialized to appreciate this change, and given their belief that romantic and passion-

*Note that the 13.5% figure for marriages of 10–14 years duration includes five separate years of marriage.

Exhibit 11.9

Sidelights on American Culture

Divorce Rates in the United States, 1900–1990

Year	Number of Divorces	Rate per 1,000 Population
1900	55,751	0.7
1910	83,045	0.9
1920	170,505	1.6
1930	195,961	1.6
1940	264,000	2.0
1950	385,144	2.6
1960	393,000	2.2
1970	715,000	3.5
1980	1,182,000	5.2
1985	1,187,000	5.0
1987	1,157,000	4.5

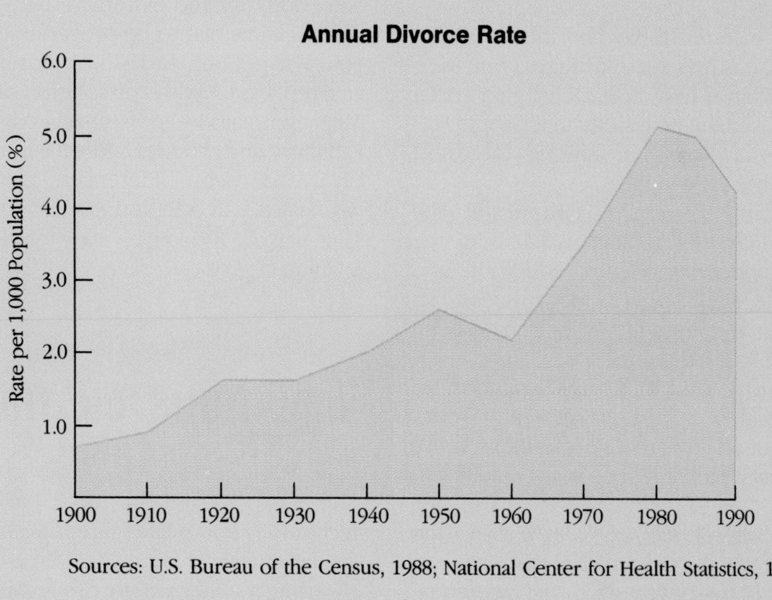

Sources: U.S. Bureau of the Census, 1988; National Center for Health Statistics, 1988.

ate love is the only basis for a successful marriage, they begin looking elsewhere.

Second, a variety of personal factors may lead to divorce. In one study of divorced women in Detroit, the most commonly cited reasons for the breakup were excessive drinking, gambling, infidelity, and nonsupport on the part of the husband, as well as "authority problems" and "personality clashes."[38] In another study of 600 couples applying for divorce, wives complained of verbal and physical abuse by the husband, inadequate financial support, the husband's drinking habits, his neglect of home and children, his lack of love, and

Exhibit 11.10

Sociological Focus

Duration of Marriage at Time of Divorce in the United States

	Percent	Cumulative Percent		Percent	Cumulative Percent
Less than 1 Year	4.4%	4.4%	Seven Years	5.7%	58.2%
One Year	8.1	12.5	Eight Years	4.7	62.9
Two Years	9.0	21.5	Nine Years	4.1	67.0
Three Years	9.2	30.7	10–14 Years	13.5	80.5
Four Years	8.4	39.1	15–19 Years	8.0	88.5
Five Years	7.2	46.3	20–29 Years	8.9	97.2
Six Years	6.2	52.5	30 or More Years	2.8	100.0

Sources: U.S. Bureau of the Census, 1986; National Center for Health Statistics, 1986.

"mental cruelty." The two most common complaints from husbands were sexual incompatibility and in-law troubles.[39]

Third, personal incompatibility and the tarnishing of romantic love place stress on marriages, but such things are not new. What *is* new is that changing social conditions have increased the possibility that people will divorce rather than stay together. Among the most important factors are the following:

■ *Changing Family Functions.* Historically, the traditional nuclear family was a functional unit in the areas of economic productivity, religion, education, and recreation. This is less the case in modern times; thus some of the reasons for keeping a family intact have been removed.

■ *Decline in Moral and Religious Sanctions.* In generations past, the *divorcée* was a "deviant." Today such stigma have all but disappeared. Furthermore, more religions now recognize divorce and do not consider it to be sinful.

■ *Economic Independence for Women.* With the increasing numbers of women entering the labor force in pursuit of occupational careers, fewer women are dependent on their husbands for support, thus lowering a long-standing economic barrier to divorce.

■ *The Changing Role of Women.* In previous generations, the role of the "American wife" was that of cook, housekeeper, and child-rearer. More American women have come to reject this role and may abandon those husbands who insist on perpetuating the idea that "a woman's place is in the home."

■ *More Liberal Divorce Laws.* In past generations, acceptable grounds for divorce in the eyes of the law were adultery and extreme cruelty (mental or physical). These claims had to be proven in court before a divorce could be granted. In 1970, California abolished "divorce" and replaced it with "dissolution of marriage." That state also eliminated the fault-related grounds for divorce (adultery and cruelty) and substituted a no-fault standard of "irreconcilable differences." By the early 1980s, all but two states had adopted similar "no-fault" divorce laws, thus making it relatively easy for almost anyone to obtain a divorce.

VARIATIONS ON THE AMERICAN FAMILY

Shifting social and economic patterns, and advances in technology and health care have had a significant impact on the American family. People are living longer and are choosing a wider variety of life-styles. They are marrying later, divorcing more often, and having fewer children. An increasing number of married mothers are pursuing full-time professional careers, while others are choosing to either delay child rearing or avoid it altogether. And still others have made the voluntary decision never to marry, yet to be mothers nevertheless. In short, marriage, the family, and American couples have changed (see Exhibit 11.11). What do these alternatives mean for the integrity of the nuclear family? How have these profound changes affected the family as a social institution?

Cohabitation

The sexual revolution of the 1960s brought about several notable changes in American life-styles. Not only were people initiating heterosexual activity at a younger age, but greater sexual permissiveness and changing attitudes towards sex brought about a wider acceptance of **cohabitation**—living together out of wedlock. Census figures for 1987 estimated that some 2.3 million cohabiting couples live in the United States, quadruple the 1970 figure. And cohabitation is not a life-style adopted only by young adults; it has become a characteristic pattern among all age categories.

Several reasons have been given for why people choose to live together when not married. Many younger couples see cohabitation as a "trial marriage"—an opportunity to learn whether or not they are compatible before entering into a more binding contract. For others it is a long-term substitute for marriage. Many older couples are forced into cohabitation by the structure of Social Security regulations. An elderly widow receiving her deceased husband's Social Security benefits will find her monthly checks reduced in size if she remarries.

Cohabiting couples live together as a family or quasi-family, yet they generally do not have children. Cohabitation helps to account for the tendency among many to defer marriage. It would appear, however, that it has not emerged as a replacement for marriage in the majority of cases, but is rather, merely a new stage in the premarital sequence.[40]

The Rise of the Singles

In the earlier discussion of love and marriage we pointed out that the median age at first marriage for both men and women has changed over the past few decades. In 1960 the ages for men and women were 22.8 and 20.3 years, respectively. By the latter half of the 1980s men were marrying for the first time at 25.5 years of age and women at 23.3. Exhibit 11.12 demonstrates just how significant that change has been in terms of the number of unmarried adults. In 1960, 28.4% of all women and 53.1% of all men in the 20–24 year-old age cohort were unmarried; by 1987, the proportion of "singles" in the same age group had increased to 60.8% for women and 77.7% for men. Significant changes can also be observed in the other age cohorts.

Thus, large numbers of people are remaining single well into their twenties. One can only speculate as to the reasons for this shift, but some agreement has been reached regarding a number of influential factors. First, many young adults are disillusioned about marriage. As the offspring of marriages that took place in the 1950s—a time when marriage, home, and family were accepted symbols of the "good life"—these individuals witnessed the marital discord and stress experienced by their parents. In their minds the image of marriage may carry a bit of tarnish.[41] Second, for many women the feminist movement defined the traditional marriage as an undesirable exchange. As one observer of marriage trends explained it, "Men no longer had to get married to get sex. Women no longer had to marry to get financial or even social support. . . . The old deal of sex for support has long been a dead letter."[42]

Third, and more important with respect to the feminist movement, women have been encouraged to remain unmarried and pursue their own careers. Fourth, being unmarried today has less stigma associated with it than in years past. A generation ago the single person of marriageable age was a "loser," a "bachelor," a "spinster," an "old maid." In more contemporary American society being "single" carries the connotation of being "independent" and "on the move."

Will all of these singles remain unmarried permanently? Some of them probably will, but the vast majority will not. Studies indicate that most Americans wish to marry, eventually. In terms of absolute numbers marriage still seems to be in style. Although 51,000 fewer marriages took place in 1985 than in 1982 (the first decline since 1975), during the balance of the 1980s some 2.4 million couples were married each year.[43]

For years, research on marriage trends has given attention to the rise of the singles. In 1986, the preliminary findings of one of these studies became an international media event. The study suggested that a "man shortage" existed in the United States and that most career-oriented women were doomed to spending their lives single. As the June 2, 1986 issue of *Newsweek* opened its feature story:

> Her sister had heard about it from a friend who had heard about it on "Phil Donahue" that morning.

SOCIAL INDICATOR

Unmarried Couples in the United States by Age (in thousands)

Age	1979	1980	1986
Under 25	55	411	489
25–44	103	837	1,344
45–64	186	221	277
65 and Over	178	119	110
Total	523	1,569	2,220

Research in Sociology

American Couples in the 1980s

With the increased number of divorces and the many social changes affecting contemporary marital life-styles, University of Washington sociologists Philip Blumstein and Pepper Schwartz decided to initiate an in-depth study of 6,000 American couples to determine if modern relationships were different in some way. With the support of $236,000 in grants from public and private sources, they distributed a 38-page questionnaire that probed a variety of topics from infidelity to grocery shopping. The researchers received responses from 6,071 couples. They conducted individual personal interviews with some 300 additional pairs and did a follow-up eighteen months later with half of their original sample to find out if those couples were still together and why.

Their findings indicated that despite the women's movement, the greater acceptance of alternative life-styles, and the commotion over efforts to establish sexual equality, most American households had remained fairly traditional. Some of the more general findings were that few men believed that they should be the family's sole breadwinner, that women still do most of the housework—whether they hold full-time jobs or not—and that both men and women overwhelmingly believe in monogamy. More specific results included the following:

With Respect to Money

- To men money represents identity and power; to women it represents security and autonomy.
- Couples argue more about the way money is managed than about how much they have, regardless of their income level.
- When partners are disappointed about the amount of money they have, their relationship is less satisfying.
- Married couples fight more about money management than all other couples.
- Cohabiting women use money to achieve equality in their relationships.
- Cohabiting couples do not pool their finances if they doubt the durability of the relationship.
- Among all types of couples, when partners feel they have equal control over how money is spent, the relationship is more tranquil.
- Among married couples, the partner with the larger income rarely exercises greater control over major financial decisions.

With Respect to Sex and Companionship

- The frequency of sexual intercourse tends to decline over the years.
- When the nonsexual parts of couples' lives are going badly, their sex life suffers.
- Equality in sexual initiation and refusal goes with a happier sex life.
- Women, more than men, need to be in love to have sex.
- Most suspicions about infidelity are justified.
- A good sex life is essential to an overall good relationship.
- Couples who regularly attend some kind of religious services are no more monogamous than other couples.
- Heterosexuals who are unfaithful to their partners are as happy with their relationships as are monogamous couples, but they are not as certain that their relationships will last.
- Among young heterosexual couples, men have less desire for their partner's companionship, but this pattern reverses with age.
- Women want more time alone than men.

With Respect to Work

- A considerable difference of opinion exists over whether wives should work. Among couples who disagree, more wives want to work than husbands want them to.
- When husbands do a lot of housework, married couples argue more.
- Few men and women judge their success by comparing it with their partner's success.
- For employed wives, the happier they are with their jobs, the happier they are with their marriages.
- Wives of successful husbands are happier with their marriages, as are the husbands of successful women.

Finally, the researchers concluded that in spite of differences and difficulties:

> The couple is a basic unit of society. . . . When Americans marry, they hope they are making a lifetime commitment. . . . If these attempts at a longterm intimacy fail, the desire to be part of a couple is so strong that most try again.

SOURCE: Philip Blumstein and Pepper Schwartz, *American Couples: Money, Work, and Sex* (New York: William Morrow, 1983).

Sexual Frequency among American Couples

Married

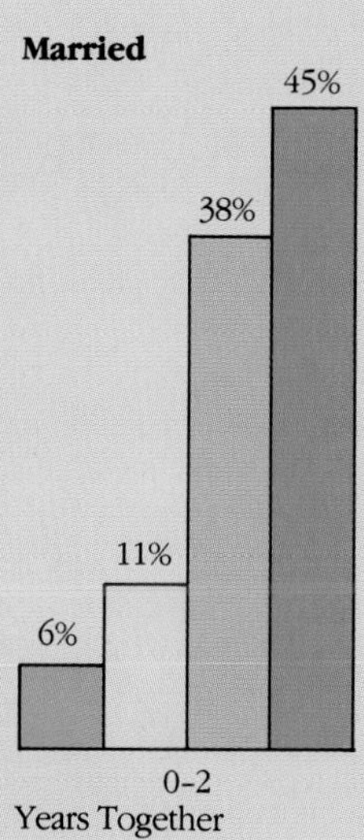

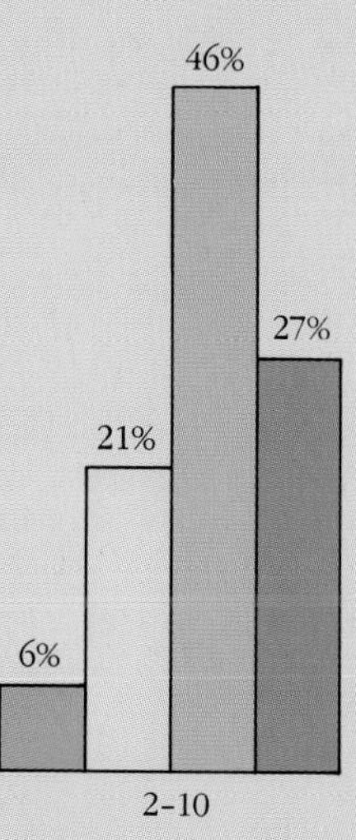

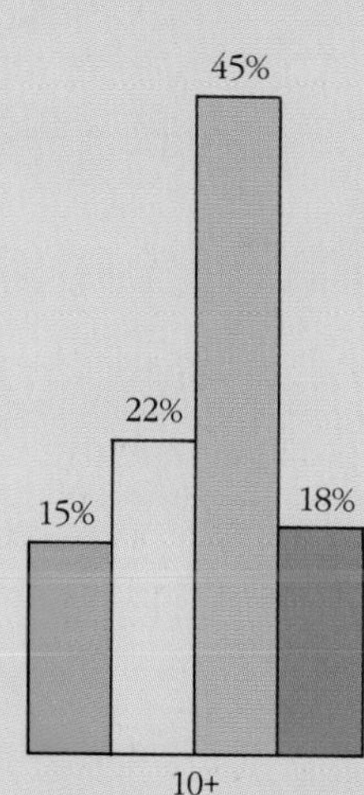

Cohabitors

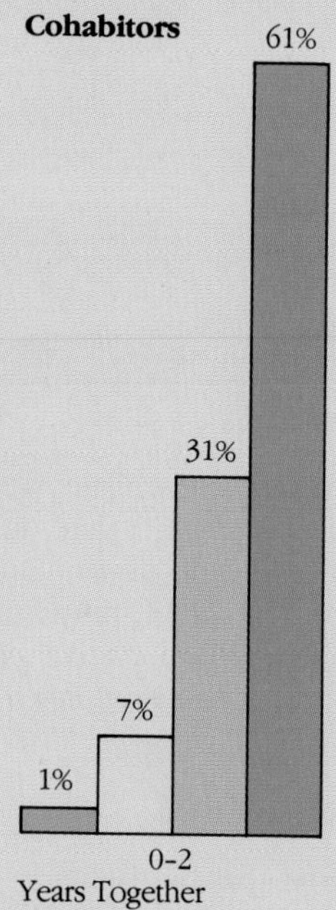

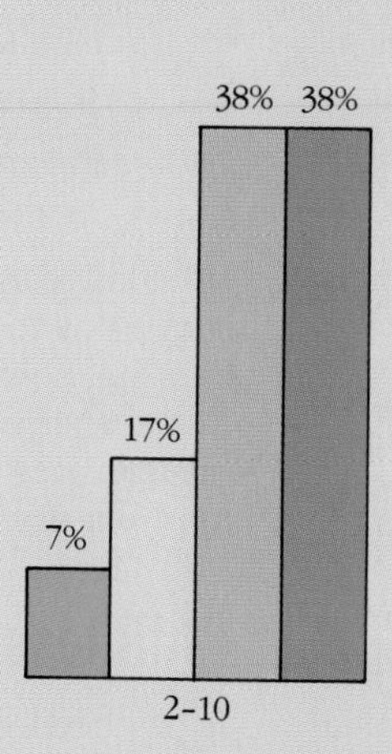

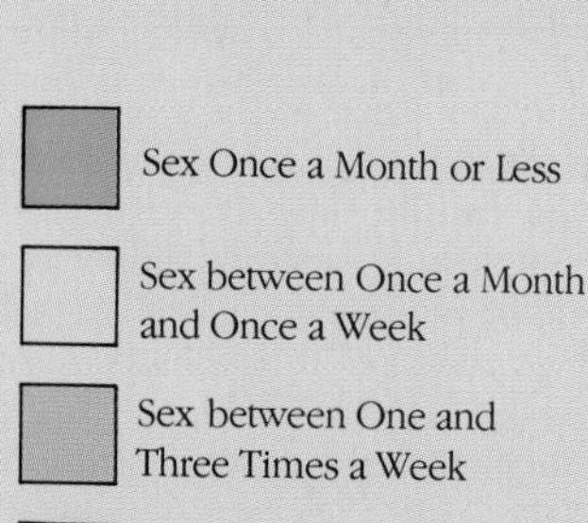

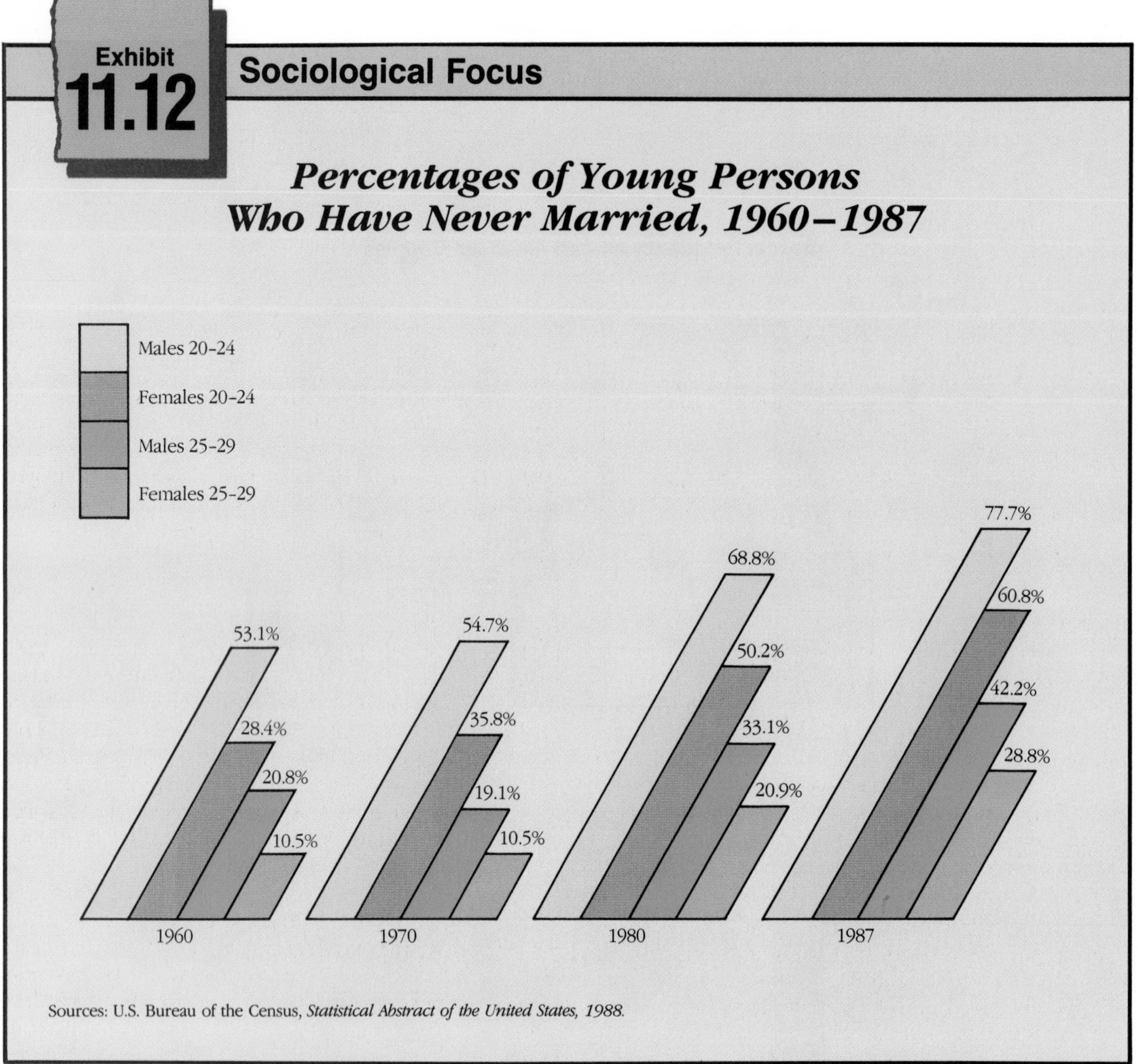

Sources: U.S. Bureau of the Census, *Statistical Abstract of the United States, 1988.*

> Her mother got the bad news via a radio talk show that afternoon. So by the time Harvard graduate Carol Owens, 23, sat down to a family dinner in Boston, the discussion of the man shortage had reached a feverish pitch. With six unmarried daughters, Carol's mother was sounding an alarm. "You've got to get out of the house and meet someone," she insisted. "Now."[44]

The *Newsweek* essay, titled "Too Late for Prince Charming?" went on to note some dismal statistics: white, college-educated women born in the mid-fifties who are still single at 30 have only a 20% chance of marrying; by age 35 the odds drop to 5%; and 40-year-olds with their minuscule 2.6% chance of tying the knot are more likely to be killed by a terrorist. The statistics were indeed grim, suggesting to those women who were delaying marriage that "not now" actually meant "never." But as pointed out in the analysis in Exhibit 11.13, much of the study was misinterpreted. It was not so much that women could not *find,* but that many were choosing *not to do so.*

Childless Households

It has been estimated that by the early 1990s, the total number of childless households will total nearly 59 million, or about two-thirds of all households.[45] Does this mean that the majority of American couples are choosing not to have children?

SOCIAL INDICATOR

Number of Children Women Ages 18–34 Expect To Have

Percentage of Women Citing

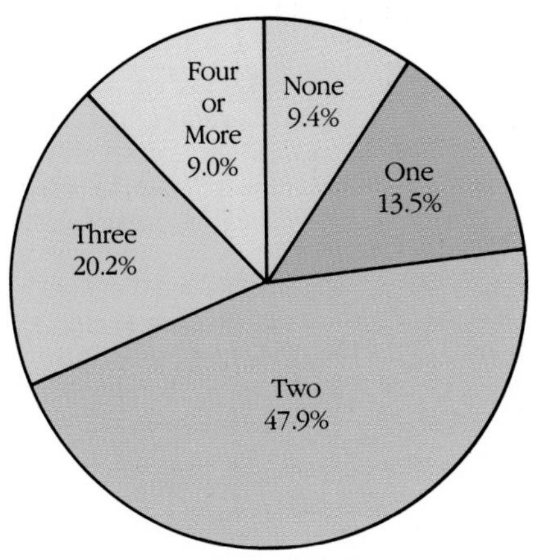

Before answering this question, the definition of what a "household" is requires some clarification to make the two-thirds estimate more meaningful. In U.S. Bureau of the Census terms, there are three types of households: *family households* consist of two or more persons living together who are related by birth or marriage; *nonfamily households* consist of two or more unrelated individuals who share living quarters; and *single-person households* consist of individuals who live alone in their own separate residential units. The 1990s estimate includes all three types of households. Furthermore, the number of childless households is expected to expand dramatically due to increasing life expectancies and hence, a greater number of units containing elderly persons in the postparental and retirement stages of the family life cycle whose children have their own residences.

Nevertheless, there appears to be an increase in voluntarily childless marriages. It is estimated that 5% of all married women choose to remain childless. The decision for those not wanting children has been facilitated by more effective contraceptive methods. In the long view, however, more women are able to have children today than in previous generations. In 1950, 20% of all women were still childless by the time they reached the age of 40.[46] The great majority of these women were childless involuntarily, and their proportions have been reduced over the years by more advanced methods of fertility control.

The few studies that have focused on contemporary women who choose to be childless have concluded that for some wives the whole idea of children is a negative experience; they prefer the exclusive company and companionship of their husbands.[47] This position stands in sharp contrast to the functionalist view of the family and its emphasis on reproduction, socialization, and placement. It also opens to question the alleged "maternal instinct," the belief that *all* women wish to have and care for children.

SOCIAL INDICATOR

Average Number of People in American Households

1950	3.37
1960	3.33
1970	3.14
1980	2.76
1987	2.62

Delaying Parenthood

Growing numbers of couples are postponing child rearing. Since 1970, the number of first births to women ages 25 and older has doubled while first births to women under 25 have declined. The largest increase has been among women in the 30–34 year-old age cohort, whose first births tripled from 42,000 in 1970 to 137,000 by the 1980s. In all, women aged 30 and over accounted for only 4% of first births in 1970, but 11% in the late 1980s.

Studies of this expanding pattern have suggested that at the root of this trend are changes in women's attitudes and expectations resulting from greater educational and employment opportunities.[48] The more education a woman has, the studies maintain, the more likely she is to postpone both marriage and childbearing. Statistics demonstrate that more than twice the number of recent first-time mothers ages 30 and older have completed at least one year of college than have their younger counterparts. Moreover, almost four times the proportion of new mothers in the over-30 group are college graduates and three times the proportion are in the labor force with managerial or professional positions.

Several reasons have been offered for the delayed childbearing among "mature mothers." As Judith Langer, president of a New York–based consumer research firm indicated concerning her own investigations of the phenomenon:

> With the exception of women who had not been able to conceive earlier, all women shared the strong sense of having made a deliberate choice to become mothers. A woman today, they said, has the

Exhibit 11.13 Sociology in the Media

Who's Winding the Matrimonial Clock?

The American public is given little opportunity to read about demographic studies. Media attention is often an elusive commodity for demographic researchers, but in the "publish or perish" academic world in which many research-oriented demographers thrive, the media spotlight can be an important barometer of success.

Once in a blue moon the media seize on a demographic topic and turn it into an *event*. Such was the case with a study of "Marriage Patterns in the United States," by Neil G. Bennett, David E. Bloom, and Patricia H. Craig. In this—as yet unpublished—study, Bennett and Craig, sociologists at Yale University, and Bloom, a Harvard economist, investigated why period marriage rates were declining: Was it a result of women delaying marriage or foregoing it entirely? They concluded that to a surprising extent women were, in fact, foregoing marriage. . . .

The most widely reported of the study's conclusions seemed tailor-made for the media: The study showed that only 20 percent of college-educated women born in the mid-1950s who reach the age of 30 without marrying can expect to marry. . . .

The Media Blitz

The popular media turned [the study's] conclusions into one of those rare stories that permeates the public consciousness. The authors put out no news release on the study. Instead, the story got out last February when a reporter from a Stamford, Connecticut, newspaper phoned Bennett for some help interpreting some marriage statistics. He told her about the new statistics he and his colleagues had come up with, and it made the front page of the *Stamford Advocate*. The Associated Press then picked it up and it spread throughout the country. Thus, what started with an innocuous phone call turned into a *Newsweek* cover story and appearances by the authors on . . . "Donahue" and "Good Morning America.". . .

The *Newsweek* story was what caused the public to sit up and take notice—and prompted millions of women to start worrying. On June 2, 1986, for the first time since the high inflation of the mid-1970s, the weekly magazine used a graph as its cover illustration. This graph showed marriage probabilities for college-educated women.

A grim, underlying message of the *Newsweek* article and others like it is that women have brought on their own marital woes by foregoing marriage when they were young in favor of pursuing a career. Strike while the iron is hot, the story implicitly warned, or risk a lifetime without a husband. This conclusion does not sit well with the study's authors. "You can't talk about this nonmarriage trend looking at women alone," says Bennett. "The fact that they haven't married may be due to men maintaining a sexist position, demanding sacrifices of women that they would never make themselves," such as interrupting a career to raise children. . . .

option to decide if and when she will become a mother. Contraception and abortion give her physical control; reduced social pressure [to conceive early in marriage] gives her greater freedom. Most of the women said they had always wanted children. . . .[49]

Single-parent Families

The high divorce rate and the greater number of women who have chosen to become unmarried mothers have resulted in a sharp rise in the number of one-parent families. The total number of one-parent families increased from 2.2 million in 1960 to almost 8 million in the latter half of the 1980s, representing more than a fourth of all families with children (Exhibit 11.14). This number means that in the early 1980s almost 14 million children in the United States lived with a single parent—20.5% of all children under the age of six—and it has been estimated that half of all children born in the eighties will spend at least a portion of their childhood in a one-parent situation.[50]

The single-parent family has emerged as the most common alternative to the traditional nuclear unit, and in most cases it is an economically disadvantageous option. The majority of single parents are ex-spouses who have retained custody of their minor children. A great many of these are dependent on child support and alimony. Many ex-spouses become delinquent in their payments

As the study points out, women today are less motivated to marry than ever before. The need and desire for economic support prompted women to marry in the past—but that factor has been all but eliminated for career women today. Meanwhile, contraception, legal abortion, and relaxed social taboos on single parenthood have made childbearing a less compelling reason for marriage.

In short, the authors say, women today don't "need" marriage as they once did, though the widespread reaction to the study's conclusions indicates that marriage is an important topic to women today.

The story even made the foreign press, with articles appearing in the *Jakarta Post* and the *South China Morning Post.* Back in the U.S. *People* magazine jumped on the bandwagon with an article in their March 31 issue asking the burning question "Old Maids?" about glamorous, aging, unmarried female celebrities. . . .

Just as the authors didn't expect their study to receive the media hype it did, they did not foresee the extent to which it would be misinterpreted. "My main gripe is that so much of the press has taken the angle that women who aren't married are dejected, unfulfilled human beings," says Bennett. Many of the articles "assume marriage is a measure of success" for women, he asserts.

Unhappily for the authors, this "antiwoman" attitude has been attributed to the study, which the magazines insisted upon referring to as "the Yale-Harvard" study. The result was a media backlash of sorts. A spate of articles about the study appeared in August and September issues of many women's magazines. In general, these articles sought to reassure women that hope for marriage is not lost. . . .

Why Marriage?

Why this study? Certainly many other demographic topics deserve equal, if not more extensive, treatment than the marriage patterns of American women. "As far as other demographic issues go, in no way did this study deserve all the attention it received," says Bennett, adding that other population-related topics, such as the recent study on population and development by the National Academy of Sciences or the world's high rates of infant mortality merit, but do not receive, national media attention. "I am glad that people are discussing the issue and that a demographic, socioeconomic study has come to the fore.". . .

SOURCE: Janine Adams, "Demography as a Media Event: Who's Winding the Matrimonial Clock?" *Population Today* (Washington, DC), September 1986, pp. 3, 8. Reprinted by permission.

because they are either unwilling or unable to fully comply, and enforcement of support orders is a low priority in many jurisdictions. Other single parents are displaced homemakers who have recently entered the labor force without the skills or experience to compete for the higher-paying positions. In either case, the result can be serious emotional and economic hardships.

The U.S. Commission on Civil Rights reported in the early 1980s that children in single-parent families are more likely than other Americans to suffer from malnutrition and shortened life spans, and they often do poorly in school and struggle with behavioral problems.[51] The parents in these families are concentrated in low-paying jobs and are faced with the unrelenting pressures of trying to cope with the needs of both the home and the job, and the children.

Two-career Marriages and Latchkey Children

The two-career marriage began to emerge as a major phenomenon during the decade of the sixties. In 1960, both spouses worked in 40% of all American families. By the 1980s, this figure had increased to 62%, representing 26.3 million couples.[52]

Two-career marriages occur at all points of the socioeconomic spectrum, but they seem to be more

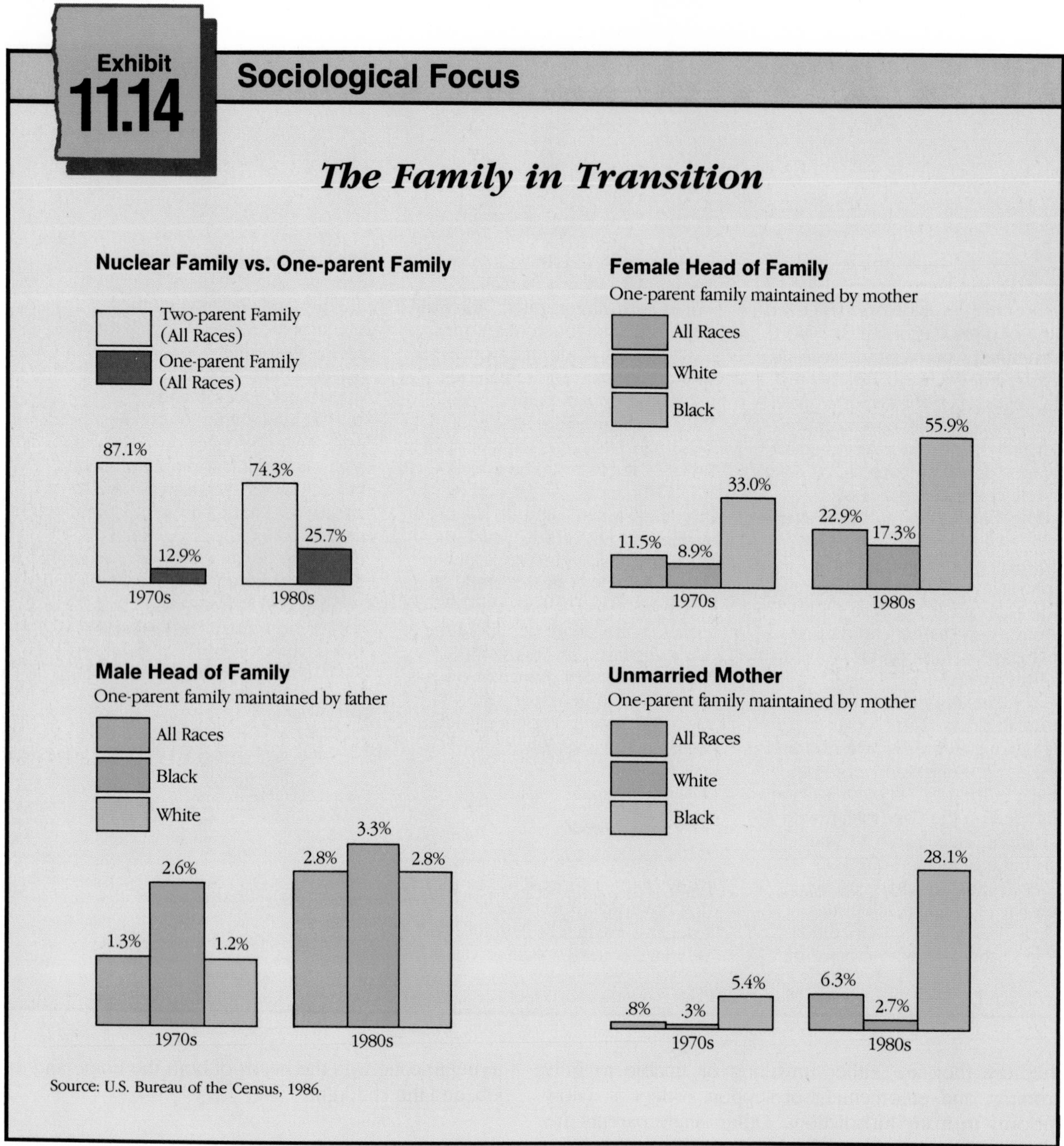

common among middle-class professionals and semi-professionals. Moreover, although in the 1970s women with young children at home were less likely to have an active career, a decade later half of them worked outside the home. Not surprisingly, this change has caused strain and conflict in many marriages. Combining domestic tasks with the daily work routine requires organization, cooperation, and compromise between partners, yet many spouses are unwilling to make the necessary adjustments. The situation becomes even more complicated when the family includes young children. Most working wives, including those in professional positions, seem to feel that mothers have the primary responsibility for child care, and that the burden of the household is theirs as well.[53] Yet many women have been successful in deprogramming themselves in this regard and no longer feel guilty for expecting their husbands to share in domestic responsibilities.

Many single parents have been forced to develop creative ways of reconciling the competing demands of child rearing and working.

The proliferation of two-career marriages and single-parent families in recent years has given rise to what many observers refer to as *the* new social problem of the 1980s and 1990s. In 1987, more than half of all children in both single or dual-parent households had parents who worked outside the home. These parents need adequate day-care arrangements for their children, but organized facilities are not a viable option to all parents, either for financial reasons or because day-care centers are simply not available. Licensing requirements for existing day-care programs are often lax or nonexistent, leaving parents with the worry of whether they must entrust their children to strangers. Even the "good" day-care centers have caused concern. The problem came to national attention in 1984 with revelations of activities at the McMartin Preschool in Manhattan Beach, California. The owner of the school, 76-year-old Virginia McMartin, along with three members of her family and three teachers, were indicted on charges of sexual child abuse. The district attorney in the case contended that over a ten-year period, as many as 125 children, some as

SOCIAL INDICATOR

Children and Working Mothers

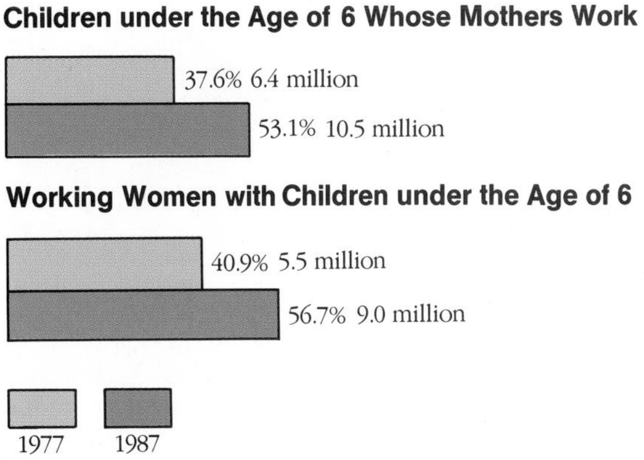

Children under the Age of 6 Whose Mothers Work

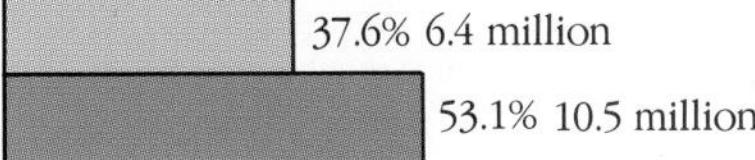

Working Women with Children under the Age of 6

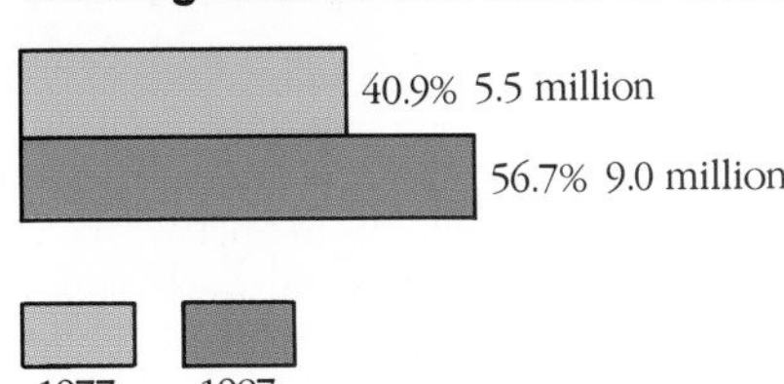

Source: Bureau of Labor Statistics, 1988.

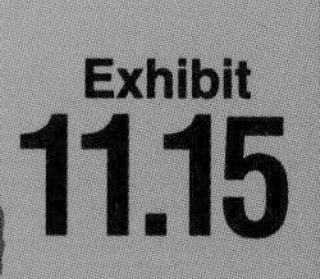

Applied Sociology

The Chances of Divorce

No one can really predict whether a marriage will last. Far too many personal and social factors enter into the decision to divorce to make a fully accurate prediction possible. On the other hand, however, human behavior seems to follow certain patterns. By combining these behavior patterns and statistical trends, one can at least speculate as to what the *chances* of divorce may be.

In 1980, the National Center for Health Statistics completed a study projecting the chances of "marriage dissolution and survivorship" in the United States. Researchers determined how many of the marriages contracted in 1952, 1962, and 1972 had actually ended in divorce by 1977. On the basis of current trends they then projected how many more divorces would occur among the remaining marriages subsequent to 1977. The initial results were as follows:

	1952	**1962**	**1972**
Already Divorced by 1977	28.9%	29.7%	19.6%
Probable Post-1977 Divorces	3.2	10.3	29.6
Total to Be Divorced	**32.1**	**40.0**	**49.2**

Represented graphically, the projections would look something like the graphs below.

The general finding, at least for the marriage years 1952, 1962, and 1972, was the more recent the marriage, the greater the likelihood of divorce. The study then went on to project the outcomes of marriages contracted in 1977, based on the assumption that the existing trends would continue (which they have). The projections suggested that by 1980, 10.8% of all marriages that took place in 1977 would have ended in divorce and by 1982 that percentage would have almost doubled to 19.2%. Extending the projections to the year 2007 and beyond, the percentages came out as shown in the table on page 357. This

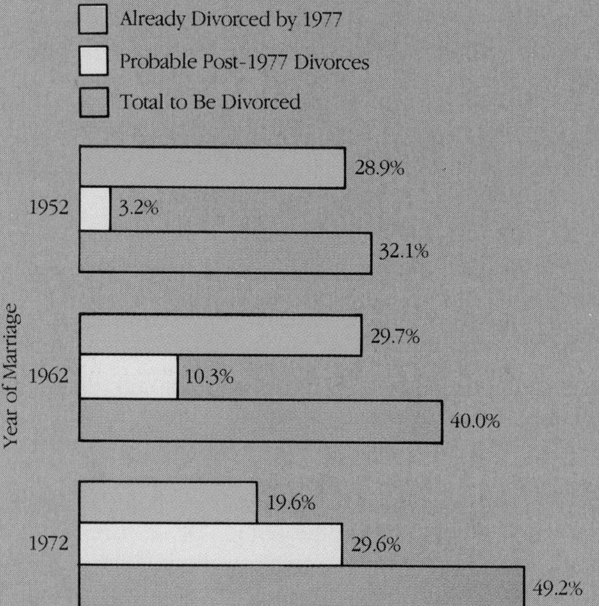

young as age two, had been raped, sodomized, or otherwise sexually abused at the school.[54] Although indictments against the majority of the defendants in the McMartin case were eventually dropped for a lack of evidence,[55] the sensationalism the event generated cast a shroud of suspicion over the child-care industry as a whole.

The alternative to child care for working parents is leaving the children at home alone—a practice that has given rise to the media term "latchkey kids, so-named because when they return home from school each day to empty houses and apartments, they must let themselves in with their own keys and wait alone until their parents return from work."[56] It has been estimated that as many

	Percent Divorced	Cumulative Percent
1977–1982	19.2%	19.2%
1983–1987	13.7	32.9
1988–1992	7.3	40.2
1993–1997	4.2	44.4
1998–2007	4.0	48.4
After 2007	1.2	49.6

information is illustrated graphically in the figure below.

How can these figures be utilized for predicting the chances of divorce? Since they were projected from 1977 data and from the assumption of "continuing trends," can they predict the chances of divorce for marriages in the 1980s? The answer to both questions is yes! Since 1976, the divorce rate per 1,000 population has remained much the same. The rate was 5.0 in 1976, 5.1 in 1977 and 1978, 5.3 in 1979, 5.2 in 1980, and during the latter part of the 1980s it appears to have leveled off at just below 5.0. Since the social changes that drove up the divorce rate in the 1960s and 1970s have become more or less accepted American social patterns (more liberal divorce laws, greater economic independence of women, reduced stigma attached to divorce), the divorce rate will probably not change drastically in either direction in the near future. Thus, it is safe to say that for marriages that take place during the 1980s and early 1990s, almost half of them are likely to end in divorce, and some two-thirds of these divorces will take place before the marriage has endured for ten years. Indeed, the chances of a broken marriage are actually higher than these figures suggest. The projections do not include the many desertions and separations that never result in formal divorce proceedings. If those figures were included, the chances for divorce would be somewhat greater.

Given the factors most commonly present in those marital relationships that do end in dissolution, one can measurably increase their chances of divorce by marrying young, being young and immature, marrying hastily, and being a woman (or marrying one) in the labor force who is not dependent on a spouse for economic support. To almost guarantee a marital breakup, one should add to these factors such items as excessive drinking, drug use, infidelity, spouse abuse, and child neglect.

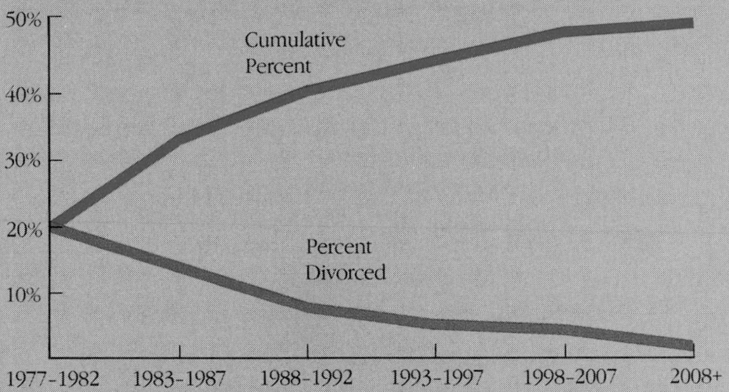

SOURCE: National Center for Health Statistics, *National Estimates of Marriage Dissolution and Survivorship,* Health and Vital Statistics: Series 3, No. 19, November 1980.

as 10 million latchkey children may currently live in the United States, but research findings tend to be inconclusive as to whether or not this phenomenon has a negative impact on children and family functioning.[57]

As a curious historical and linguistic anecdote, children fending for themselves while their parents worked is nothing new in the United States. At the turn of the century, they were known as "door-key children" and often regarded as maladjusted and somehow "different" from other youths. As the decades passed, the term "door-key" child (and its negative connotations) took on a life of its own, becoming *dorky,* or simply *dork* in today's slang usage, meaning someone strange or unusual.[58]

The high costs of child care mean that the children of many lower-income families are "latchkey kids."

THE FUTURE OF THE FAMILY

The history of human evolution, written in the dusty fossils of ancient skulls, jaw bones, and skeletons, fades into obscurity at a point somewhere between three and four million years ago. That is the age of the oldest *homo sapiens* fossil—the skeleton of "Lucy," discovered in 1974 and believed to belong to a member of an early human family. If paleontologists are correct, this finding suggests that the human condition is very old, having survived the geologic, meteorological, and social changes of perhaps 40,000 centuries.

A number of observers of contemporary family life argue that after these many millenia, the family currently is in a state of rapid decay—that the "death" of the family as a social institution may come within the next generation or two. Does cause for such concern really exist? Is it possible that the "family" as we know it may disappear?

Sociologists do not question that the family, and particularly the American family, is in a state of flux. Half of all marriages end in divorce; one-parent families and dual-career marriages have become common; delayed marriage and cohabitation are manifest at all levels of the socioeconomic spectrum; and rates of family violence seem to be on the rise. Family size has also diminished, steadily declining over the past quarter century. In addition to these changes, a variety of alternatives to the traditional nuclear family household have become increasingly more visible. *Gay-parent families* are composed of a homosexual couple and sometimes children from one or both of the partners' prior marriages. In *communes* the task of raising children is shared by all members. *Open marriages* are characterized by sanctioned extramarital relationships and a "do-it-yourself" approach to making family life conform to the needs of the life-style. In *swinging marriages* couples exchange partners for the purpose of periodic extramarital sex. Each partner's career pursuits in *commuter marriages* require that the individuals live in geographically separate locations with only periodic get-togethers.

Various social and economic shifts are indeed affecting family structures. Family composition and patterns are clearly in a state of change. But "change" and "flux" do not necessarily mean "decay" and "death." The institution of the family has endured for hundreds of thousands of years; it has proven itself to be extremely flexible and persistent; it has flourished in all human societies, adapting itself to every new and imaginable condition. In fact, the family appears to be the most indestructible of all social forms. Civilizations have come and gone, governments and nations have risen and fallen,

SOCIAL INDICATOR

Average Number of People Living in a U.S. Household

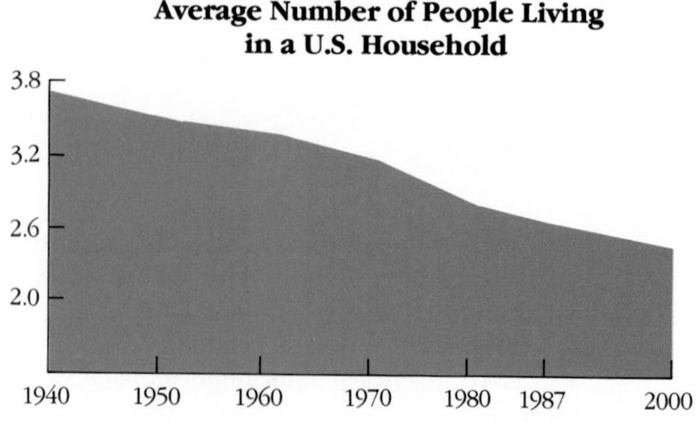

but the family remains. The family of today is undergoing a period of transformation, but the new forms of family structure should not be interpreted as decay. Rather, they are adaptations to those social changes and conditions that served to make "traditional" married life and the "typical" nuclear family unworkable in this evolving postindustrial society.

MARRIAGE, THE FAMILY, AND APPLIED SOCIOLOGY

An understanding of the structure and functions of the family and the changing patterns of marriage and household organization has some very practical applications. Marital and family interactions do not exist in a vacuum. As has been seen, they are very much tied to the wider social order. It is social change that has altered the structure of the family in recent years; it is change that often places marital and family ties in jeopardy.

Studies of the nature of family functioning and the impact of social change on the family lie at the basis of successful *family counseling* programs. Informal marriage and family counseling has probably been tendered for centuries by members of the clergy, physicians, lawyers, teachers, and parents. During the early decades of the twentieth century, however, family counseling emerged as a specialized career, and currently, structured agencies and programs designed to strengthen marital and family ties exist throughout the United States. Counselors serve an important function in offering married couples, parents, and children the opportunity to present difficult problems, to understand the nature and source of those problems, and to make decisions for promoting adjustment.

Related to counseling agencies are marriage and family *enrichment programs.* Started in the 1960s, their purpose is to make marriage better and more rewarding for those couples whose marriages may be in jeopardy, and also for those couples whose relationships are viable but do not seem to be reaching their potential. Studies have demonstrated that the impact of social change on the family has required that modern couples develop new orientations toward marital companionship, intimacy, equity, and interpersonal interaction, and that family enrichment programs can play a positive role in this transformation.[59]

Recent studies by social scientists specializing in family issues have examined the possible connection between the growing number of women in the work force and America's high divorce rates. Research conducted at the State University of New York may have practical applications for reducing the rates of dual-earner divorces.[60] These studies indicated that when the wife works, more conflict develops in the family over the division of household tasks, especially since the husbands of working wives do little more housework than other husbands. Related to this problem was the fact that busy working wives also had less time to spend with their husbands, and low levels of interaction between the two increased the probability of divorce. Most important, among couples in which the husband did a considerable amount of housework, contemplation of divorce was much less likely. A variety of other studies have examined divorce rates, and the findings have demonstrated that people can roughly calculate their chances of divorce (see Exhibit 11.15, pages 356–57).

Research on marriage and the family is also actively pursued in the business sector, specifically to determine how the effects of social change on the family might affect spending habits. A recent effort in this regard found that American consumers are split into two camps—those who have children and those who do not.[61] The most interesting finding was that married couples, regardless of whether or not they have children, spend proportionately the same amount of money relative to their income each year. However, childless couples spend significantly more on household furnishings and equipment, clothing, entertainment, and transportation. In addition, childless couples tend to be more egalitarian when it comes to household chores and all purchasing decisions, and they have considerably less housework and fewer family responsibilities (and hence, more leisure time). The implications of these findings for business suggest that childless couples should be identified and targeted in the development of marketing strategies by manufacturers and retailers of luxury items.

Finally, the government also has a focused interest in family trends, not only for the sake of planning for social programs, but also for other significant, but less obvious reasons. A report in 1986 demonstrated how the family in transition will require special strategies on the part of the Internal Revenue Service (IRS) for many years to come.[62] The greater number of persons living alone or in nonfamily households, the rapid increase of dual-earner families, the expanding number of women in the work force, the declining marriage rate and the high divorce rate will all combine to increase the size and complexity of the tax-return processing workload. More specifically the sheer volume of tax returns being filed will increase as couples divorce and file separately, and as elderly persons continue to work part time and continue to file returns well into old age. The complexity of returns also will increase as couples report dual, but separate, incomes and assets; as divorced parents claim exemptions for children that may not be in their households; and as the greater incomes of working couples increase the tendency to itemize deductions.

SUMMARY

Any definition of the family must be broad enough to encompass all of the many different patterns of family structure in all societies. Thus, the family might be defined as two or more persons related by blood, marriage, adoption, or some other socially recognized arrangement, who live together and share a variety of social and economic responsibilities. The primary family functions include reproduction, sexual regulation, socialization, economic support, social placement, and emotional support.

Families can be nuclear or extended, and marriages can be monogamous or polygamous. Polygamy is permitted in the majority of societies, but for various economic and social reasons, most married people live in monogamous relationships. Marriage and family patterns are guided by norms governing mate selection, authority patterns, and descent and inheritance.

In the United States, marriages are monogamous, most families are nuclear, authority patterns are increasingly egalitarian, and descent and inheritance are bilateral. The belief in romantic love is the guiding factor in most American marriages, but mate selection is also directed by endogamous norms with regard to race, religion, social class, and education. Contemporary divorce rates suggest that romantic love as a basis for marriage has its weaknesses. Personal reasons for divorce have proliferated in recent years, and rates have risen over the decades as a result of changing family functions, a decline in the stigma associated with divorce, the greater economic independence of women, the changing role of women, and more liberal divorce laws.

An increasingly visible problem in the family is violence. Significant rates of murder occur among family members. Marital violence in the forms of "battered wives," "battered husbands," and marital rape affects millions of couples annually. Child abuse by parents, in the form of physical and sexual assault, is estimated to involve over two million children each year.

Shifting social and economic patterns, combined with advances in technology and health care, have had a significant impact on the American family. These changes have brought about an increase in the number of cohabiting couples, single persons of marriageable age who live alone, childless households, single-parent families, and two-career marriages. The family, however, is the most enduring social institution, and while change has put the family into a state of transformation, it appears to be adapting well.

KEY TERMS/CONCEPTS

bilateral system of descent
cohabitation
divorce rate
egalitarian authority
endogamy
exogamy
extended family
family
family life cycle
family of orientation
family of procreation
homogamy
incest taboo
kinship
marriage
marriage rate
miscegenation
monogamy
nuclear family
polygamy
principle of legitimacy
serial monogamy
social institution

DISCUSSION QUESTIONS

1. The family has been defined as two or more persons related by blood, marriage, adoption, or some other socially recognized arrangement, who live together and share a variety of social and economic responsibilities. At the same time the functions of the family have been discussed as including reproduction, sexual regulation, socialization, economic support, and social placement. Would it be more appropriate to define the family in terms of the functions it serves rather than the structure of its organization? Why?
2. How different would the organization of society be if the institution of the family did not exist? In answering this question, think about the functions of the family. In the absence of the family, what other social institutions could fill the gap? Would new social institutions have to be created?
3. In the closing paragraphs of this chapter, a fairly optimistic outlook is presented for the future of the family. But on the basis of the high rates of divorce, widespread family violence, and the increasing number of alternative life-styles and family forms, do you share this hopeful prognosis?
4. Of the new and emerging family and marriage forms discussed in the chapter, do you think that any of them are destructive to the institutions of marriage and the family?

SUGGESTED READINGS

Jessie Bernard, *The Future of Marriage* (New York: Bantam, 1973). A discussion and perspective on current and future changes in marriage and the family.

Philip Blumstein and Pepper Schwartz, *American Couples: Money, Work, and Sex* (New York: William Morrow, 1983). The results of an eight-year survey of over 6,000 American couples focusing on the nature of their relationships and their practices and attitudes regarding money, work, and sex.

Carl N. Degler, *At Odds* (New York: Oxford University Press, 1980). An examination of the American woman and the American family, suggesting that despite various changes in society, women's roles in the family reflect gender inequality in the larger society.

Richard J. Gelles, *Family Violence* (Beverly Hills: Sage, 1979). An overview of family violence and the abuse of children. Data are presented on the prevalence of violence in the family, and particular attention is given to marital rape, violence and pregnancy, and husband abuse.

Melford E. Spiro, "Is the Family Universal?" *American Anthropologist* 56 (October 1954), pp. 839–46. Although more than three decades old, this classic essay describes the nature of the family and communal life in the Israeli kibbutz.

Virginia Tufte and Barbara Myerhoff (eds.), *Changing Images of the Family* (New Haven, CT: Yale University Press, 1979). A collection of essays on the changing nature of the family, including images of the family as it appears in history, the arts, law, and contemporary society.

NOTES

1. Kingsley Davis, *Human Society* (New York: Macmillan, 1949), p. 395; George P. Murdock, *Social Structure* (New York: Macmillan, 1949); William F. Ogburn and Clark Tibbits, "The Family and Its Functions," in President's Research Committee on Social Trends, *Social Trends in the United States* (New York: McGraw-Hill, 1934), pp. 661–708.
2. Bronislaw Malinowski, "Parenthood, the Basis of Social Structure," in V. F. Calverton and Samuel D. Schmalhausen (eds.), *The New Generation* (New York: Macaulay, 1930).
3. *USA Today,* February 21, 1984, p. 3D.
4. Rachel Rosenfeld, "U.S. Farm Women," *Work and Occupations,* 13 (November 1986), pp. 179–202.
5. George P. Murdock, "World Ethnographic Sample," *American Anthropologist,* 59 (August 1957), p. 686.
6. J. C. Furnas, *The Americans: A Social History of the United States, 1587–1914* (New York: G. P. Putnam's Sons, 1969), p. 405.
7. Loving v. Virginia, 388 U.S. 1 (1967).
8. S. K. Weinberg, *Incest Behavior* (New York: Citadel, 1955).
9. William H. Masters, Virginia E. Johnson, and Robert C. Kolodny, *Human Sexuality* (Boston: Little, Brown, 1982), pp. 437–40.
10. Randall Collins, *Conflict Sociology* (New York: Academic Press, 1975), p. 236.
11. R. F. Winch, *The Modern Family* (New York: Holt, Rinehart and Winston, 1971).
12. Andrew Hacker, *U.S.: A Statistical Portrait of the American People* (New York: Viking, 1983), p. 105.
13. Andrew Hacker, *U.S.: A Statistical Portrait.*
14. Gerald R. Leslie, *The Family in Social Context* (New York: Oxford University Press, 1982), pp. 399–422.
15. Carle C. Zimmerman and Lucius F. Cervantes, *Successful American Families* (New York: Pageant, 1960).
16. See Evelyn Duvall, *Family Development* (Philadelphia: Lippincott, 1971).
17. Irwin Deutscher, "Socialization and Postparental Life," in Arnold Rose (ed.), *Human Behavior and Social Process* (Boston: Houghton Mifflin, 1967), p. 516.
18. Marvin Sussman, "Intergenerational Family Relationships and Social Role Changes in Middle Age," *Journal of Gerontology,* 15 (1960), pp. 71–75.
19. United States Department of Commerce, Bureau of the Census, *Statistical Abstract of the United States, 1986* (Washington, DC: U.S. Government Printing Office, 1985), p. 69.
20. Murray A. Straus, Richard J. Gelles, and Suzanne K. Steinmetz, *Behind Closed Doors* (New York: Doubleday, 1980), p. 86.
21. Richard J. Gelles, *Family Violence* (Beverly Hills: Sage, 1979), p. 140.
22. *Justice Assistance News,* February/March 1984, p. 2; Richard J. Gelles, *The Violent Home: A Study of Physical Aggression Between Husbands and Wives* (Beverly Hills: Sage, 1974).
23. Cited in Susan Brownmiller, *Against Our Will: Men, Women and Rape* (New York: Simon and Schuster, 1975), p. 380.
24. *West Virginia Code,* 61–8B–3.
25. Gerald R. Leslie, *The Family in Social Context,* p. 442.
26. Richard J. Gelles, Murray A. Straus, and Suzanne K. Steinmetz, *Violence in the American Family* (Garden City, NY: Doubleday, 1978); *Justice Assistance News,* February/March 1984, p. 2.
27. Richard J. Gelles, *Family Violence,* p. 77.
28. Richard J. Gelles, *Family Violence,* p. 37.
29. *The Miami Herald,* April 25, 1983, p. 3B; April 30, 1983, p. 2B.
30. Wilmington (Delaware) *News-Journal,* February 22, 1984, p. B5.
31. Robert L. Geiser, *Hidden Victims: The Sexual Abuse of Children* (Boston: Beacon, 1979). See also James A. Inciardi, "Little Girls and Sex: A Glimpse at the World of the 'Baby Pro'," *Deviant Behavior,* 5 (1984), pp. 71–78.
32. Wilmington (Delaware) *News-Journal,* December 4, 1983, p. B3.

33. *New York Times,* March 4, 1984, p. 31.
34. *Time,* December 13, 1982, p. 34.
35. *USA Today,* March 24, 1986, p. 1A.
36. Personal communication, June 20, 1975.
37. R. Bell and P. Bell, "Sexual Satisfaction Among Married Women," *Medical Aspects of Human Sexuality,* 6 (1972), pp. 136–44; Philip Blumstein and Pepper Schwartz, *American Couples: Money, Work, and Sex* (New York: William Morrow, 1983), p. 196; Morton Hunt, *Sexual Behavior in the 1970s* (New York: Dell, 1975); Robert J. Levin and Amy Levin, "Sexual Pleasure: The Surprising Preferences of 100,000 Women," *Redbook,* September 1975, pp. 51–58; J. Trussell and C. F. Westoff, "Contraceptive Practice and Trends in Coital Frequency," *Family Planning Perspectives,* 12 (1980), pp. 246–49.
38. William J. Goode, *After Divorce* (New York: Free Press, 1956).
39. George Levinger, "Sources of Marital Dissatisfaction Among Applicants for Divorce," in Paul H. Glasser and Lois N. Glasser (eds.), *Families in Crisis* (New York: Harper & Row, 1970).
40. Andrew Cherlin, *Marriage, Divorce, and Remarriage* (Cambridge: Harvard University Press, 1981).
41. Genevieve Knupfer, Walter Clark, and Robin Room, "The Mental Health of the Unmarried," *American Journal of Psychiatry,* 122 (1966), pp. 841–51.
42. Caroline Bird, "Women Should Stay Single," in Harold Hart (ed.), *Marriage: For and Against* (New York: Hart, 1972), pp. 36, 39.
43. National Center for Health Statistics News Release, 1988.
44. *Newsweek,* June 2, 1986, p. 55.
45. George Masnick and Mary Jo Bane, *The Nation's Families, 1960–1990* (Cambridge: Joint Center for Urban Studies of MIT and Harvard University, 1980).
46. Robert R. Bell, *Marriage and Family Interaction* (Homewood, IL: Dorsey, 1983), p. 405.
47. Christine A. Bachrach, "Childlessness and Social Isolation Among the Elderly," *Journal of Marriage and Family,* August 1980, p. 627; Jean E. Veevers, "The Moral Careers of Voluntary Childless Wives: Notes on the Defense of a Variant World View," *The Family Coordinator,* October 1975, p. 473.
48. See, for example, Judith Langer, "The New Mature Mothers," *American Demographics,* July 1985, pp. 29–31, 50.
49. Judith Langer, "The New Mature Mothers," p. 30.
50. Paul C. Glick and Arthur J. Norton, "Marrying, Divorcing, and Living Together in the U.S. Today," *Population Bulletin,* 32 (Washington, DC: Population Reference Bureau, 1979), p. 5.
51. *U.S. News & World Report,* November 28, 1983, p. 57.
52. *USA Today,* April 2, 1984, p. 1A.
53. Brian F. Pendleton, Margaret M. Poloma, and T. Neal Garland, "Scales for Investigation of the Dual-Career Family," *Journal of Marriage and the Family,* 42 (May 1980), pp. 269–75.
54. *Time,* April 23, 1984, p. 72.
55. *Newsweek,* January 27, 1986, p. 26.
56. *Good Housekeeping,* September 1984, p. 254; *Harper's Bazaar,* December 1983, pp. 222–24, 229; *McCalls,* May 1982, p. 36; *Newsweek,* December 26, 1983, p. 9; *Redbook,* April 1985, pp. 75–77; *Seventeen,* September 1983, pp. 136–38, 172–73.
57. Sandra Scarr, *Mother Care/Other Care* (New York: Basic Books, 1984).
58. Robert L. Chapman, *New Dictionary of American Slang* (New York: Harper & Row, 1986), p. 110; Richard A. Spears, *Slang and Euphemism* (Middle Village, NY: Jonathan David, 1981), p. 111.
59. David Mace and Vera Mace, "Counter-epilogue," in R. W. Libby and R. N. Whitehurst (eds.), *Marriage and Alternatives: Exploring Intimate Relationships* (Glenview, IL: Scott, Foresman, 1977); Herbert A. Otto, "Marriage and Family Enrichment Programs in North America—Report and Analysis," *The Family Coordinator,* 24 (April 1975), pp. 137–42.
60. Glenna Spitze and Scott J. South, "Women's Employment, Time Expenditure, and Divorce," *Journal of Family Issues,* 6 (September 1985), pp. 307–29.
61. *American Demographics,* August 1986, pp. 23–25.
62. Peter A. Morrison and Paola Scommenga, *Demographic Trends Tax the IRS* (Santa Monica: Population Reference Bureau, 1986).

Religion: The Sacred and the Secular

By almost any criteria, the United States can be considered a powerfully religious nation. Surveys suggest that 60% of adult Americans identify themselves as members of some religious group, with four out of ten reporting recent church or synagogue attendance.[1] In addition, almost all Americans (96%) say they pray at least occasionally, with 75% reporting weekly prayer and most believing that their prayers are heard.[2] Finally, a nationwide poll conducted during the mid-eighties found that 43% of the population felt that they had had an unusual or inexplicable spiritual experience—either direct contact with the presence of God, or a profound sense of peace, well-being, or contentment.[3]

The manifestations and symbols of religion are everywhere. In addition to the many houses of worship across the nation, the days of the week and months of the year are named after ancient gods. Years are counted from the presumed date of the birth of Jesus; coins proclaim trust in God; public officials swear fidelity to the Constitution and the American system of government by placing a hand on the Bible; and citizens of the United States pledge allegiance to "one nation, under God. . . ."

Unquestionably, religion plays an important role in American life—at both an individual and a collective level—as it does in most other parts of the world. Religion is deeply imbedded in the cultural traditions of society, shaping attitudes, beliefs, and behavior. It also has the power and potential to divide or unite the members of a community, society, or nation.

Given the place of religion in society, it would appear that it represents a logical and important topic for sociological analysis. However, many individuals perceive an inherent contradiction between religious belief

SOCIAL INDICATOR

Religious Membership in the United States

Religious Body	Membership (in thousands)						Number of Churches, 1985
	1960	1970	1975	1980	1984	1985	
Total	**114,449**	**131,045**	**131,013**	**134,817**	**142,172**	**142,926**	**345,961**
Members as Percent of Population*	64	63	61	59	60	60	—
Average Members per Local Church	359	399	393	401	409	413	—
Buddhist Churches of America	20	100	60	60	100	100	100
Eastern Churches	2,699	3,850	3,696	3,823	4,053	4,026	1,659
Jews (Orthodox, Conservative, and Reformed)	5,367	5,870	6,115	5,920	5,817	5,835	3,416
Old Catholic, Polish national Catholic, and Armenian Churches	590	848	846	924	1,024	1,024	428
The Roman Catholic Church	42,105	48,215	48,882	50,450	52,286	52,655	24,251
Protestants†	} 63,669	71,713	71,043	73,479	78,702	79,096	314,983
Miscellaneous‡		449	372	161	190	191	1,124

Source: U.S. Bureau of the Census, 1988.
*Based on Bureau of the Census estimated total population as of July 1. †Includes nonprotestant bodies such as "Latter-day Saints" and "Jehovah's Witnesses." ‡Includes non-Christian bodies such as "Spiritualists," "Ethical Culture Movement," and "Unitarian-Universalists."

and practice on the one hand, and the professed goals of social science on the other. Critics argue that religious beliefs are not, and indeed cannot be, confirmed or denied by the logic and method of science. And although this conclusion is correct, it totally misses the point of the sociology of religion. The goal is not to test the *validity* of religious doctrines, but rather to investigate the place of religion in society. Thus, for our purposes no inconsistencies really exist between the goals of religion and social science.

RELIGION: THE SACRED AND THE PROFANE

Feeling the presence of God is not an everyday event, nor is having prayers answered, or carrying a "good luck" charm to class on the day of an exam. All involve uncommon situations. Central to any understanding of religion is the observation made by the French sociologist Emile Durkheim, that people divide the world into two categories, the *sacred* and the *profane*.[4] In addition to its definitional association with irreverence and desecration, **profane** also refers to the common, ordinary, everyday elements of human life, those that are easily explained and understood. The more modern term for Durkheim's "profane" is **secular**—not concerned with religion or under the control of a church. By contrast, the **sacred** are the uncommon or extraordinary dimensions of social life, things that transcend the physical world in which people live, inspiring awe and respect.

Sacredness involves a special feeling or meaning. Many parts of the physical environment are considered sacred—specific places, foods, drinks, buildings, and objects. The special meanings lie not in the objects themselves, but in the way people perceive the objects. Wine used by Catholic priests when they celebrate the Mass, for example, is not quite the same beverage as that consumed at a restaurant or local tavern, even though it may have originated in the very same vineyard. Similarly, the sacred cow of the Hindu is no ordinary cow, even though it is physically indistinguishable from cows in other places.

Going beyond physical objects, special meanings are attached to other things as well. Many ideas that cannot be explained scientifically, for example, are considered sacred. The sentiment that Jesus Christ is the Messiah is a special kind of belief—certainly different from the conviction that Babe Ruth or Ted Williams was the greatest major league baseball player. Behavior also can be sacred. The acts of kneeling at an altar or praying before Jerusalem's Western Wall have a different significance than standing for the singing of a national anthem.

What makes the Mass, sacramental wine, cows, Christ, and the Western Wall "sacred" is the fact that people associate them with supernatural power. Religious statues are considered sacred because they are

The same objects may be viewed as sacred or secular in different religions. Cows are merely a source of food in many parts of the world, but have religious meaning for the Hindu.

symbols of the supernatural; Jerusalem and Mecca are viewed as sacred and holy cities because they are associated with supernatural personages; and hymns and prayers are regarded as sacred because they represent ways of communicating with supernatural beings.

Defining Religion

At the heart of understanding the role of religion in society is developing a useful definition of the term, one that is not only precise but that also acknowledges religions of many diverse types. Thus, sociologists identify **religion** as a system of *shared beliefs* and *standardized practices* relating to *supernatural forces* or *beings* that cannot be explained rationally but nevertheless give meaning to life by illuminating complex human questions. Each of these three dimensions of religion is important and requires focused explanation.

Shared Beliefs

Every religion includes beliefs about the nature of the world and the place of people in it. Complex modern religions have formalized these beliefs into "doctrines" or "creeds," which are contained in special books such as the Bible, the Talmud, or the Koran. Religions also may have oral traditions that are passed down from one generation to the next. Yet regardless of the medium, religious beliefs focus on the unknown and unpredictable dimensions of human life—its origins, the possibility of a "life" after physical death, and supernatural beings. The Hindu belief system, for example, is organized around the idea that the soul is eternal, undergoing a continuous process of rebirth. Every action influences the future of the soul. By living a good life and doing good works, people can anticipate a better incarnation (rebirth), perhaps even as a god. The ideal is to achieve spiritual perfection, a point where the soul permanently attains a new level of existence, in full harmony with the universe.

Standardized Practices

Members of religions regularly participate in social **rituals**—carefully designated patterns of behavior involving the sacred and supernatural—such as praying, singing sacred songs, preparing offerings, or making pilgrimages or sacrifices. Sociological analysis has suggested that rituals can be grouped into three basic types: prayer, magic, and ceremonies.

SOCIAL INDICATOR

Estimated Religious Population of the World

Religion	North America*	South America	Europe†	Asia‡	Africa	Oceania‖	Totals
Total Christian	262,870,400	195,431,000	329,380,000	106,230,000	149,200,200	18,600,000	1,061,711,600
Roman Catholic	143,850,000	185,100,200	177,140,200	58,100,200	59,700,000	5,100,200	628,990,900
Eastern Orthodox	5,320,400	330,400	43,430,300	2,800,000	6,700,200	370,000	58,951,100
Protestant**	113,700,000	10,000,400	108,809,500	45,329,800	82,800,100	13,129,800	373,769,600
Jewish	7,630,000	720,200	3,800,100	4,480,200	227,500	74,000	16,932,000
Moslem††	1,820,000	390,100	20,400,000	381,700,800	150,300,000	89,000	554,700,200
Zoroastrian	2,700	2,600	14,000	230,000	1,500	—	250,800
Shinto	48,000	—	—	32,000,000	—	—	32,048,000
Taoist	30,000	11,000	12,000	20,000,000	—	3,000	20,056,000
Confucian	100,000	56,000	410,000	150,400,000	—	18,000	150,984,000
Buddhist	350,200	248,000	210,000	246,740,300	15,000	24,000	247,587,500
Hindu	380,000	615,200	390,000	461,300,000	800,000	325,000	463,815,200
Totals	273,231,600	197,474,100	354,616,100	1,403,081,300	300,544,200	19,138,000	2,548,085,200
Population‡‡	400,802,000	268,825,000	775,310,000	2,819,081,000	553,210,000	24,820,000	4,842,048,000

Source: *Statistical Abstract of the United States, 1989.*

*Includes Central America and West Indies. †Includes communist countries where it is difficult to determine religious affiliation. ‡Includes areas in which persons have traditionally enrolled in several religions, as well as China, with an official communist establishment. ‖Includes Australia, New Zealand, and islands of the South Pacific. **Protestant figures outside Europe usually include "full members" (adults) rather than all baptized persons and are not comparable to those of ethnic religions or churches counting all adherents. ††According to the Islamic Center, Washington, DC, there are 1 billion Moslems worldwide. ‡‡United Nations data, midyear 1985.

Prayer **Prayer,** a form of communication with supernatural beings for the purpose of requesting their aid, is a part of almost every religion. As a ritual, praying involves a number of ceremonial formalities, particularly in terms of posture—a bowed head, kneeling, clasped hands, or upraised arms. Frequently, praying is appropriate only in certain places such as a temple or other formal house of worship. Prayers also may require a specific sequence of words, with no others permitted.

Although prayer is common in the home, places of worship, and even some public places, it has been quite controversial in a few locations, particularly the public-school classroom. The debate over school prayer has its roots in the establishment clause of the First Amendment of the Constitution of the United States, which prohibits Congress from making any law "respecting an establishment of religion." The U.S. Supreme Court has interpreted this statement to mean that the government is not only forbidden to designate a national church but also to support directly one or all religions in any way. Religious exercises, even prayer, in tax-supported schools have been viewed as a violation of the establishment clause because when they are *denominational,* they favor one religion over another; when they are *nondenominational,* they favor all religions over nonreligious beliefs.

For almost two centuries after the framing of the Constitution, prayer recitations, Bible readings, and religious instruction were found in many public schools throughout the United States. Yet the Supreme Court was silent about school prayer and the establishment clause. This situation started to change in the 1960s when a series of court cases began to challenge traditional practice. A leading case in this regard was *Engle v. Vitale* in 1962,[5] a response to a New York State Board of Regents recommendation that school districts adopt a specified nondenominational prayer to be recited voluntarily at the beginning of each school day. When the school board of

SOCIAL INDICATOR

Socioeconomic Status and Frequency of Prayer

Frequency of Prayer	Socioeconomic Status: Upper Class	Middle Class	Working Class	Lower Class
Several Times a Day	22.6%	24.5%	27.2%	35.4%
Once a Day	29.6	29.2	29.3	30.8
Several Times a Week	14.5	14.3	13.9	9.4
Once a Week	29.5	29.9	27.4	22.6
Less than Once a Week or Never	3.8	2.1	2.2	1.8

Source: NORC General Social Surveys, 1984. Reprinted by permission.

New Hyde Park, New York, adopted the prayer, the parents of ten students, with the support of the American Civil Liberties Union, brought the case to court. Ultimately, the Supreme Court ruled that the prayer was "wholly inconsistent with the Establishment Clause." The following year, the High Court affirmed its "school prayer" decision, declaring unconstitutional the practice of daily Bible readings in public-school classrooms.[6]

Reactions to the Supreme Court's rulings on school prayer have been significant. Almost immediately after the Court's decision in *Engle v. Vitale,* North Carolina Senator Sam Ervin was quoted as saying, "The Supreme Court has made God unconstitutional."[7] In the years since 1962 congressional proposals have been made for a constitutional amendment allowing school prayer and thus abolishing the Supreme Court rulings. Yet even with the full support of President Reagan during the 1980s, the school-prayer amendment never accumulated overwhelming support, perhaps a reflection of the fact that most Americans favor church-state separation.[8]

In 1985, while the hopes for a constitutional amendment continued to languish, another school prayer challenge reached the Supreme Court. The issue was an Alabama law—with similar statutes in 16 other states at the time—that allowed moments of silence "for meditation or voluntary prayer." Not unexpectedly, the High Court struck down the moment-of-silence practice. Justice Stevens commented on the ruling: "The state intended to characterize prayer as a favored practice. That clashed with the principle that the government must pursue a course of complete neutrality toward religion."[9]

SOCIAL INDICATOR

Silence and Prayer Laws

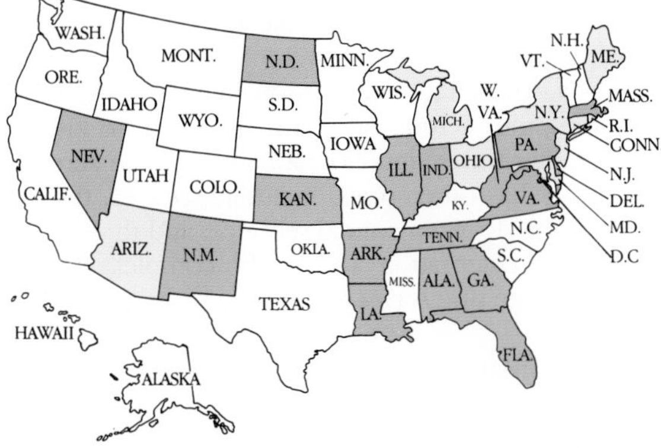

Source: *U.S. News & World Report,* June 17, 1985, p. 9.

SOCIAL INDICATOR

Religious Practices in Japan

Regularly go to pray, meditate	17%
Often pray	20
Visit ancestors' graves once or twice a year	68
Often read the Bible, sutras, and other religious literature	10
Visited a shrine to pray for safety, prosperity, or success in entrance exams during the past one or two years	32
Carry charms to repel evil or bad luck	36
Have gone to a fortune teller during the past one or two years	22
Practice nothing religious	10

Source: *Index to International Public Opinion* (Westport, CT: Greenwood, 1986), p. 531 from Yomiuri Shimbun, Tokyo.

Magic **Magic** is a ritual for controlling the physical and social worlds. It is based on the belief that if certain procedures are followed precisely, they will inevitably produce specific results. Societies dependent upon farming for subsistence, for example, often have rituals aimed at affecting the weather, such as the Hopi Rain Dance.[10]

For years, people on Bali believed that witches could harm a person by fashioning a mud or clay doll, adding something that once belonged to that person (a bit of hair, saliva, nail-cuttings, or the soil from a footprint), and injuring the doll.[11] A knife wound to the leg of the doll was believed to cause leg pains in the victim. Such beliefs in the power of magic on doll images in Bali and in other cultures led people in these societies to take special care to bury their feces, gather up and dispose of hair cuttings, and refrain from spitting.[12]

Magic is not limited to small out-of-the way societies. Many contemporary superstitions involve what is believed to be magic. As mentioned briefly in Chapter 6 (Exhibit 6.4), for example, professional athletes are well-known believers in magic. Many have been known to repeat precisely the same behavior patterns that led to victories, in the belief that doing so might produce future victories. To cite a recent case in point, as the New York Giants' winning streak moved them toward the Super Bowl in January 1987, both players and coach followed several carefully prescribed forms of magic ritual. The coach's office was littered with pennies, all with the tails facing upward. One player refused to shave. Each practice play had to be repeated at the same time of the day, at the same yard-marker, and running in the same direction. And the coach had to take a cab, rather than

Magic rituals are often believed to control human destiny. The New York Mets balance baseballs on their caps to score runs, while the Apache use body paint, masks, and dances to cure illness.

riding the team bus, because on the day of the first win he had done so and was the first member of the Giant organization to arrive at the stadium.[13]

Ceremonies **Ceremonies** involve a number of interconnected and related rituals performed at a given time. Widely known examples include such Roman Catholic sacraments as baptism, communion, and last rites. Each involves a specific set of activities, with the various participants following a carefully documented script. Baptism is organized around the induction of new members into the church. It requires a specific complement of people—the inductee, sponsors called "godparents," and a priest—each performing certain parts in the ceremony. Only the priest, for example, can anoint the infant with oil and water and invoke the intervention of God.

The Muslim *hajj,* the annual trip to Mecca, is another example of a religious ceremony. Muhammad, the seventh-century prophet of Islam, performed his farewell pilgrimage to the Holy City of Mecca just a few months before his death in A.D. 632, and his performance of the rite has become the model for contemporary Muslims. While a Muslim may visit Mecca at any time, the *hajj* may be performed only during the twelfth lunar month. It begins with the pilgrim's departure from home after settling all personal affairs and praying for God's protection on the journey. Before entering the sacred territory that surrounds Mecca, the pilgrim performs an elaborate rite that includes the donning of the simple white garment worn by all pilgrims, regardless of status. At this point the pilgrim becomes subject to certain prohibitions, including one forbidding sexual relations. After arriving in Mecca the pilgrim goes to the Ka'ba (a sacred building) to perform the circumambulation of arrival, which consists of marching seven times around the Ka'ba. The circumambulation begins at the corner containing the sacred black stone, which one kisses or touches, after the example of Muhammad. The ceremony of the *hajj* has other parts, including prayer, throwing stones at the devil, an animal sacrifice, and three days of feasting and celebration. Those who complete the ceremony earn the title *hajji* (pilgrim).

Supernatural Forces and Beings: The Types of Religion

Central to religion is a belief in supernatural beings—gods, spirits, ghosts—that have the ability to control one or more aspects of the physical world and influence human destiny. Some have human form; a few are vague, almost impersonal spirits; and still others are ghosts of deceased ancestors. In an effort to provide some conceptual order to this diversity of beliefs and supernatural beings, sociologists and anthropologists studying the world's religions have classified them into a few basic types. Although not all-inclusive, a classification based on a religion's central belief suggests three basic types: *animatism, animism,* and *theism.*

Animatism Suggested by the early twentieth-century anthropologist Robert A. Marett, **animatism** is the belief in an impersonal and unseen supernatural force or power that is thought to be everywhere.[14]

Animatism is fairly common in simple preindustrial societies. Believers conceive of a massive reservoir of power that may infuse or possess, and perhaps even be used by, gods and spirits, individuals, the forces of nature, and even natural objects. The concept of *mana* in the cultures of Melanesia and Polynesia is an example of such a force.[15] Mana has been described as a force that resided in Polynesian royalty, making direct contact with them fatal to commoners. It constituted the special abilities of great artists, orators, artisans, and warriors, and objects in which it resided were considered dangerous. But mana could be lost, and the person or object possessing it would thereby become ordinary once again.

Forces similar to mana have been identified in many cultures, and a modern parallel is the late French philosopher Henri Bergson's *elan vital,* a spirit of energy and life that moves all living things.

Animism The pioneer English anthropologist Edward Tylor found the center and origin of primitive religions to lie in what he termed **animism,** a belief in the existence of almost numberless spirits that dwell in animals and places or simply wander about the earth.[16] These spirits can be souls, ghosts, angels, gods, demons, or any other invisible creature, and they can inhabit any part of the physical world—rocks, trees, streams, or mountains. Should these spirits be mischievous, they may cause harm (for example, an unsuspecting person wandering too near a stream may be dragged down, swept away, and drowned). A spirit offended by some personal or tribal action may become angry and punish the offenders with a flood, failed crops, or a poor hunting season.

The number of categories of animistic spirits tends to vary from one primitive culture to the next. The Apache believe in only two spirits: the Controller of Water who does good things, and the Water Monster who causes harm.[17] By contrast, the Javanese have many categories, including frightening spirits, possessing spirits, familiar spirits, place spirits, and guardian spirits.[18] Regardless of the number of spirits, few have clear, well-defined features. Rather, they are evident by their actions—they cause storms, floods, fire, or drought. Most cultures have developed ceremonies to appease these spirits, or to summon their help. Knocking on wood is a simple animistic response designed to mollify the wood spirit, who might otherwise bring bad luck.

Theism **Theism** is the belief in one or more gods. The most common form of theism is *polytheism,* the belief in many gods. The ancient Greeks believed in a number of gods and goddesses, each having some special power or responsibility for a specific place or phenomenon. Zeus was the ruler of the Olympian gods and lord of the sky. His sister, Demeter, was the earth goddess, lady of growing things. His sister (and wife), Hera, was queen of the gods. Other gods included Poseidon, god of the sea; Hades, ruler of the dark domain; Ares, the god of war; Hephaestus, the god of weapons; and Eris, the goddess of discord.

The majority of the larger religions in the world today are *monotheistic,* emphasizing a single supreme being. The powers that polytheistic religions divide among many different gods and spirits are centered in a single being in monotheistic religions. Such a deity has supreme power, although some theologians note that even monotheistic religions must grant a degree of power to a devil in order to explain why evil occurs.[19]

Interestingly, the three monotheistic religions in the world today—Christianity, Judaism, and Islam—have the greatest number of adherents among all religions. Most Americans profess a belief in a single supreme being, but they do not share the same image of God, even within a particular religious tradition. Recent surveys have attempted to develop an image of how Americans think of God, and in one study some 1,569 respondents were asked how they view God and given a number of possible descriptions. Their responses are tabulated in Exhibit 12.1. On a less formal note, young children seem to have ideas about God that combine formal religious teachings with their own experiences. For example:

> "He has a black robe and he's really tall and he's got brown hair and has a cross around his neck and has big brown eyelashes and he wears big shoes—Nikes."
>
> "He looks like a giant; he's big but he doesn't talk on the phone. He wears red clothes—his favorite color."
>
> "He wears a red robe, because I like red. He has long, pretty black hair. Like mine."[20]

Other Forms of Religion Animatism, animism, and theism certainly do not account for all types of religious beliefs. Another notable category includes those beliefs that focus on abstract ideals rather than the worship of a god or the belief in spirits. Buddhism, the system of religion inaugurated by Siddhartha Gautama, the Buddha

Exhibit 12.1 Research in Sociology

Images of God among Americans

(percent answering "extremely likely")

	Creator	Healer	Friend	Redeemer	Father	Master	King	Judge	Lover	Liberator	Mother	Spouse
Protestant (970)	87	76	68	67	68	64	58	52	50	50	28	18
Baptist (303)	90	80	75	70	77	72	66	60	49	56	34	21
Methodist (147)	86	69	63	64	55	54	48	44	47	41	23	14
Lutheran 9143)	79	70	59	64	59	55	50	41	45	38	19	16
Presbyterian (64)	82	67	53	48	49	49	36	30	30	38	16	12
Episcopalian (37)	78	60	60	50	46	41	35	35	44	27	20	8
Catholic (439)	81	68	59	62	60	45	47	43	41	39	24	17
Jewish (43)	54	21	13	15	15	10	18	23	10	8	13	11
None (117)	45	35	36	26	28	30	28	29	18	17	13	8

Source: Wade Clark Roof and Jenifer L. Roof, "Review of Polls: Images of God among Americans," *Journal for the Scientific Study of Religion,* 23:2 (June 1984), p. 203. Reprinted by permission.

(enlightened one) of India, in the sixth century B.C., is most prominent in this respect and is based on four sublime truths:

1. Pain exists.
2. The cause of pain is "birth sin"—the accumulation of all the sins committed during each person's many previous existences.
3. Pain is ended only by *nirvana*—enlightenment and deliverance achieved through the complete annihilation of the drives for money, fame, and immortality.
4. The way that leads to nirvana is the Eightfold Path: right faith, right judgment, right language, right purpose, right practice, right obedience, right memory, and right meditation.[21]

The Sources of Evil Usually spirits, ghosts, or supernatural beings are believed to cause "good" and "evil" things to happen. Within the context of religious expression and experience, *evil* includes the whole range of puzzling and unjust troubles that plague human societies. The very nature of existence brings with it countless injustices: wars, failed crops and famine; natural disasters; the undeserved suffering of innocent children; and illnesses that unmercifully strike those who lead exemplary lives. In short, people wonder why the world is not perfect and just, and it is usual for religions to explain these events as the acts of supernatural beings.

In Greek mythology, all evil was attributed to Pandora, the first woman. In one of the many versions of the story, Pandora was created to bring about the ruin of man, and she was presented by Zeus with a box that was never to be opened. Pandora's curiosity overcame her, and she opened the box, thus releasing all the world's sins, troubles, and diseases.

A more typical explanation of evil is the belief in **dualism,** the struggle of supernatural beings working for "good" against the awesome forces of "evil." The "devil" (Satan or Lucifer) long has dominated Western thought as the personification of evil, forming a central part of contemporary religions. Among the more recent reminders of the existence of the devil came one from the Vatican in 1987. Speaking to Catholics throughout the world, Pope John Paul II emphasized that "the struggle against the demon [Satan] which marked the life of the Archangel Michael, is present even today because the demon is alive and functioning in the world."[22]

Dualism implies the presence of more than one supernatural being, suggesting that Christianity, Judaism, and Islam are not purely monotheistic. Although each emphasizes a single supreme being, all have lesser gods or semidivine figures—angels (good and evil), saints and other celestial personages (who are prayed to or even worshipped), and devils (with varying powers).[23]

The Functions of Religion

Not too long after his initial involvement in the founding of sociology, Emile Durkheim argued that society and religion could not exist without one another.[24] Society, he commented, would be impossible without religion, and to attempt to understand religion independent of the social context would be a meaningless exercise. In fact, Durkheim claimed that the worship of a god was a way of worshiping the society. A number of sociologists have elaborated on this fundamental insight.[25]

The Religious Community and Social Solidarity

Durkheim was interested in the social bonds that link members of society together, and he noted that religion promoted social solidarity in several ways. The mere fact that a group of individuals shares a set of religious values and beliefs serves to tie them together, generating unity. These values also create a sense of common identity and linkage that extends even to those with whom no direct contact exists. Thus, all Catholics, Jews, Hindus, Buddhists, Baptists, Mormons, and Muslims, wherever in the world they reside, are joined to others in their faith.

Religious rituals promote solidarity in an even more direct and meaningful way. Each religion has regular ceremonies, whether daily, weekly, or annually. Being together on a regular basis and reenacting religious rituals reinforces a sense of group history and belonging.

Consecrating Crises

Religion and ritual are especially important at times when a group is threatened. Warfare represents a crisis in almost every society, and as soldiers prepare to face their enemies on the battlefield, their priests, shamans, or commanders lead them in prayer. Victory is often celebrated with prayers of thanksgiving.

Every society also faces predictable crises that threaten survival. In farming communities, the annual planting of crops is a crisis point. Thus, religious festivals are common in the spring of the year as groups face the uncertainties of another harvest season.

Many modern religious celebrations typically include elements inherited from the pre-Christian era. All-Saints Day (November 1) is but one example. The Druids, an ancient religious group that once inhabited the British Isles, had a festival called "Samhain" (summer's end), which marked the end of the growing season and the dangers of the approaching winter. One of the traditions practiced during Samhain as a way of predicting who would prosper or fail in the coming year was bobbing for apples. The Druids also believed that the dead returned to roam the land as ghosts and witches, and that cats were sacred because they had once been humans. Around A.D. 700, the Catholic church, which had honored its saints during the spring of each year, changed the commemoration to November 1, creating Allhallows Eve (eve of the Holy One's day). The ensuing celebrations incorporated both Christian and Druid customs, and survive today as Halloween.[26]

SOCIAL INDICATOR

The Contemporary Relevance of Religion

Do you believe that religion can answer all or most of today's problems, or that religion is largely old-fashioned and out of date?

	Can Answer	Out of Date	No Opinion
1957	81%	7%	12%
1974	62	20	18
1981	65	15	20
1982	60	22	18
1984	56	21	23
1985	61	22	17

Source: The Gallup Poll, 1985. Reprinted by permission.

Meaning and Morale: Providing Sacred Answers

As people confront illness, the risks of war, the loss of loved ones, and technological and natural disasters, frustration and anxiety become regular aspects of social living. These events are of important religious significance to both the individual and the group, for religious faith offers comfort and solace, affirming that life has meaning beyond immediate problems. A person's death, for example, may be a personal tragedy for loved ones, but it is also a community loss. Funerals are religious rituals that bring the members of the community together and encourage them to carry on the life of the society. This point was most poignantly evident in the ceremonies and national mourning following the deaths of the *Challenger* astronauts in 1986. It should come as no surprise that religion also takes on special meaning in times of war. Research among combat soldiers confirmed that many (over 75%) admitted that prayer was a great help during combat.[27] Such behavior, often referred to as "foxhole religion," suggests that faith takes on new meaning in the face of danger, enabling people to function more effectively.

Social Control: Reinforcing the Moral Order

Norms are a central dimension of the social order of any society, a broad dimension of its culture. Most of the

Exhibit 12.2

Sociological Focus

Social Control and Voodoo in Haiti

Voodoo ritual is a way of contacting spirits who are believed to control human events.

Although voodoo is portrayed in movies as a form of black magic, in reality, voodoo is more religion than anything else.

The basic features of voodoo came from West Africa (principally from the area now known as Dahomey) with slaves being transported to Haiti and other Caribbean islands. Forbidden by their French masters to practice their religion, by the late seventeenth century the slaves had been forced to accept Catholicism. Yet they never deserted their spirits, secretly worshiping them in the guise of Catholic saints. The blending of the two sets of beliefs is the basis of modern voodoo.

As the following report suggests, voodoo is an important mechanism of social control in societies where it is practiced.

HAITI, VOODOO, AND DRUG MISUSE

Six years ago, a man walked into a small Haitian village, approached a peasant woman and introduced himself as her brother Clairvius. Had he not used his boyhood nickname and mentioned facts only known to intimate family members, she would not have believed him since she had watched her brother Clairvius lowered into his grave and covered with earth. The burial had taken place 18 years earlier.

Clairvius told his sister that he remembered the night he was lowered into his grave because he was fully conscious but could not speak or move. He remembered experiencing an out-of-body sensation as if he were floating over his grave while earth was thrown over his coffin.

He told his sister that he was removed from the grave later that night by a voodoo priest. He was beaten and carried off to a sugar plantation where, with other zombies, he was forced to work as a slave. Until the death of the zombie master, Clairvius had been unable to escape and return to his village.

Most Haitians believe in zombies and events such as this are not unique. This case, however, was different in one critical aspect. The death had been documented by physicians at the American-directed Schweitzer Hospital in Deschapelles on April 30, 1962. The records show that Clairvius was initially treated in the hospital's emergency room and was subsequently admitted to the hospital for fever, aches, and, spitting up blood. The doctors could not diagnose his illness. Three days after entering the hospital he was pronounced dead by his attending physicians.

Zombie Research

Dr. Lemarque Douyon, a Haitian-born, Canadian-trained psychiatrist, has been investigating all reports of zombies since 1961 at the Centre de Psychiatrie et Neurologie in Port-au-Prince. The event described by Clairvius convinced Dr. Douyon to search for an ethnobotanist who would determine if a potion existed which could dramatically slow metabolism to such a degree that a victim could be buried, dug up in a short time, and somehow be revived.

The search ended at the Harvard Botanical Museum with Wade Davis, a 28-year-old Canadian pursuing a doctorate in biology. Although Davis knew nothing about Haiti or the African traditions which are the basis of the country's culture, he arrived in Haiti a week later to seek the existence of a zombie drug and how the drug might be made.

Davis describes Haiti as a country materially impoverished, rich in culture and mystery. He found a cohesion in Haitian society; one in which crime, social disorder and rampant drug and alcohol abuse did not exist. Davis believes this cohesion is the result of the country's turbulent history. Haiti was occupied by the French in the late eighteenth century. During this period, African-born slaves were imported. In 1791, the slaves formed secret societies and launched a successful revolt against the French. Haiti thereafter remained an independent black republic and the population did not forget its African heritage.

Davis discovered that the majority of Haitian peasants still practice voodoo, a religion with strong African roots. He found the voodoo (sometimes called *vodoun* by cultural anthropologists) society to be a system of education, law, medicine, and a code of ethics regulating social behavior. In rural areas, voodoo societies control life in Haiti as much as the government. . . .

The Voodoo Potion

When Davis arrived in Haiti, he immersed himself in the local culture. Through various contacts he arranged a meeting with a voodoo sorcerer from whom he obtained a vial of ingredients. . . .

The formula proved inexact since the ingredients often varied in the samples, although the basic ingredients remained the same. The effects produced by the potion also varied but, overall, it worked well enough to establish that zombies were more than a figment of Haitian imagination. When the poison is rubbed into the subject's skin, nausea and difficulty in breathing occur in a few hours. Pins-and-needles sensations first afflict the extremities and progress throughout the body. The victim becomes paralyzed and the lips turn blue from a lack of oxygen. After six hours, metabolism is lowered to a level almost indistinguishable from death.

The ingredients consist of a variety of dried toads, sea worms, lizards, tarantulas, human bones, and dried fish from a species of puffer or blowfish. These fish contain a powerful poison known as tetrodotoxin, one of the most powerful non-protein poisons known. Tetrodotoxin was found in every batch of poison acquired by Davis. . . .

Davis was certain he had resolved the zombie mystery but identification of the poison was, in fact, just the starting point.

Tetrodotoxin alone does not produce zombies. . . . If a victim survives the first few hours following tetrodotoxin poisoning, he is likely to revive spontaneously and fully recover. However, zombies remain without a will, in a trance-like state. Davis believes that the psychological trauma of zombification is augmented by the use of *Datura* species found in Haiti which are also used in various ritual activities. *Datura* (various Solanaceae species which produce belladonna alkaloids) could produce a stupor when administered in large doses (possibly fed to zombies in a paste form) which would accentuate their disorientation. Tetrodotoxin and *Datura* can thus serve as templates on which cultural beliefs may be amplified a thousandfold.

Upon further investigation Davis found that the combination of drugs could prime the subject for a series of psychological pressures which were deeply rooted in Haitian culture.

Social Control in Voodoo Societies

Davis finally came to understand the social matrix within which zombies were created. He believes the secret societies were responsible for policing Haitian villages and the threat of zombification was one way in which they maintained order. To the unfamiliar, the practice appears as a random criminal act, but within rural voodoo society it is a sanction imposed by recognized authorities as a form of capital punishment. Zombification is an even more severe punishment than death to rural Haitians because it robs the subject of his most valued possessions: free will and independence.

These exotic discoveries by Davis provide a glimpse into the varied cultural uses and misuses of drugs by primitive societies. Today these societies are rapidly becoming modernized and the cultural wealth of knowledge on plant and animal toxins accumulated over the years is also rapidly disappearing.

SOURCE: Deborah A. Handrinos, *Street Pharmacologist,* April 1987, Up Front Drug Information.

more important norms have religious legitimation, making them moral imperatives. For example, many of the central laws of western societies—the prohibitions against murder, suicide, and theft—are also part of the teachings of Christianity, Judaism, and other religions. Thus, murderers face not only such secular punishments as imprisonment or execution, but the threat of punishment in the afterlife as well. In Haiti, voodoo is used as a form of social control (see Exhibit 12.2).

In retrospect, it would appear that Durkheim was quite correct to observe the meaningful links between the sacred and the secular dimensions of society. In fact, it would be difficult to draw a meaningful line between the two. This statement has special validity in small, homogeneous societies, where religion is a powerful force that holds people together and reinforces fundamental ideas and beliefs. However, the power of religion also has a disruptive potential.

The Dysfunctions of Religion

While religion may be an important source of group or social solidarity, it also can be a powerful force in separating groups, as well as a major source of conflict. Devotees to any particular religion often exhibit a tenacious adherence to their belief system, with an equally intolerant view of other religions.

It is well documented that many of the major wars in human history have been attempts to impose one religion upon adherents of some other faith. No example is more famous than the Crusades of the Middle Ages, mounted by Christians at the behest of various popes to "liberate" Jerusalem from domination by the Moslems. More recently, the smoldering conflict in Northern Ireland has pitted Protestants against Catholics for the control of a few hundred square miles of land.

Similarly, the pages of history books are filled with the names of people forced to suffer or even die for their religious faiths. Joan of Arc was burned at the stake. Galileo's scientific teachings caused his books to be banned for two centuries. In the contemporary world fanatic terrorists often are willing to sacrifice their lives in pursuit of their religious beliefs (see Chapter 20).

The emphasis on religious solidarity should not mask the fact that divisions exist within society. Complex industrial societies generally contain many different religious groups, and even subdivisions within individual religions. Too, changing social conditions may draw the sacred and secular spheres apart, as is strongly apparent

SOCIAL INDICATOR

The Decision in *Roe v. Wade*

	Favor	Oppose	No Opinion
1974	47%	44%	9%
1981	45	46	9
1983	50	43	7
1985	45	45	10

Source: *The Gallup Report*, 1986.

Religious differences may contribute to intergroup conflict. Hundreds have died in Northern Ireland, where Protestants are pitted against Catholics.

SOCIAL INDICATOR

Abortion Clinic Arsons and Bombings

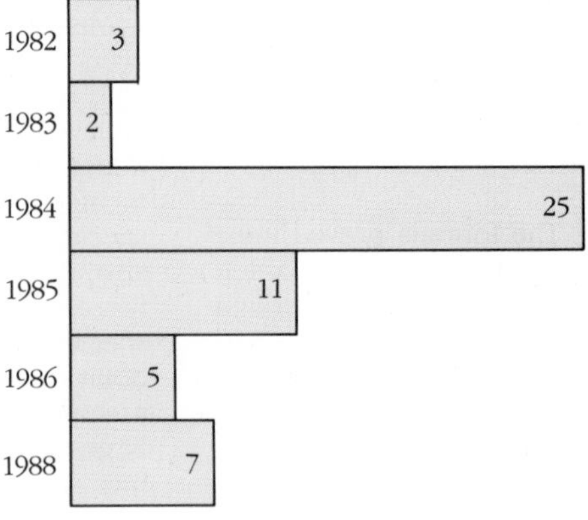

Source: Bureau of Alcohol, Tobacco and Firearms, 1989.

Exhibit 12.3

Sidelights on American Culture

"Secular Humanism," Textbooks, and Judge W. Brevard Hand

"It wasn't quite a sequence from *Amerika,*" wrote the editors of *USA Today* on March 9, 1987; nor "a scene from a Nazi war film. But it was close." What they were referring to was an event that took place just a few days earlier in an Alabama courtroom. Under a decision by U.S. District Judge W. Brevard Hand, students were ordered to turn over banned textbooks—books on history, biology, social studies, home economics, and other disciplines.

Judge Hand's decision was the result of a long-brewing controversy over *secular humanism,* a fundamentalist term for the belief that man is answerable only to himself. Secular humanism, many religious fundamentalists have argued, is the number one disease afflicting the United States; it is the doctrine of those who are pluralistic in their concept of morality and in their economic and political ideology and practice. And it is because of secular humanism, they add, that prayer has been banned from public school classrooms, that pornography and abortion are legal across America, and that the rates of crime, premarital sex, drug abuse, and AIDS are so high.

Textbooks and other publications targeted as reflections of secular humanism are numerous. They include the following perplexing mixture:

- *Ms.* magazine, because it contains articles on abortion
- *Today's Teen* magazine, because one edition stated that "too strict a conscience may make you afraid to try new ventures"
- John Steinbeck's *Of Mice and Men,* because it contains "profanity"
- *Funk & Wagnalls Standard Desk Dictionary,* because it contains "inappropriate words," including *fag,* defined as slang for a male homosexual
- Hundreds of textbooks, because they discuss such topics as feminism, witchcraft, telepathy, and evolution
- Most curiously, James A. Inciardi's *The War on Drugs,* because it mentions *The Wizard of Oz* and Jesus Christ in the same discussion

The two sides of the secular humanism debate ultimately met in Judge Hand's court, one seeking to ban the objectionable publications and the other arguing the First Amendment right to free speech. Interestingly, Judge Hand upheld the argument *for* book banning on First Amendment grounds, ruling that secular humanism was a religion, and as such, was a violation of the amendment's establishment clause. More specifically, the judge held that since the books in question promoted the "religion" of secular humanism to the exclusion of theistic religions, they could be used only as reference materials in courses on comparative religion.

On the day following Judge Hand's decision, school officials in Mobile County, Alabama, began removing the designated books from classrooms and libraries. But the victory was but a brief one for the plaintiffs in the case. In 1988 fundamentalist Christian parents throughout the United States lost their crusade to prevent their children from reading "godless" textbooks when the Supreme Court refused to hear the case of *Bob Mozert v. Hawkins County Public Schools.* By refusing to hear the *Mozert* case the High Court let stand a federal court of appeals ruling that permitted the use of such texts in Tennessee schools.

SOURCES: Samuel S. Hill and Dennis E. Owen, *The New Religious Political Right in America* (Nashville: Abington, 1982); Jaffree v. Wallace, 705 F. 2d, 1526, 1535–1536 (CA 11, 1983); *Miami Herald,* February 23, 1988, p. 1A; *National Law Journal,* March 23, 1987, pp. 3, 10; *Time,* March 16, 1987, p. 66; *USA Today,* March 9, 1987, p. 6A.

in the debate over abortion. The 1973 Supreme Court decision in ***Roe v. Wade***[28] held that the right to privacy extended to the qualified right of a woman to have an abortion. Pro-choice advocates faced a serious setback in 1989, however, when the Court ruled that each state has the right to regulate abortions. Americans are equally divided on the abortion issue, and the standoff continues. Primarily on the basis of religious views, the antiabortion forces hold that life begins at conception, and that abortion is thus tantamount to murder. On the other side of the argument is the more relativist view that human life is achieved by degrees over nine months of gestation. Therefore, the decision to abort during the early months of pregnancy is a matter of choice rather than public morality. And while the issues have been argued in places of worship, homes, and at political gatherings, the controversy also has spilled into the streets. In 1985, for example, of the almost 700 nonhospital abortion clinics in the United States, some 88% experienced harassment in the forms of picketing, vandalism, death or bomb threats, invasions by demonstrators, or bombings.[29] Stated with almost equal vigor are the arguments surrounding the often mentioned but rarely defined concept of *secular humanism* (see Exhibit 12.3).

Religion and the Conflict Perspective

While Durkheim emphasized the positive consequences of religion, Karl Marx and other conflict theorists have offered a rather different perspective. Because Marx saw groups as divided into the privileged and the underprivileged, he attempted to understand how social institutions served to maintain such inequality. It is not surprising that he included religion in his analysis, commenting that religion was ". . . the opium of the people."[30]

The reference to opium, a narcotic drug with stupifying effects that was widely used in over-the-counter medications during the nineteenth century, suggested that religion tranquilized the poor and powerless. Marx felt that by emphasizing rewards in the "next world," religion deflected attention away from the hardships of daily life. Moreover, religion stressed an acceptance of the world as it was, rather than encouraging change. In this regard Marx noted that while religion has sometimes *caused* revolutionary change, it generally does not preach revolution.

The position taken by Marx is readily supported in Christian teachings. In Luke 6:20–21, for example, the poverty of Christians is celebrated:

> **Blessed are the poor, the reign of God is yours.**
> **Blessed are you who hunger; you shall be filled.**
> **Blessed are you who are weeping; you shall laugh.**

Luke 6:29–30 preaches an acceptance of adversity without rebellion:

> **When someone slaps you upon the cheek, turn and give him the other.**
> **When a man takes what is yours, do not demand it back.**

From these and other teachings, Marx concluded that Christianity endorsed inequality and contributed to the spread of capitalism. He noted further that under *socialism,* an economic structure in which private property is abolished and the tools of production are held by the state (see Chapter 14), class distinctions disappear and "religion dies a natural death."[31]

Other conflict theorists have sanctioned the Marxist notion that religion fosters an endorsement of secular systems of inequality. The caste system in India is perhaps the most often cited example of a religious system that supports the economic and political orders of a society. As noted earlier in Chapter 8, the privileged position of those in the highest Hindu caste—the Brahmins—is explained by their behavior in an earlier life, as is the segregation of the "untouchables." Similarly, in sixteenth-century England, followers of the French Protestant reformer, John Calvin, readily accepted the belief that the rich and powerful were God's "elect," those destined to rule.

The point espoused by the conflict perspective is that religion tends to support the political and economic *status quo.* When social institutions are supported by religious beliefs, any attempt to overthrow the existing order is not simply a political revolution, but a moral revolution as well.[32] Thus, Marx and other proponents of the conflict tradition would argue that religion is dysfunctional for society, not simply because it endorses structured inequality, but also because it inhibits social change.

THE SOCIAL ORGANIZATION OF RELIGIONS

Religions display a variety of different structural arrangements. Some, such as Catholicism, qualify as bureaucracies, with a formal system of rules, a hierarchy of authority, and a relatively organized division of labor. Others lack any formal structure and are best understood as collections of believers welded together by a single influential leader. Sociologists have developed a set of *ideal types* to describe three major forms of religious organization—churches, cults, and sects. The purpose of the typology is to facilitate the analysis of the role of religion in society.

Churches

The most familiar type of religious arrangement in the United States is the **church,** a large organization with a formal structure, an official clergy, an elaborate theology, and a broad membership of people who are generally the children of members. All of the major religions of the world—Christianity, Judaism, Islam, and Buddhism—are organized as churches. Each of the major divisions within a religious tradition (such as Catholicism, Eastern Orthodox, Mormon, and Lutheran within Christianity, for example) also takes this form.

Churches also are characterized by the fact that they have established stable relations with other social institutions in the society. Exceptions exist, of course, as seen in the case of the "sanctuary movement." In 1986 a number of clergy and lay workers, operating with the official sanction of their churches, were found guilty in federal court of transporting, harboring, and conspiring to smuggle illegal aliens from Guatemala and San Salvador.[33]

On the whole, religions organized as churches tend to be tolerant of other religious beliefs. Protestants, Catholics, and Jews peacefully coexist in most parts of the United States, and disagreements over doctrine do not usually produce conflict. Moreover, a strong correspondence usually is evident between the values and perspectives of a church and the society from which it draws its members. Churches tend to support and reinforce society. Thus, the "church" typifies the integration between the sacred and the secular emphasized by Durkheim (see Exhibit 12.4).

SOCIAL INDICATOR

Stability of Church Membership

The majority of Americans are raised with some religious faith, and most remain in it. Some churches have very stable memberships, with affiliation inherited. In others, many members are acquired through conversion.

Church	Percent Raised in Same Faith
Jews	93.3
Catholics	89.7
Southern Baptists	86.0
Other Baptists	77.3
Lutherans	75.7
Methodists	72.4
Presbyterians	59.8
Episcopalians	54.0
All Religions	69.7

Source: *American Demographics,* June 1984, p. 23.

Cults

New religious ideas and doctrines are always emerging. When they appear for the first time they attract small numbers of adherents, often merely a handful. Most such groups are organized around individuals who claim special insights or a unique relationship with the supernatural, uniting people through charismatic leadership. Sociologists refer to these groups as cults. More formally, a **cult** is a loosely organized spiritual movement that offers "new" religious ideas and beliefs.

As the result of their support for doctrines that are generally at odds with those of more conventional religions or the society at large, cults are often met with suspicion, disbelief, or even outright hostility. The Reverend Sun Myung Moon's Unification Church, the

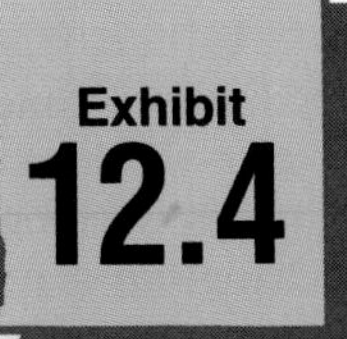

Sociological Focus

Churches, Cults, and Sects

Characteristic	Church	Cult	Sect
Size	Large	Small	Small
Services	Formal, Passive	Varies	Emotional, Active
Interpretation of Writings	Broad	Literal	Literal
Membership Criteria	Birth, or Ritual Ceremony	Conversion Experience	Conversion Experience
Clergy	Professional Role	Charisma	Unspecialized, Part-time
Relationship with Other Religions	Tolerant, Accepting	Emphasizes Errors of Others	Emphasizes Correctness of Own View
Relationship with Secular Society	Integrated	Rejects, and Is Rejected	Opposes or Rejects

New members of the Rajneesh cult undergo a conversion experience.

International Society for Krishna Consciousness, the Scientology of L. Ron Hubbard, and the movement of Bhagwan Shree Rajneesh all have had their doctrines attacked, their leaders labeled as either frauds, fools, or opportunists, and their members ridiculed. And while these attacks are sometimes justified, it also must be remembered that although cults may be unusual and unconventional when they first appear, many evolve into established religions.

A key characteristic of all cults is the personal magnetism of their leaders. Leaders capable of guiding others through force of personality are said to have **charisma,** or the ability to inspire faith. Thus, when based on charismatic leadership alone, many cults fail to survive after their leaders die. However, a few manage to flourish, continuing to attract adherents and ultimately becoming recognizable forces in society. This continuity is accomplished through what might be called a **routinization of charisma:** the teachings of the founder are formalized and preserved; a new leader is selected; and others are trained to assume positions of leadership and carry on the work of the founder. As cults grow in size and complexity, they tend to develop an increasingly organized structure. In time, they become "churches"—religions having a formal doctrine, a bureaucratic organization, and a clergy.

As a cult evolves into a church, its stance toward the larger society also begins to shift. Many cults are founded for the purpose of instigating social change. Some have managed to accomplish this goal, at least to a limited extent. But as they grow, in order to increase their power and influence, they must accommodate to the secular society and demonstrate greater tolerance for diversity.

All major world religions originated as cults (at least in terms of the sociological definition of a cult). Jesus Christ, for example, propounded ideas that were at odds with the polytheism of Roman society. He was, of course, a charismatic leader, attracting followers as he moved about the land as both teacher and preacher. Upon his death, it fell to his followers to establish and maintain Christianity.

Cults and Conversion

Members of cults must be attracted from existing religions or the ranks of nonbelievers. In short, they must be converted. Conversion is a deep, personal, and private experience. As a convert to Sun Myung Moon's Unification Church once recalled it: "I looked up at the sky and all at once everything just sort of melted together; it all just unified. Everything was everything, nothing was separate. The guru said 'That's it—you just saw God!'"[34]

The conversion experience is also an important sociological event—one of acceptance and rejection. Converts publicly announce acceptance of a new religious faith (and the group publicly accepts them), and at the same time they reject their former selves. Many times conversion is spoken of as a new life. For example, as reported by the same convert to the Unification Church: "I was reborn. I experienced myself as a transformed, totally reconstructed person. I died to my old self, Barbara, and became Lael."[35]

Socialization into Cults

As discussed briefly in Chapter 6 (Exhibit 6.7), indoctrination and conversion to a cult occur within a social context. Cults, like most other groups seeking new members, work to bring about a change in a recruit's outlook and perspective, and they often accomplish this change through a variety of mechanisms employing any of a number of socialization and resocialization techniques.

First (and crucial to the process) is *milieu control,* the physical and social isolation of the recruit. This technique makes the cult the center of activity, a situation in which certain doctrines are more easily emphasized.

Second, cults impose a *demand for purity.* The cult demands the impossible—perfection—and creates a sense of incompetence and imperfection by constantly criticizing the recruit's behavior.

Third is the *cult of confession,* demands for constant public admission of imperfections. Admission of personal shortcomings can have therapeutic value, but it also renders an individual more vulnerable to conversion. The emphasis on individual failings teaches recruits one vital lesson—they cannot improve themselves by their own actions alone; they must depend upon the group.

Fourth, cults tend to promote the concept of *absolute truth,* the assertion that their message has special inspiration and cannot be questioned. Former Unification Church members report that they were silenced by being told any suspicions they had about the cult had come from Satan. Others were reminded that they were thinking too much.

Thus, cult socialization emphasizes the importance of the group over the individual and demands total commitment. It is only through the group, it is stressed, that the individual can hope to realize the inner peace offered by the cult. In a few cults, some final public ritual, such as the surrendering of worldly possessions, is required as a prerequisite to full membership. To cite a case in point, between 1983 and 1986, a wealthy heiress was persuaded to contribute almost $7 million to the religious group known as The Bible Speaks. Although it was argued by the founder of The Bible Speaks that the heiress had donated the money willingly, she nevertheless won full restitution after a three-week trial in 1987.[36]

A Theory of Cult Formation

A major interest of many sociologists over the years has been uncovering the process through which people are influenced to reject one set of beliefs and to replace it with a radically different system. At a broad social level, it has been observed that cults are more likely to flourish during the periods of social upheaval caused by wars, revolutions, urbanization, industrialization, or economic dislocation.[37] Dramatic social change can create a sense of alienation and a questioning of traditional social values and goals. Within this context, research has demonstrated that many cult members have been young, middle-class whites who grew up during the upheavals of the 1960s and early 1970s. Those years of antiwar protests, civil rights unrest, political protests, and the women's movement may well have alienated them from traditional values, including traditional religions.[38]

Since alienation is a general societal condition, not all people are equally effected. For this reason, an additional factor must be considered with reference to cult formation. People who are attracted to contemporary cults are very likely to have experienced a period of severe stress, which was brought about by the disruption of meaningful social relations—the death or illness of a relative or close friend, the breakup of a romantic relationship, even the dislocation produced by starting college.[39] Thus, many cult members are lonely, alienated, unhappy people. They often are referred to as "seekers"—individuals who are seeking new meaning for their lives. A cult's doctrine may offer a fresh approach to the world, and existing members provide strong social support. And finally, cults give the recruit the opportunity to assume a new role with a clear break from a past that has proven to be both unsatisfactory and unrewarding.

Sects

A **sect** is a religious group that has split off from some other established church or denomination. Sects generally are founded by a strong, charismatic leader, and the basis for the split is the belief that the "church" has deviated from its historical origins or mission; thus the sect represents a return to fundamental principles. For this reason, members of sects place great emphasis on reading the sacred texts and following them closely. The beginnings of the Mormon Church illustrate the dynamics of sect formation (see Exhibit 12.5).

During the early part of the twentieth century, H. Richard Niebuhr offered a compelling theory of the origin of sects that contrasts markedly with the Mormon experience.[40] Puzzled by the proliferation of diverse religious groups throughout history, Niebuhr concluded that sect formation and social inequality were interrelated. Most religions originated, he argued, to serve the needs of the poor and underprivileged. This role is certainly clear in Christian teachings, as has been noted already. As sects grow, Niebuhr continued, they begin to attract members of the middle and upper classes. Their doctrines shift to accommodate to the needs of society's more advantaged groups, just as Marx had observed, and in the process the sects become less relevant to the lower classes. An example of the shift to middle-class interests might be seen in greater emphasis on secular concerns to the exclusion of the sacred. The evolution of Calvinist doctrines tends to reflect this pattern; early emphases on salvation gradually shift toward a greater affirmation of worldly success.

THE RELIGIOUS MOSAIC: CONTEMPORARY RELIGION IN THE UNITED STATES

Religions—grouped as churches, cults, and sects—are ideal types that are useful for classification purposes. However, it is also useful to identify the contours of actual religions that fall into these categories. The major religions in the United States are Judaism, Catholicism, and Protestantism. Each has millions of adherents and a variety of different beliefs and rituals.

Exhibit 12.5

Case Study

Polygamy and the Mormons vs. Celibacy and the Shakers

The history of the Mormons recounts that the angel Moroni appeared to Joseph Smith, a religious seeker living near Palmyra, New York, in a vision in 1822 and told Smith where golden tablets containing God's revelation were buried. Smith unearthed the tablets, translated them, and published them as the Book of Mormon. On April 6, 1830, Smith and five others gathered together on a hillside near Palmyra and founded the Mormons, first known as the Church of Christ and later as the Church of Jesus Christ of Latter Day Saints. From its humble beginnings with but six believers, the church has grown to 5 million members worldwide, and has become well established.

Although Christian in perspective, Mormon teaching diverges from orthodoxy in a number of ways. The Bible was viewed as the word of God, but it was incomplete until the discovery of the Book of Mormon, which clarified various elements of dogma. The first Mormons faced persecution from the very beginning. Some were arrested, and many were beaten. They fled westward to Ohio in 1831, to Missouri in 1837, and to Illinois in 1844, where Smith and his brother were attacked and killed by a mob. Leadership then passed to Brigham Young, who led his followers further west in search of refuge, eventually settling in Utah in 1847.

Much of the opposition to the Mormons came from their acceptance of polygamy. In 1882, Congress passed legislation prohibiting polygamy, defining it as "lewd cohabitation." Subsequently, over 500 Mormons were convicted under the new law. In 1887 Congress dissolved the church as a legal entity and provided for the confiscation of its property in an additional repressive measure. Curiously, more than a half-century later the polygamy issue emerged once again, generating a new sect that broke with the Mormon Church. In 1943 several Mormons founded the United Effort Plan, based on the belief that polygamy was central to true Mormonism. The leader, Leroy S. Johnson, was excommunicated, and he and his followers eventually migrated to Arizona. Johnson died in 1986, at age 98, leaving 13 widows, but some 3,000 members of the United Effort Plan sect remain.

While the early Mormons practiced polygamy, the Shakers practiced celibacy. The Shakers were founded in 1758 by Ann Lee of Manchester, England, a member of the Shaking Quakers—a Quaker sect whose members practiced ritualistic dancing. At age 22, Lee had a revelation that she was Christ in female form, that sexual activity was the cause of sin, and that she was to establish a church in the New World. After convincing eight others to follow her, she established the first Shaker community just north of Albany, New York, in 1776.

Celibacy, communal ownership of property, separation from the world, and communal confession of sin—with emphasis on its sexual origins—were the defining practices of the Shakers. Worship was based on silent group meditation and distinctive dances and songs. The strictures against sex, marriage, and procreation could be traced back to Ann Lee's childhood, when she saw how excessive childbearing wore women out and caused them to die young. Her early life also left her with the images of how too many, or unwanted, children inflicted hardships on parents and children alike.

The Shakers expanded slowly, with some 6,000 members in 20 communities by 1850. In the aftermath of the Civil War, however, their numbers declined rapidly, dropping to less than 600 by 1901. Today, the Shakers are all but extinct. In 1986 less than a dozen members remained, most quite elderly, and living in Sabbathday Lake, Maine.

SOURCES: H. Paul Chalfant, Robert E. Beckley, and C. Eddie Palmer, *Religion in Contemporary Society* (Palo Alto, CA: Mayfield. 1981); William M. Kephart, *Extraordinary Groups: An Examination of Unconventional Life-Styles* (New York: St. Martins, 1987); Martin Marty, *Modern American Religion* (Chicago: University of Chicago Press, 1986); Martin Marty, *Righteous Empire: The Protestant Experience in America* (New York: Dial, 1970).

Judaism

Judaism was the first major religion to teach *monotheism,* the belief in one God. Judaic beliefs are contained in the Hebrew Bible (the Christian Old Testament), plus a body of scholarship and interpretation called the Talmud. Houses of worship are called *synagogues,* and services are led by a *cantor* (by virtue of his expertise in Hebrew liturgical chant). *Rabbis* are spiritual leaders, schooled in religious law and tradition. Judaism may be divided into three major "churches" or "branches"—orthodox, reform, and conservative.

Orthodox Judaism

Orthodox Judaism emphasizes the divine inspiration of the holy books. Thus, members organize their behavior around strict adherence to Judaic laws. Men wear caps at all times as a sign of respect for God, and all Orthodox Jews follow strict dietary laws and observe the Sabbath by abstaining from work, travel, and the carrying of money.[41]

The sacred and secular worlds of Orthodox Jews are sometimes at odds with one another. For example, biblical law grants the right to dissolve marriages only to husbands, and *not* to civil authorities. As a result, many Jewish women—15,000 in New York alone—have won divorces in the courts but have not been able to obtain the consent of their husbands.[42] As a result, they may remarry, but not within their faith.

Orthodox Jews consider themselves to be the only "true" Jews. They are willing to accommodate to the secular world, but only if no conflict arises as a result of such accommodation with the teachings contained in the Torah.

Reform Judaism

Reform Judaism had its origins in Europe during the nineteenth century as a response to the social and political transformations of Western society. The mood of the era had encouraged growth and change, and Reform Jews took the position that each generation had the right to interpret religious teachings in the light of contemporary events and developments.[43] Under such circumstances ethical teachings retain their original meanings while rituals are subject to change. Among contemporary Reform Jews, older dietary laws are often ignored and English has replaced Hebrew in worship services. Moreover, the orthodox idea that calls for the segregation of the sexes has been abandoned, and women have been permitted to become rabbis since the 1970s. Each of these changes has served to separate the Orthodox and Reform branches of Judaism, sometimes introducing intergenerational divisions and conflict within families.

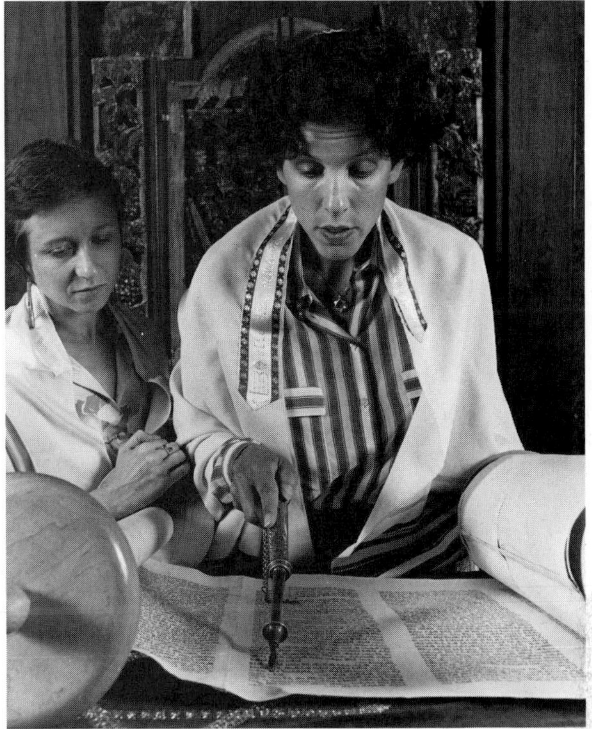

The basic beliefs and values of some religions are contained in sacred books. Here, a rabbi reads from the Torah.

Conservative Judaism

Conservative Judaism represents an attempt to respond to secular change while retaining the proud traditions of the faith. In some ways Conservative Judaism stands part way between the Orthodox and Reform branches, yet it does not have any "official" doctrine. Rather, attempts to harmonize Jewish beliefs are respected and encouraged. Hence, some congregations observe dietary laws, while others do not. Among all Conservative groups, however, a strong emphasis is placed on the maintenance of Jewish tradition.[44]

Catholicism

Catholicism is the branch of Christianity that accepts the supreme authority of the Pope as successor to Peter, the fisherman designated by Christ to found his church on earth. The Pope is the head of a large bureaucracy, with authority delegated to cardinals, bishops, and priests. *Priests* are the direct link between believers and God, and can administer baptism, communion, matrimony, and the other sacraments of the church.

Exhibit 12.6 Sociological Focus

Profiling America's Catholics

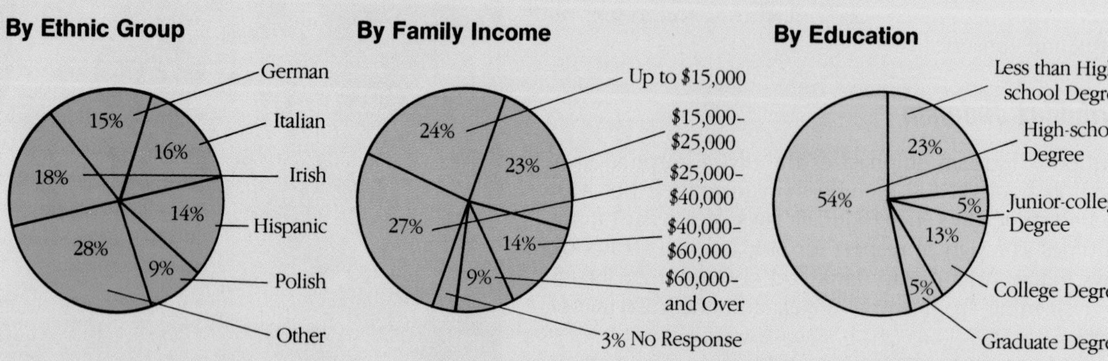

Source: *Newsweek*, September 21, 1987, p. 25.

On Being Catholic

	All Catholics	18–49 Years	50 and Older
Opinion of Pope John Paul II			
Favorable	59%	54%	69%
Not Favorable	5	5	4
On Social and Political Issues, the Pope Is:			
More Liberal Than You	14	14	14
More Conservative	50	58	34
On Personal Morality Issues, the Pope Is:			
More Liberal Than You	10	11	8
More Conservative	47	54	31
Church Should Change Some Teachings to Reflect Opinions of Most Catholics	58	65	42
Should Continue to Hold to Its Teachings Regardless of What Most Catholics Think	36	30	49
Favor Artificial Birth Control	64	74	43
Oppose	27	20	43
Favor Permitting Divorce and Remarriage	66	72	54
Oppose	27	23	35

Catholic Population in U.S.

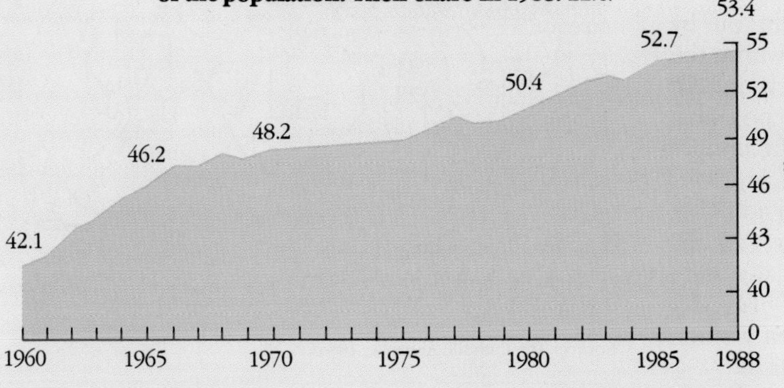

Sources: *The American Catholic People,* 1987; National Opinion Research Center, 1987; *New York Times*/CBS News Poll, 1987; *Catholic Almanac,* 1989.

The Changing Church

	1960	1985	1988
Parishes	16,996	19,313	19,596
Grade Schools	10,594	7,865	7,659
High Schools	2,433	1,418	1,391
Colleges	267	243	233
Seminaries	537	319	250
Hospitals	949	737	646
Homes for Aged	339	615	688
Nuns	170,438	113,658	106,912
Seminarians	41,871	10,440	7,512
Priests	54,682*	57,183	53,522
Infant Bapitisms	1,313,653	953,323	937,947
Converts	131,641	87,996	81,739
Deaths	348,529	448,822	453,290

*Peak was 59,892 in 1967.

	All Catholics	18–49 Years	50 and Older
Favor Legal Abortion	29	35	17
Favor Only to Save Mother or in Cases of Rape or Incest	48	48	49
Should not Be Permitted	19	12	31
A Woman Who Has an Abortion Can Still Be a Good Catholic	85	91	71
Cannot	8	5	15
Unmarried Men and Unmarried Women Who Have Sexual Relations with Each Other Can Still Be Good Catholics	80	88	61
Cannot	16	10	29
Someone Who Engages in Homosexual Relations Can Still Be a Good Catholic	55	62	40
Cannot	35	31	44
Married Couples Who Can't Have Children and Use a Surrogate Mother to Have a Child Can Still Be Good Catholics	74	85	52
Cannot	16	9	29

Source: *New York Times,* CBS News Poll, 1987.

Basic Catholic doctrine is found in the Bible, but the Vatican—the Pope and his College of Cardinals—has responsibility for its interpretation. Thus, all Catholics are united by a single set of beliefs and rituals. Many may disagree with the teachings of their church, violating them in private. However, those who openly offer alternative interpretations run the risk of finding themselves in direct conflict with the Pope. A recent case in point was Father Charles Curran, barred in 1986 from teaching at Catholic University because he challenged his church's absolute ban on birth control and abortion.[45]

In many ways, the controversy brought on by Father Curran was a reflection of the discord within the general membership of the Catholic Church in the United States. As indicated in the opinion poll that appears as part of Exhibit 12.6, the majority of Catholics are at odds with their church's unyielding positions against abortion, birth control, and divorce. In addition, dissension has been widespread among many Catholic women who hold that the Church's patriarchal system discriminates against their full participation.[46] The fact that the priesthood is "for men only" has given women feelings of second-class citizenship (see Exhibit 12.7).

Difficulties also are evident in other areas. As pointed out briefly in Chapter 4, from the 1950s through the 1980s the numbers of people becoming Catholic priests, nuns, and brothers have declined significantly. Several factors are responsible for this decline. First, the Church is unwilling to permit priests and nuns to publicly express their views on abortion and other matters when they oppose those of the Vatican. Second, the strict vows of poverty and celibacy required of the Catholic clergy have become increasingly unpopular. Third, as mentioned above, many female Catholics resent the Church's paternal attitude toward women. And it is in the priesthood that the most significant changes are anticipated. Although the total number of priests has increased slightly during the past 30 years, few new recruits have joined in the 1980s. It is anticipated that by the year 2000 there will be less than 25,000 priests in the United States, and the majority of these will be over the age of 60.

The dissension and controversy also have caused a decline in the number of American Catholics. Although the number has increased worldwide in recent decades, the growth of Catholicism in the United States has stagnated, declining by about 100,000 members since the early 1980s.[47]

SOCIAL INDICATOR

World Roman Catholic Population by Region

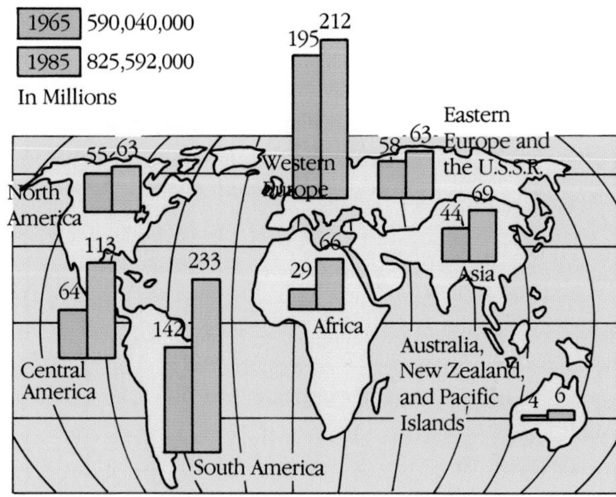

Source: The Catholic Almanac, 1986.

SOCIAL INDICATOR

Fewer Nuns and Priests

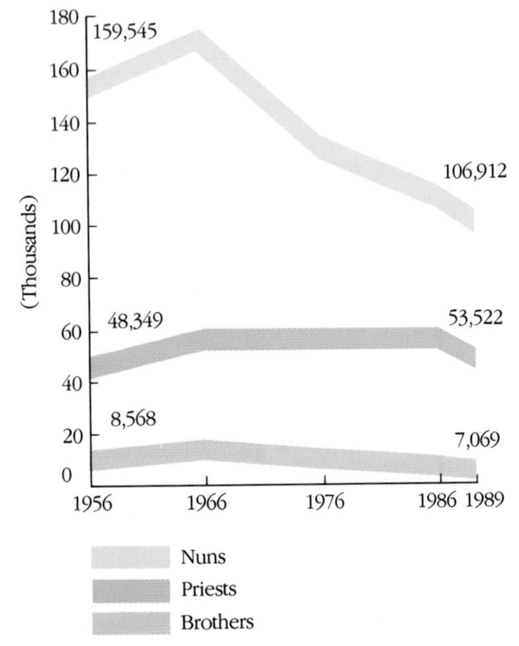

Source: The Official Catholic Directory, 1986.

Protestantism

Christianity encompasses all religions that believe in and follow the teachings of Jesus Christ, and Protestantism includes all Christian religions other than Catholicism.

Exhibit 12.7 **Types & Stereotypes**

Scrubbing the Scriptures

The women's movement of the 1970s brought forth feminist critics of the Holy Scriptures, claiming that something was terribly wrong with the Old and New Testaments. Both were riddled with sexism, feminists argued, requiring a new, even-handed rendering. By the close of the decade, the National Council of Churches (NCC) had embarked on the task of generating a nonsexist version, a task they accomplished by rewriting some 313 biblical passages. The NCC version was finally published in 1984. The "male bias" had been removed, but a new controversy was sparked—that of tampering with the word of God. Contrast the two examples to the right.

Revised Standard Version	***New NCC Lectionary***
Then the Lord God said, "It is not good that the man should be alone; I will make him a helper fit for him." . . . And the rib which the Lord God had taken from the man he made into a woman and brought her to the man. ***Genesis 2:18–24.***	Then God the Sovereign One said, "It is not good that the human being should be alone; I will make a companion corresponding to the human being." . . . And God the Sovereign One made the rib taken from that human being into a woman and brought her to the man. ***Genesis 2:18–24.***
The Lord is my shepherd, I shall not want; he makes me lie down in green pastures. ***Psalms 23:1–2***	God is my shepherd, I shall not want; God makes me lie down in green pastures. ***Psalms 23:1–2.***
For God so loved the world that he gave his only Son, that whoever believes in him should not perish but have eternal life. ***John 3:16.***	For God so loved the world that God gave God's only Child, that whoever believes in that Child should not perish but have eternal life. ***John 3:16.***

The feminist critique of the wording of particular passages should not divert attention from the more complex issues they raise. It is not just the words that are troublesome, but rather the underlying roles, values, and attitudes reinforced and perpetuated by much traditional religious theology. The role of Christian women is subordinate, for example, as evidenced by the marital admonition that wives "love, honor and *obey,*" and the exclusion of women from positions of leadership in many churches. Jewish feminists have taken exception to a traditional prayer in which men bless God for not creating them as women.

SOURCES: Mary Daly, *Beyond God the Father* (Boston: Beacon, 1973); Mary McGuire, *Religion: The Social Context* (Belmont, CA: Wadsworth, 1981); Rosemary Reuter and R. Keller, *Women and Religion* (New York: Harper & Row, 1986).

The origins of Protestantism may be traced to a challenge of the supreme authority of Rome during the sixteenth century, and in the years since more than a hundred major and minor denominations have evolved. All branches of Protestantism place great emphasis on personal interpretation of the Bible and individual responsibility for salvation, in sharp contrast with the Catholic requirement concerning the role of the church in such matters.

The many evangelical branches of Protestantism stress faith in Jesus Christ and the necessity of individual repentance if one is to achieve salvation. Among the Evangelicals, fundamentalist groups emphasize a strict and literal interpretation of the words of the Bible, and pentecostals believe that every Christian should personally experience being touched by the Holy Spirit.

A number of Protestant denominations occasionally have been in conflict with the wider society, primarily because of their emphasis on freedom in the interpretation of the Bible. The teachings of some Protestant denominations put their members at odds with modern medical care. Jehovah's Witnesses may not receive blood transfusions; the leadership of the Worldwide Church of God considers vaccines to be "monkey pus" and likens the use of physicians to the worship of pagan gods; and both the Church of God of the Union

Exhibit 12.8

Sociology in the Media

Are Some Cuddly Dolls the Devil's Playthings?

Care Bears and Rainbow Brite look cuddly and adorable, but some people believe that these toys—when linked to television cartoons—can be morally and spiritually unhealthy for children.

Sweet-looking toys are not necessarily "innocent," writes Phil Phillips, evangelist and author of "Turmoil in the Toy Box," which has been selling briskly at Christian bookstores around the country.

"Many of these toys, even the ones that tug on our heartstrings as being adorable, portray occult symbolisms, while others offer witchcraft, magic, and sorcery," Phillips writes.

Phillips, 25, lives in Rockwall, Texas, a suburb of Dallas. He believes that most toys are harmless when a child uses his own imagination to determine the toy's role or personality. The problem, as Phillips sees it, is that many toys today are linked with television cartoons that present non-Christian story lines.

When children play with toys based on a cartoon program, they're apt not to use their own imagination, writes Phillips. They will re-enact scenes straight from the cartoons, incorporating the themes that are presented.

For instance, Phillips argues that Care Bears, as depicted in television cartoons, "play an almost God-like, or at least an angelic, role when helping out children in trouble and in establishing their own religious order and rituals."

Although Care Bears share a caring attitude through symbols emblazoned on their stomachs, the symbols "are not Christian," writes Phillips.

Phillips sees Rainbow Brite's chief symbol as the rainbow, which he writes is also a "symbol of God's covenant that He never again would destroy the earth by flood."

However, Phillips warns that for followers of the tenets of the New Age Movement or humanistic psychology, rainbows "signify their building of the 'Rainbow Bridge' between man and Lucifer." Phillips believes that humanistic teachings are contradictory to God's word.

Even Cabbage Patch Kids are not immune to Phillips' scrutiny. Children are encouraged to pretend that these soft-sculptured dolls are real babies, he writes. As a result, he says, "The line separating fantasy from the real world has become distorted."

Other toys deemed dangerous by Phillips are Gummi Bears, My Little Pony, Smurfs, and Barbie dolls.

Phillips also denounces war-oriented toys such as G.I. Joe and Masters of the Universe.

SOURCE: Stephanie Wyche, Wilmington (Delaware) *News-Journal,* March 7, 1987, pp. D1, D4. Reprinted with permission of the *News-Journal,* Wilmington, Delaware.

Assembly and the Faith Assembly Church forbid their members from obtaining medical treatment of any type. The courts have ordered treatment for some members, and criminal prosecution has been used against other church members whose children died for the want of simple medications.[48]

As noted earlier in Exhibit 12.3, the issue of secular humanism involves conflict of a different sort. A recent Tennessee case illustrates this point. In 1986, a group of parents who believed strongly in the literal reading of the Bible sued the local school board, objecting to the "anti-Christian" messages contained in certain schoolbooks.[49] Specific examples raised at the trial included *The Wizard of Oz,* because it contains "good" witches; *Cinderella,* because of the magic performed by the fairy godmother; and *The Diary of Anne Frank,* because it implies an equality of all religious beliefs. Most recently, such anti-Christian messages have also been reported in association with Cabbage Patch Kids, Care Bears, Rainbow Brite, and other contemporary toys (see Exhibit 12.8).

While the dilemma for Catholicism in recent years has been accusations of rigidity, Protestantism has been plagued by a doctrine of individual interpretation that creates the potential for limitless versions of the same faith and disunity and conflict among its many branches. The number of different Protestant sects and cults provides ample testimony for this point.

Sects, as noted earlier, originate by breaking off from an existing church. One of the more untraditional examples involved the serpent-handlers, who flourished for decades until states prohibited their actions.[50] This group emerged through a literal interpretation of the biblical message to "take up serpents" (Mark 16:18). Using poisonous snakes as part of their services, many were bitten, and some died. Yet they persisted because their faith was strong enough that they placed their lives in the hands of God.

Along with the many different Protestant sects, Christian cults may be even more numerous, with estimates reaching as high as 600 in the mid-eighties.[51] Among those that have achieved high public visibility in recent years are the Unification Church and Scientology. The Unification Church was founded during the 1950s by Reverend Sun Myung Moon, a Korean industrialist, and now has some 50,000 members. Some observers see this group as a sect, because it incorporates some elements of conventional Protestant doctrine, yet in practice it operates as a cult. The Unification Church identifies Koreans as God's chosen people and Reverend Moon as successor to Christ.[52] Another prominent cult, the Church of Scientology was founded in 1954, based on the writings of L. Ron Hubbard.[53] His doctrine stresses individual attainment of a high mental and moral state that yields good health, financial success, and personal happiness. These elements, in turn, eliminate all of the evils and problems of the secular world.[54] Scientology shares with more conventional religions such social norms as "Love Thy Neighbor," but it also teaches the existence of supernatural spirits called "theta beings." Scientology is a nonexclusive religion in the sense that members are free to simultaneously belong to other faiths.

Serpent-handlers in Kentucky placed their faith in the supernatural to protect them from harm when handling poisonous snakes.

THE ELECTRONIC CHURCH

On an August day in 1801 in the small village of Cane Ridge, Kentucky, a small group of settlers joined together in America's first known "camp meeting." The gathering was seen as a way to revive religious spirit along a frontier where formal churches were rare.[55] The idea soon spread across the American plains and the trans-Mississippi west. Camp meetings were typically outdoor services that lasted several days and were often conducted by visiting preachers. Religious doctrine played a secondary role in the services after emotionalism. Laughter, singing, and dancing were prominent features. Although they originated as a rural tradition, by 1900 revival meetings could be found throughout urban America as well.

The invention of radio in the 1920s added a new element to religion in general and to revivals in particular. Members of the clergy could now take their messages directly into the homes of their parishioners. Among the first to use the new media was Dr. Charles Fuller, a minister whose "Old-Fashioned Revival Hour" premiered in 1923. During the 1940s and 1950s Reverend Billy Graham called hundreds of thousands of people to reaffirm their faith over the airwaves or at huge outdoor rallies.

Then, on February 12, 1952, a dramatic change occurred in the delivery of religious messages. That date marked the first telecast of "Life Is Worth Living," a half-hour, prime-time television program featuring a charming and well-spoken Catholic priest who offered anecdotes and little lessons in morality. "Life Is Worth Living" generated a large and devoted following and was in all probability the most widely viewed religious series in the history of television. Its "star" and only "regular" was the Most Reverend Fulton J. Sheen, Auxiliary Bishop of New York, a modest middle-level cleric who managed to keep his show a prime-time success for more than half a decade.* In so doing, Sheen made it possible for

*At least a part of Sheen's success can be attributed to a rather dramatic event early in 1953. A number of his talks focused on the evils of world communism, and on one occasion he delivered a hair-raising reading of the burial scene from *Julius Caesar,* with the names of Caesar, Cassius, Brutus, and Marc Antony replaced by Stalin and three other high-ranking Soviets of the era. "Stalin," Sheen intoned with hypnotic forcefulness, "must one day meet his judgment." A few days later the Soviet dictator suffered a stroke, and in less than a week he was dead.

television to emerge as a means of reaching hundreds of thousands, and then millions of people. At the peak of their popularity in the early 1980s, the electronic churches were able to claim 13.5 million viewers.[56]

Although Bishop Sheen is probably unknown to most young Americans today, the ministers of the major contemporary electronic churches are familiar to nearly everyone (see Exhibit 12.9). While few of the ministers have become international figures and the rest target mostly local audiences, three themes are shared by almost all electronic ministers: a belief in the absolute authority of the Bible; salvation through repentance; and the importance of being "born again,"—a reaffirmation of the central importance of Jesus Christ in the individual's life. Beyond this shared message, the most popular TV ministers are very different personalities, and they

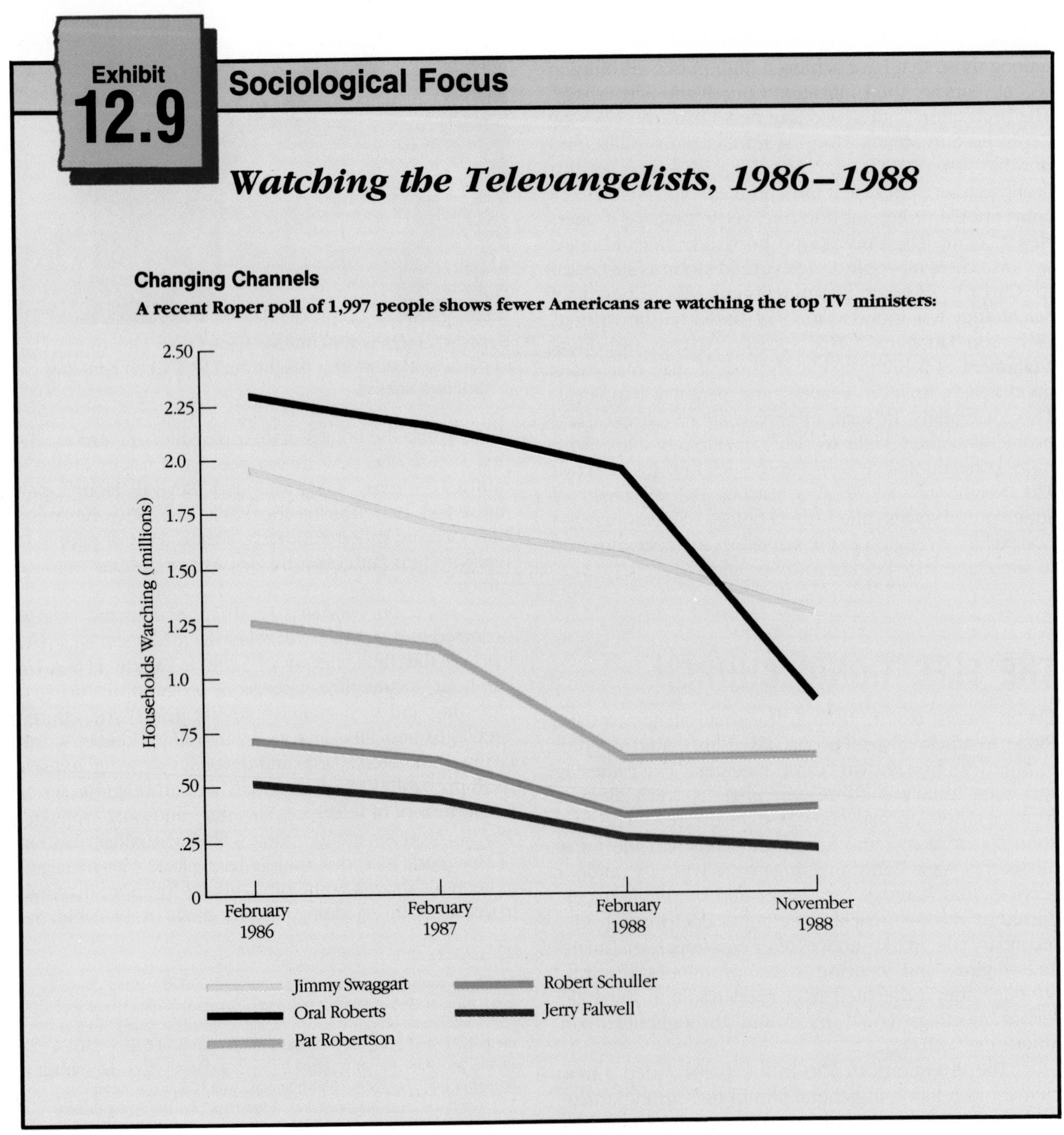

Television has fostered the growth of electronic churches. The Reverend Robert Schuller, broadcasting from the $18-million Crystal Cathedral, reaches an audience of three-quarters of a million households.

represent a wide range of perspectives. M.G. "Pat" Robertson is a Southern Baptist and Jerry Falwell, a fundamental Baptist. Jim Bakker and Jimmy Swaggert are Pentecostal ministers (adherents to a group in which faith healing and speaking in tongues play a central role). Robert Schuller is a minister in the Reformed Church of America and emphasizes the power of positive thinking. All of these ministers are personable, forceful, and have a strong element of charisma in their sermons.

Electronic churches are, in part, a product of demographic changes in the twentieth century. As American society became larger, more impersonal, and more highly mobile in the decades following World War II, traditional congregations were no longer the stable communities that Durkheim had envisioned. For some, the television church replaced the traditional church service. Currently, televangelists appeal most to an older, rural, lower-income, and disproportionately female audience.[57] These viewers generally are attracted to conservative, fundamentalist Christian teachings and look to the electronic church to reinforce their beliefs. For others, television religion seems to supplement "regular" religion; almost one-fourth of the viewers say they have increased their participation in local church activities as a consequence of exposure to electronic religion.[58]

As the electronic ministries grew in popularity, they became big business, raising millions of dollars by appealing directly to their viewers for financial support. It has been estimated, for example, that $500 million was being donated annually during the early 1980s, at the peak of electronic church popularity.[59] The TV ministers have used their revenues to finance their missionary work, as well as to build churches, universities, hospitals, and clinics. Robert Schuller broadcasts his Sunday services from the Crystal Cathedral, a twelve-story glass and steel edifice that cost $18 million to construct. Oral Roberts founded Oral Roberts University and the $150-million City of Faith Medical Center in Tulsa. In addition, Roberts has clinics and missions in many Third World nations.

In recent years a number of the television evangelists have extended their fund-raising endeavors into some nontraditional areas. Jim Bakker of the PTL Club (the initials stand for "Praise The Lord" and "People That Love") wrote *The Exodus Diet Plan* and several other books on weight control, while his wife Tammy Faye Bakker marketed a line of cosmetics. The Bakkers also built Heritage USA, a 2,300-acre Christian theme park near Charlotte, North Carolina, that combined religious activities (daily communion services, weekly baptisms) with secular diversions (tennis, horseback riding, swimming pools, and water slides). In 1985, five million people visited the park. Many of them were "Lifetime Partners," who enjoyed the right to free weekends at Heritage USA for the cost of $1,000.[60]

The electronic church in the United States fell on difficult times during the second half of the 1980s. Oral Roberts attracted both publicity and criticism in 1987 when he announced that God had spoken to him, warning him that he would die if he failed in an $8-million fund-raising endeavor.[61] Later in the year Jim and Tammy Bakker were forced to resign from their PTL Club ministry when earlier incidents of drug abuse, adultery, and allegations of blackmail surfaced. Their departure led to an investigation of organizational finances that revealed salaries of over a million dollars per year and extravagant life-styles.[62] In 1988 Jimmy Swaggart was dropped from the Assemblies of God ministry in the aftermath of his alleged "please-pose-for-me" scandal with a Baton Rouge prostitute.[63]

The Bakker and Roberts incidents of 1987 and the Swaggart scandal in 1988 had negative effects on all television ministries. Polls taken soon after the revelations of impropriety found that the majority of the general population felt that TV evangelists were not truly in the service of God; half of those who actually watched TV ministers held an unfavorable picture of them; and a fourth reported that they would curtail their contributions.[64] Yet, a strong element of support remained as evidenced by the fact that PTL was able to raise millions of dollars to maintain its program during the height of the scandal. It is certainly too soon to predict the long-term implications of the Bakker and Swaggart scandals, but they seem certain to have negative implications for TV evangelism.

RELIGION AND APPLIED SOCIOLOGY

The scientific study of religion presents the sociologist with a problem. Survey research can provide a picture of religious beliefs, attitudes, rates of attendance at services, and related information, and such information has value for understanding the role of religion in the everyday lives of people. Yet critics argue that science and religion are at odds, for the very nature of religious beliefs defies verification by means of the scientific method. To some extent the point is valid, for after all, the existence of one or more supreme beings can neither be proven nor denied with any of the tools that social science can muster. But all of this misses the point of sociological research. The goal is to understand the interaction between religion and other aspects of social behavior, not to prove or disqualify the validity of deeply held personal convictions.

Actually, a considerable amount of social research suggests clues to the dynamics of religious behavior. In a classic study undertaken several decades ago, for example, researchers conducted participant observations in a cult that had predicted world destruction. Cult members believed they would be the only group saved; salvation was to take the form of extraterrestrials in a flying saucer.[65] The observers watched the group prepare for the predicted day of reckoning. Ultimately, the believers gathered at the appointed site to wait, confident that the obliteration of the world was close at hand. As the day passed and it became evident that the prophecy had failed, the undaunted cult leader announced that judgment day had been postponed. Some followers wandered off, but those who remained in the group accepted the new prediction. The research demonstrated that religious beliefs—like *all* deeply held beliefs—are not merely individual matters but are maintained in the social context of a group. Those whose faith was shaken by the failure of the prophecy were able to have it reaffirmed and restored by the support of others. Thus, the group survived, its beliefs modified and reoriented—an achievement that would have been difficult for isolated individuals to accomplish.

Sociological research findings also have direct utility to religions in assessing the impact of their teachings by monitoring the attitudes and behaviors of their congregations. Despite pronouncements from the Vatican, for example, a recent study found that among young, unmarried, sexually active women, devout Catholics were more likely than any other group to use birth control. Fully 98% of the Catholic women who attend Mass and receive communion at least once a week were found to use contraceptives, as compared to 86% of non-Catholic women.[66] This finding suggests two things: first, the Catholic Church in the United States needs to reevaluate either its position on birth control or the mechanisms through which it preaches against it; second, since Catholic women seem to be "more careful" when it comes to sexual activity, family planning groups need to find out why, and to use that information when targeting sex education messages to other groups.

Basic demographic data have been used for decades by advertising and market research groups, but rarely have they been analyzed by religious organizations for fund-raising purposes. In fact, if churches and television evangelists were to examine the data on who gives the most to charity, they would find that—at least from a financial point of view—they need to be targeting wider audiences. While the audiences currently attracted by TV ministers are primarily older, low-income women, the major contributors to charity are middle-aged, middle-income women *and* men.[67] In short, churches and other religious groups in need of funds to support their endeavors can make use of sociological research techniques and data to identify and cultivate donors.

As a final note to the applied side of sociology and religion, it is useful to recall the election of John F. Kennedy. Prior to 1960, only Protestant candidates were elected, and consequently his campaign needed to focus directly on the religious affiliations of voters (see Exhibit 12.10).

Exhibit 12.10 **Applied Sociology**

Sociology, Religion, and the Election of JFK

Since the founding of the nation more than two centuries ago, presidential campaign managers have been strategists—individuals who put forth the *best* in their own candidates while highlighting the *worst* in the opposing candidates. Attention focused on a candidate's experience and voting record, and as many speeches were delivered, hands shaken, and babies kissed—in as many parts of the nation—as time and finances permitted.

Campaign strategies in the United States expanded during the twentieth century—primarily through the use of the media to better shape and present a candidate's image, and by means of the collection and use of demographic and sociological data to identify appropriate target groups for political messages. All of the recent presidential candidates have used these approaches to a greater or lesser degree, but the issue of religion was of special interest and concern to the Kennedy team in the election of 1960.

John Fitzgerald Kennedy had many advantages as a presidential candidate: he was the nominee of the Democratic party; he had charisma and a leader's stature and image; he had been awarded a Pulitzer Prize for his book, *Profiles in Courage;* he had the support of organized labor; and he had his family's great wealth to supplement his campaign funds.

But Kennedy had to run as far and as hard as he possibly could, for he had many disadvantages as well. He was opposing Richard M. Nixon, the Vice-President of the United States. He was young for a presidential candidate (43 years old to Nixon's 47), and he was less experienced. And finally, Kennedy was a Catholic, and a widespread conviction dating from Al Smith's candidacy in 1928 maintained that a Roman Catholic could not be elected President of the United States. True, Kennedy was a different sort of Irish-Catholic—New England "society," Harvard-trained, immaculately tailored, and superbly eloquent. Nevertheless, Kennedy *was* a Roman Catholic, and his campaign team worried about it.

On the basis of preliminary census tabulations and projections from earlier years, the Kennedy campaign strategy was to divide the country into four groups—Catholic Democrats, non-Catholic Democrats, Catholic Republicans, and non-Catholic Republicans. Since Kennedy was both a Catholic and a Democrat, his staff gambled that the majority of the Catholic Democrat votes could be counted on. Thus, only minimal campaign time and expense were focused on that group. The converse was decided for non-Catholic Republicans. Little could be done to make Kennedy attractive to them, so they were all but ignored. That left non-Catholic Democrats and Catholic Republicans—the two groups that Kennedy had the best chance of winning over.

It would appear that the strategy worked, at least in part. Kennedy won the election by a margin of 118,550 votes out of some 68 million cast. While he attracted only 5% of the Republican votes, he amassed 84% of the Democrat votes—enough to carry him into the White House.

SOURCES: Robert D. Cantor, *Voting Behavior and Presidential Elections* (Itasca, IL: F. E. Peacock, 1975); William Manchester, *The Glory and the Dream: A Narrative History of America, 1932–1972* (Boston: Little, Brown, 1973); Richard M. Pious, *The American Presidency* (New York: Basic Books, 1979); Theodore H. White, *The Making of a President 1960* (New York: Atheneum, 1961).

SUMMARY

Religion plays a central role in all known human societies. At the most general level, religion means that certain objects and places are deemed sacred, thus separating them from the secular or profane world. Despite the diversity that characterizes the world's many religions, each is organized around a set of beliefs and rituals, and various concepts involving one or more supernatural beings.

Emile Durkheim was convinced that religion was vital to the survival of society, for it established and reaffirmed group solidarity, enforced social norms, and eased individuals and groups through the stressful crises that are so much a part of life in organized society. By contrast, Marx and other theorists viewed religion as a source of conflict and disunity, and as a mechanism through which the elite classes could manipulate the lower classes. Thus, while Durkheim emphasized solidarity within the group and Marx focused on divisions, both agreed on two things: first, that religion is a powerful force in human affairs; and second, that religion reflects existing arrangements of the social structure.

Organized religion takes many forms, ranging from tiny cults and sects to large-scale organizations that employ thousands of people and encompass millions of followers. The *church* represents the end product of a long process of evolution extending over many years. Churches are bureaucracies. Like secular bureaucracies, they are created to achieve goals—to minister to the faith of followers and to guide them toward salvation. *Cults* are groups dedicated to entirely new or radically different ideas. A *sect* splits off from a church when a group of believers feels that the church has strayed from the original religious doctrines or intent, or when new ideas are discovered.

Religion often creates difficulties in a society as complex as that in the United States. The very religious diversity that makes America attractive to immigrants simultaneously generates social divisions and introduces the potential for conflict. Laws designed to govern millions of people may inevitably encroach on the beliefs of some faiths.

KEY TERMS/CONCEPTS

animatism
animism
ceremonies
charisma
church
cult
dualism
magic
prayer
profane
religion
rituals
Roe v. Wade
routinization of charisma
sacred
sect
secular
theism

DISCUSSION QUESTIONS

1. Durkheim and Marx offered different interpretations of the role of religion in society. How are their views similar and different?
2. What do you think might be the long-term implications of the Bakker scandal for the future of television religion?
3. Should religious "cults," such as the Unification Church, be outlawed because people disagree with their ideas and methods?
4. Does magic ever play a role in the lives of students as they prepare for final examinations?
5. How might the concepts of *church, cult,* or *sect* apply to the religious group of which you are a member?

SUGGESTED READINGS

Peter L. Berger, *A Rumor of Angels: Modern Society and the Rediscovery of the Supernatural* (New York: Doubleday, 1969). A noted sociologist develops a theory of religion in the tradition of Emile Durkheim, and his analysis makes it clear that sociology can coexist with religious faith.

Theodore M. Caplow, Howard M. Bahr, and Bruce A. Chadwick, *All Faithful People* (Minneapolis: University of Minnesota Press, 1983). This study focuses on the role and meaning of religion in the lives of the residents of the midwestern city "Middletown," first systematically studied by sociologists in the 1920s.

H. Paul Chalfant, Robert E. Beckley, and C. Eddie Palmer, *Religion in Contemporary Society* (Palo Alto, CA: Mayfield, 1986). This textbook provides the beginning student with a thorough and systematic overview of the sociological study of religion.

Jeffrey K. Hadden and Anson Shupe, *Televangelism: Power and Politics on God's Frontier* (New York: Henry Holt, 1988). A thorough and systematic examination of the electronic church and an analysis of how televangelists and their followers are creating a cultural revolution in America.

Robert C. Liebman and Robert Wuthnow (eds.), *The New Christian Right* (New York: Aldine, 1983). This collection of original articles examines the political activity of fundamentalist Christian groups. It sheds light on both religion and culture in American society.

Rodney Stark and W. S. Bainbridge, *The Future of Religion: Secularization, Revival and Cult Formation* (Berkeley, CA: University of California Press, 1985). The authors argue that western society is undergoing a period of dramatic religious change as many people experiment with new religions because established churches have failed to respond to the modern world.

NOTES

1. "Church Attendance," The Gallup Poll (Wilmington, DE: Scholarly Research Inc., 1985), p. 291.
2. Rodney Stark and William Sims Bainbridge, *The Future of Religion* (Berkeley: University of California Press, 1985), p. 85.
3. "Religion: Spiritual Experiences," The Gallup Poll (Wilmington, DE: Scholarly Research Inc., 1986), pp. 108–109.
4. Emile Durkheim, *The Elementary Forms of Religious Life* (New York: Free Press, 1926), p. 46.
5. Engle v. Vitale, 370 U.S. 421 (1962).
6. School District of Abington Township v. Schempp, Murray and Curlett, 374 U.S. 203 (1963).
7. See Leo Pfeffer, *Church, State and Freedom* (Boston: Beacon, 1967), p. 466.
8. See *Business Week*, September 24, 1984, p. 24; *Newsweek*, March 19, 1984, p. 31; *U.S. News & World Report*, March 5, 1984, p. 42; *U.S. News & World Report*, April 2, 1984, p. 11.
9. *U.S. News & World Report*, June 17, 1985, p. 9.
10. Fred Eggan, *Social Organization of the Western Pueblos* (Chicago: University of Chicago Press, 1950).
11. Miguel Covarrubias, *Island of Bali* (New York: Alfred A. Knopf, 1938), p. 351.
12. Carole Devillers, "Of Spirits and Saints," *National Geographic*, 167 (March 1985), pp. 394–408.
13. *USA Today*, November 25, 1986, p. 3C.
14. Robert A. Marett, *The Threshold of Religion* (London: Methuen, 1909).
15. R. H. Codrington, *The Melanesians* (Oxford: Oxford University Press, 1891).
16. Edward B. Tylor, *Primitive Culture* (London: John Murray, 1891).
17. Morris Opler, *An Apache Life-Way* (Chicago: University of Chicago Press, 1941), p. 280.
18. Clifford Geertz, *The Religion of Java* (Glencoe, IL: Free Press, 1960), pp. 16–29.
19. Wallace Murphree, "Can Theism Survive Without the Devil?" *Religious Studies*, 21 (June 1985), pp. 231–44.
20. *USA Today*, April 16, 1987, p. 6D.
21. See Geoffrey Parrinder, *World Religions: From Ancient History to the Present* (New York: Facts on File, 1984), pp. 262–303.
22. Wilmington (Delaware) *News-Journal*, May 25, 1987, p. 2A.
23. For the argument against monotheism, see Jeffrey Burton Russell, *The Devil: Perceptions of Evil from Antiquity to Primitive Christianity* (Ithaca, NY: Cornell University Press, 1977).
24. Emile Durkheim, *The Elementary Forms.*
25. For example, see Harry Alpert, *Emile Durkheim and His Sociology* (New York: Columbia University Press, 1939), pp. 198–203.
26. Ward Rutherford, *The Druids and Their Heritage* (London: Gordon and Cremonesi, 1978).
27. M. B. Smith, "Combat Motivation Among Ground Troops," pp. 179–91 in Samuel A. Stouffer, et al, *The American Soldier* (Princeton, NJ: Princeton University Press, 1949).
28. Roe v. Wade, 410 U.S. 113 (1973).
29. *Newsweek*, January 14, 1985, pp. 20–28; *Time*, January 14, 1985, pp. 16–17; *USA Today*, October 30, 1986, p. 3A; *USA Today*, March 27, 1987, p. 3A; *U.S. News & World Report*, December 3, 1984, p. 72.
30. See Karl Marx, *Selected Writings in Sociology and Social Philosophy*, trans. and ed. by Tom Bottomore and Maximillian Rubel (Baltimore: Penguin, 1964), p. 42.
31. M. M. Bober, *Karl Marx's Interpretation of History* (New York: W. W. Norton, 1965), p. 156.
32. Elizabeth Nottingham, *Religion and Society* (Garden City, NJ: Doubleday, 1954), p. 51.
33. *Time*, May 12, 1986, p. 82.
34. Philip Cushman, "The Self-Besieged: Recruitment-Indoctrination Processes in Restrictive Groups," *Journal for the Theory of Social Behavior*, 16 (March 1986), p. 21.
35. Philip Cushman, "The Self-Besieged."
36. Wilmington (Delaware) *News-Journal*, May 21, 1987, p. 2C.
37. Philip Cushman, "The Self-Besieged."
38. Teresa Donati Marciano, "Families and Cults," in Florence Kaslow and Marvin Sussman (eds.), *Cults and the Family* (Boston: Haworth, 1982), pp. 101–118.
39. See John Clark, Michael D. Langone, Robert E. Schacter, and Roger C. G. Daly, *Destructive Cult Conversion* (Weston, MA: American Family Foundation, 1981); Marvin Galper, "The Cult Phenomena," in Florence Kaslow and Marvin B. Sussman (eds.), *Cults and the Family* (Boston: Haworth, 1982), pp. 141–50; John Lofland and Rodney Stark, "Becoming a World-saver: A Theory of Conversion to a Deviant Perspective," *American Sociological Review* 30 (December 1965), pp. 862–75; John Lofland, "'Becoming a World-saver' Revisited," *American Behavioral Scientist*, 20 (July-August 1977), pp. 805–18.
40. H. Richard Niebuhr, *The Social Sources of Denominationalism* (New York: Henry Holt, 1929).
41. Reuben Kaufman, *Great Sects and Schisms in Judaism* (New York: Jonathan David, 1967).
42. *New York Times*, December 28, 1986, p. 35.
43. Jacob Neusner, *Death and Birth of Judaism: The Impact of Christianity, Secularism, and the Holocaust on the Jewish Faith* (New York: Basic Books, 1987).
44. Bernard Lazerwitz and Michael Harrison, "American Jewish Denominations: A Social and Religious Profile," *American Sociological Review*, 44 (August 1979), pp. 656–66; Marc Lee

Raphael, *Profiles in American Judaism* (San Francisco: Harper & Row, 1984).

45. *New York Times,* August 24, 1986, p. 7E.
46. *New York Times,* March 16, 1986, p. 29; *Time,* February 4, 1985, p. 62; *USA Today,* March 15, 1985, p. 3A; *USA Today,* September 17, 1987, p. 5A.
47. *New York Times,* May 23, 1985, p. A24.
48. *Miami Herald,* June 24, 1984, pp. 1A, 5A; *Time,* April 16, 1984, p. 42.
49. *Newsweek,* July 28, 1986, pp. 18–20.
50. Weston LaBarre, *They Shall Take Up Serpents* (Minneapolis: University of Minnesota Press, 1962).
51. *Chronicle of Higher Education,* March 9, 1983, p. 5.
52. Eileen Barker, *The Making of a Moonie* (Oxford: Basil Blackwell, 1984).
53. L. Ron Hubbard, *Dianetics: The Modern Science of Mental Health* (Los Angeles: Bridge, 1950).
54. William Sims Bainbridge and Rodney Stark, "Scientology: To Be Perfectly Clear," *Sociological Analysis,* 41 (1980), pp. 128–36.
55. Sydney E. Ahlstrom, *A Religious History of the American People* (New Haven: Yale University Press, 1972), p. 435; see also Ben Armstrong, *The Electronic Church* (Nashville: Thomas Nelson, 1979).
56. *USA Today,* March 26, 1987, p. 5D.
57. Jeffrey K. Hadden and Anson Shupe, *Televangelism: Power and Politics on God's Frontier* (New York: Henry Holt, 1988); Jeffrey K. Hadden and Charles E. Swann, *Prime Time Preachers: The Rising Power of Televangelism* (Reading, MA: Addison-Wesley, 1981).
58. *Religion in America* (Princeton, NJ: The Gallup Organization, 1981), pp. 65–66.
59. *USA Today,* March 27, 1987, p. 12A.
60. *Newsweek,* August 11, 1986, p. 47.
61. *Time,* January 26, 1987, p. 63.
62. *Newsweek,* March 30, 1987, p. 28; *Newsweek,* April 6, 1987, pp. 16–21; *Time,* April 6, 1987, pp. 60–67; *U.S. News & World Report,* April 13, 1987, p. 15.
63. *Time,* June 6, 1988, p. 7.
64. *New York Times,* March 31, 1987, pp. 1A, 8B; *Time,* June 6, 1988, p. 7; *USA Today,* April 1, 1987, p. 3A.
65. Leon Festinger, Henry W. Rieken, and Kent Back, *Social Pressures in Informal Groups* (New York: Harper & Row, 1950).
66. *American Demographics,* October 1985, pp. 13–14.
67. *American Demographics,* November 1986, pp. 45–49.

Education: Controversy and Crisis

Every September, millions of American children march off to school for their first day in a formal classroom. Anticipation is tinged with a bit of apprehension as they approach a new adventure. Yet few of these 5- and 6-year-olds are aware of the controversy that swirls around their teachers and schools, or the public criticism directed at educational systems throughout the nation. American education, at every level, continuously is examined and evaluated, praised and damned, challenged and defended, and even taken to court and sued. It frequently would appear that few people are satisfied with the American educational system.

Education is a social institution, the formal process by which society transmits its knowledge, skills, and values from one person or group to another. As such, education is a mechanism of socialization, a responsibility shared with the family, the community, and other social institutions (see Chapter 5).

While most Americans might agree that primary schools should teach basic writing and mathematical skills, beyond that they exhibit a considerable diversity of opinion. Each of the many different social, cultural, ethnic, religious, and political groups in a democratic society attempts to force school systems to reflect its own particular values and beliefs. In addition to the basics, many ask, should the schools be teaching students about sex and reproduction, drugs, religion, driver training, typing, and even cheerleading? As American society grows more complex and heterogeneous, education is called upon to expand its scope well beyond a teaching of the basics.

Beyond the debates over the basic subject matter of formal learning, education generates controversy because activities in schools often violate the ideals of particular social groups. As noted earlier in Chapter 12 (Exhibit 12.3), for example, the contents of textbooks and library books are heatedly debated in many locales. Teachers' groups and publishers regularly report on objections to certain courses and books, along with attempts to have them removed from schools.

Education also can reflect the biases of the larger society. In Chapter 10, for example, we noted that women were long barred from admission to medical schools. Education also may be openly manipulated to maintain inequality. When segregation was the law of the land, blacks were shunted off into second-rate schools, virtually guaranteeing that they would be unable to compete equally with whites in the job market after they finished school.*

If education is to be judged on the basis of how much students have learned by the time they leave school, then many people would argue that the United States is facing a major educational crisis. Estimates of the incidence of **functional illiteracy,** the inability to read and comprehend at the fourth-grade level, range as high as 27 million persons.[1] Other studies indicate that most high-school students are unable to identify such notable personages as Henry David Thoreau and Joseph Stalin. In 1983 a study commission labeled the United States a "nation at risk" because of the "mediocre" performance of American education.[2]

Quite clearly, this situation poses a challenge for social scientists who seek to understand and explain what

*Although progress has been made in overcoming obstacles to formal education for minorities, many serious problems still remain. Black participation in higher education is shrinking, for example, with rates of college attendance having declined from 50% to 42% from 1977 through 1988. See *New York Times,* April 19, 1987, p. 1.

SOCIAL INDICATOR

Books Challenged Most Often during the 1980s

The Chocolate War, by Robert Cormier
The Catcher in the Rye, by J. D. Salinger
Of Mice and Men, by John Steinbeck
The Adventures of Huckleberry Finn, by Mark Twain
Deenie, by Judy Blume
Go Ask Alice, by unlisted author
A Light in the Attic, by Shel Silverstein

has been happening in society, in its schools, and in its classrooms—where the actual teaching and learning processes take place—that has produced the crisis and controversy. Within this context, and since the present often tends to reflect the past, perhaps the most logical place to begin this sociological analysis of education is with its emergence and growth in American society.

THE GROWTH OF EDUCATION IN AMERICA

Colonial America was first populated and ruled by British settlers who held to the aristocratic ideal that since members of the upper classes were destined to become leaders, education should be reserved for them. As a result, education in the United States evolved in a somewhat erratic manner, first in the Northeast and later in the South and West. A number of social, political, and economic factors operating in the larger society also influenced the way education evolved. Considerations of religion, social class, race and ethnicity, and gender shaped the process at every stage of development.[3]

Education in Colonial America

Organized education developed early in the American colonies, at least in the Northeast, primarily because the first settlers tended to be a rather bookish lot. Most of them were Congregationalists who believed that religious truth was incomprehensible to those who did not read the Scriptures. Despite their life in the wilderness, they wanted to read, and they wanted their children to be educated. "How," they asked, "can the next generation find salvation if it cannot read the Bible?"

SOCIAL INDICATOR

The First Colleges and Universities in the United States

1636	John Harvard College
1693	College of William and Mary
1701	Collegiate School of Connecticut (renamed Yale in 1718)
1746	College of New Jersey (renamed Princeton in 1896)
1751	Franklin's Academy (renamed University of Pennsylvania in 1779)
1754	King's College (renamed Columbia in 1784)
1764	Rhode Island College (renamed Brown in 1804)
1766	Queen's College (renamed Rutgers in 1825)
1769	Dartmouth College
1795	University of North Carolina (the first *state* university)

Thus, within sixteen years of the founding of the Massachusetts Bay Colony in 1620, Harvard College was founded. In addition, colonial Massachusetts laws required that every town of 50 families maintain a schoolmaster and every town of 100 families have someone able to teach Latin and Greek. Other New England colonies had similar laws. Although they were not always enforced, literacy rates from the very beginning exceeded those found in England, and by the middle of the 1700s, almost all adult males could read and write.

Other colonial regions lagged far behind New England. In the South, particularly, a tremendous gap developed in educational opportunities between the upper classes and all others. Well-to-do plantation owners could afford private tutors for their children, and occasionally several families would band together to hire a teacher. The College of William and Mary was established at Williamsburg, Virginia, in 1693 for the education of the children of plantation owners, but no effective primary or secondary school system for the middle classes appeared until much later. Many of the wealthy also continued the tradition of sending their children to England for higher education.

Colonial schools typically were small—often a single room in the teacher's home.

From the beginning, slavery also shaped education and the school systems. Many politicians argued that slaves were uneducable, and this myth was reinforced by laws that prohibited people from teaching slaves to read and write.[4] A few did teach their slaves some basic skills, but most did not. Only a handful of whites at the time were willing to run the risks of prosecution and social disapproval for the sake of making slaves fully literate. Certain schools in the South had been set up for slaves, but since their education in formal schools was considered a serious violation of law, such institutions were few in number.

Education in Post-Revolutionary America

With the exception of those in Massachusetts, in the decades immediately following the Revolutionary War, most people, both rural and urban, were at best only semiliterate. Even during the early years of the nineteenth century, the children of the poor obtained their elementary education at home or in church or charity schools, while the children of the rich had access to private schools and tutors. This gap was exacerbated by two rather significant factors: first, little public support existed for mass education; second, most teaching was done by poorly paid, minimally trained young men who regarded the enterprise merely as a temporary occupation. A good bit of what *was* taught was considerably out of date. As late as 1810, for example, some widely used arithmetic texts still employed problems based on British shillings and pence as well as systems of weights and measures that had no practical application for Americans.[5]

As the nineteenth century progressed, however, stronger support for public education came from several sources. Practical merchants, business owners, and politicians recognized that their increasingly commercial society was creating occupations that required that people be able to read, write, and cipher. Additional support came from political and social reformers who viewed education as a mechanism for upward mobility and the means for achieving a more general diffusion of property ownership. Finally, in a society based on the principles of democracy, many felt that to understand political issues, the electorate needed to be literate.

Just before mid-century, things began to change noticeably. A drive to build a compulsory, tax-supported, public-school system was underway. Horace Mann, the first head of the Massachusetts Board of Education, along with his lesser-known counterparts in other northern states, had become convinced that the future of America depended on the education of its children. These individuals worked to develop an elaborate system of schools open to *all* children—including those of indigent parents. Public schools, they argued, would equalize opportunities to get ahead in society, provide the educated citizenry needed for a democratic elective government, stimulate economic productivity, and instill social discipline.

By the early 1850s most states had some public elementary schools, and by the close of the decade free secondary schools had also been opened in Massachusetts, New York, and Ohio. The attitude that public schools were only for paupers was changing too, and the foundations were being laid for the development of teaching as an acknowledged profession.

Yet despite these advances, the very idea of public education in a multinational society posed a dilemma. Schools tend to reflect the traditions and values of dominant social groups, perhaps violating the beliefs of certain minorities. Thus, for example, amidst the sudden growth of public education, opposition arose from large segments of the Irish-American community. Most lived in such poverty that they needed to put their children to work at an early age just to insure that their families had basic necessities. Their primary objections, however, were religious. The Irish regarded educational reform as anti-Catholic. Although the public schools claimed to be nonsectarian, they were viewed as thinly disguised Protestant schools that would alienate Irish children from Catholicism. Holding that religion and education could not be separated, yet failing in their attempts to secure public funding for a system of Catholic schools, Irish-Americans were influential in having independent parochial schools established by the Catholic Church where their children could avoid the dangerous influence of Protestant fervor.

In the South, educational progress reflected a perpetuation of ignorance as well as a rather curious contradiction. For the children of the wealthy, a formal education that extended through college was the norm. In 1860, for example, the number of college students per 1,000 whites was three times higher in the South than in the North. At the primary and secondary levels, however, the South lagged far behind. As indicated in Exhibit 13.1, fewer southern white children were enrolled in school, and those that were spent little time in class. As a result, illiteracy rates among whites were high. When slavery and its legacy are factored in, the regional differences in education were even more striking.

The push for mass education that was beginning to open education to ever-wider numbers of students had considerably less influence on higher education during this period. However, many new denominational colleges developed, with 80 being founded between 1830 and 1850 alone. Numerous state universities also were founded, primarily in the South and West. Yet the quality

Exhibit 13.1

Sociological Focus

Regional Differences in Education for Whites, Ages 5–19, 1861

Region	Percent Enrolled in School	Average Percent of Enrolled Attending	Number of Days in School Year	Days of School per Child Ages 5–19 in Region
Northeast	62	59	150	55
West	76	57	116	50
South	30	45	80	11

Source: Stephan Thernstrom, *A History of the American People*, 2nd ed., vol. 1 (San Diego: Harcourt Brace Jovanovich, 1989), p. 286.

of higher education was seriously deficient. With the exception of the largest and oldest institutions, most colleges and universities had meager budgets and lacked the libraries and personnel necessary to become centers of intellectual life.

Coeducational higher learning for women was openly ignored during most of this period, and the majority of professional schools were closed to females. Despite repeated attempts to gain entry to law schools, women were consistently rebuffed. Gender stereotypes suggested that education would be wasted on women or even harmful to them. A Supreme Court justice made the following comments in 1873:

> The natural and proper timidity and delicacy which belongs to the female sex evidently unfits it for many occupations of civil life. . . . The paramount destiny and mission of women are to fulfill the noble and benign offices of wife and mother. This is the law of the creator.[6]

By the 1930s, the American schoolhouse had changed drastically, but the one-room school persisted in some rural areas.

The Era of Mass Education

The era of mass education in the United States began during the early 1870s. The foundations had been established years earlier by reformers like Horace Mann and by the impetus for state-supported school systems, but it was during the Industrial Revolution that the process actually began in earnest. Industrialization and the consequent growth of cities provided concentrated populations that made mass education economical (see Chapter 17); industrialization and concomitant increases in human productivity generated the revenues that universal education required.

As late as 1870 the average American had received only four years of formal schooling, but shortly thereafter steady growth became readily apparent. Attendance in public schools increased from 6.9 million in 1870 to 9.9 million in 1880 and 15.5 million by 1900.[7] Public expenditures for education increased from $63 million in 1870 to $250 million by the turn of the century and over $1 billion by 1920. The national illiteracy rate declined from 20% to 6.0% over the same fifty-year period.

During this period the goals and philosophy of education also shifted quite dramatically. John Dewey is credited with fostering the movement toward "progressive education," a philosophy that suggests that education be concerned not only with intellectual skills, but with social skills as well. The goal was "education for life," as Dewey put it, in addition to the academic skills of reading and counting. His idea was that schools had a responsibility to prepare each new generation for participation in the community. Linked to this idea was the belief that schools ought to teach what was relevant and interesting to children, and schools responded by introducing new courses to supplement the traditional basic curriculum.

By 1938, the emphasis in the schools, and particularly in high schools, was clearly on "life adjustment." The National Educational Association, in its report *The Purposes of Education in American Democracy,* announced four goals of education: self-realization, human relations, civic efficiency, and economic competence.[8] In this document "economic competence" meant preparation for the world of work. The economic devastation of the Great Depression that left millions of Americans unemployed led many to argue that schools should accept greater responsibility for preparing people for productive work.

Southern schools, however, continued to lag behind the rest of the nation, in large part because the region was poor and predominantly rural. For blacks the situation was even worse. The southern practice of segregating white and black students in public schools, buttressed by the United States Supreme Court's "separate but equal" decision in *Plessy v. Ferguson* in 1896 (see Chapter 9, Exhibit 9.1) insured inferior educational opportunities. In small communities where financial resources were limited, the practical result of segregation was a "white only" school system. Northern blacks were somewhat better off, although not on a par with whites. Most schools there were segregated as well, however

Exhibit 13.2

Sociological Focus

White/Nonwhite Illiteracy Rates, 1870–1950

	1870	1880	1890	1900	1910	1920	1930	1940	1950
White	20%	17%	13%	11%	8%	6%	4%	3%	3%
Nonwhite	80	70	57	45	31	23	16	12	11

Source: *Historical Statistics of the United States, Colonial Times to 1957,* 1960.

unofficially, and had inadequate resources and insufficiently trained staffs. The overall result was the almost wholesale disenfranchisement of blacks from quality education in much of the nation well into the twentieth century—a fact that is easily observed by comparing illiteracy rates (see Exhibit 13.2).

It was during the post–Civil War era that institutions of higher education evolved into centers for intellectual development and research. The number of colleges and universities expanded from 563 in 1870 to well over a thousand by the turn of the century.[9] Enrollments increased as well, from 52,000 in 1870 to 238,000 by 1900 and almost 600,000 by 1920.

By the first decade of the twentieth century, all of the pieces of the American educational system seemed to be in place. A commitment had been made that every child was entitled to a free, quality education, and as time passed opportunities for minorities slowly began to increase and greater proportions of individuals from all class levels and regions of the country were obtaining undergraduate and graduate degrees.

Education in the 1950s through the 1990s

Education faced two major new challenges in the aftermath of World War II. The most dramatic was the demand for equal education for ethnic and racial minorities. As noted in Chapter 9 (Exhibit 9.13), court challenges to the "separate but equal" segregated school systems for blacks led to the case of *Brown v. Board of Education of Topeka* in 1954. The Supreme Court's decision in *Brown* met with strong resistence in many locales throughout the 1960s and part of the 1970s. In fact, public schools in one southern jurisdiction closed for four years rather than admit blacks, while in the north many schools remained segregated due to housing patterns.

The other challenge centered on demands that the tenets of "progressive education" be abandoned in favor of a return to a strict academic curriculum. This challenge had been spirited by many factors. None was more dramatic than the launch of the Soviet's *Sputnik* space capsule in 1957, which suggested that the United States had fallen behind in scientific competition. A new generation of middle-class parents also was concerned that their children be able to succeed in college and careers. Schools responded by creating college preparatory tracks and other related programs.

Contemporary education faces a number of new challenges and crises that reflect the legacy of its three centuries of development. The demand for equal opportunity has not yet been realized. Moreover, concerns over the quality of American education now embrace anxieties about foreign competition and the threat it poses to entire industries.

THE FUNCTIONS OF EDUCATION

The functional perspective serves as a reminder that social institutions play a major role in the life of a society. In small, homogeneous societies all children typically step into adult roles similar to those of their parents. Consequently, socialization for these roles can take place in the family and the community. Formal education emerges when informal mechanisms of training become inadequate, and once established as a social institution, education takes on functions once performed by family and community.

It is possible to identify five major functions of education. First, education teaches the basic cognitive skills (reading and mathematics) necessary for individuals to participate in a complex industrial society. Second (and reflecting the influence of the "progressive movement"), is the broader goal of preparing individuals to participate in the social and political life of society. Third is the matter of what is usually called "cultural transmission," with the objective of passing on the history, traditions, and values of the society. Fourth, and usually limited to democratic societies, is the creation of opportunities for social mobility. When education is the exclusive province of the elites in society, lower classes are excluded from any opportunity to rise above the status of their parents. Fifth, and finally, educational institutions have become sources of social change by instilling progressive attitudes and by creating new knowledge through research and development.

Thus, education is called upon to accomplish many different objectives. An evaluation of education involves judging the level of success or failure in realizing each of these functions and attempting to understand the problems that produce less than ideal results.

Cognitive Skills and the Back-to-basics Movement

Reading and writing skills are so basic to modern social functioning that those who have already mastered them typically forget how vital they really are. Consider, for example, the importance of basic communication and computational skills—the ability to read newspapers, train schedules, recipes, maps, contracts, and income tax forms; to fill out job applications, prepare memos, and write letters and cards; to count money, compute prices, figure interest rates, or balance a checkbook. To these skills should be added the acquisition of knowledge about the physical and social worlds—the fundamentals of science and technology, government and politics, and the principles of human behavior offered by psychology, sociology, and the other social sciences.

For generations, the basic skills that educational systems needed to focus on were easily summed up in the old "three Rs" cliché (readin', 'ritin' and 'rithmetic). However, as society became more complex, new definitions of essential skills evolved. To the three Rs were added the fundamentals of science, history, and social studies; the computer revolution of the past decade has complicated the situation even further.

During recent years it has been argued that the American system of education may not be teaching basic skills. In fact, in 1983 a nationwide study by the National Commission on Excellence in Education viewed the declining SAT scores of high-school students as an indication of the failure of the educational system to accomplish its fundamental goal. The Commission warned that "the educational foundations of our society are presently being eroded by a rising tide of mediocrity that threatens the very future as a nation and a people."[10] The indictment may be somewhat justified, for many students do indeed finish school with only limited cognitive abilities. A striking example occurred in New York City during 1987 when the local telephone company had 2,000 job openings to fill. A high-school diploma was not a requirement; applicants needed only to demonstrate their abilities to read, write, and speak clearly. Some 90,000 candidates had to be interviewed before the positions could be filled.[11] As a consequence of this and similar situations, many corporations have been forced to create their own training programs to teach employees the basic principles of the three Rs.

Many reasons beyond declining SAT scores have served to fuel the argument for a return to the basics of education. As noted earlier in this chapter, it has been estimated that perhaps as many as 27 million Americans—more than one in eight nationwide—are *functionally illiterate.* This means that these individuals cannot look up a friend's number in a telephone book, address an envelope, or write a check. Another 20–30 million people are estimated to be only *semiliterate,* with reading abilities that fall short of the routine demands of an industrial society. Consider, for example, that one must read at a ninth-grade reading level to understand antidote instructions on a bottle of poison, a tenth-grade level to follow even the most simple income-tax forms, and a twelfth-grade level to read a life-insurance form.[12]

Many students are leaving school deficient in the basic cognitive skills—a key component of America's illiteracy problem. This fact has generated a strong back-to-basics movement in many parts of the nation.

SOCIAL INDICATOR

Average SAT (Scholastic Aptitude Test) Scores of College-bound Seniors, 1968–1987

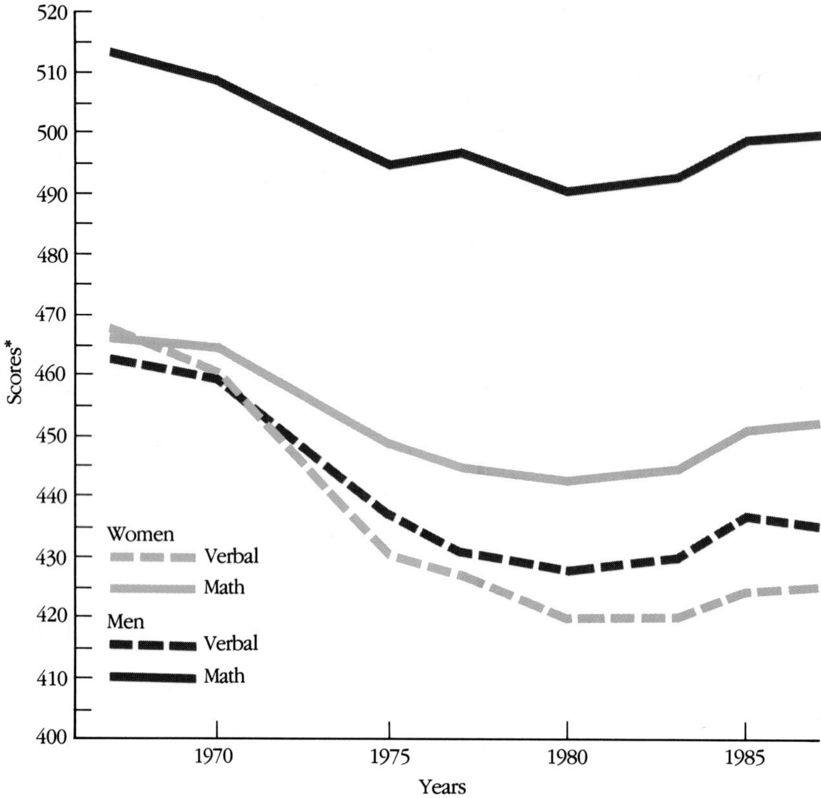

*Minimum score 200; maximum score 800.

Source: College Entrance Examination Board, 1988.

Although it would be difficult to provide an explicit definition of back to basics, the concept embraces the notion that the cause of underachievement in school is a lack of hard work in the classroom and concentrated study at home. To deal with the problem, a number of school districts are instituting longer school days, mandating more homework, or extending the school year. However, back-to-basics programs alone are unlikely to solve America's educational difficulties, for other, more complex issues also contribute to the problems.

Several studies place much of the blame on large, overcrowded schools and classrooms. The majority of high-school students reportedly are being educated in institutions with enrollments of 5,000 or more. Class sizes range as high as 40 students.[13] Under such crowded conditions instructors may spend more time keeping order than teaching. Moreover, they have virtually no time to give students personal attention. Historian Raymond E. Callahan has argued that school administrators have been influenced by the principles of "scientific management" that transformed American business early in this century (see Chapter 5).[14] In accordance with that line of thinking, schools have been viewed as giant educational factories designed to process ever-larger numbers of students at lower cost.

It might be mentioned here that many schools not only look like factories, but are run like factories as well, with constantly ringing bells to announce class changes and endless trivial announcements over public-address systems. In the educational factories, students are judged on the basis of their ability to regurgitate answers; they need not demonstrate an understanding of the impor-

Scott is dropping in his studie's he acts as if he don't Care. Scott want pass in his assignment at all, he a had a poem to learn and he fell to do it.

A poor educational foundation in one generation can have an impact on the next. For example, this note was written by a teacher with a master's degree. Obviously, some teachers are incompetent and do not have a complete grasp of even the most basic skills.

tance of the information involved or indicate the relationship of that information to other facts and events.[15] It appears that in many educational systems today, the mere memorization of a sufficient number of facts allows the student to pass on to the next grade level.

To this factor might be added what University of Virginia professor E. D. Hirsch referred to in 1987 as a declining level of "cultural literacy" in the United States.[16] Hirsch's point was that newspaper and magazine articles, television news reports, and all other general information sources take for granted prior knowledge of the events, people, and places to which they refer. He noted, however, that based on surveys of students' basic knowledge of history, geography, literature, and politics, young Americans do not seem to be familiar with this body of facts. Large gaps in the knowledge of young students are evidenced by such mistakes as indicating that Leningrad is a city in Jamaica, that the Alamo is an epic poem written by Homer, that Socrates was a native American chief, and that the Great Gatsby was a magician. Finally, as illustrated by some rather pointed comments by the noted television producer and social commentator, Norman Lear, American students appear to have fallen behind in science as well (see Exhibit 13.3), which has serious implications for the United States in the world economy.

It would appear that America's educational shortcomings are rooted in broader social changes and trends occurring in the larger society. Among the most evident sources are the impact of television, rapid technological changes, and demographic shifts.

Contemporary students enter school already strongly influenced by television. This influence continues throughout their lives. Television has many positive consequences, such as giving people more immediate access to news and wider exposure to social and cultural events. At the same time, however, television programming has influenced the way people learn. It tends to focus on the brief and strongly visual, thus encouraging superficial rather than in-depth knowledge. In addition, the ever-changing television image may have limited the attention span of students, leaving them unprepared for the longer time demands of the classroom.

The rate of technological change has become so rapid that oftentimes it is difficult for schools to prepare students for the world they will soon be entering. Children entering kindergarten in 1990 will graduate from high school in a new century, probably in the year 2003. Given rapid changes in science and technology, it is impossible for the schools to anticipate what kind of world these children will be entering and what skills they will need.

Finally, society is also being reshaped by demographic changes that have important consequences for education. For example, marriages end in divorce more often than a generation ago, thus producing more children with at least some level of emotional disruption. Similarly, geographic mobility also is more common, causing interruptions in children's educational careers. Both of these factors have an impact on educational performance that typically is difficult to measure but is present nevertheless.

Exhibit 13.3

Sociology in the Media

Why Johnny Can't Think

The author of the following essay, Norman Lear, is one of the better-known television producers in the United States. As the creator of such serials as "All in the Family," "Maude," "The Jeffersons," "Good Times," and "Mary Hartman, Mary Hartman," Lear was the first to deal with issues previously considered taboo on television, such as racial bias, homosexuality, and current political problems. Lear is also founder of People for the American Way, an organization that opposes the Moral Majority.

When it comes to science education, my personal experience—and, now, my worries for the future—may be typical of my generation.

I'm a man in my sixties. I learned a little about science in school, several decades before the era of spaceflight, computers, and genetic engineering. During World War II, I had the opportunity to study applied aerodynamics as a radio operator/gunner in the Air Force. For the past three decades, I've been a television writer and producer and have learned something about the daily miracle of TV production and broadcasting.

In other words, when it comes to science, like most people of my generation, I might charitably be classified as marginally literate.

Here's what worries me: The generation of Americans that's growing up now will need to cope with a world much more technologically advanced than the one I entered. But they're even more ill-prepared than I was. And I fear that the inadequacies of the science education that they've received are typical of their schooling in other important subjects as well.

Recently, I've had the opportunity to learn about the state of science education—and education in general. Through my work in People for the American Way, I came to learn about how textbooks and curricula have deteriorated, largely as a result of pressure by the religious right and other groups to avoid mention of controversial subjects.

It came as a little bit of a surprise to me that more than six decades after the Scopes trial, the teaching of evolution is still on trial. For a scientific theory to be banished from the textbooks and banned from classrooms—not because it has been disproved but because it offends some people—is an alarming indication of the state of science education.

Many educators have told me that alarm *is* warranted. Our textbook reviews have discovered that the censorship of evolution is typical of the declining quality of science textbooks. Instead of serving as intellectually stimulating classroom materials that encourage students to learn by themselves about the natural world, science texts have degenerated into pedagogical pabulum that encourages memorization and rote learning.

These facts explain why we may be in the process of producing a generation of scientific illiterates. Consider these recent news stories:

- In a survey conducted for the National Science Foundation, only one-third of the public understood what a molecule is, fewer than one-third

Education for Life

One result of the progressive movement was that the American school system began to assume the responsibility of preparing students for adult life. Curriculum changes in this direction meant that the fundamental reading and writing skills were supplemented by other skills demanded by life in modern society. If the goal is preparation for adulthood, it is logical to ask how, for example, a person can live in society without knowing how to drive a car. Similar questions were asked about other "skills," and in time school systems either accepted or had imposed upon them the responsibility for teaching a whole variety of new subjects. What emerged was a "cafeteria" or "shopping mall" approach to education wherein students could choose from a variety of subjects. One practical outcome was that high-school students were able to accumulate credits for courses such as driver education, career development, sex education, and in some cases even cheerleading and weight lifting. A second result was that less time was available to instruct students in the fundamental cognitive skills.

understood radiation, and only one-sixth understood DNA.

- The same study found Americans suspicious of science and embracing pseudoscience and even superstition. Fifty-three percent declared scientists are dangerous because they know too much, 46 percent rejected the theory of evolution, 43 percent believed UFOs carry visitors from outer space, and a significant number expressed a belief in astrology.
- During 1986, Japan—a country half our size—graduated twice as many science Ph.D's as the United States did.

Not only science, but also hundreds of controversial subjects have been downplayed—or eliminated entirely. Censorship by organized pressure groups—and self-censoring by textbook publishers—affect treatment of such tragic chapters of history as slavery, the Holocaust, the Great Depression, and even such literary classics as *Romeo and Juliet.*

Curiously enough, there's one issue on which I find myself agreeing with Jerry Falwell and Pat Robertson: Textbooks and curricula *do* shortchange the subject of religion. This view was confirmed by a review of high-school textbooks conducted by a panel of historians and educators for People for the American Way; they found history texts minimize the important role religious people, religious values, religious leaders, and religious institutions have played—and continue to play—in American life.

What's lacking in science curricula is lacking in education in other subjects as well—not only specific information but respect for the spirit of free inquiry, which is at the heart of the scientific method and any education worthy of the name.

For anyone to be denied an education is a personal tragedy, but if this generation grows up uneducated, it will be a national tragedy as well. Today's high-school students will inherit awesome responsibilities: to revive our stagnant industrial base and develop new industries; to find a way that the world's nations can live in peace at a time when a growing number of countries have the capacity to destroy the world; and to preserve and expand our democracy at a time when an anxious people may be vulnerable to demagogues preaching a politics of scapegoating and simple solutions. These challenges will certainly overwhelm a generation cheated of the opportunity to study modern science, to read the classics, or even to think for themselves.

Thirty years ago, when the Soviet *Sputnik* launch started Americans thinking about the failures of our educational system, there was a popular book called *Why Johnny Can't Read.* Three decades later, a similar book might be entitled *Why Johnny and Janey Can't Think.*

SOURCE: "Why Johnny Can't Think," by Norman Lear. Reprinted by permission of The People for the American Way.

Some of the additions to the curriculum were initiated by educators, and others were prompted by influential parent groups. This situation poses a significant educational dilemma, for in a society as heterogeneous as that in the United States, what is relevant for some may not be relevant for others. Moreover, topics and ideas presented in the classroom may violate some groups' cultural values and beliefs. Sex education not only provides students with vital information about their emerging sexual consciousness and changing reproductive capacity but also has the potential for lowering rates of teenage pregnancy. Yet not everyone concurs that sex education should be taught in the schools. Many hold that it is a parental responsibility to instruct children about sexuality. As for cheerleading, weight lifting, football, and similar activities, some argue that physical fitness is "basic" to a well-rounded education, while others counter that it is irrelevant to the mission of the public schools.

A final dimension of the education-for-life question is the belief that education should be interesting for students. While this principle is fundamentally sound,

With the growing threat of AIDS, sex education in American schools has a strong emphasis on "safe sex" and the prevention of the transmission of disease.

when carried to extremes, it means that class time could be diverted to any activity that might catch the fancy of students. Teachers, especially during the 1970s, became "facilitators" and "resource persons," directing students in a variety of activities of doubtful educational value. As author Jonathan Kozol reported in 1985:

> "Wow!" I heard one of those cheerful teachers say. "We made an Iroquois canoe out of an oak log!" I will offend the memories of many of my friends by stating . . . what I replied: Nobody needs an Iroquois canoe in Boston or Chicago. Even Iroquois do not.[17]

Schooling and Cultural Transmission

Complex industrial societies depend on their educational systems to maintain and preserve their cultural heritage. The cultural heritage of a society is the body of values, beliefs, and traditions to which it adheres. When it is taught, it tends to instill a sense of national pride and unity. A culture's history is evident in any cursory examination of school curricula. Art, music, and literature courses celebrate the great creative geniuses of a nation's past and present, and history courses emphasize cultural heroes and accomplishments. Students in classrooms across the United States learn much about George Washington and Abraham Lincoln, but how many of them know anything about the historical significance of Simón Bolívar? How many North American students even know the country from which he came or the century in which he lived? By contrast, it is likely that few South American students know much, if anything about Washington or Lincoln, but South Americans know Bolívar was "El Libertador," the early ninteenth-century Venezuelan revolutionary leader who liberated Venezuela from Spanish domination and led the fight for freedom in Colombia, Ecuador, Bolivia, and Peru. Citizens of Bolivia are especially aware of him, for in 1825 General Bolívar rather immodestly named their country after himself.[18]

Cultural Transmission and Selective Education

While the educational system functions to transmit a nation's cultural heritage, it often does so in a number of very selective ways.

First, historical "facts" that appear in high-school textbooks are sometimes altered in accordance with intellectual and political fashions. Journalist Frances FitzGerald has pointed out, for example, that the reported character of the American Indian seems to have changed drastically over the generations.[19] She notes that in texts written during the 1830s, the Indians were deemed "friendly" and "brave," yet later in the century they were "savage," "barbarous," "cruel," and "lazy." By the middle of the twentieth century they were not mentioned at all, almost as if they had never existed. However, starting in the 1960s "Indians" reemerged as "native Americans," a brave and persecuted people with a unique cultural identity.

Second, national pride often falls prey to bias. For example, stories of a nation's wars seldom admit to episodes of brutality and unwarranted aggression (see Exhibit 13.4). Similarly, in the West the virtues of democracy are extolled while the characteristics of socialism are denigrated. Thus, the possibility exists that the cultural transmission function of education might foster *ethnocentrism,* the tendency to judge other cultures by the standards of one's own.

Social Solidarity

The functionalist perspective emphasizes that a shared cultural heritage plays an important role in bringing about a sense of group solidarity. Without some sense of belonging or social consciousness, people are less likely to share, to cooperate, or to make sacrifices for one another. Solidarity is especially crucial in a nation characterized by a diversity of ethnic, racial, or regional groups. In fact, it was a lack of such solidarity that contributed in great part to the outbreak of the American Civil War.

One of the functions of education is to promote social solidarity, but evidence suggests that the American school system may not be fulfilling this role very well. In a recent study conducted by the National Endowment for the Humanities, for example, thousands of 17-year-olds from across the United States were tested and found lacking in their basic knowledge of history and literature.[20] Interestingly, half did not know *when* the Civil War was fought. Without a basic understanding of historical events, students fail to grasp important ideas and trends. Researchers at the National Endowment for the Humanities argued that if people have no knowledge of the Civil War, Emancipation, the Reconstruction era, and related events in American history, they cannot possibly comprehend the significance and meaning of racial confrontations in contemporary America.

History, furthermore, is not the only subject in which student understanding is lacking. As illustrated in Exhibit 13.5, an even greater problem may exist with regard to geography.

Education and Social Mobility

Most people have potential talents and abilities that go well beyond basic skills. The avowed purposes of both free public education and financial-aid programs include the identification and development of these talents for the sake of helping individuals to advance themselves socially, economically, and politically. Or as the American educator and legislator Horace Mann expressed this function of education in 1848, "Education, beyond all other devices of human origin, is the great equalizer of the conditions of men—the balance wheel of the social machinery."[21]

The significance of Mann's comment becomes clear when the concept of mass public education is contrasted with societies in which access to education is controlled by one's social class, race, or religion. The history of American education reflects instances where this principle was violated—the episodes of exclusion or segregation of blacks into inferior schools. At its best, on the other hand, public education has provided opportunities for those unable to afford private education. Also important is the related, yet special role that education has played in the lives of immigrant groups. The history of the United States to a great extent is the story of millions of foreign-born individuals flooding across its borders and into its cities and countryside in search of freedom and security. From the countries of Asia, Africa, Europe, and Latin America, immigrants brought not only themselves, but their languages and cultures as well. The burden of teaching their children the ways of their new country was shouldered by the American school system (a situation that has endured). Thus, education functions to assist immigrants in **assimilation,** the process of learning to fit in and be accepted into the host culture.[22]

Education and Social Change

Educational institutions help to preserve the past, but they also contribute to social change, both directly and indirectly. They promote change by instilling generally progressive attitudes, and by challenging ideas, beliefs, and behaviors based on invalid assumptions. Some educational institutions teach people to question, to be skeptical, and to be critical. At the same time, education has a direct effect on social change through its chief

Exhibit 13.4

Case Study

The "My Lai Massacre" and the Revision of American History

Many great tragedies were associated with American involvement in the war in Vietnam. Atrocities took place as well—perpetrated by both sides—the most visible of which became known as the My Lai Massacre.

My Lai was a small Vietnamese town believed to be held by the 48th Battalion of the Viet Cong (the Vietnamese pro-Communist guerrillas). To the members of Lt. William L. Calley's platoon it was known as "Pinkville," for the area was colored pink on the military maps that had been issued the night before the unit's occupation of My Lai. Calley was ordered to "clean the village out," and on March 16, 1968, he and his platoon were flown in in helicopters, armed with M-16 automatic rifles. When they entered the settlement, however, they found no members of the Viet Cong battalion but only several

hundred defenseless civilians. The American soldiers herded their captives to the center of the village where Lt. Calley reportedly ordered them shot. By the end of the day an estimated 567 civilians had been executed. Some were shot at point-blank range; others were pushed into huts which were then blown up with hand grenades; still another group was thrown into a ditch where they were cut down in assembly-line fashion.

Many soldiers refused to take part in the massacre, claiming that it was an unlawful command. One American serviceman even shot himself in the foot rather than participate in the killings. Others, however, took an active part, including Calley. In addition to his rapid firing on the victims in the ditch and in the village square, one witness recalled how he had personally dealt with a Buddhist priest and a baby:

> The priest, who was wearing the flowing white robe of his office, held out supplicating hands as though in prayer. He kept repeating, "No Viet, no Viet." Calley, according to testimony, smashed in the man's mouth with the butt of his M-16, reversed the rifle, "and pulled the trigger in the priest's face. Half of his head was blown off."

Many historical accounts of the Vietnam War leave out mention of the massacre at My Lai. Over 500 Vietnamese civilians, including women and children, were killed by U.S. soldiers.

> As for the infant, "Lieutenant Calley grabbed it by the arm and threw it into the ditch and fired."

When news of the incident in My Lai arrived in the United States, it became a *cause célèbre.* Played up in all of its gruesomeness in the media and investigated by Congress, My Lai also became a kind of oriflamme for the antiwar movement. Too, it shook a nation convinced of its own humanity. To realize that their own soldiers were no better than the Communists in their treatment of prisoners was so damaging to American self-esteem that many refused to believe the massacre had actually happened.

As for Lt. Calley, he was court-martialed and convicted of the murder of 22 civilians. Although he was sentenced to life imprisonment, after serving a few years under house arrest, confined to quarters, his life term was commuted and he was released. To many, for whatever reasons, Calley was a hero. In fact, just three days after his conviction in military court a record entitled "The Battle Hymn of Lieutenant Calley" sold over 200,000 copies.

In the history books, little can be found about My Lai. A case in point is Stanley Karnow's *Vietnam: A History.* Published in 1983, *Vietnam* became a national bestseller. It was acclaimed as "the definitive history" of the war in Vietnam and served as the basis of a PBS television series. Yet in all of its 752 pages, My Lai received only a few lines. In fact, the most that was said was offered as a counterpoint to Viet Cong murders of civilians:

> Paradoxically, the American public barely noticed these atrocities, preoccupied as it was by the incident at My Lai—in which American soldiers had massacred a hundred Vietnamese peasants, women and children among them.

SOURCES: Stanley Karnow, *Vietnam: A History* (New York: Viking Press, 1983); Robert Leckie, *The Wars of America* (New York: Harper & Row, 1981); William Manchester, *The Glory and the Dream* (Boston: Little, Brown, 1974), pp. 1441–42; United States v. Calley, 46 C. M. R.1131 (1973, Military Review Court).

Exhibit 13.5

Sidelights on American Culture

Geography: The Forgotton Subject

Ask American college students where the state of Delaware is and many will tell you it is somewhere in New England. Ask them to point out Haiti on a map of the world and they will begin to scrutinize the nations in Africa. One survey of college students in 1986 put Africa in North America, the U.S.S.R. down near Panama, and Texas on the Pacific coast (see map at right). In another study Brazil was mistaken for the United States on world maps, and Costa Rica was placed on the Persian Gulf. In a study conducted in 1988, young adults in nine countries were given an unlabeled world map (see map below) and asked to identify 16 spots: the United States, the Soviet Union, Japan, Canada, France, Mexico, Italy, Sweden, the United Kingdom, South Africa, West Germany, Egypt, Vietnam, Central America, the Persian Gulf, and the Pacific Ocean. The accompanying graph shows the average number of locations correctly identified by the respondents in each nation.

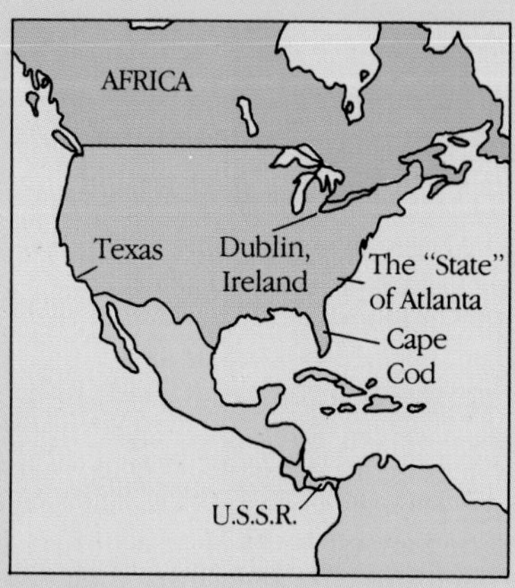

While the errors in these experiments may seem rather far-fetched, they are an outgrowth of a trend in education that began shortly after the close of World War II and gained prominence in the 1960s. Rather than exposing students to separate geography classes as in the past, what evolved was a hybrid course known as "social studies," which included geography, history, government, economics, psychology, anthropology, sociology, and law. Geography tended to be neglected in the new curriculum because it was the subject that everybody "loved to hate," and because it was assumed that important locations would be learned through history lessons. In recent years geography has been given more emphasis, but for a whole generation of Americans the ordering of states, countries, and bodies of water on the globe is a mystery.

SOURCES: *Miami Herald,* July 28, 1988, pp. 1A; *Newsweek,* September 1, 1986, p. 67; *New York Times,* July 28, 1988, p. A16; *U.S. News & World Report,* March 25, 1985, p. 50.

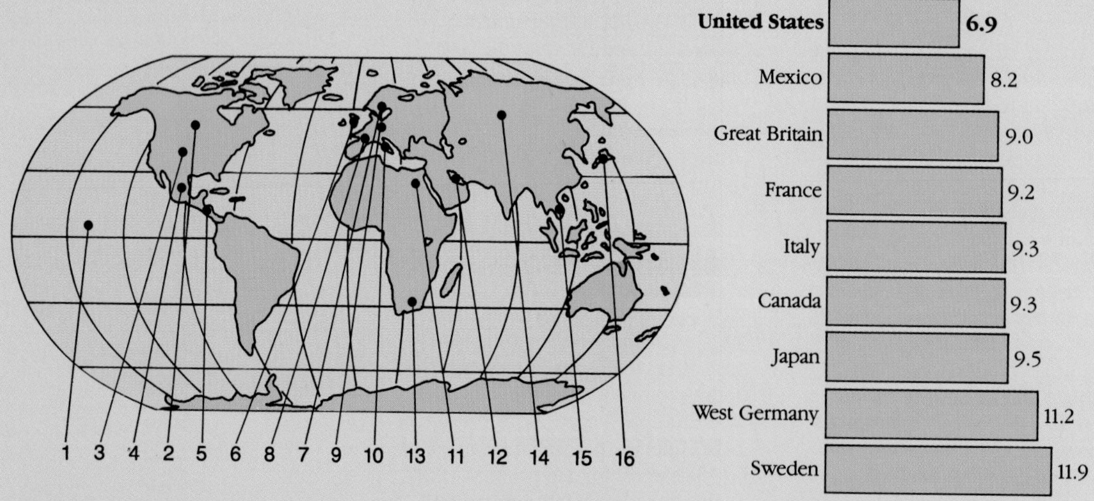

Answers: 1. Pacific Ocean 2. Canada 3. United States 4. Mexico 5. Central America 6. United Kingdom 7. Sweden 8. France 9. West Germany 10. Italy 11. Egypt 12. Persian Gulf 13. South Africa 14. Soviet Union 15. Vietnam 16. Japan activity of passing on knowledge. To cite but one example, consider the comments made about the death penalty in the early pages of Chapter 1. The assumption that the imposition of the death penalty deters others from committing murder is *not* supported by social research. This finding, in turn, has instigated pressure for the elimination of capital punishment in the United States.

Moreover, educational institutions, largely colleges and universities, also promote social change by generating new knowledge through basic research. The efforts of individual faculty members or various types of research centers based in universities have been responsible for most of the important scientific breakthroughs of modern times, including new knowledge in the social sciences. Research, however, tends to be a rather expensive enterprise for educational institutions, leading many of them to some rather questionable expenditures (see Exhibit 13.6).

In summary, schools have taken on a number of social functions since their modest beginnings in colonial America. Society depends on schools to prepare the next generation, but recent evaluations of education in America have been anything but positive. Many of the difficulties have emerged slowly, as the schools have evolved. Others are tied to the fact that educational systems must serve diverse and varied populations, each with different values and beliefs.

THE HIDDEN CURRICULUM: THE LATENT FUNCTIONS OF EDUCATION

As noted in Chapter 1, it is often useful to delve into the less obvious implications of social arrangements. *Manifest* functions of education are openly professed by educators and the public, but education's *latent* functions have unanticipated and unintended consequences. Research on the dynamics of education has shown that many lessons taught in school are not part of the "official curricula" of history, English, mathematics, and other subjects. Instead these lessons are part of the **hidden curriculum,** a subtle configuration of norms and attitudes instilled during the educational process.[23]

The majority of students, for example, have learned how to raise their hands before speaking, take turns at the chalkboard, and line up for gym class. On the surface it can be argued that such behaviors have no counterpart in the adult world. Except for journalists at presidential news conferences, no one else raises a hand in anticipation of speaking. It may be argued that such activities teach discipline and self-control, necessary traits in the adult world. A different interpretation, however, would be that the hidden lesson of such a rule is to obey teachers (and other authority figures) and to follow rules without question.

Is this a manifestation of the "hidden curriculum"?

Exhibit 13.6

Types & Stereotypes

The Ratings Game

College and university research expenditures, in the form of faculty salaries, equipment, and facilities tend to be rather high. Given the high costs of running institutions of higher education, it would seem logical, even requisite, that fiscal administrators make every research dollar count. Yet in recent testimony before Congress, it has been argued that American colleges waste a considerable amount of research money on the quest for high rankings in the hierarchy of "the best schools."

Various rating criteria have been used to arrive at a list of so-called best schools. One common criteria over the years has been a count of the number of books in an institution's library, the assumption being that the better schools have the most complete libraries (see Table 1). A second mechanism has been to consider the size of an institution's endowment (money or property donated for the permanent use of an institution), with the rationale that the financially "better off" schools had the resources needed to purchase the best facilities, and hence, attract the best faculty (see Table 2).

Almost all colleges and universities tend to operate on the principle that the best single way to improve ratings is to attract a famous person to campus. The winners of Nobel Prizes (Nobel laureates) are especially sought after; they bring instant recognition and visibility to a school. Although not all institutions of higher learning play the ratings game in the quest for prestige, a significant number do. But not just prestige is at stake; student recruitment, alumni contributions, government funding, and good scholars also are.

In recent years it would appear that some schools have been willing to spend significant sums of money on almost *any* person with high visibility. Former U.S. presidents are highly sought after, despite the fact that their credentials as scholars or researchers may be minimal or even nonexistent. (Jimmy Carter holds a distinguished professorship at Emory University in Atlanta and Gerald Ford has lectured at Michigan.) On occasion, the costs of "stars" can be controversial. The University of South Carolina met with some criticism when it was revealed that Jihan Sadat, widow of Anwar Sadat, earned $325,000 for lecturing once a week during the 1985–86 academic year. The university president tried to explain the expense, claiming that "she helped the university achieve national recognition way beyond our capacity to reimburse her."

Large expenditures for internationally visible figures may increase a university's rating in the eyes of both the government and the public at large, but they also generate questions from the

Table 1
Major U.S. College and University Libraries

Institution	Volumes	Microforms
Harvard	11,136,662	4,154,154
Yale	8,236,679	2,395,015
University of Illinois	7,000,170	2,894,312
University of California—Berkeley	6,845,732	3,385,553
University of Michigan	5,920,576	3,090,623
University of Texas	5,579,326	3,672,370
Columbia	5,551,739	3,388,230
University of California—Los Angeles	5,486,955	3,835,492
Stanford	5,447,869	3,036,169
Cornell	4,870,570	3,989,843
University of Chicago	4,756,076	1,474,116
University of Wisconsin	4,607,542	1,156,515
University of Washington	4,549,114	4,558,183
University of Minnesota	4,286,431	2,642,377
Ohio State	4,077,575	2,552,137
Princeton	3,856,638	1,991,432
Indiana	3,786,962	1,256,323
Duke	3,510,645	1,332,419
University of Pennsylvania	3,376,901	1,972,178
North Carolina	3,301,751	2,622,754
Northwestern	3,206,698	1,669,565
University of Arizona	3,139,481	3,149,171
Michigan State	3,129,802	2,192,757
New York	2,932,055	2,097,678
University of Virginia	2,812,167	3,578,749

legislators and benefactors providing the support. It is likely, too, that such expenditures impact on the morale of an institution's regular faculty, the majority of whom have only moderate incomes (see Table 3).

Table 2
College and University Endowments, 1985–1986
(top 35 in millions of dollars)

Institution	Endowment (Market Value)	Institution	Endowment (Market Value)
Harvard	$3,865.7	Johns Hopkins	$491.5
Princeton	1,900.0	Rockefeller	475.7
Yale	1,750.7	Vanderbilt	446.5
Columbia	1,282.8	University of Notre Dame	388.1
Texas A&M	1,195.3	University of Southern California	361.8
Stanford	1,183.9	California Institute of Technology	349.0
Washington University	972.5	University of Virginia	340.0
Massachusetts Institute of Technology	971.3	Duke	338.7
University of Chicago	800.7	Brown	315.4
Rice	795.8	Case Western Reserve	307.3
Northwestern	738.5	University of Michigan	291.7
Emory	731.8	Princeton Theological Seminary	284.2
University of Minnesota	730.6	Southern Methodist	282.1
Cornell	711.7	Smith	272.7
University of Rochester	583.2	Wellesley	265.0
University of Pennsylvania	540.1	Williams College	247.8
New York University	521.3	University of Texas—Austin	244.6
Dartmouth	520.6		

Table 3
Average Salaries and Fringe Benefits for Faculty Members, 1986
(in thousands of dollars)

Control and Academic Rank 1986			
Average Salaries			
Public: All Ranks	33.4	Private: All ranks	35.4
Professor	42.3	Professor	47.0
Associate Professor	32.2	Associate Professor	32.9
Assistant Professor	26.7	Assistant Professor	26.8
Instructor	20.9	Instructor	19.8
Average Fringe Benefits—All Ranks Combined			
Public	7.3	Private	8.0

SOURCES: Harry Anderson, "Tracking the Faculty Stars," *Newsweek on Campus,* September, 1987, pp. 8–12; *Statistical Abstract of the United States—1988* (Washington, DC: U.S. Bureau of the Census, 1987), p. 8; Robin Wilson, "Critics Tell House Panel that Colleges Waste Money on Overpaid Professors and Duplicate Programs," *The Chronicle of Higher Education,* 34 (September 23, 1987), pp. 1, 27; Harriet Zuckerman, *The Scientific Elite: Nobel Laureates in the United States* (New York: Free Press, 1976).

Quite clearly, the hidden curriculum involves learning behaviors that are conducive to the smooth functioning of schools, but some observers argue that in the process children are taught to be docile and unquestioning of authority. This contention led sociologist Richard Flacks to question the broader implications of such lessons. "Can people," he contemplated, "be capable of self-government if most of their daily lives is spent in situations of submissive authority and most of the authority they encounter is not legitimately accountable to them?"[24]

The idea of the hidden curriculum takes on concrete meaning when it is applied to specific cases and situations. For example, college faculty are often plagued by the low level of student participation in class. As demonstrated in Exhibit 13.7, perhaps the difficulty is that the students have learned an unanticipated set of lessons.

Schooling and Work

The idea that education should prepare people for work roles is one that many people would endorse, but the hidden curriculum may teach students lessons that are of little practical use in the world of work. The discontinuities between education and the world of work may be observed in a variety of areas, including individual versus group efforts, abstract versus practical knowledge, and fixed versus shifting deadlines.[25]

Individual versus Group Efforts. Schools tend to be organized around individual effort and performance; students complete assignments and take exams as individuals. Although students may be assessed for their "ability to get along with others" in many group activities, the grades and grade-point averages that play such a major role in job seeking are essentially a measure of individual effort. By contrast, the world of work is largely collaborative, and the ability of most workers to get their jobs done depends on how well their work coordinates with the work of others. A flight crew in a cockpit, a research team designing a new car, a shift of coal miners, or the members of a ball team represent individuals involved in a group effort.

Abstract versus Practical Knowledge. On the assumption that the purpose of school is to *educate* rather than *train,* much of the material presented in classrooms deals with abstract ideas and concepts. This tends to be particularly the case in the area of law. Law students spend most of their time learning "the law," with little time being devoted to the skills needed for actually "practicing law"—structuring arguments, writing briefs, and dealing with clients and the courtroom work group.

Fixed versus Shifting Deadlines. School days, semesters, and academic years are organized into tidy blocks of time with fixed deadlines. Most students plan their work in anticipation of such commands as "*Macbeth* should be read by Thursday," "mathematics homework is due a week from today," and "your Western Civ paper will be due at the end of the marking period." All of these mandates teach students that they will generally have a considerable amount of time before assignments are due. Unfortunately, however, the work place often operates on shifting deadlines and without the luxury of long preparation periods. Reports are often due "yesterday," or "immediately, if not sooner."

In retrospect, schools are large organizations that must develop the rules and procedures necessary to proper functioning. Order must be maintained, timetables established, and grades assigned. Yet in the process, and in subtle and indirect ways, schools instill perspectives that are sometimes at odds with the goals of education.

CONFLICT PERSPECTIVES ON EDUCATION

Conflict sociologists argue that, in general, social institutions tend to work to the advantage of the privileged in society, and that the educational process is very much a part of this overall phenomenon. Research in the conflict tradition has emphasized, for example, the direct and subtle ways that education serves to maintain and perpetuate the existing patterns of social inequality and stratification that are apparent in the larger society. This line of research is of vital concern to both social scientists and educators, for it raises questions about the availability of equal educational opportunities for all Americans.

One of the more extreme views of conflict theory holds that those in power use the educational system to maintain their position of control. Adherents to this view claim that the upper classes deliberately try to preserve a monopoly over the most valuable kinds of knowledge and skills by ensuring that only they and their children have access to them. Taking this view one step further, higher education, and thus training for better jobs, is seen as the exclusive domain of the rich, with the consequence that lower-class children have been prevented from advancing beyond the social levels of their parents.[26]

The tradition of free public education in the United States has made it impossible for the upper class to control access to education. However, the fact remains that inequalities among parents have a profound impact on the educational attainments of their children. For some, this impact is inevitable, or as conflict theorists

Exhibit 13.7

Research in Sociology

The Hidden Curriculum in the College Classroom

The classroom is the basic locus of scholastic education. It is in the classroom that formal and informal lessons are taught, that students succeed or fail, and that people accumulate the grades and other measures of achievement that shape the direction of their subsequent careers. These experiences are affected, furthermore, by the subtle norms of the classroom, and the social dynamics of the college classroom clearly illustrate this.

College faculty frequently observe that students fail to come to class prepared, which results in classroom interaction dominated by only a handful of students. One explanation for this lack of preparation is that most students are lazy and apathetic. Another explanation is that students feel uncomfortable about speaking out—one result of the encouraged passivity fostered by the lessons of the hidden curriculum. In this view, students see instructors as experts on their subjects—individuals who have read extensively, learned all the facts, and mastered the issues. Students wonder if there is anything new that they could add to the instructor's lecture by participating in class discussions.

Although these explanations appear plausible, classroom behavior is far more complex than they suggest. Like all other forms of group activity, classroom behavior is guided by social norms and beliefs, and research suggests that the lack of student preparation and participation may be the result of a different form of the hidden curriculum—one involving the social dynamics of the classroom.

It would appear that students "believe" that it is safe to remain silent, "knowing" they will not be called upon directly in class. Sociologists David A. Karp and William C. Yoles have studied this phenomenon and have concluded that ill-prepared students are indeed safe under most circumstances as a result of teachers' classroom norms. Instructors avoid making students look unintelligent in front of their peers. Hence, they refrain from any direct questioning that has the potential to embarrass.

A second classroom dynamic seems to operate as well. Students believe that just a few people can be counted on to carry the burden of participation in any class, so they apply social pressure on these individuals to do so. When a question is posed, they glance toward persons who have spoken earlier. They may even turn their chairs toward them, thus "giving them the floor." But classroom norms also place limits on how much the "talkers" may say. Should they drone on too long, other students let them know by sighing, shuffling papers, and even whispering to one another.

Thus, both students and faculty have sets of norms and beliefs that result in classes dominated by instructors who lecture while students listen passively. A few students may participate regularly, protecting the majority from having to worry about speaking. Freed from the risk of public involvement, most have no incentive to complete assignments and readings. In turn, their lack of preparation virtually guarantees they will not participate.

SOURCE: David A. Karp and William C. Yoles, "The College Classroom: Some Observations on the Meanings of Student Participation," *Sociology and Social Research,* 60 (1976), pp. 421–39. Reprinted by permission of *Sociology and Social Research: An International Journal.*

Samuel Bowles and Herbert Gintis suggest, "Education is powerless to correct economic inequality. The class, sex, and race biases in schooling do not produce, but rather reflect the structure of privilege in society at large."[27] One pattern, for example, established in a number of studies, shows that children of upper-income parents have a much greater chance of getting into college and getting better-paying jobs than lower-income students with the same level of measured ability.[28] This tendency occurs, furthermore, not necessarily as the result of discriminatory intent, but due to the way that education has evolved and that schools are organized. Sociologists have focused specifically on two educational techniques—*ability groupings* and *curriculum tracking.* Both techniques evolved as a means of dealing with the heterogeneous student populations found in American

SOCIAL INDICATOR

The Economic Benefits of Education

It is often said that education pays—in jobs and income. That is clearly true. Income rises noticeably with each higher level of educational attainment.

Average monthly income of people with these educational attainments:

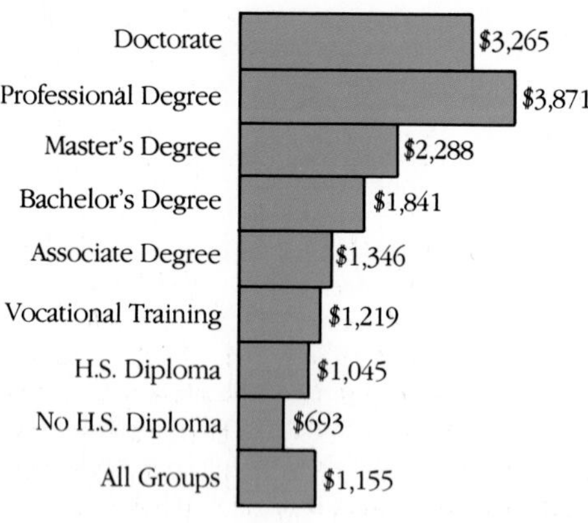

However, the rewards of education are not equally distributed. At every level, women and minorities earn less than men and white individuals with a comparable education.

By Sex and Race

Education	**Men**	**Women**	**White**	**Black**
Doctorate	$3,667	n/a	$3,342	n/a
Professional	$4,309	$1,864	$3,927	n/a
Master's	$2,843	$1,645	$2,287	$1,966
Bachelor's	$2,455	$1,148	$1,881	$1,388
Associate	$1,755	$ 959	$1,367	$1,158
Vocational	$1,822	$ 923	$1,248	$ 860
H.S. Diploma	$1,510	$ 684	$1,080	$ 765
No H.S. Diploma	$ 973	$ 453	$ 734	$ 513
All Groups	$1,620	$ 734	$1,208	$ 754

Note: n/a—too few people in category for representative sample.

Source: U.S. Bureau of the Census, 1987.

schools. Advocates claim they facilitate the educational process while detractors maintain they subvert the goals of education. The main criticism is that both seem to work to the disadvantage of minorities, women, and lower-class children.

Ability Groupings

The ideal educational arrangement might be visualized as a situation in which one instructor is assigned to every student. However, the reality of the primary- and secondary-school classroom is one teacher and no less than 20 or 30 students at different levels. In most such cases, instruction conducted at only one level is quite inappropriate: faster students are bored and distracted while slower ones are frustrated. With few exceptions, the solution is **ability groupings,** small clusters of students of similar ability. Teachers can then gear their instruction to each group's level, and ideally, both students and teachers benefit. But while ability groupings may facilitate classroom organization and function, critics argue that they also stifle or hinder the achievement of certain students.

Ability groupings have been criticized for two major reasons. First, research confirms that criteria other than academic performance play a role in the makeup of ability groupings. Teachers, for example, often use their judgments of such student characteristics as attentiveness, maturity, self-confidence, cooperativeness, and independence in making up groupings.[29] Such selection criteria are not an unreasonable mechanism, for disruptive students do indeed hinder the learning process. Yet a problem emerges when lower-class or minority children are unintentionally discriminated against because their values and behaviors do not coincide with the "middle-class" norms of many schools.

A second unanticipated consequence of ability groupings is that they are subtly influenced by the beliefs and stereotypes prevalent in the larger society. We noted in Chapter 10 that in primary grades males are much more likely to be assigned to high-ability math groups, reflecting widely held expectations about gender roles.[30] This factor, interestingly, may also contribute to women's unequal access to scientific and technical careers.

Curriculum Tracking

Curriculum tracks group high-school students into different programs on the basis of their abilities and aspirations. About one-third of contemporary students are enrolled in academic programs, typically referred to as "college prep" or "AG" (academically gifted). The balance are distributed into a "general" track or a bottom track labeled "vocational" or "career."

Tracks are a form of educational specialization. They are designed to provide the appropriate preparation for students heading for college, while at the same time keeping potential dropouts in school by directing them toward viable vocational routes. Assignment to different tracks is based on a variety of factors. Academic performance is important, but so too are perceptions of ability and aspirations. Heated debates have occurred over the educational value of tracking, with conflict sociologists claiming that such arrangements result in lower-class children's being channeled into vocational or general curricula, thus reducing their educational accomplishments and ultimate career opportunities.[31]

No one questions the fact that track placement results in differential educational experiences. All too often the better teachers are assigned to college-prep tracks. Moreover, the educational experiences of students once they have been assigned to a track tend to emphasize inequality and privilege—constantly reminding students of their alternative futures. Students in college-bound academic tracks read Shakespeare and are encouraged to grow and develop intellectually. Vocational-track curricula include almost no exposure to serious literature. Rather, instructional time in vocational-track English classes is devoted to filling out job applications and acquiring good work habits. Several studies have found that most vocational preparation is not only weak, but does little to prepare students for the world of work. In one school, career education students in "food service" spent time mopping cafeteria floors.[32]

A number of sociologists have used the classic symbolic interactionist approach to explain how ability grouping and tracking affect academic performance. Central to their research is the notion of the self-fulfilling prophecy. A **self-fulfilling prophecy** is an incorrect definition of a situation that becomes true because people (1) accept the incorrect definition, and (2) act in such a way as to make it come true. Stated differently, things sometimes become real because people believe they will, and thus act to make them happen. If, for example, a police anti-riot troop believes that strikers on a picket line are hostile and violent agitators, the troop's behavior may incite the strikers to be hostile and violent.

Within this context, consider a rather well-known classroom experiment.[33] Elementary-school teachers were told that all of their students had achieved high test scores and could be expected to perform well during the upcoming year. Yet in fact, the students had been randomly assigned to classes. However, over the course of the year, student IQ scores in these "high-achiever" classes improved more than those of students in other classes. The self-fulfilling prophecy may have led teachers to treat the "high-achiever" students as especially bright, thus causing the improvement.

Other research suggests that tracking may sometimes have the same result. Sociologist James Rosenbaum compared the IQ scores of students in five different curriculum tracks, first in eighth grade and again in tenth grade. As indicated in the accompanying table, he found improvement in the two upper tracks and a decline in the rest, leading him to conclude that teachers paid more attention to those they thought were going on to college than to those headed directly into the labor market.[34]

Track	Mean IQ Scores Eighth Grade	Tenth Grade
Upper College	123	127
Lower College	107	109
Upper Noncollege	104	102
Middle Noncollege	99	95
Low Noncollege	97	93

Source: James R. Rosenbaum, "Stratification of the Socialization Process," *American Sociological Review,* vol. 40, 1975, table 1. Reprinted by permission.

In summary, then, it would appear that social groupings in schools combine scholastic, social, and behavioral characteristics. The goal of groups and tracks may be to maintain order and facilitate the educational process, but the results often work to the advantage of only upper- and middle-class children.

CHALLENGES TO EDUCATION: RECURRING AND EMERGING ISSUES

Educational systems, like other social institutions, evolve and change in response to shifting social conditions and values. Many new issues face American school systems at the dawn of the 1990s, combining with problems that have endured as legacies of the past.

Nontraditional Students: Extending Education throughout the Life Cycle

For most Americans formal education follows a fairly predictable pattern. It begins at about age five with enrollment in kindergarten and ends either in the late teenage years with high-school graduation or in the early twenties with the completion of college. Although the many exceptions range from dropouts at one end of the continuum to recipients of graduate degrees at the other, this progression is the typical pattern, inherited from the era of mass public education. However, in recent years demographic and social changes have begun to place new demands on the educational system. Increasing numbers of "nontraditional students" are having an unexpected impact on educational institutions. These students include preschoolers and "after school" students and large numbers of returning students.

The demands created by paid employment outside the home may leave very young children unattended for extended periods of time. Poorer families have coped with this situation for many years, typically depending on friends and relatives to assist with child-care responsibilities. In recent years, however, a whole variety of organizations—ranging from commercial day-care centers to company sponsored, on-site facilities—have responded to this problem. Many individuals argue, however, that such activities should take place in the schools and that schools should be reorganized to accommodate such situations. First, placing these children in the school system would provide some minimum standards for curriculum and staffing. It also would guarantee that access to child-care facilities would not be limited only to those who could afford them or happened to work for companies that offered them.

In 1985 the federal government started an experimental program designed to meet the needs of these young children of working parents. Several hundred children are enrolled in a Maryland school, for example, that operates from 7 A.M. to 6 P.M. and provides enrichment courses in art and music as well as the basics of the traditional curriculum.[35] Unsupervised after-school time that might be lost to unproductive activities is thus directed toward more meaningful pursuits.

In addition to the growing cohorts of pre-schoolers and "after-school" students, school systems are also being called upon to deal with returning students. A sizable number of older people are enrolling at colleges and universities. Some, mainly women, are returning to school to resume an education postponed (or prematurely terminated) by the demands of marriage and child rearing. Others are people in mid-career, seeking to upgrade their knowledge and skills to qualify for promotion or a job change.

Returning students present special problems for educational institutions. Many of these individuals have jobs or family responsibilities that demand more flexible schedules. Returning students also favor more concentrated work, objecting to the leisurely pace of traditional academics organized around a single class meeting once-a-week for 14 weeks. Programs oriented toward young adults also often have little or no relevance for older students. The interests of returning students frequently focus more on material that has direct practical relevance. This fact places pressure on schools to restructure courses in the direction of application rather than abstract knowledge. Too, institutions have an additional burden in that many returning students need to be

Nontraditional students at local community colleges and four-year institutions include women returning to resume a postponed education and mid-career individuals seeking to improve skills or switch jobs.

redirected to the skills of studying and preparing for exams.

Yet not all returning students have a vocational focus. Increases in the amount of leisure time available to people have led many to return to school for coursework that will enrich the quality of their lives—music and literature as well as such practical subjects as financial planning and money management. Currently, much of this need is being met by local community colleges, but four-year institutions are also responding by offering programs for these nontraditional students.[36]

Minorities and Higher Education

The end of formal racial segregation in educational facilities in the United States began with the Supreme Court's decision in *Brown v. Board of Education* in 1954. While all barriers did not immediately fall, the High Court ruling cleared the way for the expansion of educational opportunities for black Americans. One of the more promising indications of progress was the increased number of blacks graduating from both high school and college. In fact, as indicated in Exhibit 13.8, the proportions of blacks completing both high school and college increased from 1940 to 1985 to a much greater extent than among whites. However, it would appear that some of the gains of the 1950s, 1960s, and 1970s are being eroded. As indicated in Exhibit 13.9, since 1975 the proportion of blacks enrolled in college has declined.

Behind this decline is a shortage of money. Since 1980, for example, college costs have outstripped the inflation rate. In addition, requirements for financial aid have tightened. During much of the 1970s, most black students needing money for higher education could readily obtain government grants covering almost 75% of their college expenses. Currently, educational assistance largely takes the form of loans that cover less than half of the requisite costs.[37]

A second factor discouraging black enrollments involves the perceived inhospitality of many university environments. Incidents of open racial confrontation have increased. Perhaps the most widely reported incident in recent years occurred during 1986 at the Citadel, a military university in South Carolina, where five white cadets dressed in Ku-Klux-Klan-type regalia broke into the room of a black student and burned a paper cross.[38] Such racially motivated incidents have no geographic boundaries, having occurred at institutions in Massachusetts, New York, Michigan, and elsewhere. Although college administrators maintain that the actual number of incidents is low, they admit that instances occur often

Exhibit 13.8 Sociological Focus

Proportion of White and Black High-School and College Graduates, 1940 and 1985

		1940	1985
Whites:	High-school Graduates	26%	76%
	College Gradutes	5	20
Blacks:	High-school Graduates	7	60
	College Graduates	1	11

Note: Data is for persons age 25 and older.

Source: Adapted from *Educational Attainment in the United States* (Washington, DC: U.S. Bureau of the Census, 1987).

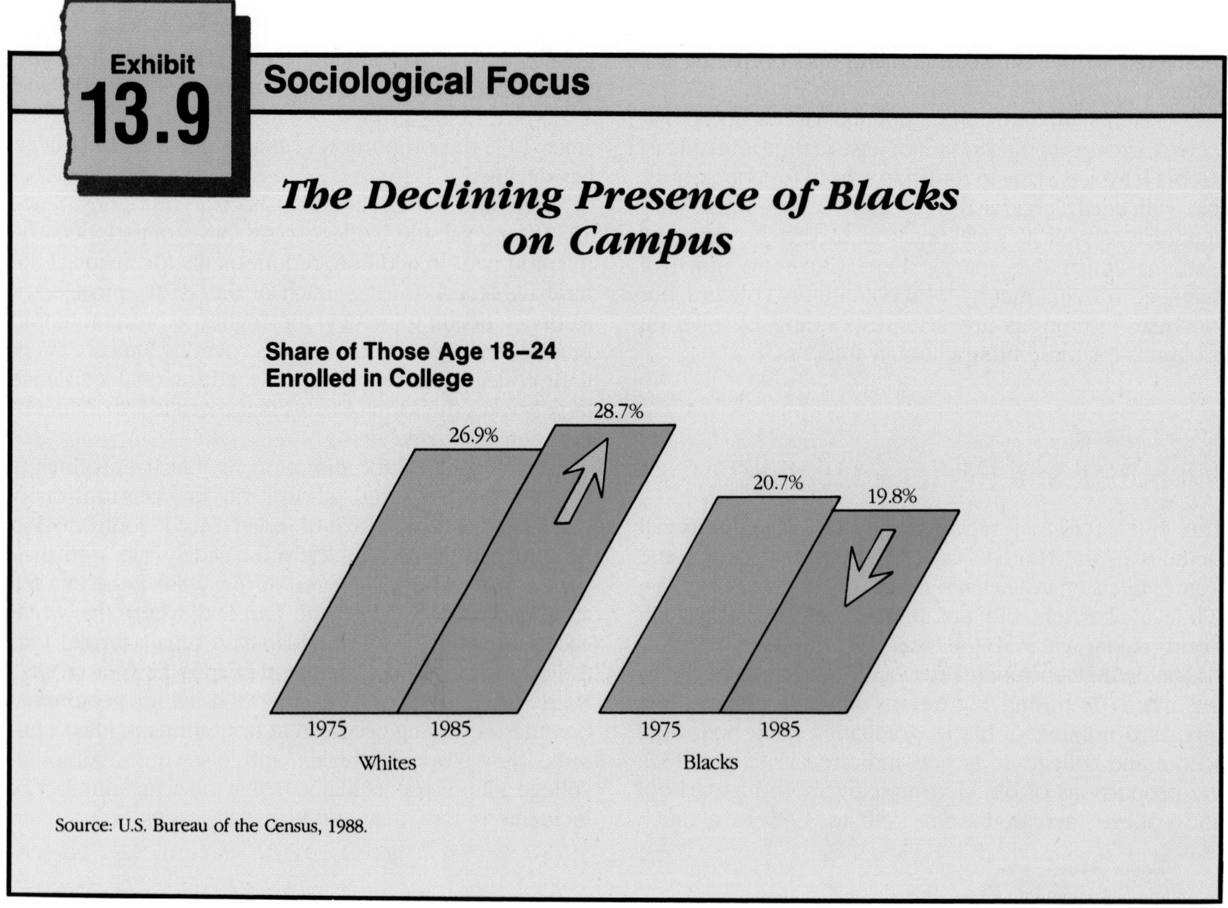

enough to create an unpleasant environment for blacks.[39] The long-term consequences of this situation include smaller numbers of college-educated blacks, and ultimately, fewer blacks with the educational qualifications for professional and managerial careers.

School Segregation in the 1990s: The Case of Hispanic Students

The segregation of any group into separate schools has the potential to limit the achievements of an entire generation of students. Many times minority schools slip below the standards prevailing in other schools, resulting in lower quality education. More importantly, the public and prospective employers may perceive these schools as inferior and downgrade the achievements of their graduates. Research has indicated, for example, that employers give preference to minorities from integrated suburban schools over those with the same educational credentials from segregated center-city schools.[40] Then too, minority children often are isolated socially from mainstream American society, deprived of contacts with students and teachers who are more likely to have been socialized from birth into the expectations of the larger society.

According to a recent study, the same pattern of segregation that channeled black students into separate schools is now being repeated with Hispanics.[41] The research indicated that 70% of all Hispanic students were enrolled in schools where more than half the students were also Hispanic. Levels of segregation were found to be highest in urban areas that had recently experienced significant infusions of Hispanic immigrants. A circular pattern of poverty, discrimination, and educational segregation is also evident. Handicapped by both discrimination and limited educational attainment, Hispanics are attracted to the cities with the opportunity for low-income jobs in the service and unskilled sectors. This, in turn, leads to patterns of segregation in both housing and schools. The pattern tends to be further accentuated by

Americans overwhelmingly favor racially integrated schools, but they have little enthusiasm for the use of busing to achieve integration. Bus loads of black students had to be escorted by police to an all-white school in Boston in 1971.

the movement of more affluent families out of center cities toward suburban areas. Unless this pattern is broken, second-generation Hispanics will grow up with the same handicaps as their parents.

EDUCATION AND APPLIED SOCIOLOGY

Sociologists have long been active in bringing their knowledge to bear on the educational system. We noted in Chapter 9, for example, that research conducted by sociologists and other social scientists was used by the United States Supreme Court in arriving at its landmark decision in *Brown v. Board of Education.* Since that time sociologists have been involved in research evaluating the impact of various plans for desegregating the schools.

One widely discussed remedy for segregation has been the use of busing to achieve racial balance in the schools. Actually, despite the controversy surrounding this issue, it should be noted that very few students are currently bused to other schools. Less than 10% of all high-school students, for example, are bused.[42] Research suggests that school integration can have beneficial long-term consequences—lower-income children earn improved test scores as a result of exposure to the more middle-class environment of suburban schools, without depressing the scores of white children.[43]

Perhaps the more significant long-term advantage of desegregation is that it helps to break down the social isolation of minority students. As already noted in Chapter 8, interracial contacts often expose minorities to discrimination, hostility, and personal indignities, encouraging them to avoid such encounters. Yet segregated neighborhoods and schools foster even greater social isolation of the races. By contrast, mixed schools have the potential to lessen such isolation. Hartford, Connecticut, experimentally desegregated some schools and followed the progress of 660 black students after they graduated. Those from desegregated schools were more likely to have white friends and work associates, and to live in white neighborhoods. Thus, integration aids both groups—black and white—to live and work together. As the authors of the research put it, "School desegregation is not simply an educational reform; it also reforms the socialization function of the schools."[44]

The tools of sociology, furthermore, have generally been used for the evaluation of a whole spectrum of education programs, ranging from general education efforts to specialized educational endeavors attempting

Exhibit 13.10 Applied Sociology

Responding to Social Change

If the Census Bureau's population projections are correct, there will never again be as many children in the United States as in 1970. During that year, almost 70 million people under age 18, representing more than a third of the national population, resided within our national boundaries. The number of children fell to a low of 62 million in 1983, but is expected to level off at about 64 million in 2010 when only 21% of the U.S. population will be younger than age 18.

All of these population changes involve the "baby boom" generation, a phenomenon that is discussed at length in Chapter 18. Briefly, for two decades following World War II, the birth rate was exceedingly high, bringing about overcrowding in the nation's classrooms for much of the 1960s and early 1970s. Now that the baby-boom generation has begun to come of age and have children of its own, it is expected that classrooms will again become crowded, but not to the same extent and not for as long. The reason is that baby boomers are having fewer children than their parents did. Therefore, the number of children in the U.S. is expected to peak at about 67 million in the late 1990s and then decline. This means that as school districts begin to prepare for the future, they must be aware of some important sociological facts. Any plans to build new schools, hire additional personnel, and raise money for educational purposes must take into account a variety of social and demographic changes.

The first and most obvious issue is that the size of the student population within the next several decades will not always be on the rise. With 3 million more children in the late 1990s than a decade or so later, it becomes clear that school systems cannot build new facilities and hire new teachers simply on an "as needed" basis. Assuming a 30:1 student–teacher ratio, by 2010 we could conceivably be faced with a surplus of 100,000 teachers, hired to cover the late 1990s peak but no longer needed twelve years later.

Even more crucial are issues related to the changing social patterns noted earlier in this text. We noted in Chapter 10, for example, that more elderly people are currently living in the United States than ever before. In addition, the Chapter 11 discussion of the changing family pointed out that the number of married couples with children has been shrinking and that the number of people electing to remain single and not raise a family is on the rise. The result of all of these factors is the addition of many more adults in today's population, and even more in tomorrow's, who do not have school-aged children. The consequence for schools is that the proportion of people willing to vote in favor of expanding school budgets is decreasing.

Finally, other social changes impact on school systems. Children born during the last decade or so are experiencing a family environment unknown to any other generation. More live with mothers only, and nearly two-thirds of all school children live in dual-earner or single-working-parent households. The needs of children, therefore, are different than before, placing an even greater demand on schools. Education also faces the problems of balancing the requirements of the back-to-basics movement with the innovations of a technological revolution, a situation that creates a need for "cultural literacy" and "computer literacy" at the same time.

In the final analysis, the lesson for applied sociology is that school systems need to be conscious of the changing social and demographic landscape and to structure programs and policies relevant to the needs of children with funding levels acceptable to taxpaying adults.

to reduce the prevalence of such phenomena as drug abuse, drunk driving, AIDS, anorexia, and teenage pregnancy.[45]

As a final note here, the importance of sociological knowledge and the sociological perspective might be best illustrated through a brief analysis of their roles in educational planning. Exhibit 13.10 illustrates how social changes have affected and will continue to affect the American schoolhouse, and a consciousness of these changes on the part of educational planners and administrators will affect the course of schooling in the years to come.

SUMMARY

Organized education in the United States emerged in the Massachusetts Bay Colony where settlers felt that their children needed to read the Bible if they were to find religious truth. By the time of the Revolution some sentiment for mass public education had developed, with Thomas Jefferson calling for "general education to enable every man to judge for himself what will secure or endanger his freedom." Changes in society produced by industrialization, combined with broadly based educational reform, led to the implementation of free public education in the nineteenth century.

Education has a number of different functions in industrial societies, and a great deal of the criticism leveled at the American educational system involves perceptions of how well it has been able to achieve its goals. Perhaps the most important goal of education is teaching the basic cognitive skills of reading, writing, and arithmetic. Despite the availability of public education, however, tens of millions of Americans are functionally illiterate. Schools also function to prepare students for adult roles. Here, controversy continues over the content and values that ought to be taught.

The many unanticipated and unintended consequences of education and the structure of schools often work to subvert the goals of education. For example, while the Jeffersonian ideal of responsible self-government is a frequently sought goal, the way that schools are organized actually encourages passivity.

Schools serve to transmit the broader cultural heritage of a society—its values, myths, customs, and traditions. Schools foster national pride and loyalty, as well as help to overcome racial and ethnic diversity that might otherwise promote disunity. Educational institutions also promote social change, not only by the creation and transmission of knowledge, but also by attempting to instill critical and questioning approaches that challenge existing beliefs.

Conflict-oriented sociologists have pointed out that education maintains patterns of inequality in society. These patterns are nowhere more evident than in the secondary school practice of tracking, which diverts students into alternative directions. It provides an enriched curriculum for the children of advantaged parents by preparing them for further education and better jobs. By contrast, children of working-class parents are likely to end up in tracks that assure they will hold jobs similar to those of their parents.

During the 1990s the American educational system faces a number of continuing challenges. Social and demographic changes have produced increasing numbers of "nontraditional students"—preschoolers, after-school students, and returning students. Accommodating these students will require considerable restructuring on the part of educational networks. The problems of segregation remain in some school districts, not only for blacks, but for growing numbers of Hispanics as well. And finally, the back-to-basics movement seeks to upgrade the quality of education across the United States.

KEY TERMS/CONCEPTS

ability groupings
assimilation
curriculum tracks
education
functional illiteracy
hidden curriculum
self-fulfilling prophecy

DISCUSSION QUESTIONS

1. How do you view the back-to-basics movement, and what kind of a curriculum do you think would be best for the nation's high schools?
2. Conflict sociologists argue that an educational system reflects the biases of the larger society in which it exists. Do you agree? Do you think that it is possible for an educational system to be active in bringing about social justice?
3. Education has many different functions. What are they, and do they tend to conflict with one another?
4. Has the hidden curriculum ever hindered your educational activities? How?
5. Should public educational systems provide day care for preschoolers whose parents work, or should this be a family responsibility?

SUGGESTED READINGS

Samuel Bowles and Herbert Gintis, *Schooling and Capitalist America* (New York: Basic Books, 1976). A conflict approach to education, in which the authors argue that public and private schools are the primary mechanisms through which inequality in capitalist societies is transmitted from generation to generation.

Ernest L. Boyer and the Carnegie Foundation for the Advancement of Teaching, *High School: A Report on Secondary Education in America* (New York: Harper & Row, 1983). This study provides a comprehensive analysis of high schools in America, with special attention being given to the social consequences of curriculum tracking.

Mark Chesler and William Cave, *A Sociology of Education* (New York: Macmillan, 1981). This text provides an overview of sociological studies of educational institutions.

John I. Goodlad, *A Place Called School* (New York: McGraw-Hill, 1983). A critical evaluation of American education based on an eight-year study of 38 public schools. The emphasis in this book is on the dynamics of the classroom.

E. D. Hirsch, Jr., *Cultural Literacy: What Every American Needs to Know* (Boston: Houghton Mifflin, 1987). The author stresses that every person must possess a body of knowledge for effective participation in the life of society. The book concludes with a "cultural literacy" checklist.

Vincent Tinto, *Leaving College* (Chicago: University of Chicago Press, 1987). This volume addresses the issue of the escalating college dropout rate, surveying the causes and offering ideas for dealing with the problem.

NOTES

1. Jonathan Kozol, *Illiterate America* (Garden City, NY: Doubleday/Anchor, 1985), p. 1.
2. National Commission on Excellence in Education, *A Nation at Risk* (Washington, DC: U.S. Government Printing Office, 1983).
3. This summary is based on John M. Blum, Arthur M. Schlesinger, Jr., William S. McFeely, Kenneth M. Stampp, Edmund S. Morgan, and C. Vann Woodward, *The National Experience: A History of the United States,* 7th ed. (San Diego: Harcourt Brace Jovanovich, 1989); Daniel Calhoun, *The Educating of Americans* (New York: Houghton Mifflin, 1969); George R. Cressman and Harold W. Benda, *Public Education in America* (New York: Appleton-Century-Crofts, 1966); H. G. Good, *A History of American Education* (New York: Macmillan, 1962); Ruskin Teeter, *The Opening Up of American Education* (Lanham, MD: University Press of America, 1983).
4. John Hope Franklin, *From Slavery to Freedom: A History of Negro Americans* (New York: Alfred A. Knopf, 1967), p. 202.
5. John A. Garraty, *The American Nation* (New York: Harper & Row, 1966), p. 247.
6. Robert Stevens, *Law School: Legal Education in America from the 1850s to the 1980s* (Chapel Hill: University of North Carolina Press, 1983), p. 82.
7. Social Science Research Council, *The Statistical History of the United States, from Colonial Times to the Present* (Stamford, CT: Fairfield, 1965), pp. 207–13.
8. Robert L. Church, *Education in the United States* (New York: Free Press, 1976), p. 403.
9. Social Science Research Council, *The Statistical History of the United States* pp. 210–11.
10. National Commission on Excellence in Education, *A Nation at Risk.*
11. *Newsweek,* September 21, 1987, pp. 54–55.
12. Jonathan Kozol, *Illiterate America,* p. 10.
13. Ernest L. Boyer and the Carnegie Foundation for the Advancement of Teaching, *High School: A Report on Secondary Education in America* (New York: Harper & Row, 1983).
14. Raymond E. Callahan, *Education and the Cult of Efficiency* (Chicago: University of Chicago Press, 1962).
15. John I. Goodlad, *A Place Called School* (New York: McGraw-Hill, 1983).
16. E. D. Hirsch, *Cultural Literacy: What Every American Needs to Know* (Boston: Houghton Mifflin, 1987).
17. Jonathan Kozol, *Illiterate America* p. 208.
18. See Herbert S. Klein, *Bolivia: The Evolution of a Multi-Ethnic Society* (New York: Oxford, 1982).
19. Frances FitzGerald, *America Revised: History Schoolbooks in the Twentieth Century* (New York: Random House, 1980).
20. Lynne V. Cheney, *American Memory* (Washington, DC: National Endowment for the Humanities, 1987).
21. For an analysis of the role of Horace Mann in the development of American public education, see Robert B. Downs, *Horace Mann: Champion of Public Schools* (New York: Twayne, 1974).
22. For example, see Richard D. Alba, *Italian Americans: Into the Twilight of Ethnicity* (Englewood Cliffs, NJ: Prentice-Hall, 1985).
23. Philip W. Jackson, *Life in Classrooms* (New York: Holt, Rinehart and Winston, 1968).
24. Richard Flacks, *Conformity, Resistance, and Self-Determination* (Boston: Little, Brown, 1973), p. 18.
25. Howard Becker, "A School Is a Lousy Place to Learn Anything," *American Behavioral Scientist,* 16 (1972), pp. 89–109; Lauren Resnick, "Learning in School and Out," *Educational Researcher,* December 1987; Robert A. Rothman, *Working: Sociological Perspectives* (Englewood Cliffs, NJ: Prentice-Hall, 1987), pp. 310–12.
26. Pierre Bourdieu, *Outline of a Theory of Practice* (Cambridge: Cambridge University Press, 1977).
27. Samuel Bowles and Herbert Gintis, *Schooling in a Capitalist Society* (New York: Basic Books, 1976).
28. See, for example, Jerome Karabel and A. H. Halsey (eds.), *Power and Ideology in Education* (New York: Oxford University Press, 1977); William Sewell and Robert M. Hauser, *Education, Occupations and Earnings* (New York: Academic Press, 1976).
29. For a review of this research, see Ray W. Cooksey, Peter Freebody, and Graham R. Davidson, "Teachers' Predictions of Children's Early Reading Achievement," *American Educational Research Journal,* 23 (September 1986), pp. 41–64.
30. Maureen T. Hallinan and Aage B. Sorensen, "Ability Grouping and Sex Differences in Mathematics Achievement," *Sociology of Education,* 60 (April 1987), pp. 63–72.

31. See Beth E. Vanfossen, James D. Jones, and Joan Z. Spade, "Curriculum Tracking and Status Maintenance," *Sociology of Education,* 60 (April 1987), pp. 104–22.
32. Sarah Lawrence Lightfoot, *The Good High School* (New York: Basic Books, 1983).
33. Robert Rosenthal and Lenore Jacobson, *Pygmalion in the Classroom: Teacher Expectations and Pupils' Intellectual Development* (New York: Holt, Rinehart and Winston, 1968).
34. James F. Rosenbaum, "The Stratification of the Socialization Process," *American Sociological Review,* 40 (February 1975), pp. 48–54.
35. *New York Times,* August 11, 1985, p. 9E.
36. Arthur Cohen and Florence Brawer, "Community College as a College," *Change Magazine,* March 1982, pp. 39–42.
37. *New York Times,* January 3, 1987, p. A23; Brent Staples, "The Dwindling Black Presence on Campus," *New York Times Magazine,* April 27, 1986, pp. 46–62.
38. *New York Times,* November 23, 1986, p. 26.
39. See *New York Times,* April 19, 1987, p. 1.
40. Robert L. Crain, *The Quality of American High School Graduates* (Baltimore: Johns Hopkins University, Center for Social Education of Schools, 1984).
41. Gary Orfield, Franklin Monfort, and Rosemary George, *School Segregation in the 1980s* (Chicago: National School Desegregation Project, 1987).
42. United States Department of Education, *The Condition of Education* (Washington, DC: U.S. Government Printing Office, 1982).
43. See Robert L. Crain, Rita Mahard, and Ruth E. Narot, *Making Desegregation Work* (Cambridge, MA: Ballinger, 1982); Ray C. Rist (ed.), *Desegregated Schools* (New York: Academic Press, 1979).
44. Jomills Henry Braddock II, Robert L. Crain, and James M. McPartland, "A Long-Term View of School Desegregation," *Phi Kappa Deltan,* 66 (1984), pp. 44–48.
45. Evan L. Baker, "Can Educational Research Inform Educational Practice? Yes!" *Phi Delta Kappan,* 65 (March 1984), pp. 453–59; Robert A . Dentler, "Research on Educational Programs," in Howard E. Freeman, Russell R. Dynes, Peter H. Rossi, and William Foote Whyte (eds.), *Applied Sociology: Roles and Activities of Sociologists in Diverse Settings* (San Francisco: Jossey-Bass, 1983), pp. 251–60.

14 Power, Politics, and the Economic Order

World history has recorded the exploits of such well-known individuals as Alexander the Great, Adolph Hitler, the Shah of Iran, Ronald Reagan, and Margaret Thatcher. Alexander the Great, the king of Macedonia from 336 to 323 B.C., is considered one of the greatest leaders of all time. He conquered much of Asia, and at one point in his short life of only 33 years he mused that his empire would some day encompass all of civilization. Hitler was the Fuhrer of the Third Reich from 1933 to 1945. He ordered the systematic extermination of six million Jews in an attempt to establish racial purity, and his ultimate dream was world conquest. Mohammed Reza Pahlavi, the Shah of Iran, was the absolute dictator of his nation until he was overthrown in 1979 by Ayatollah Khomeini and his Arab fundamentalist forces. The Shah was also one of the wealthiest men in the world and perhaps history's greatest proponent of monopolistic economic power. Reagan, first known to the American public as a film star, defied his celluloid beginnings to enter politics. He served as governor of California for almost a decade, and in 1980 he was elected to the first of two terms as the fortieth president of the United States. Thatcher, the daughter of a grocer and Methodist lay preacher, first worked as a research chemist and then studied law. In 1959, she entered the British Parliament, and twenty years later she became her nation's prime minister.

Somewhat less conspicuous in world affairs were John D. Rockefeller and Meyer Lansky. Rockefeller was an American industrialist. He created the Standard Oil Company in 1870, a corporate institution that quickly acquired control of virtually all facilities for the refining and transportation of petroleum in the United States. So great was his personal wealth that even in the 1990s his many descendants are listed among the nation's richest families. Meyer Lansky was a gangster. A Russian immigrant, Lansky worked his way up through the ranks of organized crime during the turbulent years of Prohibition. When he died of natural causes in 1983, he had not only outlived his peers from the early days of syndicate racketeering—Al Capone, Lucky Luciano, Joe Adonis, and "Bugsy" Siegel—but he also had amassed a personal fortune of some $600 million and had turned "organized crime" into an internationally powerful institution.

The factor that links these personalities is the fact that they all possessed great power. Each was able to command large numbers of people, sometimes even entire nations. But each individual also was different from the others in the way that he amassed and exercised his power. Reagan was elected to direct the executive branch of a stable and ongoing democratic government; his power was limited by both the Congress and the federal courts. The Shah was a monarch, a despot whose *will* was the positive law of the land. Khomeini was a spiritual leader, but he was able to influence the government of his nation profoundly. Alexander the Great commanded allegiance through military might, and Lansky used murder and intimidation. The Rockefeller organization was built on the economic power associated with the accumulation of vast amounts of capital. In short, the sources of power vary as do the ways in which power is used.

These brief profiles of persons and exploits of national and international significance focus attention on two of the major institutional centers of power in world society—politics and economics—both of which typically are interlinked. Yet what *is* power and what are its sources in the political and economic sectors? How is power distributed in society? And importantly, whether it is political or economic, how does power affect people's lives and the course of world affairs?

THE NATURE OF POWER

In 1972, political columnist William Safire was among a delegation of journalists who accompanied Richard Nixon on a visit to Teheran after a summit meeting in Moscow. At a state dinner shortly after their arrival, White House staff members were presented to His Majesty, the Shah of Iran. When the Shah asked his guests if they were enjoying their overnight stay, Safire expressed his dismay at not having the time to go shopping. The Shah nodded, turned to his grand vizier and ordered that all shops stay open all night. And so they did. At every shop at every hotel accommodating the traveling party and press corps, groggy storekeepers stood on hand throughout the night and far into the morning hours.[1] It had been the Shah's command and grand testimony to his absolute power (see Exhibit 14.1).

Power, Legitimacy, and Authority

According to Max Weber, **power** is the ability to control the behavior of others, even if they resist.[2] That is, individuals and groups have power when they can make other people behave in a desired manner, even if the other people do not wish to do so. The halting of traffic by a police officer's raised hand is a demonstration of power; a university's ability to determine the requirements for a college degree is a demonstration of power; a worker's observance of a corporation's time and attendance rules is a demonstration of power; and the Teheran shopkeepers' compliance with the Shah's order to remain open all night was a demonstration of power.

These few examples suggest that power can be of several types and can come from many sources. Power, for example, is not necessarily *legitimate* in all situations. It is legitimate only when those subject to it recognize that the people in charge have the right or authority to be there. Authority exists when people voluntarily comply with the directives of a superior or some other person with a designated rank. Thus, **authority** is legitimate power. A police officer has the authority to halt traffic, a university has the authority to determine academic standards for students, and a corporation has the authority to require its workers to comply with time and attendance rules. On the other hand, power is *illegitimate* when people feel that those applying it do not have the right to do so. **Coercion,** to use Weber's term, is illegitimate power. An armed robber's demand that a

Students demonstrated in Beijing's Tiananmen Square in July 1989, because they felt that their government's power was illegitimate. Other protesters included a Chinese worker who said, "Tell the United Nations, tell the world what has happened in China. Tell them that the Chinese government is killing the Chinese people."

Exhibit 14.1 **Types & Stereotypes**

The Dynamics of Power

In a letter dated April 3, 1887, to the Bishop of London, the British historian and Member of Parliament John Emerich Edward Dalberg-Acton, made the comment: "Power tends to corrupt and absolute power corrupts absolutely." In the years since, Lord Acton's phrase has become quite famous and is often repeated. Curiously, it has been used by contemporary public figures with a variety of modifications:

Power corrupts, but the lack of power corrupts absolutely.

—Adlai Stevenson

Power does not corrupt. Fear corrupts, perhaps the fear of a loss of power.

—John Steinbeck

Power does not corrupt men; but fools, if they get into a position of power, corrupt power.

—George Bernard Shaw

Power corrupts the few, while weakness corrupts the many.

—Eric Hoffer

Power dements even more than it corrupts, lowering the guard of foresight and raising the haste of action.

—Will Durant

In addition to the wisdom of Lord Acton and the opinions of his mimics, others also have commented on the nature and implications of power:

Power means not needing to raise your voice.

—George F. Will

Power is the ability not to have to please.

—Elizabeth Janeway

Never forget that as Parks Commissioner you have a weapon possessed by very few people—something that even Bobby Kennedy doesn't have—you have 800 trucks.

—New York City Parks Commissioner

bank teller open a cash drawer and fill a bag with money is an exercise in coercion. In the case of the Shah, few believed in the legitimacy of his leadership. As a result, his power was based on political dominance and coercion rather than on authority.

It should be noted that *power based on authority* tends to be accepted by the majority of those subject to it. Compliance becomes the social norm and those who refuse to recognize authority and follow the rules are considered deviant. Power based on coercion, however, tends to be unstable. Again, consider the case of the Shah. His father, Reza Khan Pahlavi, had been prime minister of Iran and was crowned "shah" (king) in 1926. He proceeded to improve his country's finances, but abdicated in 1941 at the age of 67. He was succeeded by his son, who continued to implement the changes begun by Reza Khan. The new Shah did much to wrench his people out of the Middle Ages and push them into the modern world. He raised the literacy rate and standard of living, advanced women's rights, and worked to maintain stability in the Middle East. For a time, although he had absolute power over his people, his rule was deemed legitimate. Yet when it suited his economic interests, the Shah was a traitor to the well-being of his kingdom. His pursuit of wealth, power, and influence led to corruption and the use of terror tactics by his secret police. His people then obeyed him only out of fear and ultimately revolted and overthrew him.

The Types of Authority

A variety of different reasons explains why people obey the orders and commands of others. In addition, some very clear limits may be placed on the extent of people's authority. University professors, as legitimate representatives of educational institutions, have the authority to require that their students attend classes and take examinations, but professors have absolutely no authority with regard to students' registering for the draft or driving safely. Similarly, while police officers have the authority to halt traffic, they cannot demand that motorists attend church or remain faithful to their spouses. These differences are rooted in the alternative bases for the legitimacy of authority. Max Weber identified three general types of authority: *traditional, legal-rational,* and *charismatic.*

Traditional Authority

The basis of legitimacy for traditional authority is custom or habit. **Traditional authority** is rooted in the assumption that the habits and customs of the past legitimize the present—that things *are* as they are because they have always been that way and will likely remain so. Traditional authority, moreover, is typically based on birthright or social position. Young children generally do as their parents tell them, subjects follow the rules of their monarch, and students study their professor's assignments. Where traditional authority prevails, both superiors and subordinates view their positions as legitimate, and alternative forms of authority are resisted because they lack the legitimacy of established custom.

Legal-rational Authority

Max Weber once described legal-rational authority as the belief in the legality of patterns of normative rules and the right of those elevated to authority under such rules to issue commands.[3] Thus, **legal-rational authority** is based on procedures that define the rights, duties, and obligations of those in power and the willingness of subordinates to follow the rules. For example, people abide by the authority of the state to establish laws; they respect the authority of the police to enforce the laws; and they recognize the authority of the judicial system to deal with those who violate the laws. Legal-rational authority stresses a "government of laws, not of people." If it were left up to each individual citizen to decide what behaviors should be under the control of laws, which rules should be enforced, and what ought to be done with the lawbreakers, the uncertainty and chaos of life would be a bit too much to manage. Rather than opt for this kind of disorder, citizens have decided that it is legitimate for the state to establish laws that may not allow them to do exactly as they wish. Yet such a system insures that others will be similarly prohibited, thus making the society a more orderly and predictable place in which to live.

It should be pointed out that legal-rational authority is not limited to political systems that elect leaders. The concept was applied by Weber to *any* system involving belief in the "legality" of patterns of normative rules and the right of those elevated to authority under such rules to issue commands. Thus, teachers have legal-rational authority, as do police officers and employers.

Charismatic Authority

The basis of legitimacy for charismatic authority is the belief that the ruler has been "graced" in some way. Thus, **charismatic authority** is the power that derives from a ruler's force of personality—one that can inspire devotion and loyalty among followers. The charismatic leader is seen as an individual who is inspired by an unusual vision, by lofty ideals, or even by God. Julius Caesar of ancient Rome, Pancho Villa of Mexico, Adolph Hitler of Nazi Germany, Fidel Castro of Cuba, Mohandas Gandhi of India, Ayatollah Khomeini of Iran, and Lech Walesa of Poland were (or are) all charismatic leaders. They inspired loyalty, passion, and devotion among their followers and their charisma alone was enough to make their authority seem legitimate. It should be emphasized, however, that unlike traditional and legal-rational authority, which are attached to some impersonal office, charismatic authority is vested in a particular individual and is not readily transferable to another. As a result, charismatic authority often can lead to instability. When the charismatic figure is no longer available to lead, the subjects may not view the new ruler as legitimate.

Lech Walesa, head of Poland's Solidarity Union, is a well-known charismatic leader.

Each of these three types—traditional, legal-rational, and charismatic—should be viewed as no more than "ideal types" of authority. Moreover, it is not likely that any given political system rests totally on any one type to the exclusion of the others. Rather, the three typically function in combination. In addition, various groups in a population may extend different forms of legitimacy to an authority system. In post-revolutionary America, for example, evidence points to the existence of both legal-rational and charismatic authority. The Constitution of the United States and the Bill of Rights provided the legal-rational authority basis for the new political system. The charismatic appeal of George Washington, however, also added legitimacy to the new government. The same might be said of Corazon Aquino, who defeated Ferdinand Marcos for the presidency of the Philippines in 1986. What happened to Marcos was a loss of *legitimacy*—he broke the rules by attempting to fix the election against Aquino.[4]

States, Nations, and Power

Several decades ago, anthropologist George P. Murdock observed that for the better part of human history, societies developed and people thrived in the absence of any true forms of government. He also noted that as recently as a century ago, half the world's societies ordered the lives of their members exclusively through informal controls and without the benefit of political institutions.[5] This situation certainly does not hold today; the modern world is made up of a complex of states, nations, and governments that feature varying political regimes.

The terms "state," "nation," "government," and "political regime" are often used interchangeably. However, they are actually separate entities that coexist in every complex society that has a political system and seat of power. The **state** is a social institution that has a monopoly on the legitimate right to use force within a given territory. A **nation** is a geographically distinct collection of people within the territory of a state. The **government** consists of the individuals or groups who control the political power of the state at any given time. A **regime** is the *system* of rules that determines how power and authority are organized. Thus, in any complex society where official rules determine how things ought to be done, the *state* is the institutional seat of power that enforces the rules, while the *nation* is the territory of people subject to those rules, the *government* is the individuals or groups that make the rules and direct their enforcement, and the *regime* reflects the policies and rules and how they are established and carried out. To cite a concrete example, the United States is a "nation" under a democratic "regime." The Constitution and its Bill of Rights represent the "state"—the institutional seat of power and authority—and the "government" is whatever presidential (or gubernatorial or mayoral in the case of states and cities) administration happens to be in office.

Cataloging the various kinds of political regimes can be a difficult exercise, for every classification system seems to exclude particular characteristics of some while overemphasizing those of others. The Greek conception of the state, advanced by both Plato and Aristotle, classified regimes according to the number of persons included in the rule making. In a *monarchy* a single ruler ruled; in *autocracies* and *oligarchies* a small group of people ruled; and in the *polity,* the majority of the citizens decided on who would rule and what the rules would be. These, of course, were also "ideal types" that never existed in their pure forms. However, their evolutionary counterparts can be observed in the autocracies, oligarchies, and democracies of the modern world.

Autocratic Regimes

In an **autocracy,** the ultimate authority and rule of government rest with one person; power is vested in the hands of a monarch or dictator who rules by force. Although similar in many ways to totalitarian states, autocracies tend to be less restrictive in controlling the private lives of citizens. The family, the church, and other traditional social institutions rarely are interfered with, and individuals have some personal freedom to pursue their own lives. However, autocratic rule requires absolute loyalty and devotion to the head of state, and dissent and criticism of the government and the person in power are strictly forbidden. The regime of Francisco Franco in Spain, the rule of Haile Selassie in Ethiopia, and the dictatorships of Juan Perón of Argentina and the Shah of Iran were autocracies. Autocratic rule recently existed under former President Jean-Claude "Baby Doc" Duvalier in Haiti and former President Ferdinand Marcos in the Philippines, and continues today on the Arabian Peninsula.

> ***Dictators are rulers who look good until the last 10 minutes.***
>
> **—Ferdinand Marcos**

Oligarchic Regimes

In an **oligarchy,** leadership and authority are vested in the hands of a small elite group. Oligarchical systems usually are based on wealth, military power, or social position, and rule with absolute power, unencumbered by democratic restraints. According to the *iron law of oligarchy,* the practice of democratic principles is impossible because of the tendency of the elite ruling group to dominate and control the majority of the people.[6]

Oligarchic regimes are in some ways similar to autocracies in that although they are not fully totalitarian, they enforce loyalty and compliance requirements through coercion. In addition, various segments of the population may be excluded from the decision-making processes of government or rights of residence on the basis of race, religion, or other social characteristics. Examples of these regimes can be found in the post-colonial governments of several African nations. In 1972, for example, President Idi Amin of Uganda expelled all Asians from his country. A variety of oligarchic government also exists in contemporary South Africa, where only whites may vote in parliamentary elections; the principles of apartheid bar the black majority from political participation. The ruling military juntas of many Latin American nations also reflect oligarchic forms of government.

Democratic Regimes

Democracy, which is discussed in more detail later in this chapter, is a system of government in which political authority is vested in the people. Democracy involves decision making based on majority rule, but it provides protection for minority rights as well. Democratic systems are often characterized by the effective guarantees of freedom of speech, the press, religion, assembly, petition, and equality before the law.

To a very great extent, the autocratic, oligarchic, and democratic systems of government are ideal types, as were the classical Greek conceptions of the state. In *real* political systems, any one type may have elements of one or more of the others. In the constitutional monarchy of Nepal, for example, the system of government reflects elements of both a democracy and an autocracy. For more than 200 years, Nepal was ruled by a succession of kings, and in recent years its citizens also have enjoyed many of the privileges found in democracies. On May 2, 1980, elections were held in which voters voluntarily approved the continued autocratic rule of King Birendra Bir Bikram. By contrast, although the United States has been a democracy since its founding, the "machine politics" of New York's Tammany Hall and other big city political organizations have been reflections of autocratic rule (see Exhibit 14.2).

SOCIAL INDICATOR

South America: Democracy's New Allure

In 1975, all but a few South American countries were oligarchies and autocracies, led by military regimes. By the late 1980s, democratic governments prevailed in all but Guyana, Chile, Paraguay, and Surinam. A coup in Paraguay in February of 1989 ended the 34-year dictatorship of Alfredo Stroessner, but the future of democratic government in that nation remains uncertain.

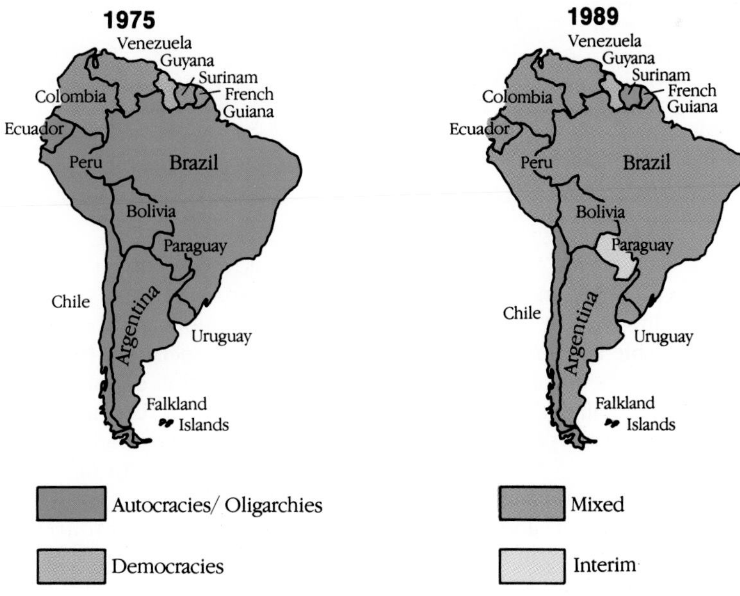

Exhibit 14.2 Case Study

Machine Politics and New York's Tammany Hall

"Machine politics" refers to the election of officials and the passage of legislation accomplished by means of the power of an organization created specifically for political action. It involves a strict and rigid structure, with rewards of one kind or another going to those who loyally work for the organization and observe its disciplines. The political machine has a long history in the United States, but it is most associated with the urban politics of Tammany Hall in nineteenth-century New York City.

The Tammany organization, originally a Jeffersonian political club founded in New York City in 1789 as the Society of St. Tammany, was mobilized in army fashion within the city wards (electoral districts) during the 1820s and early 1830s. It backed those issues that were popular among the groups living in low-income tenement housing, and distributed fuel, food, and clothing throughout poverty areas during times of economic crisis. Tammany also gained popularity and power through political patronage. The organization was regularly consulted in the choice of Democratic candidates. Officials who were placed in office through Tammany support, in turn, consulted with the Society regarding the distribution of municipal, state, and federal jobs.

Sometime during the 1850s, the Society of St. Tammany became functionally entangled with the emergent colonies of Irish immigrants, organized gambling and prostitution in New York's vice districts, and the vast mosaic of street gangs throughout the city. Tammany politics utilized the Irish immigrants and street gangs to maintain their power base by providing the members of these sectors with opportunities for upward mobility through employment or the spoils of graft. Initially, the pattern of Irish settlement, characterized by disembarkation through the New York port without the means for dispersion further into the continent, surrendered to the city some 130,000 Irish-born people before mid-century. By 1855 this minority collective represented one-third of the potential voters. Tammany, in organizing for its own survival, offered hospitality to the newly arriving Irish. Irishmen were naturalized by the thousands with the understanding that they would vote Democratic, and scores were guaranteed positions within the sectors of public administration.

Tammany entanglements with the Irish-dominated street gangs of lower Manhattan's Bowery and Five Points areas and other city wards were also structured into highly functional operations. Gang leaders and line members were dispatched to the polls to serve as bullies. They intimidated voters and were paid nominal sums to vote three and four times for

Totalitarianism

The concepts of autocracy, oligarchy, and democracy reflect the number of people involved in the decision-making processes. Another variable concerns the *extent* of control. Totalitarianism exists when political control extends to virtually every aspect of life. Totalitarianism can be present in any of the three ideal types—even in a democracy.

Totalitarianism is typified by restricted access to the decision-making process of the state and the total control of social institutions by one group. In totalitarian societies, a one-party political system monopolizes the offices of government and the sources of power, prestige, and wealth. An ideology is accentuated in which a particular set of social goals and valued behaviors is communicated, often in distorted terms. The group in power exercises control over the economy, weapons, the media, and public and private activities, and attempts to obliterate the social ties between individuals and groups other than those endorsed by the state. Totalitarian regimes employ force and terror to maintain full control; individual liberties, rights, and dissent are forcefully stifled. The Soviet Union—which considers itself a democracy—and the world of Big Brother in George Orwell's *1984* are clear reflections of totalitarianism (see Exhibit 14.3). The same can be said of Castro's Cuba. Similarly, the autocratic leadership of Duvalier in Haiti and Marcos in the Philippines, as well as the oligarchy in Idi Amin's Uganda exhibited many of the aspects of totalitarianism.

Tammany candidates. District leaders and ward heelers (workers for the local political "boss") provided protection for gang henchmen by keeping them out of jail and extending immunities to gang-operated houses of prostitution and gambling establishments.

Tammany bosses at all levels, given enduring survival power through patronage and election manipulation, defrauded the city treasury of immense sums of cash and property. The more notorious of the machine politicians were William Marcy Tweed and Richard Croker. Tweed is estimated to have cheated the city out of $30 million in cash and an additional $170 million in bribes and other types of graft between 1850 and the early 1870s. Croker, the "boss" of Tammany Hall from 1886 to 1902, became perhaps the most powerful figure in the history of New York politics and personally accumulated some $7 million a year through the extension of police protection to almost every form of vice and crime.

Despite a series of investigations that led to Tweed's arrest and conviction in 1873 and Croker's flight to Ireland in 1903 to live out his years as a country gentleman, Tammany nevertheless persisted with organized graft and corruption enduring through the early 1930s. But by then, Tammany's influence as a political machine had already begun to decline as the result of women's suffrage, immigration restrictions, and the social programs of the New Deal. It finally passed out of existence during the late 1960s under the mayoralty of John V. Lindsay.

Political machines were not limited to New York City. Counterparts of Tammany Hall were active at one time in San Francisco, Philadelphia, St. Louis, New Orleans, and other major American cities. The most recent held sway in Chicago under the leadership of Mayor Richard J. Daley. Daley's Cook County Democratic organization was the largest, richest, and *last* of the great urban political machines, remaining fully unchallenged until Daley's death in 1976.

SOURCES: Daniel J. Boorstin, *The Americans: The Democratic Experience* (New York: Random House, 1973), pp. 256–61; Charles N. Glaab and A. Theodore Brown, *A History of Urban America* (New York: Macmillan, 1967), pp. 201–27; Alfred Henry Lewis, *Richard Croker* (New York: Life, 1901); *New York Times,* December 21, 1976, p. 1; Len O'Connor, *Clout: Mayor Daley and His City* (New York: Avon, 1975); Mike Royko, *Boss: Richard J. Daley of Chicago* (New York: Signet, 1971); Alfred Steinberg, *The Bosses* (New York: Macmillan, 1972); M. R. Werner, *Tammany Hall* (Garden City, NY: Doubleday, Doran, 1928); Harold Zink, *City Bosses in the U.S.* (Durham, NC: Duke University Press, 1930).

WHO GOVERNS? DIFFERING PERSPECTIVES ON THE STATE

As every student who has taken a high-school civics course understands, the United States is a democracy, with leadership and decision making divided among the executive, legislative, and judicial branches of government. The president and vice-president, senators and members of the House of Representatives, and governors, mayors, city councils, and some judges are all elected officials, suggesting that "the people" have the final say in determining *who governs* them. However, when sociologists pose the question of who governs they are asking an altogether different question: within the framework of the democracy, *who* actually *makes* the important decisions and *how* are they made?

Four basic perspectives on, or models of, decision making have been proposed. "Pluralists" argue that power resides in various organized *interest groups* that seek to influence Congress and the Executive Branch. Each interest group, they suggest, oftentimes has the ability to affect government actions, but no one group is ever able to impose consistently its goals on all other groups. The "power-elite" perspective views the government (and society) as dominated by a small group of elite individuals who are able to determine the course of events by virtue of occupying high-level positions in government, industry, or the military. It is the attitudes, values, and goals of these "elites" that determine the

Exhibit 14.3

Sociological Focus

Big Brother and 1984

The totalitarian state, a distinctly twentieth-century phenomenon, does not tolerate the existence of autonomous institutions—such as churches, universities, or clubs—without the explicit approval of the government and in accordance with rigidly specific instructions and procedures. Totalitarianism involves the total control of peoples' lives by a monolithic and authoritarian state empowered to require instant obedience. This type of political order is currently apparent to a considerable degree in the Soviet Union and other iron-curtain countries, but the most extreme manifestation of the complete and relentless control of totalitarianism was depicted in George Orwell's novel, *1984*.

Orwell's book is the story of a grim Utopia, or more appropriately, an anti-utopia. The society of *1984* emerges in Oceania, one of the three superstates into which the world is divided, and it is composed of three classes—the Inner Party, the Outer Party, and the Proles. The Inner Party is the ruling class, a selective aristocracy of talent numbering no more than two percent of the population. Big Brother, whose pictures and statues appear everywhere, is the imaginary representative of the power elite of the Inner Party, and the symbolic, yet all-powerful, leader of the state. Under the complete control of the Inner Party is the Outer Party, a relatively small and powerless middle group that handles all the routine administration of the state. The Proles are the faceless masses—the lower class. They exist simply to serve the state as workers and soldiers and to breed more workers and soldiers. The government of *1984* is monolithic and centralized. It is composed of four basic structures: the Ministry of Truth, which controls the news, entertainment, education, and the arts; the Ministry of Peace, which concerns itself with war; the Ministry of Plenty, which is responsible for economic affairs; and the Ministry of Love, which maintains law and order through an all-powerful secret police.

The slogan, "BIG BROTHER IS WATCHING YOU," is the essence of social control in *1984*, and is realized through the "telescreen"—a built-in television monitor found almost everywhere in Oceania. The telescreen has a dual purpose: it continually drones on in a rapid monologue about the economic and political affairs of the state, and it is a transmitter, sending to some central police observation station a picture of everything in its view. Telescreens are mounted on every street corner and square in Oceania, in every office, every apartment, and every room, and they cannot be shut off.

The machinery of social control is the Ministry of Love's

nature and direction of decision making. The economic theories of Karl Marx suggest a third perspective—domination of the government by capitalists. In this model the industrial leaders of society control the government *directly,* by supplying the people who hold office, and *indirectly,* by influencing public officials. Finally, a "functionalist" point of view suggests that all members of a society benefit from the state's position of power.

Political Pluralism

In the political sense, **pluralism** is the diffusion of power among various groups and interests. Many decades ago, sociologist David Riesman and his associates described the American political system as pluralistic, composed of many interest groups—collections of individuals sharing similar goals and concerns who organize for the purpose of influencing legislation and public policy. Thus, the **pluralist theory of politics** holds that power is distributed among many different groups which compete with one another in both government and the private sectors of the economy.[7]

Many interest groups currently function in the United States—the American Medical Association, the National Rifle Association, the Chamber of Commerce, the United Auto Workers, and literally hundreds of others at the national level alone. Each seeks to introduce legislation that would be beneficial to its interests, while opposing laws that might do them harm. The National Rifle Association, for example, has consistently been effective in opposing legislation that it feels will infringe on the rights and activities of gun owners. Similarly,

Thought Police. All crimes in *1984* are comprehended as one master offense—"*Thoughtcrime,*" which consists in having an improper mental or inner attitude toward the Party and Big Brother. To speak out against the Party is *Thoughtcrime;* to hate Big Brother, even unconsciously, is *Thoughtcrime;* to question the history or policy of the Party is *Thoughtcrime.*

The hero of *1984* is Winston Smith, and the story revolves around his revolt against the straitjacket society of Oceania and the end to which his revolt leads him. Winston Smith is Everyman. He is a member of the Outer Party and a minor employee of the Ministry of Truth. Smith is also a "Thoughtcriminal," for he hates Big Brother.

George Orwell, in writing *1984,* was offering an exaggerated projection of a future which, given the logical outcome of certain tendencies that existed at the time of his writing, *might* come to pass. Thus, the book was not a portrayal of the shape of things to come, but simply a warning to the present. And the reactions to *1984* were mixed. It was belittled by many, alternatively dismissed as "cynical rot," "propaganda," and a "depressing hatred of everything approaching progress." By others, Orwell's book was described as "terrifying," "brilliant," and "relevant." Most interesting in the commentaries was that a select group of Orwell's contemporaries was quick to recognize that his imaginary world had already arrived. Sociologist Daniel Bell, in his remarks about *1984* shortly after its publication in 1949, commented:

> Is, for example, the action of the British Labour government in creating a wage freeze the imposition of controls whose consequence is the acceleration of power concentration and the total state? Or is the creation of a central intelligence agency in the United States—voted recently by Congress—with the power to plant agents in every voluntary association in the country, including trade unions, another step toward that end? Are these not irreversible steps, and hence, the danger that we are being warned against?

Although the year 1984 has come and gone, the realities of Orwell's *1984* have not come to pass. Orwell's book is a classic reminder that the creation of government also creates the potential for abuse of individual rights.

SOURCES: Isaac Deutscher, "1984: The Mysticism of Cruelty," in Isaac Deutscher, *Heretics and Renegades* (London: Hamilton, 1956); Jeffrey Meyers (ed.), *George Orwell: The Critical Heritage* (London: Routledge & Kegan Paul, 1975); *New Leader,* June 25, 1949; George Orwell, *1984* (New York: Harcourt, Brace & World, 1949).

businesses and industries that felt they were being economically victimized by imported microchips formed the Semiconductor Industry Association. In 1987, their lobbying—the practice of directly trying to pursuade decision makers to adopt policies that favor one's own interests—convinced the President of the United States to impose tariffs on certain Japanese imports.[8] Interest groups pursue their own self-interest. Consequently the victories of any particular interest group are rarely beneficial to all members of society. The fact that the National Rifle Association has been able to thwart strict controls on handguns has had the effect of putting guns in the possession of many people who should not have them—criminals, the mentally ill, individuals who use violence as a mechanism to settle disputes, and homeowners untrained in the use of weapons. Similarly, trade restrictions that are imposed as the result of interest group lobbying can have an adverse economic impact on many individuals by forcing up the prices of certain needed goods.

Pluralists note that no single interest group is ever powerful enough to dominate every issue that affects them. Therefore, no single group's total interests prevail. What often happens, however, is that different interest groups form temporary coalitions to fight for activities that benefit all of the members of the coalition. These are generally temporary liaisons, which break up after the specific issue is resolved.

Interest groups also lobby to prevent unfavorable actions. Acting as "veto groups," they attempt to protect their interests by blocking proposals of other groups that might encroach on their aims. Many of the lobbying activities of the National Rifle Association have been of a veto nature.

Exhibit 14.4

Research in Sociology

The Power Elite in the United States

C. Wright Mills' claim that a "power elite" of corporate executives, military officers, and political officials—leaders who share similar upper-class origins, social values, and economic prosperity—makes all decisions of national significance in the United States, has been put to considerable empirical testing over the years. The findings suggest that the power elite did not just develop in this country in recent years; small elite groups of influential decision makers reflect a pattern that dates back to the early years of the American republic.

Among the more unique contributions to research in support of a long history for the existence of the power elite was the work of historical sociologist Sidney Aronson, who tested some of the historical assumptions about Jacksonian democracy. Much twentieth-century American historical writing has reiterated the idea that Jacksonian democracy was a farmer-labor coalition, a distinctively frontier product. This view was not without basis. Pro-Jackson editors and politicians, in predicting the defeat of the Adams administration in the election of 1828, persuaded the people that the first task of their new president would be the removal of enough office holders to make way for the deserving Democrats. Jackson, moreover, in his first annual message, stressed the notion that "the duties of all public offices [were so] plain and simple" that even the average man was qualified. His appeal was to the mass electorate, and his philosophy reflected on the virtues of the common man. Thus, history has suggested that it was Jackson's intention to remove existing office holders and replace them with Democrats of simple origins. Aronson's examinations of the social backgrounds of the higher civil servants in the administrations of John Adams, Thomas Jefferson, John Quincy Adams, and Andrew Jackson demonstrated that the overwhelming majority of these government workers in all four administrations had come from the socioeconomic elite. These findings received support from Harvard University historian Samuel Eliot Morison who found that Jackson actually removed very few of the presidential appointees named by his predecessors. And finally, historian Richard Hofstadter demonstrated that Jackson was even aligned against the Democratic movement in his home state of Tennessee.

Psychologist G. William Domhoff, in his book, *Who Rules America?,* published in 1967, argued for the existence of a "governing class" in the United States that controls the corporate economy, opinion-making organizations, the federal

The Power Elites

As he was leaving the presidency in 1960, Dwight David Eisenhower warned of the emergence of a "military-industrial complex" that had gained unusual power in American governmental affairs. Sociologist C. Wright Mills had spoken of the same thing a few years earlier.[9] Both worried that the United States was dominated by a small group of individuals, only a portion of whom were elected officials (the President and members of the Cabinet). Others develop significant levels of influence by achieving top positions in the military (the Joint Chiefs of Staff) and business and industry (the top officers in the nation's largest corporations). Thus, the **power elite** is a small network of influential individuals who are alleged to make the most important political decisions in American society.

As a result of their backgrounds (they are largely white, upper-middle and upper class, Protestant males), the members of the power elite have certain common values and perspectives. Moreover, because they regularly associate with one another, they tend to reinforce commonly held points of view. They also tend to circulate between positions in the three spheres—the military, industry, and government. Eisenhower himself had been a member of the power elite as a five-star general in the United States Army and a university president, before being elected to the presidency. Sociologists and other social scientists have attempted to demonstrate that a power elite existed much earlier than colonial times and continues in contemporary society (see Exhibit 14.4).

government, the CIA, and the FBI. He defined this governing class as:

> A social upper class which owns a disproportionate amount of a country's wealth, receives a disproportionate amount of the country's annual income, and contributes a disproportionate number of its members to the controlling institutions and key decision-making groups of the country.

Domhoff's analysis was heavily criticized on the grounds that his research was incomplete, his statistics were muddled, his argument was without theoretical foundation, and his definition of "social class" was unclear. Despite these criticisms, however, other researchers were arriving at basically the same conclusions.

In 1975, studies by sociologist Peter J. Freitag, undertaken with considerably more care than Domhoff's work, examined the social backgrounds of United States cabinet members who served at some point during the years from 1897 to 1973. His findings demonstrated that throughout this period, 76.1% of all cabinet members had been associated with corporations, either as directors, officers, or attorneys. During recent administrations, this "interlock" was even more pronounced: 85.7% under Eisenhower, 76.9% under Kennedy, 85.7% under Johnson, and 95.7% under Nixon.

In the 1980s, a glance at the top cabinet officers in the Reagan administration tends to support the power-elite view. Secretary of State George Shultz was a director of the banking giant Morgan Guaranty Trust, and president of Bechtel Corporation, one of the largest construction firms in the world prior to his government appointment. Secretary of Defense Casper Weinberger had been a vice-president and general counsel of Bechtel, and Secretary of the Treasury Donald Regan had been the chief executive officer of Wall Street's Merrill Lynch, Pierce, Fenner and Smith, Inc. In addition, according to Domhoff's *Who Rules America Now?,* the balance of the Reagan decision makers came from corporate backgrounds.

SOURCES: Sidney Aronson, *Status and Kinship in the Higher Civil Service* (Cambridge: Harvard University Press, 1964); G. William Domhoff, *Who Rules America?* (Englewood Cliffs, NJ: Prentice-Hall, 1967); G. William Domhoff, *Who Rules America Now?* (Englewood Cliffs, NJ: Prentice-Hall, 1983); Peter J. Freitag, "The Cabinet and Big Business: A Study of Interlocks," *Social Problems,* 2 (December 1975), pp. 137–52; Richard Hofstadter, *The Progressive Historians* (New York: Alfred A. Knopf, 1969), p. 441; Samuel Eliot Morison, *The Oxford History of the American People* (New York: Oxford, 1965), p. 426.

Karl Marx and the Conflict Perspective

Adherents of the **conflict theory of politics** argue that the state is biased in favor of the interests of wealthy and powerful economic groups and that the interests of the upper classes dominate it. The most influential proponent of this view was Karl Marx, who held that except for the most primitive of societies, all others are divided into two or more classes, based on the existing economic system.[10] One of these classes dominates and exploits the others, and uses various social institutions, including the state, to secure and maintain its privileges. This ruling class, furthermore, also controls the forces of economic production. Thus, Marx held that the nature of the means of production determined which class would control not only the economy, but the state and other social and cultural institutions as well.

The position taken by Marx also held that the transition from one form of economic production to another was the major source of change for all political, social, and cultural systems. Transitions took place in a predictable series of stages:

1. from *primitive communal society* in which no class dominates and all productive property is held in common by members of the social group
2. to *slavery,* in which the ruling class owns the laborers
3. to *feudalism,* in which the ruling class holds the workers through bondage by law and tradition

4. to *capitalism,* in which the ruling class controls the workers through law and economic necessity
5. to *socialism,* in which private property is abolished
6. to *communism,* in which society returns once again to the communal ownership of all productive property

In the socialist stage, Marx believed that certain "reactionary" groups in society would attempt to reimpose the right to ownership of private property. To prevent this from happening, he maintained that the socialist state might be forced temporarily to become a "dictatorship of the proletariat"—that is, a dictatorship that would act to suppress nonsocialist values. As for the final stage in the cycle, Marx felt that the state would eventually "wither away"; that under communism, the state, as a complex hierarchy of offices, would become useless and vanish.

Marx focused his view on "capitalists," whom he saw as using the government to dominate workers. In contrast to Marx's position, however, modern advocates of his conflict theory of politics argue that government decisions are dominated by a small ruling class composed of the individuals and families that own vast wealth, as well as the top managers of large corporations and financial institutions who use the state to further their own economic interests.

The ruling class, according to modern conflict theory, exercises its power in several ways. The first, and perhaps the most obvious way, is by having representatives of the industrial sector move into positions of political power. Interestingly, such names as Kennedy, Du Pont, and Rockefeller are not all that uncommon in government. A second dimension of ruling class domination is more subtle, occurring behind the scenes. On this point, T. Boone Pickens, an industrialist who accumulated vast wealth in the oil business, has claimed that a little known group known as the "Business Roundtable," composed of the CEOs (chief executive officers) of some of America's largest corporations, influences both the President of the United States and the Federal Reserve Board through direct personal contacts.[11]

The Functionalist Perspective

Proponents of the **functionalist theory of politics** hold that the state's position of power provides benefits to all members of society, not just the upper classes. Particularly important to an understanding of this view is the examination of the *functions* of the state for the society as a whole. A noted adherent of the functionalist perspective was the well-known American sociologist Talcott Parsons, who maintained that the political system must (1) adapt society to its environment, (2) attain goals for society, (3) integrate the various elements of society, and (4) maintain the values and patterns in a society.[12]

The Adaptive Function

The adaptive function of the state is to maintain responsible political, economic, and military relations with other states and societies. Since the "environment" of any given society is all other societies, and since this environment is in a constant state of change as the result of trading agreements, alliances of all kinds, and wars, a state must adapt to these changes. Thus, to survive, any state or nation must defend its population against aggressors and negotiate agreements to maintain its economic stability. Recent history suggests that such adaptation can be quite complex and typically involves a variety of arrangements with both antagonistic and friendly societies. Since the United States and the Soviet Union are staunch political adversaries, for example, throughout his two terms President Ronald Reagan increased military appropriations and pursued his *Star Wars* defense initiative. At the same time, however, for the sake of the economic security of certain sectors of the American farm industry, arrangements were made to sell wheat to the Soviet Union. By contrast, although the United States and Japan are firm allies, to protect American auto workers and the industries that depend on automobile production, quotas were placed on the importation of Japanese vehicles.

The Goal-attainment Function

The goal-attainment function of the state is to coordinate the planning and direction of its development and to facilitate the achievement of the plans, goals, and directions it prescribes. If a state is to have a technologically based economic system, for example, then it also must have a technically skilled labor force to provide the workers necessary for the occupational structure. Thus, an effective educational system must be available. In addition, the state also must foster adequate transportation and communication systems. Supporting this goal-attainment function in the United States is a complex tax system. Tax revenues are necessary for the construction of schools and hospitals, the building and maintenance of highways, the establishment of public health programs, the care of the aged and the poor, the strengthening of the military, and the general running of the government.

At times, the goal-attainment function of the state suffers a breakdown. In June 1989, an error by Soviet technicians in responding to the lowered pressure reading along one section of a gas pipeline resulted in the deaths of hundreds of people.

Ever since taxes were first imposed in the Puritan colony of Massachusetts Bay in 1643, the government has wrestled with the problems of setting rates that match peoples' ability to pay, compliance with the tax laws, and convenience and economy of collection. In 1913, the progressive income tax was introduced, and since that time no less than two dozen revisions have been enacted by Congress. Progressive taxation is based on the idea that the more people earn, the more they should pay; not too long ago, the highest tax bracket was assessed at a rate of 90%. During the 1980 presidential campaign, candidate Ronald Reagan, reflecting on the high rates imposed, commented that the progressive income tax must have been an invention of Karl Marx. After his election to the presidency, despite a high federal deficit, he reduced tax rates for individuals and for businesses. *Reaganomics*—the president's conception of how to exercise the goal-attainment function of the government—was based on the idea that if people have more to spend and if businesses have greater profits, investment and spending will increase, thus stimulating the economy as a whole and increasing the tax base and revenues collected.

The Integrative Function

The integrative function of the state is to arbitrate the conflicts that arise among its various elements and groups. Since most societies are composed of a variety of groups with conflicting interests—workers and management, liberals and conservatives, rich and poor, producers and consumers—the state must serve to resolve these differences, and to do so in a manner biased toward the welfare of the society as a whole. Indeed, if the state consistently favored one group over another, those left out would eventually view the state as illegitimate, thus undermining the authority of the political leadership. Acting to fulfill the integrative function are the various governmental regulations controlling public utility rates, minimum wages, consumer product safety, workmen's compensation, corporate monopolies, political campaign funds, and environmental pollution.

The Pattern-maintenance Function

The pattern-maintenance function of the state is the enforcement of the established rules of conduct—that is, law enforcement. Since a society's laws derive from its customs and values, the state must enforce the laws to ensure that the customs and values are maintained and *anomie* is avoided. By using negative sanctions—arrest, fines, imprisonment, or perhaps execution—the state is able to suppress threats to the social order. The state's enforcement of the law also protects the rights of individuals and groups, thereby reinforcing their perception of the state as legitimate. Any attempt to classify a given system of politics as either "conflict," "power-elite," "functionalist," or "pluralist" would indeed be difficult, since many of the elements of each may be operative at any given time. This observation seems to be true even of a democracy such as the United States.

With respect to the Marxist view of monopoly capitalism, the American industrial complex is indeed controlled by the bastions of financial wealth. At the same time, as already made clear in Exhibit 14.4, the United States government has always been in the hands of a power-elite with only a small segment of the population involved in major decision making. In support of the functionalist view, over the past several decades the government has exerted more and more power over the private sector with respect to pollution regulations, increased emphasis on employee safety, discrimination in housing and employment, and monopolistic controls. Moreover, the pluralistic position is clearly evident in the fact that many policies are the result of conflict and bargaining among people and organizations that represent specific interest groups. And finally, none of these theories of political power can adequately explain the extraordinary role that is played by the judiciary, an institution that would be difficult to describe as a "group" with "interests." Rather, the courts are a constitutionally based source of power and authority, the exercise of which depends crucially on the ideas and beliefs of its individual members (see Chapter 15). Thus, we find no simple answer to the question, "Who governs?" Authority and decision making seem to depend on what policy is being proposed and on the opportunities different proponents and opponents have to mobilize support for their position.

American women had to campaign for the right to vote in the early 1900s.

POLITICAL POWER IN DEMOCRATIC SOCIETIES

The term, *democracy,* is of Greek origin and means "the rule of the people." While the word conjures up images of the widespread participation of the population in decision making, in actual practice most democratic societies must function as *representative democracies.* That is, most democratic states, because they are far too large to allow all persons to become involved in every resolution, have periodic elections in which designates are selected to represent the interests of their constituencies in the decision-making process. Moreover, in most democracies only certain segments of the population are *enfranchised*—that is, allowed to vote. In early American politics, blacks, women, and nonproperty holders were barred from voting. Up until the passage of the Voting Rights Act of 1965, literacy and other tests placed restrictions on voting, often for the purpose of discriminating against minority groups. Even today, only those persons age 18 and over have the right to vote. Nevertheless, most modern democracies have near **universal suffrage**—the right of *all* to vote. Yet critics argue that the structure of the political process can make a democracy anything *but* representative because of the fact that candidates are chosen by small numbers of voters (see Exhibit 14.5).

For many decades, social and political scientists have had considerable interest in two major issues regarding democratic political systems. The first issue focuses on the reasons why some states are democratic while others tend toward totalitarianism, asking the question, "What are the prerequisites for democracy?" The second issue is concerned with the distribution of power within democracies, asking, "Does universal suffrage insure that all groups and points of view are equally represented?" The answers to these questions have led observers and researchers to examine the influences of economics, social class, interest groups, and cultural institutions on politics.

The Prerequisites for Democracy

Americans typically take democracy for granted. Yet even the most casual review of the world's political systems makes clear that democracies are in the minority. Most of Asia and parts of Africa, Latin America, and Eastern Europe are composed of various types of totalitarian states, military dictatorships, constitutional monarchies, and other forms of government in which total power resides in the hands of an absolute and select few. Such a review also would suggest that experiments with democracy do not always work well; only some nations that attempt to extend suffrage to the population at large actually succeed. These phenomena have led a number of social and political theorists to ask what conditions promote democracy. The work of political sociologist Seymour Martin Lipset suggests that three factors play an important role: (1) advanced economic development, (2) a balance and diffusion of power, and (3) a cultural heritage of tolerance for dissenting views.[13]

1. *Democratic institutions are most likely to flourish in nations with advanced economic development.* This observation appears to be true because of two major factors. First, economically advanced nations tend to have literate, urbanized populations that are well informed, sophisticated, and less likely to be seduced by charismatic, would-be despots. Second, these nations are likely to have large middle classes, able to resist political upheavals that would threaten their economic well-being. Thus, in economically advanced societies the political and economic stake of the literate middle class is too great to risk a civil war or revolution. In nations with large impoverished classes, on the other hand, the ruling class resists granting the extension of democratic privileges to all social groups. In these nations, the disadvantaged frequently resort to nondemocratic methods of social change, such as civil disorder, rioting, or outright rebellion.

2. *Democratic institutions are most likely to flourish in nations where a balance and diffusion of power develop.* If one social group can control the major segments of power within a society, then it is quite unlikely that this ruling body will voluntarily allow others to share its privileged position of political leadership. This observation suggests three important points. First, in a community or state that is dominated by one assemblage (either an industry or social group), it is likely that such power will overshadow the existing political leadership and limit attempts at democracy. Second, societies with major social or political cleavages—deep divisions between groups characterized by antipathy, distrust, and even outright hostility—do not provide a fertile environment for the growth of democratic values and institutions. A major cleavage in any society typically indicates an unwillingness to resolve the conflict at the expense of the established political system. The contemporary situations of religious cleavage in Lebanon and Northern Ireland, and of racial division in South Africa, suggest that democratic institutions tend to be unstable when they exist in societies with deep social fission. A most recent example was apparent in India with the opposition of the Sikhs to the government of Indira Gandhi.

The Sikhs are members of a casteless religion who scorn India's Hindus and Muslims. Though the 15 million Sikhs represent only 2% of India's population, they account for 15% of the nation's army and a similar proportion of its civil servants. Moreover, their efficient farming in Punjab, India's richest state, has made this once starving nation almost self-sufficient in food production. Too, the Sikhs have a binding sense of community and a determination to protect their rights.

The trouble began with the nation's independence from the British in 1947 and its partitioning into India and Pakistan: India went to the Hindus, Pakistan to the Muslims, and the Sikhs were left in the middle. Their home state of Punjab was cut to a third of its former size. In recent decades, Sikh moderates pressed the Indian government for greater autonomy in the Punjab, while extremists agitated for a separate Sikh state of Khalistan. In June 1984, 500 Sikhs armed themselves within the walls of the Golden Temple of Amritsar, their holiest shrine. Their demand was to have their independent state, or die. On the order of Indira Gandhi, the Golden Temple and 40 other Sikh shrines were simultaneously attacked. This action resulted in the deaths of thousands of Sikhs, the assassination of Gandhi several months later, rioting and many more thousands of deaths, even greater cleavages between Sikhs, Muslims, and Hindus, and a general weakening of India's democratic government.[14]

The lesson in India and other nations in which cleavages exist suggests that competing groups must share in the governing of the state in such a way that no single sector can dominate the others. This condition has been realized in a number of democratic nations through the division of governmental power between executive, legislative, and judicial branches, and through a system of "checks and balances" in which each component of the

Exhibit 14.5

Sidelights on American Culture

The American Presidential Election: A Frustration of the Representative Democratic Process?

Democracy, quite literally, is government by the people. But the theory of democracy is immensely complicated, partly because of difficulties in understanding who the "people" are, and which acts of government are truly "theirs" rather than those of some dominant group. In the representative democracy where people choose designates who are then answerable to them, the issue becomes even more clouded. In many instances, the selection of these designates is so complex that in the end it is not altogether clear as to who is representing whom. This is particularly the case in American presidential elections.

The selection of the President of the United States begins, at least officially, with the *primaries*—elections carried out by political parties to determine who will stand as their candidates in the national election. Primary winners claim to be the choice of the people, but this is not really so, and for a variety of reasons. First, not all states hold primaries. Second, in those states that do, *all* of the candidates do not appear on *all* of the ballots. Third, in most states, in a sense, the primaries are "closed." That is, the Democratic primaries are open only to registered Democrats, with a corresponding arrangement in Republican primaries. Few states permit "crossovers." In 1988, 26% of all registered voters were registered Independents, most of whom could not participate in the primary process. Fourth, voter turnout is generally low. In the 1988 presidential election, almost 90 million votes were cast, yet less than 35 million voters participated in the primaries.

Delegates to the national nominating convention for each party are generally party leaders, chosen during the primaries and elected at state conventions. They, in turn, cast a ballot at the nominating convention to determine their party's candidate. But whom do these delegates really represent? Through some mathematical manipulation understood by political scientists and election specialists, delegates are assigned to a candidate according to the number of popular votes received by that candidate at a given primary. These delegates are thus "committed" to vote for their candidate at the nominating convention, at least on the first ballot. Two major problems arise in connection with this segment of the process. First, the number of delegates assigned to a given candidate is disproportionate to the number of actual votes received. During the Democratic primaries in 1984, for example, Reverend Jesse Jackson, who complained vigorously about delegate selection rules, wound up with 18.4% of the popular vote but only 9.6% of the delegates.

Second, the party activists and leaders who become delegates often have views that are different from those of the rank and file they represent. At both the 1972 and 1976 Democratic national conventions, for example, the delegates who chose the candidates had views on welfare, military policy, school desegregation, crime, and abortion that were diametrically opposed to those of most Democrats.

Finally, the winner-take-all principle of the American Electoral College casts additional doubt on the representative nature of the political process in this country. Under the electoral vote system, each state has a given number of electoral votes based on its population size as of the most recent decennial census. A total of 538 electoral votes are at stake, with 270 needed for victory. The candidate for president who wins the most popular votes in a state wins *all* of that state's electoral votes. In consequence, the winner of the popular vote can lose the election in the electoral college. Has this ever happened? In 1824, Andrew Jackson won a plurality but lost to John Quincy Adams; in 1876, Rutherford B. Hayes was elected with a minority of the popular vote, as was Benjamin Harrison in 1888; and in 1960, John F. Kennedy won the election with 34,049,096 votes—59,061 popular votes less than the number cast for Richard Nixon. In this way, the American Electoral College system disenfranchises those who voted for the loser in any given state, in effect permitting the majority to cast their own votes as well as those of the losers. Moreover, this system can give the perception of a "landslide" for the winning candidate, when such may not necessarily be the case. In 1984, for example, Ronald Reagan clearly won both the popular vote and electoral counts. However, while Walter Mondale won 41% of the popular vote, he accumulated only 2.4% of the electoral vote. And in the 1988 presidential election, George Bush's victory over Michael Dukakis occurred with 54% of the popular vote and 79% of the electoral vote.

SOURCES: James David Barber, *The Pulse of Politics* (New York: W. W. Norton, 1980); Richard M. Pious, *The American Presidency* (New York: Basic Books, 1970); James Q. Wilson, *American Government: Institutions and Policies* (Lexington, MA: D.C. Heath, 1983), pp. 151–55; *U.S. News & World Report,* November 19, 1984, pp. 24–28.

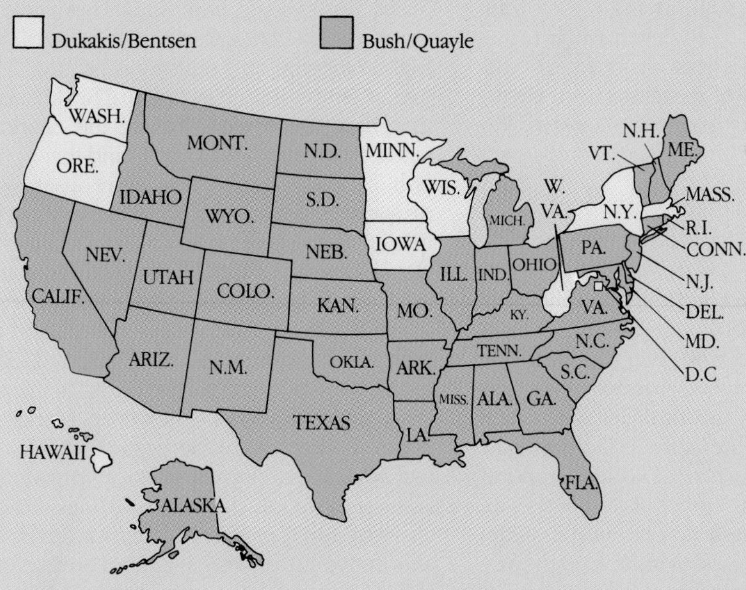

democratic regime keeps a close watch on all of the others.

3. *Democratic institutions are most likely to flourish in nations with a cultural heritage of tolerance for dissenting views.* Citizens of democracies generally form opinions regarding their own self-interests. If existing social and cultural institutions support the right of all citizens to express their views freely, even when these views conflict with prevailing ideas or those of the governing party, the conditions of repression and cleavage that challenge democratic leadership tend to be minimized.

Social Class and Democracy

Advocates of the conflict, or Marxist theory of politics, as noted earlier, maintain that governments are the servants of the upper classes, that those who own the means of production also are able to control the government, and that such control often results in domination of other social institutions, such as art, literature, education, and religion. In short, the entire structure of society supports the continued dominance of the upper class.

By contrast, others maintain that political systems cannot be democratic if one class does indeed reign over all others, particularly if that prevailing class accounts for only a small segment of the population.[15] It is apparent, however, that political party systems in most democratic states rest, at least in part, on the class division in their societies. A **political party** is a collectivity of people organized for the specific purpose of gaining legitimate control of the government. In the United States a *two-party system* developed. Voter loyalties are usually divided between two major political parties, a situation that often results in the virtual exclusion of minor parties from seriously competing with the major parties or sharing in political power. For the most part, wealthier individuals in professional, managerial, and white-collar occupations more often identify with the Republican party, while the majority Democratic party tends to appeal to the less wealthy in the nonprofessional and blue-collar occupations. Similarly, support for England's Conservative party comes almost exclusively from the upper classes, while that of the Labour party comes mostly from the working classes. As a result, the ballot box becomes a battleground for the class interests in society. Moreover, as opposed to the extreme class differences suggested by conflict theorists, democracies are characterized by varying levels of social fragmentation based on race, religion, ethnicity, geographical region, and other social differences that cut across all class divisions, thus limiting the ability of one class to use the government to dominate other classes.

Still, all evidence suggests that those who are more comfortable economically have a larger share of political power. Virtually all political and social observers agree that this is so. *How,* then, can middle- and lower-income citizens gain leverage within democratic political systems? In one study of voting patterns in Nigeria, Austria, Japan, Yugoslavia, India, the Netherlands, and the United States, individuals with limited wealth and education were less likely to participate in politics than those in the higher income and education groups.[16] Thus, the messages communicated to political leaders were more likely to reflect the preferences of the economically advantaged. However, it was also found that upper-class bias in political participation was often offset by political organizations and institutions that actively encouraged participation by the economically and socially disadvantaged. A clear example of this kind of influence has occurred in the United States during recent years. Historically, as part of the legacy of slavery, segregation, and discrimination, most black communities have reflected low levels of both income and political participation. In the aftermath of the civil rights movement, however, blacks began to seek political power. As blacks began to run for political office, the NAACP and other political organizations initiated voter registration drives throughout the country. By the close of 1983, of the 17.6 million blacks of voting age, almost two-thirds were included on the voter registration rolls.[17] Several important developments have resulted. Prior to the civil rights movement, the election of a black person to public office in the U.S. was a strikingly rare phenomenon. By 1970, however, 1,472 black officials had been elected, and by the 1980s (as noted in Chapter 9), this figure had risen to over 6,000. In 1988, 23 blacks were elected to the House of Representatives. None have been elected to serve as senators, although some blacks have been candidates for the Senate in Virginia and

SOCIAL INDICATOR

Portrait of the Electorate

Percent 1988 Total		Vote in 1980			Vote in 1984		Vote in 1988	
		Reagan	Carter	Anderson	Reagan	Mondale	Bush	Dukakis
—	Total	51%	41%	7%	59%	40%	53%	45%
48	Men	55	36	7	62	37	57	41
52	Women	47	45	7	56	44	50	49
85	Whites	55	36	7	64	35	59	40
10	Blacks	11	85	3	9	89	12	86
3	Hispanics	35	56	8	37	61	30	69
69	Married	—	—	—	62	38	57	42
31	Not Married	—	—	—	52	46	46	53
20	18–29 Years Old	43	44	11	59	40	52	47
35	30–44 Years Old	54	36	8	57	42	54	45
22	45–59 Years Old	55	39	5	59	39	57	42
22	60 and Older	54	41	4	60	39	50	49
8	Not a High-school Graduate	46	51	2	49	50	43	56
27	High-school Graduate	51	43	4	60	39	50	49
30	Some College Education	55	35	8	61	37	57	42
35	College Graduate or More	52	35	11	58	41	56	43
19	College Graduate	—	—	—	—	—	62	37
16	Post-graduate Education	—	—	—	—	—	50	48
48	White Protestant	63	31	6	72	27	66	33
28	Catholic	49	42	7	54	45	52	47
4	Jewish	39	45	15	31	67	35	64
9	White Fundamentalist or Evangelical Christian	63	33	3	78	22	81	18
35	Republicans	86	8	4	93	6	91	8
37	Democrats	26	67	6	24	75	17	82
26	Independents	55	30	12	63	35	55	43
25	Union Household	43	48	6	46	53	42	57
12	Family Income under $12,500	42	51	6	45	54	37	62
20	$12,500–$24,999	44	46	7	57	42	49	50
20	$25,000–$34,999	52	39	7	59	40	56	44
20	$35,000–$49,999	59	32	8	66	33	56	42
24	$50,000 and Over	63	26	9	69	30	62	37
19	$50,000–$100,000	—	—	—	—	—	61	38
5	Over $100,000	—	—	—	—	—	65	32
25	From the East	47	42	9	52	47	50	49
28	From the Midwest	51	40	7	58	40	52	47
28	From the South	52	44	3	64	36	58	41
19	From the West	53	34	10	61	38	52	46
18	Liberals	25	60	11	28	70	18	81
45	Moderates	48	42	8	53	47	49	50
33	Conservatives	72	23	4	82	17	80	19
31	Professional or Manager	57	32	9	62	37	59	40
11	White-collar Worker	50	41	8	59	40	57	42
13	Blue-collar Worker	47	46	5	54	45	49	50
4	Full-time Student	—	—	—	52	47	44	54
5	Teacher	46	42	10	51	48	47	51
5	Unemployed	39	51	8	32	67	37	62
10	Homemaker	—	—	—	61	38	58	41
2	Agricultural Worker	36	59	4	—	—	55	44
16	Retired	—	—	—	60	40	50	49

Maryland. In addition, early in 1989, Ron Brown, a black man, was chosen to chair the Democratic National Committee. Moreover, Reverend Jesse Jackson's bid for the Democratic presidential nomination in 1984 and 1988 represented the first time in the history of the United States that a minority group member seeking the nation's highest office was taken seriously by voters, his political opponents, and the media.

Political Participation and the American Voter

Like all democracies, the American political system is based on the idea of mass participation, particularly with respect to voting. The principle of *one person one vote* is meant to provide each citizen with the ability to influence the political process. Compared with other democracies, however, political participation in the United States is relatively low. As indicated in Exhibit 14.6, which compares voter turnout in 13 Western nations for the period 1960–1978—the most recent composite data available on this issue—the United States ranked twelfth with 59%, while in eleven other nations 70% or more of the voting-age population cast ballots. Moreover, low voter turnout in the United States has been a consistent pattern during most of the twentieth century. As indicated in Exhibit 14.7, from 1860 to 1896, more than 70% of the voting-age population participated in presidential elections. A decline began with the election of 1900, and during the last several elections participation has been below 60%.

Political scholars have vigorously debated the meaning of these figures. The majority view holds that the decline in turnout is the result of a loss of popular interest in elections combined with a weakening in the competitive nature of the major political parties.[18] According to this argument, during the nineteenth century the parties fought hard to promote their ideas, worked energetically to get the voters to the polls, kept the legal barriers to participation at a minimum, and gave large numbers of citizens the chance to get involved in party politics through caucuses and conventions. The typical result was close, exciting elections. By 1896, however, the South had become predominantly Democratic and the North heavily Republican. Both parties gradually became more conservative, national elections resulted in one-sided victories for the Republicans, and citizens lost interest in politics since it no longer seemed to meet their needs. In addition, as the parties fell under the control of mostly conservative leaders who resisted mass participation, political organizations functioned less frequently to mobilize a greater number of voters.

Advocates of an alternative argument hold that the political parties were no more democratic in generations past than they are today, and that the greater voter turnout of the nineteenth century was more apparent than real due to inflated figures and fraud.[19] Specifically, until around the beginning of the twentieth century, election fraud was both easy and commonplace. Efforts to decide who was eligible to vote were at best haphazard. Votes typically were cast in public, not in private booths, and sometimes votes were cast orally. It was difficult to prevent people from voting more than once; polling places were poorly policed, permitting threats of retaliation if voters failed to choose the "correct" candidate. The political parties also often controlled the counting of votes. As implied in Exhibit 14.2, the stuffing of ballot

SOCIAL INDICATOR

Percent of People Who Vote, by Age

18–24 Years	41%
25–44 Years	58
45–64 Years	70
65 Years and Over	68

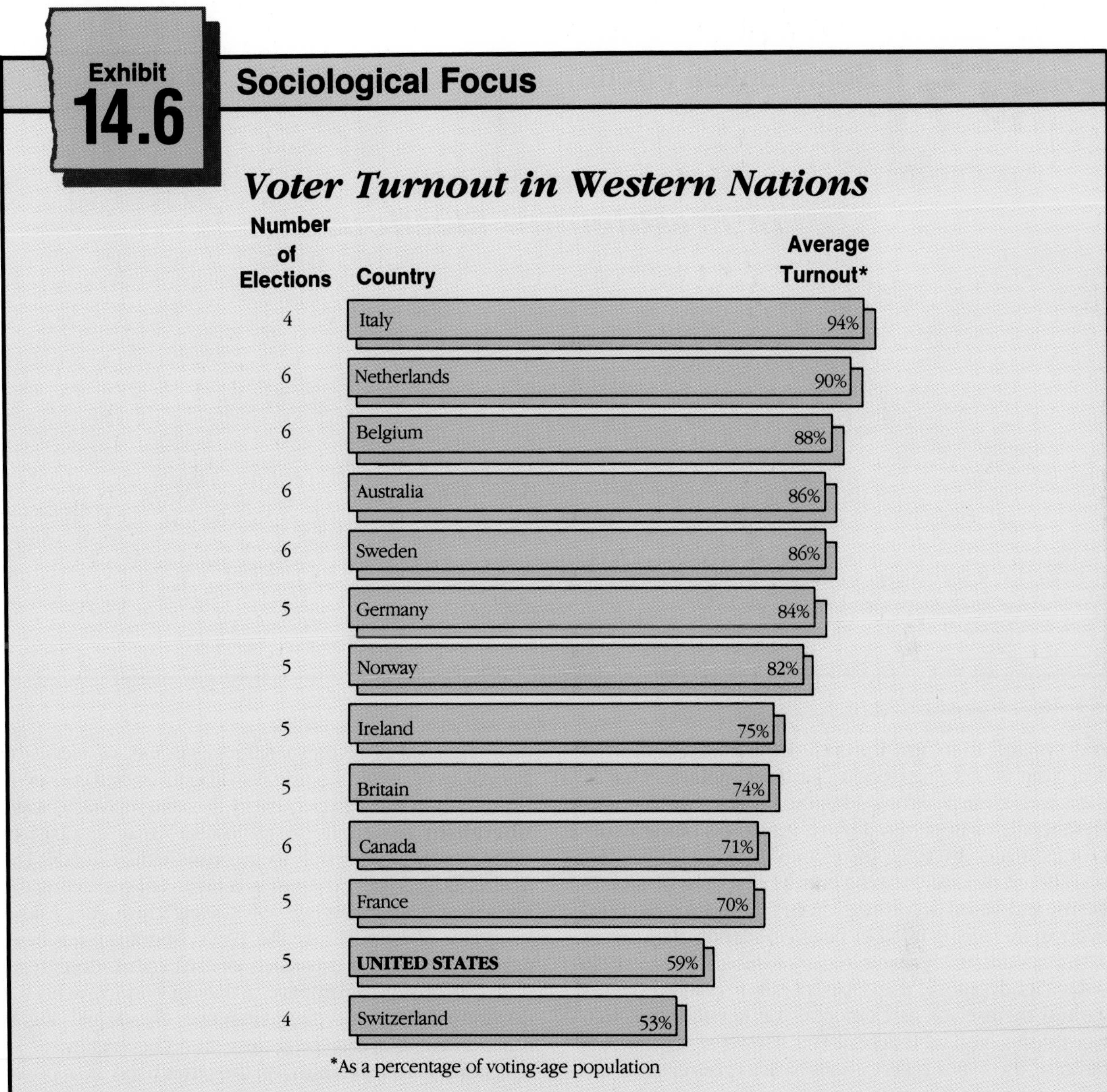

Source: G. Bingham Powell, Jr., "Voting Turnout in Thirty Democracies," in Richard Rose (ed.), *Electoral Participation: A Comparative Analysis* (London and Beverly Hills: Sage, 1980), p. 6.

boxes was common. In the election of 1888, West Virginia officially claimed that 147,408 persons in the state were eligible to vote. After the election, however, a count revealed that 159,440 ballots had been cast—a remarkable 108% voter turnout.[20] With the onset of the twentieth century, most states had adopted the **Australian ballot system**, a secret ballot that was prepared, distributed, and tabulated by government officials at public expense. In addition, more organized registration procedures and better policing of the polls inhibited repeat voting. In short, then, if votes had been legally cast and honestly counted during the nineteenth century, the statistics on voter turnout would be less inflated and more similar to those of recent years.

The contemporary American voter also is characterized by change—change with respect to *partisanship*

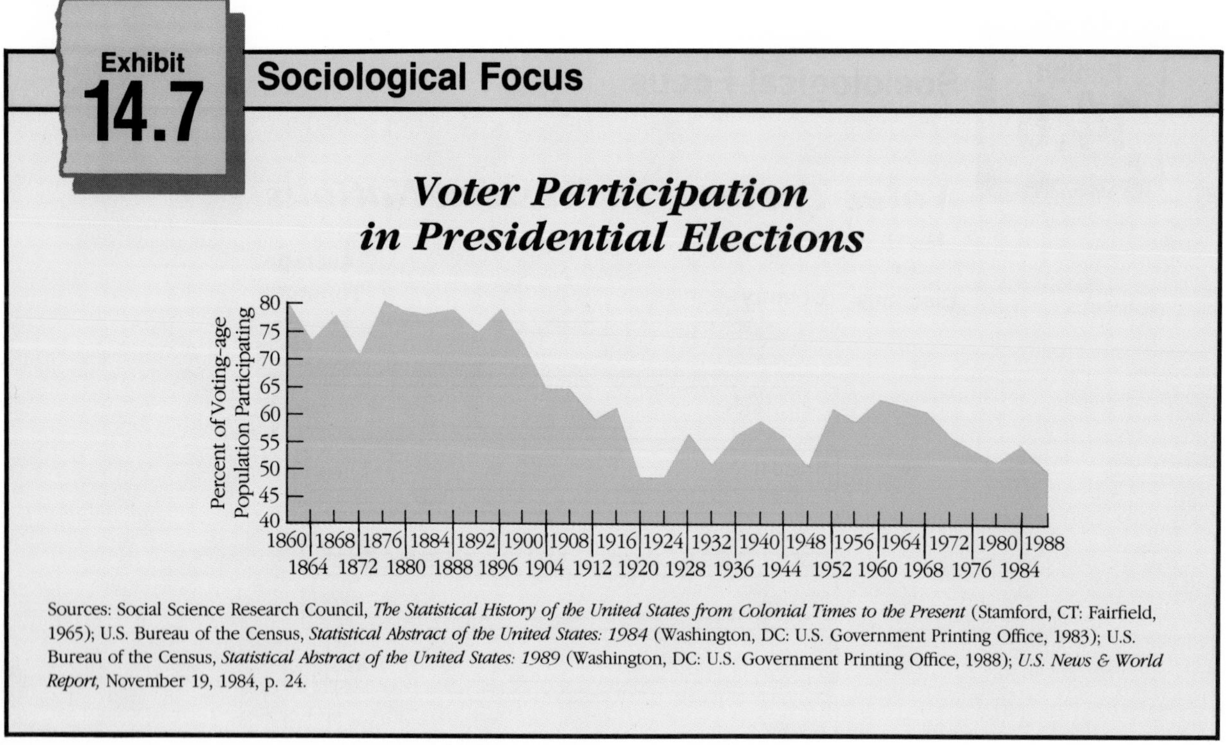

Sources: Social Science Research Council, *The Statistical History of the United States from Colonial Times to the Present* (Stamford, CT: Fairfield, 1965); U.S. Bureau of the Census, *Statistical Abstract of the United States: 1984* (Washington, DC: U.S. Government Printing Office, 1983); U.S. Bureau of the Census, *Statistical Abstract of the United States: 1989* (Washington, DC: U.S. Government Printing Office, 1988); *U.S. News & World Report,* November 19, 1984, p. 24.

and political ideology. Up until a generation ago, most American voters engaged in "partisan" politics. That is, they had a fairly strong identification with either the Democratic or Republican party, regardless of the issues or candidates. In 1952, for example, 75% of all voters considered themselves to be either Democrats or Republicans, and voted accordingly.[21] In the mid-sixties, however, an increasing number began to identify themselves as Independents. As indicated in Exhibit 14.8, by 1976 only slightly more than half of all registered voters viewed themselves as Democrats or Republicans; 46% were designated as Independents. However, as the data indicate, the 1980s reflect a shift back to greater partisanship, as the number of Independents dropped to below one-third.

This fluctuation in party ties has been viewed with alarm by some political observers. Instead of using their party affiliations to guide their voting behavior, political scientists argue that voters may be more influenced by transitory issues and candidates' images, resulting in greater uncertainty in American politics and less stability in the overall political structure.[22] On the other hand, it also can be argued that as an outgrowth of the expansion of higher education in the United States and the wider exposure of political issues in the electronic media, Americans today may be more informed about domestic and foreign policy issues and have even more explicit views than in decades past.

Regardless of these differing points of view, the categories of political opinion—liberalism and conservatism—have shifted in popularity. In contemporary usage, **liberalism** is a political philosophy that emphasizes more government action to meet individual needs. The *liberal* looks to government as a means of correcting the abuses and shortcomings of society through positive programs of action. Since the 1960s, liberalism has been associated with the expansion of civil rights, desegregation and busing, affirmative action in employment, the decriminalization of marijuana use, the Equal Rights Amendment, poverty programs, and the legitimacy of abortions. **Conservatism,** on the other hand, is opposed to major changes in the political, economic, and social institutions of society. The *conservative* philosophy in American politics opposes governmental regulation of the economy and civil rights legislation, and favors state over federal action, fiscal responsibility, decreased government spending, and lower taxes. One might contrast liberalism and conservatism with moderation, a position that falls somewhere between the other two. *Moderates* believe that political transformations should be gradual and involve no great violence to social institutions.

Although liberal traditions in American politics have been apparent for generations, they came to the forefront in their most potent forms during the 1960s, spirited by those who opposed the war in Vietman, were tolerant of protest demonstrations, and took part in civil

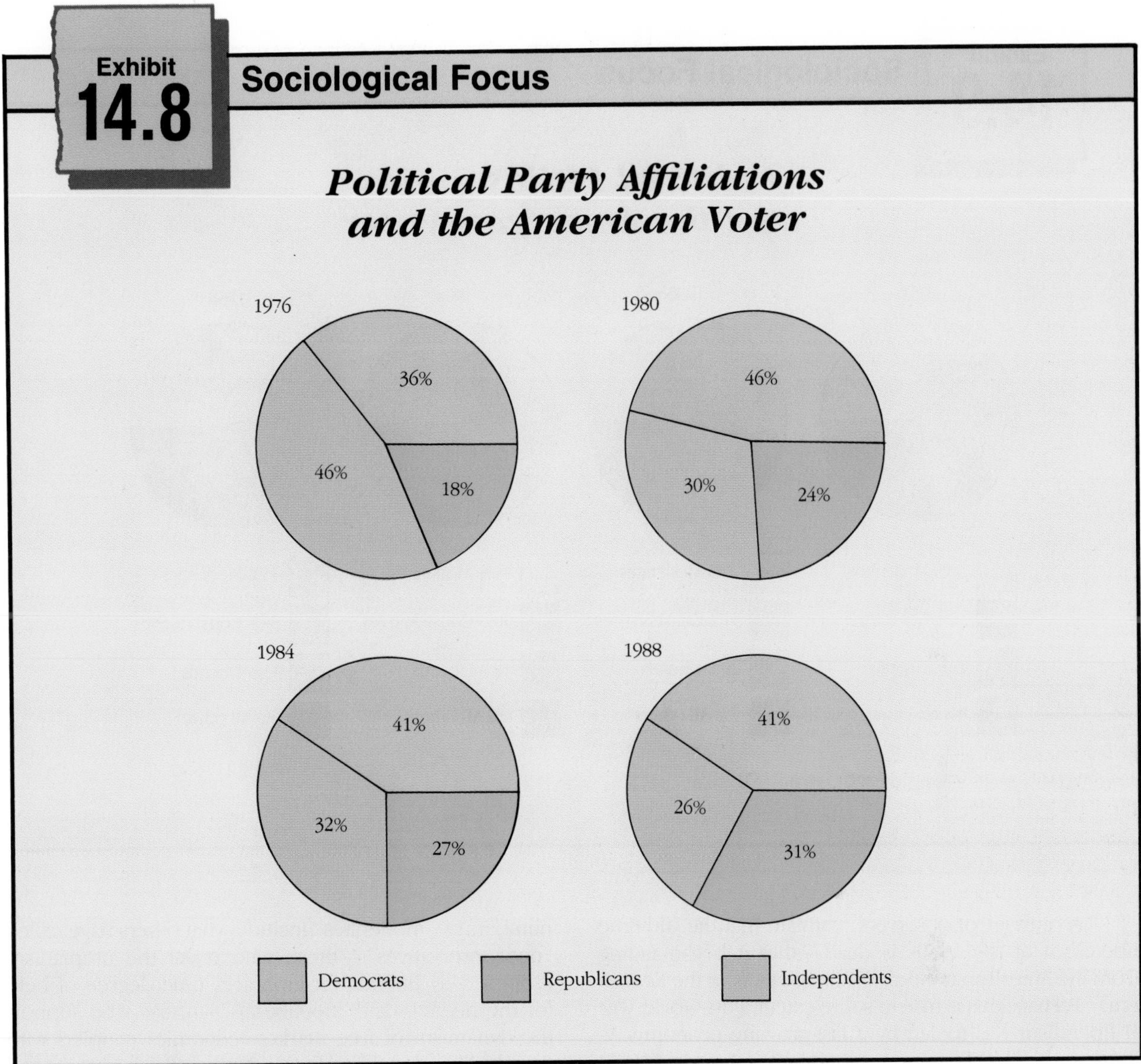

rights marches. These individuals believed that drug use was a personal decision and should not be a matter of law; they emphasized the rights of the accused over the punishment of criminals, and saw the solution to crime in eliminating its causes rather than in getting tough with offenders. During the administrations of John F. Kennedy and Lyndon B. Johnson, liberalism was a significant factor in American political life. In a Gallup Poll undertaken during the latter part of 1963, some 49% of those surveyed identified themselves as "liberals," but as indicated in Exhibit 14.9, during the 1970s and 1980s, liberalism has declined significantly. Just prior to the presidential election of 1984, less than one-fifth of registered voters considered themselves to be "liberals." Almost half designated themselves as "moderates," a segment that tends toward a conservative position on some issues while professing liberalism on others, combined with individuals in the "middle-of-the-road," who wander neither to the "left" nor the "right" on most political and social matters. Perhaps the greatest political shift in recent years has been among young adults. Traditionally in the center of liberal politics since the early 1960s, a clear majority supported the conservative and moderate principles of Ronald Reagan in the presidential election of 1984. Moreover, so conservative have many college students become in recent years that some have become campus watchdogs, reporting on Marxist and other left-wing professors (see Exhibit 14.10).

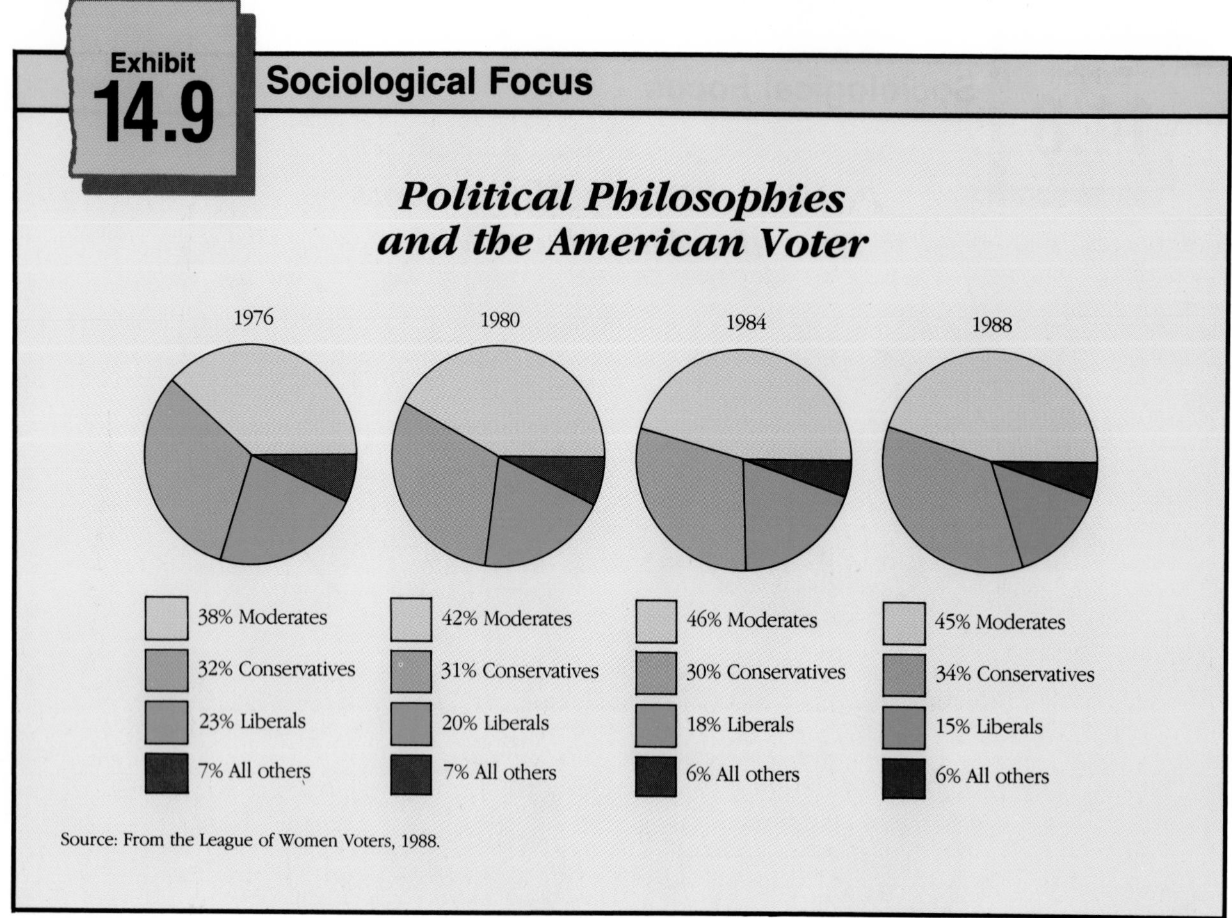

A number of observers maintain that the old-time liberalism of the 1960s is dead—that it began fading from the American political landscape early in the Reagan era.[23] Perhaps this is true to some extent. Post-World War II liberalism was fueled by a fast-growing economy. As long as wealth increased rapidly, it was considered progressive to expand the social safety net, democratize higher education, and target underprivileged pockets of society. But when economic productivity slowed in the 1970s, liberalism faced a crisis. As the size of government and the growing welfare state became a ball and chain on the creation of wealth, the addition of more government spending and expanded social programs was judged to be *regressive;* not progressive, by many observers. Yet others maintain that the liberal coalitions are still there, but that the term "liberal" has simply fallen on hard times. During the 1976 presidential primaries, the Democratic Representative from Arizona, Morris K. Udall, commented that liberalism was associated with abortion, drugs, busing, and wasteful government. "When a word takes on connotations you don't like," he noted, "it's time to change the label."[24] Similarly, perhaps the growing numbers of "moderates" include what others have called "neoconservatives"—those who reject the utopianism espoused by liberals yet embrace some degree of help for the needy—and "neoliberals"—those who support the dynamism of free market economics coupled with the old liberal compassion and concern for fairness.[25]

POWER, POLITICS, AND THE ECONOMIC ORDER

All sociopolitical systems share the same set of basic economic problems. Each must somehow resolve various complex issues. How are limited natural resources to be utilized? Which of the resources are to be developed? What goods will be produced? How will they be produced? How will the limited goods and services be distributed throughout the society?

The manner in which these questions are addressed and answered defines the character of a society's **economy,** the social institution that specializes in the production and exchange of goods and services to satisfy the needs and wants of the population. An examination of modern societies suggests that two major, and conflicting, systems are used to deal with economic questions. In the *capitalist market economy*, decisions are the result of individual consumer preferences; in the *socialist command economy,* decisions are the result of centralized planning by the political leadership.

The Capitalist Market Economy

Capitalism is an economic system based on private ownership of productive resources and allocation of goods according to the signals provided by free markets. Thus, the **capitalist market economy** is characterized by a competitive marketplace, private ownership of the means of production, and a profit motive.

More specifically, the idea behind the capitalist market economy is that the best way to resolve the basic economic problems of society is to allow individual consumers to purchase freely the goods and services they prefer in a competitive marketplace. Therefore, it follows that the means of production be owned by individuals, not the state, so that producers can compete for consumer expenditures. Moreover, since the means of production are held as private property, owners determine what is to be produced. Ostensibly, the profit motive insures that owners will produce those goods and services most desired by consumers. Capitalist ideology also suggests that producers who can sell goods for less than their competitors are more likely to find a greater number of buyers. This promotes efficiency in production, since lower production costs promote lower prices, and in the end society benefits, for the most desired goods will be produced at the lowest possible price.

Few observers hold to the idea that a *pure* capitalist market economy actually exists anywhere in the world. Rather, the capitalist market economy, like many other concepts is an ideal type whose features are never fully reflected in any economic system. The United States is generally described as having a capitalist market economy, yet many aspects of the American economic system deviate considerably from the capitalist design. For example, government subsidies are granted to many businesses to relieve them of the risks associated with producing unusable, undesirable, or surplus products. In the aerospace industry, the Department of Defense has underwritten the development costs of new military aircraft, and in the agriculture and dairy industries, direct cash payments are made to cover surplus production.

The government also has protected a number of other industries as well. Tariffs and negotiated agreements have served to shield the American automobile industry from the full impact of foreign competition. Consider, too, the government bailout of Chrysler Corporation in 1980. Moreover, in direct opposition to the capitalist ideology, the United States government has gone into business for itself, directly competing with free enterprise. Many of the programs of the National Aeronautics and Space Administration in the deployment and rescue of telecommunication satellites and in pharmaceutical experimentation are conducted on behalf of private firms and in competition with other private companies. The Government Printing Office's publication of many books and periodicals operates in direct competition with the commercial sector, and the Central Intelligence Agency is involved in the commercial mapmaking industry.

The abundance of food seen in the markets of capitalist nations stands in sharp contrast to the situation in many communist countries. Even in times of plenty in the U.S.S.R., Soviet consumers must often stand in line for hours to make a purchase.

Exhibit 14.10 **Sociology in the Media**

Students, Professors, and Political Ideologies

"Liberal arts colleges turn out little liberals who go knee-jerking their way through life."

—Reed Irvine, Founder of Accuracy in Academia

Perhaps the most controversial political development on college campuses during the last half of the 1980s was triggered by Accuracy in Academia, a Washington, D.C.–based organization formed for the avowed purpose of challenging liberal professors who it claims feed biased information to students.

Supporters of Accuracy in Academia (AIA) hold that students are impressionable, that academic freedom has limits, and that students should not be exposed to a steady diet of liberal doctrine. So AIA has recruited students on 110 college campuses to turn in left-wing professors, who are then mentioned in *The Campus Report*—a nationally circulated publication specifically created to expose and castigate academics with whose opinions the group does not agree.

The following commentaries, first published in *USA Today,* offer points of view for and against AIA tactics.

Pro

It's Time to Balance the Intellectual Diet

COLUMBUS, Ohio—As '60s and '70s graduates of liberal arts colleges know, almost all professors who politicize their lectures lean left.

This became clear to me in 1931: I entered Kent State believing in God and country. Within six months, a corps of faculty fagins converted me into an agnostic and card-carrying Communist.

For many years, liberal professors and their student stooges have shouted down conservative speakers like Jeane Kirkpatrick and Caspar Weinberger. It's as true as it is trite: The name of the game in liberal arts is "liberal."

Accuracy in Media has served well as a feisty watchdog of the press. Its newsletters, films, books, and speeches expose brainwashing in news columns and on TV. But its greatest contribution has not been the errors exposed and corrected. It is the bias it has *prevented* by warning the media that someone is watching and ready to blow the whistle in case of deliberate foul. This Nader-like deterrent effect can also be applied to classrooms.

Accuracy in Academia, an offshoot of AIM, may be just in time to combat the new wave of Marxist professors, described in the *Wall Street Journal* as "political agents in academic robes." AIA can also oppose the traditional southpaw slants of student newspapers (I was a revolting student editor at Kent State, God forgive me).

For reasons I've never understood, journalism and academe attract congenital critics who are far left of mainstream U.S. A 1981 survey of leading New York–Washington journalists proved most are liberals. In 1976, the Carnegie Commission found 49 percent of professors said they were "left" and only 25 percent said "right."

It's not surprising that many newspapers have leaped to denigrate Accuracy in Academia, as though free speech is not for conservatives. For years, our press has fought for open meetings and full disclosure for everyone except itself. In some states, the media have bludgeoned legislatures to adopt "shield" laws that exempt journalists from laws that govern the rest of us. *The*

The Socialist Command Economy

Socialism is a system of economic organization in which the ownership and control of the basic means of production rest with the state and resource allocation is determined by centralized planning rather than free market forces. Thus, in the **socialist command economy** free enterprise is prohibited and the government determines which goods are to be produced and who will produce them.

The basic ideology of the socialist command economy suggests that far too many resources are consumed by competition, and that capitalist producers must continually create demand for goods through

Washington Post keeps giving prime examples of news bias. After draining every drop out of Watergate, its investigative reporters haven't told us yet what really happened at the Bay of Pigs or Chappaquiddick.

Now academicians claim they, too, are a breed apart. They want their lectures shielded from public scrutiny, their classrooms closed to reportage. They deny that professors, like journalists, tend to view the world through the prism of their own prejudices.

I think freedom is indivisible, that none of our citizens is on a songbird list, and that Accuracy in Academia can help balance the intellectual diet on college campuses.

Con

My Students Regularly Outvote Me

BOULDER, Colo.—I was born in 1951, in the midst of the McCarthy era. Good timing, I've thought; at least infants were safe from the witch hunts, Red-baiting, and trumped-up charges.

Evidently my timing was not as good as I thought. With its curious new crusade, Accuracy in Academia has resurrected much of the old nightmare of concealed spies setting out in pursuit of ideological sins.

In 18 years as a university student and teacher, I've learned nearly as much from people with whom I disagreed as from intellectual allies. Diversity of opinion is the heartbeat of the University, a beat Accuracy in Academia evidently would like to stop.

The most important lesson you learn in graduate school is that the world is terribly complicated. Properly trained professors could not offer their classes a simple party line even if they wanted to, because they know nothing is simple.

To acknowledge this complexity and to encourage independent thinking, I often pause in a lecture to have students vote on their interpretation of particular events. Anyone who trembles at the image of tyrannical, leftward-steering hands at the tiller of the academic ship ought to come watch me being regularly outvoted.

Students, these exercises show me, are not very malleable. Psychologists say the first years of life form human character; nothing I've seen causes me to doubt that. Discussing voting patterns of the nineteenth century in one class, I asked the students if they held political opinions similar to those of their parents. Out of the 90 students, 80 stood with their parents. It's a pattern I can't quarrel with. It describes me, too.

Ideology aside, a much more basic problem of pure ignorance far outweighs any problem of bias. In a recent poll, only 44 percent of high school seniors knew the Cold War involves the U.S. and the Soviet Union. If over half the country's young people think the Cold War is some war fought by somebody during a cruel winter, then it hardly matters how they interpret it.

A well-informed, conservative former student called the other night. "Did I make it hard on you guys?" I asked. "Did you feel oppressed?"

"No," he said, "not at all. You always liked fighters who took a stand."

I still like fighters—fair ones. But Accuracy in Academia with its sneaky underground tactics has embraced an unfair and literally un-American way to fight.

SOURCE: Patricia Nelson Limerick, "My Students Regularly Outvote Me," reprinted by permission of the author. Walt Seifert, "It's Time to Balance the Intellectual Diet," reprinted by permission of Professor Emeritus Walt Seifert, School of Journalism, Ohio State University.

advertising if profits are to be made. Because such competition is so wasteful, the socialist perspective argues that the state must assure that the maximum number of citizens receive the greatest possible benefits from the productive apparatus of society.

The economy of the Soviet Union is an example of the socialist command system (see Exhibit 14.11), but just as the U.S. is not a pure capitalist market economy, the Soviet economy is not a pure type either. In Moscow and elsewhere in the Soviet Union, an active underground economy known as *na levo* has developed. Meaning "on the left," *na levo* is another name for free enterprise, which accounts for as much as 15% of the Soviet Union's gross national product.[26] Rather than a black market

Exhibit 14.11 Case Study

The Soviet Economy

The economy of the Soviet Union is of the authoritarian socialist type, characterized by central planning, detailed directives to all production systems, and few discretionary decision-making powers extended to individual enterprises. The Soviet government owns and operates almost all of the industrial sector, foreign trade, transportation and communications, banking and financial institutions, a sizable portion of the agricultural sector, and most of the wholesale and retail networks. The state sector of the Soviet economy is the largest economic unit in the world. It employs approximately 100 million white- and blue-collar workers.

In a sense, the state-operated Soviet economy is akin to a giant corporation, with Communist party members acting as stockholders. The party establishes the basic economic objectives, strives to ensure their execution, and oversees the bureaucracy necessary to carry out the details of the planning directives. As in Western economies, the basic unit of economic activity is the business firm, which the Soviets call an "enterprise." Soviet enterprises, much like individual factories or units of a large U.S. corporation, take their orders from the central planning authorities.

The state sector of the Soviet economy functions through the *Gosplan,* the government's central planning agency, which drafts the basic economic plans for the entire nation. These plans focus on short- and long-range objectives. They are constructed annually and are written into law by the Soviet government. The plans are directed toward the enterprises, and they set production targets as well as establish resource constraints. Thus, each enterprise knows how much it is supposed to produce. The resource allotments, the amount of raw materials, labor, machines, and other productive inputs that the enterprise is permitted to utilize also are provided for in the central plans. The problem of the enterprise is to transform its allotted inputs into the target output.

Although the central economic plans are constructed by the Gosplan, it is the responsibility of the enterprise managers to carry them out. An incentive structure combining the carrot and the stick is used to motivate managers, and both pecuniary and nonpecuniary factors play a role. Managers who meet their production quotas are rewarded with bonuses, promotions, and medals. When the output of an enterprise is falling short of production quotas, it is up to the manager to exhort employees to work harder and longer, to obtain additional labor and material inputs, or to persuade higher authorities that the production quota should be lowered. If these efforts are insufficient and the enterprise fails to meet its production targets, the manager can expect a demotion.

The performance evaluations and rewards of enterprise managers are based largely on output. Since product quality, innovativeness, and experimentation are both costly and difficult to measure, they usually are not rewarded by the Soviet system. The emphasis is on quantity of output relative to the output target. This kind of emphasis creates two important problems. Widespread falsification of records exaggerates actual output, and inflated production plans promise much more than realistically can be delivered. Those who have analyzed the performance of the Soviet economy hold that the detailed planning results in perverse decision making and organizational inefficiency.

SOURCE: Adapted from Richard D. Gwartney and Richard Stroup, *Economics: Private and Public Choice* (New York: Academic Press, 1980), pp. 817–21.

(which also exists), *na levo* involves craft workers, professionals, and farmers who sell their services for a fee—a practice that is forbidden by official state policy. Participants include tutors who help students prepare for university entrance exams, seamstresses who make patterns to reproduce Western designer jeans, electronics specialists who repair television sets (that were originally purchased on the black market), and farmers who produce and bottle *samogon* (moonshine)—all for a profit. Alternatively, the People's Republic of China, historically a socialist nation, in 1984 designated 14 key coastal cities as special trade zones. As a part of China's economic modernization program, the new "zones" offer special tax breaks, cheap land and rentals, and relaxed trade restrictions to attract foreign investment.[27]

In practice, all modern nations employ some combination of capitalist and socialist economic organization. Primarily capitalist economies use government

SOCIAL INDICATOR

Nations at Risk for Economic Breakdown

According to the British publication *The Economist,* the countries depicted below are considered to be "at risk" for economic breakdown. The various risk levels were calculated on the basis of each country's foreign debt, falling gross domestic product, inflation rate, ethnic tensions, involvement in wars, and the nature of its political system.

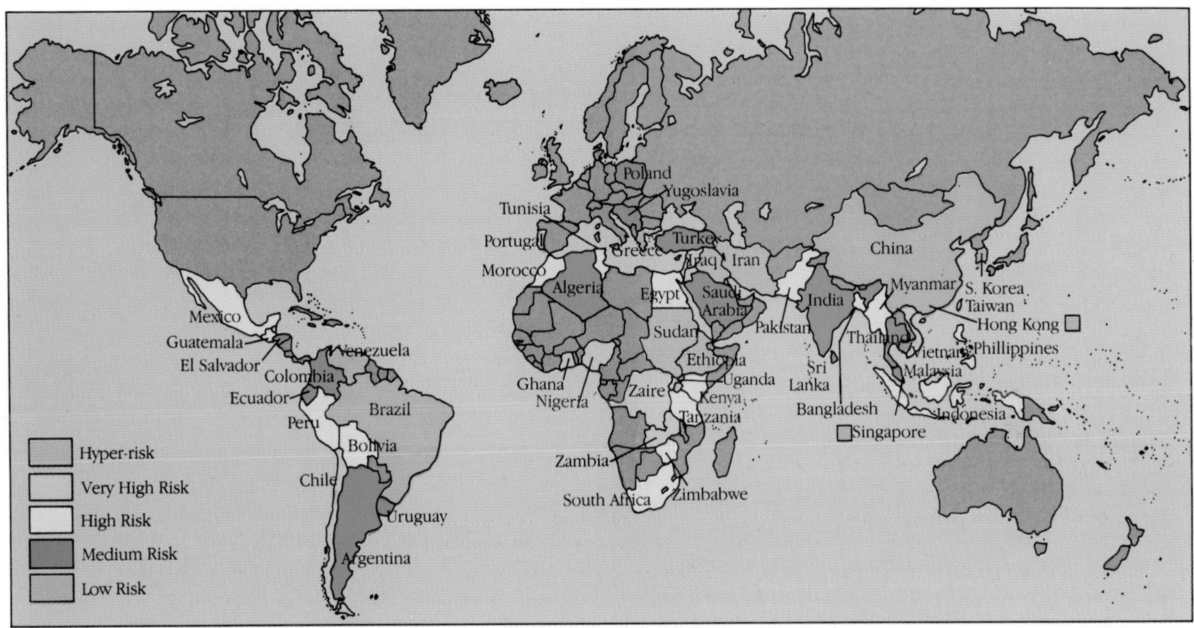

Source: *The Economist,* December 12, 1986, p. 69.

regulation, selective government ownership, and taxation to modify the forces of supply and demand. In socialist countries, central planning and administrative control exist side by side with a small but often highly significant market system. To these should be added the market-directed socialist economies of Sweden, India, Israel, and Yugoslavia, which fall between the extremes of capitalism and socialism (see Exhibit 14.12).

CORPORATIONS AND SOCIETY

Perhaps the most striking single feature of industrial economic organization is its enormous variety. Well over 11 million business enterprises are currently operating in the United States. They may be categorized into three basic structures. A *single proprietorship* is a business organization in which an individual operator invests his or her personal capital and runs the firm. These owner-employer firms account for the vast majority of American businesses and range from the corner grocery store to manufacturing plants of various sizes. In *partnerships,* two or more people pool their resources and share the profits and obligations of the enterprise. Partnerships currently account for some 10% of American businesses and are generally small in size. Although single proprietorships and partnerships collectively employ and support millions of people, their decision-making activities have only minimal social impact. **Corporations,** on the other hand—business organizations chartered by the state as legal entities that can own property, sell stock, enter into contracts, and extend privileges of limited financial liability to their shareholders—generate economic implications of national and international scale.

The Evolution of Corporations

The corporation as it is known today is an outgrowth of the eighteenth-century "joint stock company," an instrument developed in England for amassing large amounts of capital from numerous investors.[28] Corporations attracted widespread interest because of the advantages they provided for both their organizers and investors.

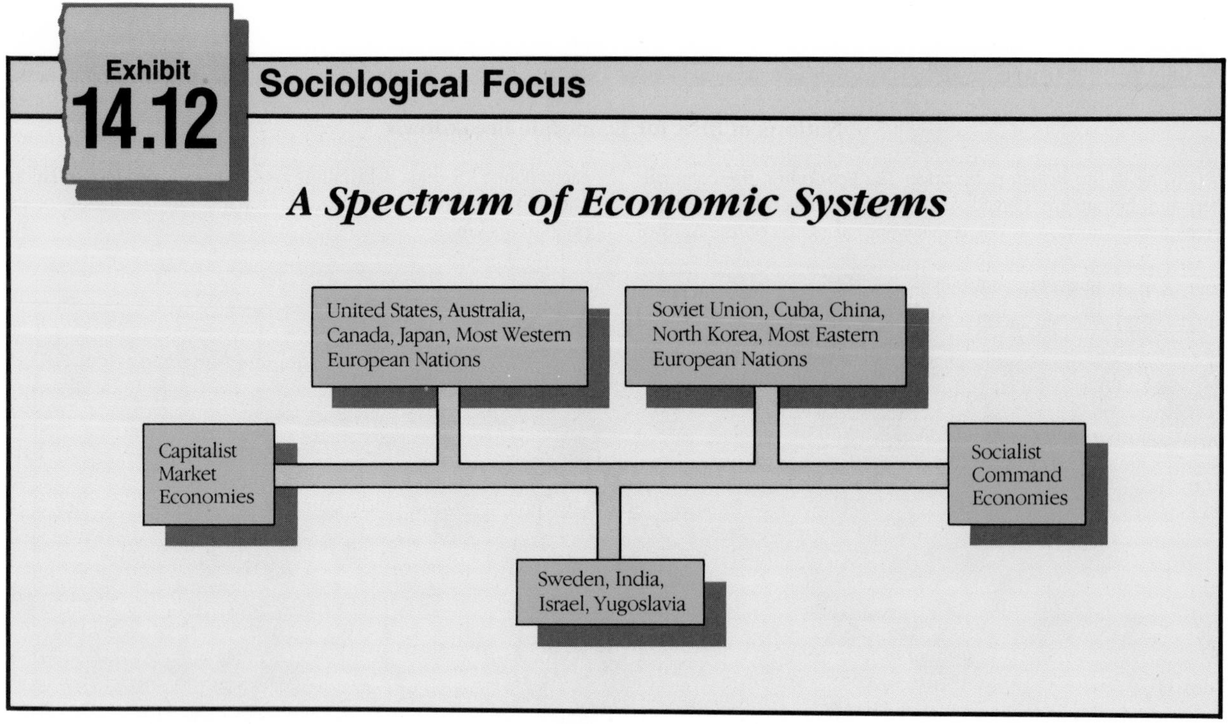

They had obvious advantages for financing vast and risky undertakings. Ownership interests, in the form of shares of stock, could be offered to thousands of small investors, who, because of the "limited liability" of corporations, could be confident that they would not be liable for the debts of the company, and so could lose no more than the amount paid for the stock. The investment units could be divided and multiplied according to the needs of the enterprise and the extent of public interest. State laws of incorporation, together with the bylaws that each corporation was empowered to make for its own governance, could delegate the running of an enterprise to a few managers. Stockholders could share windfall profits, yet because of "limited liability," they were protected from unpredictable losses.

The growth of corporations in America was slow at first. Only seven firms existed in 1775, and by 1800 their numbers had risen to barely 300. Few of these companies were involved in manufacturing, for prevailing opinion held that only groups engaged in projects of a quasi-public character, such as road building, canal construction, insurance sales, and waterworks installation were entitled to the privilege of incorporation.

Despite early resistance, by the beginning of the nineteenth century corporations had begun to proliferate. Their expansion necessitated the establishment of stock exchanges—marts where corporate securities could readily be bought and sold. Places were needed where new issues could be launched, where those with savings could place their funds, change their portfolios, or turn their holdings into cash. In 1817, brokers founded the New York Stock Exchange. Their business flourished so that only a few decades later they were buying and selling securities worth tens of billions of dollars annually.[29]

The major impetus for the expansion of corporate America was industrialization, and by the close of the Civil War the corporation had become a familiar business entity throughout the country. At the turn of the twentieth century, two-thirds of all manufactured goods were produced by corporations. By 1930, this figure was well over 90%, and corporations employed more than 90% of all persons working in manufacturing[30] By the 1980s, more than 2.7 million corporations were in business in the United States, with assets totaling almost $8 trillion. More than 60% of America's manufacturing assets were concentrated in its 200 largest corporations.[31]

SOCIAL INDICATOR

How Much Is $8,000,000,000,000?

Eight trillion dollars in $1 bills placed end to end would stretch 745 million miles—from the earth to the sun and back four times. An 8-trillion-dollar spending spree, at a rate of $1,000 a minute, would take 16,000 years.

New York merchants gathered on the now-famous Wall Street in 1817 to found the first stock exchange.

The Implications of Corporate Power

The relatively rapid rise of the American corporation has generated considerable interest among political, social, and economic observers. Common concerns include the separation of ownership from the control of corporations, their domination of certain industries, and their impact on the social and political structures of society.

Ownership versus Control

As has already been noted, the central idea of capitalist enterprise is that owners of firms will attempt to make the maximum possible profit. In doing so, they make decisions that influence how purchasing, production techniques, and marketing will best serve the profit motive. Corporations, however, are legal entities that sell shares in their ownership. Thus, they separate ownership from control of the productive enterprise: stockholders *own* the corporation while management and the board of directors *control* the corporation. Since many of those in control may not own shares in the enterprise, decisions do not necessarily reflect an attempt to maximize profits—the very essence of the capitalist market ideology. Rather, as some analysts have noted, corporate managers may use their power to advance or secure their own individual interests.[32]

Recent observations in this regard have focused on the problem of *greenmail.*[33] Greenmail occurs when a wealthy investor purchases a large block of stock in a corporation and threatens to use his or her shareholding power to fire the existing managers and replace them with others. Fearing the loss of their positions, the managers offer to buy back a large segment of the stock from the investor at a price higher than that originally paid. Since the funds for this buy-back come from the corporate treasury, the value of general stockholders' shares declines because the corporation becomes worth somewhat less. The wealthy investor receives part of the corporate profits, management retains its position, but the rank-and-file shareholders lose out because they fail to get the maximum profit to which they are entitled.

Oligopolies

Capitalist market economics assumes that producers will compete with one another for the consumer dollar. This arrangement guarantees that goods will be provided at minimum cost. One of the best examples of this principle occurred in the early years of the century and involved industrialist Henry Ford. Ford's motto was "Get the prices down to the buying power," an insight that initiated his mass production of automobiles. In 1908, he designed his famous Model T—a simple, tough little box on wheels, powered by a light, durable, easily repaired engine. Ford proved his point by relentlessly cutting costs and by installing the assembly-line system to increase efficiency. By 1914 he could put a car together in his plant in 93 minutes; by 1925 he was turning out over 9,000 cars a day, one approximately every 10 seconds, and the price of the Model T had been reduced to below $300.[34]

Ford's efforts to produce a durable and efficient vehicle were the result of the competitive spirit that raged during the early years of the automobile industry. In 1904, 35 separate manufacturers were producing automobiles, and by the late 1940s, some 2,000 different makes of cars had been manufactured in the United States.[35] However, the majority of these competitors did not survive; they either failed or were absorbed by Ford, General Motors, and Chrysler, the three firms that now comprise the American automobile industry. This domination of the industry and market by only a few monolithic corporations is referred to as an **oligopoly.** In oligopolies, firms do not have the same pressure to keep prices low and quality high as in more competitive situations where numerous producers offer the consumer more choices. The result can be inferior merchandise, a situation that certainly occurred within the American automobile industry, at least until it was invaded by more efficient German and Japanese vehicles, beginning in the mid-sixties.

In American industry, oligopolies are not necessarily limited to such large and expensive products as automobiles. The more than one-half billion American-made cigarettes that are smoked in the United States each year, for example, are manufactured by only six corporations.[36] Similarly, as illustrated in Exhibit 14.13, the more than $6-billion-a-year overnight mail service industry is controlled by only a few competitors, with Federal Express holding nearly a 53% share.

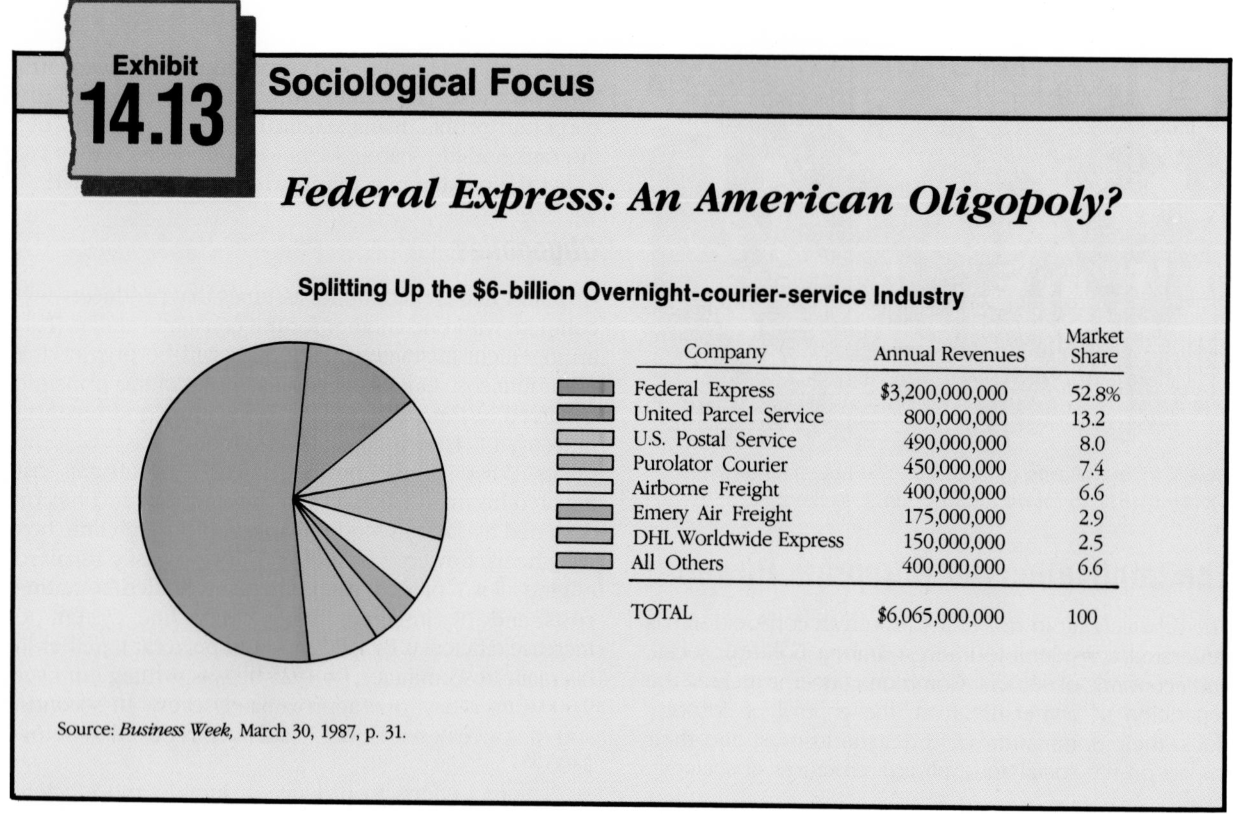

Exhibit 14.13 Sociological Focus

Federal Express: An American Oligopoly?

Splitting Up the $6-billion Overnight-courier-service Industry

Company	Annual Revenues	Market Share
Federal Express	$3,200,000,000	52.8%
United Parcel Service	800,000,000	13.2
U.S. Postal Service	490,000,000	8.0
Purolator Courier	450,000,000	7.4
Airborne Freight	400,000,000	6.6
Emery Air Freight	175,000,000	2.9
DHL Worldwide Express	150,000,000	2.5
All Others	400,000,000	6.6
TOTAL	$6,065,000,000	100

Source: *Business Week,* March 30, 1987, p. 31.

Monopolies

Uncontrolled corporate growth brings with it the potential for the creation of monopolies. A **monopoly** is a market condition in which only one seller is actively marketing a given commodity. By virtue of its control over supply, a firm with a monopoly position is able to exert almost total command over prices. In the "pure monopoly," the single seller can restrict supplies, thus forcing prices up and maximizing profits. Pure monopolies in unregulated conditions do not exist in the United States; they are expressly forbidden by various antitrust laws. Yet the U.S. government has created other kinds of monopolies through the passage of laws that exclude competition from an industry. The result has been either public monopolies, such as that presided over by the U.S. Postal Service, or publicly regulated private monopolies, such as most local power and lighting companies.

Conglomerates

The most common direction of massive corporate growth involves expansion into conglomerates. A **conglomerate** is a corporation that controls many other firms in vastly diversified markets. Conglomerates are created by means of the conglomerate merger, the combining under one ownership of two or more firms that produce unrelated products. Although conglomerate mergers began during the 1920s, the first giant corporation to devote itself exclusively to the buying and selling of other companies came into existence during World War II. Based in Rhode Island, Textron Incorporated was founded in 1943 to provide blankets and other textile products to the United States Army. Textron went on to set an international standard as the first fully integrated conglomerate. Between 1943 and 1980 the firm bought and sold over one hundred different companies in industries as diversified as textile, aerospace, machinery, metals, shoes, optical instruments, pens, paints, tools, and furniture, to name but a few. Conglomerate mergers have continued, and such activity became so common during the 1980s that the prediction of mergers has become a Wall Street specialty.

From a corporation's point of view, conglomerate mergers have positive effects. They create *cash*, flexibility, and the ability to shift gears in whatever new directions the rapidly changing world situation may present. Moreover, mergers offer the potential for considerable personal gain for top management. The editors of *Forbes Magazine,* for example, writing about Xerox Corporation's contemplated takeover of C.I.T. Financial Corporation in 1968, commented, "Among the biggest gainers will be C.I.T.'s top management . . . if the merger goes through, they could end up with a combined stock

J. Morin/The Miami Herald

market gain on their own personal stock options of approximately $10 million, a gain which C.I.T. on its own probably couldn't have achieved for many, many years."[37]

Yet conglomerate mergers can also create social and economic fallout by establishing favorable environments for monopolization and the destruction of industries. The tremendous assets held by some conglomerates enable them to sustain long predatory price wars, whereas smaller firms cannot. Moreover, "merger movement" can have economic impact on a national scale. The United States Federal Trade Commission estimated that during the merger boom of 1968, if the capital that went into acquiring existing companies had been spent on new plants and equipment, national investment would have been 46% higher.[38] And finally, conglomerates can bring about job loss and the undermining of workers' security, the reduction of productivity, and the disruption of total communities. In their book, *The Deindustrialization of America,* economists Barry Bluestone of Boston College and Bennett Harrison of Massachusetts Institute of Technology point to the fact that since 1970, millions of jobs have been lost and numerous communities have been destroyed as a result of the closures of profitable plants, all because of conglomerate needs for additional cash for further mergers and diversification.[39]

Multinationals

Multinational corporations also pose questions relative to the impact of business on society because by definition, these corporations operate within several national jurisdictions. Multinationals tend to dominate the economies of the Western world. Some of the larger ones have annual net profits larger than the entire gross national product of many developing nations. In 1980, for example, Exxon had a net profit of nearly $4.3 billion from over $79 billion in sales, and an operating budget larger than those of all nations except the United States and the Soviet Union.

SOCIAL INDICATOR

Deindustrialization and the Decline of the Steel Industry

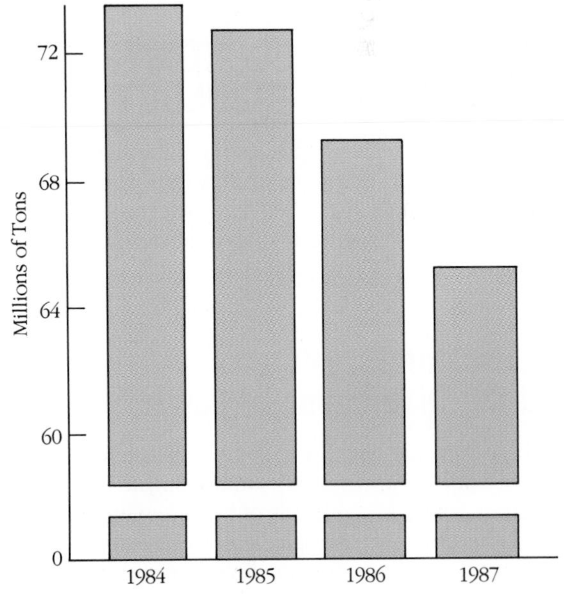

Source: American Iron and Steel Institute, 1987.

The size and wealth of corporations, particularly the multinationals, have far-reaching implications for the social and political structures of societies. Large corporations frequently decide what types of scientific research will receive funds—decisions typically based on economic rather than humanitarian criteria. Some observers also have suggested that corporations have knowingly altered the traditional patterns of behavior and cultural forms in some developing countries in order to create new markets for inferior, and sometimes dangerous products.

At the local community level, a number of observers have noted that when one corporation dominates the economy, decision making is likely to be more centralized and less democratic than elsewhere.[40] In recent years corporations have used the threat of moving to obtain tax breaks from local political leaders and concessions from labor unions.[41] In the instance of multinationals, corporations are in a position to pressure high governmental officials to extend special privileges through similar relocation threats. And finally, because they often are operating beyond the supervision and control of U.S. government agencies, some multinationals may employ less rigid procedures for environmental, community, and worker safety. One need only recall the tragedy in Bhopal, India, in December 1984, when the leak of lethal gas from a Union Carbide insecticide plant impacted thousands of people, causing death, brain damage, blindness, neurological disorders, and secondary infections.[42]

POLITICS, THE ECONOMY, AND APPLIED SOCIOLOGY

The study of political and economic institutions has raised important questions that sociologists have attempted to answer with their research, the findings of which are often important to both political and economic strategists.

Interlocking Directorates and the Distribution of Power

Concern with the issue of who governs has led sociologists and other social scientists to investigate the concentration of power in the hands of but a few individuals. It was sociologists, for example, who were responsible for first uncovering interlocking directorates in the corporate sector. An **interlocking directorate** exists when the members of the board of directors of one corporation are also members of the boards of other corpora-

SOCIAL INDICATOR

The Interlocking Directorate of General Motors*

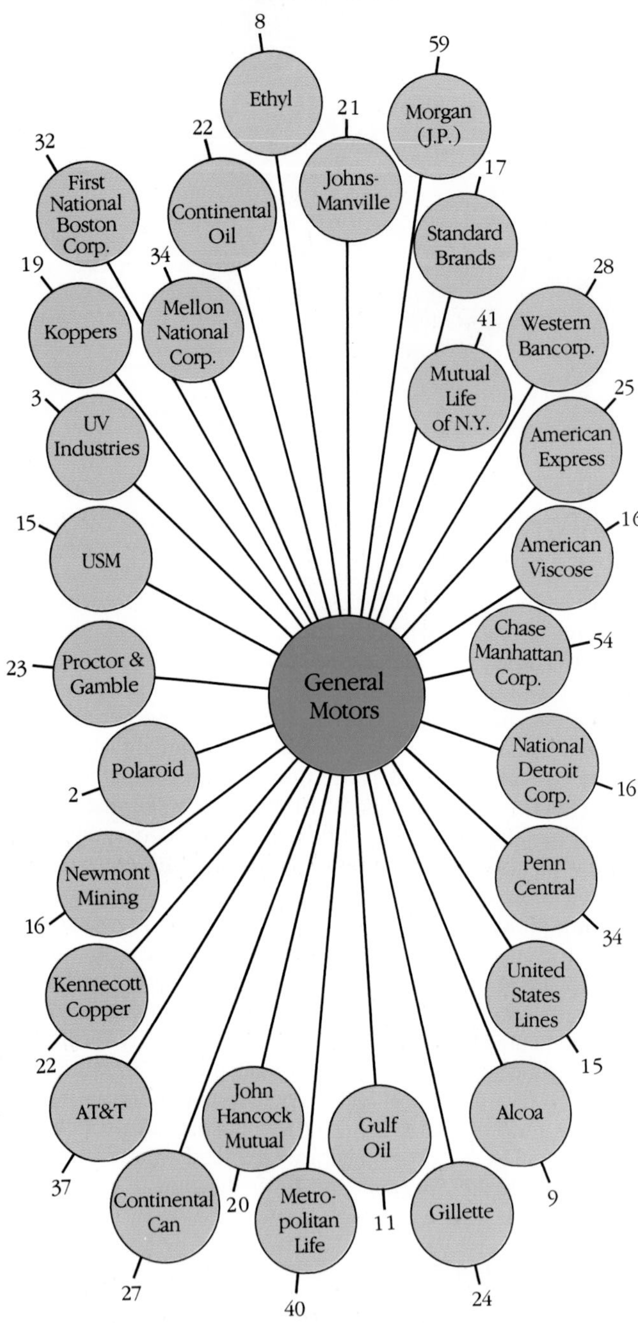

Source: Beth Mintz and Michael Schwartz, "Interlocking Directorates and Interest Group Formation," *American Sociological Review,* 46 (December 1981), pp. 851–69.

*The numbers next to firm names represent the total number of corporations to which the organization is intertied.

tions. In one sociological investigation published during the 1980s, for example, it was found that those who sit on the Board of Directors of General Motors are members of 29 other boards—including such lesser giants as Proctor & Gamble, John Hancock Mutual, Chase Manhattan, Gulf Oil, Alcoa, and American Express.[43] Moreover, the research demonstrated that the board members of these lesser giants were also members of other corporate boards, so that a tabulation of all of the individuals involved would result in an interlocking directorate involving almost 700 major corporations. This type of research dramatically illustrates that a vast amount of power is concentrated within the hands of a few individuals. It also suggests that the stability of the overall network is far more important than the profitability of any individual corporate member. Each corporation in the directorate may hold large amounts of stock in the others, making a giant interlocking economic structure that must not be allowed to fail. It is for this reason that the government stepped in to support the economic difficulties of Chrysler Corporation during the early part of the 1980s. If it had not, the entire financial network to which Chrysler was tied, as well as the communities they supported, would have been in jeopardy.

Television, Elections, and Voter Turnout

One of the more dramatic changes in the political process over the last four decades has been the emergence of television as a powerful force in the selection of political leaders. John F. Kennedy was the first presidential candidate to use the video media effectively; his nationally televised debates with Richard Nixon played a significant role in winning him the White House.

Although television has helped certain candidates, however, some observers feel that it also has weakened the leadership of the nation by exposing politicians to constant scrutiny.[44] Currently, everything a political leader does, especially if he is the president, is defined as newsworthy. In consequence, a pool of mobile television cameras follow him everywhere. This constant coverage permitted the American people to have a record of the assassination attempt on President Reagan in 1982. But the situation also tends to reveal a politician's every human error and mistake. Gerald Ford's tendency to literally trip over his own feet, for example, was televised so often that it has become a matter of American folklore. And too, it was the focused attention of the media in 1987 that contributed to the demise of both Gary Hart and Joseph Biden as viable nominees in the most recent race for the presidency.

In short, the result is that public leaders no longer have that special aura of power and dignity that earlier candidates seemed to project through their "managed" appearances on film. Observers have speculated that it is for this reason—the fact that candidates appear more as real people than as distant leaders—that voter turnout may be on the decline. Sociologists and other social scientists are among the key researchers studying this phenomenon, attempting to learn who does not vote, why, and what must be done to change the pattern.[45]

In an alternative area of political participation, sociological findings are frequently used by candidates and campaign strategists to map out pre-election tactics. After the 1984 Presidential election, for example, the Democratic Party realized that they had misread the public mood, having misunderstood that many of their constituents were divided between liberal attitudes on social and foreign policy issues on the one hand, and more conservative attitudes on domestic economic issues on the other. What the Democrats (and Republicans as well) did for the balance of the decade was to focus on sociological data—the attitudes and values of their constituents, in each age cohort, tailoring their political messages to the changing political trends (see Exhibit 14.14).

Former President Gerald Ford's tendency to slip, trip, fall, or bump his head was immortalized by the media. Ford's son Jack kept him from falling into a crowd of GOP supporters in 1976.

Exhibit 14.14

Applied Sociology

Changing American Conservatism as a Factor in Election Strategies

Conservative Issues

Americans were more conservative about capital punishment and public school prayer in the 1980s than in the 1970s, but less conservative about spending for foreign aid and crime control. Opinion differences by age diminished most for social issues, but shifted most for spending issues.

(Percent* with Conservative Response by Age)	Total		20–29		30–39		40–49		50–59		60–69	
Percent who Think	**1980s**	**1970s**	**1980s**	**1970s**	**1980s**	**1970s**	**1980s**	**1970s**	**1980s**	**1970s**	**1980s**	**1970s**
Courts Are Too Lenient	87%	85%	83%	78%	86%	83%	89%	87%	91%	88%	90%	93%
Capital Punishment Is Needed	79	64	79	57	82	66	79	65	79	68	83	69
Foreign Aid Spending Is Excessive	68	77	56	74	66	82	77	78	69	85	71	75
Crime Spending Is Inadequate	66	70	69	66	67	69	61	65	66	75	63	75
Welfare Spending Is Excessive	47	45	43	41	48	49	56	49	43	49	44	44
Public School Prayer Should Be Allowed	45	37	58	49	50	37	42	30	36	34	31	25
Pornography Should Be Illegal for All†	41	41	22	21	30	33	40	43	58	48	64	61
Gun Control Legislation Is Unnecessary	27	25	26	20	25	26	34	29	26	23	28	24
Spending on Blacks Is Excessive	22	26	21	10	23	18	21	25	24	31	13	29
Spending on Cities Is Excessive	19	14	15	8	15	17	23	15	19	15	16	15
Defense Spending Is Inadequate	15	18	17	13	13	18	10	21	16	22	17	20
Space Spending Is Inadequate	12	8	11	9	16	10	18	14	11	6	4	3
Spending on Environment Is Excessive	8	10	8	4	6	12	7	12	11	10	6	17
Spending on Education Is Excessive	5	12	4	6	4	9	3	12	8	13	5	19

Source: *American Demographics,* November 1986, p. 33. Reprinted with permission. Copyright © November 1986 American Demographics.
*"Don't know" responses not included in percentage base. †Responses from 1975 and 1984.

SUMMARY

Power is the ability to control others, even in the absence of their consent. But power is not legitimate in all situations. Power based on authority is accepted without question by the majority of those who are subject to it. When it is based only on fear, however, it tends to be unstable.

People can exercise various kinds of authority in society. Traditional authority, that of parents, for example, is rooted in the assumption that the habits and customs of the past legitimize the present. Legal-rational authority is based on official rules and procedures and is given to leaders by their subordinates, typically through appointment or election. Charismatic authority evolves from a ruler's force of personality.

In any complex society where official rules determine how things ought to be done, the state is the institutional seat of power that enforces the rules, the nation is the territory of people subject to those rules, the government includes the individuals and groups that make the rules and direct their enforcement, and the regime reflects the way those rules are created and enforced. Regimes can be totalitarian, autocratic, oligarchic, or democratic in type. None of these exist in their pure forms, however, but more typically occur in some combination.

Politics has often been defined as "who gets what, when, and how much." In other words, all societies must decide what, when, and how valued resources will be distributed, and politics is the chief mechanism through which these decisions are accomplished. Various theories have been offered to explain how politics operates, including the conflict, power-elite, functionalist, and pluralist perspectives. Yet any attempt to classify any political system exclusively in these terms would be difficult since elements of several tend to operate simultaneously.

Most democratic societies must function as representative democracies. That is, since most democratic states are far too large to allow all citizens to participate in every decision, elections are used to designate representatives who will be directly involved in the decision-making process. Although most Americans take democracy for granted, democracies are in the minority among world political systems. Democratic institutions are most likely to flourish in nations with advanced economic development, a cultural heritage of tolerance for dissenting views, and a balance and diffusion of power.

All sociopolitical systems share the same set of basic economic problems. Each must decide how limited natural resources should be utilized, which resources should be developed, what goods ought to be produced, and how goods and services should be distributed. The decisions on these issues determine the character of a society's economy. The capitalist market economy, clearly apparent in the United States, is characterized by a competitive marketplace, private ownership of the means of production, and a profit motive. The socialist command economy, evident in the Soviet Union, formally prohibits free enterprise; the government determines which goods will be produced and who will produce them.

A striking feature of industrial economic organization is its variety of business forms. Business enterprises are either single proprietorships, partnerships, or corporations. Single proprietorships are the most common, but corporations are the most powerful. Corporations tend to dominate certain industries, and their size and wealth can have far-reaching implications for the social and political structures of societies.

KEY TERMS/CONCEPTS

Australian ballot system
authority
autocracy
capitalist market economy
charismatic authority
coercion
conflict theory of politics
conglomerate
conservatism
corporation
democracy
economy
functionalist theory of politics
government
interlocking directorates
legal-rational authority
liberalism
monopoly
multinational corporations
nation
oligarchy
oligopoly
pluralism
pluralist theory of politics
political party
power
power elite
regime
socialist command economy
state
totalitarianism
traditional authority
universal suffrage

DISCUSSION QUESTIONS

1. What theory (or theories) of politics best explain the structure and process of the American political systems? What groups exercise the most power in the American political system?
2. Where in American society can aspects of socialism be found? Is socialism workable in any other areas of American life?

3. What kinds of power and authority are exercised within the university setting?
4. Sir Winston Churchill once commented that "democracy is the worst system devised by the wit of man, except for all others." What do you think Churchill had in mind when he made this statement?
5. Is it possible to increase voter turnout in the United States? If yes, how? If not, why?
6. It has been argued in this chapter that the process through which American presidents are elected fails to fully reflect the will of the people. Do you agree? Should changes be made in our system of elections? If yes, what kinds of changes?
7. Since large corporations have such a great impact on social, economic, and political life, how might they be better controlled? Should they be controlled at all?

SUGGESTED READINGS

Barry Bluestone and Bennett Harrison, *The Deindustrialization of America: Plant Closings, Community Abandonment, and the Dismantling of Basic Industry* (New York: Basic Books, 1982). Based on data gathered from more than five million establishments, the authors argue that during the 1970s, more than 30 million jobs were lost as a direct result of plant closures—reflecting a process that has continued into the 1980s. They point to the fact that corporations have been pulling their capital out of the nation's basic industries, and discuss the implications of such actions for the nation's future industrial growth.

C. Wright Mills, *The Power Elite* (New York: Oxford University Press, 1956). A modern sociological classic, Mills' thesis is that American society is ruled by a small, powerful elite formed of business, military, and government leaders.

Thomas J. Peters and Robert H. Waterman, Jr., *In Search of Excellence: Lessons from American's Best-Run Companies* (New York: Harper & Row, 1982). A national best-seller in 1983 and 1984, this volume examines the planning strategies of American corporations. The authors argue that a major problem with many corporations is an unwillingness to experiment and innovate, combined with the inability of universities to turn out MBAs well versed in the art of management.

Arnold M. Rose, *The Power Structure* (New York: Oxford University Press, 1967). In contrast to Mills' power-elite perspective, this volume provides a detailed exposition of the pluralist theory of politics.

Randall Rothenberg, *The Neo-Liberals: Creating the New American Politics* (New York: Simon and Schuster, 1984). The author, a journalist, argues that the emergence of the neo-liberals represents the most significant political development of the 1980s. While they profess a liberal ideology, the neo-liberals reject many traditional liberal programs as unworkable, emphasizing instead a new philosophy that incorporates ideas from across the political spectrum.

William Safire, *Safire's Washington* (New York: Times Books, 1980). Written by a Pulitzer Prize winning staffer from the *New York Times,* this volume is a collection of the author's political columns from recent years. Much of it is investigative commentary and discusses leadership that has been either corrupted or ennobled by power.

NOTES

1. William Safire, *Safire's Washington* (New York: Times Books, 1980), p. 494.
2. Max Weber, "Class, Status and Party," in Hans W. Gerth and C. Wright Mills (eds.), *Max Weber: Essays in Sociology* (New York: Oxford University Press, 1946), pp. 180–95.
3. Max Weber, *Theory of Social and Economic Organization,* translated by Talcott Parsons (New York: Free Press, 1947), p. 32.
4. *Time,* February 17, 1986, pp. 34–39.
5. George P. Murdock, *Social Structure* (New York: Macmillan, 1949).
6. Robert M. MacIver, *The Web of Government* (New York: Macmillan, 1951), pp. 140–41.
7. David Riesman, *The Lonely Crowd* (New Haven: Yale University Press, 1950). See also, Robert A. Dahl, *Who Governs? Democracy and Power in an American City* (New Haven: Yale University Press, 1961).
8. *New York Times,* April 19, 1987, p. E2.
9. C. Wright Mills, *The Power Elite* (New York: Oxford University Press, 1956).
10. Karl Marx, *Wage Labor and Capital* (New York: International Publishers, 1933); Karl Marx and Friedrich Engels, *The Communist Manifesto* (Middlesex: Penguin, 1848, 1967); Ralph Miliband, *Marxism and Politics* (New York: Oxford University Press, 1977).
11. T. Boone Pickens, *Boone* (New York: Houghton Mifflin, 1987).
12. Talcott Parsons, *The Social System* (New York: Free Press, 1951).
13. Seymour Martin Lipset, *Political Man: The Social Bases of Politics* (Garden City, NY: Doubleday, 1959).
14. *Business Week,* November 12, 1984, p. 61; *Newsweek,* June 18, 1984, pp. 44–46; *Time,* November 12, 1984, pp. 53–55.
15. See, for example, Martin Lipset, *Political Man.*
16. Norman H. Nie, Sidney Verba, and Jae-on Kim, *Participation and Political Equality* (Cambridge: Cambridge University Press, 1978).
17. Paul Delaney, "Voting: The New Black Power," *New York Times Magazine,* November 27, 1983, p. 35.
18. William H. Flanigan and Nancy H. Zingale, *Political Behavior of the American Electorate* (Boston: Allyn and Bacon, 1975); E. E. Schattsschneider, *The Semisovereign People* (New York: Holt, Rinehart and Winston, 1960).
19. Morton Keller, *Affairs of State* (Cambridge: Harvard University Press, 1977), pp. 523–24.

20. Morton Keller, *Affairs of State.*
21. Paul R. Abramson, "Generational Change and the Decline of Party Identification in America," *American Political Science Review,* 70 (1976), pp. 469–78.
22. Norman H. Nie, Sidney Verba, and John R. Petrocik, *The Changing American Voter* (Cambridge: Harvard University Press, 1976); Gerald M. Pomper, *Voters Choice* (New York: Dodd, Mead, 1975).
23. William Johnson, "Old Liberalism Dead," *World Press Review,* December 1984, p. 37.
24. William Safire, *Safire's Political Dictionary* (New York: Random House, 1978), p. 373.
25. See Randall Rothenberg, *The Neo-Liberals: Creating the New American Politcs:* (New York: Simon and Schuster, 1984).
26. *U.S. News & World Report,* June 25, 1984, pp. 35–36.
27. *Business Week,* October 15, 1984, pp. 183–84.
28. Shepard B. Clough, *The Economic Development of Western Civilization* (New York: McGraw-Hill, 1959), p. 344.
29. Clough, *The Economic Development of Western Civilization,* p. 347.
30. Daniel J. Boorstin, *The Americans: The Democratic Experience* (New York: Random House, 1973), p. 420
31. *Statistical Abstract of the United States: 1984,* pp. 538–39.
32. Adolf A. Berle and G. C. Means, *The Modern Corporation and Private Property* (New York: Harcourt Brace Jovanovich, 1968).
33. See *Newsweek,* June 25, 1984, p. 56.
34. Carol Gelderman, *Henry Ford: The Wayward Capitalist* (New York: Dial, 1981).
35. Daniel J. Boorstin, *The Americans,* p. 475.
36. *Business Week,* December 17, 1984, p. 57.
37. *Forbes Magazine,* October 15, 1968, p. 30.
38. United States Federal Trade Commission, Bureau of Economics, *Statistical Report on Mergers and Acquisitions,* Washington, D.C., July 1981, pp. 104, 115.
39. Barry Bluestone and Bennett Harrison, *The Deindustrialization of America: Plant Closings, Community Abandonment, and the Dismantling of Basic Industry* (New York: Basic Books, 1982).
40. See Terry N. Clark and Robert L. Linehart, *Community Politics* (New York: Free Press, 1971).
41. Michael Buroway, "Between the Labor Process and the State: The Changing Face of Factory Regimes Under Advanced Capitalism," *American Sociological Review,* 48 (1983), pp. 587–605.
42. *New York Times,* December 9, 1984, p. 22.
43. Beth Mintz and Michael Schwartz, "Interlocking Directorates and Interest Group Formation," *American Sociological Review,* 46 (December 1981), pp. 851–69.
44. Joshua Meyerowitz, "Where Have All the Heroes Gone?" *Psychology Today,* 18 (July 1984), pp. 46–51.
45. See Gary W. R. Patton and Cathleen E. Kaericher, "Effect of Characteristics of the Candidate on Voters' Preference," *Psychological Reports,* 47 (August 1980), pp. 171–82; Raymond E. Wolfinger and Steven J. Rosenstone, *Who Votes?* (New Haven: Yale University Press, 1980).

Criminal Justice: Maintaining the Social Order

If a society has laws, then it is only logical that it also has mechanisms for enforcing them, penalties for their violation, procedures for determining suspects' guilt or innocence, and alternatives for dealing with those convicted of crimes. This complex of mechanisms, penalties, procedures, and alternatives is part of a process—the **criminal justice process**—a complex system of agencies and operations organized to manage crime and those accused of violating criminal laws. The criminal justice process includes the agencies of law enforcement charged with the prevention of crime and the apprehension of criminal offenders. It includes the court systems charged with determining the guilt or innocence of accused offenders and the sentencing of convicted criminals. And it includes the network of correctional organizations charged with the control, custody, supervision, and treatment of those who have violated criminal laws.

On the surface, all of this seems fairly simple. If people violate the criminal law, the police attempt to locate and arrest them. After they are taken into custody, the "offenders" are brought before the courts. If they are found not guilty, they are released. But in the event of a guilty verdict, they are punished with a fine, probation, jail, prison, or even execution. Such a scenario raises many crucial questions. Can the police arrest anyone they "think" may have violated the law? Do any controls exist on police activity in this regard? Who determines innocence or guilt, and what criteria are used? How are different punishments decided, and what are the purposes of punishment? Do the accused and the guilty have any rights at all? Do guiding principles determine what is "fair" in the administration of justice?

To these questions can be added a variety of sociological inquiries about the institutions of justice processing. Is "justice" applied uniformly regardless of a suspect's race, sex, or age? Why is it that America's prisons house a disproportionate number of minority group members? And in an alternative direction, can the tools of sociology be used effectively for studying and improving the criminal justice process?

Few easy answers can be found to any of these questions, and the issues they raise point to the complexity of criminal justice processing in America. The police, the courts, and the correctional processes of which the criminal justice system is composed—even the legislatures involved in the creation of laws—do not have ultimate authority. All are advised and controlled, at least in theory, by the rather abstract principles of justice, fairness, and equity—principles embodied in the concept of *due process of law.* This notion of due process of law, written into the Constitution of the United States and enforced by the United States Supreme Court, establishes the general guidelines of criminal justice processing. Due process of law places limitations on the use of police powers and the discretionary behavior of the courts; it fashions the checks and balances in the administration of justice that serve to protect the innocent and separate them from the guilty; it determines and guarantees the rights of the accused and the convicted; and it restricts the imposition of arbitrary or cruel and unusual punishments.

Due process of law, however, is an elusive concept, one that has been evolving for many centuries. Moreover, even where the principles of due process have been made clear, they are sometimes ignored or misunderstood. Of crucial importance then, is an understanding of how the criminal justice system in America works, how it is grounded in the principle of due process of law, and what due process means for those accused of committing crimes.

CRIMINAL DUE PROCESS

Throughout history, processes of justice have emerged in numerous and varied forms. During the early centuries of Christianity, for example, when a thief was caught in the act of stealing, no trial was considered necessary. If he was a poor man who could not pay even the smallest of fines, he was simply put to death. But in the more doubtful cases, some degree of innocence or guilt had to be determined. Typical in such instances was the **trial by ordeal.** The accused was ordered to immerse a bandaged arm into a vat of boiling water, walk barefoot over red-hot ploughshares, or place a hand into a glove of near-molten metal. It was believed that Almighty God would make the truth known, and the accused, if innocent, would not be burned. Another common alternative was a trial by battle, in which the defendant would be pitted against his accuser, with victory going to the side of the truth.[1]

Inquisitorial, Inquiry, and Adversary Systems of Justice

Trials by ordeal or battle represented the cornerstone of the **inquisitorial system of justice.** The assumption of guilt was the guiding principle, and the accused was considered guilty until he could prove himself innocent. Inquisitorial "justice" became manifest when some form of divine intervention spared the accused from pain, suffering, and death, or when the accused admitted guilt—an admission usually elicited through torture or other forms of corporal punishment.

During the Golden Age of Chivalry inquisitorial justice was dominant and torture was the most common method of ascertaining guilt. Periods of torture usually followed imprisonment in some foul dungeon. Defendants were left to contemplate the infinitely worse treatment that awaited them. Eventually, they were brought to the torture room to face their accusers and those in charge of the gruesome ceremonies.

The inquisitorial system, now referred to as the **inquiry system of justice** so as to remove the aura of terror so often associated with its past history, still exists in modified form in most countries of the world that did not evolve from English or American colonial rule. In the modern inquiry court, all persons—judge, prosecutor, defense attorney, accused, and witnesses—are obliged

Inquisitorial prisons during the Golden Age of Chivalry used torture to determine guilt.

to cooperate with the court in its inquiry into the crime. Out of this inquiry, it is believed the truth will emerge.

By contrast, the American judicial process is an **adversary system of justice,** in which the innocence of the accused is assumed, and the burden of proof is placed on the court. In the adversary court, the judge is an impartial arbiter or referee between battling adversaries—the prosecution and the defense. Within strict rules of procedure, the opposing parties fight to win, believing that the position with truth on its side will be victorious. Adversary proceedings are grounded in the right of the defendant to refrain from hurting him- or herself (a right lacking in the inquiry court), and in the elusive notion of due process of law, a concept that asserts fundamental principles of justice and implies the administration of laws that do not violate privacy rights.

Due Process of Law

During the First Congress, just two years after the signing of the Constitution of the United States, James Madison of Virginia, who was later to become the nation's fourth president, proposed a dozen constitutional amendments. Congress approved ten of the amendments in September 1791, and they took effect after ratification by the requisite number of states. These first ten amendments to the Constitution have become known as the Bill of Rights.

The significance of the Bill of Rights is that it restricts government rather than individuals and private groups. It was added to the Constitution at the insistence of those who feared a strong central government, or, as U.S. Supreme Court Chief Justice Earl Warren noted more than a century and a half later:

> The men of our First Congress knew that whatever form it may assume, government is potentially as dangerous a thing as it is a necessary one. They knew that power must be lodged somewhere to prevent anarchy within and conquest from without, but that this power could be abused to the detriment of their liberties.[2]

Within the Bill of Rights, the amendments protect the freedoms of speech, religion, assembly, the press, the redress of grievances and the right to bear arms; they forbid the use of force to compel self-incrimination, excessive bail, cruel and unusual punishments, and the unreasonable search and seizure of persons and property; and they set out certain requirements for criminal trials.

The Fifth Amendment contained the first constitutional statement on due process of law: "No person shall . . . be deprived of life, liberty, or property, without due process of law. . . ." But since no rights are absolute, due process is subject to reasonable regulation through law. Moreover, the original intent of the due-process clause is neither self-evident nor explained in any detail. Furthermore, the Bill of Rights provided no protection against state actions. The protections afforded by these first ten amendments served only to curtail federal authority, and the requirements for criminal trials and protections of private rights did not apply in state prosecutions. The due-process clause also appeared in the Fourteenth Amendment in 1868, but once again it was not explained. Moreover, it too failed to extend all the guarantees of the Bill of Rights to state defendants.

The meaning and intent of the due-process concept has been debated for almost two centuries. Although **due process of law** may be impossible to define precisely, in contemporary American law it asserts a fundamental principle of justice rather than a specific rule of law. It implies and comprehends the administration of laws that do not violate the very foundations of civil liberties; it requires in each case an evaluation based on disinterested inquiry, a balanced order of facts exactly and fairly stated, the detached consideration of conflicting claims, and a judgment mindful of reconciling the needs of continuity and change in a complex society.[3] The application of the due-process requirements to state criminal proceedings did not begin until the 1930s, and as is detailed in the following discussions of the police, courts, and corrections, the majority of these rights and requirements were not extended to state defendants until the 1960s.

POLICE AND LAW ENFORCEMENT

Modern policing as we know it today can be traced to the latter part of the ninth century when England's Alfred the Great was structuring the defenses of his kingdom against a Danish invasion. Part of Alfred's strategy depended on the internal stability of his empire. To guarantee this stability, he instituted a system of **mutual pledge,** which organized the country at several levels. At the lowest level were *tithings,* ten families grouped together who each assumed responsibility for the acts of their members. At the next level, ten tithings, or one hundred families, were grouped together into a *hundred;* the hundred was under the charge of a *constable.* Hundreds within a specific geographic area were combined to form *shires*—administrative units (now called counties) under royal authority that were governed by a *shire-reeve,* or sheriff.[4] In thirteenth-century England, the *night watch* appeared in urban areas to patrol late-night city streets, thus representing the most rudimentary form of metropolitan policing.[5] Various forms of the constable, sheriff, and night-watch systems persisted for centuries. For the most part, however, they were poorly organized and ineffective. In 1829, the London Metropolitan Police system was established, and it became the first centralized law enforcement agency charged with the dual responsibilities of preventing crime and apprehending offenders. New York City established the first organized police force in the United States in 1845, and by the turn of the twentieth century, metropolitan police systems had become quite common.[6]

Police Systems in the United States

With a population well in excess of 240 million people, under the authority of competing political jurisdictions at federal, state, county, and local levels, law enforcement in the United States today reflects a structure more complex than that of any other society. More than 40,000 professional police agencies currently are found in the public sector alone—each representing the enforcement area of a specific judicial body. To these can be added the numerous others in the private sphere. The duties and authority of each agency are generally quite clear, but oftentimes these can be muddled by jurisdictional disputes, agency rivalries, and lack of coordination and communication.

Federal law enforcement agencies have two features that make them unique within the spectrum of police activity. First, because they were structured to enforce specific statutes—those contained in the U.S. Criminal Code—their units are highly specialized, often with distinctive resources and training. Second, because they are the enforcement arms of the federal government, their jurisdictional boundaries have been limited by congressional authority. Best known of these agencies is the Federal Bureau of Investigation (FBI), the chief investigative body of the United States Department of Justice, whose legal jurisdiction extends to such crimes as kidnapping, bank robbery, aircraft piracy, violations of the Civil Rights Act, interstate gambling, and organized crime. Among the other visible federal police agencies are the Drug Enforcement Administration, the Immigration and Naturalization Service, the Intelligence Division of the Internal Revenue Service, and the United States Secret Service.

New York City Police Department personnel pose in front of the 20th Precinct Station on West 37th Street in 1910.

State law enforcement bodies emerged in response to basic deficiencies in rural crime control. In the decades that followed the Civil War and Reconstruction, population growth, combined with changing economic conditions and the numerous complexities characteristic of any pluralistic society, resulted in a dramatic increase in crime. In many communities, local sheriffs and constables lacked the personnel, training, and resources to combat crime. Moreover, crime had become more global in nature and was less localized in particular communities. Yet no effective communication and cooperation existed between the police force of one municipality and those of other cities and towns. The emergence of state police agencies came about in direct response to these issues.[7] Currently, each state has its own law enforcement apparatus, and although the structure and functions of these fifty state organizations vary somewhat, they all generally fulfill a number of the regulatory and investigative roles carried out by the federal government groups, as well as some of the uniformed patrol duties of local police.

Despite the existence of the large federal enforcement bureaucracies and the state police agencies, most law enforcement and peacekeeping in rural and urban areas is provided by county and municipal authorities. It is policing at these local levels that best characterizes

SOCIAL INDICATOR

Full-time Law Enforcement Officers in the United States

Year	Officers
1965	271,659
1970	343,669
1975	476,324
1980	438,442
1987	480,383

Source: United States Department of Justice, 1987.

Exhibit 15.1

Sidelights on American Culture

The Pinkertons

In history, folklore, and popular culture, both the significance and impact of private police in the United States are profound. Perhaps the most famous private police force in the entire world is the Pinkerton National Detective Agency, founded in 1850 in a small Chicago office by Scottish immigrant Allan Pinkerton. "The Pinkertons," as they were called, initially gained notoriety just before the Civil War by thwarting the alleged "Baltimore Plot" to assassinate president-elect Abraham Lincoln. During the decades that followed, Pinkerton agents played a major role in numerous industrial clashes between workers and management. The Pinkertons also had their impact on crime control in America's trans-Mississippi West. Hired to protect the railroads during the outlaw era, they were responsible for the arrests of John and Simeon Reno, who were credited with having organized the nation's first band of bank robbers. Pinkertons were the persistent adversaries of Jesse James, Cole Younger, and other members of the James-Younger gang. In Texas, they were retained by railroad executives to hunt down the legendary Sam Bass. Pinkerton agents also appear in the annals of Western Americana as the group who rid Montana and Wyoming of Robert Leroy Parker (Butch Cassidy), Harry Longbaugh (the Sundance Kid), Etta Place, Blackjack Ketchum, and other members of the romanticized Wild Bunch from Robbers' Roost.

Allan Pinkerton himself, with his insistence on detailed descriptions of known criminals—including physical characteristics, background, companions, and hideouts—devised the rogues' gallery, the precursor of today's "mug books." And curiously, the Pinkerton National Detective Agency is responsible for the term *private eye* in American slang usage. The firm's trademark is an open eye, underlined with the slogan "We never sleep."

Today, known simply as Pinkerton's, Inc., the agency continues as one of the largest private police forces in the United States, with offices in most major cities.

SOURCES: James D. Horan, *The Pinkertons: The Detective Dynasty That Made History* (New York: Crown, 1967); James D. Horan and Howard Swiggett, *The Pinkerton Story* (New York: G. P. Putnam's Sons, 1951).

policing in the United States today. More than 90% of all arrests are made by local law enforcement officers, and local police are responsible for the day-to-day aspects of crime control and community protection.

Private policing began during the middle of the last century (see Exhibit 15.1), and continues today in the form of nonpublic organizations that provide guard, patrol, detection, protection, and alarm services, as well as armored car transportation, insurance investigation, and retail and industrial security. In general, these activities fall into areas of criminal and noncriminal activity that conventional law enforcement is either ill-equipped to deal with or otherwise prohibited from handling.

The Functions of Police

"Police work" is a term that conjures up dramatic confrontations between police and lawbreakers. It suggests initiation of the process of justice, an enterprise bounded by the dusting for fingerprints and the search for elusive clues, the investigation and chase, and the ultimate apprehension and arrest of the suspected offender. Police work might also suggest that the functions of law enforcement only involve the control of crime and the protection of society. But police work goes well beyond these tasks.

The Peacekeeping Role of the Police

Although policing does include the dangerous task of apprehending criminals, officers assigned to patrol duties, even in large cities, are typically confronted with few, if any, serious crimes during the course of a single assignment. Most police work is a *peacekeeping operation*. In this guise it can include a wide spectrum of activities: the enforcement of traffic laws and other civil ordinances; general areas of public service such as

SOCIAL INDICATOR

Total Estimated Arrests,*
United States, 1987

Total†	**12,711,600**	**100.0%**
Murder and Nonnegligent Manslaughter	19,200	0.2
Forcible Rape	36,310	0.3
Robbery	138,290	1.1
Aggravated Assault	352,450	2.8
Burglary	443,400	3.5
Larceny-theft	1,469,200	11.6
Motor Vehicle Theft	169,300	1.3
Arson	18,000	0.1
Other Assaults	787,200	6.2
Forgery and Counterfeiting	93,900	0.7
Fraud	341,900	2.7
Embezzlement	12,700	0.1
Stolen Property; Buying, Receiving, Possessing	139,300	1.1
Vandalism	273,500	2.2
Weapons; Carrying, Possessing, etc.	191,700	1.5
Prostitution and Commercialized Vice	110,100	0.9
Sex Offenses (except forcible rape and prostitution)	100,100	0.8
Drug Abuse Violations	937,400	7.4
Gambling	25,400	0.2
Offenses against Family and Children	58,700	0.5
Driving under the Influence	1,727,200	13.6
Liquor Laws	616,700	4.9
Drunkenness	828,300	6.5
Disorderly Conduct	698,700	5.5
Vagrancy	36,100	0.3
All Other Offenses (except traffic)	2,836,700	22.3
Suspicion (not included in totals)	13,500	0.1
Curfew and Loitering Law Violations	89,500	0.7
Runaways	160,400	1.3
Violent Crime‡	546,300	4.3
Property Crime§	2,099,900	16.5
Crime Index Total//	2,646,200	20.8

Source: *Uniform Crime Reports, 1987,* p. 164.

*Arrest totals based on all reporting agencies and estimates for unreported areas.

†Becaue of rounding, items may not add to totals.

‡Violent crimes are offenses of murder, forcible rape, robbery, and aggravated assault.

§Property crimes are offenses of burglary, larceny-theft, motor vehicle theft, and arson.

//Includes arson.

directing traffic, settling disputes, locating missing children, and providing directions to confused pedestrians. This **peacekeeping role** includes preventive and protective roles as well; the presence of police on patrol lessens opportunities and discourages individuals intent on committing crimes.

Studies of various municipal law-enforcement agencies have demonstrated repeatedly that only a small portion of police activity involves the exercise of law-enforcement functions. Yale sociologist Albert J. Reiss, Jr., conducting research on the Chicago police in 1966, indicated that 83% of the incidents handled by that organization were considered to be of a noncriminal nature.[8] Similarly, Richard J. Lundman's examination of police operations in five separate jurisdictions during the late 1970s found that most of the time spent on patrol was taken up by traffic control, service calls, and dealing with minor disturbances.[9] Even when attention *is* focused on the *law-enforcement* aspects of police work, a significant proportion of the activity does not involve "dangerous crime." Of the almost 13 million arrests made by law-enforcement agents in the United States in 1987, for example, only 4.3% involved the serious offenses of homicide, forcible rape, robbery, aggravated assault, burglary, larceny-theft, vehicle theft, and arson. By contrast, more than a third of the arrests were for the "lesser" crimes of gambling, driving while intoxicated, liquor law violations, disorderly conduct, prostitution, vagrancy, and drunkenness.[10]

The Right to Use Force

Although police work involves more of "keeping the peace" than "enforcing the law," this difference should

Police work is primarily a peacekeeping operation.

not suggest that policing is not without its risks. Each year, for example, more than 50,000 assaults on police officers are reported in the United States.[11] While a fourth of these occur when officers are responding to robbery and burglary calls and attempting other arrests, a significantly greater proportion take place when officers are following up on disputes and other "disturbance" calls—the more common areas of keeping the peace.

This peacekeeping role is the main factor that separates the functions of police from those of private citizens. This role involves the legitimate right to use force in situations whose urgency requires it. Although modern democratic society severely restricts the right of private citizens to use force, the law does recognize that situations may develop about which something must be done *immediately*—situations in which resorting to the courts and other forms of dispute settlement would simply take too long. It is just for such situations that we have police. This idea is based on the notion that it is better to have a small group of people (police) with a monopoly on the right to use force than to allow every individual to use a club, knife, or gun in situations that *they* may perceive to be immediately demanding. This right to use force is what justifies the role of the police in peacekeeping, crime control, order maintenance, and everything else they do.

Not surprisingly, police use of deadly force has been a controversial issue over the years. Of particular sociological interest in this regard are the allegations that police officers discriminate in the use of deadly force—that they are more likely to shoot blacks than whites. This viewpoint has been expressed by a number of black leaders.[12] Even one sociologist, Paul Takagi, has stated that "police have one trigger finger for whites and another for blacks,"[13] suggesting that police are engaged in a form of genocide against minority groups.

It has been well documented that while blacks account for only 12% of the population of the United States, approximately 60% of the citizens killed by the police are black—clearly a disproportionate share.[14] In spite of this fact, however, research evidence fails to confirm the allegation of police discrimination.[15] The only exception to this conclusion was James J. Fyfe's study in Memphis during the period 1969–1976, in which he found that all factors considered, blacks were at far greater risk of becoming victims of police shootings than were whites.[16]

The right of the police to use force and the opportunity to abuse that right have long been controversial issues.

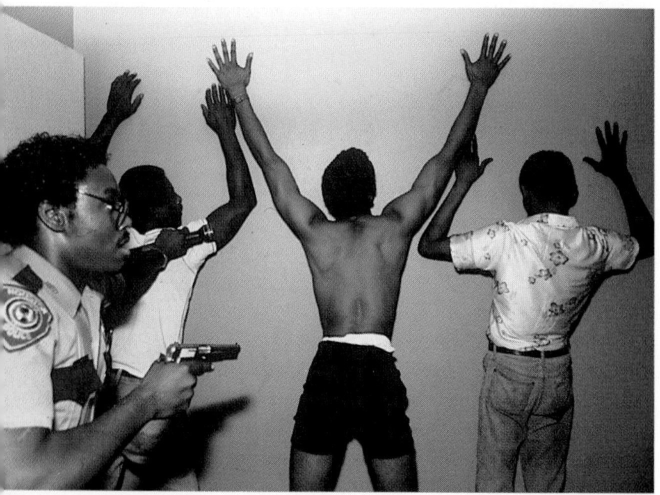

Police Discretion

In carrying out their duties, police stand at the forefront of the criminal justice system and must serve as chief interpreters of the law. Based on their knowledge of criminal codes, they must make immediate judgments as to whether a law has been violated, whether to make an arrest, and whether to exercise the use of force in making that arrest. Decision making in these situations tends to be exceedingly complex, especially since laws *are not,* and *cannot* be, written to take into account the specific circumstances surrounding every police confrontation. Moreover, all laws cannot be fully enforced, and most police officers, having only minimal legal training, are not equipped to deal with the intricacies of law. Therefore, police must exercise a great deal of discretion in deciding *what* constitutes a violation of the law, *which* laws to enforce, and *how* and *when* to enforce them. Thus, **police discretion** exists in situations where a police officer is free to choose among various alternatives—to enforce the law and to do so selectively, to use force, and to deal with some citizens differently than with others.

Irving Piliavin and Scott Briar's well-known study, "Police Encounters with Juveniles," gives a particularly useful perspective on discretion and differential law enforcement.[17] These researchers demonstrated that, with the exception of offenders who had committed serious crimes or who were already wanted by the authorities, the disposition of juvenile cases depended largely on how a youth's character was evaluated by an officer. Such evaluations and decisions typically were limited to the information gathered by police during their actual encounters with juveniles. This fact, the researchers found, had serious implications for the accused, the criminal justice system, and the concept of due process of law. When police officers believed that a youth's demeanor, race, or style of dress were good indicators of future behavior or criminality, arrests became totally discriminatory—the youths who were arrested were those who typically did not fit the officer's idea of normalcy. Police conceptions of "normalcy" and other values and beliefs are shaped during the socialization of the police personality (see Exhibit 15.2).

The Police and Due Process

The peacekeeping role of the police gives them tremendous powers—powers to stop, to frisk, to order someone out of a car, to question, to detain, to use force, and to exercise seizure and restraint.[18] Yet the Constitution of the United States was designed to protect each citizen's rights, and thus, it placed certain restrictions on the exercise of these powers. As noted earlier, however, the guarantees of the Bill of Rights only applied to federal authority. Moreover, even at the federal level, the specific provisions of the Bill of Rights were applicable only after they were interpreted by the United States Supreme Court. As a result, for a great part of the history of policing in America, law enforcement was in a position to operate independently of the Constitution.

Throughout the twentieth century, and particularly since the beginning of the 1960s, hundreds of Supreme Court decisions have been handed down that regulate police powers. Many of these decisions have been highly significant. Of these, three have had the greatest impact on policing: *Mapp v. Ohio* in 1961,[19] *Escobedo v. Illinois* in 1964,[20] and *Miranda v. Arizona* in 1966.[21]

Mapp v. Ohio

In criminal investigations, evidence gathering depends on the *search* of persons and property for the purpose of discovering stolen items or other indications of guilt. Associated with search is *seizure*—taking a person or property into custody in consequence of a violation of the public law. Thus, **search and seizure** involves means for the detection and accusation of crime.

The Fourth Amendment prohibits "unreasonable searches and seizures." The term "unreasonable" is rather elastic, however, and was never defined by the framers of the Constitution. Search warrants obviate much of the problematic nature of search and seizure; they reflect the formal authority of the law in their sanctioning of the use of police search powers. Warrantless searches are permitted during the course of an arrest, but historically in most other instances, including those within the privacy of one's own home, the use of the powers of search and seizure was left to police discretion.

In 1914, more than a century after the Bill of Rights had been incorporated into the Constitution, the United States Supreme Court announced its well-known **exclusionary rule,** which prohibited or excluded the use of evidence seized in violation of the Fourth Amendment. At the time, however, because the Justices of the High Court interpreted the Bill of Rights as applying solely to federal authority, the new rule pertained only to evidence seized illegally by federal agents for use in federal courts. It was not until almost five decades later that the exclusionary rule was applied universally. The precipitating case was ***Mapp v. Ohio,*** decided in 1961 (see Exhibit 15.3).

Mrs. Dollree Mapp, a resident of Cleveland, had been convicted in an Ohio trial court of knowingly having in her possession obscene materials in violation of state law. Although the Supreme Court of Ohio found that the evidence of her crime had been seized during an unlawful search of her home, her conviction was nevertheless upheld. On her appeal to the United States Supreme Court, the Justices ruled in favor of Mapp, thus extending the exclusionary rule to state prosecutions as a necessary safeguard against unreasonable searches and seizures.

Escobedo v. Illinois

Confessions, the Supreme Court stated more than a century ago, are "among the most effectual proofs of the law," but by constitutional implication, they are admissible as evidence only when given voluntarily.[22] This has long been the rule in the federal courts where the Fifth Amendment privilege against self-incrimination clearly applies. In 1936 the Supreme Court extended this privilege to state defendants, but only with respect to confessions exacted under torture.[23] The 1964 decision in ***Escobedo v. Illinois*** extended the Fifth Amendment to all state cases, and at the same time linked it in some measure to the Sixth Amendment right to counsel.

On January 19, 1960, 22-year-old Danny Escobedo was arrested by Chicago police for the fatal shooting of his brother-in-law. He was interrogated for 15 hours, made no statements, and was eventually released. Eleven days later, he was arrested for a second time and taken to a police station for questioning. Escobedo's attorney arrived shortly thereafter but was denied access to his client. Both the attorney and Escobedo repeatedly requested to see one another, but to no avail. Escobedo was told that he could not see his attorney until the police had finished their questioning. It was during this second period of interrogation that Escobedo made certain incriminating statements that would be construed as his voluntary confession to the crime.

Danny Escobedo was convicted of murder and sentenced to a 22-year prison term. His attorney appealed the decision, and on June 22, 1964, the United States Supreme Court ruled in favor of Escobedo. The High

Exhibit 15.2 **Types & Stereotypes**

Socialization and the Police Personality

Why is it that all cops seem to think the same way?
—A Miami attorney, 1984

Police officers are members of a subculture. Their system of shared norms, values, goals, career patterns, and life-style is essentially different from those of the wider society in which they function. Entry into the police subculture begins with a process of socialization whereby police recruits learn the values and behavior patterns characteristic of experienced officers. Ultimately, many develop an occupational or "working personality" characterized by authoritarianism, suspicion, racism, hostility, insecurity, conservatism, and cynicism.

Perhaps the most definitive statement on the development of the police personality comes from sociologist Jerome H. Skolnick, who summarized the process:

Police officers may develop the "police personality," characterized by authoritarianism, suspicion, hostility, and cynicism.

> The policeman's role contains two principal variables, danger and authority, which should be interpreted in the light of a "constant" pressure to appear efficient. The element of danger seems to make the policeman especially attentive to signs indicating a potential for violence and lawbreaking. As a result, the policeman is generally a "suspicious" person. Furthermore, the character of the policeman's work makes him less desirable as

Court's position required that an individual accused of a crime be permitted to have an attorney present during police interrogation. The Court's view was that the adversary system of justice had traditionally been restricted to the trial stage, and that changes were long overdue that would extend the adversary nature of the system back into the earlier stages of criminal proceedings. Thus, no longer were police in a position to engage in "third-degree" methods of interrogation, brow-beating their suspects until the desired statement was elicited.

Miranda v. Arizona

Ernesto Miranda, a 23-year-old Mexican with less than a ninth-grade education, was arrested in Phoenix on March 13, 1963. He was suspected of kidnapping and raping an 18-year-old girl. At the police station, he was placed in a line-up and identified by the victim, after which he was interrogated for several hours. At the close of the interrogation, the questioning officers emerged with a confession signed by Miranda. Over his objections, the

> a friend, since norms of friendship implicate others in his work. Accordingly, the element of danger isolates the policeman socially from that segment of the citizenry which he regards as symbolically dangerous and also from the conventional citizenry with whom he identifies.

Skolnick goes on to suggest that the element of authority reinforces the element of danger in isolating the police officer. Police are required to enforce laws that often reflect a puritanical morality, such as those prohibiting gambling and drunkenness—although in their personal lives they often are known not to uphold the values that they are called upon to enforce. In addition, police are charged with enforcing the traffic laws and other codes that regulate the flow of public activity. In these situations, where police direct the citizenry and enforce unpopular laws that stem from some idealized middle-class morality, they come to be viewed as adversaries. The public prefers to ignore these instances of police authority, stressing the police obligation to respond to danger.

Skolnick and others have elaborated on additional elements that contribute to the development and crystallization of the police personality. All officers, for example, enter the police profession by the same route—academy training followed by the constabulary role of the "cop on the beat" (or the cop in the cruising squad car). Because of this early experience, officers share various elements of similarity, routine, and predictability. Furthermore, as functionaries charged with enforcing the law and keeping the peace, police are required to respond to all assaults against persons and property. Thus, in an occupation characterized by an ever-present potential for violence, many police develop a perceptual shorthand that enables them to identify certain kinds of people as "symbolic assailants." As a consequence, police develop conceptions that are shaped by exaggerated caution. In fact, police are trained to be suspicious.

In sum, the police personality emerges as a result of the very nature of police work and the kindred socialization processes in which most police officers seem to be involved. Furthermore, to combat the social isolation that results from the authoritarian role of the police, they develop resources within their own world—other police officers—to combat their social rejection. In the end, most police become part of a closely knit subculture that is protective and supportive of its members and shares similar attitudes, values, understandings, and views of the world. This sense of isolation and the resulting solidarity are typified in a comment in 1989 by a police officer in Albany, New York:

> It's tough being a cop when in the beginning most of the people you know are ordinary citizens. Friends, neighbors, and sometimes even family don't seem to be all that comfortable when you're around. After a while you hear less and less from them.

SOURCES: Jonathan Rubenstein, *City Police* (New York: Farrar, Straus & Giroux, 1973); Jerome H. Skolnick, *Justice Without Trial: Law Enforcement in Democratic Society* (New York: Wiley, 1966).

confession was introduced at trial, and Miranda was convicted and given a 20–30 year sentence.

The issue in ***Miranda v. Arizona*** was that custodial interrogation is inherently coercive, and that the procedures for providing suspects with knowledge of their rights—even if explained—were rarely sufficiently clear. Miranda's conviction was overturned by the High Court, and from this decision came the well-known *Miranda* warning rules, (see Exhibit 15.4), which every officer must recite to a suspect prior to interrogation.

Police Corruption

Research in the area of white-collar crime, combined with government inquiries targeting the internal operations of organized crime, labor unions, and various business enterprises have demonstrated that work-related lawbreaking can be found within every occupation and profession. Within the ranks of law enforcement officers, illegal job-related activities involving graft, corruption, theft, and other practices are comparatively evident. Yet

Exhibit 15.3 Case Study

Mapp v. Ohio

The *Mapp* case began on May 23, 1957, when three Cleveland police officers arrived at the residence of Dollree "Dolly" Mapp. The police had been given information that a suspect, wanted for questioning in a recent bombing, was hiding out in Mapp's home, and also that a large amount of gambling paraphernalia was being concealed at the residence. Mapp and her daughter by a former marriage resided on the top floor of the two-family dwelling. Upon arrival, the police knocked at the door and demanded entry. Mapp, after telephoning her attorney, refused to admit them without a warrant. The officers then advised their superiors of the situation and undertook a surveillance of the house.

The police again sought entrance some three hours later when at least four additional officers arrived on the scene. When Mapp did not come to the door immediately, the police forced their way into the dwelling. Meanwhile, Mapp's attorney arrived, but the police prohibited him from seeing his client or entering the house.

From the testimony in the case, Dolly Mapp was apparently about halfway down the stairs from the second floor when the police broke into the lower hall. She demanded to see the search warrant. Thereupon, a paper, claimed to be a warrant, was held up by one of the officers. Mapp grabbed the alleged warrant and stuffed it into her blouse. A struggle ensued during which the officers recovered the paper and at the same time handcuffed Mapp because she had reportedly been "belligerent" in resisting their official rescue of the "warrant" from her person. The officers then took her forcibly, in handcuffs, to her bedroom where they searched a chest of drawers, a dresser, a closet, and some suitcases. The search then spread to the remainder of the second floor and the basement. Neither the bombing suspect nor the gambling paraphernalia was found, but the search did turn up an unspecified amount of pornographic literature.

Following the search, Dolly Mapp was arrested for possessing "lewd and lascivious books, pictures, and photographs," and was subsequently convicted for possession of obscene materials. At the trial, no search warrant was produced by the prosecution, nor was the failure to produce one ever explained.

The issue in *Mapp,* of course, was the legality of the arrest, search, and seizure. No search warrant existed and Mapp had not given her consent to a search, but one could argue, as the prosecution heatedly did, that at the time the police applied force and searched her apartment, Dolly Mapp was indeed under arrest—hence, it was a lawful search, incident to arrest. Yet, as the defense pointed out and the facts of the case substantiated, no reasonable cause could be put forth for arrest. The only background data the police had was "information that a fugitive was hiding in her home."

On the basis of these facts, the Supreme Court reversed the decision of the Ohio Court and extended the exclusionary rule to all 50 states. The Supreme Court indicated that from the day of its decision, June 19, 1961, any evidence that was obtained illegally by the police would be inadmissible in every courtroom in the nation.

SOURCE: Mapp v. Ohio, 367 U.S. 643 (1961).

police crime and corruption may be considerably more widespread than crime and corruption in most other occupations. Virtually every urban police department in the United States has experienced both organized corruption and some form of scandal, and similar problems have been found in small towns and rural sheriffs' departments as well.[24]

Studies of police organizations and activities have found that the problem lies in the fact that policing is rich in opportunities for corruption. In a nation where crime rates are high and where the demands for illegal goods and services are widespread, police officers find themselves in a situation where they are confronted almost daily with opportunities for accepting payments in lieu of fully discharging their duties.

In its broadest sense, police corruption involves job-related illegal activities *for economic gain,* including payment for services that police are sworn to carry out as part of their law enforcement role. Police corruption can occur in many forms, but most observers and researchers

Sociological Focus

The Miranda *Warning Rules*

1. You have a right to remain silent.
2. Anything you say can and will be used against you in a court of law.
3. You have the right to consult with a lawyer and to have the lawyer present during any questioning.
4. If you cannot afford a lawyer, one will be obtained for you if you so desire.

of police behavior tend to agree that it is found most often in nine specific areas:

1. Free or discount meals, goods, or services provided by business owners in return for police "good will."
2. Kickbacks and fees from attorneys, bail bondsmen, tow truck operators, and others to whom police officers can refer individuals asking for help.
3. The "opportunistic theft" of jewelry, money, narcotics, and other items of value found on suspects and at burglary and other crime scenes.
4. Planned theft in the form of the direct involvement of police in predatory criminal activities—either on their own or through complicity with established criminals.
5. "Shakedowns" and other forms of extortion in which police officers accept money from citizens in lieu of enforcing the law.
6. "Protection" through the acceptance of graft on a regular basis from organized prostitution, gambling, and narcotics rackets.
7. Case fixing through the acceptance of money in exchange for not making an arrest, perjury, reducing the seriousness of a charge, or agreeing to drop an investigation.
8. Providing bodyguard and other security services for a fee.
9. Patronage, through the granting of promotions or transfers, in return for money.[25]

Various techniques have been used in attempts to control police corruption, including civilian review of police activity, tighter supervision of police officers by administrators, and internal police units that investigate citizen complaints against police. Current thinking about police behavior suggests, however, that the best means for reducing corruption is probably greater police professionalism. Police professionalism serves to establish group norms of pride and dignity of occupation that will make police intolerant of fellow officers who taint and tarnish their profession.

THE COURTS

On the surface, the American court system seems confusing and complex. It appears as a perplexing mosaic of names and functions, with structures varying from one jurisdiction to the next. The system consists of superior courts and inferior courts, lower courts and supreme courts, as well as night, police, justice of the peace, municipal, mayor's, and magistrates' courts. Moreover, the United States has what is known as a **dual court system**—one at the federal level and one at the state level. Yet despite the many kinds of courts, the structure

SOCIAL INDICATOR

Proportion of U.S. Population Who Feel That the Courts Do Not Deal Harshly Enough with Criminals

1975	85.1%
1980	88.4
1985	87.1

Source: National Opinion Research Center, 1985.

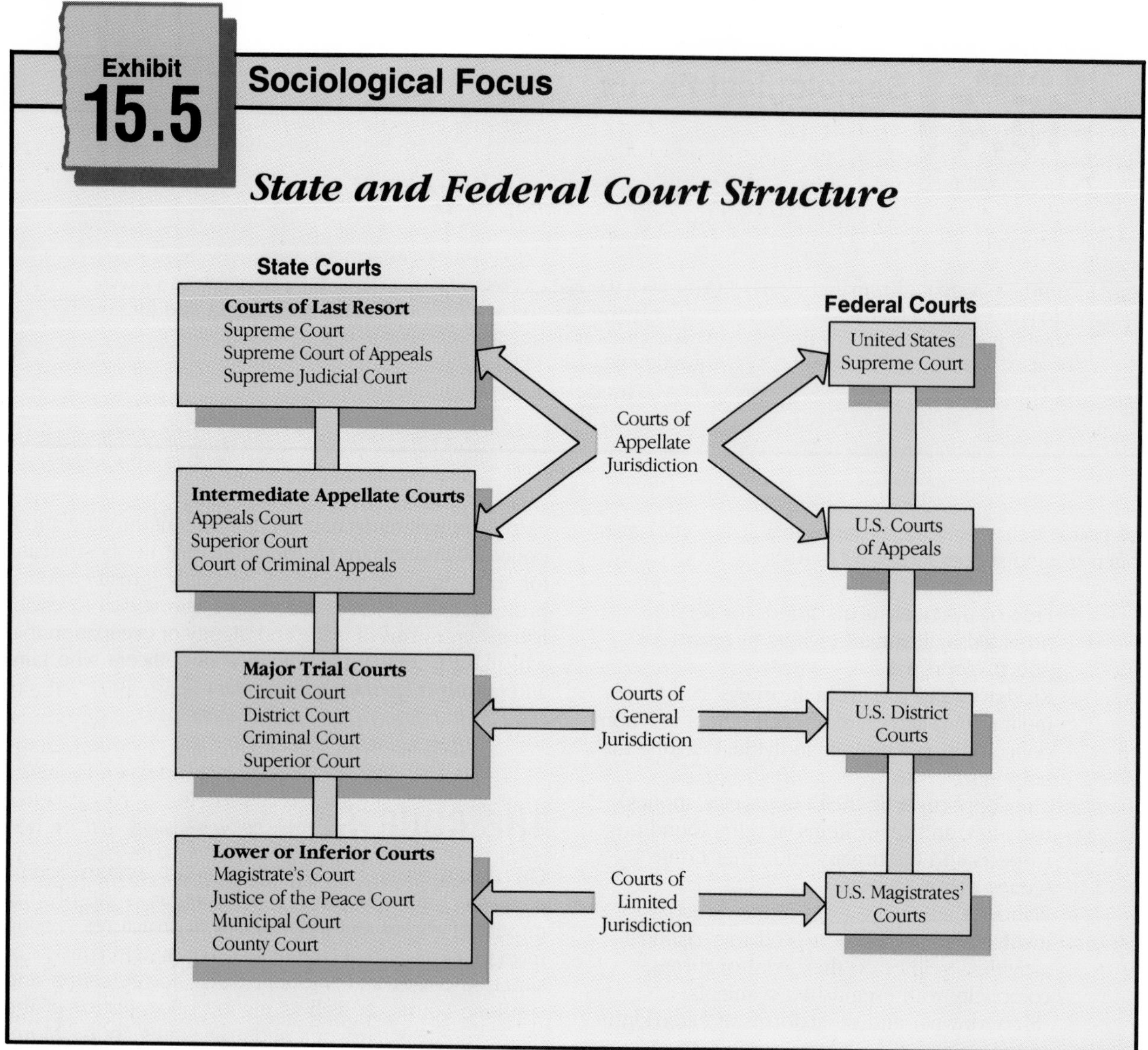

of the American courts, at least in terms of criminal judicial processing, is simple and clear, with almost identical arrangements in the federal system and all 50 states.

American Court Structure

As illustrated in Exhibit 15.5, in the federal courts and in most of the state courts, a four-tier system is divided into three levels of jurisdiction: limited, general, and appellate.

At the lowest level are the **courts of limited jurisdiction.** More than 13,000 of these courts are found across the nation. They are the entry point for all criminal justice processing. In the federal system they are called U.S. Magistrates' Courts, and in the states they may be known as county, municipal, or justice of the peace courts. They handle all minor criminal offenses —misdemeanors, and the myriad violations of traffic laws and city and county ordinances. For felony cases, their jurisdiction is *limited.* That is, they are restricted to the preliminary hearings of felony defendants. Although they can make bail decisions, these courts cannot conduct felony trials nor do they possess appellate authority.

The **courts of general jurisdiction** are the major trial courts. Known as U.S. District Courts at the federal level, in the state systems they are known by many different names—perhaps circuit, superior, or simply criminal courts. They have the power to try and decide any criminal case, including appeals from a lower court.

At the uppermost levels of the court hierarchy are the **courts of appellate jurisdiction.** As their name implies, they are limited to conducting appeals. (The only exception in this regard involves the United States Supreme Court, which can serve as a trial court in cases involving suits between two states, issues that test the constitutionality of state laws, and matters relating to ambassadors.) The intermediate appellate courts in the states and the U.S. Courts of Appeals in the federal system serve to ease the work load of the highest courts in the land—the state courts of last resort and the United States Supreme Court.

The United States Supreme Court is the highest court in the nation, the final authority on legal matters. It is truly the court of last resort. Yet the Supreme Court does not hear every case. It has the discretion to decide which cases it will review and typically opts to examine only those of "substantial federal question"—that is, matters dealing directly with interpretations of the Constitution.

Before a case can be appealed to the High Court, the petitioner must exhaust all other remedies. Thus, federal cases must first proceed up through the U.S. Court of Appeals, while state cases must be decided upon by the state's highest court.

The Supreme Court's authority to exercise its own discretion in deciding which cases it will hear is known as its *certiorari power,* and comes from the **writ of *certiorari,*** a writ of review issued by the High Court, ordering some lower court to "forward up the record" of a case it has tried for Supreme Court review. Prior to this granting of *certiorari,* the potential case must pass the **Rule of Four;** that is, a case is accepted for review only if four of the nine Supreme Court Justices feel that it merits consideration. Currently, more than 4,000 cases are filed annually for review. However, the Supreme Court limits itself to deciding about 150 cases each year.

Bail and the Pretrial Process

As suggested by Exhibit 15.6, the criminal judicial process is an intricate one, involving many steps and stages that can lead off into a variety of alternative paths. The complexity exists because of the many checks and balances built into the American system of justice to guarantee due process of law.

The criminal justice process begins with an *initial appearance* in one of the courts of limited jurisdiction. The accused is given a formal notification of the charges, his or her legal rights are explained, and bail or some other form of temporary release is determined.

Due to the complexity of criminal processing and the delays generated by overloaded court calendars, many jurisdictions have abolished the initial appearance and go directly to the next step in the process, the preliminary hearing. The major purpose of the *preliminary hearing* is to protect defendants from unwarranted prosecutions. Thus, the presiding judge seeks to

- determine whether a crime has been committed
- determine whether the evidence establishes probable cause to believe that the defendant committed it
- inquire into the reasonableness of the arrest and search
- determine appropriate bail or temporary release, if these issues have not already been addressed

Of considerable sociological interest during these early stages of court processing are bail and temporary release decisions. **Bail** is a form of security that guarantees that a defendant will appear in court when required to do so. Thus, bail is an assurance. In return for being released from jail, the accused guarantees his or her future appearance by posting funds or some other form of security with the court. When the defendant appears as required, the security is returned; if the defendant fails to appear, the security is forfeited.

One of the principal difficulties with bail is its relationship to financial well-being. It is difficult to argue that the bail system does not discriminate against the poor. The indigent defendant's loss of freedom, however, is often one of several problems. Pretrial detention prevents the accused from locating evidence and witnesses, and having complete access to counsel. It disrupts employment and family relations. It coerces defendants into plea negotiation as they seek to settle the matter more rapidly. And too, pretrial detainees are confined in city and county jails—the worst penal institutions in the country. Most of these facilities are overcrowded, unsanitary, and poorly equipped. Few have sufficient space for inmates to confer with their attorneys or visit with their families, and because jails are populated with many violent offenders, scores of detainees are beaten, raped, and murdered each year while awaiting trial. Finally, research has repeatedly demonstrated that detainees are more likely to be indicted, convicted, and sentenced harshly than are bailed defendants. As illustrated in

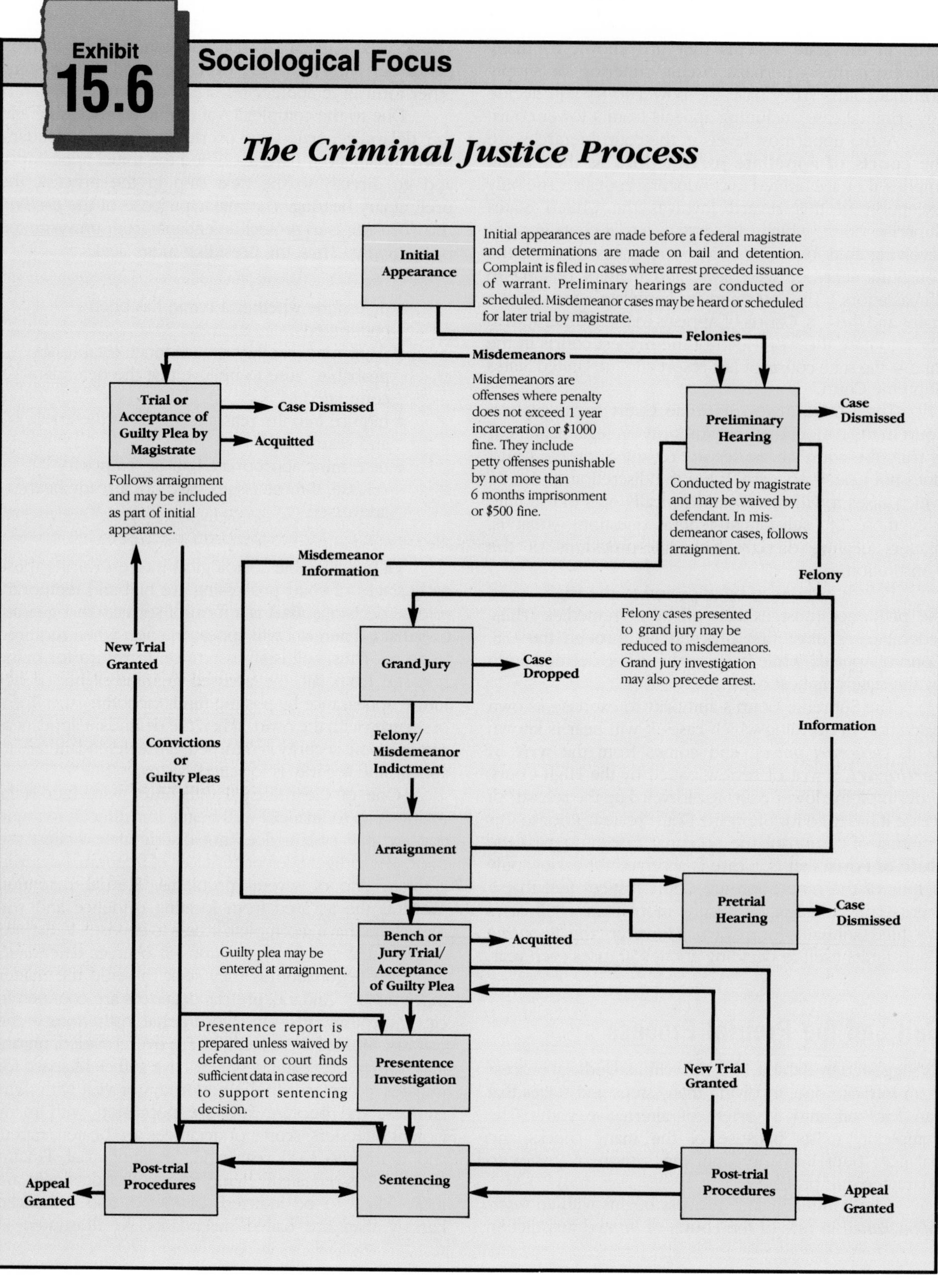
Exhibit 15.6
Sociological Focus
The Criminal Justice Process
Initial Appearance
Initial appearances are made before a federal magistrate and determinations are made on bail and detention. Complaint is filed in cases where arrest preceded issuance of warrant. Preliminary hearings are conducted or scheduled. Misdemeanor cases may be heard or scheduled for later trial by magistrate.
Felonies
Misdemeanors
Misdemeanors are offenses where penalty does not exceed 1 year incarceration or $1000 fine. They include petty offenses punishable by not more than 6 months imprisonment or $500 fine.
Trial or Acceptance of Guilty Plea by Magistrate
Case Dismissed
Acquitted
Follows arraignment and may be included as part of initial appearance.
Preliminary Hearing
Case Dismissed
Conducted by magistrate and may be waived by defendant. In misdemeanor cases, follows arraignment.
Misdemeanor Information
Felony
Felony cases presented to grand jury may be reduced to misdemeanors. Grand jury investigation may also precede arrest.
New Trial Granted
Grand Jury
Case Dropped
Information
Convictions or Guilty Pleas
Felony/ Misdemeanor Indictment
Arraignment
Pretrial Hearing
Case Dismissed
Bench or Jury Trial/ Acceptance of Guilty Plea
Acquitted
Guilty plea may be entered at arraignment.
Presentence report is prepared unless waived by defendant or court finds sufficient data in case record to support sentencing decision.
Presentence Investigation
New Trial Granted
Post-trial Procedures
Sentencing
Post-trial Procedures
Appeal Granted
Appeal Granted

Exhibit 15.7, for example, a study based on almost 3,500 cases from New York's Court of General Sessions highlighted the fact that when the nature of the offense, previous record, and other factors were roughly equivalent, detainees were more often convicted and sentenced to prison than were defendants released on bail.[26]

In recent years, increasing dissatisfactions with the bail system have led to experiments with a variety of release-on-recognizance programs in which defendants are released without any money bail requirement. Those arrested for murder, robbery, rape, and other serious felony offenses are routinely excluded from such release programs, and on the whole, follow-up studies have deemed these experimental programs successful.[27]

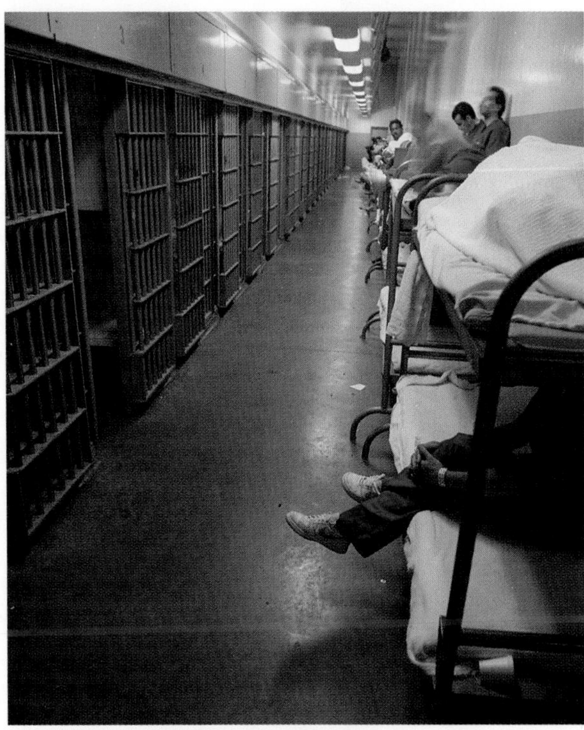

Overcrowded conditions are typical of local jails.

Plea Negotiation

Whether or not the initial court processing includes an initial appearance or preliminary hearing, the next step in the process is the formalization of charges. One mechanism used to accomplish this step is indictment by a grand jury. The *indictment* is a formal charging document based on the grand jury's determination that sufficient cause for a trial is evident. Grand juries are available in about half the states and in the federal system, but in only a limited number of jurisdictions are they the exclusive mechanism for sending a defendant to trial. The most common method for bringing formal charges is the *information,* a charging document drafted by a prosecutor and tested before a judge.

After the formal determination of charges is brought through the indictment or information, the actual trial procedures begin and the process shifts from the lower court to the court of original jurisdiction. At the *arraignment,* the accused is taken before a judge, the formal charges are read, and the defendant is asked to enter a plea.

Perhaps the most heavily debated issue associated with the arraignment phase of criminal justice processing is plea negotiation, better known as plea bargaining or "copping a plea." *Plea negotiation* takes place between the prosecutor and the defense counsel or the accused, and involves discussions that are directed toward reaching an agreement under which the defendant will enter a plea of guilty in exchange for some prosecutorial or judicial concession. These concessions are of four possible types:

1. The initial charges may be reduced to some lesser offense, thus insuring a reduction in the sentence imposed.
2. In instances of multiple criminal charges, the number of counts may be reduced.
3. A recommendation for leniency may be made by the prosecutor, thus reducing the potential sentence from incarceration to probation.
4. In instances where the charges involve a negative label, such as child molesting, the complaint may be altered to a less repugnant charge, such as assault.[28]

The widespread use of negotiated pleas of guilt comes about as a result of overcrowded case loads in American criminal courts, and at present, more than 90% of all criminal convictions are the result of negotiated pleas. Proponents of this bargaining process maintain that it is beneficial to both the accused and the state. *For the accused,* for example, plea negotiation:

- reduces the possibility of detention during extensive pretrial and trial processing
- extends the potential for a reduced sentence
- reduces the financial costs of legal representation

For the State, plea negotiation:

- reduces the overall costs of criminal prosecution

Exhibit 15.7

Research in Sociology

Conviction Rates and Prison Sentences for Released and Detained Criminal Defendants, New York Court of General Sessions

Offense	Convictions		Prison Sentences	
	Bailed Defendants	Jailed Defendants	Bailed Defendants	Jailed Defendants
Assault	23%	59%	58%	94%
Grand Larceny	43	72	48	93
Robbery	51	58	78	97
Dangerous Weapons	43	57	70	91
Narcotics	52	38	59	100
Sex Crimes	10	14	—	—
Others	30	78	56	88

Source: Daniel J. Freed and Patricia M. Wald, *Bail in the United States* (Washington, DC: National Conference on Bail and Criminal Justice, 1964), p. 47.

- improves the administrative efficiency of the courts by requiring that few cases go to a full and time-consuming trial
- enables the prosecution to devote more time and resources to cases of greater importance and seriousness

While plea negotiation is common, it is also highly controversial. First, it encourages an accused to waive the constitutional right to trial. Second, it enables the defendant to receive a generally less severe sentence. In the eyes of the public, the criminal has "beaten the system" and the judicial system becomes even further tarnished. Third, it sacrifices the legislative policies reflected in the criminal law for the sake of tactical accommodations between the prosecution and the defense. Fourth, it ignores the correctional needs of the bulk of offenders; in many instances the accused may ultimately plead guilty to a charge far removed from that of the original crime. Fifth, it raises the danger that an innocent person, fearing a determination of guilt and a harsh sentence if the case goes to trial, will accept conviction for a lesser crime if convinced that a guilty plea will result in lighter treatment. In this regard, one can only wonder about the guilt or innocence and state of mind of Harry Seigler, the defendant in a 1982 Virgina murder case who was caught up in the pitfalls of "to plea or not to plea" (see Exhibit 15.8).

The Criminal Trial

The trial process can be lengthy, beginning with a hearing on pretrial motions entered by the defense to suppress evidence (if Fourth Amendment violations are claimed), to relocate the trial to another city (if pretrial publicity suggests that a fully impartial trial is not possible locally), to discover the nature of the state's evidence, or to postpone the trial itself. The jury is then selected, and the trial proceeds.

The jury is of primary sociological significance throughout the trial; its composition can have a direct impact on the outcome of a case. The Sixth Amendment to the Constitution guarantees a trial by an impartial jury. "Impartial" is interpreted to mean a representative cross section of a community's citizens, yet research has conclusively demonstrated that juries are anything but representative, and for a variety of reasons.

Exhibit 15.8 Sociology in the Media

Gamble of a Lifetime

Harry Seigler, on trial in Richmond for robbery and murder, was sitting in a courthouse jail cell one afternoon last week, awaiting the jury's verdict. Charged with robbing a local insurance salesman last December and then slashing his throat, Seigler, 30, had pleaded not guilty.

The jurors had begun deliberating around 3:00 in the afternoon, and it was now around 6:30 P.M. Prosecutor Warren Von Schuch was worried. As he later put it, "The longer a [jury] panel is out, the worse shape we're in." And so he proposed a deal to Seigler's attorneys: their client would plead guilty to first-degree murder and robbery and receive a 60-year prison term, with 20 years suspended.

Perhaps Seigler, already convicted three times for robbery, calculated that if he was convicted for capital murder, he might be sent to the electric chair like Frank Coppola, a fellow Virginian executed two weeks ago. At 7:25 P.M., Seigler, ushered into the courtroom of Judge William E. Spain, accepted the deal. The jury, which had sent word of a verdict, was kept waiting while Spain approved the new plea. After Seigler was led away, the judge invited the jury into the room and informed them of the guilty plea. One juror slumped in a chair, while several others just moaned. What was the matter? The jurors had already reached a verdict: *not guilty*.

Seigler must serve his sentence and will not be eligible for parole for 12 years. Said Defense Attorney John Dodson: "I can't tell you how badly he feels."

SOURCE: *Time*, August 30, 1982, p. 22.

First, the master list from which jurors are drawn rarely reflects a representative cross section. In most jurisdictions the list is based on voter registration rolls because they do not systematically exclude people on the basis of age, sex, ethnicity, political affiliation, or socioeconomic status. However, studies have shown that the indigent, the young, the poorly educated, and members of minority groups often ignore the electoral process, or have been excluded from it by legal or extra-legal means.[29] Second, the structure of the jury selection process permits the elimination of certain jurors. On the one hand, *challenges for cause* permit both the defense and the prosecution to eliminate a potential juror for some sound legal reason. Membership in the Ku Klux Klan, for example, would certainly suggest a juror's inability to judge a black defendant fairly. On the other hand, *peremptory challenges* are objections to prospective jurors for which no explanation need be given. Although the number of peremptory challenges permitted the defense or prosecution is controlled by statute, such challenges still may create jury imbalance.

Peremptory challenges generally reflect the biases and strategies of an attorney to eliminate certain types of individuals from a jury, and to overload it with others. Therefore, some limits have been placed on their use. In 1986, for example, the Supreme Court of the United States held that peremptory challenges were not to be used solely on the basis of race.[30] It was the High Court's view that the exclusion from a jury of members of a defendant's own race violated the constitutional rights of both the defendant and the excluded jurors.

Although the Bill of Rights guarantees a trial by jury, an accused may prefer a *trial by judge*. In such a circumstance, those elements involving the jury are eliminated, and the judge makes the determination of innocence or guilt. Interestingly, however, research suggests that defendants may be better off with juries than judges. In one analysis of over 3,000 cases, for example, investigators compared actual jury verdicts with

SOCIAL INDICATOR

Women and Juries

Until it was struck down by the United States Supreme Court in 1975, a Louisiana law systematically barred women from juries, unless they specifically requested participation, *in writing*. See Taylor v. Louisiana, 419 U.S. 522 (1975).

the hypothetical verdicts of the judges involved in the cases. Although the judges and juries agreed in some 80% of the cases, when they did not agree, the juries tended to be more lenient than the judges.[31]

The Right to Counsel

Despite the unambiguous language of the Sixth Amendment, for almost a century and a half after the framing of the Constitution, only persons charged with federal crimes punishable by death were guaranteed the right to counsel. The right of all other defendants—both state and federal—to have the help of an attorney typically depended on their ability to retain their own defense lawyer. If they were indigent, and could not afford their own attorney, they went to trial unrepresented. Thus, the poor were clearly at a disadvantage in the courts. During the 1930s, the Supreme Court extended the Sixth Amendment right to all federal defendants,[32] and to certain state defendants in capital cases (see Exhibit 15.9).[33] The major broadening of this right did not occur, however, until 1963, in *Gideon v. Wainwright*.[34]

Gideon v. Wainwright

Gideon v. Wainwright is among the most significant cases decided by the Supreme Court in its 200-plus year history. This case not only extended the right to counsel to all state defendants facing felony trials, but it also dramatically demonstrated that even the least influential of citizens could persuade those in charge to reexamine the basic premises of justice in America.

Clarence Earl Gideon was charged with breaking and entering with intent to commit a misdemeanor in Panama City, Florida—a charge of petty larceny, which under Florida law is treated as a felony. The year was 1961, and Gideon was a 51-year-old white man who had been in and out of prisons much of his life. He was not a violent man, but he had served time for four previous felonies. He was a drifter who never seemed to settle down, making his way through life gambling and occasionally stealing. Those who knew him, even the officers who had arrested him, considered Gideon a harmless and rather likeable person, but one tossed aside by life.[35]

On August 4, 1961, when Clarence Earl Gideon was taken before Judge Robert L. McCrary, Jr., in the Bay County, Florida, Circuit Court for trial, he stated that he was not ready. Gideon said to Judge McCrary: "The United States Supreme Court says I am entitled to be represented by counsel." Gideon, of course, was wrong, for the High Court had *not* said that he was entitled to counsel. Some 20 years earlier, the Supreme Court had specifically stated quite the opposite.[36]

Judge McCrary apologetically informed Gideon of his mistake, and put to trial before a jury, Gideon conducted his own defense. He made an opening statement to the jury, cross-examined the State's witnesses, presented witnesses in his own defense, declined to testify himself, and made a short closing statement emphasizing his innocence. But Gideon's defense was ineffective; he was found guilty and sentenced to serve five years in state prison.

In the morning mail on January 8, 1962, the Supreme Court of the United States received a large envelope from Clarence Earl Gideon, Prisoner No. 003826, Florida State Prison. The envelope contained Gideon's petition. It was prepared in pencil, with carefully formed printing on lined sheets provided by the Florida prison.

Certiorari was granted to Gideon's petition. The Supreme Court assigned Washington, D.C., attorney Abe Fortas, who was later appointed to the Supreme Court by President Lyndon B. Johnson, to argue Gideon's claim. Fortas contended that counsel in a criminal trial is a fundamental right of due process enforced on the states by the Fourteenth Amendment's "equal protection" clause. In the Court's unanimous decision in favor of Gideon, Justice Hugo Black wrote: "Any person hailed into court, who is too poor to hire a lawyer, cannot be assured a fair trial unless counsel is provided for him. This seems to us an obvious truth."[37]

This ruling of the Supreme Court on March 18, 1963, after Gideon had served almost two years in prison, entitled him to a new trial. He was immediately retried in the same court and by the same judge as in the initial trial, but this time he was represented by counsel and was acquitted. Gideon was set free, as were thousands of other prisoners in Florida and elsewhere because they had been tried without an attorney.[38]

In extending the right to counsel to all state defendants facing felony trials, *Gideon* also represented the beginning of a trend that ultimately expanded Sixth Amendment rights to most phases of criminal justice proceedings, including misdemeanor trials for offenses serious enough to warrant a jail sentence. The decision in *Escobedo v. Illinois,* examined earlier, was part of this trend.

"The fit's O.K., but does it say 'Not guilty'?"

Drawing by Schoenbaum © 1988 *The New Yorker Magazine,* Inc.

Sentencing

What should be done with criminal offenders after they have been convicted? The answer is a difficult one for a sentencing judge, because the administration of justice has a number of conflicting goals: the rehabilitation of offenders, the discouragement of potential lawbreakers, the isolation of dangerous criminals who pose a threat to community safety, the condemnation of extralegal conduct, and the reinforcement of accepted social norms. The burden on the judge is to choose one or more of these goals.

Sentencing Objectives

Throughout American history, no single and clearly defined rationale has been developed to serve as a guiding principle in sentencing. The public has alternated between revulsion at inhumane sentencing practices and prison conditions on the one hand, and overly compassionate treatment on the other. While the former is denounced as "barbaric" and "uncivilized" and the latter is termed "coddling," the fate of convicted offenders has repeatedly shifted according to prevailing national values and current perceptions of danger and the fear of crime. As a result, sentencing objectives are based on at least four competing philosophies: retribution, isolation, deterrence, and rehabilitation.

Punishment takes many forms. Here, a DWI work force cleans litter along the highway.

Retribution is societal vengeance. It is concerned exclusively with making the punishment fit the crime, and is grounded on the notion that criminals are wicked, evil people who are responsible for their actions and deserve to be punished.

Isolation is the removal of dangerous persons from the community. Its object is community protection rather than revenge. By removing offenders from society through exile, imprisonment, or execution, the community is protected against future criminal acts.

Deterrence refers to the prevention of criminal acts by making examples of persons convicted of crimes. This notion is best illustrated in the words of an eighteenth-century judge who reportedly stated to an offender at sentencing: "You are to be hanged not because you have stolen a sheep, but in order that others may not steal sheep."[39]

Rehabilitation rests on the premise that persons who commit crimes have identifiable reasons for doing so, and that these can be discovered, addressed, and altered. The aim is to change behavior and reintegrate

Exhibit 15.9 Case Study

The Scottsboro Boys

On March 25, 1931, a group of nine young black men and boys, ranging in age from 13 to 21 years, were riding in an open gondola car aboard a freight train as it made its way across the state of Alabama. Also aboard the train were seven other boys and two young women, all of whom were white. At some point during the journey, and for whatever reason, a fight broke out between the two groups of men, during the course of which a number of the white men were thrown from the train. A message was relayed ahead reporting the incident and requesting that all of the blacks be taken from the train. As it pulled into the station at Paint Rock, a small town in northeast Alabama, a sheriff's posse was waiting. The two white women, Victoria Price and Ruby Bates, claimed that they had been raped by a number of the black youths, and all nine were immediately taken into custody. Amidst the hostility of a growing crowd, the youths were taken some 20 miles east and placed under military guard in the local jail at Scottsboro, the seat of Jackson County, Alabama.

The Scottsboro boys and their attorney, Samuel Leibowitz, are flanked by two National Guardsmen in 1932.

The Scottsboro boys, as they became known to history, were indicted on March 31, arraigned on the same day, and entered pleas of not guilty. Until the morning of the trial, no lawyer had been

the lawbreaker into the wider society as a productive citizen.

Disparities in Sentencing

Every state has sentencing guidelines that are established by statute. These reflect the range of possible alternatives available to a judge, demonstrating that considerable discretion rests in the hands of the court. As a result, the sanctions imposed can vary widely according to the jurisdiction, the community, and the punishment philosophy of a particular judge. Moreover, the dynamics of plea negotiation enable various defendants accused of the same crime to be convicted and sentenced differentially. These problems exist both within an individual court and across jurisdictions, because sentencing statutes can differ drastically from one state to the next.

One could argue that in apparent cases of sentencing disparity, judges are dealing with crimes of varying degrees of seriousness and with offenders who are deserving of more or less punishment. But some data contradict such an argument. In one study, conducted by the Federal Judicial Center during 1974, each of 50 federal judges from the same geographical circuit were given 20 identical presentence reports, drawn from actual cases, and asked to render sentences. The outcome clearly indicated disparate sentencing. In one case of a defendant convicted of extortion, the sentences ranged designated by name to represent any of the defendants. On April 6, a visiting lawyer from Tennessee expressed an interest in assisting any counsel the court might designate for the defense. A local Scottsboro attorney then offered to represent the defendants, whereupon the proceedings immediately began.

Of the nine youths arrested, one had not been indicted because he was only 13 years old. The remaining eight were divided into three groups for separate trials, each lasting a single day. Medical and other evidence was presented that established that the two women, who were alleged to be prostitutes, had not been raped. Nevertheless, the eight Scottsboro boys were convicted of rape. Under the existing Alabama statute, the punishment for rape was to be fixed by the jury at anywhere from ten years' imprisonment to death. The jury chose death for all eight defendants.

The court overruled all motions for new trials and sentenced the defendants in accordance with the jury's recommendation. Subsequently, the Supreme Court of Alabama reversed the conviction of one defendant, but affirmed the convictions of the remaining seven. Upon appeal to the United States Supreme Court, the Scottsboro defendants, in *Powell v. Alabama,* alleged a denial of Fourteenth Amendment due process and equal protection of the laws because (1) they had not been given a fair trial, (2) they had been denied the right to counsel, and (3) they had been denied a trial by an impartial jury because blacks were systematically excluded from jury service.

In reversing the rape convictions, the Supreme Court observed that Powell and his codefendants were denied their right to the effective assistance of legal counsel and, in turn, that this denial contravened the due process clause of the Fourteenth Amendment. In the Court's 7–2 majority opinion, Justice George Sutherland noted: "It is hardly necessary to say that . . . a defendant should be afforded a fair opportunity to secure counsel of his own choice. Not only was that not done here, but such designation of counsel as was attempted was either so indefinite or so close upon the trial as to amount to a denial of effective and substantial aid in that regard."

The decision in *Powell* was a very narrow ruling, for it limited its application to defendants who were indigent, accused of a crime for which the death penalty could be imposed, and incapable of defending themselves because of low intelligence, illiteracy, or some similar handicap. Nevertheless, *Powell* was the first in a series of Supreme Court cases that would extend the Sixth Amendment right to counsel.

SOURCES: Dan T. Carter, *Scottsboro: A Tragedy of the American South* (New York: Oxford University Press, 1969), Robert Leibowitz, *The Defender: The Life and Career of Samuel S. Leibowitz, 1893–1933* (Englewood Cliffs, NJ: Prentice-Hall, 1981), pp. 186–249; Powell v. Alabama, 287 U.S. 45 (1932).

from 3 years' imprisonment to 20 years plus a $65,000 fine.[40] More recently, 41 New York judges drawn from across the state participated in a similar experiment, and the results further confirmed disparate sentencing practices (see Exhibit 15.10).

The Death Penalty

For the greater part of U.S. history, the death penalty was used as a punishment for crime, with little thought as to its legitimacy or justification. It was simply accepted as an efficient mechanism for dealing with criminal offenders. When the framers of the Constitution incorporated the Eighth Amendment ban against cruel and unusual punishment, the death penalty per se was apparently not an issue. From the earliest days of the colonial experience, capital punishment was considered neither "cruel" nor "unusual."

Death and the Supreme Court

The Supreme Court's position on the death penalty and its relation to the Eighth Amendment has remained flexible. Although the Court has supported the general constitutionality of capital punishment, it has often taken a dim view of other issues related to this extreme penalty. The most significant case in this regard—*Furman v. Georgia*[41]—occurred in 1972. The decision in *Furman*

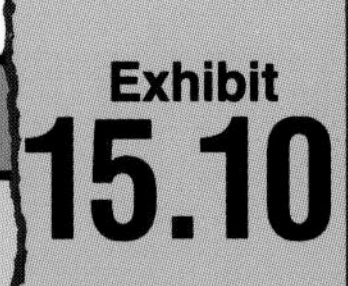

Research in Sociology

Disparate Sentencing

Forty-one New York judges from across the state were asked to review files on actual cases and then indicate the sentences they would impose.

In this case, an elderly man was robbed at gunpoint by a heroin addict. The defendant was convicted of first degree robbery. He was unemployed, lived with his pregnant wife and had a minor criminal record. Actual Sentence: 0–5 years. Each bar represents a judge's sentence.

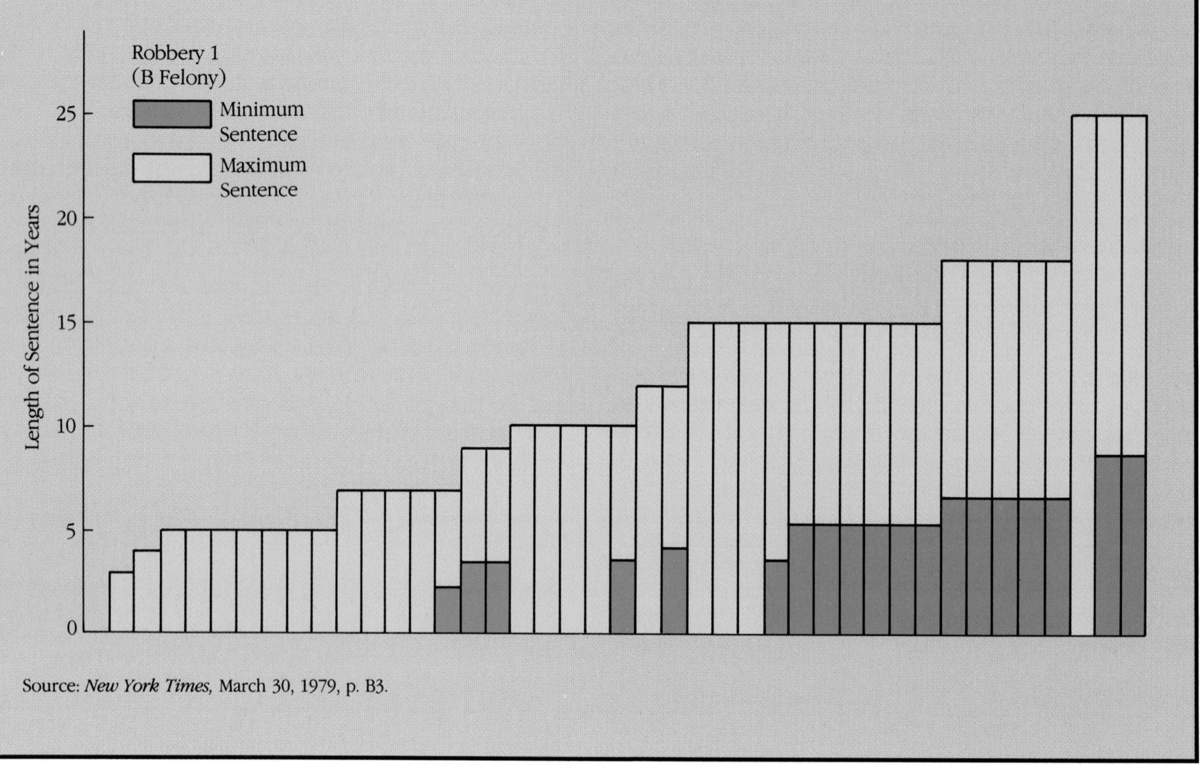

Source: *New York Times,* March 30, 1979, p. B3.

attacked all state and federal death penalty statutes, holding that they were too arbitrary, capricious, and discriminatory to withstand constitutional scrutiny. The Court declared all existing death penalty laws to be violations of the Eighth Amendment because they offered judges and juries no standards and guidelines to consider in deciding between life and death. Subsequent to *Furman,* capital statutes were rewritten to conform with Supreme Court guidelines.

A second major decision came with *Coker v. Georgia*[42] in 1977, when the court declared that death was an excessive penalty for the crime of rape. The ruling in *Coker* was long overdue. Research has demonstrated that for well over a century, capital punishment had been an instrument of racial discrimination in the United States, particularly with respect to sentences for rape.[43] More specifically, from 1864 to 1982, a total of 5,643 executions were imposed under state authority and in the District of Columbia. Of these, 50% were of non-whites, in a country that is predominantly white. Moreover, of the 560 executions for rape, only 10% were of whites.[44]

The Death Penalty Debate

Largely a matter of personal opinion and philosophy, the death penalty debate revolves around a variety of issues. Proponents of the *economic argument* hold that execu-

SOCIAL INDICATOR

Proportion of U.S. Population in Favor of the Death Penalty

1975	64.4%
1980	71.6
1988	76.3

Source: National Opinion Research Center, 1988.

tion is far less expensive than maintaining a prisoner behind bars for a lifetime. Advocates of the *retribution argument* assert that the kidnapper, the murderer, and the rapist, as vile and despicable human beings, deserve to die. Adherents to the *community protection argument* maintain that the finality of execution is necessary to keep the murderer from further ravaging society. Those who support the *deterrence argument* hold that capital punishment not only prevents the offender from committing additional crimes, but deters others as well. Conversely, individuals who adhere to the *irreversibility argument* contend that the possibility always exists that an innocent person may be put to death. People who favor the *discrimination argument* contend that the death penalty is a lottery system, with the odds stacked heavily against those less capable of defending themselves. And finally, supporters of the *cruel and unusual punishment argument* hold that, despite the Supreme Court's rulings to the contrary, the death penalty is a violation of the Eighth Amendment.[45]

Those who feel that the death penalty should be the final resort for truly evil crime seem to be in the majority in the United States today. By contrast, however, the United States is one of the few industrialized nations outside of the Communist bloc that still executes people. England banned the death penalty in 1965, joining such nations as West Germany, Israel, and Italy, which changed their laws in the 1940s and 1950s. Canada followed suit in 1976 and France in 1981, leaving the United States and Turkey as the only NATO nations still permitting executions.

SOCIAL INDICATOR

Persons under Sentence of Death, and Persons Executed, 1955–1989

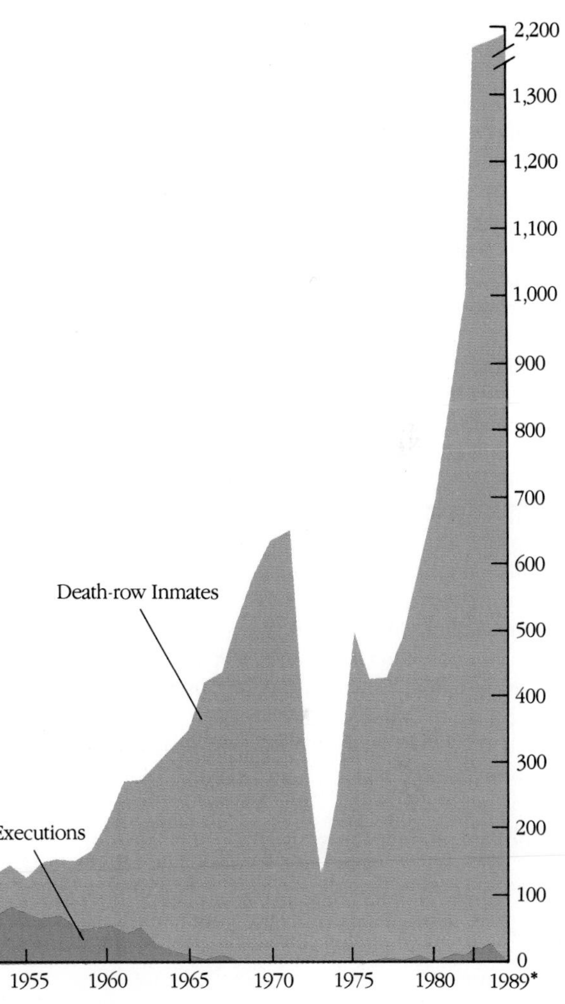

*Through mid-May.

CORRECTIONS

Criminal sanctions are numerous. Convicted offenders may be fined, placed on probation, ordered to pay restitution, and sometimes subjected to a combination of the three. Others may be sentenced to a short period of incarceration in a local jail. If they have been confined since arrest because of an inability to make bail and their offense is slight, perhaps they will be sentenced to "time served." For the more serious offenders, particularly those convicted of violent crimes, prison is the usual sentence.

Prisons

The first prison in the American prison system began with the solitary confinement of hardened offenders in Philadelphia's Walnut Street Jail in 1776. "Corrections," during these first days of the Republic, was based on the idea that **recidivism,** the repetition of criminal behavior, could be stopped and the offender reformed by preventing the evil associations that characteristically developed in crowded jail cells. It was believed that confinement in an isolated cell—a confinement procedure known as the **separate system**—would give the inmate the opportunity to contemplate the evils of his past life, thereby leading him to resolve "in the spiritual presence of his Maker" to reform his future conduct.[46] From this idea of being penitent, prisons became known as penitentiaries.

At New York State's Auburn Prison in 1823, the **silent system** emerged as a more humane and economically sound penitentiary program. Inmates were put to work in groups during the day under a rigid rule of absolute silence at all times; solitary confinement was used only at night. Hard labor was considered essential to the reformation of character. Perpetual silence was seen as mandatory when inmates were near each other in order to avoid their corruption of one another and to reduce any opportunities for the hatching of plots for insurrection, riot, or escape.

By the early years of the twentieth century, the American prison system had evolved into a collection of maximum security institutions. Many reflected the architecture of medieval dungeons and Gothic castles. They were walled fortresses of iron and stone, operated on the principle of mass congregate incarceration with rigid discipline and security. The prisons that are being built today are of more modern design, but many of the monuments of the past still stand and house inmates. Auburn Prison (now known as Auburn Correctional Facility) will be 167 years old in 1990. Sing Sing, built in 1825 and renamed Ossining Correctional Facility in 1970, is undoubtedly the most famous prison in the world. Located on the banks of the Hudson River in New York state it is the origin of such terms as "the big house" and "up the river."

Communication between inmates in segregation cells, where the most violent offenders are held, is severely restricted.

Prisons as Total Institutions

All prisons are what sociologist Erving Goffman referred to as total institutions. As noted earlier in Chapter 6, total institutions are places that furnish barriers to social interchange with the rest of society. In total institutions, large groups of people live together, day and night, in a fixed area, operating under a tightly scheduled sequence of activities imposed by a central authority. Everyone is either a "subject" or a "manager." Subjects are the large class of individuals who have restricted contact with the world outside. Managers, who are socially integrated into the world outside the walls, are the small class that supervises the subjects. In total institutions, the social distance is great, and communication is tightly restricted. Each group conceives of the members of the other in terms of narrow hostile stereotypes, resulting in the development of alternate social and cultural worlds that remain in continuous conflict with one another. In total institutions, an elaborate system of formal rules is structured to achieve the organization's official aim and to maintain the distance between subjects and managers.[47] At the close of 1987, nearly 600,000 persons were being housed in the total institution of the American prison (see Exhibit 15.11).

Institutional Routines

The American penitentiary as a contemporary total institution is designed to achieve all of the competing sentencing philosophies of retribution, isolation, deterrence, and rehabilitation.

A prison sentence carries with it a considerable measure of retribution. Inmates experience a severe loss of freedom and a major portion of their time is spent confined to small cells. Outside of their cells, their movements are restricted to certain sections of the prison compound. They are permitted few personal possessions and are subject to strict discipline.

Isolation is achieved through the placement of inmates in a controlled environment, with little chance of escape. New York's Green Haven epitomizes, if not exaggerates, the mechanisms of isolation. Built as a military prison and acquired by New York State in 1949, Green Haven was designed to be an escape-proof institution. Its outer wall of reinforced concrete is 30 feet

Exhibit 15.11 Sociological Focus

Number of Sentenced State and Federal Prisoners, 1930–1987

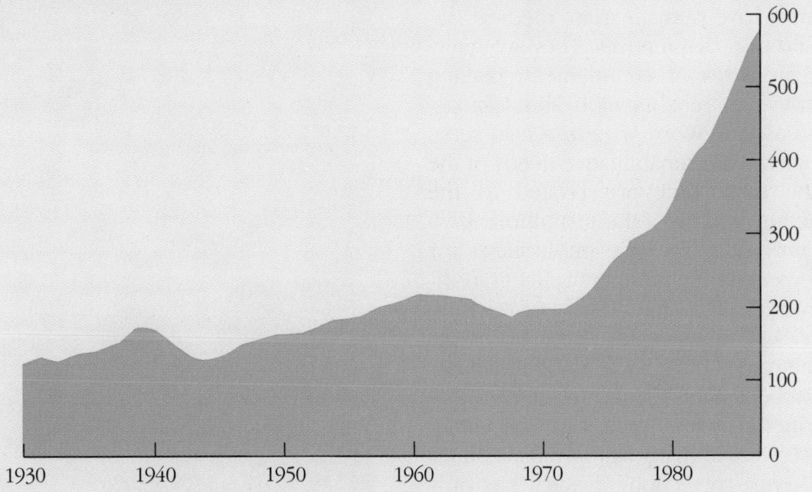

600
500
400
300
200
100
0
Thousands
1930
1940
1950
1960
1970
1980

SOCIAL INDICATOR

Women Behind Bars, 1976–1987

30,000
28,000
26,000
24,000
22,000
20,000
18,000
16,000
14,000
12,000
10,000
1976
1978
1980
1982
1984
1986

Typical women in prison

- 54% white; 46% nonwhite
- Between the ages of 25 and 34
- 75% not married
- 51% committed property crimes; 40% crimes against persons
- Likely to have had children
- Unemployed at time of arrest
- Women make up 4.9% of the U.S. prison population

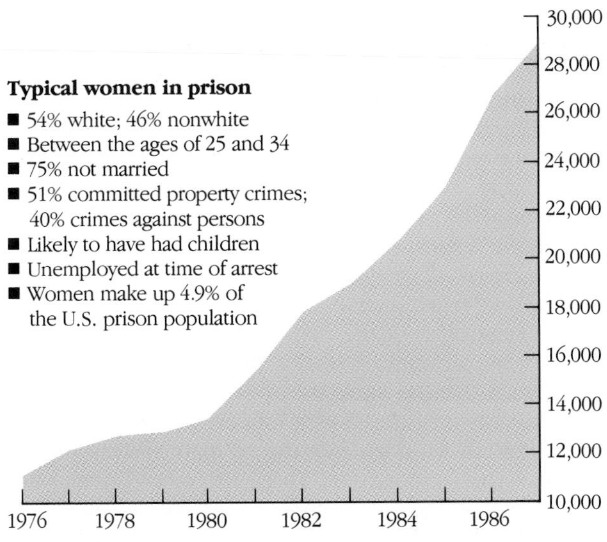

high, almost 3 feet thick, and reportedly extends 30 feet below the ground. Its twelve towers, reaching 40 feet above the ground, are evenly positioned along the mile-long wall around the perimeter of the prison. Tower guards, armed with an array of shotguns, rifles, and tear-gas guns, have a sweeping view of both sides of the wall. The towers also provide focused surveillance of "no man's land," a 100-foot-wide stretch of open space between the inner and outer walls of the prison, across which no one can pass unobserved. No prisoner has ever managed to escape over the wall at Green Haven.[48]

For some, the prison experience does indeed suggest that "crime does not pay"; thus, the deterrence goal of sentencing is achieved. Yet for many, the deterrent value of correctional placement can be called into question. The high recidivism rates among many ex-inmates, combined with the high rates of crime in all segments of the social order imply that prisons are not doing well at "making examples" of persons convicted of crimes.

The rehabilitation philosophy of sentencing has been readily operationalized in many correctional institutions. A considerable variety of institutional programs can have an impact, either directly or indirectly, on offender rehabilitation and the successful reintegration of prisoners into the free community. *Treatment programs* focus primarily on behavioral change. Programs of this type attempt to remove what are often considered "defects" in an inmate's socialization and psychological development—"defects" that have been assigned responsibility for lawbreaking behaviors. *Academic and vocational programs* serve to provide inmates with the skills necessary for adequate employment after release. *Recreational programs* have humanitarian, medical, social-psychological, and custodial motives. They are structured to ease the pressures of confinement, making inmates more receptive to rehabilitation and less depressed, hostile, and asocial. *Work programs* also serve many of the humanitarian and rehabilitative needs of the offender, yet at the same time are related to the successful economic functioning of the institution. *Medical and religious programs* too have implications for institutional management and community reintegration.

Despite its practical goals, the efficacy of rehabilitation has been seriously questioned. Some observers suggest that since the causes of crime are not altogether understood, efforts at behavioral change are of questionable value. Other critics maintain that since the availability of rehabilitative services in many institutions is either minimal or nonexistent, "correction" as such has only limited practical value. Still a third group espouses a "nothing works" philosophy, arguing that rehabilitation has not demonstrated and never will demonstrate its ability to prevent or reduce crime.[49]

A soldier in riot gear stands over one of the casualties from the New Mexico State Penitentiary riot in 1980.

The Inmate Social System

The internal order of the prison is maintained by strictly controlling the inmates and regimenting every aspect of their lives. In addition to their loss of freedom and basic liberties, goods and services, heterosexual relationships, and autonomy, they are deprived of personal identity. Upon entering prison, inmates are stripped of their clothing and most of their personal possessions; they are examined, inspected, weighed, documented, and given a number. Thus, the prison becomes painful, both physically and psychologically, and as noted earlier in Chapter 4 (Exhibit 4.5), inmates respond by becoming part of the social system of the penitentiary.

Exposure to the social system of the prison community is almost immediate. All new inmates quickly become aware of the norms and values shared by their fellow captives. The internalization of these prison norms and values is known as **prisonization.** More specifically, prisonization refers to the socializing process by which the inmate learns the rules and regulations of the institution and the informal rules, values, customs, and general culture of the penitentiary.[50] Not all prisoners are fully socialized into the inmate social system. Prisonization is affected by an inmate's priority, duration, frequency, and intensity of contact with the prison subculture and the values of varying segments of the convict population. However, it is generally agreed that once the norms and values of the prison community are internalized, the prisonized inmate becomes immune, for the most part, to the influences of conventional value systems. This process suggests that prisonization transforms the novitiate inmate into a fully accredited convict; it is a *criminalization* process that militates against any chances of rehabilitation or reform.

Regardless of the degree of prisonization experienced by an inmate, every penitentiary—as a total institution—has a subculture. Every prison subculture has its system of norms that influence prisoners' behavior, typically to a greater extent than the institution's formally prescribed rules. These subcultural rules, often referred to as the inmate code, have remained essentially unchanged for well over a century, and include such proscriptions as "never rat on another con," "don't steal from cons or welsh on debts or break your word," "don't give respect to guards or the world for which they stand."[51]

The norms of the inmate social system—the inmate code—are informal, unwritten rules, but their violation can evoke sanctions from fellow inmates that range from ostracism to physical violence, rape, torture, and even death. Such was the case when New Mexico State Penitentiary distinguished itself for having the most gruesome riot in U.S. history. During the course of the uprising that took place on February 1, 1980, a seven-man inmate execution squad exacted revenge on convict informers. One prisoner was beheaded; another was found with a metal rod driven through his head; several had their arms and legs cut off or their eyes gouged out; and still others were charred with blowtorches or beaten beyond recognition. In all, 33 prisoners were brutally murdered during this one episode.[52]

Community-based Correction

Most Americans consider imprisonment to be the most typical sentence given to serious felony offenders. However, as noted earlier in this section, sentencing judges have a variety of alternatives, and the *criminal justice funnel* (see Exhibit 15.12) suggests that proportionately few offenders actually go to prison.

At the top of the funnel is the "dark figure" of crime, those many millions of offenses which, for one reason or another, never come to the attention of the police. At the next level, for each 1 million Part I offenses (the serious felonies—homicide, forcible rape, robbery, aggravated assault, larceny-theft, burglary, motor vehicle theft, and arson) that *do* become known to law enforcement authorities, some 26% (about 260,000) result in arrest. Of those persons arrested, more than a third are juveniles who, as minors, are diverted out of the criminal process into the juvenile justice system. This diversion leaves 190,000 suspects available for prosecution. Yet of these, only about 63,000 appear before the courts on formal felony complaints. The others are released due to decisions *not* to prosecute, usually because of a lack of evidence or some illegal arrest or interrogation practice on the part of the police, or because they plea negotiate their charges down to the misdemeanor level. Of these 63,000 felony prosecutions, 57,000 are convicted and sentenced, and 22,000 actually go to prison. Thus, of every 63,000 felony prosecutions, only about one-third result in prison terms. What happens to the rest? Some are acquitted, but most are channeled into some form of community-based correctional program.

Community-based correction includes activities and programs within the community that have effective ties with the local environment. These ties are generally of a rehabilitative rather than a punitive nature, and can include arrangements for employment, education, social activities, and health care. The most typical forms of community-based correctional services include pretrial diversion projects and probation. As with all types of community-based correction, it is generally agreed that the rehabilitation of offenders is more realistically possible in the natural environment of the free community than behind prison walls.

Criminal Justice Diversion

Criminal justice diversion refers to the removal of offenders from direct contact with the criminal law at any stage of the police and court processes. It implies the formal halting or suspending of traditional criminal proceedings against persons who have violated the law, in favor of processing them through some *noncriminal* disposition or means. Thus, through diversion, the defendant does not become convicted of a crime.

The arguments in favor of diversion are numerous. Many observers feel that diversion programs can reduce court backlog, provide early treatment intervention before the offender develops a full-fledged criminal career, reduce the costs of criminal processing, and enhance the offender's chances of community reintegration. More importantly, it has been the conclusion of many social scientists that the criminal justice process, which was designed to protect society from criminals, often contributes to the very behavior it is trying to eliminate. This typically is accomplished by sending novice offenders to prison, where they come into direct contact with experienced and hardened criminals, and are thus socialized into a wide variety of criminal roles.[53]

Formal diversion programs began in 1914 at the Chicago Boys' Court.[54] The Boys' Court system placed young defendants under the authority and supervision of a local community agency. After a time, the court requested a report on the defendant's community activities and adjustment, and if it was favorable, the defendant would be discharged from court without a criminal record.

Primarily as a result of massive federal funding allocated by the United States Department of Justice for the prevention and reduction of crime, diversion programs of many types emerged and expanded throughout the country during the 1970s. Most were designed for youths, and for special offenders whose crimes were deemed to be related to problem drinking or drug use.

Probation

Probation is a sentence. It is a sentence of conditional release to the community. While not involving confinement, probation imposes conditions and retains authority

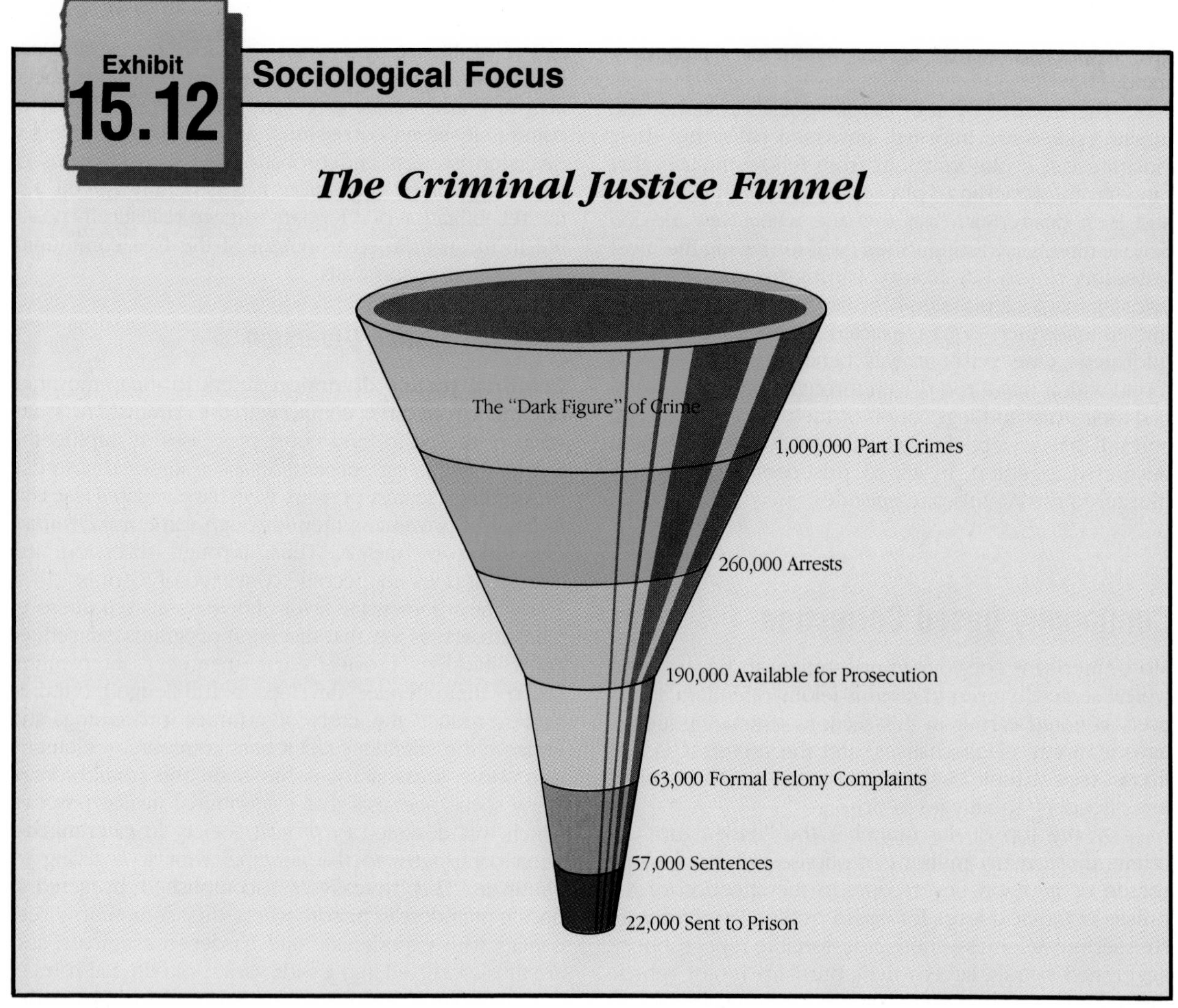

in the sentencing court. Should the probationer fail to live up to the conditions and requirements imposed, he or she can be brought back to court for resentencing.

The philosophical issue underlying the use of probation is that many offenders are not dangerous and represent little, if any, menace to society. It has been argued that when defendants are institutionalized, the prison community becomes their new reference point. They are forced into contact with hard-core criminals, the prison experience generates embitterment and hostility, and the "ex-con" label becomes a stigma that impedes social adjustment. Probation, on the other hand, provides a more therapeutic alternative. The term comes from the Latin *probare,* meaning to test or prove, and probationers are given the opportunity to demonstrate that if given a second chance, they will adopt more socially acceptable behavior patterns.[55]

The probation philosophy also includes elements of community protection and offender rehabilitation. Probationers are supervised by agents of the court or probation agency. These trained personnel perform dual roles. They are present to insure that the conditions of probation are fulfilled and to provide counseling and assistance in community reintegration.

While these are the ideal philosophical underpinnings of probation, several more pragmatic issues have developed in connection with its widespread use as an alternative to incarceration. First, American prisons have become painfully overcrowded in recent years, and the high costs of new construction have made probation an economically more viable alternative. Second, the probation process is cheaper than the prison process. In Texas, for example, the costs of supervising a probationer are less than one-tenth the revenues needed to house an offender in a penitentiary.[56] Third, within some sectors of the criminal justice community, imprisonment is being viewed more and more as cruel and unusual punishment. Prisons are dangerous places to live. Inmates may be physically, sexually, or emotionally victimized. Probation, in this context, is considered to be the more humane avenue of correctional intervention.

The probation process begins with a **presentence investigation,** an investigation into the background and characteristics of the defendant, which serves as a guide for sentencing. Should the judge deem probation appropriate, the defendant is conditionally released into the community.

As part of the probation agreement, the probationer is required to abide by a variety of regulations and conditions. These conditions exhort the probationer to live a law-abiding and productive life, to work, to support his or her dependants, to maintain contact with the supervising probation officer, and to remain within the jurisdiction of the court. Violation of these conditions can result in revocation of probation, followed by a sentence of imprisonment.

At least in theory, the probation process incorporates a casework approach to treatment. During the probationer's initial interview with his or her probation officer, an evaluation is made to determine what type of treatment supervision is most appropriate. A treatment schedule is then designed to allow the probationer to make a reasonable community adjustment. In practice, however, few probationers actually receive such individualized treatment and supervision. Many probation officers do not possess the skills, training, and experience appropriate for the tasks they are called upon to perform. Furthermore, while the case loads in some agencies may be as small as a dozen probationers per officer, in many others these loads are as high as two and three hundred. Under such circumstances, even the most proficient and dedicated probation officer does not possess the time to provide worthwhile individualized treatment.

Parole

Unlike criminal justice diversion and probation, which provide community services and supervision in lieu of imprisonment, parole is a form of community-based correction that occurs *after* a portion of a prison term has been served. From the French meaning "word of honor," **parole** is conditional release from a correctional institution after serving part of the sentence, based on the parolee's maintaining good behavior and remaining in the custody and under the guidance of the institution or some other agency approved by the state until a final discharge is granted.[57]

For almost a century, parole has been an established part of American correctional practice and theory. It serves the ostensible purposes of (1) ensuring that imprisonment is tailored to the needs of the inmate, (2) ameliorating the harshness of long prison sentences, and (3) hastening the offender's reintegration into the community when it appears that he or she is able to function as a law-abiding citizen. In addition, it fulfills the more subtle functions of (4) alleviating the overcrowded conditions of correctional institutions, and (5) assisting in the maintenance of prison social control through the threat of parole denial for instances of misbehavior.

To understand the dynamics of parole, one must first contemplate the structure of indeterminate sentencing laws. The **indeterminate sentence,** the most common sentence handed down by the courts, has a fixed minimum and a fixed maximum term for incarceration, rather than a definite period of time. Sentences of 1–5 years and 10–20 years are indeterminate sentences. Inmates are generally eligible for a parole hearing after completion of the minimum sentence or some portion of the maximum sentence, as specified by state parole eligibility laws.

When an inmate becomes eligible for parole he or she receives a hearing before the parole board. If the board's decision is to release the inmate, the supervision process is similar to that of probation. The parolee lives in the community under the supervision and service of a parole officer, subject to a series of conditions. The violation of these conditions can result in return to prison for all or part of the remainder of the sentence, at the parole board's discretion.

CRIMINAL JUSTICE AS A "SYSTEM"

In 1967, the President's Commission on Law Enforcement and Administration of Justice, appointed by Lyndon B. Johnson to examine the nature and structure of crime and the administration of justice in the United States, described the criminal justice process as a "system"—some orderly flow of managerial decision making that begins with the investigation of a criminal offense and ends with a correctional placement.[58] However, the notion of criminal justice operating as an orderly "system" is essentially a myth. The unity of purpose and organized interrelationships among the police, the courts, and corrections are beset with inefficiency, fallout, and failure. In most jurisdictions, the courts are dumping grounds for arrested offenders; correctional systems serve as holding pens for convicted offenders;

and the free community—under the protection and patrol of law enforcement—is the reentry point for those released from corrections. Rarely does each segment of the criminal justice "system" operate with a full awareness of the long-term cyclical implications of its activities.

Yet on the other hand, the justice system generally does an effective job of separating the innocent from the guilty. Although most of those guilty of crimes are never arrested, the perpetrators of the majority of the most serious ones are eventually caught by the police. Moreover, most of those coming to the courts who should be convicted *are* convicted, and most of those who should be punished *are* punished. Most importantly, under the adversary system of justice based on "due process of law"—where the process of justice typically does function as an "ideal system"—it is only on the most rare of occasions that the innocent are punished for the crimes of others.

CRIMINAL JUSTICE AND APPLIED SOCIOLOGY

The criminal justice process is a fertile area for sociological applications—for designing and testing new programs, for evaluating existing programs, and for enhancing the effectiveness of functioning programs and procedures.

The Kansas City Patrol Experiment

In the area of policing, one of the recent classic applications of the tools of social science occurred in what has become known as the Kansas City Patrol Experiment. Conducted by the Police Foundation during the early 1970s, three levels of police patrol were compared to determine the effectiveness of patrol in the prevention and suppression of crime.[59] Fifteen police beats were divided into five groups on the basis of similarities in neighborhoods. One beat in each of the five groups was randomly selected for each of the three levels of patrol: "normal," "proactive," and "reactive." *Normal* patrol involved a single car cruising the streets when not responding to calls. The *proactive* patrol strategy involved increasing the level of preventive patrol and police visibility by doubling or tripling the number of cruising cars. *Reactive* patrol was characterized by the virtual elimination of cruising cars with police entering the designated areas only in response to specific requests. At the conclusion of the study, no significant differences were found in any of the areas—regardless of the level of patrol—in the amount of crime reported to the police or according to victim surveys, in the observed criminal activity, in citizen fear of crime, or in the degree of citizen satisfaction with police.

The Death Penalty and Racial Discrimination

Given the disproportionate number of blacks in the United States who have received sentences of death over the years, the issue of capital punishment as an instrument of racial discrimination has received the concerted attention of sociological research and analysis. Most recently, two death penalty cases receiving Supreme Court attention were argued, albeit unsuccessfully, on the basis of social science research findings.

In 1968, the Supreme Court had ruled that in capital cases *all* persons opposed to the death penalty could not be excluded from juries.[60] To do this, the Court argued, would result in a jury that could not speak for the community. Such a jury was "death-qualified" and represented a violation of due process of law. However, the Court also held that jurors could be excluded for cause if their scruples against the death penalty were so strong that they would automatically vote against the imposition of capital punishment—*regardless of the evidence.* The ruling, furthermore, applied only to juries involved in sentencing decisions, leaving open the question of whether "death qualification" tainted a guilty or not guilty verdict. *Lockhart v. McCree,*[61] decided by the Court in 1986, addressed this latter issue, and much of the argument revolved around the social science evidence presented to the High Court.

In 1978, Ardia McCree had been charged with capital felony murder. In accordance with Arkansas law the trial judge removed for cause, over McCree's objections, those prospective jurors who stated that they could not under any circumstances vote for the imposition of the death penalty. McCree was convicted, and although the prosecution had requested a capital sentence, the jury set the punishment at life imprisonment without the possibility of parole. On appeal, McCree argued that the removal of prospective jurors who had scruples about the death penalty violated his right under the Sixth and Fourteenth Amendments to have his guilt or innocence determined by an impartial jury selected from a representative cross-section of the community. McCree also maintained that the absence of jurors opposed to the death penalty slanted the jury in favor of conviction. Support for his position came from the findings of a variety of social science studies which suggested that the juries in question were indeed conviction-prone.[62]

SOCIAL INDICATOR

Total Sentenced to Death in the United States, 1976–1988, and Methods of Execution

	Total		Method		Total		Method
Alabama	94		E	Montana	7		I,H
Alaska		No Death Penalty		Nebraska	13		E
Arizona	83		G	Nevada	45		I
Arkansas	30		I,E	New Hampshire	0		H
California	238		G	New Jersey	25		I
Colorado	3		G	New Mexico	2		I
Connecticut	1		E	New York		No Death Penalty	
Delaware	7		H,I	North Carolina	81		G,I
District of Columbia		No Death Penalty		North Dakota		No Death Penalty	
Florida	296		E	Ohio	85		E
Georgia	106		E	Oklahoma	99		I
Hawaii		No Death Penalty		Oregon	14		I
Idaho	15		I,F	Pennsylvania	115		E
Illinois	119		I	Rhode Island		No Death Penalty	
Indiana	51		E	South Carolina	42		E
Iowa		No Death Penalty		South Dakota	0		I
Kansas		No Death Penalty		Tennessee	70		E
Kentucky	31		E	Texas	284		I
Louisiana	41		E	Utah	6		F,I
Maine		No Death Penalty		Vermont	0		E
Maryland	18		G	Virginia	39		E
Massachusetts		No Death Penalty		Washington	7		I
Michigan		No Death Penalty		West Virginia		No Death Penalty	
Minnesota		No Death Penalty		Wisconsin		No Death Penalty	
Mississippi	47		G,I	Wyoming	3		G,I
Missouri	71		G				

E = Electrocution; G = Gas; I = Lethal Injection; H = Hanging; F = Firing Squad.
Source: Bureau of Justice Statistics; NAACP Legal Defense and Educational Fund, 1989.

The research data were convincing, but to the bewilderment of social scientists and civil libertarians across the country, the Supreme Court ruled against Ardia McCree. It was the opinion of the High Court that the death qualification process did not cast doubt on the impartiality of any individuals chosen to be on a jury, and that the Constitution does not require that a trial jury, as a group, hold a balance of viewpoints or attitudes.

As to the many social science studies which addressed the purported conviction-prone nature of death-qualified juries, the Court had examined them closely, but commented, ". . . we will assume for purposes of this opinion that the studies are both methodologically valid and adequate to establish that "death qualification" in fact produces juries somewhat more "conviction-prone" than "non-death-qualified" juries. We hold, nonetheless, that the Constitution does not prohibit the States from "death qualifying" juries in capital cases." In essence, the Court had accepted the validity of the research findings, but chose to ignore them.

In 1987, a second death penalty case was argued on the basis of social research data. It involved Warren McCleskey, a black man, sentenced to death in 1978 after conviction in a Georgia court for killing a white police officer.[63] McCleskey appealed his sentence on the grounds that Georgia's capital punishment system discriminated against blacks, and was therefore unconstitutional. In support of his contention, McCleskey produced the findings of a comprehensive study of 724 offenders arrested and convicted of murder in the state of Georgia between January 1, 1970 and June 30, 1978, who later received life imprisonment or a death sentence.[64] The study conclusively demonstrated that, even taking into

Applied Sociology

The Salient Factor Score Matrix

The Salient Factor Score Matrix is a statistical prediction method used by the United States Board of Parole for determining an inmate's suitability for parole. The *salient factor score,* which ranges from 0 to 11, is based on a number of elements (education, employment history, marital status, prior convictions and imprisonments, plus a number of other factors) combined to suggest four categories of parole prognosis: very good, good, fair, or poor. The case is then given an offense severity rating, which is taken from a structured schedule that designates various crimes as having specific levels of severity. These factors are combined into a matrix that suggests how many months an inmate ought to remain incarcerated prior to being paroled. As indicated in the accompanying table, an inmate incarcerated for motor vehicle theft (moderate severity) with a "very good" Salient Factor Score (11–9 points) could conceivably be paroled after 12 to 16 months.

Salient Factor Score Matrix for Adult Inmates

		Parole Prognosis (Salient Factor Score)			
Severity of Offense (examples)		**Very Good (11–9)**	**Good (8–6)**	**Fair (5–4)**	**Poor (3–0)**
Low	Immigration Law Violations Minor Theft (under $1,000)	6–10 months	8–12 months	10–14 months	12–16 months
Low Moderate	Alcohol Law Violations Marijuana Possession (under $500) Forgery, Fraud (under $1,000)	8–12 months	12–16 months	16–20 months	20–25 months
Moderate	Bribery of Public Official Possession of Hard Drugs by User (under $500) Possession of Marijuana (over $500) Sale of Marijuana (under $5,000) Receiving Stolen Property to Resell (under $20,000) Motor Vehicle Theft	12–16 months	16–20 months	20–24 months	24–30 months
High	Burglary or Larceny from Bank or Post Office Sale of Hard Drugs to Support Habit	16–20 months	20–26 months	26–32 months	32–38 months

account many variables that could have explained capital sentencing disparities on nonracial grounds (for example, the aggravating and mitigating circumstances of the offenses), defendants charged with killing whites were more than four times as likely to receive the death sentence as those charged with killing blacks.

Although the research was scientifically sound, the High Court rejected McCleskey's argument by a margin of 5–4, focusing on the problem of generalizing from retrospective social science data to specific cases involving particular offenders and juries. In other words, the Court held, each capital jury is unique. It is faced with innumerable factors that it must take into account, and the statistical evidence presented could not be accepted as "proof" that intent to discriminate existed in McCleskey's case.

However, a forcible sex offender (very high severity) with a "poor" Salient Factor Score (3–0 points) might be held for 55 to 65 months. The index is a guide that can be overridden by the parole board's judgment.

The advantage to the Salient Factor Score Matrix is that it makes parole decision making more consistent by controlling discretion. It eliminates negative input from institutional treatment and custodial staff, and curbs the influences of board members' whims, prejudices, and hunches. On the other hand, it precludes the idea of individualized justice and makes potential parolees "prisoners" of their past mistakes.

SOURCES: William E. Amos and Charles L. Newman (eds.), *Parole: Legal Issues/Decision-Making/Research* (New York: Federal Legal Publications, 1975), pp. 169–210; Peter B. Hoffman and Lucille K. DeGosten, "Parole Decision-Making: Structuring Discretion," *Federal Probation*, 38 (December 1974), p. 12.

		Parole Prognosis (Salient Factor Score)			
Severity of Offense (examples)		**Very Good (11–9)**	**Good (8–6)**	**Fair (5–4)**	**Poor (3–0)**
High *(cont.)*	Sale of Marijuana (over $5,000) Possession of Soft Drugs (over $5,000) Embezzlement ($20,000–$100,000) Organized Vehicle Theft Receiving Stolen Property $20,000–$100,000) Robbery (no weapon or injury) Theft, Forgery, Fraud ($20,000–$100,000)				
Very High	Robbery (weapon) Sale of Soft Drugs (over $5,000) Extortion Sexual Act (force)	26–36 months	36–45 months	45–55 months	55–65 months
Greatest	Aggravated Felony (weapon fired or serious injury) Aircraft Hijacking Kidnapping Willful Homicide	Greater than above. However, specific ranges are not given due to the limited number of cases and the extreme variations in severity possible within the category.			

Parole Prediction

Finally, the tools of sociology have been put to use for making parole release decisions. An overview of contemporary parole practice suggests that parole board members typically rely on "intuitive prognosis" and "common sense" in deciding when to release an inmate from a correctional institution. This practice would indicate that in many jurisdictions, parole decision making is an arbitrary process. Parole prediction is a statistical estimate of the probability of success on parole.[65] Perhaps the most developed of the contemporary prediction approaches is the Salient Factor Score Index, a technique that has rendered release decisions far more objective than those obtained by means of personal judgment (see Exhibit 15.13).

SUMMARY

The criminal justice process includes the agencies of law enforcement charged with the prevention of crime and the apprehension of criminal offenders; it includes the court systems charged with determining the guilt or innocence of accused offenders and with the sentencing of convicted criminals; and it includes the network of corrections agencies charged with the control, custody, supervision, and treatment of those found guilty of violations of the law. American justice is an adversary system, grounded in due process of law, where the accused is considered innocent until proven guilty and where the rights of the accused are guaranteed by the Constitution.

Police systems in the United States exist at the federal, state, and local levels, as well as in the private sector. Most police work is a peacekeeping operation, and the peacekeeping role of the police is what separates their functions from those of private citizens. This peacekeeping role gives the police the right to use force in situations whose urgency demands it. In conducting their work, police have wide discretionary powers. The Supreme Court of the United States has made numerous decisions over the years intended to control police powers and ensure the rights of the accused, the most significant of which were *Mapp v. Ohio, Escobedo v. Illinois,* and *Miranda v. Arizona.* Corruption has been visible throughout policing, primarily because policing is rife in opportunities for corruption. The most effective mechanism for controlling such corruption appears to be greater police professionalism.

The United States has a dual court system, one at the federal level and one at the state level. Courts can be of limited, general, or appellate jurisdiction, and the United States Supreme Court is the highest court in the nation. The criminal judicial process has many stages including initial appearance, preliminary hearing, formalization of charges, arraignment, and trial. The controversial issue of plea negotiation, which accounts for more than 90% of all guilty pleas occurs at the point of arraignment. At trial, the right to counsel is guaranteed. The most significant Supreme Court decision in this regard was *Gideon v. Wainwright* in 1963.

Sentencing objectives are based on the competing philosophies of retribution, isolation, deterrence, and rehabilitation. In contemporary sentencing practices, whether the sentence involves the imposition of a fine, payment of restitution, assignment to community service work, jail, prison, or execution, one or more of these philosophies is apparent. However, widespread disparities occur in sentencing, due to the discretionary powers of judges. With respect to the death penalty as a form of punishment, the Supreme Court has remained flexible in its interpretation of the Eighth Amendment ban against cruel and unusual punishment. In *Furman v. Georgia,* the Court invalidated all state and federal death penalty statutes.

Prisons are total institutions that are designed to achieve the goals of the various sentencing philosophies. Prisons have various types of inmate self-development programs, an inmate social system, and an inmate code. Inmates are socialized into the prison community through the process of prisonization.

Most convicted criminals do not go to prison. The majority are placed in community-based correctional programs that are believed to enhance the offenders' chances of reintegration into the community. Criminal justice diversion is a noncriminal disposition. Probation is a conditional release to the community not involving confinement. Parole is a conditional release from prison after a portion of the sentence has been served.

The criminal justice process has been described as a "system," but fails to operate as one. However, it does manage generally to separate the innocent from the guilty and guarantee due process of law.

KEY TERMS/CONCEPTS

adversary system of justice
bail
courts of appellate jurisdiction
courts of general jurisdiction
courts of limited jurisdiction
criminal justice diversion
criminal justice process
dual court system
due process of law
Escobedo v. Illinois
exclusionary rule
Gideon v. Wainwright
indeterminate sentence
inquisitorial system of justice
inquiry system of justice
Mapp v. Ohio
Miranda v. Arizona
mutual pledge
parole
peacekeeping role
police discretion
presentence investigation
prisonization
probation
recidivism
Rule of Four
search and seizure
separate system
silent system
trial by ordeal
writ of *certiorari*

DISCUSSION QUESTIONS

1. People have argued that due process of law and the rights of the accused as guaranteed by the Constitution and enforced by the Supreme Court result in the release of far too many serious criminals on technicalities of law. In order to make crime control more effective and prevent this "coddling of criminals," which of the guarantees of the Bill of Rights would you be willing to give up?
2. What do you feel should be the primary purpose of sentencing? Why?
3. Do you feel that the death penalty is a rational and effective form of punishment? Why?
4. In addition to prisons, what other institutions might be considered total institutions?
5. Which theory of crime and deviance discussed in Chapter 7 best explains the dynamics of the prisonization process?

SUGGESTED READINGS

Lee H. Bowker, *Prison Victimization* (New York: Elsevier, 1980). Based on his observations of prison life in Washington State Penitentiary, the author details the nature of prison violence and rape, the psychological, economic, and social victimizations among prisoners, and staff-inmate victimization.

Donald Clemmer, *The Prison Community* (New York: Rinehart, 1958). Originally published in 1940, this study stands as a classic analysis of the social organization of a maximum security penitentiary, providing a detailed examination of the inmate subculture and the social relations in the prison community.

Kenneth C. Haas and James A. Inciardi (eds.), *Adjudicating Death: Law and Social Science Confront the Death Penalty* (Newbury Park, CA: Sage, 1988). A collection of essays by social scientists and legal scholars arguing on the basis of social science research and constitutional law that the death penalty is discriminatory and a violation of due process of law.

Anthony Lewis, *Gideon's Trumpet* (New York: Vintage, 1966). The story of Clarence Earl Gideon and the Supreme Court's landmark decision in *Gideon v. Wainwright.*

Steven Phillips, *No Heroes, No Villains: The Story of a Murder Trial* (New York: Vintage, 1978). Written by the prosecuting attorney in the case and as absorbing as a mystery novel, this short paperback outlines the various steps in the criminal justice process and examines the intricacies and problems in the administration of justice.

Jonathan Rubenstein, *City Police* (New York: Farrar, Straus and Giroux, 1973). A detailed description of the way that big-city police work "on the street," the way they regard their work, the way they deal day by day with suspects and criminals, with colleagues and superiors, and with the general public.

NOTES

1. Christopher Hibbert, *The Roots of Evil* (Boston: Little, Brown, 1963), pp. 5–8; Luke Owen Pike, *A History of Crime in England,* vol. 1 (London: Smith, Elder, 1873–1876), pp. 52–55.
2. Henry M. Christman (ed.), *The Public Papers of Chief Justice Earl Warren* (New York: Simon and Schuster, 1959), p. 70.
3. See Charles Rembar, *The Law of the Land: The Evolution of Our Legal System* (New York: Simon and Schuster, 1980).
4. Luke Owen Pike, *Crime in England,* vol. 2, pp. 457–62.
5. Luke Owen Pike, *Crime in England,* vol. 1, p. 218.
6. Thomas A. Reppetto, *The Blue Parade* (New York: Free Press, 1978); James F. Richardson, *The New York Police: Colonial Times to 1901* (New York: Oxford University Press, 1970); Bruce Smith, *Police Systems in the United States* (New York: Harper & Brothers, 1949).
7. Bruce Smith, *The State Police: Organization and Administration* (New York: Columbia University Institute of Public Administration, 1925), pp. 1–40.
8. Albert J. Reiss, Jr., *The Police and the Public* (New Haven, CT: Yale University Press, 1971).
9. Richard J. Lundman, "Police Patrol Work: A Comparative Perspective," in Richard J. Lundman (ed.), *Police Behavior: A Sociological Perspective* (New York: Oxford University Press, 1980), pp. 52–65.
10. Federal Bureau of Investigation, *Uniform Crime Reports—1987* (Washington, DC: U.S. Government Printing Office, 1988), p. 164.
11. For example, see FBI, *Uniform Crime Reports—1987,* p. 333.
12. James J. Fyfe, "Who Shoots? A Look at Officer Race and Police Shooting," *Journal of Police Science Administration,* 9 (1981), p. 367; Lennox S. Hinds, "The Police Use of Excessive and Deadly Force: Racial Implications," in Robert N. Brenner and Majorie Kravitz (eds.), *A Community Concern: Police Use of Deadly Force* (Washington, DC: United States Department of Justice, 1979), pp. 7–11; K. J. Matulia, *A Balance of Forces* (Gaithersburg, MD: International Association of Chiefs of Police, 1982), p. 58.
13. Paul Takagi, "A Garrison State in a 'Democratic' Society," *Crime and Social Justice,* 1 (Spring-Summer 1974), pp. 27–33.
14. William Wilbanks, *The Myth of a Racist Criminal Justice System* (Monterey, CA: Brooks/Cole, 1987), p. 76.
15. James J. Fyfe, *Readings on the Police Use of Deadly Force* (Washington, DC: Police Foundation, 1982); Arthur L. Kobler,

"Police Homicide in a Democracy," *Journal of Social Issues,* 31 (Winter 1975), pp. 163–84; Gerald D. Robin, "Justifiable Homicides by Police Officers," *Journal of Criminal Law, Criminology, and Police Science,* June 1963, pp. 225–31; Cynthia G. Sulton and Philip Cooper, "Summary of Research on Police Use of Deadly Force," in Brenner and Kravitz, *A Community Concern,* pp. 69–94.

16. James J. Fyfe, "Blind Justice: Police Shootings in Memphis," *Journal of Criminal Law and Criminology,* 73 (1982), pp. 707–22.
17. Irving Piliavin and Scott Briar, "Police Encounters with Juveniles," *American Journal of Sociology,* 70 (September 1964), pp. 206–14.
18. J. Shane Creamer, *The Law of Arrest, Search and Seizure* (New York: Holt, Rinehart and Winston, 1980), p. 3.
19. Mapp v. Ohio, 367 U.S. 643 (1961).
20. Escobedo v. Illinois, 378 U.S. 478 (1964).
21. Miranda v. Arizona, 384 U.S. 436 (1966).
22. Hopt v. Utah, 110 U.S. 574 (1884).
23. Brown v. Mississippi, 297 U.S. 278 (1936).
24. Lawrence W. Sherman, *Scandal and Reform* (Berkeley: University of California Press, 1978), p. xxii.
25. See, for example, Thomas Barker and Julian Roebuck, *An Empirical Typology of Police Corruption: A Study in Organizational Deviance* (Springfield, IL: Charles C. Thomas, 1973); Herman Goldstein, *Policing a Free Society* (Cambridge, MA: Ballinger, 1977), pp. 194–95; Richard J. Lundman, *Police and Policing* (New York: Holt, Rinehart and Winston, 1980), pp. 142–48; Jonathan Rubinstein, *City Police* (New York: Farrar, Straus and Giroux, 1973).
26. See Daniel J. Freed and Patricia M. Wald, *Bail in the United States* (Washington, DC: National Conference on Bail and Criminal Justice, 1964).
27. For a summary of the research on alternatives to bail, see James A. Inciardi, *Criminal Justice,* 3rd ed. (San Diego: Harcourt Brace Jovanovich, 1987), pp. 422–25.
28. See Arthur Rosett and Donald R. Cressey, *Justice by Consent: Plea Bargains in the American Courthouse* (Philadelphia: Lippincott, 1976).
29. Laura Rose Handman, "Underrepresentation of Economic Groups in Federal Juries," *Boston University Law Review,* 57 (January 1977), pp. 198–224.
30. Batson v. Kentucky, 39 CrL 3061 (1986).
31. Harry Kalven and Hans Zeisel, *The American Jury* (Boston: Little, Brown, 1966), pp. 55–56.
32. Johnson v. Zerbst, 304 U.S. 458 (1938).
33. Powell v. Alabama, 287 U.S. 45 (1932).
34. Gideon v. Wainwright, 372 U.S. 335 (1963).
35. Anthony Lewis, *Gideon's Trumpet* (New York: Vintage, 1966).
36. Betts v. Brady, 316 U.S. 455 (1942).
37. Gideon v. Wainwright, 372 U.S. 335 (1963).
38. Howard N. Meyer, *XIV: The Amendment That Refused to Die* (Boston: Beacon, 1978).
39. Quoted in Sanford H. Kadish and Monrad G. Paulsen, *Criminal Law and Its Processes* (Boston: Little, Brown, 1969), p. 85.
40. *National Observer,* September 14, 1974, p. 5.
41. Furman v. Georgia, 408 U.S. 238 (1972).
42. Coker v. Georgia, 433 U.S. 583 (1977).
43. Marvin E. Wolfgang and Marc Riedel, "Race, Judicial Discretion, and the Death Penalty," *Annals of the American Academy of Political and Social Sciences,* 407 (May 1973), pp. 119–29.
44. William J. Bowers, *Legal Homicide: Death as Punishment in America, 1864–1982* (Boston: Northeastern University Press, 1984), p. 74.
45. Hugo Adam Bedau and Chester M. Pierce (eds.), *Capital Punishment in the United States* (New York: AMS, 1976); William J. Bowers, *Legal Homicide;* Charles L. Black, *Capital Punishment: The Inevitability of Caprice and Mistake* (New York: W. W. Norton, 1978); Ernest van den Haag, "In Defense of the Death Penalty: A Legal-Practical-Moral Analysis," *Criminal Law Bulletin,* 14 (January-February 1978), pp. 51–68; Kenneth C. Haas and James A. Inciardi (eds.), *Adjudicating Death: Law and Social Science Confront the Death Penalty* (Newbury Park, CA: Sage, 1988).
46. Harry Elmer Barnes, *The Repression of Crime* (New York: George H. Doran, 1926); Orlando F. Lewis, *The Development of American Prisons and Prison Customs, 1776–1845* (Albany, NY: Prison Association of New York, 1922).
47. Erving Goffman, *Asylums* (Garden City, NY: Anchor, 1961), pp. 1–8.
48. For a description of life at Green Haven, see Susan Sheehan, *A Prison and a Prisoner* (Boston: Houghton Mifflin, 1978).
49. Robert Martinson, "What Works?—Questions and Answers About Prison Reform," *The Public Interest,* 35 (Spring 1974), pp. 22–54.
50. Donald Clemmer, *The Prison Community* (New York: Holt, Rinehart, and Winston, 1958), p. 299.
51. Gresham M. Sykes and Sheldon L. Messenger, "The Inmate Social System," in *Theoretical Studies in the Social Organization of the Prison* (New York: Social Science Research Council, 1960), pp. 6–8.
52. Kinesley Hammett, *Holocaust at New Mexico State Penitentiary* (Lubbock, TX: C. F. Boone, 1980); *New York Times,* February 2, 1980, p. 1; *U.S. News & World Report,* February 18, 1980, p. 68.
53. Duane C. McBride, "Criminal Justice Diversion," in James A. Inciardi and Kenneth C. Haas (eds.), *Crime and the Criminal Justice Process* (Dubuque, IA: Kendall/Hunt, 1978), pp. 246–59.
54. Jacob M. Braude, "Boys' Court: Individualized Justice for the Youthful Offender," *Federal Probation,* 12 (June 1948), pp. 9–14.
55. David Dressler, *Practice and Theory of Probation and Parole* (New York: Columbia University Press, 1969).
56. Division of Information Services, *TACP Shock Probation Survey* (Austin: Texas Adult Probation Commission, 1980).
57. Edwin H. Sutherland, *Principles of Criminology* (Philadelphia: Lippincott, 1947), p. 534.
58. President's Commission on Law Enforcement and the Administration of Justice, *The Challenge of Crime in a Free Society* (Washington, DC: U.S. Government Printing Office, 1967), p. 7.
59. George L. Kelling, *The Kansas City Preventive Patrol Experiment: A Summary Report* (Washington, DC: Police Foundation, 1974).
60. Witherspoon v. Illinois, 391 U.S. 510 (1968).

61. Lockhart v. McCree, 38 CrL 4014 (1985).
62. See Brief for *Amicus Curiae,* American Psychological Association in support of Respondent, *Lockhart v. McCree,* on Writ of *Certiorari* to the United States Court of Appeals for the Eighth Circuit.
63. McCleskey v. Kemp, 41 CrL 3047 (1987).
64. David C. Baldus, Charles Pulaski, and George Woodworth, "Comparative Review of Death Sentences: An Empirical Study of the Georgia Experience," *Journal of Criminal Law and Criminology,* 74 (1983), pp. 661–753.
65. James A. Inciardi, "The Use of Parole Prediction with Institutionalized Narcotic Addicts," *Journal of Research in Crime and Delinquency,* 8 (January 1971), pp. 65–73.

PART
SIX

The Dynamics of Change

16 Collective Behavior and Social Movements

History is marked with events of a most curious and bizarre nature. On Halloween night in 1938, Orson Welles and Columbia Broadcasting System's Mercury Theater dramatized the H. G. Wells fantasy "War of the Worlds." The dramatization was an hour-long program in which a series of "news bulletins" interrupted a regular program of dance music. The bulletins described a "Martian war cylinder" some 38 yards in diameter, which was said to have landed at a farm in New Jersey. "Creatures" emerged from the space vehicle, armed with a "flame ray" that instantly killed 40 onlookers and 6 state troopers. An army of 7,000 men eventually battled the Martian machine, and all but 120 of them were mercilessly slaughtered.

In spite of four announcements by CBS during the broadcast indicating the fictitious nature of the incident being described, the events were understood as being real by almost two million listeners. People from Maine to California thought that hideous monsters with death rays were destroying all armed resistance sent against them. In New York, CBS and police telephone switchboards were jammed; Riverside Drive became impassable, packed with mobs of sobbing people. In northern New Jersey, conditions were even worse. Weeping families clung to one another; terrified men ran blindly across fields; train terminals and bus stations were filled with wild-eyed people demanding tickets to anywhere. Elsewhere mobs roamed the streets, women and children huddled in churches, and violence and looting went on unchecked.[1]

On a Wednesday evening in June 1962, a six o'clock news broadcast reported the closing of a local clothing plant in a small city in the South. At least ten women who worked in the plant had been admitted to the hospital for the treatment of severe nausea, allegedly the result of bites from some small insect that had come from England in a shipment of cloth. Within a few days, a total of sixty-two people had been affected by the "June Bug" epidemic. A task force composed of plant officials, representatives of insurance companies, entomologists (insect specialists), and experts from the U.S. Public Health Service Communicable Disease Center searched the entire textile plant for anything that might have caused the "illness." Although a thorough vacuuming of the premises turned up a common housefly, one black ant, several gnats, a chigger, and a small variety of beetles, the cause of the epidemic was never found.[2]

On May 28, 1977, between 3,500 and 4,000 people gathered in the immense Beverly Hills Supper Club, a popular nightspot in Southgate, Kentucky, just across the Ohio River from downtown Cincinnati. It was the beginning of the long Memorial Day weekend. Some had come to hear singer John Davidson perform, others to begin the holiday festivities, but most simply wished to have dinner in one of the facility's 21 private dining rooms. At approximately 9 P.M., the club seemed suddenly to burst into flames, and a total of 164 people perished. It was the worst nightclub fire since 1942, when 491 persons died in Boston's Coconut Grove Supper Club. In both cases, while most of the victims died of smoke inhalation, *panic* had been the real cause of the majority of the deaths. At the first signs of danger, the crowds charged the exits. Many bodies were found trampled; others were stuffed in doorways, preventing everyone else from escaping.[3]

At 6 P.M. on December 28, 1982, 20-year-old Nevell Johnson, Jr., a black man, was shot to death in a video-game arcade by a white police officer. The incident occurred in the Overtown section of Miami, Florida, a district populated primarily by low-income blacks. Almost immediately, word of the shooting raced through the dark streets of Overtown. First, a police car parked in front of the arcade was torched by the gathering crowd, and within minutes, a full-fledged riot was in progress.[4]

Miami police officers in full riot gear patrolled city streets during that city's 1980 outbreak of racial violence.

The riot, furthermore, was the second to occur in Miami in less than three years. On December 17, 1979, 33-year-old Arthur McDuffie, an insurance salesman and ex-Marine, was beaten to death during an altercation with police. Indicted for manslaughter were four white patrolmen, all previously cited in civilian complaints of police brutality. On May 17, 1980, the officers were acquitted by an all-white jury, and the response was the worst outbreak of racial violence the country had seen since the ghetto riots of the 1960s. After three days of fury, fifteen people were dead and the city had suffered a financial loss of $200 million.[5]

In early July, 1987, several congressional committees, led by Democrats, began questioning Lieutenant Colonel Oliver L. North of the United States Marine Corps about what was called the "Iran-Contra affair." Contrary to the wishes of Congress (and apparently the secretaries of state and defense as well) and in violation of several laws, a plan had been secretly implemented to ship weapons to Iran in exchange for Americans being held hostage in Lebanon. In addition, the profits from the arms sales were to be channeled to anti-Communist rebels in Central America. The operation did not remain a secret and despite several investigating committees, no one could quite figure it all out. Lieutenant Colonel North seemed to be the key, but he was not talking. In the media and in Congress he was often depicted as an "evil wizard," who had masterminded the entire operation. Finally, North agreed to testify, and the hearings were televised live and in their entirety.

What followed was what several commentators called "Olliemania." People from all over the United States supported Lieutenant Colonel North. Polls demonstrated that while the majority of Americans considered him to be a super patriot, a few even saw North as a national hero.[6]

What accounts for these behaviors? Throughout history people have participated in riots, lynchings, revivals, panics, fads, protest marches, manias, and social movements to the extent that such activities have come to be accepted as a natural part of social living. What is known about these seemingly uncontrolled behaviors? How are they a part of the structure of society and culture?

THE NATURE OF COLLECTIVE BEHAVIOR

Collective behavior is the relatively spontaneous behavior of a group of people who are reacting to a common influence in an undefined or ambiguous, and often emotional, situation. Collectivities are impermanent and for the most part not formally organized. They are responses to a set of immediate circumstances that unfold gradually in ways that fall outside of conventional norms. Collective behavior can take a variety of forms. It can develop as a protest demonstration against the opening of a nuclear power plant or the policies of some political figure. It can emerge as the group excitement often seen at rock concerts or the Super Bowl. It can appear as highly visible and dramatic forms of behavior, such as riots, lynchings, panics, and social movements.

Collective behavior, however, is not limited only to group actions of a highly emotional character. It can occur in the form of a crowd watching a fire, an audience viewing a motion picture, or a group of students listening to a sociology lecture. It is apparent in the form of fads in patterns of dress and manners of speech. Furthermore, collective behavior need not involve the formation of actual physical groups. The members of the collective can share a common interest but may be physically dispersed. A curious example occurred in Brazil during the closing months of 1987. In the town of Goiania, just southwest of Brasilia, scrap metal dealers discovered a mysterious capsule at an abandoned clinic. Marveling at what they had found, but totally baffled by the mysterious force that made it shine in the dark, they believed they had unearthed a precious stone with special powers. They brought it home, showed it to family, friends, peers, workmates, and others. They removed the glowing powder from the surface of the capsule, sharing it with friends, and even sprinkling it on floors and in food. But the capsule had been found in a discarded cancer treatment machine, and it contained radioactive cesium-137. The effects of radioactive contamination promptly began to set in. The skin of those who had touched the capsule began to swell and blister; hair began to fall out; teeth began to loosen. Burning pains developed. Quickly, Brazilian health authorities isolated all of the radioactive material and began treating the contaminated victims. But fear of radiation rapidly spread across Brazil. Every day for months, anxious and confused citizens lined up for tests with radiation detectors. In fact, within two months of the finding of the capsule, one-tenth of Brazil's population had been screened. Fearing discrimination, thousands of people carried certificates stating that they bore no radioactivity.[7]

Thus, collective behavior can appear in many forms, on a continuum ranging from the most unstructured and spontaneous (the panicking diners at the burning Beverly Hills Supper Club), to the most structured and planned (a group of strikers forming an orderly picket line). In all instances, it involves a collection of people who share some common interest or concern and whose actions fall to some extent outside of conventional norms. For the sake of systematic discussion, collective behavior can be broken down into three

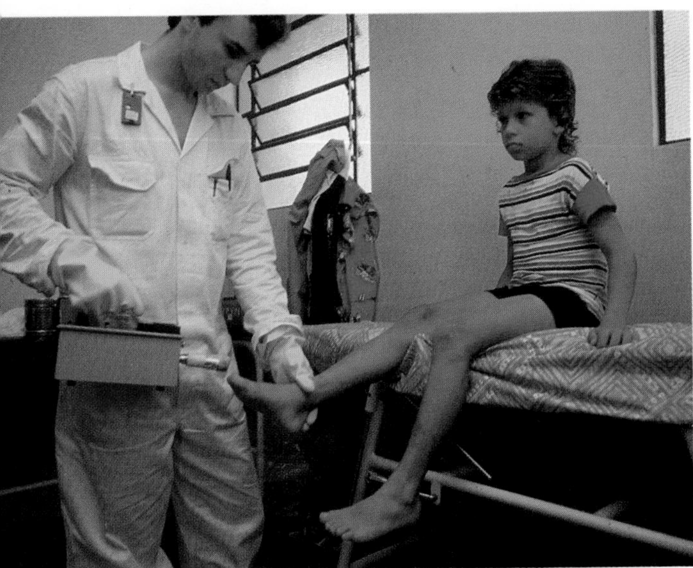

Nearly one-tenth of Brazil's population was screened for radiation exposure in the two months following the cesium-137 calamity in 1987.

general categories: *crowds, mass behavior,* and later in this chapter, *social movements.*

CROWDS

Crowds are temporary collections of people who have a united focus on some person or event and who are conscious of and are influenced by one another's presence. Crowds seem to have a magnetic quality and tend to grow very quickly. How often at the scene of an accident, a fire, or a fight do people appear to come "out of nowhere" and gather to watch? Moreover, when people see a crowd, they tend to interrupt whatever they are doing to join. Crowds seem to have a number of unique characteristics.

First, crowds are self-generating; they have no natural boundaries. Every New Year's Eve, hundreds of thousands of people gather in New York's Times Square to watch the "big apple" descend a pole and to welcome in a new year. Because normal barriers fail to contain the self-generating character of crowds, merchants in the Times Square area must shield their storefronts with plywood in order to prevent people from being pushed through display windows.

Second, crowds are characterized by equality, in that social differences are quickly ignored by their members. In a crowd, even the most avid bigots comingle with members of the groups they despise.

Third, crowds have high density. The amount of private space that a person normally occupies is reduced to nothing in a crowd. On a mass transit bus or subway car during rush hours, people are often packed shoulder to shoulder, back to back, and even front to front, sometimes inadvertently touching in ways that would be considered sexually abusive in other circumstances.

Fourth, crowds do not have a past or future. They are relatively unstructured events, and their members may have no other interchanges beyond the specific moment of common focus. People who gather at an accident cease interacting once they leave the scene. The individuals who comprise some crowds may indeed have a common history, such as the participants in a prison riot. However, as an acting collectivity, the rioting crowd has no past or future.

Fifth, the members of a crowd feel a sense of anonymity but are conscious of and are influenced by one another's presence. Thus, crowds can be volatile, emotional, and highly spontaneous in their behavior. Participants in a crowd are more suggestible than individuals are, and they can easily get "swept along" into doing things that they would never have done by themselves. Crowd situations often generate feelings of invulnerability in individual crowd members.

Thus, the characteristics of a crowd make crowds different from most other group situations. A crowd's lack of history prevents group norms from developing. The relative anonymity of a crowd tends to weaken both norms and social conventions. Moreover, violations of personal space increase levels of emotion. These characteristics suggest that crowds possess the potential for unpredictable and unreasonable behavior. A well-known example of such behavior is seen in the activities of the lynch mob, a band of normally law-abiding citizens who take the law into their own hands and commit murder in the name of "justice" (see Exhibit 16.1).

Types of Crowds

The unpredictability and explosive nature of crowd behavior has brought focused attention to the phenomenon from social scientists, and at least four types of crowds have been identified and studied.[8]

Casual crowds are short-lived and have little or no sense of unity. The throngs of people who appear daily in urban business districts are casual crowds. Their members come and go as they please, and they are there for any number of reasons—to work, to shop, to meet friends, to do business. Only when some precipitating event catches their attention, such as an automobile accident, do they develop any common identity.

Conventional crowds come together for some specific purpose and the behavior of their members

Exhibit 16.1

Sociology in the Media

A Crime Rise Spurs Brazil Lynch Mobs

Vigilantism Is Said to Reflect Dissatisfaction with the Police and the Courts

RIO DE JANEIRO—During the wake for a taxi driver killed in late December in the western town of Amambaí, word reached mourners that a murder suspect had been found. A few hours later, his bullet-riddled and mutilated body was dumped beside an outlying road. He was the victim of a lynch mob.

Days earlier, in the southern town of Umuarama, three young men who were arrested on charges of murdering a local photographer and raping his fiancée were pulled out of jail and beaten to death in front of several hundred people. Their bodies were then tied to a car and dragged through the town before being burned.

A few days later, on December 27, five men in the eastern town of Ipiaú who had been accused of assaulting and wounding a local taxi driver were also pulled from their cells and murdered, to the applause of a crowd estimated at around 1,000. "I saw hate in the eyes of those people," one local official later told reporters.

With small variations, these scenes have been repeated on scores of occasions in recent years as communities in both large cities and small towns have reacted angrily to Brazil's rising crime rate. "A lynching is a grave symptom," Justice Minister Paulo Brossard said. "It reflects dissatisfaction with the police and with delays in the application of justice."

A Victim Who Was Not Guilty

The latest incidents of mob justice—four others have occurred since late November—won headlines here for one macabre reason: in the case of Amambaí, just hours after the 25-year-old former policeman, Josa Nestor, was killed by colleagues of the slain taxi driver, it became apparent that he was not guilty.

Witnesses said that while being beaten and tortured, Mr. Nestor insisted that he had been some 40 miles away with a friend and her mother at the time of the murder. And although three taxi drivers were dispatched to verify the alibi, Mr. Nestor was shot to death before they returned to Amambaí with confirmation of his story.

As with previous lynchings, however, there was little expectation that those responsible for Mr. Nestor's death would themselves be brought to trial. In some cases, in fact, such has been the anger of communities besieged by crime that hundreds of people have come forward to say they took part in lynchings. In other cases, small police units have simply preferred to prolong investigations until the incidents have been forgotten.

Nonetheless, the frequency of lynchings reflects the extent to which violent crime has come to dominate the urban way of life here. In polls published before nationwide elections here in November, a lack of security was identified as Rio de Janeiro's most serious problem, while 60 percent of those questioned in São Paulo favored the death penalty. A radio commentator who regularly calls for the death penalty won the most votes in an election in São Paulo.

Sociologists here have linked the sharp rise in crime to a four-year recession that began in 1981 and left millions of people out of work. But they also blamed the neglect of education and other social priorities that marked the economic strategy adopted by the military regime that ruled Brazil between 1964 and 1985. At the same time, the police in most cities lack either the resources or the experience to deal with the situation.

As a result, Brazilians have grown accustomed to hearing hair-raising stories of assaults or even witnessing crime in action.

Sunbathers outside the Sheraton Hotel here recently heard a gun battle between the police and criminals, and then saw dozens of heavily armed police officers combing an adjacent slum while a submachine gun was fired into nearby undergrowth from a helicopter flying overhead.

In Brazil's largest cities, São Paulo and Rio de Janeiro, ways of life have also changed to adjust to the insecurity. Women, for example, avoid wearing jewelry on the street, and at night drivers rarely stop for traffic lights for fear of assault.

In addition, the number of people carrying firearms is said to have grown, and in the last five years the price of buying or renting houses has fallen in relative terms because apartment buildings are considered safer.

SOURCE: Alan Riding, *New York Times,* January 21, 1987, p. A10.

Ninety-three people died when soccer fans in Sheffield, England, surged forward against a security fence in April 1989. Crowd behavior can be highly spontaneous.

conforms to a well-established set of cultural rules. Even excitement in the conventional crowd is governed by a set of accepted social norms. Students attending a lecture, an audience listening to an opera, people watching a football game, and mourners at a funeral are conventional crowds. In each case, the people have gathered for a particular reason and generally behave according to established norms. Applause at the conclusion of an opera is the norm, but it would be considered extremely inappropriate at a funeral.

Expressive crowds are emotionally charged gatherings in which collective excitement is common as a form of release and members often behave in ways that they themselves would consider unacceptable in other settings. Audience members at rock concerts often exhibit expressive crowd behavior. Common at such gatherings are screaming and shouting and the open use of drugs.

Acting crowds are excited, highly volatile collections of people provoked by some focal event in which passions and tempers are fed by one another and often result in spontaneous acts of violence. Unlike expressive crowds, for whom the release of feelings is an end in and of itself, members of an acting crowd see redress of some "wrong" as their ultimate goal. A lynch mob is an acting crowd. The Iranian demonstrators who stormed the U.S. Embassy in Tehran on November 4, 1979, shouting "Death to America" and taking hostages, were an acting crowd. Acting crowds form and disperse quickly after achieving their goal.

Profile of a Riot

Mass uprisings, mob revolts, and angry riots have been part of American history for more than three hundred years. This country has witnessed farmers' revolts, slave insurrections, miners' rebellions, battles between unions and police, draft riots, lynchings, race and ghetto riots, and numerous other types of violent confrontations. A **riot** is a specific form of an acting crowd, one involving confrontations with authority aimed at creating disorder through attacks on people or property. Among the more well-known of the nation's bloody uprisings was the riot at New York's Attica Prison in September 1971.[9]

For prisoners at Attica at that time, "correction" meant little more than daily degradation and humiliation. They were locked in their cells for 14–16 hours each day; they worked for wages that averaged 30 cents a day at jobs with little or no vocational value; and they had to abide by hundreds of petty rules for which they could see no justification. In addition, their mail was read, their radio programs and reading materials were screened, their movements outside their cells were tightly regulated, they were told when to turn out the lights and when to wake up, their toilet needs had to be taken care of in the full view of patrolling officers, and their visits from family and friends took place through a mesh screen and were preceded and followed by strip searches.

In prison, inmates found deprivations worse than those they had encountered on the streets of the urban slums from which they had come. Meals were unappetizing, poorly prepared, and not up to nutritional standards. Clothing was old, ill-fitting, and inadequate. Most inmates could take showers only once a week. State-issued clothing, toilet articles, and other personal items had to be supplemented by purchases at a commissary where prices did not reflect the meager wages inmates were given to spend. To get along in the prison economy, inmates resorted to "hustling."

For officers, "correction" meant a steady but monotonous 40-hour-a-week job, with a pension after 25 years of service. It meant maintaining custody and control over an inmate population largely composed of young blacks and Puerto Ricans from the urban ghettos, unwilling to conform to the restrictions of prison life and ready to provoke confrontation—men whom the officers could not understand and were not trained to handle. It meant keeping the inmates in line, seeing that everything ran smoothly, and enforcing the rules. It did *not* mean, for most officers, helping inmates to solve their problems or to become citizens capable of returning to society. For the corrections officers, who were always outnumbered by inmates, security was a legitimate concern, but the concern was not served by policies that created frustration and tension far more dangerous than the security risks they were intended to avert.

Above all, for both inmates and officers, "correction" meant an atmosphere charged with racism. Racism was manifest in job assignments, discipline, self-segregation in the inmate mess halls, and in the daily interactions of inmates and officers and inmates and

Inmate negotiators bargained with prison officials in a penitentiary corridor prior to the final stages of the Attica riots in 1971.

other inmates. Within the walls of the prison it was impossible to escape from the growing mistrust between white, middle America and the residents of urban ghettos. Indeed, at Attica, racial polarity and mistrust were magnified by the constant reminder that the keepers were white and the kept were largely black or Spanish speaking. The young black inmate tended to see the white officer as the symbol of a racist, oppressive system that put him behind bars. The officer, his perspective shaped by his experience on the job, knew blacks only as belligerent, unrepentant criminals. The result was a mutual lack of respect that made communication all but impossible.

The uprising against the conditions in Attica was not the result of a planned revolt inspired by a core of inmate revolutionaries. Rather, it was the product of escalating frustration and dissatisfaction and was sparked by two related incidents. On September 8, an event occurred that provoked particular resentment and anger in two sections of a particular cell block. A misunderstanding in the exercise yard led to an unusually intense confrontation between officers and inmates, during which inmate Leroy Dewer struck a lieutenant. The officers were forced to back down. That evening, however, Dewer and another inmate were removed from their cells and placed in solitary confinement. It was widely believed that several of the guards subsequently beat the two inmates.

On the following morning, officers found the men of the section to which Dewer belonged to be especially belligerent and troublesome. Thus, they decided to return them to their cells immediately after breakfast without allowing them their usual time in the exercise yard. This decision came at a point when the inmates were lined up in one of the prison's many tunnels—corridors which ran from each cell block to a junction room known as "Times Square" that controlled access to all of Attica's cell blocks.

As the inmates of Dewer's section were being escorted through the tunnels back to their cells, several attacked the officer on duty. Others joined in, and after an initial outburst of violence, the inmates regrouped and set upon the locked gate at Times Square. A defective weld, unknown to officers and inmates alike, broke and the gate gave way. This provided the prisoners access to Times Square and the keys that unlocked the gates to all other tunnels. From Times Square the inmates spread throughout the prison, attacking officers, taking hostages, and destroying property.

By afternoon, the New York State Police had regained control of part of the prison, but most of the inmates assembled in one of the exercise yards, along with their 39 hostages, whom the rioters threatened to kill if their demands were not met.

For four days negotiations dragged on with little progress. Governor Nelson Rockefeller was asked to make a personal appearance at Attica to help with the negotiations and to prevent a bloodbath, but he refused. Instead, he authorized Corrections Commissioner Russell Oswald to end the rebellion, by force, if necessary.

On the morning of September 13, 1971, a second riot of a sort took place. A local New York State Police troop commander planned and led an assault to retake Attica Prison. The troop went in with guns blazing, and within 15 minutes, the Attica uprising was over. The troopers had killed 29 inmates and 10 of the officer hostages, and wounded hundreds more. Ironically, it was the bloodiest one-day encounter between Americans since the Civil War.*

MASS BEHAVIOR

Mass behavior is dispersed collective behavior. **Masses** are collections of people who are widely scattered yet participate in some event either physically or with a common concern or interest. Mass behavior, made possible by media technology, which communicates information instantaneously throughout an entire population, generally lasts over a period of time—weeks, months, and even years. The most common examples of mass behavior include fads, fashions, crazes, rumors, mass hysteria and panics, and public opinion.

Fads, Fashions, and Crazes

Fads consist of markedly novel, trivial, and short-lived behaviors that spread rapidly throughout whichever portions of society choose to adopt them. Fads seem to focus on highly superficial areas of life and have restricted appeal. Adolescents appear to be especially prone to fad behavior, particularly with respect to slang, movie and rock idols, dance steps, and amusements. Some examples of fads from the 1980s include punk hairstyles, Pac-Man, *The Rocky Horror Picture Show, Flashdance* and rock-video fashions, pit-bull terriers, Garbage Pail Kids, Dove Bars and other pricey ice creams, breakdancing, and teddy bears. Fads, however, are not limited only to the younger generations. For two years in the 1920s, mah-jongg held the nation captive as the game of choice; in the 1950s it was canasta; and in 1984 Trivial Pursuit arrived in American living rooms.

*The Attica riot is analyzed later in this chapter within the context of Neil J. Smelser's theory of collective behavior.

The Rocky Horror Picture Show has developed a fanatic following—the audience becomes the characters.

Fads also appear in the business and industrial sectors of American life. During the seventies, a portfolio management system that enjoyed widespread popularity identified businesses as either cash cows, stars, dogs, or question marks.

Crazes are short-lived fads that become very central to the lives of their adherents. While unraveling the mystery of Rubik's Cube was a fad during the early 1980s for some, for example, for others it became a craze. Purists who approached the cube as the ultimate challenge spent most of their waking hours attacking the puzzle. In the process, they often damaged their careers by missing work, their marriages by ignoring their spouses, and their health by poor eating and sleeping habits. One of the more interesting crazes of the 1980s involved emulation of the behaviors of California's Valley Girls (see Exhibit 16.2).

Fashions are fluctuating styles in appearance and behavior that generally relate to standards of dress and manners. Fashions differ from fads and crazes in that they tend to last somewhat longer and have more widespread acceptance. Moreover, fashions are "customary" departures from custom—that is, attempts to be different in a way that is within the bounds of accepted dress and behavior. Fashions from the 1980s included stone-washed jeans, down coats, jogging suits, the "preppy look," and the return of the "mini skirt" (from the 1920s and late 1960s).

Fads, crazes, and fashions are looked upon by many simply as fun; they tend to break the monotony of an otherwise drab existence. But forms of mass behavior also serve important social functions. Some fads and crazes capture audiences seeking to solve their life problems—primal scream therapy, *The Joy of Sex, Jane Fonda's Workout Book,* Dr. Ruth, the Scarsdale Diet, the Beverly Hills Diet, the Cambridge Diet, aerobics, body wrapping, tanning salons, breast implants, hair transplants, and mood rings.

Many fads and fashions are mechanisms of identification and differentiation.[10] By adopting a fad or fashion, whether it be a hairstyle, a musical preference, or a particular pattern of dress, people are identifying with one group and holding themselves apart from others. Clothing, particularly, has a language all its own. Long before individuals are near enough to talk to on the street, in a meeting, or at a party, they announce their sex, age, and class by what they are wearing—and very possibly give information as to their occupation, origin, personality, tastes, sexual desires, and current mood.[11]

As a postscript to this discussion, fads and fashion can have a negative side. A case in point involved Cazal eyeglass frames during the mid-eighties. The West German imports, made of a heavy, dark plastic molded into square lens frames linked by a broad gold nosepiece, sold for as high as $200 a pair. As fashion, the frames spread from celebrities to the streets, first in New York and then to Philadelphia and points south and west. In Philadelphia, the frames initiated a crime wave. People were being robbed and killed for them. The craze over Cazals caused many youths to arm themselves with handguns whenever they wore their glasses.[12]

A more recent controversy involves pit-bull terriers. During the 1980s the pit bull seemed to emerge as the macho dog to have. Descended from old English lines and once bred to attack bulls for sport, they are powerful animals with jaws that can clamp down with a grip of 1,500 pounds of pressure. Throughout the 1980s attacks by pit-bull terriers became more frequent, and as the mauling incidents increased, so too did lawsuits and anti-pit-bull legislation.[13]

Rumors

Rumors are unconfirmed stories that are shared informally and spread rapidly through a mass or crowd. They may be true, partially true, or false, but they are difficult or impossible to verify and represent "improvised news."[14] Rumors seem to emerge when people have no reliable source of information in an uncertain situation, and their communication tends to be spontaneous and unpredictable. Rumors of Leroy Dewer's being beaten by prison guards while in solitary confinement fanned the flames of revolt at Attica in 1971; rumors of heart attacks or ill-health on the part of the President of the United

Exhibit 16.2 Sidelights on American Culture

It Was a Bitchen Twitchen Blowchoice Down in the Valley

They were the sensation of the summer of 1982. Like the "flappers" of the 1920s and the "chipwiches" and "bobby soxers" of later years, *Puella americana valensis*—the Valley Girls—were a new subspecies from Teenage Land.

Valley Girls were first identified in that beige outreach of Los Angeles—California's San Fernando Valley—and then they were seen in almost every major city and suburban area. They came from fairly well-to-do families, were between the ages of 13 and 17, and had passions for pigging-out on junk food and piling on cosmetics. Too, they distinguished themselves by the amount of money they spent on clothing, tanning oil, sunglasses, lip gloss, Tab, Doritos, Kahlua brownies, Bubblicious chewing gum, movies, records, Harlequin romances, and other necessities such as blow dryers, Sony Walkmans, and gold chains. The Val Gals were also obsessed with fashion, and their top status possessions included horses, health-club memberships, and monthly clothing allowances.

What really differentiated Valley Girls from the preppies and bobby soxers of old was their arcane language and the enunciation that went with it. Their strange new language borrowed much from 1960s hippie slang, surfer lingo, and the street jargon of black inner-city youths: *scarf-out* meant overeat, *zod* or *goober* meant weird, *mondo* was great, and *groovy* meant out of fashion. All of the verbiage was accentuated by a blasé delivery, and most declarative statements were offered as sardonic questions. "Oh My God" (pronounced *omigod* and stretched over two octaves in a pinched nasal drawl) meant that something was just plain *raspy* or *spaz*. The overuse of the word *like* was part of the Val Gal slang that still carries over today among teenagers.

Why did "Valism" come into vogue? It developed for the same reasons as all other fads, particularly those that revolve around patterns of adolescent dress and speech. One group initiated the fad, probably for the purpose of setting itself apart. Others followed the trend because it represented a new in-group and afforded a type of prestige. Once the fad became highly visible, still more took part in order not to be left out or be considered "square." And like all fads, Valism persisted for only a short time.

Some Valley Girl Lingo

bagpipe it—forget it
Barf City—awful, bad, the worst
bitchen—the best
bitchen twitchen—more than the best
chill out—calm down
crank—to do something, like crank to school or crank up the TV
goober—a really dumb guy or something weird
grody—the worst, the most disgusting
live—great; "he's live," means he's great
Melvin—a weird person
Poindexter—someone who reads a lot of books
raspy—like bitchen
real smart—real dumb
shred the tube—going surfing
take it easy—to sit in the sun
trippy—outrageous
bag some Z's—to take a nap
zeeked out—acting crazy
zooned out—zeeked out, only worse
blowchoice—the thing to do
mondo—really great
outrageous—like mondo bitchen

SOURCES: *Newsweek,* August 2, 1982, p. 61; Mini Pond, *The Valley Girls' Guide to Life* (New York: Dell, 1982); *Time,* September 27, 1982, p. 56.

States have caused sudden and sharp declines in the stock market; rumors of war in the Middle East have abruptly altered the prices of gold and other precious metals.

One of the more interesting rumors in recent history involved the alleged death of Beatle Paul McCartney. On October 12, 1969, Detroit disc jockey Russ Gibbs received a telephone call on the air from a listener who described some curious evidence that suggested that Paul McCartney was dead:

> In the album *Revolution* [actually it was *The White Album*], if one listens carefully to the voice saying, "Number Nine, Number Nine, Number Nine" being played backwards, the words become: "Turn Me On Dead Man!" At the end of the song "Strawberry

Exhibit 16.3

Sociological Focus

Rumors: Test Yourself

1. True or False?
Actress Marilyn Monroe was killed by the CIA because she knew of their plot to assassinate President John F. Kennedy.

2. True or False?
Alligators roam the sewers under the streets of New York City.

3. True or False?
Singer Michael Jackson is actually Donna Summer in drag.
Singer Michael Jackson and his sister LaToya are the same person.

4. True or False?
McDonald's hamburgers contain spider eggs, and their milkshakes are made with seaweed.

5. True or False?
Cocaine is, and always has been, an ingredient in Coca-Cola.

Michael and LaToya Jackson appeared together at the Grammy Awards. LaToya later posed for *Playboy*, dispelling all rumors that she and Michael were one person.

Fields" in the *Magical Mystery Tour* album, there is someone saying: "I buried Paul!" when the background noises are filtered out.[15]

Several days later a review of the Beatles' album *Abbey Road* appeared in the *Michigan Daily,* accompanied by a picture of a bloody, decapitated head. The article presented additional evidence from recent Beatles albums suggesting McCartney's demise:

> *Sgt. Pepper* shows the lower part of a grave with yellow flowers shaped as Paul McCartney's bass guitar—or, if one prefers, the initial P. Inside the cover, McCartney wears an arm patch reading O.P.D., for Officially Pronounced Dead. The medal on his chest commemorates heroic death. On the back cover, everyone is facing forward—except, of course, Paul McCartney!
>
> *Abbey Road* shows John Lennon garbed in white to resemble an anthropomorphic god (or a minister), Ringo Starr dressed as an undertaker, George Harrison resembling a grave digger, and McCartney barefoot to suggest the way corpses are sometimes buried in England. They are leaving a cemetery. The license plate on the Volkswagen parked along the road reads "28IF," the age McCartney would have been if he had lived.[16]

The rumor spread quickly that McCartney had been killed some years earlier in an automobile accident and that the record company had substituted a double, urging John, George, and Ringo to go along with the scheme in the interests of future album sales. But the Beatles, it was believed, always faithful to their fans, had worked clues to Paul's death into their records in order to let the tragedy be known. Thousands of Beatles' enthusiasts examined

Answers

1. **False.** Monroe's death occurred a year before the Kennedy assassination. No evidence exists that the CIA was involved in his death. Lee Harvey Oswald, Kennedy's accused assassin, seemed to be too minor a character to have committed such a world-shaking act on his own. As a result, rumors began to fill the gap. At various times rumors attributed Kennedy's killing not only to the CIA, but to the FBI, the Cuban government, the Mafia, and even Lyndon Johnson.

2. **True, at least at one time.** Between 1932 and 1938, the *New York Times* printed several documented reports of alligators caught in the sewers in and around the city. How they got there no one really knows for sure. Records indicate that in 1936 the alligators were cleaned out by sewer workers under the orders of New York City's Sewer Superintendent, Teddy May.

3. **False and false.** Actually, with Jackson's rise to superstar status in the 1980s, many rumors circulated about him: that he sang the high notes for Diana Ross on many of her recordings, and that he was her illegitimate son. It was once rumored that Donna Summer was a transsexual, and if all of the rumors about Jackson and Summer were true, that would make Jackson a previously male/female impersonating a male. Does that make sense? As for Michael and LaToya Jackson being one and the same person, the rumor evolved because the two were never seen together. Although they are photographed together on the cover of the *We Are the World* album, true believers claim that trick photography was used and point out that the two look alike, are the same size, and have the same stature and demeanor (which, they probably do not consider, is very common among brothers and sisters).

4. **False and true.** Many rumors have developed about McDonald's. The spider egg rumor is the most curious since spider eggs are not a readily available commodity. On the other hand, the milkshakes do indeed contain a by-product of seaweed, used as a thickening agent.

5. **False and false.** In the late 1800s, most cola drinks contained extracts of the coca leaf—the natural product from which cocaine is derived. With the passage of the Pure Food and Drug Act in 1906, the coca extract had to be removed from all of the drinks. As a flavoring, however, Coca-Cola still contains a drug-free extract of the coca leaf.

SOURCES: Robert Daley, *The World Beneath the City* (New York: Lippincott, 1959); Hal Morgan and Kerry Tucker, *Rumor* (New York: Penguin, 1984); *New York Times,* February 10, 1935; Andrew Weil and Winifred Rosen, *From Chocolate to Morphine* (Boston: Houghton Mifflin, 1983).

album covers and other Beatles' memorabilia in search of additional clues. McCartney, of course, was not dead, and made the following comment about the rumor to a *Life* magazine correspondent:

> It is all bloody stupid. I picked up that O.P.D. badge in Canada. It was a police badge. Perhaps it means Ontario Police Department or something. I was wearing a black flower because they ran out of red ones. It is John, not me, dressed in black on the cover and inside of *Magical Mystery Tour*. On *Abbey Road* we were wearing our ordinary clothes. I was walking barefoot because it was a hot day. The Volkswagen just happened to be parked there. Perhaps the rumor started because I haven't been much in the press lately. . . . Can you spread it around that I am just an ordinary person and want to live in peace?[17]

Rumor thrives on ambiguous situations where it is either difficult or impossible to get accurate information, but where people are keenly interested in knowing what is going on. Celebrities and famous products are frequently the subject of rumors (see Exhibit 16.3).

Panic and Mass Hysteria

A **panic** is an uncoordinated and irrational flight from some threat—real or otherwise. Panic is a collective break for safety, and studies of panic behavior have made two important observations about this type of collective action.

First, panic depends on the availability of information about the danger involved. Hence, it takes place only if people believe that escape routes are available, but are either limited or closing. The former was the case in the stampedes for the exits in both the Beverly Hills Supper Club and Coconut Grove Night Club fires mentioned in the opening section of this chapter. Within this context, research by sociologist Neil J. Smelser has demonstrated a converse point: panic will *not* occur when people know that escape is not possible and that they are facing certain death.[18] This observation was clearly substantiated in the loss of the nuclear submarine *Thresher* in 1963. During a deep test dive, the $45-million vessel sprang a leak and was unable to return to the surface. As it slowly sank to a depth of 8,400 feet some 240 miles at sea east of Boston, its escort vessel, the subchaser *Skylark,* was in constant communication. While the underwater telephone transmissions between the two vessels indicated that fear and even terror characterized the emotions on the *Thresher*, no evidence of panic was apparent.[19]

Second, panic depends on people's sense of whether or not those present will help one another. Thus, the possibility of panic is diminished in a threatening situation if strong leadership is evident.[20] In a burning building, for example, panic would be almost certain if someone simply screamed, "Let's get out of here!" However, a rather different outcome would be likely if a leader emerged and shouted, "Line up quickly and follow me!"

Mass hysteria involves widespread and contagious anxiety, a highly emotional fear of a potentially threatening situation. It is a variety of panic that tends to be spread over longer periods of time or wider geographical areas than the fire-in-theater type of panic. The "June Bug" epidemic in 1962 and the radiation testing in Brazil in 1987 described at the beginning of this chapter were clear cases of mass hysteria. The witch hunting by the early Puritans of Massachusetts Bay Colony described in Chapter 7 (Exhibit 7.4) was a several-year-long incident of mass hysteria.

Unlike fads, fashions, and other forms of collective behavior, mass hysteria is less frequent and rarely has been studied. The *War of the Worlds* episode in 1938 was documented thoroughly, however, yielding a number of important insights into the dynamics of mass hysteria. At least 6 million people heard the broadcast, and no less than 1 million were frightened by it. As researcher Hadley Cantril described the hysteria:

> Long before the broadcast had ended, people all over the United States were praying, crying, fleeing frantically to escape death from Martians. Some ran to rescue loved ones. Others telephoned farewells or warnings, hurried to inform neighbors, sought information from newspapers or radio stations, summoned ambulances and police cars.[21]

On the basis of detailed interviews conducted soon after the radio broadcast, Cantril uncovered two characteristics, at least one of which was apparent among most of those who believed the broadcast. First, given world events in 1938, many people imagined that an invasion from someone—Germans or Japanese—was imminent. The fact that it was an alien from outer space rather than an enemy from Europe or Asia that was attacking seemed to be unimportant. For those who had a morbid fear of war, it appears that invaders were invaders, regardless of their origins. Second, many people questioned their own judgment. While an invasion from outer space seemed incredible, the announcers and government people on the radio were saying it was so. Less-educated people, primarily, lost confidence in their own wisdom and good sense.

Publics and Public Opinion

A **public** is a spatially diffuse collective of individuals who have a shared interest in some issue about which differing opinions are possible. Members of the population who are opposed to abortion are a *public.* Individuals who favor school prayer, the death penalty, the legalization of marijuana, or equal rights for women, are different *publics.*

Public opinion begins to emerge when the issue in question is discussed in order to resolve differences in point of view. Thus, **public opinion** is the dominant opinion of any given population on a particular issue. To cite specific examples of publics and public opinion, each year the American Council on Education and the University of California at Los Angeles conduct a national survey of first-year college students. The survey focuses on background characteristics, educational goals, interests and activities, career plans, personal objectives, and attitudes on contemporary social issues. The attitudes on social issues for the class of 1992 appear in Exhibit 16.4. Over 200,000 students were polled for this survey. Note that each issue reflects a different public. Public opinion, the dominant opinion for this particular population, is quite clear for a number of issues: the death penalty, equality for women, and the rights of criminals.

The "Two-step Flow" Hypothesis

Public opinion does not arise spontaneously, emerging as if from some vacuum, nor is it the result of independently formed judgments. Rather, it comes about informally through a series of social processes involving the influence of family members, close friends, peer groups, public figures, and the media. Public figures and the mass media may be the most vital factors in the formation of

Exhibit 16.4

Sociological Focus

Opinions of the Class of 1992: A National Profile Based on Students Entering College in 1988

Agree Strongly or Somewhat That:	Men	Women	Total
Government isn't protecting the consumer	61.0%	69.1%	65.4%
Government isn't doing enough to promote disarmament	56.9	75.2	66.7
Government isn't doing enough to control environmental pollution	82.3	85.3	83.9
Government should raise taxes to help reduce the deficit	32.0	24.1	27.8
There is too much concern for the rights of criminals	72.7	66.0	69.1
Military spending should be increased	33.1	20.5	26.3
Nuclear disarmament is attainable	59.5	61.2	60.4
Abortion should be legalized	56.8	57.2	57.0
The death penalty should be abolished	19.6	26.0	23.0
If two people really like each other, it's all right for them to have sex, even if they've known each other for only a very short time	65.1	37.1	50.0
The activities of married women are best confined to the home and family	32.1	20.1	25.6
Couples should live together for some time before deciding to get married	57.3	46.3	51.3
Students might appreciate the value of college more if they had to pay a greater share of the costs	56.2	50.8	53.3
Marijuana should be legalized	22.8	16.4	19.3
Busing to achieve racial balance in schools is all right	52.3	54.9	53.7
It is important to have laws prohibiting homosexual relations	59.7	39.9	49.0
Colleges should not invest funds in companies that do business with South Africa	51.4	42.1	46.4
The chief benefit of college is that it increases one's earning power	73.9	64.7	69.0
Employers should be allowed to require employees or job applicants to take drug tests	69.8	72.0	71.0
The best way to control AIDS is through widespread, mandatory testing	67.7	67.7	67.7
Just because a man thinks that a woman has "led him on" does not entitle him to have sex with her	75.3	91.0	83.8
Only volunteers should serve in the armed forces	52.7	53.9	53.4

Source: Adapted from *Chronicle on Higher Education,* January 11, 1989, p. A34. Reprinted by permission of the Higher Education Research Institute, UCLA.

public opinion. Some decades ago, this hypothesis was stressed by researchers Elihu Katz and Paul Lazarsfeld, who suggested that the media influences general public opinion in a "two-step flow" of communication.[22] In their view, the media has its primary impact on the opinion leaders and "influentials" of a community—the most respected political, professional, and business leaders. They, in turn, influence the more general public opinion. Thus, information and ideas flow directly from the media to community leaders and respected citizens, and then to the public at large through networks of interaction involving those influentials. In later studies by Katz, Lazarsfeld, and others, this two-step flow hypothesis was confirmed.[23]

Advertisements and Propaganda

Without question, the mass media has a tremendous impact on the formation of public opinion, specifically with respect to its communication of advertisements and propaganda. **Advertisements** are commercial messages that attempt to mold public opinion in the area of consumption. They may create a "need" where none existed previously, as was the case in 1983 with the introduction of Cabbage Patch Kids (see Exhibit 16.5), or they may try to convince consumers that one product is better than the next, when no difference really exists at all (as is the situation with most nonprescription pain relief preparations).

A George Bush campaign ad dealing with the Massachusetts prison furlough program left the impression that Michael Dukakis was soft on crime. Many observers believe the effective use of such propaganda was pivotal in Bush's election success.

SOCIAL INDICATOR

Public Opinion and the Legalization of Drugs

Given the perceptions of a failing war on drugs during 1988, debates emerged in Congress, the media, and academic circles. The possibility of legalizing *any* illicit drugs quickly died however, because *public opinion,* both before and during the debates, reflected nationwide opposition to the idea. For example, as indicated in a national survey of 1,003 adults conducted for *Parents Magazine* by Kane, Parsone & Associates during May 1987, most Americans are against legalization.

	Yes	No	Not Sure
Do you think prescription drugs such as valium or amphetamines should be legally available to any adult who wants them?	29%	65%	6%
Do you think that marijuana should be legally available to any adult who wants it?	14	81	5
Do you think cocaine or crack should be legally available to any adult who wants it?	2	97	1
Do you think other illegal drugs, such as heroin, should be legally available to any adult who wants them?	2	96	2

And according to a nationwide *Washington Post* poll of 1,012 randomly selected adults during June 1988, 90% opposed the legalization of drugs.

Advertisements become **propaganda** when they are of a political nature, seeking to mobilize public support behind a particular political party, candidate, or point of view by means of selective, limited, or even false information.

Public-opinion Polls

Knowledge of public opinion is generally obtained through the use of polls. A **public-opinion poll** involves a sampling of a population that is representative of a geographical area, a specific public, or a society as a whole. Such polls are used primarily in market research and the political arena. The pollster asks the sample population a series of questions about the product, issue, or candidate of concern. Polls can track many dimensions of public opinion, such as different views of Oliver North (Exhibit 16.6). With a properly chosen sample, a limited number of respondents can predict the likes and dislikes of the entire population they represent. A sample of as few as 3,000 voters can predict the outcome of a national election, usually within 2 percentage points of the final result.

SOCIAL INDICATOR

Gallup Poll Accuracy in 14 Presidential Elections

Year	Final Gallup Survey		Election Result	
1988	51.0%	Bush	53.9%	Bush
1984	59.0	Reagan	59.2	Reagan
1980	47.0	Reagan	50.8	Reagan
1976	48.0	Carter	50.0	Carter
1972	62.0	Nixon	61.8	Nixon
1968	43.0	Nixon	43.5	Nixon
1964	64.0	Johnson	61.3	Johnson
1960	51.0	Kennedy	50.1	Kennedy
1956	59.5	Eisenhower	57.8	Eisenhower
1952	51.0	Eisenhower	55.5	Eisenhower
1948	44.5	Truman	49.9	Truman
1944	51.5	Roosevelt	53.3	Roosevelt
1940	52.0	Roosevelt	55.0	Roosevelt
1936	55.7	Roosevelt	62.5	Roosevelt

This statement suggests the extreme power of political polling in particular, a matter that has caused considerable debate in recent years. Since the 1960s, the major television networks—ABC, NBC, and CBS—have made projections as to the outcome of elections based on actual results in sample key precincts, after the polls closed. Although it took the suspense out of watching the election returns, no one seemed to mind. But during the 1980 presidential election between Jimmy Carter and Ronald Reagan, exit polling was used. At key locations, voters leaving their polling places were asked by television reporters how they voted and why. The result was that by 8:15 P.M. eastern time, the networks had predicted Reagan's landslide victory over Carter several hours before the polls had closed in the West. Subsequent studies after the 1980 election found that many people did not vote because of the news. Critics of the procedure question its news value and argue that it thwarts the democratic process by discouraging citizens from voting.[24] The networks, on the other hand, maintain that it is their job to report and not withhold news. In 1985, the networks agreed not to use exit-poll data to even hint at the outcome of elections until after all state polls closed.[25]

THEORIES OF COLLECTIVE BEHAVIOR

What causes collective behavior? In some instances, like the Beverly Hills Supper Club fire, the stimulus is quite clear. The building was ablaze and the situation was a matter of self-preservation. But even in those circumstances, why did the people stampede—an action that insured increased casualties? Why did the residents of Miami's Overtown riot after the shooting of Nevell Johnson, Jr.? Again, their anger is easily understood. But why burning, looting, and assault? Why was so much hysteria associated with Orson Welles' broadcast of "War of the Worlds"? And what is it that pushes people into other types of collective behavior, such as demonstrations, social movements, fads and fashions, lynchings, and other mass episodes?

Smelser's Value-added Theory

Just as no one theory of disease can explain all forms of illness, no single approach can point to the reasons for all forms of collective behavior. However, Neil Smelser's analysis of these phenomena—his **value-added theory**—is regarded as one of the most important statements on this subject, one which is considered the most systematic theoretical treatment of collective behavior.[26] It is based on the idea that each stage in the process contributes something (adds value) to the end result.

Collective behavior, according to Smelser, is "mobilization on the basis of a belief which redefines social action," and moves through a series of six stages: (1) structural conduciveness, (2) structural strain, (3) a generalized belief, (4) precipitating events, (5) mobilization for action, and (6) operation of social control.

Structural Conduciveness

The first stage, structural conduciveness, suggests that the fabric of society must be conducive to a manifestation of collective behavior. That is, the social organization of society must lend itself to the occurrence of collective behavior. In a society with only one race, for example, race riots could not occur. The stampede at the Beverly Hills Supper Club could not happen in La Paz, Bolivia, for at an altitude of almost 13,000 feet, the amount of oxygen in the air is barely enough to keep a cigarette lighted and would never support a raging fire. On the other hand, the United States contains many urban areas in which socially isolated inner-city neighborhoods are characterized by poverty, crowding, and minority groups victimized by institutionalized patterns of racial or ethnic discrimination. These areas are structurally conducive to rioting.

Structural Strain

Structural strains are those conflicts caused by frustration, stress, and tension. They may be initiated by contradictions between real and ideal norms, by the deficit between desired goals and the institutionalized means

Exhibit 16.5

Case Study

The Saga of the Cabbage Patch Kids

We create the market. We create the demand.

—Arnold C. Greenberg, President, Coleco Industries

The Cabbage Patch Kids show the power of creative advertising. In fact, more than just a simple fad, these dough-faced, chinless, homely dolls with their touching runt-of-the-litter charm became the Holy Grail of the 1983 Christmas shopping season. They caused more crowds, fights, ravening mobs, riots, mass hysteria, and other forms of collective behavior than any other product in recent history.

The story of Cabbage Patch Kids actually began some years earlier, in 1977, with Georgia artist Xavier Roberts. Back in those days, the dolls were handmade and were known simply as "little people." Roberts had a rather mawkish ritual for selling his dolls. They were not "made," but "delivered" and "adopted" at what had once been a medical clinic in Cleveland, Georgia, a small rural town some 80 miles northeast of Atlanta. At the "adoption," Roberts' employees wore white nurse's uniforms, and each prospective "parent" had to vow undying love to the little cloth creature. Some of the dolls sold for as high as $1,000, and many of the "parents" were adults.

All of this changed when Roberts negotiated a contract with Coleco Industries of Hartford, Connecticut. From handmade "little people," the dolls became mass-produced Cabbage Patch Kids. When they first appeared on the shelves of American toy stores in February 1983, little notice was taken of them. The few shoppers that did happen to give them a second look saw them as no more than ugly little apparitions that did not walk, talk, cry, wet, or look pretty like the other dolls with which children were accustomed. Then media hype took over.

Coleco Industries built on the "adoption" theme. The company promoted the idea that the dolls were foundlings left in a cabbage patch, and each doll came with its own set of adoption papers. Moreover, by means of minute differentiation in a computer program, each one of the dolls had one-of-a-kind features. The Cabbage Patch Kids projected a caricature of almost every characteristic of real babies—blunt, chubby, round cheeks, big eyes, and pudgy little arms and legs—without actually resembling any real baby. The advertising blitz included every form of mass communication, and the public relations campaign included a paper by a Brandeis University psychologist that pointed out that the doll's features constituted a "releasing mechanism" that triggered the instinct for nurturing in both adults and children.

As the 1983 Christmas season drew near, it became apparent that the promotion had worked; Cabbage Patch hysteria was in full swing. Shoppers engaged in some rather bizarre behaviors in their attempts to obtain dolls:

- In Wilkes-Barre, Pennsylvania, a crowd of 1,000 turned to

The 1983 Christmas shopping craze for Cabbage Patch Kids is evident here. Shoppers stand outside a Zayre discount store in Virginia waiting to purchase one of the sought-after dolls.

violence after waiting eight hours to get into a Zayre store. One shopper suffered a broken leg in the melee and the store manager had to arm himself with a baseball bat to defend his position behind the counter.

- At a Hills Department Store in Charleston, West Virginia, 5,000 people turned into a Christmas mob and staged a near riot. Said the store manager: "They knocked over the display table. People were grabbing at each other, pushing and shoving. It got ugly."
- Groups of Wisconsinites appeared at Milwaukee County Stadium when it was rumored that a B-29 bomber would be making an airborne delivery of 2,000 Cabbage Patch Kids. All the customers had to do, it was believed, was bring catcher's mitts and credit cards, which would be photographed from the air.
- In Lansing, Michigan, shoppers angry about not winning dolls in a drawing refused to leave a store until police threatened to arrest them.
- A Kansas City postman, despairing of finding one of the dolls in the Western Hemisphere, flew to London to get a Cabbage Patch Kid for his five-year-old daughter.
- Just days before Christmas, the newspaper want ads became a new hope for anxious customers. On one Sunday, the *Boston Globe* listed 22 ads, one asking $3,000 for a doll signed by creator Xavier Roberts; a *Chicago Tribune* ad offered to trade two Rose Bowl tickets for a doll; and in the *Washington Post,* 48 ads on one day included two dolls for $2,500—with one offering a free 1948 pickup truck in which to take them home.

But why did Cabbage Patch dolls create such havoc? Psychologists quickly offered a blizzard of explanations. Dr. Joyce Brothers held that it was the very homeliness of the doll that was appealing. "It is comforting," Brothers commented, "to feel the Cabbage Patch doll can be loved with all your might—even though it isn't pretty." Dr. Bruce Axelrod of Milwaukee's Comprehensive Mental Health Services focused on an alternative theory, emphasizing the adoption ritual. "Most children between the ages of six and twelve fantasize that they were really adopted," explained Axelrod. "A child who adopts a Cabbage Patch Kid can act out that fantasy."

Whether the psychological theories are correct is difficult to tell. From the sociological perspective, perhaps children wanted their Cabbage Patch Kids because other children wanted them or because the television ads said other children wanted them. Or perhaps children didn't really want them as much as their parents did. One customer commented, "If each girl on either side of us had one, and my girl didn't, I'd never hear the end of it." And another offered, "If my girl has one and the others don't, just think of how their parents will eat their hearts out." But less grand motives were also involved. A *New York Times* reporter asked one five-year-old girl why she liked her Cabbage Patch doll so much. Said the child: "She has a real belly button."

As a postscript to this saga, the Cabbage Patch Kids fad tended to be short-lived. Although interest in the dolls endured for another Christmas season, the number of Cabbage Patch seekers declined radically. By the middle of 1984 the dolls could be had almost anywhere, even at discount prices. Coleco Industries then introduced spin-off products—Cabbage Patch fashions, strollers, games, and numerous other items, but these too failed to maintain interest in the pudgy-faced creations. By 1988 Coleco had accumulated some $335 million in debts and was forced to declare bankruptcy.

SOURCES: *Business Week,* January 16, 1984, pp. 27, 31; *National Law Journal,* January 2, 1984, p. 43; *Newsweek,* December 12, 1983, pp. 78–82, 85; *Time,* December 12, 1983, pp. 64, 67; *USA Today,* December 18, 1983, p. 1A; *USA Today,* July 13, 1988, p. 3B; *U.S. News & World Report,* July 25, 1988, p. 48; *Wall Street Journal,* December 8, 1983, p. 34; Wilmington (Delaware) *News-Journal,* December 20, 1983, p. A14.

Exhibit 16.6

Types & Stereotypes

Ollie's Follies

Starring Lieutenant Colonel Oliver L. North as the Swashbuckling Diplomat, Fawn Hall as the Shredding Secretary, Ronald Reagan as the Commander-in-Chief, and a Cast of Contras

Throughout late 1986 and the better part of 1987, the U.S. Congress, the news media, and even a segment of the American people seemed to be obsessed with what became known as the "Iran-Contra affair." Oliver North resurfaced again in 1989 when he was sentenced.

The principals in the episode were many. In addition to a shadowy collection of arms merchants, foreign government officials, and international financiers, the government of Iran, two warring factions in Nicaragua (the Sandinistas and the Contras), President Ronald Reagan, and members of the U.S. intelligence community all played a role.

Although all of the Iran-Contra events probably will never be fully known, the general thrust of the initiative was relatively clear. First, and contrary to the wisdom and logic of good foreign policy, weapons were sold secretly to Iran with the apparent understanding that American hostages being held in Lebanon would be freed. Second, and contrary to the wishes and mandates of Congress, the profits from the arms sales were channeled secretly to Nicaragua for the support of the Contras and their guerrilla war against the Marxist Sandinista government. Third, the effort had been engineered by the American intelligence community, and contrary to the principles of democratic government, it would appear that a "secret government" had been developing in the United States that was creating and implementing foreign policy without the approval of Congress and the President. Fourth, when news of the Iran-Contra venture began to leak out, several members of the intelligence community scrambled to hide the truth: false accounts of the weapons and financial transactions were prepared; papers documenting the operations were either hidden or shredded; and incorrect statements were made to those investigating the operation and cover-up.

Early on, it appeared that a key character in the whole sordid affair was Lieutenant Colonel Oliver L. North, a member of the National Security Council. North had been linked to many aspects of the arms sales and diversion of funds, and testimony by his secretary Fawn Hall implicated him in the shredding of documents and other aspects of the cover-up. But North was not talking, and initial press and television coverage of the Iran-Contra events portrayed North as either an overzealous patriot or a lone wolf villain. When North ultimately testified before a national television audience,

for achieving them, or by the gap between social ideals and social realities. Many of the race riots of years past involved structural strains that developed as the result of frustrations experienced in black communities where a huge disparity exists between the American dream of equality and the hunger and poverty of the ghetto. Similarly, the protests against the United States' placement of nuclear missiles in various parts of Europe involves concerns and strains over the threat of nuclear annihilation.

Generalized Beliefs

Structural conduciveness and strain are not enough to generate collective behavior. A third determinant involves the growth and spread of generalized beliefs as to the conditions that are causing the strain. That is, people must identify a problem and share a common interpretation of it before the scene is set for collective behavior to develop. Consider again the case of Miami's Overtown riot in 1982. Overtown was (and still is) a socially isolated

Which of these descriptions do you feel describes Lieutenant Colonel North?

	Describes	Does Not Describe	Not Sure
A Reckless Adventurer	15%	72%	13%
A National Hero	29	61	10
A True Patriot	67	24	9
Someone We Need in Government	37	49	14
A Scapegoat for Higher-ups	77	15	8
Someone I Would Want to Marry My Daughter	26	57	17

however, he became an American social phenomenon.

In his four days of testimony before the congressional committee investigating the Iran-Contra controversy, Lieutenant Colonel North put on a bravura performance that was rooted in American tradition. While admitting that he had run his own brand of foreign policy from the White House basement, he emerged as an underdog, a true believer, a patriot, and an honest man facing down the politicians. Pensive, passionate, sanctimonious, sincere, impatient, impenitent, articulate, aggressive, cocky, contrite—he was all of those things and more. His telegenic charm put the investigating committee on the defensive and touched off a tidal wave of telegrams, letters, and flowers. T-shirts and bumper stickers sporting "Give 'em Hell, Ollie" appeared across the nation. North had sparked the American imagination, spiriting an "Olliemania" craze that elevated him to the status of an American folk hero.

Interestingly, although Oliver North had been catapulted to the status of a cultural hero, polls taken in July 1987 during and after his testimony suggested that the American people actually had a rather qualified opinion of him and his exploits. In a poll conducted for *Time,* for example, most thought of him as both a "patriot" and a "scapegoat."

SOURCES: *Christian Science Monitor,* July 17, 1987, p. 4; *New York Times,* July 11, 1987, pp. 1, 5; *Newsweek,* July 13, 1987, pp. 14–20; *Newsweek,* July 20, 1987, p. 10; *New York Times,* July 18, 1987, pp. 1, 7; *Time,* July 20, 1987, p. 15.

inner-city environment characterized by poverty, hunger, and unemployment. The area was populated by minorities who had experienced varieties of discrimination for a good part of their lives (structural conduciveness). Their neighborhood was situated at the center of a metropolitan area well-known for affluence and highly mobile wealth. But for the people of Overtown the American Dream was but a charade (structural strain). Within this setting, residents developed the *generalized belief* that part of their problem was a continual victimization of blacks by a ruthless, white police force. Whether this generalized belief, or any other for that matter, was accurate, is not the point; people act on their beliefs. Generalized beliefs may be based on known facts, shared attitudes, or some common ideology.

Precipitating Events

In all instances of collective behavior, some event, or set of related events, triggers a collective response. The precipitating event itself need not be particularly significant. A seemingly unwarranted search in a prison exercise yard can precipitate a collective action by inmates. In the case of the Overtown riot, the precipitating event was indeed significant—the shooting of Nevell Johnson, Jr., by a white police officer. And too, the event(s) in question need not have even taken place. Looking back to the discussion of the Watts riot in Chapter 7, it is apparent that a whole series of precipitating events took place, the major one being a false rumor that the police had roughed up an innocent, pregnant woman.

Mobilization for Action

As soon as the precipitating event occurs, people must be persuaded to join the movement. This mobilization may be structured or may emerge spontaneously. In the more structured instances of mobilization, it is usually group leaders who initiate the collective action. In 1978, it was the leadership of the Ayatollah Khomeini that brought about the Islamic Revolution in Iran; in 1980, it was the influence of Lech Walesa that led to the formation of the Solidarity labor movement in Poland; in 1986 it was the challenge of Corazon Aquino, widow of a murdered opposition politician that resulted in the fall of Philippine president Ferdinand Marcos. Leaders such as these are not always necessary. Mobilization can occur spontaneously: in Overtown, expressive acts took place in the form of stone throwing and destruction of property; at the Beverly Hills Supper Club the crowd stampeded when black smoke began to pour into the dining rooms. In both cases, it was the precipitating event itself that mobilized the people into collective action.

Operation of Social Control

The course and persistence of the collective action are shaped by the available mechanisms of social control. If the mechanisms are absent or ineffective, the collective action will continue to run its course. In Watts, Overtown, and numerous other inner-city settings where riots have occurred, the police were either outnumbered or disorganized, thus allowing the riots to expand and continue.

By contrast, social control also can prevent an episode of collective behavior. After the incident in Overtown in late 1982, Patrolman Luis Alvarez, the officer who had slain Nevell Johnson, Jr., was charged with manslaughter. During his trial, a variety of social control elements mobilized in Overtown to defuse the potential for disruptive collective action that could result from an unpopular verdict. Religious leaders, community figures, black disc jockeys, black police officers, the county community relations board, and even members of the Miami Dolphins' football team, worked in the area counseling residents to remain calm. Radio stations sponsored programs and talk shows to explain the trial, and to allow people to vent frustrations. Nevell Johnson, Jr.'s, family urged calm. The judge presiding at the trial delayed announcing the verdict for one hour in order to allow 1,000 police to deploy in Overtown, and among them were all of Miami's 174 black officers—assigned to high-visibility patrols in an attempt to make police a less provocative target. Luis Alvarez was found not guilty of manslaughter by an all-white jury. But due to the preparations, no riot ever developed. Some scattered violence and looting occurred, but no lives were lost. No serious injuries resulted, and damage estimates were put at less than $100,000.[27]

Smelser's theory does not explain why specific incidents of collective behavior occur, but it does suggest what the preconditions of collective behavior generally are. And it readily can be applied to numerous episodes of collective action. Consider the riot at New York's Attica Prison, described earlier, in light of Smelser's "value-added" theory:

- In 1971 Attica was a maximum-security prison that housed many of New York's toughest and most serious offenders *(structural conduciveness).*
- The conditions of incarceration involved daily degradation and humiliation; deprivations were numerous; and the prison atmosphere was charged with racism *(structural strain).*
- When Leroy Dewer and another inmate were removed from their cells and placed in solitary confinement on the evening of September 8, it was widely believed that subsequently several of the guards beat the two *(generalized belief).*
- On the morning of September 9, custodial officers found the inmates of Leroy Dewer's section to be especially belligerant; the officers decided it would be best to return the inmates directly to their cells without allowing them their usual time in the exercise yard; as the inmates were being escorted to their cells, several attacked the officer on duty *(precipitating factors).*
- Spontaneously, other inmates joined in the violence; they set upon the gate at Times Square, which gave way, thus giving them access to the entire prison complex *(mobilization for action).*
- State officials attempted to negotiate an end to the inmate revolt, thus permitting the prison takeover to endure for several days; when negotiations broke down, state troopers mounted an armed assault on the prison

complex, ending the uprising fifteen minutes later and killing 39 inmates and hostages in the process *(social control).*

Thus, for many episodes of collective behavior to occur, a series of conditions must be present. Clearly these preconditions need not be present for all types of collective behavior to emerge; after all, some varieties are common, everyday occurrences. Nothing is unusual, for example, about casual or conventional crowds. They occur every day and are dictated by the very structure of organized society—customers accumulating in a shopping mall, commuters packing themselves into a bus or subway car, students attending a lecture. All of these collectivities are necessary for a society to function and remain dynamic. But why do some crowds, fads, crazes, and forms of mass behavior diminish their members' individualism and encourage people to accept the attitudes and behavior of the group? Why will otherwise law-abiding citizens participate in a riot or lynch mob? Why will others participate in a fad, become hostage to mass hysteria, or strip themselves naked at a rock concert?

The Contagion Perspective

In *The Crowd,* published in 1895, French sociologist Gustave Le Bon held that members of a crowd have a mental unity, a collective mind that replaces conscious personalities:

> Whoever be the individuals that compose it, however like or unlike be their mode of life, their occupations, their character, or their intelligence, the fact that they have been transformed into a crowd puts them in possession of a sort of collective mind which makes them feel, think, and act in a manner quite different from that in which each individual of them would feel, think, and act were he in a state of isolation.[28]

Thus, in Le Bon's **contagion perspective,** people undergo some radical transformation under the influence of a crowd. Le Bon believed that crowds cause people to regress, that crowds are guided by instinct, not by rational decisions. Furthermore, the anonymity of the collective gives each member a certain feeling of power—the participants become suggestible as if they had been hypnotized, and a contagion effectively sweeps through them. The result is the unquestioning approval of and submission to the crowd's leadership.

Le Bon's work is considered "classic" by many and has had a significant influence on collective behavior as a field of study. However, it has analytical weaknesses. It fails to explain why some crowds form and operate in the absence of leadership, why some people do not join crowds while others do, and why crowd action stops. Moreover, it is a bit simplistic to assume that the members of a crowd act as if they were mindless cattle.

The Interactionist Perspective

Sociologist Herbert Blumer, while rejecting Le Bon's notion of a "collective mind," expressed an **interactionist perspective** on collective behavior, holding that the contagion that sweeps through crowds is the result of "circular reactions" operating in a situation of "social unrest":

> [Circular reaction] refers to a type of interstimulation wherein the response of one individual reproduces the stimulation that has come from another individual and in being reflected back to this individual reinforces the stimulation. Thus the interstimulation assumes a circular form in which individuals reflect one another's states of feeling and in so doing intensify this feeling.[29]

In other words, circular reaction involves a process whereby the emotions of others generate the same emotions in oneself, in turn intensifying the emotions of others. Imagine that a Boeing 747 is flying through a severe electrical storm; the lightning is fierce, the air is choppy, and the flight is anything but smooth. It is the first flight for a couple in the third row. They are afraid of flying and both of them are quite nervous. They become highly agitated, thus shaking the solitude of those around them. The other passengers, conscious of the storm and observing the growing frenzy of the frightened couple, begin to feel and appear nervous themselves. The couple, in seeing that they are not alone in their plight, become even more stricken, further influencing those nearby. In time, the anguish spreads from row to row, until the entire cabin is in a state of near hysteria.

The Convergence Perspective

Le Bon's contagion theory and Blumer's interactionist approach stress the transformation of individuals under the influence of the crowd situation. By contrast, supporters of the **convergence perspective** hold that people who share certain tendencies come together to act out their common predispositions. Thus, the members of an acting crowd, the participants in a craze, or the individuals caught up in some mass hysteria are merely revealing their "true selves." Those who argue this perspective maintain that the emergent action of certain collectivities results, at the very least, from what people bring to the scene, as well as what occurs at the scene. Or as social psychologist Floyd Allport once explained it: "The individual in the crowd behaves as he would behave alone, *only more so.*"[30]

The convergence perspective has been criticized on several grounds. It assumes too much predictability on the part of individuals and too little human complexity. More importantly, it has been argued that individuals in a crowd may have more than one latent tendency toward the same object, and convergence theory fails to predict which will be expressed.[31]

The Emergent Norm Perspective

Challenging the bases of the contagion, interactionist, and convergence theories, proponents of the **emergent norm perspective** stress the differences in motives, attitudes, and actions of the members of collectivities, particularly those in crowds. First, adherents of this point of view reject the idea that a crowd behaves as some homogeneous entity. Rather, they argue, "crowd unanimity" is an illusion. Observers may think that the members of a crowd act as a unit, but divergent behaviors may go unrecognized or be dismissed as unimportant. What actually happens in a crowd, theorists Ralph Turner and Lewis Killian maintain, is that new norms emerge during the course of social interaction. These norms define appropriate behavior in the crowd situation and arise from the visible actions of but a few individuals. These few activists are able to define the norms—whether they are norms regarding when to applaud a performer, boo an umpire, jump to the music of a rock group, throw stones at a police car, destroy the interior of a prison compound, or lynch an accused offender—for most of the other members. While many of the members of the collective may not agree with the direction group behavior is taking, they refrain from offering opposition and sometimes even participate in the action out of fear of ridicule, coercion, or perhaps personal injury.[32]

Although the Turner-Killian perspective is plausible, it suffers from a major weakness. It fails to explain how behavior that is at one moment *deviant* (assault, lynching, looting) is somehow transformed into normative behavior. This perspective implies that social norms may be very weak, and that the members of certain collectivities have no real commitment to them (see Exhibit 16.7).

Some Considerations of Theory

Historically, collective behavior has been stereotyped as being completely unplanned, spontaneous, and unorganized. As a result, it has suffered from neglect by the social sciences in terms of theoretical development. Recent research and theory, however, particularly the contributions of Smelser, and Turner and Killian, have emphasized the rationality and organizational characteristics of collective behavior. Smelser's value-added theory demonstrates that the emergence of collective behavior involves a process—a series of stages—and that each stage is necessary for collective action to occur. Turner and Killian's emergent norm perspective suggests that while the members of collectivities may have different motives and attitudes, the norms that emerge from activists may be imposed on other members.

Within this context, one can speculate as to whether or not certain events typically identified as the individual actions of cruel, depraved, asocial predators were actually incidents of collective behavior. A case in point involves the infamous New Bedford rape incident of 1983. According to police reports and trial testimony, the 21-year-old victim had entered Big Dan's—a rather seedy bar in the North End of New Bedford, Massachusetts—to buy cigarettes. Before she could leave, one of the tavern patrons grabbed her, stripped her of most of her clothes, and raped her on the barroom floor. No one came to her aid. Instead, she was lifted onto a pool table and raped repeatedly by at least four men to the cheers and applause of the bar patrons. The victim ultimately fled, and four of the suspects were later convicted of rape.[33]

Although theories of collective behavior do not serve to mitigate or even lessen the seriousness of the actions of the offenders and the cheering bystanders, to what extent were the norms of the participants and onlookers influenced by contagion, convergence, interactionism, or emergent norms? A number of those who observed the rape maintained that they did not intervene out of fear. Was Turner and Killian's emergent norm perspective operative here? On the other hand, was the group participation in the rape the result of some *convergence* of individuals with predispositions to sexual assault? Regardless of which explanation, if any, is appropriate, the New Bedford case points to an important consideration about theories of collective behavior. That consideration is that it is likely no one theory is either right or wrong. While one perspective may be appropriate for explaining certain types of crazes, riots, or mob actions, other types are better understood by other theories. Furthermore, in many instances of collective behavior, contagion, convergence, interactionism, *and* emergent norms may be operating side by side.

SOCIAL MOVEMENTS

Most instances of collective behavior involve time-bound episodes. Crowds form and disperse rather quickly. Riots,

By campaigning for the right to vote, these women were part of a social movement.

mob actions, panics, mass hysteria, and rumors may last a few hours or days. Even fads and fashions tend to be transient. Some may last for up to a year or two, but they are nevertheless time bound. Social movements, on the other hand, persist over time. **Social movements** are attempts to bring about or resist social change. Important social movements in the United States have focused on the abolition of slavery, civil rights, voting rights, women's rights, resistance to war, employee unionism, the prosecution of drunk drivers, the state of the environment, and many other issues.

One of the more interesting social movements of recent decades focuses on the planet Earth—the environmental movement. This movement is curious, not because of the type of change it attempts to bring about, but because one of its components was responsible for the largest demonstration in the nation's history.

The thrust of the environmental movement began during the 1960s, primarily with the publication of Rachel Carson's landmark book, *Silent Spring,* a devastating indictment of the use of chemical insecticides. Carson's words were dramatic and quickly caught the attention of a wide audience. As she so poignantly wrote:

> The world of systemic insecticides is a weird world, surpassing the imaginings of the brothers Grimm. It is a world where the enchanted forest of the fairy tales has become a poisonous forest in which an insect that chews a leaf or sucks the sap of a plant is doomed. It is a world where a flea bites a dog, and dies because the dog's blood has been made poisonous, where an insect may die from vapors emanating from a plant it has never touched, where a bee may carry poisonous nectar back to its hive and presently produce poisonous honey.[34]

Following Rachel Carson's lead, others spoke of the environmental crisis as a major American tragedy. Ecologists documented the destruction of ecosystems; independent observers noted the pollution of air and waterways; conservationists cried for the preservation of the wilderness; and the press kept the nation informed as to the latest reports of water, air, soil, sound, and thermal pollution. Friends of the Earth, the Environmental Defense Fund, and other "save the environment" groups emerged, and *The Environmental Handbook* became a national bestseller.[35] The first decade of the movement reached its climax on April 22, 1970,—the date of the nation's first "Earth Day." Huge rallies were held in high schools, on college campuses, and in the streets; state governors and assemblies enacted environmental legislation; industries announced pollution control measures; and in Washington, D.C., both houses of Congress were adjourned as senators and representatives spoke at gatherings across the country. In all, more than 20 millions Americans participated in Earth Day, and it was the largest, cleanest, safest, and most peaceful demonstration in American history.[36]

Environmentalism is but one example of an extremely visible social movement. It is a highly successful social movement as well, one that not only persists, but that has achieved many of its goals. Many social movements, however, fail to survive or have any impact. Social movements can be of many different types and can come into being for many different reasons. Thus, the important questions to ask about social movements include the following: what are the different types of social movements? why and how do they emerge? why are some successful while others are not?

Types of Social Movements

Sociologists have put forth any number of ways to categorize social movements. Perhaps the most useful is the typology offered by William Cameron, who sees social movements as *reactionary, conservative, revisionary, revolutionary, escapist,* or *expressive,* depending on the degree of change the movement seeks.[37]

Reactionary social movements seek to restore society, or at least some part of it, to its former condition or state—to "the good old days." The members of reactionary social movements look fondly to the past and hope to relinquish the changes that have transformed

Exhibit 16.7

Research in Sociology

Blackout Looting

The New York City skyline is pictured at the time of the November 9, 1963, blackout. Buildings with lights have emergency power generators.

In 1963, at a Canadian hydrogenerating installation four miles west of Niagara Falls, a small electrical relay was adjusted for existing power loads. Although power requirements continued to increase as time passed, the relay was never readjusted.

At 5 P.M. on November 9, 1965, the power load for Toronto increased just enough to trip the relay adjusted two years earlier. That, in turn, activated a circuit breaker, putting one power line out of action. Under most circumstances, the incident would have caused a small electrical blackout in a localized area, which could be quickly remedied by an adjustment of the relay. In this case, the relay was connected to the Northeast Power Grid, an electrical pool covering an area of 80,000 square miles.

When the first power line was put out of action, its load was shifted to others. They, however, could not handle it. Suddenly, 1.6 million kilowatts of energy destined for Toronto but unable to get there surged southward into upper New York State and New England. Years earlier, several senior engineers of the Northeast Power Grid had speculated about what they called a "cascade effect," in which an enormous, unexpected demand for power by one member on the grid would suck up the electricity of all the others. If that happened, every generator in the grid would shut itself down in order to avoid damage to the equipment. That's exactly what happened on November 9, 1965. All 80,000 square miles of the Northeast Power Grid were plunged into darkness—from Canada to the Carolinas, including New York City. Thus began the worst power failure in the history of technology.

Although one would expect that chaos might break out on the streets of New York at such a time, the reverse seemed to be the case. New Yorkers of all classes, backgrounds, and neighborhoods reacted in a way that became part of the city's folklore. Not only did people feel a sudden surge of community spirit, but they also had a remarkably diminished urge to commit crimes. Only a few stores were looted, and the crime rate declined appreciably. Instead of crime, New York experienced an 800% increase in local telephone calls, and nine months later to the day all hospitals reported a sharp increase in the number of births.

At 9:35 P.M. on July 13, 1977, New York City experienced its second blackout. Almost spontaneously, and in contrast to the 1965 episode, looting broke out in all five boroughs of the city within ten minutes after the lights went out. Moreover, the looting continued throughout the night and into the following afternoon. In all, 1,576 businesses were looted with losses estimated at almost $40 million. Why such radically different reactions to two seemingly similar incidents?

A number of explanations were offered, the most common

being that the event in 1965 marked the city's first large-scale blackout and few figured that the power would be off for an extended period of time. In the 1977 incident, New Yorkers had already lived through a blackout. People seemed to "know" that the city was in for a long spell without light and with diminished law enforcement capability.

A *New York Times*/CBS poll of attitudes found that 60% of New Yorkers thought the looters were criminals to start with—"the kind of people that steal anyway." More liberal explanations maintained that since the majority of the looters were inner-city residents, they were deprived citizens who were rebelling against their desperate circumstances. Research commissioned by the Ford Foundation in the wake of the 1977 blackout revealed a considerably more complex picture.

Analyses of arrest statistics and other official reports, combined with interviews with looters, bystanders, business owners, and police indicated that the looting occurred in three stages. During Stage I, the first hour after the lights went out, looting was carried out almost exclusively by individuals who quickly broke into stores to steal the most valuable merchandise. These looters were primarily men between the ages of 20 and 30. They were street types who normally lived by various forms of theft and street hustling. Law enforcement activity on the streets during Stage I was minimal.

Stage II lasted from about 10:30 to 11:30 P.M. During this phase, the looters were joined by bands of youths—primarily alienated adolescents who were looking for fun and excitement, but who also seized the opportunity to secure money and goods. Once involved, these youths participated extensively in the looting for the remainder of the blackout. Also arriving on the scene to loot in Stage II were the generally unemployed, badly educated, ghetto poor under 35 years of age who saw no reason not to join in on the stealing.

The Stage III looting started at approximately midnight and stretched into the next afternoon. Stage III looters included the stable poor and working-class members of the community who were caught up by the near hysteria in the streets. Legal constraints against theft had suddenly been lifted for them; social pressure to "dip in" and take something was far greater than the more normal pressures to obey the law. The chaos of Stage III also drew in better-off, employed neighborhood residents who seemed to be motivated by greed. The Stage III looters, moreover, had been encouraged by the early blackout situation during which they perceived no risk of arrest. However, they appeared on the scene at the same time that the police had mobilized sufficient strength to regain control of the streets.

The ultimate conclusion of the research was that it would be too simplistic to refer to the looters as neighborhood riff-raff. Although street criminals played an important part in initiating the disturbances, the main cause of the upheaval was the serious national economic decline that had created exceedingly high levels of unemployment in the inner-city, combined with the high prices of food and other necessary goods that resulted from a decade of inflation. As the Ford Foundation concluded:

> What the looting seemed to say was that the issue is a general spiritual kind of hunger, deeply felt by citizens of the ghetto because they simply lack the goods, the material things, and the power to consume what is so thoroughly emphasized by the media in our society. In other words, the welfare check or the unemployment allotment is important for survival, but just surviving is not important enough in a society that is constantly beating into the minds of all its citizens that all kinds of goods and luxuries are necessary for a decent life.

SOURCES: Robert Curvin and Bruce Porter, *Blackout Looting* (New York: Gardner Press, 1979); William Manchester, *The Glory and the Dream* (Boston: Little, Brown, 1974), pp. 1327–31; *New York Times*, July 13, 1987, pp. B1, B3; A. M. Rosenthal and Arthur Gelb, *The Night the Lights Went Out* (New York: Signet, 1965).

society. Highly visible in this regard during the 1960s was the John Birch Society, an ultraconservative, anticommunist organization founded in 1958 to honor a U.S. intelligence officer killed by communists in China in 1945. Although the original goal of the society was to fight subversive communism in the United States, the organization was also solidly opposed to integration. Other reactionary movements include the American Nazi Party, the Ku Klux Klan, and similar groups that espouse extremist racial and religious values more characteristic of a bigoted past.

A more current (and considerably less extremist) example of a reactionary social movement is the Moral Majority, a religious ethic that seeks a return to those values that considered premarital sex a sin, homosexuality a disease, and abortion a crime.

Conservative social movements seek to maintain the status quo, to keep society's current values. Conservative movements tend to emerge when change threatens. A current example involves the participants in the American handgun war. When the first remarks about gun control appeared in the press, the National Rifle Association mobilized its forces into a "magnum-force lobby." With its $30-million annual budget and 1.8 million members, it became an effective interest group and managed to block all efforts to strengthen federal gun legislation. The success of the National Rifle Association brought about the formation of Handgun Control, Inc., a group of gun-control advocates who began to push the commonsense argument that fewer guns result in fewer killings. The Moral Majority, while already characterized as a type of *reactionary* social movement, is in many ways *conservative* as well. In its attempt to preserve what it considered the traditional values of family, religion, and womanhood that had not yet been lost to social change, it engineered campaigns against sex and violence on television, equal rights for women, and political candidates who opposed its views.

Revisionary social movements pursue moderate changes in a society's present state of affairs. They do not threaten the social order, but rather, seek to alter its course. The psycho-medical redefinitions of alcoholism and homosexuality as diseases were revisionary in nature, as have been attempts to change the laws that prohibit the use of marijuana.

Revolutionary social movements seek large-scale social change. Their goal is to overthrow part or all of the existing social order and replace it with a system they consider to be more appropriate. The civil rights and women's movements in the United States and the emergence of Solidarity in Poland were revolutionary in that their goals involved making substantial changes in the law and social structure. More extreme examples of revolutionary social movements include the Islamic Revolution in Iran, the terrorist killings of the Irish Republican Army in Northern Ireland, and the conflicts in Lebanon and El Salvador.

Not all members of violent revolutionary social movements participate in or even condone terrorist acts; revolutionary movements need not involve war and bloodshed. Furthermore, some social movements can have both "revolutionary" and "revisionary" factions at the same time. The women's movement represents such a case. While many members of the movement seek equal pay and equal rights for women, others argue for more sweeping social changes, including a restructuring of the nature of sex roles and sex relations as well as the ways in which men think—not only about women, but about themselves—and the ways men express their emotions.

Escapist social movements involve a withdrawal from society rather than attempts to alter it. Dissatisfied with the way society is structured, members of these movements remove themselves from it physically, emotionally, or socially. Marcus Garvey's back-to-Africa movement for American blacks (discussed in Chapter 9) and Jim Jones' establishment of the People's Temple in the jungles of South America (discussed in Chapter 12) were clearly escapist movements. Attempts by the Beats and hippies to decriminalize marijuana use was an escapist social movement of a different sort (see Exhibit 16.8).

Expressive social movements seek to distract people from the dissatisfactions in their lives or society by changing the psychic or emotional states of their members. Thus, such movements do not attempt to alter social conditions. A variety of religious movements are of an expressive nature. A case in point is the Hare Krishna sect. The International Society for Krishna Consciousness was founded in the United States in 1965. Establishing its first "temple" in New York's East Village, it attracted disciples from local "hippies" and "flower children." They quickly became a familiar sight on busy city streets, where—clothed in saffron-colored robes and to the accompaniment of tambourines and tinkling bells—they chanted "Hare Krishna" (beloved Krishna) in homage to their Hindu god. "Krishna consciousness" demands a life-style that forbids gambling, smoking, drug use, the eating of meat, fish, or eggs, and the indulgence in sex for any reason other than procreation.

MADD: The Genesis of a Social Movement

The drunk driver has been a problem on American streets and highways ever since the inception of automobile travel. According to National Safety Council figures of a decade ago, at a time prior to the mobilization against

Hare Krishnas, a familiar sight on the streets of urban America, form an expressive social movement.

SOCIAL INDICATOR

Charting the Effects

Drinks, Body Weight and Blood Alcohol Percentage

Drinks*	Body Weight in Pounds								
	100	**120**	**140**	**160**	**180**	**200**	**220**	**240**	
1	.04	.03	.03	.02	.02	.02	.02	.02	**Possibly**
2	.08	.06	.05	.05	.04	.04	.03	.03	**Influenced**
3	.11	.09	.08	.07	.06	.06	.05	.05	
4	.15	.12	.11	.09	.08	.08	.07	.06	**Under the**
5	.19	.16	.13	.12	.11	.09	.09	.08	**Influence**
6	.22	.19	.16	.14	.13	.11	.10	.09	
7	.26	.22	.19	.16	.15	.13	.12	.11	
8	.30	.25	.21	.19	.17	.15	.14	.13	**Intoxicated**
9	.34	.28	.24	.21	.19	.17	.15	.14	
10	.38	.31	.27	.23	.21	.19	.17	.16	

(Based on approximately 1 hour)

*One drink equals: 1 oz. of 80 proof liquor, 12 oz. of beer, 4 oz. of wine (12% alcohol)

At:	A Person Generally Experiences:
0.02% BAC	Some Loss of Judgment and Efficiency
0.05% BAC	Poor Judgment, Loss of Control over Actions
0.10% BAC	Judgment Seriously Affected, Impaired Coordination
0.15% BAC	Staggering, Disoriented, All Faculties Seriously Affected
0.30% BAC	In a Stupor, Barely Conscious
0.40% BAC	Unconscious, in a Coma, and Possibly on the Verge of Death

Source: Connecticut Department of Transportation.

the alcohol-automobile connection, drunk driving was the cause of half the country's 50,000 car deaths, 800,000 crashes, and 750,000 serious injuries.[38] Historically, however, despite such high levels of roadway carnage, the general public seemed willing to tolerate the matter. Legal penalties were light, and rarely would a conviction for drunk driving result in a jail sentence—even when death was involved. Consider, for example, an incident that occurred in Bowie, Maryland, during the summer of 1980. Fifteen-year-old Tom Sexton was driving home from a day of fishing when a car driven by David Watkins swerved into his lane and hit him. Sexton was killed instantly. Watkins, who was drunk and at fault in the accident, was not injured. In court, he was fined $200.[39] Even more tragic was the case of Cindy Ferguson, who, accompanied by her twin sons, her baby, and a close friend were smashed in the rear. The car she was driving burst into flames and her 2-year-old son and her friend were burned to death. One of her other sons spent six months in the hospital in critical condition. He lost all use of his kidneys and most of his hearing. The other driver, who was drunk at the time, suffered a broken nose. Moreover, he had had at least seven drunk driving arrests in the previous four years and never spent a day in jail. As far as Cindy Ferguson was concerned, it was a matter of "socially accepted murder."[40]

The leniency towards drunk drivers might be explained, at least in part, by the fact that the typical offender is generally a law-abiding citizen in all other respects and does not cause harm intentionally. Thus, the courts have been reluctant to impose penalties that could wreck careers and make worse the already overcrowded conditions in jails. An Ohio prosecutor explained the situation with what he called the "good old boy" mentality: A jury would say, "he's just a good old boy out having some fun."[41]

Many campaigns have been launched against drunk drivers, but few communities ever made it a major enforcement issue. Attempts at reforming the drunk driving laws never had any real constituency. All of this seemed to change one spring afternoon in 1980 when 13-year-old Cari Lightner of Fair Oaks, California, was struck down and killed by a hit-and-run driver as she walked to a church carnival. Candy Lightner, the victim's mother, was stunned when she learned that the driver had been drunk, that he had two previous convictions for driving while intoxicated, that he was out on bail after a third drunk driving arrest, that he had previously spent only two days in jail, and that he was unlikely to be punished for killing Cari. Lightner gave impetus to drunk driving law reform by providing the constituency it had always needed—the victims. She launched Mothers

Exhibit 16.8

Sociological Focus

Beats, Hippies, Marijuana, and the Failure of a Social Movement

The marijuana debate has involved a variety of arguments, all revolving around notions of prohibition, repeal, selective legalization and control, and decriminalization. The American public initially had been alerted to the intoxicating effects of marijuana smoking as early as the 1880s. By the 1920s legislative efforts to outlaw marijuana had accelerated, with sixteen states prohibiting the use of the drug by 1930. The Marijuana Tax Act of 1937 represented the first federal effort to control the possession, sale, and distribution of marijuana on a nationwide scale. Subsequent decades witnessed new legislation, expanded enforcement activities, and harsh punishment for marijuana users, combined with an increasing and spirited opposition to the wisdom and philosophy of the original laws.

The beginnings of what has become known as "the marijuana epidemic" occurred during the 1960s, at a time when *any* possession of the drug was a felony under federal and *all* state laws. A movement towards "decriminalization" (the removal of criminal penalties for the possession of small amounts for personal use) began during the sixties, and by the mid-seventies a number of states had enacted decriminalization laws. But the movement stalled for several reasons: the United States Congress failed to pass legislation that would decriminalize marijuana under federal statutes; the issue never became salient enough throughout the nation as a whole to result in a wider social movement; the lobbying on behalf of marijuana law reform never demonstrated any significant power and influence; and as a drug traditionally associated with youth, marijuana failed to acquire broad support among other members of society. Most importantly, however, the movement was tainted—tainted by the very persons who formally sought the law's reform.

For decades, marijuana was considered the "weed of madness," an "assassin of youth." Then it became associated with the "Beats" of America's bohemian underground. *Beat,* in American slang, originated in *harlem jive,* the jargon of the black musicians of the 1920s and 1930s. Meaning "exhausted and worn out," beat was descriptive of a part social, part literary phenomenon of the late 1940s and 1950s initiated by the post–World War II disaffected and a cult of West Coast writers. They were of a generation that was trying to make sense of a postwar world, a world that seemed to offer no respite, only an eternal state of chaos.

The Beats believed that the path to harmony in a chaotic world could not be had by the more traditional consolations of success and achievement, which demanded a feigning of beliefs, feelings, and virtues, and a relentless obligation to the prevailing social forms and customs. Many Beats, in their attempt to more readily attain the success of setting themselves right with nature, pursued their "true" reality through an effort of the mind that required a rejection of life in organized society. For most, it involved a movement away from everyday existence through a casting off of social conventions and restraints, separation into urban bohemias, and high-frequency long-duration marijuana and hashish use.

The chief spokespersons of the Beat movement were authors Allen Ginsberg, Jack Kerouac, William Burroughs, and Lawrence Ferlinghetti, but the most celebrated of these was Ginsberg, whose writings were so often charged with obscenity that they brought awkward national attention to the movement. The best known of Ginsberg's works was *Howl,* written, for the most part while he was under the influence of drugs. In its 75 lines of inelegant poetry aimed at dismaying the middle class, *Howl* condemned American society and suggested a new set of values that were almost totally antisocial. It was from this context that Ginsberg emerged during the early 1960s to make the rounds on Capitol Hill lobbying for

Against Drunk Driving (MADD) and initiated a campaign of public outcry.[42]

The efforts of MADD—lobbying, personal appearances, contacts with drunk driving victims and their relatives, and the organization of chapters in other states—seemed to consolidate into a social movement. Existing organizations and other new groups joined in—SADD (Students Against Drunk Driving), RID (Remove Intoxicated Drivers), CSD (Citizens for Safe Drivers), and PARK (Prevent Alcohol Related Killings). The result was a flurry of new legislation in more than half the states. The reforms included mandatory jail terms in reform of the marijuana laws. Understandably, a change in the law could be viewed as nothing more than the radical politics of the time, and Ginsberg's appearance in the midst of the issue did much to confirm the persisting negative images of the marijuana user.

As the 1960s progressed, the nonconformist notions of the tiny minority of Beats in the 1950s emerged as the common social currency of the new youth movement. And the new counterculture contained a variety of types. It included what social critic Norman Mailer called the "philosophical psychopaths" who had found a need to throw off the political and social restraints of their generation. They lived immoderately and for the moment, congregated in communes, spoke a special avant-garde language, experimented with sex, and smoked marijuana. And too, the new counterculture included the tens of thousands of "plastic" or weekend "hippies" and "heads" whose social schizophrenia placed them partially in the straight world and partially in this "new underground"—children of two cultures, never wholly in phase with one or the other, and not believing fully in the values and mores of either.

With the rise of the counterculture came a revolution in the technology and handling of drugs, which had begun at mid-century and served to designate the sixties as a "new chemical age." Recently compounded mind-altering agents were introduced enthusiastically and promoted effectively, with the consequence of exposing the national consciousness to an impressive catalog of chemical temptations that could offer fresh inspiration as well as simple and immediate relief from fear, anxiety, tension, frustration, and boredom. Exploiting the new hallucinogenic, stimulant, and sedative drugs that emerged during this period, the new counterculture became the new drug culture, and the image of marijuana users and their drug was further denigrated.

It was not until the 1970s that the nation became fully aware of the fact that marijuana use went well beyond the "dangerous and criminal classes." In 1965, less than ten million Americans were estimated to have ever used the drug, but by the mid-seventies this figure had more than tripled, and a large and rapidly expanding segment of the American population had become the target of legal concern.

The initial surge of decriminalization statutes that did occur developed, for the most part, in those states where marijuana use was most prevalent, and the movement toward decriminalization emerged primarily as an attempt to implement antimarijuana statutes of reduced severity that were more likely to produce arrests and court processing. In the main, however, public attitudes toward marijuana continued to reflect much of the stigma that had been attached to the drug formerly, and the decriminalization movement came to a halt.

With the onset of the 1980s, the growing number of users within the youthful population at all class and social levels drew much attention away from the earlier images of the marijuana user, but the depiction of marijuana as the "devil drug," "weed of madness," and "assassin of youth" seemed to be reinforced. Promotion of promarijuana legislation became political suicide for any member of Congress, and the movement toward decriminalization came to an abrupt end. While the spokespersons for the promarijuana crusade still presented their arguments, their messages were unheard; the national opinion about marijuana, even within new generations of youth, had become more negative than ever before.

SOURCE: Adapted from James A. Inciardi, "Marijuana Decriminalization Research: A Perspective and Commentary," *Criminology*, 19 (May 1981), pp. 145–59.

many instances, combined with a more serious treatment of prosecutions in cases where a death was involved. In some instances, convictions of second-degree murder resulted.[43]

As the movement continued into the mid-eighties, it began to have its impact in other areas as well. One was the drinking age. During the 1970s (perhaps influenced by the battle cry: "Old enough to fight, old enough to drink!"), 29 states lowered the drinking age. The rediscovery of the drunk driver by the new social movement, however, brought to light some rather grim statistics: almost one-half of the fatal alcohol-related automobile

SOCIAL INDICATOR

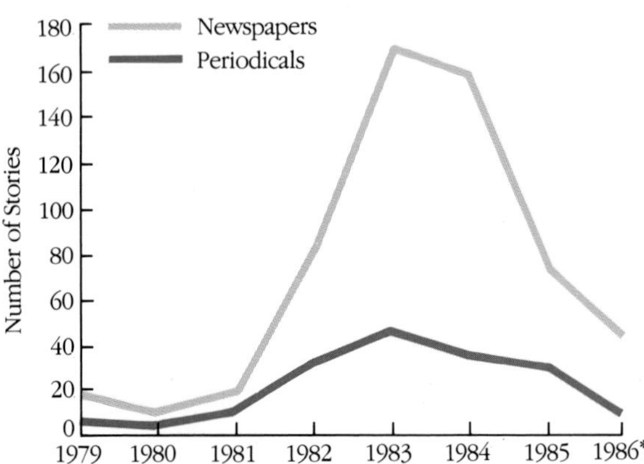

*Newspaper volume is based on a count of stories in the National Newspaper Index, 1979–1986 (Information Access Corporation, Menlo Park, CA). This data base indexes stories in the *Christian Science Monitor*, the *Los Angeles Times*, the *New York Times*, the *Wall Street Journal*, and the *Washington Post*. Periodical volume is based on counts of stories in the Magazine Index, 1978–1986 (Information Access Corporation, Menlo Park, CA). The magazine data base indexes stories in 370 popular periodicals.

Source: John D. McCarthy, Mark Wolfson, David P. Baker, and Elaine M. Mosakowski, "The Founding of Social Movement Organizations: Local Citizens' Groups Opposing Drunken Driving," in Glenn R. Carroll (ed.), *Ecological Models of Organizations* (Cambridge, MA: Ballinger-forthcoming).

accidents occurring at night were caused by persons under age 25, a group that constituted only one-fifth of all licensed drivers; and drunk-driving accidents were the leading cause of death of persons between the ages of 16 and 24. Half the states reconsidered the legal drinking age, and in many instances, the minimum age was raised.

The Life Cycle of Social Movements

Social movements, like all other forms of collective behavior, are temporary. If a movement fails to coalesce and gain an active constituency, it tends to disintegrate, often rather quickly. Even those that succeed do not go on forever. Social movements evolve through a natural history. Among the more recent treatments of the natural history of social movements is the work of Armand Mauss, who identified a life cycle involving five stages: (1) incipiency, (2) coalescence, (3) institutionalization, (4) fragmentation, and (5) demise (see Exhibit 16.9).[44]

Incipiency. In the incipiency stage, some situation is defined as a problem. The members of the public that are concerned with the situation comment about it. Their commentaries are generally visible—meetings, speeches and presentations to groups, contacts with the media and local political figures. Leaders also emerge during this incipiency stage, generally on the basis of their persistence and charisma.

Coalescence. In this second stage, groups begin to gather and form about the leaders for the sake of developing policies and promoting programs. Competing groups in the same movement either join forces with the dominant group or coalition of groups, or they fragment due to an inability to recruit or hold members. Coalescence typically comes about as a consequence of society's failure to correct the problem in question, or in response to repressive action by an opposition group.

Institutionalization. When the social movement reaches institutionalization, society has responded to it with standardized patterns of action. Furthermore, at this point the movement has the most strength and influence, and can achieve the most success. The movement is organized, it has a large membership base and significant resources, it can impact on social and political processes, and society takes it seriously.

Fragmentation. After a period of success, the movement begins to break down, primarily through a process of co-optation. The early supporters of the movement often find that the social problem at issue has been improved significantly, thus allowing them to turn their attention to other matters. Those who remain behind in the movement may struggle among themselves and establish splinter organizations.

Demise. Social movements eventually cease to exist, even though the organizations they created, the reforms they initiated, and the institutions they introduced may survive. In fact, the goals of the successful social movement become official policy. Having achieved its goals, the movement loses its purpose, so it reaches the end of its cycle.

A Theory of Social Movements: Resource Mobilization

Theorists have been attempting to discover why people join social movements for almost a century. Among the earliest to contemplate the issue was Gustave Le Bon, whose contagion theory has already been examined with respect to crowd behavior. Le Bon was one of many psychological theorists who regarded participation in a social movement as irrational individual behavior. Moreover, the proponents of this *psychological* approach viewed such movements as satisfying the needs of their members—reactions to their own discontent. The major problem with this perspective is that it totally ignores the possibility that the sources of social movements may be

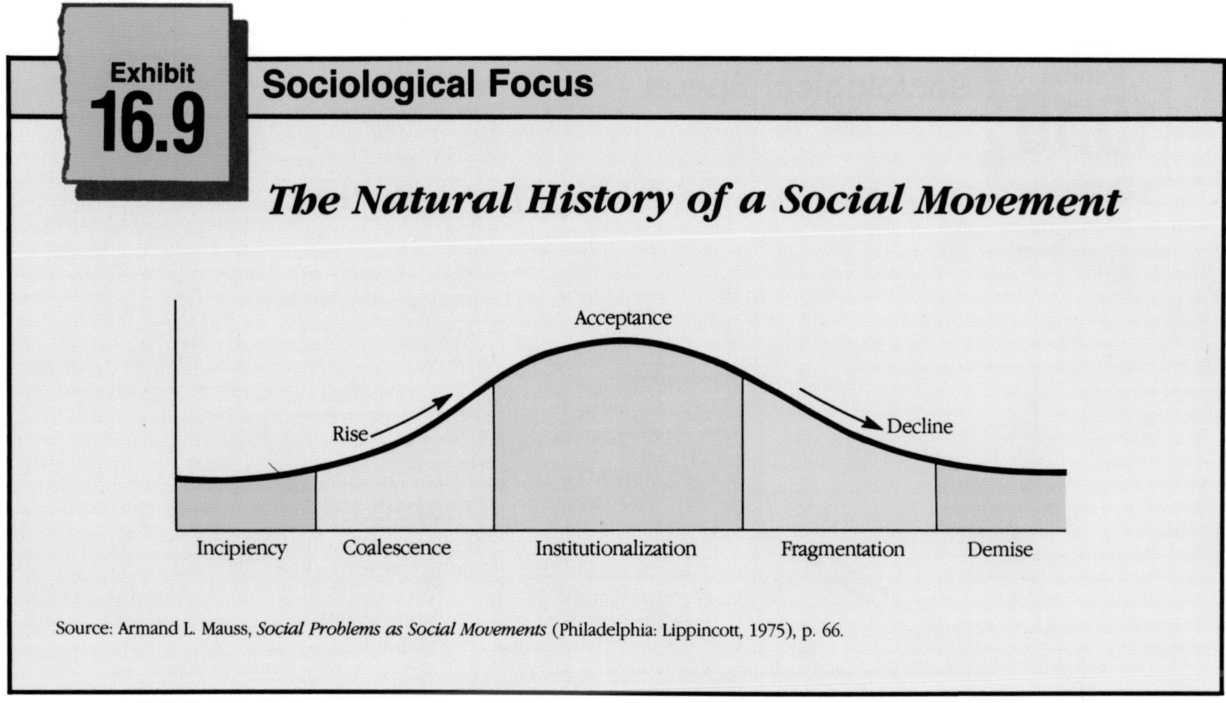

Source: Armand L. Mauss, *Social Problems as Social Movements* (Philadelphia: Lippincott, 1975), p. 66.

social; it disregards the prospect that something may indeed be "wrong" with society and that individuals participate in movements to bring about needed social change.

With the onset of the 1960s, sociologists began to develop new explanations of social movements. Smelser's value-added theory, which did much to clarify the preconditions of collective behavior in general, also suggested that the crucial element in the genesis of social movements was *social strain.* The strain caused by certain unfavorable social conditions leads to movements to alleviate the strain. Using similar reasoning, others have maintained that social movements emerge as attempts to reduce *social deprivation.* But strain and deprivation theories also have a serious shortcoming. Most, if not all societies, experience some sort of strain and deprivation at any given time, yet social movements do not regularly become manifest. Blacks in America experienced strain and deprivation long before the civil rights movement began to emerge in the late 1950s. The same can be said of the women's movement, the gay liberation movement, the antiwar movement, the antinuclear movement, and the other contemporary movements involving drunk drivers, abortion, school prayer, and the rights of native Americans. Why did all of these social movements arise when they did, and not earlier?

James C. Davies' *J-curve of rising expectations* represented one attempt to explain why social movements emerge when they do (see Exhibit 16.10).[45] He noted that people may be able to tolerate a small gap between expectations and satisfactions. Davies argued that improving conditions in society generated expectations of further improvements at the same rate. However, he continued, the rising expectations of many deprived groups may be frustrated by their failure to be realized, creating an intolerable gap between expectations and satisfactions, which is the direct cause of collective behavior. Davies' theory was derived from his studies of the French and Russian Revolutions, and his J-curve is more suitable for examining forms of collective violence. However, as a theory of social movements, he did attempt to apply it to the black and student movements of the 1960s, holding that when signs of progress were unmistakable, but did not quickly come to pass, collective actions were a natural consequence. The difficulty here is that few social movements fit into such a mold. Was it a matter of rising expectations that instigated the movements relative to abortion, nuclear power plants, war, and environmental pollution? Did Candy Lightner organize MADD out of her rising expectations? Probably not!

Resource mobilization theory, in contrast with the psychological, strain and deprivation, and J-curve points of view, involves the study of social movement organization and the uses of available resources. In the view of theorists John D. McCarthy and Mayer N. Zald, such things as psychological frustrations, social strains and deprivations, rising expectations, or any other reason for that matter are only secondary in the emergence of social movements.[46] The major factor involves a series of politically and economically rational decisions. Social

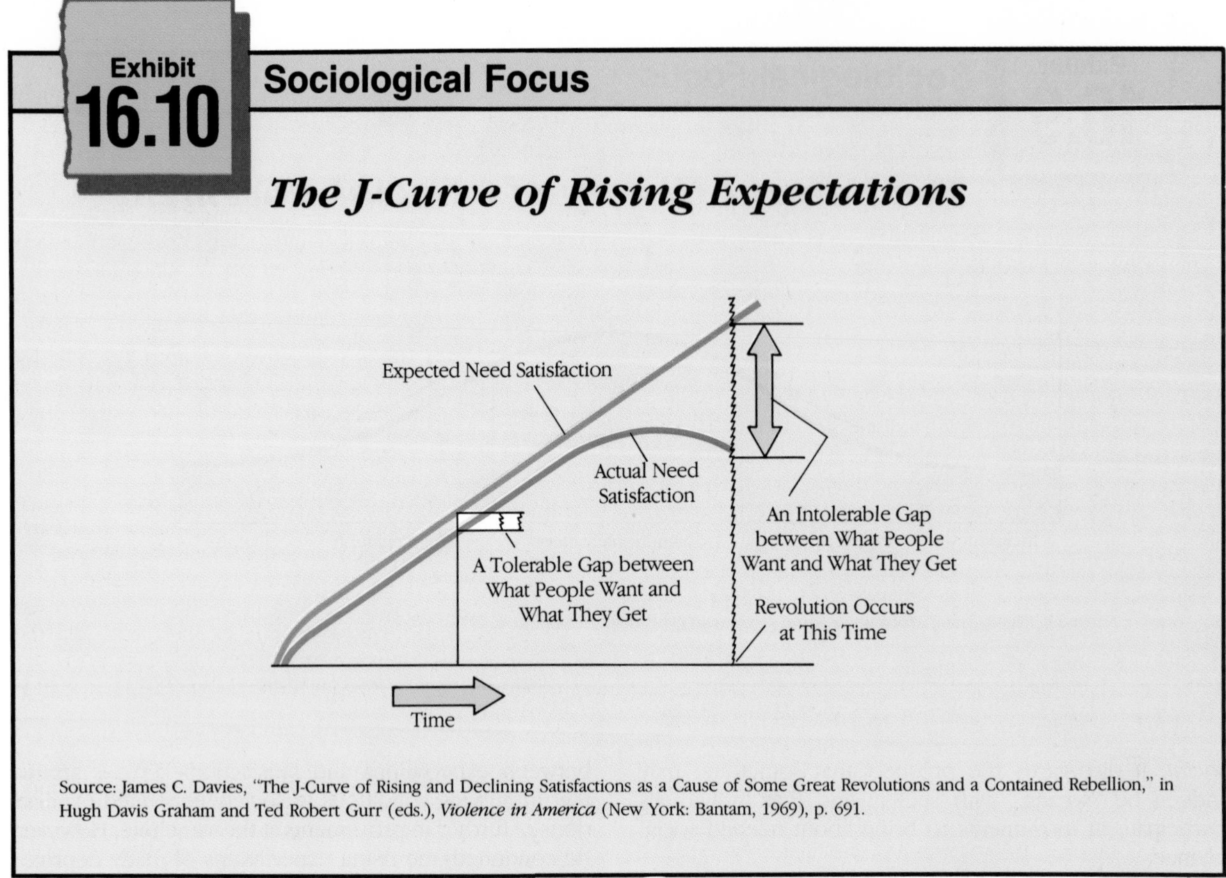

The J-Curve of Rising Expectations

Source: James C. Davies, "The J-Curve of Rising and Declining Satisfactions as a Cause of Some Great Revolutions and a Contained Rebellion," in Hugh Davis Graham and Ted Robert Gurr (eds.), *Violence in America* (New York: Bantam, 1969), p. 691.

movements come about when people organize and take action by using whatever *resources* they can muster—when individuals have the political and economic capabilities to turn grievances into action. The resources can be of many kinds: access to the media, access to political figures, charismatic leadership qualities that attract sympathizers to devote time and money to the cause, the services of professional organizers or fund raisers, or perhaps even linkages with other social movements that can help to propel the cause at hand.

The contemporary social movement against drunk drivers has been cited as a clear example of resource mobilization. For decades grievances about the high number of alcohol-related traffic deaths and the apathy of the courts in their handling of convicted drunk drivers fell on deaf ears. Organizations even existed whose goals were to get drunk drivers off the road. However, it was not until Candy Lightner came on the scene that a "real" movement developed. Lightner's resources included a variety of charismatic qualities and a growing constituency of victims who enabled her to get the attention of the media, the polity, and the public to tell her tragic story and to mobilize a following.[47]

COLLECTIVE BEHAVIOR AND APPLIED SOCIOLOGY

A number of the incidents of collective behavior reported in this chapter emphasize the importance of applied sociology. At a very practical level, the consequences of certain forms of collective behavior can be costly, devastating, and even deadly, and the tools of sociology have had applications for ameliorating the behaviors of acting crowds. In alternative directions, collective behavior and applied sociology have come together in the fields of market research, consumer behavior, opinion polling, and advertising.

Controlling Crowds

More than four decades ago, a sociologist prepared a riot manual for the Chicago Police Department. It offered the following suggestions for dealing with acting crowds:

1. Remove or isolate the individuals involved in the precipitating incident before the crowd has begun to achieve substantial unity.

2. Interrupt communication during the milling about process by dividing the crowd into smaller units.
3. Remove crowd leaders if it can be done without force.
4. Distract the attention of the crowd from its focal point by creating diversions at other places.
5. Prevent the spread and reinforcement of the crowd by containing it.[48]

Based on principles found in the contagion and emergent-norm theories of collective behavior, in the years since their formulation these five suggestions have become the basis of crowd control throughout much of the United States and Western Europe.[49] Perhaps the most unique and dramatic application of one of these principles was employed, for a time, by London's Metropolitan Police. Their secret weapon for crowd control was not water cannons, tear gas, rubber bullets, or brute force, but public sympathy for the purpose of appearing to lose. To this end they had an especially handsome show-quality police horse, specifically trained to collapse, feigning death on command. Put into play before an erupting crowd, the sympathies of the animal-loving British public were immediately aroused, resulting in public support instead of violence.[50]

Controlling Social Movements

The principles of crowd control focus on disruption —the disruption of an emerging process. Combining these principles with ideas borrowed from resource mobilization theory results in direct applications for altering the course of threatening social movements. Based on what sociology suggested about the structure of social movements and the dynamics of rumor, during the 1960s and 1970s the Federal Bureau of Investigation (FBI) set out to damage the momentum that the Ku Klux Klan had gathered in the South in its war against blacks. The FBI technique was to use rumor to create paranoia within the leadership of the Klan and to undermine the solidarity of its membership. In addition, it was felt that if the levels of paranoia could be pushed to a high enough degree of intensity, the Klan would shift its resources from the activities of propagandizing and recruitment into self-protection.[51]

One FBI technique during the 1960s involved having informants infiltrate the Klan for the purpose of creating informal confusion and suspicion. Rumors, true and false, were spread about Klan members, exposing their financial manipulations and personal foibles. On another occasion, FBI informants accumulated the names of *every* Klan member in the state of Mississippi. Agents then proceeded to interview every person on the list, just to let them know that they had been identified and were being watched.

Perhaps the most pervasive effort against the Klan was a two-step process initiated in Alabama. Initially, a series of rumors were planted suggesting that so many FBI informants had infiltrated the membership of the Ku Klux Klan that an FBI agent probably was to be found behind every Klan member's mailbox. FBI informants inside the Klan then suggested that all members be subjected to lie detector tests to weed out informers. Former FBI official William C. Sullivan later explained what happened:

> We suggested that because we knew that the test is an expensive process that would drain them of funds and a lot of time. Our informant said that if anybody opposed the test he would be a suspect. Because of the expense and effort involved, a lot of them backed down on submitting to a lie detector test, and the more they backpedaled, the more our informant would raise hell. They all ended up suspecting each other.[52]

The FBI effort had been effective. When it started in the mid-sixties, an estimated 14,000 Ku Klux Klan members resided in the United States. By 1971, membership had dropped to a disorganized 4,300.[53]

Collective Behavior and Business

Perhaps the best example of applied sociology in connection with collective behavior involves consumer and advertising research. Although this field of inquiry is not generally associated with sociology, sociological tools are used in advertising agencies, public-relations firms, and market-research companies for studies of wholesale and retail markets.[54]

Although advertising and consumer research appear to focus on a range of rather esoteric concerns —teenagers' television viewing habits, why "yuppies" prefer to drive Saabs and BMWs, single parents' evaluations of children's breakfast foods—at closer glance all of these activities are collective behaviors.

From a somewhat different perspective, the worlds of business and industry often have made use of sociological theory and research on fads and fashions when making decisions about what products to develop and market, when to discontinue production, and when to sell off certain assets. The recent history of video arcades illustrates the importance of understanding the life cycle of fads (see Exhibit 16.11).

Exhibit 16.11 Applied Sociology

Want to Buy a Video Arcade? Cheap? Real Cheap?

As America approached the beginning of the 1990s, observers of the Sunday classified ads in newspapers across the nation found ads for "investment opportunities" and "business ventures" in the video game field. The advertisements often stated:

> VIDEO ARCADE, prime location, $800,000 annual gross, get in for only $50,000 cash down.
>
> ARCADE, all major games, in active shopping mall, solid income, grab this opportunity before it's too late—$75,000 cash.

In 1983, the bottom fell out of the video-arcade business. About 3,000 arcades closed and sales of game machines dropped 65%.

	1982	1983
Number of Arcades	10,000	7,000
Video Game Machines Sold	480,000	170,000
Value of Machines Sold	$1 billion	$350 million

To an interested investor anxious to make a quick profit in the entertainment market, video games would certainly seem to be a good idea. In the early 1970s, the microchip was perfected and the video game was introduced. The first to arrive was Pong, a simplistic version of table tennis played on a TV screen. Then the genre became more sophisticated. As the games grew more popular, video arcades appeared. Packed with dozens of different and challenging recreational contests, the game arcades attracted young and old alike. Parents were wondering where their children were and why the weekly allowances they gave them disappeared so quickly.

When the secret was revealed and the arcade was discovered, the inevitable debate ensued. Some critics maintained that the new machines were the work of the devil; that they kept children away from their studies and more "normal" outlets; that the games engendered feelings of aggression, dominance, and hostility; and that the arcades attracted an undesirable element that would expose children to drugs, and perhaps even sex. Others argued the reverse. If youths were at the arcades, then you *knew* where they were. At least they were off the streets and not getting into trouble.

Despite the controversy, the arcades flourished. The early 1980s witnessed the arrival of Pac-Man. Pac-Man became a craze. Players were stacked four and five deep behind the new machines waiting their chance to gobble up the little blue ghosts of mazeland. To cash in on the Pac-Man video mania, game developers also introduced Asteroids, Frogger, Donkey Kong, Tron, and hundreds more. By 1982, arcade games had become a multi-billion dollar industry. In that year alone, almost 500,000 machines were sold at prices ranging as high as $3,000 each. Bally, the largest maker of the machines, earned $91 million on video games during that year alone.

Within this context, jumping into the video-arcade business would appear to be a wise

(continued)

SALES SLUMP

Coin-operated games and rides are losing their zip. Revenue has dropped since its 1981 high.

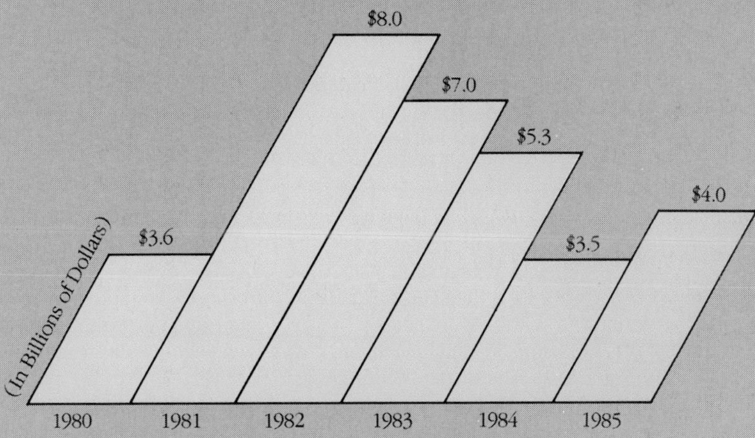

Video games have taken the worst beating. Pinball games and pool tables are gaining slightly. Weekly revenues have dropped from the 1981 high.

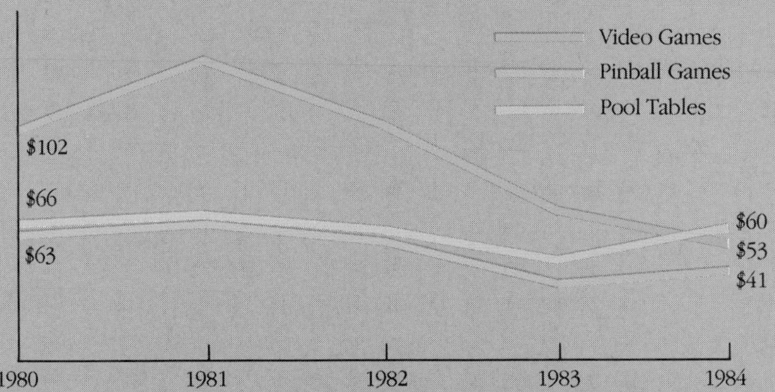

Exhibit 16.11 (continued)

investment. But given the dynamics of fads and crazes, would a response to the late 1980s classified ads be an appropriate venture?

Fads and crazes refer to an exceptional preoccupation with a single viewpoint, a single interest, or a single line of behavior. The preoccupation is exceptional in its intensity, in the uniformity with which it is exhibited, and in the number of people it includes. But most importantly, this preoccupation is of limited duration.

The typical fad or craze runs through a cycle of five phases. First is a latent period during which the idea, although present in the minds of a few, shows little sign of spreading. Second, the idea begins to spread rapidly. The number of people who participate in the fad or craze mounts with an increasing velocity. Third, as the market of susceptible minds becomes saturated, the velocity of the wave begins to slacken. Fourth, a mental resistance to the idea, interest, or behavior that propelled the fad begins to develop. During this phase, the mental infection wanes; among those already infected, the enthusiasm lessens and fewer new recruits are found. Fifth, and last, if the idea or interest persists, it does so in the activities of only a few. Either it becomes incorporated into the occasional habits of many, or it is kept alive in the minds of only a few avid enthusiasts.

How does all of this apply to video arcades? An overview by market observers offers a rather clear picture. Despite the incredible success of the electronic games, suddenly, by early 1983, the bottom seemed to be falling out of the video game industry. The number of arcades was declining by the thousands; the number of machines being sold dropped by more than 50%; and per machine revenues fell in some cases by as much as 80%—all in a matter of a few months. Why?

To start with, many customers were not getting their quarter's worth. More than 80% of those playing M.A.C.H. 3, for example, a complicated laser game, were lasting less than 60 seconds efore being blasted out of combat. It seems that video game designers, in their high-tech frenzy to make the games more and more difficult and challenging, had forgotten that over 80% of the players were nonregulars, many of whom were adults and all of whom were amateurs. Even Pac-Man, the only game that drew women into the arcades, had been replaced by the more complex games to attract what was believed to be a mass of avid players. Thus, the amateurs and nonregulars abandoned the arcades for records, movies, home computers, television, and even books!

It seems that when the classified ads suggesting opportunities to "get in" on the arcade revolution began appearing, the fad that had propelled the revolution was already in its fourth phase—hardly the time to view the phenomenon as a unique investment. Thus, video games and the arcades that housed them were part of a fad. And as with all fads and crazes, they could endure for just so long. Moreover, their doom was hastened by other segments of the high-tech revolution—home computers and video-cassette players, and by M-TV and subscription television. By the late 1980s, Pac-Man and the arcade that had so proudly housed him had begun to go the way of hula-hoops, roller-disco, and Rubik's cube. In fact, during 1988, Bally sold its video game division to its closest competitor for $8 million, a small sum in contrast to what the industry had earned earlier in the decade.

SOURCES: *Business Week,* May 21, 1984, p. 46; L. S. Penrose, *On the Objective Side of Crowd Behavior* (London: H. K. Lewis, 1952), pp. 18–22; *Psychology Today,* December 1983, pp. 72–73; *Time,* July 25, 1988, p. 63; Ralph H. Turner and Lewis M. Killian, *Collective Behavior* (Englewood Cliffs, NJ: Prentice-Hall, 1957), pp. 207–208; *USA Today,* March 2, 1984, p. 3B; *USA Today,* October 3, 1984, p. 3B; *USA Today,* March 1, 1985, p. 1B.

SUMMARY

Collective behavior refers to the actions of relatively large numbers of people that emerge and develop in undefined and often emotional situations. The collectivities are impermanent and for the most part unstructured, and they are responding to a set of immediate circumstances in ways that fall outside of conventional norms. The more common forms of collective behavior fall into the categories of crowds, masses, and social movements.

Crowds are temporary collections of people who have a united focus and who are conscious of and influenced by one another's presence. Crowds are self-generating. They have no natural boundaries, and are characterized by equality and a high density. They have no past or future, and their members have a sense of anonymity. Crowds can be classified as casual, conventional, expressive, or acting.

Mass behavior is dispersed collective behavior. Masses are collections of people who are widely scattered yet participate in some event either physically or with a common concern or interest. The common examples of mass behavior are fads, fashions, crazes, rumors, panics, mass hysteria, and public opinion.

According to sociologist Neil Smelser, collective behavior involves a process of mobilization through six stages: structural conduciveness, structural strain, generalized beliefs, precipitating events, mobilization for action, and operation of social control. These preconditions are necessary for collective behavior to occur.

Theories explaining collective behavior vary considerably in focus. Le Bon's contagion perspective suggests that members of collectivities, particularly crowds, are guided by instinct rather than rational decisions. Adherents of Blumer's interactionist perspective hold that contagion sweeps through crowds because of "circular reactions" operating in a situation of "social unrest." Supporters of the convergence perspective argue that people who share certain tendencies come together to collectively act out their common predispositions. Turner and Killian's emergent norm perspective suggests that new norms arise in a collective situation, and although members of the collective may not agree with them, they refrain from offering opposition and may even participate in the action out of fear of ridicule or coercion.

Social movements are attempts to resist or bring about social change, and can be reactionary, conservative, revisionary, revolutionary, escapist, or expressive. Social movements, furthermore, run through a cycle involving stages of incipiency, coalescence, institutionalization, fragmentation, and demise. Resource mobilization theory suggests that social movements come about when people organize and take action using whatever resources they have to turn grievances into change.

KEY TERMS/CONCEPTS

acting crowds
advertisements
casual crowds
coalescence
collective behavior
conservative social movements
contagion perspective
conventional crowds
convergence perspective
crazes
crowds
demise
emergent norm perspective
escapist social movements
expressive crowds
expressive social movements
fads
fashions
fragmentation
generalized beliefs
incipiency
institutionalization
interactionist perspective
masses
mass hysteria
mobilization for action
operation of social control
panic
precipitating events
propaganda
public
public opinion
public-opinion poll
reactionary social movements
resource mobilization theory
revisionary social movements
revolutionary social movements
riot
rumors
social movements
structural conduciveness
structural strain
value-added theory

DISCUSSION QUESTIONS

1. Do people act differently in crowds than in other social situations? Why?
2. What factors explain why some social movements seem to succeed (MADD), while others fail (legalization of marijuana)?
3. Recalling the descriptions of the collective behaviors exhibited at Attica and certain cities in Brazil, what accounts for the differences in each?
4. What different forms of collective behavior became apparent in 1983 during the quest for Cabbage Patch Kids?
5. What kind of a social movement is the anti-drunk-driver crusade? What stages in the life cycle of social movements has it gone through?
6. Which theories of collective behavior seem to apply directly to the blackout looting in New York City in 1977?

SUGGESTED READINGS

Robert Curvin and Bruce Porter, *Blackout Looting!* (New York: Gardner, 1979). The result of the Ford Foundation's research into the looting that occurred during New York City's blackout in 1977, this book analyzes the stages of the looting, the characteristics of the looters, the police response, and the proliferation of poverty that may have been the root cause of the phenomenon.

Howard Koch, *The Panic Broadcast: Portrait of an Event* (Boston: Little, Brown, 1970). An analysis of the mass hysteria that erupted in 1938 from the radio broadcast of H. G. Wells' "War of the Worlds."

Joseph Perry and M. D. Pugh, *Collective Behavior: Response to Stress* (St. Paul, MN: West, 1978). An introduction to the study of collective behavior, including a discussion of the various forms and theories of collective behavior, with particular attention to crowd violence and social movements.

Tom Wicker, *A Time to Die* (New York: Ballantine, 1975). A recounting of the riot at New York's Attica Prison in 1971, written by a journalist who was chosen to be one of the mediators in the negotiations with the rebelling inmates.

NOTES

1. Hadley Cantril, *The Invasion from Mars: A Study in the Psychology of Panic* (New York: Harper & Row, 1966).
2. Alan C. Kerckhoff and Kurt W. Back, *The June Bug* (New York: Appleton-Century-Crofts, 1968).
3. Donald Paneth (ed.), *1977 News Dictionary* (New York: Facts on File, 1978), p. 105.
4. *Time,* January 10, 1983, pp. 20–21; *Time,* January 17, 1983, p. 18; *Newsweek,* March 28, 1983, p. 18.
5. *U.S. News & World Report,* June 2, 1980, pp. 19–22.
6. *New York Times,* July 11, 1987, pp. 1, 5.
7. *New York Times,* October 19, 1987, p. A4; *New York Times,* October 29, 1987, p. A3; *New York Times,* December 2, 1987, p. A7.
8. Herbert Blumer, "Collective Behavior," in Alfred McClung Lee (ed.), *Principles of Sociology* (New York: Barnes and Noble, 1951), pp. 167–222.
9. See *Attica: The Official Report of the New York State Special Commission on Attica* (New York: Bantam, 1972).
10. Kurt Land and Gladys Land, *Collective Dynamics* (New York: Crowell, 1961), p. 480.
11. Alison Lurie, *The Language of Clothes* (New York: Vintage, 1981).
12. *New York Times,* April 1, 1984, p. 25.
13. *Christian Science Monitor,* July 23, 1987, pp. 1, 28; *National Law Journal,* November 10, 1986, pp. 1, 28–29; *National Law Journal,* March 16, 1987, p. 9; *Newsweek,* July 11, 1986, p. 40; *USA Today,* December 5, 1986, p. 3A; *USA Today,* February 27, 1987, p. 3A; *USA Today,* June 23, 1987, p. 3A; Wilmington (Delaware) *News-Journal,* November 3, 1986, p. 1B.
14. Tamotsu Shibutani, *Improvised News: A Sociological Study of Rumor* (Indianapolis, IN: Bobbs-Merrill, 1966).
15. Ralph Rownow and Gary Alan Fine, "Inside Rumors," *Human Behavior,* 3 (1974), p. 66.
16. Rownaw and Fine, "Inside Rumors."
17. Hal Morgan and Kerry Tucker, *Rumor!* (New York: Penguin, 1984), p. 87.
18. Neil J. Smelser, *Theory of Collective Behavior* (New York: Free Press, 1962).
19. The circumstances of the *Thresher* disaster are reported in *New York Times,* April 11, 1963, pp. 1, 14; *New York Times,* April 14, 1963, pp. 1, 80.
20. Michael Brown and Amy Goldin, *Collective Behavior* (Pacific Palisades, CA: Goodyear, 1973); Andrew L. Klein, "Changes of Leadership Appraisal as a Function of the Stress of a Simulated Panic Situation," *Journal of Personality and Social Psychology,* 34 (December 1976), pp. 1143–54; S. L. Marshall, *Men Under Fire* (New York: William Morrow, 1947).
21. Hadley Cantril, *The Invasion from Mars,* p. 47.
22. Elihu Katz and Paul Lazarsfeld, *Personal Influence* (New York: Free Press, 1955).
23. Irving Allen, "Social Relations and the Two-Step Flow: A Defense of the Tradition," in Alan Wells (ed.), *Mass Media and Society* (Palo Alto, CA: Mayfield, 1975); Elihu Katz, "The Two-Step Flow of Communication: An Up-to-Date Report on an Hypothesis," *Public Opinion Quarterly,* 21 (1957), pp. 61–78.
24. *USA Today,* March 13, 1984, pp. 1–2A; *U.S. News & World Report,* March 19, 1984, p. 27.
25. *USA Today,* January 18, 1985, p 3A.
26. Neil J. Smelser, *Theory of Collective Behavior.*
27. *Miami Herald,* March 17, 1984, pp. 1A, 24–25A; *New York Times,* March 18, 1984, p. 23; *USA Today,* March 13, 1984, p. 3A; *USA Today,* March 16, 1984, p. 3A; Wilmington (Delaware) *News-Journal,* March 20, 1984, p. A7.
28. Gustave Le Bon, *The Crowd: A Study of the Popular Mind* (New York: Viking, 1960), p. 27.
29. Herbert Blumer, "Collective Behavior."
30. Floyd H. Allport, *Social Psychology* (Boston: Houghton Mifflin, 1924).
31. Joseph B. Perry, Jr., and M. D. Pugh, *Collective Behavior: Response to Social Stress* (St. Paul, MN: West, 1978), p. 33.
32. Ralph H. Turner, "Collective Behavior," in Robert E. L. Faris (ed.), *Handbook of Modern Sociology* (Chicago: Rand McNally, 1964), pp. 389–92; Ralph H. Turner and Lewis M. Killian, *Collective Behavior* (Englewood Cliffs, NJ: Prentice-Hall, 1972).

33. *Newsweek,* March 21, 1983, p. 25; *New York Times,* March 4, 1984, p. 22; *USA Today,* February 8, 1984, p. 3A; *USA Today,* March 23, 1984, p. 3A.
34. Rachel Carson, *Silent Spring* (Greenwich, CT: Fawcett, 1962), p. 39.
35. Garrett De Bell (ed.), *The Environmental Handbook* (New York: Ballantine, 1970).
36. See National Staff of Environmental Action, *Earth Day—The Beginning* (New York: Bantam, 1970).
37. William Bruce Cameron, *Modern Social Movements* (New York: Random House, 1966).
38. *New York Times,* May 23, 1982, p. 37.
39. *Time,* August 3, 1981, p. 64.
40. *Newsweek,* September 13, 1982, p. 34.
41. *Changing Times,* July 1982, p. 51.
42. *Newsweek,* September 13, 1982, p. 36; *Time,* August 3, 1981, p. 64.
43. See *Miami Herald,* June 21, 1983, p. 2B; *National Law Journal,* August 2, 1982, p. 11.
44. Armand L. Mauss, *Social Problems as Social Movements* (Philadelphia: Lippincott, 1975), pp. 61–66.
45. James C. Davies, "Toward a Theory of Revolution," *American Sociological Review,* 27 (1962), pp. 5–19; James C. Davies, "The J-Curve of Rising and Declining Satisfactions as a Cause of Some Great Revolutions and a Contained Rebellion," in Hugh Davis Graham and Ted Robert Gurr (eds.), *Violence in America* (New York: Bantam, 1969), pp. 690–730.
46. John D. McCarthy and Mayer N. Zald, *The Trend of Social Movements in America* (Morristown, NJ: General Learning Press, 1973); John D. McCarthy and Mayer N. Zald "Resource Mobilization and Social Movements: A Partial Theory," *American Journal of Sociology,* 82 (1977), pp. 1212–41.
47. Craig Reinarman, "Social Movements and Social Problems: 'Mothers Against Drunk Driving,' Restrictive Alcohol Laws, and Social Control in the 1980s," *Paper Presented at the 35th Annual Meeting of the Society for the Study of Social Problems,* Washington, DC, August 1985; Frank J. Weed, "Grass-Roots Activism and the Drunk Driving Issue: A Survey of MADD Chapters," *Paper Presented at the 80th Annual Meeting of the American Sociological Association,* Washington, DC, August 1985.
48. Cited by Ralph Turner and Lewis Killian, *Collective Behavior* (Englewood Cliffs, NJ: Prentice-Hall, 1972), p. 165.
49. See John V. Lindsay, *The City* (New York: W. W. Norton, 1970), pp. 91–114.
50. Robert Reiner, *The Politics of the Police* (New York: St. Martin's, 1985), pp. 54–55.
51. See Sanford J. Unger, *FBI: An Uncensored Look Behind the Walls* (Boston: Little, Brown, 1976), pp. 414–18.
52. William C. Sullivan, *The Bureau: My Thirty Years in Hoover's FBI* (New York: W. W. Norton, 1979), pp. 130–31.
53. David Wise, *The American Police State* (New York: Random House, 1976), p. 320.
54. A. Emerson Smith, "Consumer and Advertising Research," in Howard E. Freeman, Russell R. Dynes, Peter H. Rossi, and William Foote Whyte (eds.), *Applied Sociology: Roles and Activities of Sociologists in Diverse Settings* (San Francisco: Jossey-Bass, 1983), pp. 189–99.

Urbanization, Industrialization, and Life in the City

The city has been viewed as the epitome of the social world, as the decisive battleground of civilization and religion, and as a place with a million forms of hidden life. Yet the vision of the city in the minds of most people is that of streets, parks, rivers, bridges, and endless bustling crowds. The common imagery of the city suggested in literature and by the networks of mass communication is a place teeming with people of different origins, cultures, and beliefs; a mosaic of worlds with many classes, communities, and neighborhoods; a skyline, dress and fashion, restaurants, street scenes, sounds, and city lights; an exciting place and a land of opportunity and upward mobility. The vision also includes bars and brothels, tough cops and street crime, hobos, tramps, bums, and the poor and homeless. Yet such a collective image of the urban scene and city life is chiefly folklore, for in many ways each city is unique, each having a separate identity, history, and existence. Contrast, for example, the cities of La Paz and San Francisco.

Straddling the Andes of western South America, Bolivia is a land of gaunt mountains, cold desolate plains, and semitropical lowlands. Some 70% of Bolivia's 6 million people live on its bleak, treeless, windswept altiplano—a lofty plateau over 13,000 feet above sea level. Rising from the floor of a shallow canyon in the middle of the altiplano stands the city of La Paz, Bolivia's capital and major urban area. Living in La Paz is in some ways like living on the moon. The city rests in a barren crater of naked land, and moreover, at an altitude of more than two miles, the air is so thin that for the newcomer it is difficult to breathe. In fact, so little oxygen is present in La Paz's rarefied atmosphere that fires are quite uncommon.

La Paz is unusual in other ways as well. The city's almost one million residents are packed into but a few square miles. La Paz hosts a small population of financial elites—merchants, professionals, and politicians who see to the needs of the city and country; executives and landowners made affluent by Bolivia's rich mineral resources; and the *narcotrafficantes,* whose extravagant wealth comes from the cultivation of the coca leaf and the processing of cocaine. Yet more than half of the people in La Paz are impoverished Aymara Indians. The men wear work clothes, often of the type worn by laborers in the United States, but the few who can find jobs typically are employed at the most menial of tasks. The Indian women present a striking contrast. Jamming the streets and sidewalk stalls to sell the few fruits and vegetables that can be grown on the altiplano wasteland, they are always in the most colorful of costumes. Almost all seem to be carrying babies, each tied in an ingenious bundle of striped blanket on their backs.

For the Indians of La Paz, life is spare and bitter, with almost no comforts. They live in the hills surrounding the city where the air is even thinner. Their homes, even the better ones, are shanties made of discarded signboards, doors, and other debris, or mud that has been shaped into bricks and dried in the sun. The houses have no windows, electricity, or plumbing, and are dank, dark, musty, and unpleasant. The life expectancy of the Indians is only 33 years. Financial security is unknown, and tuberculosis and other diseases take a tremendous toll on children and adults. Most Indian mothers expect to have two of three children die in the first few years of life.

In contrast to the bleak landscape of La Paz is the city of San Francisco. On a different part of the planet geographically, culturally, and historically, San Francisco has a quality that makes it one of the most well-loved cities in the world. Its commercial hub matches Paris for smartness. The window displays of its department stores and small shops rival New York's finest for style. Many gingerbread houses cling to the steep hillsides like displaced Alpine cottages, and the golden pagoda roofs of Chinatown, the unexpected glimpses of the Pacific Ocean, and the toylike cable cars complete a fantasy scene.

Composed of the very same groups found in other American cities—Italians, Germans, Irish, blacks, British, and Asians—San Francisco seems to have developed an urban sophistication based on tolerance. Many of the people have an easygoing broad-mindedness that combines with an eminently stretchable moral outlook. No other city in the United States looks so benevolently on saints and sinners alike.

La Paz is an urban center perched in a crater over two miles above sea level.

Unlike the urban imagery that fosters the sameness of a collection of cosmopolitan masses and classes, of wealth and haste, and of poverty and sin, these few glimpses suggest the kinds of characteristics that make each city of the world rather unique. Yet in sharp contradiction, cities do indeed have many things in common, and it is these elements of commonality—in urban growth, structure, and process—that constitute the sociology of cities.

CITIES AND THE URBAN TRANSFORMATION

What, first of all, is a city? At the outset, this may seem like a simple question to answer, but the concept of *a city* can be rather difficult to unravel. A native of the rural Northeast once referred to the city as a place where the mountains are gone. The ordinary dictionary defines the city as a town of significant size. Philosophers of the urban way of life, on the other hand, see the city as a state of mind. These, of course, are oversimplifications, for a city possesses a complex of characteristics: a physical plant, population concentration and size, economic centrality, political autonomy, and sociocultural features. *Physically,* the city is a compact cluster of relatively permanent buildings. *Demographically,* a city is a large concentration of people in a relatively small area (although no specific definition of the minimal size of a city has been agreed upon consensually). *Economically,* the city is a place where much of the work force is concentrated. *Politically,* a city exists under the administrative structure of a government and is defined by that government as "a city." In fact, the term *city* comes from "citizen," or member of a political unit; the city is thus the place where citizens reside.[1] *Socioculturally,* the city represents a relatively large, heterogeneous, and diverse set of interrelationships. Thus, a **city** is not simply a town of sufficient size, but rather, a dense and permanent concentration of people with distinct forms of social organization and economic relationships, located in a geographical area delineated by physical and political boundaries.

Cities are viewed generally in light of the larger urbanization process. **Urbanization** is the progressive movement of people from rural areas to cities, resulting in city growth and a shift in the relative proportions of rural versus urban populations.

The Emergence of Cities

Cities began to develop sometime between 6000 and 5000 B.C. Because so few written records exist concerning early civilizations, much of what is known about the cities of antiquity comes from the work of archeologists. Research on the city is hampered by the fact that writing was not developed until well after the emergence of the first cities.[2] In consequence, the early history of the urban phenomenon is somewhat speculative.

Cities first appeared in the Fertile Crescent, an area arcing across the northern part of the Syrian desert, now occupied by parts of present-day Israel, Lebanon, Syria, Jordan, and Iraq (see Exhibit 17.1). Others cities emerged in the fertile valleys of the Yellow (China) and Indus (India) rivers, and in Mesoamerica (Mexico and Central America) with the Mayan culture. They were hardly "cities" in the modern sense since they were more like small villages. Yet they were different in that nothing like them had existed previously.

The development of cities began during the Neolithic era, that period in archeological time when people first domesticated plants and animals. Agriculture had slowly taken precedence over the hunting and gathering forms of subsistence that had characterized the preceding age. This shift to agriculture was among the most important factors in the development of cities; an agricultural surplus is vital to the support of any urban population. The early cities also developed social and political systems characterized by a specialized division of labor that fostered the creation of writing and such occupations as craftsmen, traders, officials, priests, and other nonsubsistence workers.[3]

Early cities were small by contemporary standards, containing less than 5% of the local populations. Those in the Fertile Crescent had from 2,000 to 20,000 inhabitants, although Erech in Babylonia is believed to have contained some 50,000 residents on approximately 1,000 acres.[4]

Early Greek and Roman Cities

Perhaps the best known of early urban and city developments were found in the Greek and Roman cultures. Greek cities first appeared some 4,000 years ago and reached their summit during that nation's Golden Age, around the fifth century B.C. The Greeks were famous for their *polis,* or city-state. The **city-state** was an autonomous political unit consisting of a city and the surrounding countryside. Citizenship in the Greek city involved the sharing of a common religion and place of protection. Full-fledged citizenship, however, was accorded only to males. In Athens, by far the largest of the ancient Greek cities, some 40,000 citizens, possibly 150,000 free people (women, children, and foreigners), and 100,000 slaves were all concentrated in an area no larger than one square mile.[5]

The Roman Empire began during the fifth century B.C. and endured for almost 1,000 years. Throughout that

Exhibit 17.1 Sociological Focus

The Fertile Crescent

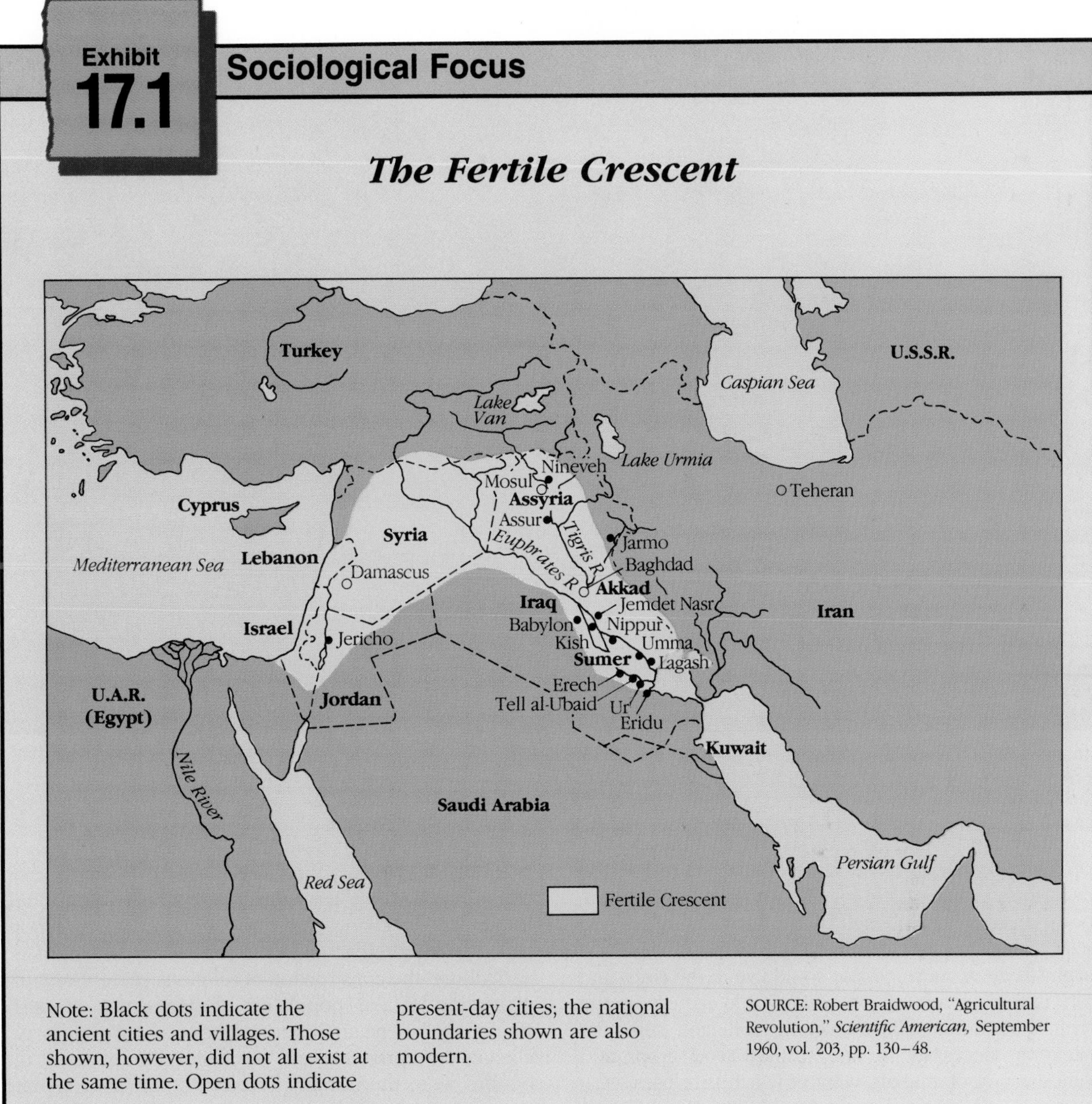

Note: Black dots indicate the ancient cities and villages. Those shown, however, did not all exist at the same time. Open dots indicate present-day cities; the national boundaries shown are also modern.

SOURCE: Robert Braidwood, "Agricultural Revolution," *Scientific American*, September 1960, vol. 203, pp. 130–48.

millennium, the empire and city of Rome grew, and at its peak, the city had perhaps as many as 1 million inhabitants. The Romans made many contributions to the advancement of civilization and constructed a variety of technological wonders that still stand. Examples include the aqueducts used to transport water to urban Rome and tens of thousands of well-maintained roads, many of which surpass contemporary U.S. standards. Yet the city also had many of the problems that plague modern urban areas: deteriorating buildings, political corruption, traffic congestion, and poverty. Rome, however, was more advanced than earlier Neolithic villages; early Rome was directed by a strong urban government and supported by an agricultural surplus produced by farmers.[6]

Preindustrial Cities

Rome and Athens were preindustrial cities (a designation that indicates their establishment prior to the Industrial Revolution), and four conditions are generally recognized as necessary for their emergence and development: an adequate population base, a favorable ecology,

Athens, one of the world's oldest cities, boasted a population of nearly 300,000 during the fifth century B.C.

technology, and some degree of social organization.[7] The population base had to be large enough to supply the labor force appropriate for the production of food, goods, and services needed by the urban dwellers and those living in the surrounding hinterland. As food surpluses grew, more people could live in the cities and work in nonagricultural jobs. A favorable ecology, in the form of moderate climate, arable soil, and sufficient water was necessary for the cultivation of crops and domestication of animals, without which surpluses were impossible. For this reason the first cities appeared in the valleys and along the silted flood plains of the Tigris, Euphrates, Indus, Nile, and Yellow rivers. Technology enabled urban settlements to expand in size, density, and importance. The discovery of irrigation, for example, served to extend croplands. The domestication of animals, along with the introduction of the plow and yoke, increased the efficiency of agricultural production. Pottery permitted the storage and transportation of food, while the discovery of metallurgy and the rise of metal work stimulated trade in fashioned weapons and ornaments.

The structured social organization of preindustrial cities, characterized by a sharp division of labor, clearly distinguished them from rural settlements. In most preindustrial cities, a three-class system of stratification was adopted. At the top a small core of elites supported themselves by taxing everyone else. They were responsible for city administration, the supervision of hinterland agriculture, the construction of religious centers, and the protection of the population during times of peril. Immediately beneath this aristocracy was a slightly larger class of entrepreneurs and successful merchants. At the bottom were the farmers, artisans, other laborers, and outcasts who sold their crops and artifacts and traded with other settlements. Thus, **preindustrial cities** were those urban centers established prior to the Industrial Revolution that were based on agricultural and trade economies, and characterized by a core ruling elite, a small middle class, and a large impoverished population of manual laborers.

Medieval Cities

After the demise of the Roman Empire in the fifth century, life in Europe came to be dominated by the feudal system and rural agriculture. The **feudal system** was a sociopolitical structure based on a rural economy and characterized by a dispersal of power to a variety of semi-independent domains in which land was held by serfs on the condition of their service and homage to the landowning lords. With the emergence of feudal relations, urban development ceased for almost five hundred years.

The reappearance of cities in Europe was tangibly affected by the political conditions of the eighth through eleventh centuries. The Moslem and Norman invasions, the cavalry raids of the Hungarians, and the struggles of rival lords during those four centuries influenced feudal princes to build large fortified castles or *burgs,* frequently on the sites of earlier towns. As trade increased, traveling merchants sought shelter and security at night in these castles and often conducted business with the local inhabitants. With greater advances in trade and commerce, the number of merchants increased to the point where the feudal castles could no longer hold them, thus stimulating settlement outside the burg. As their numbers continued to increase, they built walls, creating a new burg, and accordingly, the princes became known as burghers, burgesses, or *bourgeois.*[8]

The concentration of merchants and trade in these locations lured the artisans, causing cloth-makers, weavers, and the entire clothing industry to shift from a rural to an urban setting. The continued demand for agricultural tools and weapons attracted copper-, bronze-, and stoneworkers, with consequent needs for more labor. Rural population was growing simultaneously, and many a feudal manor was unable to support the larger families, leading laborers to the developing markets in search of other work.

During the Renaissance, from the mid-fourteenth century to the end of the sixteenth century, no more than 5% of the population lived in cities. Most cities had less than 30,000 inhabitants, although it has been estimated that Paris, Florence, Venice, and Milan reached population levels of 100,000 or more. Although the rich lived in spacious homes, life for most medieval city dwellers was anything but elegant. Rich and poor alike faced the problems of congestion, poor sanitation, filth, and contaminated water. Moreover, the cities were ripe for epidemics. During the outbreak of the Black Plague in 1347, at least one-fourth of the European population perished, and in the cities populations were cut in half.

The Industrial Revolution and Modern Urbanization

The term **industrial revolution** applies to the social and economic changes that marked the transition from a stable agricultural and commercial society to a modern industrial society, reliant on complex machinery rather than on tools.

Industrialization, which began in England during the middle of the eighteenth century, was the result of a variety of factors. First, political consolidation fostered nationalism and the establishment of nation-states. The dispersed feudal estates were unified under permanent and centrally located government bureaucracies, courts of justice, and archives. Second, transportation routes became safer, uniform coinage systems were expanded, and tax and toll collections became less frequent. Third, the Protestant Reformation, which swept Western Europe during the sixteenth century, supported the new ideology of capitalism. According to Max Weber, Protestantism fostered beliefs in hard work, individualism, frugality, deferral of rewards, and a purposeful life.[9] The new religious values of this **Protestant ethic** were tied directly to the economic orientations of industrial capitalism. Fourth, technological advancements in agriculture freed people from the soil for other productive activities.

The most important change during this period of transformation was the decline of home and craft production and the rise of the factory system. Machinery and the use of steam for power transferred most types of home industries to the factory. Coupled with agricultural advancements, the shift to labor-saving devices initiated an exodus from the countryside as displaced workers flocked to the cities seeking work in the rapidly expanding factories.[10]

The end product of these various factors was the modern **industrial city,** a large urban settlement situated near an energy source or raw materials, dependent on manufacturing, banking, and transportation. In contrast to their preindustrial counterparts, the new industrial complexes tended to have flexible class systems that offered opportunities for social mobility and were administrated by officials selected on the basis of experience and expertise.

The Urbanization of America

The growth of cities and urbanization in America can be characterized by several stages. During the *preindustrial stage,* which lasted from colonization until around 1850, the cities were quite small. New York, the Dutch outpost of New Amsterdam, had a population of only 18,000 in 1760.[11] The most important cities were east coast seaports, particularly Philadelphia, New York, Boston, Charles Town (now Charleston), and Newport.

The *urban industrial stage* of American urbanization lasted from just prior to the Civil War until the end of World War I (1850–1920). During this period of transition cities grew and gained an increasing share of

SOCIAL INDICATOR

Population of Colonial Cities, 1743 and 1760

	1743	1760
Philadelphia	13,000	23,750
New York	11,000	18,000
Boston	16,382	15,631
Charles Town	6,800	8,000
Newport	6,200	7,500

Source: Carl Bridenbaugh, *Cities in Revolt* (New York: Alfred A. Knopf, 1965), p. 5. Copyright ©1965 Alfred A. Knopf.

the total population. As large-scale manufacturing emerged, cities expanded dramatically and became more differentiated, with areas of retail trade, residences, industry, and entertainment. This period even witnessed the introduction of vice areas—areas in which many forms of crime flourish together—in numerous cities (see Exhibit 17.2). City governments assumed more responsibility and provided police, fire, and water services, as well as sanitation and health-care systems. The new, large-scale urban societies provided a level of economic opportunity never seen before, but at the same time they created the many problems characteristic of contemporary urban areas.

The Metropolis

The *metropolitan stage* of American cities began around 1920 and continues today. The period is characterized by massive gains in population and productive capacity, combined with a shift from agriculture and factory labor to service industries. In the metropolitanization process, a gradual decentralization away from center cities occurs, as factories, retail facilities, and residences move to suburban areas. Currently, the metropolis, or **metropolitan area,** composed of one or more central cities, together with surrounding suburbs, has become a characteristic of the national urban scene.

The rise of metropolitan areas brought profound changes in the American way of life. Prior to the era of the metropolis, cities were centers of industrial and commercial activity. Workers lived in houses or tenements within walking distance of factories or trolley and subway lines that went out only relatively short distances from the city hub. Few questioned where the city ended and the country began. Outside of city boundaries, large population concentrations did not occur, and government structure beyond these borders was designed for basically rural conditions. The metropolitan area became, in effect, a new community. Its boundaries were often hard to define; in some instances they changed frequently. These new communities reflected a different kind of society that was largely the result of higher average incomes, the development of new tastes in living standards, and the technological means for releasing people from old patterns.[12]

The Megalopolis

Many contemporary observers hold that American cities have entered a new stage of development—the *postindustrial stage*—characterized by the emergence of the megalopolis. The term **megalopolis** was introduced by French geographer Jean Gottman and is generally applied to an urban region that contains several metropolitan centers:

> The Northeastern seaboard of the United States is today the site of a remarkable development—an almost continuous stretch of urban and suburban areas from southern New Hampshire to northern Virginia and from the Atlantic shore to the Appalachian foothills. . . .
>
> As one follows the main highways or railroads between Boston and Washington, D.C., one hardly loses sight of built-up areas, tightly woven residential communities, or powerful concentrations of manufacturing plants. Flying this same route one discovers, on the other hand, that behind the ribbons of densely occupied land . . . there still remain large areas covered with woods and brush. . . . These green spaces, however, when inspected at closer range, appear stuffed with a loose but immense scattering of buildings. . . . That is, many of these sections that look rural actually function largely as suburbs in the orbit of some city's downtown. . . .
>
> Thus, the distinctions between rural and urban do not apply here any more.[13]

What Gottman was describing was what has become known as the Northeast Corridor and the phenomenon of urban sprawl. As metropolitan areas spread outward, in a totally unplanned fashion, they contact one another to form a continuous chain of metropolitan regions. Twenty-eight of these massive urban regions known as "strip cities," are to be found in the United States today, containing more than two-thirds of the American population (see Exhibit 17.3). Shopping malls now stand on pastures where cows grazed only a decade ago; subdivisions and developments of suburban tract housing occupy farms where corn and other produce were grown; and six- and eight-lane interstate highway systems bisect once deserted fields, forests, and marshlands.

Exhibit 17.2

Sidelights on American Culture

Urbanization and the Emergence of Vice Areas

The history of urban America suggests that although the growth of city populations and crime were associated with industrialization, trans-Atlantic migrations, and demographic shifts, the evolutionary development of the urban vice area or criminal district, was usually guided by one or more specific, often unique and cataclysmic, factors. Whether the city was a great seaport or an interior exchange point, this notion is generally applicable. In San Francisco the crucial factor was the discovery of gold in 1848; in Chicago it was extremely rapid population growth combined with the city's role as a focal point for the American railroad complex; for the cities along the Mississippi it was the keelmen along the river and the wagoners heading west; and for New York it was the Revolutionary War followed by successive population movements. The growth of vice areas and criminal districts in New Orleans, stimulated by piracy and the riverboat, illustrates the general evolutionary process.

The city of New Orleans, a Gulf Coast seaport, gained sudden significance with the Louisiana Purchase. The French had used New Orleans as a depository for deported convicts from the early 1700s through 1803, when the United States purchased the Louisiana Territory. During the next twenty years, the population of New Orleans more than quadrupled; large numbers of the new settlers were thieves, vagabonds, and prostitutes from all parts of the civilized world.

Geography also contributed to the rise of New Orleans' criminal districts and vice areas. The early immigrants to the rich lands of the Louisiana Territory in the first years after its purchase required manufactured goods. Commerce developed along the Mississippi River with New Orleans as its central port, both for riverboats and ocean-going cargo ships. The central means of transportation down the Mississippi was the crude flatboat. It was primarily designed for the transportation of goods, with no provision for the comfort of its crew, who ate and slept on the open decks. Only the strongest could survive work on this craft, and as a class, the riverboat men were among the roughest, toughest, and most pugnacious of the early pioneers. The men of the river developed a life-style based on the survival of the fittest. The shores of the Ohio and Mississippi rivers were infested with gangs of "land pirates." These individuals and the riverboat men periodically invaded New Orleans.

The emerging underworld of the growing port city entertained both pirates and boatmen in a section known as "the Swamp." It was composed of six blocks of saloons, dance halls, hotels, brothels, and gambling houses where, as one observer described it, "a roving keelboat man could obtain a bed, a bottle of whiskey, and a woman for six cents, and, should he have more in his pockets, might also have his throat cut."

Piracy in the manner of Blackbeard, and privateering as a later counterpart, began in the eighteenth century in the Gulf of Mexico and continued until the late 1800s. Smugglers and other merchants of contraband used New Orleans as a point of rendezvous, and others created their permanent headquarters in the criminal areas of the city.

In 1807, Robert Fulton propelled the *Clermont,* the first steamboat, up the Hudson River. On January 12, 1812, steamboats came to New Orleans, initiating the disappearance of the keelmen. The newer vessels were of greater size and speed than the flatboats, which had been powered only by human muscle, and large crews and swivel guns mounted at the bow overcame any landside invaders. By 1815 passenger travel was instituted along the Mississippi, followed by the era of riverboat gamblers. More gaudy than the earlier "Swamp" gamblers, this group brought their reputations and skills to New Orleans' growing centers of vice.

By the 1880s, certain districts in New Orleans had become highly developed centers of vice and contained well-organized gangs of pickpockets, burglars, and sneak thieves. Not only were these individuals organized and specialized, but their political connections were strong enough to prevent prosecution by the courts.

SOURCE: James A. Inciardi, *Careers in Crime* (Chicago: Rand McNally, 1975) p. 165.

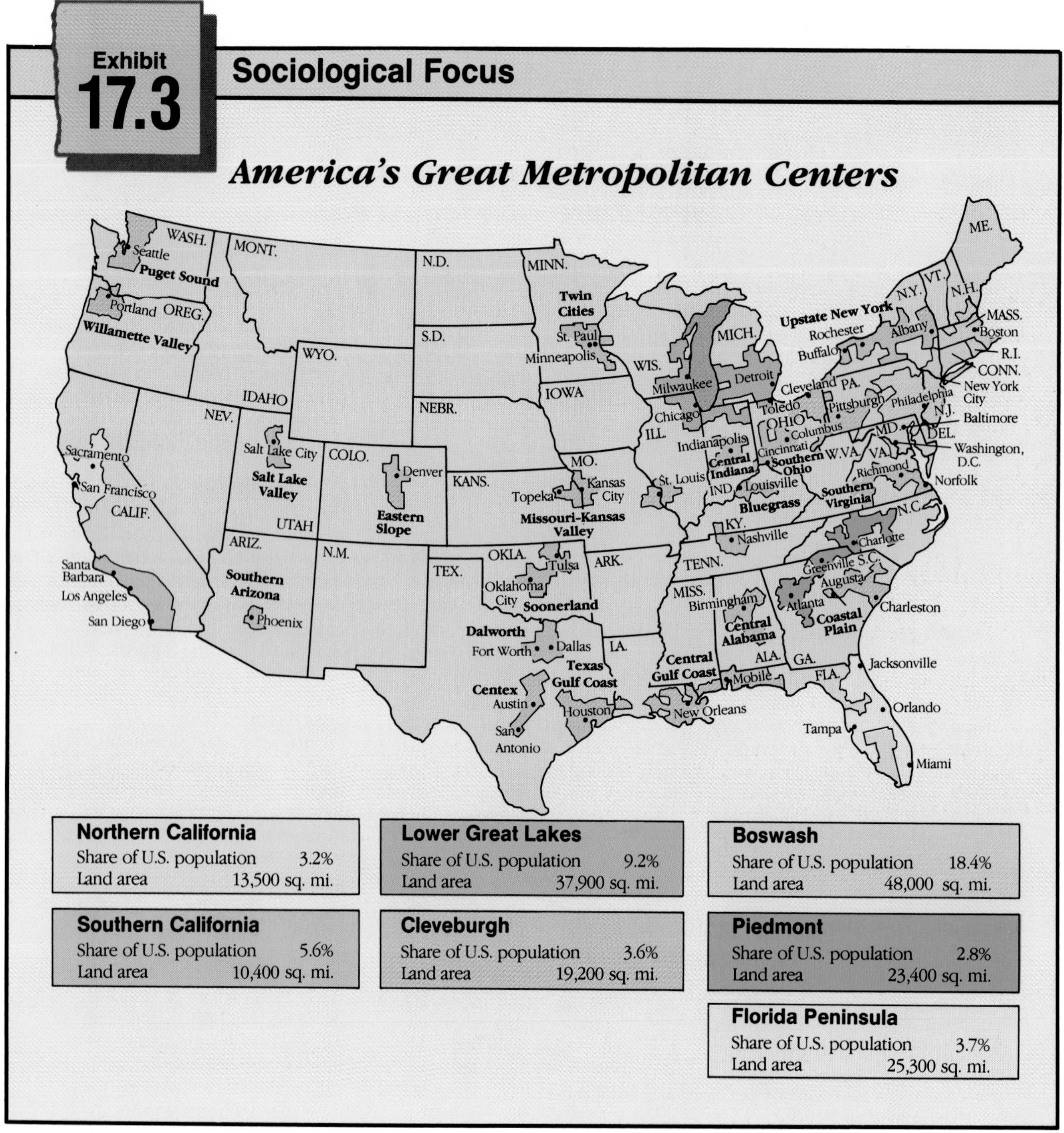

Exhibit 17.3 Sociological Focus

America's Great Metropolitan Centers

Urbanization and Population Movements

Although the shift from agricultural and other rural occupations to the industrial work and support services found in the cities was the major factor in urban growth, other elements were involved as well. Immigration and migration also served to increase the size of cities. Between 1800 and 1925, some 40 million immigrants entered the United States through eastern port cities, with the majority settling in Boston, New York, Philadelphia, Baltimore, and Chicago. Between 1901 and 1910 alone almost 9 million immigrants were added to city populations. The first large wave of immigrants, primarily of northern and western European extraction, came during the 1850s. The Irish, fleeing the potato famine of the 1840s, accounted for the largest proportion of this group. The second wave, commencing around 1880, was composed of large numbers of Italian, Jewish, Slavic, Polish, and Greek immigrants.[14]

A suspender merchant at the turn of the century in the Lower East Side of New York City sold his wares to a community composed entirely of immigrants.

Internal migrations also added to city growth and metropolitan expansion. During World War I, a shortage of labor in the industrial North attracted many blacks away from the rural South, with another wave occurring during World War II. Although the numbers involved were not great in comparison to European immigration, the 5 million migrants between 1910 and 1960 did have an impact on New York, Detroit, Chicago, and Los Angeles.[15] In an effort to escape from the congestion, pollution, crime, and harsher climate of the Northeastern and Midwestern cities, during the 1970s millions of Americans emigrated from these areas to the South and West. From 1970 to 1980 New York, Newark, Philadelphia, Cleveland, Pittsburgh, and several other cities actually lost population, while the population of Phoenix went up by 63%, that of the Florida Peninsula increased by 45%, and the Texas Gulf Coast and the Salt Lake Valley both grew by 33%.[16] Since the beginning of the 1980s additional shifts have occurred. While growth continued in the South and Southwest, many of the Northeastern cities began to grow once more, with corresponding declines in the older Midwestern industrial cities (see Exhibit 17.4).

WORLD URBANIZATION

With the exceptions of the Arctic and Antarctic regions of high ice plateaus, glaciated mountains, and frozen tundra, where urban development is virtually impossible, cities appear throughout the world—on every continent, in every major area, and in every country.

Yet despite the presence of cities almost everywhere, the distribution of urban areas is rather uneven. Moreover, at the international level, coming to grips with what constitutes an "urban area" can be problematic. Some nations define a locale as urban only if it is an administrative center of some kind; others use population size as the basis of definition. In Korea, urban status applies to places with 40,000 or more inhabitants; in Denmark, any place with as few as 250 people is considered a city.

In view of these definitional differences, discussions of world urbanization tend to use as the standard of

SOCIAL INDICATOR

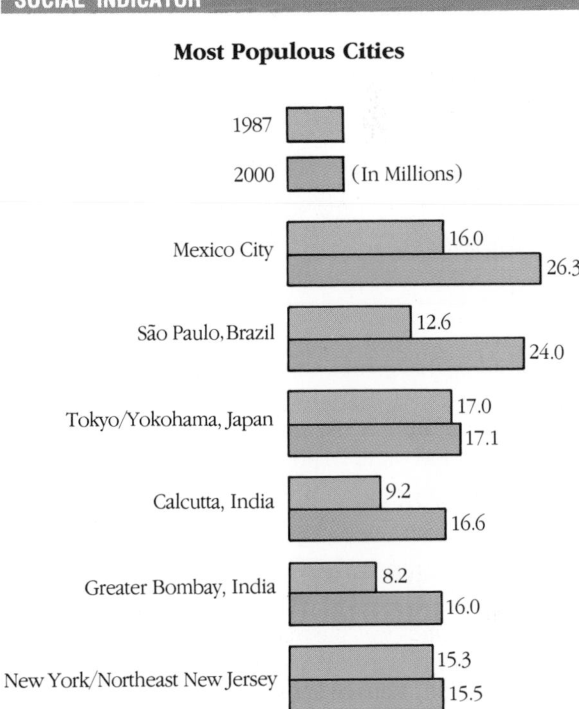

Exhibit 17.4

Sociological Focus

Forecasting Metropolitan Growth

The Top 50 — **Ranked by Growth, in Thousands**

MSAs and PMSAs	1985	2005	Growth	Percent Change
Washington, District of Columbia–Maryland–Virginia	3,477.5	6,103.9	2,626.4	75.5%
Houston, Texas	3,378.3	5,910.3	2,532.0	74.9
Anaheim–Santa Ana, California	2,214.3	4,451.0	2,236.7	101.0
Los Angeles–Long Beach, California	7,967.4	9,842.8	1,875.4	23.5
San Diego, California	2,131.0	3,528.5	1,397.5	65.6
Denver, Colorado	1,671.6	2,987.8	1,316.2	78.7
Dallas, Texas	2,294.7	3,592.1	1,297.4	56.5
Atlanta, Georgia	2,405.6	3,537.4	1,131.8	47.0
San Francisco, California	1,562.0	2,670.3	1,108.3	71.0
Phoenix, Arizona	1,806.5	2,727.4	920.9	51.0
San Jose, California	1,419.1	2,302.6	883.5	62.3
Tampa–St. Petersburg–Clearwater, Florida	1,863.1	2,613.9	750.8	40.3
San Antonio, Texas	1,219.0	1,956.4	737.4	60.5
Austin, Texas	656.2	1,371.1	714.9	108.9
Ft. Lauderdale–Hollywood–Pompano Beach, Florida	1,185.8	1,866.8	681.0	57.4
Oakland, California	1,898.2	2,501.7	603.5	31.8
Chicago, Illinois	6,114.6	6,712.2	597.6	9.8
Oklahoma City, Oklahoma	1,009.8	1,588.5	578.7	57.3
Orlando, Florida	852.1	1,426.2	574.1	67.4
Seattle, Washington	1,797.0	2,364.1	567.1	31.6
Sacramento, California	1,261.3	1,812.0	550.7	43.7
Minneapolis–St. Paul, Minnesota–Wisconsin	2,279.8	2,829.0	549.2	24.1
Middlesex–Somerset–Hunterdon, New Jersey	945.1	1,473.5	528.4	55.9
New Orleans, Louisiana	1,372.1	1,889.5	517.4	37.7
Nassau–Suffolk, New York	2,678.4	3,178.0	499.6	18.7
Miami–Hialeah, Florida	1,771.5	2,250.2	478.7	27.0
Norfolk–Virginia Beach–Newport News, Virginia	1,242.9	1,719.0	476.1	38.3
Portland, Oregon	1,203.4	1,678.0	474.6	39.4

urbanization the proportion of a country's population living in cities of 100,000 or more. This yardstick is employed because of the high correlation between the proportion of a country's population living in large cities and other measures and characteristics of urbanization.[17]

World Urbanization and the Industrial Order

The established urban-industrial nations—the United States, England, Canada, Australia, New Zealand, West Germany, and the Netherlands—are primarily those countries in which industrialization originated. Urbanization and industrialization occurred during the nineteenth century, and the growth of cities was typically a response to labor demands of the factory system. A similar process occurred early in the twentieth century among the newly industrial nations—Japan, the Soviet Union, the countries of Eastern Europe, and a few areas of the Middle East and Southeast Asia. The process reflected elements of stability. Rural populations were drawn to the cities in search of work, and new social forms in government, family, economics, and education emerged and adapted. In most other parts of the world, however, urbanization occurred differently and with alternative implications.

The Top 50	Ranked by Growth, in Thousands			
MSAs and PMSAs*	1985	2005	Growth	Percent Change
Tucson, Arizona	609.1	1,076.2	467.1	76.7
Detroit, Michigan	4,354.5	4,811.6	457.1	10.5
Las Vegas, Nevada	551.9	1,008.5	456.6	82.7
Boston–Lawrence–Salem–Lowell–Brockton, Massachusetts–New Hampshire	3,679.4	4,124.6	445.2	12.1
Honolulu, Hawaii	782.3	1,198.1	415.8	53.2
Baltimore, Maryland	2,257.6	2,663.4	405.8	18.0
Monmouth–Ocean, New Jersey	915.3	1,311.7	396.4	43.3
Salt Lake City–Ogden, Utah	1,053.5	1,440.7	387.2	36.8
Raleigh–Durham, North Carolina	621.3	995.1	373.8	60.2
Fort Worth–Arlington, Texas	1,144.6	1,479.1	334.5	29.2
Kansas City, Missouri–Kansas City, Kansas	1,489.5	1,823.1	333.6	22.4
Portsmouth–Dover–Rochester, New Hampshire–Maine	313.8	629.0	315.2	100.4
Newark, New Jersey	1,889.7	2,197.0	307.3	16.3
Columbus, Ohio	1,303.4	1,604.3	300.9	23.1
Riverside–San Bernardino, California	1,746.7	2,016.2	269.5	15.4
Bridgeport–Stamford–Norwalk–Danbury, Connecticut	845.8	1,109.0	263.2	31.1
Colorado Springs, Colorado	361.2	624.2	263.0	72.8
Nashville, Tennessee	913.8	1,175.9	262.1	28.7
Oxnard–Ventura, California	611.5	872.1	260.6	42.6
Philadelphia, Pennsylvania–New Jersey	4,774.4	5,026.7	252.3	5.3
Lafayette, Louisiana	236.9	484.0	247.1	104.3
Santa Rosa–Petaluma, California	345.4	589.3	243.9	70.6

Source: Population Reference Bureau, 1987.

*The Metropolitan Statistical Area (MSA) is either one or more central cities, each with a population of at least 50,000, or a single urbanized area that has at least 50,000 people and that is part of an MSA with a total population of 100,000. The Primary Metropolitan Statistical Area (PMSA) is a large urbanized county or cluster of counties that is part of a metropolitan statistical area with one million people or more.

In the **Third World*** countries of Latin America, Africa, the Middle East, and India, early colonization by more established nations resulted in urban systems with underdeveloped economies. In most instances, the social and economic structures were established for the benefit of the ruling elite and the citizenry of the "mother country."[18] While under colonial rule, the cities specialized in exports, with only minimal energy, if any, focused on generating wealth and opportunities for the bulk of

*Third World is a political and economic designation that is commonly used but rarely explained. Third World nations were originally those that were not aligned politically with the western, capitalistic democracies (the "first" world) or the Communist bloc (the "second" world). The term now refers to those nations that recently gained their freedom from colonial rule and are seeking to develop and modernize. With the exception of some oil-producing countries, most are relatively poor, have low per-capita incomes, and are characterized by a markedly unequal distribution of wealth.

SOCIAL INDICATOR

The Largest City

What is the largest city in the world? New York? Tokyo? Los Angeles? Mexico City? Hong Kong? Some other city? See page 559 for answer.

the indigenous population or in developing industrial capabilities. Thus, when independence came, the nations of the Third World were characterized by subsistence economies, urbanization in the absence of the technical know-how for efficient and rapid industrialization, and political instability.

At one time not too long ago, many urban researchers and theorists believed that cities in the less-developed nations of the world would ultimately follow the industrialization-urbanization pattern formulated in the United States and Western Europe. That is, industrialization would be followed by rural to urban migration and city growth. Yet contrary to these expectations, Third World urbanization has been extremely rapid, at rates well beyond those experienced in the United States. Furthermore, as noted in Chapter 18, the populations of Third World nations have been increasing at an explosive pace. As a result, many of these developing countries have fallen victim to serious economic hardship. While their productive capacities have increased at a respectable rate, the populations that must be supported and maintained are absorbing resources at an even faster rate. Many Western nations, furthermore, were able to handle their surplus population through expansion to new territories; today's developing countries, however, have no new territories or colonies. And in addition to these problems, some countries, such as Nigeria, are also plagued by levels of waste, mismanagement, and corruption that serve to further divert precious economic resources (see Exhibit 17.5).

Primate Cities and Overurbanization

Most of the developing nations contain a **primate city**, a city that grows in population and influence far beyond the other cities in the region or nation. In many countries of the Third World, the largest city may have several times the combined population of the next largest two or three urban areas and may also have a significant share of the national population. Mexico City's population of 16 million, for example, accounts for 20% of that nation's population, while the other major cities are considerably smaller: Guadalajara (1.8 million), Monterrey (1.1 million), and Puebla de Zaragoza (678,000).

Primate cities typically are located on the coast or in other areas close to transportation, since many were political and economic centers when under colonial rule. The orientation of such cities had been toward supplying the developed nations with raw materials and other goods, rather than toward the urban areas and hinterland of their own country.

Among the greatest difficulties experienced by cities in the less developed countries are those of stimulating industrialization and providing employment. People who move into urban areas do so, not because of the employment opportunities the cities provide, but because the living conditions in rural areas seem so much worse. Recent research has suggested that rural populations have been "forced" to relocate because of increasing agricultural density and the inability of the land to support its people.[19] Rural-urban migrants believe that the cities offer a better life and at least the hope for employment. Some do find work in small enterprises, but the lack of sophisticated technology and industrial production methods does not provide for the large pool of unskilled labor that characterized the Western industrial revolution. As a result, the unemployment rates in the cities of many developing nations exceed 25% of the labor force.

Common features of the city landscape are the sections comprised of shanties, shacks, and makeshift huts inhabited by those who have no other shelter. Known as "barriadas," "favelas," "kampongs," and "bustees," depending on the nation, these squatter settlements have been estimated to house as much as one-third of the urban population.[20] Mexico City currently has in excess of 4 million squatters; Seoul and Calcutta have more than 2 million each. The United Nations has estimated that squatter villages double their populations every six years.[21] This proliferation of squatter settlements is the natural outgrowth of **overurbanization,** the inability of the economic and industrial bases of a city to support its population. Overurbanization is essentially the level of population in excess of that which can "normally" be sustained by the existing level of urbanization.

Garbage pickers established a squatter community in Mexico City's Santa Fe dump, a common occurrence in Third World cities.

Modernization and Dependency Theory

A current debate in the literature on world urbanization and industrialization involves the conflicting perspectives of the modernization and dependency theories of Third World urbanization.[22] Proponents of **modernization theory** contend that the traditional social and political arrangements in developing nations must be altered if modern industrial benefits are to be derived. Advocates of this position argue that a modern sector and a traditional sector exist in every developing society, and the contemporary social structure has failed to achieve the benefits of modernization in the form of low birth rates, education, industrialization, employment, and a more equitable distribution of wealth, because industrialization has been resisted. This resistance has come from two sources. First, cultural traditions inhibit development of an impersonal industrial economy because values stress close interpersonal relationships over opportunities to earn more money. Second, native elites resist modernization because of the perceived threat it poses to the power and status that the existing socioeconomic arrangements accord them. In *both* instances, the forces of "tradition" impede industrialization and the focus of change.

Dependency theory is a more recent perspective, one whose adherents maintain that the underdevelopment characteristic of most Third World nations is not the result of existing cultural values, but rather, a consequence of the worldwide capitalist structure. Dependence is the natural outcome of a world system that perpetuates the relationships between developed and less-developed countries and hence, hampers the economic growth of the emerging industrial nations.

The advocates of dependency theory suggest that dependency relationships emerge and are sustained by means of a two-phase process. First, during the colonial era, European powers established cities in their frontier settlements as outlets for manufactured goods and as points of export for raw materials being shipped to industrialized nations. Political and economic control prevented the colonies from developing their own industrial base to process raw materials and export finished goods. Thus, the colonial cities were designed for export; resources were concentrated in the primate cities to the exclusion of rural areas. The interior regions stagnated as the primate cities grew, a situation that still characterizes many contemporary Third World nations.

Second, since the close of World War II, a phase of neocolonialism has emerged. Current dependencies focus on multinational corporations and the economic and political power they exercise in developing nations. The argument here is that investments and political meddling have locked the Third World into a subordinate role in the capitalist system. Typical practices include the use of Third World nations as sites for the manufacture of goods to be exported to developed nations. This practice is economically advantageous to foreign corporations because of the cheap labor costs abroad. A most recent case in point is Mexico. In 1982, Mexico was on the verge of almost total economic collapse. With a near-default on its $80-billion foreign debt that placed the international financial community at the brink of disaster, President Miguel de la Madrid was forced to devalue the Mexican peso. In 1982, before the economic crisis, the peso was worth 1.8 cents in American currency; by 1983, after the devaluation, the peso had dropped to 0.7 of a cent; in late 1984 it was worth half a cent, and by 1988 one U.S. penny could buy 23 Mexican pesos. In addition, income dropped by 25% and unemployment increased.[23] In an effort to capitalize on the Mexican economic crisis, the multinational corporations began to move into Mexico. By the middle of the decade, a colony of new factories was in operation in Juarez, just across the U.S.–Mexico border from El Paso, Texas, producing goods for export and paying Mexican laborers wages of less than $5 a day.

SOCIAL INDICATOR

The Largest City

The largest city in the world is Chongqing, a sprawling urban area perched on a bluff above the confluence of the Yangtze and Jialing Rivers. Once known as Chungking, it was China's capital city during World War II.

Chongqing has a population of 14 million people. Although greater metropolitan Mexico City has a larger population, Mexico City itself has under 12 million people.

Exhibit 17.5

Sociology in the Media

". . . A City Like No Other"

The back streets of Lagos are characterized by poverty and a notable lack of basic city services, such as piped water.

It should be the showplace of Africa, the capital of the most populous country on the continent, and—for a decade now—one of the oil and financial centers of the world. It is a city like no other: Lagos, the capital of the Federal Republic of Nigeria. Up until the world oil surplus, Nigeria was earning, on average, $15 billion a year as a major partner in OPEC.

That income has dropped, but still the dollars continue to roll in, not just in oil revenues, but from the big international banks and the World Bank. Democratic by African standards, rich by any standards, Lagos is the most expensive city in the world to visit.

Of all the cities a traveler might visit, be he European or from some other African state, he comes to no city with a heavier heart than to Lagos. Here he is beset almost everywhere by filth, contamination, incompetence, broken everything, and a bureaucracy that is a constant grievance to the soul—by lawlessness and by corruption on a scale so massive that it is not a crime but a condition.

Standing back, you see an impressive skyline, but enter into it and you find that the Lagos most of its citizens live in is an open sewer that is overflowing, clogged with human waste that is washed through the streets when the ditches can take no more—an abomination of a place. Mostly, it is without piped water, and the water that is available should not be drunk. It is a city that is a casualty of an oil boom, a victim of the wealth that attracts 35 people an hour, 25,000 a month—rural people who gave up scratching the earth for a living for survival in exchange for this.

Bodies can lie in the streets of Lagos for a week before they are removed. We were fortunate enough not to see any—or maybe not to notice any. Not noticing is a habit you easily acquire in Lagos. Men work in fetid waters, in the creeks and lagoons in the city, in conditions that seem reminiscent of the worst of slavery. Lagos is a diseased place, and it always has been a white man's and a black man's graveyard, a devil's cauldron.

A Nigerian wealthy enough not to have to use the free Lagos General Hospital said the only reason to go there is to die—one doctor for every 10,000 people in the country. The doctors who are there to treat often have to be bribed to treat. It is front-page news in the local press when a shipment of medicine arrives.

Lagos is also suffering from a thrombosis of traffic. The 20 miles between airport and town take three hours to accomplish. It is traffic beyond mere annoyance, a-choke with hawkers, dead and dying vehicles, and policemen gone hysterical. They tried ages ago putting traffic lights in, but they only made things worse and were cut off. They still stare unblinking out at Lagos, dusty monuments to a bad idea.

Lagos, the most populous city in Africa, maybe 5.5 million, has the power supply for a city of less than half a million. That poses a problem for international businessmen who still flock to Lagos to share the wealth: how does a European bank like the Société Général keep its computer brain safe from the power loss and power surge? The answer would have made Rube Goldberg envious.

In the computer room itself, all is well. The brain coolly registers its fortunes back to Paris and Zurich and other less-blighted cities. But just look at the almost fail-safe system that keeps it humming. The heart of it, the belt that holds up the computer's trousers, is a series of 250 car batteries kept cool by three spastic fans. The suspenders, just in case the belt breaks, are a generator that huffs away, but might also break down because everything breaks down in Lagos' misbegotten climate.

In Lagos, sweaty men from everywhere share the Lagos miseries with the locals, drinking beer by the liter, while they see this minister or that, fighting half a day's worth of traffic, and back, for a meeting that does not happen—exhausted, debilitated, stomachs suffering the special pangs of Lagos diarrhea—attaché cases solid with hundred-dollar bills for "Dash," the small bribe that you must pay almost everyone, and just for living—frightened silly of saying publicly that they hate the place for fear of losing an edge or a whole contract. Meantime, it's $150 a day for a Holiday Inn room, $75 for dinner for one, a dinner worth mentioning only to your doctor. And if you're "lucky" enough to bribe yourself a residency permit, the rent for a fairly modest house is $150,000 a year, three years in advance—all deposited, of course, in Switzerland.

An understated government report says, "Perennial traffic jams, intolerable congestion, the chaotic sanitary situation, inadequate social amenities and alarming crime rates have become Lagos' trademark. It defies all solutions." So, the Nigerian government, in its wisdom, decided eight years ago to abandon Lagos.

A new capital would be built at Abuja, 300 miles away from the mangrove swamps, up in the savannah land in central Nigeria. The roads up there, after Lagos, are a delight to all the senses. But it has cost $2 billion so far and they're spending at a rate of $50 million a month. The corruption is legendary. Hundreds of millions have disappeared. Luxury hotels go up—the room rate is to be $300 a day, single. The purpose of this venture is to take the pressure off Lagos. But it's a Catch-22. If no one comes—and a lot of the political and financial fat cats say they have no intention of coming—then all this is an unconscionable waste. If anyone comes, then everyone will come—urban drift and instant slum.

And there's the cost. The latest upward estimate of the cost is $16 billion. And it was supposed to have been ready to move into by September of 1983. Of course, it's going to cost more, and of course, it may not be ready until the year 2000. And if they ever do move into this vast, overpriced, concrete bureaucratic jungle, it still will be necessary to maintain the steamy old one back in the lagoons of Lagos. So, it'll be the familiar Lagos nightmare twice over, and at a nightmare price, and with no visible benefit to a hundred million Nigerians.

Note: In the years since this description was first broadcast on *60 Minutes*, the problems in Lagos have become worse. With the sliding price of oil, Nigeria's wealth faded, and in 1988 the World Bank reclassified it from a "middle" to a "low income" country. Much of the corruption and high prices have disappeared, primarily because of Nigeria's shattered economy. And for the same reasons, the unrepaired ravages of decay have become far worse, further enhancing Lagos' image as "a city like no other." See *New York Times*, August 14, 1988, p. L15.

SOURCE: *60 Minutes*, Volume XVI, Number 11, CBS Television Network, Sunday, November 27, 1983, 7:34–8:34 PM, EST.

URBAN ECOLOGY

Within cities are many subareas that have specialized functions or unique characteristics. Financial districts, such as New York's Wall Street, house the stock exchanges, the headquarters of banking firms, brokerage houses, and the head offices of national and international businesses. Entertainment centers—New York's Times Square, New Orleans' French Quarter, and the "downtowns" of other urban areas—are composed of arcades, theaters, restaurants, and perhaps a host of alternative attractions. The so-called "inner cities" house the urban poor and are characterized by deteriorating buildings and high rates of crime, drug addiction, truancy, and unemployment. Other subareas include the suburbs, ethnic enclaves, shopping districts, areas of heavy industry, centers of vice, and skid rows. It is clear that cities are composed of separate subareas. Large shopping malls are rarely found within the financial district, or similarly, the plush high-rise apartment complexes of the wealthy are quite separate from the skid rows or entertainment centers. How do these patterns of urban land use emerge and develop?

Urban ecology, the study of the ways that cities are patterned by their social and economic systems and the availability of land, emerged during the early part of the twentieth century as part of an attempt to explain the peculiarities of the spatial distribution of urban groups. An outgrowth of *ecology,* the natural science concerned with the relationship of living organisms to their environment, urban ecology demonstrates that the subareas of cities do not appear at random, nor do cities themselves grow randomly.

Ecological Succession

Anyone who lives in a city or visits the same city often enough will notice that changes take place: a street lined with six-story *walk-ups* and *railroad flats** becomes a promenade of luxury condominiums; industries move to the suburbs and their abandoned factories become warehouses or residential lofts; neighborhoods deteriorate, change hands, and decay further, or they are renovated or disappear entirely; business and entertainment districts lose their luster and become vice areas or skid rows. These kinds of changes are readily visible over time and many sociologists hold that a pattern is evident in their evolution.

Research in urban ecology at the University of Chicago during the 1920s and 1930s was influenced by the thinking of sociologist Robert E. Park and his conception of the "natural areas" of the city (see Exhibit 1.1).

Natural areas, in Park's view, were geographic zones characterized by physical individuality and by the cultural characteristics of those who lived in them. They were essentially *unplanned* segments of urban development that were both geographically limited and socioculturally homogeneous, and they represented the initial thread of Park's theory of urban ecology. Park and other sociologists at the University of Chicago introduced the concepts of "invasion" and "succession" to explain the character of certain natural areas, to describe how neighborhoods change hands or deteriorate, and to illustrate how some groups are segregated into certain parts of a city.[24] Because of competition for space, better housing, nearby work, or perhaps other reasons, a group begins to move into a neighborhood that is occupied by some other group. This is **invasion,** and the "invaders" are met initially with hostility and resistance. In time, as the invasion progresses, the original residents begin to leave, making more room for additional invaders. Ultimately, the invading group becomes dominant, and **succession** has occurred.

Examples of ecological invasion and succession abound, particularly with respect to the emergence of Italian, Jewish, Irish, black, and other racial and ethnic neighborhoods in many American cities. The term "white flight" has often been used to describe the process through which all-white neighborhoods rapidly become predominantly black neighborhoods. More unique examples may be cited as well. Many observers of state correctional systems have commented, for example, that blacks are overrepresented in prison populations. This phenomenon has generated communities of blacks —initially settled by the wives and children of inmates—in the vicinities of many correctional institutions. A case in point is Ossining, New York, the site of Sing Sing Correctional Facility. New York's Bowery became a skid-row area during the nineteenth century as the result of the invasion of an entertainment district by homeless men (see Exhibit 17.6). Perhaps a most unique example of ecological succession exists in Medellín, Colombia. At the edge of this industrial city of 2 million people, a massive shantytown with many thousands of residents has developed. This settlement stands at the site of a city garbage dump, which attracted vagrants, the destitute poor, and scavengers in search of food and the

*Six-story *walk-ups* and *railroad flats* are distinctively turn-of-the century Northeastern designations for urban tenement housing. The tenement, often above a retail store, was a cheap and narrow apartment house whose facilities and maintenance barely met minimum standards. The *walk-ups* were those tenement apartments in buildings equipped only with stairways. They were typically limited to six stories because local ordinances required buildings any higher to have elevators. *Railroad flats,* often found in the walk-up-type tenements, were narrow apartments with one room situated behind the other, much like the arrangement in nineteenth-century railroad cars.

Exhibit 17.6

Case Study

Urban Ecology and Skid Row

When Skid Rows began to appear in major American cities a few years after the close of the Civil War, many observers at the time felt that these areas were accidents of history, that they had been chosen at random, and that as the first hobos and tramps arbitrarily drifted into them, others simply followed. The perspective of urban ecology suggests quite a different story, as can be illustrated by the history of New York's infamous Bowery.

The emergence of the New York Skid Row on a street known as the Bowery had much to do with geography, for its specific geographical arrangement was primary among the influences that led to its degeneration. Briefly, the Bowery was the first road through the early colonies, and its southernmost tip (where the Skid Row appeared), was the only straight pathway of any significant length in lower Manhattan. The arrangement of hills and ponds on Manhattan Island had allowed an unbending road at only one place in the growing colony. In time, the Bowery's straight and level character was recognized by the more aristocratic sportsmen who wished to test the speed of their horses. Their regular Sunday morning races attracted many spectators and gamblers. Ale houses, taverns, and restaurants followed the expanding crowds, and as the population grew, racing extended beyond Sundays.

The atmosphere and sport that attended these racing events encouraged other types of amusements and small hotels along the Bowery. During the early part of the nineteenth century, the Bowery was supreme as an entertainment center. In 1826 the Bowery Theater was opened. Seating 3,000 persons, it was the nation's first gaslit playhouse and attracted performers of international fame.

By 1850, the Bowery began to lose its luster as an entertainment center. Times Square in midtown Manhattan had become popular as a theater and restaurant district. Coney Island in Brooklyn was emerging as a spectacular seaside resort. When the crowds stopped coming to the Bowery and other businesses failed to move in because of its essentially gaudy character, the area began to deteriorate and urban decay set in. The deterioration and decay along the Bowery were affected by its close proximity to the Five Points, a section just a few blocks south, which was considered to be the worst slum in nineteenth-century America.

After the Civil War the Bowery became the logical choice for homeless men who were appearing in New York. Hobos, tramps, and bums preferred it over other decaying areas because, in contrast to the essentially residential character of most slums and low-rent districts, the more commercial nature of this particular section met the needs of the homeless. Lodging, food, alcohol, and amusement were all provided by the holdovers and hangers-on from the time when the Bowery was a purveyor of entertainment. Once the poor and destitute became a visible fixture on the Bowery, a mold was cast that would endure for more than a century. Having developed a reputation as "a place where the bums live," the Bowery could attract only the most marginal of visitors and the businesses that catered to them—the missions, cheap restaurants, soup kitchens, and ten-cent flophouses. Despite social changes and attempts at urban renewal that have caused the disappearance of Skid Rows in other American cities, New York's Bowery is still to a very great extent "a place where the bums live."

SOURCES: Howard Bahr and Theodore Caplow, *Old Men Drunk and Sober* (New York: New York University Press, 1973); Edward Robb Ellis, *The Epic of New York City* (New York: Coward-McCann, 1966); Alvin F. Harlow, *Old Bowery Days* (New York: D. Appleton, 1931); Edo McCollough, *Good Old Coney Island* (New York: Charles Scribner's and Sons, 1957); Lloyd Morris, *Incredible New York* (New York: Bonanza, 1951); Oliver Pilat and Jo Ranson, *Sodom by the Sea* (Garden City, NY: Garden City, 1943); Harvey A. Siegal and James A. Inciardi, "The Demise of Skid Row," *Society/Transaction,* 19 (January–February 1982), pp. 39–45; Bayrd Still, *Mirror for Gotham* (New York: New York University Press, 1956).

discarded essentials of living. With nowhere else to go and a meager means of survival available in the form of garbage and other waste, many stayed, building themselves a community from the refuse of the more fortunate.

Patterns of Urban Growth

Given the rise and decline of natural areas and the processes of invasion and succession, Park and his associates at the University of Chicago saw cities as constantly changing, evolving into larger, more complex social systems. But are there indeed general trends that cities follow as they undergo change? Do cities manifest specific and predictable growth patterns? To answer these questions, urban ecologists have proposed a number of growth models.

The Concentric Zone Model

During the 1920s, University of Chicago professor Ernest W. Burgess devised the **concentric zone model** of urban growth which suggested that a city develops by spreading outward. It evolves as a series of concentric rings or zones that are added to the city as it grows.[25] Using Chicago as his model, Burgess held that cities have five general zones, each characterized by typical land use patterns (see Exhibit 17.7):

I. *The Central Business District.* The inner zone (or "Loop" in Chicago) is composed of retail businesses, light manufacturing, skyscrapers, entertainment, and commercialized recreation areas.

II. *Zone in Transition.* Surrounding the central business district is a transitional zone composed of low-income, crowded, and unstable residential housing characterized by high crime rates, prostitution, gambling, and other social problems. This zone is considered transitional because it sits in the immediate path of urban expansion.

III. *Zone of Workingmen's Homes.* Superior to the transitional zone but less attractive than middle-class residential areas, this zone is inhabited by industrial workers who escaped the more deteriorated areas to enjoy some of the comforts that the city had to offer.

IV. *Residential Zone.* Occupied by professionals, owners of small businesses, and managerial and clerical workers, this is the zone of the middle class. It contains apartment complexes, single-family homes, and some hotels.

V. *Commuters' Zone.* Located beyond the city limits and composed of small towns in which the more affluent live and from which they travel to the city to work, this is the suburban region.

The concentric zone model was well received when it was first proposed. It did indeed reflect the structure and growth pattern of certain cities, particularly those, like Chicago, that had emerged and developed quickly in the early stages of the Industrial Revolution, before the automobile and mass transportation introduced the complicating factor of increased geographical mobility. However, as an "ideal type," the concentric zone model did not fit any city perfectly. Furthermore, it in no way characterized the growth of newer cities, and other models were soon introduced.

The Sector Model

As a modification of the concentric zone model, in the 1930s Homer Hoyt's **sector model** was an attempt to account for the influences of urban transportation systems. In this scheme, Hoyt divided the city into sectors, or quadrants, which radiated out from the center, with growth following transportation routes and expanding away from already built-up areas (see Exhibit 17.8).[26] Each sector is typified by similar land use patterns such as lower-class residences, light manufacturing, or high-income housing. Hoyt contended that as cities grow, high-rent districts, for example, move outward along a sector. Industrial areas develop along sectors adjoining rivers, truck routes, railroad lines, and other geographical features, rather than forming rings around the central business district. But this model, too, while explaining some cities quite well, fell short of having universal applicability. Furthermore, many cities present striking exceptions to its central thesis. Boston's Beacon Hill and Manhattan's fashionable East Side are mid-town upper-class residential areas that have managed to retain their character for several generations.

The Multiple-nuclei Model

During the 1940s Chauncey Harris and Edward Ullman proposed the **multiple-nuclei model,** in which they posited that cities have not one, but several "core" or central business districts. Each of these core districts specializes in a particular activity, such as retailing, wholesaling, or manufacturing. These zones of activity and residence take on various shapes, and their locales depend on the resources available, nearness of markets, topography, transportation routes, and the city's past history of settlement and development (see Exhibit 17.9). Harris and Ullman also contended that the number and location of nuclei would vary from city to city. Thus, they concluded that seeking an ideal urban pattern may be a fruitless venture since historic and not necessarily predictable patterns may account for city shape, size, and structure.[27]

Exhibit 17.7 Sociological Focus

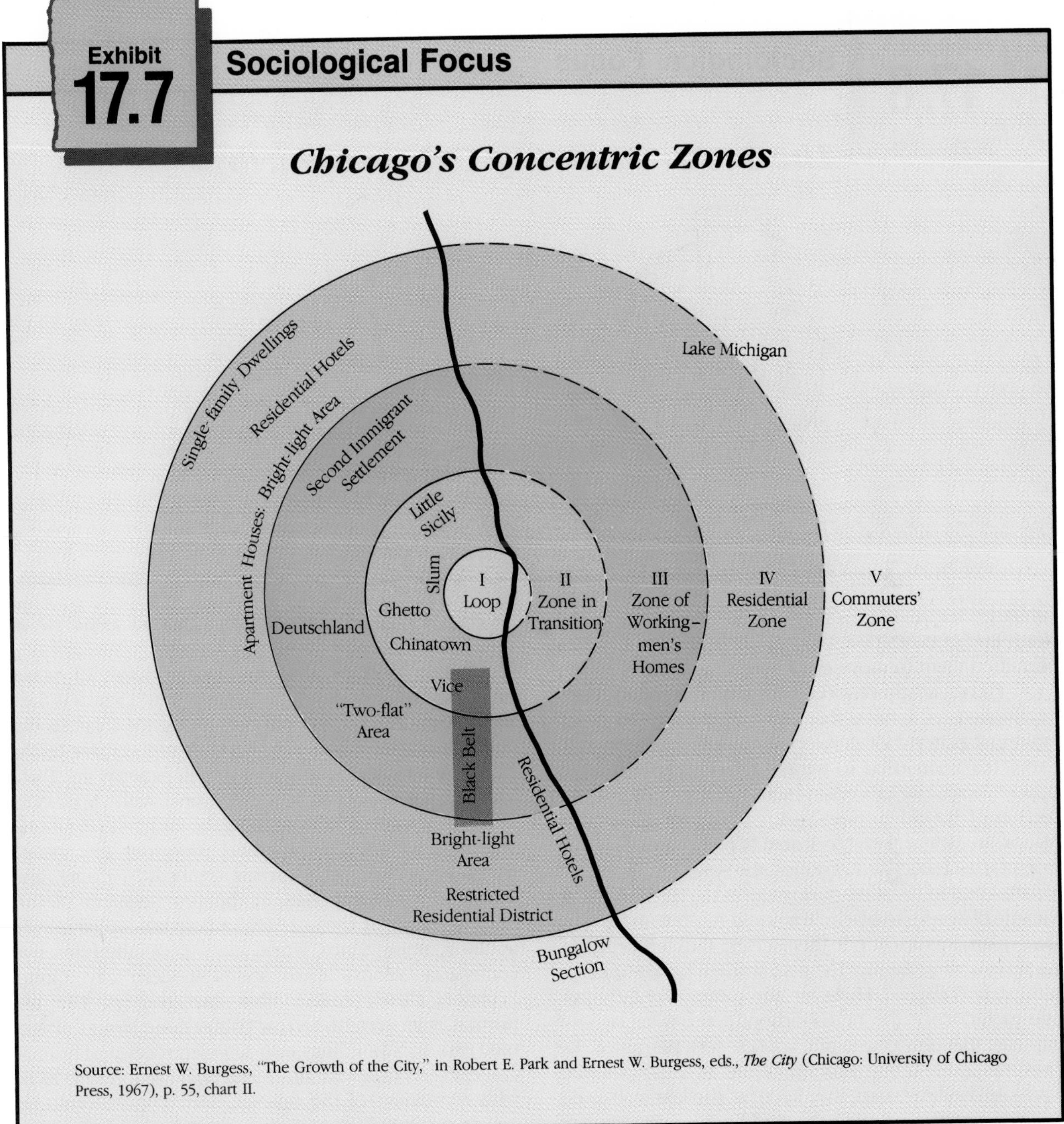

Source: Ernest W. Burgess, "The Growth of the City," in Robert E. Park and Ernest W. Burgess, eds., *The City* (Chicago: University of Chicago Press, 1967), p. 55, chart II.

Criticisms of Urban Land-use Models

Various criticisms of the ecological models used to explain city growth and urban land use patterns have developed in the decades since the models were first suggested.[28]

First, a number of the models have been based on the notions of invasion-succession and economic competition for space. Many observers feel that these approaches are overly simplistic, and that they are inaccurate since their applicability is limited to the American experience.

Second, most models ignore the role that social values play in decisions regarding urban land use. Walter Firey's extensive studies of Boston, for example, demonstrated that despite the high commercial value of the land occupied by Boston Common in the center of the city, it will always be a public park because of its historic value.

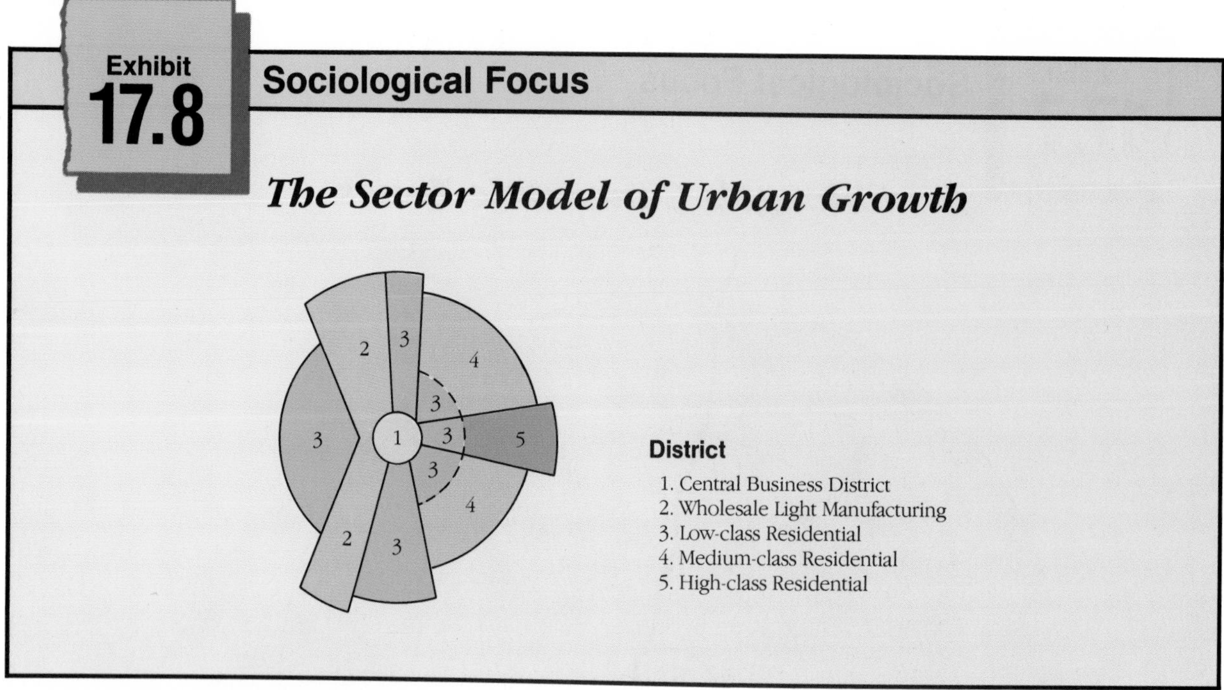

Similarly, Italian immigrants tended to remain in the North End of Boston even though their economic means permitted them to move elsewhere.[29]

Third, neighborhood cohesion has often been overlooked as a force that has the capacity to block emergent patterns of development. Neighborhood solidarity has been used to fight expansion as well as to oppose "invasion" by certain racial or ethnic groups. In a section of Brooklyn, New York, still known as Lefferts Manor, an eight-square-block area of predominately large turn-of-the-century brownstones, the neighborhood physicians banded together during the early 1950s to block the sale of houses to blacks. If a house was put up for sale, their plan was to buy it themselves, thus ensuring its resale to a white family. The plan worked for a while, but ultimately collapsed. However, the community did manage to influence the neighborhood's rezoning laws to stipulate that only one-family houses were permitted. By preventing any transformation of the large houses into multiple-dwelling units, they kept out the less well-to-do renters, thus maintaining the middle-class character of the area.

Fourth, among the most important factors influencing urban ecology are local and national politics. Implementation of rent control as a World War II emergency measure in New York City, for example, initiated a policy that has continued to affect rents and urban development. Similarly, ever since zoning was introduced early in the twentieth century, it has allowed government and other interests to effectively alter the "natural forces" of ecological change. Urban renewal is another nonnatural force that alters urban spatial development.

Fifth, perhaps the strongest criticism of urban ecological models developed in the United States is their inapplicability to other countries. Evidence suggests that contemporary cities in the Third World do not fit the North American design. Residential patterns in Third World urban areas are often the reverse, with upper-class neighborhoods to be found in the inner-city sections, while slums ring the periphery. Consider the shantytowns composed of discarded signboards, doors, and other debris (mentioned in the first segment of this chapter) that ring the outskirts of Bolivia's capital city. In addition, many Third World cities generally have two centers: a colonial town and a modern city. Quito, Ecuador, clearly reflects this dual pattern. The old portion is an area of narrow cobblestone streets, balconied two-story buildings with red-tiled roofs, and historic churches; its business and residential sections are filled with reminders of the Spanish dominion of centuries ago. New Quito, on the other hand, has wide avenues, fine private residences, parks, embassies, villas, and modern high-rise office buildings.

THE URBAN EXPERIENCE

Descriptions of cities and city life reflect many sentiments. To American novelist and journalist Christopher Morley, all cities were both mad and beautiful, but the

Exhibit 17.9

Sociological Focus

The Multiple-nuclei Model of Urban Growth

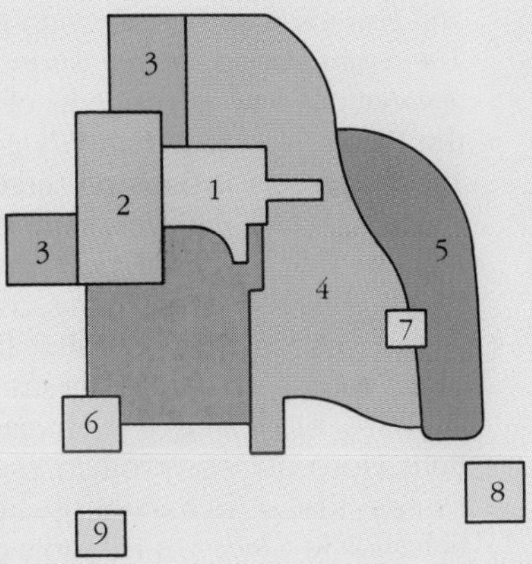

3
3
2
1
4
5
7
6
8
9

District

1. Central Business District
2. Wholesale Light Manufacturing
3. Low-class Residential
4. Medium-class Residential
5. High-class Residential
6. Heavy Manufacturing
7. Outlying Business District
8. Residential Suburb
9. Industrial Suburb

madness was gallant and the beauty was grim. Some have praised cities as the centers of civilization, the nurseries of intellectual curiosity, and places rich in humanity, culture, and pride; while others have ridiculed them as cemeteries with lights, graves uncheered by any gleam of promise, and warrens where the inmates are in charge of the asylum. Given these many optimistic and pessimistic views, what can really be said about the nature and quality of urban life?

Theoretical Perspectives on Urban Life

Since their discipline was in its infancy, sociologists have attempted to determine whether urban and rural life differ, and if so, how. The earliest theoretical perspectives to capture the essence of rural-urban differences were apparent in Ferdinand Tonnies' concepts of *gemeinschaft-gesellschaft,* Emile Durkheim's *mechanical and organic societies,* and Max Weber's *traditional and rational societies.* A similar but later formulation of the rural-urban scheme was constructed by anthropologist Robert Redfield in his *folk-urban* typology.[30] Redfield viewed the folk society as small, sacred and religious, and nonmarket oriented. Group solidarity, homogeneity, and personal interaction characteristically were common. Although he never actually specified his typology's urban

Crowded conditions in Tokyo have led to the creation of a new occupation—subway station "pushers."

component, Redfield implied that it was the opposite of the folk society. Thus, urban society was characterized by market economies, dependence on rational thought, impersonal social relationships, and an erosion of traditional values.

Scholars at the University of Chicago during the 1920s also were concerned with the complex social relationships that developed in connection with industrialization, and it was their work that stimulated the most comprehensive examinations of the urban way of life.

Louis Wirth's "Urbanism as a Way of Life"

Based on extensive research in the city of Chicago, Louis Wirth's well-known essay, "Urbanism as a Way of Life," defined urbanism in terms of three traits: size, density, and the heterogeneity of the population. These traits served to shape the experiences of urban dwellers.[31] Wirth contended that despite close physical contact in densely populated urban areas, the social distance of urban relationships made people quite lonely, while congestion and the fast pace of life brought on irritability and nervous strain. He went on to argue that the distinctive features of life in the city included the substitution of secondary for primary contacts, the weakening of kinship bonds, the declining social significance of the family, a disappearance of "neighborhoods" and sense of "community," an increased diversity of values and opinions, and the emergence of subcultures that were at variance with the larger society.

In more concrete terms, Wirth was suggesting that life in the city, with its lights, sounds, blinking signs, streets congested with both human and mechanical traffic, and massive population, is not particularly simple. The distractions, competition, and variations from day to day force urban dwellers to adapt by embracing more calculated and rational approaches to their daily routines. To simply get through the day, city residents must maintain stable and impersonal time schedules and be exact in everything they do, lest ill consequences occur. Moreover, with all of the hustle, movement, and jostling amid profusions of unfamiliar people, urban dwellers are nudged into a perennial state of distrust and reserve characterized by relationships that are anonymous, superficial, and transitory.

Compositional Theory

Wirth's views of the city and urban life were contradicted by many studies which contended that city living is indeed personal and integrative. Challenging Wirth's assumption that once a community attains a certain size, density, and population mix differentiation begins to erode primary ties, compositionalists argued that city life revolves around a series of "social worlds" that people construct. William F. Whyte's *Street Corner Society,* an investigation of street life in an Italian slum in Boston during the 1940s, illustrated that culture and traditional relationships were important forces in urban life.[32] W. Lloyd Warner and Paul S. Lunt's studies of "Yankee City" (Newburyport, Massachusetts) during the same period found that informal cliques were socially significant in maintaining class structure, providing social mobility, and lending members a group identity.[33] Gerald Suttles' *The Social Order of the Slum* found strong voluntary associations among residents of a Chicago ghetto during the 1960s.[34] In *The Urban Villagers,* also published in the 1960s, Herbert J. Gans presented a portrait of a social system in which the lives of the Italian working class were regulated by informal peer groups. Socialization into these groups began during childhood and continued throughout one's life.[35] Elliot Liebow's *Talley's Corner* discovered a rich network of street-corner social relationships in a black area of Washington, D.C.[36] Most recently, Ruth Horowitz observed in *Honor and the American Dream* that a rich culture and strong values guide behavior in Chicago's Hispanic community.[37]

These studies demonstrate that culture, and community and primary relationships, are indeed very real facets of city life, and that alienation and depersonalization per se do not result from urbanization. Perhaps the most explicit illustration of this compositional perspective came from Columbia University sociologist Herbert J. Gans in 1968.[38] Gans maintained that many life-styles are found in the city, and that only some bear the stamp of anonymity as a fundamental urban characteristic. Urban diversity, he contended, is best understood by considering the effects of the more general social factors of age, sex, income, and educational level on people's lives. Using this orientation, Gans identified five basic life-styles in the American city (see Exhibit 17.10). And it might be suggested here that the "yuppies" (young urban professionals) of the 1980s are a popular, public view of one kind of urban dweller (see Exhibit 17.11).

Subcultural Theory

Borrowing elements from the perspectives of both Wirth and the compositionalists, Claude Fischer's subcultural view maintains that urban environments indeed affect the lives of their residents.[39] Fischer argues that urban residents differ significantly from those who live in rural areas, and they do so to a degree not accounted for by the individual traits that each group brings to its locale. Fischer points out that cities are more often centers of innovation and places where behaviors and attitudes contrast sharply with more conventional "middle-American" morality. It is this greater level of unconventional behavior that Fischer attributes to city organization and living. Large community size promotes subcultures. Moreover, it nurtures them as a result of the differentiation, isolation, and conflict that Wirth discussed. Where else but in the city would one find such primary groups as gay-rights activitists, fashion designers, entertainers, and heroin addicts? Once a certain number of any given type takes up residence in an urban area, they find out about one another, establish meeting places, create their own rituals, and begin to elaborate their activities. And as in the case of Gans' "ethnic villagers," these individuals tend to live in the same neighborhoods.

An early commuter train in Stamford, Connecticut, in the 1870s foreshadowed one of the busy commuter routes of the 1980s in the Northeastern Corridor.

The City and Suburbanization

The city, as Robert E. Park pointed out, is a mosaic of minor communities—central business districts, areas of industry, middle-class and exclusive residential neighborhoods, more or less isolated ethnic enclaves and low-income slums, entertainment and restaurant districts, wholesale and retail marketplaces, and perhaps vice areas and skid rows. Almost every urban community also had its **suburbs,** those politically independent areas immediately outside of the city that have substantial population densities, a preponderance of nonrural occupations, and distinctly urban forms of education, recreation, and family life.

Suburbs have existed on the outskirts of America's largest cities for more than a century but remained relatively unnoticed for many decades. After World War II, suburbanization spread rapidly as the result of the successful expansion of a variety of commercial and industrial enterprises, and the consequent creation of a rising middle class; improvements in communication and transportation; and the efforts of real estate developers who tantalized the urban dweller with a concept of "gracious living" formerly limited to the more affluent. Other factors luring people to the suburbs included the desire for space, scenery, and home ownership; a communal identity and proximity to social equals; and escape from the crime, congestion, and controls of the big city.

SOCIAL INDICATOR

Commuting Routes in the United States

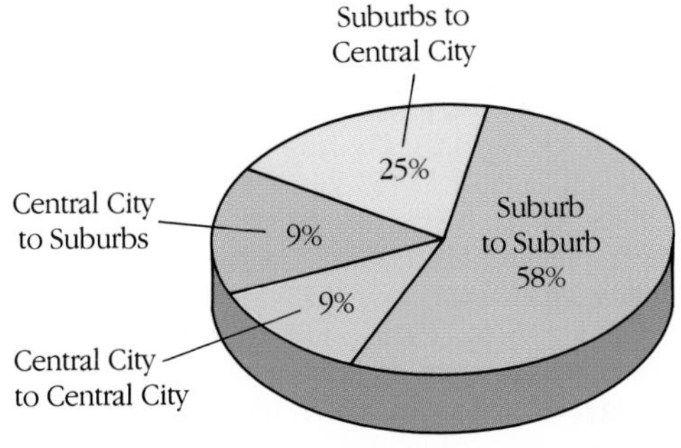

History of Suburban Growth

Suburbanization seemingly evolved through a series of five stages.[40] The first stage stretched from the late 1800s through the close of World War I. During this horse-and-buggy period, suburbs contained the homes of the wealthy, who lived in them for only part of the year. With the advent of the electric streetcar at the turn of the century, the concept of commuter zones emerged. Some urban dwellers moved to the rim of the city, settling in residential clusters at the end of trolley and railway lines.

The 1920s marked the beginning of the second stage of suburban development, when personal transportation was revolutionized by the proliferation of the automobile. From 1915 to 1930, automobile registrations jumped from less than 3 million to more than 26 million, and cars made it possible for people to establish residences in locales through which trains and trolleys did not pass. From the Great Depression through World War II, the third stage, suburbanization was essentially stalled. Little new construction took place during the depression years, and governmental restrictions on building and transportation imposed by the war limited growth to the empty gaps along existing thoroughfares near the city.

Exhibit 17.10

Research in Sociology

Urbanism as Many Ways of Life

The social and cultural moorings of inner-city life are best described by a brief analysis of five types of inner-city residents first proposed by Herbert Gans in 1962. Gans' classifications include (1) the "cosmopolites," (2) the "unmarried or childless," (3) the "ethnic villagers," (4) the "deprived," and (5) the "trapped" and "downward-mobile." These categories are still quite useful, even though Gans' research was done nearly 30 years ago.

The *cosmopolites* include students, artists, writers, musicians, and entertainers, as well as other intellectuals and professionals. They live in the city in order to be near the special cultural facilities that can be located only near the center of the city. Many cosmopolites are unmarried or childless. Others rear children in the city, especially if they have the income to afford the aid of servants and governesses. The less affluent may move to the suburbs to raise their children, continuing to live as cosmopolites under considerable strain, especially in the lower-middle-class suburbs. Many very rich and powerful people are also cosmopolites, although they are likely to have at least two residences, one of which is suburban or exurban.

The *unmarried or childless* must be divided into two subtypes, depending on the permanence or transience of their status. The temporarily unmarried or childless live in the inner city for only a limited time. Young adults may team up to rent an apartment away from their parents and close to job or entertainment opportunities. When they marry, they may move to an apartment in a transient neighborhood, but if they can afford to do so, they leave for the outer city or the suburbs with the arrival of the first or second child. The permanently unmarried may stay in the inner city for the remainder of their lives, their housing depending on their income.

The *ethnic villagers* are ethnic groups that are found in such inner-city neighborhoods as New York's Lower East Side. In some ways they live as they did when they were peasants in European or Puerto Rican villages. Although they reside in the city, they isolate themselves from significant contact with most city facilities, aside from work places. Their way of life differs sharply from Wirth's urbanism in its emphasis on kinship and the primary group, the lack of anonymity and secondary-group contacts, the weakness of formal organizations, and the suspicion of anything and anyone outside their neighborhood.

Gans' first two types of inner-city residents live in the inner city by choice; the third resides there partly out of necessity, partly because of tradition. The final two types are in the inner city because they have no other choice. One is the *deprived* population: the very poor; the emotionally disturbed or otherwise handicapped; members of broken families; and, most important, the nonwhite population. These urban dwellers reside in the dilapidated housing and blighted neighborhoods to which the housing market relegates them, although for some of them the slum is a hiding place or a temporary stopover to save money for a house in the outer city or the suburbs.

The *trapped* are the people who stay behind when their

The fourth stage was an explosive period of suburban expansion. Born of the post-war housing shortage, housing projects were mass-produced, with whole new communities added to the landscape. This was the origin of "suburbia," as it came to be called. An almost legendary figure in connection with this phenomenon was William J. Levitt, who began Levittown with the purchase of a 1,500-acre potato field in Long Island's Nassau County and spurred the building of 17,500 homes. As William Manchester described it:

> On signal his bulldozers moved across the landscape in echelon, pivoting at red flags. Street pavers followed, then electricians with light poles and men bearing stamped street signs. Next, house lots were marked off. Convoys of trucks moved over the hardened pavements, tossing out prefabricated sidings at 8:00 A.M., toilets at 9:30, sinks and tubs at ten, sheetrock at 10:45, flooring at 11:00. . . . Everything was uniform. . . . Picket fences were prohibited. Lawns had to be cut regularly. It was all in the deed. Even pleasant innovations conformed to Levitt's game plans. Trees were introduced at the rate of one every 28 feet (2.5 for each house), and the distance from trunk to trunk was precise to the inch. . . . Families struggling to assert their identity were limited to interior decorating and the pitch of the door chime. (It had to be a chime, though; buzzers and bellpulls were out.)[41]

neighborhood is invaded by nonresidential land uses or lower-class immigrants. They cannot afford to move or are otherwise bound to their present location. The *downward-mobiles* are a related type; they may have started life in a higher class position, but they have been forced to a lower level in the socioeconomic hierarchy and must accept a concomitant change in the quality of their accommodations. Many of them are old people, living out their existence on small pensions.

These five types all live in dense and heterogeneous surroundings, yet they have such diverse ways of life that it is hard to see how density and heterogeneity could exert a common influence. Moreover, all but the last two types are isolated or detached from their neighborhood and thus from the social consequences that Wirth described.

When people who live together have social ties based on criteria other than common occupancy, they can set up social barriers, regardless of the physical closeness or the heterogeneity of their neighbors. The ethnic villagers are the best illustration. While a number of ethnic groups are usually found living together in the same neighborhood, they are able to isolate themselves from one another through a variety of social devices.

The cosmopolites, the unmarried, and the childless are *detached* from neighborhood life. The cosmopolites possess a distinct subculture that causes them to be uninterested in all but the most superficial contacts with their neighbors, somewhat like the ethnic villagers. The unmarried and childless are detached from the neighborhood because of their life-cycle stage, which frees them from the routine family responsibilities that entail some relationship with the local area.

The deprived and the trapped do seem to be affected by some of the consequences of number, density, and heterogeneity. The deprived population suffers considerably from overcrowding, but this is a consequence of low income, racial discrimination, and other handicaps and cannot be considered an inevitable result of the ecological makeup of the city. Because the deprived have no residential choice, they also are forced to live amid neighbors not of their own choosing, with ways of life different and even contradictory to their own. If familial defenses against the neighborhood climate are weak, as may happen among broken families and downward-mobile individuals, parents may lose their children to the culture of "the street." The trapped are the unhappy people who remain behind when their more advantaged neighbors move on; they must endure the heterogeneity that results from neighborhood change.

SOURCE: Adapted from Herbert J. Gans, *People and Plans: Essays on Urban Problems and Solutions* (New York: Basic Books, 1968), pp. 36–39. Reprinted with permission of Herbert J. Gans, Robert S. Lynd Professor of Sociology at Columbia.

Although architects and sociologists were aghast at the whole arrangement, the prospective Levittowners were delighted. Levitt made no announcement of the development and bought no advertising space. The only communication was word of mouth. Among young families with modest incomes and veteran status who could buy the homes with GI mortgages, word spread quickly. When Levitt's sales office was opened on March 7, 1949, over a thousand couples were already waiting. In fact, some had been there for four days and four nights, living in the cold on coffee and doughnuts, resolved to be among the first to purchase the basic four-room houses for $6,990 plus closing fees. And the regimentation imposed by the Levitt plan was nothing out of the ordinary to the new settlers. After all, the first Levittowners were veterans, well-accustomed to life according to standard specifications.

The fifth stage of suburbanization, which began in the 1950s and continues even now, involved the discovery of the suburbs by business and industry. Both the manufacturing and retail sectors increasingly have moved out of the cities, with the result that the majority of workers who live in the suburbs also work in the suburbs. Significant indicators of this transformation include the increased numbers of shopping malls, office buildings, and rental apartments in suburban areas,

Levittown, William J. Levitt's community on Long Island (shown here in 1954), was representative of an explosive period of suburban expansion born of the post-war housing shortage.

combined with the movement of many businesses and industries away from the cities.

The reasons for this post-war suburban expansion are numerous.[42] First, by 1950, particularly in the Northeast, almost all of the available land within the cities had been developed. The demand for additional housing pushed new construction to the suburbs by default. Second, after World War II the government, through the Federal Housing Authority (FHA) and the Veterans Administration (VA), provided low-interest mortgage loans for new homes in the suburbs. The new FHA and VA loans were considerably less costly than those available in the cities. This impetus, specifically, was behind the development of Levittown on New York's Long Island. Third, the post-war marriage and baby booms resulted in the creation of 10 million new households. Existing housing in the cities could not absorb the swell of new families, forcing a movement to the suburbs. And fourth, most Americans seem to prefer living in single family homes outside the city. In fact, many young couples residing in apartment houses view their tenancy as a temporary step before moving into a privately owned, single-family dwelling unit.[43] Home ownership is part of the so-called American dream, and the majority of affordable housing exists in the suburbs.

Exhibit 17.11 **Types & Stereotypes**

Yuppies, Dinks, Dumps, and Other Assorted Characters

In the 1960s Americans spoke of hippies, and in the 1970s it was preppies, but the 1980s was certainly the decade of the yuppies—young urban professionals. The term caught on because it was a convenient, shorthand description of a growing segment of the urban population. This group was created by a number of social and economic trends that included the expansion of professional and managerial jobs, an influx of women into the work force, and the fact that young people were delaying marriage and childbearing. These trends also provided yuppies with high levels of income.

The term "yuppie" quickly was used to stereotype a whole range of behaviors and attitudes. The stereotype included the expenditure of large sums of money for conspicuous consumer goods, which was interpreted as supermaterialism. Yuppies were characterized by designer clothing and an interest in jogging and health-club memberships.

Although yuppies never constituted a very large segment of the total population, the term "yuppie" was often used to describe most members of the baby-boom generation. Journalists responded by inventing labels for other groups: dinks (double income, no kids); dumps (downwardly mobile professionals—for those who fail in the quest for success); pups (poor urban professionals—for teachers and other underpaid professionals); and tips (tiny income, parents supporting—for those just starting in middle-class jobs).

The Myth of Suburbia

With the spectacular growth of the suburbs in the years after World War II, it was perhaps inevitable that social scientists and social commentators would discover suburbia as something new to study, interpret, and critique. The result was a flood of suburban literature, much of which served to present rather oversimplified images of suburban life. Certainly William H. Whyte's *The Organization Man* did much to establish the psychological and literary matrix from which these images emerged.[44]

Discussed briefly in Chapter 5 (Exhibit 5.5), *The Organization Man* was a study of Park Forest, a middle-class commuting suburb near Chicago, and an analysis of the lives its residents led, particularly those on their way up the executive ladder in large corporations during the early 1950s. Park Forest was a planned community, and most of the houses were similar, although not identical. A segment of the population was upwardly mobile—junior executives and their families who lived in Park Forest only temporarily, until progress in their careers enabled them to move elsewhere. Whyte indicted the suburban culture and social ethic of this group as redundant, premature, delusory, static, and self-destructive. He found that families focused their attention almost exclusively on gaining approval. They made a conscious effort to appear happy and neighborly, believing that fulfillment came only through group participation. Getting along with others was a prime virtue, while the desire to be alone was considered neurotic and childish.

The "social impressionists" who came after Whyte overgeneralized his findings to include all of suburbia. As a result, the emergent portrait of the middle-class suburban way of life was one of overbearing conformity. Just as the houses were standardized in appearance, so too were the lives and families within them. All suburbanites were young and had small children who ate the same breakfast cereal and went to the same nursery school; they socialized with each other aggressively and endlessly; and they obsessively copied each other in tastes, styles, and material possessions.

The collective image of the suburb, of course, was incorrect. Although Whyte's "organization man" and his family were temporary fixtures in Park Forest and other suburban developments, many other types also resided there and in numerous different kinds of suburbs elsewhere as well. Even in the 1950s, some satellite communities were devoted to industrial employment and populated primarily by blue-collar workers; other affluent "bedroom communities" housed high-income managers and professionals; the middle-income developments, like Park Forest and Levittown, catered to a variety of middle-class types in both white- and blue-collar occupations; and the more stagnant older suburban zones had many of the problems that characterized the central cities. These same types of suburbs exist today. And beyond suburbia are the regions of the "exurbanites."[45] The "exurbs" are residential districts in the hinterland, well past the traditional suburbs. Most exurban dwellers tend to be relatively wealthy, highly educated, and professional, and consider themselves "urbanites" at heart.

Black Suburbanization

Historically, racial and ethnic minorities have been concentrated in American cities and are a characteristic feature of urban life. Blacks, particularly, are among the oldest and largest minorities in the United States, yet their patterns of urbanization differ significantly from other minority groups, especially white European ethnic immigrants. Blacks were originally brought to this country involuntarily and were enslaved; they moved to urban areas in search of jobs almost exclusively during the twentieth century. In the cities racism and segregation drastically reduced opportunities for education, housing, employment, and general social mobility. These factors also account for the relatively small number of blacks involved in the suburbanization process.

Black Americans currently account for 12% of the national population, with half living in metropolitan areas. As an outgrowth of court-enforced desegregation and the advantages accorded by the civil rights movement, rates of black suburbanization are now proportionately greater than those of whites. Those moving to suburban areas are typically younger, and have higher levels of income, education, and occupational status than their counterparts in the cities. Yet despite the fact that most suburban blacks hold the same middle-class values as whites, they are still not welcomed or integrated into many white suburbs. The majority of those moving to the suburbs settle in older areas near the large cities, with few joining the ranks of the "exurbanites." McHenry County, Illinois, for example, an exurban area beyond the ring of Chicago's suburbs, increased by 32% from 1970 to 1980, yet less than one-tenth of 1% of its 1980 population of 148,000 was black. Similarly, near Atlanta, Georgia, the black population of the inner suburban area of DeKalb County increased from 57,000 in 1970 to 131,000 in 1980, yet by contrast, in exurban Forsythe County, blacks were outnumbered by a ratio of over 27,000 to 1.[46]

Gentrification

Despite the popularity and continued growth of the suburbs, the tendency of members of the middle class to move from the central cities to suburban areas has reversed itself slightly. This reversal, known as

Chicago's Old Town is one of many gentrified neighborhoods that were refurbished by middle- and upper-class suburbanites returning to the cities during the second half of the twentieth century.

gentrification, began during the mid-seventies and involved the renovation of inner-city neighborhoods by middle- and upper-class suburbanites who moved back to the city. In most American cities where the process of gentrification is occurring, it appears that those individuals moving into and refurbishing the older city neighborhoods are predominantly young, white, childless, well-educated, professional and managerial types. They move to areas close to central business districts with a high proportion of renter-occupied dwelling units that are deteriorated or abandoned, yet architecturally interesting.[47]

Gentrification seems to be most typical in the older, more exciting and desirable cities in the United States—New York, Boston, Philadelphia, Chicago, San Francisco, and Washington, D.C. Moreover, the process is not simply a return of suburban families to the city. Rather, the "gentry"—a British term referring to people of superior social position—is composed largely of persons who were originally raised in the suburbs, but as young adults, moved to the city and do not want to leave for various reasons. First, housing in center city neighborhoods is often less costly than that in the suburbs, and it is definitely more convenient for those who work in the city. Second, among the members of the currently maturing baby-boom generation, many have postponed marriage and most couples either have remained childless or have chosen to have small families. As a result, the additional space for child rearing that suburban developments provide is of minimal importance. Third, the Internal Revenue Service began offering tax incentives during the 1970s for the restoration of "historic" buildings. In most cities, this refers to buildings more than a century old, and renovation expenses are tax deductable. Fourth, from a social-psychological point of view, many young city dwellers do not necessarily equate "better" with "new;" they prefer living in an upgraded, solidly built "old house" to a cheaply constructed, mass-produced suburban home. And fifth, among many of the young urban professionals—including the yuppies and dinks mentioned in Exhibit 17.11—renovating and living in a nineteenth-century home in the city is simply more "fashionable" than occupying a "tract house" in the suburbs.

Critics argue that the gentrification process can have only a negative effect on the inner-city poor. They maintain that as the more affluent move into and renovate deteriorated neighborhoods, property values will increase and the poor will be further displaced. This has already happened in New York City, where entire communities of low-income groups have been pushed out for the sake of condominium development.[48] Other observers suggest that gentrification has little, if any, effect on the urban disadvantaged, since many of the buildings involved were not occupied by the poor before they were taken over by the "gentry." A trend in many cities, for example, and particularly in New York, is to renovate old industrial sites into condominium "lofts."

Similarly, gentrification sometimes focuses on "disinvested" property. **Disinvestment** occurs when tax, utility, and maintenance costs outstrip rental income, making properties unprofitable and causing landlords to abandon them. Once abandoned, the buildings fall into disrepair and become the targets of vandals or are transformed into "shooting galleries" for heroin users. They are then no longer livable. The many burned-out buildings of New York City's South Bronx have become the national symbols of this process. The poor are not dislocated in gentrification cases involving either factory sites or disinvested buildings, and some evidence indicates that gentrification even can have a positive impact on the displaced poor. In one investigation of 112 inner-city residents who were forced to relocate, 87% found living quarters either comparable to or better than those they left behind.[49] Moreover, some low-income residents are actually offered significant economic incentives to move so that landlords can more easily restore their properties and make them more profitable. On New York's Lower East Side during late 1984, for example, one urban speculator purchased a run-down 33-unit apartment building with the intention of converting it into "gentrified" luxury condominiums. Each tenant family was given $5,000 to compensate for their inconvenience and relocation costs. This incentive enabled many of the poor families in the building to upgrade the quality of their lives.[50]

URBANIZATION AND APPLIED SOCIOLOGY

The so-called urban crisis of recent years is not particularly new. Anyone who has had the opportunity to review the history of American cities has probably noticed that urban problems have been around for quite some time.

If transportation is an aspect of the urban crisis, considerable evidence suggests that it was a problem of acute proportions for the residents of many cities as long as a century ago. Even before the Civil War, the streets of downtown New York City were a congested jungle of brewery drays, horse trolleys, hackney coaches, and even steam locomotives. So desperate were the citizens that they built overhead crosswalks to bridge the equestrian battlefield of lower Broadway.[51] At the turn of the century, the congestion of the streets had become so profound that city planners initiated the construction of electric railways under the sidewalks of New York.[52] By the 1920s in all of the major cities in the East, the growing popularity of the automobile had created intolerable conditions on the streets of central business and shopping districts.

If poor housing and slums are aspects of the urban crisis, by today's standards the quality of life in the nineteenth-century American ghetto was the ultimate tragedy. New York's Five Points area, briefly mentioned in Exhibit 17.6, was once characterized as the nation's most abominable slum.[53] During the early 1800s, tens of thousands of European immigrants settled annually in the Five Points, a locale that drew its name from the intersection of Cross, Anthony, Little Water, Orange, and Mulberry Streets (now the intersection of Baxter and Worth Streets). As early as 1815, the housing there was composed of clapboard tenements. The poor conditions were compounded by the fact that the weak structures had been built on the former site of The Collect, a marshy area of pond and meadow extending from contemporary Chambers Street to Canal Street, east of Broadway. The marsh had been poorly drained and filled with garbage, and the inadequate foundations were sinking into the ground. The results included pollution, standing water, mosquitoes, crawling insects, rats and other vermin, and disease. In combination with poverty, malnutrition, poor sanitation, and crime, the conditions in Five Points in the 1800s make today's Harlem, South Bronx, East St. Louis, and sections of South Philadelphia appear somewhat benign. And conditions in areas of nineteenth-century Chicago and San Francisco were barely better.

Contemporary Urban Problems

Even in this age of advanced technological accomplishment, the seemingly endless course of urban decay and the ever-changing nature of the American socioeconomic structure have created a multitude of problems for cities.

Business districts increasingly are losing dominance as centers of retail trade. The suburbanization process, along with the growth of shopping malls in outlying areas and expansions in the mail-order industry, have brought about the neglect of aging downtown facilities.

Fiscal crises are also a prominent feature of contemporary cities, particularly those in the Northeast and Midwest. As homeowners and businesses leave the cities for the suburbs or migrate to the "sunbelt" states of Florida, Arizona, and New Mexico, the urban tax base becomes smaller. Most of those left behind are the less economically fortunate, which places limitations on city governments' ability to raise revenues through additional taxation. Yet essential police, fire, hospital, and other public-service networks must continue. Moreover, the aging infrastructure of the older cities—the streets, bridges, power and water lines, and transportation systems—continue to decay and require repair. Boston, for example, loses a staggering 29 billion gallons of water each year because of leaks in its water lines; New York has over 100,000 potholes, with new ones appearing each day at a rate faster than the old ones can be filled. During the 1970s, moreover, inflation not only increased the costs of governing cities but also drove up interest rates and borrowing costs.

Inadequate housing is an unremitting urban dilemma that is exacerbated by the persistent ravages of decay in aging structures, the lack of maintenance resources by the inner-city poor, and the inability or unwillingness of many landlords and "slum lords" to make repairs. Added to these problems is the practice of *redlining** and the unwillingness of lenders to give mortgages to inner-city residents. Closely linked to inadequate housing is poverty. A significant proportion of those living at or below the poverty level are inner-city residents who create special demands for both protective and social services.

**Redlining* gets its name from bank officials who, years ago, drew red lines on city maps around those neighborhoods considered unsafe for mortgage lending.

Transportation, as noted earlier, has been the basis of many an urban problem for more than a century. A dependence on the automobile is a characteristic of both city and suburban living. Government highway construction policies and special interest lobbies in the auto industry have promoted the use of the family car over mass transportation. Decades ago, for example, General Motors, Firestone Tire, and Standard Oil engineered a successful effort to eliminate electric street cars and replace them with less reliable diesel buses for the purpose of stimulating auto sales. Yet the private automobile, particularly when it is used for daily commuting, entails high operating and energy costs. In addition, it creates traffic congestion and pollution, and plays a crucial role in transforming the city landscape into a contorted and inefficient system of blighted freeways. The automobile also works against the interests of the poor, who generally do not own cars and are often displaced by highway construction. During the 1970s and early 1980s, renewed interest was focused on mass transit and other mechanisms for alleviating roadway congestion. Washington, D.C., and Miami built totally new systems; other cities revamped subway and bus lines, set aside special lanes on existing highways for the exclusive use of buses and car-pooling commuters, and built special parking lots to encourage the use of "park and ride" routes by suburban commuters. But these measures seem to have had only minimal effect on the problems of urban congestion and air pollution. Suburbanization has made mass transit a less than practical alternative for the commuter, since living and work locations are widely dispersed. Moreover, Americans have been involved in a love affair with the automobile for more than four decades, and creating a preference for mass transit has moved, at best, rather slowly.

Finally, cities must face the problem of crime. According to the FBI's *Uniform Crime Reports,* in 1987 serious crimes were considerably overrepresented in metropolitan areas—85% of all homicides, 85% of all burglaries, 87% of all rapes, 94% of all vehicle thefts, and 97% of all robberies occurred in cities.[54] Furthermore, as indicated in Exhibit 17.12), a rather straightforward correlation exists between crime rates and population density.

Urban Renewal and City Planning

No easy solutions to the basic problems of cities have been found. In fact, solutions ultimately may never be found. Cities throughout the world are the result of human settlement that simply grew, with no conscious planning. The expansion of settlements into villages and towns, and then cities, was haphazard. Business districts

Exhibit 17.12

Sociological Focus

Crime Rates in Metropolitan Areas, Other Cities, and Rural Counties, 1987

Crimes Known to the Police	Crime Rates per 100,000 Population			
	Total U.S.	Metropolitan Areas	Other Cities	Rural Counties
Total Crime	5,550.0	6,294.5	4,898.5	1,900.4
Violent Crime*	609.7	720.0	350.8	177.7
Property Crime*	4,940.3	5,574.5	4,547.7	1,722.8
Murder and Nonnegligent Manslaughter	8.3	9.2	4.5	5.7
Forcible Rape	37.4	42.5	24.4	18.5
Robbery	212.7	268.6	49.9	14.7
Aggravated Assault	351.3	399.7	272.0	138.7
Burglary	1,329.6	1,484.8	1,042.0	670.1
Larceny-Theft	3,081.3	3,444.0	3,302.7	942.7
Motor-vehicle Theft	529.4	645.7	203.0	110.0

Source: Federal Bureau of Investigation, *Uniform Crime Reports, Crime in the United States—1987* (Washington, DC: U.S. Government Printing Office, 1988), p. 42.

*Violent crimes are offenses of murder, forcible rape, robbery, and aggravated assault. Property crimes are offenses of burglary, larceny-theft, and motor-vehicle theft. Data are not included for the property crime of arson.

were extended and residential precincts branched out in all possible directions. Primal cow paths, trails, and byways, regardless of their layout or pattern, were paved over into streets. As rural and other immigrant populations descended upon the cities, their boundaries were pushed further into the hinterlands.

In the United States, "urban planning" did not occur until well after most cities had been built. Moreover, much of the planning focused on architecture and design rather than on socially and environmentally constructive land use. During the "city beautiful" period in the nineteenth century, for example, parks were sculptured and cast, and designs for new buildings in downtown areas were patterned after classical and Gothic structures. Splendid tree-lined streets were laid out and ornate public edifices of imposing proportions were constructed of stone. At the same time, multi-family tenements were introduced. The first were built in 1835 on Cherry Street in New York City, for the lowest of income groups.[55] They covered 90% of the lots on which they were constructed, and standardized the concept of airless and unsanitary conditions. With an indifference to hygiene and the quality of life, developers had a one-sided preoccupation with rent and profit. Incorporating a population density that corresponded, not to human needs, but to the cost of land, the apartments quickly turned into slums. Late in the century they were recognized as such, and the idea emerged that cleaning up the slums was the way to clean up the city. The tenements were seen as the breeding grounds of urban social problems.

With the onset of the twentieth century, the first attempts at systematic planning came to some American cities. The new orientation viewed urban design not as an exercise in beautification, but as an engineering problem involving traffic patterns, sewage and water systems, and land use. Zoning, introduced by New York City in 1916 and at the federal level five years later, was used as a tool to segregate land and maintain its value in the face of "invading" immigrants and business use. In later decades urban master planning was developed as a fitful attempt to control the nature and direction of future urban growth, and to coordinate the design of entirely new cities (see Exhibit 17.13).

Exhibit 17.13

Applied Sociology

The Search for New Jerusalem

They have been called "garden cities," "greenbelt towns," "socialist cities," and "new towns," but by any name, they all represent aspects of the search for a New Jerusalem—that visionary quest for the new city that would embrace the essentials of quality urban life.

More than a century ago, Sir Ebenezer Howard, a social reformer and reporter in the London law courts, had a dream. Deeply influenced by Edward Bellamy's novel, *Looking Backward,* a utopian vision of the year 2000 in which all of the problems of the city had been eliminated and people lived together in joyous harmony, Howard imagined a city without the misery, despair, and overcrowded conditions that characterized the urban panorama of his day. In his book, *Garden Cities of To-Morrow,* published in 1898, he argued that the city had the advantages of opportunity and diversity, while the country offered a healthful environment and a sense of freedom. Thus, the New Jerusalem could be found in the creation of a city that combined the benefits of each:

> The two magnets must be one. As man and woman by their varied gifts and faculties supplement each other, so should town and country. The town is the symbol of society—of mutual help and friendly cooperation, of fatherhood, motherhood, brotherhood, sisterhood, of wide relations. . . . The country is the symbol of God's love and care. . . . All that we are and all that we have comes from it. Our bodies are formed of it; to it they return. We are fed by it, clothed by it, and by it we are warmed and sheltered. . . . Town and country must be married, and out of this joyous union will spring a new hope, a new life, a new civilization.

Howard's design called for self-contained communities that would have residential employment, and recreational facilities for 30,000 residents on 6,000 acres of land. To prevent speculators, all land would be publicly owned. The community would be designed in concentric circle fashion with a central commercial area, residential ring, industrial area, and a greenbelt of cow pastures, farms, and forests. Shortly after the turn of the century, with the support of several businessmen, Howard established his first garden city, Letchworth, some 35 miles outside of London. In 1919, the second garden city of Welwyn was built. Yet neither turned out to be the fulfillment of Howard's dream. Although they did serve to alleviate population pressures in London, at least for a time, the planners failed to account for the individual preferences of potential residents. Nor could they manage to attract the business, industry, and varying levels of human diversity and other positive qualities that are so crucial to a rewarding urban experience.

Sir Ebenezer Howard's work did not go unnoticed in the United States. Heavily influenced by the garden-city plan, Constance Austin of Santa Barbara, California, designed her "Socialist City." Based on a conviction that housework relegated women to an oppressed role, her design emphasized communal living and an economy of labor. Kitchenless houses would relieve the drudgery of preparing over 1,000 meals a year and cleaning up after each one; built-in furniture, roll-away beds, carpetless tile floors, and curtainless windows would reduce dusting to a minimum; each kitchenless house would be connected to a central kitchen and laundry by an underground network of tunnels through which small electric cars would deliver cooked food and other necessities. The city could be made efficient through a socialist political economy.

With the help of several investors, Austin actually began construction of her dream at Llano del Rio, in California. After but a brief tenure, however, her mission collapsed in 1917 as a result of inadequate financing. Her followers later settled Newllano in rural west-central Louisiana, but even there Austin's "Socialist City" dream was never realized. In the early 1980s, Newllano was still on the map, with an estimated population of 2,213.

As an outgrowth of the Emergency Relief Appropriation Act and the National Industrial Recovery Act, both signed into law in 1935 by President Franklin D. Roosevelt to counteract the effects of the Great Depression, the United States government stepped into the new cities movement. The acts sponsored the Greenbelt Towns project, designed to provide work for men on unemployment relief and low-rent housing in physically and socially robust environments. Three towns were constructed: Greenbelt, Maryland

(13 miles northeast of Washington, D.C.), Greendale, Wisconsin (7 miles outside of Milwaukee), and Green Hills, Ohio (5 miles north of Cincinnati). Established under Ebenezer Howard's garden city principles, it was hoped that the new communities would thrive, and do so without the problems associated with big cities. But like all previous efforts, the new greenbelt towns never achieved their goals. They failed to attract sufficient industrial development and business activity, and evolved into suburban communities of the large cities nearby.

A more recent and concerted effort in the search for New Jerusalem is Columbia, Maryland, situated between the nation's capital and Baltimore. Columbia was the idea of developer James Rouse, who wanted "to create a social and physical environment which works for people and nourishes human growth and to allow private venture capital to make a profit in land development and sale." Thus, Columbia was a profit-motivated "new city" endeavor. The planning involved representatives from the fields of sociology, psychology, family counseling, education, and city planning. The design included the establishment of seven villages centered around a downtown area, as well as housing for middle-class and low- to moderate-income groups. Urban sociologist Herbert Gans, a consultant to the project, commented in 1968 as the first residents of Columbia moved into their new homes:

> I felt that most people would not want the village life, intense community participation, and adult education being proposed for them, and that they would be more interested in developing their personal and familial lives, and in getting along with their neighbors. Sharing Rouse's goal that Columbia should be "a garden of people," I attempted instead to deal with these interests, and to suggest solutions for all the problems of home, block and community life which I expected to come up based on what I had observed in Park Forest and Levittown. In other words, I tried to plan the garden in terms of goals and problems which mattered most to the people who would occupy it.

How well has Columbia done after two decades? The long-term hope was that it would evolve into a garden city with a population of 110,000 by 1981 and ultimately would house some 250,000 inhabitants. In 1970 it had 8,815 residents, and according to Bureau of Census data this figure was up to 56,100 in 1980. In addition to not attracting the population its planners had hoped for, other problems have emerged. Like other new towns before it, Columbia failed to attract the diversity of business necessary to support its labor force. As a result, many of its residents commute to work in the Baltimore and Washington areas. In fact, a significant number of its residents are U.S. government employees who travel on a daily basis to the nation's capital. Columbia also seems to have an emerging crime problem. Although it is not listed in the FBI's *Uniform Crime Reports*, figures for Howard County, Maryland, for which Columbia represents half of the population, showed a crime rate of 4,753.4 per 100,000 in 1982, about 20% higher than the national average for suburban counties. Finally, the mix of middle- and low-income residents has not had encouraging results.

And so, as Columbia grows and continues to struggle, and as others have their visions of the garden cities and new towns that will solve the problems of urban life, the search for the New Jerusalem endures.

SOURCES: Herbert J. Gans, *People and Plans: Essays on Urban Problems and Solutions* (New York: Basic Books, 1967), pp. 130, 183–201; Dolores Hayden, "Two Utopian Feminists and Their Campaigns for Kitchenless Houses," *Signs*, 4 (Winter 1978), pp. 274–90; Ebenezer Howard, *Garden Cities of To-Morrow* (Cambridge, MA: MIT Press, 1965); Neil Sandberg, *Stairwell 7: Family Life in the Welfare State* (Beverly Hills: Sage, 1978); James L. Spates and John J. Macionis, *The Sociology of Cities* (New York: St. Martin's, 1982), pp. 455–71; Clarence Stein, *Toward New Towns for America* (Cambridge, MA: MIT Press, 1957); U.S. Department of Commerce, Bureau of the Census, *Statistical Abstract of the United States: 1984* (Washington, DC: U.S. Government Printing Office, 1983).

The great urban tragedy is that cities, in their early years, were never viewed as places that should evolve as socially well-balanced and attractive places in which to live. What often seemed to many people to be healthy evidence of social activity and economic dynamism was too often, like ascending land values and congested streets, a symptom of social malfunction and organic defects in planning. Most of the "evils" so gravely evident in contemporary urban areas were already visible more than a century ago—chronic poverty, blighted areas, filthy slums, gangsterism and street crime, race riots, police corruption and brutality, and persistent deficiencies in medical, social, and educational services.

But the essential proof that something was radically wrong with the whole pattern of urban life was that those who could afford to leave the city were deserting it. Indeed, they had begun to desert long before, seeking in the residential suburb qualities that were steadily disappearing from the metropolis. Yet instead of taking this defection as a command to transform the city, the leaders of urban communities vigorously grasped it as an invitation to invest profitably in multiplying the means of escape—first by railroads, subways, and trolleys, then by automobiles, bridges, and tunnels, and finally with beltways, freeways, and heliports. The daily congestion of the city then became counterbalanced by decongestion and dispersal, and as living conditions grew worse in the overcrowded central city, the regions of suburban sprawl expanded, until the overflow of one metropolis mingled with that of others to form disorganized masses of formless, low-grade urban-suburban sprawl.

The typical approaches to urban planning and revitalization can be viewed as conventional, ameliorative, allocative, exploitive, and normative. The *conventional approach* assumes that urban problems can be solved by the existing system with but few modifications. This thinking is most manifest in the campaign platforms of big-city mayoralty candidates. Bring in new leadership and an efficient administration that has a better understanding of urban problems and the situation will improve. The *ameliorative approach* is a Band-Aid technique that ignores problems until they become significant enough to attract widespread attention. As has been the case with local transportation planning and the filling of potholes, this method seeks solutions only to emergent problems. The *allocative approach* is a future-oriented method that involves the identification of current trends and projects them into the future. Resources are then allocated through the manipulation of tax and interest rates and other governmental expenditures to produce the desired outcomes. The *exploitive approach* involves the search for new growth and promotable opportunities. Rather than problem solving, it involves the identification of means and goals, and most

SOCIAL INDICATOR

The Future of Cities

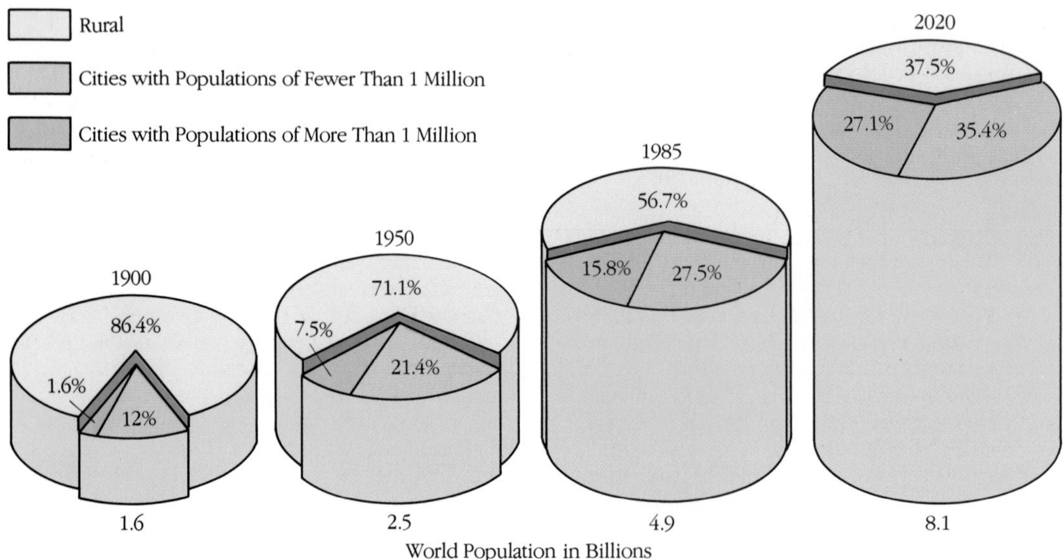

Source: Population Reference Bureau, 1985.

typically focuses on economic and industrial development. A typical example is found in Brazil, where the opportunistic development of the Amazon basin is being undertaken as a means of advancing the national economy, and ultimately, the problems of the cities. The *normative approach* deals with the creation of the "ideal" urban area. It is a radical approach in that it assumes that problems cannot be solved by the existing system and that total revision or replacement is necessary. In this regard, Harvard University economist Raymond Vernon once commented:

> If a major object of our existence were to create great cities of beauty and grace, there would be something to be said in favor of dictatorship. As a rule, the great cities of the past have been the cities of the powerful state—cities in which a dominant king or governing body has had the power and the will to impose its land-use strictures upon an obedient populace.[56]

To some extent, this is being tried in contemporary times. Consider, for example, the desperate attempt to build Abuja as the new capital of Nigeria, described earlier in Exhibit 17.5.

Throughout the American urban landscape, a combination of the conventional, ameliorative, and allocative approaches often are employed simultaneously. In many large cities—New York, Baltimore, St. Louis, Detroit, and others—urban renewal and revitalization programs have involved the long-term planning of new political and economic leadership. Ten-, thirty-, and fifty-year plans include the razing of slums and the removal of the social conditions that perpetuate them, the renovation of business and entertainment districts, the rehabilitation of roadways and bridges, the replacement of aging power and water lines, the modernization of transportation systems, and the enticement of people and commerce back into the city. And the real challenge here involves the ability of urban environments to match their resources to their needs, and to generate the political, intellectual, technological, and financial resources necessary for long-term change. Only with these resources and vision can cities become the socially concentrated, varied, stimulating, and rewarding human environments that they were intended to be.

SUMMARY

The history of urban life dates back many thousands of years to the Neolithic period when plants and animals were initially domesticated. The first cities appeared in the Fertile Crescent, with populations ranging from 2,000 to 20,000 inhabitants. Urban settlements established prior to the early part of the eighteenth century were preindustrial cities, characterized by agricultural and trade economies, a core ruling elite, a small middle class, and a large impoverished population.

The Industrial Revolution spurred the emergence of modern industrial cities, large urban settlements dependent on manufacturing and with flexible class systems. Industrialization stimulated urbanization, which involved the progressive movement of people from rural areas to the cities in search of work. As cities grew, metropolitan areas appeared, followed by urban sprawl and the advent of the megalopolis.

Industrialization and urbanization began in the United States and Western Europe during the eighteenth century, but in many parts of the world these processes have been relatively recent. Moreover, particularly in the Third World nations, urbanization has been extremely rapid, resulting in serious economic hardships for the majority of city residents. Many observers contend that the existing political and social arrangements in these urbanizing nations must be altered before they can reap the benefits of industrialization. Others argue that Third World urban problems are the result of dependence on worldwide capitalist arrangements, rather than on existing cultural values.

Urban ecologists have attempted to explain the structure of cities on the basis of land use patterns. Urban ecology began at the University of Chicago during the 1920s, and the theoretical perspectives of natural areas, invasion-succession, and urban concentric zones have had a lasting impact on the study of cities. Significant contributions of the Chicago School were made by urban sociologists Robert E. Park, Ernest W. Burgess, and Louis Wirth.

Wirth's essay, "Urbanism as a Way of Life," stimulated considerable research into the urban experience. Wirth contended that city life was cold and isolated. Later studies contradicted his position, finding that cities display a variety of life-styles, that the differentiation of urban life promoted the development of subcultures, and that community and primary relationships are very real aspects of the urban way of life.

Suburbanization began in the United States during the latter part of the nineteenth century, but explosive growth came with the close of World War II. As a result of the post-war housing shortage and the GI mortgage, people began moving out of the city at an unprecedented rate. Despite myths of suburbia that depicted the new way of life as one of overbearing conformity, many types of suburbs are populated by many different classes and types of people. In contrast to suburbanization, the mid-seventies witnessed the emergence of gentrification—the refurbishment of inner-city neighborhoods by a younger generation of Americans who were raised in the suburbs.

Continuous urban decay, along with the ever-changing nature of the American social structure has created a multitude of problems—congestion, crime, poor housing, pollution, and other crises. Numerous attempts at city revitalization have been conducted, yet no easy solutions have been found. The real challenge involves the ability of urban environments to match their resources with their needs.

KEY TERMS

city
city-state
concentric zone model
dependency theory
disinvestment
feudal system
gentrification
industrial cities
industrial revolution
invasion-succession
megalopolis
metropolitan area
modernization theory
multiple-nuclei model
natural areas
overurbanization
preindustrial cities
primate city
Protestant ethic
sector model
suburbs
Third World
urban ecology
urbanization

DISCUSSION QUESTIONS

1. The history of American life and culture demonstrates that generations of European immigrants came to the cities, were assimilated, and ultimately moved into the mainstream of urban life. Why is it that blacks, many Hispanic groups, and recent Asian immigrants have been less successful in their attempts at assimilation into mainstream city life?
2. Herbert J. Gans of Columbia University suggested that inner-city residents may be classified as one of five types: the cosmopolites, the unmarried or childless, the ethnic villagers, the deprived, and the trapped or downward-mobile. Where would today's yuppies, the young urban professionals, fit into this categorization? Why?
3. Considering that the overurbanization of Third World primate cities involves the dynamics of population, economics, politics, technology, and culture, can anything be done to reverse this trend?
4. Have you seen the gentrification process in any urban areas with which you are familiar? What have you observed? Do you think that, in the long run, gentrification will affect the urban poor? Why?

SUGGESTED READINGS

Gunther Barth, *City People* (New York: Oxford University Press, 1980). With anecdotes and a wealth of information drawn from the records of real people, this book is an engrossing social history that traces the invention and dissemination of big-city culture in the last century. Special emphasis is given to such urban innovations as the ball park, apartment house, department store, and metropolitan press.

Douglas Butterworth and John Chance, *Latin American Urbanization* (Cambridge: Cambridge University Press, 1981). Offering an in-depth look at the processes of social change in the Third World, the authors concentrate on the rural-urban migration of the lower classes and the adaptation of migrants to city life.

Ruth Horowitz, *Honor and the American Dream* (New Brunswick, NJ: Rutgers University Press, 1983). In the intellectual tradition of urban-community participant observation studies that came to be identified with the Chicago School of Sociology, this study of gang membership in Chicago's contemporary Chicano community focuses on the culture and social values of an urban "ethnic village."

Jane Jacobs, *The Death and Life of Great American Cities* (New York: Random House, 1961). An innovative analysis of urban decay and attempts at urban renewal and revitalization in which the author explains why cities decline and why urban renewal has failed.

Lewis Mumford, *The City in History* (New York: Harcourt Brace Jovanovich, 1961). Perhaps the classic description and analysis of the conditions that led to the development of American and Western European cities. The author traces the evolution of the city from ancient Egypt and Mesopotamia to Greece and Rome, and examines cities in the Middle Ages and in modern times.

Gideon Sjoberg, *The Preindustrial City* (New York: Free Press, 1960). Not just a history of early cities, this volume analyzes the structure of preindustrial urban societies, including such things as social class, the family, religion, politics, education, economics, and communication.

Louis Wirth, "Urbanism as a Way of Life," *American Journal of Sociology,* 44 (July 1938), pp. 1–24. One of the most influential essays in the field of urban sociology, Wirth puts forth his views on how and why life in the city is cold and desolate.

NOTES

1. Amos Hawley, *Urban Society* (New York: Wiley, 1981), pp. 3–4.
2. John J. Palen, *The Urban World* (New York: McGraw-Hill, 1981), p. 19.
3. Noel P. Gist and Sylvia F. Fava, *Urban Society* (New York: Crowell, 1974), p. 10.
4. Robert Adams, "The Origin of Cities," *Scientific American,* 203 (September 1960), p. 168.
5. Lewis Mumford, *The City in History* (New York: Harcourt Brace Jovanovich, 1961), p. 153.
6. See Mark LaGory and John Pipkin, *Urban Social Space* (Belmont, CA: Wadsworth, 1981), pp. 57–59; Lewis Mumford, *The City in History,* pp. 205–42.
7. Philip M. Hauser, "Urbanization: An Overview," in Philip M. Hauser and Leo F. Schnore (eds.), *The Study of Urbanization* (New York: Wiley, 1965), pp. 1–47; Gideon Sjoberg, *The Preindustrial City* (New York: Free Press, 1960).
8. James A. Inciardi, *Careers in Crime* (Chicago: Rand McNally, 1975), p. 8.
9. Max Weber, *The Protestant Ethic and the Spirit of Capitalism* (New York: Charles Scribner's and Sons, 1958).
10. Gist and Fava, *Urban Society,* pp. 27–32.
11. Carl Bridenbough, *Cities in Revolt* (New York: Alfred A. Knopf, 1965), p. 5; Charles N. Glaab and A. Theodore Brown, *A History of Urban America* (New York: Macmillan, 1967), p. 9.
12. Charles N. Glaab, *The American City: A Documentary History* (Homewood, IL: Dorsey, 1963), pp. 461–62.
13. Jean Gottman, *Megalopolis: The Urbanized Northeastern Seaboard of the United States* (New York: Twentieth-Century Fund, 1961), pp. 3–5.
14. John J. Palen, *The Urban World,* p. 185.
15. John J. Palen, *The Urban World,* p. 197.
16. *U.S. News & World Report,* October 3, 1983, p. 56.
17. Gist and Fava, *Urban Society,* p. 58.
18. James L. Spates and John J. Macionis, *The Sociology of Cities* (New York: St. Martin's, 1982), p. 313.
19. Glenn Firebaugh, "Structural Determinants of Urbanization in Asia and Latin America," *American Sociological Review,* 44 (1979), pp. 199–215.
20. Douglas Butterworth and John K. Chance, *Latin American Urbanization* (Cambridge: Cambridge University Press, 1981), pp. 151–57.
21. John J. Palen, *The Urban World,* p. 342.
22. Daniel Chirot and Thomas D. Hall, "World System Theory," *Annual Review of Sociology,* 8 (1982), pp. 81–106.
23. *Business Week,* October 1, 1984, pp. 74–79, *U.S. News & World Report,* February 13, 1984, p. 38.
24. Ernest W. Burgess, "The Growth of the City," in Robert E. Park and Ernest W. Burgess (eds.), *The City* (Chicago: University of Chicago Press, 1967), pp. 55.
25. Park and Burgess, *The City.*
26. Homer Hoyt, *The Structure and Growth of Residential Neighborhoods in American Cities* (Washington, DC: Federal Housing Administration, 1939).
27. Chauncey D. Harris and Edward L. Ullman, "The Nature of Cities," *The Annals,* 242 (November 1945), pp. 7–17.
28. Ivan Light, *Cities in World Perspective* (New York: Macmillan, 1983), pp. 253–65.
29. Walter Firey, "Sentiment and Symbolism as Ecological Variables," *American Sociological Review,* 10 (April 1945), pp. 140–48.
30. Robert Redfield, "The Folk Society," *American Journal of Sociology,* 52 (January 1947), pp. 293–308.
31. Louis Wirth, "Urbanism as a Way of Life," *American Journal of Sociology,* 44 (July 1938), pp. 3–24.
32. William F. Whyte, *Street Corner Society* (Chicago: University of Chicago Press, 1943).
33. W. Lloyd Warner and Paul S. Lunt, *The Social Life of a Modern Community* (New Haven, CT: Yale University Press, 1942).
34. Gerald Suttles, *The Social Order of the Slum* (Chicago: University of Chicago Press, 1968).
35. H. J. Gans, *The Urban Villagers* (Glencoe, IL: Free Press, 1962).
36. Elliot Liebow, *Talley's Corner* (Boston: Little, Brown, 1967).
37. Ruth Horowitz, *Honor and the American Dream* (New Brunswick, NJ: Rutgers University Press, 1983).
38. Herbert J. Gans, *People and Plans: Essays on Urban Problems and Solutions* (New York: Basic Books, 1968), pp. 34–52.
39. Claude Fischer, "Towards a Subcultural Theory of Urbanism," *American Journal of Sociology,* 80 (May 1975), pp. 1319–1341; Fischer, *The Urban Experience* (New York: Harcourt Brace Jovanovich, 1976).
40. Frederick L. Allen, "The Big Change in Suburbia," *Harper's Magazine,* 208 (June 1954), pp. 21–28.
41. William Manchester, *The Glory and the Dream* (Boston: Little, Brown, 1974), pp. 527–28.
42. Ivan Light, *Cities in World Perspective,* pp. 396–402; John J. Palen, *The Urban World,* pp. 161–62.
43. William Michelson, *Environmental Choice, Human Behavior, and Residential Satisfaction* (New York: Oxford University Press, 1977).
44. William H. Whyte, Jr., *The Organization Man* (New York: Simon and Schuster, 1956).
45. A. C. Spectorsky, *The Exurbanites* (Philadelphia: Lippincott, 1955); *New York Times,* May 5, 1985, p. 6E.
46. *New York Times,* May 31, 1981, p. 46.
47. Jeffrey Henig, "Gentrification and Misplacement Within Cities: A Comparative Analysis," *Social Science Quarterly,* 61 (1980), pp. 638–52.
48. Neil Smith and Peter Williams (eds.), *Gentrification of the City* (Boston: Allen & Unwin, 1986), *World Press Review,* April 1987, p. 44.
49. John J. Palen, *The Urban World,* p. 291.
50. Personal communication, October 26, 1984.
51. Raymond Vernon, *The Myth and Reality of Our Urban Problems* (Cambridge: Harvard University Press, 1966), p. 4.
52. See Brian J. Cudahy, *Under the Sidewalks of New York* (Brattleboro, VT: Stephen Greene, 1979).
53. Herbert Asbury, *The Gangs of New York* (Garden City, NY: Garden City, 1927), pp. 1–45; Alvin F. Harlow, *Old Bowery Days* (New York: D. Appleton, 1931), pp. 80–98; Joel Tyler Headley, *The Great Riots of New York: 1712–1873* (New York: E. B. Treat, 1873), pp. 131–34; Courtenay Tarrett, *Only Saps Work* (New York: Vanguard, 1930), pp. 54–64.
54. *Uniform Crime Reports: 1987,* p. 42.
55. Lewis Mumford, *The City in History,* p. 433.
56. Raymond Vernon, *The Myth and Reality of Our Urban Problems,* p. 47.

Population and World Affairs

To those unfamiliar with it, the study of population must sound like a horribly boring enterprise. Birth rates? Death rates? Fertility and mortality ratios? Family planning practices? Are these issues of interest to anyone except the statisticians who spend their lives compiling such information? Of what interest is population research? How is it all related to the way people live? Or to ask the same question in a more sociological fashion, what is the relationship of population size and distribution to social structure? And even more significantly, of what *use* is population data? How important, really, is a knowledge of population trends? For a glimpse at the answers to these questions, consider the following:

- The Live-Aid concert in 1985 and the heavily promoted *We Are the World* album released in the same year were devised to assist victims of the devastating drought that crept across Africa, leaving in its path 35 million starving people. Albums and concerts alleviated the problem for some of the victims, at least temporarily, but one of the root problems remains—uncontrolled population growth.
- It has been estimated that by the year 2000, as many as 20 nations will be unable to grow enough food to feed their people, even if they use the most current agricultural technologies available. In addition, most of the poor countries of the world will have only half the water per person that they had a decade ago. By the year 2035, the availability of water will be halved again.
- A total of 600 million new jobs will be needed in developing countries by the year 2000, just to employ people who have already been born and will then be ready to enter the work force.

Focusing on things a little closer to home:

- Chapter 10 examined how the elderly population in the United States is increasing. In 1985 some 2.7 million persons in this country

More than 90,000 people attended the Live-Aid concert at JFK Stadium in Philadelphia on July 13, 1985. Similar concerts were held in other parts of the world on the same day to raise awareness and funds for the victims of famine. In Ethiopia, famine victims waited in food lines for hours each day.

were 85 years of age or older—not too many, it would seem, in a nation whose total population was 238.6 million people. By the year 2000, however, the number over 85 will have almost doubled. By 2030, when today's college students are in their sixties, the number of people 85 and older will have tripled. Who is going to take care of them? The trend certainly suggests that investing in a nursing home might be a good idea, but where is the money for elderly health care going to come from? Medical costs are high now. Imagine what they will be like 40 years from now.

Other population issues have a direct impact on social structure and social organization. Changes in the makeup and character of the population sometimes stimulate change in society. Population affects where people live and the quality of their lives. Population issues and changes can influence the economy, politics, the status of women in society, and even the crime rate. Population structure affects the availability of work; it dictates marketing directions in business and industry; and when properly analyzed, population data can be used to make useful predictions for choosing careers and making worthwhile investments. Population and health problems also are closely linked, suggesting that the study of population might indeed be far more worthwhile than one might initially suspect.

THE STUDY OF POPULATION

Demography is the scientific study of human populations, including their size, composition, distribution, density, growth, socioeconomic characteristics, and the causes and consequences of changes in these factors. As such, demography involves far more than simply extending lines on population graphs. It takes into account all sorts of cultural, social, environmental, and historical phenomena. What this might suggest for newcomers to the study of population is that perhaps the best place to start is at the very beginning.

Exhibit 18.1, perhaps the most familiar graph in the field of demography, demonstrates that the rapid changes in world population growth only have been recent. For millions of years, world population remained relatively small—an estimated 5–10 million until 8000 B.C. The harsh conditions of life during the Old Stone Age militated against survival, resulting in high death rates and thus, extremely slow growth. Population then began to increase, but relatively slowly—reaching some 300 million by A.D 1, a level that endured until about A.D. 1650. During these many millennia prior to the advent of written records, large segments of the population shifted away from the nomadic way of life to form agricultural societies. This change increased the food supply and stimulated the emergence of more stable forms of social organization. The growth pattern was not always steady; in the fourteenth century the Black Plague reduced the population of Europe by half.[1]

The year 1650 has been designated as marking the onset of the modern era, when the population began to expand dramatically. While it took millions of years for the world population to reach the billion mark in 1850, it took only another 75 years to top two billion. This rapid expansion was the result of urbanization, the Industrial Revolution, technological changes, advances in medical care, and a variety of other factors. At a less abstract level, this population "explosion" was the result of changes in *fertility* and *mortality,* two of the most basic concepts in the science of demography. The third variable in the demographic equation, which will be discussed later in this section, is *migration*.

SOCIAL INDICATOR

Crude Birth Rates in Selected Regions and Nations, 1988

World	**28**
Africa	44
Asia	28
North America	16
Latin America	29
Europe	13
Oceania*	20
Egypt	38
Ethiopia	46
Kenya	54
Malawi	53
Zaire	45
Iraq	45
Laos	41
United States	**16**
China	21
Japan	11
Cuba	16
Haiti	41
Bolivia	40
Mexico	30
Norway	13
West Germany	10
Italy	10
Australia	15
Fiji	28
U.S.S.R.	20

Source: Carl Haub and Mary Mederios Kent, *1988 World Population Data Sheet* (Washington DC: Population Reference Bureau, Inc., April 1988).

*Oceania includes Fiji, Australia, French Polynesia, New Caledonia, New Zealand, Papua-New Guinea, Solomon Islands, Vanuatu, and Western Samoa.

Fertility

Fertility refers to the actual number of births in a population and is expressed typically as a *rate.* The **crude birth rate,** for example, is the annual number of births per 1,000 population, calculated as follows:

$$\text{Crude Birth Rate} = \frac{\text{Number of Births in Year}}{\text{Total Population}} \times 1000$$

For the demographer, a society's or community's crude birth rate can suggest much about its social structure. The crude birth rate in the United States is 16, as compared with 11 in Denmark, 17 in Ireland, 41 in Haiti, and 54 in Kenya.[2] The difference between the rate in Kenya and that in the United States may not sound like much, but a fuller analysis demonstrates that the differences are indeed profound.

A crude birth rate of 54 means that out of 1,000 Kenyans, 54 of the women spent most of the year pregnant and ultimately gave birth. This figure may appear to be a limited burden, but the true picture is a bit more complex. One way of looking at it is to start out with 1,000 Kenyans, approximately half of whom are males, thus reducing the pool to about 500 women. Roughly 60% of these are not of childbearing age, further reducing the pool to 200. Since about a fourth of these women are either unmarried, widowed, or otherwise not engaged in sexual unions, only 150 remain, 10% of whom are involuntarily sterile. That reduction leaves 135 potential mothers. A crude birth rate of 54 means that of these 135 Kenyan women, 54 produce a child every year. Even if they take turns, with each bearing a child once every 2.5 or 3 years, it means a lifetime of childbearing for the average woman and potentially 8 to 10 children.

Exhibit 18.1 Sociological Focus

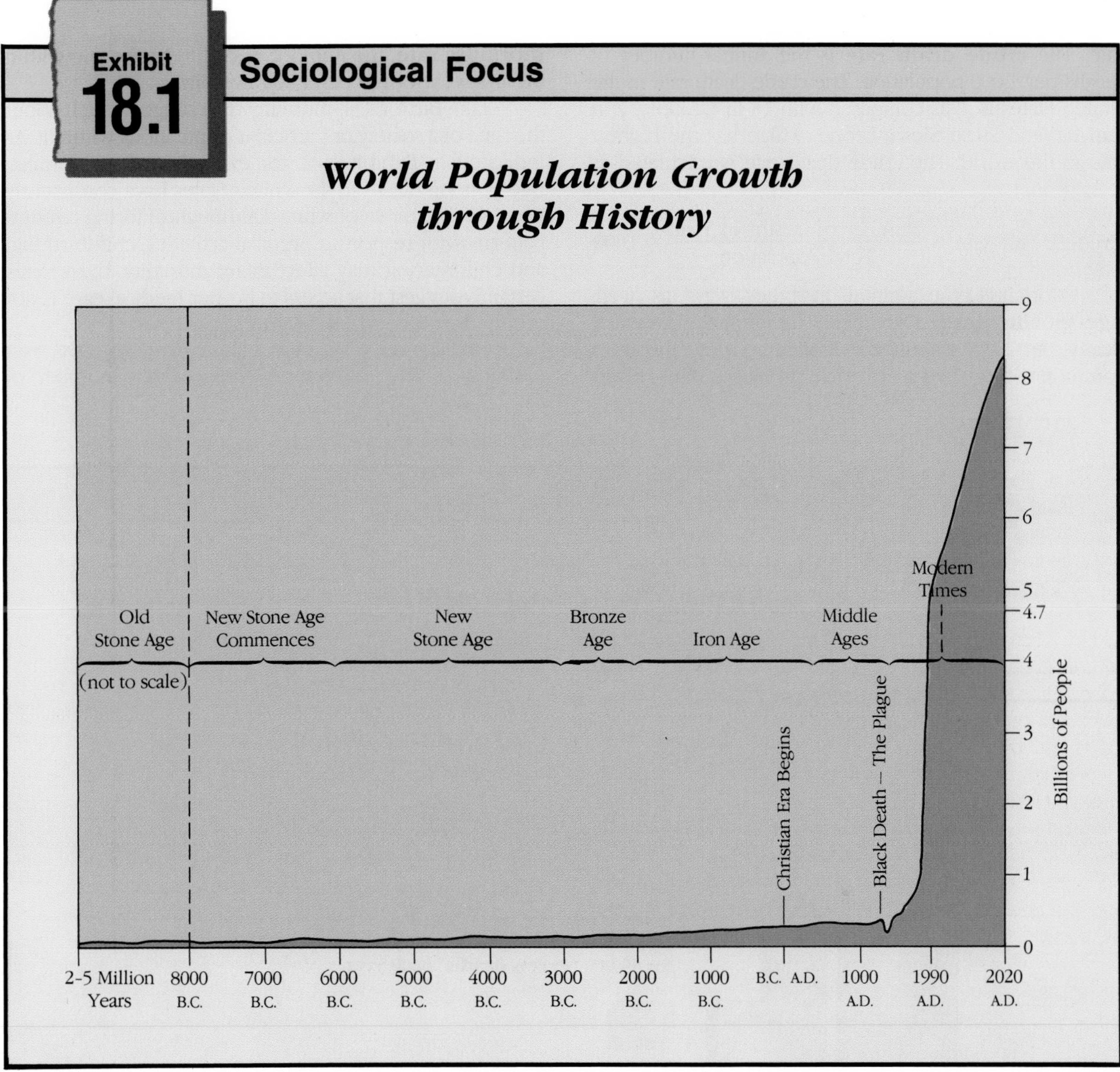

What then, does a crude birth rate of 54 suggest about the social structure, at least as far as women are concerned? Typically, a lifetime of childbearing would have a profound effect on their social roles. If they are tied closely to the home for most of their lives, women's involvement in careers or in political or economic affairs would be drastically reduced, if not totally precluded. The crude birth rate of 16 in the United States suggests vastly different social effects—only 16 women from the eligible pool of mothers will produce a child each year. Even in this country this low rate is relatively recent; the crude birth rate in the United States was higher than the current rate in Kenya throughout the first half of the last century.[3]

The crude birth rate is not the most accurate measure of fertility, but it is commonly used, particularly with international data, because it requires only two pieces of information—total population and births per year. A more accurate way of expressing fertility is the **fertility rate,** the number of annual births per 1,000 women of childbearing age in a population. The fertility rate in the United States is 1.8; the rate in Kenya is 8.0.

Mortality

Mortality is the frequency of the actual deaths in a population. Like fertility, mortality is also expressed as a rate. The **crude death rate** is the annual number of deaths per 1,000 population. The crude death rate in the United States is 9, as compared with 15 in Ethiopia, 7 in Canada, and 29 in Sierra Leone, which has the highest rate in the world. The crude death rate is calculated as follows:

$$\text{Crude Death Rate} = \frac{\text{Number of Deaths in Year}}{\text{Total Population}} \times 1000$$

Mortality is examined in other ways as well. **Age-specific death rates** detail the annual number of deaths per 1,000 population at specific ages. The most commonly used age-specific death rate is the **infant mortality rate,** the number of children who die within the first year of life per 1,000 live births.

Like birth rates, mortality data suggest much about the state of a society or particular populations within it. As indicated in Exhibit 18.2, for example, infant mortality rates among blacks in the United States have consistently been double those of whites. Although differing cultural patterns with respect to prenatal activities, childbirthing, and childrearing may affect infant mortality, these rates certainly suggest that access to proper medical care is not evenly distributed in the United States.

Perhaps the term most commonly associated with mortality is **life expectancy,** the average number of

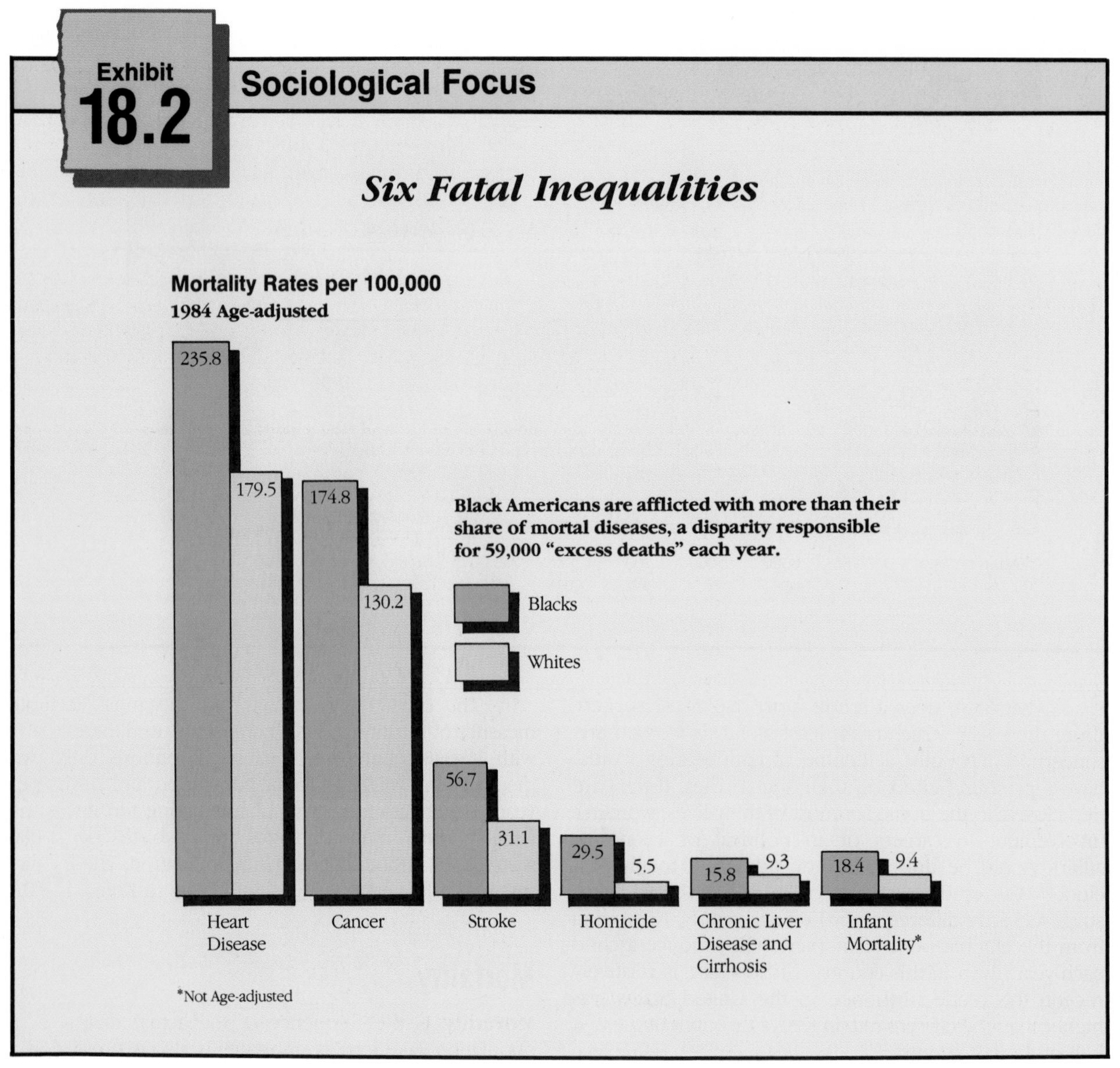

years that a person born in a particular year can expect to live. Like birth and death rates, life expectancy varies dramatically from one nation and part of the world to the next. In 1988, life expectancy ranged from highs of 78 years in Japan and 77 years in Switzerland, Sweden, and Iceland, to lows of 36 in Gambia and 35 in Sierra Leone.[4] Typically, life expectancy is determined more by infant than adult mortality. In most societies, once people survive infancy, their chances of survival increase.

Migration

Migration is the movement of population from one geographical area to another. As the third variable in the demographic equation, it differs from fertility and mortality in two distinct ways. First, fertility and mortality rates involve one-time biological events, whereas migration is generally unrelated to physiological processes. Second, fertility and mortality are social universals, for birth and death are inevitable. Yet migration is neither inevitable nor necessary for population survival, although instances occur when it appears to be. Nevertheless, migration is as tied to the structure of most societies as are birth and death.

For as long as human groups have existed on the planet, they have taken part in population migrations. Hunting and gathering societies were often nomadic, continually moving from place to place without any permanent settlements. After the rise of agricultural settlements and the first cities (topics already addressed in some detail in Chapter 17), communities—sometimes even whole societies—still shifted locations in search of subsistence or work; or moved in retreat from famine, slavery, disease, or war.

Population migrations have been classified in a variety of ways, but the simple dichotomy of *international* versus *internal* seems to be used most often by demographers. In terms of the direction of population shifts, **immigration** is the movement of people into a society, while **emigration** is their movement out.

International Migration

International migration refers to the movement of a population from one nation to another, and in modern times many such movements have taken place. Beginning with the early years of the sixteenth century and for a

SOCIAL INDICATOR

Life Expectancy at Birth (in years) in Selected Regions and Nations, 1988

World	**63**
Africa	52
Asia	61
North America	75
Latin America	66
Europe	74
Oceania	72
Egypt	59
Ethiopia	50
Kenya	54
Gambia	36
Zaire	51
Iraq	62
Laos	50
United States	**75**
China	66
Japan	78
Cuba	74
Haiti	54
Bolivia	53
Mexico	66
Norway	76
West Germany	75
Italy	75
Australia	76
Fiji	67
U.S.S.R.	69

Source: Carl Haub and Mary Mederios Kent, *1988 World Population Data Sheet* (Washington, DC: Population Reference Bureau, April 1988).

SOCIAL INDICATOR

U.S. Swells with Naturalized Citizens

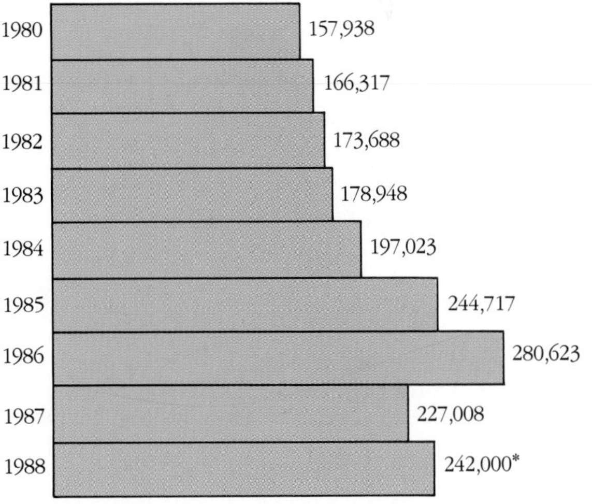

*Estimate

Source: Immigration and Naturalization Service, 1988.

period of three hundred years, more than 85 million Europeans left their homelands and emigrated to North America, Central America, South America, South Africa, Australia, and the South Pacific. While part of this movement was the result of an ecological push, due to a deterioration in the resources necessary for population support, much of it was *free* migration—free in the sense that it was undertaken by individual choice, and not forced by war or famine.[5] And too, a great part of it was *collective,* in much the same way that a social movement is collective. While the first European migrants were pioneers who made individual decisions to emigrate, entire communities later were swept into migration streams that seemed to have a momentum of their own.

The migration from Europe was unique in human history. A number of events converged, making it possible. First, a population explosion occurred in Europe at a time when existing institutions were unable to absorb the growing numbers of people. Second, the New World was opened to Europeans, offering promises of riches, adventure, and escape from increasingly crowded homelands. Third, the invention of the steamship made mass transportation to the New World possible. And finally, the Industrial Revolution and the increased need for labor beckoned workers to cross the oceans.

Not all migration was free. Between 1451 and 1870 an estimated 10 million Africans were brought to the New World as slaves. Others came as indentured servants, kidnap victims, and convicts deported from their native lands (see Exhibit 18.3).

In recent years important international migrations have occurred in the Middle East with population shifts involving Israel, Jordan, Lebanon, and Syria as a result of the partitioning of Palestine after World War II (see Chapter 20). Many peoples of European ancestry have migrated from the recently liberated African countries. Refugee movements in the war-torn areas of Southeast Asia have sent Laotians, Vietnamese, and Cambodians to many nations worldwide, and in the Western Hemisphere the seemingly endless waves of immigration from Latin America continue to impact on the United States.

Internal Migration

Internal migration is the movement of a population *within* a nation's boundary lines. Historically, internal

Exhibit 18.3 Case Study

Indentured Servitude and International Migration

When slavery was abolished in the British Empire in 1833, the British, who controlled a large share of the world's tropical lands, substituted indentured labor, and the Dutch did the same. Instead of coming from Africa, however, indentured plantation labor came overwhelmingly from densely settled areas such as southern China, Java, and India, which not only were closer to new zones of plantation agriculture in Malaya, Sumatra, Burma, Ceylon and Fiji, but also were societies in which thousands of illiterate and landless workers could be induced to risk their fate in unknown places. Usually the indenture contract guaranteed the return fare after three to five years of service, but plantation managers often escaped this clause by paying a bonus for reenlistment. Migrants coming under a short-term *kangani* agreement (group recruitment under a leader, a form used for areas near the place of origin) were normally free to leave employment after a month if they paid back the cost of their journey. In some places labor recruitment, ostensibly by contract, was achieved by force. In the later half of the nineteenth century, the practice of kidnapping Melanesians to work in Queensland and Fiji was notorious under the name of "blackbirding" and the impressment of Chinese coolies for naval duty gave rise to the verb "shanghai." Abusive or not, the contract system fueled plantation agriculture in tropical areas around the world. I have estimated that 16.8 million Indians left India, of whom 4.4 million stayed away permanently. It seems probable that several million Chinese left China and hundreds of thousands left Java. Although the coolie migration was historically brief, its volume probably exceeded that of slave migration.

SOURCE: Quoted from Kingsley Davis, "The Migration of Human Populations," *Scientific American,* 321 (1974), p. 97.

migration in the United States is like that in other nations. As is detailed in Chapter 17, a common pattern involves shifts from rural to urban areas and subsequent migrations to the suburbs.

The factors affecting internal migrations, at least in terms of large-scale movements, are similar to those spiriting international migration. The ecological advantages of one locale over another (seen in the movement of so many Americans to Florida in recent years for the sake of its warm climate) pull individuals into relocating. An even more important factor, however, is the economic dimension.[6] The shifting of business and industry to the Sunbelt regions of Texas, Arizona, and southern California, combined with disinvestment and hard times in the manufacturing sectors of the Rustbelt areas of Ohio, Michigan, Illinois, and western Pennsylvania, caused many internal population shifts during the 1980s.

Studies have demonstrated that two factors both inhibit and induce internal migration. The first factor is *age,* with younger people more likely to move. The highest rates of migration are generally found among those 18–38 years old. As age increases, the probability of migration decreases. Although many elderly Americans seem to migrate to warm climates after retirement, the vast majority do not. The second variable involves *community and kinship attachments.* When family and friends are located in some other part of the nation, the probability of migration is increased; those with relatives close by are less likely to emigrate.[7] Regardless of the reasons for migration, it would appear that the mobility of Americans is higher than elsewhere. The average number of lifetime moves per resident of the United States is thirteen, as compared with eight for Great Britain, seven for Japan, and six for Taiwan.[8]

SOCIAL INDICATOR

The Shift to the Sunshine State: Florida Population, 1986 and 2000

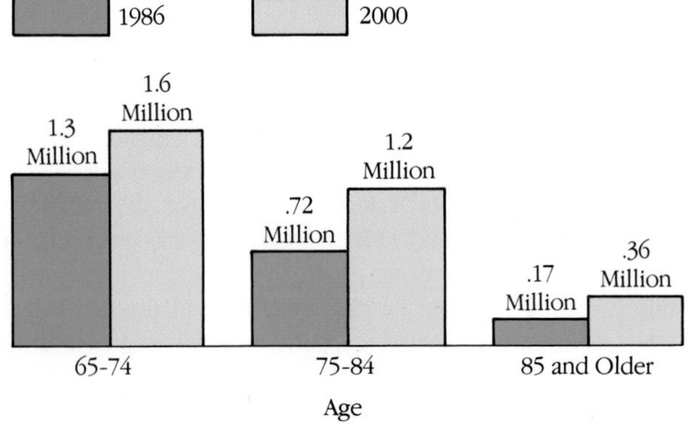

Source: *USA Today,* July 27, 1987, p. 1A.

POPULATION AND SOCIETY

Fertility rates, mortality rates, and population movements do not exist in a vacuum. All are *caused* by social events, and in turn bring about varying degrees of social change.

Fertility and Social Structure

Global population has been growing at an annual rate of 1.7% in recent years, down from its peak of 2% during the late 1960s and early 1970s. And while birth rates appear to be in a downward global trend, even the small 1.7% rate of increase results in over 90 million additional people on the planet each year (see Exhibit 18.4). Assuming that this downward trend continues for at least the next few decades, it is estimated that world population will nevertheless increase by almost 3 billion people by A.D. 2020, reaching a total of some 7.9 billion.

Currently, 92% of the global population growth is concentrated in the less developed countries of Africa, Asia, and Latin America, and in general, a strong relationship exists between the level of a nation's economic development and its birth rate. Sub-Saharan Africa provides a striking example. It is the poorest region of

SOCIAL INDICATOR

World Population Growth

While the growth rate for the world population has dropped, the numbers added to the population continue to grow.

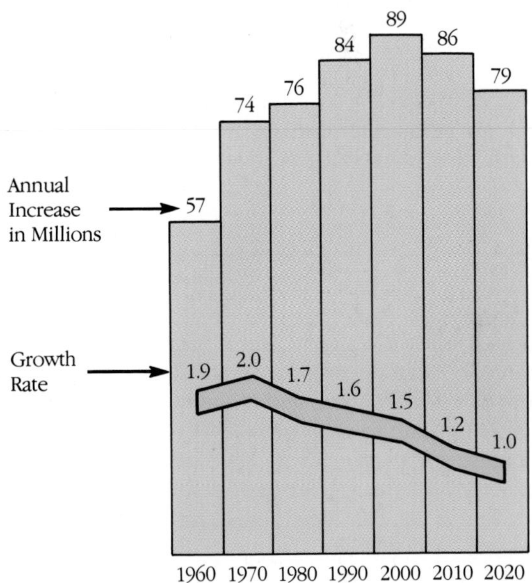

Source: Population Reference Bureau, 1989.

Exhibit 18.4

Sociological Focus

The Population Clock

1988 Population Clock	World	MDCs	LDCs
Births per Year	143,584,000	17,970,000	121,861,000
Month	11,965,334	1,497,500	11,071,750
Week	2,761,231	345,577	2,343,481
Day	393,381	49,233	333,866
Hour	16,391	2,051	13,911
Minute	274	34	232
Second	4.6	0.6	3.9
Deaths per Year	51,280,000	10,972,000	39,310,000
Month	4,273,333	914,333	3,275,833
Week	986,154	211,000	755,962
Day	140,493	30,060	107,699
Hour	5,854	1,253	4,488
Minute	98	21	75
Second	1.6	0.4	1.3
Natural Increase per Year	92,304,000	6,998,000	82,551,000
Month	7,692,000	583,167	6,879,250
Week	1,775,077	134,577	1,587,519
Day	252,888	19,173	226,167
Hour	10,537	799	9,424
Minute	176	13	157
Second	2.9	0.2	2.6
Infant Deaths per Year	11,056,000	269,550	10,480,000
Month	921,333	22,463	873,333
Week	212,615	5,184	201,539
Day	30,290	739	28,712
Hour	1,262	31	1,196
Minute	21	0.5	20
Second	0.4	0.0	0.3

Note: MDCs = More Developed Countries, LDCs = Less Developed Countries. MDCs plus LDCs do not total to world population due to independent rounding of individual countries on *World Population Data Sheet*.

Source: *1988 World Population Data Sheet* (Washington DC: Population Reference Bureau, Inc., 1988).

the world, yet its population grows 3.2% annually. Scarcely 5% of the women of childbearing age use any form of contraception, and it appears that governments are doing little to limit growth. Per capita earnings are decreasing 2% annually and life expectancy is only 49 years. Conditions are not expected to improve much in the future. It has been predicted that famines will become increasingly frequent in the Sub-Saharan region.[9] In attempting to provide food for the growing population, much of the land has been cleared for agriculture. Yet the continual depletion of trees contributes to rapid soil erosion, resulting in reduced water retention and the rapid development of desert areas. The outcome of this cycle is famine, death for the weakest, and an exodus toward urban areas. But this population movement, too, compounds the problem; as a result of migration the number of city dwellers will increase at a rate faster than food producers in a region already unable to feed its people. These observations make clear how firmly fertility is tied to social structure and organization.

What is happening in Sub-Saharan Africa may be extreme, but it is hardly unique. Given the known consequences of population excess, why is it so difficult to bring about change? In the face of famine, malnutrition, deteriorating natural resources, overcrowding, and all of the other social problems associated with these difficulties, why do fertility rates in developing countries remain high?

Various elements contribute to the perpetuation of high fertility figures and the concomitant problems, but most significant are the sociocultural factors that for generations have emphasized the importance of large families. In agricultural societies, having a considerable number of children insures a large enough labor force to work the fields. Also, many cultural traditions stress the greater desirability of male offspring, thus prompting more frequent pregnancies.[10] Nor is the influence of religion a minor factor. Many religions encourage large families, and as already noted in Chapter 12 with regard to Catholicism, artificial birth control measures are forbidden.

Low fertility rates are frequently used as the major indicator of social modernization, a logical conclusion given the uniformly lower birth rates in all of the industrialized nations. The United States, Japan, and Sweden are often cited as examples of how industrialization can influence a reduction in fertility, and the American experience is especially illustrative in this regard. With the exception of the "baby boom" years (see Exhibit 18.5), the fertility rates of American women have been declining steadily since 1800—hand in hand with the growth of industrialization. The growth of cities that was tied to the Industrial Revolution drew families from agricultural work into manufacturing. This change tended to reduce the need for large families for purposes of economic security. In turn, the greater availability of work—first in manufacturing and later in the white-collar sector—enabled women to participate in the paid labor force. As already noted in Chapters 4 and 11, the involvement of women in work careers brought about a redefinition of their roles in American society, particularly with regard to childbearing and childrearing.

Industrialization, urbanization, the decreased importance of large families, the number of women entering the labor force, the redefinition of women's roles—all of these factors can have an impact on the birth rate. Equally important, however, are effective mechanisms of fertility control and measures through which such mechanisms can be readily introduced and implemented.

Fertility Control

The control of population growth is directly related to a number of variables. The first variable is **fecundity,** the physiological capacity to reproduce. A second level of variables includes age at entry into sexual unions, voluntary abstinence, and coital frequency. Third are gestation and birthing factors affecting fetal and infant mortality—elements typically related to nutrition and the availability of medical care. Fourth is the society's acceptence of abortion and the availability of abortion services, and finally, the most important factor is contraception.

The use of contraceptive techniques varies considerably around the globe, and not unexpectedly, usage rates are highest in the developed nations. As for the extent of contraceptive use in developing nations, some 500,000 women in 61 such countries were questioned on the matter between 1975 and 1985.[11] The study focused only on married women ages 15–44 years of age, and rates of usage were found to be under 5% in Sub-Saharan Africa and generally under 40% in most other developing nations.

The effectiveness of fertility control in most developing nations seems to be directly related to government involvement in family planning. One of the more effective, and certainly the most dramatic, attempts at national control of fertility occurred in India. As the first nation to adopt a family planning program, India recognized almost four decades ago that it was headed toward population disaster. During the early 1950s India's crude birth rate of 40 per 1,000 and a death rate of 16 per 1,000 had already outstripped the country's ability to provide for its population. Contraceptives were distributed throughout the 1950s and incentives for voluntary sterilization were introduced during the 1960s. But these efforts met with only minimal success. Government

SOCIAL INDICATOR

International Birth Control

With the world population expected to nearly double by 2025, studies indicate that 270 million people worldwide—two thirds of whom live in developed nations—use contraception or abortion to control population growth.

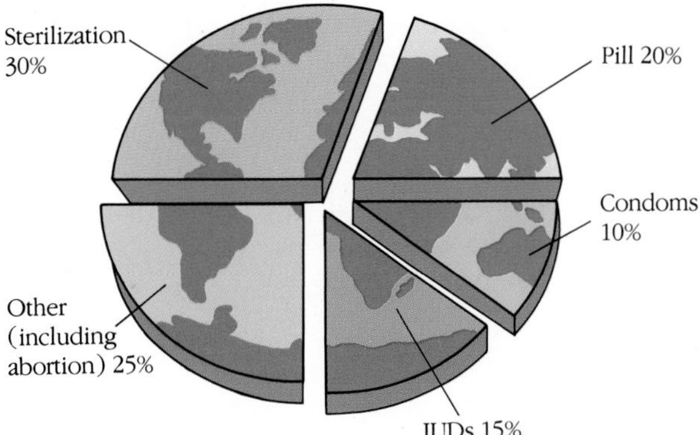

Source: International Planned Parenthood Foundation, 1987.

Exhibit 18.5 Sidelights on American Culture

The Baby Boom

They say that it all started on V-J Day.* In fact, in May 1946—some nine months after V-J Day—an unprecedented 233,452 babies were born in the United States. By year's end, an all-time United States record of 3.4 million babies had been born, and the biggest baby boom in the nation's history had begun.

As indicated in Figure 1 the birth rate in the United States actually began to rise during the early 1940s, but the major increases were seen during the second half of the decade, peaking in the 1950s but lasting into the early 1960s.

The baby boom has often been viewed as a "catching up" by American men who had been away at war and by others who had delayed marriage or childbearing in response to the financial insecurities brought on by the Great Depression of the 1930s. But these factors are only a partial explanation. Numerous other influences were also at work, among them the following:

1. By the mid-thirties the crude birth rate in the U.S. had declined from 30.1 births per 1,000 in 1910 to 18.7. Thus, the higher fertility prior to the 1930s, relative to that during the depression, resulted in a higher proportion of women reaching their childbearing years during the baby-boom era.
2. In the years immediately after World War II, the marriage rate increased from a low of 7.9 per 1,000 in 1932 to a high of 16.4 in 1946. Although the 1946 figure was in part the catching up mentioned earlier, for almost ten years greater numbers of women were getting married than in previous years. In addition, the age at first marriage for both men and women declined, and people began having children sooner after marriage and closer together than the previous generation.
3. The post-war economic boom, combined with the growth of suburban America, made perhaps the greatest contributions to the baby boom. The prosperity of the 1950s encouraged families to have an extra child, and as families moved to the suburbs and had more space in which to raise children, three- and four-child families became the norm.

Figure 1 U.S. Fertility and the Baby Boom

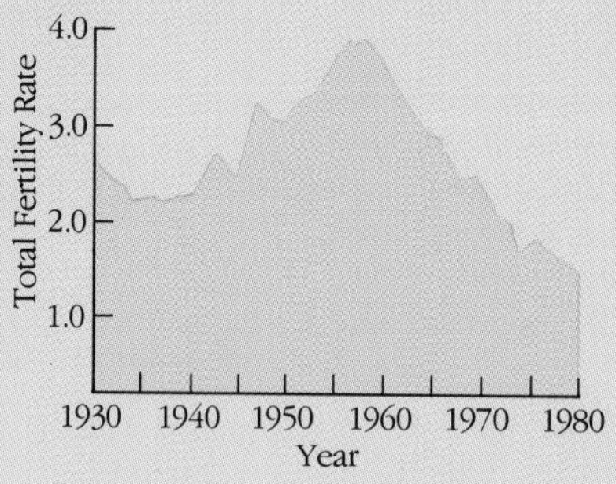

Total Fertility Rate: 1.0, 2.0, 3.0, 4.0
Year: 1930, 1940, 1950, 1960, 1970, 1980

The baby-boom cohort has often been likened to a watermelon swallowed whole by a snake—it constitutes a bulge in the age composition of the nation's population and creates problems all along the way. Between 1950 and 1970 the number of children ages 5–17 increased by some 70%, resulting in school enrollments that created large and crowded classrooms, double sessions, shortages of qualified teachers, and inadequate school facilities. Baby boomers also clogged college campuses. In 1960, for example, when the baby boomers were in their early teens, or were still toddlers, or were yet unborn, the number of persons enrolled in colleges and universities in the United States was only slightly more than 3 million. By 1978, however, this figure had more than tripled.

As the baby boomers entered the labor force from the mid-sixties through the early eighties, many encountered a scarcity of suitable jobs. When they started families, they also found that housing had become scarce and expensive in many parts of the country. As indicated in Figure 2, they now have middle-age clout in that they represent almost half of America's adults and the majority of its managers. However, their problems are still not over. In the year 2011 they will begin to reach retirement age. The demands they will place on Social Security will inevitably produce strain and conflict with the younger generations of workers who will have to finance the system.

If the baby boom made population predictions difficult for demographers, the so-called baby

**V-J Day* is an abbreviation for "Victory-in-Japan Day," August 14, 1945, marking the end of World War II.

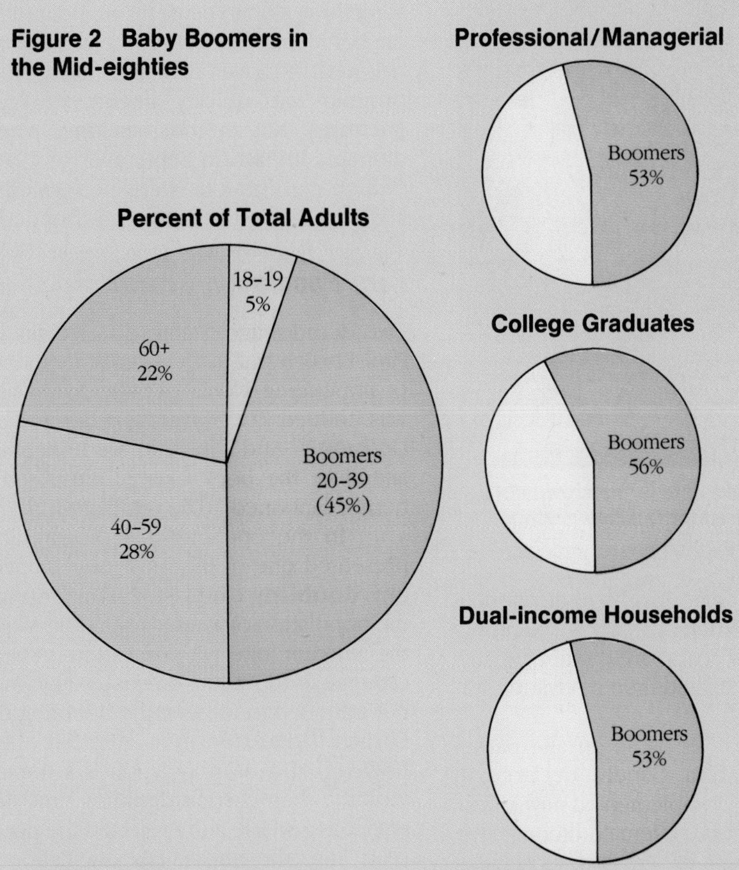

bust was no easier. Beginning in 1970 the birthrate began to decline significantly. In fact, throughout the seventies only some 33 million births occurred in the United States, less than half the number during the baby boom years. And while this statistic may have generated uncertainty for demographic forecasting, what *was* certain was that members of the baby-bust cohort would be in a favored position throughout their lives. As the noted demographer Conrad Taeuber once put it, "Not only will there be fewer of them competing for jobs, services, and attention, but there will also have been an increase in public services and provisions made to accommodate the demands of the larger number of people that preceded them. They will be the beneficiaries of the baby boom."

SOURCES: Landon Y. Jones, *Great Expectations: America and the Baby Boom Generation* (New York: Coward, McCann and Geoghegan, 1980); Population Reference Bureau, " 'Boom Babies' Come of Age: The American Family at the Crossroads," *Population Bulletin,* 3 (August 1966), pp. 61–79; Conrad Taeuber, "A Changing America," *American Demographics,* 1 (January 1979), pp. 6–16; *USA Today,* April 20, 1987, p. 1A; Robert H. Weller and Leon F. Bouvier, *Population: Demography and Policy* (New York: St. Martin's, 1981), pp. 251–75.

Overpopulation in India, reflected here in the crowds of Bombay, has brought on the need for radical solutions and created a national state of emergency.

commitment was lacking, and many problems developed in connection with the delivery of family planning information and techniques to rural areas where many different languages were spoken and little motivation for change existed.

During the 1970s, India set off in an alternative direction. Prime Minister Indira Gandhi declared a national state of emergency and implemented new rules: a priority was placed on increasing female literacy, the minimum age for marriage was raised, and substantial monetary rewards for sterilization were introduced. In addition to the national proclamation, a variety of rules and incentives were established in individual Indian states. They included but were not limited to the following:

1. Government employees were guaranteed raises for undergoing sterilization.
2. Maternity leave was limited to two months.
3. People having more than three children were barred from government employment unless they underwent sterilization.
4. Teachers had to be sterilized or lose an entire month's wages.
5. Government workers were given quotas as to the number of people they had to persuade to be sterilized.
6. Food rations were denied to those with more than three children.
7. Government loans were granted only to those who had small families or who were sterilized.[12]

Needless to say, Gandhi's proclamation caused something akin to panic throughout India. It also brought on her defeat in the 1977 elections, although she was restored to power two years later. Her family planning program was quickly amended to reinstate voluntary measures, but in the meantime planning had had a dramatic impact. In September of 1976 alone, almost 2 million sterilizations were performed in India, and by 1987 the crude birth rate had dropped to 33 per 1,000.

Zero Population Growth

Two decades ago, Stanford University biology professor Paul Ehrlich put forth a rather melodramatic exposition of impending world population problems. His treatise was entitled *The Population Bomb: Control or Race to Oblivion?*[13] And if the title was not enough to catch one's attention, the book's cover illustrated a facsimile of a bomb, captioned: "The population bomb keeps ticking."

In the opening of Professor Ehrlich's book, he presented one of the most basic concepts in demography: **doubling time**—the number of years required for the population of an area to double its present size, given the current rate of population growth. Although the estimate for doubling time is a rough indicator of a trend, not intended to forecast the doubling of any population, Ehrlich had to rely on it. "After all," he said, "no matter how you slice it, population is a numbers game."[14] He took the then current doubling time of 37 years for the planet as a whole and projected the population some 900 years into the future. His calculation yielded a world population of some 60,000,000,000,000,000 (sixty quadrillion). That figure works out to about 100 persons for each square yard of the earth's surface, land and sea. Many readers accepted *The Population Bomb* as a prophecy, initiating a zero population growth movement in the United States.

To demographers, **zero population growth** is a population in equilibrium, with a growth rate of zero achieved when births plus immigration equal deaths plus emigration. To many others, a fertility replacement level of 2.1 means zero population growth. That is, if all couples have about 2 children, then population growth will cease. Yet attaining zero population growth is far more complicated than that, for the fertility replacement level in the United States is already 2.1, but the population continues to increase. The reasons involve the age structure and immigration.[15] Age structure is

SOCIAL INDICATOR

Population Projections

In contrast to Paul Ehrlich's projection, in 1984 the World Bank projected that the global population would stabilize at just over 11 billion people in the year 2150 (see *USA Today*, July 11, 1984, p. 4A). As indicated below, rates of population increase for key countries were also projected to the middle of the twenty-second century.

Rate of Population Increase

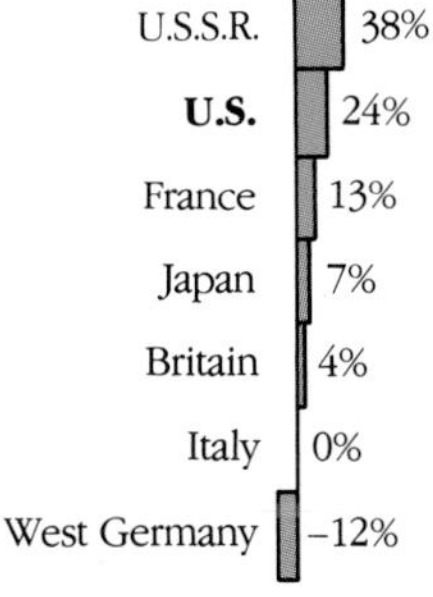

Developing Countries

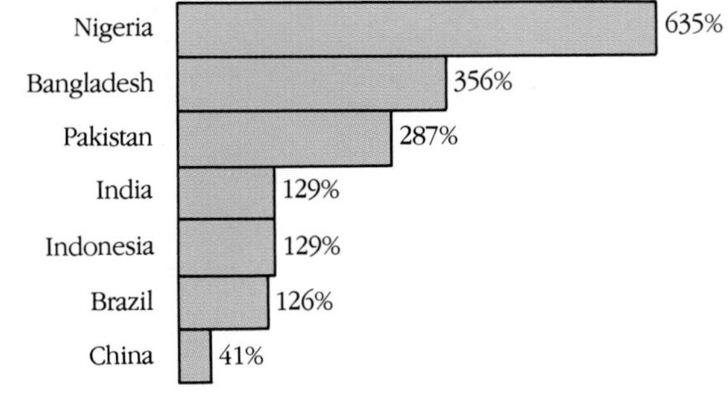

constantly changing. Its current effect on the fertility replacement level has to do with the baby boom. During the post-war boom from 1946 to 1961 (refer back to Exhibit 18.5), 70 million babies were born in the United States. As a result, a relatively high proportion of women reached their prime childbearing years during the late 1960s to the close of the 1980s. An average of two children each born to women in this age cohort would generate a considerable population increase. Thus, even in the short run, replacement level fertility would not produce zero population growth. In the long run, the continuing effect of immigration on population growth also precludes a zero growth level.

Famine and overpopulation in Sudan have forced some people to trap rats for food.

Population Composition and Dependency

Size is not the only population variable important to social structure. Two additional factors that are repeatedly examined by demographers are sex and age composition—both of which vary in any population.

Age-Sex Distribution

It has been estimated that for every 100 females born throughout the world, approximately 105 males are also born.[16] Yet it seems to be common knowledge that women outnumber men. Why is this? In the United States and numerous other countries, the male death rate seems to exceed that of females, so that by age 19, females slightly outnumber males. As people age, the increase of women over men accelerates; by age 65 women far outnumber men. Explanations for this phenomenon include the facts that war casualties fall more heavily on males, that men are more vulnerable to violence, and that, as noted earlier in Chapter 10, masculine gender roles impose a greater emphasis on risk-taking. Mythology also has it that men die earlier because they work harder. Although risk taking is indeed more apparent among men, especially young men, it is unlikely that they really do work harder. More realistically, it would appear that women live longer because they take better care of themselves and because the female organism is far more durable than that of the male.

Age distributions in a population are affected by past and recent trends in fertility, mortality, and migration. Taken together, age and sex distributions are important not only as both causes and consequences of population change, but because various combinations of the two can generate some special effects on social stability.

The Population Pyramid

Perhaps the most useful device for illustrating the past, present, and future age-sex distributions in a population is the age-sex pyramid. Typically referred to as the **population pyramid,** it is a graphic representation of age and sex groups in a society. As is readily apparent in Exhibit 18.6, "pyramids" take on different shapes depending on the age structure, with some only remotely resembling the traditional notions of a pyramid.

Exhibit 18.6 Sociological Focus

Three Patterns of Population Change

Morocco's population pyramid is like that of many developing countries with rapid growth; it is broad at the base because of past high fertility. West Germany, on the other hand, must deal with a decreasing population, and more people at the older ages.

SOURCE: Carl Haub, *Understanding Population Projections* (Washington, DC: Population Reference Bureau, 1987), p. 21.

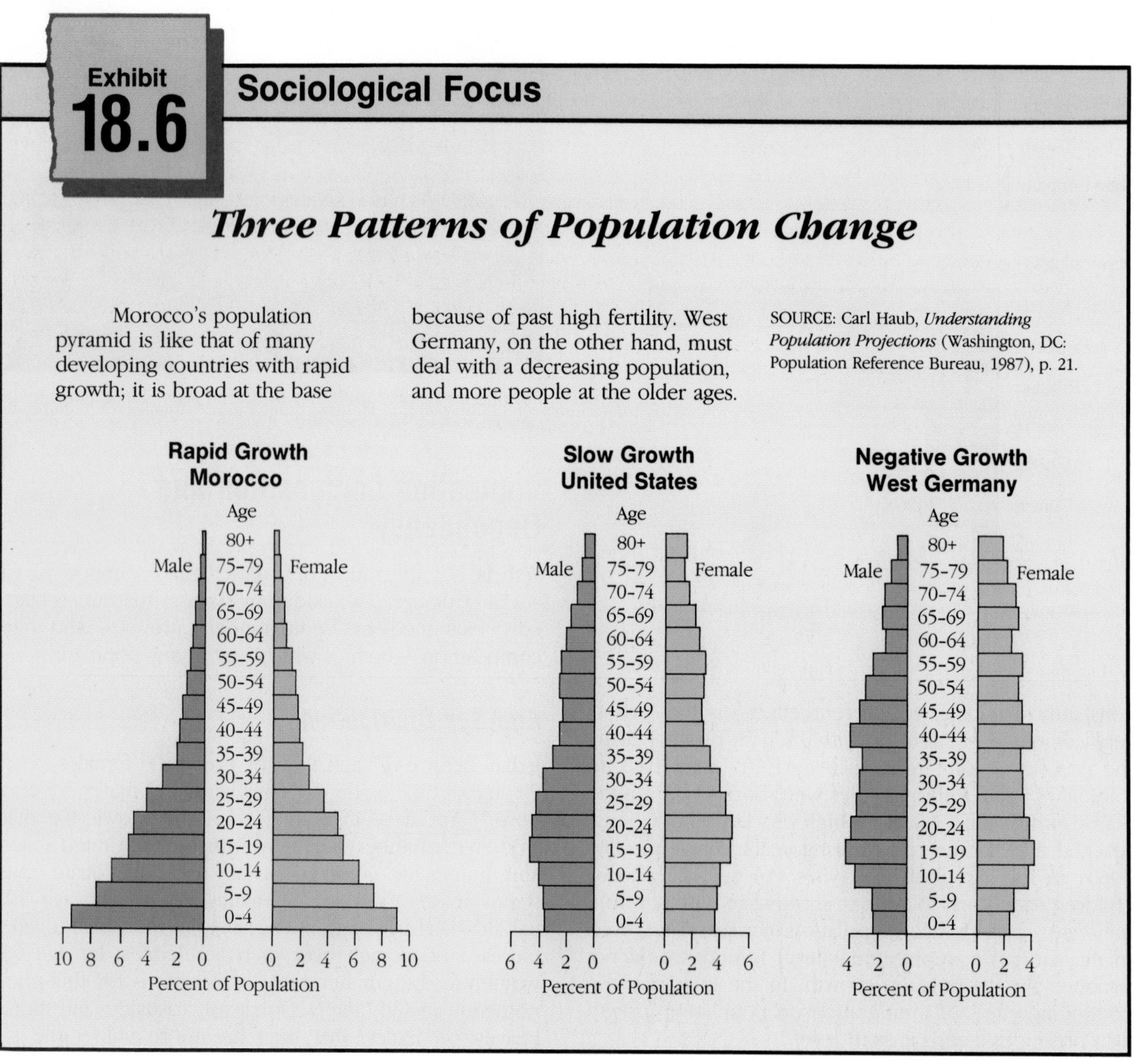

Each of the three shapes in Exhibit 18.6 has a distinct meaning. It should be noticed that Morocco's population is a rather "young" one. As the result of Morocco's high fertility, combined with lower rates of infant mortality, almost 20% of the population is extremely young (under age 5), giving the pyramid a large base. Falling mortality rates also contribute to the number of infants and children who survive to the reproductive ages, further increasing the base of the pyramid by the number of children they bear. The small proportion of elderly people in the Morocco pyramid is a reflection of the high mortality rates experienced in generations past. It should be noted here as well that Morocco's population pyramid, characterized by a pattern of rapid population growth due to high fertility and declining mortality, is typical of most developing nations.

The population pyramid for the United States reflects a slow rate of population growth. Rates of fertility have been declining in recent years, reducing the size of the base of the pyramid. The "bulge" in the lower half of the pyramid reflects the baby boom generation, a cohort that will affect the shape of the pyramid for many years to come.

The pyramidal pattern for West Germany reflects an "old" population, characterized by an extended period of low fertility and mortality. While fewer children are being born, most survive birth to reach middle and old age. This West German pattern is what one would expect for a nation approaching zero population growth.

The Dependency Ratio

Although population pyramids have visual usefulness for understanding a society's age structure, a better measure is the **dependency ratio**—the ratio of the number of people under age 15 and over age 65 per persons ages 15 through 65. This ratio is a rough measure of the number of dependents per productive adult. Stated differently, the dependency ratio indicates the number of individuals dependent on each economically active person, calculated as follows:

$$\text{Dependency Ratio} = \frac{\text{People Ages } 0-14 + 65 \text{ and Above}}{\text{People Ages } 15-64}$$

The lower the dependency ratio, the more economically sound a society appears to be. In 1988, dependency ratios ranged from a high of 1.0 in East Africa to lows of 0.52 in the United States and 0.47 in Canada and Western Europe. That works out to 1 dependent for every producer in East Africa, as opposed to about two dependents per producer in the United States.

Although high fertility rates and their corresponding high dependency ratios are concerns for developing nations, dependency ratios that are extremely low may also be problematic. In contrast to Paul Ehrlich's "population bomb" in the late 1960s, Ben Wattenberg's "birth dearth" in the late 1980s warned of the consequences of a collapsing birth rate (see Exhibit 18.7).

Awareness is a major factor in population-control efforts. A French population-control poster urging people to have children reads, "There is more to life than sex." A poster used in Kenya encourages families to limit their size to two children per family.

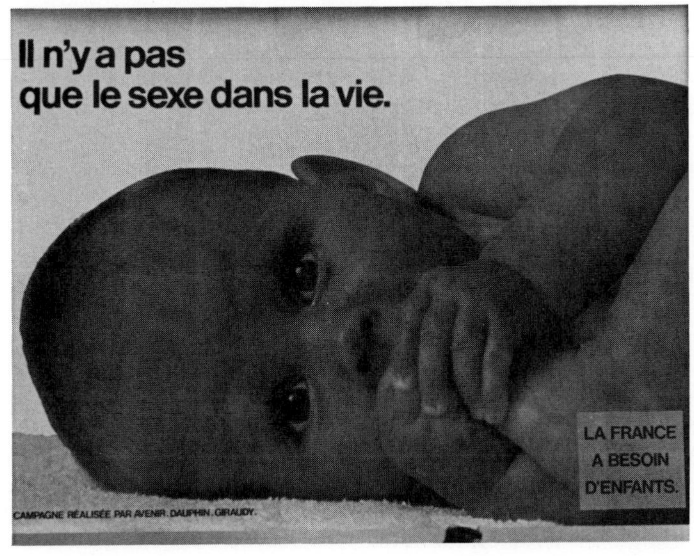

Exhibit 18.7

Research in Sociology

"Birth Dearth" and the West

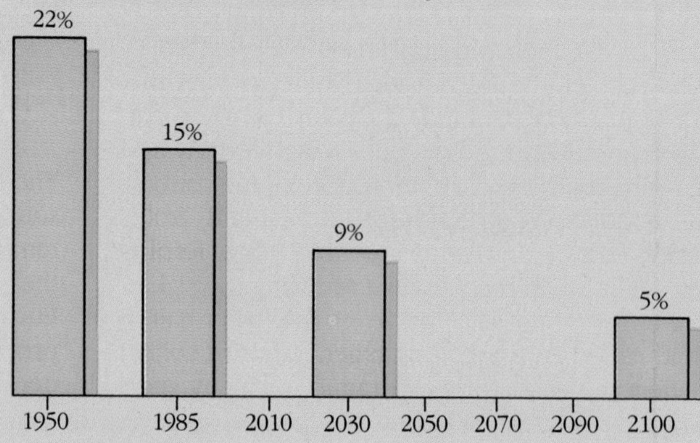

*Industrial democracies include United States, Canada, Western Europe, Scandinavia, Australia, New Zealand, and Japan

There was nothing fancy about it: a bit of cardboard, hand-lettered in felt-tip pen and propped in a shop window in Bar Harbor, Maine. Its message echoed hundreds of signs up and down America's East Coast this summer: Help Wanted.

But behind the message stands a new reality. The United States is running out of teenagers. Employers, accustomed to a ready pool of labor during the school-vacation months, have had to comb the landscape for workers: The news this season has been full of accounts of $7-an-hour jobs slinging hamburgers.

What has yet to dawn on the public, however, is the bigger picture. These "Help Wanted" signs are tiny portents, no bigger than a man's hand, of a deeply disturbing trend. They may be the first ripples of what demographers call the "birth dearth"—the collapse of the birthrate among Western nations.

In a book published this week by Pharos Books in New York, Ben J. Wattenberg argues with great persuasion that "The Birth Dearth" (as he titles his study) is an unprecedented phenomenon. So relentless has been what he calls the "free fall" of birthrates in the Western industrial nations—and so serious are the consequences for economies dependent on an ever-expanding market and work force—that the West risks putting itself, quite literally, out of business. Most important, it risks producing a world in which the Western values of democracy, freedom, and equality will be held by such a tiny fraction of the population (see chart) that they may not prevail.

But how on earth, ask the wide-eyed baby-boomers now in their childbearing years, can this be so? Hasn't it been pounded into us, ever since we all gasped at Paul Ehrlich's "The Population Bomb" in 1968, that we're about to crowd one another off the planet? Aren't we being warned that in this very month—July 1987—the world's population will pass the 5 billion mark?

Didn't we Americans do what was right by slicing our fertility

PEOPLE AND RESOURCES: THE POPULATION DEBATE

Population studies do not lack empirical data on fertility, mortality, age and sex composition, migration, and other variables. Yet as a relatively new scholarly undertaking, demography seems to be limited in its theoretical analyses of the dynamics of population change. Several ideas have been widely debated, however, particularly those of Thomas Malthus and Karl Marx.

The Malthusian Trap

Thomas Robert Malthus, an early nineteenth-century economist, is generally considered to be the father of population study as a field of scholarship.[17] Since the publication of the first edition of his *An Essay on the Principle of Population* in 1798, his views have been the subject of heated discussion.

Malthus contended that human populations tend to increase at a more rapid rate than the food supply needed to sustain them. He reached this conclusion on rate from 3.77 births per woman in 1957 to 1.8 in 1986? And now you're telling us that at this rate the nation will dwindle away—since we're well below the magic 2.1 figure needed just to replace each couple? How has this happened?

Very quietly and with great complexity, replies Wattenberg, a senior fellow at the American Enterprise Institute in Washington, D.C. He reminds us that, although most Western nations are still growing slowly, West Germany is already experiencing an absolute decline in population—and may well be the bellwether for the rest of the West.

Immigration, according to his carefully marshaled numbers, will come nowhere near closing the gap. The population implosion, he warns, will be felt everywhere from fast-food counters to the housing industry, as markets dwindle and nations age.

Causes of the birth dearth? Urbanization, education, higher incomes, more working women, better contraception, easier abortion, delayed marriage, increasing divorce, the higher costs of children—these and other factors all conspire, he argues, to depress fertility. Result: The nations most able to provide leadership and economic support for the growing populations in the less-developed countries (LDCs) may be handicapping themselves just when their assistance is most needed.

Wattenberg's thesis, as he regularly reminds us, is speculative—and the reader will want to subject some of its assumptions to tough scrutiny. First is the assumption that today's LDCs will still be LDCs in 2100—that the next 113 years, in other words, will see no progress at all in the spread of Western values. Second is the apparent assumption that, while most demographers view the "baby boom" itself as a wild aberration, the current birth dearth (which may be no more than a reaction to it) is inevitable and irreversible.

Third is the notion, so common among economists, that *markets* are measured by *warm bodies*—as though the size of a population, rather than the magnitude of its ideas and inventiveness, was what mattered.

That said, however, the book remains a forceful, readable, and much-needed awakening—especially when, at the very end, Wattenberg puts his finger on the fundamental issue. "Our central problem," he concludes, "is in the realm of spirit."

"If our young people remain a generation that can be characterized as 'me-oriented' or 'self-actualizing,' they probably will continue to have few children.

"But suppose we could re-enspirit this generation to understand and take pride in the fact that they are part of a remarkable, potent, productive, humane, beneficent culture. . . . Suppose it was explained that only they can preserve it and that there is something real to fear if they don't."

Does that sound rather grand? So it is. The effort to "re-enspirit" the West is the real "Help Wanted." Nothing less will do.

SOURCE: Reprinted from Rushworth M. Kidder, *The Christian Science Monitor,* July 6, 1987, p. 23. Reprinted by permission from *The Christian Science Monitor.*

the basis of several postulates about people's material needs, sexual instincts, and reproductive capacities. His basic theory was stated in three distinct principles:

> 1. Population is necessarily limited to the means of subsistence. 2. Population invariably increases where the means of subsistence increases, unless prevented by some powerful and obvious checks. 3. These checks, and the checks which repress the superior power of population, and keep its effects on a level with the means of subsistence, are all resolvable into moral restraint, vice and misery.[18]

Principles 1 and 2 suggest that if population always increases to the point where any further increase is checked by the limits of the food supply, then quite obviously, material progress can generate no significant improvements in living conditions. Malthus was asserting here that instead of permitting the existing population to lead a better life, increases in food production merely allow a *larger* population to subsist at the same low level that prevailed prior to increased food output. "Moral restraint," he added in principle three, in the forms of "late marriage and abstinence [from sex] in marriage," was a preventive check against population growth, but so too were "vice and misery" (war, infanticide, plague, and famine). Malthus concluded:

> Assuming then, my postula as granted, I say, that the power of population is indefinitely greater than the power in the earth to produce subsistence for man.
>
> Population, when unchecked, increases in a geometrical ratio. Subsistence increases in only an arithmetical ratio.* A slight acquaintance with numbers will show the immensity of the first power in comparison with the second.[19]

When viewed from the vantage point of the twentieth century, Malthus' theory reflects four significant weaknesses.[20] First, he placed undue emphasis on the limited amount of food that the land could yield. He did not anticipate the nineteenth-century revolution in agricultural methods—crop rotation, chemical fertilizers, plant and animal breeding, and improved livestock feed. During the twentieth century many new scientific techniques were applied to agriculture and animal reproduction that enabled "subsistence," to use Malthus' term, to increase at a geometric rate.

Second, Malthus had the misfortune—from the standpoint of the plausibility of his theory—to formulate his ideas on the eve of the Industrial Revolution. He failed to recognize the possibilities for improvements in the standard of living that would be made possible by industrialization, especially more efficient methods of production. In short, he fully underestimated the potential for invention and innovation.

Third, and also related to industrialization, Malthus' argument did not take into consideration the faster and more reliable modes of transport that helped colonial empires to provide additional raw materials, an exploitable labor supply, and new markets for manufactured products. The emergence of a flourishing international trade and the tide of emigrants from Europe brought relief from population pressures on the European continent and a needed labor supply in the United States.

Fourth, and perhaps most importantly, Malthus had closed his eyes to the possibilities of birth control. His religious beliefs defined contraception as immoral, so he never gave consideration to its widespread use.

Numerous written responses, both supporting and opposing Malthus' theory appeared immediately following the publication of his book.[21] Yet following his death in 1834, his theory quickly dropped from favor. By then the Industrial Revolution had begun, and the vast grassy plains of North America had been opened to cultivation. The new lands and more efficient means of production and distribution had eliminated from people's thoughts the mass destitution that had given Malthus' doctrines meaning during his lifetime.

On the other hand, Malthus' contributions to the development of population theory were far greater than the criticisms of his work suggest. His essay aroused a storm of controversy which long outlived him and made both his followers and opponents conscious of the need for adequate information about population trends and for painstaking investigation of the relationship between such trends and social and economic conditions.[22] In short, Malthus had stimulated the growth of the scientific study of population.

Marx and Population

The Malthusian view of population still was being debated heavily throughout Europe when Karl Marx and Friedrich Engels began to formulate their political philosophy. They were very much aware of the debate. The idea that any single law of population could be applied universally, no matter what the nature of the societal organization, was necessarily inconsistent with the socialist theories that they were contemplating.[23]

The Marxist approach argues that "overpopulation" and "population limits" are social creations that are neither inevitable nor necessary. Rather, the apparent existence of population problems is not caused by a lack of resources, but is instead a facet of their unequal distribution in capitalist economies. While the productive capacity of society increases to meet population levels, it is the processes of distribution in class-based social systems that generate poverty, hunger, and misery.

This Marxist view specifically contends that population dynamics can be understood only in terms of the class structure within the political economy of capitalism. It is in the relationship between bourgeoisie and proletariat, through the exploitation of labor and extraction of surplus value, that the working class and poverty populations are created. Stated differently, capitalism requires a surplus population of labor to keep wages down. Thus, the population problems that Malthus viewed as inevitable were in Marx's opinion actually the result of the economic system that created them, and the exploitative class structure.

Although it was Marx's view that population growth was not the root source of poverty, it would appear that in China, the Soviet Union, and other Communist nations where socialist policies are based on the writings of Marx and Engels, the governments have taken a rather relativistic view of the Marxist perspective. Witness the fact that

*Arithmetical ratios increase in the form of 1, 2, 3, 4, 5, 6, 7, and so forth. Geometrical ratios increase in the form of a geometric progression: 1, 2, 4, 8, 16, 32, 64, and so on.

Communist China now points to its huge population as a cause of its continued underdevelopment, a conclusion that Malthus might applaud from his grave. However, Engels once elaborated on the Marxian view of population, holding that in a planned socialist society, fertility could be controlled.[24]

Demographic Transition Theory

While Malthus addressed the inevitability of population pressures and Marx examined the relationships among population, capitalism, and the distribution of resources, demographic transition theory was an attempt to explain the rates of population growth in Europe following the Industrial Revolution.

Demographic transition theory is used to chart the evolution of societies through various stages, as evidenced by changes in their fertility and mortality rates. Proposed by sociologist Warren S. Thompson in 1929, the theory suggests that population growth passes through three stages (see Exhibit 18.8).[25] During Stage I, the *preindustrial stage,* high fertility rates are counterbalanced by high mortality rates as the result of disease, starvation, and natural disasters. The many births and deaths counterbalance each other, resulting in population stability. The *transitional stage* (Stage II) is ushered in with better living conditions and rising public health standards. Higher standards of living reduce infant mortality rates, while improvements in sanitation reduce the impact of disease. Because fertility remains high, the population grows. Finally, in the *industrial stage* (Stage III), low mortality rates are matched by a corresponding decline in fertility rates. As noted earlier, industrialization weakens the economic value of large families, and this, combined with the wide dissemination of family planning information, lowers birth rates.

From an historical point of view, the theory of demographic transition offers an interesting descriptive model of the evolution of many societies. However, the

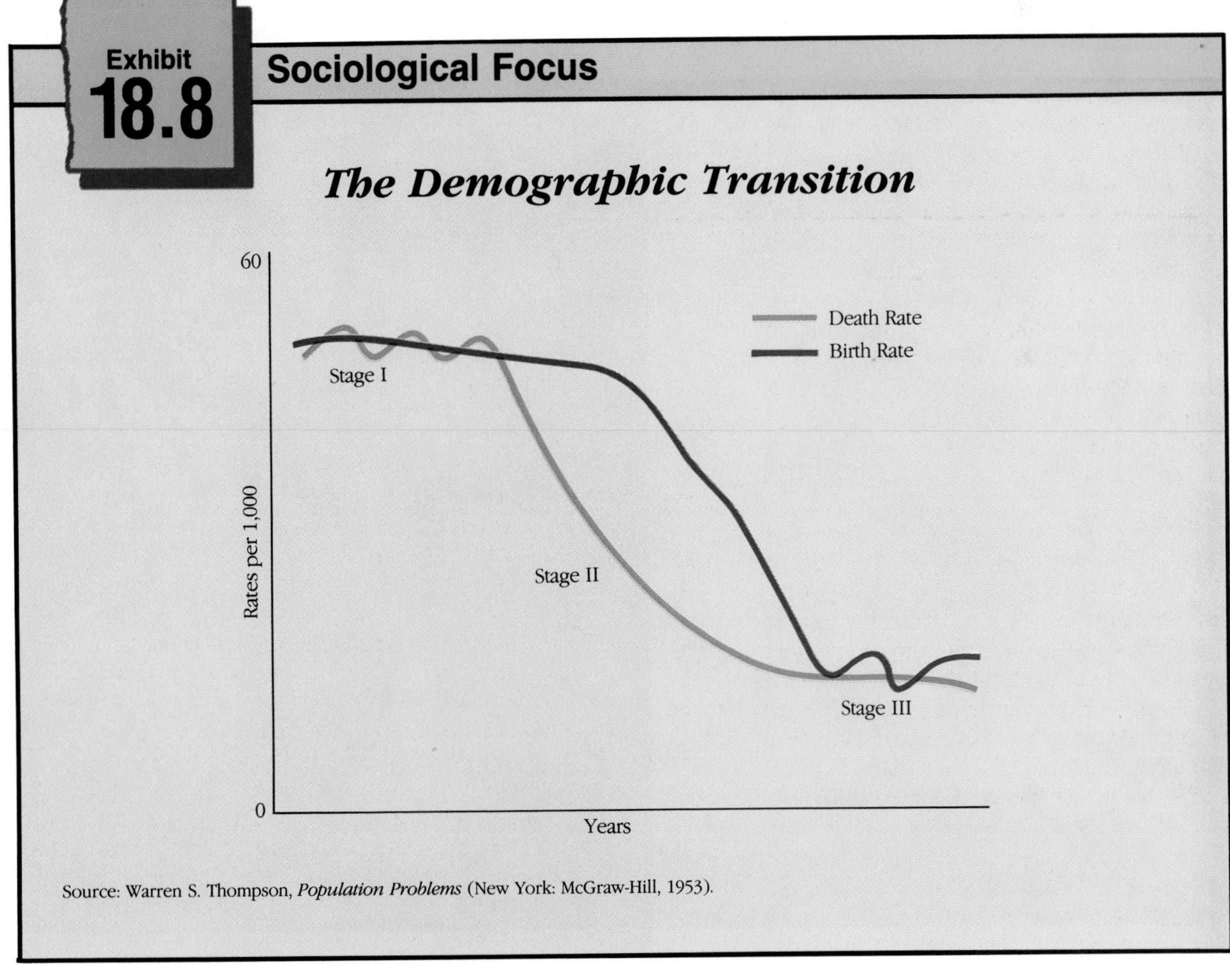

Source: Warren S. Thompson, *Population Problems* (New York: McGraw-Hill, 1953).

theory has received considerable criticism.[26] While it provides a general reflection of population change as it occurred in much of Western Europe, the United States, and Canada, it does not account for the post–World War II baby boom. According to demographic transition theory, fertility should have been falling at the end of World War II, but that certainly was not the case. In addition, demographic transition theory does not seem to apply to many developing nations, where mortality rates are presently declining but in the absence of corresponding declines in fertility. In short, the theory is interesting, but simplistic, for its greatest defect lies in an overall failure to account for the myriad social factors that can impact on family planning and hence, population change.

POPULATION AND AIDS

Writing at the turn of the seventeenth century, the English metaphysical poet and cleric John Donne reminded us in his *Devotions Upon Emergent Occasions* that "no man is an island." He used the island image to convey people's dependence on their neighbors. In 1965, in a speech delivered in Switzerland shortly before his death, United Nations Ambassador Adlai E. Stevenson changed the parable somewhat: "We all travel together, passengers on a little space ship, dependent on its vulnerable supplies of air and soil; all committed for our safety to its security and peace, preserved from annihilation only by the care, the work, and I will say the love we give our fragile craft."[27]

In identifying the human condition with life on a spaceship, Stevenson had poignantly noted how interdependent all aspects of creation tend to be. His concept of the "spaceship *Earth*" became a rallying cry for the environmental movement in the years that followed,[28] and it remains equally important to the understanding of population-related problems in a global perspective. In this regard, the population-AIDS connection has been chosen for analysis here because of the topic's currency and the many sociological issues associated with it. AIDS' recent invasion of Stevenson's spaceship *Earth* serves as a reminder of the fact that the planet is a closed system

within which all of the segments of the population are interconnected. AIDS also serves as a lesson on how epidemic diseases quickly become meshed with the workings of fertility, mortality, and migration.

The Nature of AIDS

Since the early 1980s, the American public has been exposed to dozens, if not hundreds, of accounts of the most widely publicized disease of the twentieth century—AIDS (Acquired Immune Deficiency Syndrome). AIDS cripples the body's defense mechanisms, leaving them unable to fight even the least aggressive bacteria and other microorganisms. **AIDS,** caused by **HIV** (Human Immunodeficiency Virus), is best defined as a severe late manifestation of infection with HIV, which destroys or incapacitates various important components of the human immune system. The actual causes of death among AIDS victims include a variety of somewhat rare infections and other diseases that an otherwise healthy immune system can effectively combat.

The Transmission of AIDS

HIV is transmitted when virus particles or infected cells gain direct access to the bloodstream. Transmission can occur during all forms of sexual intercourse that involve the transmission of body fluids, and presumably during oral or genital intercourse with an infected partner as well. The other major routes of transmission include the sharing of needles among intravenous (IV) drug users, the passing of the virus to unborn or newborn children by infected mothers, and the receipt of transfusions from an infected blood supply.[29]

Given these methods of transmission, the "high risk" groups for AIDS include homosexual and bisexual men, intravenous drug users, persons with hemophilia, and the sexual partners of members of these groups (see Exhibit 18.9). The highest rates of AIDS in the United States are found among homosexual and bisexual men, followed by IV heroin and cocaine users.*

No evidence exists that indicates that AIDS can be transmitted by "casual" contact. The AIDS virus does not penetrate the skin, the cells lining the respiratory tract, or the mucosa of the digestive tract. Thus, the disease cannot be transmitted by a handshake or from a toilet seat, by a cough or sneeze, or by the consumption of food prepared by someone who has AIDS. In fact, long-term studies of the families of adult and pediatric AIDS patients and thousands of health-care workers demonstrate that the AIDS virus is not transmitted by any daily activity related to living with or caring for an infected patient.[30] The virus is concentrated in such body fluids as blood and semen, and in some cases it has been detected in tears and saliva. In these two latter cases, however, the levels of the virus appear to be too low to play a role in infection.

*Since the transmission of HIV is common through "needle-sharing" by IV-drug users, this would suggest that other types of needle-sharing—such as those found in tattoo parlors and ear-piercing establishments—also should be avoided.

Tracking the AIDS Epidemic

George Gordon Byron, the nineteenth-century English poet better known as Lord Byron, is credited with having coined the phrase about truth being stranger than fiction. Two decades ago science-fiction author Michael Crichton wrote *The Andromeda Strain.* It was a gripping story of a space-borne organism that wiped out an entire American town before mutating into a harmless germ. Little would the readers of Crichton's book have believed what reality had in store for humankind.

As the medical community in the United States and Western Europe first became aware of AIDS, many of the characteristics of the *Andromeda* mystery certainly seemed to be evident. Not only did AIDS appear to be a *new* disease, but in conventional medical terms, it was not even a disease at all. Rather, it was a *syndrome,* a collection of symptoms that seemingly opened the body to the ravages of a whole set of rather unusual infections, which *always* proved fatal.[31] The so-called disease, furthermore, was neither airborne nor spread by casual contact, but through blood and semen. To complicate the enigma even further, no one seemed to know where it all had started. And perhaps most mysterious to medical scientists around the globe was the fact that AIDS apparently had moved from the status of being virtually unknown to the status of an epidemic within a period of only four years.

The first cases of what is now known as Acquired Immune Deficiency Syndrome were reported in the medical literature in the late 1970s.* At the time,

*Medical experts now believe that earlier cases have been documented. One report in *The Lancet* speculated that a case treated in 1959 may have been AIDS. (See G. Williams, T. B. Stretton, and J. C. Leonard, "AIDS in 1959?" *The Lancet,* November 12, 1983.) Moreover, the death of a St. Louis teenager in 1969 from a disease that was determined in 1987 to be AIDS has suggested that the virus may have entered the U.S. population on a variety of occasions. Two theories have been advanced to explain why the disease did not spread in the 1960s. Some researchers suggest that it mutated during the 1970s into a more virulent and contagious form. Others point to the increased number of carriers of the disease associated with the rapid increase in homosexual activity in New York and San Francisco during the 1970s. (See *Newsweek,* November 9, 1987, p. 62; *New York Times,* October 28, 1987, p. A15.)

Exhibit 18.9

Sociological Focus

AIDS Cases in the United States Reported to the Centers for Disease Control through August 1989

Transmission Category*	Total
Adult Male	
Homosexual/Bisexual Only	63,497
IV-drug Abuser Only	16,523
Both Homosexual/IV-drug Abuser	7,379
Hemophilia/Coagulation Disorder	971
Heterosexual Contact	1,998
Transfusion	1,598
Other/Undetermined	2,898
Male Subtotal	94,864

Transmission Category*	Total
Adult Female	
IV-drug Abuser Only	4,847
Hemophilia/Coagulation Disorder	25
Heterosexual Contact	2,809
Transfusion	968
Other/Undetermined	697
Female Subtotal	9,346
Adult Subtotal	104,210
Pediatric	1,780
Total	**105,990**

Source: Centers for Disease Control, 1989.

*Transmission categories are hierarchically ordered; patients with multiple risk factors are tabulated only in the category listed first.

however, the disease had yet to be identified, so only minimal attention was paid to the earliest medical commentaries. The official tracking of the disease began in 1981 when the Centers for Disease Control (CDC) in Atlanta reported on a new disease syndrome in the June 5 issue of its *Morbidity and Mortality Weekly Report.*[32] Five young men, all active homosexuals, had been treated in Los Angeles hospitals for a rare infection—*Pneumocystis carinii* pneumonia. Two of the patients had already died, and all had evidence of other infections and a defective immune system. An editorial note in the CDC report gave a hint of the puzzle that has since developed into one of the major public health and scientific challenges of the generation:

> *Pneumocystis* pneumonia in the United States is almost exclusively limited to severely immunosuppressed patients. The occurrence of *pneumocystosis* in 5 previously healthy individuals without a clinically apparent underlying immunodeficiency is unusual. The fact that these patients were all homosexuals suggests some association between some aspect of a homosexual life-style, or disease acquired through sexual contact, and *Pneumocystis* pneumonia in this population.[33]

Then the mystery became even more perplexing. At about the same time that the CDC issued its report, physicians had diagnosed Kaposi's sarcoma, then an exceedingly rare form of cancer in the United States, in more than two dozen homosexual men in New York and California. Surveillance of other unusual infections by the Centers for Disease Control led to the discovery that all of the conditions in question were the result of an underlying immune defect. This prompted the adoption of the name, Acquired Immune Deficiency Syndrome (AIDS), late in the summer of 1981.[34]

As to where AIDS originated, the matter remains unsettled, but the most widely accepted theories point to central Africa. The AIDS problem in Africa first became evident in 1982 when physicians in Belgium began seeing patients from Zaire and Burundi.* These patients had signs and symptoms virtually identical to those being identified as AIDS in the United States. Further investigation led to two separate theories. The first proposal was

*Prior to gaining their independence in the early 1960s, Zaire and Burundi were part of the Belgian Congo, and those citizens with financial means still travel to Belgium for major medical care.

that AIDS had long been nestled in a remote area of Africa and then spread when thousands of people moved from rural to urban areas after countries gained their independence. The alternative idea suggested that the natural home of the AIDS virus is in an animal, most likely the African green monkey, and that somehow, the virus mutated and jumped species; entering the human population when monkeys bit hunters who were attempting to capture them for food.[35]

Further investigation has suggested that AIDS made its way to North America from Africa via Haiti. More specifically, from the early sixties through the mid-seventies, considerable migration took place between Zaire and Haiti, and many of these immigrants are believed to have resettled in the United States.[36] In addition, it has been argued that African green monkeys were imported from Zaire to Haiti and kept as pets in male houses of prostitution.[37] Other speculators suggest that Haiti was a popular vacation spot for gay Americans, who brought the disease home with them and infected the mainland population.[38] Whatever the source, by 1983 it was clear that AIDS was an epidemic disease with a 100% mortality rate.

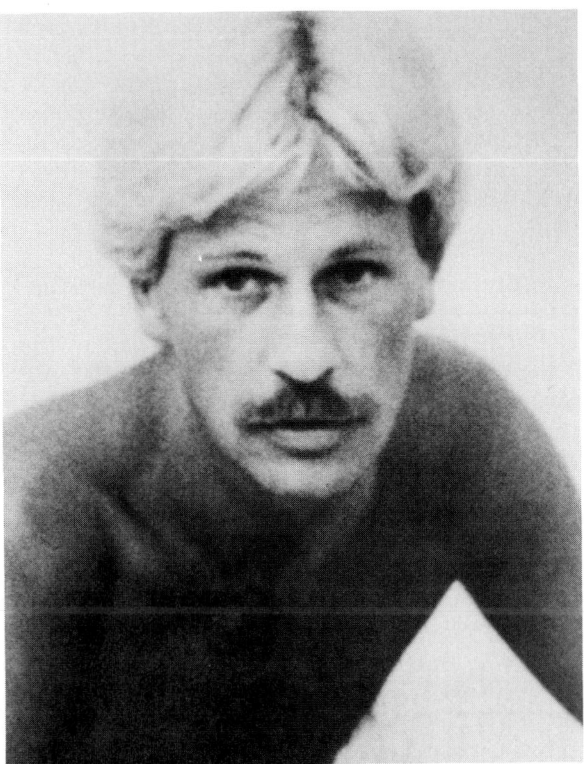

Gaetan Dugas, the infamous "Patient Zero," was an Air Canada flight attendant believed to have played a major role in the early spread of AIDS in the United States. At least 40 of the first 248 gay men diagnosed with AIDS by early April 1982 had either been involved with Dugas or with someone else who had been involved with Dugas. A statistician from the Centers for Disease Control calculated that the odds of these 40 men getting AIDS by simple coincidence were *zero*.

AIDS and Social Structure

No one has captured the unique exile that an epidemic imposes better than the French novelist Albert Camus. In *The Plague,* published in 1947, Camus wrote:

> There was always something missing in their lives. Hostile to the past, impatient of the present, and cheated of the future, we were much like those whom men's justice, or hatred, forces to live behind prison bars. . . . The plague had swallowed everything and everyone. No longer were there individual destinies, only a collective destiny, made of plague and the emotions shared by all. Strongest of these emotions was the sense of exile and of deprivation, with all the crosscurrents of revolt and fear set up by these.[39]

As AIDS spread throughout America, no doubt many of its victims were made to feel the isolation Camus described.

Exponential Growth

Malthus spoke of exponential growth, and so have many others. Remember the problem: if you place a penny on the first square of a checkerboard and double the number of coins on each subsequent square—2,4,8,16. . .—how big is the stack by the time you reach square 64? The answer: about as high as the universe is wide. That kind of growth, as was pointed out earlier in this chapter, was one of the problems of population increase contemplated by Malthus. Exponential growth has been similarly contemplated with respect to the spread of AIDS and its impact on population.

What was clear about AIDS from the outset was its exponential growth rate—8 cases prior to 1979, then 10 new cases in 1979, 46 more in 1980, another 252 in 1981, and so on, until by late 1989 the number of diagnosed cases in the United States alone was 105,990.[40]

At times, a "doubling" of known AIDS cases was taking place every five months, and it was then that people began to wonder where it would all end. Adherents of doomsday prophecies held that AIDS was nature's answer to overpopulation. Religious fanatics argued that the disease had been wrought by God to punish the sodomites, perverts, junkies, and whores who were infecting the world with sin. But as the demographers and other scientists who came after Malthus have learned, exponential growth in a finite world has its limits. It either destroys the entire system, or the process slows down.

By 1987, in the United States at any rate, signs of a slowing were beginning to appear—at least in terms of the doubling time. The number of newly diagnosed AIDS cases was still increasing rapidly, with a projection of over a quarter of a million victims expected by 1991.[41] But the doubling time had gone from 5 months early in the decade to 13 months five years later.

Elsewhere in the world, however, and particularly in the developing nations of Central and West Africa, a rather different picture was emerging. While the World Health Organization was reporting less than 12,000 AIDS cases on the entire continent of Africa in mid-1988, that figure referred only to "known" diagnosed cases. Estimates as to the numbers of Africans infected by the AIDS virus were as high as 100 million.[42] And to make matters worse, in 1987 a second strain of HIV was found to be spreading on the African continent.[43]

Other factors add to the severity of AIDS in Central and West Africa. First, the pattern of AIDS in that region of the world is different than in the United States. While the majority of American AIDS victims have been IV-drug users and male homosexuals and bisexuals, in Africa almost half of the known AIDS patients are women. This statistic certainly reinforces the belief that AIDS can be transmitted heterosexually. Second, and ironically, evidence indicates that the epidemic character of AIDS in Africa may be in part the result of existing health-care practices. Many such practices tend to be unsanitary, such as the reuse of unsterilized hypodermic needles for inoculations and transfusions.[44] Third, a strong link exists in Africa between AIDS and prostitution. As one observer recently explained the situation:

> A study at Nairobi's Kenyatta Hospital shows just how fast a virus can spread in a society where sexual partners change frequently. Within six years, 60 percent of all prostitutes examined were carriers [of the AIDS virus]. In the slums of Nairobi today, there is almost no prostitute who is not infected with the virus. The women, most of whom were forced by poverty to leave their native villages, have about 1,000 customers a year. After spending a while in the slums, the women return to their families on the land. They bring the deadly plague with them.[45]

A fourth element in the AIDS–Central Africa connection is the fact that the disease has been compounded by other infections—malaria, yellow fever, tuberculosis, and leprosy—and by undernourishment and pregnancy. All of these burdens weaken the immune system, making it easier for the AIDS virus to establish itself (see Exhibit 18.10). Fifth, and finally, it has been calculated that the *average* lag time between initial infection with the AIDS virus and the development of AIDS may be 15 years.[46] What this suggests is that perhaps 90% of the AIDS epidemic will not emerge until the mid-nineties.

The Start of a Plague Mentality?

The 1956 science-fiction film *The Invasion of the Body Snatchers* and its 1978 remake with Donald Sutherland and Brooke Adams told the story of alien "pods" taking over human bodies, and in so doing destroying personality and individuality. Those who were still normal would peer intently at one another as if to detect the telltale change, the sign that one had crossed over and had become one of them—alien and lethal. *The Invasion of the Body Snatchers* offered a vivid portrait of the plague mentality.

In the plague mentality, one belongs to the kingdom of life or the kingdom of death. During the Black Death in the fourteenth century, people were afraid to approach one another; parents abandoned children,

SOCIAL INDICATOR

Total U.S. AIDS Cases and Deaths, 1981–1988, and Projections to 1991

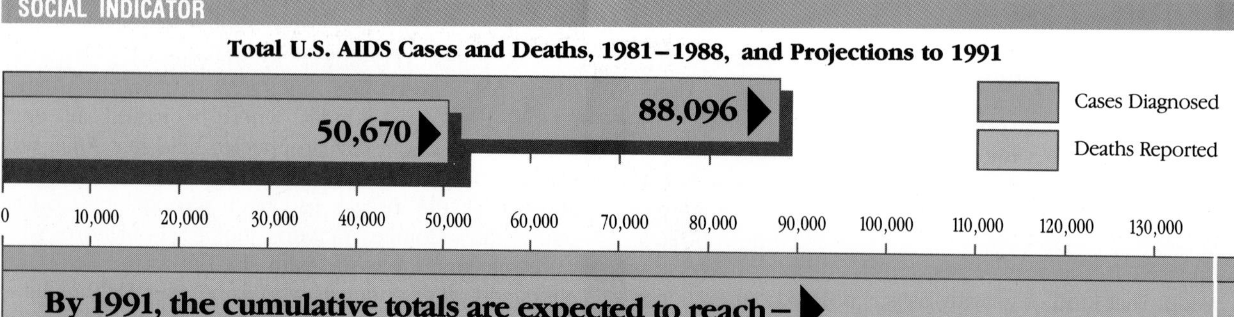

SOCIAL INDICATOR

AIDS Cases Reported to WHO, 1988

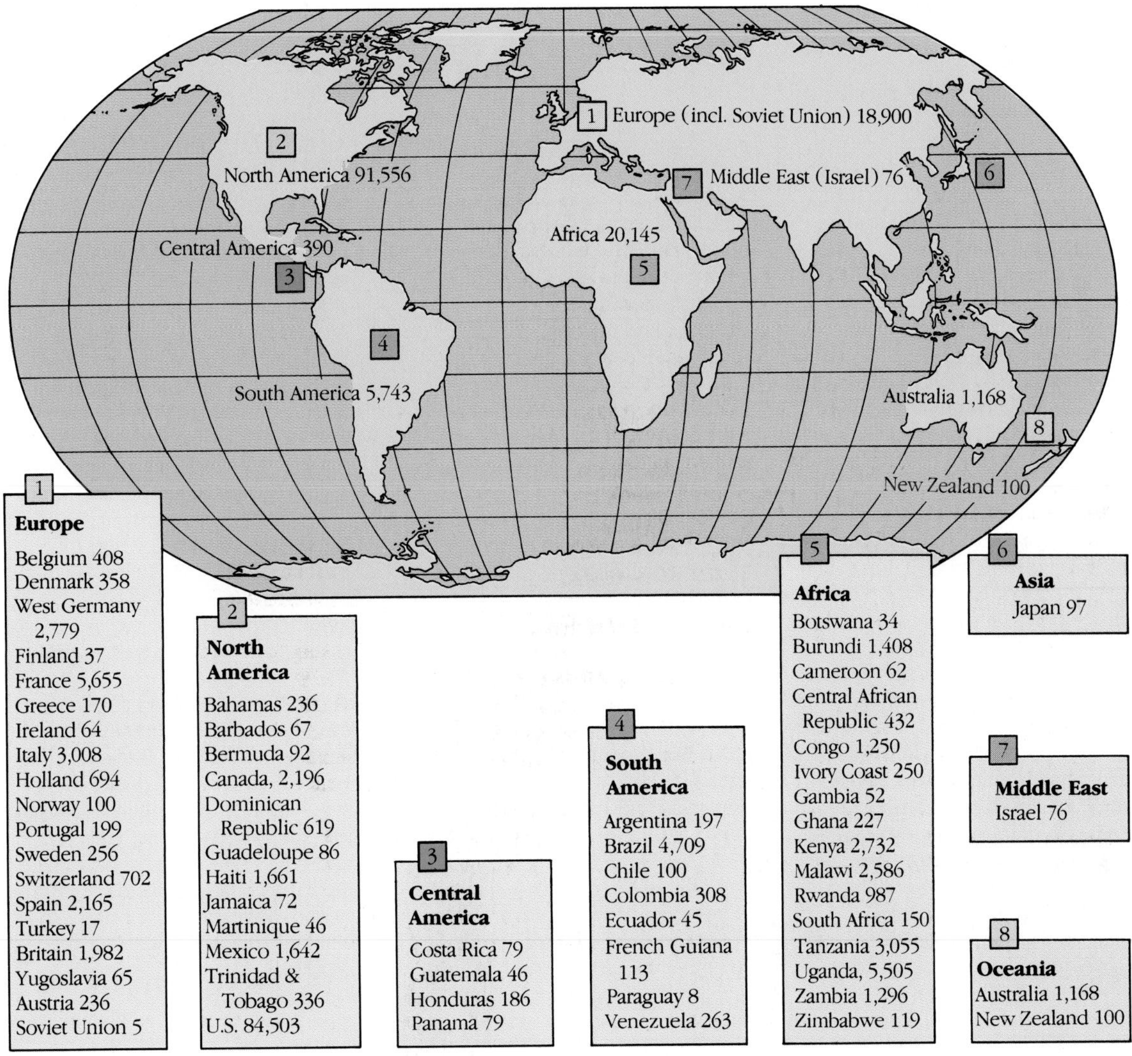

1 Europe (incl. Soviet Union) 18,900
2 North America 91,556
3 Central America 390
4 South America 5,743
5 Africa 20,145
6
7 Middle East (Israel) 76
8 Australia 1,168
New Zealand 100

1 Europe

Belgium 408
Denmark 358
West Germany 2,779
Finland 37
France 5,655
Greece 170
Ireland 64
Italy 3,008
Holland 694
Norway 100
Portugal 199
Sweden 256
Switzerland 702
Spain 2,165
Turkey 17
Britain 1,982
Yugoslavia 65
Austria 236
Soviet Union 5

2 North America

Bahamas 236
Barbados 67
Bermuda 92
Canada, 2,196
Dominican Republic 619
Guadeloupe 86
Haiti 1,661
Jamaica 72
Martinique 46
Mexico 1,642
Trinidad & Tobago 336
U.S. 84,503

3 Central America

Costa Rica 79
Guatemala 46
Honduras 186
Panama 79

4 South America

Argentina 197
Brazil 4,709
Chile 100
Colombia 308
Ecuador 45
French Guiana 113
Paraguay 8
Venezuela 263

5 Africa

Botswana 34
Burundi 1,408
Cameroon 62
Central African Republic 432
Congo 1,250
Ivory Coast 250
Gambia 52
Ghana 227
Kenya 2,732
Malawi 2,586
Rwanda 987
South Africa 150
Tanzania 3,055
Uganda, 5,505
Zambia 1,296
Zimbabwe 119

6 Asia

Japan 97

7 Middle East

Israel 76

8 Oceania

Australia 1,168
New Zealand 100

140,000 150,000 160,000 170,000 180,000 190,000 200,000 210,000 220,000 230,000 240,000 250,000 260,000 270,000

179,000 deaths

270,000 cases

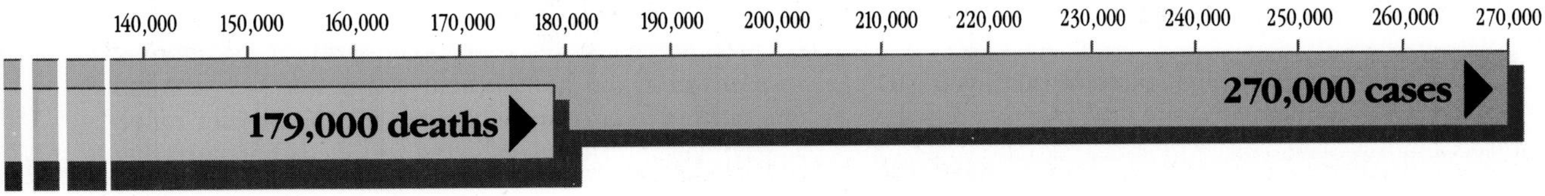

Exhibit 18.10

Sociology in the Media

Stunting Progress in Africa

AIDS has begun to undermine the fragile economies of Africa, to undo the work of training people to carry out the technical and administrative tasks that were once the preserve of their colonial masters.

Zambia is typical of the central African countries that are worst affected by AIDS. Every week brings news of another government official, another employee at a foreign embassy, who had a cough that would not heal. Then comes the inevitable announcement that the patient has succumbed to a "long illness."

A survey last year in Zambia's copper belt, the mining region that is the mainstay of the country's economy, showed that more than 68 percent of men who tested positively for the virus were skilled professionals. Trade unions have been urged to help prevent the spread of the disease, and businessmen have called in AIDS experts to address their meetings.

In Zaire, companies started to worry in 1983 about the prohibitively high price of sick pay, of pensions for workers' relatives, and of the wasted investment in skilled employees. The cost in lost work time through AIDS-related illnesses, coupled with the understandable lack of motivation among its victims, is incalculable. Even the funerals of AIDS victims—such rituals are important social events—are proving too time-consuming.

Although industry has been affected first—the infection rate in industrialized towns is far higher than in the countryside—agriculture is unlikely to be spared. In Zambia, the disease seems to be spreading outside the cities; in Tanzania and Uganda, it is already severe in some rural areas. "AIDS in Africa," says a report by the Panos Institute, an international information and research organization based in London, "does not threaten only individual lives. The survival of whole industries and national economies may be at stake."

African governments are generally willing to acknowledge only the tip of what doctors are convinced is an iceberg, and many have reacted half-heartedly to the AIDS crisis. The governments have little money to spare to fight a rare, incurable disease when their citizens are dying by the thousands from easily preventable ailments such as cholera, measles, and malaria. The budget of an average African hospital would fund a year's treatment for only a handful of American or European AIDS patients. In Africa, victims are often sent home to make room for people who can be cured.

The continent is also afraid of losing its valuable tourists. Kenya was outraged when the British Ministry of Defense banned visiting members of the Parachute Regiment from going to the coastal resorts of Mombasa and Malindi.

While the spread of AIDS may be slowing in the West after the onslaught of publicity about the disease, it seems to be as rapid as ever in parts of Africa. But the news is not uniformly bad. Rwanda, for example, is said to have the best AIDS education campaign in the Third World. Uganda, with the slogan "love carefully," has also been relatively open about the problem.

---

wives left husbands, and all normal social relationships stopped. When children in the streets saw the telltale signs of the plague, they sang, "Ring around a rosie!" That line meant that they saw a ring on the skin that surrounded a red spot—an indication of the onset of the disease. "A pocket full of posies" stood for the fresh flowers that plague victims carried to mask the stench of the disease. The verse ended with the apocalyptic, "All fall down." The Black Death ultimately killed half the population of Europe.

Despite its rather benign-sounding acronym, AIDS seems to have rekindled aspects of the plague mentality. The recognition of AIDS as a new disease phenomenon was somewhat like the process of the three blind men describing an elephant. All had touched different parts of the huge beast, and alternately suggested that it was like a snake (the trunk), a tree (a leg), and a pair of spears (the tusks). To those physicians who first observed an extraordinarily rare form of skin malignancy—Kaposi's sarcoma—occurring in a cluster of young homosexual men, it appeared that a new "gay cancer" had surfaced in the United States. To those who began reporting unprecedented instances of a peculiar form of pneumonia—also within the homosexual community—it seemed that they were encountering what the media later called a "gay plague." However, when reports began surfacing

Many Africans are convinced that the international publicity given to their outbreaks of AIDS, known in some places as "slim" because of the wasted appearance of its victims, is no more than a malicious campaign waged by racists. The unfortunate result of this conviction, strengthened by the explosion of infected African students from various countries, is that the African media devote much time and space to bitter arguments about where AIDS originated as well as to reports on the progress of the disease in the U.S., while virtually ignoring its increasingly serious impact at home.

It is true that there have been sensationalist stories in the West about AIDS in Africa, and that mistakes were made in the early days of research that gave incorrect and very high figures for the incidence of the virus in stored samples of African blood. It is also true that some scientists believe AIDS originated in African green monkeys.

But none of this seems to justify the secrecy and near-paranoia with which some African governments tackle, or fail to tackle, a crisis of potentially catastrophic proportions. Ignorance, rumor, and speculation are widespread.

The AIDS epidemic poses dangers even for those who are not infected by the virus, because it can reactivate dormant tuberculosis in its victims, causing the spread of that illness. Other infectious diseases common in Africa may also increase in incidence.

AIDS thus represents an unwelcome challenge to the creaking structures of government in Africa. The first step is to admit the problem—difficult when those countries that are honest are singled out by the foreign media for attention not because their problems are worse but because their information is accessible. The second step is to educate—again, not an easy task in countries with poor communications, many languages, a reluctance to talk openly about sex, and sometimes with unstable refugee populations.

Africa hates to be portrayed as a continent of disasters, but AIDS is a disaster that cannot be ignored, a disease that is not just killing people but also culling Africa's future leaders from the population. African governments are already cooperating in research that could eventually lead to a cure. If they do not also take the right precautions against AIDS, says Dr. Sam Nyaywa of the Zambian Ministry of Health, "It is possible that quite a large population in Africa will be wiped out—not by war or hunger, but by this deadly disease."

SOURCE: Reprinted from Victor Mallet, *World Press Review,* September 1987, p. 53. Reprinted with permission.

of cases with similar symptoms in groups as diverse as intravenous drug users of both sexes, heterosexual Haitian immigrants, hemophiliac recipients of blood clotting material, infants of affected mothers, and odd cases that failed to fit into any of the logical groups, it quickly became clear that AIDS was anything but a homosexual epidemic.

Although there have been far more serious epidemics, the initial association of AIDS with homosexuals created a population of "new untouchables." Opinion polls reflected changed attitudes about homosexuals,[47] and an editorial in a 1984 edition of the *Southern Medical Journal* went so far as to comment, "Might we be witnessing, in fact, in the form of a modern communicable disorder, a fulfillment of St. Paul's pronouncement: 'the due penalty of their error.' "[48]

As reports of AIDS spread and it became apparent that other populations were involved as well, irrational fear, paranoia, and discrimination surfaced (see Exhibit 18.11). Haitians and homosexuals have suffered employment and housing discrimination as a result of their association with the disease.[49] Children infected with the AIDS virus, even those who have not actually contracted AIDS, are shunned from classrooms, play groups, and foster homes.[50] Prisoners with AIDS are being segregated from other inmates, and in some jurisdictions, local jails

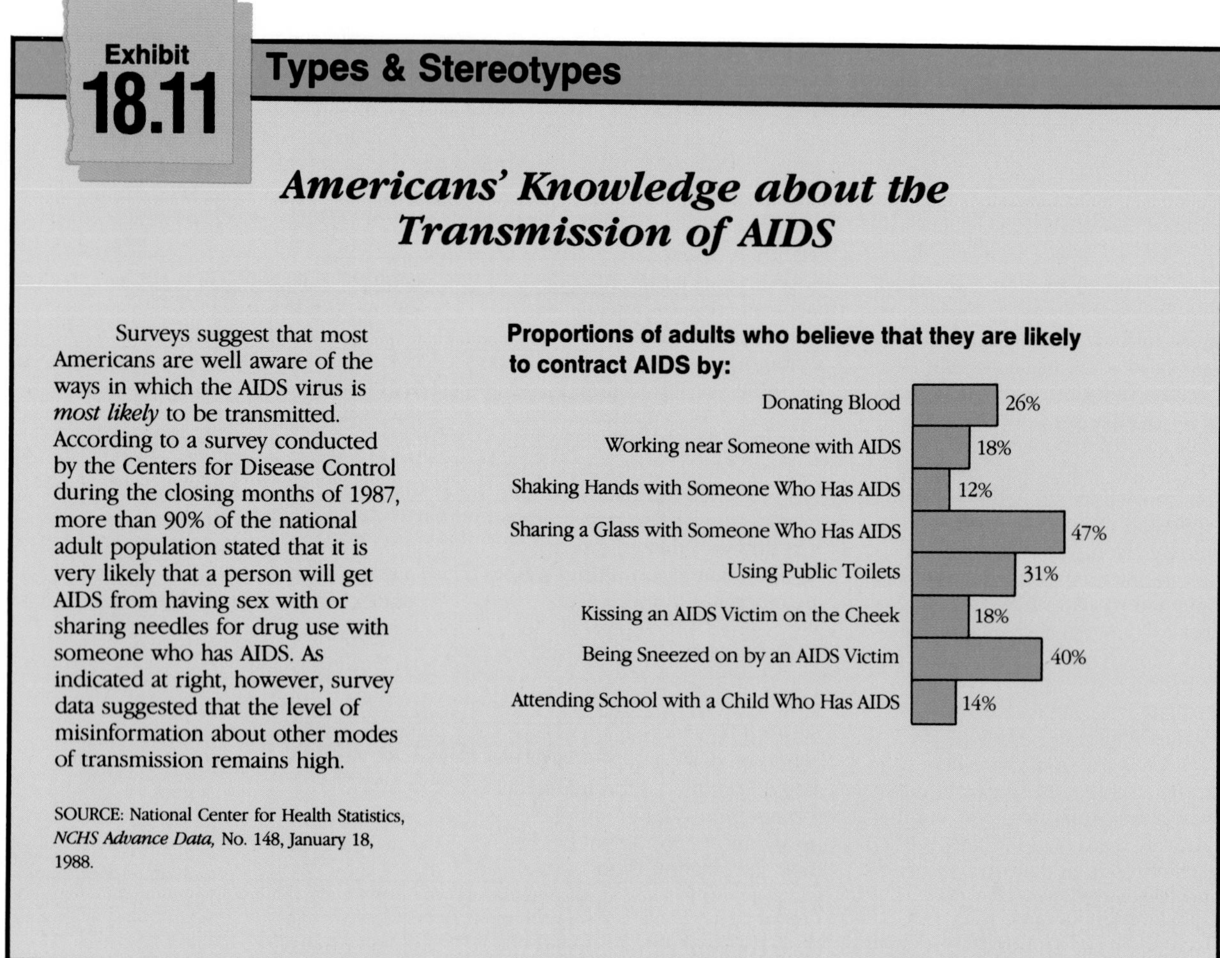

have "leper cells," in which AIDS victims are held.[51] Throughout the world, Africans, Haitians, Americans, and all others associated with the virus have become the targets of a new type of xenophobia, and the discrimination against entire population groups in several parts of the world.[52]

POPULATION AND APPLIED SOCIOLOGY

In a speech to the National Sheriffs' Association in 1984, Ronald Reagan noted that his presidency saw the first two-year-in-a-row decline in the rate of serious crimes since 1950. The reversal came, he said, once Americans turned away from "years of liberal leniency" and "pseudo-intellectual apologies for crime."[53] Perhaps that was so, but without even a glimmer of what might be the state of the nation as the result of a Reagan presidency, in 1977 the declining crime rate of the early 1980s had been predicted. Based on his projections of the makeup of the American population in coming decades, sociologist Jackson Toby of Rutgers University announced in 1977 that a reduction in serious crimes would occur by 1984.[54] He made his prediction on the basis of the fact that the number of 15–29-year-old males in the United States —the most crime-prone segment of the population— would be declining in the early eighties as the result of the falling birth rate that began in the 1970s.

Without question, the changing demographic composition of the nation was probably not the only reason for the falling crime rate, and one could easily argue that criminal statistics are so riddled with error and political manipulation that no one ever really knows for sure when rates of crime go up *or* down. Nevertheless, the incident points to the significance of demographic data—to the fact that such data can be used to forecast certain types of trends, based on the characteristics of populations already born.

Within this context, it is evident that the cold, dry statistics of demography take on new meanings when their implications for the social organization of society are examined. Thus, applied sociology has an important role in attempts to generate information and strategies to cope with population dynamics.

The primary agenda for the applied side of demography is *planning*. Consider, for example, some of the trends that will evolve in the United States in the years to come as the result of the declining birth rate. Without more children to follow the baby-boom generation, for example, the "aging" of the population will accelerate. By the year 2035, 1 out of every 5 Americans will be 65 years old or older, a situation that will put severe stress on Social Security and other retirement systems. By one estimate, in 2035 only 1.5 workers will support each Social Security beneficiary, as compared with 3.4 workers per beneficiary in the mid-eighties.[55] All segments of the economy and society that depend on youth for survival will be similarly effected. Already, for example, as the number of students decline, both public and private universities have had to increase their recruiting activities and budgets.[56]

Perhaps the greatest impact of the demographic changes in the United States will be on the labor market (see Exhibit 18.12, Figures 1–4). As population growth levels off—from a growth rate of 1.8% per year in 1980 to less than 1% by the mid-nineties (Figure 1), the number of new workers will decline significantly (Figure 2). Yet as the economy expands in the years approaching the twenty-first century, the number of jobs will increase (Figure 3). Instead of a solution to the unemployment problem, we will actually have a serious shortage of younger workers (Figure 4). Few occupations and professions will be unaffected. As the number of college-age Americans drops, for example, the number of highly educated employees will decrease. This phenomenon will probably cause shortfalls of scientists, engineers, and others in highly specialized technical fields. In fact, based on the work of demographers at the United States Bureau of Labor Statistics, predictions are already available as to the occupations and professions in which the largest growth will take place and the greatest need for workers will arise.

Researchers predict dire social and economic consequences for cities such as Miami in the twenty-first century as a result of the growing numbers of elderly citizens in our society. Applied sociology can make major contributions to solving such problems by generating information and designing strategies to deal with changes in population dynamics.

Exhibit 18.12

Applied Sociology

The Coming Era of Worker Scarcity

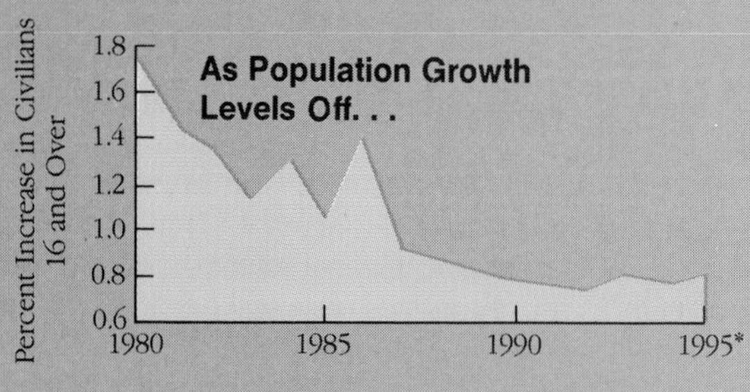

Figure 1

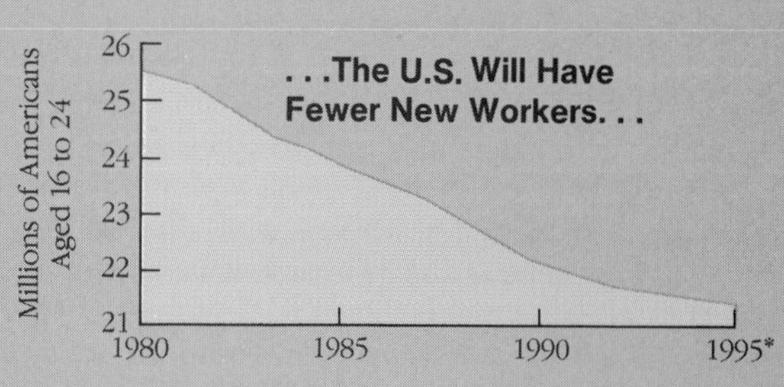

Figure 2

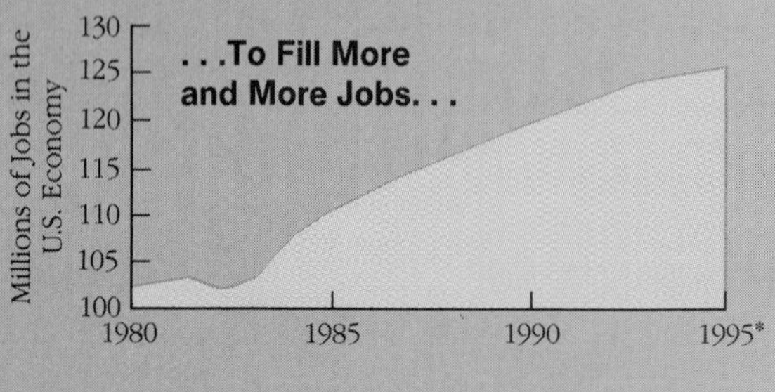

Figure 3

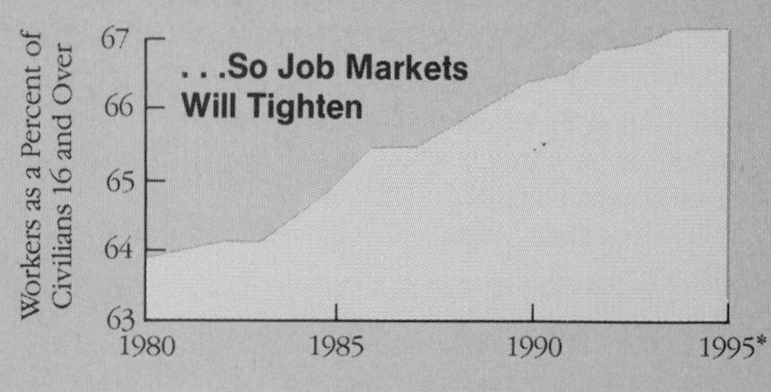

Figure 4

*Projected

Where the Jobs Will Be, 1990–2000

Largest Absolute Growth

Occupation	Number of New Jobs	Percent Change
Retail Sales	1,200,000	33%
Waiter/Waitress	752,000	44
Nursing	612,000	44
Janitor	604,000	23
General Manager	582,000	24
Cashier	575,000	26
Truck Driver	525,000	24
Office Clerk	462,000	20
Food Counter Worker	449,000	30
Nursing Aide	433,000	35

Fastest Growth Rates

Occupation	Number of New Jobs	Percent Change
Paralegal	64,000	104%
Medical Assistant	119,000	90
Physical Therapist	53,000	87
Physical Therapy Aide	29,000	82
Data Processing Equipment Repair	56,000	81
Home Health Aide	111,000	80
Systems Analyst	251,000	76
Medical Records Technician	30,000	75
Employment Interviewer	54,000	71
Computer Programmer	35,000	70

SUMMARY

Demography is the scientific study of human populations, and it is an important field because of the way that population composition and change can affect most areas of social life.

For millions of years, the population of the world remained relatively small. Approximately 300 million people populated the Earth in A.D. 1; their numbers increased to 1 billion by 1850. Since that time the population has expanded dramatically, primarily as the result of high fertility rates and declining mortality rates.

Population migrations have occurred throughout the history of humans on the planet. Hunting and gathering societies continually moved across the land in search of food. After the rise of agricultural settlements and the first cities, people shifted locations in search of subsistence or work, or in retreat from famine. International migration involves movement from one nation to another, and internal migration is the movement of a population within a nation's boundaries.

Global population growth is currently increasing at an annual rate of 1.7%, down from its peak of 2% during the early 1970s. Assuming that this downward trend continues, world population will nevertheless increase by some 3 billion persons by A.D. 2020. Much of this growth will be concentrated in the developing nations, and in many of these countries the people will face famine, malnutrition, overcrowding, and the deterioration of natural resources. In spite of the difficulties posed by such expansive population growth, cultural traditions tend to inhibit the use of birth control techniques.

Population size is not the only demographic variable of importance to social structure. Of almost equal significance is the age distribution, typically illustrated by the population pyramid. Another measure is the dependency ratio—the ratio of the number of people dependent on each economically active person.

Thomas Malthus is generally considered to be the father of population study as a field of scholarship. His much debated theory held that human populations tend to increase at a more rapid rate than the food supply needed to sustain them. By contrast, supporters of the Marxist view argued that population problems were a facet of the unequal distribution of resources in capitalist economies. While Malthus addressed the inevitability of population pressures and Marx examined the relationships between population, capitalism, and the distribution of resources, demographic transition theory was an attempt to explain the rates of population growth in Europe following the Industrial Revolution.

One of the more pressing concerns in the study of population is the growing AIDS epidemic. It is a disease that destroys or incapacitates the human immune system and is transmitted primarily through blood and semen. It is generally believed that the AIDS epidemic originated in Central Africa, and currently, the "high risk" groups in the United States include intravenous drug users, homosexual and bisexual males, hemophiliacs, the unborn and newborn infants of affected mothers, and the sexual partners of infected individuals.

KEY TERMS/CONCEPTS

age-specific death rates
AIDS
crude birth rate
crude death rate
demographic transition theory
demography
dependency ratio
doubling time
emigration
fecundity
fertility
fertility rate
HIV
immigration
infant mortality rate
internal migration
international migration
life expectancy
migration
mortality
population pyramid
zero population growth

DISCUSSION QUESTIONS

1. Life expectancy in some parts of the world ranges between 35 and 40 years. Given this, how would *you* reorganize your life and future plans if you knew that you had only 15 more years to live?
2. Given the rate of population growth in many developing nations, do you think that the importance of Malthus' theory of population should be reevaluated?
3. What would the implications of zero population growth be on the economic, occupational, and health dimensions of American society? What would be the implications of another baby boom?
4. Family planning and religion are sometimes at odds with one another. How is a government with the responsibility for the public welfare to deal with this issue without violating the rights of certain groups?
5. The idea of socially and physically isolating people suffering from certain illnesses is an ancient one. Leper colonies existed for this explicit purpose. What are the implications of isolating people who have AIDS? What about those who do not have the disease but have been exposed to it?

SUGGESTED READINGS

Dennis Altman, *AIDS in the Mind of America: The Social, Political, and Psychological Impact of a New Epidemic* (Garden City, NY: Doubleday, 1987). One of the few nontechnical books on AIDS, this volume, written in an engaging style, traces the history of the disease, America's reactions to the epidemic, and the stigma that AIDS victims suffer.

Landon Y. Jones, *Great Expectations: America and the Baby Boom Generation* (New York: Coward, McCann and Geoghegan, 1980). Both historical and contemporary, this analysis of the baby boom examines how it all started, its impact on America, and the hopes and expectations of those who are members of the baby-boom generation.

Thomas W. Merrick, "World Population in Transition," *Population Bulletin,* 41 (April 1986), pp. 1–51. This short pamphlet, published by the Population Reference Bureau, examines world population trends and their implications for living standards and economic growth.

Ben J. Wattenberg, *The Birth Dearth: What Happens When People in Free Countries Don't Have Enough Babies* (New York: Pharos, 1987). In this widely debated book, the author provides a detailed analysis examining the long-term implications of low fertility.

Dennis Wrong, *Population and Society,* 4th ed. (New York: Random House, 1977). This book is an excellent and short paperback that offers an overview of the study of population.

NOTES

1. Warren S. Thompson, *Population Problems* (New York: McGraw-Hill, 1953), pp. 55–57.
2. *1987 World Population Data Sheet* (Washington, DC: Population Reference Bureau, 1987).
3. *The Statistical History of the United States from Colonial Times to the Present* (Stamford, CT: Fairfield, 1965), p. 23.
4. *1987 World Population Data Sheet.*
5. William Peterson, *Population* (New York: Macmillan, 1961).
6. P. Neal Ritchey, "Explanations of Migration," *Annual Review of Sociology,* 2 (1976), pp. 363–404.
7. P. Neal Ritchey, "Explanations of Migration," pp. 363–404.
8. Charles B. Nam and Susan G. Philliber, *Population: A Basic Orientation,* 2nd ed. (Englewood Cliffs, NJ: Prentice-Hall, 1984), p. 182.
9. John R. Weeks, *Population: An Introduction to Concepts and Issues* (Belmont, CA: Wadsworth, 1978), p. 80.
10. K. Widmer, G. McClelland, and C. Nickerson, "Determining the Impact of Sex Preferences on Fertility: A Demonstration Study," *Demography,* 18 (1981), pp. 27–37.
11. *Population Today,* January 1986, p. 7.
12. Davidson R. Gwatkin, "Political Will and Family Planning: The Implications of India's Emergency Experience," *Population and Development Review,* 5 (March 1979), pp. 29–59.
13. Paul R. Ehrlich, *The Population Bomb: Control or Race to Oblivion?* (New York: Ballantine, 1968).
14. Paul R. Ehrlich, *The Population Bomb,* p. 17.
15. Robert H. Weller and Leon F. Bouvier, *Population: Demography and Policy* (New York: St. Martin's, 1981), p. 68.
16. G. E. Markle, "Sex Ratios at Birth: Values, Variance, and Some Determinants," *Demography,* 11 (1974), pp. 131–42.
17. Dennis H. Wrong, *Population and Society,* 3rd ed. (New York: Random House, 1967), p. 100.
18. Cited by Dennis H. Wrong, *Population and Society*, p. 101.
19. Cited by Warren S. Thompson, *Population Problems*, p. 20.
20. For a discussion of the population debate, see E. P. Hutchinson, *The Population Debate: The Development of Conflicting Theories Up to 1900* (New York: Houghton Mifflin, 1967).
21. Ralph Thomlinson, *Population Dynamics: Causes and Consequences of World Demographic Change* (New York: Random House, 1965), pp. 56–57.
22. See Neil W. Chamberlain, *Beyond Malthus: Population and Power* (New York: Basic Books, 1970); E. P. Hutchinson, *The Population Debate.*
23. See T. Bottomore, L. Harris, V. Kiernan, and R. Miliband (eds.), *A Dictionary of Marxist Thought* (Cambridge: Harvard University Press, 1983), pp. 378–80.
24. John F. Besemeres, *Socialist Population Policies: The Political Implications of Demographic Trends in the USSR and Eastern Europe* (White Plains, NY: Sharp, 1980).
25. Warren S. Thompson, "Recent Trends in World Population," *American Journal of Sociology* 34 (May 1929), pp. 959–75.
26. See, for example, Kingsley Davis, "The Controversial Future of Underdeveloped Areas," in Paul K. Hatt (ed.), *World Population and Future Resources* (New York: American, 1952), pp. 22–24; Philip M. Hauser and Otis Dudley Duncan (eds.), *The Study of Population: An Inventory and Appraisal* (Chicago: University of Chicago Press, 1959), pp. 93–96; Leighton van Nort, "On Values in Population Theory," *The Milbank Memorial Fund Quarterly,* 38 (October 1960), pp. 387–95.
27. Adlai E. Stevenson, *Speech Delivered before the United Nations Economic and Social Council,* Geneva, Switzerland, July 9, 1965.
28. Kenneth E. Boulding, "The Economics of the Coming Spaceship Earth," in Garrett De Bell (ed.), *The Environmental Handbook* (New York: Ballantine, 1970), pp. 96–101; Rene Dubos, *So Human an Animal* (New York: Charles Scribner's and Sons, 1968).
29. William Foege, "The National Pattern of AIDS," in Kevin M. Cahill (ed.), *The AIDS Epidemic* (New York: St. Martin's, 1983), pp. 7–17; Frederick P. Siegal and Marta Siegal, *AIDS: The Medical Mystery* (New York: Grove, 1983), pp. 68–103.
30. National Academy of Sciences, *Mobilizing Against AIDS: The Unfinished Story of a Virus* (Cambridge: Harvard University Press, 1986), p. 10.

31. Dennis Altman, *AIDS in the Mind of America: The Social, Political, and Psychological Impact of a New Epidemic* (Garden City, NY: Doubleday, 1987), p. 30.
32. William Foege, "The National Pattern of AIDS."
33. Cited by William Foege, "The National Pattern of AIDS."
34. Stuart E. Nichols and David G. Ostrow, *Psychiatric Implications of Acquired Immune Deficiency Syndrome* (Washington, DC: American Psychiatric Press, 1984), p. 4.
35. National Academy of Sciences, *Mobilizing Against AIDS*, p. 72; *New York Times,* November 21, 1985, p. A1.
36. Vincent T. DeVita, Samuel Hellman, and Steven A. Rosenberg, *AIDS: Etiology, Diagnosis, Treatment, and Prevention* (Philadelphia: Lippincott, 1985), p. 304.
37. Dennis Altman, *AIDS in the Mind of America,* p. 72.
38. Dennis Altman, *AIDS in the Mind of America,* p. 72.
39. Albert Camus, *The Plague* (New York: Alfred A. Knopf, 1947), p. 47.
40. Centers for Disease Control, *AIDS Weekly Surveillance Report,* August 1, 1988, p. 1.
41. *U.S. News & World Report,* January 12, 1987, p. 61.
42. *The Economist,* November 22, 1986, p. 16; *New York Times,* August 15, 1987, p. A12; *Time,* December 1, 1986, p. 45; *U.S. News & World Report,* January 12, 1987, p. 64.
43. *New York Times,* June 5, 1987, p. A17.
44. Thomas C. Quinn, Jonathan M. Mann, James W. Curren, and Peter Piot, "AIDS in Africa: An Epidemiologic Paradigm," *Science,* 234 (November 21, 1986), pp. 955–63; Thomas C. Quinn, "AIDS in Africa: Evidence for Heterosexual Transmission of the Human Immunodeficiency Virus," *New York State Journal of Medicine* 87 (May 1987), pp. 286–89.
45. *World Press Review,* February 1987, p. 57.
46. *Population Today,* June 1987, p. 4.
47. *New York Times,* December 15, 1985, p. 41; *USA Today,* March 26, 1984, p. 3A.
48. Cited by Dennis Altman, *AIDS in the Mind of America,* p. 13.
49. *Newsweek,* June 6, 1983, p. 95; *Newsweek,* September 23, 1985, pp. 18–23; *Time,* August 12, 1985, pp. 40–47; Wilmington (Delaware) *News-Journal,* December 8, 1983, p. A14. See also David Black, *The Plague Years* (New York: Simon and Schuster, 1986).
50. *New York Times,* June 17, 1984, p. 22; *Time,* September 23, 1985, pp. 24–26; *USA Today,* August 24, 1987, p. 3A.
51. For example, see *Miami Herald,* August 14, 1986, p. 1B.
52. *Newsweek,* April 6, 1987, p. 36; *Time,* November 28, 1985, p. 50; *U.S. News & World Report,* February 16, 1987, p. 25.
53. *U.S. News & World Report,* July 2, 1984, p. 11.
54. Honolulu *Star-Bulletin,* December 17, 1977, p. A10. See also Jackson Toby, "A Prospect of Less Crime in the 1980s," *New York Times,* October 26, 1977.
55. *U.S. News & World Report,* December 16, 1985, pp. 66–67.
56. *New York Times,* August 26, 1984, pp. F1, F6.

The World of Work: Prospects and Problems

In the 1980s the world of work has been transformed by a variety of social, economic, demographic, and technological changes. Change in the American work place has improved the lives of people in many occupations and professions, yet while thousands prosper, others suffer considerably. A few of the more dramatic contrasts illustrate the nature of the problem.

ITEM: The American economy is in a state of constant flux. During the second half of the 1980s, for example, the American automobile industry was emerging from an extended crisis brought on by escalating oil prices and foreign competition. The situation had been so severe that in 1980 Chrysler Corporation Chairman Lee Iacocca agreed to work for one dollar (plus stock options). Automobile plants were then modernized and American cars became more competitive. One measure of the subsequent recovery is apparent in the salaries paid in 1988 to the industry's chief executive officers: $2.4 million to Roger Smith of General Motors; $3.3 million to Donald Peterson of Ford; and $1.4 million to Lee Iacocca of Chrysler.[1] The down side of the restructuring involves the number of jobs lost through efforts to scale back production costs. Consequently, while executive salaries soared, some 200,000 assembly-line workers lost their jobs.[2]

ITEM: Social and economic change are reshaping the occupational activities of women in American society. Increasing numbers of women have abandoned their full-time roles in the home to join the paid labor force, introducing the need to balance the demands of their work against those of their roles as wives and mothers. This trend has brought on a variety of practical problems. Over half of all women with young children now have jobs. The fact that many are single parents has created an unmet need for suitable child-care facilities. And despite the influx of women into the world of paid work, their average income lags behind that of men.

ITEM: The computer revolution has touched almost every aspect of society, including the creation of new occupations in the design, manufacturing, sales and distribution, servicing, programming, and operation of computers, both large and small. While many of these new positions provide excellent career opportunities for workers, this story also has another side. Consider, for example, the operators of the computer terminals that handle airline reservations. While the computer keeps track of schedules, seats, and fares, it also keeps track of the operators. The computer records when they answer calls and when they appear to be away from their stations. They may take only 11 seconds between calls and cannot spend more than 109 seconds with any individual caller. Most importantly, operators are permitted 72 minutes away from their terminals during an 8.5 hour shift. The computer assigns points if operators exceed these limits and keeps a running total that determines whether employees keep their jobs; an accumulation of 37 points means dismissal.[3]

What these cases suggest is that while the future of work holds great promise for many workers, problems will persist for others. Income discrepancies separate workers in different parts of the system, and many are constantly threatened with unemployment. As new jobs are created, old ones are either transformed or eliminated. Although computers and robotics may be freeing some people from the drudgery of unrewarding employment, other workers have either lost their jobs or have been pushed into tasks that eliminate opportunities to use their skills and abilities.

Within this context, work is a complex social activity that may be analyzed within the sociological perspective in a number of different ways. Individual jobs, for example, are *social roles.* Moreover, they are linked to many other social roles. Workers have regular interpersonal relations with a variety of individuals—customers, clients, co-workers, superiors, and subordinates. Employees must be able to satisfy their superiors, please their customers or clients, supervise those who work for them, and get along with co-workers if they are to succeed in their careers. The nature of these relationships—whether they are cooperative or conflictual—shapes the way jobs are performed and influences how people feel about their work and themselves.

Workers also are members of *social groups.* Those doing the same type of work join together to form unions or associations for the sake of improving the conditions of their employment. Furthermore, although labor unions and professional associations may be quite different in many ways, they nevertheless have one feature in common: they act to protect and enhance the interests of their members.

In short, the world of work is an area of considerable sociological significance, and as is demonstrated in this chapter, it is fully tied to the many changes that characterize contemporary life in industrial society.

THEORETICAL APPROACHES TO THE SOCIOLOGY OF WORK

From the vantage point of sociological theory, both the functional and conflict perspectives are of significance for exploring the role of work in modern society. The functionalist view focuses on society as a system. It seeks to understand those social arrangements that contribute to group solidarity, and it notes the social institutions that evolve to meet changing societal needs. The conflict approach, in contrast, calls attention to competition among groups. Both perspectives are useful in the study of work and occupations.

Durkheim and Functionalism

Not unexpectedly, French sociologist Emile Durkheim was among the first researchers to apply the functionalist approach to the world of work. For Durkheim, the most important dimension of society was the degree of specialization within it—what he called "the division of labor." He believed, furthermore, that historically societies have moved from a low to a high degree of specialization in work, a trend that is most evident in the contrasts that separate industrial from agricultural societies.[4] In fact, Durkheim delineated societies on the basis of how far they had progressed on the division of labor question. Earlier societies, those based on small-scale agriculture, depended on what he called *mechanical solidarity,* typified by a limited degree of specialization. In these societies almost every family was a self-contained unit that produced its own food, clothing, and tools. People were held together by bonds that emerged from their primary institutions—the family and religion.

The other type of society differentiated by Durkheim was that based on what he called *organic solidarity.* Relations were less intimate; people were tied together by contracts, common interests, and social symbols. It was Durkheim's belief that the second type always evolved from and succeeded the first as the degree of specialization—the divison of labor—increased. This evolution occurred because it was functional for society. Every urban dweller, for example, is dependent upon a whole array of other individuals who provide needed goods and services. Thus, each person always depends on many others. This interdependence functionally links all members of a society together through their work; each job is a vital aspect of the functioning and survival of the total society. From Durkheim's functionalist view, occupational interdependence would counteract the disruptive social trends caused by urbanization and industrialization, and divisions based on race, ethnic background, and gender.

Contemporary functionalists point out that social roles and institutions evolve to fill social needs as change creates gaps that must be filled, either by inventing new roles or by borrowing substitutes from other societies. Occupational roles are a good example of this process, for they are constantly emerging and vanishing. Within the last few years, for example, American society has adopted the role of the nanny, a fixture in British society for many decades. A nanny is simply a person hired to care for children in the home, and in generations past the role focused on the etiquette and demeanor expected of children in wealthy families. The American version of the job developed during the mid-eighties in response to the need for quality child care. The influx of upper-middle-class women into the paid labor force created a void not filled by schools or day-care centers. Although working-class families traditionally depend upon friends and relatives to care for their young children, this arrangement has never been widely utilized by the more affluent middle class. Rather, the tendency among middle-class families is toward professionalized care. In response, nanny schools began to appear during the early part of the decade, and by 1987 nearly two dozen such schools were scattered across the country. As a reflection of the expectations of middle-class parents, the curricula emphasize courses in infant care, child psychology, and nutrition, rather than discipline. Not unexpectedly, the supply of qualified nannies in the United States is limited.* Waiting lists are long, and today's expert nanny is able to command a substantial salary.[5]

Occupations: Competition and Conflict

As we have seen in earlier chapters, the conflict perspective envisions society in a competitive context, with individuals and groups contending for social status, income, and influence. Work, like other social arrangements, can easily be viewed from this perspective because every occupation is at the center of a network of groups, each with different goals, interests, and points of view.[6] Members of particular occupations often join together to improve their wages and working conditions. The most visible of these groups are the formal trade unions and professional associations. The American Medical Association, the National Association of Teachers, and the Teamsters' Union are among the largest.

The competition and conflict associated with the world of work are readily evident in many ways. The job interview reflects the competitive nature of the world of work; several individuals typically are contending for any given job. The history of work in industrial societies is marked as well by disputes between workers and managers, and between unions and corporate officials. Similarly, the malpractice crisis pits professionals against clients.

Competition and conflict can be more subtle. Consider, for example, how a pharmacist is impacted by outside groups. Governments charged with protecting the public set rules for the handling and dispensing of drugs; pharmaceutical companies in the pursuit of profits set prices for the products they supply; customers concerned with quality care are a potential source of malpractice suits; hospitals and clinics that employ pharmacists seek to impose work rules in the interests of efficiency; and physicians in their role as primary health-care providers seek to control the writing of prescriptions.

Competition with Employers

Historically, workers and managers have long been at odds over wages and working conditions. Employers typically have sought to increase output and profits by

This 1912 strike shows that in the early stages of industrialization, workers and employers were often in open conflict.

*A more recent development has been the *manny*—the employment of a man for the family that wants a male role model for its children.

SOCIAL INDICATOR

Labor Strikes, 1960–1988

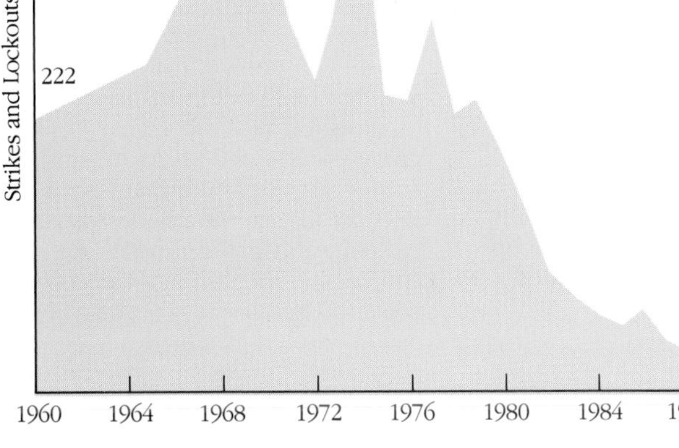

Source: Bureau of Labor Statistics, 1988.

paying the lowest possible wages, while workers have fought for higher wages and more inclusive fringe benefits. Factors other than wages are also contested—hours, working conditions, and safety and health matters.

Workers use the work stoppage as a major weapon in fighting for beneficial change. Strikes by printers over wages and working conditions were recorded as early as 1539 in France. Tailors in New York City in 1768 called the first known work stoppage in the American colonies. Employers battled back by using nonunionized workers, who were willing to work for lower wages.

Malpractice

Malpractice is a direct and open form of conflict that appears to be occurring with greater frequency in recent years. In the malpractice suit, victims must prove that appropriate standards of practice were not used, and that they have suffered damage (physical or economic, and sometimes emotional) as a direct result. Both claims are difficult to prove, and as a result, only a few of the complaints that are filed ever reach trial (see Exhibit 19.1).

Competition among Professions: Boundary Disputes

Competition for the right to perform certain tasks results from the fact that no absolute boundaries delineate the work of different professional groups. Conflicts involving the limits of work tasks and roles are known as **boundary disputes.** Such conflicts typically are based on different professions' beliefs as to which group is better qualified, but often the issue also involves money and social status. Unlike work stoppages or strikes, which take place in the streets, contests among professionals are usually fought in the courts and the legislatures.

The long-standing dispute between physicians and other groups for the right to prescribe drugs is a prime example of a boundary dispute.[7] In the American colonies, the prescribing, compounding, and selling of drugs were done by both physicians and pharmacists (then called apothecaries). By the early nineteenth century, however, the medical profession had begun to exclude pharmacists from prescribing drugs by convincing state legislatures that physicians were better qualified to prescribe for medical needs. By the 1920s a clear division of labor had been established, with physicians enjoying a legal monopoly over the prescription of drugs. Although they could, they did not sell drugs, leaving that to the pharmacist. In the last decade the dispute has resurfaced, and once again the rules are being modified. The revolution in the technology of drugs, combined with the nature of pharmacy education and specialization in the medical profession, now make the pharmacist the most knowledgeable individual when it comes to questions of which drugs to prescribe. Clinical pharmacists in hospitals currently act as advisors and consultants to physicians, which is just short of actually having the right to prescribe.[8] In 1986, Florida pharmacists actually won the legal right to prescribe certain drugs.[9] On the other side of the conflict, some physicians sell prescription drugs out of their offices, thus infringing on the territory of druggists. Pharmacists have lobbied state legislatures, and in 1987 they were able to impose limits on doctors' rights to sell drugs in at least six states.[10]

WORK AND SOCIAL EXPECTATIONS

The American work place has changed, and so too have individuals' expectations about *their* work. People want many things from their jobs. Money is important, but so are the less tangible rewards such as opportunities for personal growth and development. Other considerations are also involved. In 1986, for example, high-school seniors from across the United States were asked to rate the importance of a number of job characteristics. Their answers reflected the same array of needs that research has suggested apply to workers in the society as a whole—financial rewards, social relationships, social value, social prestige, and advancement.

Exhibit 19.1

Sidelights on American Culture

The Malpractice Crisis

The consumer movement is a powerful force in American society. Activist Ralph Nader became an American folk hero when he initiated the consumer movement years ago, and over the years efforts on behalf of consumer protection and product safety have had numerous successes. A recent chapter in the same vein involves the proliferation of medical malpractice suits filed by patients who feel that their care was inappropriate or otherwise inadequate. In 1985, for example, some 40,000 lawsuits were filed against physicians in the United States, a 300% increase over the previous decade.

The legal right to bring suit is not new. However, the number of malpractice suits, jury awards, and responses to the phenomenon is unprecedented. Physicians are not the only professionals who are at risk. Educational malpractice suits have been filed against teachers for allegedly failing to provide students with basic skills. Architects have found themselves in court for improperly designed buildings. Malpractice has even approached the pulpit; a clergyman was sued because a young man he had counseled eventually committed suicide. Jury awards in malpractice cases range from thousands to millions of dollars. Not surprisingly, these awards have resulted in soaring insurance costs, with premiums doubling and tripling. Some physicians have been forced to curtail their practices, and in one city, a different sort of response emerged. Local physicians developed a controversial computer system that enabled them to review whether or not potential patients had ever filed a malpractice suit.

Malpractice has had direct and measurable effects on all professionals, but its most dramatic impact has been on health-care practitioners. Although the wider use of malpractice suits has given patients needed recourse against

The Price of Malpractice

The average award for the costliest suits:

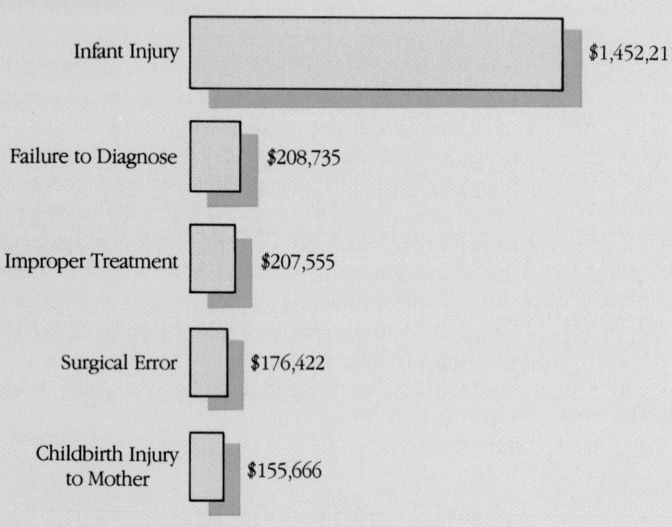

Financial Rewards

It should come as no surprise that money is an important reason why most people work. Aside from basic subsistence, people hope to earn enough money to support a family in a nice home with a few creature comforts. But to focus exclusively on the financial rewards of work is to miss the social significance of work in modern industrial society. Work fills many other needs and offers a wide range of dividends beyond the dollars earned. Most people report they would continue to work even if they had enough money to live comfortably.[11] The winners of big lottery jackpots generally remain in some form of paid work. The lure of work beyond any monetary need is explained by the meanings attached to it in modern industrial societies.

Social Relationships

Co-workers are an important part of any job. Not only do they depend on one another in getting the job done, but sloppy medical care, it would appear that, as many physicians have suggested, "the cure is worse than the illness." Most physicians have turned to "defensive medicine," with an emphasis on detailed record keeping and the increased use of tests and second opinions. This practice, quite understandably, has driven up the cost of medical care. Some physicians are leaving high-risk medical specialties, such as obstetrics. In fact, during 1986, 12% of American doctors cut out their obstetrical practice. In extreme cases services are totally eliminated. In Florida, where malpractice insurance rates are unusually high, a number of hospitals have actually closed their trauma units.

It is increasingly difficult to ascertain who is to blame for the problem. Physicians blame attorneys, claiming that they provoke malpractice suits in hopes of winning large contingency fees. Ralph Nader's Public Citizen Group claims that the cause of the malpractice crisis is the failure of the medical profession to discipline incompetent performance. Some patients may be at fault for viewing malpractice suits as a way of getting rich quickly. Other analysts criticize the juries that hand down large awards. Regardless of the source of the problem, what the malpractice crisis really means is a decline in the availability of health care for many segments of the population.

Rising Rates

These are malpractice insurance premiums charged in Dade and Broward counties by the Physicians Protective Trust Fund, the largest insurer of South Florida doctors. Doctors in other Florida counties pay one-half to three-fourths these rates, depending on the company.

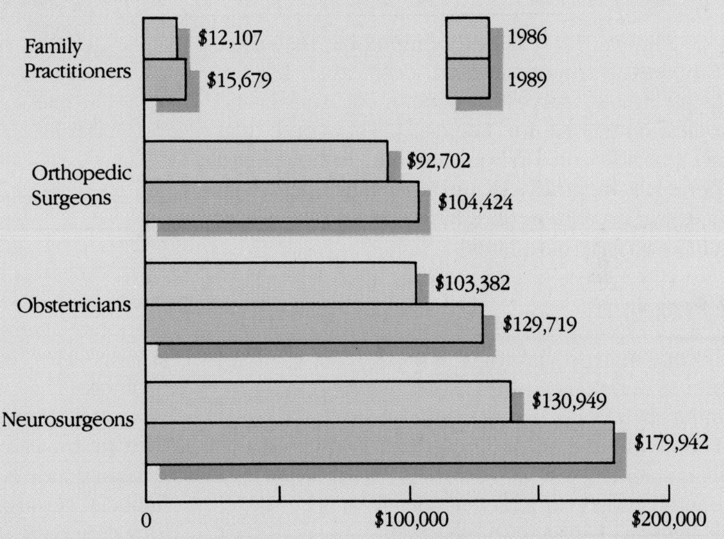

SOURCES: *ABC News*, "Medical Malpractice," May 13, 1985; *Miami Herald*, December 9, 1986, p. 3A; *Newsweek*, February 17, 1986, p. 75; *USA Today*, November 17, 1986, p. 3A; Wilmington (Delaware) *News-Journal*, April 3, 1985, p. 15A.

work-based friendships often extend beyond the office doors or factory gates. Studies have demonstrated repeatedly that local bars are often an extension of the work place, where people congregate on a regular basis to enjoy a drink and friendly conversation. While sports and current events may be discussed, the dominant theme is usually work, and the reason is quite simple: only people who share the same work situation can fully appreciate its problems and prospects. Teachers, for example, may use the informal setting of a nearby tavern to share strategies for handling unruly students,[12] while police officers may meet at the saloon across the street to compare tactics for dealing with domestic disputes.[13]

Social Value

Most young adults entering the American work place look forward to embarking on their careers, not only for the things that their salaries will buy, but also for the importance that their work has for society. And this feeling seems to apply to almost everyone, not just to those in the performing arts, politics, and health care.

SOCIAL INDICATOR

Attitudes toward Work

U.S. High-school Seniors Rate "Very Important" Job Characteristics:

Interesting Work	87%
A Chance to Earn a Great Deal of Money	58
A Chance to Make Friends	53
Worthwhile to Society	41
High Social Status	32

Source: Adapted from Jerald G. Bachman, "An Eye on the Future," *Psychology Today,* 21 (July 1987), pp. 6–8. By permission.

SOCIAL INDICATOR

Winning the Lottery

As of 1986, more than 1,200 people had won $1 million or more in a lottery. A survey of a sample of them suggests the impact of their luck on their jobs one year after winning.

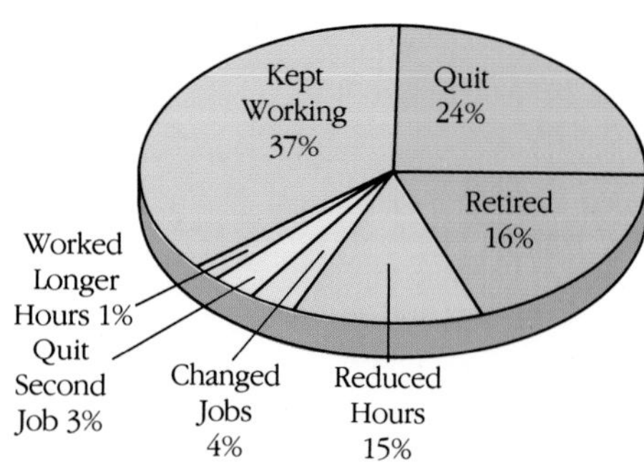

Source: Institute for Socioeconomic Studies, 1986.

Women prostitutes, for example, emphasize that their work, although disreputable and despicable by the standards of many, serves a number of social and psychological functions for society.[14] They note that prostitutes provide comfort to many men handicapped by inexperience, ineptness, or unattractiveness, and that the services that prostitutes offer have salvaged marriages that would otherwise have failed.

Social Prestige

People occupy many social roles in society, but as noted in Chapter 8, none seems to be more important in determining social prestige than is an individual's occupation. People judge their peers, friends, neighbors, and other acquaintances by the kinds of work they do. Consequently, people in jobs that society might dismiss as low in status will attempt to elevate the importance of what they do. For example, a grave digger once commented, "Not anybody can be a grave digger. . . . You have to make a neat job. . . . A human body is going in that grave. That's why you need skill when you're gonna dig a grave. . . . It's like a trade. It's the same as a mechanic or a doctor. . . . A grave digger is a very important person."[15]

Advancement Opportunities

Most workers are interested in opportunities for advancement—the chances of being promoted to higher positions as their careers progress. The value of promotions is obvious. They lead directly to other things that are important—more money (through pay raises), increased social status and prestige (a larger office in a better part of the building), and greater power (in the form of increased responsibility and authority). But promotions also have a value that cannot always be measured by dollars or titles. Promotions extend a form of public recognition. They are announced in company newspapers or marked by a ceremony or party. At the same time, promotions usually bring recognition from peers and co-workers, friends and relatives. As one corporate executive put it, "Money is not a motivator anyway. The reward we really control is the ability to promote."[16]

It becomes clear, then, that work involves far more than simply earning a living. It fills a variety of social and symbolic needs for people in complex societies. The financial rewards of employment are important because they define the style of life that workers and their families can enjoy, but the fact that most individuals would continue to work even if they did not need the money emphasizes how powerful the social and symbolic dimensions of working tend to be.

MAJOR KINDS OF WORK

Tens of thousands of diverse jobs and occupations are recognized by the government.[17] Each one is different, but they can be grouped into smaller categories based on the dominant features of the work. Each of the following groups—professionals, executives and managers, clerical workers, service workers, and blue-collar workers—has certain distinctive features.

The Professions: Self-regulation

The term **profession** is reserved for occupations based on extensive and specialized formal education, and licensed by the states. Law and medicine demand the most training. Law school is three years beyond the bachelor's degree. In addition, most law students spend another year of self-study preparing for the bar examinations. The training to be a physician typically takes almost a decade beyond college by the time medical school, internships, and residencies are completed. The requirements for such professions as nursing and pharmacy do not involve quite as much time, but they still demand more education than other types of work.

In short, professionals are *experts*. And because they are experts they enjoy a legal monopoly over their work. In the United States, for example, only licensed physicians may perform surgery, prescribe drugs, and certify births and deaths. Only a licensed attorney may represent another person for pay in a court of law or prepare certain kinds of legal documents.

In many ways the professions compose the occupational elite. A number of professions command extremely high financial compensation, far above that accorded other white-collar work. This is, of course, not true for all professions; nurses and teachers earn only average incomes. However, all professions *do* have very high levels of social prestige. Physicians, lawyers, dentists, college professors, scientists, engineers, teachers, and members of the clergy enjoy a high degree of public esteem.

A key characteristic of the professions is their emphasis on *self-regulation*. Medical and legal professionals are clear examples. Each group acting through well-organized and well-financed professional associations, has been able to win the right to regulate itself, free from outside intervention. Self-regulation includes authority to set the standards for membership, accredit training schools, examine applicants, establish professional norms, and enforce discipline. This system would appear to make sense, because the work is so highly specialized that only professionals seem competent to judge other professionals.

Analysts see two sides to the problem of professional self-regulation. On the positive side, self-regulation functions in the public interest. The professions are continually upgrading the quality of education and standards for admission. These measures help to guarantee that practitioners will be competent and that the unscrupulous will be weeded out. Professional associations also enforce codes of ethics that ensure that their members behave responsibly.

Alternatively, critics of professional self-regulation point out that such power may also be used for self-enhancement.[18] Economics are a powerful incentive. Because physicians, attorneys, and other professional groups have a monopoly over the services they provide, prices may be artificially high. Thus, in states where both optometrists (those who examine the eye for defects of refraction and prescribe corrective lenses) and ophthalmologists (physicians who specialize in the structure, functions, and diseases of the eye) perform eye examinations, prices are lower than in states where such competition does not exist.[19]

Executives and Managers: Organizational People

The people who run the vast bureaucratic apparatus of large-scale organizations are collectively referred to as "managers." **Managers** direct and evaluate the activities of workers below them in a bureaucratic hierarchy. Each managerial level has wider authority and broader responsibility than the level below it. At the lowest levels are *supervisors*, who oversee the work of the clerical staff or production workers. They generally have limited authority and are expected to assure that productivity is maintained. *Middle-managers* usually have authority over a larger number of workers. They are usually responsible for a specialized set of operations within the organization, as is reflected in such representative job titles as plant superintendent, production manager, or personnel director. At the top of the managerial hierarchy are the **executives,** those responsible for making policy for the entire organization—president, chief executive officer, senior vice-president.

The executive level is the most important rank of management. By virtue of their positions, executives have authority over all members of the organization. They formulate policies and make decisions that influence people, products, and organizations. A common image of corporate executives is one of efficiency and decisiveness. They are often pictured behind well-organized desks, isolated and protected from intrusions, studying lengthy computer printouts or pondering crucial long-term decisions. Yet the reality of the situation differs from the images rather substantially. Managing the activities of a large organization is a complex social process. Two elements of this task command special attention: one is the amazing number of people involved, and the other is the way that executives relate to these people.[20]

Interpersonal Networks

Large-scale organizations often have complex bureaucratic-looking charts that indicate that a handful of vice-presidents report to the top person—the president or CEO (chief executive officer). In actual practice, however, the best chief executives routinely violate this bureaucratic principle. Researchers who have followed the daily activities of chief executives found that those individuals deal with an extensive network of people on a regular basis. They have contacts that extend far down in the organization, and across the boundaries of the organization to bankers, customers, union leaders, stockholders, journalists, government officials, and executives in other firms. In short, they may deal with as many as a thousand people in the course of running a company. Each of these people affects the way the organization functions.

Interpersonal Relations

Probably the most striking characteristic of the executive workday is the amount of time spent talking and listening. Major executives typically work long hours—over 60 hours per week—and three-fourths of that time is devoted to meetings, phone conversations, chatting with people in hallways and elevators, and business discussions over lunch or dinner.

Virtually every conversation is seen as an opportunity to gather information. Executives are constantly asking questions, sometimes posing dozens of inquiries during a single brief encounter. Effective managers want to know what is happening in their organizations, and they depend on the people they come in contact with to alert them as to what is happening. The thing that distinguishes the successful executive or manager is the ability to sort through this mass of information and choose the items that require attention.

It should be pointed out here that not all of the conversations and discussions that managers and executives participate in focus on the functioning of the organization. Subordinates may want to share family vacation pictures. Customers may want to talk about baseball. A lot of humor also is injected into these activities—joking, teasing, storytelling. Such pursuits may seem to be a waste of valuable time, but actually they are very important for maintaining cooperative working relationships.

In reality, it is rare to find executives issuing orders to subordinates. Such situations usually occur only when a decision must be made quickly. In most cases executives prefer to suggest, convince, or persuade subordinates of a particular course of action. Clearly, they have the authority to decide, but seldom do. They are aware that issuing commands may accomplish a specific task, but it also creates hostility.

Some executives succeed, but others do not. Research conducted over a period of 30 years with many executives of the Sears Roebuck chain of retail department stores has identified several unsuccessful types, all of whom failed to master the executive role described above.[21] Perhaps the most obvious failures are those who push "too many buttons," as the saying goes. That is, they simply cannot cope with the complexities of running an organization. Because they have too much information to sort through, they flounder, incapable of separating the unimportant from the important. "Rudderless leaders," on the other hand, leave too much to their subordinates. Never taking full control of the direction of the organization, they let things drift. Failure also results from "undisciplined judgment"—a reliance on methods that worked in the past rather than trying new approaches. And finally, the "strong personality/weak administrator" executive failure types, who take charge and give orders. They seem to get things done in the short run but cause so many problems with subordinates along the way that the organization ultimately fails.

Executive Earnings

American executives are rather well paid. They earn more than executives in other countries. The average income, including salary, bonuses, and stock plans for leaders of the largest firms is well over a million dollars per year, with some individual salaries far exceeding the $10 million mark. In 1988 Michael Eisner, chairperson of the Walt Disney Company, earned a $7 million salary and an extra $32 million in bonuses. Frank Wells, president of the same company, was the next highest paid executive, with a total of $32,125,000. In view of such high salaries, many people often ask whether executives are really worth what they are paid (see Exhibit 19.2).

SOCIAL INDICATOR

U.S. Chief Executives' Earnings as Compared to their European Peers

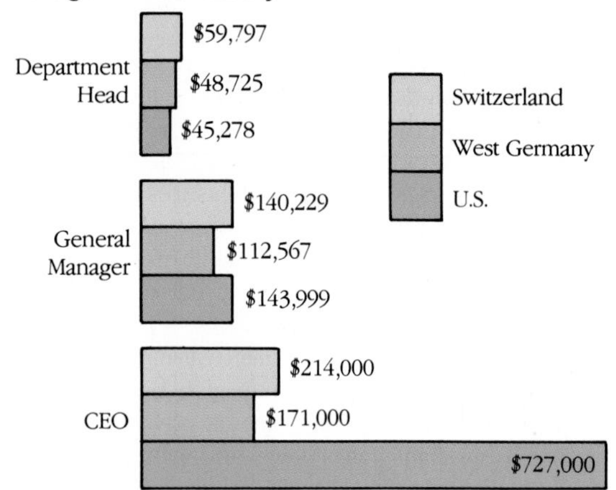

Source: Business International Corporation, 1986 survey of 2,000 U.S. and European companies of all sizes.

Clerical Workers: A Pink-collar Ghetto

Clerical workers—secretaries, bookkeepers, receptionists, timekeepers, file clerks, and key-punch operators—staff the offices of modern organizations. The work they do is vital; they manage the flow of information, maintain the records, and organize the activities of executives and managers. The demand for clerical work in modern industrial society is strong, increasing steadily during the twentieth century as governments and business firms expand.

Early in the nineteenth century, office work was among the best of jobs.[23] Offices were simple operations in those early days of industrialization, and clerks enjoyed a privileged position in the organization and in society. They were paid better than blue-collar workers, their jobs were cleaner and less hazardous than factory jobs, many had a great deal of authority, and they worked directly with the owners and managers. Hence, clerical work was a high status position, and attracted middle-class men. As late as 1880, men held 90% of all clerical positions.

Most clerical workers are women, performing routine, repetitive tasks.

In time, however, the conditions of work changed in many different ways, all of which served to reduce the desirability of clerical work. Offices grew larger and more impersonal, and clerks grew more distant from the owners and executives. Blue-collar workers unionized and successfully fought for better pay and working conditions, thus narrowing the gaps between themselves and clerical workers—in most cases surpassing clerical pay scales. A wide array of new office machines were invented and each worker began to perform a single, repetitive job—typing, billing, copying, or filing.

As clerical work became less attractive in the 1880s and subsequent decades, men began to abandon it. Gradually it became a female work domain. The transition was a natural one. Working women in those early years had few other options. They were excluded from managerial and professional jobs (except teaching and nursing), and factory work was considered too dirty and dangerous for the "fair sex" (unless they were immigrants). By the 1930s women outnumbered men in clerical positions, and currently a majority of secretaries, bank tellers, receptionists, bookkeepers, and file clerks in the United States are women.

Today, social status of clerical work is only modest, and the pay rarely compares well with many blue-collar jobs. Most workers find their tasks neither challenging nor rewarding. Many report that they end up acting as an "office wife" to their male superiors—fixing and serving coffee, cleaning coffeepots, running personal errands, and getting lunch.[24] Probably the most frequently voiced complaint among clerical workers concerns the paucity of opportunities for advancement or promotion. Consequently, many people think of secretarial and other clerical occupations as part of a "pink-collar ghetto," forever separated from professional and managerial work, and with little or no chance of upward mobility.[25]

Service Workers: Support and Subordination

More than 20 million people in the United States in the 1980s could be classified as service workers—retail salespeople, fast-food servers, janitors, waiters and waitresses, barbers, housekeepers and other domestics, flight attendants, and numerous others. Each of these occupations involves personal contact between worker and customer. Many workers report that this is an uncomfortable and unpleasant arrangement. Because their jobs depend on satisfied customers, service workers must be

Exhibit 19.2

Research in Sociology

Are Executives Worth the Money?

"That's the American way. If little kids don't aspire to make money like I did, what the hell good is this country?"
—Lee Iacocca, commenting on his $20 million-plus income, in salary, bonuses, and stock options in 1986

Is *any* employee worth $30 million a year to a corporation? Or $10 million? Or even $1 million? This question is often asked by stockholders, union leaders, lower-level employees who receive considerably smaller paychecks, and consumers—the people who actually pay the company salaries. A union official argued in 1987 that "No one individual can be worth that much money to a corporation. . . . [It] sends a message of greed and complacency."

Some people feel that executives do deserve what they are paid. Among this group are some of the executives themselves, plus a few pay consultants who emphasize executives' efforts and abilities. When questioned about his multimillion dollar salary in 1984, for example, DuPont president Edward Jefferson was quoted as saying, "You wouldn't want to buy a minor league team to run your company, would you?" The effective leadership of a large industry demands dedication, hard work, experience, talent, and the ability to make decisions that involve millions of dollars and thousands of people.

Still, the question lingers. Is any executive worth a million dollars? Unfortunately, it is a question that cannot be answered through any type of rigorous scientific research, because it is a question that involves no more than simple value judgments. However, sociologists interested in the issue have posed a different sort of question, one that has generated some interesting insights into the nature of executive pay: "What personal, organizational, and market variables are associated with the levels of executive pay?"

Research conducted by Naresh Agarwal indicated that only two factors appeared to be significant to an understanding of the income levels of executive officers. The first was economic (profitability), and the second was organizational (the number of management levels in the company). The observed relationship between profit and salary was expected for two reasons. On the one hand, corporations raise salaries in years that they are profitable. On the other, bonuses are typically built into compensation packages. What all of this seems to mean is that organizations reward top executives and managers who are able to make money for their shareholders. In a sense, then, this would confirm the executives' own estimation of their importance to their firms.

The fact that salaries increase with the number of management levels is based on a more complex hypothesis. It seems that many corporations follow a social norm in paying managers and executives that dictates that people at each higher level must receive twice as much as those immediately below them. This equation apparently evolved because of the prestige and symbolic value attached to money in corporate cultures. Thus, the greater the number of organizational levels between executives and managers, the greater the discrepancy in pay between upper and lower management.

Studies such as this demonstrate how sociological research can explain certain matters. Whether any given executive is actually worth what he or she receives is still a value judgment. In 1986, *Business Week* analysts attempted to make this judgment by establishing a "pay performance index" for top executives in each of the nation's major corporations. The index was a numerical figure based on the relationship between an executive's cumulative salary during 1983–1985 and company shareholder returns during the same period of time. The lower the pay performance index, *Business Week* analysts suggested, the more each executive delivered for the pay received. As indicated in the accompanying table, such well-known executives as Lee Iacocca of Chrysler Corporation, An Wang of Wang Laboratories, and T. Boone Pickens of Mesa Petroleum were among those who apparently did the least for their pay.

Yet even this seemingly scientific analysis leaves much that is judgmental. Although the pay performance index may be accurate, it remains a sterile figure that fails to reflect the social and economic factors involved in executive performance. C. Edward Packer of Pan American Airlines, for example, who ranked third among those who did the most for their pay, was rarely praised by Pan

Am shareholders during the period in question. Although he managed to keep the airline from going bankrupt, he did so by selling off a good part of its assets. Moreover, during the year that *Business Week* computed its rankings, Pan Am lost in excess of $100 million and shareholders were still no better off. On the other hand, consider Lee Iacocca. He returned Chrysler from the brink of disaster amidst the economic chaos in the automobile industry brought about by high fuel costs and foreign competition.

SOURCES: Naresh C. Agarwal, "Determinates of Executive Compensation," *Industrial Relations,* 20 (Winter 1981), pp. 36–46; *Business Week,* May 4, 1987, pp. 53, 58; *USA Today,* April 25, 1986, p. 2B; Wilmington (Delaware) *News-Journal,* June 10, 1984, p. 1C.

Most for the Pay

Executive/Company	3 Years' Pay	Total Shareholder Return	Pay Performance Index
1. Floyd. D. Gottwald Jr./Ethyl	$ 1,685,000	288.7%	38
2. Joseph L. Jones/Armstrong World Inds.	$ 1,151,000	94.6%	42
3. C. Edward Acker/Pan Am	$ 1,425,000	113.8%	43
4. William J. McCune Jr./Polaroid	$ 1,131,000	83.2%	43
5. Philip Kramer/Amerada Hess	$ 1,410,000	14.7%	43
6. Lew R. Wasserman/MCA	$ 1,409,000	116.0%	45
7. Edward J. Noha/CNA Financial	$ 1,719,000	271.2%	47
8. R. Gordon McGovern/Campbell Soup	$ 1,879,000	19.6%	52
9. Frederick W. Smith/Federal Express	$ 1,249,000	63.3%	52
10. Philip E. Lippincott/Scott Paper	$ 1,954,000	166.4%	53

Least for the Pay

Executive/Company	3 Years' Pay	Total Shareholder Return	Pay Performance Index
1. Victor Posner/DWG	$12,739,000	−4.3%	820
2. T. Boone Pickens Jr./Mesa Petroleum	$31,729,000	40.2%	645
3. Edson D. deCastro/Data General	$ 9,999,000	128.3%	353
4. An Wang/Wang Laboratories	$ 5,340,000	−32.1%	317
5. John Sculley/Apple Computer	$ 5,223,000	−26.4%	317
6. Lee A. Iacocca/Chrysler	$17,585,000	173.1%	302
7. James F. Bere/Borg-Warner	$ 7,108,000	43.6%	271
8. Charles R. Palmer/Rowan	$ 2,057,000	−21.5%	271
9. William S. Cook/Union Pacific	$ 7,141,000	26.1%	259
10. John G. Breen/Sherwin-Williams	$ 7,163,000	111.5%	238

Source: Reprinted from May 4, 1987 issue of *Business Week* by special permission, copyright © 1987 by McGraw-Hill, Inc.

pleasant at all times. Yet customers can generate all types of difficult situations.[26] Workers are confronted continually with patterns of unpleasantness, having to deal repeatedly with complaints, drunkenness, belligerence, humiliation, and (in the case of women more often than men) unwanted sexual advances and sometimes physical abuse. Sociologists trace the origins of this conflict to the very nature of the social relationship between worker and customer.

American culture encourages customers to feel superior and to treat service workers as subordinates. Everyone *knows*, for example, that "the customer is always right." Moreover, many Americans think of these people as their own personal servants and expect them to cater to their every whim. Employers emphasize subordination and courteous response to the wishes of the customer. Workers are compelled to address people politely and to display fixed smiles as if they were part of their uniforms. Most do indeed wear uniforms and name tags. Customers, in turn, are well aware of the fact that they control the income of many service workers. Waiters, waitresses, and numerous others depend on tips to supplement meager wages. Customers also can always cause trouble by complaining to a worker's boss.

Service workers must smile even when customers are rude and unpleasant.

Blue-collar Workers: Deskilling and Displacement

Blue-collar workers are the laborers, operatives, and craft workers of complex industrial society. They operate machines and heavy equipment; drive trucks and make deliveries; assemble automobiles and refrigerators; make clothing and toys; repair bicycles and telephone lines; dig graves and fill potholes; erect buildings and factories; and pick fruit and harvest crops. Their skill levels vary, a factor that has a variety of implications for pay, prestige, and job security.

Unskilled laborers, at the bottom of the blue-collar pay and prestige scales, are employed at heavy physical work or routine repetitive tasks. Although this type of labor in one form or another has always been a part of organized society, the Industrial Revolution created a need for increased numbers of unskilled workers for the building of railroads and canal systems, and for factory assembly-line tasks. Unskilled laborers continue to be used in modern society, but only at the most menial of tasks—cleaning, moving stock, harvesting fields.

Industrialization also created a new category of blue-collar work involving the operation of complex machinery. A large pool of workers are needed to operate vehicles (trucks and bulldozers), run machines (lathes and stamping presses), and assemble products (automobiles, radios, and refrigerators). More than average skills are required for such tasks, resulting in better wages and benefits, as well as greater social recognition than that accorded unskilled workers.

The final segment of the blue-collar labor force involves the skilled trades, often called *crafts*. Skilled manual workers have always formed exclusive and elite groups. As early as the eleventh century they united to form *guilds* for the purpose of training apprentices and setting standards. Guilds included the entire range of manual workers: butchers, bakers, glovers, silversmiths, weavers, tailors, tanners, shoemakers, and printers. Later, blue-collar workers turned to trade unions as a means of mutual protection and bargaining strength. The skilled trades represent the aristocracy of labor, having the most prestige and earning the highest wages of all blue-collar workers—sometimes higher than those of white-collar, managerial, or professional workers.

Although the Industrial Revolution and the machinery it created increased the need for laborers in the construction and manufacturing sectors, they caused the displacement and deskilling of skilled workers. **Displacement,** the replacement of workers with machines,

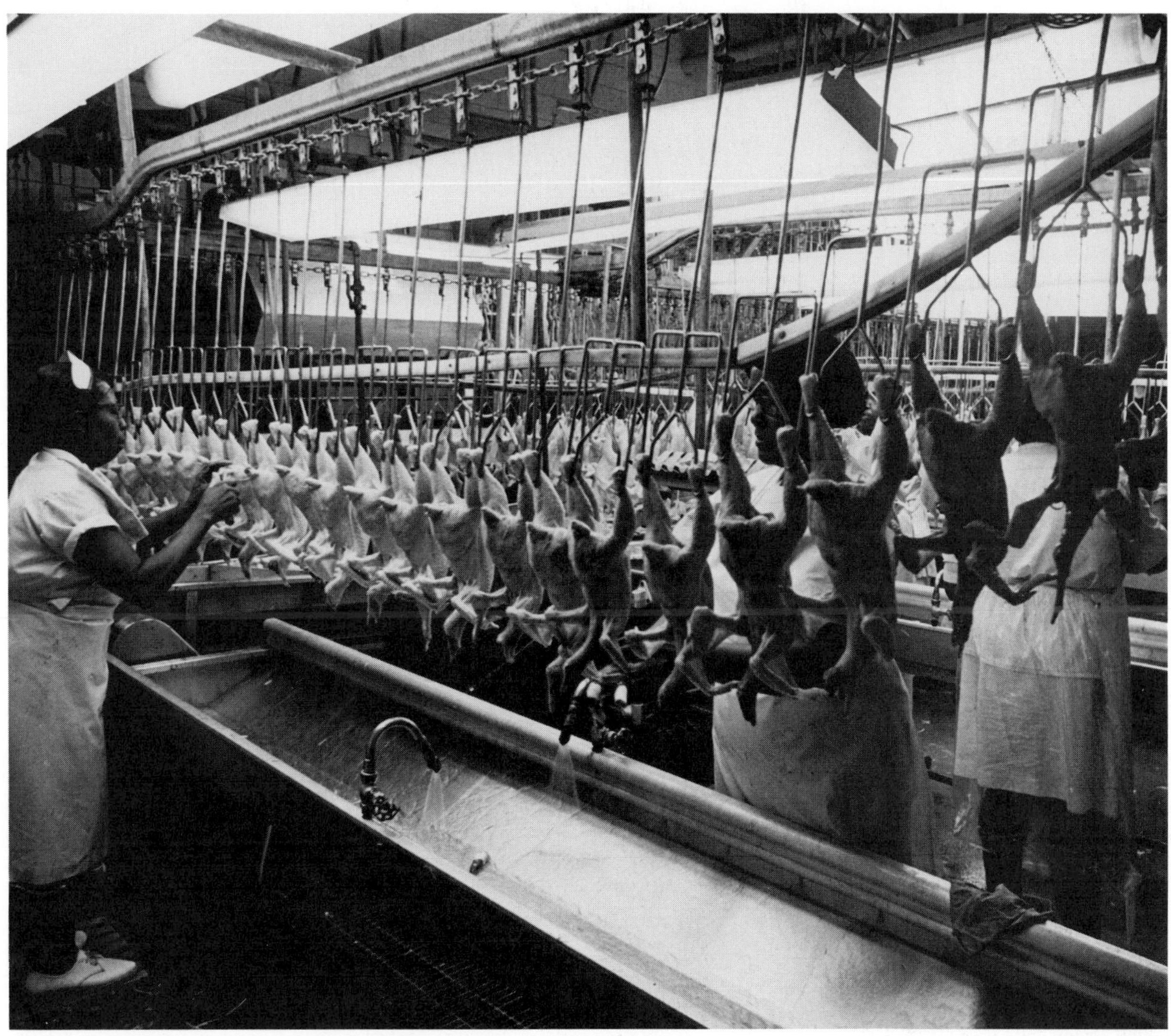

Cars or chickens can be processed on assembly lines. In either case, the work is not very challenging.

occurred in the early years of industrialization as sewing machines and other labor-saving devices were introduced. More recently jobs have been lost to sophisticated machinery capable of cutting glass, riveting sheet metal, or assembling a piano. Industrialization also initiated the **deskilling of work,** the reduction of skilled workers to machine operators or unskilled laborers. The implications of deskilling are readily illustrated by the experience of shoemakers in the middle of the nineteenth century.[27] As late as 1840, skilled cobblers still made most footwear by hand. Within two decades, however, the entire process had been mechanized, and workers who previously had made shoes had become operators of machines that cut, sewed, shaped, and polished shoes. The same thing happened to glass blowers, hatters, cigar makers, blacksmiths, and tailors.

Today's robotics, computers, and lasers threaten to displace a whole new array of skilled workers (see Exhibit 19.3). Printers who once set type and laid out pages are being displaced by advances in computer technology. At the offices of large newspapers reporters compose their stories at video display terminals, editors call the stories up on computer monitors to check and edit them, and the final copy is prepared for printing by computer software. Printers are unnecessary. This development, combined with changes in the structure of the industry, has produced steady declines in wage levels and the number of jobs.[28]

Exhibit 19.3

Case Study

Working with a Robot

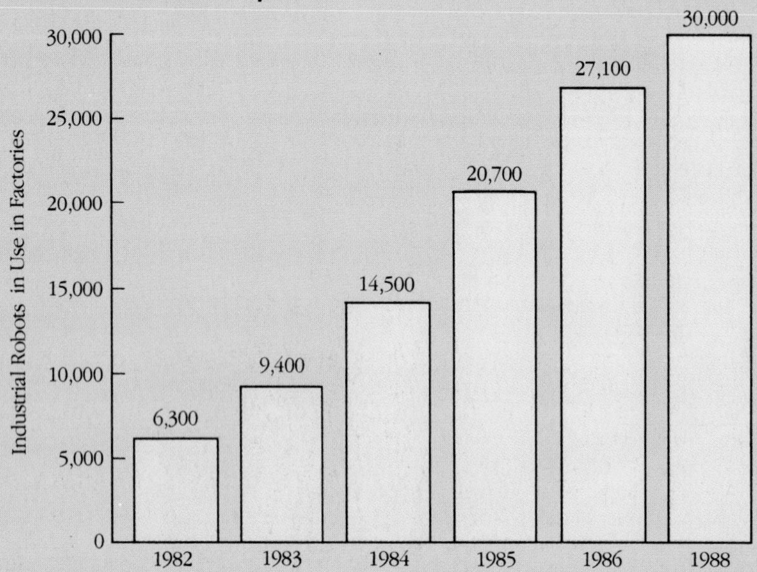

During the second half of the 1980s more than 20,000 robots were at work in factories and offices across America. By 1999, some 20,000 new robots will be added to the work force each year.

Employers claim that robots have the potential to improve the quality of life in the world of work by eliminating the repetitive and hazardous jobs that workers find unpleasant and employing the same individuals to build, repair, and maintain robots. Factories without workers are rare, but more and more people are confronting a new situation—laboring alongside a mechanical worker.

Social scientists have already begun to look at the effects that working with robots has on people, and their research has found both positive and negative impacts. Robots indeed reduce the physical demands of work, but working with machines increases the threat of injury. A worker in Japan, the world leader in robotics, was crushed to death by a robot in 1981. In some cases the introduction of mechanical workers improves feelings of job satisfaction. One survey of office workers, for example, found that 41% preferred a computer to a personal assistant. In other cases, feelings of alienation were evident. Numerous cases of machine sabotage have been reported.

Some interesting insights into how workers interact with machines have also become

Karl Marx, Work, and Alienation

The plight of blue-collar workers during the early years of the Industrial Revolution led Karl Marx to formulate an important insight about work in industrial society. It was the way that factory work was organized, Marx argued, that generated *alienation*—the general term he used to express a sense of loss of meaningful relationships. Industrialization severed workers' contacts not only with what they produced, but also with themselves and their co-workers.[29] The most important thing to understand about Marx in this context is that he believed that the impulse to work is a basic human trait. He felt that only through the process of working and the creation of physical objects could a person become a complete human being.

People become disassociated from the things or *products* they make because they no longer own them. Blacksmiths and potters, for example, could sell or keep what they made as they saw fit. Yet in the factory system workers do not own the cars or televisions or widgets they build—the company that employs them does. People are dissociated from the *process of production* because they no longer control it. The assembly line determines the speed at which they must toil and the supervisor instructs them on what to do and how to do it. Thus, mechanization strips workers of the freedom to use evident. In one factory a robot was added to a work group composed of forty people. All did the same tasks—shaping and polishing metal parts. Perhaps the most significant observation was that most of the workers viewed the machine in human terms. They gave it a name and attributed human characteristics to it. When it broke down, it was labeled as "temperamental." Workers also pitted themselves against their mechanized workmate in one-to-one competition to see who could produce more. Not surprisingly, the people always lost; the robot took no breaks and never went to lunch. In retrospect, perhaps the tendency to think of machines in personal terms is a part of American culture, a product of Hollywood's inclination to people its films with humanlike robots as in *Star Wars,* or androids as in *Aliens.*

The study also found that although some workers feared displacement by robots, most generally accepted that robots were more efficient than people, and that the machines held the potential for revitalizing American industry. Curiously, however, most industrial workers felt reassured that machines would never take over their particular jobs. Such a sense of security would appear to be unfounded, however, since almost all factory jobs can be automated.

Finally, the robot imposed new forms of stress on the factory workers. At first, the people had more work, trying to learn to operate the machine. Once they had mastered it, however, they became concerned with the potential for accidents from working near a nonhuman associate. Too, they recognized that the machine functioned more efficiently than they could. It is likely that these are the kinds of problems and stress that will confront all workers who toil beside machines in the factories of the next few decades.

SOURCES: Linda Argote, Paul S. Goodman, and David Schkade; "The Human Side of Robotics: How Workers React to a Robot," *Sloan Industrial Review,* 24 (Spring 1983), pp. 31–41; H. McIlvaine Parsons, "Automation and the Individual," *Human Factors,* 27 February 1985) pp. 99–112; Harvey Shaiken, *Work Transformed: Automation and Labor in the Computer Age* (New York: Holt, Rinehart and Winston, 1985).

their skills and judgment, and this process, in turn, alienates people from *themselves.* Without the ability to express themselves through their work, they cannot fully develop their personalities. As Marx put it, the worker "does not belong to himself but to another person." As they become alienated from themselves they become alienated from each other and thus, the *society* in which they live.[30]

Modern sociological research focusing on the various dimensions of alienation has tended to support Marx's views about the effects of work in industrial society. Studies have demonstrated that assembly-line workers show the highest levels of alienation. This conclusion would be expected, given the fact that they have the least control over their jobs. By contrast, those in managerial and professional jobs have more control over their work, and hence, express less alienation.[31]

Housework: Occupation or Servitude?

Almost three decades ago feminist Betty Friedan referred to the home as a "comfortable concentration camp" that imprisoned women in an endless round of dull, monotonous, and unrewarding work.[32] One of the most profound social changes to have occurred in the years

SOCIAL INDICATOR

How Much Are People Worth?

Reporter $66,435
Washington Post; *senior position, national staff*

Reporter $77,567
National Enquirer; *senior position*

Ticket Host/Hostess $18,103
Disneyland; 3 years' experience

Aerospace Executive R. Anderson $3,636,000
CEO, Rockwell International Corp.

Air-traffic Controller $44,430
O'Hare Airport; 2 years' experience

Airline Captain $125,000
Pan American Airways 747; 15 years' experience

Secretary $15,000
Unemployment office, Youngstown, Ohio; 3 years' experience

Attorney $25,000
Public defender's office, New Orleans

Attorney $150,000
Partner, 50-member firm, Kansas City, Missouri

Bartender $20,000
Sloppy Joe's Bar, Key West; including tips

Merger-and-acquisition Adviser $1,000,000
Major Wall Street firm

Model Christie Brinkley per day, $50,000
Typical guarantee

Movie-camera Grip per week, $1,960
Production assistant for Eddie Murphy's movie, "Golden Child," Los Angeles

Surgeon $67,940
National Institutes of Health; top salary

Telephone Lineman $32,189
Chicago

Playmate of the Month fee, $15,000
Playboy *magazine*

Plastic Surgeon $830,000
Beverly Hills

Police Officer $22,801
Pittsburgh; 1 year's experience

Football Player James Lofton $835,000
Wide receiver, formerly of the Green Bay Packers; not including bonuses

Gardener $36,000
Beverly Hills; self-employed

U.S. Senator $75,100
Washington, D.C.

Ferryboat Captain $34,052
New York City

Meatcutter $15,288
Esskay Co., Baltimore

Mechanic $31,472
United Airlines; 3 years' experience

Supreme Court Justice $104,100
Associate Justice Sandra Day O'Connor

Cruise-missile Assembler $18,770
San Diego

Fisherman on Scalloper $30,000
New Bedford, Massachusetts

Gravedigger $30,360
San Francisco

Interpreter $47,972
United Nations, New York City

Source: Adapted from *U.S. News & World Report,* pp. 62–63. Copyright © February 23, 1986, *U.S. News & World Report.*

since the publication of *The Feminine Mystique* has been the dramatic increase in the number of women entering the paid labor force. Yet even with dual-earner couples, *someone* must do the housework. Housework remains, as always, the largest single occupation in the United States for women (and a few men), with approximately 30 million people working full time, operating homes and caring for dependent children.[33]

For the better part of the twentieth century, the socially sanctioned division of labor in the home was clear, understood, and accepted. Husbands' responsibilities centered on earning a living through a paid occupation, while housework and child rearing were the domain of women. This arrangement was an overwhelmingly middle-class image, however, because upper-class households enjoyed the luxury of servants, and working-class women frequently also worked outside the home to supplement the family income.

Modern ideas of housework were first introduced early in the current century under the titles of "domestic science" and "home economics." Prior to then, housework was a haphazard practice. Cleaning was an annual event (in the spring); dirty clothes often accumulated for weeks between washings; and meals were basic. Young women were encouraged to devote themselves to home decoration, nutrition, complex food preparation, and scientific child rearing, but scrupulous cleanliness was valued above all else. The first systematic studies of housework were done in the 1920s and demonstrated that urban women were devoting over fifty hours per week to home and children.[34]

Domestic labor-saving devices (vacuum cleaners, electric irons and automatic washing machines), which began to appear during the 1920s, had fully invaded the American home early in the post–World War II era. Each invention was a potential time saver, yet the number of hours devoted to housework actually *increased* to more than 60 hours during this period. It appears that articles in women's magazines and the mass-market advertising media had raised the standards of cleanliness. Producers of vacuum cleaners exhorted women to seek out and destroy the slightest hint of dirt,[35] and the new range of household cleansers provided women with the tools to make their homes sparkling clean.

Early in the 1960s, a new configuration of social and economic forces began to reshape housework. The increasing educational attainments of middle- and working-class women rendered the routine and repetitive rounds of cooking and cleaning less satisfying. More women were entering the paid labor force, and even those who remained at home expanded their horizons into leisure pursuits or community-service activities. A new generation of technological advances had also been utilized to provide women with such additional labor-saving items as wash-and-wear fabrics, self-cleaning ovens, convenience foods, and microwave ovens. By the 1980s, standards of household cleanliness had declined "a great deal" for the majority of women, with the result that even full-time homemakers were devoting only some 25 hours each week to domestic tasks.[36]

Advertising in the 1950s glamorized the routine tasks of keeping homes clean.

The social changes associated with the emancipation of women in American society also have had an impact on housework, most particularly in the division of household chores. Women, whether they work outside the home or not, expect their husbands to share the household duties. And, an ever increasing proportion of men are doing at least some tasks in the home. However, it is difficult to generalize on this point, since considerable variation seems to occur on the basis of age, geography, and socioeconomic status.[37] On the whole, it would appear that women still do most of the household chores (men are least likely to do laundry and cooking) and most couples share child-rearing responsibilities.[38]

SOCIAL INDICATOR

Average Hours per Day Spent on Housework (married with 2 children)

	Employed Outside the Home	
	No	**Yes**
Food Preparation	2.3	1.8
Home Care	1.7	1.1
Washing/Ironing	1.4	0.9
Family Care	2.1	1.1
Marketing	0.9	0.9
Total	8.4	5.8

Source: K. E. Walker, "Household Work Time," *Journal of Home Economics* (1983). Reprinted by permission.

WORK AND FAMILY ROLES

The two most salient social roles that people occupy in contemporary society focus on work and the family. The two cannot be separated, even under the best of circumstances. The joys and frustrations experienced at home always seem to carry over to the job, just as disappointments and successes at work influence family relationships. Because both roles are so important and so time consuming, one of the greatest challenges facing people is the need to somehow balance the demands of

SOCIAL INDICATOR

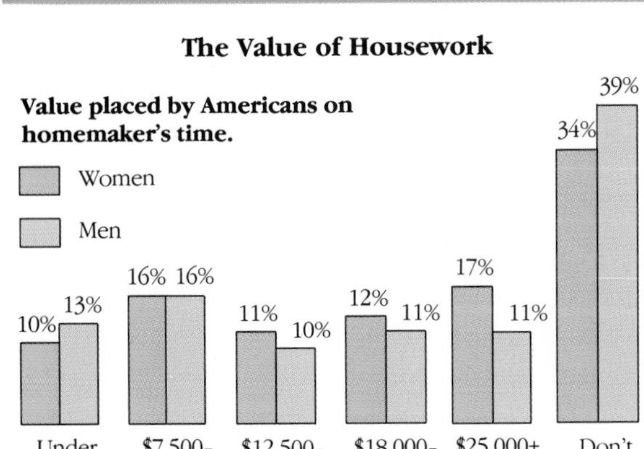

Source: 1985 Virginia Slims American Women's Opinion Poll, survey of 3,000 women and 1,000 men.

the two. A recent survey reveals that a majority of people admit to having problems handling both work and family roles. Those having the most problems were single mothers (84%), followed by single fathers (77%), married mothers (77%), and married fathers (40%).[39]

Single Parents and Work

It is not surprising that single parents face the most complex problems in balancing work and family roles, for they have complex roles to manage on their own. They must satisfactorily perform their jobs, care for their children, and keep house. Research has suggested that when conflicts emerge, it is the job that almost invariably suffers. One recent study found that child-care problems caused absenteeism and unproductive time on the job. More specifically, some 40% of single parents had taken time off from work to care for a sick child or similar matter, while others were often late because of the need to deliver children to school.[40]

The problems of being a working single parent are not simply a matter of time lost from work. Many women are forced into part-time or low-paying jobs because such positions offer the advantage of flexible hours. Others refuse promotions and better positions because they fear the negative impact increased responsibilities may have on their families.

Men and women confront alternative sets of problems because they have grown up in a society that continues to separate male and female social roles. Men are at a disadvantage in child rearing because their socialization experiences generally have not prepared them for the everyday routine of caring for, nurturing, supervising, and directing young children.[41] By contrast, women's socialization experiences emphasize their primary responsibility to family obligations, a phenomenon that is likely to produce feelings of guilt about time devoted to work at the expense of that spent with children.[42]

Families and Dual Careers

As noted earlier in this chapter, the division of housework tasks is often a source of dissension within many households, with wives generally expecting far more sharing than husbands are prepared to offer.[43] This issue is a serious one, but other more fundamental problems also are produced by the participation of husband and wife in the paid labor market.

A major difficulty involves the problem of career priorities. It is not uncommon for couples to face a serious dilemma when the career of one impinges on that of the other. The most common situation involves one partner being transferred to another location. It may be a major career move for that individual, but for his or her partner it means starting over in some other place. Research has shown that when couples are confronted with this situation, women are more likely to make accommodations to facilitate their husbands' careers.[44]

Two factors combine to explain this accomodation. First, the persistence of traditional gender roles dictates that a husband's career is more important. The second consideration is the more practical matter that on the average, men have better jobs, more career opportunities, and higher salaries than women. The loss of the wife's job causes less of a financial burden. Of course, not all families are forced to make this choice, and some men do forego transfers so as not to disrupt their wives' careers.[45]

A second major difficulty in the dual-career family involves the undermining of the husband's role. Socially defined gender roles are a powerful force in society. They may be changing, but the process has been very slow. A long-surviving aspect of the husband's role in the family has been the expectation that financial responsibility is *his*. Two incomes produce opportunities for a better life-style, and many husbands approve of their wives' working and make an effort to help with household chores. And yet, a dilemma persists. Some husbands may have difficulty with the idea of being one of two breadwinners in the family. They interpret this as a form of personal failure, which often manifests itself in feelings of poor self-esteem.[46] The situation becomes even more

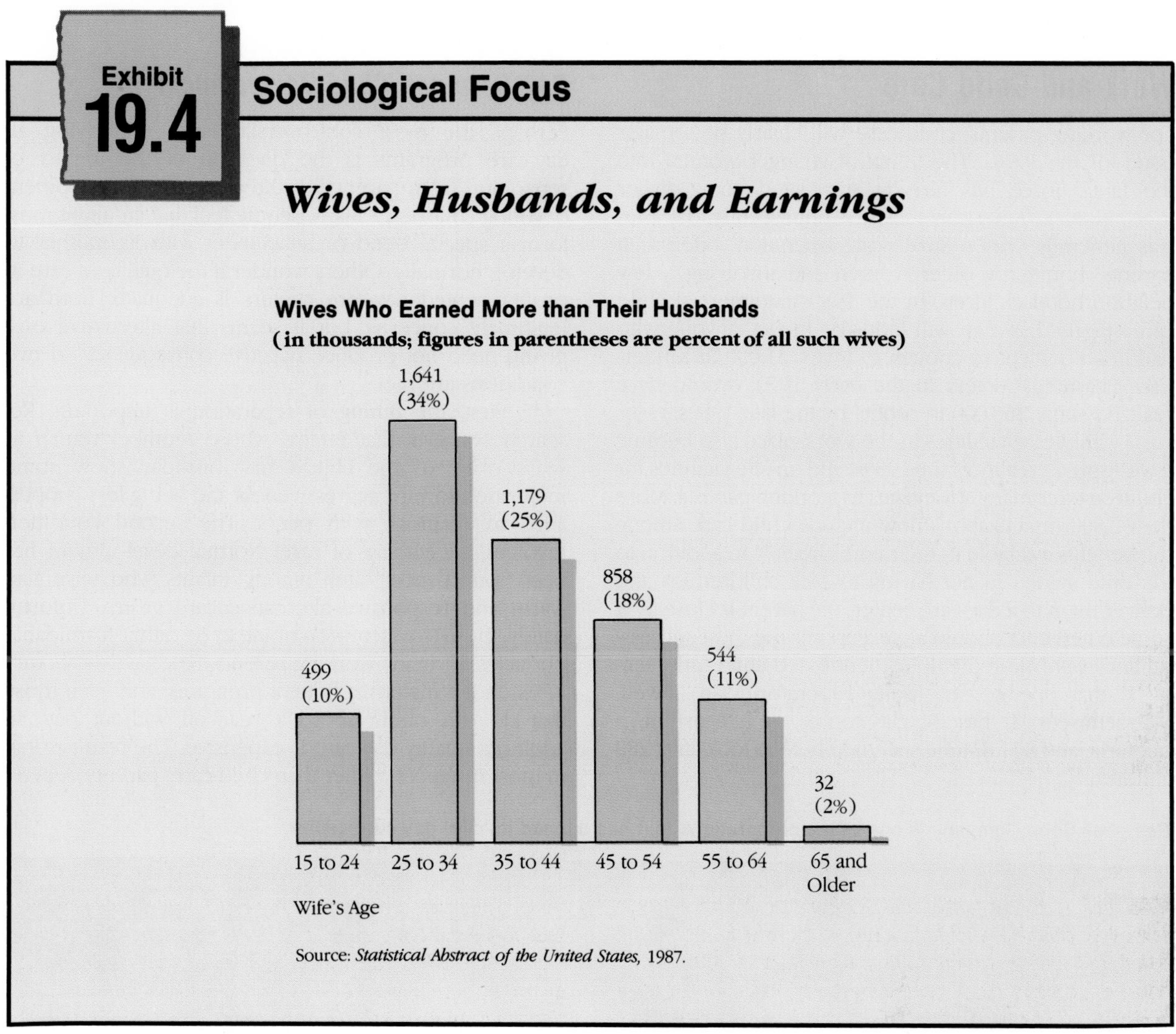

problematic when the wife's income is higher than the husband's, or when he loses his job and must look to his spouse for total support.

Finally, the issue of occupational competition more often comes into consideration in dual-career families. For some couples, their separate jobs become the basis of internal rivalry. They strive to outdo one another in promotions, income, and social status (see Exhibit 19.4). One study of managerial personnel found that half the respondents admitted some feelings of competitiveness.[47] Viewing a marriage partner as a competitor unquestionably places an additional strain on the relationship, increasing the likelihood of a breakup.

Dual careers are not an endless series of problems. They do have positive aspects. The rewards include the potential for improved life-styles and personal growth as well as enhanced husband-wife relationships. Two incomes allow people to enjoy life-styles that would otherwise be impossible. In addition, the second income can be used to solve some of the problems of insufficient time with expenditures for paid child care, cleaning services, and restaurant meals. Social relations between dual-career couples also often are enhanced. The sharing of child-care responsibilities typically builds solidarity. Moreover, when both wife and husband work, each is likely to be sensitive to the problems the other faces on the job. And finally, the very dilemmas that plague dual-career families eventually can produce a heightened sense of accomplishment among those who cope successfully.

Work and Child Care

For working parents, child care will clearly be a major issue for the 1990s. The influx of younger women into the labor force has already stimulated some major innovations in American society. Until recently, day care was generally only a small-scale operation, offered in parents' homes by older women and involving a few neighborhood children. In the 1980s commercial child care emerged as a growth industry. In fact, anyone who had been perceptive enough to invest $1,000 in Kinder-Care Learning Centers in the early 1970s would have realized some $65,000 in profits by the late 1980s.

Child-care facilities in the work place also became a widespread reality of the 1980s, and on-site facilities for children offer many advantages to working parents. More than 2,500 organizations now include child care among the benefits available to their employees.[48] In addition to the time gained in not having to pick children up and deliver them to a day-care center, the parent is close by if some emergency should arise. Perhaps the most successful and sophisticated employment-based child-care facility is that operated by Wang Laboratories in Lowell, Massachusetts. It has 24 classrooms, a gymnasium, a cafeteria, and 80 full-time staff members to look after 280 children.[49]

Day Care and Child Development

Perhaps the most controversial issue underlying all day-care programs is the question of the impact of separation from parents on the emotional development of young children.[50] Many people feel that an infant must form a special bond or attachment with its mother to develop normally. Others wonder if the quality of care in profit-oriented day-care centers is adequate. Both are legitimate concerns, but it seems that alternative care giving need not produce negative consequences if two conditions are met.[51]

First, the timing of separation is important. Research suggests that infants whose mothers return to work prior to the child's first birthday show some inclination toward aggressiveness and being less cooperative in relations with peers. The second condition involves the *quality* of care. Normal development has been found most often among infants who have had warm and responsive alternative care givers. Unfortunately, these two factors combine to be rather formidable obstacles for many working parents. Few have the luxury of extended maternity benefit programs, and even those that do can rarely afford a year off without pay. In addition, quality day care is expensive. The result is that in most instances, rather than child care, parents depend

Campbell Soup Company is one of the corporations that has opened its own day-care center.

SOCIAL INDICATOR

Government-supported Child Care in Europe

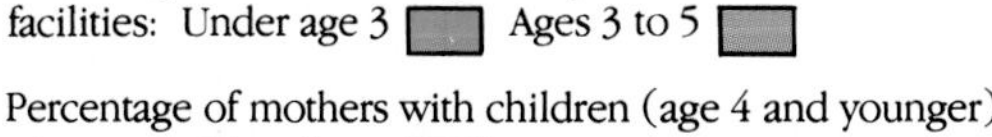

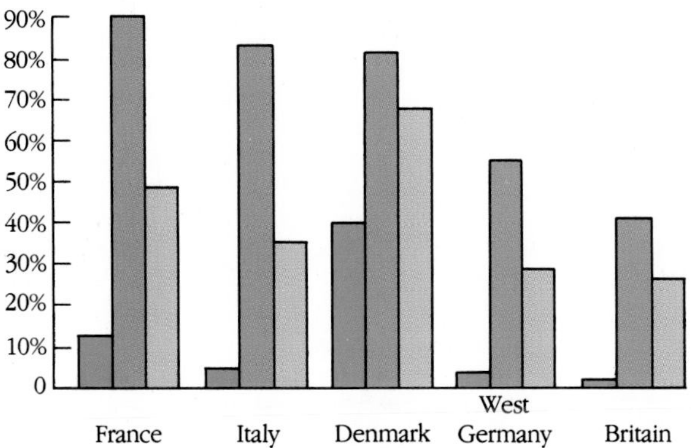

Source: U.S. News & World Report, August 22, 1988, p. 36.

on baby-sitting provided by siblings, other relatives, or trustworthy neighbors.

WORK CAREERS

A work history involves a life-long accumulation of experiences. Most workers encounter changes, transfers, promotions, and maybe even demotions and periods of joblessness along the way. A work history also involves a **work career,** the stages through which people must progress in any occupation.

Each step in every work career presents an array of challenges and opportunities. The first step in the process is simply getting a job—negotiating one's way through a *job application* and then a *job interview.* The next step is the crucial first assignment—the *entry level* position. When a worker is settled into a job, negotiating a *career path* and working with *mentors* must be considered. Finally, at any stage in the work career, people may have to cope with the setback of sudden or extended *unemployment.*

Job Applications: A Symbolic-interactionist Approach

Getting a job is rarely a simple affair. Even obtaining the least skilled or most temporary positions requires submitting an application and passing a personal interview. On the surface, applying for a job appears to be a rather straightforward process, an opportunity for one person to assess the objective work qualifications of another. However, it really is a much more complex procedure than that. Social symbols and stereotypes, and culturally defined perceptions all play a major role in determining the outcome of the process.

Evaluating Experience

The first step in the application process is the filling out of a job application, the submission of a résumé, or both. All applicants emphasize their training and experience. For many positions education and grades are even more important. Often, however, things having little to do with qualifications play major roles in decisions concerning who is hired.

The manner in which a person completes an application form is vital. Disqualification is almost certain for mistakes, inconsistencies, misspelled words, or spaces left blank. In American culture, these errors loom large because people have been socialized to associate them with such undesirable personal traits as sloppiness, inattention, and laziness.

Social stereotyping may also enter into the evaluation of a written job application. One form is **trait stereotyping,** the assumption that all members of given social categories—women, racial or ethnic minorities—have certain characteristics or traits (see Exhibit 19.5). Some varieties of gender trait stereotyping, for example, assume that all women behave in a particular way, or have particular attitudes.

An alternative form of stereotyping relevant to the world of work is **occupational stereotyping,** the assumption that some jobs are automatically appropriate for certain groups. Thus, those who stereotype "men's jobs" or "women's jobs" typically identify them on the basis of which group usually occupies them. For example, when identical applicants are compared, women receive higher ratings for jobs as grocery clerks or telephone operators, while men are rated more favorably for auto or hardware clerk positions.[52] Racially based occupational stereotypes also exist, with blacks favored for custodial work and whites for skilled trades.

The Interview

Interviews last from 30 minutes to an hour, but in most cases a conclusion is reached very early in the process—usually within the first four minutes. Interviewers are seldom influenced by things that happen later in the interview. This fact confirms the importance of first impressions and visual clues.

First impressions are based in large part on physical appearance—height, weight, and facial features.

Exhibit 19.5

Types & Stereotypes

Women and Gender Stereotypes

Research conducted in actual employment interviews and under experimental conditions has frequently highlighted that female applicants are evaluated less positively than males, even when women's qualifications match those of the men. Thus, it appears that gender stereotypes are among the factors contributing to the devaluation of women candidates. Stereotypes are, as already noted, tacit and often unrecognized assumptions about the traits of a group of people.

Gender stereotypes in American society give men the advantage over women in competition for many jobs. For example, intelligence, responsibility, leadership, independence, and ambition are all traits more likely to be attributed to males. This differentiation would clearly place women at a disadvantage for such jobs as attorney or police officer—careers that seem to demand so-called male traits.

In an ironic twist, stereotypes of gender and physical beauty may interact to produce negative consequences for women in specific jobs. A study of candidates for managerial jobs found that attractive women rated lower than unattractive women. The authors of the research suggest that people think more beautiful women are more "feminine," and thus, more "indecisive" and "gentle," not the traits of good managers.

Stereotypes are part of the cultural heritage of a society and are generally slow to change. They influence how people think about many things, including men and women. Stereotypes are most likely to come into play in ambiguous situations, particularly when not much information is available about the people involved. Use of stereotypes applies in particular to job application forms that do not ask for much information about job candidates. In time, however, it is likely that gender stereotypes will play a less important role in the evaluation of job applicants as more women enter the labor force and function successfully in diverse career fields.

SOURCES: Richard D. Arvey, "Unfair Discrimination in the Employment Interview: Legal and Psychological Aspects," *Psychological Bulletin* 86 (1979), pp. 736–65; Richard D. Arvey and James E. Champion, "The Employment Interview," *Personnel Psychology,* 35 (1982), pp. 281–83; Madeline Heilman and Lois E. Saruwatari, "When Beauty Is Beastly: The Effects of Appearance and Sex on Evaluations of Job Applicants for Managerial and Nonmanagerial Jobs," *Organizational Behavior and Human Performance,* 23 (June 1979), pp. 360–72.

Thus, in a country like the United States, which places a high premium on beauty, it is not surprising to find that attractive people have an advantage.[53] In fact, physically attractive people are almost always given preference over unattractive ones. People who typify cultural standards of beauty are obviously more pleasing to look at, but other factors are also involved. Attractive people are assumed to have more desirable personality traits. For example, for white women, facial beauty is defined by such things as high cheekbones, a small, narrow nose, and widely set eyes. Women with such features are not only considered more attractive, but "brighter," more "assertive," and more "sociable" as well.[54]

Among men, being tall seems to be an advantage.[55] Taller women do not enjoy this benefit because similar cultural value is not placed on the stature of females.[56] Taller men do better not only during the employment interview, but apparently throughout their careers. Studies indicate that taller men tend to earn more than their shorter peers, and overweight men earn less than men of average build.[57] A degree of personal-characteristic stereotyping often also is involved. Tall men are assumed to be more "responsible" and "self-confident," while overweight people are assumed to be "lazy" and less personable. One recruiting firm reports being told not to send overweight candidates because "fat people steal."[58]

As the job interview progresses, other nonverbal behaviors may affect the impression candidates project. Maintaining good posture, smiling, and making eye contact with the interviewer tend to project more favorable images to a prospective employer. Specifically, direct eye contact is believed to reflect confidence, dependability, initiative, and responsibility.[59]

In short, an employment interview is a brief social encounter in which the interviewer tries to evaluate a candidate. Interviewers are looking for indications of maturity, reliability, and responsibility that are not easy to gauge. Consequently, their judgment may well be influenced by social stereotypes and assumptions about personal traits based on physical appearance and nonverbal clues—often to the disadvantage of well-qualified people.

Testing Applicants

The Sphinx was a monster of Greek mythology that had the face of a woman, the body of a lion, and the wings of a bird. For years she perched on Mount Phicium, near the ancient city of Thebes, posing a riddle to all passersby. "What goes on four feet," she would ask, "on two feet, and three, but the more feet it goes on the weaker it be?" Those who could not answer her riddle—all respondents, save one—were promptly devoured. Oedipus answered her directly. "It is a *man,*" he stated, "for he crawls as an infant, walks upright as an adult, and totters with a staff in old age." Upon hearing this, the Sphinx slew herself. Oedipus was made king of Thebes, and as such, it might be said that he was the first person to have passed an employment test. Pilots, police officers, and fire fighters have long since been subjected to batteries of tests designed to measure physical capacity and personality traits. In recent years similar testing has been adopted for more routine forms of employment. In addition, modern industrial societies have added other mechanisms of testing. For many jobs today, it is standard practice to require job applicants and employees to take tests, including urinalysis, the polygraph, graphoanalysis, and character assessment.

Urinalysis

The proliferation of recreational drug use in the United States has produced widespread experimentation with drug testing as part of the job-application process. The economic cost of employees who use drugs is very large. An annual $36.7 billion-loss in productivity is attributed to drug abuse.[60] Consequently, by 1987, 20% of all firms were conducting tests, with urinalysis testing concentrated among the large industrial firms.[61]

Firms that do urine tests on job applicants and employees have reported that the procedures have brought about drastic reductions in absenteeism and industrial accidents. The procedures screen out drug users, and discourage drug use among employees. Yet drug testing is controversial. One argument holds that urinalysis represents a violation of privacy rights guaranteed by the Constitution of the United States.[62] Differing opinions have been handed down by state and federal courts, and in 1989 the Supreme Court ruled drug tests permissible for members of some occupations. Another criticism revolves around the accuracy of urine testing. Studies have demonstrated that the tests are quite fallible. Several over-the-counter drugs have shown up in tests as morphine, marijuana, or amphetamines.[63] Although this complaint is quite valid, newer methods for testing have been developed that appear to make the process foolproof (see Exhibit 19.6).

SOCIAL INDICATOR

Drug Tests at Work: Crackdown on Cocaine

Forty-seven percent of adults approve of mandatory drug tests for all workers. They also believe work-place tests should focus on these drugs:

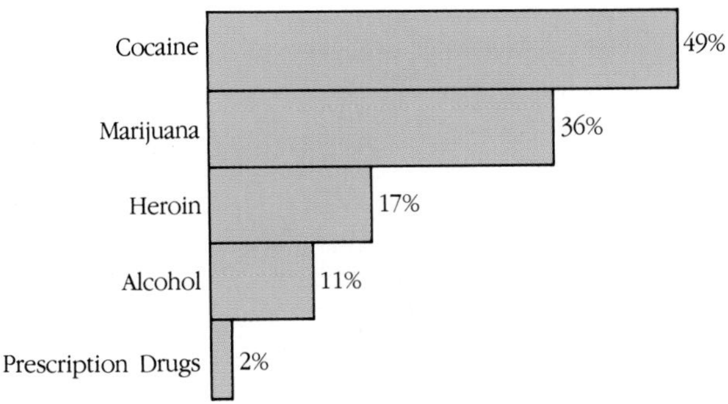

Note: Respondents could choose more than one response.
Source: *USA Today,* September 23, 1986, p. 1A.

The Polygraph

A number of employment experts have estimated that one-fourth of all job candidates are not fully honest on application forms, either misrepresenting or distorting their files.[64] Employee theft in private industry and espionage in the government sector have also made employers wary. These factors have stimulated the use of the polygraph, better known as the lie detector. As many as 2 million polygraph tests are administered each year in the United States.[65] One hotel chain claims that lie detectors helped to reduce losses from employee theft from $1 million in 1975 to $115,000 in 1985. Like urinalysis, however, the accuracy of the polygraph is problematic—so much so that its results remain inadmissible as evidence in American courts, and in 1988 Congress severely limited its use in the job-application process.

Graphoanalysis

Graphoanalysis, more commonly known as handwriting analysis, is popular in a number of European nations. In Germany, for example, employment announcements may request a sample of handwriting, and about half of all German industries require it of their top executives.[66] In the United States it is estimated that some 200 graphologists are working as full-time consultants to business firms, analyzing job applicants' handwriting.

Exhibit 19.6

Sociology in the Media

Analysis of Hair Traces Drug Use

Indicted for cocaine use, Municipal Judge Michael J. Scott of Santa Maria, California, called a press conference in April to proclaim his innocence and to offer to take a drug test.

The judge had 11 years' criminal justice experience and so must have known the urinalysis universally used to test for cocaine can check only the immediate past 36 to 72 hours. But the prosecutor had something else in mind. He mailed the defense a draft of a court application for samples of the judge's hair—together with the credentials of an expert who would testify that five-inch strands of hair give a month-by-month record of cocaine or other drug use reaching back nearly a year.

Judge Scott quickly changed his story. He pleaded guilty to two counts of possession and gave up his judgeship. On July 2, he received a 90-day jail sentence.

Those few who have heard of the use of radioimmunoassay (RIA) on hair (RIA-H) consider it an emerging exculpatory device to challenge a false-positive drug-test urinalysis, to discredit witnesses, or to show that a drug-using defendant was not responsible for his actions.

However, the Scott prosecution is typical of RIA-H success stories: the case ended quietly in a way that keeps it out of the law books, and courtroom usefulness of the scientific technique remained open to debate.

Indelible Record

The rationale behind RIA-H is relatively simple. A person's bloodstream briefly carries a drug or its identifiable by-product, feeding all cells including those forming head hair. Some residue is locked in the strand, and the new increment of hair carrying its minute but indelible record is pushed out through the scalp at the predictable rate of about 1 centimeter a month for men and 1.3 centimeters a month for women. Body hair also is testable and carries a more condensed record, but its growth rates are less standard.

The tester cuts sample strands into segments representing a month's growth, backdating from that closest to the scalp. The cleaned samples are treated to break down the hair structure and produce an extract. From there, the procedure corresponds to the radioimmunoassay technique widely accepted in urinalysis: antibodies and a radioactive version of the drug being sought are introduced to the extract, and the extent of bonding between antibodies and drugs is measured.

Nuclear chemist Werner A. Baumgartner, a researcher at Wadsworth Veterans Administration Hospital in Los Angeles, says he and his wife, Annette, pioneered the application of RIA to hair a decade ago. He says he has refined the technique through more than 700 human tests to the point where he can read not only the history but also the quantity of drug use. Currently, he has a National Institute of Justice grant to monitor parolees and probationers.

One booster is Marine Captain Arthur Adams, a defense lawyer at Camp Pendleton in San Diego. He heard about Mr. Baumgartner while preparing for a court-martial earlier this year in which his client, Lance Corporal Steven Piccolo, insisted he was the victim of a false positive in a routine urinalysis.

His hair tested clean.

The military judge did not allow RIA-H into evidence, basing his acquittal on the corporal's exemplary record—and leaving the inference the urine sample somehow was tainted. Given the Navy's claim that its 600,000 annual urinalyses are foolproof, Captain Adams is elated and says he plans to use RIA-H with the next client who has enough hair and confidence.

SOURCE: Extracted from Gail Diane Cox, *National Law Journal,* July 27, 1987, pp. 3, 8.

Graphologists claim that certain features of a person's writing reveal underlying personality traits that are of interest to potential employers. For instance, heavy pressure on a pen indicates aggressiveness, while a bold script shows self-confidence. One firm hired a person despite a graphologist's warning that the applicant was potentially dishonest. The worker was later convicted of robbery. Some critics dismiss the whole idea of handwriting analysis, comparing it to tea-leaf reading or other forms of carnival magic. While that may be an unfair assessment of graphoanalysis, it must be recognized that the technique is highly subjective, with different practitioners of graphoanalysis often reaching completely different conclusions.

Character Assessments

Many employers, particularly those in defense and high-technology industries, are interested in such employee traits as honesty, loyalty, dedication, and performance potential—none of which is easily evaluated. Among the most controversial mechanisms in this regard are the personality tests devised by psychologists to assess individual character. Critics advise that human personality is far too complex and multidimensional to uncover with a simple paper-and-pencil test. Nevertheless, many firms use such tests to screen candidates for positions requiring unusual abilities (see Exhibit 19.7).

In summary, it is easy to understand the motivation to subject potential employees to various types of testing. The very real issues of public safety have surfaced in connection with workers who are responsible for the lives of others. Early in 1987, for example, 16 persons were killed and 175 were injured in a train accident near Baltimore, Maryland. Tests indicated that the operators of the locomotive that caused the accident had traces of marijuana in their blood. In fact, between 1975 and 1984, drug or alcohol use by rail workers was reportedly a factor in 48 accidents that caused 37 deaths, 80 injuries, and more than $34 million in property damage.[67]

The practical, legal, and moral issues surrounding testing are even more complex. Critics point out that all tests have some margin of error. "False positives" on drug and lie-detector tests could result in negative outcomes for innocent victims. Accurate interpretation of the results of personality tests and handwriting analyses may also be problematic. Neither qualifies as an exact science. The issue ultimately is one of individual privacy

Rescue workers remove bodies from the wreckage of an Amtrak passenger train. After the death of 16 people in the 1987 accident, the drug-testing of transportation workers became commonplace.

Exhibit 19.7

Sociological Focus

The Personality Test: Are You the Right One for the Job?

Personality tests often require job applicants to respond to hundreds of self-descriptive items designed to help employers determine an individual's traits. No single answer, or group of answers, is considered significant without taking into account the total pattern of responses. An individual's test score is measured against the response patterns of normal persons as well as those clinically diagnosed as suffering from such psychiatric disorders as depression, hysteria, paranoia, and schizophrenia. Some personality tests also can predict, according to W. Grant Dahlstrom, professor of psychology at the University of North Carolina. For example, some tests may suggest which applicants are at risk of drug abuse; those who are unsuitable for employment in stressful positions at flight-control centers or nuclear power plants; or even those who would function well in jobs that involve frequent rejection (sales) or physical threat (psychiatric nursing). Questions similar to those below—which focus on experiences, relations, and attitudes—are often incorporated in personality tests. Whether they are answered "true" or "false" may help detect the following traits and others.

	True	False	Can't Say	
I have trouble going to sleep at night. I feel unhappy most of the time. I rarely see the bright side of things.	☐ ☐ ☐	☐ ☐ ☐	☐ ☐ ☐	True responses to a large number of items similar to these could reveal extreme despondency.
Sometimes there is a feeling like something is pressing in on my head. My fingers sometimes feel numb.	☐ ☐	☐ ☐	☐ ☐	Physical complaints that have no organic causes may be symptomatic of underlying emotional problems.
I used to like to do the dances in gym class. I do not like sports. I like visiting art museums.	☐ ☐ ☐	☐ ☐ ☐	☐ ☐ ☐	The answers to these questions are used to gauge traditionally masculine and feminine interests.

and the right to be left alone. At what point do employers' legitimate concerns infringe upon employees' civil and personal rights? These are not merely abstract issues.

Entry-level Jobs

The second step in work careers is the entry-level job. These jobs are logically called "entry-level" because they represent the point at which new employees get their first real experience with the world of work. This stage is probably the most difficult one in any worker's career. First, they must learn how to fit into the social structure of the organization. They will meet many new people within but a few days and will have to figure out the status and role of each. A whole new set of formal and informal norms also must be mastered. These include relatively minor things, such as how to dress and how long to take for lunch, but more important concerns also are involved, particularly those relating to work expectations. It usually takes new workers about six months to reach a point at which they feel competent on the job. Many fail to last that long.[68]

One reason why the first few months of a job are so difficult is that newly hired workers have only vague ideas about the knowledge and skills needed to accomplish their tasks. Sometimes perceptions are biased by stereotypes or mass media portrayals of the work. As a result, new workers are often disappointed by the realities of daily job activities. Work in law enforcement

	True	False	Can't Say	
It distresses me that people have the wrong ideas about me.	☐	☐	☐	True responses, reflecting extreme suspiciousness and fears of persecution, may signal paranoid traits.
There are those out there who want to get me.	☐	☐	☐	
I am often very tense on the job.	☐	☐	☐	True responses to such questions may indicate anxiety, indecisiveness, and obsessive-compulsive tendencies.
I wish I could do over some of the things I have done.	☐	☐	☐	
I worry about sexual matters.	☐	☐	☐	
I can't keep my mind on what I'm doing.	☐	☐	☐	
The things that run through my head sometimes are horrible.	☐	☐	☐	True responses to many items such as these may contribute to a pattern of a schizophrenic personality.
I sometimes smell strange odors.	☐	☐	☐	
I never told a lie.	☐	☐	☐	These items may help to determine if a person comprehends the testing task, is lying, or is trying to influence the outcome.
Everything tastes salty.	☐	☐	☐	
I never had a bad night's sleep.	☐	☐	☐	
I'm more satisfied with life than my friends are.	☐	☐	☐	

Source: From *Newsweek,* May 5, 1986, p. 48.

readily illustrates this point. Recruits are often attracted to police work because they believe it will offer them a chance to do something important and meaningful in the community. In addition, they anticipate the opportunity for adventurous, dramatic, and exciting work. These rewards are always possible, but as already pointed out in Chapter 15, most police work involves fairly routine peacekeeping operations. Once in the field, rookies quickly find themselves devoting the majority of their time to filing reports, directing traffic, issuing summonses, handling crowds, settling minor disputes, and processing drunks.

New workers also find their entry-level jobs disappointing because of insufficient challenge. Organizations expect people to start at the bottom, intending to promote them only after they have proven themselves. Consequently, entry-level jobs seldom involve much responsibility or authority. For example, highly trained law-school graduates may find themselves doing simple legal research in the library. A highly educated, but bitter and frustrated employee of an insurance company illustrates the problem with the comment, "This work could be done by a high-school graduate with a calculator. They didn't tell me in the MBA program that I'd be doing this routine work."[69]

Consequently, it is not unusual for many workers' first few years in the labor force to be periods of experimentation with many different entry-level jobs as they try to find work that is meaningful and rewarding to them. During this career phase, individuals devote much of their effort searching for work that matches their talents and abilities.

Career Paths

As soon as people finally become settled in their new occupations, most devote their energies to improving their positions. They become concerned with performance evaluations and promotions. In short, they become career conscious. Opportunities in organizations involve jobs of ever-increasing responsibility and income. The majority of American workers follow one of four basic types of career paths—fixed, developmental, fast track, or low ceiling.

Fixed Paths

A **fixed career path** is a specific set of occupations or positions that a worker must follow for occupational mobility. Fixed career paths are evident in the military, for example, since officers must pass through a regular series of ranks. Similarly, most college and university faculty members progress through a fixed set of positions—from assistant professor to associate professor and then full professor. Professors typically must serve a minimum number of years in each position and demonstrate certain kinds of competence along the way. In most universities, entry-level assistant professors typically have six years in which to demonstrate an ability to do independent research. Thus, professors face pressures to conduct research and publish articles and books. Emphasis on publications continues after promotion to associate professor, but the pressure is eased somewhat by the fact that no fixed deadline is set for promotion to the next level and the threat of dismissal declines. Associate professors typically devote more time to graduate education. Promotion to full professor usually carries with it the expectation that more time will be devoted to committee work and other forms of service to the university.

Developmental Paths

In most business structures, organizational levels, rather than particular positions, represent the measure of upward mobility and increasing success. That is, workers must accumulate experience and skills in certain *types* of work to qualify for promotions. Thus, **developmental career paths** involve movement through jobs requiring ever higher levels of skill and responsibility. For example, the route to superintendent of a public school system includes different positions in which specific capabilities may be learned and demonstrated—curriculum development, supervision of teachers, community relations, and administrative skills. Thus, any number of specific jobs might provide those experiences.[70]

Fast-track Paths

Most organizations seem to have **fast-track career paths** that involve a series of jobs leading directly to upper-level positions. Movement along this path is reserved for those who have been identified as having unusual potential. Their progress is rapid and continuous as they circulate in and out of positions, moving upward with each change.

Being placed on a fast track often seems to be a self-fulfilling prophecy. That is, because fast-track employees are expected to be successful, they are treated in a way that assures their success. Having been labeled as fast trackers, they are granted special experiences and opportunities that help them to perform better. Thus, fast trackers receive more frequent performance reviews and a wider range of jobs. They are treated more leniently and are integrated into the network of senior executives who control future promotions.[71]

Low-ceiling Paths

In contrast to the other types of career paths, in the **low-ceiling career path** little or no potential for advancement exists. Workers on this path may qualify for annual merit and cost-of-living salary increases, but they have no chances for moving up, despite the fact that they may be talented, competent, and productive people.

The factor that determines whether a person falls into a low-ceiling career path is not his or her age, sex, or any other sociodemographic characteristic, nor is it the type of organization within which he or she works. Rather, the determining issue is the relationship of qualifications to specific occupational careers. Recall the fixed career pattern of the university professor. Career mobility begins at the assistant professor level. However, in most universities, a necessary qualification for employment as an assistant professor is the PhD degree. In many cases a non-PhD is hired at the instructor or lecturer rank. If that individual ultimately fails to obtain the PhD, he or she will never obtain a professorship. The most common low-ceiling occupation is that of secretary. Secretaries, no matter how talented and efficient, have little chance of ever qualifying for promotion into management. Management positions are reserved for people with specialized training.

Blocked Mobility

Most workers, usually by the time they have reached age 45, experience **blocked mobility,** a point in the work career at which they have progressed as far as their opportunities and abilities will permit.[72] Different explanations have been given for this phenomenon. The most apparent is that the majority of workers do not have the abilities to handle more complex tasks. However, many may be blocked by factors over which they have no control. For example, fewer opportunities for promotion are available to people as they move up in an organization. Hierarchies are shaped like pyramids, and only one president is chosen from the ranks of all the vice-presidents. Thus, even very competent people find themselves stalled.

A specific type of blocked mobility often confronts women and minority group members. They are able to achieve a modest degree of upward mobility, winning promotions and sometimes attaining high levels of responsibility and influence. Ultimately, however, they fail to reach the very top organizational positions. They can *see* into the board rooms and executive suites, but cannot move *into* them. They are blocked by a **glass ceiling,** an informal boundary that stops them from reaching the uppermost positions. For example, women have been moving into managerial positions in significant numbers since the 1970s. However, according to one survey few attain executive status, and on the average, when they do, they earn 42% less than their male counterparts.[73]

Glass ceilings and other invisible barriers persist for many reasons. Gender stereotypes burden women with the image that they lack the leadership skills necessary for managerial roles. Many men are resistent to the idea of being supervised by a woman. Too, women tend to be excluded from informal, business-related social activities (such as golf) and meetings at bars and clubs, where information is traded and deals are made.[74]

Responses to Blocked Mobility

In a landmark study of corporate men and women conducted during the 1970s, Rosabeth Moss Kanter identified several different responses to blocked mobility that manifest themselves in the form of personal dissatisfactions. These responses hinder organizational effectiveness.[75] Some employees become "zombies." They lose interest in their work, and their level of effort drifts to the acceptable minimum. Although they do enough to keep their jobs, they make no real contribution to the functioning of the organization. Others become "chronic complainers" about the organization and its leadership. Their anger and frustrations about having become stalled in their careers is channeled into criticism of company policy. Consequently, they often hinder the operations of the firm by opposing the decisions of superiors.

SOCIAL INDICATOR

What It Takes to Succeed

Horatio Alger would blanch at the thought. Americans believe that to get ahead only one thing counts: whom you know. Hard work, creative ability, and idealism, for most, play almost no role.

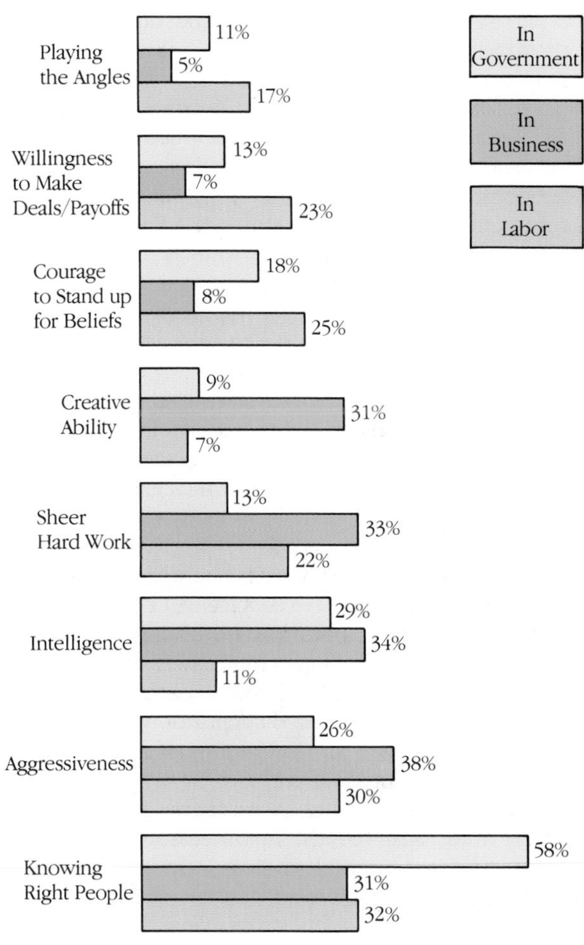

Source: *Newsweek,* February 24, 1986, p. 4.

Careers and Mentors

At times, senior members of an organization play an active role in guiding the career development of junior employees. These high-ranking individuals, known as mentors (or "sponsors," "patrons," "rabbis" and "godfathers") can exert considerable influence in shaping careers. Reports by senior-level managers and executives reveal that they benefited from the help of others in their climb up the organizational ladder.[76] In fact, it appears that executives with mentors enjoy higher salaries and win more promotions than executives who do not have mentors. Moreover, mentors can play different roles—teachers, counselors, facilitators, and advocates.

When sharing their knowledge and experience with new people, mentors serve as teachers and help novices to learn the realities of work quickly and to avoid mistakes. Perhaps the most important thing mentors can provide is "insider information,"—the details of the informal workings of the organization—how to circumvent minor rules, what is tolerated and what must be avoided, who has the real power in an office (see Exhibit 19.8). Such information is usually not public, and those who have it are at an advantage over those who do not.

Mentors offer encouragement, emotional support, and friendly advice. Having someone to talk with, to share problems and frustrations with, is an important source of strength for many inexperienced workers. This relationship can be especially important for women breaking into nontraditional jobs, where only men have been employed previously.[77]

Mentors may use their contacts and positions to provide a selected few with the opportunity to demonstrate their ability. They may introduce them to senior people or include them in a project which gives them the chance to excel. Many famous scientists report their mentors included them in ongoing research projects that set them on the road to future accomplishments.[78]

Mentors may use their contacts with upper management to praise the prodigy's work, point out their abilities, or suggest them for promotions. In certain types of careers it is virtually impossible to achieve success without the aid of a well-placed supporter. This observation is especially valid for occupations that depend on subjective judgments of ability, such as the performing arts. For example, many good musicians have proven themselves in small bands, but access to the more desirable work in recording studios is open only to those who "have a hook" (a mentor).[79]

The existence of mentors emphasizes the social dimensions of careers. Individual effort and ability may be prerequisites to upward mobility, but they do not always guarantee it. The reality of the situation is that many qualified people are at work in every occupation; it is important that they somehow come to the attention of superiors, and mentors can accomplish that.

Unemployment

Most workers, regardless of their occupation, face the possibility of losing their jobs. Because work plays such an important role in people's lives—shaping their social identities, contributing to their social status, and determining their life-style—unemployment can be a painful experience, disrupting social relationships and sometimes destroying careers and families.

The Unemployment Rate

The unemployment rate is a measure of the health of a society—its ability to provide work for those who want to work. The **unemployment rate,** expressed as a percentage, is the proportion of the civilian labor force that is unemployed and looking for work.

Unquestionably, the worst period of unemployment in American history was the Great Depression of the 1930s, when approximately one in four people was out of work. During the late 1980s, unemployment hovered around 6 to 8 percent, suggesting that 8 million people in the United States were looking for a job, but were unable to find one. Typically, the unemployment situation is generally worse than the official figures indicate. The unemployment rate does not include those who have been classified as "discouraged workers"—people who want work, but have ceased looking for a job because they are convinced that they will not find one.[80]

Reasons for Unemployment

The legions of the unemployed include four general categories of people—job leavers, new entrants, reentrants, and job losers. *Job leavers* are idle as a matter of personal choice, having left a job because of poor pay, undesirable working conditions, or a paucity of chances for promotion and career growth. This category is a part of the normal circulation among jobs as people seek to improve themselves.

New entrants have completed their schooling and have not yet been able to find permanent work. The unemployment rates are always very high for young people, largely because they lack marketable skills. By contrast, *reentrants* are those trying to get back into the labor force after having been away for a time. Many are mature women seeking to resume their careers after their children are no longer fully dependent on them. Others are displaced homemakers, divorceés, or widows. These people are at a real disadvantage because their skills have become outdated over time and few have kept abreast of changes in their fields.

The largest single category of the unemployed are the *job losers.* As the label implies, these are people dismissed from jobs for one reason or another. Most are out of work because jobs simply disappear due to changes in technology, consumer preferences, or foreign competition. Too, the American economy is undergoing a period of rapid change. As a result, some industries have become smaller; they are offering fewer jobs.

Exhibit 19.8 Sociological Focus

Mentors as Teachers: The Police Signal-box System

A rather well-known personality in the ranks of modern policing is Patrick V. Murphy, former police chief in the cities of New York, Detroit, and Washington, D.C. In his book, *Commissioner,* Murphy recalls his early days as a rookie cop during World War II. His discussion of the police signal-box system, quoted below, clearly illustrates the concept of *mentors as teachers.*

Learning to use the signal box is an important part of the socialization of police officers.

Take the police signal-box system. Its official purpose was to maintain a management check on the movement of officers out on patrol. Each precinct had a large number of call boxes that were laid out in the pattern of an electronic grid, more or less in a logical schematic pattern across the territory of the precinct. However, there was a hitch in the scheme's logic which required all officers to phone the precinct switchboard once an hour, the line on which the call was received identifying the caller's location.

The hitch was that there might be two to four boxes on the same line. One learned this beat-the-system fact on the first day. "Kid," one veteran explained, "you can call in on any one of these three boxes, and for all they know at the switchboard, you could be at any one of the three locations. They're all on the same line. You can call up and say, 'This is Murphy on Box Four,' and since Four is connected to Six and Eight, be at either place." What the experienced hand was saying was that Murphy could be playing poker in a "coop" (sleeping or loafing location kept by officers) near Box Four, but could call in and give the impression that he was blocks away. An hour later, to give the impression that he was on the move, he could call back from the same box and give a different location entirely. Yet the system was designed, and publicized, as a management control measure to insure constant movement; this was the great police omnipresence.

SOURCE: Patrick V. Murphy and Thomas Plate, *Commissioner: A View From the Top of American Law Enforcement* (New York: Simon and Schuster, 1977), pp. 32–33.

SOCIAL INDICATOR

Unemployment in the United States, 1890–1988

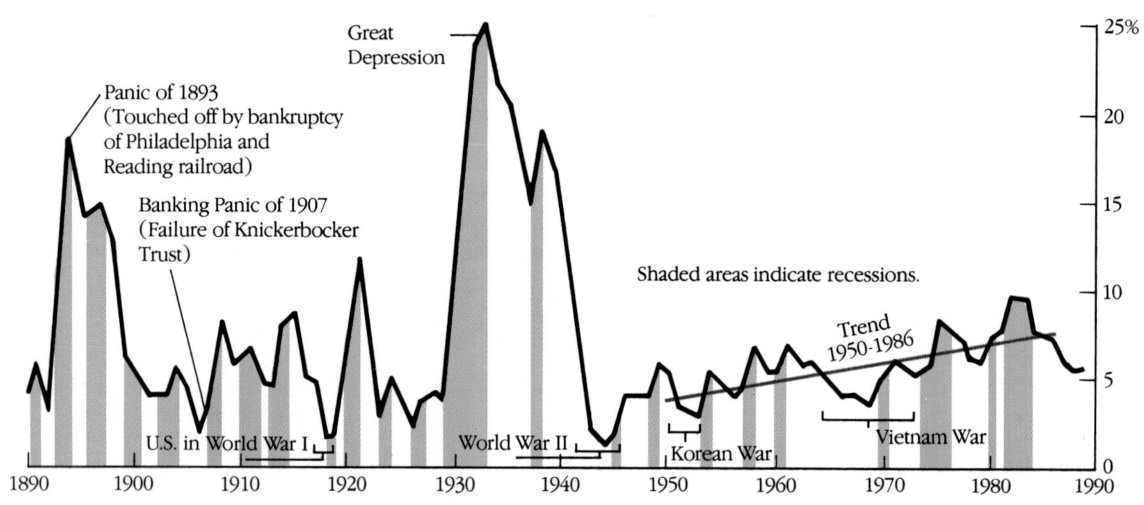

Source: Bureau of Labor Statistics, 1988.

The automobile industry, where some 200,000 jobs were lost between 1975 and 1984, represents an acute example.[81] Social, technological, and economic changes also bring about the elimination of entire industries. Other industries emerge to fill the gaps created by social change, but most displaced workers lack the skills to compete for the new positions.

Consequences of Unemployment

The personal and social costs of unemployment can be harsh, affecting many aspects of people's lives. Job loss imposes a financial burden, alters life-styles, threatens the individual's sense of personal worth, and disrupts personal relations with friends and family.

The financial costs of unemployment are the most immediate. Unemployment benefits protect some workers, but not all individuals are covered and others exhaust their payments. Thus, in any given year, only one-third of the unemployed are actually receiving benefits. The rest must depend on savings, assistance from other family members, or public-aid programs.

Almost all unemployed workers adjust their life-styles to compensate for lost income. Entertainment, vacations, and new clothing are the first casualties.[82] If unemployment persists, appliances and automobiles may be sold. More than a few of the unemployed end up among the ranks of the homeless, wandering the streets in search of a place to stay.

Self-esteem is also likely to suffer. Even when people lose their jobs because of plant closings or some other factor beyond their control, they nevertheless are likely to blame themselves. They wonder if they had somehow worked harder or had been more diligent, they might have kept their jobs. Men may feel that they are unable to live up to their role of being financial provider for wife and children.

People may also lose the esteem of their peers. Many people blame the individual rather than the economic system for all forms of unemployment. Those without work are assumed to be lazy and unwilling to put forth sufficient effort.[83] Thus, the jobless are assumed to be people who have undesirable traits.

Social relations become strained, or in some cases destroyed. The most immediate consequence is that the worker is cut off from co-workers and peers. Some close friends will stay in touch and even try to help by providing job leads, but others become elusive for fear of being asked for money. Still others avoid their unemployed friends and relatives because they feel uncomfortable, not knowing how to treat them.[84] Husband-wife relationships also are likely to be altered. At first, unemployment can draw couples closer as they confront their problems together, but over time frustrations may drive them apart.

It should be remembered as well that financial, personal, and social problems can take a toll on physical and mental health. Most of the unemployed suffer from

SOCIAL INDICATOR

Occupations That Will Suffer Significant Declines during the Period 1982–1995

Occupation	Percent Decline in Employment
Railroad Conductors	−32.0
Shoemaking Machine Operatives	−30.2
Aircraft Structure Assemblers	−21.0
Central Telephone Office Operators	−20.0
Taxi Drivers	−18.9
Postal Clerks	−17.9
Private Household Workers	−16.9
Farm Laborers	−15.9
College and University Faculty	−15.0
Roustabouts	−14.4
Postmasters and Mail Superintendents	−13.8
Rotary Drill Operator Helpers	−11.6
Graduate Assistants	−11.2
Data Entry Operators	−10.6
Railroad Brake Operators	−9.8
Fallers and Buckers	−8.7
Stenographers	−7.4
Farm Owners and Tenants	−7.3
Typesetters and Compositors	−7.3
Butchers and Meatcutters	−6.3

Source: Bureau of Labor Statistics, 1987.

bouts of nervousness, tension, and fear, reporting frequent headaches, sleepless nights, and stomach upsets. A few report that they drink and smoke more than usual after losing their jobs.[85] M. Harvey Brenner's research suggests that these problems have long-term consequences, showing up in mental illness, deaths due to heart disease, and even in suicide rates.[86]

Coping with Unemployment

Unemployment can drag on for weeks or months, and in a few circumstances, may last for years. The average period of joblessness is 15.6 weeks.[87] This figure tends to vary, however, depending on a worker's age, skill level, and segment of the industry. In any case, research has suggested that peoples' responses change as their unemployment endures and they attempt to adjust to their losses. The first stage is crisis, followed by search, doubt, and apathy.[88]

Crisis. Some workers start other jobs, or at least start looking for work immediately, but for most the first week or two following a job loss is a time of personal crisis. They experience waves of disbelief, bitterness, anger, frustration, confusion, and fear. Many experience

An abandoned steel mill in Pennsylvania symbolizes the changing economy, which causes widespread unemployment.

sleepless nights and severe depression often may overwhelm them.

Search. The initial shock is usually followed by a period of rising optimism that may last for weeks. During this stage unemployed people actively search the newspapers for leads, make telephone calls, and ask friends

SOCIAL INDICATOR

White-collar Layoffs

Out of Work
Unemployed White-collar Workers

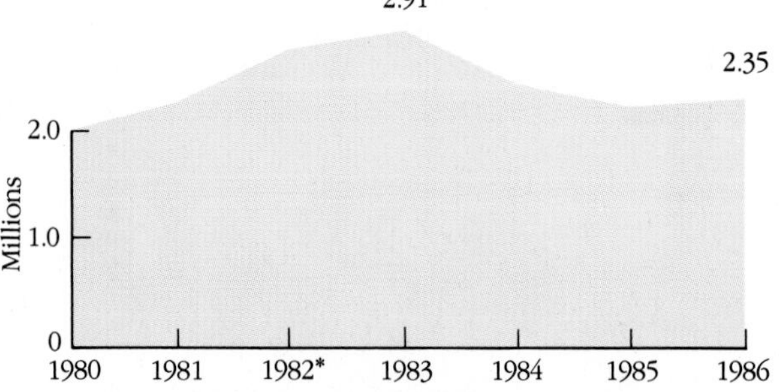

***Changes in occupational classifications make pre-1982 figures not strictly comparable with later years.**

The Age Factor
Average Weeks of Unemployment by Age

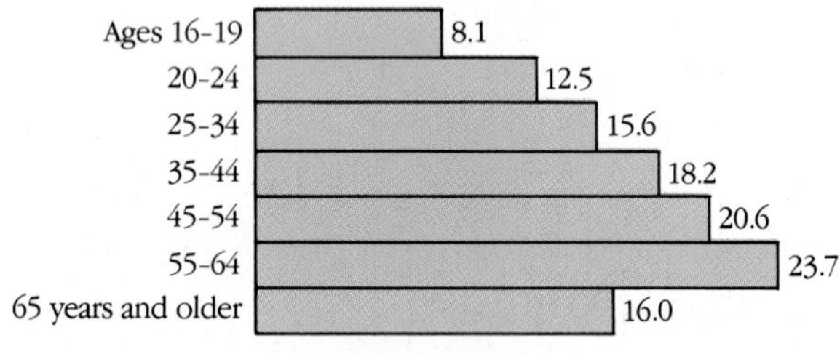

Back on the Job
Laid-off White-collar Workers Who Found New Jobs

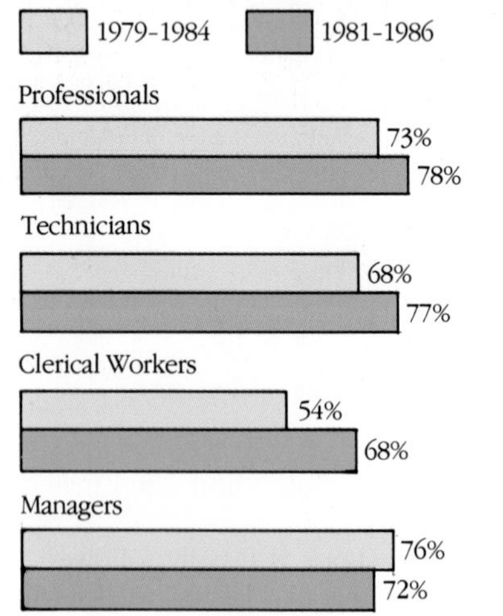

Source: *U.S. News & World Report,* March 23, 1987, p. 53.

for ideas. Their own optimism is reinforced by family and friends who are extremely supportive as they explore the job market. Social support is a major factor in keeping them going.

Doubt. After about 6–8 weeks optimism begins to fade. When job-seeking efforts fail to produce employment, increasingly less time and trouble is devoted to the search. Failure weakens resolve and erodes self-confidence. Self-doubt emerges, social relationships begin to deteriorate, and levels of stress rise. Friends feel guilty because *they* are employed but are unable to help. The unemployed feel envy. Frustration may lead to domestic violence. Some people even contemplate suicide.

Apathy. After weeks of disappointment, the unemployed are likely to drift into apathy and feelings of hopelessness. Many lose all contact with old friends. It is rare to find them looking for work, and older workers may say they are "retired" to avoid the constant embarrassment of failure.

APPLIED SOCIOLOGY AND THE WORLD OF WORK

Sociologists have long been actively involved in the study of roles and social relations in the work place. The Hawthorne studies of the 1930s (as noted in Chapter 2) were some of the earliest applied research efforts in this area. More recently, sociologists have become involved with efforts to improve employee productivity by reorganizing jobs (Chapter 5). Today, sociologists continue to be included among a whole range of social scientists attempting to improve productivity, make the work place a more satisfying place to be, and reduce conflicts between work and family roles (see Exhibit 19.9). In addition, the data of sociological research has some direct applications for selecting a career, negotiating one's way through a job interview, and coping with unemployment.

Selecting a Job

Complex industrial societies reflect the dynamics of a rapidly changing world. Alterations in technology, the economy, and various social phenomena cause businesses and industries to come and go. Social and demographic changes also affect particular occupational careers. A knowledge of these trends can sometimes go a long way in suggesting career choices. As already pointed out in Chapter 18, for students entering college, an examination of the sizes of various birth cohorts can

Exhibit 19.9

Applied Sociology

Experimenting with Flexible Work Schedules

The demands of work and family roles have the potential to produce many forms of conflict. One of the most common is *role overload,* conflicting time demands that make it impossible to meet two schedules. This special problem is faced by certain categories of workers. Employed mothers or fathers with school-age children simply cannot get their children off to school and still report for an eight o'clock job. At the other end of the day the parent wants to be at home when the child gets home from school.

Research with flexible work schedules suggests that they are able to lessen the problems of workers without disrupting the operations of firms. In fact, flexible schedules have turned out to be one of the most widely adopted organizational innovations of the last decade. Flextime, as it is called, is most easily adopted in the insurance and banking industries, which permit people to work at their own pace.

Flexible schedules permit workers to choose their own hours, within some limits. "Core hours" are established—usually 10:00 A.M. to 3:00 P.M.—during which all workers must be present, but people are free to arrange remaining hours at their own convenience so that they can care for children, engage in hobbies or other leisure activities, or just have free time to spend with their families.

Flexible Schedules Catch On

The use of flexible workday schedules at U.S. companies has doubled in the last 10 years.

Percentage Using Flextime

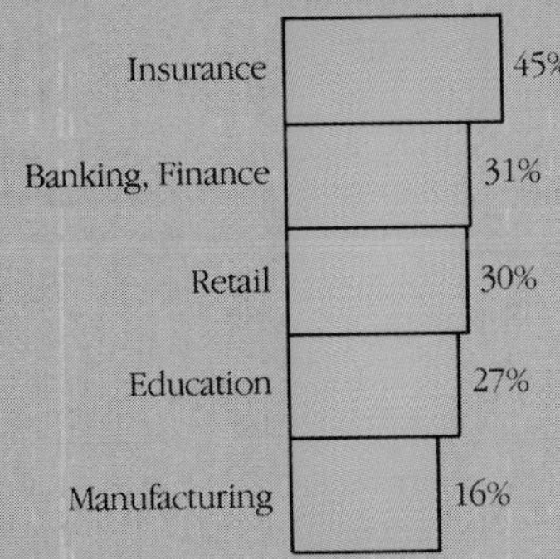

Flexible work schedules have some very positive consequences. One definite result is that they eliminate a major source of conflict between employees and supervisors—tardiness. Delinquent workers can simply make up lost time at the end of the day. Workers also gain some sense of control over their work situations. The most pronounced result is a reduction in the feelings of stress produced by the simultaneous demands of work and family. Overall, some 80% of the workers involved like the innovation.

SOURCES: Robert T. Golembiewski, Rick Hilles, and Michael Kagno, "A Longitudinal Study of Flextime Effects," *Journal of Applied Behavioral Science,* 10 (October-November 1974), pp. 503–32; Robert A. Lee, "Flextime and Conjugal Roles," *Journal of Occupational Behavior,* 4 (January 1983), pp. 297–315; Simcha Rohen, *Flexible Working Hours: An Innovation in the Quality of Work Life* (New York: McGraw-Hill, 1981).

suggest the right time to enter careers or businesses dependent on infant and school-age children.

Alternatively, sociological insights into the culture, fads, and foibles of certain occupations and industries can provide useful data for career decision making. Analyses of the culture of big business advertising suggest that as a field it might be the wrong direction for people seeking long-term professional careers. It is a fast-paced industry emphasizing glamor, youth, and vitality. As advertising executives begin to age, their careers begin to falter. A 32-year-old female junior executive in a Philadelphia advertising agency commented:

> What you are saying is very real. All you have to do is look around the industry and you'll know you are right. I doubt if you'll find any gray-haired women. . . . As for my own career, I look at it this way. When I get to the point where I look better *in* clothes than out of them, then I know it's time to get out of advertising—before I'm thrown out and am too old to shift elsewhere.[89]

Employment Interviews

Employment interviews have consistently been shown to be affected by social factors and physical appearance. It is evident that many people do not understand the process, and therefore can profit from simple advice on filing applications, dress, and the conduct of the interview. As noted already in Chapter 8 (Exhibit 8.9), "dressing for success" is a real consideration. For management and executive positions in large corporations, the business clothing styles that were deemed appropriate for men and women in the 1970s also applied in the late 1980s.

In addition, research has shown that coaching on some simple things like sitting up, looking directly at an interviewer, and being animated—suggestions based on social science research—can improve the chances of success.

Another dimension of the interview is the role of social stereotypes. Recalling the discussion earlier in this chapter in Exhibit 19.5, stereotypes in the world of work most often work to the disadvantage of women and minorities. What social science research consistently has demonstrated in this regard is that stereotypes play a greater role *when little is known about the person being judged.* When a woman or minority group member applies for a job that typically has been filled by a white male—engineer, for example—social stereotypes lead people to believe that men are more qualified. This result would suggest that when such a situation arises, a simple and direct solution would be to provide more information about the candidates' qualifications and experience, thus helping to neutralize the negative consequences of stereotypes.

Dealing with Unemployment

Social scientists have devoted a great deal of effort to understanding the problems of unemployment. A good bit of their research offers suggestions that serve to reduce difficulties facing the unemployed. Obviously, the key is to facilitate the process of finding new work, and a number of personal strategies can be taught in this regard.[90] Although the research targeted displaced workers, it also offers useful clues for those entering the job market for the first time.

Learning *how* to look for a job is the first step, and discussion groups have proven to be a useful means for teaching people the basic skills of job search and interview preparation. In one effort groups were broken down into pairs, each helping the other to follow up job leads. They also provided each other with emotional support in the process.

It is also vital that workers fully understand their individual qualifications. Self-images are shaped by the responses of others, and all too often people have only a vague sense of their strengths and weaknesses. Counselors can aid job hunters in structuring a realistic picture of their capabilities. The outcome is a more accurate list of potential job areas, and the elimination of frustration and wasted time and effort associated with applying for the wrong job.

Important too is the need to instill the motivation for a sustained job search. Some people approach job hunting in a haphazard manner. Employment counselors frequently use a simple technique to remind people of the need to systematically seek work. They encourage people to "hire themselves to find themselves a job." The point is that a successful job search requires the same strategies as a regular job—regular hours, hard work, and continuous effort. In other words, looking for a job is a full-time job.

Dealing with the frustrations caused by a continued lack of success is a more complex problem. Failure destroys the incentive to look for work, adding to the ranks of discouraged workers. It produces what social scientists call **learned helplessness,** the sense of apathy or helplessness that emerges when people feel they have no control over events.[91] Research in the laboratory has shown some success in combating learned helplessness. One strategy has been to engage people in experiments that reward competence and effort. Whether this approach can work with discouraged workers is untested, but it does illustrate the potential of applied sociology to aid in resolving the problems of unemployment.

SUMMARY

Jobs involve one of the most salient roles that people in industrial societies occupy. Although important, jobs mean quite a bit more than earning a living. People have many expectations about work that offers them meaningful and challenging experiences and the chance to improve themselves.

Conflict and competition are an integral part of the world of work. Members of occupations join together to improve their income and working conditions. This often brings labor and management into conflict. It also produces conflicts over the scope of work tasks, as illustrated in physician-pharmacist debate over prescribing medicines. Conflict may be more individualized as when service workers and customers meet.

Major social and technological forces are reshaping the nature of work in contemporary society. This point is nowhere more evident than in blue-collar occupations where skilled craft workers face the dual threat of displacement and deskilling. Established professions, once largely self-regulating, face a massive number of lawsuits as their clients turn to the courts to protect their interests. Housework, traditionally accepted by both men and women as part of the female role, has become a center of controversy as increasing numbers of wives enter the paid work force.

Careers in any occupation can be viewed in terms of a number of steps. The first step is getting the job, that is, completing applications and negotiating employment interviews. Then come the entry-level jobs, the learning of job skills, and figuring out how to get along with co-workers. Later stages in the career path involve the pursuit of positions of increasing rewards and responsibility. Success along the way can be aided by the help of informal teachers or mentors. Often unrecognized is the fact that blocked mobility and unemployment are often a regular part of most work careers. Both are difficult experiences, and workers must learn to cope with such setbacks if they are to continue to function in society.

KEY TERMS/CONCEPTS

blocked mobility
boundary disputes
developmental career path
deskilling
displacement
executives
fast-track career path
fixed career path
glass ceiling
learned helplessness
low-ceiling career path
managers
occupational stereotyping
profession
trait stereotyping
unemployment rate
work careers

DISCUSSION QUESTIONS

1. Is it a good idea to monitor employees' behavior with computers, or does it violate some basic employee rights? What rights do workers have? What rights do you think they should have?
2. Will robots be able to replace every worker, or will some jobs always require human beings? If so, which ones?
3. Many people talk about "dressing for success." What does that mean for a woman today? A man? Given the manner in which the average college student dresses most (if not all) of the time, how easy do you think it will be to "dress successfully"?
4. If you were an executive, forced to close a plant because it was unprofitable, how could you help the workers who would lose their jobs?
5. Generally only physicians are legally permitted to write prescriptions, but pharmacists, nurses, and even optometrists claim they should have the right to prescribe certain drugs. Are such people qualified? Why or why not?

SUGGESTED READINGS

Richard N. Bolles, *What Color Is Your Parachute?* (New York: Ten Speed, 1986). A popular manual for the person looking for their first job or thinking about changing careers.

Eliot Freidson, *Professional Powers* (Chicago: University of Chicago Press, 1986). This book examines the way in which formal knowledge is created, acquired, used, and translated into political power.

Richard H. Hall, *Dimensions of Work* (Beverly Hills, CA: Sage, 1987). The most thorough and comprehensive survey of sociological theory and research available on the world of work.

Robert A. Rothman, *Working: Sociological Perspectives* (Englewood Cliffs, NJ: Prentice-Hall, 1987). A textbook focusing on the social context of jobs and occupational careers.

Studs Terkel, *Working* (New York: Avon, 1974). This modern classic contains interviews with dozens of people in which they reveal, in their own words, the rewards and frustrations of their jobs.

NOTES

1. *Business Week,* May 1, 1989, p. 53.
2. *New York Times,* July 7, 1987, p. 1D.
3. *USA Today,* July 7, 1986, p. 6B.
4. Emile Durkheim, *The Division of Labor in Society* (New York: Free Press, 1956).
5. *New York Times,* June 15, 1986, p. 1F; *USA Today,* November 14, 1985, pp. 1D–2D. See also Sue Arnold, "The British Nanny Carries On, Though She's Being Updated," *Smithsonian,* 14 (January 1984), pp. 97–105.
6. This perspective on work and occupations is developed in Eliot Freidson, *The Profession of Medicine* (New York: Dodd, Mead, 1972); Magali Sarfatti Larson, *The Rise of Professionalism* (Berkeley, CA: University of California Press, 1977); Robert A. Rothman, "Occupational Roles: Power and

Negotiation in the Division of Labor," *Sociological Quarterly,* 20 (Autumn 1979), pp. 495–515.
7. Carol L. Kronus, "The Evolution of Occupational Power: A Historical Study of Task Boundaries Between Physicians and Pharmacists," *Sociology of Work and Occupations,* 3 (1976), pp. 3–37.
8. Robert S. Broadhead and Neil J. Facchinetti, "Drug Iatrogenesis and Clinical Pharmacy," *Social Problems,* 32 (June 1985), pp. 426–36.
9. *USA Today,* May 14, 1986, p. 5D.
10. See *Newsweek,* May 25, 1987, pp. 32–33.
11. See, for example, Nancy C. Morse and Robert S. Weiss, "The Function and Meaning of Work and the Job," *American Sociological Review,* 30 (April 1955), pp. 191–98; *New York Times,* December 4, 1983, pp. 1, 66; Barbara Renwick and Edward E. Lawler III, "What Do You Really Want From Your Job?" *Psychology Today,* 11 (May 1978), pp. 53–65.
12. Edward F. Pajak and Joseph J. Blase, "Teachers in Bars," *Sociology of Education,* 57 (July 1983), pp. 164–73.
13. See, for example, Mark Baker, *Cops: Their Lives in Their Own Words* (New York: Simon and Schuster, 1985); Robert M. Fogelson, *Big-City Police* (Cambridge, MA: Harvard University Press, 1977); Jonathan Rubinstein, *City Police* (New York: Farrar, Straus and Giroux, 1973).
14. James Bryan, "Occupational Ideologies and Individual Attitudes of Call Girls," *Social Problems,* 13 (1966), pp. 441–50.
15. Studs Terkel, *Working* (New York: Random House, 1972), p. 685.
16. Rosabeth Moss Kanter, *Men and Women of the Corporation* (New York: Basic Books, 1977), p. 129.
17. United States Employment and Training Administration, *Dictionary of Occupational Titles* (Washington, DC: U.S. Government Printing Office, 1977).
18. See, for example, Eliot Freidson, *Professional Powers* (Chicago: University of Chicago Press, 1986); Magali Sarfatti Larson, *The Rise of Professionalism* (Berkeley: University of California Press, 1977).
19. James W. Begun and Ronald D. Feldman, *A Social and Economic Analysis of Professional Regulation in Optometry* (Washington, DC: National Center for Health Services Research, 1981), p. 21.
20. The following description of the activities of corporate executives is drawn from John P. Kotter, *The General Managers* (New York: Free Press, 1982).
21. Jack C. Horn, "Executive Action," *Psychology Today,* 14 (January 1986), p. 14.
22. Executive compensation data from *Business Week,* May 1, 1989, p. 47.
23. See David Lockwood, *The Blackcoated Worker* (London: Allen and Unwin, 1958); C. Wright Mills, *White Collar* (New York: Oxford, 1951).
24. Julia Kagan and Julianne Malveau, "The Uneasy Alliance of the Boss and Secretary," *Working Woman,* 11 (May 1986), p. 106.
25. Mary Kathleen Benet, *The Secretarial Ghetto* (New York: McGraw-Hill, 1972).
26. George Ritzer and David Walczak, *Working: Conflict and Change* (Englewood Cliffs, NJ: Prentice-Hall, 1986), p. 318.
27. See Daniel T. Rodgers, *The Work Ethic in Industrial America, 1850–1920* (Chicago: University of Chicago Press, 1978), p. 23.
28. Michael Wallace and Arne Kalleberg, "Industrial Transformation and the Decline of Craft: The Decomposition of Skill in the Printing Industry," *American Sociological Review,* 47 (June 1982), pp. 307–24.
29. Karl Marx, *Karl Marx: Early Writings,* translated and edited by T. B. Bottomore (New York: McGraw-Hill, 1964), pp. 124–26.
30. Karl Marx, *Karl Marx,* p. 125.
31. Robert Blauner, *Alienation and Freedom* (Chicago: University of Chicago Press, 1964); Melvin L. Kohn, *Class and Conformity* (Homewood, IL: Dorsey, 1972); Jon Sheppard, *Alienation and Automation* (Cambridge, MA: MIT Press, 1971).
32. Betty Friedan, *The Feminine Mystique,* (New York: Dell, 1963).
33. *American Demographics,* October 1985, pp. 23–27.
34. Joann Vanek, "Time Spent in Housework," *Scientific American,* 231 (November 1974), pp. 116–20.
35. Erik Arnold, "The Appliance of Science: Technology and Housework," *New Scientist,* 18 (April 1985), pp. 12–15.
36. *American Demographics,* October 1985, pp. 23–27.
37. Dana V. Hiller and William W. Philliber, "The Division of Labor in Contemporary Marriage," *Social Problems,* 23 (February 1986), pp. 191–201.
38. Joseph H. Pleck, *Working Wives, Working Husbands* (Beverly Hills, CA: Sage, 1985).
39. *USA Today,* May 10, 1985, p. 1A.
40. *Fortune,* February 16, 1987, p. 36.
41. Geoffrey Greif, *Single Fathers* (Lexington, MA: Lexington, 1985).
42. Barbara Berg, *The Crisis of the Working Mother* (New York: Summit, 1986).
43. Dana V. Hiller and William W. Philliber, "The Division of Labor."
44. Glenna Spitze, "Family Migration Largely Unresponsive to Wives' Employment," *Sociology and Social Research,* 70 (April 1986), pp. 231–34.
45. Bam Dev Sharada and Barry E. Nangle, "Marital Effects on Occupational Attainment," *Journal of Family Issues,* 2 (February 1981), pp. 148–56.
46. Zick Rubin, "Are Working Wives Hazardous to Their Husbands' Mental Health," *Psychology Today,* 17 (May 1983), pp. 70–72.
47. *USA Today,* June 4, 1987, p. 7D.
48. *New York Times,* December 7, 1986, p. 33.
49. *Newsweek,* September 2, 1985, p. 59.
50. A review of the issues may be found in Anne E. Rothman, "Day Care," Unpublished paper, (Newark, DE: University of Delaware, 1985).
51. Lois Hoffman, "Maternal Employment," *American Psychologist,* 34 (1979), pp. 859–65.
52. Richard D. Arvey and James E. Champion, "The Employment Interview," *Personnel Psychology,* 25 (1982), pp. 281–83.
53. Robert L. Dipole, H. L. Fromkin and K. Wiback, "Relative Importance of Applicant Sex, Attractiveness, and Scholastic Standing in Evaluation of Job Applicant Résumés," *Journal of Applied Psychology,* 60 (1975), pp. 39–43.
54. Michael R. Cunningham, "Measuring the Physical in Physical Attractiveness: Quasi-Experiments on the Sociobiology of Female Physical Beauty," *Journal of Personality and Social Psychology,* 50 (1986), pp. 925–35.
55. David Kurtz, "Physical Appearance and Stature," *Personnel Journal,* 48 (1969), pp. 981–83.

56. Gail Tom and Jeanne Shevell, "The Height of Success," *Sociology and Social Research,* 71 (October 1986), pp. 15–19.
57. Robert A. Rothman, *Working: Sociological Perspectives* (Englewood Cliffs: Prentice-Hall, 1987), pp. 271–72.
58. *USA Today,* May 28, 1985, p. 5B.
59. Richard D. Arvey and James E. Champion, "The Employment Interview."
60. *USA Today,* November 6, 1986, p. 1B.
61. *USA Today,* June 17, 1987, p. 7B.
62. See, for example, Paul R. Joseph, "Fourth Amendment Implications of Public Sector Workplace Drug Testing," *Nova Law Review,* 11 (Winter 1987), pp. 605–45.
63. Arthur J. McBay, "Efficient Drug Testing: Addressing the Basic Issues," *Nova Law Review,* 11 (Winter 1987), pp. 647–52.
64. *USA Today,* May 28, 1985, p. 7B.
65. *Newsweek,* May 5, 1986, p. 47.
66. *New York Times,* February 24, 1985, p. 17F.
67. *USA Today,* February 3, 1987, p. 8A.
68. Daniel C. Feldman, "A Contingency Theory of Socialization," *Administrative Science Quarterly,* 21 (September 1976), pp. 433–52.
69. Gene Dalton, Paul Thompson and Raymond Price, "The Four Stages of Professional Careers," *Organizational Dynamics,* 8 (Spring 1977), p. 24.
70. Karen N. Gaertner, "The Structure of Organizational Careers," *Sociology of Education,* January 1980, p. 17.
71. See Rosabeth Moss Kanter, *Men and Women of the Corporation,* pp. 133–34.
72. See James E. Rosenbaum, "Organizational Career Mobility," *American Journal of Sociology,* 85 (July 1979), pp. 21–48.
73. *Business Week,* June 22, 1987, p. 73.
74. See, for example, Linda K. Brown, "Women and Business Management," *Signs,* 5 (Winter 1979), pp. 267–88.
75. Rosabeth Moss Kanter, *Men and Women of the Corporation,* pp. 155–57.
76. R. Gerald Roche, "Much Ado About Mentors," *Harvard Business Review,* 57 (January-February 1979), pp. 14–24.
77. Helen J. McLane, *Selecting, Developing, and Retaining Women Executives* (New York: Von Nostrand, 1980).
78. Harriet Zuckerman, *Scientific Elite* (New York: Free Press, 1977).
79. Robert R. Faulkner, *Hollywood Studio Musicians* (Chicago: Aldine-Atherton, 1977).
80. *Handbook of Labor Statistics* (Washington, DC: United States Bureau of Labor Statistics, 1985), Table 14, p. 38.
81. Richard M. Devens, Jr., "Employment and Unemployment in 1984," *Monthly Labor Review,* 108 (February 1985), pp. 3–15.
82. Peter B. Warr, "Reported Behavioral Changes After Job Loss," *British Journal of Social Psychology,* 13 (1983), pp. 271–75.
83. Joe E. Feagin first proposed this idea in "Poverty, We Still Believe That God Helps Those Who Help Themselves," *Psychology Today,* 6 (1977), pp. 101–29. Adrian Furham has extended this research to Britain in, "Why Are The Poor Always With Us?" *British Journal of Social Psychology,* 21 (1982), pp. 311–22.
84. Nancy K. Schlossberg and Zandy Leibowitz, "Organizational Support Systems as a Buffer Against Job Loss," *Journal of Vocational Behavior,* 17 (1980), pp. 204–17.
85. Roy Payne, Peter B. Warr, and Jean Hartley, "Social Class and Psychological Ill-health during Unemployment," *Sociology of Health and Illness,* 6 (July 1984), pp. 152–74.
86. M. Harvey Brenner, *Mental Illness and the Economy* (Cambridge: Harvard University Press, 1973).
87. *Monthly Labor Review,* 109 (November 1986), Table 10, p. 74.
88. Schlossberg and Leibowitz, "Organizational Support Systems."
89. Personal communication, June 1, 1987.
90. Sue J. Hepworth, "Moderating Factors of the Psychological Impact of Unemployment," *Journal of Occupational Psychology,* 53 (January 1980), pp. 139–45.
91. M. E. P. Seligman, *Learned Helplessness* (San Francisco: Freeman, 1975).

Terrorism, War, and Peace

If anything has been learned from the study of society, it is that while groups, communities, and nations endeavor toward harmonious relationships with one another, social contact also tends to produce conflict. Conflict manifests itself in many ways. Social conflict in its more innocuous and relatively common forms may involve the simple rivalries between siblings or peers, and the competition among students and work mates for achievement. More disruptive forms of conflict have been studied throughout this textbook. The extremes include terrorism and war, manifestations of social conflict at a level that can be disruptive to the order of entire societies and nations.

Although terrorism is a rare phenomenon within the borders of the United States, Americans abroad have had their share of exposure to terrorist activities throughout the 1980s. As the decade began, 52 Americans were being held hostage at the U.S. Embassy in Teheran, where they had been seized more than a year earlier. Other highly visible terrorist events included the bombing of the U.S. Embassy and military barracks in Beirut in 1983 and a second bombing of the embassy annex the following year. In 1985 an Athens nightclub frequented by American service personnel was bombed, TWA flight 847 was hijacked by Shiite Muslims after takeoff from Athens, and the Italian cruise ship *Achille Lauro* was hijacked in the Mediterranean by Palestinian terrorists, who also conducted follow-up attacks on the Rome and Vienna airports some months later. During the rest of the decade car bombings and kidnappings continued, and Americans frequently were among the victims.

While the United States was not at war at any time during the 1980s, Americans were bombarded on an almost daily basis, however indirectly, with news of the violence and destruction imposed by other nations at war. Throughout the decade, the national media devoted a considerable amount of its reporting time to the Iran-Iraq war, the troubles between Israel and the Palestinians (see Exhibit 20.1), the attacks and counterattacks between Libya and Chad, the struggles involving the British and

Exhibit 20.1

Case Study

Israeli-Palestinian Conflict

The conflicts between contemporary Jews and Arabs are directly linked to the establishment of the state of Israel in 1948—an event rooted deeply in history. Palestine is an historic region on the eastern shore of the Mediterranean Sea, comprising parts of modern Israel, Jordan, and Egypt. Palestine is also the "Holy Land" of the Jews, having been promised to them by God as recorded in the Old Testament. The area is venerated by Christians because it was the place where Jesus Christ lived and died. It also holds special importance for Moslems because they consider Islam to be the heir of Judaism and Christianity, and because according to Moslem tradition, Jerusalem is the site of Muhammad's ascent to heaven.

The lands embracing Palestine have been disputed for millennia. Early in its history the region was inhabited by the Jews, but it was conquered and occupied at various times by forces from Mesopotamia, Babylonia, Persia, and the Roman Empire. Under Rome's Emperor Constantine, Palestine became a center of Christian pilgrimage in the fourth century A.D., thus initiating Jewish emigration. By the seventh century, Palestine had come under Arab rule, and the region became important to Moslems for the first time. Arab domination spirited further emigration. During the next thousand years, Palestine was ruled by Egypt and twice by the Ottoman Turks.

In the meantime, as the result of various antisemitic pogroms in late-nineteenth-century Russia, the Zionist movement was born. Founded by Theodor Herzl in 1897, it was a crusade for reconstituting the Jewish nation—*in Palestine*. As Turkish rule of Palestine crumbled and was finally dismantled by the Allies after World War I, new opportunities emerged for the Zionist initiative. The Balfour Declaration in 1917 was a pledge of British support for Zionist hopes in Palestine, provided that the integrity of non-Jewish communities already there be respected. Then, in 1922, the League of Nations gave Britain a mandate over Palestine. The terms of the arrangement included the establishment of an agency to advise on the creation of a Jewish nation.

For the next two decades Jewish immigration to Palestine and colonization of the region increased, but only in accordance with strict quotas established by the British government. Numerous clashes took place between Arabs and politically militant Jews, primarily because of Arab fears with regard to the political and economic implications of Jewish immigration and land purchase. The rise of Nazism and antisemitism in Europe during the 1930s, however, resulted in an easing of the restrictions on immigration. Whereas only 5,000 Jews were authorized for entry into Palestine in 1932, by 1935 that figure was up to over 60,000. By the end of World War II the Jewish population of Palestine numbered over half a million, as compared with only 56,000 in 1922.

To protect themselves from increasing Arab hostility, the *Hashomer* (watchman) and *Haganah* (defense organization) were established—Jewish vigilante groups that served as informal, but highly visible, internal defense forces. Militant Zionists in Palestine, however, turned to terrorism—attacking both Arabs and British rule. In 1947, the United Nations voted to divide the region into two ethnically based states, and the following year Britain withdrew from the area. Both Jews and Arabs objected to the partitioning of Palestine, and during the ensuing conflicts Jewish forces drove 400,000 Arabs out of the region. The Jews established the independent state of Israel, to which both the United States and the Soviet Union accorded immediate recognition.

The exodus of Palestinians from Israel fostered a new sense of Palestinian consciousness, and what had once been communal violence was quickly transformed into a national liberation movement. Since that time, Israel and a variety of pro-Palestinian groups have battled one another for possession of the Holy Land.

SOURCES: Peter Janke, *Guerrilla and Terrorist Organizations: A World Dictionary and Bibliography* (New York: Macmillan, 1983), pp. 239–46; David K. Shipler, *Arab and Jew: Wounded Spirits in a Promised Land* (New York: Times, 1986).

the Irish Republican Army, and the conflicts in Central America. Late in the decade the so-called tanker wars occurred in the Persian Gulf. The purposes of this chapter are to examine the dimensions of terrorism and warfare, their sociological significance, their relationships to the general social order, and the steps that societies and governments take to attain peace.

TERRORISM

As they issued their final report in 1986, after hearing testimony from hundreds of witnesses and reviewing 2,375 magazines, 725 books, and 2,370 films, the members of the Attorney General's Commission on Pornography confessed that they had no better definition of pornography than the one offered years earlier by the late Supreme Court Justice Potter Stewart, who stated, "I know it when I see it."[1] The same statement might be made concerning terrorism, for when analyzing television, press, and wire service reports on terrorism, it is never quite clear exactly what the phenomenon in question really is. From reading much of the terrorism literature, it would appear that terrorism, most of the time, is *terrorism* when people think it is terrorism.

Defining Terrorism

Political scientists and specialists in international affairs have struggled for decades with the problems of defining terrorism; almost every treatise on the topic begins with the definitional question.[2] One result has been a lack of agreement on exactly what terrorism is. In fact, a recent research guide on the topic listed more than 100

The cockpit of Pan Am flight 103 landed in a field in Scotland after the plane was blown apart by a terrorist bomb in December 1988.

definitions of terrorism offered between 1936 and 1981.[3] The difficulty stems from the fact that many forms of political violence have been called "terrorism" at one time or another. In the broadest sense, terrorism is the use of violence for political ends, but such a definition has a variety of shortcomings because reality is far more complicated than any generalization.

At various times terrorism has included the indiscriminate acts of aggression that seem to be a by-product of all forms of war, violent repression on the part of governments to quell opposition to its rule, acts of protest of all types when violence is involved, and perhaps most conspicuously, the coordinated activities of revolutionary groups organized to bring about political change—activities such as those of the Irish Republican Army, Italy's Red Brigades, and the many Middle Eastern groups operating under the umbrella of the Islamic Jihad (see Exhibit 20.2).[4]

Certainly what has been called "terrorism" is not a uniquely isolated form of political activity. Rather, terrorism exists on a continuum ranging from aspects of conventional warfare, through assassination, **guerrilla warfare** and **insurgency** (aggression by small military units for the purpose of creating liberated zones in which an alternative government can be established), sabotage, state repression, persecution, and torture. But despite these many differences in perspective, all terrorism specialists seem to agree on a few points. First, terrorism is almost exclusively a *political* weapon. Second, it is grounded in ideological politics. Third, it is a technique of psychological warfare, accomplished primarily through violence directed against innocent, civilian victims. Fourth, the victims of terrorist violence are not necessarily the primary targets. And fifth, the effects of relatively small amounts of violence tend to be disproportionate to the number of people terrorized,[5] or to cite an ancient Chinese proverb, "kill one, frighten ten thousand."

Observers of terrorism also agree on several other points. Terrorists are not simply vandals. They always have a purpose. They do what they do in the name of "justice," although their conception of justice often may be at odds with that of the rest of the world. From the "Assassins" of eleventh- and twelfth-century Islam to the contemporary M-19 guerrillas in Colombia or the Islamic Jihad in the Middle East, terrorists always have a cause for which they are willing to destroy or kill. Moreover, the cause need not be something immediate. Armenians murder Turkish diplomats today because thousands of Turks exterminated thousands of Armenians long ago. None of the original killers are still alive, but no matter. Some feuds survive in the culture. Irish Catholics are still avenging themselves on Oliver Cromwell.

Keeping these general guidelines in mind, **terrorism** is probably best defined as the systematic use or threat of extreme violence directed against innocent victims, and typically performed for psychological rather than material effects, with the aim of coercing individuals, groups, communities, or governments into making political concessions.

Terrorist Organization and Operations

Terrorism is a phenomenon that does not lend itself well to social scientific analysis. Unlike studies of bureaucracy, narcotics addiction, labor-management relations, incest taboos, and the many other activities, organizations, and behavior patterns that sociologists study, accessing terrorists in the field itself often involves a number of potential obstacles, including the safety of the researcher. Nevertheless, much has been learned about terrorists and their organizations, primarily through observations of overt terrorist operations and the interrogation of captured participants.

Terrorist Ideology

Terrorism, as noted earlier, is grounded in ideological politics. That is, it is rooted in a specific political doctrine and the beliefs on which that doctrine is based. The ideology may reflect nationalist ideas of liberation from colonial rule or Marxist opposition to a class-based power structure. Terrorist ideologies have been pro-Communist and anti-Communist, leftist and rightist, liberal and conservative. To cite but one specific example, consider the ideological politics of Peru's *Sendero Luminoso* (Shining Path) insurgents.

Sendero Luminoso emerged from a tangled web of Peruvian politics in 1970 in the ancient colonial city of Ayacucho—a community of 70,000 residents located some 200 miles southeast of Lima. The force behind Sendero's creation was Abimael Guzmán, a philosophy professor at the San Cristobal de Huamanga University.[6] Noting the striking class differences in his society, Guzmán concluded that as Peru approached the twenty-first century, it was still a semifeudal and semicolonial society. Moreover, the government embodied a fascist structure masquerading as a democracy and engaging in the construction of a corporate state and the development of bureaucratic capitalism. Guzmán's political ideology was predominantly *Maoist,* the militant Communist philosophy of China's Mao Tse-Tung, which teaches "uninterrupted revolution" and the overwhelming role of the human will in history. Guzmán held that social reform could be achieved only by making revolutionaries out of Peruvian peasants for the purpose of overthrowing the established government.

Sendero Luminoso first came to widespread public attention after a full decade of dogmatic self-examination

Exhibit 20.2 Sociological Focus

Terrorist Organizations

Literally hundreds of guerrilla and terrorist organizations are located throughout the world. Those described here include a few that have received media attention in recent years, as well as groups referred to later in this chapter.

Palestine Liberation Organization (PLO)

The PLO was an outgrowth of an Arab summit conference held in 1964 at which delegates decided to establish a formal Palestinian entity with the objective of supporting armed struggle to regain lands held by Israel. All Palestinians are considered natural members of the PLO, and dues and taxes were regularly paid to the organization. The PLO has a constitution and an elected executive committee. Since 1969 the chairman of the PLO's executive committee has been Yasser Arafat, a Palestinian born in Jerusalem in 1929 and educated as an engineer at Cairo University during the early 1950s. Over the years the PLO executive committee has been dominated by many guerrilla factions, of which *Fatah* is the most powerful.

Al-Fatah

Fatah, better known to Westerners as the Palestine National Liberation Movement, was the first Palestinian commando organization. Established in the mid-fifties, it was a nationalist movement whose purpose was to liberate Palestine from Israeli occupation by waging low-intensity warfare. Under the command of PLO leader, Yasser Arafat, Fatah attacked Israeli settlements and quickly grew in organizational capacity. The Palestine Liberation Organization intially confronted Fatah as a rival group, but emnity ended in 1969 when Arafat became the chairman of the PLO.

Amal

The Islamic religion has many branches, of which the Shiites are the most militant. Shiite Muslims constitute 40% of the population of Lebanon, but they have long been considered second-class citizens. During the late 1960s, however, a council to represent Shiite interests in Lebanon was founded by Moussa Sadr, a highly educated Shiite cleric. In 1975, having been granted the title of *Imam* (a spiritual leader whose authority is derived directly from the Prophet Muhammad), Sadr established *Amal* (hope), an armed militia that has played a continuing role in the Lebanese civil war. Amal has ties with Iran and the PLO, and it was originally neutral vis-à-vis Israel. However, following Israel's invasion of South Lebanon during the early 1980s, Amal turned against the Jews and their political and military supporters (including the United States).

The Islamic Jihad

Several radical groups split from Amal in 1982 and became known as the Islamic *Jihad* (holy war). The Islamic Jihad is a Shiite cover organization that unites a host of Lebanese, Iranian, and Iraqi terrorist groups for the purpose of making war on the West and spreading a Shiite Islamic revolution throughout the Middle East. It was this terrorist organization that was responsible for the suicide bombings against the U.S. embassies in Beirut and Kuwait and the U.S. Marine Corps barracks in Lebanon.

Abu Nidal Group

Conflict and terrorism in the Middle East are not simply matters of Arab-Israeli differences and related hostilities. Nationalist, ethnic, and religious groups throughout the region seek to avenge and rectify past wrongs. Religious fundamentalists hold strong longings for national redemption, national power, self-purification, and revenge. Extremist factions within all of the active groups support goals and methods that are often at odds with those of the parent organization. Political groups, both right wing and left wing, strive to increase their power. Religious zealots hope to purge infidels from Islam. The result is not just terrorism against Israel and the West, but terrorism that also pits Arab against Arab. It is within this context that the infamous Abu Nidal group has played a major role.

Sabri al Banna, better known as Abu Nidal, attained fame in the 1980s as the most ruthless and radical Palestinian leader—a man who did not shy away from any act or form of terrorism. Originally a member of the PLO, Abu Nidal ultimately formed his own group. Often changing his alliances, his activities have been directed against other Arab leaders, and over the years his operations have targeted the PLO, Syria, Jordan, and Israel. Although active in the Middle East since the early 1970s, Abu Nidal did not come to the attention of mainstream America

Abu Nidal, photographed in Tripoli in 1983, is perhaps the world's most active and elusive terrorist.

until 1985 when he acknowledged his responsibility in the coordination of the terrorist bombings at the Rome and Vienna airports—activities undertaken at the behest of Libya.

ETA (Basque Homeland and Liberty)

The ETA stems from a century-old struggle for nationhood waged by the Basques in Spain. ETA dates to 1959, having evolved from a radical group that split from a Basque political party. The group draws its strength from the Basque people, who are spread throughout the provinces in northern Spain along the Bay of Biscay and the French border. ETA political violence has accounted for some 450 terrorist murders and numerous acts of sabotage.

IRA (Irish Republican Army)

The emergence of the IRA is an outgrowth of the treaty with Great Britain in 1922 that partitioned Ireland into the Irish Free State and Northern Ireland. The IRA evolved as a militant group seeking reunification. The IRA's terrorist activities throughout the British Isles resulted in hundreds of deaths.

The Red Brigades

Emerging in Italy in the early 1970s, the *Brigate Rosse,* or Red Brigades, was formed by disillusioned middle-class students seeking to establish Communism through armed struggle. The group's activities have included arson, murder, kidnapping, bombing, and industrial sabotage. Their most well-known terrorist act was the kidnap-murder of former Italian prime minister Aldo Moro in 1978. The killing of Moro aroused universal indignation throughout Italy. Antiterrorist squads captured many of the leading members of the Red Brigades in the aftermath of the Moro assassination. The organization has nevertheless persisted, but with only minimal strength.

Movimiento 19 de Abril (M-19)

Colombia's M-19 is a Marxist insurgent-terrorist group that has become quite visible in South America in recent years. Its origins are rooted in the National Popular Alliance (ANP), a minor political party that had been successful enough in the 1960s to be represented in the Colombian parliament. In the much disputed presidential election of April 19, 1970, however, the ANP suffered serious losses. To extremists in the party, the only solution appeared to be an armed struggle aimed at achieving political ends. Named after the date of the disputed election, M-19 (*Movimiento 19 de Abril* or 19th of April Movement) officially announced its birth in 1974 by raiding the Simón Bolívar Museum outside Bogotá, making off with the sword and spurs of the man who is revered as "the Liberator" in much of Latin America.

After its theatrical debut as an insurgent-guerrilla movement, M-19 followed the normal terrorist course of bank robberies, raids on military armories, kidnappings, and killings. Yet it has always had a touch of flamboyance about its activities for which it has received considerable international publicity. In 1979, M-19 tunneled into a Bogotá arsenal to steal armaments; in 1980 group members kidnapped all of the guests, including a U.S. ambassador, attending a cocktail party at the embassy of the Dominican Republic in Bogotá; and in 1981 the group kidnapped and executed a missionary from the United States.

Throughout the 1980s, M-19 continued to gain strength, threatening the integrity of democracy in Colombia and extending its operations to neighboring Brazil.

SOURCES: Christopher Dobson and Ronald Payne, *The Never-Ending War: Terrorism in the 80's* (New York: Facts on File, 1987); Peter Janke, *Guerrilla and Terrorist Organizations: A World Directory and Bibliography* (New York: Macmillan, 1983); Walter Laqueur, *The Age of Terrorism* (Boston: Little, Brown, 1987).

and rigorously selective recruitment. The violence against the government began in July 1980, and by the end of that year some 240 terrorist incidents had been recorded, including the destruction of local tax records, bombings of government offices, and sabotage of electricity pylons.[7] By 1981, the number of incidents had increased, expanding to include such activities as the raiding of banks, mines, and police posts. Kidnapping was added the following year. Sendero's most spectacular action took place early in 1982 when 150 guerrillas attacked the Ayacucho jail, freeing some 300 prisoners.

The ideological politics of the Sendero Luminoso became most evident in the focus of its terrorist activities during 1986. In southern Peru, Sendero guerrillas captured plantations and haciendas, sometimes killing their owners and employees, and distributing cattle, sheep, alpacas, and other goods to local peasants.[8]

Terrorist Membership

Students new to terrorism and the politics of the Middle East have often been introduced to these topics with the fable of the scorpion and the frog that one day find themselves together on a riverbank. The scorpion asks the frog to carry him across to the other shore.

"Don't be ridiculous," answers the frog. "If I let you on my back, you'll sting me!"

But the scorpion points out that he cannot swim, and if he were to sting the frog in midriver, they would both drown.

So the frog, persuaded by the logic of the argument, allows the scorpion to climb up on his back, and they set out into the river. When they reach the middle, the scorpion stings the frog and the paralyzed amphibian starts to sink beneath the water.

"Why did you do that?" the frog feebly croaks. "Now we'll both die."

"Oh well," the scorpion sighs, shrugging his carapace. "After all, this is the Middle East, and *I* am a terrorist."[9]

This fable seems to suggest that terrorists are individuals with severe emotional disturbances—individuals who may harbor intense suicidal impulses or repressed hatreds for all that humanity represents. Other images conjure up the stereotypical villains of television and Hollywood: enraged lunatics, mercenary assassins, or emotionless robots. But research suggests that these impressions are not necessarily valid, for as one observer of the phenomenon noted: "A psychological profile of a model terrorist cannot be drawn. The personalities are disparate. The context and circumstances within which terrorism . . . has been carried out are diverse in chronology, geography, and motive."[10] Examining the nature of the terrorist in a somewhat different light, a Chicago journalist quite familiar with the matter once described the terrorist as "the guy next door."[11] Most other observers seem to agree with this assessment,[12] and the logic of it is deeply rooted in the politics and ideologies of the groups from which terrorists emerge. Perhaps this point is best illustrated through a brief examination of the situation in the Middle East.

As the fable of the frog and the scorpion clearly suggests, Middle Eastern politics are violent and vengeful. However, they are not quite so irrational. The key element in the relationship between terrorism and rationality is Islam, the religion of the overwhelming majority of the people in the Arab states and Iran. Islam is not merely a set of beliefs about God, but a very specific program for individual behavior and social organization. Drawn from precepts found in the Koran and other writings, Islamic regulations cover almost all aspects of private and public life. Islamic fundamentalists hold that religious law must be implemented in its every detail, and that the fulfillment of God's commands is a duty incumbent on all believers.

To these beliefs should be added the fact that from the point of view of Islamic fundamentalists, the culture and politics of the West (and those of Israel) are considered to be not only ethically and morally corrupt, but are viewed as threats to the very existence of Islamic civilization as well. In the minds of many Middle Easterners a life-and-death struggle characterizes relations between the East and the West. Since extremism has always been an aspect of Arab politics, subversion, aggression, and terrorism are justified. In addition, Islamic law teaches that believers who sacrifice their lives in pursuit of religious ends are guaranteed a place in eternity with Allah.[13]

Within this context, one begins to understand why Lebanese terrorists were willing to sacrifice themselves by driving a dynamite-laden truck into the Beirut headquarters of the United States Marines on August 23, 1983, and why an Egyptian soldier in the Sinai was deemed a hero by several Arab governments in 1985 after he murdered seven Israeli tourists, including five children, in cold blood.

In the Middle East and elsewhere, terrorists generally *are* the "people next door," but other things are known about them as well. On the basis of comprehensive studies of terrorist profiles conducted by Charles Russell and Bowman Miller, most members of terrorist groups tend to be young adults between the ages of 18 and 35.[14] Although the vast majority are males, women now and then play leading roles. These individuals generally come from middle-class or upwardly mobile working-class families. Russell and Miller also have pointed out that many terrorists have been recruited from the ranks of college students, white-collar workers,

Drawing by Englehart, *The Hartford Courant.*

and professionals who were involved in nonviolent political activity on the fringes of mainstream political parties. The major recruiting grounds tend to be Western university campuses staffed with Marxist professors and Marxist-dominated student federations.

The most recent terrorist profile was developed by Risks International, Inc. of Alexandria, Virginia, in 1985.[15] It found the average terrorist to be a single or separated male between the ages of 20 and 23, who typically had attended college for a few years, was from a middle- or upper-class urban family, and was recruited from a university campus. Moreover, the Risks profile indicated that today's terrorists support a Marxist ideology and are either students, government workers, nurses, or sociologists.

Thus, terrorism seems to be explained not by individual pathologies, but rather, by the social context within which it occurs. Cultural traditions define certain groups as enemies, often keeping ancient animosities alive. As noted earlier in Chapter 4, the world is divided into clusters of in-groups and out-groups—an arrangement that is clearly evident in the politics of terrorism. Members of terrorist organizations are recruited from groups that are already politically active, typically at universities where the appropriate political ideals flourish. Most terrorists are single men and women, because such individuals lack the strong social ties that might cause divided loyalties.

Terrorist Financing

Many acts of terrorism are limited by national boundaries and seldom receive much attention in the international media. Those incidents that do receive attention often are committed by members of large-scale, international terrorist organizations active worldwide. Such terrorist organizations cannot be run on ideology and enthusiasm alone, for international terrorism is an expensive proposition. Money is needed for logistic purposes, for travel, for information, and perhaps most importantly, for the day-to-day living expenses of the members of the organizations who generally have no other income.

Equipment, arms, vehicles, and housing also must be secured. Weapons and dynamite can be stolen, but large-scale thefts of arms tend to be risky and opportunities for such thefts are limited. While an active underground arms market operates internationally to provide terrorists with virtually every conceivable armament, black-market weaponry does not come cheaply. Trucks and other vehicles also can be stolen, but again, it is far less risky to purchase them. Safe houses, of course, cannot be stolen.

Without question, weapons and related field equipment account for the largest segment of terrorist expenditures. When Israel defeated the Palestine Liberation Organization (PLO) during the "Peace in Galilee" operation in 1982, the Israeli Defense Force seized 4,670 tons of artillery and small arms ammunition; 80 tanks and almost 1,000 other combat vehicles; 28,304 pistols, rifles, and other small arms; 1,352 antitank weapons; 202 mortars; 56 rocket launchers; 158 antiaircraft weapons; and 70 pieces of heavy artillery.[16] No doubt these weapons had been obtained by the PLO at great cost.

Historically, many terrorist groups operated with limited funding, depending primarily on theft income and donations from sympathizers. In the modern world of international terrorism these sources have been supplemented by income from legitimate businesses, ransom kidnapping, and most recently **narco-terrorism**—the financing of terrorist activities through direct or indirect involvement in illegal drug trafficking (see Exhibit 20.3).

Finally, the mechanism of terrorist financing of perhaps the most far-reaching significance has little to do with the traditional criminal activities engaged in by most terrorist groups. In recent years, terrorism frequently has been one of the instruments used in conflicts of varying intensity between Arabs and Israelis. It has been an adjunct to the Iran-Iraq war and has played a role in Iran's efforts to subvert or sway the policies of various Arab governments. Terrorists have perpetrated the kaleidoscopic violence in Lebanon and have moved against Western targets in the Middle East and in Europe.[17] These situations have included numerous instances of **state-sponsored terrorism**—the strategic and financial support of terrorist organizations by national governments.

Several factors explain state sponsorship of international terrorism. Journalists Christopher Dobson and Ronald Payne made the following observations early in the 1980s concerning the wealth of the PLO:

> In one of the classic paradoxes of terrorism, the richest terrorists are the Palestinians, who come from the poverty of the refugee camps. . . . This paradox stems from the fact that their movement attracted support from the Arab world at precisely the moment when the oil states of the Middle East were beginning to enjoy their immense, newly acquired wealth. Because even conservative and antirevolutionary Arabs could not resist the emotional appeals to help free Palestine of the Israelis and to recover the holy places of Islam lost to the Jews, money poured into the coffers of the Palestinian organizations.[18]

Libyan involvement in international terrorism is more complex. Libya's leader, Moammar El-Gadhafi, is clearly in sympathy with the Palestinian cause. In addition, however, as a Muslim, he regards Westerners as infidels. Thus, a major aim of Gadhafi's sponsorship of terrorism is the destabilization of Western democracies—to be accomplished by creating anarchy within the targeted nations.[19]

SOCIAL INDICATOR

Terrorism and Finance

Year	Terrorist Group	Country	Income in 1980 U.S. Dollars	Sources
1975	Al-Fatah	Middle East	150–200 Million	Arab Oil-producing Countries
1980	ETA	Spain	1–2 Million	Robbery, Donations
1980	Red Brigades	Italy	5–10 Million	Ransom, Bank Robbery
1985	Abu Nidal Group	Middle East	30–40 Million	State-sponsorship (Libya & Syria)
1985	FARC	Colombia	50–150 Million	Narco-terrorism
1985	M-19	Colombia	50–150 Million	Narco-terrorism

Note: The terrorist groups noted in this table are identified in Exhibit 20.2.

Sources: James Adams, *The Financing of Terror* (New York: Simon and Schuster, 1986); Christopher Dobson and Ronald Payne, *The Terrorists: Their Weapons, Leaders and Tactics* (New York: Facts On File, 1982); Walter Laqueur, *The Age of Terrorism* (Boston: Little, Brown, 1987).

Terrorism and Society

Throughout the past two decades, Americans have been extremely conscious of terrorism, continually ranking it among the nation's top concerns. During the mid-eighties in particular, Americans were especially frightened by terrorism, but they also were angered, calling for vigorous action by the White House. During those years, the psychological warfare conducted by international terrorists had become more brutal and deadly. Hostage taking in Iran, hijackings, and the bloody attacks at the Rome and Vienna airports were capped by an in-flight explosion aboard Pan Am flight 103 over Scotland in December of 1988, during which Americans were killed. It appears that terrorism has become almost commonplace.

SOCIAL INDICATOR

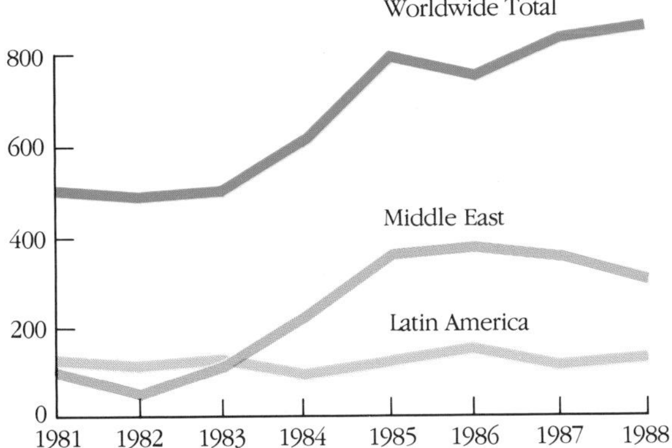

Source: U.S. Department of State, 1988.

*Terrorism involving citizens or territory of more than one country. Numbers refer to incidents only, and not to numbers of people killed in each incident.

Terrorism and Government

Terrorism has clearly changed the way that governments do business and the way that political leaders live. During the early 1960s when President John F. Kennedy visited Galway, a small seaport on the western shore of Ireland, his open car moved at a walking pace through the huge throngs of local citizens. Some two decades later Ronald Reagan was driven through the very same streets, but on that occasion they were almost deserted and the motorcade moved at high speed—almost as if the president's bodyguards were expecting something to happen. Although the restrictions placed on the movement of Reagan and other American politicians are in part reactions to the assassinations of John and Robert Kennedy and Reverend Martin Luther King, Jr., and the unsuccessful attempts on the lives of Gerald R. Ford and Reagan, much awareness of security matters also has to do with terrorism.

Because of terrorism, the machinery of both local and international politics has had to alter course. As an outgrowth of the embassy takeover in Iran and bombing of the American Embassy in Lebanon, the United States no longer has official, direct contact with either of those nations, making delicate negotiations difficult to conduct. Political leaders and other influential persons in many parts of the Middle East are prisoners of their positions, generally confined to fortified houses sealed off with sandbags and iron pipes as defenses against car bombs.[20]

Because of terrorism, political leaders in most parts of Latin America and other parts of the world rarely meet in public places, which makes consensus building quite difficult and tends to reduce politics to very private affairs conducted in well-guarded homes, offices, and embassies.

Terrorism and Hostages

While terrorism has brought greater isolation to national leaders around the world, one of its more curious effects has been noticed among terrorist victims being held hostage. In many instances a bonding—known as the **Stockholm syndrome**—evolves between captor and captive, with the result that each group identifies with the beliefs and goals of the other. The syndrome was first noticed in the aftermath of a 1973 bank robbery in Stockholm, Sweden, during which the hostages came to idolize their captors and ultimately refused to testify against them.[21]

According to psychologists, the bonding is an outgrowth of strain and the fact that the hostages are placed in an infantile and dependent position. It is suggested that the syndrome occurs in three stages. In the first stage, the hostages come to have positive feelings about their captors. In the second phase, they begin to have negative feelings about the authorities trying to rescue them, and in the final stage, the terrorists begin to develop positive feelings toward their victims. Feeling isolated, the members of both groups come to believe, "We're in this together."

Perhaps the best-known instance of the Stockholm syndrome involved Patricia Hearst, granddaughter of

California heiress Patty Hearst was believed to be a member of the Symbionese Liberation Army in the mid-1970s. She was later termed a victim of the Stockholm syndrome.

Exhibit 20.3

Sociological Focus

Narco-terrorism

Not too long after the Colombian cocaine entrepreneur, Carlos Lehder Rivas, was arrested and extradited to the United States during the early weeks of 1987, *U.S. News & World Report* published a rather dramatic feature. The lead-in to the article, headlined "Narcotics: Terror's New Ally," commented, "With cash from global drug trafficking bankrolling the agendas of governments and insurgents bent on destabilizing democracies, spawning anarchy, and exporting revolution, the specter of narco-terrorism is a powerful threat on the international stage as dope becomes the newest political weapon."

The article, fraught with journalistic innuendo, presented a rather melodramatic discussion of the "deadly new threat on the international stage"—trafficking in drugs for the purpose of underwriting insurgencies on four continents. The *U.S. News* report went on to speculate on the stake the Soviets, Bulgarians, and Cubans had in the international drug trades. The implication was that a conspiracy existed among several nations whose strategic and tactical goals were far more threatening than those of either illegal drug distribution or political terrorism alone. By fostering, and even supporting, the trafficking of heroin and cocaine to the United States and other Western countries, conspiring nations increased the potential for spreading drug abuse and thereby weakening the very fabric of democratic society on a global scale.

The *U.S. News* story offered no conclusions in connection with its speculations, but for researchers and students of crime and world affairs, it posed a variety of questions. What, first of all, is narco-terrorism? Is it a subspecies of terrorism or some new form of political violence? Where is it concentrated and how is it manifested?

At the outset, it would appear that narco-terrorism, a term reportedly invented by former Peruvian President Fernando Belaúnde Terry, has never been properly defined but suggests some unholy alliance between drugs and terrorism, or at the very least a link between drug trafficking and the activities of terrorist groups. In all likelihood, the term narco-terrorism has remained undefined because it applies to a number of different groups and activities.

One approach to unraveling the meaning of narco-terrorism is to point out that while terrorism is a *political* concept, narco-terrorism is an *economic* concept. As such, narco-terrorism is not some new form of terrorist activity, but rather, a shorthand label used to identify the many different ways that the economics of illegal drug production and distribution can be tied to violence and terrorist activities.

Drugs and terrorism seem to be linked in two significant ways. First, terroristlike activities are used by some drug trafficking groups for the sake of intimidation and deterrence. Although these violent activities have no connection with what is typically understood as terrorism, they have been labeled as narco-terrorism nevertheless. Second, some insurgent groups and national governments are directly or indirectly involved in drug trafficking for the purpose of financing their revolutionary ventures. In both cases, narco-terrorism is an *economic,* rather than a *political,* concept.

The large profits associated with drug trafficking instigate brutal aggression and extraordinary violence against people, property, and institutions. Although these activities are clearly types of criminal behavior, they generally are referred to as narco-terrorism by the South American media and by government officials on both sides of the equator. Throughout the trafficking regions of South America, for example, killings are quite commonly undertaken in a terroristlike fashion for the sake of deterrence and intimidation. In the cocaine business in particular, a typical pattern involves the execution of not only the rival dealer, but of his entire family as well, to serve as a warning to others.

The violence is not always directed against other traffickers. In Sierra Nevada de Santa Marta, Colombia, the people of the Arhuacos tribe had grown coca for generations, using it for the mild stimulant effects. In 1982, however, the men of the tribe were murdered and their women raped by traffickers seeking the aborigines' coca plantings, and in 1983, Colombian soldiers found the remains of 60 peasants who had refused to cooperate with drug traffickers.

Killings occur in other sectors as well. In Medellín and other Colombian drug centers, prosecutors and judges seeking convictions of traffickers have been systematically executed. One of the victims was that nation's justice minister, Rodrigo Lara Bonilla, assassinated in 1984 after he made the mistake of publicly demanding stronger measures against local *narcotrafficantes.* The President of Colombia also has been threatened, and the President of Bolivia has been kidnapped.

Although traditional criminal organizations continue to dominate the international heroin, cocaine, and other illegal drug trades, in recent years a growing number of insurgent and revolutionary groups have become involved in drug-related operations. These activities, all undertaken for economic purposes, have been referred to in the South American media as narco-terrorism and include (1) the extortion of money from low-level producers (such as peasants who grow opium poppies or coca leaves), (2) the provision of protection services to refining and trafficking organizations, (3) direct involvement in illegal drug production and distribution, and (4) outright control of drug-producing regions. These activities are the most direct links between drugs and terrorism. Moreover, it is from these insurgent activities that "narco-terrorism" likely gets its name.

The more visible involvement of revolutionary organizations in the drug trades is relatively recent, in part as a result of expansion in the international demand for narcotics, cocaine, Quaalude and Mandrax tablets, and other illicit substances. With greater demand came oppotunities for nontraditional suppliers who range from presidents and representatives of sovereign governments, to officials of political parties, business entrepreneurs, law-enforcement agents, *and* members of insurgent-terrorist groups.

Perhaps most closely associated with narco-terrorism is FARC, the Armed Revolutionary Forces of Colombia, a pro-Marxist revolutionary group with some 4,000–7,000 members and supporters, divided into perhaps two dozen guerrilla fronts, half of which operate in the regions of Colombia's marijuana and cocaine industries. After its formation in 1966, FARC had little impact on the Colombian political scene for a number of years, limiting its activities to a symbolic occupation of some remote rural villages. In the mid-seventies, however, FARC went into the ransom-kidnapping business. As its income grew, so did its ambitions.

FARC's entry into the drug trades came in the early 1980s, and since that time its narco-terrorist activities have been focused in four areas: (1) the regular collection of protection money from marijuana and coca growers in its operating territories; (2) the overseeing of drug trafficking in certain areas with collections based on specific quotas; (3) the provision of guaranteed access to clandestine airfields for smuggling; and, (4) direct involvement in coca growing and refining. Payments for these activities are received in the form of cash or armaments.

The drug trafficking-terrorism connection is an important one, primarily because one activity tends to facilitate the other. In addition, narco-terrorism can threaten the stability of local government.

SOURCE: Adapted from James A. Inciardi, "Narco-terrorism: Cocaine, Insurgency, and the Links Between Political and Economic Violence in South America," *Paper Presented at the Defense Academic Research Support Program Conference,* "International Drugs: Threat and Response," National Defense College, Defense Intelligence Analysis Center, Washington, DC, June 2–3, 1987.

SOCIAL INDICATOR

The Lebanese Roll Call

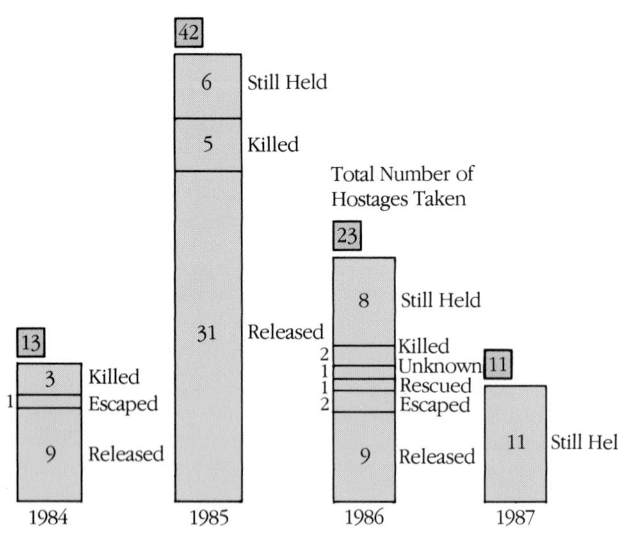

From:	1984	1985	1986	1987	Total
Syria		15	2		17 (1)*
France	1	6	8	1	16 (5)
Britain	1	8	5		14 (4)
United States	5	2	3	3	13 (6)
West Germany				4	4 (4)
Soviet Union		4			4
Saudi Arabia	1		1	2	4 (2)
Kuwait	2	1			3
Cyprus			2		2
Libya	2				2
Spain	1		1		2
Canada		1			1
Holland		1			1
India				1	1 (1)
Iran		1			1
Ireland		1			1
Italy		1			1 (1)
South Korea			1		1 (1)
Switzerland		1			1
Total	13	42	23	11	89 (25)

Source: *The Economist,* January 31, 1987, p. 32.

newspaper tycoon William Randolph Hearst, who was kidnapped from her Berkeley, California, apartment in 1974 by members of the Symbionese Liberation Army (SLA). After but a few months of captivity, Hearst disowned her family, broke her engagement, formed a liaison with a member of the group, and participated in a San Francisco bank robbery.[22] More recently, a number of the American hostages being held in the embassy takeover in Iran at the close of the 1970s suffered the same type of strain.[23]

Social Response to Terrorism

While hostages may sometimes identify with their captors, observers have considerably different reactions. One reaction is fear, characterized by exaggerated efforts to avoid places and situations that might harbor terrorists. A case in point is what the travel and tourism industries refer to as the "Panic of 1986." In the aftermath of the hijackings of TWA Flight 847 and the *Achille Lauro* and the terrorist attacks on the Rome and Vienna airports, Americans began avoiding travel abroad. Specifically, in 1986 virtually every major Hollywood figure decided to miss the Cannes Film Festival; U.S. junior tennis players skipped the French Open in Paris; U.S. travel to England dropped by 30%; travel to Italy dropped by 70%; and travel to Greece dropped by 85%. European tourism alone suffered losses of billions of American dollars.[24]

A second reaction is anger, combined with a renewed spirit of nationalism. On April 5, 1986, a bomb planted in a West Berlin discotheque killed an American soldier and a Turkish woman, and wounded more than 200 others. Messages intercepted between Tripoli and the Libyan Peoples Bureau in East Berlin established Libyan involvement in the bombing.[25] Ten days later, in retaliation for this and other Libyan-inspired attacks on Americans, U.S. aircraft from carriers and British bases bombed strategic targets in and around the Libyan cities of Tripoli and Benghazi. Polls taken after the bombing demonstrated clearly that the American people overwhelmingly supported their government's actions. Also apparent across the United States was an attitude that Durkheim had referred to a century earlier as the "collective consciousness," a renewed solidarity in the face of the nation's determination to thwart an enemy.

Terrorism and the Media

Reflections on terrorism present a rather peculiar contradiction. In many ways, terrorism has become theater;

Media coverage of terrorist incidents, such as the TWA hijacking in 1985, has turned terrorism into theater.

in a very real sense the modern media has made all the world a stage for the terrorist. The print and electronic media are as important to terrorism as are bombs and artillery.

Terrorists both need and seek publicity; if terrorism is propaganda by deed, then the success of a campaign depends decisively on the amount of attention it receives. The media provides leverage. Like the Wizard of Oz, who was menacing and frightening from a distance, behind the scenes, terrorists are principally inconsequential figures pulling at a set of levers. The mass media is their primary lever.

It might be added here that in many ways terrorism and the media exist in a symbiotic relationship. Violence is news; peace and harmony are not. Putting it quite bluntly, terrorism sells newspapers and boosts television news ratings. The seemingly excessive time devoted to episodes of terrorism was strikingly apparent during the 1985 Beirut hostage crisis associated with the hijacking of TWA Flight 847. All three of the major TV networks devoted at least two-thirds of their evening news time to the story. On four nights ABC spent less than two minutes on *all* nonhostage news.[26] Even more interesting, U.S. television networks reportedly paid over $1 million each week to the terrorists to assure their monopoly over access to the hostage spectacular. ABC supposedly paid the Amal militia $30,000 for sole access to a hostage interview session and another $50,000 for the so-called final banquet before the hostages' release.[27]

Given these situations, it would appear that the media acts in complicity with terrorism in a very direct way. Faced with this criticism, however, the media generally responds that in a democracy where freedom of speech and the press go hand in hand, the public has a right to know, and it is the journalist's duty to report, without fear or favor. Freedom of the press, along with other freedoms in a democracy, may facilitate terrorist acts (see Exhibit 20.4).

Exhibit 20.4 Sociology in the Media

Terror and Democracy: Security through Repression?

The greatest proportion of terrorist operations—36 percent of the world total—occur in Western Europe, according to statistics on terrorism in the early 1980s. The Middle East is second with 21 percent, followed by Latin America with 19 percent, North America with 9 percent, Asia with 5 percent, and Africa with 3 percent. Terrorism in the U.S.S.R. and Eastern Europe accounts for only 3 percent of the total, with the remainder distributed among other countries such as Australia and Oceania.

These figures suggest that about half of all terrorist operations occur in countries with democratic governments. Students of terrorism offer several reasons for the low incidence of terrorism in totalitarian countries.

The first reason is that most terrorist groups are leftist and therefore are not inclined to commit terrorist acts in Communist countries. Another reason is that totalitarian governments directly control the press and broadcast media in their countries and have an iron grip on the gathering and diffusion of news. These governments are in a position to suppress any information concerning terrorist acts committed against them. Finally, security provisions and police powers are unrestricted in Communist countries, making the apprehension of terrorists and the suppression of their activities relatively easy.

Should democratic governments violate democratic principles and individual freedoms in order to fight terrorism? This is an extremely important question, because if the answer is yes, these governments face a difficult choice. Either they must maintain the rule of uncompromising democracy and tolerate the evils of terrorism, or they must sacrifice some democratic freedoms to eliminate terrorism.

Citizens of today's democratic societies have voluntarily relinquished certain personal freedoms to protect themselves from terrorism. Airplane passengers, for example, permit searches of their persons and of their baggage. They know that this inconvenience may save them from hijackers who would commandeer their planes to unwanted destinations and hold them hostage for a cause they neither support nor understand.

This logic has prompted many democratic governments to take security measures against terrorism. Such provisions compromise constitutional freedoms, but they have been enacted without public protest because they protect national

WAR

Although terrorism is often referred to as "unconventional" warfare, or as a variety of "psychological" warfare sometimes accomplished by the mechanisms of "guerrilla" warfare, terrorism technically is not war. Both terrorism and war have their origins in the dynamics of intergroup relations, and their causes are often identical—the pursuit of land or political or ethnic sovereignty, and perhaps the expansion of religious or secular ideals. But a key observation about war is that it is not *random* violence. It is not conducted by small groups within a state as a one-sided affair, and the targets are not exclusively civilian, nor are they limited to one particular social sector. As the former British diplomat and foreign office minister Evan Luard recently emphasized:

> Organised violence may take many forms: skirmishes among disorganized groups, whether of the same or different states; sporadic incidents along a border over a long period, each relatively limited in scale; a single raid or naval bombardment against the territory of another state; an invasion by large-scale forces that is unresisted; a **coup d'etat** [a sudden seizure of government typically undertaken by a nation's existing military forces] involving substantial loss of life but rapidly accomplished; intermittent terrorist activity between or within states, directed at specific targets. . . . [None] of these, even if they lead to substantial loss of life, would normally be classified as "wars."[28]

The Nature of War

War may be broadly defined as socially organized violent conflict involving large social groups. The groups may be nations, alliances of nations, or subgroups within a nation security and the cause of democracy.

It is significant that, except for popular movements of national liberation and self-determination, most terrorist organizations represent intellectual or ideological minorities that can impose their beliefs on society at large only through terrorism, "the weapon of the weak." These groups pursue two goals vis-à-vis democratic government.

They want to demonstrate the weakness of a regime that is powerless to protect its citizens and institutions at home and abroad. They also want to force the regime to fight terrorism by adopting the repressive measures of a police state, legitimizing the terrorists' actions as just resistance to tyranny.

To protect national security and democracy, many democratic governments have enacted special laws to fight terrorism. Britain and West Germany, both known for their respect for freedom, have passed such laws.

In 1973 the British Parliament approved the Emergency Measures Law to deal with terrorist organizations in Northern Ireland. In 1974 the law was amended and a committee was appointed to study antiterrorist measures and their effects on civilian and human rights. British law enforcement agencies were given wider powers of search, arrest, and detainment, and judicial procedures were changed to relax the rules of evidence in cases relating to terrorist crimes.

In the same year, after a terrorist attack in Birmingham killed twenty-one people, the House of Commons granted British police additional powers, including the right to deport those connected with terrorist activities in other countries, and to hold citizens and aliens without trial for up to seven days.

West Germany enacted laws that widened governmental powers of search, arrest, and detainment so that, for example, suspects accused of terrorist crimes could be tried without legal counsel. German antiterrorist laws are similar to their British counterparts, with one critical difference. The British provisions are temporary and come up for renewal at regular intervals, while Germany's are permanent.

SOURCE: Reprinted from Amhed Jalal Izzeddin, of Al-Ahram (Cairo), *World Press Review,* September 1985, pp. 37–38. Reprinted by permission from *World Press Review.*

(as in a civil war). A key feature of this definition is its simplicity. It makes no mention of either the number of casualties involved or the duration of the fighting. The Iran-Iraq war and the Soviet invasion of Afghanistan both endured for most of the 1980s. Even longer was the Hundred Years' War, when England and France fought sporadically from 1337 to 1454. At the other end of the spectrum in both time and number of casualties was the conflict in 1967 between Israel and the Arab nations of Egypt, Jordan, and Syria, which lasted for such a short period of time that it came to be known as the Six-day War.

Wars typically involve combat among nations, but they also may involve religious or ethnic groups. For example, in a remote region of the Middle East lies Kurdistan, the ethnic homeland of the Kurds, an Islamic society of some seven million persons. Kurdistan occupies parts of Turkey, Iran, Iraq, Syria, and Soviet Armenia, and for centuries, the Kurds have struggled for national sovereignty.[29] They are involved in an undeclared war with all of these nations, because the nations' borders encroach on Kurdish cultural boundaries. Curiously, however, this is an unpublicized war, overshadowed by the Iran-Iraq war, despite the fact that it has endured now for many decades.

Whether wars involve nations, religious groups, or ethnic groups, they technically begin with the outbreak of hostilities, but they do not begin randomly. Their sources are deeply rooted in events that precede actual fighting. On this point, a British political scientist commented just prior to American involvement in World War II, "The immediate reasons of war are manifold and, maybe, trivial—an "insult to the flag," the murder of an official personage, the rash act of some panic-stricken commander of troops. . . . But these occasions are not the causes of war. They are the match to the powder magazine."[30]

The Sources of War

Specific events do not set wars in motion, although they often serve as rallying cries for a nation already engaged in warfare. "Remember Pearl Harbor," for example, echoed across the United States throughout World War II, reminding soldiers and civilians alike of what had triggered American involvement in the conflict. Dramatic events also fail to explain the sources of tension that typically initiate the outbreak of war, and philosophers and social scientists have debated two questions in connection with this observation. First, and quite simply, they wonder if war is inevitable. Second, they ask, "What are the causes of wars?" Many commentators have argued that wars are a universal because their source is to be found in human nature. Social science critics counter with the notion that aggressive behavior, like other forms of social behavior, is learned. Still others have suggested that nations always seek to expand, making conflict inevitable.

An Instinct for War?

The frequency of war in the history of the world has led many observers to suggest that people must have some innate propensity toward conflict and aggression. The many different versions of this approach all seem to focus, at least at the outset, on the notion of instincts.[31]

Sigmund Freud was a notable figure in the early discussions of the relationship between war and innate aggressive tendencies. Early in his career, Freud maintained that human aggression was the result of the frustration of sexual drives. Witnessing the destruction of Europe during World War I, however, led him to revise his views and claim that a "lust for aggression and destruction" was part of a basic destructive "death drive," which caused people to seek to return to a state of nonbeing.[32] In Freud's view, warfare channels this "death drive" or "death wish" toward external social groups.

An alternative form of the aggression instinct approach became popular in the 1960s as part of sociobiology. The most influential contemporary adherent to this view has been Robert Ardrey, who argues that organized warfare is a modern invention rooted in the evolutionary development of the human species.[33] Ardrey claims that when human societies were small and survival precarious, aggressive behavior was necessary for hunting success and for armed combat in defense of territory. According to Ardrey, aggression thus aided the survival of the species, and modern peoples carry this genetic baggage of their fighting ancestors with them.

Sociologists and other social scientists are not convinced, however, that aggression is biologically based. They note that instinct theories are very general and do not explain why particular wars occur. Moreover, this approach fails to explain peace, for although war is common, societies also exist for prolonged periods without engaging in armed conflict. Some societies do not engage in war at all.

Aggression as Learned Behavior

Social scientists point out that all instinct theories ignore the social environment of conflict and the social relationships that precede it. They emphasize the fact that some societies overtly reject the display of aggression against others. The Zapotec Indians of Mexico have cultural mechanisms for controlling violence and producing peaceful resolution of any conflicts that might arise.[34] Cultural standards emphasize respect for others, responsibility, and cooperation, all of which prevent violence from becoming accepted as normal behavior. If someone physically attacks a Zapotec, he or she turns to group leaders for help in resolving the matter.

From this and similar examples, it could be concluded that warfare is, like any other form of social behavior, a human invention. Despite the dismal statistics and the grim casualty reports from conflicts around the globe, not all societies accept (or even understand) the concept of organized warfare. Anthropologists generally agree on a list of "peaceful societies" that includes the Hopi, Mbuti Pygmies, K'ung Bushmen, Copper Eskimos, and the Amish. These groups qualify as **peaceful societies** because they do not engage in war or systematic violence. According to one observer, the trait that distinguishes these groups from others is ". . . that they have no idea of brave, aggressive masculinity, . . . have no heros or martyrs to emulate or cowards or traitors to despise; their religious life lacks significant personalized gods and devils; [and] a happy, hard-working and productive life is within reach of all."[35]

By contrast, some societies are characterized by cultural traditions that actually *teach* aggression. Young men of the Sambia tribe of New Guinea pass through a number of ceremonies and experiences that encourage militant behavior.[36] Hostility, bravery, and the ability to fight are considered ideals for Sambia males. Aggressive socialization is developed during initiation into manhood, a long process that begins at age 7 and continues for some 20 years.

The application of the *culture* concept to explanations of war suggests that people are neither submissive nor warlike by nature. Instead, adherents to this position believe that cultural traditions encourage or inhibit violence.

War and National Expansionism

Expansionism, also referred to as imperialism, may be defined as a national policy of extending control over other societies.[37] In reflecting on expansionism, the Prussian military thinker, Karl Von Clausewitz, once suggested that "war is nothing but the continuation of politics by other means."[38] His comment was based on the fact that all the great empires of history were built at the expense of other social systems. History has witnessed many different forms of imperialism, but it is convenient to divide them into three categories—economic, sociocultural, and militaristic.

Economic Expansionism In instances of **economic expansionism** imperialistic motives target natural and material resources (wealth, raw materials, land, markets). Karl Marx emphasized that colonial exploitation was a necessary part of the development of capitalism, with undeveloped nations providing slaves, precious metals, cheap raw materials, and markets for the products of early industrial production.[39] Moreover, Marx argued that the sources of the imperialist impulse were linked to the class system, with the upper classes benefiting from economic expansion.

Both Marxists and non-Marxists alike point to various incidents in American history to illustrate economic imperialism. Quite clearly, the lure of the raw materials found in the Philippines (forests and precious metals) contributed heavily to the outbreak of the Spanish-American War in 1898. One advocate of the war spoke openly on the issue: "If this be commercialism, for God's sake let us have commercialism."[40]

Sociocultural Expansionism **Sociocultural expansionism** is evident when nations use war as a device to impose their values and beliefs on other nations. This form of expansionism has brought "true religion" to "pagans" and imposed the benefits of democracy on unwilling societies. The Christian countries of Europe devoted three centuries to the Crusades in an attempt to rescue the Holy Land. Perhaps sociocultural imperialism is best summed up by the words of Rudyard Kipling:

> Take up the White's burden—
> Ye dare not stoop to less.

Sociocultural imperialism may be merely another form of *ethnocentrism,* or, as is suggested by Kipling's words, it may take the form of *racism.* Sometimes it is used as an official rationale for economic or military ventures.

Militaristic Expansionism Proponents of the military expansionism perspective on the causes of war recognize that societies must have a military as a means of protection, but they hypothesize that the mere existence of the military may become a cause of warfare. Some studies have shown that levels of military activity in a society correlate directly with the outbreak of wars.[41] The basic idea is that the military may become powerful enough to influence political decisions, or it may gain control of the civilian government and use war as an instrument of policy rather than attempting to resolve conflicts through peaceful means. Within this context, a nation controlled by the armed forces is generally referred to as a **militarized society.** Chile, Guatemala, Nigeria, and Uganda currently are militarized societies.

Military budgets can absorb a large share of the total resources of a nation. The United States devotes some 7% of the Gross Domestic Product (the total value of goods and services produced for internal consumption) to defense. The Soviet Union, Saudi Arabia, Iran, and Iraq invest a much larger share, and Israel spends nearly one-third of its resources on defense.

Even if the military does not use armed violence as a mechanism for the implementation of social policy, the very act of building up a military establishment creates a dangerous international environment, encouraging other nations to engage in what has become known as an "arms race." As the race escalates, one nation may interpret some minor gesture as a hostile act, thus initiating conflict and perhaps war.[42] In the United States, public opinion is clearly divided on this issue. Surveys taken during the 1980s suggest that the population is rather evenly divided between those who feel that the arms race increases the likelihood of nuclear war and those who

SOCIAL INDICATOR

The Top 15 Military Spenders

Country	Rank	Military Budget (in billions of dollars)	Percentage of GDP
United States	**1**	**255.0**	**7.5**
Soviet Union	2	214.0	14.8
Britain	3	25.2	5.3
China	4	22.8	6.3
Saudi Arabia	5	22.0	14.4
France	6	21.4	4.0
West Germany	7	18.9	2.9
Iran	8	15.0	14.7
Japan	9	10.4	1.0
Italy	10	9.8	2.8
Iraq	11	7.7	21.7
East Germany	12	7.7	7.7
Israel	13	6.5	31.4
Canada	14	6.4	2.2
Poland	15	6.3	5.2

Source: Adapted from James F. Dunnigan and Austin Bay, *A Quick and Dirty Guide to War* (New York: William Morrow, 1985), p. 392.

Israel spends nearly one-third of its resources to deploy troops and equipment in southern Lebanon and for other defense-related projects in protecting its borders against its Arab neighbors.

worry that conflict is possible if America falls behind the Soviet Union.[43]

In summary, although it is useful to identify three different forms of expansionism—economic, sociocultural, and militaristic—in most cases the three coexist and reinforce one another. All three forms of expansionism appeared to be involved in the Soviet intervention in Afghanistan between 1979 and 1988. The Soviet Union would definitely reap economic advantages by having year-round, warm-water ports on the Indian Ocean. Those same ports have obvious military significance, and sociocultural expansion comes into play because opposition in Afghanistan centers among Afghan-Islam guerrillas (the Mujahadeen), who oppose Soviet socialist ideology.

The approaches we have looked at only begin to cover the many explanations that have been developed to identify the sources of war. Many observers continue to develop abstract theories of war, but the contribution that sociology makes to these endeavors is to focus on the social environment and social processes that lead to war or to the maintenance of peace.

Making War: The Institutionalization of Violence

A declaration of war sets in motion a whole complex of social processes. Since modern warfare generally involves almost every member of a society in one way or another, social support must be mobilized to sustain the war effort. Some people may be called upon to fight, while others will have to make various material sacrifices. The entire society bears the war burden through taxation and reduced social resources.

Who Fights Wars?

Governments declare wars, but who fights and dies in them? Men? Women? Minorities? Does the military discriminate in selecting leadership personnel as opposed to those chosen for combat roles? Are some people specialists in fighting wars?

In the United States an enduring cliché states that "old men send boys to war." At age 18 all males are

SOCIAL INDICATOR

Attitudes on Arms Control

How likely are we to get into a nuclear war within the next 10 years?

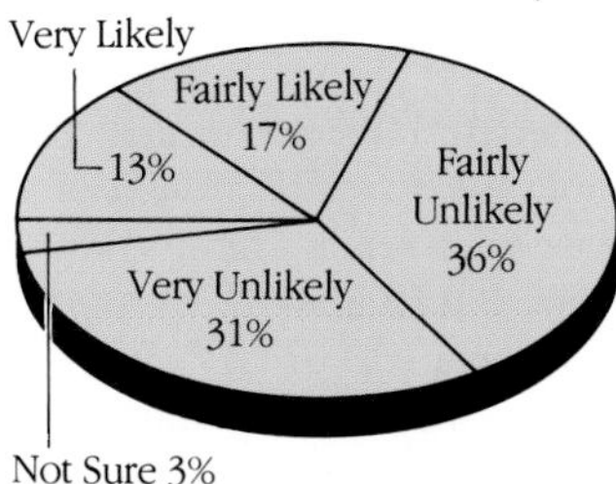

Which one or more of these countries would be most likely to explode a nuclear weapon?

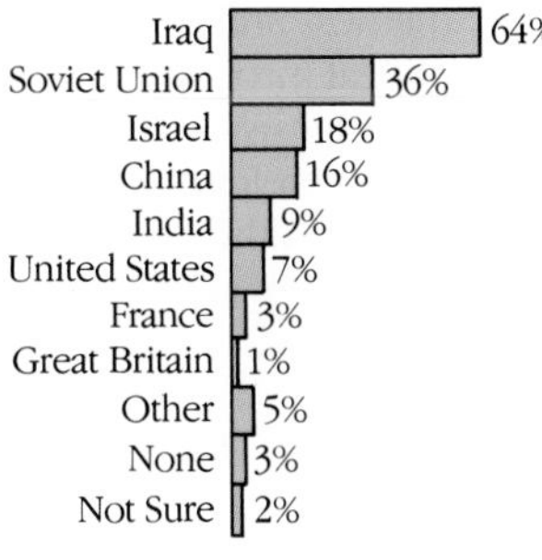

How likely is nuclear war within the next 25 years?

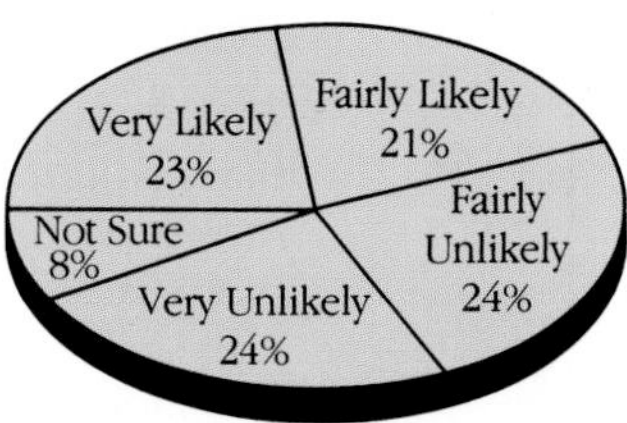

Should the United States take a new step to reverse the arms race?

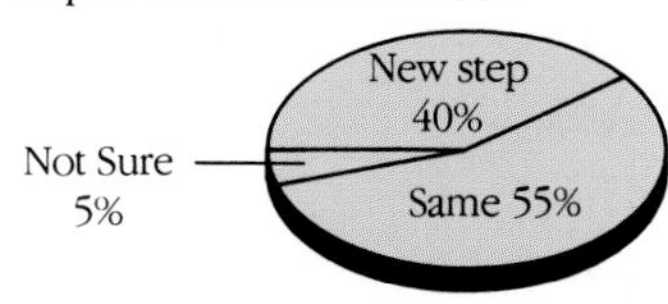

The Soviets now are more serious about arms control.

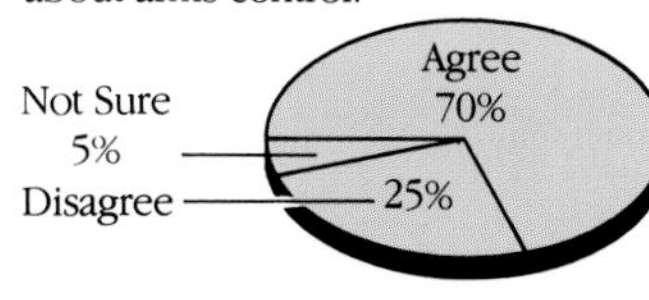

What about continued development of "star wars"?

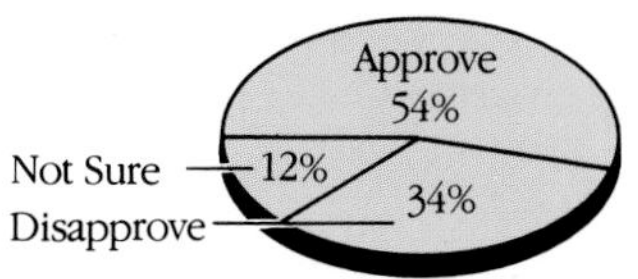

"Star wars" is already an effective bargaining issue.

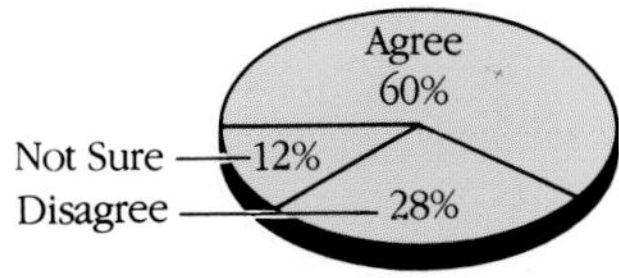

Do you agree with tentative pact to eliminate mid-range nuclear missiles?

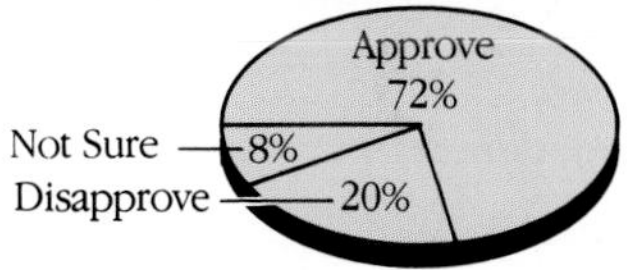

Which country gave up more—the United States or the Soviet Union?

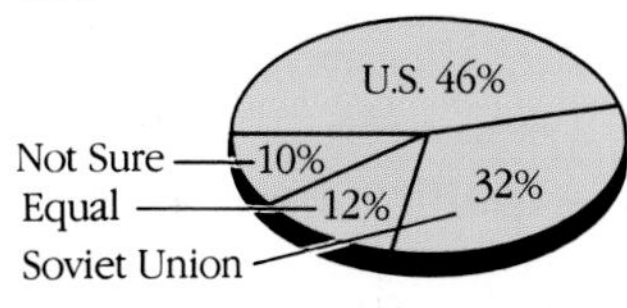

required to register for possible induction. Women are exempt from involuntary military service, although this nation currently has more than 218,000 women in uniform—about 10% of the total American armed forces.

Since 1948 women have been excluded from most combat-related roles in the military. In earlier times it was considered socially appropriate to argue that women should be protected from the dangers of combat. Some observers even argued that women lacked the attitudes and skills necessary to be fighters. Today, the exclusionary rule has become an issue because it often results in women's being treated as second-class members of the military. In addition, it serves as a barrier to career advancement. Women in the military, for example, are not permitted to be fighter pilots—one of the more prestigious specialties. Service in combat-related positions is also an advantage in the promotion process. Less than a dozen women currently occupy the highest military ranks.

However, the cliché should also be amended to read, "Old men send lower-class and minority boys to war." Records from all of America's recent wars show that poor and minority males are more likely to be drafted and are overrepresented among the casualties. Several factors explain why this occurs. One reason is simple economics. Parents with higher incomes can afford to keep their children in college, where they are protected by student deferments. Then, too, draft laws often exempt members of "middle-class" occupations (teachers, for example) from military service.[44]

In addition to the draft, many warring nations also use **mercenaries**—professional soldiers in the employ

SOCIAL INDICATOR

Women in the Military

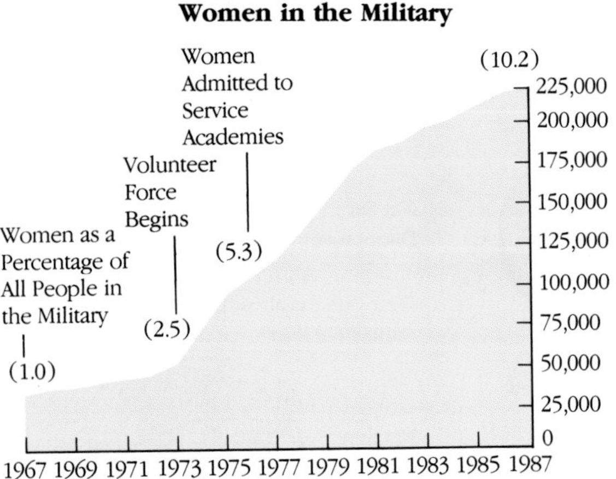

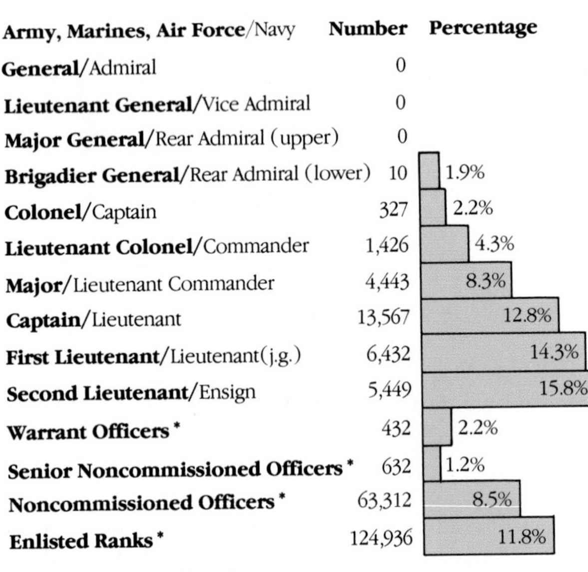

Army, Marines, Air Force/Navy	**Number**	**Percentage**
General/Admiral	0	
Lieutenant General/Vice Admiral	0	
Major General/Rear Admiral (upper)	0	
Brigadier General/Rear Admiral (lower)	10	1.9%
Colonel/Captain	327	2.2%
Lieutenant Colonel/Commander	1,426	4.3%
Major/Lieutenant Commander	4,443	8.3%
Captain/Lieutenant	13,567	12.8%
First Lieutenant/Lieutenant(j.g.)	6,432	14.3%
Second Lieutenant/Ensign	5,449	15.8%
Warrant Officers*	432	2.2%
Senior Noncommissioned Officers*	632	1.2%
Noncommissioned Officers*	63,312	8.5%
Enlisted Ranks*	124,936	11.8%

*Applies to all branches of the military

of foreign governments who fight in wars for a fee. Little is known about mercenaries. Available data suggest that perhaps as few as 200 Americans fell into this category during the 1980s.[45] They included older men, typically combat veterans of the war in Vietnam, who apparently thrived on the risks and thrills of the battles they had once experienced. Others were young men, who evidently felt they had no chance to demonstrate their courage and bravery in a peacetime military. Regardless of age, all seemingly shared a need for personal challenge and the opportunity to demonstrate their masculinity through violent, risk-taking behaviors.*

Propaganda and the Legitimation of War

The people who are drafted, trained for combat, and sent into battle may represent only a small segment of a total society, yet many of those who remain behind must also mobilize for the war effort. For civilians to support a war, it must be viewed as legitimate.

One of the ways that governments attempt to mold public opinion is through *propaganda,* which was defined in Chapter 16 as messages of a political nature that are used to mobilize public support behind a particular political party, candidate, or point of view by means of selective, limited, or false information. When used to legitimate a war effort, propaganda is stark and bold, invoking powerful themes and images—quite unlike the rather bland political propaganda typically used to elect people to office. The usual forms include posters, newspaper cartoons, and television spots. War propaganda almost always identifies the enemy as *alien, pagan, barbarian,* or *rapist,* and in all of its varieties propaganda carries the same message—the very survival of the society and culture is in peril.[46]

Some war propaganda uses a shadowy, faceless figure to represent the enemy, suggesting that the danger posed by an unknown force is far greater than that brought to bear by a known foe. When the enemy has a face, it is a strange and alien face, and cultural stereotypes single out unusual customs or religious practices to emphasize this fact (see Exhibit 20.5). In virtually every war the enemy comes to be identified by a single term that serves as a symbol for all of the differences that separate warring societies. During World War II, the Germans were collectively referred to as "Krauts" (from sauerkraut), and the cold war of the 1950s resulted in the label "Reds" being applied to the Soviets (from the red flag used by the international Communist movement).

The emphasis in identifying the enemy as an alien rests on the differences that exist among people. Such propaganda takes advantage of the tendency toward ethnocentrism, a common feature of human societies,

*Although the actual number of Americans employed as mercenaries may be small, the *lure* of mercenary life would appear to be much greater. *Soldier of Fortune,* a magazine founded in 1975 by a former Green Beret, claimed a monthly circulation in 1986 of some 171,000. In addition, the magazine sponsors a convention each year that offers military seminars on various topics, to which upwards of 1,000 participants are attracted. See *Newsweek,* November 3, 1986, pp. 35–39.

Exhibit 20.5 Types & Stereotypes

The Enemy as Alien

Drawing by Scrawls. Atlanta *Constitution*. Used by special permission.

and turns the tendency into outright hostility toward the enemy. It creates the impression of a world divided into just two camps, "us" and "them," or as presented in Chapter 5, *in-groups* and *out-groups*.

Religious beliefs are seldom taken lightly, dealing as they do with God, morality, and salvation. The enemy in propaganda is pictured either as godless or as worshipping some primitive spirit. War thus becomes a form of religious crusade—a war against pagans is seen as God's work. Different rules apply when the enemy is godless. For example, in 1139 the Catholic Church prohibited some uses of the crossbow. It was criticized as a weapon that was "hateful to God and unfit for Christians," but appropriate for use against infidels.[47]

It also is popular to portray the enemy as cruel, with special emphasis placed on alleged injuries to the vulnerable (children, the elderly) and categories of people usually viewed as "neutral" (religious figures, medical personnel, and the wounded). During World War I German war propaganda claimed that Belgians carried pails filled with eyeballs gouged from dead German soldiers.[48] During World War II, American propaganda aimed at the Japanese alleged that they practiced bizarre and inhumanly brutal torture on prisoners of war.

The enemy disrobing a woman is a common propaganda image. This image takes the barbarian one step further and turns him into a *rapist*. In part, this happens because the customs of Western society free women from any active role in combat. The gender stereotype of women portrays them as peaceful, gentle, weak, and defenseless. Far deeper emotions and images are also targeted—the violation of mothers, wives, and daughters. Violent rape is, as noted in Chapter 7, among the most serious crimes in society, and it is thus a powerful tool in the arsenal of war propaganda.

With all of these themes, the typical strategy is to emphasize that the very survival of the society is at stake, and it often is. This emphasis serves to create group solidarity and to reinforce group identification.

Rallying Popular Support

At the same time that the enemy is being painted in gross negative terms, the war effort is encouraged and endorsed by the use of positive symbols. Sociologist Orrin E. Klapp has noted that dramatic encounters are the stuff of which heroes are made.[49] In peacetime, heroes are usually the men and women who press the frontiers of technology (the Wright brothers and the early space explorers). In wartime heroes are people who make a decisive contribution to the survival of the society. Beginning with World War I, for example, the military and representatives of the press counted the number of enemy planes a fighter pilot destroyed, thus creating the flying "ace." Medals for bravery and courage are still awarded for those who act "above and beyond the call of duty." The war effort is also supported by people who are willing to work industriously, be watchful for spies and saboteurs, and contribute financially to the war.

One campaign to encourage public participation in the war effort in 1917 urged Americans to contribute peach stones.

The "Just" War

When a nation is attacked, it acts in self-defense, and the external threat is usually enough to maintain public support. Patriotism and propaganda can rally popular support, but a very different situation exists when no direct hostile attack has taken place. On those occasions, it must somehow be shown that war is *right*. Philosophers since Plato have wrestled with the idea of a **just war,** one fought because it is morally right, seeks ethical goals, and protects national interests.[50]

When governments wage wars they must convince their citizens that the conflicts are just. World War I, for example, was fought by the Western powers "to make the world safe for democracy," as the politicians and propagandists put it. Much of World War II was widely seen as a struggle against a facist regime that was bent on world domination. The Korean conflict, contested on an obscure peninsula in Asia, was labeled as "just" because it could be viewed as the first step in the global expansion of Communism. Troops were sent to the Caribbean island of Grenada in 1983 "at the request of the local government" and "to protect American students and citizens" there.

The vitality of the concept of a just war is best illustrated when a government fails to make its case. Vietnam is a perfect example. Those favoring American involvement in Southeast Asia felt that the conflict was not simply a civil war among Vietnamese factions. They viewed it more as a matter of global interest since other nations in that part of the world would quickly fall like "dominoes" if Vietnam were lost. The failure of the proponents of the conflict to convince all Americans of the validity of this point led to the erosion of the war's legitimacy. Countless draft-age men became objectors or fled to Canada. The unconvinced took their opposition to the streets, attracting widespread media coverage and expanding their questioning attitude to even wider segments of society. The war came to be perceived as unjust not only because many Americans felt that there was no direct threat to the United States, but also because the enemy did not appear to be following the accepted rules of war. In many ways Vietnam reflects a case study in the failure to rally popular support for a war.

War in the Nuclear Era

The explosion that destroyed Hiroshima in 1945 ushered in both the nuclear age and a new era in the evolution of weapons systems (see Exhibit 20.6). The **nuclear era**

Exhibit 20.6 Sociological Focus

The Evolution of Weapons Systems

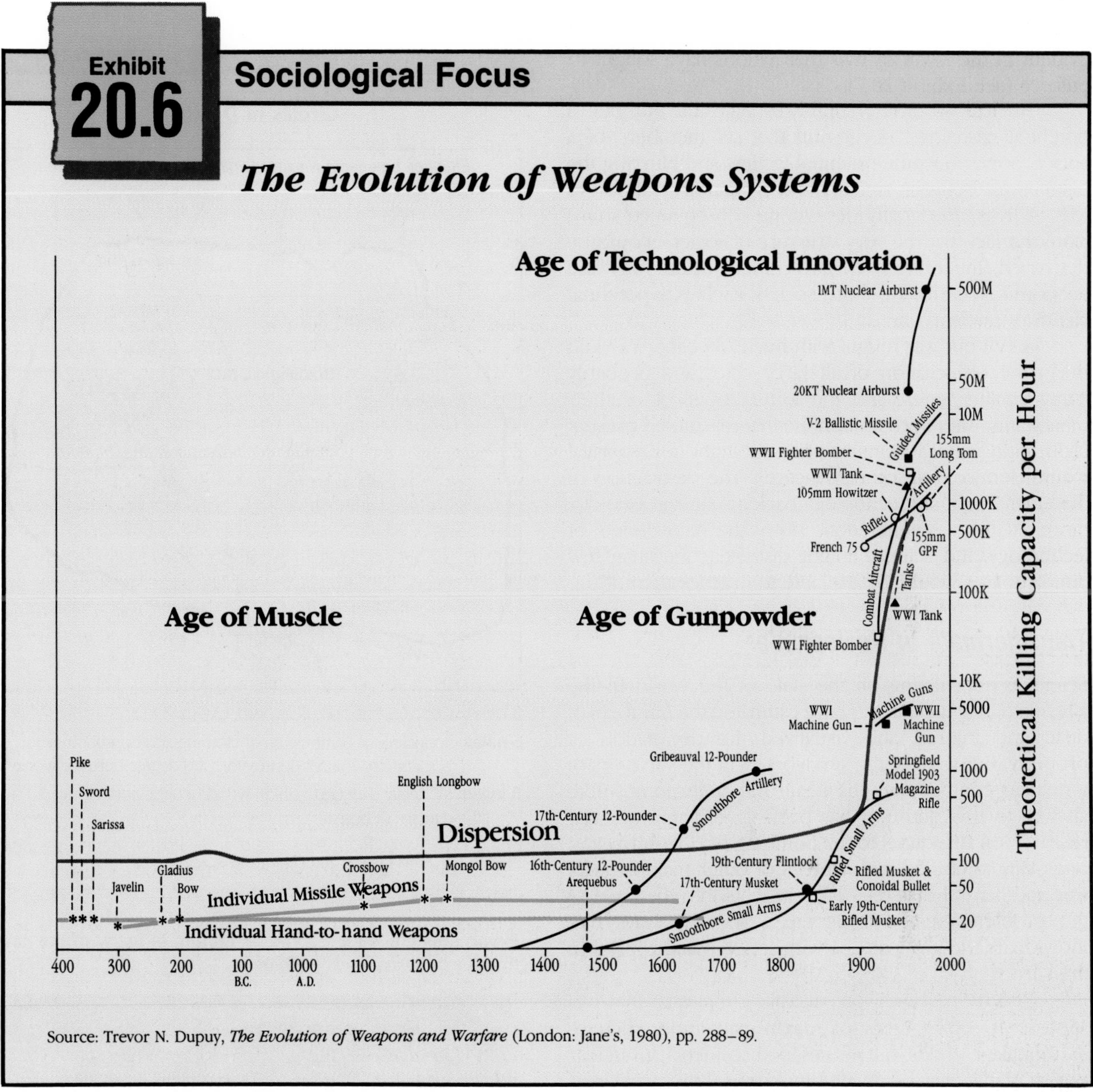

Source: Trevor N. Dupuy, *The Evolution of Weapons and Warfare* (London: Jane's, 1980), pp. 288–89.

represents the ultimate step in the "dispersion" of war. *Dispersion* is a measure of the impact of war on the society. It can be seen when tracing the evolution of war from the point in early history when battles were essentially hand-to-hand combat between relatively small numbers of individuals using swords and other hand-held weapons. Battles took place within very narrow physical limits. Longer range weapons, such as the crossbow (and later the cannon and rifle), extended the range of war-making capacity. However, wars tended still to be contested within specific physical boundaries and by the military component of the society. Land battles were fought by soldiers occupying fixed battle lines while sea battles pitted the cannon of one set of ships against those of another. Civilian casualties tended to be incidental.

Such twentieth-century innovations as aircraft and long-range artillery rendered the idea of fixed battle lines obsolete as they made it easy to attack an enemy behind its lines of defense. These developments also blurred the distinction between *military* and *civilians,* as an attack on civilian targets became an accepted means of weakening a nation's morale and destroying its war-making capacity. In twentieth-century wars whole cities have been military targets. However, recognition of the distinction between civilians and combatants is still generally recognized, as is evident in the *Rules of War* that nations have sought to enforce (see Exhibit 20.7).

Nuclear war immeasurably escalates the number of potential casualties, suggesting that *all* members of a society at war become potential victims and blurring the distinctions between military and civilian. In addition to loss of lives, an equally devastating consequence stems from the fact that the very structure of society would be destroyed, including both government institutions and economic systems. In short, society itself is a potential victim of nuclear war.

An all-out war fought with nuclear weapons would mean the obliteration of all large cities and probably many smaller ones, and the killing of most of their inhabitants. After such a war, little that resembled present civilization would remain, and the fight for survival would dominate all other concerns. The destruction of the cities might set technology back a hundred years or more. Within a generation, even the knowledge of technology and science might disappear, because few opportunities would be available to practice them.

The Aftermath of Nuclear War

Scientists speculating on the state of the world in the aftermath of a nuclear war have estimated the numbers of dead and injured and visualized the devastation of property. But what of the survivors? Will the survivors of a nuclear conflict envy the dead? Although no absolute answer to this question has been agreed upon, social research on responses to the bombing of Hiroshima and Nagasaki, combined with studies of other major acts of war and natural disasters, offer insights into the scale of the problems that will be faced and the ways that individuals and groups cope with serious catastrophes in their lives.

Recent research on disasters suggests that responses to every crisis of major magnitude, such as earthquakes, floods, hurricanes, and accidents at nuclear power plants, may be divided into several distinct stages. These response stages likely parallel those that would occur following a nuclear attack (see Exhibit 20.8). Sometimes a *warning phase* announces the possibility of disaster, followed by the intense activity of the "impact", which combines taking stock of events and dealing with immediate problems. This period typically overlaps the so-called *honeymoon phase,* which focuses on the initial tasks of rebuilding. People affected by disaster often fall into a period of declining effort, aptly called *disillusionment,* as they begin to understand the kinds of long-term problems that they face. These issues may be so great as to qualify as a "second disaster."

The Warning Phase The threat of catastrophe underscores the importance of the family unit. During the

SOCIAL INDICATOR

Circles of Death

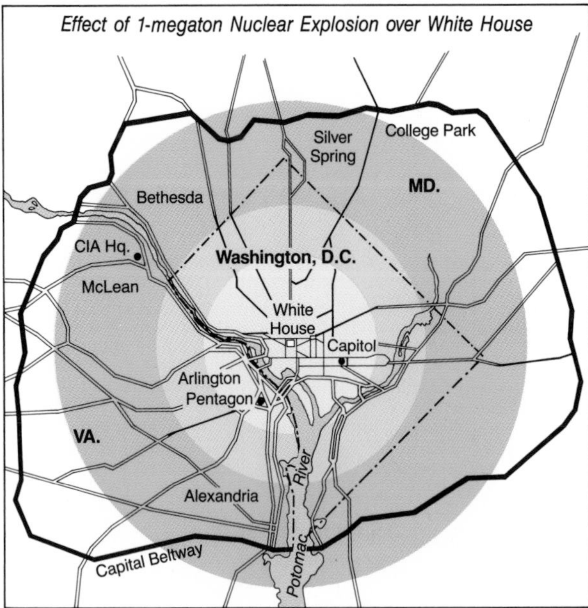

3 miles: Concrete buildings destroyed; few survivors.

5 miles: Spontaneous combustion of clothing and household items; brick, wood houses destroyed; third-degree burns or worse.

8 miles: Moderate damage to brick, wood houses; possible eye damage or burns.

Source: U.S. Arms Control and Disarmament Agency, 1988.

Bomb shelters were a common feature in many of the new houses built during the 1950s.

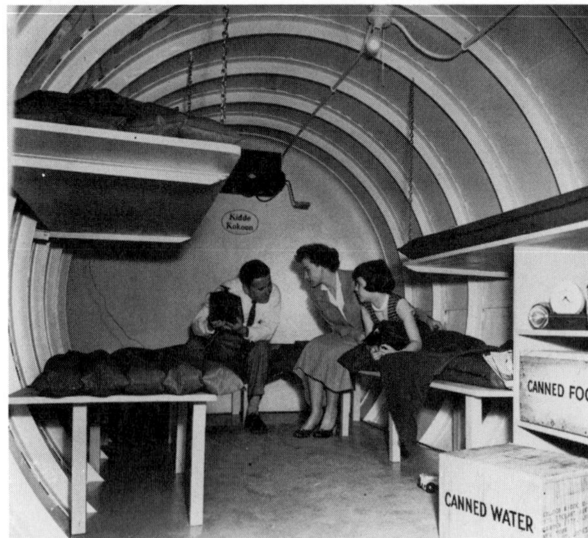

Exhibit 20.7

Sociological Focus

The Rules of War

Unlike terrorism, *war* does not involve random, unfettered violence focused primarily on civilians. Therefore, nations have sought to impose limits on the conduct of wars, using the following guidelines:

Whom a Soldier May Kill. A soldier may kill any troops who belong to the armed forces of the enemy, except for those mentioned below. He may always kill in self-defense any enemy troops who seek to attack him, including those belonging to categories normally protected, but who forfeit their immunity by acting as combatants. Enemy civilians who engage him in combat may be killed.

Whom a Soldier May Not Kill. A soldier may not kill

- Enemy troops who have surrendered, or have been captured.
- Sick, wounded, or shipwrecked enemy troops who do not engage in active hostilities.
- Personnel exclusively engaged in caring for, finding, collecting, or transporting the wounded and sick; they are identified by Red Cross armlets and identity cards.
- Personnel engaged in safeguarding cultural property (defined below); they are identified by an armlet . . . and identity cards.
- Enemies who appear under the (white) flag of truce.
- Enemy airmen bailing out of disabled aircraft.
- Enemy troops protected by a truce or armistice.
- Peaceful enemy civilians.

Forbidden Weapons of War. Arms, projectiles, or material which are calculated to cause unnecessary suffering (for example, uselessly aggravate the sufferings of disabled men, or render their deaths inevitable) are forbidden. Included are

- Poison and poisoned weapons.
- Dumdum bullets—bullets designed to expand or flatten easily in the human body.
- Suffocating and poisonous gases.
- Bacteriological warfare.
- Radiological weapons.

Forbidden Methods of Warfare. To kill or wound the enemy by treachery is forbidden. Examples are

- Pretending to surrender in order to attack the enemy.
- Use of the flag of truce for this purpose.
- Use of the Red Cross emblem to cover acts of hostility.
- Use of signals or messages of distress to put the enemy off guard, such as a false distress signal at sea.
- Opening fire while dressed in enemy or neutral uniform.
- Pretending death, wounds, or sickness to attack the enemy.
- Requesting quarter (mercy) for the same purpose.
- Assassination—the use of murder as a means of war (for instance, poisoning an enemy political leader).
- Contaminating food and water which it is intended that the enemy shall use.

It is also forbidden to declare that no quarter will be given to enemy troops captured or surrendered. Torture of the enemy is prohibited.

Places and Objects Which May Not Be Attacked. The following may not be attacked

- Hospitals and places for the care of the sick and wounded.
- Hospital ships.
- Coastal rescue craft and their installations ashore.
- Hospital and safety zones and localities that may be agreed upon between the states at war.
- Neutralized zones agreed upon by the states at war.
- Buildings dedicated to public worship, art, science, or charitable purposes.
- Cultural property—namely, movable or immovable property of great importance to the heritage of every people, including the buildings and centers where they are housed or situated. Historic monuments are comprised in the term.
- Coastal fishing boats.
- Boats engaged in petty local navigation.
- Vessels charged with religious, scientific, or philanthropic missions.

SOURCE: Morris Greenspan, *The Soldier's Guide to the Laws of War* (Washington, DC: Public Affairs Press, 1969), pp. 3–6.

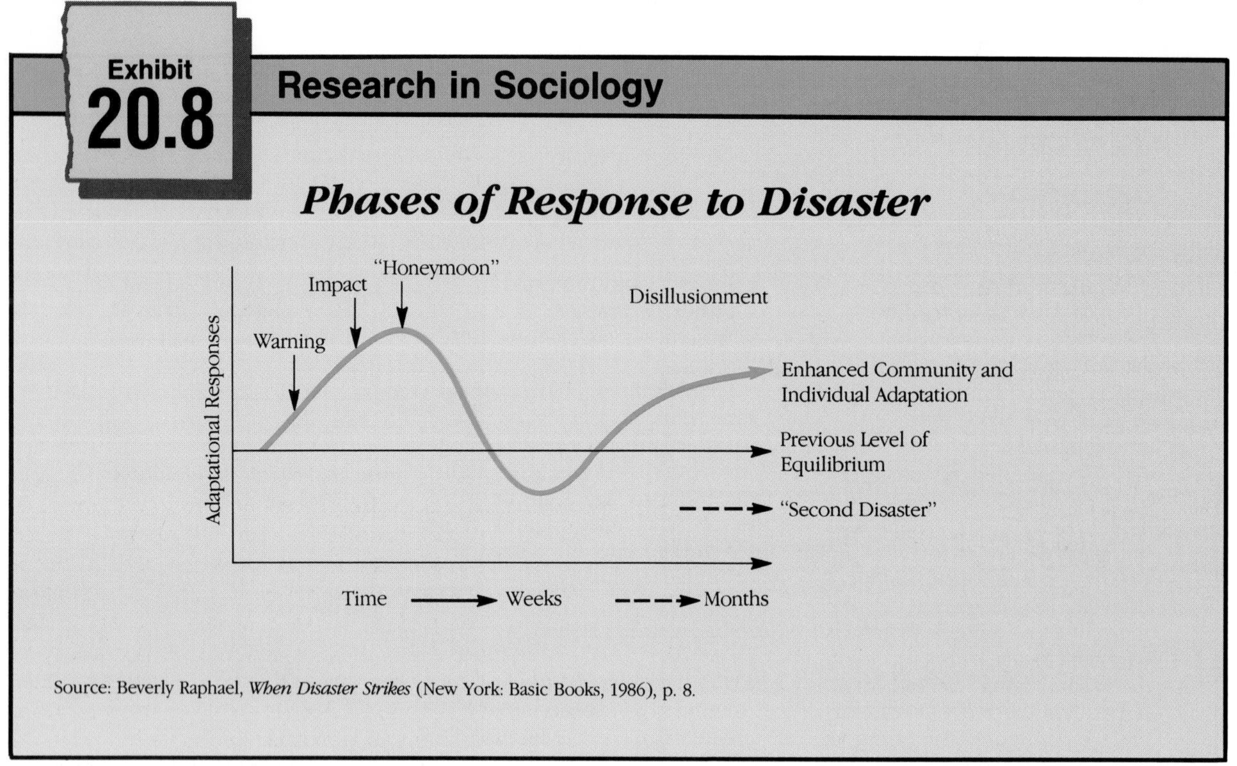

Source: Beverly Raphael, *When Disaster Strikes* (New York: Basic Books, 1986), p. 8.

warning phase, if any forewarning of the impending disaster is given, people's first thoughts are for family members and relatives. Fear draws families together—to protect themselves or plan escape routes. If they are uncertain or unsure as to the reality of the alert, close relatives depend on one another for advice. If evacuation occurs, they leave as a family unit, heading for the homes of more distant relatives.[51]

Not all people respond to warnings: some refuse to believe them; many more ignore them; and still others do not take them seriously. Studies of reactions to warnings of cyclones and tornadoes reveal that all social groups do not respond in the same way.[52] Women are more likely than men to accept the validity of the warning and take action, largely because they have been socialized to accept the major responsibility for the family. Older people are less likely to respond, because of the inconvenience and difficulties associated with relocation.

The existing social context also exerts an influence on responses to warnings, with individuals behaving differently than groups. Being with family members increases the probability of evacuation. The shared sense of danger heightens and reinforces the threat. By contrast, groups of individuals tend to ignore warnings; they are more sensitive about looking foolish if the alert turns out to be a false alarm. Members of groups reinforce this behavior in each other.

Inventory and Rescue Most disasters create death and devastation. During the first few hours after a disaster strikes—the inventory phase—people immediately begin an inventory of the damage. First thoughts focus on an individual's personal injuries and the well-being of loved ones. Activities then shift to the care of victims, mobilizing searches for survivors, and burying the dead. In major disasters the usual medical and rescue institutions are often destroyed or disrupted. The securing of these services is vital, for those that do survive are generally unprepared if the destruction is expansive. It is also imperative to reestablish mechanisms for the provision of water, food, and shelter for the survivors. Following the inventory phase is the rescue phase, during which other victims are sought out and order is restored.

All survivors experience a rush of emotions. The first is typically elation at being alive. Elation is followed quickly by confusion, pain over the loss of loved ones, sadness, rage, and fear. A strong sense of guilt—for being alive while others are dead—also is reported.[53] On the whole, however, while all survivors are bewildered, most nevertheless are able to help themselves and those around them. They may experience emotional scars for the rest of their lives, but their functioning remains stable. A few survivors may experience what has been referred to as the **disaster syndrome**—a state of

Ruins and caskets, the aftermath of the earthquake in Armenia in 1988, are common sights after almost every disaster.

shock characterized by trancelike and emotionless behavior.[54]

The "Honeymoon" Phase Rescue and restoration activities generally continue to build for hours and days, even weeks. Governmental and private relief agencies appear on the scene. People not directly affected attempt to provide assistance, joined by others searching for loved ones. This stage is referred to as the honeymoon phase because many people expend unusual effort, often well beyond their anticipated capabilities. However, at this point, finding some way to direct and mobilize the survival efforts of a shocked and dazed population is the most immediate social dilemma. It is a complex problem that involves establishing communication, coordination, and social control in a situation in which the conventional social structure has been distorted.[55]

The Disillusionment Phase Studies of disasters indicate that while most survivors experience an impulse to cope with immediate problems, in the days and weeks following a disaster, a series of delayed reactions begin to emerge. During this disillusionment phase, a growing sense of loss is compounded by the fact that the survivors find themselves in an alien physical and social environment, stripped of all social support mechanisms. While the "first disaster" is in the past, a "second disaster" emerges, one characterized by the problems of coping, relocation, reconstruction, and recovery.

In summary, the nuclear era has changed the nature of both war and peace. Research on conventional disasters reveals how important groups and agencies outside of affected areas can be in helping casualties to cope with the trauma of war. The massive scale of nuclear weaponry has the potential to disrupt the very fabric of society everywhere. Thus, every person on earth lives in the shadow of potential death, but also with the possibility that the survivors will be unable to rebuild.

PEACE

The birth of the nuclear era lent new impetus and urgency to the quest for peace. The destructive power of nuclear weaponry suddenly made the need for peace seem more urgent. But then, what is peace? Certainly, it involves more than the absence of war. That definition suggests that violence is the normal condition and ignores the fact that powerful nations often are able to intimidate less powerful nations to avoid open conflict. Thus, **peace** is better defined as a status evolving from groups or nations that maintain cooperative relations with one another. Interestingly, one observer of war and peace has recently noted that since the year 3600 B.C., 14,500 wars have been fought, but the world has experienced only 292 years of peace.[56]

Many societies have maintained peace for long periods of time. A few have even managed to survive for more than a century without resorting to violence against any other nation. Many nations have peacefully coexisted with neighbors for even longer periods. The governments of the United States and Canada, for example, frequently boast that the two nations share the world's longest undefended boundary, reflecting two centuries of cooperation.

Pacifism and the Peace Movement

The search for peace in America has a long history, one characterized by the activities of both *pacifists* and *peace movements.*

Pacifism is opposition to war and violence as mechanisms for settling disputes. Some pacifists are opposed not only to war, but to military preparedness as well. Others, **conscientious objectors,** are against their own personal involvement in war. Pacifism has now and then been a matter of religious conviction. Among the first advocates of pacifism were the Quakers, and in later periods the Amish and several other religious groups have adopted highly pacifistic positions.[57] More recently, pacifism has become a social or political philosophy, attracting people with a variety of reasons for opposing war.

By contrast, a **peace movement** is a loose confederation of people organized for peace. Following the patterns of other social movements (see Chapter 16), they donate money, lobby legislatures, and take to the streets in pursuit of their cause. Opposition to war is usually a matter of religious conviction. Most leaders in the Judeo-Christian tradition emphasize peace; Buddha preached nonviolence; Martin Luther King, Jr., and many other religious figures also have counseled nonviolent resistance as a means of gaining support for widely divergent causes. Many wars have indeed been fought in the name of religion, but strong antiwar elements are to be found in the teachings of many faiths.

Motives other than religion also support peace movements. The well-known industrialist Andrew Carnegie (1835–1919), for example, believed that education was the key to peace, and he donated millions of dollars to fund studies of peace. Social reformer and suffragette Jane Addams (1860–1935) condemned war, arguing that it destroyed family life. American political leader and socialist Norman Thomas (1884–1968) spoke out against war on the grounds that it diverted money from the eradication of poverty. Physicist Albert Einstein (1879–1955) also was an advocate of peace, fearing nuclear destruction. King, Carnegie, Addams, Thomas, and Einstein, as well as current peace activists and most other citizens around the globe seem to share two things. The first is the goal of preventing war. The second is the notion that war endangers the social goals of freedom, security, and justice.

Strategies for Peace

The dangers of the nuclear era have accelerated efforts for assuring peace, with measures ranging from the establishment of international law and world courts for dispute arbitration to the development of defensive armaments for the sake of inhibiting attack, and selective disarmament in the hope of reducing tension and hostility.

International Courts

The International Court of Justice, founded as part of the United Nations, has been in operation since shortly after the close of World War II. Although it has helped to settle some disputes between nations, for the most part its success has been limited. The difficulty is a sociocultural one. The norms, customs, and social patterns of the nations of the world differ so dramatically that it is impossible to establish one standard that is applicable to all. As a result, most nations tend to ignore international court rulings with which they do not agree.

Deterrence Theory and Military Buildup

The **deterrence theory of military buildup** is based on the belief that since nuclear wars carry the certainty of mutual destruction, no nation will start a war that it cannot finish. In the early years of the nuclear era this led nations into an **arms race,** the building and accumulation of more and more weaponry to assure massive retaliation if attacked. Among the **nuclear powers,** the nations of the world that possess nuclear armaments, the theory has its advocates. The governments of both the United States and the Soviet Union seem to agree that the logical outgrowth of nuclear war is world annihilation. Thus, each nation's stockpile of nuclear arms deters the others from launching a nuclear attack (see Exhibit 20.9).

Critics of this policy worry that if a nation felt it was going to be defeated in a conventional war, it would have nothing to lose by unleashing a nuclear attack. Then too, and despite the many fail-safe mechanisms built into the nuclear structure, the possibility always exists that war might be started by computer error or some other technical malfunction. However, the most serious flaw in the deterrence theory is its failure to fully account for social behavior. Deterrence theory assumes that groups always act rationally, that concern with survival will override any other intention. Yet as already illustrated in the analysis of terrorism, patriotism or religious fervor may cause a nation or group to use *any* means it considers necessary to destroy its enemy.

Disarmament and Arms Reduction

Proponents of the arms reduction approach to the quest for peace view disarmament as a way of reducing tensions among nations and eliminating the chances of unintentional war. Some of the scientists who created the first atomic bomb were in the forefront of those originally working for disarmament (see Exhibit 20.10). In more recent years in the United States it has become a broader national issue. Yet attempts at arms reduction have always had their problems, primarily because one nation fears that it will put itself at a disadvantage, rendering it more vulnerable to attack. The United States and the Soviet Union have been discussing approaches for the reduction of nuclear arms for decades, with some very significant accomplishments in mid-1989. And while both nations claim that the ultimate goal is the elimination of all such weapons, it would appear that the deep political and social divisions between the two nations will make it a slow process, requiring that they overcome more than three decades of distrust and competition.

Exhibit 20.9

Sociological Focus

Who Has the Bomb?

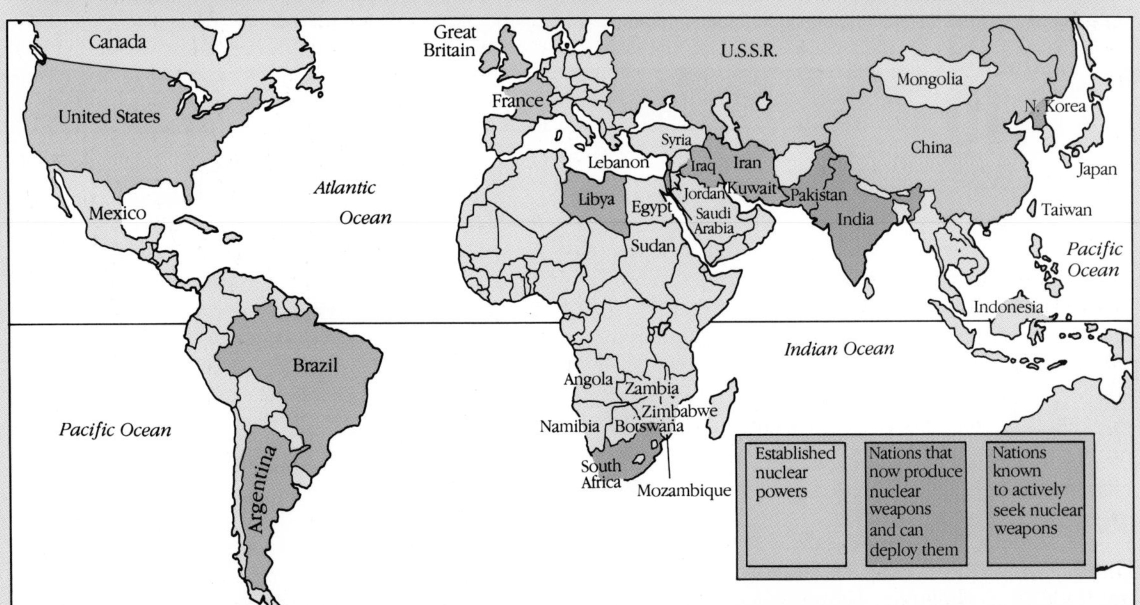

Source: *Time,* June 3, 1985, p. 41.

SOCIAL INDICATOR

Defense Buildup in the United States

Buildup
Fiscal Years

Surface Ships
1981: 201
1988: 239

Submarines
1981: 128
1988: 137

Bombers
1981: 376
1988: 291

ICBM's
1981: 1,054
1988: 1,000

Tanks
1981: 12,821
1988: 15,600

Source: Arms Control Association, 1988.

Spending
In Billions of 1982 Dollars, Fiscal Years

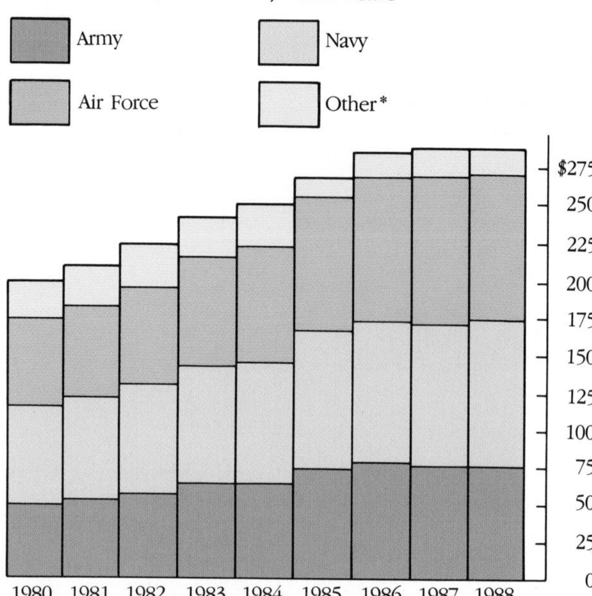

*Includes expenses for joint services and for the Office of Secretary of Defense.

Exhibit 20.10

Sidelights on American Culture

The Doomsday Clock

Many of the scientists who participated in the development of nuclear weapons were among the first to foresee the implications of an arms race and nuclear war. In 1947 they founded the *Bulletin of the Atomic Scientists* as a vehicle for promoting world peace and discussing the issues associated with war and its aftermath.

To demonstrate graphically how close nuclear scientists believe the world is to nuclear holocaust, the cover of each monthly issue of the *Bulletin* is dominated by the *doomsday clock.* Midnight may have been the witching hour for

Cinderella, but for atomic scientists midnight symbolizes nuclear war—"doomsday" for the human race. The hands of the clock move closer to midnight as world tensions rise and retreat during more peaceful periods.

The doomsday clock was set at 7 minutes to midnight in 1947. It was set at 2 minutes to midnight in 1953, when the Soviets detonated their first hydrogen bomb, and at 12 minutes to midnight in 1972, when the United States and the Soviet Union signed SALT I, the arms limitation agreement. In 1987, in anticipation of the 1988 arms-reduction summit between Ronald Reagan and Mikhail Gorbachev, the doomsday clock was set at 6 minutes to midnight.

TERRORISM, WAR, PEACE, AND APPLIED SOCIOLOGY

Violence is a common feature of human life and a matter of great concern for numerous reasons. The loss of human life is never trivial. Whether organized, as in war, or isolated, as in terrorism, violence disrupts the structures and arrangements that are basic to cooperative social life. For that reason, the application of sociological knowledge to the study of war, peace, and terrorism represents a meaningful and practical endeavor.

Although war and peace are topics typically associated with the field of political science, sociologists have not been absent from this crucial area of inquiry. More than a half-century ago sociologist Pitirim A. Sorokin analyzed the relationships between cycles in cultural patterns and fluctuations in war over thousands of years.[58] His conclusions have provided many useful insights into why wars begin and how hostilities are sustained. In addition, analyses by C: Wright Mills and Amitai Etzioni have focused on the social causes of war,[59] and sociologists have joined forces with economists, anthropologists, political scientists, and others in the emerging field of **peace science,** the study of the sources, management, and resolution of conflict.

On the whole, however, the tools of social science have been put to little use in the study of war.[60] Sociology can be most productive in the future in investigating any systematic connections between cultural conditions and the incidence of war. It is the field of sociology, too, that is best equipped to explain why no two elective democratic governments have ever fought a war with one another. The answer to this question might offer important insights to the whole area of conflict resolution. Sociology already *has* had a significant applied impact in the area of disaster research (see Exhibit 20.11).

Exhibit 20.11 **Applied Sociology**

Disaster Research

Although disaster research is generally undertaken by sociologists and other social scientists interested in the area of collective behavior, it has direct applications to a variety of areas. As a subfield of sociology, disaster research evolved in the aftermath of World War II. Its primary interests have included human and social responses to disaster, citizen reactions to disaster warnings, and techniques for moving or relocating people who cannot be otherwise protected from environmental threats and loss of life.

Almost all research on disaster behaviors is based on responses to natural disasters—floods, hurricanes, tornadoes, earthquakes, and volcanic eruptions. However, much of what has been learned about coping with these situations also applies to man-made disasters, including war and terrorism. In fact, primary research topics include crisis relocation planning in connection with threats of nuclear war and relief strategies in the event of terrorist attacks. A recent effort in Rochester, New York, illustrates one of these applications.

Early on in the study of disasters it was realized that preparedness is much like playing a game of Clue. The victim, weapon, crime scene, and guilty party are unknown. Relief agencies and groups that are to deal with the effects of disasters must assess the number of victims, their needs, and the appropriate responses—without knowing in advance where, how, or with what force tragedy will strike. These conditions are especially characteristic of terrorist bombings.

Researchers in Rochester conducted an exercise in which they mapped high-risk locations and populations. By determining in advance the characteristics of each neighborhood—including population densities and demographics, evacuation routes, and available services—the research team was able to pinpoint disaster management needs in terms of transportation, medical care, child care, economic assistance, and bilingual instructions.

SOURCES: Ronald W. Perry and Alvin H. Mushkatel, *Disaster Management: Warning Response and Community Relocation* (Westport, CT: Quorum Books, 1987); Darrell A. Norris, "Disaster Demographics," *American Demographics,* August 1987, pp. 39–41; Dennis E. Wenger, James D. Dykes, Thomas D. Sebok, and Joan L. Neff, "It's a Matter of Myths: An Empirical Examination of Individual Insight into Disaster Response," *Mass Emergencies,* 1 (1975), pp. 33–46.

SUMMARY

Terrorism and war are extreme forms of social conflict. Terrorism is the systematic use or threat of extreme violence directed against symbolic victims, and typically performed for psychological rather than material effects, with the aim of coercing groups or governments into making political concessions. Terrorism is rooted in ideological politics, while the terrorists themselves are generally the "people next door"—young adults from middle-class or upwardly mobile working-class families.

Terrorism is financed through a variety of sources, including donations, robbery, ransom kidnapping, and state-sponsorship. The financing of terrorist activities by means of direct involvement in illegal drug trafficking—narco-terrorism—has recently become a more important funding source. In the last several decades terrorism has changed the ways that governments do business. In addition, it has affected the machinery of both local and international politics. Most curious is the relationship between terrorism and the media. Violence is news, and the extensive media coverage given to terrorism at times makes it appear that the media acts in complicity with terrorists.

In contrast to the random nature of terrorism, war is systematic, organized violence. War is as old as recorded history, representing a phenomenon that has marred the relationships between nations, both ancient and modern.

The regularity with which wars occur has led many observers to suggest that aggressive instincts buried deep within human genes cause wars, but in fact, many different sources of war have been traced. The differences that separate people—economically, socially, and culturally—tend to produce hostilities and antagonisms that groups and nations feel they cannot resolve without open conflict.

The sheer destructiveness of war often masks the fact that nations have long sought to develop rules for the conduct of war. The most significant development in the history of warfare was the harnessing of nuclear power. Like terrorism, nuclear war blurs the distinctions between combatants and civilians. However unthinkable nuclear war may seem, it is nevertheless possible, forcing societies to focus on processes of peace.

KEY TERMS/CONCEPTS

arms race
conscientious objectors
coup d'etat
deterrence theory of military build-up
disaster syndrome
economic expansionism
expansionism
guerrilla war/insurgency
just war
mercenaries
militarized expansionism
militarized society
narco-terrorism
nuclear era
nuclear powers
pacifism
peace
peaceful societies
peace movement
peace science
sociocultural expansionism
state-sponsored terrorism
Stockholm syndrome
terrorism
war

DISCUSSION QUESTIONS

1. Is war the result of innate aggressive drives?
2. Popular support for war is often based on images. According to current images, what nations are presently foes of the United States and how are those countries portrayed in the media?
3. How do you think the United States should respond to terrorism?
4. It was stated in this chapter that no two elective democratic governments have ever fought a war against one another. Why do you think this is so?
5. What do you think would constitute a just war?

SUGGESTED READINGS

Sam Keen, *Faces of the Enemy* (New York: Harper & Row, 1986). A review of a century of war-time propaganda, well-illustrated with cartoons and posters.

Walter Laqueur and Yonah Alexander (eds.), *The Terrorism Reader: An Historical Anthology* (New York: Penguin, 1987). This collection of readings brings together the most notable proponents, critics, and analysts of terrorism from ancient times through the 1980s, and includes a discussion of sociological interpretations of terrorism.

Robert J. Lifton, *Death in Life: Survivors of Hiroshima* (New York: Random House, 1967). A sensitive and humane portrait of the survivors of the Hiroshima atomic bomb blast, who were forever left with the "imprint of death." The victims relate their response to the horror of the disaster.

Beverly Raphael, *When Disaster Strikes* (New York: Basic Books, 1986). This comprehensive volume reveals how individuals and communities cope with the catastrophes of war and natural disaster.

Paul Wilkinson, *Terrorism and the Liberal State,* 2nd ed. (New York: New York University Press, 1986). Written by a British professor of international relations, this volume addresses three sets of problems: the relation of terrorism to the basic values and processes of liberal democracies; the underlying and precipitative causes of terrorist action and the internal and external defenses against terrorism open to liberal governments; and the growth and implications of international terrorism.

NOTES

1. *Newsweek,* July 21, 1986, p. 18.
2. For example, see Ronald D. Crelinsten, Kanielle Laberge-Altmejd, and Dennis Szabo, *Terrorism and Criminal Justice* (Lexington, MA: Lexington Books, 1978); Noel O'Sullivan (ed.), *Terrorism, Ideology, and Revolution* (Brighton, East Sussex, England: Wheatsheaf, 1986); Paul Wilkinson, *Terrorism and the Liberal State* (New York: New York University Press, 1986).
3. Alex Schmid, *Political Terrorism: A Research Guide* (New Brunswick, NJ: Transaction, 1984).
4. Chalmers Johnson, "Interpretations of Terrorism," in Walter Laqueur and Yonah Alexander (eds.), *The Terrorism Reader* (New York: Penguin, 1987), pp. 267–85.
5. For example, see Christopher Dobson and Ronald Payne, *The Never-Ending War: Terrorism in the 80's* (New York: Facts On File, 1987); Beau Grosscup, *The Explosion of Terrorism* (Far Hills, NJ: New Horizon Press, 1987); Richard E. Rubenstein, *Alchemists of Revolution: Terrorism in the Modern World* (New York: Basic Books, 1987).
6. Michael Reid, *Peru: Paths to Poverty* (London: Latin America Bureau, 1985), p. 108.
7. Peter Janke, *Guerrilla and Terrorist Organizations: A World Directory and Bibliography* (New York: Macmillan, 1983), p. 505.
8. *Latin American Regional Reports, Andean Group Report,* 31 July 1986, pp. 2–3; *New York Times,* June 15, 1986, p. 7.
9. Noted by Barry Rubin, *Modern Dictators: Third World Coup Makers, Strongmen, and Populist Tyrants* (New York: McGraw-Hill, 1987), p. 201.
10. Lawrence Zelic Freedman, "Why Does Terrorism Terrorize?" *Terrorism: An International Journal,* 6 (1983), pp. 399–400.
11. Paul Galloway, "Red Brigades: Like the Guy Next Door," Chicago *Sun-Times,* June 5, 1978, pp. 7, 16.
12. For example, see Stephen Segaller, *Invisible Armies: Terrorism into the 1990s* (San Diego: Harcourt Brace Jovanovich, 1987), pp. 290–92; Richard E. Rubenstein, *Alchemists of Revolution,* p. 6.
13. See Richard Falk, *Revolutionaries and Functionaries: The Dual Face of Terrorism* (New York: E. P. Dutton, 1988); Daniel Pipes, "Fundamentalist Muslims Between America and Russia," *Foreign Affairs,* 64 (Summer 1986), pp. 939–59; Emmanuel Sivan, *Radical Islam: Medieval Theology and Modern Politics* (New Haven: Yale University Press, 1985); Robert O. Slater and Michael Stohl (eds.), *Current Perspectives on International Terrorism* (New York: St. Martin's, 1988).
14. Charles A. Russell and Bowman H. Miller, "Profile of a Terrorist," *Terrorism: An International Journal,* 1 (1978), pp. 17–27.
15. *U.S. News & World Report,* July 8, 1985, p. 27.
16. James Adams, *The Financing of Terror* (New York: Simon and Schuster, 1986), p. 46; Paul Wilkinson, *Terrorism and the Liberal State*, pp. 201–202.
17. Robert Oakley, "International Terrorism," *Foreign Affairs,* 65 (1986), p. 623; Amir Taheri, *Holy Terror: Inside the World of Islamic Terrorism* (Bethesda, MD: Adler & Adler, 1987).
18. Christopher Dobson and Ronald Payne, *The Terrorists: Their Weapons, Leaders and Tactics* (New York: Facts On File, 1982), p. 88.
19. Desmond McForan, *The World Held Hostage: The War Waged by International Terrorism* (New York: St. Martin's, 1986), pp. 129–45; *World Press Review,* March 1986, pp. 25–27.
20. See *USA Today,* January 29, 1985, p. 4A.
21. Abraham Miller, "Hostage Negotiations and the Concept of Transference," in Yonal Alexander, David Carlton, and Paul Wilkinson (eds.), *Terrorism: Theory and Practice* (Boulder, CO: Westview, 1979), p. 114; Frank Ochberg, "The Victim of Terrorism—Psychiatric Considerations," in Ronald D. Crelinsten (ed.), *The Dimensions of Victimization in the Context of Terroristic Acts* (Montreal: University of Montreal Monograph, 1977), p. 27.
22. Peter Janke, *Guerilla and Terrorist Organizations,* p. 407.
23. Clive C. Aston, "Political Hostage-taking in Western Europe," in William Gutteridge (ed.), *Contemporary Terrorism* (New York: Facts On File, 1986), pp. 76–77.
24. *U.S. News & World Report,* February 3, 1986, p. 55; *USA Today,* May 30, 1986, p. 10A.
25. Dobson and Payne, *The Never-Ending War,* p. 340.
26. William C. Adams, "The Beirut Hostages: ABC and CBS Seize an Opportunity," *Public Opinion,* August-September 1985, pp. 43–44.
27. Marvin Maurer, "The TWA Hijack," *Midstream,* November 1985, p. 10.
28. Evan Luard, *War in International Society: A Study in International Sociology* (New Haven, CT: Yale University Press, 1987), p. 1.
29. James F. Dunnigan and Austin Bay, *A Quick and Dirty Guide to War* (New York: William Morrow, 1985), pp. 67–79; *Newsweek,* March 10, 1987, p. 45; *New York Times,* October 22, 1987, p. A9; *U.S. News & World Report,* November 9, 1987.
30. A. C. Pigou, *The Political Economy of War* (New York: Macmillan, 1941), p. 19.
31. For varying approaches to the study of war, see Nicholas S. Timasheff, *War and Revolution* (New York: Sheed and Ward, 1965), pp. 271–76.
32. Sigmund Freud, "Why War?" in Leon Bramson and G. Goethals (eds.), *War: Studies from Psychology, Sociology and Anthropology* (New York: Basic Books, 1964), pp. 71–80.
33. Robert Ardrey, *African Genesis* (New York: Dell, 1961); Robert Ardrey, *The Territorial Imperative* (New York: Atheneum, 1966).

34. Carl W. O'Neil, "Primary and Secondary Effects of Violence Control Among the Nonviolent Zapotec," *Anthropological Quarterly,* 59 (October 1986), pp. 184–90.
35. Geoffrey Gorer, "Man Has No Killer Instinct," in Ashley Montagu (ed.), *Man and Aggression* (New York: Oxford University Press, 1968), p. 34.
36. Gilbert Herdt, *Sambia: Ritual and Gender in New Guinea* (New York: Holt, Rinehart and Winston, 1987).
37. For alternative definitions and ideas about imperialism, see Lewis Feuer, *Imperialism and the Anti-Imperialist Mind* (Buffalo, NY: Prometheus, 1986).
38. Karl Von Clausewitz, *On War* (London: Pelican Books, 1971), p. 402.
39. M. M. Bober, *Karl Marx's Interpretation of History* (New York: W. W. Norton, 1948), p. 226.
40. Thomas A. Bailey, *The American Pageant* (Boston: D.C. Heath, 1956), p. 625.
41. Raoul Naroll, Vern Bullough and Frada Naroll, *Military Deterrence in History* (Albany: State University of New York Press, 1974).
42. Francis Beer, *Peace Against War* (San Francisco: Freeman, 1981).
43. *USA Today,* November 18, 1987, p. 10A.
44. Duane E. Leigh and Robert E. Berney, "The Distribution of Hostile Casualties on Draft-Eligible Males with Differing Socioeconomic Characteristics," *Social Science Quarterly* 52 (March 1971), pp. 932–40.
45. *Newsweek,* November 3, 1986, pp. 35–39. See also Anthony Mockler, *The Mercenaries* (New York: Macmillan, 1969).
46. See, for example, Jacques Ellul, *Propaganda* (New York: Vintage Books, 1973); Sam Keen, *Faces of the Enemy* (San Francisco: Harper & Row, 1986); Sanford Nevitt, *Sanctions for Evil* (San Francisco: Jossey-Bass, 1971).
47. Robert L. Phillips, *War and Justice* (Norman: University of Oklahoma Press, 1984), p. i.
48. Fernand van Langehove, *The Growth of a Legend* (New York: G. P. Putnam's and Sons, 1916).
49. Orrin E. Klapp, *Heroes, Villains and Fools: The Changing American Character* (Englewood Cliffs, NJ: Aegis 1972).
50. John D. Jones and Marc F. Griesbach, *Just War* (New York: University Press of America, 1985), p. viii; Phillips, *War and Justice,* p. ix.
51. Beverly Raphael, *When Disaster Strikes* (New York: Basic Books, 1986), p. 47.
52. Dennis S. Mileti, Thomas E. Drabeck, and J. Eugene Haas, *Human Systems in Extreme Environments* (Boulder, CO: University of Colorado Institute of Behavioral Sciences, 1975).
53. Enrico L. Quarantelli and Russell Dynes, "When Disaster Strikes," *New Society,* 23 (1973), pp. 5–9.
54. Robert J. Lifton, *Death in Life: Survivors of Hiroshima* (New York: Random House, 1967); Hachiya Michihiko, *Hiroshima Diary* (Chapel Hill: University of North Carolina Press, 1955); J. S. Tyhurst, "Individual Reactions to Community Disasters," *American Journal of Psychiatry,* 107 (1950), pp. 764–69.
55. Edward A. Tiryakian, "Aftermath of a Thermonuclear Attack on the United States: Some Sociological Considerations," *Social Problems,* 4 (Spring 1959), pp. 291–303.
56. Francis A. Beer, *Peace Against War,* p. 20.
57. Charles DeBenedetti, *Peace Heroes in Twentieth-Century America* (Bloomington, Indiana University Press, 1986).
58. See Philip A. Allen (ed.), *Pitirim A. Sorokin in Review* (Durham, NC: Duke University Press, 1963); Pitirim A. Sorokin, *Social and Cultural Dynamics: Fluctuations of Social Relationships, War and Revolution,* Vol. 3 (New York: American Books, 1937).
59. Amitai Etzioni, *The Hard Way to Peace* (New York: Collier, 1962); C. Wright Mills, *The Causes of World War Three* (New York: Ballantine, 1960).
60. Ronald C. Kramer and Sam Marullo, "Toward a Sociology of Nuclear Weapons," *Sociological Quarterly,* 26 (1985), pp. 277–92; J. David Singer, "Accounting for International War: The State of the Discipline," *Annual Review of Sociology,* 6 (1980), pp. 349–67.

GLOSSARY

This glossary includes all key terms and is followed by pertinent sections of amendments to the United States Constitution that are discussed in the text. Numbers following each definition refer to the page on which the term is defined.

ability groupings Small clusters of students of similar ability. **416**

achieved status A status acquired through personal effort, choice, or merit. **93**

acting crowds An excited and highly volatile collection of people provoked by some focal event in which passions and temper are fed by one another; the result may be spontaneous acts of violence. **511**

administrative law The branch of public law that deals with the powers and duties of government agencies. **205**

adversary system of justice A system of justice in which the accused is considered innocent until proven guilty and the judge serves as a referee between adversaries—the prosecution and the defense. **468**

advertisements Commercial messages that attempt to mold public opinion in the area of consumption. **521**

ageism Prejudice and discrimination directed against older people. **315**

age roles Social segments involving different rights and privileges. **294**

age-specific death rate The annual number of deaths per 1,000 population at specific ages. **588**

AIDS (acquired immune deficiency syndrome) A late manifestation of infection with HIV. **605**

anglo conformity Conformity to a style of life that has its origins in a white, middle-class, Christian, northwestern European society. **269**

animatism The belief in an impersonal and unseen supernatural force or power that is thought to be everywhere. **369**

animism The belief in the existence of almost numberless spirits that dwell in animals and places or simply wander about the earth. **369**

anomie A condition of normative confusion or "normlessness" in which the existing rules and values have little impact. **195**

antagonistic negotiations Negotiations that occur when the players are pursuing diverse interests that must be compromised. **104**

anthropology The scientific study of small-scale or primitive societies. **8**

anticipatory socialization The process of preparing for a new role in anticipation of being in it. **171**

apartheid "Apartness" in Afrikaans; the South African government's policies of racial segregation. **261**

applied science In sociology, knowledge collected and organized to solve practical problems, guide policy decisions, or serve particular clients or groups. **25**

arms race The building and accumulation of more and more weaponry to assure massive retaliation if attacked. **686**

ascribed status A status assigned to an individual without regard for innate differences or abilities. **92**

assimilation The process of learning to fit in and be accepted into the host culture; the eventual disappearance of a minority group as a separate and unique culture when its members adopt the culture of the majority. **268, 407**

assimilation dilemma Social acceptance gained at the cost of a group's unique identity. **271**

atavism A "throwback" to an earlier stage in human evolution. **191**

attribute A single characteristic of a person or group. **35**

Australian ballot system A secret ballot that is prepared, distributed, and tabulated by government officials at public expense. **447**

authority Power that is considered legitimate by those exercising it. **427**

autocracy A system of government in which ultimate authority and the rule of government rest with one person. **430**

bail A form of security guaranteeing that the defendant will appear in court when required to do so. **479**

basic science In sociology, the accumulation of fundamental knowledge about human behavior, the structure of society, and social phenomena. **25**

Bem Sex-Role Inventory A list of adjectives that people have identified as either desirable or sexually neutral traits for men and women. **295**

bilateral system of descent A system whereby kinship lines are traced through both parents equally and the sex of the child is not of consequence in determining inheritance. **335**

biological determinism A notion that suggests that the causes of deviance are the result of some biological or physical element. **191**

blocked mobility A point in work careers at which people have progressed as far as their opportunities and abilities will permit. **646**

boundary disputes Conflicts between different professional groups involving the limits of work tasks and roles. **621**

bourgeois capitalist In Marxist terminology, the owner of the means of production. **252**

bureaucracy A rationally organized formal organization that emphasizes a logical and efficient pursuit of goals achieved through a highly structured network of statuses and roles, an explicit hierarchy of authority, and clearly defined patterns of activity. **125**

bystander effect The unwillingness of bystanders to "get involved" in the problems of others. **115**

capitalist market economy An economy characterized by a competitive marketplace, private ownership of the means of production, and a profit motive. **451**

caste A ranked hereditary grouping within a rigid system of stratification. **224**

caste system A system of social stratification in which individuals are permanently positioned at a given social level on the basis of inherited characteristics. **224**

casual crowds A short-lived crowd with little or no sense of unity, composed of individuals who just happen to be in the same place at the same time. **509**

ceremonies A number of interconnected and related rituals performed at a given time. **368**

charisma The ability to inspire faith. **378**

charismatic authority Power that derives from a ruler's force of personality. **429**

Chinese Exclusion Acts A series of laws passed between 1882 and 1892 that prohibited Chinese laborers from entering the United States. **280**

chromosomes The structural carriers of hereditary characteristics that are found in the nucleus of every cell. **294**

church A large religious organization with a formal structure, an official clergy, an elaborate theology, and a broad membership of people who are generally the children of members. **376**

city A dense and permanent concentration of people with distinctive forms of social organization and economic relationships. **549**

city-state An autonomous political unit consisting of a city and the surrounding countryside. **549**

class consciousness According to Karl Marx, the recognition by a group of its role in the production process; in more current usage, the recognition by a group of its membership in a particular social class. **231**

class system A system of social stratification composed of numerous and typically vague categories of social position that are generally determined by individual achievement, particularly economic achievement. **228**

coalescence The second stage of a social movement; the stage during which groups begin to gather and form about leaders for the sake of developing policies and promoting programs. **536**

coercion Power that is considered illegitimate by those over whom it is exercised. **427**

coercive organizations Organizations, such as prisons or mental institutions, into which people are forced against their will. **123**

cohabitation Living together out of wedlock. **347**

collective behavior The relatively spontaneous behavior of a group of people who are reacting to a common influence in an undefined or ambiguous, and often emotional situation. **508**

collective conscience The collection of values held in common by the members of any relatively well-integrated social system. **204**

collectivist organization A formal organization characterized by an emphasis on participation and shared values. **140**

comparable worth Equal pay for males and females doing work requiring comparable skill, effort, and responsibility under similar working conditions. **309**

Comte, Auguste In seeking ways of structuring a stable society, Comte founded the field of sociology as a scientific discipline. His "positivism" held that standards of empirical observation and logical understanding could unravel the workings of social affairs and lead to the creation of a better society. Comte's major works included *A Discourse on the Positive Spirit* (1844). **11**

concentric zone model A theory of urban growth that suggests that as a city expands in size, it evolves in a series of concentric rings or zones characterized by typical land-use patterns. **564**

concept A term that describes or identifies a specific category of behaviors, characteristics, or events. **6**

conflict A theoretical perspective in sociology that directs attention to the struggles for wealth, power, and social prestige that occur within society. **19**

conflict theory of politics A political theory that argues that the state is biased in favor of the wealthy and powerful, that it is dominated by the interests of the upper classes, and that those of high social position legitimate the holders of political office. **437**

conformity The acceptance of cultural goals and the approved means for achieving them. **196**

conglomerate A corporation that controls many other firms in vastly diversified markets. **458**

conscientious objectors Individuals who oppose their own personal involvement in war. **685**

consciousness of kind The feeling of being bound together by common traits, views, or situations. **106**

conservatism A political philosophy that opposes changes in the political, economic, and social institutions of society. **448**

conservative social movements Social movements that seek to maintain a society's current values. **532**

contagion perspective The theory of French sociologist Gustave LeBon, which held that people undergo some radical change under the influence of a crowd that causes them to regress and act by instinct. **527**

content analysis A research technique that examines communications in an objective and quantitative way for the purpose of measuring certain variables. **48**

control group In a research experiment, the group that is not subjected to the stimulus or event. **39**

conventional crowds A crowd composed of individuals who come together for some specific purpose and whose behavior conforms to a well-established set of cultural rules. **509**

convergence perspective The theory of collective behavior that holds that people who share certain tendencies come together to act out their common predispositions. **527**

cooperative negotiations Negotiations that occur when role partners agree on a goal and develop plans for its realization. **104**

core culture The kaleidoscope of values, norms, beliefs, and practices that are ascribed to by the majority of a society's constituents. **77**

corporate crime. *See* **white-collar crime**

corporation A business organization that is chartered by the state as a legal entity that can own property, sell stock, enter into contracts, and extend privileges of limited financial liability to its shareholders. **455**

correlational techniques Analytical techniques that focus on the extent to which a change in the independent variable is accompanied by a change in the dependent variable. **53**

counterculture A group whose total system of norms, values, and life-styles intentionally deviates from or is in conflict with that of the wider society. **79**

coup d'etat A sudden seizure of government typically undertaken by existing military forces. **672**

courts of appellate jurisdiction Courts whose jurisdiction is limited to conducting appeals. **479**

courts of general jurisdiction The major trial courts—those with the authority to try and decide any criminal case, including appeals from a lower court. **479**

courts of limited jurisdiction The entry point for all criminal proceedings; courts that handle all minor criminal offenses but whose jurisdiction is limited in felony cases to pretrial proceedings. **478**

crazes Short-lived fads that become very central to the lives of their followers. **514**

crime Any intentional act or omission in violation of the criminal law, committed without defense or justification, and sanctioned by the state as a felony or misdemeanor. **202**

crime index The total number of serious crimes that became known to the police during the course of a year. **210**

crime rate Number of Part I offenses that occurred in any given area for every 100,000 persons living in that area. **210**

criminal justice diversion A noncriminal disposition involving the removal of offenders from direct contact with the criminal law at any stage of the police and court processes. **493**

criminal justice process The agencies and operations organized to manage crime and those accused of violating criminal laws. **466**

criminal law The collection of legal codes that deals with offenses committed against the safety and order of the state. **202**

crowds Temporary collections of people who have a united focus on some person or event and who are conscious of and are influenced by one another's presence. **509**

crude birth rate The annual number of births per 1,000 population. **586**

crude death rate The annual number of deaths per 1,000 population. **588**

cult A loosely organized spiritual movement that offers "new" religious ideas and beliefs. **377**

cultural beliefs Strongly held convictions that define social and physical reality for the members of a society. **76**

cultural relativity The principle that any culture must be understood in terms of its own values and in its own context. **66**

cultural universals Traits and patterns that are found in all known societies. **66**

cultural values Shared standards of desirability that define what is good or bad, important or unimportant, and vital or trivial. **72**

culture The customary manner in which human groups learn to organize their behavior in relation to their environment. **63**

culture shock The psychic stress brought on by the strain of adjusting to a different culture. **63**

cumulative socialization The process whereby life transitions build on existing social skills and abilities. **171**

curriculum tracks The grouping of high-school students into different programs on the basis of their abilities and aspirations. **416**

"dark figure" of crime The amount of unknown crime that is not included in official criminal statistics. **211**

***de facto* segregation** Segregationist policies based on custom, tradition, and social practice. **261**

deindividuation The sense of anonymity provided by involvement in a large group. **114**

***de jure* segregation** Segregationist policies based on law. **261**

demise The fifth and last stage of a social movement; the stage during which, having achieved its goals, there is no need for the movement to continue and it ceases to exist. **536**

democracy A system of government in which ultimate political authority is vested in the people. **431**

demographic transition theory A population theory that charts the evolution of societies through various stages, as evidenced by changes in their fertility and mortality rates. **603**

demography The scientific study of human populations, including their size, composition, distribution, density, growth, socioeconomic characteristics, and the causes and consequences of changes in these factors. **585**

dependency ratio The ratio of the number of people under age 15 and over age 65 per person ages 15–65. **599**

dependency theory A perspective on Third World urbanization that contends that the underdevelopment characteristic of such nations is not the result of existing cultural values, but is rather, a consequence of the worldwide capitalist structure. **582**

dependent variable A variable that is the result of a cause-and-effect relationship. **35**

descriptive statistics Arithmetic methods of reporting general patterns of social behavior. **52**

deskilling of work An impact of industrialization that reduces skilled workers to the status of machine operators or unskilled laborers. **631**

deterrence theory of military buildup The theory that no nation will start a war that it cannot finish. **686**

developmental career paths Movement through jobs requiring ever higher levels of skill and responsibility. **646**

deviant behavior Behavior that fails to conform with the significant social norms and expectations of society. **183**

differential association The theory of deviance that suggests that criminal and deviant behaviors are learned through the same processes that nondeviant behaviors are learned. **199**

diffusion The movement of cultural traits from one group or culture to another. **78**

diffusion of responsibility The tendency for no one individual to feel responsible for acting when others are present. **116**

disaster syndrome A state of shock characterized by trancelike and emotionless behavior. **684**

discrimination The acting out of prejudice by depriving minority group members of equal access to rights, privileges, and opportunities. **275**

disinvestment The abandonment of housing by landlords when tax, utility, and maintenance costs outstrip rental income. **575**

displacement The elimination of jobs by machines. **630**

divorce rate The number of divorces per 1,000 population. **344**

doubling time The number of years required for the population of an area to double in size, given the current rate of population growth. **596**

dual court system The court system in the United States in which courts operate at both the federal and state levels. **477**

dualism The struggle of supernatural beings working for "good" against the forces of "evil." **371**

due process of law A principle of American justice that implies and comprehends the administration of laws and judicial procedures that do not violate the very foundations of civil liberties. **468**

Durkheim, Emile One of the initial proponents of the "functionalist" perspective in sociology; Durkheim held that individuals are the exclusive product of their social environment; that society shapes people in every possible way. He also introduced quantitative research methods to sociology. Durkheim's major works included *The Division of Labor in Society* (1893), *The Rules of Sociological Method* (1895), *Suicide: A Study in Sociology* (1897), and *The Elementary Forms of Religious Life* (1915). **15**

earnings gap The lower pay accorded to women as compared to men. **306**

economic determinism The contention that every aspect of social life is patterned on economic relationships. **14**

economic expansionism Expansionism that targets the natural and material resources of nations. **675**

economics A specialized social science that focuses on the production and distribution of goods and services, and patterns of consumption throughout society. **9**

economy The social institution that specializes in the production and exchange of goods and services to satisfy the needs and wants of the population. **9, 450**

education The formal process by which society transmits its knowledge, skills, and values from one person or group to another. **395**

egalitarian authority Authority pattern in which power is equally vested among men and women. **334**

ego The mediator of the id and superego that seeks to find socially acceptable outlets for instinctual drives. **159**

elder abuse Physical violence directed toward older family members. **315**

emergent norm perspective The theory postulated by Ralph Turner and Lewis Killian, which argues that new norms emerge during the course of social interaction, thus defining the appropriate behavior for the situation. **528**

emigration The movement of people out of a society. **589**

endogamy The obligation to marry within the group. **334**

enslavement A pattern of domination that involves the reduction of a group to the status of property. **260**

escapist social movements A social movement in which the participants withdraw from society rather than trying to alter it. **532**

Escobedo v. Illinois The 1964 Supreme Court decision that extended the Fifth Amendment privilege against self-incrimination to the states and mandated that an accused have the right to have an attorney present during police interrogation. **473**

estate A ranked division of a society whose members have rights and duties that are prescribed by law. **226**

estate system A system of social stratification in which social position is based on birth, relationship to the land, and political or military strength. **226**

ethnic enclaves/ethnic villages Small communities or neighborhoods made up of members of a single racial or ethnic group. **270**

ethnicity/ethnic group A sociological concept referring to the members of a group who share a distinctive cultural tradition. **257**

ethnocentrism The tendency to judge other cultures by the standards of one's own. **64**

ethnogenesis The tendency in recent years of minority groups to be conscious about reviving their cultural traditions. **271**

ethnomethodology The study of the unwritten rules of social behavior. **23**

exchange negotiations Negotiations that occur between individuals with equal authority and result in trading behavior. **105**

exclusionary rule The Supreme Court doctrine that prohibits the use of evidence seized in violation of the Fourth Amendment. **473**

executives Those responsible for making policy for an entire organization. **625**

exogamy The obligation to marry outside the group. **360**

expansionism A national policy of extending control over other societies. **674**

experiment In social science research, a technique used to ascertain the effects of some specific experience or event on individuals or groups. **39**

experimental design A research technique exposing two groups of people (who are similar in every respect) to alternative experiences and measuring the consequences. **39**

experimental group In a research experiment, the group that is subjected to some stimulus or event. **39**

exploratory study A study conducted for the sole purpose of generating baseline information that can describe a social process or event. **36**

expressive crowds An emotionally charged gathering in which collective excitement is common as a form of release and members often behave in ways that they themselves would consider unacceptable in other settings. **511**

expressive social movements Social movements that seek to distract people from the dissatisfactions in their lives or society by changing their psychic or emotional states. **532**

expulsion A pattern of domination that involves a policy for eliminating minorities by forcibly removing them from the territory of the dominant society. **259**

extended family A family that includes at least three generations—children, parents, and grandparents—living together in the same household or a single family formed by the joining of siblings, their spouses, and children. **332**

extermination A pattern of domination that involves a policy of systematic destruction aimed at the members of a particular minority group. **259**

fads Novel, trivial, and short-lived patterns of behavior that spread rapidly throughout those portions of society that choose to adopt them. **513**

family Two or more persons related by blood, marriage, adoption, or some other socially recognized arrangement, who live together and share a variety of social and economic responsibilities. **327**

family life cycle The progression of expansions and contractions that almost every family undergoes during the course of time. **339**

family of orientation The nuclear family into which an individual is born. **332**

family of procreation The new nuclear family—composed of self, spouse, and perhaps children—that develops when an individual marries. **332**

fashions Fluctuating styles in appearance or behavior that typically relate to standards of dress and manners. **514**

fast-track career path The rapid movement through a series of jobs that lead directly to upper-level positions. **646**

fecundity The physiological capacity to reproduce. **593**

felony Any serious crime punishable by death or imprisonment in a federal or state penitentiary. **202**

feral children Infants and youths growing up in isolation from meaningful human contact. **154**

fertility The actual number of births in a population. **586**

fertility rate The number of annual births per 1,000 women of childbearing age in a population. **587**

feudal system A sociopolitical structure based on a rural economy and characterized by a dispersal of power in a variety of semi-independent domains in which land was held by serfs on the condition of their service and homage to the landowning lords. **550**

fixed career path A specific set of occupations or positions that a worker must follow for occupational mobility. **646**

folkways Norms that guide the customary, normal, and habitual ways in which the peoples of a society or group do things. **69**

formal organizations The relatively large social groups created to pursue specific goals. **122**

formal sanctions Institutionalized means of rewarding for conformity and punishing for deviance. **187**

fragmentation The fourth stage of a social movement; the stage during which, after a period of success, the movement begins to break down, primarily through a process of co-optation. **536**

frustration-aggression hypothesis The argument that aggression *is* a common response to frustration **271**

functional illiteracy The inability to read and comprehend at the fourth-grade level. **396**

functionalist theory of politics A political theory that holds that the state's position of power provides benefits to all members of society, not just the upper classes. **438**

gender The sociological, psychological, and cultural aspects of being male or female. **294**

gender identity The awareness of being a member of one sex or the other. **294**

gender inequality Unequal rewards and opportunities associated with being a man or woman in contemporary society. **303**

gender roles The social expectations held for boys and girls and men and women in any given society. **294**

generalized beliefs In Smelser's theory of collective behavior, the identification and common interpretation of the problems that are causing strain in a society. **524**

generalized other The composite of attitudes, values, and expectations shared by an entire group. **159**

generational inversion The process whereby parents and children reverse roles in terms of physical care and emotional support. **316**

genocide The systematic destruction of an entire ethnic or national group. **59**

gentrification A process involving the renovation and settlement of inner-city neighborhoods by middle- and upper-class suburbanites who have moved back to the city. **574**

Gideon v. Wainwright The 1963 Supreme Court decision that extended the Sixth Amendment right to counsel to all state defendants facing felony trials. **484**

glass ceiling An informal boundary that stops workers from reaching the uppermost positions. **647**

government The individuals or groups who control the political power of the state at any given time. **430**

group A collection of two or more people who interact with one another on the basis of a shared social identity. **105**

guerrilla warfare/insurgency Aggression by small military units for the purpose of establishing liberated zones in which an alternative government can be established. **661**

Hawthorne effect The possibility of influencing subjects in an experiment simply by giving them the satisfaction of being noticed and studied. **39**

helping behavior Any positive act aimed at aiding another or preventing a criminal act. **115**

hidden curriculum A subtle configuration of norms and attitudes instilled during the educational process. **411**

history The scientific study of the events of the past. **10**

HIV (human immunodeficiency virus) A virus that destroys or incapacitates important components of the human immune system. **605**

homogamy The tendency of an individual to choose a spouse with a similar background. **337**

horizontal mobility Social mobility from one position in the stratification system to another at the same level. **244**

hypothesis A precise statement of the anticipated relationship between two or more concepts. **6, 35**

I As described by sociologist George Herbert Mead, the unpredictable and unique aspect of an individual's personality. **159**

id The unconscious drive or instincts that represent the unsocialized side of the human animal. **159**

ideal type An abstract model or a social phenomenon based on observations of many actual cases. **125**

ideology of inferiority A cultural belief system that suggests that minorities are somehow (socially, culturally, or intellectually) inferior. **268**

immigration The movement of people into a society. **589**

incest taboo A rule that forbids sexual contacts between closely related individuals. **328**

incipiency The first stage of the life cycle of a social movement; the stage during which some situation is defined as a problem. **536**

independent variable A variable that does not bring about a cause-and-effect relationship. **35**

indeterminate sentence The most common sentence handed down by the courts; a sentence with a fixed minimum and a fixed maximum term for incarceration, rather than a definite period of time. **495**

industrial cities Large urban settlements situated near sources of energy or raw materials, and dependent on manufacturing, banking, and transportation. **551**

industrial revolution The social and economic changes that marked the transition from a stable agricultural and commercial society to a modern industrial society reliant on complex machinery rather than on tools. **551**

infant mortality rate The number of children who die within the first year of life per 1,000 live births. **588**

informal sanctions Responses by members of a group to an individual's behavior that arise spontaneously with little or no institutionalized leadership. **187**

in-group A group of individuals characterized by a strong sense of identification, loyalty, and the exclusion of nonmembers. **108**

innovation The acceptance of cultural goals but rejection of the means a society deems proper for reaching them. **196**

inquiry system of justice A system of justice in which all persons are obligated to cooperate with the court in its inquiry into a crime. **467**

inquisitorial system of justice A system of justice in which the accused was considered guilty until he could prove himself innocent. **467**

instincts Fixed and unalterable behaviors that are inherited as part of one's fundamental physical/biological makeup. **159**

institutionalization The third stage of a social movement; the stage during which society has responded with standardized patterns of action. **536**

institutionalized sexism Social patterns and elements of social organization that limit opportunity and access for the members of a particular sex. **300**

interactionist perspective Herbert Blumer's theory that contagion spreads through a collective because the emotions of others generate the same emotions in oneself, in turn intensifying the emotions of those nearby. **527**

intergenerational mobility Movement in the stratification system from the level occupied by one's parents. **245**

interlocking directorate A structure in which the members of the board of directors of one corporation are also members of the boards of other corporations. **460**

internal migration The movement of a population *within* a nation's boundary lines. **590**

international migration The movement of a population from one nation to another. **589**

invasion-succession A theory of urban ecology that suggests that as a new group moves into, or "invades" a neighborhood occupied by some other group, the invaders are initially met with resistance and hostility, but as the invasion progresses, the original residents begin to move out, thus making room for additional invaders. **562**

just war A war that is fought because it is morally right, seeks ethical goals, and protects national interests. **680**

kinship A socially recognized link based on ancestry, marriage, or adoption. **330**

labeling theory The theory of deviance that focuses on the processes of interaction through which behaviors become defined as deviant and the ways in which the labeling process can bring about more deviance. **197**

laissez faire The economic doctrine that holds that systems work best when there is no government interference. **11**

latent functions Consequences that are neither intended nor recognized by the participants of a society or group. **19**

laws Norms that are enacted and enforced by a specific group within a society. **71**

learned helplessness The sense of apathy or helplessness that emerges when people feel they have no control over events. **654**

legal-rational authority Power that is rooted in the prudent decision making of those subject to official rules founded on procedures that define the rights, duties, and obligations of those in power. **429**

liberalism A political philosophy that emphasizes more government action to meet individual needs. **448**

life expectancy The average number of years that a person born in a particular year can expect to live. **588**

looking-glass self The concept that a person's self-image is a reflection of what others see. **157**

low ceiling career path A career path in which little or no potential for advancement exists. **646**

lumpenproletariat In Marxist terminology, the poorest and most degraded members of capitalist society. **231**

magic A ritual for controlling the physical and social worlds. **367**

managers Those who direct and evaluate the activities of workers below them in a bureaucratic hierarchy. **625**

manifest functions Consequences that are intended and recognized by the participants of a society or group. **19**

Mapp v. Ohio The 1961 Supreme Court decision that extended the exclusionary rule to the states by barring the use of illegally seized evidence in state prosecutions. **473**

marginality Participation in two cultures without being a full member of either. **270**

marriage A socially recognized union between men and women that permits sexual relations and childbirth. **332**

marriage rate The number of marriages per 1,000 population. **338**

Marx, Karl The popularizer of socialism; Marx saw human history as the history of class conflict—conflict between those who own and control the means of production and those who work for them. He also maintained that all aspects of the emerging social industrial society were shaped by the economic system and used by those in control to maintain and consolidate their power. Marx's major work was *Das Kapital* (3 vols—1867, 1885, 1895). **14**

masses Collections of people who are widely scattered yet participate in some event either physically or with a common concern or interest. **513**

mass hysteria A highly emotional fear of a potentially threatening situation; involves widespread and contagious anxiety. **518**

master status The status that dominates a person's social identity. **95**

material culture All the tangible objects that a society produces and uses. **68**

me As described by sociologist George Herbert Mead, the aspect of the personality that represents the conventional side of human behavior and responds to the expectations of society. **159**

mean Arithmetic average computed by adding all scores and dividing by the number of cases. **55**

median The value that divides a group exactly in half. **55**

megalopolis An urban region that contains one or more metropolitan centers. **552**

mercenaries Professional soldiers in the employ of foreign governments who fight in wars for a fee. **677**

metropolitan area A complex of one or more central cities, together with their surrounding suburbs. **552**

migration The movement of population from one geographical area to another. **589**

militarized society A nation controlled by its armed forces. **675**

Miranda v. Arizona The 1966 Supreme Court decision that ruled that prior to any questioning, police must advise suspects that they have a right to remain silent, that anything they say can and will be used against them in a court of law, that they have a right to consult with a lawyer and to have a lawyer present during any questioning, and that if they cannot afford a lawyer, one will be obtained for them if they so desire. **475**

miscegenation The interbreeding of what are presumed to be distinctly different races. **334**

misdemeanor Any minor offense punishable by no more than a $1,000 fine or a term of up to one year in a local jail. **202**

mobilization for action In Smelser's theory of collective behavior, the movement into a collective action, either spontaneously or as a result of persuasion by group leaders. **526**

mode The number that occurs most frequently in a collection of scores. **55**

modernization The social, demographic, and economic changes that accompany the transition of societies from agricultural to industrial production. **312**

modernization theory A perspective on Third World urbanization that contends that the traditional social and political arrangements in the developing nations must be altered if modern industrial benefits are to accrue. **559**

monogamy The marriage of one man to one woman at a time. **332**

monopoly A market condition in which only one seller is actively marketing a given commodity. **458**

mores Strongly held norms that generally have a moral connotation and are based on a culture's central values. **70**

mortality The frequency of the actual deaths in a population. **587**

multinational corporation A corporation that operates within several national jurisdictions. **459**

multiple-nuclei model A theory of urban growth that contends that a city has several core business districts, each of which specializes in a particular activity and takes on various shapes (with their locales depending on resources, history, topography, and the nearness of markets and transportation). **564**

mutual pledge A method of policing instituted by England's Alfred the Great, which places responsibility in the hands of the community. **468**

narco-terrorism The financing of terrorist activities through direct or indirect involvement in illegal drug trafficking. **666**

nation A geographically distinct collection of people within the territory of a state. **430**

natural areas Geographic zones characterized by physical individuality and the cultural characteristics of the people who live in them. **562**

nepotism Favoritism toward a relative (generally avoided in bureaucratic organizations by rules that forbid a worker to supervise his or her spouse or children). **128**

norm of objectivity A rule demanding that the collection of information in scientific investigations not be influenced by the values and beliefs of the investigator. **48**

norms The various rules, standards, and expectations that regulate an individual's interactions with other members of his or her culture and society. **69**

nuclear family A family composed of a husband, wife, and children, usually living apart from other relatives. **330**

nuclear powers Nations that possess nuclear armaments. **686**

occasional property crime The types and instances of burglary, larceny, forgery, and other thefts undertaken infrequently or irregularly, and often quite crudely. **206**

occupational stereotyping The assumption that some jobs are automatically appropriate for certain groups. **639**

oligarchy A system of government in which leadership and authority are vested in the hands of a small elite group. **430**

oligopoly A market condition in which an industry is dominated by a few monolithic corporations. **457**

operation of social control In Smelser's theory of collective behavior, the availability and actions of mechanisms of social control which shape the course and persistence of an episode of collective behavior. **526**

operationalizing concepts Defining concepts in measurable forms. **34**

organized crime Business activities directed toward economic gain through unlawful means, typically in the form of the provision of illegal goods and services. **207**

organized robbery and gang theft Highly skilled criminal activities using or threatening force, violence, coercion, or property damage, and accomplished by planning, surprise, and speed in order to diminish the risks of apprehension. **207**

out-group All people outside the in-group. **108**

overurbanization The level of population in excess of that which can normally be sustained by the existing level of urbanization. **558**

pacifism Opposition to war and violence as mechanism for settling disputes. **685**

panic An uncoordinated and irrational flight from some threat, real or otherwise. **517**

Parkinson's law The principle which holds that "work expands to fill the time available for its completion." **133**

parole A conditional release from a correctional institution after a portion of the sentence has been served. **495**

Part I offenses The FBI category of "serious" crimes, including criminal homicide, forcible rape, aggravated assault, robbery, burglary, larceny-theft, motor-vehicle theft, and arson. **205**

Part II offenses The FBI category of crimes considered "less serious" than the Part I offenses. **205**

participant observation A research technique that requires the investigator to become personally involved in a group in order to observe the group's behavior. **41**

patterned social interaction Social relations among people based on group membership and social position. **7**

peace A status evolving from groups or nations that maintain cooperative relations with one another. **685**

peaceful societies Societies that do not engage in war or systematic violence. **674**

peacekeeping role The role that separates the functions of the police from those of the private citizen and gives the police the legitimate right to use force in situations whose urgency demands it. **471**

peace movement A loose confederation of people organized for peace. **686**

peace science The study of the sources, management, and resolution of conflict. **689**

peer group A loose, unstable collection of individuals of roughly the same age, linked by common interests and preferences. **165**

perfect correlation A correlation in which every change in the independent variable is accompanied by a change in the dependent variable. **53**

personal identity kit The ways in which people decorate their bodies to express their individuality. **174**

Peter Principle The argument that "in a hierarchy every employee tends to rise to his level of incompetence." **133**

petit bourgeois In Marxist terminology, craftsmen and shopkeepers who own their own tools and shops. **231**

pluralism Peaceful coexistence and equality among peoples with differing racial, ethnic, and religious backgrounds; the diffusion of power among various groups and interests. **259, 434**

pluralist theory of politics A political theory which holds that power is distributed among many different groups that compete with one another in both government and the private sectors of the economy. **434**

police discretion The option held by the police to choose between various alternatives in their role as peacekeepers. **472**

political crime Law violations committed by persons who feel that their criminal activities are necessary in order to achieve needed changes in society. **208**

political party A collectivity of people organized for the specific purpose of gaining legitimate control of the government. **444**

political science The study of the ways in which governmental power is acquired, channeled, and used in society. **9**

polygamy Marriage to more than one spouse. **333**

population pyramid A graphic representation of age and sex groups in a society. **598**

poverty A condition in which people have too little money and too few resources to afford the basic necessities of life. **240**

poverty line The designated level of income deemed necessary for the provision of basic nutrition, clothing, and shelter. **240**

power The ability to control the behavior of others, even if they resist. **427**

power elite A small network of influential individuals who are alleged to make the most important political decisions in American society. **436**

prayer A form of communication with supernatural beings for the purpose of requesting their aid. **366**

precipitating events In Smelser's theory of collective behavior, the event or set of related events that trigger a collective response. **525**

preindustrial cities Cities established prior to the Industrial Revolution, based on agricultural and trade economics, and characterized by a core ruling elite, a small middle class, and a large impoverished population of manual laborers. **550**

prejudice A negative attitude toward a group or individual members of a group. **271**

presentence investigation An investigation into the background and characteristics of an offender that serves as a guide for sentencing. **495**

prestige The honor, respectability, or worth that a person's position in society commands. **222**

primary deviation The term used in labeling theory to describe the violation of some norm. **198**

primary group A group characterized by intimate, face-to-face association and cooperation. **109**

primary socialization The learning processes of infants and children that occur as a result of contacts with the family, peers, school, and the media. **170**

primate city A city that grows in population and influence far beyond the other cities in the region or nation. **558**

principle of legitimacy A norm that states that every child should have a legitimate father to act as the child's guardian, protector, and representative in society. **327**

prisonization The process of socialization in which inmates learn the rules and regulations of a correctional institution and the informal rules, values, customs, and general culture of a penitentiary. **492**

probation A sentence of conditional release to the community that does not involve confinement. **492**

profane The common, ordinary, everyday elements of human life; those that are easily explained and understood. **364**

profession An occupation based on extensive and specialized formal education, and licensed by the states. **624**

professional theft Nonviolent forms of criminal occupation pursued with a high degree of skill to maximize financial gain and minimize the risks of apprehension. **208**

proletariat In Marxist terminology, the nonowners of the means of production. **231**

propaganda Messages of a political nature that attempt to mobilize public support behind a particular political party, candidate, or point of view by means of selective, limited, or false information. **520**

Protestant ethic Religious values tied directly to the economic orientations of industrial capitalism; the values include hard work, individualism, frugality, deferral of rewards, and a purposeful life. **551**

psychoanalytic theory Sigmund Freud's theory that every human action has a psychological basis, and that a function of society is to tame the savage beast within the unconscious mind. **159**

psychology The study of individual behavior and human mental processes. **10**

public A spatially diffuse collective of individuals who have a shared interest in some issue about which differing opinions are possible. **518**

public opinion The dominant opinion of any given population on a particular issue. **518**

public-opinion poll The questioning on a particular topic of a sample of people who are representative of a geographical area, a specific public, or a society as a whole. **520**

race An ascribed status defined on the basis of visible physical characteristics. **258**

racism The belief that the human population is made up of different genetic groups that can be identified by distinctive physical characteristics and are distinguished by unequal intellectual capacity. **268**

random sample A selection method that assures that every person in the population under study has an equal chance of being included. **51**

reactionary social movements Social movements that seek to restore society, or at least part of it, to its former condition or state. **529**

rebellion The rejection of the goals and means of society and an attempt to establish some new social order. **196**

recidivism The repetition of criminal behavior. **489**

red tape The finicky and often exasperating procedures used by bureaucrats in handling papers. **133**

reference groups A group that exhibits attitudes and standards of behavior that provide comparison points against which persons measure themselves and others. **111**

regime The system of power and authority that determines how rules will be made and enforced. **430**

reliability The extent to which a research operation will yield the same results every time it is repeated. **35**

religion A system of shared beliefs and standardized practices relating to supernatural forces or beings that cannot be explained rationally but nevertheless gives meaning to life by illuminating complex human questions. **365**

representative sample A sample that represents the population from which it is drawn and can be used to generalize research findings to an entire population. **51**

research design An orderly plan for collecting, analyzing, and interpreting data. **37**

resocialization The process of learning new roles that simultaneously requires the surrendering of old ones. **171**

resource mobilization theory A theory of social movements which holds that movements come about when people organize and take action because they have the resources to turn grievances into action. **537**

retreatism The rejection of both the goals and the means for attaining them that a society has established. **196**

revisionary social movements Social movements that pursue only moderate changes in a society's state of affairs. **532**

revolutionary social movements Social movements that seek large-scale social change with the goal of overthrowing most or all of the existing social order and replacing it with a new system. **532**

riot A specific form of an acting crowd that involves confrontations with authority aimed at creating disorder through attacks on people or property. **511**

ritualism The rejection of society's goals but the acceptance of the means of achieving them. **196**

rituals In religious practice, carefully designated patterns of behavior involving the sacred and supernatural. **365**

Roe v. Wade The 1973 Supreme Court decision that held that the right to privacy extended to the qualified right of a woman to have an abortion. **375**

role conflict A situation in which the expectations associated with a person's multiple-status positions impose inconsistent, contradictory, or impossible demands. **94**

role making The process of individualizing, creating, and enlarging social roles. **104**

role partners The cluster of people a person must relate to when performing any given role. **95**

role playing The acting out of socially defined roles. **101**

role set The array of social roles an individual occupies. **95**

role strain Any difficulty a person encounters in performing a particular role. **93**

role taking Taking on the role or position of another. **158**

routinization of charisma A process in the evolution of a cult in which the teachings of the founder are preserved, a new leader is selected, and others are trained to carry on the work of the founder. **378**

Rule of Four The United States Supreme Court procedure that requires that at least four of the nine Justices of the Court agree that a case merits consideration before it can be accepted for review. **479**

rumors Unconfirmed stories that are shared informally and spread rapidly through a crowd or mass. **514**

sacred The uncommon or extraordinary dimensions of social life; things that transcend the physical world in which people live, inspiring awe and respect. **364**

sample A smaller group selected to represent the whole from which it is drawn. **48**

sanctions Rewards for conformity and punishments for nonconformity or deviance. **102, 187**

Sapir-Whorf hypothesis The proposition that language shapes the way people perceive and experience the world around them. **68**

scapegoat A substitute for the real cause of frustration. **272**

science A system of rational inquiry disciplined by methodically precise testing. **30**

scientific management A tradition in bureaucratic organizations aimed at increasing productivity through the minute specialization of jobs, the precise specification of how they are to be carried out, and the assumption that workers are irresponsible while managers are not. **134**

scientific method A set of procedures and rules for gathering systematic information about the social or physical world. **30**

search and seizure The means for the detection and accusation of crime; evidence gathering in the form of the discovery of stolen items or other indications of guilt and the taking into custody of a person in consequence of law violation. **473**

secondary deviation The term used in labeling theory to describe the behavior that people develop as a result of being labeled as deviant. **198**

secondary group A group composed of individuals who cooperate with one another for distinct, practical reasons and generally maintain few strong emotional ties. **110**

sect A religious group that has split off from a more established church or denomination. **379**

sector model A theory of urban growth that suggests that as a city expands, it becomes divided into sectors with growth taking place along transportation routes and expanding away from already built-up areas. **564**

secular Not concerned with religion or under the control of a church. **364**

segregation A pattern of domination that involves the physical and social separation of the members of a minority within a society. **261**

self A person's sense of identity and awareness as a unique human being. **156**

self-concepts People's perceptions, beliefs, and ideas about themselves as persons. **156**

self-fulfilling prophecy An incorrect definition of a situation that becomes true because people (1) accept the incorrect definition, and (2) act in such a way as to make it come true. **417**

separate system A method of correctional practice in which the inmate was confined in an isolated cell for the purpose of enabling him to contemplate his wrongdoing and resolve to reform his future behavior. **490**

separatist movements Attempts to escape oppression and gain political autonomy by forming separate nations. **264**

serial monogamy The pattern of having several spouses, one after another. **333**

sex A biological category defined on the basis of chromosomes, hormones, and anatomy. **293**

sex discrimination Open and covert limitations placed on opportunities because of an individual's sex. **299**

sexual harassment Unwelcome and unreciprocated sexual advances or contacts, or requests for sexual favors. **310**

significant others Persons that are considered important in one's life. **158**

silent system A method of correctional practice in which inmates were put to work in groups during the day under a rigid rule of absolute silence at all times, with solitary confinement at night. **490**

slave systems Systems of social stratification in which some individuals are regarded as property that can be bought, sold, traded, or destroyed. **225**

slavery The holding of people as property or chattel. **225**

snowball sample A sample wherein each person selects the next person. **51**

social aggregate A collectivity of individuals who meet by chance or circumstance; individuals who are gathered together in the same place but share little else. **108**

social classes Abstract categories of social position composed of individuals who share similar opportunities, economics levels, life-styles, attitudes, and behavior. **228**

social Darwinism The application of evolutionary theory to human social life. **11**

social distance The degree of closeness or intimacy people are willing to extend to members of dissimilar groups. **271**

social fact An element in the overall pattern of social structure that shaped human behavior. **15**

social group A collection of people who live or work together for extended periods of time. **7**

social institution A relatively stable organization of social groups, roles, and norms that exists to deal with fundamental issues in social living. **330**

socialist command economy An economy in which free enterprise is prohibited and the government determines which goods are to be produced and who will produce them. **452**

socialization The process by which people learn the behavior and attitudes appropriate to their roles in society; becoming a member of society and developing a self-concept. **92, 153**

social loafing The reduced productivity of individuals that results from participation in group activity. **114**

social mobility The movement of people from one position in the stratification system to another. **244**

social movement A form of collective behavior that persists over time and attempts to resist or bring about social change. **529**

social organization The arrangement of positions within a group of people and the social relations among these positions. **90**

social protest movements The unconventional actions undertaken to show disapproval of, and the need for change in, some social policy or condition. **264**

social role The behavior expected of a person in a particular social position. **91**

social status A socially recognized position within some larger social unit. **91**

social stratification The division of society into levels based on wealth, prestige, and power. **224**

social structure A concept that refers to stable and enduring social arrangements. **8**

society A group of interacting individuals who share the same territory. **63**

sociobiology The systematic study of the biological basis of social behavior. **164**

sociocultural expansionism The use of war as a device for imposing one nation's values and beliefs on other nations. **675**

sociological perspective An approach to social phenomena that considers the group context of individual behaviors, patterned social interactions, and the impact of social structure. **6**

sociology The scientific study of society, including the relationships between people and patterns of social life. **4**

Spencer, Herbert Defined the initial subject matter of sociology, including in it the study of such things as the family, politics, religion, social control, work, and stratification. Spencer saw society as analogous to a living organism and explained its processes of change in biological terms. Spencer's major works included *First Principles* (1860–1862) and *Sociology* (1876). **11**

split labor market A labor market in which one group dominates the higher paying and higher prestige jobs, while the members of the minority groups are limited to the less desirable positions. **268**

state A social institution that has a monopoly on the legitimate right to use force within a given territory. **430**

state-sponsored terrorism Strategic and financial support of terrorist organizations by national governments. **666**

statistical category People classified together because they share certain characteristics. **108**

status set The array of social positions an individual occupies. **95**

status symbols Visible identifiers of a person's social status, often material goods associated with superior social rank. **93, 247**

stereotypes Rigid beliefs or assumptions about a whole category of people. **273**

Stockholm syndrome In hostage situations, a bonding between captor and captive that results in each group's identifying with the beliefs and goals of the other. **667**

structural conduciveness In Smelser's theory of collective behavior, the conditions within a society that lend themselves to an occurrence of collective behavior. **521**

structural-functionalism A theoretical perspective in sociology whose proponents view society as an integrated system in which each part contributes to the functioning of the whole. **18**

structural inequality The unequal distribution of wealth and other rewards in society. **221**

structural strain In Smelser's theory of collective behavior, the conflicts within a society that promote stress, frustration, and tension. **521**

subculture The way of life of a group of people whose backgrounds, experiences, and/or norms and values make them culturally distinct from the rest of the society in which they live. **79**

subjugation Forced control of lives and activities, combined with denial of the rights and privileges available to others. **260**

suburbs Politically independent areas immediately outside of a city, which are characterized by substantial population densities, a preponderance of nonrural occupations, and distinctly urban forms of education, recreation, and family life. **569**

superego The norms and values that serve as an internal censor to control the id. **159**

survey A study in which a group of people is asked to answer a prepared list of questions. **37**

symbolic-interactionism A theoretical perspective in sociology that examines social relationships and the meanings that people communicate with their actions. **23**

terrorism The systematic use or threat of extreme violence directed against symbolic victims; typically performed for psychological rather than material effects, with the aim of coercing individuals, groups, communities, or governments into making political concessions. **661**

theism The belief in one or more gods. **369**

theory A general description or explanation of relationships among concepts. **6**

Theory X A theory of formal organizations that emphasizes an elaborate division of labor and the social control of workers. **134**

Theory Y A theory of formal organizations that emphasizes directing human resources toward the goals of the organization. **137**

Theory Z A theory of formal organizations found in Japan that emphasizes group decision making and cooperative activities. **138**

Third World Nations that recently gained freedom from colonial rule and are now seeking to develop and modernize. **557**

total institutions Places that furnish barriers to social interchange with the world at large, thus isolating and dominating individuals' lives. **171**

totalitarianism A system of government typified by restricted access to the decision-making processes of the state and the total control of social institutions by one group. **432**

traditional authority Power that is rooted in the assumption that the habits and customs of the past legitimize the present. **428**

trait stereotyping The assumption that all members of a given social category have certain characteristics or traits. **639**

trial by ordeal A method of determining innocence or guilt in which divine intervention spares the innocent of any suffering in an ordeal, or gives victory in battle with one's accuser. **467**

undervaluation The placing of a lower monetary value on the work tasks of women. **309**

unemployment rate A percentage representing the proportion of the civilian labor force that is unemployed and looking for work. **646**

Uniform Crime Reports The annual publication of the FBI that details the magnitude and trends of crime in the United States. **210**

universal suffrage The right of *all* people to vote. **440**

unobtrusive measures Data collection methods that do not impinge directly on the subjects under study. **44**

urban ecology The study of the ways in which cities are patterned by their social and economic systems and the availability of land. **562**

urbanization The progressive movement of people from rural areas to cities, resulting in city growth and a shift in the relative proportions of rural versus urban populations. **549**

utilitarian organizations Organizations, such as the Ford Motor Company, which motivate their members (employees) by offering material rewards in the forms of wages and fringe benefits. **125**

validity The extent to which research measures what the investigator claims to be measuring. **34**

value-added theory Neil Smelser's theory of collective behavior which holds that collective behavior is the end result of a six-stage process involving structural conduciveness, structural strain, generalized beliefs, precipitating factors, mobilization for action, and the operation of social control. **521**

variables Characteristics or properties of individuals, groups, events, objects, or processes that are present in differing degrees. **35**

verstehen A term referring to the subjective meanings that people associate with their own behavior and that of others. **15**

vertical mobility Social mobility in an upward or downward direction. **244**

victimless crime Public safety, drug, sex, and nuisance offenses in which no real injury to another person or theft of goods or services is involved. **210**

violent personal crime Criminal acts resulting from differences in personal relations in which death or physical injury is inflicted. **206**

voluntary organizations Organizations, such as local parent-teacher associations, which people freely join because they are interested in helping to achieve the organization's goals. **124**

war Socially organized violent conflict involving large social groups. **672**

Weber, Max Explored the history of Western civilization through the study of social classes, religion, and formal organizations, but his primary foci were the individual and the subjective meaning of social behavior. His major works include *The Protestant Ethic and the Spirit of Capitalism* (1904–1905), and *Theory of Social and Economic Organization* (1922). **15**

white-collar crime (corporate crime) Offenses committed by persons acting in their legitimate occupational roles. **207**

white supremacy The doctrine that racial purity should be maintained, and that members of the "white race" are, and should be, dominant. **287**

work careers The stages through which people must progress in any occupation. **639**

writ of *certiorari* A writ of review issued by the United States Supreme Court ordering some lower court to "forward up the record" of a case it has tried. **479**

XYY chromosome The chromosomal pattern with an extra Y ("maleness") chromosome. **194**

zero population growth A population in equilibrium with a growth rate of zero, achieved when births plus immigration equals deaths plus emigration. **596**

Amendments

The Fourth Amendment

The right of the people to be secure in their persons, houses, papers, and effects, against unreasonable searches and seizures, shall not be violated, and no Warrants shall issue, but upon probable cause, supported by Oath or affirmation, and particularly describing the place to be searched, and the persons or things to be seized.

The Fifth Amendment

No person shall be held to answer for a capital or otherwise infamous crime, unless on a presentment or indictment of a Grand Jury . . . ; nor shall any person be subject for the same offense to be twice put in jeopardy of life or limb; nor shall be compelled in any criminal case to be a witness against himself, nor be deprived of life, liberty, or property, without due process of law. . . .

The Sixth Amendment

In all criminal prosecutions, the accused shall enjoy the right to a speedy and public trial, by an impartial jury of the State and district wherein the crime shall have been committed . . . and to be informed of the nature and cause of the accusation; to be confronted with the witnesses against him; to have compulsory process for obtaining witnesses in his favor; and to have the assistance of Counsel for his defense.

The Eighth Amendment

Excessive bail shall not be required, nor excessive fines imposed, nor cruel and unusual punishments inflicted.

The Fourteenth Amendment (Section 1)

. . . No State shall make or enforce any law which shall abridge the privilege or immunities of citizens of the United States; nor shall any State deprive any person of life, liberty, or property, without due process of law; nor deny to any person within its jurisdiction the equal protection of the laws.

PHOTO CREDITS

PART OPENING PHOTOS One: © Phil Hulier/Black Star; **Two:** © George C. Hight/ FPG; **Three:** © Rick Browne/Stock, Boston; **Four:** © Jan Castro/FPG; **Five:** © S. M. Estvanik/FPG; **Six:** Novosti Press Agency

CHAPTER 1: Page 3: © Ann Marie Rousseau/Image Works; **9:** Kevah Golestan/TIME MAGAZINE; **11:** Museum of the City of New York; **12:** © Bill Gentile/Picture Group; **17:** (left) AP/Wide World; (center) AP/Wide World; (right) AP/Wide World; **18:** © Brad Bower/Picture Group; **19:** Sygma; **21:** © John P. Filo; **24:** © Susan Holtz

CHAPTER 2: Page 30: © Steve Starr/Picture Group; **31:** © Steve Starr/Picture Group; **35:** © Arthur Tress/Photo Researchers; **37:** © Billy E. Barner/Stock, Boston; **42:** Courtesy Western Electric; **44:** © Bill Gallery/Stock, Boston; **46:** Philip G. Zimbardo; **47:** Philip G. Zimbardo; **50:** AP/Wide World

CHAPTER 3: Page 63: © Kal Muller/Woodfin Camp & Assoc.; **64:** (top) Robert Harding Assoc., London; (bottom) © Kennedy/TexaStock; **65:** © Jeff Rotman/Picture Cube; **66:** (right) © Zephyr Pictures; (left) © George Holton/Photo Researchers; **68:** (top) Courtesy General Motors Corp.; (center) Courtesy NBC; **69:** © Hugh Rogers/Monkmeyer; **70:** Courtesy Procter & Gamble; **71:** AP/Wide World; **74:** © Bruce Davidson/Magnum; **77:** AP/Wide World; **81:** © Cynthia W. Sterling/Picture Cube

CHAPTER 4: Page 90: © Bill Gentile/Picture Cube; **93:** © 1987 Nathan Holtz; **94:** Courtesy Sarasota County, Florida; **95:** (left) Used with permission of General Mills, Inc.; (right) Used with permission of General Mills, Inc.; **100:** © Barbara Alper/Stock, Boston; **102:** (left) AP/Wide World; (right) Sygma; **103:** © Jean-Pierre Laffont/Sygma; **111:** Taurus; **112:** Museum of the City of New York; **114:** AP/Wide World

CHAPTER 5: Page 122: © Vandiver/TexaStock; **123:** (left) © Guy Gillette/Photo Researchers; (right) © Susan Holtz; **124:** © Bob Daemmrich/Image Works; **126:** Art Resource; **127:** © George Whiteley/Photo Researchers; **129:** *The New York Times*; **133:** © Richard Falco/Photo Researchers; **134:** © Dennis Brack/Black Star; **136:** © Rick Friedman/Picture Cube; **144:** AP/Wide World

CHAPTER 6: Page 153: © Jeffrey Myers/Stock, Boston; **154:** HBJ Collection; **156:** Fred Sponholz; **157:** © Reed Kaestner/Zephyr; **165:** © Bob Daemmrich/Image Works; **167:** Brown Brothers; **169:** Culver Pictures; **170:** © Robert Eckert/Picture Cube; **172:** UPI/Bettmann Newsphotos; **174:** © Anne M. Grobet/Black Star; **175:** © Bob Krist/Black Star; **176:** © Menschen Freund/Taurus

CHAPTER 7: Page 182: (top) © Liane Enkelis/Stock, Boston; (bottom) © Tony Savino/Image Works; **184:** G. Marche/FPG; **185:** © Karen Preuss/Taurus; **187:** © Charles Gatewood/Image Works; **190:** (left) UPI/Bettmann Newsphotos; (right) © Rob Nelson/Picture Group; **193:** Culver Pictures; **200:** © Jerome Delay/Gamma-Liaison; **204:** Charles Mason/Black Star; **206:** © Bob Daemmrich/Image Works

CHAPTER 8: Page 225: © Alan Sussman/Image Works; **226:** National Maritime Museum; **230:** © Patrick Ward/Stock, Boston; **231:** © IPA/Image Works; **233:** (left) © Brian Drake/EKM Nepenthe; (right) © Duomo/Dan Helms; **235:** © Benno Friedman/Outline Press; **243:** © Michael Uffer/Photo Researchers; **244:** © Herb Levart/Photo Researchers; **249:** © Nik Wheeler/Black Star

CHAPTER 9: Page 256: Jacob Lawrence, *No. 15: Another cause was lynching. It was found that where there had been a lynching, the people who were reluctant to leave at first left immediately after this* from the "Migration of the Negro" series, 1940–41, tempera on hardboard, 12″ × 18″. Phillips Collection, Washington, DC; **257:** © Rob Nelson/Picture Group; **258:** Culver Pictures; **260:** Robert Lidneux, *Trail of Tears,* 20th century, oil on canvas. Woolaroc Museum, Bartlesville, OK; **266:** AP/Wide World; **270:** © Margot Granitsas/Image Works; **273:** © Eric Kroll/Taurus; **277:** © Marc Pokempner/TSW-Click Chicago, Ltd.; **279:** HBJ Collection; **280:** © Chuck Nacke/Picture Group; **284:** UPI/Bettmann Newsphotos; **286:** © Mark Richards/Picture Group

CHAPTER 10: Page 295: © Paul Damien/TSW-Click Chicago, Ltd.; **302:** Library of Congress; **303:** Margaret Bourke-White, LIFE Magazine © 1943 Time Inc.; **306:** © Mimi Forsyth/Monkmeyer; **310:** © Frank Siteman/Taurus; **312:** © Paul Conklin; **314:** Jerry & Addie Solheid; **315:** © David Wells/Image Works

CHAPTER 11: Page 329: (top) © Henley & Savage/TSW-Click Chicago, Ltd.; (left) Taurus; (bottom right) © Tim Carlson/Stock, Boston; **332:** © Eric Kroll/Taurus; **335:** Ward H. Goodenough, Univ. of Pennsylvania; **337:** © Charles Feil/Stock, Boston; **341:** © Scott Dietrich/TSW-Click Chicago, Ltd.; **355:** © Cathy Cheney/EKM Nepenthe; **358:** © Michael Sullivan/TexaStock

CHAPTER 12: Page 365: © (left) Catherine Noren/Photo Researchers; (right) © Rapho/Photo Researchers; **368:** (right) © Marvin Newman; (left) UPI/Bettmann Newsphotos; **372:** © Odetti Mennesson-Rigaud/Photo Researchers; **374:** © David Turnley/Black Star; **378:** © Laffont/Sygma; **381:** © Bill Aron/Photo Researchers; **387:** National Archives; **389:** © Tom Zimberoff/Sygma

CHAPTER 13: Page 396: © 1989 Rogers/Pittsburgh Press; **397:** Bettmann Archive; **399:** Bettmann Archive; **400:** © Elizabeth Crews/Image Works; **403:** TIME MAGAZINE, June 16, 1980,

p. 59; **406:** © Mario Ruiz/Picture Group; **408:** Ron Haerberle, LIFE Magazine © 1969 Time, Inc.; **411:** © Barrera/TexaStock; **418:** © Bob Daemmrich/Image Works; **420:** © Spencer Grant/Picture Cube

CHAPTER 14: Page 429: © Alain Keler/Sygma; **439:** © Blanche/Gamma-Liaison; **440:** Brown Brothers; **446:** Linda L. Creighton/USN&WR; **451:** (top) AP/Wide World; (bottom) Cameron Davidson/Wheeler Pictures; **457:** Culver Pictures; **459:** J. Morin/THE MIAMI HERALD; **461:** UPI/Bettmann Newsphotos

CHAPTER 15: Page 467: Culver Pictures; **469:** Bettmann Archive; **471:** © Rob Nelson/Picture Group; **472:** © Dan Ford Connolly/Picture Group; **474:** © Bill Gallery/Stock, Boston; **484:** © Jim Pickerell/Stock, Boston; **485:** © Tom Lankes/TexaStock; **486:** Brown Brothers; **490:** © Robert R. McElroy/Woodfin Camp & Assoc.; **492:** AP/Wide World

CHAPTER 16: Page 507: AP/Wide World; **509:** © Cytrynowicz/Picture Group; **511:** © David Cannon/Allsport; **512:** AP/Wide World; **514:** © Mario Ruiz/Picture Group; **516:** AP/Wide World; **520:** Republican National Committee; **522:** AP/Wide World; **529:** Culver Pictures; **530:** AP/Wide World; **533:** © Paul Conklin/Monkmeyer

CHAPTER 17: Page 547: © Colin Jones/Picture Group; **550:** © Ken Lambert/FPG; **555:** Bettmann Archive; **558:** © Tony O'Brien/Picture Group; **559:** Ed Reingold/TIME MAGAZINE; **560:** AP/Wide World; **563:** © Bonnie Freer/Photo Researchers; **567:** Peter Bowles; **569:** Edward Lamson Henry, *The 9:45 Accommodation, Stratford, Conn.,* oil on canvas, 30 5/8″ × 16″. The Metropolitan Museum of Art, Bequest of Moses Tanenbaum, 1937; **572:** UPI/Bettmann Newsphotos; **574:** © Margot Granitsas/Image Works; **576:** © Joe Munroe/Photo Researchers

CHAPTER 18: Page 585: (left) AP/Wide World; (right) © Betty Press/Monkmeyer; **596:** © Cornelius Meffert/Black Star; **597:** © Philip Jones Griffith/Magnum; **599:** (right) Reuters/Bettmann Newsphotos; **604:** © Bettina Cirone/Photo Researchers; **607:** AP/Wide World and CBS News-*60 Minutes;* **613:** © Rick Kopstein/Monkmeyer

CHAPTER 19: Page 620: Library of Congress; **627:** © Andrew Popper/Picture Group; **630:** © J. Schweiker/Photo Researchers; **631:** © Robert J. Bennett/FPG; **638:** © Robert Knowles/Black Star; **643:** AP/Wide World; **649:** © Charles Gatewood/Stock, Boston; **651:** © Dennis Brack/Black Star

CHAPTER 20: Page 660: © RDR Productions, All Rights Reserved.; **663:** © Ledru/Sygma; **667:** UPI/Bettmann Newsphotos; **671:** © 1985 American Newsphotos; **685:** AP/Wide World; **687:** © E.C.P. Armees/NEWSWEEK

AUTHOR INDEX

SUBJECT INDEX